APA Handbook of

Forensic
Psychology

APA Handbooks in Psychology® Series

APA Handbook of Industrial and Organizational Psychology—three volumes
    Sheldon Zedeck, Editor-in-Chief
APA Handbook of Ethics in Psychology—two volumes
    Samuel J. Knapp, Editor-in-Chief
APA Educational Psychology Handbook—three volumes
    Karen R. Harris, Steve Graham, and Tim Urdan, Editors-in-Chief
APA Handbook of Research Methods in Psychology—three volumes
    Harris Cooper, Editor-in-Chief
APA Addiction Syndrome Handbook—two volumes
    Howard J. Shaffer, Editor-in-Chief
APA Handbook of Counseling Psychology—two volumes
    Nadya A. Fouad, Editor-in-Chief
APA Handbook of Behavior Analysis—two volumes
    Gregory J. Madden, Editor-in-Chief
APA Handbook of Psychology, Religion, and Spirituality—two volumes
    Kenneth I. Pargament, Editor-in-Chief
APA Handbook of Testing and Assessment in Psychology—three volumes
    Kurt F. Geisinger, Editor-in-Chief
APA Handbook of Multicultural Psychology—two volumes
    Frederick T. L. Leong, Editor-in-Chief
APA Handbook of Sexuality and Psychology—two volumes
    Deborah L. Tolman and Lisa M. Diamond, Editors-in-Chief
APA Handbook of Personality and Social Psychology—four volumes
    Mario Mikulincer and Phillip R. Shaver, Editors-in-Chief
APA Handbook of Career Intervention—two volumes
    Paul J. Hartung, Mark L. Savickas, and W. Bruce Walsh, Editors-in-Chief
APA Handbook of Forensic Psychology—two volumes
    Brian L. Cutler and Patricia A. Zapf, Editors-in-Chief

APA Handbooks in Psychology

APA Handbook of
Forensic
Psychology

VOLUME 2

Criminal Investigation, Adjudication,
and Sentencing Outcomes

Brian L. Cutler and Patricia A. Zapf, *Editors-in-Chief*

American Psychological Association • Washington, DC

Copyright © 2015 by the American Psychological Association. All rights reserved. Except as permitted under the United States Copyright Act of 1976, no part of this publication may be reproduced or distributed in any form or by any means, including, but not limited to, the process of scanning and digitization, or stored in a database or retrieval system, without the prior written permission of the publisher.

Published by
American Psychological Association
750 First Street, NE
Washington, DC 20002-4242
www.apa.org

To order
APA Order Department
P.O. Box 92984
Washington, DC 20090-2984
Tel: (800) 374-2721; Direct: (202) 336-5510
Fax: (202) 336-5502; TDD/TTY: (202) 336-6123
Online: www.apa.org/books/
E-mail: order@apa.org

In the U.K., Europe, Africa, and the Middle East, copies may be ordered from
American Psychological Association
3 Henrietta Street
Covent Garden, London
WC2E 8LU England

AMERICAN PSYCHOLOGICAL ASSOCIATION STAFF
Gary R. VandenBos, *Publisher*
Julia Frank-McNeil, *Senior Director, APA Books*
Theodore J. Baroody, *Director, Reference, APA Books*
Patricia D. Mathis, *Reference Editorial Manager, APA Books*
Lisa T. Corry, *Project Editor, APA Books*

Typeset in Berkeley by Cenveo Publisher Services, Columbia, MD

Printer: Maple Press, York, PA
Cover Designer: Naylor Design, Washington, DC

Library of Congress Cataloging-in-Publication Data

APA handbook of forensic psychology / Brian L. Cutler and Patricia A. Zapf,
Editors-in-Chief.
     pages   cm. — (APA handbooks in psychology)
   Includes bibliographical references and index.
   ISBN 978-1-4338-1793-9 — ISBN 1-4338-1793-4
   1. Forensic psychology—Handbooks, manuals, etc. I. Cutler, Brian L.,
editor of compilation. II. Zapf, Patricia A., 1971– editor of compilation.
   RA1148.A63 2014
   614′.1—dc23
                                         2014014393

British Library Cataloguing-in-Publication Data
A CIP record is available from the British Library.

Printed in the United States of America
First Edition

http://dx.doi.org/10.1037/14462-000

Contents

Editorial Board

EDITORS-IN-CHIEF

Brian L. Cutler, PhD, Professor and Associate Dean, Faculty of Social Sciences and Humanities, University of Ontario Institute of Technology, Oshawa, Ontario, Canada

Patricia A. Zapf, PhD, Professor, Department of Psychology, John Jay College of Criminal Justice, City University of New York

HANDBOOK EDITORIAL MANAGER

Lisa T. Corry, American Psychological Association, Washington, DC

PART I

VICTIM AND OFFENDER GROUPS

CHAPTER 1

CHILDREN AS WITNESSES

Debra Ann Poole, Sonja P. Brubacher, and Jason J. Dickinson

This chapter reviews three knowledge sets that professionals rely on to navigate cases involving child witnesses. The first set includes psychological principles that explain why children's testimony can be amazingly rich and accurate in some instances and disturbingly inaccurate at other times. Children recall events from the time they start talking, but episodic memory (memory for details of personally experienced events) has a protracted developmental course. In early development, neurological immaturity contributes to poor source monitoring (the confusion of information from various sources), a propensity for false recognition (saying, "Yes, that is familiar" to novel stimuli), confabulations (wild tales that are interjected into event narratives), a tendency to drift off the topic of conversation, and impulsive responding. Broad knowledge of development is necessary for working with child witnesses because many facets of development influence testimony, and basic processes are affected by individual children's life experiences, temperaments, and developmental trajectories.

The second knowledge set consists of findings about autobiographical recall and suggestibility that describe how developmental principles translate into children's capabilities and limitations as witnesses. Even at young ages, children's reports of personally significant events are logically structured and include basic information about who was involved and what happened. Episodic memories are fragile when children are just learning to talk, however, and event reports contain some inaccuracies at all ages and delays. Accuracy declines when

interviewers ask specific and yes–no questions, and the passage of time both hurts testimony (because accuracy declines) and helps testimony (because children's accounts become more detailed as they mature). Children develop scripts when they experience multiple instances of similar events (i.e., general representations that describe what usually happens), but young children are less likely than older children to retrieve details that vary across repeated events and are more likely to make errors when matching these details to the correct occurrence.

Compared to adults, children are at a disadvantage when it comes to resisting suggestions. Influences that compromise testimonial accuracy include asking specific and misleading questions, pairing props with specific questions, using social incentives during conversations (e.g., verbally reinforcing desired responses), voicing negative stereotypes about an individual prior to interviews, and exposing children to narratives about events they did not experience (either through adults or by mere contact with peers who spontaneously talk about those events). Preschoolers and school-aged children sometimes come to believe fictitious events, and false information acquired before interviews often appears in responses to open-ended questions. Contrary to myth, it does not take heavy-handed techniques to distort children's testimony, and no features have been found that reliably distinguish narratives about suggested versus experienced events. Children's vulnerability to suggestion is also evident when they are asked to identify

http://dx.doi.org/10.1037/14462-001
APA Handbook of Forensic Psychology: Vol. 2. Criminal Investigation, Adjudication, and Sentencing Outcomes,
B. L. Cutler and P. A. Zapf (Editors-in-Chief)
Copyright © 2015 by the American Psychological Association. All rights reserved.

a perpetrator in a lineup: Even into adolescence, children frequently make errors by selecting a photo from target-absent lineups.

The third knowledge set involves four principles of skilled practice: Expert practice is informed by knowledge of human development, embeds testimony in the context of children's lives, considers the strength of case evidence when making practice decisions, and is guided by standards and evidence-based protocols. Examples for each of these four principles of skilled practice explain how forensic thinking and practice differ from the habits adults acquire in their everyday lives. Experts need a comprehensive, detailed approach to cases involving child witnesses because autobiographical reports are dynamic products of a developing cognitive architecture interacting with a social world.

IMPORTANCE OF THE PROBLEM

It has been said that the legal system "has not known quite what to make of child witnesses" (McGough, 1994, p. 4). Depending on the time and place, young children have been excluded as witnesses, treated in the same manner as other witnesses, or viewed as "testimonial cripples" (McGough, 1994, p. 5) who could serve fact-finding efforts reliably only when special procedures addressed their emotional and developmental needs. The inability to construct a stable view of child witnesses stems partly from the range of decisions that hinge on their testimony and partly from the complex pattern of their capacities and limitations.

Because discussions about children and the law are discussions about their involvement in particular types of cases, deep knowledge of a specialty area is crucial for understanding young witnesses. Consider the following example, in which seasoned detectives relied on their experiences to protect a child and her community:[1]

Jon took his 5-year-old daughter to a medical clinic after noticing stains on

her underwear. Although the doctor diagnosed an infection, Jon was uncomfortable and researched his ex-wife's boyfriend on the Internet. He quickly discovered that the man was a registered sex offender and contacted the local police department.

The girl was reluctant to talk when a detective first visited. Nonetheless, an investigative team went to the mother's home to interview the adults and to inquire about computers, which the boyfriend was prohibited from using as part of his probation conditions. After seizing a computer, a forensic examination revealed videos of abuse, which were then registered with the National Center for Missing and Exploited Children. During a subsequent interview, the girl described events consistent with the video-recorded evidence.

This investigative team knew a great deal about sexual offenders, realized that victims are not always forthcoming about abuse, and operated under the assumption that statements from child witnesses are only one part of an investigation (see Volume 1, Chapter 11, this handbook for a review of sexual offending). They carefully researched the child's caregivers, interviewed these caregivers separately, looked quickly and thoroughly for corroborating evidence, and were guided by a protocol that encourages children to express themselves in their own words. In a similar fashion, experts in other fields of criminal investigation—along with child protective services workers and professionals involved in family law and civil cases—close files each day that illustrate best-practice standards for cases involving child witnesses.

When case features overwhelm professionals' knowledge, however, the result can be what one judge called a "runaway train" (Brasier & Wisely, 2011, para. 5). Consider the cascade of events that impacted this Midwestern family:

---

[1]We created this composite case by combining features from multiple cases; this example and the others that follow do not describe any single case that we know of and are not intended to reference a particular case.

Julian and Thal Wendrow wanted the best life possible for their mute, autistic daughter. When a retired education professor introduced them to facilitated communication, the couple thought the technique would open up a world of opportunities for their child. They pressured the school district to hire a full-time aide, and soon the girl who had tested at the cognitive level of a 2-year-old was mastering middle-school coursework with an adult supporting her hands over a keyboard.

School officials and the Wendrows had reached a truce—until one fall day, when the girl's hands typed that her father had been sexually abusing her. In the words of two journalists who followed the trial, "Within hours, police, prosecutors and social workers were on the move. Within two days, the children were wards of the state. Within a week, the Wendrows were in jail . . . The ordeal didn't end when it was clear that the girl wasn't communicating, after all. It didn't end when a sexual assault exam found no proof of abuse. And it didn't end when a prosecution witness insisted the abuse never happened" (Brasier & Wisely, 2011, "The allegations," para. 7–9, and "Introduction to the series," para. 8). By the time the prosecutor filed for dismissal, the case had slowly unraveled in the face of evidence that the girl's responses originated solely from the facilitator.

The majority of cases lie between the textbook cases, in which children were quickly understood, and those like the Wendrow's, where misunderstanding prevailed.[2] Most of the time, professionals live with varying degrees of uncertainty as they work to make sense of children's behaviors and reports. Making sense often involves three types of information. First is education about basic psychological theory and principles, which we address by answering a series of questions about memory, development, and individual differences. Next is knowledge of how these principles translate into children's capabilities and limitations as witnesses. Finally, four practice recommendations provide guidance for navigating a world in which no two children and sets of circumstances are exactly alike.

RELEVANT PSYCHOLOGICAL THEORY AND PRINCIPLES

Principles of cognition and development give experts the vocabulary to explain why children's testimony can be amazingly rich and accurate in some instances and disturbingly inaccurate at other times. Memory research is the foundation for analyzing testimony because the research tell us how testimony is altered by the passage of time, the way memory is assessed, and other influences. However, event reports reflect more than just the ability to encode (lay down), store, and retrieve memories. Neurological immaturity in early childhood interjects some interesting phenomena into the process of talking about life, and developmental milestones in language and other facets of cognition also affect the accuracy and cohesiveness of children's reports. Finally, children are social creatures as well as individuals from birth, so their environments and unique characteristics produce large variability in performance, even among children of the same age. These foundational issues lay the groundwork for understanding the expanding literature on children as witnesses (see Chapter 7, this volume for a review of research on adult eyewitnesses).

---

[2]There are no figures on the number of children who serve as witnesses each year, but it is clear that children frequently provide testimony for a variety of reasons. In the United States alone, nearly 3 million children are involved in child protective services investigations each year (U.S. Department of Health and Human Services, 2011), and children are frequently present during intimate partner violence (e.g., more than one third of the cases in one sample; U.S. Department of Justice, 2012). Children are also interviewed for arson and other criminal investigations, for civil cases (e.g., wrongful death and product liability), and for child custody evaluations.

What Is the Architecture of Human Memory?

While you are reading this chapter, you are holding words and sentences in mind while you work with this information to understand what you are reading. The memory system that processes online information while you are reading, conducting a conversation, planning a future task, or solving a problem is called *working memory*.

The human brain records experiences for longer periods of time through two long-term memory systems that recruit different parts of the brain, lay down memories in different ways, and develop at different rates. *Implicit memory* involves learning that occurs without conscious awareness but is observed by changes in behavior. (*Implicit* means implied but not expressed directly.) This system includes procedural memories (memories for skills that usually develop with repeated practice, such as riding a bike or reading), priming (in which exposure to something shifts your later perceptions or judgments), associative learning (such as classical conditioning, in which certain stimuli, through associations with other stimuli, come to elicit certain responses), and nonassociative learning (such as when children gradually pay less attention to repeated stimuli). The circuitry that subserves implicit memory is functional at birth, so this primitive memory system allows even young infants to begin learning about their environments (Richmond & Nelson, 2007).

Adults who infer that abuse occurred because children show fear of particular individuals are claiming that this behavior reflects implicit learning. The problem with inferences like this is not that children are incapable of such learning but that direct experience is not the only possible source of the behavior. For example, young children engage in social referencing, in which they attend to others' emotional reactions to decide how they should react to a situation (Klinnert, Emde, Butterfield, & Campos, 1986), and they rapidly pick up information through conversations. As a result, a child's fear of a person or place could be instilled by an adult's behavior.

The second long-term memory system, and the focus of research on children's testimony, is explicit (also called declarative) memory. *Explicit memory* includes episodic memory, which stores details of events experienced at particular times and places, and semantic memory, which is the repository for facts and general knowledge of the world. Autobiographical memory is often described as episodic memories that are especially personal (Newcombe, Lloyd, & Ratliff, 2007). For example, you could remember the items on a short to-do list without remembering your involvement in producing the list (i.e., an impersonal episodic memory), or you could remember writing the list (i.e., a personal episodic, or autobiographical, memory). Alternatively, autobiographical memory may involve semantic information along with the contextual information that specifies personalized episodes (see Burianova, McIntosh, & Grady, 2010, for evidence of a unified view of declarative memory).

Most accounts of autobiographical memory agree that event memories hinge on the brain's ability to link different aspects of an experience together through binding processes (see Raj & Bell, 2010). Remarkably, brain-imaging studies have found that the process of retrieving an event activates some of the neural circuitry that was activated when the event was originally experienced. Together with other findings, this suggests that the hippocampus, a critical brain area for recording new episodic memories and retrieving episodic memories of the past, acts as a directory that specifies which subsets of neocortical neurons compose a given memory. This process, however, is far from static. Instead, each act of memory retrieval is an opportunity for memories to become stronger, weaker, or to change in ways that better align the memory with newly learned information. As Miller (2012) summarized, "Our repository of memories may be less like a library and more like Wikipedia, where each entry is open to editing anytime it's pulled up" (p. 31). This highly constructive, malleable nature of event memories is what draws memory researchers to study eyewitness testimony, and it is the plastic nature of memory that raises interesting questions about the fate of memories laid down early in life, when learning is especially rapid.

Although there is no consensus on the exact age when explicit memory becomes functional, this system is clearly in place by the end of the first 2 years (Jack, Simcock, & Hayne, 2012). Thus, children talk about personally experienced events from the time they can talk, and 2- and 3-year-olds sometimes describe events from as long as a year prior (Peterson, 2002). The brain areas that support explicit memory undergo rapid changes, however, so there are striking differences in children's abilities at 2 years, 4 years, 6 years, and beyond—and in the fate of memories that date from these ages. Cases in which older children or adolescents report events from early childhood raise one of the most basic questions about testimony: Is it is possible for older individuals to remember events from their early years?

Skepticism about memories of early childhood stems from knowledge of infantile amnesia, a phenomenon in which few memories acquired before 3 1/2 years of age survive into adulthood. The term is often used broadly to describe the loss of early memories, but behavioral and neuroscience data support two related phenomena: the near total loss of memories for the first 2 years by the time adulthood arrives, and the fate of memories from the next 3 to 5 years, which are fewer and sketchier than would be predicted based on typical rates of forgetting over time (i.e., childhood amnesia, Newcombe et al., 2007).

Even though adults recall few early experiences, the fact that even young, verbal children can recall events suggests that some event memories are encoded but are then gradually lost over time. In one study, for example, the average age of the earliest memories reported by 5- to 13-year-olds was significantly less than 3.5 years, and some of the memories dating from a young age contained information about who, what, when, and where (Tustin & Hayne, 2010). Early memories tend to fade: However, when children discussed their earliest memories in one session and again 2 years later, the recollections of the younger children shifted several months later in the second session, and these children tended not to describe the same events across times (Peterson, Warren, & Short, 2011). Language development is one of the factors believed to play a role in developmental gains in event recall because it is rare for children to describe events using words that were not in their productive vocabularies at the time of the event (Jack et al., 2012; for a discussion of children's errors dating past events, see Wang, Peterson, & Hou, 2010).

Despite enormous improvements on memory tasks across childhood, some basic principles that govern adults' event reports apply to children's as well.

Dual-process theories explain important memory phenomena. People can easily sort memories into information they remember (because they have a sense of consciously recollecting contextual details of past situations) and information they merely know had occurred (because the information sparks feelings of familiarity). Because behavioral and neurological evidence confirms this distinction between remembering and knowing, memory theorists describe two types of memory traces: verbatim traces, which are rich in the vivid perceptual details that promote feelings of recollection, and gist traces, which correspond to the overall meanings that produce feelings of familiarity (Brainerd & Reyna, 2012; Gruber, Tsivilis, Giabbiconi, & Müller, 2008). Recollection is supported by a widely distributed brain network that has a protracted developmental course, with substantial improvements occurring in middle childhood followed by continued development into adolescence (Ghetti & Bunge, 2012).

Dual-process conceptualizations of memory are helpful for understanding false memories. Because children and adults extract patterns and meaning from events (albeit to different degrees in different contexts), their narratives often contain inaccurate information that is associated with event specifics. For example, an 8-year-old boy who participated in one of our memory studies produced a long description of a drop ceiling in the room where he had experienced an event, complete with information about the percentage of tiles that were replaced with light fixtures. This description reflected his knowledge of typical school buildings but did not describe the university building he had visited (which did not have drop ceilings). Realistic details like these are often regenerated when children and adults reconstruct experiences from gist (through a process called *phantom recollection*). Because relational, meaning-based information (i.e., gist traces) tends to survive longer than perceptually-based information (i.e., verbatim traces), spontaneous errors of this sort can survive longer than accurate memories do (Brainerd & Poole, 1997).

Developmental differences in memory accuracy usually favor older witnesses, but dual-process approaches explain the situations in which children are less prone to errors than adults (i.e., developmental reversals in false memories; Brainerd & Reyna, 2012). That is, because children draw upon fewer experiences than adults when reconstructing memories, they are sometimes less likely than adults to inaccurately report false but gist-consistent information. Memory theory, which summarizes principles derived from thousands of memory studies, helps professionals decide when discrepancies between testimony and other evidence are typical of memories for experienced events and when they are not.

Memory performance is influenced by the way memory is tested.   Two popular ways of testing memory are recall and recognition. During recall tests, individuals generate information in response to general prompts (free recall, e.g., "Tell me everything that happened.") or when cues direct attention to specific information (cued recall, such as "What color was the car?"). For recognition tests, individuals see or hear information and are asked whether that information was experienced (e.g., "Did you see this man?"). Recall tests require individuals to initiate mental searches and to activate memory traces prior to deciding which memories are relevant and which are not. This process activates a broader network of neural circuitry than is activated by recognition tests, which eliminates the self-directed search process (Cabeza et al., 1997). Consequently, recall is generally considered the more difficult task.

The challenges of searching memory are compounded by immaturity. In childhood, the brain areas responsible for self-initiated activity and the circuitry that supports episodic memory are not fully mature. Also, young children hold less information in working memory than do older children and adults (which makes it harder to plan a cohesive narrative), have less experience constructing event narratives, and have less developed language skills. As a result, young children's testimony usually results from a few open-ended prompts delivered by interviewers, supplemented with many directive ("When did that happen?") and option-posing questions ("Did he touch you over or under your clothes?"; Orbach, Hershkowitz, Lamb, Esplin, & Horowitz, 2000).

Preliminary instructions and the type of question can shift whether children will be more likely to access verbatim or gist memories. For example, "Tell me about the last time this happened" encourages children to retrieve a particular instance of a repeated event, whereas "Tell me what usually happens when . . ." asks only for typical features (which is called a script; Nelson, 1986). Children who have difficulty describing a specific instance may be more responsive to prompts that are worded to elicit scripts.

Despite the fact that adults often find recognition tests (e.g., multiple choice tests) easier than recall tests (e.g., essay exams), recognition questions pose problems in forensic contexts. For example, recognition questions include information witnesses have not yet generated, which could impact later memory for events. Also, questions that require only a "yes" or "no" answer are risky for young witnesses, who are prone to impulsive responding. Mapping children's accuracy across various types of instructions and questions is one of the major goals of research on interviewing children.

The content of individual event descriptions does not overlap perfectly.   Regardless of whether the to-be-remembered material involves word lists, conversations, or complex events, children and adults often remember things at one point in time that they did not recall earlier. This phenomenon, called reminiscence, occurs across questions in a single interview and across interviews, with the amount of reminiscent inconsistency being greater when interviewers use different cues to tap memory. As Gilbert and Fisher (2006) explained, "An instance of reminiscence in a real-world setting should not, by itself, give rise to concerns of having tainted the witness's memory or other extraordinary explanations" (p. 734).

Across the lifespan, reminiscent details tend to be less accurate than consistent details, especially when there is a long time between memory retrievals (La Rooy, Katz, Malloy, & Lamb, 2010), but more accurate than details that are inconsistent with prior testimony (Gilbert & Fisher, 2006; Salmon & Pipe, 1997). With children's testimony, however, special knowledge is required to decide when details are truly inconsistent, because children interpret some questions restrictively and use language differently than adults do, so their answers are influenced by the way interviewers phrase questions (Walker, 1999). When analyzing transcripts, experts disregard inconsistencies that could be due to peculiarities in the way children respond to various words or types of questions. For example, it is not remarkable when a child replies "No" to "Did anything happen?" and then, later in the interview, describes a significant event (because questions with the word "any" often elicit a "no" answer from children).

What Are the Testimonial Consequences of Neurological Immaturity?

Eyewitness testimony is not simply a product of how much information people store in memory and how effectively they access it. To participate in conversations, witnesses also need to maintain attention to the task at hand, keep the topic and recent questions in working memory (along with recently retrieved information from long-term memory), suppress irrelevant information and responses (through response inhibition), plan answers (often quickly and under pressure to respond), and monitor their performance. Cognitive psychologists use the term "cognitive control" to describe this set of skills that guides goal-directed behavior. The neural foundations of these skills are in place early in development but are not yet invoked quickly or efficiently. As a result, cognitive control improves dramatically across childhood and adolescence as individual brain regions mature, distant regions form functional circuits, and circuits become increasingly specialized (Bunge & Crone, 2009; Luna, Padmanabhan, & O'Hearn, 2010).

In early childhood, immaturity in the brain areas that support memory binding and cognitive control produce some interesting parallels between children's behavior and the behavior of adult patients with specific neurological conditions and types of brain damage (Schacter, Kagan, & Leichtman, 1995). Variability from child to child and across situations is large, however, so the most striking examples usually involve only a subset of children.

Poor source monitoring. Source monitoring is the process of specifying when, where, and how something was learned (e.g., Did you turn off the stove or only imagine turning it off? Did you see the cute puppy on television or in real life?; Johnson, Hashtroudi, & Lindsay, 1993). Accurately recalling the source of a memory depends on your ability to connect contextual information about an event at encoding and at retrieval, along with the integrity of your decision process. As a result, maturation of the hippocampus and prefrontal cortex, two brain regions that orchestrate these components of episodic memory, support large improvements in source-monitoring ability between 3 and 8 years (Roberts, 2002), with continued improvement through adolescence (Ghetti & Angelini, 2008). Across childhood and into adulthood, conditions that compromise frontal lobe function often cause deficiencies in memory source monitoring (Schacter et al., 1995).

To understand why source monitoring can be challenging, consider a child who has two competing representations of an event: one from experience and one from listening to adults talk about the event. Reporting what was actually experienced may require (a) the realization that knowledge comes from somewhere (e.g., from direct experience or being told by someone else; Wimmer, Hogrefe, & Perner, 1988), (b) the ability to simultaneously hold multiple representations (sources) in working memory (Templeton & Wilcox, 2000), (c) the ability to inhibit competing information from non-target sources (Ruffman, Rustin, Garnham, & Parkin, 2001), (d) the availability of adequate contextual detail about the conflicting events, and (e) a logical strategy for thinking about the qualities of a memory (i.e., metamemory skills, including an awareness that memories rich with perceptual detail, such as how things sounded or tasted, are likely to have been experienced rather than just overheard, suggested, or imagined; see Ghetti, Lyons, Lazzarin, & Cornoldi, 2008).

Because these skills take time to develop, young children sometimes fail to accurately report the source of their knowledge. In one study, for example, an experimenter or a puppet taught children new facts, and children who remembered each fact were asked how they had learned it (Drummey & Newcombe, 2002). More than half of the time, the 4-year-olds attributed their knowledge to a source outside the experimental setting, whereas 6- and 8-year-olds did so less frequently.

A propensity for false recognitions. Some adults with frontal lobe damage make frequent errors by saying "Yes, I saw (or heard) that" when presented with novel items (Schacter et al., 1995). Interestingly, one patient showed virtually no false recognition errors when the studied information was organized around one theme and novel test items represented another theme. The overall pattern of recognition errors suggested that deficient memory for event details (or deficient binding of details in memory), together with decision strategies that rely on general characteristics of events (i.e., gist), are responsible for expectedly high rates of false recognition (Schacter, Curran, Galluccio, Milberg, & Bates, 1996). The fact that frontal lobe deficiencies lead to reliance on gist is consistent with the fact that it is easier to induce children to report inaccurate information when they have schematic knowledge of an event (Pezdek, Finger, & Hodge, 1997).

Confabulations. Some adults with frontal lobe injuries spin grossly inaccurate tales of their lives, and young children also sometimes interject fantastic yarns into their descriptions of events. Confabulations can be plausible or clear inventions, and it is probably this process (also known as

mental surfing[3]) that colored famous day-care abuse cases with bizarre allegations.

Weak conversational skills. Language pragmatics, which refers to the social uses of language, includes conversational skills such as staying on topic, contributing appropriate amounts of information, and structuring cohesive narratives about events. Adults with Parkinson's disease who have impairments in frontal lobe function show deficits on tests of pragmatic skills (McNamara & Durso, 2003), as do young children.

One behavior that frequently causes confusion is children's tendency to drift off topic. In laboratory studies, even school-aged children sometimes begin talking about unrelated events when interviewers ask questions such as, "Can you tell me more?" rather than, "Can you tell me more about (the topic of discussion)?"—despite the fact that these children just answered numerous questions about a particular event, which should have made the intended topic obvious (Poole & Lindsay, 2001). When professionals fail to realize that children are no longer on topic, allegations can expand as unrelated stories of adults, locations, and situations become woven into investigators' hypotheses about what happened.

Greater dependence of behavior on the immediate environment. Some adults with injuries to the right frontal lobe are highly influenced by their immediate environment. Distinctive symptoms include interacting with objects when it is inappropriate to do so and imitating other people's gestures (e.g., Besnard et al., 2011).

Dependence on external cues, handling objects, and imitating other people sounds like a recipe for building a child because these are the tendencies that prompt children to learn about their physical and social worlds. The tendency to lose track of the purpose of conversations when reacting to external cues may explain why young children sometimes explore and play with objects during interviews, such as when they insert fingers into the holes of

---

[3]We picked up this phrase from Stephen Ceci and find it useful for conveying how some children creatively weave ideas together into narratives. Sometimes we can trace the origin of a child's confabulation (e.g., the plot is that of a well-known children's book, or the story incorporates themes from an upcoming holiday), but most of the time we have no idea how children came up with their invented stories.

anatomical dolls (e.g., Bruck, 2009). In the eyewitness literature, this behavior is often referred to as responding to the "affordances" of objects (i.e., actions that are possible with an object). The need to reduce unwanted exploration and imitative responses drives some of the recommendations that aim to reduce suggestive influences during interviews.

The consequences of neurological immaturity can combine to produce unexpected behavior. In one of our pilot studies, for example, a female experimenter asked children to label parts on a body outline, asked whether a man had touched them in a prior session, administered a set of developmental tests, and then asked if she had touched them on their bodies. Despite the fact that the experimenter had met each child only minutes before this interview, some children nonetheless accused her of touching. For example, one 5-year-old said that, yes, she had touched him, pointed to the belly on the diagram, and then explained that "you touched me here so you could feel me am I burning up or not." Notice that this brief interaction contained a false recognition ("Yes, that is familiar"), an impulsive point, and an on-the-spot confabulation. How often and under what circumstances behaviors like these occur are two of the questions that motivate eyewitness research with children.

Do Other Developmental Milestones Influence Children's Testimony?

While neurological development and accumulating experiences are working to improve memory and cognitive control, other facets of development are also influencing what children say about their lives. For example, research on the development of pretense has shown that preschoolers can and do lie (often, according to mothers' diaries; Stouthamer-Loeber, 1986) but that young children are poor at maintaining a ruse and generally lack a mature understanding of lying (e.g., Ahern, Lyon, & Quas, 2011; see Chapter 8, this volume for a review of deception detection). Other research has documented normative sexual behavior (Poole & Wolfe, 2009) and the silly joking about body parts and bathroom topics that is common around 6 years of age (Ames & Ilg, 1979). Perhaps

the most frequently used information comes from studies of language development, as this information helps professionals ask age-appropriate questions and make sense of children's answers (Walker, 1999). These examples illustrate why broad knowledge of development is necessary for working with child witnesses.

How Are Basic Processes Affected by Individual Differences?

Developmental psychologists have a dilemma: Professionals want to know what to expect from children of various ages, but variability ensures that rules of thumb will not apply to all children. One source of variability is individual differences in knowledge and experiences. In one study, for example, children's ages were not predictive of recalling a target event, but children who had talked to their parents more about the event after it happened were more likely to describe it than children who had not (Jack et al., 2012). Other research has found that parents who talk with their children about past experiences, and especially those who elaborate upon their children's responses, have children who report more information about events (Peterson, Sales, Rees, Fivush, 2007). In a general sense, children learn how to build memories and organize meaningful narratives, so those who engage more often in social conversation with adults about past events tend to generate richer and more complete accounts of their experiences (Fivush, Reese, & Haden, 2006).

Life experiences affect testimony in other ways. For example, gist-based memory errors reflect children's knowledge of particular topics, and willingness to discuss sexual issues is influenced by parental attitudes about nudity and sexual education. In addition to differences stemming from children's learning histories, differences in temperament and impulsivity lead to dramatic differences in the amount and accuracy of information provided by children of the same age. Finally, many school-aged children show behaviors that are typical of younger children due to conditions such as cognitive impairments and language disorders (e.g., Brown, Lewis, & Lamb, 2012).

Due to the large variability in performance during childhood, developmental norms can be highly misleading. The problem is that psychologists typically report the age when a skill is mastered as the age when some percentage of children (often 50% or 75%) have mastered that skill. As these ages infiltrate the literature, there is a tendency for professionals to forget that many children have not mastered skills by the listed ages. Due to this error, professionals sometimes believe that a particular question or technique is safe for 4-year-olds, 5-year-olds, and so forth when, in fact, this assumption disregards the significant proportion of children who have not acquired the skill by the typical age of mastery. As we move on to review how basic principles translate into trends in eyewitness testimony, keep in mind that age is not the only variable determining individual children's capabilities and limitations.

RESEARCH REVIEW

Principles of memory and development are the starting point for discussing eyewitness testimony, but this basic information does not instill a sense of how children typically report past experiences—or what happens when we ask them about events that did not happen. To address these issues, we first review studies that documented children's event reports when there were no intentional efforts to influence their memories. Next, we highlight key results from research on children's suggestibility, focusing on memory errors stemming from social interactions. Keeping these "best case" and "worst case" scenarios in mind, we then address how testimony changes across multiple interviews and describe children's ability to identify previously unfamiliar people they encountered during a past event.

Children's Reports of Meaningful Events

After a presentation on children's eyewitness testimony, an audience member asked why a child who saw a trapeze artist fall during a circus performance did not later remember this horrifying event. From a parent's perspective, the crowd's reaction and the clearing of the tent were distinctive features that should have burned the disturbing image into memory. Now consider this incident from the child's perspective: Why would a child who has no concept of a circus—which is an event containing such things

as sword-swallowing and fire throwing—realize that something had gone wrong? In situations like this one, it is not surprising that children often remember peculiar details, such as a clown's enormous shoes or the cotton candy they were allowed to eat, rather than features adults consider to be central (Poole, Warren, & Nunez, 2007).

In general, children's interest in and understanding of events predict how well they remember. Consequently, even young children demonstrate impressive memory when they are allowed to choose events to discuss or when adults ask about salient situations such as injuries and unpleasant medical procedures. Even for these types of events, however, eyewitness performance depends on children's ages, how much time has elapsed, and the types of questions that are asked.

The structure of children's event reports. The most impressive examples of children's testimonial ability involve reports of situations that evoked strong emotions because a personal goal was obtained, threatened, or blocked. Children and adults use similar language to raise such topics, as in the following examples:

> "I got my favorite Ninja toys."
> (3-year-old)
> "My grandpa is gonna die soon."
> (4-year-old)
> "He was gonna hurt me if I didn't shut up." (4 1/2-year-old)
> "She told me that I had passed the exam." (woman)
> "My dad told me that Jason had died." (man)
> "I knew the end was near, he changed so rapidly." (man) (Stein, 2002, p. 250)

In the study that generated these examples, there was amazing continuity from 3 years to adulthood in the logical structure of narratives about personally significant events (Stein, 2002). As expected, young children recalled less information than did older children and adults, but individuals of all ages conveyed the causal structure of the events, including information about what happened, who or what was responsible for the change in goals, what beliefs were violated, how the personal goals were affected, and what outcomes were unintended. Remarkably, when 3- to 6-year-olds were re-interviewed 10 years later, the majority of children still recalled these events. For example, 90% of the children remembered events that had evoked intense fear, and 76% remembered events that had provoked anger. Results were not as impressive when the researchers asked about events discussed 10 years ago that did not have the same emotional significance: Most of these happenings were not remembered years later, and the narratives children did produce about these events contained a higher percentage of clauses that were inconsistent with their initial reports.

More detailed findings come from a program of research on children's reports of injury events. For years, Carole Peterson's research assistants have greeted parents and children in an emergency room in Canada. Parents who agreed to enroll in a memory study were later interviewed about the events, and assistants then interviewed the children one or more times to map the characteristics of their reports. Unlike the children in Nancy Stein's research, who all reacted strongly to the target events, the children in these studies differed widely in their emotional reactions to unexpected injuries (Peterson, 2010). Five conclusions capture the quality and evolution of these children's testimonies over time:

1. *Even young children reported useful information soon after meaningful events.* Older 1-year-olds sometimes described events that occurred months ago (Peterson, 2002), and 2-year-olds could report (on average) nearly half of the event components when interviewed within a few days of their injuries. There was a jump in the completeness of children's recall at 3 to 4 years of age and again at 5 to 6 years of age. Remarkably, when interviewed shortly after injuries, these young but school-aged children recalled almost as many event components as 12- to 13-year-olds did (Peterson, 2011).

2. *Episodic memories were fragile when children were just learning to talk.* Among a group of children who were too young to be interviewed after an event, half recalled nothing 18 months later, and the others reported very little. Five years later, reports from former 1-year-olds, if they recalled anything, contained almost one intrusion (error) for every correct detail recalled. Memory improved greatly for events experienced when children were about 26 months of age, but delayed reports from 2-year-olds included erroneous information interwoven with accurate information (Peterson, 2002, 2012).

3. *Event reports contained inaccuracies at all ages and delays, but accuracy improved with age.* Human memory is not designed to store and retrieve literal copies of events—even when those events are very important to us. In one analysis, for example, 6% of the information that 5- and 6-year-olds reported in an initial interview was wrong, as was 2% of the information reported by the 12- and 13-year-olds. A year later, these percentages grew to 13% and 6%, respectively (Peterson, 2011).

4. *Accuracy declined when interviewers asked specific and yes–no questions.* When adults ask questions that request specific information (e.g., "What did the man do for a living—what was his job?"), it is well known that children often comply by providing a response—even when there is no reason they would know the requested information (Poole & White, 1993). The tendency to answer impulsively and to fill in for memory gaps is evident even when adults ask about personally significant events. In one study of injury reports, less than 10% of the errors children made occurred during the free recall portion of the interview; the majority of errors appeared in responses to wh- and yes–no questions (Peterson & Bell, 1996).

5. *Children's event reports got worse and better over time.* Although it is typical for memory accuracy to decline after an event (and to do so most steeply during the first year), developmental improvements in language and understanding of events produced a nuanced pattern of performance in Peterson's data. Reports of major components of injury events tended to remain constant for years after the events had occurred, but children typically recounted more elaborative detail as they matured. For example, a child

who initially said, "We were at my Nan's" later explained, "We were at my Nan's by the green shed that's next to her house" (reports from the initial interview and 2-year follow-up; Peterson, 2011, p. 289).

Other studies support these conclusions and provide additional information about variability in memory for significant events. For example, ground-breaking research on children's reports of a stressful medical procedure (urethral catheterization) found that better understanding of the event and sympathetic parental communication were associated with fewer inaccuracies (Goodman, Quas, Batterman-Faunce, Riddlesberger, & Kuhn, 1997). Surprisingly, the amount of stress that children experienced, as indexed by crying, has not been a good predictor of memory for injuries and medical events, perhaps because these events are likely to be recalled regardless of children's reactions (Goodman et al., 1997; Peterson, 2012). For discussions of relationships between stress and memory in maltreated and nonmaltreated children, see Howe (1997), Howe, Goodman, and Cicchetti (2008), and Wallin, Quas, and Yim (2009).

Recalling multiple instances of related events. We mentioned earlier that people develop scripts (i.e., general representations) that describe what usually happens when they have multiple experiences with similar events (Nelson, 1986). Young children's scripts include fewer details and are less flexible than those of older children because they have difficulty incorporating variations (i.e., predictable or typical changes from episode to episode) and deviations (i.e., exceptions that were not compatible with the event script) into their understanding of events (Hudson, Fivush, & Kuebli, 1992). Consider these examples, which illustrate how 4-year-old and 8-year-old children typically describe swimming lessons:[4]

> *Four-year old*: You put on your bathing suit, and you go in the water. Then you do, ah . . . circle time and you have to always do your kicks, and then you come out and go home.

> *Eight-year-old*: Well, once you're ready to go in the water, you come out to the pool and get your name checked off, and then you . . ., well, sometimes you start off with dives to get in the water, or jumps, like star, cannonball, spin . . ., or if there's a game at the beginning, you just get in normally. Then you have some time for practicing different swims, and usually there's always a game at the end, like Marco Polo or freeze. And then you get changed and go home, or sometimes we go for ice cream.

Note that both scripts are coherent and temporally organized, but the script from the older child contains more information and displays greater flexibility (i.e., sometimes X, sometimes Y).

Children of all ages have strong memories for details that are usually or always present across event occurrences, and even 3-year-olds are able to describe the typical details of familiar events in an organized and logical fashion (Nelson & Gruendel, 1981). Although all children show resistance to suggestions about typical details, young children are less likely than older children to retrieve details that are optional or that vary across events (Farrar & Goodman, 1990), and they are more likely to make errors when matching these details to the correct occurrence (Powell, Roberts, Ceci, & Hembrooke, 1999; Roberts & Powell, 2001).

It can be difficult to provide details associated with specific episodes because as scripts become stronger, it becomes harder to recall the specific details associated with any one event (Nelson, 1986). According to dual-process memory theories, repeated similar experiences strengthen the gist for "what usually happens," while the verbatim traces associated with specific episodes weaken (Brainerd & Reyna, 1990, 2004). Thus, retrieving gist information promotes the reporting of generic details, but there may be confusions across event occurrences as details compatible with the gist are misattributed. Only the specific verbatim traces associated with individual occurrences can aid in retrieving the correct alternative. As illustrated by the examples in Table 1.1

---

[4]These are composite examples derived from raw transcripts; summary data appeared in Brubacher, Roberts, and Powell (2011).

TABLE 1.1

Examples of Event Reports That Rely on Gist Versus Verbatim Information

Gist information	Verbatim information
Usually after school, she . . .	The last time it happened right before bed.
	One time it happened right after we ate dinner.
While mum is out of the house . . .	The first time, mum had gone to work.
	One time it happened when mum went to the shops for only 10 minutes.
He touches me when we're on the couch.	The first time he put his hand in the front of my shirt.
	The last time he took my pants down and touched my bum.
I'm usually wearing my house clothes.	The time he took my pants down I was wearing my purple pajama set.
	The first time I hadn't changed yet and still had on my school uniform.
And after, he sometimes says not to tell.	The first time he said, "If you tell anyone I'll get taken away."
	The time mum went to the shops he said, "You'd better keep quiet."

gist-based accounts preserve the general meaning and structure of what transpired but do not capture rich, incident-specific information.

A source-monitoring approach to recalling repeated events focuses on how the decision-making processes that occur at retrieval can help children accurately attribute specific details to the correct event occurrence even if memory traces have weakened. For example, children might use perceptual information to reason that a strong memory must be from a recent occurrence, or they might decide that abuse in a vacation cottage must have occurred in the summer (because the cottage is not visited at other times of the year). Although these reasoning skills improve markedly from 3 years to 8 years of age, such decisions remain challenging when event occurrences share many similar perceptual features. In the case of repeated abuse, for example, individual episodes may share the same actors (child and perpetrator), the same locations (e.g., the bedroom), similar circumstances (e.g., mother is always out of the house), and similar acts of abuse.

Source monitoring may be especially difficult for children who experienced ongoing abuse because stress can alter attention in ways that impair feature binding in memory (Mather et al., 2006). There may also be motivational reasons why some children provide little information about individual event occurrences. For example, compared to children who make

single-event allegations, children who make allegations of a repeated nature are more likely to say they expected negative consequences following disclosures of abuse (Malloy, Brubacher, & Lamb, 2011). Although many maltreated children are not motivated to share their experiences (Orbach, Shiloach, & Lamb, 2007), this finding suggests that those who have experienced abuse on multiple occasions may be even less so.

Suggestibility of Children

We trust our memory machinery to give us an accurate accounting of our lives, yet memory malleability is a fact of life across the lifespan. Seminal studies of the "misinformation effect" showed that certain question wordings altered adult witnesses' reports of event details, and narratives about fictitious childhood incidents produced false reports of having experienced those events (e.g., Frenda, Nichols, & Loftus, 2011). Sometimes, simply asking about an event leads a subset of adults to believe they were witnesses. For instance, 40% of the participants in one sample claimed to have seen nonexistent video footage of a bus exploding from a terrorist attack, and many of these suggestible adults reported details of the phantom media coverage (Ost, Granhag, Udell, & Roos af Hjelmsäter, 2008).

Compared to adults, children are at a disadvantage when it comes to resisting suggestions that threaten the reliability of their reports.[5] For

[5]Memory researchers are interested in separating reporting errors due to conformity from errors resulting from changes in underlying memory representations. Detailed discussion of the mechanisms underlying reporting errors is beyond the scope of this review, but there is evidence both for compliance-based and memory-based false reports (Otgaar, Verschuere, Meijer, & Oorsouw, 2012).

example, children under 12 years of age have difficulty reflecting on social influence (London, Bruck, Poole, & Melnyk, 2011), which can make them less aware than adults of efforts to modify their testimony. As we described earlier, the mental architecture that supports sophisticated reasoning about memory is incomplete during childhood (e.g., "How do I know this?", "Is there a contradiction between these two memories?"). A working understanding of the impact of immaturity on vulnerability to suggestion requires (a) information about the circumstances that distort children's eyewitness reports and (b) clear thinking about the many myths that circulate about children's suggestibility.

Distorting influences. Research on children's suggestibility utilizes a wide range of procedures, from videotaped events followed by tests of memory for details (e.g., "What was the boy wearing?") to studies of how well children recall central features of meaningful experiences. Although critics frequently dismiss findings from events that were not very memorable, doing so misses an important point: In most cases, researchers compared children's accuracy across two or more conditions to identify the influences that impair testimonial accuracy. Although, resistance to suggestion improves as target events increase in salience, the order of conditions generalizes from mundane to significant events, so conditions that produce a greater number of errors in the former case also tend to produce a greater number of errors in the latter.

The easiest way to foster errors is to ask specific and misleading questions. Adults and children often answer such questions—even when they do not know the correct answer, and even when interviewers have warned that it is all right to say "I don't know." After watching a videotape, for example, one sample of kindergarteners answered 43% of the specific questions inaccurately (e.g., "Can you tell me who owned the bike?"). Second and third graders performed better, but these older children still erred 31% of the time (compared to the adults' error rate of 16%). The kindergarten children also performed poorly in the face of explicitly misleading questions (a 61% error rate to questions such as, "The bike

was the girl's, wasn't it?"), and they were more likely than older children to change accurate responses when interviewers pressed them for desired but wrong answers (Cassel, Roebers, & Bjorklund, 1996). Many studies have found a gradual decline with age in interrogative suggestibility (i.e., conformance to interviewing pressures; Hünefeldt, Lucidi, Furia, & Rossi-Arnaud, 2008), with adult-like responses achieved at different ages for different procedures.

Laboratory findings generalize to interviews conducted by trained professionals. In one study, clinical psychologists with experience interviewing children for the courts were given a set of props and allowed to question children as they saw fit. Compared to police detectives who were not given props, this group spent more time off the topic, asked fewer free-recall questions, and elicited more errors from the children (Melinder et al., 2010).

Pairing props with specific questions is a two-edged sword: When interviewers ask about touching, concrete cues elicit more reports of experienced touching but also elevate false reports (for reviews, see Poole & Bruck, 2012; Poole, Bruck, & Pipe, 2011; Poole & Dickinson, 2011). Across studies, rates of false reports of genital and anal touching range from low to alarming, depending upon children's ages, the time that has elapsed since target events, and the interviewing procedures. For example, only 3% of 5- and 7-year-old children who had not experienced vaginal touching falsely said that they had when interviewed with anatomical dolls in one study (Saywitz, Goodman, Nicholas, & Moan, 1991), whereas 15% of 3- to 6-year-olds who were interviewed with props did so in another (Steward & Steward, 1996, 1-month interview). Existing studies, however, did not incorporate the atmosphere of concern about touching that characterizes sexual abuse investigations, so children's ability to resist the suggestive force of props paired with specific questions is not yet adequately tested.

There are many ways to wear down children's ability to resist suggestions. In the famous "Mousetrap" studies, assistants visited 3- to 6-year-olds multiple times to ask them if events printed on index cards had actually happened or not. ("We made this list up by talking to your mother and father to get them to tell us about things that really happened to you when you were younger, but not all of the things that I am going to read to you really happened . . . ."; Ceci, Huffman, Smith, & Loftus, 1994, p. 394.) Children assented to an unexpected number of nonexperienced events in one study, with 3- and 4-year-olds accepting 44% of the fictitious events in the first interview and 5- and 6-year-olds accepting 25% (Ceci, Huffman, et al., 1994). In a second study, instructions to picture the events in their heads led children to increase their false assent rate across repeated interviews to 45% and 40% in the last interview among younger and older children, respectively (Ceci, Loftus, Leichtman, & Bruck, 1994). Importantly, suggestible children often generated detailed narratives about these fictitious events and sometimes resisted when assistants explained that these events had not, in fact, occurred.

Drawing inspiration from techniques that interviewers used in the McMartin Preschool case, Sena Garven and her colleagues (1998) compared the testimonial accuracy of 3- to 6-year-old children in the face of a suggestive interview (with questions such as "Did Manny tear the book while he was reading it?") to accuracy rates when interviewers added social incentives to suggestive questions. In the latter condition, interviewers told children that "big kids . . . said that Manny did some bad things," verbally reinforced children for desired responses, and expressed disappointment after undesired responses. Although children of all ages sometimes went along with misleading questions, adding social incentives elevated the rate of false responses to over 50% (Garven, Wood, Malpass, & Shaw, 1998). Errors produced by interviewer pressure do not reflect just temporary cooperation on the part of children; instead, some errors persist into interviews conducted a year later (London, Bruck, & Melnyk, 2009).

Suggestive information encountered outside interviews can also infiltrate children's freely recalled narratives and compound the force of suggestive questioning. One form of influence is to convey stereotypes about other people that are consistent with the desired responses. Assistants for the Sam Stone study did this by visiting preschools, where they sometimes told stories that depicted Sam Stone as a clumsy, bumbling person (Leichtman & Ceci, 1995). After an uninteresting visit by Sam, children who had heard these stories and those who had not were repeatedly interviewed in neutral or suggestive ways. Thus some children were not exposed to stereotypes or suggestive interviewing (i.e., the control condition), some experienced only the negative stereotype, some experienced only suggestive interviewing, and others experienced both types of influence. Accuracy followed this condition order, with the best performance in the control condition and the worst performance in the stereotype-plus-suggestions condition. In the suggestion-only and stereotype-plus-suggestion groups, false accusations even infiltrated children's free-recall testimony.

To investigate what happens when adults feed children specific information prior to interviews, researchers developed the Mr. Science paradigm. After spending time with an unfamiliar man, children heard stories from their parents that described experienced and nonexperienced events, including information about events involving innocuous touching. Although the parents never explicitly said that the fictitious events actually happened, some children nonetheless described these events in response to open-ended questions about what happened with Mr. Science (Poole & Lindsay, 2001, 2002). False reports were even more frequent when interviewers progressed to specific yes–no questions: In this phase of the interview, over a third of the children confirmed recently heard information, including children who were 7 and 8 years of age (Poole & Lindsay, 2001). Unlike younger children, however, the older children were better (though not perfect) at correcting these errors when interviewers took the time to explain the difference between experienced and heard events, trained the children that it is okay to say "no" when appropriate, and revisited each question that elicited a "yes" response (i.e., "Did Mr. Science really . . . ?").

Intentional efforts are not required to spread false reports, however; naturally occurring social interactions will have the same result. In a series of studies on rumor-mongering, Principe and her colleagues arranged for some children to experience an event and tracked the spread of information through peer groups (Principe & Schindewolf, 2012). Information children could only have received from their peers consistently showed up in responses to open-ended questions, and children frequently claimed to have witnessed these events with their own eyes. Importantly, levels of false reports were higher than what is typically observed with other suggestibility paradigms, and natural social interactions produced more elaborate false narrative accounts. These findings, along with detailed information about relationships between conversations and subsequent reports (collected by belt-clipped recorders), explain how multiple children can come to describe the same, but false, events. In a similar manner, giving parents misinformation and asking them to discuss an event with their children is sufficient to foster false reports (Principe, DiPuppo, & Gammel, 2012).

Myths about children's suggestibility. Numerous misunderstandings about children's testimony crop up in articles and courtroom testimony, including the following (e.g., Ceci, Kulkofsky, Klemfuss, Sweeney, & Bruck, 2007):

Myth #1: Only young children are suggestible. Due to neurological immaturity, younger children are more likely than older children to confuse memories from difference sources, respond inappropriately to specific questions and interviewing props, and interject mind-wanderings into reports of recent events. These tendencies do not disappear suddenly, however, as is vividly illustrated by studies of false confessions by adults (see Chapter 9, this volume). Even children 11 years of age and older are susceptible to forming false memories of bizarre events, such as alien abductions (Otgaar, Candel, Merckelback, & Wade, 2009; see also Strange, Sutherland, & Garry, 2006), and to blending suggestions and reality (see Hershkowitz, 2001, for discussion of a suggestion-induced rape allegation from a 10-year-old victim of indecent exposure). Because many mechanisms contribute to false reports, age trends vary across situations

and performance measures. For example, 8-year-olds in the Mr. Science paradigm are no more accurate than younger children on some measures, perhaps because their motivation to show researchers what they know camouflages their superior source-monitoring skills (e.g., Poole & Lindsay, 2001).

Myth #2: Answers to open-ended questions are highly accurate. Rates of detail errors are low (on average) when children experience events and then respond to general prompts to describe what happened, but this is not always the case among children who have been exposed to suggestive influences before interviews (e.g., Leichtman & Ceci, 1995; Principe & Schindewolf, 2012).

Myth #3: Mild suggestions do not taint reports. Although some suggestibility studies used multiple forms of suggestive influence, children's testimony can be tainted without heavy-handed techniques. For example, the Mr. Science procedure exposed children to only minutes of narrative (most of which described experienced events; e.g., Poole & Lindsay, 2001), and natural conversation tainted testimony in Principe's studies of rumor transmission (Principe & Schindewolf, 2012).

Myth #4: True reports contain features that reliably distinguish them from false reports. A persistent myth is the idea that adults can spot suggestion-induced false reports based on features such as how elaborate or coherent the reports are. Individual studies have found mean differences between true and false narratives on various linguistic features, but no consistent patterns have been documented that enable reliable judgments (see Principe, Greenhoot, & Ceci, 2014, for a review). This is cause for concern because adults typically believe children's narratives—even when they know that children participated in a suggestibility study that produced true and false narratives (Laimon & Poole, 2008).

The fact that children sometimes deny their experiences and sometimes convincingly report nonexperienced events is the foundation of a basic principle we revisit later in this chapter: Children's reports are only one part of an investigation and, not always the most important part. Accordingly, analyses of children's testimony should always involve information about how testimony is situated in children's lives.

Recall Across Multiple Interviews

Partly due to publicity from a series of high-profile day care cases (for examples, see Ceci & Bruck, 1995), policy efforts in the 1980s and 1990s focused on two goals: findings ways to avoid suggestive influences during sexual abuse investigations and reducing the stress children experience from retelling their stories over and over again. These goals directed a two-pronged approach to reform that included the development of interviewing protocols and broader dissemination of coordinated approaches to case investigation (e.g., the child advocacy center concept). Although there was variability in how these movements played out in individual jurisdictions, the result was a widespread belief that is best to avoid interviewing children multiple times.

Even as this belief was gaining momentum, however, memory researchers were contesting the idea that multiple interviews always incurred unacceptable risks. Early reviews concluded that children's accuracy was remarkably stable when interviewers used open-ended questions, and that "misleading information, suggestive questions, or memory reconstructions due to prior stereotypes or the passage of time . . . rather than multiple interviews per se, seem to be responsible for introducing errors into testimony" (Poole & White, 1995, p. 34). In other words, multiple interviews were problematic when interviewing errors compounded, the time between interviews provided additional opportunities for adults to influence children's testimonies, and later interviews were so delayed that inconsistencies entered into evidence due to normal forgetting and memory reconstruction.

Subsequent reviews cautioned against the assumption that any misleading questioning would taint subsequent reports. Because early interviews can strengthen memories for events (at least when conducted soon after those events), even imperfect interviews sometimes produce higher accuracy rates in subsequent interviews than what is observed among children who are interviewed only once at the longer delay. As Goodman and

Quas (2008) explained, "When and how children are interviewed is at least as important for their accuracy as is how many times they are interviewed" (p. 386).

Children's Eyewitness Identification

Awareness of the frequency of false convictions that result from mistaken eyewitness identification, and the fallibility of eyewitness memory more generally, has prompted evidence-based guidelines and mandates for the collection and preservation of eyewitness evidence (e.g., Technical Working Group for Eyewitness Evidence, 1999), including guidelines for improving the accuracy of eyewitness identifications (for a discussion, see Chapter 7, this volume). However, reforms for conducting eyewitness identifications have centered on adult witnesses, perhaps reflecting the fact that most crimes against children are perpetrated by familiar adults rather than strangers (Davies & Noon, 1991).

There is another reason why children are not part of broader conversations about eyewitness identifications: Efforts to improve children's eyewitness identification performance have proven difficult, leading to few concrete practice recommendations. Existing research has, however, provided valuable insight into the strengths and limitations of child witnesses and can therefore be instructive for professionals who need to gauge the reliability of children's eyewitness identifications.

Children's difficulties with eyewitness identification begin with their descriptions of perpetrators. Before witnesses can accurately identify perpetrators, the police must first locate suspects through a process that typically involves witnesses' descriptions of perpetrators' physical appearance. Unfortunately, both archival reviews (analyses of actual cases) and laboratory studies have consistently shown that children (especially younger children) provide significantly fewer crime and person descriptors compared to adult witnesses (Pozzulo, Dempsey, & Crescini, 2009; Pozzulo & Warren, 2003). Moreover, the descriptors they do provide tend to be less accurate than those from adults. For example, although accuracy improves with age, children struggle to provide accurate descriptions of age, height, and weight—some of the most commonly requested descriptors by investigators (see also Pozzulo, 2007, 2013, for reviews).

Most research on children's identification accuracy has focused on their ability to identify a perpetrator's face from lineups. A meta-analysis found that 4-year-olds were significantly less likely than adults to correctly identify a target who was present in the lineup (47% correct vs. 67% correct, respectively), whereas children 5 years and older performed comparably (Pozzulo, 2007; Pozzulo & Lindsay, 1998). When the perpetrator was absent from the lineup, however, children across all ages were more prone to make identification errors than adults. Even adolescents 12 to 13 years of age struggled to reject target-absent lineups: Adults selected a photo only about a quarter of the time when the perpetrator was not present, whereas adolescents did so over half the time. Thus, school-aged children perform relatively well when the perpetrator is in the photo spread, but their performance decreases significantly when the perpetrator is absent (i.e., when an innocent person is included in the array). Although the phenomenology behind this choosing bias is not entirely clear, the propensity to answer when memory is weak or nonexistent mirrors children's behavior in the face of difficult questions about event details that we iscussed earlier.

Efforts to improve children's eyewitness performance have taken two approaches: (a) testing innovations that are known to improve adults' lineup performance and (b) testing innovations designed specifically for child witnesses. The most widely researched innovation for adults is the sequential lineup (the presentation of lineup photos one after the other), which was developed as an alternative to the traditional simultaneous lineup format (the presentation of lineup photos concurrently; Lindsay & Wells, 1985). With adults, sequential lineups have been found to increase correct rejections (i.e., when the target is absent) without significantly decreasing correct identifications (i.e., when the target is present; Steblay, Dysart, Fulero, & Lindsay, 2001; Steblay, Dysart, & Wells, 2011). Unfortunately, the gain in accuracy observed with adults does not apply to children, who perform poorly across both lineups formats (Pozzulo & Lindsay, 1998; Steblay et al., 2011).

One explanation for children's poor lineup performance is that they are more likely than adults to interpret the task as an investigative "demand"—that is, they believe it is their "job" to identify someone because that is what the investigator wants. Unfortunately, attempts to improve children's performance by reducing their choosing bias (e.g., giving children practice lineups, providing cautionary instructions used with adults) have had limited success (Pozzulo & Lindsay, 1998). As a result, researchers have developed more innovative techniques to alter children's strategies.

Pozzulo and Lindsay (1999) tested an "elimination" lineup approach that required children to use a two-step decision strategy: First they were asked to identify the person who most resembled the target (a relative judgment) and then were asked to compare that photograph to their memory for the target (an absolute judgment). When this procedure was paired with cautionary instructions, children's correct rejections of target-absent lineups increased significantly. Importantly, the procedure did not significantly reduce correct identifications when the target was present (Pozzulo et al., 2009).

To test a different approach, Karageorge and Zajac (2011) used a standard simultaneous lineup with one modification: the inclusion of a "wild card." The wild card was a picture with a faceless silhouetted figure, thus giving the children a salient "not there" option to choose if they did not see the target. Compared to the condition without a wild card, across delay conditions (1–2 days vs. 2 weeks) children (ages 5 to 11 years) in the wild-card condition made significantly more correct rejections when the lineup did not contain the target, and this improvement occurred without a loss in accuracy when the target was present.

In summary, although research on children's identification accuracy has lagged behind that of adults, the strengths and limitations of child witnesses are well known: Compared to adults, when the photo spread contains the perpetrator, children perform relatively well, but when the perpetrator is absent, children's lineup performance is "profoundly poorer" (Steblay et al., 2011, p. 110). These results make the use of lineups with young children a risky investigative strategy for identifying unknown per-petrators. A number of innovations designed to improve children's lineup performance have proved promising, but the reliability of these procedures has not been established to the point where they have been widely integrated into best practice guidelines for conducting eyewitness investigations. Moreover, lineup reforms that are effective with adults (e.g., sequential lineups and precautionary instructions) have not been found to significantly improve children's performance.

PRACTICE AND POLICY ISSUES

A fundamental conviction in medicine, education, and psychology is that practice should be informed by the best available research (Stuart & Lilienfeld, 2007). When professional activities involve children's testimony, the intersection of research and practice has four prongs: Expert practice (a) is informed by knowledge of human development, (b) analyzes how testimony is embedded in the context of children's lives, (c) bases decisions on the strength of case evidence, and (d) is guided by professional standards and evidence-based protocols.

Expert Practice Is Informed by Knowledge of Human Development

The tasks of eliciting and analyzing children's testimony require knowledge of language development, cognitive development more broadly, and specific topics that map onto case features (e.g., normative sexual behavior, the developmental trajectories of children with disabilities). Discussions of language development, which dominate the literature on children's testimony, explain an interesting feature of the forensic conversational style: Skilled professionals do not talk to child witnesses the way they talk to children in everyday life. Instead, the forensic style is a unique way of talking that is conceptually simple but "structured to make social and linguistic sense to children" (see Poole & Lamb, 1998, p. 153, for a review of the basic principles of talking to children).

To understand why professionals cannot rely on their natural language habits, consider one example of the difference between daily conversation and the forensic style. In most situations, it is typical to raise an issue, such as the name of a person, place, or action, and then to replace that word in subsequent utterances with a pointing word (e.g., a deictic), such as *he*, *there*, or *that*. The problem is that children do not always follow the intended meaning of these words (e.g., in questions such as "Where were you when *he* did *that*?"), especially when the question is asked many interchanges after the comment that defined the meaning of the pointing word (Walker, 1999). To help children connect thoughts across many interchanges, trained professionals repeat the topic often, use explicit transition comments when they change topics (e.g., "A few minutes ago you said that Joey took a bad picture of you. What happened?"), and avoid potentially ambiguous words.

Guidelines for talking to children also address the reasons adults sometimes misunderstand children's speech (and ways to avoid misunderstandings), how to select vocabulary and sentence structures that even young children understand, and ways to work around late-acquired concepts (e.g., how to narrow down the time of an event; Poole & Lamb, 1998). When analyzing transcripts, this knowledge helps professionals spot when children might have strayed off topic, when interviewers might have misunderstood something, and when inconsistent answers could have been due to how children interpreted or reacted to related questions that were worded differently.

Information about memory and social influence also shape best-practice guidelines. The idea that professionals should rely as much as possible on open-ended prompts is arguably the golden rule of forensic interviewing because these prompts encourage children to talk about what they remember best. Testimonial accuracy typically declines when interviewers request details that are not well-remembered, phrase questions in ways that allow children to respond by picking among a set of options (e.g., multiple choice questions) or implied options (yes–no questions), or allow young children to respond by pointing or manipulating objects (which is problematic for impulsive children; Poole & Bruck, 2012).

The way interviewers phrase questions has important implications for how children search their memories and respond. When children have alleged multiple instances of abuse, for example, interviewers try to elicit narratives about individual incidents to meet the needs of charging authorities and to provide defendants with opportunities to refute allegations. This can be difficult because, as mentioned earlier, children often confuse details that varied across repeated instances of similar events. Nevertheless, interviewers can help children separate incidents by giving them incident-specific cues (based on information the children previously mentioned; e.g., "Tell me about the day you forgot your towel at swimming"; Hudson et al., 1992). They can also use episodic prompts when episodic information is desired (e.g., "Tell me about *one time* when he touch*ed* you." versus "Tell me what *happens* when he touch*es* you."), which encourages children to respond with episodic rather than generic details (e.g., Brubacher, Roberts, & Powell, 2012; Schneider, Price, Roberts, & Hedrick, 2011). Nonsubstantive interview phases are also important: When interviewers give children practice in episodically describing neutral autobiographic events before moving on to substantive topics, the children's subsequent narratives include more episodic information compared to the narratives of children who practiced retrieving generic details prior to the substantive phase of the interview (see Roberts, Brubacher, Powell, & Price, 2011, for a review).

Some influences are subtle. For example, skilled interviewers tolerate pauses in conversation and turn conversation back to children with facilitators (comments such as "Umm hmm"), which keep children talking and reduce the need to deliver focused questions (Roberts & Duncanson, 2011). Interview transcripts usually lack detailed information about pauses, facilitators (which can be appropriate or inappropriate, as when interviewers comment only when children are offering specific types of information), and nonverbal behavior, and transcript content is not always entirely accurate. Therefore, it is best to listen to recordings (when these are available) rather than to rely solely on transcripts. Even an excellent

interview analysis is only part of the picture, though, because influences can shape children's testimony before they participate in investigations. Considering this context is the next principle of forensic work with children.

Forensic Analyses Embed Testimony in the Context of Children's Lives

When eyewitness experts agree to review a case, one of their first tasks is to review (or to construct) the case time line. A time line is a chronological record of events in the family's life (before and after an allegation emerged) that documents possible motivations and opportunities to influence reports. Time lines are useful for (a) tracking details of allegations across informants, time, and interviews; (b) developing alternative hypotheses about the origin of information in children's testimony (or in allegations brought forth by adults); and (c) suggesting what additional information would test these hypotheses. Placing children's testimony in context and engaging in hypothesis testing are the defining features of a forensic approach (Ceci & Bruck, 1995; see State of Michigan Governor's Task Force on Children's Justice and Department of Human Services, 2011, for examples of hypothesis testing during forensic interviews).

The analysis of children's testimony requires a contextual approach because interesting information is often in the details. Consider a sexual abuse case in which a young child used the word *hotdog* to refer to a penis. By itself, this comment seems developmentally appropriate, but your interpretation is different once you know that the term is not used in the child's household, that the child denied knowing that *hotdog* could refer to a penis in one interview, and that a neighbor—who initiated the sexual abuse allegation and has a history of abuse allegations—is the only adult in the child's world who uses this word.

Contextual information can cast doubt on a child's testimony (as in the *hotdog* example), help resolve misunderstandings, and counteract challenges to the reliability of a child's report. For example, suppose a child mentions a toy she does not own in a brief description of sexual contact. If this toy is at her day care center, an investigator's assumption that the child was reporting abuse in her home will need to be revisited. Time line information can also address defense challenges. For example, the fact that a girl's parents were reluctant to believe her allegation of abuse by a grandfather, and that they lost valued babysitting services as a result of the allegation, reduces the probability that they propagated her story.

Practice Decisions Consider the Strength of Evidence in a Case

The goal of an investigation is to collect information that reflects a child's experiences rather than memory errors or compliance with investigative techniques. The dilemma is that children usually do not provide all the information investigators need after a few open-ended questions, so decisions must be made about when to resort to techniques that are known to elevate rates of inaccurate information. The strength of evidence in the case should be part of these decisions.

Consider the decision to conduct multiple interviews. For cases in which adult influence and inconsistencies due to forgetting are not serious threats, there are reasons why multiple interviews can improve the quality of information obtained from child witnesses. An example at the beginning of this chapter illustrates one reason: Some children do not immediately disclose information that is potentially embarrassing (e.g., sexual abuse) or that could affect their current situation (e.g., removal of a parent from the home). Even when children do disclose in the first interview, the phenomenon of reminiscence makes it highly likely that they will report new information in a second interview (see La Rooy et al., 2010, for case examples of valuable information revealed in second interviews). Narratives also tend to be better organized in later interviews, producing more coherent accounts (Hershkowitz & Terner, 2007).

There are also practical reasons for allowing multiple interviews. Some situations are too complex to discuss in a single interview, ambiguities in children's responses may not be detected until after an initial interview is reviewed, and new evidence may arise subsequent to that interview. Finally, it can be difficult to cover needed topics in a single interview when witnesses have disabilities or or short attention spans.

On the other hand, investigative teams need to consider the risks and benefits of multiple interviews on a case-by-case basis because children's ages, their competencies as witnesses, and the delay between interviews can affect results. For example, a growing practice is the extended evaluation model, which is a multiple-session protocol for interviewing children who do not immediately verify suspicions of sexual abuse or may not be fully disclosing (Carnes, Nelson-Gardell, Wilson, & Orgassa, 2001; Carnes, Wilson, & Nelson-Gardell, 1999). Although this approach has safeguards to avoid undue influence by therapists, defense experts are receiving cases in which the concept was co-opted to justify extended quests for disclosures, using techniques that are known to produce unreliable reports, during which children were in contact with the caregivers who initiated the evaluations. Concerns about fidelity to the model illustrate the need for studies that describe how interventions are actually delivered once they have been widely distributed.

Among vulnerable groups, the risk that specific questions and props will elicit false information also increases when case evidence is weak. For example, children's tendency to point to someone in a lineup means that investigators should be cautious in their decisions to conduct lineups with child witnesses. One step investigators can take is to strengthen the evidentiary criteria (i.e., the quantity or quality of evidence) for placing a suspect in a lineup, which in turn will strengthen the prior probability that the suspect placed in the lineup is the perpetrator rather than an innocent suspect (Wells & Olson, 2003). In other words, when the decision to conduct a lineup is based on strong evidence, the probability that an innocent suspect will be identified decreases; when weak evidence forms the basis for conducting a lineup, then the probability increases. Given the lack of practical evidence-based recommendations for conducting lineups with children, and their propensity to choose even when the perpetrator is absent, police can lessen the risk of eliciting a false identification by tightening the evidentiary criteria used when deciding whether to conduct a lineup with a child witness.

Forensic Work Is Guided by Practice Standards and Evidence-Based Protocols

Gary Klein and Daniel Kahneman disagreed about the value of intuition: Klein had documented remarkable powers of intuition among highly-experienced professionals, whereas Kahneman consistently found that experts' predictions were flawed. In a rare example of an adversarial collaboration, the two joined forces to explore why data on the same issue produced such radically different conclusions. Together they asked, "When can you trust an experienced professional who claims to have an intuition?" (Kahneman, 2011, p. 235).

The answer seemed obvious in hindsight. The people Klein studied worked in environments that supported learning: (a) There were regularities in these environments (i.e., specific cues were associated with specific outcomes), (b) the tasks provided feedback, and (c) the individuals had sufficient practice to learn these regularities. For example, leaders of firefighting teams seemed to have a sixth sense about impending danger because a storehouse of knowledge told them what was likely to happen when certain conditions were present. Similarly, anesthesiologists can sense when patients are in danger because there are reliable signs of distress and quick feedback in the operating room corrects inaccurate impressions (Kahneman, 2011).

In contrast, some on-the-job experience lacks the characteristics that improve judgments over time. For example, psychologists who make custody recommendations (see Volume 1, Chapter 13, this handbook) may become increasingly confident in their decision strategies, but unless they randomly assign cases with certain characteristics to the various custody arrangements and track children's outcomes over time (which would be unethical to do outside an approved study), they would not have the needed information to correct flawed assumptions, i.e., knowledge of how individual children would have fared with a different custody arrangement (see Dawes, 1994). As Robin Hogarth (2001) explained, "We cannot learn from something that we cannot see" (p. 176).

It is difficult not to form quick impressions about the reliability of children's testimony, but judgment research helps explain why our initial beliefs may not always be accurate. For example, no amount of experience will help people distinguish coached lies from accurate reports on the basis of narratives alone if those narratives are not sufficiently different (that is, if the environment is not sufficiently regular; Warren, Dodd, Raynor, & Peterson, 2012). Even when useful indicators of truthfulness do exist, experience affords no advantage unless the work environment provides feedback about the percentage of true and false cases that have and do not have the indicator (that is, unless you know which cases are false). Practitioners overcome the limitations of their work environments by relying on knowledge gleaned from journal articles and workshops, but these sources only improve judgments when the information trained is accurate and directly relevant to the judgments being made.

When decision-making tasks involve child witnesses, the problem is clear: It is unrealistic to expect that every practitioner will supplement knowledge of their specialty area with extensive knowledge of human judgment and decision-making, child development (including neurological, cognitive, and socioemotional development), and the growing literature on children's eyewitness testimony. Two remedies help fill the gaps in individuals' knowledge: practice standards, which specify how people should conduct themselves within their professional roles, and interdisciplinary collaborations, which broaden the collective knowledge of professional teams.

One practice standard, which is embodied in ethics codes, states that people should practice within the bounds of their training and experience (e.g., American Psychological Association, 2010). In the child witness literature, this play-your-position recommendation has been augmented with the suggestion that individuals with relevant credentials should serve in either a therapeutic or a forensic role with a given child—but not both (Kuehnle & Connell, 2010).

Because different professionals bring different skill sets to the table, it is also useful to have policies that set basic expectations for various professional roles and for how professionals assuming these roles should cooperate. In the field of child protection, for instance, model investigative protocols help jurisdictions take a coordinated approach to protecting children (e.g., State of Michigan Governor's Task Force on Children's Justice and Department of Human Services, 1998).

Evidence-based protocols for specific professional tasks provide more detailed guidance. For example, interviewing protocols curtail natural but counterproductive behavior (such as not giving children time to think and asking mostly specific questions), offer suggestions for alternative approaches, address common weaknesses in interviews (for example, by modeling ways to develop and test alternative hypotheses about the origins of children's statements), and help professionals adapt procedures for children with special needs (see Poole & Dickinson, 2013).

Despite efforts to promote evidence-based practice, no formal mechanisms prevent individuals or groups from advocating procedures that have not been adequately tested, and—as we illustrated with the facilitated communication case at the beginning of this chapter—it can take decades for discredited techniques to fall out of practice. For these reasons, frequent consultation across disciplinary lines is a critical component of policy work and case management.

SUMMARY AND CONCLUSIONS

Throughout our lives, autobiographical memories are products of our mental schemas, the characteristics of events, and the social influences that surround events. Memory, however, does not always drive conversations: What we share and do not share is determined by our feelings, goals, and momentary perceptions of what behaviors will promote social harmony. In childhood as in adulthood, event reports are not intrinsically accurate or inevitably flawed; rather, they are dynamic products of a cognitive architecture interacting with a social world.

What happens when children's architecture meets the world is strikingly counterintuitive. Few developmental psychologists would have predicted the average age of earliest memories from the children in one study (a testimony to their remarkable

abilities; Tustin & Hayne, 2010) or the ease with which some 11- and 12-year-olds came to believe they were abducted by aliens in another (illustrating the malleability of memory throughout childhood; Otgaar et al., 2009). Examples such as these reinforce the central conclusion from research on children's eyewitness testimony: There is a need for careful analyses to situate children's reports in the contexts of their lives.

References

Ahern, E. C., Lyon, T. D., & Quas, J. A. (2011). Young children's emerging ability to make false statements. *Developmental Psychology, 47,* 61–66. doi:10.1037/a0021272

American Psychological Association. (2010). *Ethical principles of psychologists and code of conduct (2002, Amended June 1, 2010).* Retrieved from http://www.apa.org/ethics/code/index.aspx

Ames, L. B., & Ilg, F. (1979). *Your six-year-old.* New York, NY: Dell.

Besnard, J., Allain, P., Aubin, G., Chauviré, V., Etcharry-Bouyx, F., & Le Gall, D. (2011). A contribution to the study of environmental dependency phenomena: The social hypothesis. *Neuropsychologia, 49,* 3279–3294. doi:10.1016/j.neuropsychologia.2011.08.001

Brainerd, C. J., & Poole, D. A. (1997). Long-term survival of children's false memories: A review. *Learning and Individual Differences, 9,* 125–151. doi:10.1016/S1041-6080(97)90003-0

Brainerd, C. J., & Reyna, V. F. (1990). Gist is the grist: Fuzzy-trace theory and the new intuitionism. *Developmental Review, 10,* 3–47. doi:10.1016/0273-2297(90)90003-M

Brainerd, C. J., & Reyna, V. F. (2004). Fuzzy-trace theory and memory development. *Developmental Review, 24,* 396–439. doi:10.1016/j.dr.2004.08.005

Brainerd, C. J., & Reyna, V. F. (2012). Reliability of children's testimony in the era of developmental reversals. *Developmental Review, 32,* 224–267. doi:10.1016/j.dr.2012.06.008

Brasier, L. L., & Wisely, J. (2011, June 12). Family's life unravels with claims dad raped daughter. *Detroit Free Press.* Retrieved from http://www.freep.com/article/20110612/NEWS03/106120522/Family-s-life-unravels-claims-dad-raped-daughter

Brown, D. A., Lewis, C. N., & Lamb, M. (2012). The influences of delay and severity of intellectual disability on event memory in children. *Journal of Consulting and Clinical Psychology, 80,* 829–841. doi:10.1037/a0029388

Brubacher, S. P., Roberts, K. P., & Powell, M. B. (2011). Effects of practicing episodic versus scripted recall on children's subsequent narratives of a repeated event. *Psychology, Public Policy, and Law, 17,* 286–314. doi:10.1037/a0022793

Brubacher, S. P., Roberts, K. P., & Powell, M. (2012). Retrieval of episodic versus generic information: Does the order of recall affect the amount and accuracy of details reported by children about repeated events? *Developmental Psychology, 48,* 111–122. doi:10.1037/a0025864

Bruck, M. (2009). Human figure drawings and children's recall of touching. *Journal of Experimental Psychology: Applied, 15,* 361–374. doi:10.1037/a0017120

Bunge, S. A., & Crone, E. A. (2009). Neural correlates of the development of cognitive control. In J. Rumsey & M. Ernst (Eds.), *Neuroimaging in developmental clinical neuroscience* (pp. 22–37). New York, NY: Cambridge University Press. doi:10.1017/CBO9780511757402.005

Burianova, H., McIntosh, A. R., & Grady, C. L. (2010). A common functional brain network for autobiographical, episodic, and semantic memory retrieval. *NeuroImage, 49,* 865–874. doi:10.1016/j.neuroimage.2009.08.066

Cabeza, R., Kapur, S., Craik, F. I. M., McIntosh, A. R., Houle, S., & Tulving, E. (1997). Functional neuroanatomy of recall and recognition: A PET study of episodic memory. *Journal of Cognitive Neuroscience, 9,* 254–265. doi:10.1162/jocn.1997.9.2.254

Carnes, C. N., Nelson-Gardell, D., Wilson, C., & Orgassa, U. C. (2001). Extended forensic evaluation when sexual abuse is suspected: A multisite field study. *Child Maltreatment, 6,* 230–242. doi:10.1177/1077559501006003004

Carnes, C. N., Wilson, C., & Nelson-Gardell, D. (1999). Extended forensic evaluation when sexual abuse is suspected: A model and preliminary data. *Child Maltreatment, 4,* 242–254. doi:10.1177/1077559599004003005

Cassel, W. S., Roebers, C. E. M., & Bjorklund, D. F. (1996). Developmental patterns of eyewitness responses to repeated and increasingly suggestive questions. *Journal of Experimental Child Psychology, 61,* 116–133. doi:10.1006/jecp.1996.0008

Ceci, S. J., & Bruck, M. (1995). *Jeopardy in the courtroom: A scientific analysis of children's testimony.* Washington, DC: American Psychological Association. doi:10.1037/10180-000

Ceci, S. J., Huffman, M. L. C., Smith, E., & Loftus, E. F. (1994). Repeatedly thinking about a non-event: Source misattributions among preschool-ers. *Consciousness and Cognition, 3,* 388–407. doi:10.1006/ccog.1994.1022

Ceci, S. J., Kulkofsky, S., Klemfuss, J. Z., Sweeney, C. D., & Bruck, M. (2007). Unwarranted assumptions about children's testimonial accuracy. *Annual Review of Clinical Psychology, 3,* 311–328. doi:10.1146/annurev.clinpsy.3.022806.091354

Ceci, S. J., Loftus, E. F., Leichtman, M. D., & Bruck, M. (1994). The possible role of source misattributions in the creation of false beliefs among preschoolers. *International Journal of Clinical and Experimental Hypnosis, 42,* 304–320. doi:10.1080/00207149408409361

Davies, G., & Noon, E. (1991). *An evaluation of the live-link for child witnesses.* London, England: Home Office.

Dawes, R. M. (1994). *House of cards: Psychology and psychotherapy built on myth.* New York, NY: The Free Press.

Drummey, A. B., & Newcombe, N. S. (2002). Developmental changes in source memory. *Developmental Science, 5,* 502–513. doi:10.1111/1467-7687.00243

Farrar, M. J., & Goodman, G. S. (1990). Developmental differences in the relation between scripts and episodic memory: Do they exist? In R. Fivush & J. A. Hudson (Eds.), *Knowing and remembering in young children* (pp. 30–64). New York, NY: Cambridge University Press.

Fivush, R., Reese, E., & Haden, C. A. (2006). Elaborating on elaborations: Role of maternal reminiscing style in cognitive and socioemotional development. *Child Development, 77,* 1568–1588. doi:10.1111/j.1467-8624.2006.00960.x

Frenda, S. J., Nichols, R. M., & Loftus, E. F. (2011). Current issues and advances in misinformation research. *Current Directions in Psychological Science, 20,* 20–23. doi:10.1177/0963721410396620

Garven, S., Wood, J. M., Malpass, R. S., & Shaw, J. S., III. (1998). More than suggestion: The effect of interviewing techniques from the McMartin Preschool case. *Journal of Applied Psychology, 83,* 347–359. doi:10.1037/0021-9010.83.3.347

Ghetti, S., & Angelini, L. (2008). The development of recollection and familiarity in childhood and adolescence: Evidence from the dual-process signal detection model. *Child Development, 79,* 339–358. doi:10.1111/j.1467-8624.2007.01129.x

Ghetti, S., & Bunge, S. A. (2012). Neural changes underlying the development of episodic memory during middle childhood. *Developmental Cognitive Neuroscience, 2,* 381–395. doi:10.1016/j.dcn.2012.05.002

Ghetti, S., Lyons, K. E., Lazzarin, F., & Cornoldi, C. (2008). The development of metamemory monitoring during retrieval: The case of memory strength and memory absence. *Journal of Experimental Child Psychology, 99,* 157–181. doi:10.1016/j.jecp.2007.11.001

Gilbert, J. A. E., & Fisher, R. P. (2006). The effects of varied retrieval cues on reminiscence in eyewitness memory. *Applied Cognitive Psychology, 20,* 723–739. doi:10.1002/acp.1232

Goodman, G. S., & Quas, J. A. (2008). Repeated interviews and children's memory: It's more than just how many. *Current Directions in Psychological Science, 17,* 386–390. doi:10.1111/j.1467-8721.2008.00611.x

Goodman, G. S., Quas, J. A., Batterman-Faunce, J. M., Riddlesberger, M. M., & Kuhn, J. (1997). Children's reactions to and memory for a stressful event: Influences of age, anatomical dolls, knowledge, and parental attachment. *Applied Developmental Science, 1,* 54–75. doi:10.1207/s1532480xads0102_1

Gruber, T., Tsivilis, D., Giabbiconi, C.-M., & Müller, M. M. (2008). Induced electroencephalogram oscillations during source memory: Familiarity is reflected in the gamma band, recollection in the theta band. *Journal of Cognitive Neuroscience, 20,* 1043–1053. doi:10.1162/jocn.2008.20068

Hershkowitz, I. (2001). A case study of child sexual false allegation. *Child Abuse and Neglect, 25,* 1397–1411. doi:10.1016/S0145-2134(01)00274-5

Hershkowitz, I., & Terner, A. (2007). The effects of repeated interviewing on children's forensic statements of sexual abuse. *Applied Cognitive Psychology, 21,* 1131–1143. doi:10.1002/acp.1319

Hogarth, R. M. (2001). *Educating intuition.* Chicago, IL: University of Chicago Press.

Howe, M. L. (1997). Children's memory for traumatic experiences. *Learning and Individual Differences, 9,* 153–174. doi:10.1016/S1041-6080(97)90004-2

Howe, M. L., Goodman, G. S., & Cicchetti, D. (2008). *Stress, trauma, and children's memory development: Neurobiological, cognitive, clinical, and legal perspectives.* New York, NY: Oxford University Press. doi:10.1093/acprof:oso/9780195308457.001.0001

Hudson, J. A., Fivush, R., & Kuebli, J. (1992). Scripts and episodes: The development of event memory. *Applied Cognitive Psychology, 6,* 483–505. doi:10.1002/acp.2350060604

Hünefeldt, T., Lucidi, A., Furia, A., & Rossi-Arnaud, C. (2008). Age differences in the interrogative suggestibility of children's memory: Do shift scores peak around 5-6 years of age? *Personality and Individual Differences, 45,* 521–526. doi:10.1016/j.paid.2008.06.005

Jack, F., Simcock, G., & Hayne, H. (2012). Magic memories: Young children's verbal recall after a 6-year delay. *Child Development, 83,* 159–172. doi:10.1111/j.1467-8624.2011.01699.x

Johnson, M. K., Hashtroudi, S., & Lindsay, D. S. (1993). Source monitoring. *Psychological Bulletin, 114,* 3–28. doi:10.1037/0033-2909.114.1.3

Kahneman, D. (2011). *Thinking, fast and slow.* New York, NY: Farrar, Straus, & Giroux.

Karageorge, A., & Zajac, R. (2011). Exploring the effects of age and delay on children's person identifications: Verbal descriptions, lineup performance, and the influence of wildcards. *British Journal of Psychology, 102,* 161–183. doi:10.1348/000712610X507902

Klinnert, M. D., Emde, R. N., Butterfield, P., & Campos, J. J. (1986). Social referencing: The infant's use of emotional signals from a friendly adult with mother present. *Developmental Psychology, 22,* 427–432. doi:10.1037/0012-1649.22.4.427

Kuehnle, K., & Connell, M. (2010). Child sexual abuse suspicions: Treatment considerations during investigation. *Journal of Child Sexual Abuse, 19,* 554–571. doi:10.1080/10538712.2010.512554

La Rooy, D., Katz, C., Malloy, L. C., & Lamb, M. E. (2010). Do we need to rethink guidance on repeated interviews? *Psychology, Public Policy, and Law, 16,* 373–392. doi:10.1037/a0019909

Laimon, R. L., & Poole, D. A. (2008). Adults usually believe young children: The influence of eliciting questions and suggestibility presentations on perceptions of children's disclosures. *Law and Human Behavior, 32,* 489–501. doi:10.1007/s10979-008-9127-y

Leichtman, M. D., & Ceci, S. J. (1995). The effects of stereotypes and suggestions on preschoolers' reports. *Developmental Psychology, 31,* 568–578. doi:10.1037/0012-1649.31.4.568

Lindsay, R. C. L., & Wells, G. L. (1985). Improving eyewitness identifications from lineups: Simultaneous versus sequential lineup presentation. *Journal of Applied Psychology, 70,* 556–564. doi:10.1037/0021-9010.70.3.556

London, K., Bruck, M., & Melnyk, L. (2009). Post-event misinformation affects children's autobiographical memory after one year. *Law and Human Behavior, 33,* 344–355. doi:10.1007/s10979-008-9147-7

London, K., Bruck, M., Poole, D. A., & Melnyk, L. (2011). The development of metasuggestibility in children. *Applied Cognitive Psychology, 25,* 146–155. doi:10.1002/acp.1653

Luna, B., Padmanabhan, A., & O'Hearn, K. (2010). What has fMRI told us about the development of cognitive control through adolescence? *Brain and Cognition, 72,* 101–113. doi:10.1016/j.bandc.2009.08.005

Malloy, L. C., Brubacher, S. P., & Lamb, M. E. (2011). Expected consequences of disclosure revealed in investigative interviews with suspected victims of child sexual abuse. *Applied Developmental Science, 15*, 8–19. doi:10.1080/10888691.2011.538616

Mather, M., Mitchell, K. J., Raye, C. L., Novak, D. L., Greene, E. J., & Johnson, M. K. (2006). Emotional arousal can impair feature binding in working memory. *Journal of Cognitive Neuroscience, 18*, 614–625. doi:10.1162/jocn.2006.18.4.614

McGough, L. S. (1994). *Child witnesses: Fragile voices in the American legal system.* New Haven, CT: Yale University Press.

McNamara, P., & Durso, R. (2003). Pragmatic communication skills in patients with Parkinson's disease. *Brain and Language, 84*, 414–423. doi:10.1016/S0093-934X(02)00558-8

Melinder, A., Alexander, K., Cho, Y. I., Goodman, G. S., Thorensen, C., Lonnum, K., & Magnussen, S. (2010). Children's eyewitness memory: A comparison of two interviewing strategies as realized by forensic professionals. *Journal of Experimental Child Psychology, 105*, 156–177. doi:10.1016/j.jecp.2009.04.004

Miller, G. (2012). How are memories retrieved? *Science, 338*, 30–31. doi:10.1126/science.338.6103.30-b

Nelson, K. (Ed.). (1986). *Event knowledge: Structure and function in development.* Hillsdale, NJ: Erlbaum.

Nelson, K., & Gruendel, J. (1981). Generalized event representations: Basic building blocks of cognitive development. In M. E. Lamb & A. L. Brown (Eds.), *Advances in developmental psychology* (Vol. 1, pp. 131–158). Hillsdale, NJ: Erlbaum.

Newcombe, N. S., Lloyd, M. E., & Ratliff, K. R. (2007). Development of episodic and autobiographical memory: A cognitive neuroscience perspective. In N. S. Newcombe, M. E. Lloyd, & K. R. Ratliff (Eds.), *Advances in child development and behavior* (Vol. 35, pp. 37–85). San Diego, CA: Elsevier Academic Press. doi:10.1016/B978-0-12-009735-7.50007-4

Orbach, Y., Hershkowitz, I., Lamb, M. E., Esplin, P. W., & Horowitz, D. (2000). Assessing the value of structured protocols for forensic interviews of alleged child abuse victims. *Child Abuse and Neglect, 24*, 733–752. doi:10.1016/S0145-2134(00)00137-X

Orbach, Y., Shiloach, H., & Lamb, M. E. (2007). Reluctant disclosers of child sexual abuse. In Y. Orbach, H. Shiloach, & M. E. Lamb (Eds.), *Child sexual abuse: Disclosure, delay, and denial* (pp. 115–134). Mahwah, NJ: Erlbaum.

Ost, J., Granhag, P. A., Udell, J., & Roos af Hjelmsäter, E. (2008). Familiarity breeds distortion: The effects of media exposure on false reports concerning media coverage of the terrorist attacks in London on 7 July 2005. *Memory, 16*, 76–85. doi:10.1080/09658210701723323

Otgaar, H., Candel, I., Merckelbach, H., & Wade, K. A. (2009). Abducted by a UFO: Prevalence information affects young children's false memories for an implausible event. *Applied Cognitive Psychology, 23*, 115–125. doi:10.1002/acp.1445

Otgaar, H., Verschuere, B., Meijer, E. H., & Oorsouw, K. (2012). The origin of children's implanted false memories: Memory traces or compliance? *Acta Psychologica, 139*, 397–403. doi:10.1016/j.actpsy.2012.01.002

Peterson, C. (2002). Children's long-term memory for autobiographical events. *Developmental Review, 22*, 370–402. doi:10.1016/S0273-2297(02)00007-2

Peterson, C. (2010). "And I was very very crying": Children's self-descriptions of distress as predictors of recall. *Applied Cognitive Psychology, 24*, 909–924. doi:10.1002/acp.1636

Peterson, C. (2011). Children's memory reports over time: Getting both better and worse. *Journal of Experimental Child Psychology, 109*, 275–293. doi:10.1016/j.jecp.2011.01.009

Peterson, C. (2012). Children's autobiographical memories across the years: Forensic implications of childhood amnesia and eyewitness memory for stressful events. *Developmental Review, 32*, 287–306. doi:10.1016/j.dr.2012.06.002

Peterson, C., & Bell, M. (1996). Children's memory for traumatic injury. *Child Development, 67*, 3045–3070. doi:10.2307/1131766

Peterson, C., Sales, J. M., Rees, M., & Fivush, R. (2007). Parent-child talk and children's memory for stressful events. *Applied Cognitive Psychology, 21*, 1057–1075. doi:10.1002/acp.1314

Peterson, C., Warren, K. L., & Short, M. M. (2011). Infantile amnesia across the years: A 2-year follow-up of children's earliest memories. *Child Development, 82*, 1092–1105. doi:10.1111/j.1467-8624.2011.01597.x

Pezdek, K., Finger, K., & Hodge, D. (1997). Planting false childhood memories: The role of event plausibility. *Psychological Science, 8*, 437–441. doi:10.1111/j.1467-9280.1997.tb00457.x

Poole, D., Warren, A., & Nunez, N. (2007). *The story of human development.* Upper Saddle River, NJ: Prentice-Hall.

Poole, D. A., & Bruck, M. (2012). Divining testimony? The impact of interviewing props on children's reports of touching. *Developmental Review, 32*, 165–180. doi:10.1016/j.dr.2012.06.007

Poole, D. A., Bruck, M., & Pipe, M.-E. (2011). Forensic interviewing aids: Do props help children answer questions about touching? *Current Directions in Psychological Science, 20*, 11–15. doi:10.1177/0963721410388804

Poole, D. A., & Dickinson, J. J. (2011). Evidence supporting restrictions on uses of body diagrams in forensic interviews. *Child Abuse and Neglect*, 35, 659–669. doi:10.1016/j.chiabu.2011.05.004

Poole, D. A., & Dickinson, J. J. (2013). Investigative interviews of children. In R. Holliday & T. Marche (Eds.), *Child forensic psychology* (pp. 157–178). Houndmills, England: Palgrave Macmillan.

Poole, D. A., & Lamb, M. (1998). *Investigative interviews of children: A guide for helping professionals*. Washington, DC: American Psychological Association. doi:10.1037/10301-000

Poole, D. A., & Lindsay, D. S. (2001). Children's eyewitness reports after exposure to misinformation from parents. *Journal of Experimental Psychology: Applied*, 7, 27–50. doi:10.1037/1076-898X.7.1.27

Poole, D. A., & Lindsay, D. S. (2002). Reducing child witnesses' false reports of misinformation from parents. *Journal of Experimental Child Psychology*, 81, 117–140. doi:10.1006/jecp.2001.2648

Poole, D. A., & White, L. T. (1993). Two years later: Effect of question repetition and retention interval on the eyewitness testimony of children and adults. *Developmental Psychology*, 29, 844–853. doi:10.1037/0012-1649.29.5.844

Poole, D. A., & White, L. T. (1995). Tell me again and again: Stability and change in the repeated testimonies of children and adults. In M. S. Zaragoza, J. R. Graham, G. C. N. Hall, R. Hirschman, & Y. S. Ben-Porath (Eds.), *Memory and testimony in the child witness* (pp. 24–43). Thousand Oaks, CA: Sage.

Poole, D. A., & Wolfe, M. A. (2009). Child development: Normative sexual and non-sexual behaviors that may be confused with symptoms of sexual abuse. In K. Kuehnle & M. Connell (Eds.), *The evaluation of child sexual abuse allegations: A comprehensive guide to assessment and testimony* (pp. 101–128). Hoboken, NJ: Wiley.

Powell, M. B., Roberts, K. P., Ceci, S. J., & Hembrooke, H. (1999). The effects of repeated experience on children's suggestibility. *Developmental Psychology*, 35, 1462–1477. doi:10.1037/0012-1649.35.6.1462

Pozzulo, J. D. (2007). Person description and identification by child witnesses. In R. C. L. Lindsay, D. F. Ross, J. D. Read, & M. P. Toglia (Eds.), *Handbook of eyewitness psychology: Memory for people* (Vol. 2, pp. 283–307). East Sussex, England: Psychology Press.

Pozzulo, J. D. (2013). Child eyewitness person descriptions and lineup identifications. In R. Holliday and T. Marche (Eds.), *Child forensic psychology* (pp. 209–240). Houndmills, England: Palgrave Macmillan.

Pozzulo, J. D., Dempsey, J., & Crescini, C. (2009). Preschoolers' person description and identification accuracy: A comparison of the simultaneous and elimination lineup procedures. *Journal of Applied Developmental Psychology*, 30, 667–676. doi:10.1016/j.appdev.2009.01.004

Pozzulo, J. D., & Lindsay, R. C. L. (1998). Identification accuracy of children versus adults: A meta-analysis. *Law and Human Behavior*, 22, 549–570. doi:10.1023/A:1025739514042

Pozzulo, J. D., & Lindsay, R. C. L. (1999). Elimination lineups: An improved identification procedure for child eyewitnesses. *Journal of Applied Psychology*, 84, 167–176. doi:10.1037/0021-9010.84.2.167

Pozzulo, J. D., & Warren, K. L. (2003). Descriptions and identifications of strangers by youth and adult witnesses. *Journal of Applied Psychology*, 88, 315–323. doi:10.1037/0021-9010.88.2.315

Principe, G. F., DiPuppo, J., & Gammel, J. (2012). *Leaking misinformation to mothers: Effects of maternal style of children's suggestibility for a past event.* Manuscript submitted for publication.

Principe, G. F., Greenhoot, A. F., & Ceci, S. J. (2014). Young children's eyewitness memory. In T. J. Perfect & D. S. Lindsay (Eds.), *The Sage handbook of applied memory* (pp. 633–653). Thousand Oaks, CA: Sage.

Principe, G. F., & Schindewolf, E. (2012). Natural conversations as a source of false memories in children: Implications for the testimony of young witnesses. *Developmental Review*, 32, 205–223. doi:10.1016/j.dr.2012.06.003

Raj, V., & Bell, M. A. (2010). Cognitive processes supporting episodic memory formation in childhood: The role of source memory, binding, and executive functioning. *Developmental Review*, 30, 384–402. doi:10.1016/j.dr.2011.02.001

Richmond, J., & Nelson, C. A. (2007). Accounting for change in declarative memory: A cognitive neuroscience perspective. *Developmental Review*, 27, 349–373. doi:10.1016/j.dr.2007.04.002

Roberts, K., & Duncanson, S. (2011, March). *Enhancing children's testimony with the facilitative interview technique.* Paper presented at the meeting of the American Psychology-Law Society, Miami, FL.

Roberts, K. P. (2002). Children's ability to distinguish between memories from multiple sources: Implications for the quality and accuracy of eyewitness statements. *Developmental Review*, 22, 403–435. doi:10.1016/S0273-2297(02)00005-9

Roberts, K. P., Brubacher, S. P., Powell, M. B., & Price, H. L. (2011). Practice narratives. In M. E. Lamb, D. J. La Rooy, L. C. Malloy, & C. Katz (Eds.), *Children's testimony: A handbook of psychological research and forensic practice* (pp. 129–145). Chichester, England: Wiley. doi:10.1002/9781119998495.ch7

Roberts, K. P., & Powell, M. B. (2001). Describing individual incidents of sexual abuse: A review of research on the effects of multiple sources of information on children's reports. *Child Abuse and Neglect, 25,* 1643–1659. doi:10.1016/S0145-2134(01)00290-3

Ruffman, T., Rustin, C., Garnham, W., & Parkin, A. J. (2001). Source monitoring and false memories in children: Relation to certainty and executive functioning. *Journal of Experimental Child Psychology, 80,* 95–111. doi:10.1006/jecp.2001.2632

Salmon, K., & Pipe, M.-E. (1997). Props and children's event reports: The impact of a 1-year delay. *Journal of Experimental Child Psychology, 65,* 261–292. doi:10.1006/jecp.1996.2362

Saywitz, K. J., Goodman, G. S., Nicholas, E., & Moan, S. F. (1991). Children's memories of a physical examination involving genital touch: Implications for reports of child sexual abuse. *Journal of Consulting and Clinical Psychology, 59,* 682–691. doi:10.1037/0022-006X.59.5.682

Schacter, D. L., Curran, T., Galluccio, L., Milberg, W. P., & Bates, J. F. (1996). False recognition and the right frontal lobe: A case study. *Neuropsychologia, 34,* 793–808. doi:10.1016/0028-3932(95)00165-4

Schacter, D. L., Kagan, J., & Leichtman, M. D. (1995). True and false memories in children and adults: A cognitive neuroscience perspective. *Psychology, Public Policy, and Law, 1,* 411–428. doi:10.1037/1076-8971.1.2.411

Schneider, L., Price, H. L., Roberts, K. P., & Hedrick, A. M. (2011). Children's episodic and generic reports of alleged abuse. *Applied Cognitive Psychology, 25,* 862–870. doi:10.1002/acp.1759

State of Michigan Governor's Task Force on Children's Justice and Department of Human Services. (1998). *A model child abuse protocol: Coordinated investigative team approach.* Retrieved from http://www.michigan.gov/documents/dhs/DHS-Pub-794_206830_7.pdf

State of Michigan Governor's Task Force on Children's Justice and Department of Human Services. (2011). *Forensic interviewing protocol.* Retrieved from http://www.mi.gov/documents/dhs/DHS-PUB-0779_211637_7.pdf

Steblay, N., Dysart, J., Fulero, S., & Lindsay, R. C. L. (2001). Eyewitness accuracy rates in sequential and simultaneous lineup presentations: A meta-analytic comparison. *Law and Human Behavior, 25,* 459–473. doi:10.1023/A:1012888715007

Steblay, N. K., Dysart, J. E., & Wells, G. L. (2011). Seventy-two tests of the sequential lineups superiority effect: A meta-analysis and policy discussion. *Psychology, Public Policy, and Law, 17,* 99–139. doi:10.1037/a0021650

Stein, N. L. (2002). Memories for emotional, stressful, and traumatic events. In N. L. Stein, P. J. Bauer, M. Rabinowitz, & G. Mandler (Eds.), *Representation, memory, and development: Essays in honor of Jean Mandler* (pp. 247–265). Mahwah, NJ: Erlbaum.

Steward, M. S., & Steward, D. S. (with L. Farquhar, J. E. B. Myers, M. Reinhart, J. Welker, N. Joye, J. Driskill, & J. Morgan). (1996). Interviewing young children about body touch and handling. *Monograph of the Society for Research in Child Development, 61,* 4–5 (Serial No. 248).

Stouthamer-Loeber, M. (1986). Lying as a problem behavior in children: A review. *Clinical Psychology Review, 6,* 267–289. doi:10.1016/0272-7358(86)90002-4

Strange, D., Sutherland, R., & Garry, M. (2006). Event plausibility does not determine children's false memories. *Memory, 14,* 937–951. doi:10.1080/09658210600896105

Stuart, R. B., & Lilienfeld, S. O. (2007). The evidence missing from evidence-based practice. *American Psychologist, 62,* 615–616. doi:10.1037/0003-066X62.6.615

Technical Working Group for Eyewitness Evidence. (1999). *Eyewitness evidence: A guide for law enforcement* [Booklet]. Washington, DC: U.S. Department of Justice, Office of Justice Programs, National Institute of Justice.

Templeton, L. M., & Wilcox, S. A. (2000). A tale of two representations: The misinformation effect and children's developing theory of mind. *Child Development, 71,* 402–416. doi:10.1111/1467-8624.00153

Tustin, K., & Hayne, H. (2010). Defining the boundary: Age-related changes in childhood amnesia. *Developmental Psychology, 46,* 1049–1061. doi:10.1037/a0020105

U.S. Department of Health and Human Services. (2011). *Child maltreatment, 2010.* Retrieved from http://archive.acf.hhs.gov/programs/cb/pubs/cm10/cm10.pdf

U.S. Department of Justice, Bureau of Justice Statistics. (2012). *Intimate partner violence.* Retrieved from http://bjs.ojp.usdoj.gov/index.cfm?ty=tp&tid=971

Walker, A. G. (1999). *Handbook on questioning children: A linguistic perspective* (2nd ed.). Washington, DC: American Bar Association Center on Children and the Law.

Wallin, A. R., Quas, J. A., & Yim, I. S. (2009). Physiological stress responses and children's event memory. In J. A. Quas & R. Fivush (Eds.), *Emotion and memory in development: Biological, cognitive, and social considerations* (pp. 313–339). New York, NY: Oxford University Press. doi:10.1093/acprof:oso/9780195326932.003.0012

Wang, Q., Peterson, C., & Hou, Y. (2010). Children dating childhood memories. *Memory, 18*, 754–762. doi:10.1080/09658211.2010.508749

Warren, K. L., Dodd, E., Raynor, G., & Peterson, C. (2012). Detecting children's lies: Comparing true accounts about highly stressful injuries with unprepared, prepared, and coached lies. *Behavioral Sciences and the Law, 30*, 329–341. doi:10.1002/bsl.1994

Wells, G. L., & Olson, E. A. (2003). Eyewitness testimony. *Annual Review of Psychology, 54*, 277–295. doi:10.1146/annurev.psych.54.101601.145028

Wimmer, H., Hogrefe, G.-J., & Perner, J. (1988). Children's understanding of informational access as source of knowledge. *Child Development, 59*, 386–396. doi:10.2307/1130318

CHAPTER 2

JUVENILE OFFENDERS

Jennifer L. Woolard, Sarah Vidal, and Erika Fountain

Juvenile offenders are an important consideration in forensic psychology. This chapter begins with a description of relevant statistics about juvenile offending, which is followed by a review of the most relevant psychological theory, incorporating recent interdisciplinary developments on trajectories of juvenile offending. We then review the research, focusing on several key areas: risk and protective factors for offending at multiple ecological levels from neurobiological to contextual; offending trajectories, including onset, persistence, and desistance; and adolescents' decisional capacities in legal contexts, including competence to waive rights and effectiveness as defendants. We highlight the role of developmental science in recent U.S. Supreme Court decisions that affect juvenile culpability and punishment, and we discuss how developmental science, including neuroscience research of decision making, has and could inform policy and practice. We conclude by acknowledging the limited nature of the review and the promise of future research priorities.

IMPORTANCE OF THE PROBLEM

Although behavior by minors that could be classified as delinquent is a normative part of adolescence for many of the more than 74 million youth under age 18 (Howden & Meyer, 2011), a significant number are processed through one of the 50+ state juvenile justice systems. The FBI's Uniform Crime Reports documented over 910,000 arrests of youth under age 18 in 2012 (U.S. Department of Justice, 2012). The National Center for Juvenile Justice's Juvenile Court Statistics 2010 report (Puzzanchera & Hockenberry, 2013) provides the most comprehensive national compilation of data, and we report statistics from this report in this and the next paragraph. Over 1.3 million cases were processed through juvenile courts in 2010, consisting of 25% persons offenses, 37% property offenses, 12% drug offenses, and the remainder being various public order offenses. These numbers continue a steady decline in caseload, down 19% from 2001. Approximately half of all 2010 cases involved defendants under 16; about one quarter of the cases involved females, and about two thirds involved white youth. Although a higher absolute number of cases involved white youth compared to other groups, 87.6 African American youth per 1,000 were involved in a delinquency case, compared to 36.4 white youth per 1,000, 36.6 American Indian youth per 1,000, and 11.6 Asian youth per 1,000.

More than 80% of juvenile court cases are initiated by a referral from law enforcement. About one fifth of all cases involve some pretrial detention stay; of those, 90% were evenly distributed across person, property, and public order cases. More than half of all cases were petitioned, comparable to being charged in criminal court. Of petitioned cases, 58% were either adjudicated delinquent or waived to criminal court. Twenty-six percent of adjudicated cases resulted in out-of-home placement, but the majority of cases (61%) resulted in a sentence of some form of probation.

http://dx.doi.org/10.1037/14462-002
APA Handbook of Forensic Psychology: Vol. 2. Criminal Investigation, Adjudication, and Sentencing Outcomes,
B. L. Cutler and P. A. Zapf (Editors-in-Chief)

Copyright © 2015 by the American Psychological Association. All rights reserved.

Substantial numbers of youth experience arrest and juvenile court processing, either formal (petitioned) or informal (diversion or some voluntary services). From a developmental perspective, committing delinquent acts, whether sanctioned or not, plays a significant role in the adolescence of many youth. The effects on the youth reverberate through her family, community, and society. National fiscal impact is difficult to quantify, but state and local costs emphasize the impact of responding to juvenile offenders. New York City spent an estimated 251 million dollars on the juvenile justice system in 2008 (Wong & Spitzer, 2008).

The size of the juvenile offending problem is matched perhaps only by the sheer size of the research literature across disciplines devoted to the topic. Next we review the most relevant psychological theories of juvenile offending, and then we move to a discussion of this empirical research base.

RELEVANT PSYCHOLOGICAL THEORY AND PRINCIPLES

Entire volumes and research careers have developed theories on the causes of juvenile offending, making it difficult to summarize in a single chapter. Although psychology, sociology, and criminology are each disciplinary homes for the theoretical and empirical work undergirding this chapter, we prioritize psychology but recognize the interdisciplinary approaches that increasingly dominate the theoretical and empirical landscape of juvenile offending research. Risk and protection couched in ecological context form the heart of many contemporary interdisciplinary theories of offending.

In their review of adolescent development research, Steinberg and Morris (2001) identified four key factors driving the explosion of work on adolescent development, each of which also explains the growth of more specialized research on juvenile offending. These factors are the importance of an ecological theoretical framework that places adolescent development in its larger contexts (e.g., family, neighborhood, culture), the increasing opportunity to measure the biological bases of development, shifting research funding priorities away from basic research toward applied problems,

and the maturation of several longitudinal study samples from childhood into adolescence. In this review of theory we focus on theoretical contributions that examine the neuroscientific bases of brain and behavior, adolescent decision making and its legal contexts, and integrative and interdisciplinary theories of juvenile offending.

Several authors have proposed theories of decision making that emphasize the differential influence of psychosocial factors on adolescents compared to adults, specifically in decision contexts likely to result in justice system involvement, if not potentially harmful developmental outcomes. These theories emphasize the complementary and competing roles of cognitive and psychosocial development, arguing that their interaction is key to understanding and predicting adolescent decision making. These approaches are described in terms of culpability (i.e., blameworthiness for offending), competence (i.e., capacity to assert rights and perform effectively as defendants), and amenability (i.e., capacity to desist from offending). They provide a set of fundamental constructs thought to characterize adolescence in distinct ways from childhood and young adulthood.

Judgment and Decision Making

Judgment theory (Scott, Reppucci, & Woolard, 1995) identifies three components of normative adolescent development theory that are particularly important to understand how and why adolescents make poorer choices compared to adults—poorer choices that often bring about interaction with the justice system. These three factors—risk perception and preference, temporal perspective, and peer influence—predictably change during the course of adolescence and, according to Scott and colleagues, provide a developmental explanation for youths' delinquent behavior. They propose that adolescents are more sensitive to gains or rewards and discount both the likelihood and the extent of harm that might occur from losses. They predict that this calculus shifts as adolescents develop into young adults and consider loss potential to be more likely and more important in their decision making. Peer influence, known to increase in salience during the adolescent period, operates through social comparison and social conformity to influence risky behavior, particularly that which is labeled delinquent. Finally, adolescents are more likely than adults to focus on short-term rather than long-term consequences. Future-time perspective includes both the capacity to identify long- and short-term aspects, consequences, and implications of behaviors and decision options, as well as the capacity to integrate and value those long- and short-term consequences appropriately, i.e., in a way that optimizes outcomes or promotes positive developmental outcomes. These three factors lead to deficits or differences in adolescent decision making compared to adult decision making; these differences characterize adolescents as a class, and their influence predictably wanes for most teens as they mature into adulthood.

Building on the theory put forth by Scott, Reppucci, and Woolard, Steinberg and Cauffman (1996) frame the critical aspects of adolescent decision making and maturity of judgment somewhat differently. They identify responsibility, temperance, and perspective as the key psychosocial factors affecting adolescent judgment in a manner that is predictably different from the effect on adult decision making. The responsibility dimension incorporates an adolescent's growing sense of autonomy, particularly from parents, the need for increasing independence, and an emerging sense of identity. Temperance refers to several dimensions of risk or risk-taking, including sensation seeking, or the deliberate pursuit of intense experiences and activities. In a related, but not equivalent, manner, impulsivity and lack of consistent control also characterize this dimension. Finally, perspective refers both to the capacity to understand and view a situation from another person's perspective (self-contrast with another person) and to the capacity to identify and appreciate temporal differences (present versus future).

Several aspects of this maturity of judgment framework reference cognitive control, or the development and role of executive function in decision making and behavior. Executive function (EF) encompasses a constellation of "deliberate, top-down neurocognitive processes involved in the conscious, goal-directed control of thought, action, and emotion" (Zelazo & Carlson, 2012, p. 354). These processes include planning, self-regulating, attention, and goal selection, among others. EF processes are hypothesized to develop during adolescence and into adulthood, and to vary depending on context. Zelazo and Carlson (2012) describe a hypothesized classification of EF processes into "hot" and "cool" components. "Hot" components are active under conditions of high emotion and motivation, emphasizing affective inputs. "Cool" components include the cognitive processes without the affect-laden influences. Several authors suggest that decision contexts that explicitly involve risk, reward, and emotion are circumstances emphasizing the "hot" or affective aspects of EF, whereas decision contexts involving ambiguity and uncertainty, without risk, emphasize the "cool" or cognitive aspects of EF (e.g., Krain, Wilson, Arbuckle, Castellanos, & Milham, 2006; Zelazo & Carlson, 2012; Zelazo & Müller, 2007).

Social Neurocognitive Development

Advances in neuroscientific theory and methods have generated complementary theories that propose underlying neural mechanisms for theories of adolescent judgment and decision making. The scope of relevant literature on relevant brain bases of these behaviors is too wide to review here, but theories about adolescent brain development propose significant changes in both structure and function during this developmental period.

Steinberg (2010) describes the dual systems model of linking brain maturation and adolescent decision making as "the first new 'grand theory' of adolescence to be proposed in the last 50 years" (p. 162). At a general level, and complementing the models of maturity of judgment and executive function described above, the dual systems theory proposes that two brain systems, the cognitive control system and the socio-emotional system, develop on different timetables during adolescence. Models suggest that the regulatory systems, located primarily in the prefrontal cortex, develop on a different timetable than the areas of the brain implicated in affect regulation, including the limbic system (Sebastian, Viding, Williams, & Blakemore, 2010). The regulatory system is thought to involve the ventromedial and dorsolateral prefrontal cortex among others (Crone & Van Der Molen, 2007; Krain et al., 2006). Basic aspects of cognitive control include working memory and response inhibition (Geier & Luna, 2012). Response inhibition is the capacity to voluntarily suppress an irrelevant response that is primed or likely to occur in a given task or situation. The socio-emotional or affective system is predominantly located in the orbitofrontal cortex and is active during tasks involving risks and rewards, high motivation, and high emotion (Zelazo & Carlson, 2012).

Several models of social neurocognitive development describe underlying mechanisms for decision-making and judgment (Sebastian et al., 2010; Steinberg, 2010). Sebastian and colleagues describe two such models. The Social Information Processing Network Model focuses on the interaction of three neural *nodes* or systems: the detection node, the affective node, and the cognitive-regulatory node, each located in different parts of the brain. Each node processes different aspects of social information, and their developing integration across adolescence explain the emotional significance of stimuli. The subcortical/cortical developmental mismatch model theorizes that the increased salience of risk, reward, and peer influence results from the differential maturation of the cognitive and affective systems (Casey, Jones, & Hare, 2008). Perhaps in part due to pubertal development (Peper & Dahl, 2013; Steinberg, 2010), some researchers argue that affective systems mature early in adolescence, while the cognitive control system matures throughout adolescence. Thus, the brain structurally and functionally predisposes adolescents to have a heightened receptivity to affective information and contexts at a time when the regulatory systems remain immature. Banich and colleagues (2013) theorize that different neural systems drive the control (e.g., controlling behavior), valuation (e.g., affective features such as desirability), and prospect (e.g., capacity to imagine future outcomes) components of how we choose between immediate and delayed rewards. In keeping with other theories of adolescent development and difference, Banich et al. (2013) suggest that differences among individuals likely have an age, or developmental, component as well as an individual differences component.

Risk and Protective Factors for Offending Trajectories

Turning from a theoretical focus on the neurobiological, cognitive, and psychosocial components of adolescent decisions and behavior, next we briefly review ecological theories of crime and delinquency. The scope of theoretical work on causes of and responses to crime, even if limited to adolescents, is beyond the confines of this single chapter. Acknowledging the significant contributions of longstanding theories of crime, we focus here on recent theoretical advances that integrate sociological, criminological, and psychological causes and correlates of adolescent offending. The theoretical models of judgment and decision making reviewed in the previous section are not the only frameworks that integrate neuroscientific, cognitive, and psychosocial development to understand relevant aspects of adolescent behavior.

Derived in part from work on developmental psychopathology (e.g., O'Connor & Rutter, 1996; Rutter & Rutter, 1993), concepts of risk and protective factors inform many integrative theories of adolescent delinquency and crime. Although the specifics may vary, risks are generally defined as those factors, events, or characteristics that increase the likelihood of negative behaviors or outcomes (Guerra, Williams, Tolan, & Modecki, 2008). Risk factors can be either static (unchangeable) or dynamic (changeable or modifiable). Often but not exclusively defined as the opposite of risk, strengths-based or protective factors either decrease the likelihood of a negative behavior or alter a risk factor's effect (Guerra et al., 2008). A variety of contemporary theories can be described using a risk/protective factor framework as they focus on the variables or conditions that affect the likelihood of delinquent behavior. Each may have their factors of interest, but all recognize that delinquency is the result of multiple risk factors. Indeed, the theory of cumulative risk (G. W. Evans, Li, & Whipple, 2013; Rutter, 1981) indicates that risk is not simply a summation or count of factors. Rather, the accumulation of factors past a certain point may have multiplicative or exponential effects.

Ecological theories recognize that risk and protective factors occur and interact at multiple levels.

Theories of person–environment fit (e.g., Eccles et al., 1993) stress the bidirectional influence of person and context, predicting more positive outcomes when the expectations and needs of the individual fit the expectations and characteristics of the environments in which they operate. Other research has examined the influence of risk and protection across contexts, examining how different contexts (e.g., home and school) can interact to influence development (e.g., Steinberg & Morris, 2001). Different theories classify and categorize risk factors in different ways, but each generally adheres to characteristics of proximity, ecological level, and modifiability. Relative to the individual, a risk factor can be categorized as proximal, defined as nearby, close, or immediate. Factors can also be classified as distal, or more distant and removed from direct interaction or influence on the individual. Proximity can coincide with ecological level as well, with more proximal factors located in more immediate contexts of the individual youth (e.g., the microsystem level such as personal characteristics, home characteristics) and distal factors occurring at levels more removed from the youth (e.g., macrosystem level such as neighborhood characteristics). Risk factors can also be defined by their modifiability with risk markers, sometimes described as static factors, identifying increased risk but themselves not subject to change (e.g., male gender as increased risk for violent offending) and dynamic risk factors as potentially changeable and responsive to intervention (e.g., youth and parental attitudes, educational achievement, employment status).

Developmental life course theory combines a risk and protective factor framework with criminal career trajectory research. Guerra et al. (2008) describe five advantages of the developmental life course approach to juvenile offending: (1) includes dimensions beyond frequency, such as onset and desistance; (2) facilitates group identification using group-based trajectory modeling; (3) incorporates developmentally situated strengths as well as risk factors; (4) highlights bidirectional influence of person and context; and (5) respects the individual's influence on their subjective perspectives and realities. The focus on group trajectories shifts the emphasis from differences between individuals to modeling different paths of intraindividual change over time and the predictors of those different trajectories.

Moffitt's (1993) theory of adolescent-limited and life-course persistent offending delineates two general trajectories of adolescent offending, each with different causes and different implications for prevention and intervention. The adolescent-limited offender is what we might consider more "normative" delinquency in that onset typically coincides with puberty following a "normal" childhood development. Delinquent behavior among these youth results from a "maturity" gap between biological maturation and dependent social status. Youth mature physically and continue to mature psychosocially but remain in a societally prescribed dependent status, which fails to permit the autonomy that youth may feel their newly maturing status warrants or deserves. Delinquent behavior manifested during adolescence normatively desists as these youth mature into young adulthood with few long-term costs or consequences to development; however, "snares," such as criminal records, addictions, or other potential consequences of delinquency can delay the normal desistance and return to a nonoffending lifestyle.

For a smaller but more worrisome segment of adolescents, the life-course persistent offenders, the behavior trajectory starts with individual deficits combined with high-risk environments in early childhood. Intraindividual risks can include neuropsychological problems, cognitive limitations, or problems with temperament or behavior. These individual risks interact with environmental risks that include poor parenting or family bonds and poverty, among others, to produce a pathway of poor interpersonal relationships and personality problems through childhood into adolescence. Unlike the adolescent-limited offenders, life-course persistent offenders theoretically are not easily moved from a trajectory of consistent and persistent offending.

However, factors that contribute to offenders' desistance from crime are less well known. The age–crime curve is well recognized, with arrests peaking around age 18 and declining steeply thereafter. Theories originating from psychology, sociology, and criminology have taken different perspectives on how to identify what might play a pivotal role in distinguishing between those offenders who desist from criminal behavior and those who persist (Mulvey et al., 2004). Sampson and Laub (Laub, Nagin, & Sampson, 1998; Sampson & Laub, 2005) highlight the importance of social relationships in this process. In their theory, the development of a high-quality social relationship (e.g., through marriage) is conducive to making the transition out of antisocial behavior. Parenting styles (Hoeve et al., 2009), negative peer influence (Chung & Steinberg, 2006), and varied onset patterns (Moffitt, 1993), among others, have also been highlighted as important risk factors for adolescent antisocial behavior. In Gottfredson and Hirschi's (1990) opinion, the only explanation for the desistance of crime is aging itself. Through this theory, however, there is no clear explanation regarding what, specifically, about aging leads young adults away from criminal behavior and toward more prosocial behavior (Mulvey & Schubert, 2012; Mulvey et al., 2004).

RESEARCH REVIEW

We have many choices for a framework to review the research on juvenile offenders. One could take the juvenile justice system process as a sequence of decision points by, for, and about adolescent offenders. Another organizational option is mapping the relevant developmental psychology aspects, from cognitive to psychosocial to neurobiological, onto juvenile offending and processing. In this chapter we take a hybrid approach, using developmentally informed aspects of juvenile justice relevant to theory, policy, and practice. At the outset it is important to distinguish normative development (adolescents as a class or group distinct from children and adults) and nonnormative development that may more likely characterize youth at risk for, or who have engaged in, antisocial or delinquent behavior. We return to some of the findings of normative brain development in the section on judgment and decision making. Biological risk factors, including brain dysfunction, are reviewed in the section on risk, protection, and patterns of offending.

Then we review research on capacities for judgment and decision making in legally relevant contexts.

Structural and Functional Brain Development

Brain development during adolescence consists of changes that affect decision making, planning, and other executive functions. Developmental neuroscience findings parallel behavioral research evidence that highlights adolescent immaturity. Increasing evidence suggests that the brain continues to develop well into early adulthood, often until the mid-twenties. Relevant research on traumatic brain injury populations known for conduct-related disorders finds abnormalities in frontal and temporal regions, both in increased and reduced gray matter volume, compared to typically developing children (Portnoy et al., 2013). Specifically, studies have shown that structural changes to the prefrontal cortex, the brain area responsible for regulating executive cognitive function, occur beyond adolescence (Casey, Giedd, & Thomas, 2000; Sowell et al., 2003). During this time, white matter increases while gray matter volume decreases in the prefrontal cortex (Gogtay et al., 2004). These developmental changes are evidence of increased myelination and pruning that suggests prefrontal cortex functioning is becoming more efficient by strengthening primary neural connections and eliminating rarely used ones.

In addition to structural changes, functional connectivity changes during adolescence impact a variety of cognitive and psychosocial functions. Research with conduct-disordered youth and youth with callous-unemotional traits associated with psychopathy documents reduced amygdala activity and, in various task paradigms, reduced or impaired function in the orbitofrontal and ventromedial region, as well as the insula, hippocampus, and anterior and posterior cingulate (Portnoy et al., 2013), some of which subserve social cognition and mentalizing (Sebastian et al., 2010). Dopaminergic systems that change during this time are implicated in the research on risk taking and reward seeking (Wahlstrom, Collins, White, & Luciana, 2010). As we will see in the section on decision making, these developing systems interact with context to produce variation within adolescents as a group, in addition to between adolescents and adults (Steinberg, 2009).

Risk and Protective Factors for Offending Trajectories

Various approaches to identifying risk factors for offending have moved from consideration of global, general factors to focus on group- or pathway-specific factors that predict offending and offending patterns. Although terms such as trajectory, career, and pathway are sometimes used interchangeably, their meaning and operationalization varies across studies. Loeber et al. (2012) distinguish pathways as "orderly behavioral development between more than two problem behaviors" (p. 40), arguing that pathways focus on the idea of probabilistic behavior sequences. Developmental trajectories, they argue, describe groups of individuals with different behavioral patterns across time. These trajectories can, in turn, produce developmental types of delinquents (e.g., life-course persistent, early desister). As such, it is difficult to disentangle research on risk factors, pathways, and offending trajectories; in fact, volumes have focused on risk for persistent offending alone (e.g., Savage, 2009). Of the dominant theoretical frameworks reviewed in our earlier section, Moffitt's typology of adolescent-limited and life-course persistent offenders has garnered the most attention. We will use these broad typologies to highlight pathway-specific factors at multiple ecological levels (e.g., individual, situational, and contextual), integrating gender considerations throughout.

Persistent offenders. We describe the literature for various risk and protective factors, including biological, gender, family, and contextual factors.

Psychopathy. Although the question of whether personality disorders such as psychopathy can and should be diagnosed in adolescence remains in dispute (e.g., Seagrave & Grisso, 2002), research on the existence and predictive validity of psychopathic traits in adolescence has accelerated, including work on callous and unemotional traits and lack of empathy. Genetic studies of heritability in twins converge on a conclusion that heritability explains about half of the variance in psychopathic traits (Sylvers, Ryan, Alden, & Brennan, 2009). Several studies have demonstrated reasonable predictive validity of psychopathy assessments for behavior and conduct problems, aggression, juvenile offending, and adult offending. Lynam, Miller, Vachon, Loeber, and Stouthamer-Loeber (2009) investigated whether the psychopathy construct provided incremental validity above and beyond other established diagnoses and predictors of offending outcomes. Using data from the Pittsburgh Youth Study, they demonstrated that Childhood Psychopathy Scale scores at age 13 predicted arrests and convictions in adulthood, controlling for individual and family-level risk factors. In a meta-analysis of both published and unpublished studies, Olver, Stockdale, and Wormith (2009) found that the Level of Service Inventory, Psychopathy Checklist: Youth Version (PCL:YV), and Structured Assessment of Violence Risk in Youth (SAVRY) each successfully predicted general, violent, and nonviolent recidivism over an average 2.5-year postrelease time period during adolescence. F. Schmidt, Campbell, and Houlding (2011) compared the predictive validity of three adolescent psychopathy measures for 10-year recidivism rates in adulthood, finding that the Youth Level of Service/Case Management Inventory (YLS/CMI), SAVRY, and PCL:YV each successfully predicted recidivism but operated more effectively with male compared to female samples. Only the SAVRY demonstrated incremental validity as well.

Other biological factors. Although much of the theory on genetic and biological predictors of crime suggests that early insults to development create neuropsychological deficits that in turn predict crime, the empirical evidence is still mainly indirect with respect to linking these predictors to criminal and delinquent behavior (Sylvers et al., 2009). Even so, Sylvers et al. conclude that several factors predict early onset of conduct disorder and, indirectly, delinquent offending. These include pre- and perinatal factors such as prenatal stress brought on by a variety of maternal factors (e.g., stress, substance use), genetic markers, and neurobiological factors implicating executive function deficits.

Gender. Many of the risk factors associated with female delinquency are also related to male delinquency. The nature and correlates of delinquent behaviors, however, could be qualitatively different between male and female youth (Moretti, Odgers, & Jackson, 2004). Compared to their male counterparts, offending girls have complex needs that render their juvenile justice experience distinct and unique. For example, research shows that offending girls have higher rates and exhibit different mental health problems than offending boys (Antonishak, Reppucci, & Mulford, 2004) and their female community counterparts (Cauffman, Lexcen, Shulman, & Grisso, 2007). Offending girls are more likely to be diagnosed with posttraumatic stress disorder and depression than offending boys (Cauffman et al., 2007; Teplin, Abram, McClelland, Dulcan, & Mericle, 2002; Wasserman, McReynolds, Ko, Katz, & Carpenter, 2005). In addition, comorbidity of psychiatric disorders is also more common among offending girls than boys (Abram, Teplin, McClelland, & Dulcan, 2003). The high rates of mental health and psychological problems among offending girls may be an artifact of the high rates of victimization they experience—many of these girls have been victims of maltreatment and abuse (Maschi, Schwalbe, Morgen, Gibson, & Violette, 2009; Odgers, Robins, & Russell, 2010; Zahn et al., 2008).

Family. As Pagani (2009) emphasizes in her review, family risk factors include both static and dynamic components. She notes that family resources play a critical role, including physical and social capital available during childhood and adolescence. Greater risk for antisocial behavior (again overlapping with, but not the same as, offending behavior) occurs in children from families with a large number of children, financial circumstances of poverty, younger and more poorly educated mothers, a structure resulting from divorce or remarriage, and antisocial and substance-using parents (Pagani, 2009). Family functioning characterized by poor communication, supervision, disciplinary practices, and cohesion raises the risk for antisocial behavior as well.

In a related manner, interpersonal relationships among offending girls in particular are often characterized by conflict and hostility, including physical and emotional abuse (Downey, Irwin, Ramsay, & Ayduk, 2004; Maschi et al., 2009). For example, a greater proportion of girls experienced unstable family and housing arrangements prior to incarceration and expressed greater levels of anxiety about their living situation after their release from incarceration (Fields & Abrams, 2010). The majority of female youth also reported running away from home, and more than one third reported involvement with the child welfare services (Fields & Abrams, 2010). Indeed, female youth are more likely to be referred to the child welfare or juvenile justice system due to family-related issues and trauma as opposed to delinquent or behavioral problems (Maschi et al., 2009).

Contextual. A. A. Payne and Welch (2013) carefully examined risk factors related to school and education, finding strong support for student-level factors of academic performance and school success/failure, poor attachment and commitment to school as components of school bonding, and peer rejection. A small but growing amount of research indicates that school transitions, whether through matriculation or changes in residence, appear to increase the risk for antisocial behavior. Interestingly, Payne and Welch conclude that research on truancy and dropout is mixed. At the school level, both structural characteristics (e.g., low school-wide socioeconomic status, high teacher:student ratio) and poor school climate significantly predict higher risk for antisocial behavior. In addition to the mechanisms suggested by life course theories reviewed earlier, Payne and Welch highlight several other ways school factors could impact antisocial behavior, including negative impacts of juvenile justice involvement.

Neighborhood research has matured from considering neighborhood correlates of adolescent offending to examining how neighborhood-level stability and change over time affects offending trajectories (Foster & Brooks-Gunn, 2013). Multiple studies and reviews reinforce the importance of neighborhood characteristics, such as socioeconomic status, as having both direct and indirect risk and protective explanatory power for adolescent offending.

Adolescent-limited offenders. Moffitt's theory suggests that offending patterns limited to the adolescence period are likely due to two risk factors: the gap between biological maturity and social responsibilities, and exposure to a peer context supporting offending behavior. Piquero, Monahan, Glasheen, Schubert, and Mulvey (2013) conclude that recent research supports differentiating adolescent-limited offenders from nonoffenders on multiple risk factors predicted by the two main contributors to this trajectory: the maturity gap and the influence of delinquent peers. Compared to nonoffenders, adolescent-limited offenders demonstrate some relevant biological differences, greater prevalence of mental health disorders, distinguishing personality traits such as aggression (but not childhood temperament), larger and more conflict-prone families, and a higher likelihood of having deviant friends who engage in delinquent "adult-like" activities such as drinking, doing drugs, and theft. As expected by the theory, Piquero and colleagues' analysis of comparisons between life-course persistent and adolescent-limited offenders finds that life-course persistent offenders have a larger number of more severe risk factors.

Some research has investigated whether male and female juvenile offenders share similar trajectories of offending and desistance (Fontaine, Yang, Dodge, Pettit, & Bates, 2009). In a review of 46 studies, Fontaine and colleagues (2009) conclude that sufficient empirical support exists for multiple offending trajectories among females, although the distribution of females across those trajectories may vary. For example, they find that only 1-2% of female offenders fall in the early onset, life-course persistent trajectory, compared to 10% or more of males. Similar types of individual- and family-level risk factors predict the life-course persistent trajectory. Evidence suggests females exhibit two adolescent onset trajectories: adolescence-limited and adolescence-delayed onset, although the limitations of existing research cannot determine the risk factors that distinguish the two trajectories. Several other trajectories (e.g., childhood-limited, adult-onset) were identified less frequently but warrant further investigation.

Although much research has been done surrounding the pathways of criminal behavior and the risk factors associated with it, less has been studied on what specifically leads certain individuals to desist and others to persist in their offending (Mulvey et al., 2004). Parenting styles (Hoeve et al., 2009), negative peer influence (Chung & Steinberg, 2006), and varied onset patterns (Moffitt, 1993) have been highlighted as important risk factors for adolescent antisocial behavior. The factors that play a pivotal role in the process of changing the focus from engaging in to abstaining from criminal behavior are less well understood. The Pathways to Desistance Study followed more than 1,300 serious juvenile offenders over the course of seven years. This study highlights the fact that serious juvenile offenders are not all the same, and do not all follow the same trajectory into and out of offending. In fact, it is difficult to distinguish between "desisters" and "persisters" at any given time (Mulvey & Schubert, 2012). In their study, Mulvey and Schubert found that, consistent with the age–crime curve, the majority of their sample reduced their (self-reported) offending over time. Their analysis resulted in less than 10% of the sample consistently reporting high levels of offending (Mulvey & Schubert, 2012). Of course, as noted previously, not all offenders follow the same patterns of offending. Within their group of serious offenders, five subgroups emerged, each showing different patterns and methods of desistance. For example, some offenders' criminal behavior peaked in adolescence, while others started with very high rates of offending and decreased offending to nearly zero (Mulvey & Schubert, 2012). These results align with Moffitt's (1993) patterns of offending whereby the majority of youth "age out" of criminal behavior, leaving a small percentage that consistently offend into young adulthood.

Mental health and substance use issues are widespread in this population and also have an effect on offending behavior, both as a risk factor and a factor associated with desistance. Researchers found that adolescents' level of substance use was related to their reported levels of offending within the same time period. In other words, when adolescents reported substance usage, they also reported offending behaviors. Effective comprehensive substance use treatments that involved family members were seen to play a role in lowering non-drug offending (Mulvey & Schubert, 2012). Effective treatments were not the only mechanism by which adolescents desisted from criminal behavior. Developmental factors also played an important role in explaining what might be happening between adolescence and young adulthood.

Researchers looking at the development of psychosocial maturity in serious juvenile offenders have found that persisters and desisters differ in their development. Offenders who show increasing levels of psychosocial maturity, specifically temperance (the development of impulse control and suppression of aggression), over time show declining rates of antisocial behavior. Interestingly, those offenders who persist in their antisocial behavior show diminished performance in areas of psychosocial maturity such as impulse control, future orientation, and suppression of aggression (Monahan, Steinberg, Cauffman, & Mulvey, 2009). Similarly, research conducted on gang members found a similar pattern. Increases in psychosocial maturity are associated with increases in gang separation (Sweeten, Pyrooz, & Piquero, 2013). These findings, again, align with Moffitt's (1993) patterns of offending.

Understanding what differentiates those who persist from those who make the transition out of criminal behavior is fundamental to creating effective policies. There is still much to be learned about what mechanisms lead these individuals away from crime, but recent research has begun to shed light on the factors that are involved. It is important to note that not all serious juvenile offenders follow the same patterns into and out of criminal behavior, but as Moffitt (1993) proposed, the majority of youth "age out" of offending and a small subgroup, the persisters, continued their offending into young adulthood. Aside from the natural aging process (Gottfredson & Hirschi, 1990), research suggests that the development of psychosocial maturity, or lack thereof, affects when individuals will desist from offending (Monahan et al., 2009). Mental health and substance use also affects offending behavior such that, in the presence of substance use, adolescents also reported non-drug-related offending (Mulvey & Schubert, 2012). Despite this rather bleak outlook, when substance use interventions include family members, there appears to be

a positive effect that decreases offending among these youth.

Decisional Capacities and Legal Contexts

In this section we review research that assesses decisional capacities relevant to legal standards and decision contexts. First we begin with a brief summary of neurobiological and behavioral research on adolescent decision making more generally, and then we move to research specifically focused on legal decisions in the pretrial and trial contexts.

Normative decisional capacities. Empirical research on adolescent brain structure and function during decision making has exploded in the last decade, sparking several journals to dedicate special issues to the topic (e.g., Casey, 2013; Wahlstrom et al., 2010). Structural changes occur in white matter (e.g., Paus, 2010; Schmithorst & Yuan, 2010) and gray matter (e.g., Gogtay & Thompson, 2010) during this time in areas of the brain relevant to decision making. Converging research confirms that different parts of the brain are active during different aspects of decision making, that different brain systems mature on different time tables, and that, compared to adults, adolescents recruit different parts of the brain during decision making tasks (Steinberg, 2009, 2010). Jaeger's (2013) review of fMRI research consistently documents decreased activity in areas associated with inhibitory control.

Contextual influences, both in terms of stress and in terms of peers, appear to interact with age to differentially influence adolescents compared to adults (Steinberg, 2009). In a review of research on the teenage brain and self-control, Casey and Caudle (2013) dispel the myth that adolescents simply cannot make good decisions. Rather, adolescents perform comparably to adults in many paradigms under "cool" contexts devoid of emotionally salient cues and drawing on cognitive processes. In "hot" environments, however, adolescents have more difficulty suppressing or controlling their affective responses to task conditions and stimuli (Van Duijvenvoorde & Crone, 2013; Krain et al., 2006; Selazo & Carlson, 2012). Rewards and gains are more salient for adolescents, and risks are more attractive (e.g., Cauffman et al., 2010; Galván, 2013;

Somerville, Jones, & Casey, 2010); both tendencies are amplified in "hot" contexts. Rather than simply having an immature prefrontal cortex, Casey and Caudle (2013) argue that the immature prefrontal cortex combines with a reward-processing structure that overwhelms that prefrontal cortex, thus reducing the capacity in adolescents to control the self compared to adults, a position supportive of a dual systems model (e.g., Steinberg, 2009). For example, using the rewarded antisaccade task, Luna, Paulsen, Padmanabhan, and Geier (2013) found delayed but heightened responses in several regions of the brain. In this paradigm, participants played a game in the MRI scanner in which they were instructed not to look directly at a light that flashed randomly on the screen (i.e., inhibit the prepotent response), but instead to look in a different specific location. Some trials visually indicated potential rewards for correct performance, and others simply displayed neutral indicators. Adults performed well across all trials. Interestingly, adolescents made fewer errors on the rewarded trials compared to their performance on the neutral trials and demonstrated increased activation in the ventral striatum on reward trials compared to neutral trials. Jarcho et al. (2012) found age-based differences in brain activation during reward anticipation and feedback phases of tasks that did not require decision making but offered large versus small rewards.

One of those emotionally salient contexts for adolescents is the presence of others, including peers (Somerville, 2013). O'Brien and colleagues found that teens who played the game in the presence of peers made more risky decisions in the game and preferred more immediate rewards in a delay-discounting task (O'Brien, Albert, Chein, & Steinberg, 2011) than teens who completed the tasks alone. Similar findings were observed when teens simply believed that peers were watching from a different room (Albert, Chein, & Steinberg, 2013; Chein, Albert, O'Brien, Uckert, & Steinberg, 2011).

Normative developmental behavioral research on behavior in nonlegal contexts supports the judgment theory hypothesis that several key psychosocial factors differentiate the decision making of adolescents from adults. These factors include risk perception and preference, future time perspective,

susceptibility to peer influence, and responsibility, among others (Scott et al. 1995; Steinberg & Cauffman, 1996). Research on adolescent decisions to commit law violations and, once engaged with the justice system, to make decisions about that process complements this work by examining psychosocial factors and decision making in specific legal contexts. Some studies have related psychosocial factors to delinquent and antisocial behavior, but most research has primarily focused on the capacities relevant for waiving the right to remain silent, exhibiting adequate capacities relevant to the legal standard of competence to stand trial and, to a lesser extent, making a decision regarding a plea agreement. Important age-based differences have been demonstrated in each of these domains, consistently differentiating young juveniles from older juveniles and adults. Distinctions between older teens and young adults remain mixed, however. Overall, the research we reviewed on the differences between adolescents and adults in brain function during decision making reinforces a body of behavioral research that finds similar age-based differences.

Entire volumes are devoted to understanding the well-documented phenomenon that adolescents engage in more risky behavior than adults. The age–crime curve, health risk surveys, and self-report offending instruments create a consistent picture of risk behavior that increases and peaks in adolescence into late adulthood. We have reviewed the research on developmental trajectories of offending behavior, but here we specifically examine how psychosocial aspects of risk predict offending. Risk perception and preference is inherently connected with the reward sensitivity, or valence (Wolf, Wright, Kilford, Dolan, & Blakemore, 2013), described earlier. Research with context-neutral tasks include several variations on the Iowa Gambling Task and related measures, in which participants must choose between decks of cards that vary in the amount of their payoff or loss and the frequency with which extreme values occur. Adolescents tend to draw from the decks that offer high-value rewards compared to children and adults, but the adolescents do not demonstrate adult-like avoidance of potential losses (e.g., Cauffman et al., 2010; Wolf et al., 2013).

Legally relevant contexts.   We turn from the relevant normative brain and behavior research to examine these capacities in legally relevant context. These decisions take place in a juvenile and criminal justice context that has grown increasingly punitive in the past several decades. This "third wave" of reform follows the "due process" era, in which a series of Supreme Court cases clarified the constitutional rights guaranteed to juveniles in court. Included in the *In re Gault* (1967) decision were the rights to counsel and against self-incrimination. At that time, empirical researchers turned their attention to the capacity of juveniles to exercise the constitutional rights clarified by the Supreme Court.

At the time, it was unclear whether juveniles were able to understand these new rights being afforded to them, and doubt in this ability was supported by an early study of actual interrogations that found most juveniles waived their rights to silence and counsel (Grisso, 1981). As is true with adults, juveniles who are in custody must waive the right to silence in a "knowingly, intelligently, and voluntary" manner in order for the content of an interrogation to be accepted in court (Grisso, 1981). In *Fare v. Michael C.* (1979), the Supreme Court decided that a "totality of circumstances" approach should be taken when considering the validity of a juvenile's waiver. Under this approach, courts should consider all of the surrounding circumstances in the case to determine if a waiver of *Miranda* rights was valid. The Supreme Court never explicitly discussed whether age should be considered in that totality assessment until the *J. D. B.* case (*J. D. B. v. North Carolina*, 2011) described in the policy and practice section of this chapter.

Competence to stand trial and effective performance as a defendant rely on some of the same capacities as waiving the right to silence. A fundamental bedrock of the United States legal system (*Dusky v. United States*, 1960) is the requirement that defendants have a basic understanding of the process, and what is happening and may happen to them, in order to promote fundamental fairness and procedural justice and uphold public trust in the legal system (Grisso & Schwartz, 2003). Legal doctrine defines the relevant capacities for competence to include a basic understanding of the charges and process, the ability to appreciate one's own unique situation, and the capacity to reason about one's own case. Beyond understanding, reasoning, and appreciation, Bonnie and Grisso (2003) identify an additional component—decisional competence—as the capacity to make a choice when faced with a decision in the case. Until relatively recently, juvenile courts did not explicitly address issues of competence to stand trial, but the body of developmental research on adolescents' cognitive and psychosocial development, as well as the impact of mental illness and other impairments, has reinforced questions about youths' capacities and informed legal and statutory changes in a number of jurisdictions (see Practice and Policy Issues section below).

Given the complexity of the circumstances surrounding juvenile capacities to meet legal standards for waiving rights and being competent to stand trial, both scholars and justice system officials have wrestled with what constitutes evidence of a valid waiver of *Miranda* rights (Ferguson, 2011; Kohlman, 2012; Owen-Kostelnik, Reppucci, & Meyer, 2006; B. K. Payne, Time, & Gainey, 2006). A growing body of empirical research has examined the contours and contexts of capacities relevant to waiving the right to silence (e.g., Grisso, 1980; Abramovitch, Peterson-Badali, & Rohan, 1995; Woolard, Cleary, Harvell, & Chen, 2008). In general, juveniles under the age of 15 and both younger and older juveniles with low IQs do not understand the rights afforded to them by *Miranda* (i.e., the right to remain silent and the risk of not doing so, the right to have an attorney, the right to a free attorney, and the right exercise these rights at any time) and are more likely to recommend or actually waive the right to silence. Although youths' higher likelihood of waiving *Miranda* rights does not necessarily directly lead to a true or false confession, researchers have found that it may put juveniles at increased risk for falsely confessing (Kassin et al., 2010).

The literature on capacities relevant to competence to stand trial has produced similar results. Grisso et al. (2003) performed one of the most comprehensive comparisons of juvenile and young adult capacities relevant to competence to stand trial as well as mature judgment and decision making.

Interviewing more than 1,300 participants ages 10 to 24 in community settings and pretrial detention centers, they found that youths 15 years old and younger performed more poorly than older teens and young adults on measures assessing capacities relevant to competence to stand trial. Significant proportions of the young adolescents performed as poorly on measures of understanding and appreciation in the MacArthur Competence Assessment Tool—Criminal Adjudication (MacCAT–CA) as adults found incompetent to stand trial (Poythress, et al., 1999). These age differences did not vary by gender, race, ethnicity, or socioeconomic status. Detained and community juveniles performed comparably; justice experience did not appear to provide an advantage for juveniles, although it provided a slight difference in understanding between detained and community young adults. Subsequent analyses of these data and other original research in a variety of jurisdictions confirms the conclusion that adolescents, particularly young adults, simply do not display adult-like levels of understanding and reasoning about rights and decisions, even when taught the information they need to know.

In addition to merely understanding the components of the right to remain silent or the relevant components of the trial process in competence to stand trial, research confirms that, compared to adults, adolescents are more limited in their abilities to identify, consider, and foresee the options and consequences of decisions that face defendants in these circumstances (e.g., Grisso et al., 2003; M. Schmidt, Reppucci, & Woolard, 2003; Viljoen, Klaver, & Roesch, 2005). The ability to appreciate the implications of waivers is of utmost importance. Even adults who understand their *Miranda* rights do not always grasp their basic implications, and this is true for youth as well (Kassin et al., 2010). For example, juveniles who understand their rights might also believe that by asserting their rights, police will assume that the juvenile has something to hide or is guilty (Grisso, 1981). According to Grisso (1981), juveniles tend to believe that confessions result in leniency. Although juveniles realize confessing inevitably results in punishment of some kind, they feel that by cooperating with police, their confession could mitigate punishment. Regarding

access to counsel, research has shown that youth often believe that lawyers will only defend those who are innocent (Grisso, 1981). Adults, on the other hand, were found to be more likely to request counsel in the presence of guilt (Abramovitch et al., 1995).

Studies of hypothetical and actual decision making about police interrogation suggest that adolescents make substantively different decisions compared to adults. Grisso and colleagues (2003) presented a vignette about an individual who was involved in a crime and taken to the police station for questioning. When asked what would be the best choice in that situation, approximately one half of the 11- to 13-year-old participants identified confession as the best choice; the percentages of other age groups decreased linearly to approximately one fifth of young adults. Compared to adults, young adolescents were likely to recommend the decision choice that complied with authority across the interrogation, attorney consultation, and plea agreement vignettes. The younger adolescents identified fewer risks and found risks less likely and less detrimental than the young adults. They were more likely to emphasize short-term compared to long-term consequences. Compared to older teens and young adults, participants age 14 years and under also identified fewer long-range consequences of the vignette decision.

Viljoen et al. (2005) administered the Fitness Interview Test—Revised (FIT–R), among other instruments, to 152 adolescent pretrial detainees. In contrast to Grisso et al. (2003), this study included questions about the adolescents' own legal decisions regarding their experiences with police interrogation, communicating with attorneys, considering a plea, and considering an appeal. A majority of those teens questioned by police confessed (55%) or denied (31%) the offense. Perceptions of the strength of the evidence against them predicted older adolescents' decisions regarding police questions, but had no predictive power for young adolescents, echoing earlier studies of youths' perceptions of evidence (Abramovitch et al., 1995).

In addition to age, IQ consistently predicts poorer performance on capacities relevant to legal standards for waiver of rights (Grisso et al., 2003) and psychosocial factors and legal decision making (e.g., Grisso et al., 2003), even accounting for the general difference in average IQ between community and justice populations. These findings are consistent with a body of work that demonstrates a relationship between IQ and offending, albeit with less clarity about the mechanisms that produce the relationship (e.g., E. P. Mears & Cochran, 2013). More importantly, the impact of low IQ can be even more pronounced for younger juveniles compared to young adults with similar IQ levels (Grisso et al., 2003).

Another relevant aspect in normative adolescent development is the unique relationship with and sensitivity to parents and peers. Several studies suggest that adolescents may be differentially susceptible to parents or peers when making legally relevant decisions. Viljoen et al. (2005) found that half of the juvenile detainees in their sample knew how their parents or attorneys wanted them to plead, and one quarter reported knowing what their peers wanted them to plead. Juveniles were indeed more likely to plea if their parents, peers, or attorney recommended doing so. Viljoen et al. (2005) did not find the age difference in taking pleas that previous studies had (e.g., Grisso et al., 2003) but older adolescents (ages 15–17) again were more sensitive to evidence strength. Strong evidence increased the probability that older adolescents would plead, but it had no effect on the decisions of younger adolescents.

Simple differences among adolescent and adult populations in the choices that they make do not in and of themselves demonstrate age-based deficiencies and incapacities. Indeed, adults in laboratory and observational studies make a variety of decisions about interrogation and plea agreements that may be viewed by some as detrimental to their own interests. The legal system presumes that adults in these situations are free to make those decisions because they are rational adults without (for the most part) the kinds of impairments that render them incapable of meeting the basic requirements of competence. This body of research, however, suggests that adolescents' decisions are predicted by developmental capacities that, for many youth, will predictably change with age as a part of normative development.

Clinical impairment and competency restoration. A number of states have begun incorporating developmental immaturity into their statutes on contributors to risk for lack of competency with challenging implications for competence restoration. More than half of the states explicitly address the standard for juvenile competence evaluations (Fogel, Schiffman, Mumley, Tillbrook, & Grisso, 2013; O'Donnell & Gross, 2012). Regardless of the status of developmental immaturity in state statutory schemes, significant clinical impairments in mental health are still a consistent predictor of referrals for forensic evaluations of capacity for youth and adults (Grisso, 2004). Similar to the consistency of lower IQ among justice samples of youth compared to those in the community, justice system youth also experience more challenges to their mental health and functioning. Teplin et al. (2002) found that 60 to 70 percent of detained youth met diagnostic criteria for at least one mental health disorder, with females, non-Hispanic whites, and older adolescents demonstrating higher rates in a number of diagnostic categories. Grisso (2004) described the interaction of age and mental health disorders in juveniles as "double jeopardy" because the degree of impairment resulting from this combination is much greater for juveniles than for similarly situated adults. Research on judgment and decision making in legal contexts bears out the effects of a combination of young age and mental disorder on legally relevant decision making (Warren, Aaron, Ryan, Chauhan, & DuVal, 2003).

Restoration of competency presents unique concerns when applied to juvenile defendants. An empirical and clinical literature has emerged, highlighting special considerations for forensic evaluations of youth generally, including but not limited to questions about competence to stand trial (Hoge, 2012). Although some juvenile forensic evaluations may lack consideration of key legal or developmental issues (Christy, Douglas, Otto, & Petrila, 2004; Fogel et al., 2013), best practices for the forensic assessment process incorporate both developmental factors described above as well as concern for the developmental appropriateness, reliability, and validity of assessment tools for juvenile forensic populations (Fogel et al., 2013; Grisso, 1998; Ryba, Cooper, & Zapf, 2003). Descriptive studies suggest that the population of adolescent defendants referred for competency restoration may differ from similarly situated juveniles not referred for questions of competency in terms of age, special education histories, and diagnoses, among others (Baerger, Griffin, Lyons, & Simmons, 2003; Kruh, Sullivan, Ellis, Lexcen, & McClellan, 2006; but see T. M. Evans, 2003). Juveniles also differ from referred adults in terms of diagnoses, but, similar to adults, most adolescents were restored and returned to court proceedings within six months, or not at all (McGaha, Otto, McClaren & Petrila, 2001; Warren et al., 2009).

PRACTICE AND POLICY ISSUES

Research attention does not always match the priorities of justice practitioners who experience a wide range of policies and practices, most of which are not systematically tested or evaluated (D. P. Mears, Shollenberger, Willison, Owens, & Butts, 2010).In their national survey of practitioner views on policy priorities and effectiveness, these researchers report a consensus that policies on substance abuse treatment, sex offender treatment, mental health treatment, and reentry services and planning are effective. Perhaps not surprisingly, prosecutors and defense attorneys showed consistently conflicting perceptions of the effectiveness of a number of policies, including transfer to adult court. The entire group of prosecutors, defense attorneys, judges, and court administrators agreed on a number of recommendations, one of which is that their perspectives and experiences need to play a significant role in policy and program development. Keeping that in mind, our practice and policy section includes, but is not limited to, several issues that the D. P. Mears et al. study identified as important to practitioners. There are more topics than there is space to cover them, so we highlight changes in the law regarding culpability and punishment and how developmental science, including

neuroscience research of decision making, has and could inform policy and practice.

Culpability and Punishment

A series of U.S. Supreme Court cases in the past decade have squarely placed the science of adolescent development into the process and punishment of juvenile offenders. *Roper v. Simmons* (2005) declared the death penalty unconstitutional for offenders whose crimes were committed at ages 16 and 17. In *Graham v. Florida* (2010), Justice Kennedy continued the *Roper v. Simmons* assessment of juveniles, stating that "developments in psychology and brain science continue to show fundamental differences between juvenile and adult minds" (p. 2026), and thus declared unconstitutional sentences of life without parole for juveniles committing non-homicide offenses. In the *Miller v. Alabama; Jackson v. Hobbs* (2012) case, Justice Kagan's majority opinion struck down mandatory life without parole sentences for juveniles convicted of homicide, reaffirming the view that adolescents' lesser culpability resulted at least in part from developmental immaturity and therefore required an individualized sentencing hearing. In the wake of *Miller* and *Jackson*, 29 states must deal with the fallout for juvenile homicide offenders sentenced under the previous legal scheme (Levick & Schwartz, 2013). At issue is whether the rulings are substantive or procedural; that is, whether they should apply retroactively (substantive) or only in future cases (procedural; Jones, 2013; Levick & Schwartz, 2013).

The majority opinion in each of these cases discussed the relevance of a growing body of behavioral and brain research supporting the conclusion that adolescent offenders are qualitatively different from adults in ways that will, for most, predictably change with maturity and age. The *Roper v. Simmons* (2005) case involved a brutal homicide committed by a then 17-year-old Christopher Simmons and his friend, whose lawyers argued that his immaturity made a death sentence cruel and unusual punishment. Although the justification for the Court's decision to agree with Simmons' argument did not rely solely on social science, Justice Kennedy's majority opinion specifically noted its relevance (Haider, 2006). On behalf of the majority, Kennedy concluded that the "worst" juvenile offenders could not be reliably identified in part due to their immaturity and irresponsibility, their differential susceptibility to and impact of peer influence, and their developing character, thus diminishing their culpability and precluding the imposition of the death penalty. This line of reasoning continued in the *Graham v. Florida* (2010), and *Miller v. Alabama; Jackson v. Hobbs* (2012) cases. In the *Miller v. Alabama* majority opinion, Justice Kagan writes that *Roper v. Simmons* (2005) and *Graham v. Florida* (2010) "establish that children are constitutionally different from adults" and that these "distinctive attributes of youth diminish the penological justifications for imposing the harshest sentences on juvenile offenders, even when they commit terrible crimes" (*Miller v. Alabama*, 2012, p. 2465). As such, individual mitigating circumstances must be considered, so mandatory life without parole sentences are unconstitutional.

The acknowledgement of developmental differences carried over into *J. D. B. v. North Carolina* (2011), a case involving the interrogation of a 13-year-old boy in the school principal's office by the school resource officer and a police investigator, among others. At issue was whether the youth was in custody, and thus warranted receiving the *Miranda* warnings. The Supreme Court held that age was indeed relevant when ascertaining what a "reasonable person" might have felt in those circumstances and must be taken into account when objectively assessing the totality of the circumstances, specifically referencing what a "reasonable child" might have believed based on their ongoing yet immature development.

Not all the justices agreed with the conclusions drawn from social science in these decisions. With Chief Justice Roberts and Justice Thomas, Justice Scalia's *Roper v. Simmons* (2005) dissent accused scientists of relying on the corpus of research to justify both the need for paternalistic protection in some contexts (e.g., crime, sentencing) and autonomous decision making in others (e.g., abortion). Steinberg, Cauffman, Woolard, Graham, and Banich (2009) took to the *American Psychologist* to respond to these concerns and others (Fischer, Stein, & Heikkinen, 2009), arguing that the interaction of higher cognitive maturity and less developed psychosocial maturity could reasonably produce greater decisional competence in "cool" contexts like a deliberate medical decision and poorer competence in "hot" contexts like criminal acts. Other scholars have critiqued the scientific basis of amicus briefs in *Roper v. Simmons* (2005), suggesting that the scientific foundation was not sturdy enough at the time to support the breadth of conclusions about juvenile immaturity that the majority opinion embraced (Katt, 2009; Maroney, 2009; Morse, 2013).

The recognition by the U.S. Supreme Court of key developmental differences between adolescents and adults that are relevant to legal decision making perhaps draws to an end a period of reform beginning in the 1990s that painted quite a different picture. Two broad classes of reform pushed state justice systems into a harsher era (Scott, 2013). First, most states expanded the types of crimes, and also lowered the age of eligibility, that were able to be prosecuted in adult court in two ways. The second broad type of reform resulted in harsher and more determinate sentencing in juvenile court.

Transfer has always existed as a safety valve for youth who were unable to be treated or responded to in juvenile court. Beginning in the late 1980s, however, the scope, type, and use of transfer mechanisms expanded in virtually every state. Historically, youth who were prosecuted in adult criminal court were placed there through an adversarial hearing in front of a judge. This judicial waiver procedure considered a variety of evidence; although they varied by state, most statutes relied heavily on the *Kent v. United States* (1966) criteria. These included characteristics of the offense, offender, outcomes of previous justice system interventions for that youth, and the potential for rehabilitation and public safety through juvenile court resources. In 2010, about 6,000 cases were judicially waived to adult court (Puzzanchera & Hockenberry, 2013).

Two other mechanisms for youth to be prosecuted as adults shifted the power from the judiciary to the legislature and prosecutors. Legislative or statutory waivers delineate statutory criteria, usually based on age and offense, which mandate that youth of a certain age and charged with certain offenses must be prosecuted in criminal court. The second type, prosecutorial discretion, often statutorily specify age and offense eligibility criteria but leave the choice of venue up to the individual prosecutor. Across all three mechanisms, researchers estimate that upwards of 200,000 youthful offenders are prosecuted as adults annually (Woolard, Odgers, Lanza-Kaduce, & Daglis, 2005).

Several reviews of the early literature on transfer outcomes concluded that the policy was at best net-neutral, if not harmful to the primary outcome of interest, recidivism (Bishop & Frazier, 2000). More recently, research has moved from considering whether transfer is good or bad to considering how youth with particular individual and contextual risk factors behave after experiencing transfer, and from a focus on youth as a class to examining differential effects on subgroups of youth (Schubert et al., 2010). Serious offenders ages 14–18 in Arizona enrolled in the Pathways to Desistance study exhibited no general effect of transfer on recidivism across the entire sample after controlling for a large number of variables (Loughran et al., 2010). Once Loughran et al. created offender subgroups based on the most serious adjudicated charge (person or property) and the number of prior petitions (less than two or two and more), differential effects emerged. Transferred youth with person crimes had lower recidivism than youth in juvenile court. Youth with fewer prior petitions had a lower recidivism rate regardless of court jurisdiction. The effect of transfer on property offenders was nonsignificant. Loughran et al. (2010) suggest that the policy debate should shift from a question of whether transfer is good or bad to mechanisms for determining what parameters maximize a transfer's positive effects and minimize the negative.

In a study focused solely on the youth in the Pathways study that were transferred to criminal court, Schubert and colleagues (2010) expanded the type of outcomes considered from subsequent arrest to include overnight detention, antisocial activities, and "gainful" activities (e.g., work or school) that occurred once the youth returned to the community. In addition to legal and demographic variables, they also measured judgment factors (e.g., responsibility, perspective, resistance to peer influence), six risk/need factors (e.g., antisocial attitudes, peers, or parents; school and mental health problems), and aspects of community supervision. Most of their primarily male minority sample of transferred youth was initially arrested on an offense against persons (including 25% for murder/rape/arson and 54% for assault or weapons charges); the remainder included property and drug offenses. More than one fourth of youth had no prior petitions when they were transferred. These descriptive data emphasize that transferred youth, at least in this jurisdiction, are not a homogenous group with respect to offense type and history.

Psychological and demographic factors did not significantly predict the outcomes described above, but charge type predicted antisocial activity and recidivism. Most youth were subsequently arrested at least once upon release. The authors note that their finding that a more antisocial peer group predicts shorter time to resumption of antisocial activity and re-arrest is consistent with judgment theory hypotheses about susceptibility to peers. Interestingly, 86% of youth recalled attending school or working during one or more months of the four-year follow-up period.

Beyond transfer, other methods of harsher and more punitive treatment of juveniles do not appear to reduce recidivism; on the contrary, in some instances they appear to exacerbate it. In the latest iteration of his meta-analyses of delinquency interventions, Lipsey (2009) categorized the 548 studies in terms of program philosophy. Control-oriented programs include those that focus on discipline, deterrence through fear, and surveillance. By contrast, programs with a therapeutic philosophy include counseling, skill-building interventions, restorative interventions (e.g., restitution, mediation), and coordination of multiple services. Two of the control approaches, discipline and deterrence, produce increased recidivism among youth. Each of the therapeutic approaches, along with surveillance (primarily intensive probation), results in reductions in recidivism of five to 15% from baseline. In addition to philosophy, more effective programs focus on high-risk juveniles (who simply may have had more room to improve than low-risk juveniles), matching program type to offender need, and deliver a sufficient amount of quality service. In addition to "brand name" programs such as Multisystemic Therapy (Henggeler, Schoenwald, Borduin, Rowland, & Cunningham, 2009), with established and accepted evidence of their effectiveness, "generic" programs with a less established evidence base but a model consistent with the factors described here also effectively reduce recidivism. Factors for intervention success identified by other reviews of intervention impact draw similar conclusions (Henggeler & Schoenwald, 2011).

In addition to implementing system-wide reform that emphasizes evidence-based interventions (e.g., Greenwood, Welsh, & Rocque, 2012; Henggeler & Schoenwald, 2011) a number of states have reversed or at least tamped down the harsher statutory schemes by raising the age of juvenile court jurisdiction (Campaign for Youth Justice, 2013) and reducing incarceration, including pretrial detention (e.g., Annie E. Casey Foundation, 2013).

As reviewed above, empirical research suggests that adolescents, particularly those age 14 years and under, are less likely to understand their rights and are more likely to waive those rights. Law enforcement personnel are aware of developmental differences between youth and adults but may not translate that knowledge into interrogation practices, generally believing that similar approaches to youth and adults can be effective (Reppucci, Meyer, & Kostelnik, 2010). As the research base has grown, law enforcement organizations such as the International Association of Chiefs of Police (2012) have provided more guidance on best practices for questioning and interrogating youth.

Although the Supreme Court clarified that age is a factor in determinations of custody status, the totality of circumstances approach does not provide guidance for how to determine juveniles' abilities to understand and appreciate their rights (Grisso, 1981). Several researchers have concluded that the empirical evidence regarding the likelihood of youths' impaired capacities, including the risk of false confession, warrants policy changes to require the presence of an attorney and provide specialized training to law enforcement on developmental science and its implication for interrogating youth (Kassin et al., 2010).

Some jurisdictions have already adopted policies that require the presence of an interested adult at the interrogation of a youth. That adult could be a parent, guardian, or attorney. Research on parents' abilities to counsel their children has found that parents may not have the requisite knowledge to effectively counsel youth within the interrogation context (Woolard et al., 2008). Few parents actively participate in the interrogation process; when they do, it can be by encouraging youth to confess rather than to assert their rights (Grisso, 1981). Both parents and youth demonstrate more of what Rogers (2011) calls *metaignorance*, or false beliefs about the behavioral implications of the warning for defendants' and law enforcements' actions that in some way relates to the appreciation aspect of competence.

Recognizing that cross-sectional studies of youth and adults are inadequate because youth are not randomly assigned to parents, Woolard and her colleagues (2008) interviewed 171 pairs of parents and youths to establish whether parents have the requisite knowledge to advise and advocate for their children in an interrogation context, and to compensate for youths' knowledge and decision-making deficits. Parents did know more than their children about the four components of the *Miranda* warning, as well as a few of its implications: for example, more than 90% of parents correctly responded that one can stop answering questions from police once having started, but only two thirds of adolescents correctly responded. However, parents knew far less about police strategy or the boundaries of parental protection. One half of youth and two thirds of their parents incorrectly believed that officers must wait for parents to arrive before questioning a youth. Half of the parents and youth also incorrectly believed that the police cannot lie in interrogation. It was possible to identify four latent classes or categories of parent–youth pairs based on these and other questions about interrogation. It appears parents have some helpful knowledge that could support or advantage their children. In 41% of the families, both parent and youth demonstrated good knowledge, and 16% had parents with good knowledge and youth with poor knowledge. In 12% of families, however, the youth demonstrated good knowledge while the parent did not. Finally, and most disturbingly, neither youth nor parent demonstrated good knowledge in 31% of the participating families. This of course begs the question of whether an interested adult (e.g., a parent) is able to provide the appropriate guidance regarding waiver that a juvenile might require to make a knowing, intelligent, and voluntary decision. Parent advocacy groups have organized to fill some of these knowledge gaps (e.g., Families and Allies of Virginia's Youth, http://www.favyouth.org) but much remains to be done in research, policy, and practice (Pennell, Shapiro, & Spigner, 2011).

Neuroscience in Court

Critics of the rapidity and expansivity of the juvenile justice system's embrace point to methodological limitations that are usually mentioned in the empirical literature but not necessarily with respect to policy implications. Small sample sizes, ecological validity questions, data simplification, and assumptions underlying complicated analytic techniques reinforce that there remains some art of interpretation in the translation of neuroscience into policy recommendations (Maroney, 2009; Morse, 2005, 2013). Nonetheless, interest in and applications of these findings have gained increasing purchase in the policy and practice world. Entrepreneurs are already marketing lie detection tests (e.g., No Lie MRI, http://www.noliemri.com; Stix, 2008).

Even though scholars acknowledge both the promise and pitfalls of research technology that is not yet fully developed (Aronson, 2009), many agree that fundamental structural and functional changes in the brain happen during adolescence (Steinberg, Graham, et al., 2009). Sources of disagreement are in the interpretation and implications of those findings for policy and practice (Gruber & Yurgelun-Todd, 2006; Maroney, 2009; Steinberg, Graham, et al., 2009). Even the "policy and practice" combination needs to be disentangled. As Steinberg, Graham, et al. (2009) emphasize, using neuroscientific evidence as one of many factors to inform policy is quite different from using it to make judgments about an individual youth. The entrepreneurs notwithstanding, the methods and the data simply are not capable of conclusions about a specific youth's culpability, or where he or she falls in the distribution of adolescent capacity. Even so, it is clear that neuroscience research will continue to play a role in juvenile and criminal justice, with a need for research that continues to draw a clearer picture of the specific relationships between neurobiological functioning and capacities relevant to competence and culpability (e.g., Mayzer, Bradley, Rusinko, & Ertelt, 2009).

SUMMARY AND CONCLUSIONS

Although this review of research on juvenile offenders is necessarily limited, a number of conclusions can be drawn. First, the field has moved beyond discipline-bound dichotomous questions to interdisciplinary longitudinal research agendas spanning multiple ecological levels of development. No single study can accommodate all aspects of this complex framework, but the growing research base continues to converge on key ideas (e.g., the dual systems framework of neurobiological development, longitudinal trajectories of offending and desistance) while diving deeper into their complexities. Second, policymakers, practitioners, and scholars are in consistent if not always comprehensible dialogue about the types of research questions that push each of their respective approaches forward. The Supreme Court's embrace of a developmental differences approach to evaluating juvenile culpability might serve as validation of this collaborative effort, but much remains to be done as the practical ramifications of their decisions modify the daily legal landscape for practitioners, juveniles, and their families. Third, the rapid advances in neuroscience hold both promise and pitfall for policy relevant research. It is clear that neuroscientific research findings are now a part of the legal landscape. The polar extremes of fully embracing brain scans as the equivalent of diagnoses, and the worry that the evidence will simply eliminate the fundamental concepts of free will and responsibility, are both likely to have validity and weakness (e.g., Aronson, 2007; Gazzaniga, 2011). Empirical research has begun to elucidate the complexity of non-scientists' understanding of such evidence and its potential impact (Greene & Cahill, 2012;

McCabe & Castel, 2008; Weisberg, Keil, Goodstein, Rawson, & Gray, 2008). These three conclusions can serve as both directions and cautions. We should continue to ask complex questions about juvenile offending; remain in dialogue among scholars, policymakers, and practitioners; and understand how scientific advances are most effectively and appropriately communicated and understood. If we do, we will continue to advance the theoretical and empirical research base on juvenile offending in ways useful to those who research, those who implement, and those who live with and through the realities of juvenile offending.

References

Abram, K. M., Teplin, L. A., McClelland, G. M., & Dulcan, M. K. (2003). Comorbid psychiatric disorders in youth in juvenile detention. *Archives of General Psychiatry, 60,* 1097–1108. doi:10.1001/archpsyc.60.11.1097

Abramovitch, R., Peterson-Badali, M., & Rohan, M. (1995). Young people's understanding and assertion of their rights to silence and legal counsel. *Canadian Journal of Criminology, 1,* 1–18.

Albert, D., Chein, J., & Steinberg, L. (2013). The teenage brain: Peer influences on adolescent decision making. *Current Directions in Psychological Science, 22,* 114–120. doi:10.1177/0963721412471347

Annie E. Casey Foundation (2013). *Juvenile detention alternatives initiative 2011 results report summary.* Baltimore, MD: Author.

Antonishak, J., Reppucci, N. D., & Mulford, C. F. (2004). Girls in the justice system: Treatment and intervention. In M. M. Moretti, C. Odgers, & M. Jackson (Eds.), *Girls and aggression: Contributing factors and intervention principles* (pp. 165–180). New York, NY: Kluwer Academic/Plenum. doi:10.1007/978-1-4419-8985-7_12

Aronson, J. D. (2007). Brain imaging, culpability, and the juvenile death penalty. *Psychology, Public Policy, and Law, 13,* 115–142. doi:10.1037/1076-8971.13.2.115

Aronson, J. D. (2009). Neuroscience and juvenile justice. *Akron Law Review, 42,* 917–930.

Baerger, D. R., Griffin, E. F., Lyons, J. S., & Simmons, R. (2003). Competency to stand trial in preadjudicated and petitioned juvenile defendants. *Journal of the American Academy of Psychiatry and the Law, 31,* 314–320.

Banich, M. T., De La Vega, A., Andrews-Hanna, J. R., Mackiewicz Seghete, K., Du, Y., & Claus, E. D. (2013). Developmental trends and individual differences in brain systems involved in intertemporal choice during adolescence. *Psychology of Addictive Behaviors, 27,* 416–430. doi:10.1037/a0031991

Bishop, D., & Frazier, C. (2000). Consequences of transfer. In J. Fagan & F. E. Zimring (Eds.), *The changing borders of juvenile justice: Transfer of adolescents to criminal court* (pp. 227–276). Chicago, IL: University of Chicago Press.

Bonnie, R. J., & Grisso, T. (2003). Adjudicative competence and youthful offenders. In T. Grisso & R. J. Schwartz (Eds.), *Youth on trial: A developmental perspective on juvenile justice* (pp. 73–104). Chicago, IL: University of Chicago Press.

Campaign for Youth Justice. (2013). *State trends— Legislative victories from 2011–2013: Removing youth from the adult criminal justice system.* Washington, DC: Campaign for Youth Justice.

Casey, B. J., (2013). The teenage brain: An overview. *Current Directions in Psychological Science, 22,* 80–81. doi:10.1177/0963721413486971

Casey, B. J., & Caudle, C. (2013). The teenage brain: Self control. *Current Directions in Psychological Science, 22,* 82–87. doi:10.1177/0963721413480170

Casey, B. J., Giedd, J. N., & Thomas, K. M. (2000). Structural and functional brain development and its relation to cognitive development. *Biological Psychology, 54,* 241–257. doi:10.1016/S0301-0511(00)00058-2

Casey, B. J., Jones, R. M., & Hare, T. A. (2008). The adolescent brain. *Annals of the New York Academy of Sciences, 1124,* 111–126. doi:10.1196/annals.1440.010

Cauffman, E., Lexcen, F. A., Shulman, E., & Grisso, T. (2007). Gender differences in mental health symptoms among delinquent and community youth. *Youth Violence and Juvenile Justice, 5,* 287–307. doi:10.1177/1541204007301292

Cauffman, E., Shulman, E. P., Steinberg, L., Claus, E., Banich, M. T., Graham, S., & Woolard, J. (2010). Age differences in affective decision making as indexed by performance on the Iowa Gambling Task. *Developmental Psychology, 46,* 193–207. doi:10.1037/a0016128

Chein, J., Albert, D., O'Brien, L., Uckert, K., & Steinberg, L. (2011). Peers increase adolescent risk taking by enhancing activity in the brain's reward circuitry. *Developmental Science, 14,* F1–F10. doi:10.1111/j.1467-7687.2010.01035.x

Christy, A., Douglas, K. S., Otto, R. K., & Petrila, J. (2004). Juveniles evaluated incompetent to proceed: Characteristics and quality of mental health professionals' evaluations. *Professional Psychology: Research and Practice, 35,* 380–388. doi:10.1037/0735-7028.35.4.380

Chung, H. L., & Steinberg, L. (2006). Relations between neighborhood factors, parenting behaviors, peer deviance, and delinquency among serious juvenile offenders. *Developmental Psychology, 42*, 319–331. doi:10.1037/0012-1649.42.2.319

Crone, E. A., & Van Der Molen, M. W. (2007). Development of decision making in school-aged children and adolescents: Evidence from heart rate and skin conductance analysis. *Child Development, 78*, 1288–1301. doi:10.1111/j.1467-8624.2007.01066.x

Downey, G., Irwin, L., Ramsay, M., & Ayduk, O. (2004). Rejection sensitivity and girls' aggression. In M. M. Moretti, C. L. Odgers, & M. A. Jackson (Eds.), *Girls and aggression: Contributing factors and intervention principles* (pp. 7–25). New York, NY: Kluwer.

Dusky v. United States, 362 U.S. 402 (1960).

Eccles, J. S., Midgley, C., Wigfield, A., Buchanan, C. M., Reuman, D., Flanagan, C., & Mac Iver, D. (1993). Development during adolescence: The impact of stage-environment fit on young adolescents' experiences in schools and in families. *American Psychologist, 48*, 90–101. doi:10.1037/0003-066X.48.2.90

Evans, G. W., Li, D., & Whipple, S. S. (2013). Cumulative risk and child development. *Psychological Bulletin, 139*, 1342–1396. doi:10.1037/a0031808

Evans, T. M. (2003). Juvenile competence to stand trial: Problems and pitfalls. *American Journal of Forensic Psychology, 21*, 5–18.

Fare v. Michael C., 442 U.S. 707 (1979).

Ferguson, A. G. (2011). The dialogue approach to *Miranda* warnings and waiver. *American Criminal Law Review, 49*, 1437–1491.

Fields, D., & Abrams, L. S. (2010). Gender differences in the perceived needs and barriers of youth offenders: Preparing for community reentry. *Child and Youth Care Forum, 39*, 253–269. doi:10.1007/s10566-010-9102-x

Fischer, K. W., Stein, Z., & Heikkinen, K. (2009). Narrow assessments misrepresent development and misguide policy: Comment on Steinberg, Cauffman, Woolard, Graham, and Banich (2009). *American Psychologist, 64*, 595–600. doi:10.1037/a0017105

Fogel, M. H., Schiffman, W., Mumley, D., Tillbrook, C., & Grisso, T. (2013). Ten year research update (2001–2010): Evaluations for competence to stand trial (adjudicative competence). *Behavioral Sciences and the Law, 31*, 165–191. doi:10.1002/bsl.2051

Fontaine, R. G., Yang, C., Dodge, K. A., Pettit, G. S., & Bates, J. E. (2009). Development of response evaluation and decision (RED) and antisocial behavior in childhood and adolescence. *Developmental Psychology, 45*, 447–459. doi:10.1037/a0014142

Foster, H., & Brooks-Gunn, J. (2013). Neighborhood influences on antisocial behavior during childhood and adolescence. In C. L. Gibson & M. D. Krohn (Eds.), *Handbook of life-course criminology: Emerging trends and directions for future research* (pp. 69–90). New York, NY: Springer. doi:10.1007/978-1-4614-5113-6_5

Galván, G. (2013). The teenage brain: Sensitivity to rewards. *Current Directions in Psychological Science, 22*, 88–93. doi:10.1177/0963721413480859

Gazzaniga, M. S. (2011). Neuroscience in the courtroom. *Scientific American, 304*, 54–59. doi:10.1038/scientificamerican0411-54

Geier, C. F., & Luna, B. (2012). Developmental effects of incentives on response inhibition. *Child Development, 83*, 1262–1274. doi:10.1111/j.1467-8624.2012.01771.x

Gogtay, N., Giedd, J. N., Lusk, L., Hayashi, K. M., Greenstein, D. Vaituzis, A. C., . . . Thompson, P. M. (2004). Dynamic mapping of human cortical development during childhood through early adulthood. *Proceedings of the National Academy of Sciences, USA, 101*, 8174–8179.

Gogtay, N., & Thompson, P. M. (2010). Mapping gray matter development: Implications for typical development and vulnerability to psychopathology. *Brain and Cognition, 72*, 6–15. doi:10.1016/j.bandc.2009.08.009

Gottfredson, M. R., & Hirschi, T. (1990). *A general theory of crime*. Stanford, CA: Stanford University Press.

Graham v. Florida, 130 S. Ct. 357 (2010).

Greene, E., & Cahill, B. S. (2012). Effects of neuroimaging evidence on mock juror decision making. *Behavioral Sciences and the Law, 30*, 280–296.

Greenwood, P., Welsh, B., & Rocque, M. (2012). *Implementing proven programs for juvenile offenders: Assessing state progress*. Retrieved from http://www.advancingebp.org/wp-content/uploads/2012/01/AEBP-assessment.pdf

Grisso, T. (1980). Juveniles' capacities to waive *Miranda* rights: An empirical analysis. *California Law Review, 68*, 1134–1166. doi:10.2307/3480263

Grisso, T. (1981). *Juveniles' waiver of rights: Legal and psychological competence*. New York, NY: Plenum. doi:10.1007/978-1-4684-3815-4

Grisso, T. (1998). *Forensic evaluation of juveniles*. Sarasota, FL: Professional Resource Press.

Grisso, T. (2004). *Double jeopardy: Adolescent offenders with mental disorders*. Chicago, IL: University of Chicago Press.

Grisso, T., & Schwartz, R. G. (Eds.). (2003). *Youth on trial: A developmental perspective on juvenile justice*. Chicago, IL: University of Chicago Press.

Grisso, T., Steinberg, L., Woolard, J., Cauffman, E., Scott, E., Graham, S., . . . Schwartz, R. (2003). Juveniles' competence to stand trial: A comparison of adolescents' and adults' capacities as trial defendants. *Law and Human Behavior, 27,* 333–363. doi:10.1023/A:1024065015717

Gruber, S. A., & Yurgelun-Todd, D. A. (2006). Neurobiology and the law: A role in juvenile justice. *Ohio State Journal of Criminal Law, 3,* 321–340.

Guerra, N. G., Williams, K. R., Tolan, P. H., & Modecki, K. L. (2008). Theoretical and research advances in understanding the causes of juvenile offending. In R. D. Hoge, N. G. Guerra, & P. Boxer (Eds.), *Treating the juvenile offender* (pp. 33–53). New York, NY: Guilford Press.

Haider, A. (2006). Roper v. Simmons: The role of the science brief. *Ohio State Journal of Criminal Law, 3,* 369–377.

Henggeler, S. W., & Schoenwald, S. K. (2011). Evidence-based interventions for juvenile offenders and juvenile justice policies that support them. *Social Policy Report, 25,* 1–27.

Henggeler, S. W., Schoenwald, S. K., Borduin, C. M., Rowland, M. D., & Cunningham, P. B. (2009). *Multisystemic therapy for antisocial behavior in children and adolescents* (2nd ed.). New York, NY: Guilford Press.

Hoeve, M., Dubas, J. S., Eichelsheim, V. I., van der Laan, P. H., Smeenk, W., & Gerris, J. R. (2009). The relationship between parenting and delinquency: A meta-analysis. *Journal of Abnormal Child Psychology, 37,* 749–775. doi:10.1007/s10802-009-9310-8

Hoge, D. (2012). Forensic assessments of juveniles: Practice and legal considerations. *Criminal Justice and Behavior, 39,* 1255–1270. doi:10.1177/0093854812444024

Howden, L. M., & Meyer, J. A. (2011). *Age and sex composition: 2010.* Washington, DC: U.S. Census Bureau.

In re Gault, 387 U.S. 1 (1967).

International Association of Chiefs of Police (2012). *Reducing risks: An executive guide to effective juvenile interview and interrogation.* Alexandria, VA: Author.

Jaeger, A. (2013). Inhibitory control and the adolescent brain: A review of fMRI research. *Psychology and Neuroscience, 6,* 23–30. doi:10.3922/j.psns.2013.1.05

Jarcho, J. M., Benson, B. E., Plate, R. C., Guyer, A. E., Detloff, A. M., Pine, D. S., . . . Ernst, M. (2012). Developmental effects of decision-making on sensitivity to reward: An fMRI study. *Developmental Cognitive Neuroscience, 2,* 437–447. doi:10.1016/j.dcn.2012.04.002

J. D. B. v. North Carolina, 131 S. Ct. 2394 (2011).

Jones, A. (2013, September 4). Courts split over ruling on juvenile life sentences. *Wall Street Journal.* Retrieved from http://online.wsj.com/news/articles/SB10001424127887324906304579038610174471156

Kassin, S. M., Drizin, S. A., Grisso, T., Gudjonsson, G. H., Leo, R. A., & Redlich, A. D. (2010). Police-induced confessions: Risk factors and recommendations. *Law and Human Behavior, 34,* 3–38. doi:10.1007/s10979-009-9188-6

Katt, W. J. (2009). Roper and the scientific amicus. *Jurimetrics, 49,* 253–275.

Kent v. United States, 383 U.S. 541 (1966).

Kohlman, A. K. (2012). Kids waive the darndest constitutional rights: The impact of *J. D. B. v. North Carolina* on juvenile interrogation. *American Criminal Law Review, 49,* 1623–1643.

Krain, A. L., Wilson, A. M., Arbuckle, R., Castellanos, F. X., & Milham, M. P. (2006). Distinct neural mechanisms of risk and ambiguity: A meta-analysis of decision-making. *NeuroImage, 32,* 477–484. doi:10.1016/j.neuroimage.2006.02.047

Kruh, I. P., Sullivan, L., Ellis, M., Lexcen, F., & McClellan, J. (2006). Juvenile competence to stand trial: A historical and empirical analysis of a juvenile forensic evaluation service. *International Journal of Forensic Mental Health, 5,* 109–123. doi:10.1080/14999013.2006.10471236

Laub, J. H., Nagin, D. S., & Sampson, R. J. (1998). Trajectories of change in criminal offending: Good marriages and the desistance process. *American Sociological Review, 63,* 225–238. doi:10.2307/2657324

Levick, M. L., & Schwartz, R. G. (2013). Practical implications of *Miller v. Jackson*: Obtaining relief in court and before the parole board. *Law and Inequality, 31,* 369–409.

Lipsey, M. W. (2009). The primary factors that characterize effective interventions with juvenile offenders: A meta-analytic overview. *Victims and Offenders, 4,* 124–147. doi:10.1080/15564880802612573

Loeber, R., White, H. R., Burke, J. D., Loeber, R., White, H. R., & Burke, J. D. (2012). Developmental sequences and pathways toward serious delinquency and substance use. In T. Bliesener, A. Beelmann, & M. Stemmler (Eds.), *Antisocial behavior and crime: Contributions of developmental and evaluation research to prevention and intervention* (pp. 39–52). Cambridge, MA: Hogrefe.

Loughran, T. A., Mulvey, E. P., Schubert, C. A., Chassin, L. A., Steinberg, L., Piquero, A. R., . . . Losoya, S. (2010). Differential effects of adult court transfer on juvenile offender recidivism. *Law and Human Behavior, 34,* 476–488. doi:10.1007/s10979-009-9210-z

Luna, L., Paulsen, P., Padmanabhan, P., & Geier, G. (2013). The teenage brain: Cognitive control and motivation. *Current Directions in Psychological Science, 22,* 94–100. doi:10.1177/0963721413478416

Lynam, D. R., Miller, D. J., Vachon, D., Loeber, R., & Stouthamer-Loeber, M. (2009). Psychopathy in adolescence predicts official reports of offending in adulthood. *Youth Violence and Juvenile Justice, 7,* 189–207. doi:10.1177/1541204009333797

Maroney, T. A. (2009). False promise of adolescent brain science in juvenile justice. *Notre Dame Law Review, 85,* 89–176.

Maschi, T., Schwalbe, C., Morgen, K., Gibson, S., & Violette, N. (2009). Exploring the influence of gender on adolescents' service needs and service pathways. *Children and Youth Services Review, 31,* 257–264. doi:10.1016/j.childyouth.2008.07.018

Mayzer, R., Bradley, A. R., Rusinko, H., & Ertelt, T. W. (2009). Juvenile competency to stand trial in criminal court and brain function. *Journal of Forensic Psychiatry and Psychology, 20,* 785–800. doi:10.1080/14789940903174089

McCabe, D. P., & Castel, A. D. (2008). Seeing is believing: The effect of brain images on judgments of scientific reasoning. *Cognition, 107,* 343–352. doi:10.1016/j.cognition.2007.07.017

McGaha, A., Otto, R. K., McClaren, M. D., & Petrila, J. (2001). Juveniles adjudicated incompetent to proceed: A descriptive study of Florida's competence restoration program. *Journal of the American Academy of Psychiatry and the Law, 29,* 427–437.

Mears, D. P., Shollenberger, T. L., Willison, J. B., Owens, C. E., & Butts, J. A. (2010). Practitioner views of priorities, policies, and practices in juvenile justice. *Crime and Delinquency, 56,* 535–563. doi:10.1177/0011128708324664

Mears, E. P., & Cochran, J. C. (2013). What is the effect of IQ on offending? *Criminal Justice and Behavior, 40,* 1280–1300. doi:10.1177/0093854813485736

Miller v. Alabama; Jackson v. Hobbs, 132 S. Ct. 2455 (2012).

Moffitt, T. E. (1993). Adolescent-limited and life-course persistent antisocial behavior: A developmental taxonomy. *Psychological Review, 100,* 674–701. doi:10.1037/0033-295X.100.4.674

Monahan, K. C., Steinberg, L., Cauffman, E., & Mulvey, E. P. (2009). Trajectories of antisocial behavior and psychosocial maturity from adolescence to young adulthood. *Developmental Psychology, 45,* 1654–1668. doi:10.1037/a0015862

Moretti, M. M., Odgers, C. L., & Jackson, M. A. (Eds.). (2004). *Girls and aggression: Contributing factors and intervention principles.* New York, NY: Kluwer Academic/Plenum. doi:10.1007/978-1-4419-8985-7

Morse, S. J. (2005). Brain overclaim syndrome and criminal responsibility: A diagnostic note. *Ohio State Journal of Criminal Law, 3,* 397–412.

Morse, S. J. (2013). Brain overclaim redux. *Law and Inequality, 31,* 509–534.

Mulvey, E. P., & Schubert, C. A. (2012). Some initial findings and policy implications of the pathways to desistance study. *Victims and Offenders, 7,* 407–427. doi:10.1080/15564886.2012.713903

Mulvey, E. P., Steinberg, L., Fagan, J., Cauffman, E., Piquero, A. R., Chassin, L., . . . Losoya, S. H. (2004). Theory and research on desistance from antisocial activity among serious adolescent offenders. *Youth Violence and Juvenile Justice, 2,* 213–236. doi:10.1177/1541204004265864

O'Brien, L., Albert, D., Chein, J., & Steinberg, L. (2011). Adolescents prefer more immediate rewards when in the presence of their peers. *Journal of Research on Adolescence, 21,* 747–753. doi:10.1111/j.1532-7795.2011.00738.x

O'Connor, T. G., & Rutter, M. (1996). Risk mechanisms in development: Some conceptual and methodological considerations. *Developmental Psychology, 32,* 787–795. doi:10.1037/0012-1649.32.4.787

Odgers, C. L., Robins, S., & Russell, M. (2010). Morbidity and mortality risk among the "forgotten few": Why are girls in the justice system in such poor health? *Law and Human Behavior, 34,* 429–444. doi:10.1007/s10979-009-9199-3

O'Donnell, P. C., & Gross, B. (2012). Developmental incompetence to stand trial in juvenile courts. *Journal of Forensic Sciences, 57,* 989–996. doi:10.1111/j.1556-4029.2012.02093.x

Olver, M. E., Stockdale, K. C., & Wormith, J. S. (2009). Risk assessment with young offenders: A meta-analysis of three measures. *Criminal Justice and Behavior, 36,* 329–353. doi:10.1177/0093854809331457

Owen-Kostelnik, J., Reppucci, N. D., & Meyer, J. R. (2006). Testimony and interrogation of minors: Assumptions about maturity and morality. *American Psychologist, 61,* 286–304. doi:10.1037/0003-066X.61.4.286

Pagani, L. S. (2009). The influence of family context on the development and persistence of antisocial behavior. In J. Savage (Ed.), *The development of persistent criminality* (pp. 37–53). New York, NY: Oxford University Press. doi:10.1093/acprof:oso/9780195310313.003.0002

Paus, T. (2010). Growth of white matter in the adolescent brain: Myelin or axon? *Brain and Cognition, 72,* 26–35. doi:10.1016/j.bandc.2009.06.002

Payne, A. A., & Welch, K. (2013). The impact of schools and education on antisocial behavior during childhood and adolescence. In C. L. Gibson & M. D. Krohn (Eds.), *Handbook of life-course criminology* (pp. 93–109). New York, NY: Springer. doi:10.1007/978-1-4614-5113-6_6

Payne, B. K., Time, V., & Gainey, R. R. (2006). Police chiefs' and students' attitudes about the *Miranda* warnings. *Journal of Criminal Justice, 34,* 653–660. doi:10.1016/j.jcrimjus.2006.09.018

Pennell, J., Shapiro, C., & Spigner, C. (2011). *Safety, fairness, stability: Repositioning juvenile justice and child welfare to engage families and communities.* Washington, DC: Center for Juvenile Justice Reform, Georgetown University.

Peper, J. S., & Dahl, R. E. (2013). The teenage brain: Surging hormones—brain-behavior interactions during puberty. *Current Directions in Psychological Science, 22,* 134–139. doi:10.1177/0963721412473755

Piquero, A. R., Monahan, K. C., Glasheen, C., Schubert, C. A., & Mulvey, E. P. (2013). Does time matter? Comparing trajectory concordance and covariate association using time-based and age-based assessments. *Crime and Delinquency, 59,* 738–763. doi:10.1177/0011128712459491

Portnoy, J., Gao, Y., Glenn, A. L., Niv, S., Peskin, M., Rudo-Hutt, A., & Raine, A. (2013). The biology of childhood crime and antisocial behavior. In C. L. Gibson, M. D. Krohn (Eds.), *Handbook of life-course criminology* (pp. 21–42). New York, NY: Springer. doi:10.1007/978-1-4614-5113-6_2

Poythress, N., Nicholson, R., Otto, R., Edens, J., Bonnie, R., Monahan, J., & Hoge, S. (1999). *The MacArthur Competence Assessment Tool–Criminal adjudication: Professional manual.* Odessa, FL: Psychological Assessment Resources.

Puzzanchera, C., & Hockenberry, S. (2013). *Juvenile court statistics 2010.* Pittsburgh, PA: National Center for Juvenile Justice.

Reppucci, N. D., Meyer, J., & Kostelnik, J. (2010). Custodial interrogation of juveniles: A national survey of police. In D. G. Lassiter & C. Meissner (Eds.), *Police interrogations and false confessions: Current research, practice, and policy recommendations* (pp. 67–80). Washington, DC: American Psychological Association.

Rogers, R. (2011). Getting it wrong about *Miranda* rights: False beliefs, impaired reasoning, and professional neglect. *American Psychologist, 66,* 728–736. doi:10.1037/a0024988

Roper v. Simmons, 543 U.S. 541 (2005).

Rutter, M. (1981). Stress, coping, and development: Some issues and some questions. *Journal of Child Psychology and Psychiatry, and Allied Disciplines, 22,* 323–356. doi:10.1111/j.1469-7610.1981.tb00560.x

Rutter, M., & Rutter, M. (1993). *Developing minds: Challenge and continuity across the life span.* New York, NY: Basic Books.

Ryba, N. L., Cooper, V. G., & Zapf, P. A. (2003). Juvenile competence to stand trial evaluations: A survey of current practices and test usage among psychologists. *Professional Psychology: Research and Practice, 34,* 499–507. doi:10.1037/0735-7028.34.5.499

Sampson, R. J., & Laub, J. H. (2005). A life-course view of the development of crime. *Annals of the American Academy of Political and Social Science, 602,* 12–45. doi:10.1177/0002716205280075

Savage, J. (2009). Understanding persistent offending: Linking developmental psychology with research on the criminal career. In J. Savage (Ed.), *The development of persistent criminality* (pp. 3–34). New York, NY: Oxford University Press. doi:10.1093/acprof:oso/9780195310313.003.0001

Schmidt, F., Campbell, M. A., & Houlding, C. (2011). Comparative analyses of the YLS/CMI, SAVRY, and PCL:YV in adolescent offenders: A 10-year follow-up into adulthood. *Youth Violence and Juvenile Justice, 9,* 23–42. doi:10.1177/1541204010371793

Schmidt, M., Reppucci, N. D., & Woolard, J. L. (2003). Effectiveness of participation as a defendant: The attorney–juvenile client relationship. *Behavioral Sciences and the Law, 21,* 175–198. doi:10.1002/bsl.532

Schmithorst, V. J., & Yuan, W. (2010). White matter development during adolescence as shown by diffusion MRI. *Brain and Cognition, 72,* 16–25. doi:10.1016/j.bandc.2009.06.005

Schubert, C. A., Mulvey, E. P., Loughran, T. A., Fagan, J., Chassin, L. A., Piquero, A. R., . . . Cauffman, E. (2010). Predicting outcomes for youth transferred to adult court. *Law and Human Behavior, 34,* 460–475. doi:10.1007/s10979-009-9209-5

Scott, E. S. (2013). *Miller v. Alabama* and the (past and) future of juvenile crime regulation. *Law and Inequality, 31,* 535–558.

Scott, E. S., Reppucci, N. D., & Woolard, J. L. (1995). Evaluating adolescent decision making in legal contexts. *Law and Human Behavior, 19,* 221–244. doi:10.1007/BF01501658

Seagrave, D., & Grisso, T. (2002). Adolescent development and the measurement of juvenile psychopathy. *Law and Human Behavior, 26,* 219–239. doi:10.1023/A:1014696110850

Sebastian, C., Viding, E., Williams, K. D., & Blakemore, S. J. (2010). Social brain development and the affective consequences of ostracism in adolescence. *Brain and Cognition, 72,* 134–145. doi:10.1016/j.bandc.2009.06.008

Selazo, P. D., & Carlson, S. M. (2012). Hot and cool executive function in childhood and adolescence: Development and plasticity. *Child Development Perspectives, 6,* 354–360.

Somerville, L. H. (2013). The teenage brain: Sensitivity to social evaluation. *Current Directions in Psychological Science, 22,* 121–127. doi:10.1177/0963721413476512

Somerville, L. H., Jones, R. M., & Casey, B. J. (2010). A time of change: Behavioral and neural correlates of adolescent sensitivity to appetitive and aversive environmental cues. *Brain and Cognition, 72,* 124–133. doi:10.1016/j.bandc.2009.07.003

Sowell, E. R., Peterson, B. S., Thompson, P. M., Welcome, S. E., Henkenius, A. L., & Toga, A. W. (2003). Mapping cortical change across the human life span. *Nature Neuroscience, 6,* 309–315. doi:10.1038/nn1008

Steinberg, L. (2009). Adolescent development and juvenile justice. *Annual Review of Clinical Psychology, 5,* 459–485. doi:10.1146/annurev.clinpsy.032408.153603

Steinberg, L. (2010). A behavioral scientist looks at the science of adolescent brain development. *Brain and Cognition, 72,* 160–164. doi:10.1016/j.bandc.2009.11.003

Steinberg, L., & Cauffman, E. (1996). Maturity of judgment in adolescence. *Law and Human Behavior, 20,* 249–272. doi:10.1007/BF01499023

Steinberg, L., Cauffman, E., Woolard, J. L., Graham, S., & Banich, M. (2009). Are adolescents less mature than adults? Minors' access to abortion, the juvenile death penalty, and the alleged APA flip-flop. *American Psychologist, 64,* 583–594. doi:10.1037/a0014763

Steinberg, L., Graham, S., O'Brien, L., Woolard, J. L., Cauffman, E., & Banich, M. (2009). Age differences in future orientation and delay discounting. *Child Development, 80,* 28–44. doi:10.1111/j.1467-8624.2008.01244.x

Steinberg, L., & Morris, A. (2001). Adolescent development. *Annual Review of Psychology, 52,* 83–110. doi:10.1146/annurev.psych.52.1.83

Stix, G. (2008, July 21). Can fMRI really tell if you're lying? *Scientific American.* Retrieved from http://www.scientificamerican.com/article/new-lie-detector

Sweeten, G., Pyrooz, D. C., & Piquero, A. R. (2013). Disengaging from gangs and desistance from crime. *Justice Quarterly, 30,* 469–500. doi:10.1080/07418825.2012.723033

Sylvers, P., Ryan, S., Alden, A., & Brennan, P. A. (2009). Biological factors and the development of persistent criminality. In J. Savage (Ed.), *The development of persistent criminality* (pp. 141–162). New York, NY: Oxford University Press. doi:10.1093/acprof:oso/9780195310313.003.0007

Teplin, L. A., Abram, K. M., McClelland, G. M., Dulcan, M. K., & Mericle, A. A. (2002). Psychiatric disorders in youth in juvenile detention. *Archives of General Psychiatry, 59,* 1133–1143. doi:10.1001/archpsyc.59.12.1133

U.S. Department of Justice. (2012). *Crime in the United States, 2012.* Retrieved from http://www.fbi.gov/about-us/cjis/ucr/crime-in-the-u.s/2012

Van Duijvenvoorde, D., & Crone, C. (2013). The teenage brain: A neuroeconomic approach to adolescent decision making. *Current Directions in Psychological Science, 22,* 108–113. doi:10.1177/0963721413475446

Viljoen, J. L., Klaver, J., & Roesch, R. (2005). Legal decisions of preadolescent and adolescent defendants: Predictors of confessions, pleas, communication with attorneys, and appeals. *Law and Human Behavior, 29,* 253–277. doi:10.1007/s10979-005-3613-2

Wahlstrom, D., Collins, P., White, T., & Luciana, M. (2010). Developmental changes in dopamine neurotransmission in adolescence: Behavioral implications and issues in assessment. *Brain and Cognition, 72,* 146–159. doi:10.1016/j.bandc.2009.10.013

Warren, J. I., Aaron, J., Ryan, E., Chauhan, P., & DuVal, J. (2003). Correlates of adjudicative competence among psychiatrically impaired juveniles. *Journal of the American Academy of Psychiatry and the Law, 31,* 299–309.

Warren, J. I., DuVal, J., Komarovskaya, I., Chauhan, P., Buffington-Vollumup, J., & Ryan, E. (2009). Developing a forensic service delivery system for juveniles adjudicated incompetent to stand trial. *International Journal of Forensic Mental Health, 8,* 245–262. doi:10.1080/14999011003635670

Wasserman, G. A., McReynolds, L., Ko, S., Katz, L., & Carpenter, J. (2005). Gender differences in psychiatric disorders at juvenile probation intake. *American Journal of Public Health, 95,* 131–137. doi:10.2105/AJPH.2003.024737

Weisberg, D. S., Keil, F. C., Goodstein, J., Rawson, E., & Gray, J. R. (2008). The seductive allure of neuroscience explanations. *Journal of Cognitive Neuroscience, 20,* 470–477. doi:10.1162/jocn.2008.20040

Wolf, L. K., Wright, N. D., Kilford, E. J., Dolan, R. J., & Blakemore, S. J. (2013). Developmental changes in effects of risk and valence on adolescent decision-making. *Cognitive Development, 28,* 290–299. doi:10.1016/j.cogdev.2013.04.001

Wong, M., & Spitzer, K. (2008). *The rising costs of the city's juvenile justice system.* New York: Report of the New York City Independent Budget Office Fiscal Brief.

Woolard, J. L., Cleary, H. D., Harvell, S. S., & Chen, R. (2008). Examining adolescents' and their parents' conceptual and practical knowledge of police interrogation: A family dyad approach. *Journal of Youth and Adolescence, 37,* 685–698. doi:10.1007/s10964-008-9288-5

Woolard, J. L., Odgers, C., Lanza-Kaduce, L., & Daglis, H. (2005). Juveniles within adult correctional settings: Legal pathways and developmental considerations. *International Journal of Forensic Mental Health, 4,* 1–18. doi:10.1080/14999013.2005.10471209

Zahn, M. A., Brumbaugh, S., Steffensmeier, D., Feld, B. C., Morash, M., & Chesney-Lind, M. (2008). *Violence by teenage girls: Trends and context.* Washington, DC: U.S. Department of Justice. Retrieved from http://www.ncjrs.gov/pdffiles1/ojjdp/218905.pdf

Zelazo, P. D., & Carlson, S. M. (2012). Hot and cool executive function in childhood and adolescence: Development and plasticity. *Child Development Perspectives, 6,* 354–360.

Zelazo, P. D., & Müller, U. (2007). Executive function in typical and atypical development. In U. Goswami (Ed.), *Blackwell handbook of childhood cognitive development* (pp. 445–469). Malden, MA: Blackwell.

CHAPTER 3

ELDERS AND THE JUSTICE SYSTEM

Eve M. Brank and Lindsey E. Wylie

The broad topic of elders and the justice system requires that we address both the production and application of psychological knowledge (Bartol & Bartol, 2006). Similar to the chapter on race in the justice system (see Chapter 5, this volume), we address the justice system from multiple angles because older adult issues permeate all facets of the justice system. As such, we discuss psychological issues of importance for older adult victims, witnesses, offenders, and jurors. Given the page restrictions and the array of topics inherent in this kind of chapter, our review is not intended to be exhaustive, rather it is a selective review designed to encourage future work and exploration in this area of urgent need (Eglit, 2004).

We begin by examining the population growth of older adults, both in absolute numbers and proportionally. There is no precise criteria for a person to be considered an elder, and, unlike other groups who experience group-based discrimination, sometimes there are very good reasons for an older adult to be treated differently than a younger adult. With this in mind, we will address the relevant psychological theory and principles that focus specifically on the biological and cognitive bases for separate attention to elders within the justice system. As a group, older adults face greater physical and cognitive vulnerabilities, but some older adults continue to function cognitively and physically in much the same way as younger adults. Similarly, we address the presumption of competence and the potential

for discrimination of older adults based on ageist stereotypes. Next, we review the relevant research, focusing first on general methodological issues related to older adults. The rest of the research review section addresses older adults as victims, eyewitnesses, offenders, and jurors. In each instance, although there are some differences between older adults and younger adults, those differences are not as pronounced as people generally believe them to be. We turn next to the practice and policy section, where we recommend that the justice system should be cautious in making overly drastic adjustments for older adults: the research does not support doing so, and doing so could unintentionally send a discriminatory message to older adults (e.g., exclusion from juror service for older adults may send the message that older adults are not welcome as jurors). Our final section provides a brief summary and our conclusions from the chapter.

IMPORTANCE OF THE PROBLEM

As a society, we are getting older. This is happening because of the combined effect of higher birth rates and longer life spans (Arias, 2006). An average life span has increased approximately 10 years since the middle of the last century (National Center for Health Statistics, 2005), which is generally attributed to better medical care and living conditions. As a result, more people are reaching ages that have traditionally been considered "old"

The authors thank Liz Kneifl, Derek Grutsch, Mabry Brank, and Freida Pan for their assistance with this chapter.

http://dx.doi.org/10.1037/14462-003
APA Handbook of Forensic Psychology: Vol. 2. Criminal Investigation, Adjudication, and Sentencing Outcomes,
B. L. Cutler and P. A. Zapf (Editors-in-Chief)
Copyright © 2015 by the American Psychological Association. All rights reserved.

(Frolik & Kaplan, 2010). The first of the baby boomers turned 65 in 2011, and census predictions indicate that older adult populations will nearly double in the next few decades. According to the Pew Research Center, across the next two decades, approximately 10,000 people will have their 65th birthday every day (Cohn & Taylor, 2010). Every aspect of life, including the criminal justice system, is therefore expected to see an increase in the number of older adults (Rothman, Dunlap, & Entzel, 2000). With this comes the need for the legal system to respond with "alteration, accommodation, and innovation" (Eglit, 2004).

Two particular challenges in this area, however, are the lack of clear boundaries for who is and is not within the group considered *older adults* and what seems to be a moving target for the definition of *old age* (Brank, 2007, p. 702). The age of 65 years old or older is generally used, but that may not always apply. Sixty-five years old is the age at which a person becomes eligible to obtain Medicare in the United States, but there are a number of other age limits that could just as easily be used as a boundary. Social Security payments can start as early as 62, but the monthly payments will be reduced based on the difference between that age and the person's "full retirement age," which currently ranges from 65 to 67 years of age determined by the year of birth (Social Security, 2012). Conversely, recipients can increase their Social Security monthly benefits by delaying their benefits and waiting until they are 70 years of age (Social Security, 2012).

A number of state statutes, particularly those concerned with neglect and abuse, define *older adult* as a person 60 years of age or older (e.g., Adult Protective Services Definitions Act of 2012). The Age Discrimination in Employment Act (ADEA) generally forbids discrimination of workers 40 years of age or older. Biological evidence demonstrates that organs thicken and stiffen and become less efficient with age, and that process begins in the 20s. Maybe 30 should be the magic age at which old age begins? This age boundary mutability is just one example of the inherent difficulties in considering older adult issues. Not only is there the current variability, but we should expect this variability to be a particular problem over time as life expectancies increase and retirement ages likely increase. In other words, although 65 may seem the right age now for Medicare benefits to start, that may not be true when the majority of workers are staying in the workforce until age 80 and living until age 100. Nonetheless, for the purposes of this chapter, we generally mean anyone 65 years or older in our discussions of older adults.

Assuming that we define an older adult as someone who has achieved an age somewhere around 65 years old, probability strongly suggests that we will see a greater number of older adults throughout the justice system. In addition to the simple probability, Eglit (2004) notes that the current and upcoming generation of older adults is wealthier, more educated, and more involved in activities outside the home than previous generations have been. Combined, this makes for an even greater increased likelihood that older adults will be involved in the legal system in all facets, yet we live in a society in which there is an underlying bias against the old (Eglit, 2004). There is a general notion that older adults are in poor physical health and widely suffer from dementia; such incorrect stereotypes contribute to this age-based bias. Compared to agrarian societies that generally venerate the aged, industrialized societies are known to displace older adults from their places of authority (Butler, 2009), making old age something to be feared (Brank, 2011) and fought (Nelson, 2002).

At the same time, and unlike other categories, age can be an appropriate qualification in certain situations. For example, the age qualification for the Office of the President of the United States is 35 years of age or older (Constitution of the United States, Art. II, Sec. 1, Clause 5). There are no race or gender exclusions. We also set age restrictions in many different kinds of situations, such as military service and voting. Again, we do not have similar restrictions based on race or gender. Inasmuch as we do change developmentally as we age, this difference should not be particularly surprising, but this presents the challenging side of studying older adults as a specified group within the justice system: We cannot lump them together with all the other groups that suffer discrimination because sometimes there are very good reasons to consider age groups separately and distinctly. We now examine the psychological research that has addressed elder issues separately within the justice system, starting with the biological and cognitive reasons why it is important to do so.

RELEVANT PSYCHOLOGICAL THEORY AND PRINCIPLES

The main underlying psychological theories and principles involve the biological and cognitive bases for treating older adults differently than younger adults. Resulting from these differences are questions of competency and the potential for discrimination against older adults based on stereotypes and bias. Each of these will be addressed in the sections that follow.

Biological and Cognitive Bases for Separate Attention to Elder Issues

As we age, our bodies and minds go through developmental changes. Many of those changes are easily visible but are nonpathological (e.g., hair turning gray or skin being prone to more wrinkling). Other age-induced alterations create susceptibilities to a person's body and mind that increase risks of injury, illness, and death (Miller, 1999). Age is a known contributing factor for medical issues like heart disease, cancer, osteoporosis, and Alzheimer's disease (Amant et al., 2005; Neary & Snowden, 2003; Wilkins & Birge, 2005). Diminished hearing and vision abilities more commonly plague older adults as compared to younger adults. (Brodie, 2003; Schoenborn, Vickerie, & Powell-Griner, 2006).

Although it is true that the proportion of cognitive disabilities (e.g., dementia and Alzheimer's disease) is higher among older adults as compared to younger adults, most older adults have normal levels of cognitive functioning (Dunkin & Kasl-Godley, 2000). For example, even though the ability to solve novel problems without prior training (i.e., fluid intelligence) generally declines with age (Stuart-Hamilton, 2003, but see Beier & Ackerman, 2003), a person's crystalized intelligence (i.e., the knowledge the person has) remains stable or improves with age. Memory abilities are commonly believed to decline with age and research does suggest that there is a correlation between age and memory deterioration. Working memory, prospective memory, long-term memory, and short-term memory all show signs of degeneration (Maylor, 1998; Stuart-Hamilton, 2003). Some memory declines are fairly universal but may be influenced by a self-report inflation. For example, even when they were correct in a memory task, Parkin and Walter (1992) reported that older adult participants were significantly less confident than younger participants about their abilities.

The biological and cognitive research is clear that some developmental changes are inevitable in aging, but the rate and extent of those are not easily predicted (Jarvik & Small, 2000). Some older adults continue to function both cognitively and physically in very similar, and sometimes better, ways than do their younger counterparts. Nonetheless, as a group, older adults proportionally face greater deficits of physical capabilities, and degenerations of mental capacity, as well as more economic vulnerabilities (Frolik & Barnes, 2011). Taken together, there are important considerations the justice system must address for this subgroup of the population.

Competency and Incapacity Determinations

Within the law, all adults are presumed to be competent unless proven otherwise (see Volume 1, Chapter 16, this handbook for reviews of research on criminal and civil competencies, respectively). Contrasted to juvenile law, in which the law has defined specific milestones based on biological age (see Chapter 2, this volume), there is no specific age at which a person automatically loses legal decision-making capacity. Consider driving privileges: generally, at 16 or 17 years of age, a teenager is legally permitted to obtain a driver's license. Although some states have enacted accelerated periods or special requirements for older drivers (e.g., vision tests, road tests, and medical certification), no state automatically disallows a driver's license solely based on advanced age. Another good example is the decision to marry. Although minors are restricted from entering into a marriage or having consensual sexual relations, there is no similar restriction at the other end of the age spectrum (despite some familial concerns about late-in-life marriages). Because advanced age is not a legal proxy for competence, other determinations are required when a person may not have the requisite mental capacity to make decisions (see Volume 1, Chapter 16, this handbook).

For older adults, capacity is not a clearly defined concept (Eglit, 2004) and often cannot be determined with a simple yes-or-no answer. Rather, capacity should be thought of as a multifaceted continuum. Older adults may be competent for certain tasks, but not for others. The general topic of elder law addresses the idea of competency at relatively great length because an attorney representing an older adult must be certain that the older adult meets the requisite standards of competency in order to interact meaningfully on the particular legal issue. It is especially important to remember with older adults that bad decisions do not equal incompetence. Eccentricity is not a defining factor for incompetency (Frolik & Kaplan, 2010). Co-occurring medical issues also complicate matters because some physical conditions can manifest with mental symptoms. As an example, mental confusion is a common symptom of a urinary tract infection; it can be the only apparent symptom when the patient is elderly (MedlinePlus, 2012). This is also true when there are prescription drug treatment plans that have side effects and other indications that could be misconstrued as failing mental health. Such confusion can be misdiagnosed as chronic cognitive problems and misconstrued as incompetence, which could have serious consequences for the older adult.

Several screening tools are used to assess dementia and cognitive functioning in older adults, yet a review of the research suggests that they are not being used widely within the justice system (see Volume 1, Chapter 2, this handbook for a review of forensic assessment instruments). The Mini-Mental State Examination (MMSE) is a widely used tool for assessing older adult dementia in clinical and research settings (Friedman, Yelland, & Robinson, 2011). Although a great number of researchers have examined competence in forensic settings (see Volume 1, Chapters 5 and 16, this handbook), there has not been the kind of attention for older adults that there is for adolescents.

When older adult competency is at issue, it is generally in the context of civil competence (see Volume 1, Chapter 16, this handbook). For example, Christy, Bond, and Young (2007) studied involuntary civil commitment examinations of older adults and determined that approximately 13% of the involuntary examinations were for adults 60 years or older (the authors' definition of *older adult*) and more than 20% of those experienced more than one evaluation during the five-year period the authors examined. Although the research only reported the number of examinations and not the conclusions of those examinations, these percentages suggest that an older adult's competence could be of concern or at issue for many older adults. Ultimately, competency should receive attention when we are considering older adults in the justice system as victims, perpetrators, witnesses, or legal actors; however, incompetency should not be the expectation. Many older adults do not suffer from any cognitive deficits, yet there is a stereotype that more are incompetent than truly are.

Stereotypes and Discrimination

Ageism was first used to describe prejudice and discrimination toward older individuals by Butler (1969) and has often been referred to as the third *-ism* present in our society (after racism and sexism; Butler, 1995; see Volume 1, Chapter 15, this handbook and Chapter 5, this volume for reviews of discrimination associated with sex and race). Ageism is thought to be quite prevalent today, with age stereotypes more pronounced than gender stereotypes (Kite, Deaux, & Miele, 1991). Contrary to its apparent pervasiveness, ageism is understudied compared to racism and sexism, most likely because it is thought to be the most socially condoned form of prejudice (Nelson, 2002). Across studies examining old age stereotypes, similar themes emerge. The elderly are often ascribed as possessing both positive and negative stereotypes (Barrett & Cantwell, 2007; Cuddy, Norton, and Fiske, 2005; Kite, Stockdale, Whitley, & Johnson, 2005); however, endorsements of negative stereotypes are more prevalent (Hummert, 1993; Kite et al., 1991; Nelson, 2002).

The Stereotype Content Model (SCM), proposed by Fiske, Cuddy, Glick, and Xu (2002), is a theoretical lens through which we can understand these dichotomous positive and negative stereotypes. According to the SCM, we categorize out-groups according to two dimensions: competence and warmth. Four quadrants are formed from high and low values in each of these dimensions. According to the model, the quadrant into which a stereotyped group falls will predict the type of prejudice the group will likely experience. Older adults generally fall into the quadrant characterized by low competence and high warmth (Cuddy et al., 2005), which results in a mixed stereotype that can lead to a confusing combination of active helping and social neglecting (Fiske & Taylor, 2008).

Although we address the older eyewitness more specifically later, generally speaking, older adult stereotypes influence views of older eyewitnesses. Eyewitness research (see Chapter 7, this volume) indicates that older eyewitnesses are viewed as less accurate, less competent, but more honest than younger adult witnesses (Kwong See, Hoffman, & Wood, 2001; Mueller-Johnson, Toglia, Sweeney, & Ceci, 2007; Ross, Dunning, Toglia, & Ceci, 1990, experiment 3). Mock jurors are consequently less likely to convict defendants when the main evidence against them comes from an elderly (as opposed to a middle-aged adult) eyewitness (Neal, Christiansen, Bornstein, & Robicheaux, 2012). Although the perceived lack of credibility for older adults could in part be because older eyewitnesses often provide fewer details and lack confidence when describing crime scene information (Brimacombe, Quinton, Nance, & Garrioch, 1997), research has found that ageist attitudes may be the true reason and were related unfavorably to ratings of witnesses on convincingness, quality of observation and memory, and level of cognitive function (Mueller-Johnson et al., 2007).

Other underlying age biases also matter. Eyewitness research again provides the best example of this in research conducted by Nunez, McCoy, Clark, and Shaw (1999) in which community members read a trial summary that included testimony from an eyewitness. The descriptions of the eyewitness varied by age and by positive or negative elderly labels: a generic adult eyewitness aged 31; a generic elderly eyewitness aged 66; a senior citizen aged 66 (described to elicit a sense of vulnerability); a grandfather aged 66; and a statesman aged 66. Although results demonstrated that participants' ratings of believability of the eyewitness did not differ across conditions, participants' verdicts did vary as a function of the elderly labels. For example, participants rendered more guilty verdicts when the statesman was the eyewitness than the other elder categories. Similarly, guilty verdicts were significantly higher when the eyewitness testimony was given by the generic elder than for the vulnerable senior citizen. These results suggest that negative judgments of older adults (eyewitnesses in this research) are not only the result of the stated age, but are also due to underlying stereotypes of "old."

RESEARCH REVIEW

Although research attention to older adults in the justice system has not been as deeply or widely examined as other groups, there is a growing body of work in the specific areas related to older adult victims, eyewitnesses, and offenders. In addition, older adult jurors have garnered some attention. Each of these areas will be explored in the following sections.

General Methodological Issues

It is well documented that social psychology research relies too heavily on samples of college student participants in artificial laboratory settings (Sears, 1986). Similarly, forensic psychology research on and involving older adults has been relatively sparse, with only a very small proportion of the published research in the field having a focus on older adults, and undergraduate psychology textbooks reflect the dearth of research attention to older adults (Brank, 2007). When age comparisons do occur in forensic psychology research, it is generally a comparison of college students to other ages—often comparing college students to older adults. Inherent in such a comparison is one homogenous group with limited upper and lower age limits and one heterogeneous group with only a lower age limit. In other words, the *young adult* groups are comprised of college students who are mostly between the ages of 18 and 22. The *older adult* samples can represent a much wider variation in education level attained, and their ages can range 10, 20, or more years (e.g., 60 years and older). Such unequal comparison groups could create bias in the research findings and should be kept in mind when considering the research implications.

Often the areas that have received attention are more descriptive in nature rather than experimental, but some areas, such as eyewitness research, have used traditional experimental methods in addressing older adult issues in the justice system. In the subsections that follow we detail those areas of descriptive and experimental forensic and related psychology research that have more extensively addressed older adults within the justice system. Those areas are older adult victims, eyewitnesses, offenders, and jurors.

Victims

Older adult maltreatment by formal or informal caregivers is a relatively well hidden crime with poorly defined parameters and suggested responses (Loue, 2001). Estimates of prevalence rates range from 5% to 30% (Dong & Simon, 2011), with most incidents likely going unreported (Frolik & Kaplan, 2010). Whereas research and attention has soared in other areas of family violence (see Volume 1, Chapter 12, this handbook), attention to older adult maltreatment has trailed behind (Kohn, 2003; Rathbone-McCuan, 2000). The research that has been conducted has generally focused on detecting abuse, defining abuse, and reporting abuse rather than on preventing abuse (Kapp, 1995). One reason for the inattention can be attributed to the fact that for many years elder abuse was considered a civil rather than criminal issue (Heisler & Stiegel, 2002). Additionally, caregiver stress is the most often provided explanation for elder maltreatment (McGreevey, 2005), but focusing on this stress suggests that some level of blame rests with the older adult because they are viewed as creating the burden in an entirely different way from the explanations for child maltreatment.

An important distinction between maltreatment of older adults and children is that there is a much

greater risk and potential for financial exploitation and abuse of older adults than there is of children. In addition, because we do not have compulsory education laws for older adults in the same way we do for children, older adults can live many years in an abusive situation without any outside detection and intervention (Brank, 2007). Compounding this, many older adults are embarrassed by the abuse because often the abusers are their own adult children. Assessing abuse is more often studied within younger populations than within older populations, yet limited research suggests that interviewing methodologies traditionally used with younger populations may be successfully adapted for use with older adults (Acierno, Resnick, Kilpatrick, & Stark-Riemer, 2003).

Golding and colleagues have examined the way jurors interpret and decide cases of elder abuse, finding that there may be age effects with believability of alleged victims (E. E. Dunlap, Golding, Hodell, & Marsil, 2007) and that the health status of the elder accuser also may influence mock jurors' decisions about the case (Kinstle, Hodell, & Golding, 2008), including more guilty verdicts by mock jurors when the alleged victim had cognitive deficits compared to when they did not (Golding et al. 2004). The age of the older adult (i.e., 66, 76, or 86), however, did not have an effect on guilty verdicts or other related variables (Golding, Yozwiak, Kinstle, & Marsil, 2005).

Although there has been some recent growing attention (Heisler, 2012), it is clear that we need much more in terms of research and documentation of elder maltreatment, including longitudinal incidence studies, to examine risk and protective factors (Dong & Simon, 2011). In their vision for the next decade, Giles, Brewer, Mosqueda, Huba, and Melchior (2010) outlined five needs that will help advance the field and better address older adult maltreatment. Those needs include increased public awareness, improved identification of cases, increased integrated service models, improved justice system response, and a better utilization of resources. Of particular importance to forensic psychologists, Giles et al. (2010) note that one important area of need is the development of screening instruments to detect and respond to abuse.

Research demonstrates that elder mistreatment is related to poor self-rated health (Cisler, Amstadter, Begle, Hernandez, & Acierno, 2010) and some manifestations of abuse (e.g., bruising) can be mistakenly attributed to natural aging (Heisler, 2012). Therefore, appropriate screening is particularly important and ripe for forensic psychology research attention.

One barrier has been that older adult maltreatment statutes are mirrored after child maltreatment statutes (Brank, Wylie, & Hamm, 2012), with some states having identical statutes except for substituting "elderly person" in place of "child" (e.g., Florida). Superficially, this may seem wise and efficient because the justice system's response to child maltreatment has a longer and deeper history; however, several important issues, including self-neglect and financial exploitation, make blanket application inappropriate.

Self-neglect. Another barrier to understanding and better responding to elder maltreatment is the high prevalence of elder self-neglect (Connolly, 2008) and the difficulty of differentiating self-neglect from other neglect (Brank et al., 2012; Wylie & Brank, 2009). An autonomous adult can choose not to bathe, eat, and attend doctors' appointments, but when that adult is in the care of another person, there is a requisite level of care. Determining the difference between self-neglect and other neglect is tricky, however, and in need of much better coordination of efforts (Connolly, 2010). Indeed, in a popular legal book for elder law, the authors note that self-neglect would be better seen as an "indication of individuals who lack the necessary capacity to take care of themselves or that they suffer from a mental illness" (Frolik & Kaplan, 2010). Although that may be true some of the time, it negates the possibility that a person could competently decide to self-neglect (Loue, 2001). In addition, not allowing an older adult to be eccentrically unkempt is a form of ageism (Butler, 1969; Loue, 2001). In fact, the federal Patient Self-Determination Act (PSDA) explicitly acknowledges the patient's right to refuse medical treatment even to the point of death (*Cruzan v. Director, Missouri Department of Health*, 1990) and

a competent patient has the right to oppose reporting of abuse (Geroff & Olshaker, 2006).

Financial exploitation. Financial exploitation is a rather unique type of abuse most often targeted at older adults that does not generally have a child maltreatment counterpart. Additionally, it is one of the more common types of abuse, with perpetrators being relatives and non-relatives (Acierno, et al., 2010) and can occur by itself or with other forms of abuse (Jackson & Hafemeister, 2012). In response to the gap between clinical understanding and legal definitions of financial abuse, Kemp and Mosqueda (2005) developed an interdisciplinary framework for detecting and evaluating financial abuse of older adults. In general, the framework consists of eight elements that should be considered and weighed when evaluating a possible financial abuse situation. For example, the elements relate to a transfer of assets without an expert determination of the older adult's capacity to make such a transfer. Additionally, the transfer should not involve disproportionate benefits compared to compensation. Other research has indicated that financial exploitation can occur more "routinely" when family members comingle money or do not keep records as detailed as they should (Setterlund, Tilse, Wilson, McCawley, & Rosenman, 2007).

Eyewitnesses

The independent variables primarily investigated in applied eyewitness research are divided into two distinct avenues for research: *system variables* that can be manipulated in an actual criminal case (e.g., structure of the lineup) and *estimator variables* that predict performance but cannot be manipulated by legal authorities (e.g., witness demographics; Wells, 1978; see Chapter 7, this volume for a review of research on eyewitness memory). Although estimator variables are not within the control of the justice system, sometimes the estimator variables influence system variables that are within the justice system's control, such as witness age. Although research examining the influence on age has mostly focused on children (see Chapter 1, this volume), older adults are becoming more visible in the legal system as eyewitnesses (Eglit, 2004; Flynn, 2000), making this area ripe for empirical research. Similar to general eyewitness research, there are three main outcome variables that are of interest when studying older eyewitnesses: event recall and/or face recognition accuracy, suggestibility/susceptibility to misinformation, and perceived credibility by triers of fact (e.g., mock jurors).

Event recall and/or facial recognition accuracy.
When comparing age differences on recall tasks, research has generally shown that older eyewitnesses are less accurate than younger eyewitnesses (Coxon & Valentine, 1997; List, 1986; Yarmey, 1993). This effect, however, appears to be influenced by the type of memory task used. A review by Bornstein (1995) indicated that even though studies have found that older eyewitnesses freely recall fewer correct details than younger adults, there were fewer age differences for recognizing event details or crime perpetrators. Age comparisons within facial recognition tasks, however, depend on the type of lineup. Older adults are less accurate when the target is absent, but they perform comparably to younger adults in target-present lineups (e.g., Yarmey & Kent, 1980). Memon and Gabbert (2003) examined the effects of simultaneous and sequential lineups that were either target-absent or target-present (four different conditions). Of these four conditions, older adults were more likely to make false identifications (or choose non-target photographs) in all but the simultaneous target-present lineup. Brimacombe, Jung, Garrioch, and Allison (2003) compared older seniors (average age of 79 years old), younger seniors (average age of 69 years old), and college students on recall of event details in an eyewitness task and found that the older seniors performed considerably worse than the other two groups.

Suggestibility/susceptibility to misinformation.
The second area examines age differences on susceptibility to misinformation when older adults are subjected to a standard misinformation effect paradigm (cf. Loftus, Miller, & Burns, 1978). Over 30 years of research has found that when people receive misleading information after an event, it can lead to memory distortion for the original event. Misinformation experiments typically involve three phases in which participants are exposed to a complex event, are presented with some inaccurate information about the event that is intended to mislead them about specific details, and are tested for their memory of the original event.

A recent review and meta-analysis by Wylie and colleagues (2012) examined studies that compared younger (M age $= 22$) and older adults (M age $= 71$) on misinformation/suggestibility effects across 23 published and unpublished studies. According to this review that resulted in 39 independent effect sizes, there was a small to medium effect ($ES_m = .29$) demonstrating that older adults were more susceptible to misinformation. Of the 39 effect sizes, 31 demonstrated that older adults were more susceptible to misinformation, and eight demonstrated the opposite or null effects. Studies with a higher mean age for the older adult sample were more likely to find misinformation/suggestibility differences between younger and older adults. The review also found that studies varied by whether older adults were more confident in their false memories than younger adults.

The Modified Cognitive Interview (CI) is an approach that has been examined for reducing the misinformation effect for older adults who had difficulty with generating contextual retrieval cues (Vakil, Hornik, & Levy; 2008). The CI is thought to improve recollection by asking eyewitnesses to recreate the context and think about different perspectives (Mello & Fisher, 1996). Holliday and colleagues (2011) compared the standard structured interview and the CI with older and younger adults and tested susceptibility to misinformation. Importantly, older adults tested with the CI elicited more correct details, demonstrated greater overall accuracy, and were not susceptible to misinformation effects. Future research should examine different interviewing techniques that may improve older adults' ability to retrieve information and the source of that information.

Perceived credibility by triers of fact. Generally speaking, older adults are stereotyped as having more difficulties with cognition and memory compared to younger adults. Eyewitness research indicates older eyewitnesses are viewed as less accurate, less competent, but more honest than younger adult witnesses (Kwong See et al., 2001; Mueller-Johnson et al., 2007; Ross et al., 1990, experiment 3). Mock jurors are consequently less likely to convict defendants when the main evidence against them comes from an elderly (as opposed to a middle-aged adult) eyewitness (Neal et al., 2012). Although the perceived lack of credibility for older adults could in part be because older eyewitnesses often provide fewer details and lack confidence when describing crime scene information (Brimacombe et al., 1997), research demonstrates that ageist attitudes may also contribute to unfavorable attitudes toward older adult witnesses (Mueller-Johnson et al., 2007).

Offenders

Although older adults generally make up a small proportion of the prison population, older adults are becoming more visible in the criminal justice system as offenders. This increase is due in part to general aging trends caused by the aging of baby boomers and improvements in health care that promote longevity. It is also due to crime trends and sentencing policies, such as "three strikes" policies and mandatory sentencing policies from the 1980s and 1990s (Kerbs, 2000), yet older adults only represent a small proportion of the arrests in the United States (Flynn, 2000) and life-course criminology certainly supports the idea that criminal offending declines with age (Sampson & Laub, 1992; see Chapter 2, this volume for a review of research on juvenile offenders).

Within the criminal justice system there are three types of aging offenders. The first are aging recidivists who have been involved in the legal system most of their lives as repeat offenders. The second are the relapsing aged offenders who engaged in criminal behavior when younger but had a period of non-criminal behavior and, for a variety of reasons, lapsed into criminal behavior in old age. The third are the older adult first-time offenders who were not involved in criminal behavior until they reached older age (Frolik & Barnes, 2011).

Lemieux, Dyeson, and Castiglione (2002) comprehensively reviewed literature on older inmates and correctional responses over the preceding three

decades. In general, the authors found that, despite the increase in the proportion of older adults in prisons, there was a relatively limited amount of research examining older inmates. Unfortunately, no consistent definition of old age was used (e.g., 50 and older versus 60 and older), which makes comparisons of mental health and other effects difficult and unreliable.

Older adults incarcerated for lengthier prison sentences have committed more violent offenses (Lemieux et al., 2002), which is not to say that older adults as a population are committing more violent offenses. An examination of the Uniform Crime Report arrest data using age-standardization techniques shows that older adults are most likely to be arrested for minor offenses and alcohol-related violations and that arrests rates and the proportion of arrests to younger offenders has remained steady since 1980. Thus, trends in elder crime are generally paralleled with trends from non-elders and are likely due to legal, social, and economical changes (Feldmeyer & Steffensmeier, 2007).

Leniency in sentencing. Another issue that emerges within elder justice is whether there are any leniency effects for older adults in sentencing. Psychological research has cited anecdotal leniency effects for older adults, but to date there have not been any empirical studies examining how judges and jurors incorporate age into sentencing decisions (Gaydon & Miller, 2007; see Chapter 14, this volume for research on sentencing). Regardless of whether age is dispositive of the final sentence, age is a factor that is likely considered during sentencing. In fact, the Federal Sentencing Guidelines (U.S. Sentencing Commission, 2011) indicate that old age and infirmity are relevant factors when considering whether a downward departure from the federal guidelines is warranted—especially if home confinement might be as effective and less costly than incarceration. According to the text of the guidelines, age should be considered only if the offender's characteristics are present to an unusual degree that distinguishes it from a typical case. The sentencing guidelines have been interpreted by courts to mean that age is not a reduction in sentence per se, but leniency may be granted if age has contributed to frailness or poor physical conditions (*U.S. v. Brooke*, 2002; *U.S. v. Bullion*, 2006; *U.S. v. Johnson*, 2012). In all of these cases, although the court agreed that the defendants were elderly and infirm, the judges' decisions were based on the fact that their age and health status would not deter them from committing future crimes—the fundamental rationale for the more lenient sentence.

Inmates and aging issues. The increase in the median age of inmates has brought new challenges for the correctional system (see Chapter 15, this volume for a review of research on prison overcrowding). One of the challenges includes housing for older adults with special needs. Administrators must decide whether older adults should reside with the general population, or whether to create special units or facilities to house older adults separately. Other challenges involve physical accommodations and provisions such as safety grab bars and special dietary services (Anno, Graham, Lawrence, & Shansky, 2004).

One of the central debates surrounding aging in prison is whether older inmates should be housed separately from the general population because of health and safety concerns. Currently, most state and federal prisons do not have separate units for older adults, but the trend has increased by 40% in five years (U.S. Department of Justice, Bureau of Justice Statistics, 2004, 2009). Despite the importance of inmate housing, there are no uniform state and federal policies to date that address these housing issues. Proponents of separate housing reason that an "age-friendly" environment may be most suitable because older inmates may have more medical problems and are vulnerable to attack by other inmates. In addition, the physical environment could be altered to include fewer stairwells and upper-bunk assignments, as well as fall-proof measures such as non-waxed floors. On the other hand, opponents of separate housing reason that older inmates can benefit from services that are centralized and available to both geriatric and non-geriatric populations if housed with the general population. Furthermore, older inmates could benefit from the social interaction with younger inmates (Thivierge-Rikard & Thompson, 2007).

Although usually not successful, some inmates have brought claims against prison administration for failure to protect the older inmates under the Eighth Amendment by way of separating them from the general population (*Brown v. Pattison*, 2004; *Edney v. Kerrigan*, 2004). To establish a failure to protect under the Eighth Amendment, an inmate plaintiff must satisfy a two-prong test: that the prison conditions posed a substantial risk of serious harm and that the prison officials were deliberately indifferent (had knowledge and disregarded the potential harm) to the plaintiff's health and safety. In general, it is difficult to show that the prison or correctional officers had requisite knowledge that the older adult was at higher risk for attacks. In fact, correctional officers have testified that they thought older adults would be less vulnerable to attack because of their status as elderly inmates (*Edney v. Kerrigan*, 2004, p. 17).

Accommodations and the Americans With Disabilities Act. Prisons were designed with younger, healthier inmates in mind; thus, many prisons are not physically equipped to handle older, unhealthy inmates. In 1990, the Americans With Disabilities Act (ADA) was passed by Congress to prohibit discrimination against people with disabilities and was applied to prisoners in 1998 (*Pennsylvania Department of Corrections v. Yeskey*, 1998). Prisons must make reasonable accommodations for inmates with disabilities, which can be costly for prisons.

The financial costs associated with having older adults in jails and prisons can be significantly larger because of health care costs. In general, the prison population is one of the unhealthiest populations in the nation, in part because of the unhealthy lifestyles of criminals before and during incarceration. Older adults may be even unhealthier because of chronic physical and mental illnesses caused by advanced aging, and prison life may exacerbate medical issues that already existed (Curran, 2000). In addition, older inmates who would be age- and asset-eligible for programs such as Medicaid and Medicare are not eligible while incarcerated because inmates' health needs are mostly covered by the state prison health care system (Public Health

Chapter IV, 42 C.F.R. § 411.4, 2007). Statistics show that it costs about $70,000 a year to house an inmate over the age of 60, whereas it costs only about $22,000 a year to house younger inmates (Kinsella, 2004). Despite its expense, federal and state prisons are constitutionally required to provide reasonable medical care under the Eighth Amendment (incorporated to the states through the Fourteenth Amendment). In *Estelle v. Gamble* (1976), the Supreme Court held that the Eight Amendment was violated when corrections officials were "deliberately indifferent" to prisoners' medical needs.

Compassionate (early) release statutes. Due to the increase in older inmates and the associated costs for housing older inmates, 36 states have medical or compassionate release and 37 states have early release planning (Aday, 2003; see Chapter 16, this volume for a review of community corrections and Chapter 13, this volume for a review or parole and probation). These types of policies, however, require states to balance the rising costs of housing older inmates against ensuring that justice is served while the public is protected. Support for early release programs is based on evidence that older adults are at low risk for reoffending compared to their younger counterparts (Kerbs, 2000; see Volume 1, Chapter 3, this handbook for a review of risk assessment). Research shows that one of the best predictors of reoffending is age because the propensity to commit crime decreases with age (Sampson & Laub, 1992).

A recent federal statute called the Second Chance Act of 2008 was passed to provide prison officials with more discretion in assisting inmates with the transition back into the community. The act applies to more than just older inmates, but the bill includes a pilot program under part (g) for federal prisoners, called the Elderly and Family Reunification for Certain Nonviolent Offenders. The pilot program allowed for releasing eligible elderly inmates (e.g., over age 65, without a life-in-prison sentence for certain nonviolent crimes, no past escapes, and low risk of reoffending) from prison to home detention (see Chapter 1, this volume), which also includes nursing homes or other residential long-term care facilities. However, the Bureau of

Prisons concluded that it was more expensive to monitor the older adults through private companies contracted to monitor inmates on home detention as compared to keeping them in prison. Alternatively, others have proposed that, instead of releasing older adults to home detention, older adults could be released on *geriatric parole* (Corwin, 2001)—age-based parole programs that release older adults who pose no danger to the community (see Chapter 3, this volume). These parole programs would remove older adults from the corrections system altogether and place them on supervision that would cost far less than detaining them (American Civil Liberties Union, 2012).

Other suggestions to help pay for costs for older adults who are released on parole or home detention include filial responsibility laws (Yamamoto, 2009). Filial responsibility is a social norm that describes one's feelings of obligation to care for an aging parent. Although filial responsibility is thought of as a social value, filial responsibility laws historically have been used to mandate that adult children pay for the care of their aging parents (Brank, 2007; Wylie & Brank, 2009). Although filial responsibility laws are largely not enforced, thirty states still have filial responsibility laws on their books, and there have been recent cases requiring adult children to pay the costs of their parents' care (Yamamoto, 2009). This would certainly come with a wide range of legal and practical complications.

Death penalty. Another area of elder justice that psychology and legal scholars have examined is whether older inmates on death row, in some situations, should be deemed "too old" to execute (see Chapter 17, this volume for a review of death penalty research and Volume 1, Chapter 5, this handbook for a review of criminal competencies). According to the most recent death row statistics available from the Bureau of Justice Statistics for 2012, which include breakdowns by age, 11% of death row inmates were over the age of 60 (this increased to 37% for age 50 and older; Snell, 2014). Several notable cases have demonstrated the contentions that may emerge when executing older adults, especially in situations where the defendants are suffering from dementia, cancer, blindness, and other serious medical issues. One defendant had a heart attack and was resuscitated, just to return to death row to face execution (*Allen v. Ornoski*, 2006). The court that considered a request for a life sentence instead of a death sentence for the heart attack patient held that executing an infirm elderly person was not considered cruel and unusual punishment because a community sentiment had not been established (*Allen v. Ornoski*, 2006).

The Supreme Court has not yet ruled on whether executing an elderly person who is close to death by natural causes or suffering from dementia is considered cruel and unusual punishment. The Ninth Circuit's decision in *Allen v. Ornoski* (2006) centered on whether Allen was too physically ill to be executed under the Eighth Amendment, however, it may be possible that an older defendant may be too mentally ill to be executed because of dementia. In 2010, Viva Leroy Nash became the oldest person on death row to die of natural causes at age 94. At the time of his death, Nash was blind, confined to a wheelchair, and suffering from mental illness and dementia. Before his death, his attorneys argued that Nash could not assist in his appeal because he was mentally incapacitated as a result of a delusional disorder caused by advancing age. The Ninth Circuit agreed and held that a defendant must be able to assist his counsel in appeal. Although the Supreme Court has not granted certiorari to hear any cases involving older adults, cases that have involved capital punishment for other vulnerable populations may provide insight.

Jurors

Because most states do not collect age information about their jury panels, it is hard to know how well older adults are represented in juries. It is clear, however, that some states are willing to exclude older adults from jury service because of their age. In Florida, a state known to have a high proportion of older adults, a person 70 years old or older can be excused from jury service upon request (Persons Disqualified or Excused From Jury Service of 2011). Presumably statutes like Florida's are meant to protect older adults because there is an underlying presumption of disability based on age. The U.S. Supreme Court has not addressed the role of age in jury selection in the same way that it has forbidden peremptory challenges based on race (*Batson v. Kentucky*, 1986) or gender (*J. E. B. v. Alabama*, 1994), but we know that older adults may be more willing to serve as jurors because of their time availability (Entzel, Dunlop, & Rothman, 2000) and because they generally have a more positive attitude toward jury service (Marder, 2002; though that may be a generational effect, see Boatright, 2001).

Empirical research generally demonstrates that age has a weak or inconsistent influence in civil and criminal jury verdicts. One major issue with much of this research is the age groups used for comparison with college student samples generally forming the "younger" jurors and community samples generally forming the "older" samples. Fitzgerald (2000) examined the effect of age on juror performance by comparing a group of younger (ages 19–35) and older (ages 55–75) mock jurors in a civil mock trial after manipulating when the jurors received the jury instructions: either before watching the trial evidence video or after (the standard procedure). Older adults' memory was better when they received the instructions prior to watching the video, but the timing did not have appreciable effects for the younger adults. Several other empirical studies have examined age effects, but like Fitzgerald's study (2000), the focus is on civil and not criminal cases. Recent research described in a working paper by Anwar, Bayer, and Hjalmarsson (2012) suggests that older adults may be systematically excluded from jury service by defense attorneys, and that their analysis of actual cases demonstrates that this may be a good idea because older adult jurors were more likely to convict. In a laboratory study, Higgins, Heath, and Grannemann (2007) similarly found that older adult mock jurors compared to younger mock jurors were not only more certain of their verdicts, but were more likely to see the defendant as responsible. Although more research is certainly needed, the sparse amount that has been done suggests that defense attorneys should perhaps not heed Clarence Darrow's advice that old men are preferred for jury service because they are likely to be "more charitable and kindly disposed than young men" (Eglit, 2004, p. 99; see Chapter 10, this volume for a review of research on juries).

PRACTICE AND POLICY ISSUES

Age is often used as a way to distinguish older people from younger people, but it is not always clear that such a distinction is necessary. Such distinctions suggest that a person's age is a defining characteristic and a reason for differential treatment within the legal system. For example, if the legal response to someone who victimizes an older adult is different than if the victim was a younger adult, then there is the assumption that there is something about the age of the victim that should define and change the punishment for the perpetrator. Such policies make the underlying assumption that older adults are a homogenous group because of their age (B. D. Dunlap, Rothman, & Entzel, 2000). It is important to consider whether such differences should be highlighted and what effect doing so will have on the individuals involved and the justice system in general.

Unique courts and services have emerged that specifically address the needs of older adults. Elder Justice Centers (EJCs) are one such example, and they have the overarching goal of linking older adults to the court system and other social services. EJCs generally function as support services for the court system, rather than as advocates for individual older adults (Rothman & Dunlap, 2006). The EJC established in Florida is described as a court program that assists people over the age of 60 who are involved in the legal system because of guardianship, criminal issues, or other family or civil matters (Elder Justice Center, 2012). EJCs generally adopt a philosophy of therapeutic jurisprudence, which ascribes to the notion that the courts and legal systems are agents that may produce therapeutic or antitherapeutic consequences (Wexler & Winick, 1996). Similarly, some law schools have created clinics called Projects for Older Prisoners (POPS), which assist older adults in the criminal justice system. The POPS at George Washington University Law School works on helping adults over 55 obtain parole, pardons, or alternative forms of incarceration. If the older adults are released, the students may help with re-entry issues such as housing or community support (George Washington University Law School, 2012).

Another response for handling issues that are unique to older adults is Elder Courts. One such court emerged in California in 2008 after the recommendation of a task force aimed at coordinating the numerous services available to older adults (Center for Elders and the Courts, 2012). The County of Contra Costa Elder Court has a single judge hear all cases involving older adults, including abuse and neglect, landlord–tenant, restraining orders, criminal, probate matters, and small claims. The court accommodates older adults by designating court times later in the morning, having physical accommodations, and providing peer counselors as advocates, and the court coordinates other services such as legal advice and transportation. The intended consequences are clear for these courts and the Elder Justice Center described in the preceding paragraph, but what are the unintended consequences? The Elder Courts are unique because they address many issues relevant to older adults, but are the older adults disadvantaged because their judge does not have specialized knowledge about a certain type of case? The underlying message seems to be that age is the defining characteristic that is important to the court system rather than the legal question. Again, these separate courts also assume that the older adults are a homogenous group because of their age (B. D. Dunlap et al., 2000).

Even more important to consider than the underlying assumption of homogeneity are the resulting assumed defining characteristics of the resulting group. Is the assumption that older adults collectively are less competent or more vulnerable? What individuating factors are being ignored when older adults above a certain arbitrary age are lumped together? It is one thing if the accommodations are necessary, but is another issue entirely if accommodations are made because of incorrect stereotypes that could lead to further stigmatization of older adults (B. D. Dunlap et al., 2000).

For psychologists, these accommodations present unique research opportunities to determine the message they are sending to society generally and to older adults specifically. As mentioned above, some states allow older adults to be exempt from jury service: Is this seen as an act of state benevolence or the state patronizing older adults? It may be that it would be more beneficial to implement practices and accommodations that aid older adults in remaining active in the justice system. Clinical psychology research is needed to better assess competency of older adults in all areas of the justice system from jurors to maltreatment victims (see Volume 1, Chapters 5 and 16, this handbook for research on criminal and civil competencies, respectively). Because of the ubiquity of ageism and the great likelihood that a person's advanced age will play a role in their legal interactions (Eglit, 2004), more psychological research is needed to understand and counter its effects, especially in terms of competency determinations of older adults.

SUMMARY AND CONCLUSIONS

Although older adult issues have not always received equal attention compared to other areas within forensic psychology, the current population demographics necessitates continuing and expanding the work that has been done thus far. We should expect to see a greater proportion of older adults throughout society, which will inevitably include the justice system. They will be involved because they are victims, eyewitnesses, offenders, and jurors. As noted in the research review, older adult victimization often goes unreported, and much of the research and attention surrounding older adult maltreatment is focused on the burden of caring for an older adult as the reason for the abuse. Older adults are particularly vulnerable to financial abuse as well, and there are special circumstances related to self-neglect, yet many states have mirrored their adult protective services statutes after the child abuse statutes. Although there are some distinct differences noted in the research between older and younger eyewitnesses, research indicates that ageist attitudes may be at the core of some of the perceived differences. For the true differences, many can be reduced with appropriate law enforcement techniques. As an example, using the Modified Cognitive Interview for older eyewitnesses improves eyewitness recall. Criminal sentencing policies like mandatory minimum sentences combined with general increased longevity combine to increase the number and proportion of older adults within the prison

system. This leads to a number of issues, with two primary issues concerned with the creation of sentencing exceptions based on age and preparing prison facilities for older inmates' physical and health needs. Although older adults in many states can choose to be excluded from jury service, we should expect to see a greater number of older adults serving on juries simply because there is a greater number of older adults generally and because this generation of older adults is more active and involved than previous generations. Questions still remain concerning any real or imagined differences in jurors because of age.

No matter what role the elder holds in the justice system, research needs to focus on delineating potential age effects versus generation effects. In other words, are we finding differences because of the person's age or because of the unique life experiences that result from growing to that age during the particular time in which they did? Similarly, there should be underlying questions and concerns about competency and ageism. Unfortunately, the two can feel like they are at odds with one another: We need to consider the possibility of incompetency, but we should not assume it is based on age. This conflict exemplifies older adult issues and the need for flexibility in our ideas about older adults generally, and specifically within the justice system (B. D. Dunlap et al., 2000).

References

Acierno, R., Hernandez, M. A., Amstadter, A. B., Resnick, H. S., Steve, K., Muzzy, W., & Kilpatrick, D. G. (2010). Prevalence and correlates of emotional, physical, sexual, and financial abuse and potential neglect in the United States: The National Elder Mistreatment Study. *American Journal of Public Health, 100*, 292–297. doi:10.2105/AJPH.2009.163089

Acierno, R., Resnick, H., Kilpatrick, D., & Stark-Riemer, W. (2003). Assessing elder victimization: Demonstration of methodology. *Social Psychiatry and Psychiatric Epidemiology, 38*, 644–653. doi:10.1007/s00127-003-0686-4

Aday, R. (2003). *Aging prisoners: Crisis in American corrections.* Westport, CT: Praeger Press.

Adult Protective Services Definitions. Ohio Rev. Code Ann. §§ 5101.60 (2012).

Allen v. Ornoski, 435 F. 3d 946 (9th Cir. 2006).

Amant, F., Moerman, P., Neven, P., Timmerman, D., Van Limbergen, E., & Vergote, I. (2005). Endometrial cancer. *Lancet, 366*, 491–505. doi:10.1016/S0140-6736(05)67063-8

American Civil Liberties Union. (2012, June). *At America's expense: The mass incarceration of the elderly.* New York, NY: American Civil Liberties Union.

Anno, J., Graham, C., Lawrence, J. E., & Shansky, R. (2004). *Correctional health care: Addressing the needs of elderly, chronically ill, and terminally ill inmates.* Washington, DC: U.S. Department of Justice.

Anwar, S., Bayer, P., & Hjalmarsson, R. (2012). *A fair and impartial jury? The role of age in jury selection and trial outcomes.* Retrieved from http://www.nber.org/papers/w17887

Arias, E. (2006, April 19). United States life tables, 2003. *National Vital Statistic Reports, 54.*

Barrett, A. E., & Cantwell, L. E. (2007). Drawing on stereotypes: Using undergraduates' sketches of elders as a teaching tool. *Educational Gerontology, 33*, 327–348. doi:10.1080/03601270701198950

Bartol, C. R., & Bartol, A. M. (2006). History of forensic psychology. In I. B. Weiner & A. K. Hess (Eds.), *The handbook of forensic psychology* (pp. 3–27). Hoboken, NJ: Wiley.

Batson v. Kentucky, 476 U.S. 79 (1986).

Beier, M. E., & Ackerman, P. L. (2003). Determinants of heath knowledge: An investigation of age, gender, abilities, personality, and interests. *Journal of Personality and Social Psychology, 84*, 439–448. doi:10.1037/0022-3514.84.2.439

Boatright, R. G. (2001). Generation and age-based differences in attitudes towards jury service. *Behavioral Sciences and the Law, 19*, 285–304. doi:10.1002/bsl.440

Bornstein, B. H. (1995). Memory processes in elderly eyewitnesses: What we know and what we don't know. *Behavioral Sciences and the Law, 13*, 337–348. doi:10.1002/bsl.2370130303

Brank, E. M. (2007). Elder research: Filling an important gap in psychology and law. *Behavioral Sciences and the Law, 25*, 701–716. doi:10.1002/bsl.780

Brank, E. M. (2011). Baby boomers at work: Growing older and working more. In R. L. Wiener & S. L. Wilborn (Eds.), *Disability and aging discrimination* (pp. 93–108). New York, NY: Springer.

Brank, E. M., Wylie, L. E., & Hamm, J. A. (2012). Potential for self-reporting of older adult maltreatment: An empirical examination. *Elder Law Journal, 19*, 351–384.

Brimacombe, C. A., Quinton, N., Nance, N., & Garrioch, L. (1997). Is age irrelevant? Perceptions of young and old adult eyewitnesses. *Law and Human Behavior, 21*, 619–634.

Brimacombe, C. A., Jung, S., Garrioch, L., & Allison, M. (2003). Perceptions of older adult eyewitnesses: Will you believe me when I'm 64? *Law and Human Behavior, 27*, 507–522. doi:10.1023/A:1025486006769

Brodie, S. E. (2003). Aging and disorders of the eye. In R. C. Tallis & H. M. Fillit (Eds.), *Brocklehurst's textbook of geriatric medicine and gerontology* (6th ed., pp. 735–747). London, England: Churchill Livingston.

Brown v. Pattison, 2004 U.S. Dist. LEXIS 12204, 2004 WL 1490302 (N.D. Texas 2004)

Butler, R. N. (1969). Ageism: Another form of bigotry. *Gerontologist, 9*, 243–246. doi:10.1093/geront/9.4_Part_1.243

Butler, R. N. (1995). Ageism. In G. Maddox (Ed.), *The encyclopedia of aging* (pp. 35–36). New York, NY: Springer.

Butler, R. N. (2009). Combating ageism. *International Psychogeriatrics, 21*, 211. doi:10.1093/geront/9.4_Part_1

Center for Elders and the Courts. (2012). *Elder abuse.* Retrieved from http://www.eldersandcourts.org/elder-abuse.aspx

Christy, A., Bond, J., & Young, M. S. (2007). Short-term involuntary examination of older adults in Florida. *Behavioral Sciences and the Law, 25*, 615–628. doi:10.1002/bsl.786

Cisler, J. M., Amstadter, A. B., Begle, A. M., Hernandez, M., & Acierno, R. (2010). Elder mistreatment and physical health among older adults: The South Carolina elder mistreatment study. *Journal of Traumatic Stress, 23*, 461–467. doi:10.1002/jts.20545

Cohn, D., & Taylor, P. (2010). *Baby boomers approach 65—glumly.* Retrieved from http://pewresearch.org/pubs/1834/baby-boomers-old-age-downbeat-pessimism

Connolly, M. T. (2008). Elder self-neglect and justice system: An essay from an interdisciplinary perspective. *Journal of the American Geriatrics Society, 56*, S244–S252. doi:10.1111/j.1532-5415.2008.01976.x

Connolly, M. T. (2010). Where elder abuse and the justice system collide: Police power, parens patriae, and 12 recommendations. *Journal of Elder Abuse and Neglect, 22*, 37–93. doi:10.1080/08946560903436338

Corwin, P. S. (2001). Senioritis: Why elderly federal inmates are literally dying to get out of jail. *Journal of Contemporary Health Law and Policy, 17*, 687–714.

Coxon, P., & Valentine, T. (1997). The effects of the age of eyewitnesses on the accuracy and suggestibility of their testimony. *Applied Cognitive Psychology, 11*, 415–430. doi:10.1002/(SICI)1099-0720(199710)11:5<415::AID-ACP469>3.0.CO;2-A

Cruzan v. Director, Missouri Department of Health, 497 U.S. 261 (1990).

Cuddy, A. J. C., Norton, M. I., & Fiske, S. T. (2005). This old stereotype: The pervasiveness and persistence of the elderly stereotype. *Journal of Social Issues, 61,* 267–285. doi:10.1111/j.1540-4560.2005.00405.x

Curran, N. (2000). Blue hairs in the big house: The rise in elderly inmate population, its effects on the overcrowding dilemma and solutions to correct it. *New England Journal on Crime and Civil Confinement, 26,* 225–264.

Dong, X. Q., & Simon, M. A. (2011). Enhancing national policy and programs to address elder abuse. *JAMA, 305,* 2460–2461. doi:10.1001/jama.2011.835

Dunkin, J. J., & Kasl-Godley, J. E. (2000). Psychological changes with normal aging. In B. J. Sadock & V. A. Sadock (Eds.), *Comprehensive textbook of psychiatry* (7th ed., pp. 2980–2988). Philadelphia, PA: Lippincott, Williams & Wilkins.

Dunlap, B. D., Rothman, M. B., & Entzel, P. (2000). Policy implications for the 21st century. In M. B. Rothman, B. D. Dunlap, & P. Entzel (Eds.), *Elders, crime, and the criminal justice system: Myth, perceptions, and reality in the 21st century* (pp. 331–358). New York, NY: Springer.

Dunlap, E. E., Golding, J. M., Hodell, E. C., & Marsil, D. F. (2007). Perceptions of elder physical abuse in the courtroom: The influence of hearsay witness testimony. *Journal of Elder Abuse and Neglect, 19,* 19–39. doi:10.1300/J084v19n03_02

Edney v. Kerrigan, 2004 WL 2101907 (S.D.N.Y. Sept. 21, 2004).

Eglit, H. (2004). Elders on trial: Age and ageism in the American legal system. Gainesville: University of Florida Press.

Elder Justice Center. (2012). *About Elder Justice Center.* Retrieved from http://www.fljud13.org/Court Programs/ElderJusticeCenter/AboutElderJustice Center.aspx

Entzel, P., Dunlop, B. D., & Rothman, M. B. (2000). Elders and jury service: A case of age discrimination? In M. B. Rothman, B. D. Dunlop, & P. Entzel (Eds.), *Elders, crime, and the criminal justice system: Myth, perceptions, and reality in the 21st century* (pp. 163–184). New York, NY: Springer.

Estelle v. Gamble, 429 U.S. 97 (1976).

Feldmeyer, B., & Steffensmeier, D. (2007). Elder crime: Pattern and current trends, 1980–2004. *Research on Aging, 29.* doi:10.1177/0164027507300802

Fiske, S. T., Cuddy, A. J. C., Glick, P., & Xu, J. (2002). A model of (often mixed) stereotype content: Competence and warmth respectively follow from perceived status and competition. *Journal of Personality and Social Psychology, 82,* 878–902. doi:10.1037/0022-3514.82.6.878

Fiske, S. T., & Taylor, S. E. (2008). *Attribution processes. Social cognition: From brains to culture* (pp. 134–163). New York, NY: McGraw-Hill.

Fitzgerald, J. M. (2000). Younger and older jurors: The influence of environmental supports on memory performance and decision making in complex trials. *The Journals of Gerontology, Series B: Psychological Sciences and Social Sciences, 55,* 323–331. doi:10.1093/geronb/55.6.P323

Flynn, E. E. (2000). Elders as perpetrators. In M. B. Rothman, B. D. Dunlap, & P. Entzel (Eds.) *Elders, crime, and the criminal justice system: Myth, perceptions, and reality in the 21st century* (pp. 43–83). New York, NY: Springer.

Friedman, T. W., Yelland, G. W., & Robinson, S. R. (2011). Subtle cognitive impairments in elders with Mini-Mental State Examination scores within the 'normal' range. *International Journal of Geriatric Psychiatry, 5,* 463–471. doi:10.1002/gps.273610.1002/gps.2736

Frolik, L. A., & Barnes, A. M. (2011). *Elder law: cases and materials.* Newark, NJ: Matthew Bender.

Frolik, L. A., & Kaplan, R. L. (2010). *Elder law in a nutshell* (5th ed.), St. Paul, MN: West.

Gaydon, L. B., & Miller, M. K. (2007). Elders in the justice system: How the system treats elders in trials, during imprisonment and on death row. *Behavioral Sciences and the Law, 25,* 677–699. doi:10.1002/bsl.781

George Washington University Law School. (2012). *The Project for Older Prisoners.* Retrieved from http://www.law.gwu.edu/Academics/EL/clinics/Pages/POPS.aspx

Geroff, A. J., & Olshaker, J. S. (2006). Elder abuse. *Emergency Medicine Clinics of North America, 24,* 491–505. doi:10.1016/j.emc.2006.01.009

Giles, L., Brewer, E. T., Mosqueda, L., Huba, G. J., & Melchior, L. A. (2010). Vision for 2020. *Journal of Elder Abuse and Neglect, 22,* 375–386. doi:10.1080/08946566.2010.490193

Golding, J. M., Allen, J., Yozwiak, J. A., Marsil, D. F., Kinstle, T. S., & Stewart, T. (2004). Perceptions of elder neglect in the courtroom. *Journal of Elder Abuse and Neglect, 16,* 23–46. doi:10.1300/J084v16n01_02

Golding, J. M., Yozwiak, J. A., Kinstle, T. L., & Marsil, D. F. (2005). The effect of gender in the perception of elder physical abuse in court. *Law and Human Behavior, 29,* 605–614. doi:10.1007/s10979-005-6831-8

Heisler, C. J. (2012). Elder abuse and the criminal justice system: An uncertain future. *Journal of American Society on Aging, 36,* 83–88.

Heisler, C. J., & Stiegel, L. A. (2002). Enhancing the justice system's response to elder abuse: Discussions and recommendations of the "Improving Prosecution" working group of The National Policy

Summit on Elder Abuse. *Journal of Elder Abuse and Neglect, 14*, 31–54.

Higgins, P. L., Heath, W. P., & Grannemann, B. D. (2007). How type of excuse defense, mock juror age, and defendant age affect mock jurors' decisions. *Journal of Social Psychology, 147*, 371–392. doi:10.3200/SOCP.147.4.371-392

Holliday, R. E., Humphries, J. E., Milne, R., Memon, A., Houlder, L., Lyons, A., & Bull, R. (2012). Reducing misinformation effects in older adults with cognitive interview mnemonics. *Psychology and Aging, 27*, 1191–1203. doi:10.1037/a0022031

Hummert, M. L. (1993). Age and typicality judgments of stereotypes of the elderly: Perceptions of elderly vs. young adults. *International Journal of Aging and Human Development, 37*, 217–226. doi:10.2190/L01P-V960-8P17-PL56

Jackson, S. L., & Hafemeister, T. L. (2012). Pure financial exploitation vs. hybrid financial exploitation co-occurring with physical abuse and/or neglect of elderly persons. *Psychology of Violence, 2*, 285–296. doi:10.1037/a0027273

Jarvik, L. F., & Small, G. W. (2000). Geriatric psychiatry: Introduction. In B. J. Sadock, & V. A. Sadock (Eds.), *Comprehensive textbook of psychiatry* (7th ed., pp. 2980–2988). Philadelphia, PA: Lippincott, Williams & Wilkins.

J. E. B. v. Alabama, 511 U.S. 127 (1994).

Kapp, M. B. (1995). Elder mistreatment: legal interventions and policy uncertainties. *Behavioral Sciences and the Law, 13*, 365–380. doi:10.1002/bsl.2370130305

Kemp, B. J., & Mosqueda, L. A. (2005). Elder financial abuse: An evaluation framework and supporting evidence. *Journal of the American Geriatrics Society, 53*, 1123–1127. doi:10.1111/j.1532-5415.2005.53353.x

Kerbs, J. J. (2000). The older prisoner: Social psychological, and medical considerations. In M. B. Rothman, B. D. Dunlap, & P. Entzel (Eds.), *Elders, crime, and the criminal justice system: Myth, perceptions, and reality in the 21st century* (pp. 207–228). New York, NY: Springer.

Kinsella, C. (2004). *Corrections health care costs.* Retrieved from http://www.csg.org/knowledgecenter/docs/TA0401CorrHealth.pdf

Kinstle, T. L., Hodell, E. C., & Golding, J. M. (2008). The impact of juror characteristics and victim health status on the perception of elder physical abuse. *Journal of Interpersonal Violence, 23*, 1143–1161. doi:10.1177/0886260508314294

Kite, M. E., Deaux, K., & Miele, M. (1991). Stereotypes of young and old: Does age outweigh gender? *Psychology and Aging, 6*, 19–27. doi:10.1037/0882-7974.6.1.19.

Kite, M. E., Stockdale, G. D., Whitley, B. E., & Johnson, B. T. (2005). Attitudes toward younger and older adults: An updated meta-analytic review. *Journal of Social Issues, 61*, 241–266. doi:10.1111/j.1540-4560.2005.00404.x.

Kohn, N. A. (2003). Second childhood: What child protection systems can teach elder protection systems. *Stanford Law and Policy Review, 14*, 175–202.

Kwong See, S. T., Hoffman, H. G., & Wood, T. L. (2001). Perceptions of old female eyewitness: Is the older eyewitness believable? *Psychology and Aging, 16*, 346–350. doi:10.1037//0882-7974.16.2.346

Lemieux, C. M., Dyeson, T. B., & Castiglione, B. (2002). Revisiting the literature on prisoners who are older: Are we wiser? *Prison Journal, 82*, 440–458. doi:10.1177/0032885502238680

List, J. A. (1986). Age and schematic differences in the reliability of eyewitness testimony. *Developmental Psychology, 22*, 50–57. doi:10.1037/0012-1649.22.1.50.

Loftus, E. F., Miller, D. G., & Burns, H. J. (1978). Semantic integration of verbal information into a visual memory. *Journal of Experimental Psychology: Human Learning and Memory, 4*, 19–31. doi:10.1037//0278-7393.4.1.19

Loue, S. (2001). Elder abuse and neglect in medicine and law. *Journal of Legal Medicine, 22*, 159–209. doi:10.1080/019476401750365174

Marder, N. S. (2002). Justice and multiculturalism. *Southern California Law Review, 75*, 659–726.

Maylor, E. A. (1998). Changes in event-based prospective memory across adulthood. *Aging, Neuropsychology, and Cognition, 5*, 107–128. doi:10.1076/anec.5.2.107.599

McGreevey, J. F. (2005). Elder abuse: The physician's perspective. *Clinical Gerontologist, 28*, 83–103.

MedlinePlus. (2012). *Urinary tract infection—Adults.* Retrieved from http://www.nlm.nih.gov/medlineplus/ency/article/000521.htm

Mello, E. W., & Fisher, R. P. (1996). Enhancing older adult eyewitness memory with the cognitive interview. *Applied Cognitive Psychology, 10*, 403–417. doi:10.1002/(SICI)1099-0720(199610)10:5<403::AID-ACP395>3.0.CO;2-X

Memon, A. M., & Gabbert, F. (2003). Improving eyewitness accuracy of senior witnesses: Do prelineup questions and sequential testing help? *Journal of Applied Psychology, 88*, 341–347. doi:10.1037/0021-9010.88.2.341

Miller, R. A. (1999). Kleemeier award lecture: Are there genes for aging? *The Journals of Gerontology, Series A: Biological Sciences and Medical Sciences, 54*, 297–307. doi:10.1093/gerona/54.7.B297

Mueller-Johnson, K., Toglia, M. P., Sweeney, C. D., & Ceci, S. J. (2007). The perceived credibility of older adults as witnesses and its relation to ageism. *Behavioral Sciences and the Law, 25,* 255–375. doi:10.1002/bsl.765

National Center for Health Statistics. (2005). *Health, United States, 2005 with chart book on trends in the health of Americans.* Retrieved from http://www.cdc.gov/nchs/products/pubs/pubd/hus/2010/2010.htm#hus05

Neal, T. S., Christiansen, A., Bornstein, B. H., & Robicheaux, T. R. (2012). The effects of mock jurors' beliefs about eyewitness performance on trial judgments. *Psychology, Crime, and Law, 18,* 49–64. doi:10.1080/1068316X.2011.587815

Neary, D., & Snowden, J. S. (2003). Classification of the dementias. In R. C. Tallis, & H. M. Fillit (Eds.), *Brocklehurst's textbook of geriatric medicine and gerontology* (6th ed., pp. 775–782). London, England: Churchill Livingston.

Nelson, T. D. (2002). *Ageism: Stereotyping and prejudice against older persons.* Cambridge, MA: MIT Press.

Nunez, N., McCoy, M. L., Clark, H. L., & Shaw, L. A. (1999). The testimony of elderly victim/witnesses and their impact on juror decisions: The importance of examining multiple stereotypes. *Law and Human Behavior, 23,* 413–423. doi:10.1023/A:1022308014652

Parkin, A. J., & Walter, B. M. (1992). Recollective experiences, normal aging, and frontal dysfunction. *Psychology and Aging, 7,* 290–298. doi:10.1037//0882-7974.7.2.290

Pennsylvania Department of Corrections v. Yeskey, 524 U.S. 206 (1998)

Persons Disqualified or Excused from Jury Service, §§ 40.013, 8 F.S. (2011).

Public Health Chapter IV: Centers for Medicare and Medicaid Services, Department of Health and Human Services Subchapter B: Medicare Program 42, C.F.R. § 411.4 (1989, amended 2007).

Rathbone-McCuan, E. (2000). Elder abuse within the context of intimate violence. *University of Missouri at Kansas City Law Review, 69,* 215–226.

Ross, D. F., Dunning, D., Toglia, M. P., & Ceci, S. J. (1990). The child in the eyes of the jury: Assessing mock jurors' perceptions of the child witness. *Law and Human Behavior, 14,* 5–23. doi:10.1007/BF01055786

Rothman, M. B., & Dunlap. B. D. (2006). Elders and the courts. *Journal of Aging and Social Policy, 18* 31–46. doi:10.1300/J031v18n02_03

Rothman, M. B., Dunlap, B. D., & Entzel, P. (2000). Introduction. In M. B. Rothman, B. D. Dunlap, & P. Entzel (Eds.). *Elders, crime, and the criminal justice system: Myth, perceptions, and reality in the 21st century* (pp. xxix–xxxviii). New York, NY: Springer.

Sampson, R. J., & Laub, J. H. (1992). Crime and deviance in the life course. *Annual Review of Sociology, 18,* 63–84. doi:10.1146/annurev.soc.18.1.63

Schoenborn, C. A., Vickerie, J. L., & Powell-Griner, E. (2006). *Health characteristics of adults 55 years of age and over: United States, 2000–2003.* Retrieved from http://www.cdc.gov/nchs/data/ad/ad370.pdf

Sears, D. O. (1986). College sophomores in the laboratory: Influences of a narrow data base on psychology's view of human nature. *Journal of Personality and Social Psychology, 51,* 515–530. doi:10.1037//0022-3514.51.3.515

Second Chance Act, 42 § U.S.C. 17541 (2008).

Setterlund, D., Tilse, C., Wilson, J., McCawley, A., & Rosenman, L. (2007). Understanding financial elder abuse in families: The potential of routine activities theory. *Ageing and Society, 27,* 599–614. doi:10.1017/S0144686X07006009

Snell, T. L. (2014). *Capital punishment, 2012—Statistics table* (NCJ 245789). Washington, DC: U.S. Department of Justice, Bureau of Justice Statistics.

Social Security. (2012). Retrieved from http://www.ssa.gov

Stuart-Hamilton, I. A. (2003). Normal cognitive aging. In R. C. Tallis, & H. M. Fillit (Eds.), *Brocklehurst's textbook of geriatric medicine and gerontology* (6th ed., pp. 125–142). London, England: Churchill Livingston.

Thivierge-Rikard, R. V., & Thompson, M. S. (2007). The association between aging inmate housing management models and non-geriatric health services in state correctional institutions. *Journal of Aging and Social Policy, 19,* 39–56. doi:10.1300/J031v19n04_03

U.S. Department of Justice, Bureau of Justice Statistics. (2004). *Census of state and federal adult correctional facilities, 2000* [Computer file]. Ann Arbor, MI: Interuniversity Consortium for Political and Social Research. doi:10.3886/ICPSR04021

U.S. Department of Justice. Bureau of Justice Statistics. (2009). *Census of state and federal adult correctional facilities, 2005* [Computer file]. Ann Arbor, MI: Interuniversity Consortium for Political and Social Research. doi:10.3886/ICPSR24642

U.S. Sentencing Commission. (2011). *Determining the sentence.* Retrieved from http://www.ussc.gov/Guidelines/2011_Guidelines/Manual_HTML/5h1_1.htm

U.S. v. Brooke, 308 F.3d 17, 353 (U.S. App. D.C. 341 2002).

U.S. v. Bullion, 466 F.3d 574 (7th Cir. 2006).

U.S. v. Johnson, 685 F.3d 660 (7th Cir. 2012).

Vakil, E., Hornik, C., & Levy, D. A. (2008). Conceptual and perceptual similarity between encoding and retrieval contexts and recognition memory context effects in older and younger adults. *The Journals of Gerontology, Series B: Psychological Sciences and Social Sciences, 63,* 171–175. doi:10.1093/geronb/63.3.P171

Wells, G. L. (1978). Applied eyewitness-testimony research: System variables and estimator variables. *Journal of Personality and Social Psychology, 36,* 1546–1557. doi:10.1037//0022-3514.36.12.1546

Wexler, D. B., & Winick, B. J. (1996). *Law in a therapeutic key: Developments in therapeutic jurisprudence.* Durham, NC: Carolina Academic Press.

Wilkins, C. H., & Birge, S. J. (2005). Prevention of osteoporotic fractures in the elderly. *American Journal of Medicine, 118,* 1190–1195. doi:10.1016/j.amjmed.2005.06.046

Wylie, L. E., & Brank, E. M. (2009). Assuming elder care responsibility: Am I a caregiver? *Journal of Empirical Legal Studies, 6,* 899–924. doi:10.1111/j.1740-1461.2009.01164.x

Wylie, L. E., Patihis, L., McCuller, L. L., Davis, D., Brank, E. M., Loftus, E., & Bornsetin, B. H. (2012). Misinformation effects in older versus younger adults: A meta-analysis. In M. P. Toglia, D. F. Ross, J. Pozzulo, & E. Pica, (Eds.), *The elderly eyewitness in court.* New York, NY: Taylor & Francis.

Yamamoto, L. (2009). Overcrowded prisons and filial responsibility: Will states utilize support of the indigent statutes to solve the baby boomer and prison crises? *Rutgers Law Journal, 41,* 435–478.

Yarmey, D. A. (1993). Adult age and gender difference in eyewitness recall in field settings. *Journal of Applied Social Psychology, 23,* 1921–1932. doi.org/10.1111%2Fj.1559-1816.1993.tb01073.x

Yarmey, D. A., & Kent, J. (1980). Eyewitness identification by elderly and young adults. *Law and Human Behavior, 4,* 359–371. doi:10.1007/BF01040627

CHAPTER 4

FEMALE OFFENDERS

Tonia L. Nicholls, Keith R. Cruise, Duncan Greig, and Holly Hinz

The disproportionate growth in the involvement of women and girls in the criminal justice systems across international borders has served to bolster arguments regarding the importance of considering factors particularly relevant to the etiology, assessment, and treatment of this unique and rapidly expanding population. When compared to male offenders and inmates, women and girls are substantially less likely to come into conflict with the law, and those that do have been found to present with exceptional psychosocial and mental health needs in terms of prevalence, severity, complexity, and comorbidity. Within the context and operational requirements of correctional settings, the presenting mental health and psychosocial profile of female offenders can present significant challenges, often out of proportion to their male counterparts (e.g., emotion dysregulation expressed as aggression, suicide, self-harm; Leschied, 2011). Women offenders also more commonly have dependent children who are subsequently at risk for being placed in foster care. These characteristics accentuate the weightiness of effective assessments and interventions that do not unnecessarily place women into custodial settings, rather offering community interventions when women can be managed effectively outside of an institution. Poorly informed criminal justice policies and practices with female offenders are quite likely to be at particularly high risk of "overintervening" and inadvertently escalating adverse outcomes (Dvoskin, Skeem, Novaco, & Douglas, 2012). It has long been argued that women inmates are often housed at higher security levels than is necessary (C. D. Webster, 1999) given their often inconsequential levels of risk for serious violence, recidivism, and escape (Collie & Polaschek, 2003; van Voorhis & Presser, 2001). Attention has also been drawn to the disproportionate increase of adolescent girls being formally processed into the juvenile justice system, with the number of court cases for girls increasing by 108% for total crimes, 86% for violent crimes, 249% for person crimes, and 197% for drug offenses from 1985 to 2005 (Tracy, Kempf-Leonard, & Abramoske-James, 2009). While still representing a smaller total number, adolescent girls have been reported to receive harsher juvenile court sanctions for the same offenses committed by boys, which perpetuates cycling into the juvenile justice system (Carr, Hudson, Hanks, & Hunt, 2008). Even more concerning is the detected trend for adolescent female offenders with past traumatic experiences and higher mental health problems, a trend in which these female offenders penetrate more deeply into the juvenile justice system (Espinosa, Sorensen, & Lopez, 2013) and are placed in intervention programs either designed for adolescent male offenders or focused on putative gender-specific factors (self-esteem, empowerment) that are neither empirically tested or adequately matched to criminogenic needs (Antonishak, Reppucci, & Mulford, 2004; Miller, Leve, & Kerig, 2012).

Despite the fact that women are much less likely than men to perpetrate criminal offenses, within populations of female offenders, the entire range of criminal offenses is evident (e.g., sexual offending,

http://dx.doi.org/10.1037/14462-004
APA Handbook of Forensic Psychology: Vol. 2. Criminal Investigation, Adjudication, and Sentencing Outcomes,
B. L. Cutler and P. A. Zapf (Editors-in-Chief)
Copyright © 2015 by the American Psychological Association. All rights reserved.

assault, murder). A particular challenge cutting across diverse areas of practice has been a pervasive and prevalent societal reluctance to acknowledge the harm that can be perpetrated by females. This has been a common theme within the child abuse literature (Grayston & De Luca, 1999; Peled, 2011) and is particularly evident with regard to sexual offending (Anderson & Struckman-Johnson, 1998) and intimate partner violence (IPV; Hamel & Nicholls, 2007; Straus, 2012). Specific examples include denying access to female populations to allow for the study of controversial topics (e.g., see Laishes, 2002; Nicholls & Petrila, 2005), blocking access to research funding for IPV research (e.g., Straus, 1999, 2009) and public denunciations of academics who dare to challenge the status quo (e.g., Straus, 1999, 2009).

The implications of denying women's risk of offending and erecting obstacles to research intended to illuminate our understanding of female offending are well documented and far-reaching. Historically, the "tyranny of small numbers" has created obstacles to investigating gender-specific risk and desistence pathways for adolescent female offenders (Tracy et al., 2009, p. 174). Sadly, the largest longitudinal study to date investigating such pathways among serious adolescent offenders did not involve females (see Mulvey et al., 2010). A limited professional literature prevents the advancement of empirically informed assessment and treatment, thereby reducing the effectiveness of costly interventions. Evidence-informed policies and practices have the potential to protect both the civil liberties of female offenders and the safety and financial interests of the wider society. For instance, one of the best predictors of IPV against women is women's use of aggression (Stith, Smith, Penn, Ward, & Tritt, 2004; see Volume 1, Chapter 12, this handbook). Rectifying our inadequate knowledge base in the female offending literature is also relevant to public safety. West, Hatters, Friedman, and Kim (2011) found that, in their sample of female sex offenders from Ohio, most of the women were "opined to have unknown future risk of sexual offending due to a lack of empirically supported risk factors" (p. 738). As such, West and colleagues concluded that, without further understanding of women's risk factors, courts will

have similar difficulties determining the appropriate legal designation, especially with the standard of proof set at "clear and convincing evidence" (p. 738).

Deficiencies in our knowledge and practice also hamper our ability to offer consensus on preferred and well-validated assessment measures and state of the art, evidence-informed practice to inform treatment and management with this marginalized and needy growing population. As recently as 2012, we have seen the release of some of the first gendered assessment tools for women (Female Additional Manual; de Vogel, de Vries Robbé, van Kalmthout, & Place, 2012) and girls (Early Assessment Risk Lists for Girls, EARL-21G; Augimeri, Enebrink, Walsh, & Jiang, 2010; Levene et al., 2001), as well as the development of some of the first models of female offending (Murdoch, Vess, & Ward, 2012) and recommended treatment (van Voorhis & Salisbury, 2013; Blanchette & Brown, 2006; Lewis, 2006).

Although the fundamentals of effective correctional treatment are well-established in the literature (Gendreau & Smith, 2012; Serin, 2005; c.f., Polaschek, 2012), as with the evidence base for assessments with female offenders there remains considerable debate with regard to the extent to which present programming is sufficiently respectful of diversity (e.g., ethnicity, gender) and attuned to gender-specific treatment needs (Austin, Bloom, & Donahue, 1992; Blanchette, 2000; Goldstein et al., 2013). Blanchette (2000) maintained that "the importance of recognizing the distinctive qualities of women offenders is inestimable" ("Conclusions," para. 6). These efforts have been wholeheartedly supported in North America and abroad both by administrators (e.g., Section 77 of the Corrections and Conditional Release Act; National Commission on Correctional Health Care, 2011; National Council on Crime and Delinquency, 2006; UN Office on Drugs and Crime, 2008) and scholars (Blanchette & Brown, 2006; Franklin, 2008; Goldstein, Kemp, Leff, & Lochman, 2012; van Wormer, 2010), though they certainly have not yet been fully realized in practice.

Despite the importance of testing woman-centered interventions, most scholars agree that criminogenic variables identified through the larger forensic mental health and criminological literatures and tested largely with men and boys also have relevance to interventions with women and girls (Blanchette, 2000; Heilbrun et al., 2008; Murphy, Brecht, Huang, & Herbeck, 2012; van Voorhis, Wright, Salisbury, & Bauman, 2010). In fact, meta-analyses demonstrate that the strength of these associations is often comparable to or even exceeds the strength of the associations found with adolescent and adult male offenders (e.g., Andrews & Dowden, 2006; Bonta, Pang, & Wallace-Capretta, 1995; Cottle, Lee, & Heilbrun, 2001; Hubbard & Pratt, 2002). Moreover, efforts to identify variables unique to women tend to reveal variables that are also of relevance to men (e.g., transportation challenges, deficient educational and occupational attainment, abuse, and victimization), if to a lesser degree. Despite an acknowledgement that women are similar but distinct, there remains wide support for the urgent need to develop, implement, and systematically evaluate treatment that responds to the distinctive needs of women and girls (e.g., Heilbrun et al., 2008; Miller et al., 2012; Smith, Cullen, & Latessa, 2009). Researchers and decision-makers need to reconcile the extent to which we find incremental value when service providers abandon gender-neutral approaches and implement gender-specific or gender-responsive correctional treatment strategies. Importantly, preliminary efforts to evaluate the increased capacity to intervene effectively have some preliminary empirical support (van Voorhis et al., 2010). These developments demonstrate that advancements are on the horizon, but it largely remains to be seen to what extent gendered approaches demonstrate incremental validity in both the assessment and treatment of women and to what extent gendered theories are necessary enhancements to our clinical toolkits (Andrews et al., 2012; Heilbrun et al., 2008).

IMPORTANCE OF THE PROBLEM

Official administrative records indicate that, both nationally and internationally, women are far less likely than men to commit crimes and to be arrested, charged, convicted, and incarcerated for criminal offenses. Between 2008 and 2011, in North America, approximately one fifth of all adults accused of and charged with committing crimes were women (U.S. Department of Justice, 2010; Federal Bureau of Investigation, 2008; Statistics Canada, 2011). Women constitute just 6%–7% of U.S. and Canadian federal inmate populations. Victimization data (Greenfield & Snell, 1999; Truman & Planty, 2012) and official statistics data (U.S. Department of Justice, Bureau of Justice Statistics: http://www.ojp.usdoj.gov/bjs) continue to support the conclusion that women constitute a small proportion of all adult offenders. In 2010, male inmates were incarcerated at a rate 14 times higher than females (U.S. Department of Justice, 2011). Specifically, compared to 1.5 million male inmates there were 113,000 women offenders incarcerated in state and federal facilities in 2010 (U.S. Department of Justice, 2011). This translates to a little over one hundred females ($N = 126$) versus well over a thousand men ($N = 1,352$) per 100,000 citizens incarcerated in jails and prisons in the United States (Glaze, 2011).

Based on data reported to the Federal Bureau of Investigation's Uniform Crime Reporting (UCR) Program, 1.9 million arrests were made of individuals under the age of 18 in 2009. This rate represented a 17% decrease from 2000, and a 9% decrease from 2008 with females representing 30% of these arrests (Puzzanchera & Adams, 2011). In 2009, arrests involving females accounted for 18% of violent crime arrests, 38% of property crime arrests, and 45% of larceny-theft arrests (Puzzanchera & Adams, 2011). Data from the National Juvenile Court Data Archive indicate that trends in juvenile court cases parallel arrest trends with 1,368,200 cases being processed in juvenile courts in 2010 representing a 19% decrease from 2001 to 2010. Adolescent females were involved in 28% ($n = 381,500$) of these cases (Puzzanchera & Hockenberry, 2013). The 2010 Census of Juveniles in Residential Placement (CJRP) provides a point-prevalence estimate of juveniles in public and private facilities at three levels of custody status (committed, detained, diversion). The 2010 survey indicated 71,000 residential placements in February

2010 and represented a 33% reduction from census data obtained in 1997. Adolescent female offenders accounted for only 13% of total placements with the proportion of female placements varying little across private (14%) versus public facilities (13%; Hockenberry, 2013).

Increases in Female Offending

Official records reveal an international increase in arrests, convictions, and incarcerations of female offenders across crime categories over the past three decades; in particular, violent offense rates for adult women have nearly tripled (Federal Bureau of Investigation, 2008; Statistics Canada, 2011). Glaze (2011) reported that consistent with prior years (the growth in the female incarcerated population in the U.S has continued to outpace the growth in the male incarcerated population (2.2% vs. 1.6%, respectively).

Despite increasing rates of women's involvement in crime a consideration of raw data is a stark and important reminder that women still constitute a small proportion of individuals in conflict with the law and under the care and supervision of the criminal justice system. For instance, in the US, between 1976 and 2005 women perpetrated 74,005 homicides (12.6%), in comparison to 585,858 committed by men (U.S. Department of Justice, 2010). Similarly, between 1997 and 2009 women were implicated in 677 (13%) solved Canadian homicides in comparison to 5,195 men (Statistics Canada, 2011). Given their small numbers, percentage increases in female offenses should be considered judiciously.

Although adolescent females often represent a smaller proportion of total arrests than adolescent males, the proportion of females arrested has increased over the last decade. Between 1985 and 2010, the number of delinquency cases involving the arrest of an adolescent female increased 69% (225,800 to 381,5000 cases) relative to an increase of only 5% for males (Puzzanchera & Adams, 2011). Simple assault, larceny-theft, and disorderly conduct arrests increased for females from 2000 to 2009, while decreasing for males. Both adolescent male and female arrests for aggravated assault, vandalism, and drug abuse decreased from 2000 to 2009, but

the decrease for females was less than that of males. In 2009, females represented 18% of the 85,890 juvenile violent crime arrests (Puzzanchera & Adams, 2011). In general, the offense trends for adolescent females reflect a similar pattern for adult females. More adolescent females now come into contact and are being formally processed into the juvenile justice system yet there remains large gender discrepancies with far fewer adolescents females arrested, processed, and placed relative to the number of adolescent males.

Characteristics of Female-Perpetrated Offenses

Vast gender discrepancies are also evident when one considers the characteristics of offending. Men and women tend to be arrested for different offense categories (e.g., women are more likely than men to perpetrate embezzlement, prostitution; Federal Bureau of Investigation, 2005, 2006). Women disproportionately commit low severity, nonviolent crimes including property offenses, drug offenses, theft, and public-order failures/breaches (Federal Bureau of Investigation, 2008; McKeown, 2010; Owen & Bloom, 1995; Statistics Canada, 2011). Men generally offend at a much higher rate than women across all offense categories, but in particular, they are disproportionately likely to commit violent crimes (e.g., sexual assault, robbery, serious assault, and homicide; Lauritsen, Heimer, & Lynch, 2009; Statistics Canada, 2011; U.S. Department of Justice, 2011). For instance, the Bureau of Justice Statistics (2011) reported that 36% of incarcerated women had a violent index offense; the next most common offenses included property (30%) and drug offenses (26%). Similar trends are evident for adolescents. Adolescent males offend at higher rates than adolescent females across most crime categories, but especially violent crimes. In 2009, females represented 18% of the 85,890 juvenile violent crime arrests (Puzzanchera & Adams, 2011). Violent crime index arrest rates were 400 arrests per 100,000 juveniles age 10 to 17 for males versus 100 arrests per 100,000 juveniles age 10 to 17 for females. In 2009, adolescent females accounted for only 7% of juvenile murder arrests in 2009 while adolescent males overwhelmingly account for the number of juvenile arrests for forcible rape (98%; Puzzanchera & Adams, 2011).

It is particularly rare for women to violently victimize strangers (5.3% of murders by a female vs. 17.1% of murders by males; Statistics Canada, 2011). The most likely victims of female-perpetrated homicide, for instance are nonspousal family members including parents and children (35%; Kong & AuCoin, 2008; Statistics Canada, 2011), or romantic partners (~30%; Kong & AuCoin, 2008). A 2009 study (Roe-Sepowitz, 2009) found that adolescent females are more likely to kill someone they know, such as a parent (13.8% females versus 1.9% males) or friend (17.2% females versus 6.5% males), while males are more likely to kill strangers (56.1% males versus 17.2% females). Adolescent male homicide offenders chose guns more often than females (57.9% for males versus 13.8% for females), while females most often used vehicles. In some situations this was a result of the female losing control of the car and killing the passengers reinforcing that adolescent females may be charged with multiple homicides within a single incident and tend to have victims known to them.

Some crimes are quite unique to women (e.g., neonaticide) or men (e.g., familicide, uxoricide). To demonstrate, the vast bulk of all sexual offenses (4%–5% are women, Cortoni & Hanson, 2005; 10%, Federal Bureau of Investigation, 2006), stalking (15%–20% are women, Meloy & Boyd, 2003) and cases of familicide (95%, Daly & Wilson 1988, M. Wilson, Daly, & Daniele, 1995) are perpetrated by men. In comparison, other forms of violence are relatively evenly distributed across the sexes (e.g., partner abuse, Archer, 2000; Desmarais, Reeves, Nicholls, Telford, & Fiebert, 2012a, 2012b; child abuse, Sedlak et al., 2010; see Volume 1, Chapter 12, this handbook). Prostitution is a category in which the proportion of adolescent female arrests far exceeds that of juvenile males. In 2009, females accounted for 78% of juvenile prostitution and commercialized vice arrests (Puzzanchera & Adams, 2011). The only other category in which more females than males were arrested is runaways, with females accounting for 55% of juvenile arrests for this status offense (Puzzanchera & Adams, 2011).

Male violence is most often perpetrated against acquaintances (46%), and tends to cause greater harm to victims than female-perpetrated offenses (Denno, 1994; Nicholls, Greaves, & Moretti, 2008; Statistics Canada, 2011; U.S. Department of Justice, 2010). Conversely, female-perpetrated violent crimes, while increasing in incidence (Lauritsen, Heimer, & Lynch, 2009), more often reflect simple low-level assault, and are more likely than men's offenses to be perpetrated against intimate partners (46%; Federal Bureau of Investigation, 2008; Javdani, Sadeh, & Verona, 2011; Pollock & Davis, 2005; Statistics Canada, 2011) and children (as much as 75% of all maltreatment occurs at the hands of a female biological parent; Sedlak et al., 2010). Another strategy for benchmarking gender differences in harm is the estimated monetary costs of male perpetrated and female-perpetrated crimes. Reflecting the harm estimates reported above, Cohen, Piquero, and Jennings (2010) utilized the public's willingness-to-pay (WTP) costs estimates and calculated that one chronic male offender (inclusive of juvenile and adult offenses) imposed a cost of approximately $1.5 million relative to the $750,000 average cost associated with one chronic female offender.

Recidivism

Female offenders also are generally found to recidivate at lower rates than their male counterparts. P. Langan and Levin (2002) found that of 272,111 inmates released from federal detention centers around the US, women were less likely than men to be re-arrested (57.6% vs. 68.4%); reconvicted (39.9% vs. 47.6%); resentenced (17.3% vs. 26.2%); and re-incarcerated (39.4% vs. 53.0%) over a period of 3 years. A recent meta-analysis on sexual offending suggests that women are at substantially less risk of recidivating than male offenders with less than 3% of female sexual offenders recidivating compared to 11.5% of men (Cortoni, Hanson, & Coache, 2010; Hanson & Morton-Bourgon, 2009). Women also tend to recidivate with less serious offenses than men (Spjeldnes & Goodkind, 2009) and habitually score lower and present with different profile patterns on recidivism assessment measures (Andrews et al., 2012; van Voorhis et al., 2010). Moreover, experts assert women may even be less likely to recidivate than their risk profiles would suggest (Blanchette & Brown, 2006; Hannah-Moffat, 2009; Holtfreter & Cupp, 2007).

Recidivism rates among justice-involved youth are high, with various reports documenting rates from 8% to 85% (Minor, Wells, & Angel, 2008; H. Wilson & Hoge, 2013). Mirroring the trends noted above, adolescent female offenders recidivate at lower rates relative to adolescent males, with this trend being present across different recidivism categories. For example, rates of violent recidivism were significantly higher for adolescent males (36%) than adolescent females (11%) after release from a secure juvenile correctional facility (Lodewijks, de Ruiter, & Doreleijers, 2008). Recidivism rates of arrested youth who remain in the community after an initial juvenile court referral follow a similar pattern. In a sample of 8,132 youth (30.2% females), the overall recidivism rate for females was 27.6% compared to 35.3% for males (Baglivio, 2009). Despite variable recidivism rates, multiple studies support comparable levels of predictive validity for adolescent risk assessments across gender (see Schwalbe, 2008). When recidivism risk factors are estimated in combined samples, however, the strength and utility of gender-specific risk factors may be attenuated (Emeka & Sorensen, 2009), requiring specific methods to isolate gender-specific recidivism effects. To illustrate, Conrad, Tolou-Shams, Rizzo, Placella, and Brown (2013) found that, after controlling for other known recidivism predictors, a history of sexual abuse remained a significant predictor of recidivism for adolescent female offenders but not for adolescent male offenders. McReynolds, Schwalbe, and Wasserman (2010) found that adolescent females with comorbid substance use and affective disorders were seven times more likely to recidivate compared to adolescent males with the same risks/needs. Studies that investigate recidivism risk *within* subgroups of adolescent females have further refined our knowledge about gender-specific recidivism pathways. For example, using multi-group analysis, Chauhan, Reppucci, and Turkheimer (2009) concluded that witnessing neighborhood violence was a strong predictor of recidivism for Black females, whereas parental physical abuse was a stronger predictor for White

females. These findings reinforce that the relatively lower recidivism rate for adolescent female offenders is differentially influenced by mental health and environmental factors across and within gender.

RELEVANT PSYCHOLOGICAL THEORY AND PRINCIPLES

The female offending literature has been rife with debate about the preferred approach to the assessment and treatment of women offenders and the necessity of gender-specific risk factors in reoffending and violence risk assessments. The literature has been largely devoid of theory specific to female offending, leading some to suggest that basic descriptive work is needed to generate novel perspectives and elucidate the best means of intervening with women.

Gender-Specific Versus Gender-Neutral Theories of Female Offending and Violence

Given the discrepancies in offending and the resulting societal harm perpetrated by males and by females, it is not surprising that most research into the etiology of criminal behavior has concentrated on males. Traditional gender-neutral theories tend to reflect sociological perspectives of offending and identify systemic disadvantage in social, educational, and employment domains as causal factors that affect the genders similarly. These theories are buttressed by research indicating that male and female offenders' sociodemographic backgrounds are typically similar and include minority group membership, low socioeconomic status, lack of education, and underemployment (Chesney-Lind & Shelden, 2004; Denno, 1994; Steffensmeier & Allan, 1995). For instance, longitudinal research demonstrates that abusive and violent behaviors develop early in women and remain as aggressive traits, much like those of men (Moffitt, Caspi, Rutter, & Silva, 2001; Serbin & Karp, 2004). Further, male offending rates have been shown to be predictive of female rates, that is, high male crime rates coincide with female crime rates, and vice versa (Steffensmeier & Allan, 1988; Steffensmeier, Allan, & Streifel, 1989). Such perspectives may, however, fail to explain more micro-level gender differences in offense rates and patterns.

Howell (2003) proposed that girls and women traverse distinct pathways into serious, violent, and chronic offending. Drawing from feminist research to identify risk factors for female delinquency, he proposed five separate but interrelated risk factors—child abuse victimization, mental health problems, running away, gang involvement, and juvenile justice involvement—as the principle factors that lead to serious, violent, and chronic offending for females. Such *gender-specific* theories point to differences in genetic predisposition to antisocial behavior (Carter, 1973; Eme, 1992), development of social cognitive skills (Bennett, Farrington, & Huesmann, 2005), normative beliefs (Huesmann & Guerra, 1997), childcare needs and responsibilities (Koons, Burrow, Morash, & Bynum, 1997), and exposure to criminogenic conditions in childhood (Mears, Ploeger, & Warr, 1998) as potential explanations for the large gender gaps in offending. Women who do offend have been found to have experienced disproportionately high rates of personal/psychological maladjustment resulting from physical and sexual abuse or neglect in childhood (25%–40% in the general population; 85% in offenders), victimization in adulthood, poor coping skills, drug abuse, and major mental illness (Abram, Teplin, & McClelland, 2003; Browne, Miller, & Maguin, 1999; Byrne & Howells, 2000; McKeown, 2010; Morash, Bynum, & Koons, 1998; Rowe, Vazsonyi, & Flannery, 1995; Teplin, Abram, & McClelland, 1996; van Marle & van der Kroft, 2007).

Research suggests that, given women's greater exposure to some categories of traumatic experiences, high rates of repressive and generally dysfunctional social and intimate relationships, and a propensity for maladaptive coping strategies, substance misuse/dependence and related difficulties are proposed to be more deleterious in women than in men and are considered common conduits into offending and violence (Murdoch et al., 2012; Sorbello, Eccleston, Ward, & Jones, 2002; Thomas & Pollard, 2001). This is reflected in the greatly elevated rates of substance misuse and dependence in female offenders as compared to women in the general population (Lewis, 2006). As a result of the interplay between

severe physical and psychological trauma, emotional distress, underdeveloped coping skills, poor anger management, and low self-esteem both before and during incarceration (Loper & Levitt, 2011; Salisbury & van Voorhis, 2009; Sorbello et al., 2002), women are particularly vulnerable to the ill effects of substance misuse that, in conjunction with continued exposure to physical and psychological trauma, can serve to perpetuate a cycle of substance misuse/dependence and criminality (Sorbello et al., 2002).

Murdoch et al. (2012) postulated a model of women's violent offending as a reflection of emotion dysregulation in which women's poorly developed coping skills interact with substance misuse. The authors concluded that their exploratory research into violence perpetrated by women suggests two primary conclusions. First, female offenders might be a more homogenous population than male offenders with regard to their risks and needs (e.g., polyvictimization, emotion dysregulation, substance misuse). Second, the centrality of distal factors was highlighted (e.g., dysfunctional family systems, chronic emotion dysregulation, early and repeated exposure to abuse and interpersonal violence, the normalization of violence). Although their model is specific to women's violence, the causal mechanisms may contribute importantly to general offending as well.

RESEARCH REVIEW

Providing effective services requires an understanding of the circumstances, risks, and needs of the population to be served (Andrews et al., 2012). Justice-involved women comprise a population segment that continues to be marginalized by race, class, and gender, a circumstance that Bloom (1996) refers to as *triple jeopardy*. Black women continue to be over-represented in U.S. correctional populations, comprising only 13% of women in the United States; however, nearly half of women in prison are Black and they are eight times more likely than White women to be incarcerated (Bloom, Owen, & Covington, 2003). According to the U.S. Department of Justice (2011), Black females in the United States were three times more likely to be imprisoned in 2010. "The rate of incarceration in prisons and jails per 100,000 was 1,352 for males and 126 for females. The rates by race include Black females (260), Hispanic females (133) and White females (91)" (U.S. Department of Justice, 2011).

Similar demographic patterns have been reported within the U.S. juvenile justice system. Black youth represented 16% of the 10- to 17-year-old U.S. population but accounted for 51% of the violent crime arrests in 2009 (Puzzanchera & Adams, 2011). In 2010, 225 juvenile offenders were in custody for every 100,000 juveniles in the United States, with more than 6 out of 10 youth in residential placement being minority youth. Placement of disproportionate numbers of minority youth affected adolescent males (69%) and females (61%) similarly (Hockenberry, 2013). Vazsonyi and Chen (2010) provided developmental evidence that demonstrated greater risk of entry for Hispanic youth over Black, American Indian, Asian American, and European American youth. Entry risk increased from age 8 and peaked at age 14, with physical aggression in childhood increasing risk of entry by 23% for all groups; however, entry risk did not vary by gender. Similarly, Desai, Falzer, Chapman, and Borum (2012) found no evidence that disproportionate minority contact in one state juvenile detention differed by gender or self-reported mental health problems. The researchers reported that detained Black and Hispanic youth were more likely to be rated as low risk relative to White youth.

Mental Health Issues and Comorbidity

Mental illness. Mental illness is a well-established risk factor for all categories of offending behavior, particularly violent crime (Hodgins et al., 2011). Women exhibit higher rates of mental illness than men in the general population (Kessler, Sonnega, Bromet, Hughes, & Nelson, 1995); this trend is even more pronounced among offenders (Byrne & Howells, 2000; Sorbello et al., 2002). As many as two thirds of incarcerated female offenders require treatment for mental health issues (American Correctional Association, 1990), and more than three quarters may meet criteria for any number of psychiatric disorders including schizophrenia-spectrum disorders, bipolar disorder, generalized anxiety disorder, panic disorder and

posttraumatic stress disorder (PTSD), major depressive disorder, and personality disorders (Jordan, Schlenger, Fairbank, & Caddell, 1996; Teplin et al., 1996). Specifically, Lewis (2006) reported that, among incarcerated female offenders, 65.4% presented with substance abuse/dependency, 40.8% with PTSD, 40.8% with major depressive disorder/dysthymia, 32.3% with antisocial personality disorder (ASPD), 9.2% with anxiety related disorders, and 6.4% with schizophrenia or bipolar disorder.

A similar pattern of mental health disorders has been documented for adolescent female offenders as well. Recent prevalence studies conducted with male and female juvenile offenders have demonstrated that approximately 65% of male and female juvenile offenders meet diagnostic criteria for a mental health disorder (Teplin, Abram, McClelland, Dulcan, & Mericle, 2002; Schufelt & Coccoza, 2006; Wasserman et al., 2003). This rate surpasses prevalence estimates of male and female adolescents in community settings (42.6% in the National Comorbidity Survey Replication Adolescent Supplement study; Kessler et al., 2012). Mental health prevalence studies consistently document higher rates for female juvenile offenders (73.8%) relative to male juvenile offenders (66.3%; Teplin et al., 2002). In a large sample of detained adolescents, Teplin and colleagues reported that, among female offenders, 30.8% were identified with anxiety disorders, 27.6% with any affective disorder, 21.4% with attention deficit disorder, and 46.8% with any substance use disorder, with rates increasing modestly with age group (66.7%, <13 years; 72.2%, 14–15 years; 77.6%, >16 years). Rates of mental health disorders increase for both male and female offenders as they penetrate more deeply into the juvenile justice system; however, adolescent females' reports of affective and anxiety disorders are still two times more prevalent than reports from adolescent male offenders (odds ratios [ORs] = 2.07 and 2.04, respectively; Wasserman, McReynolds, Schwalbe, Keating, & Jones, 2010).

As we discussed with reference to substance abuse/dependence, research suggests that women's disproportionate exposure to trauma, resulting distress, and use of maladaptive coping mechanisms can precipitate the onset of mental illness, which in turn can perpetuate a cycle of behavioral dysfunction (e.g., self-harm) and offending behavior (Lewis, 2000; Sorbello et al., 2002). Such difficulties are, of course, compounded in the case of an individual with characteristics of (or diagnosed with) a comorbid mental disorder, particularly a personality disorder—the prevalence of which is higher in women than men in both general and offender populations (Singleton, Meltzer, Gatward, Coid, & Deasey, 1998; Sorbello et al., 2002; Thomas & Pollard, 2001).

Victimization and trauma.   Exposure to potential traumatic events is nearly universal among juvenile offenders, with 90% of male and female offenders in detention settings reporting exposure to at least one lifetime potentially traumatic event (Abram et al., 2004; Ford, Hartman, Hawke, & Chapman, 2008) and 56.8% reporting ≥6 exposures (Abram et al., 2004). Maltreatment and violence exposure account for the vast majority of traumatic event exposures (Kerig, Ward, Vanderzee, & Moeddel, 2009), with adolescent female offenders reporting high rates of witnessing violent crimes (70% total sample; 78% in those with PTSD), witnessing IPV (51% total sample; 68% among those with PTSD), sexual abuse (50% total sample; 81% among those with PTSD), and physical abuse (49% total sample; 49% among those with PTSD; see Dixon, Howie, & Starling, 2005). Female adolescent offenders report much higher rates of exposures to interpersonal traumas including sexual abuse ($OR = 10.78$) relative to male adolescent offenders (Wasserman & McReynolds, 2011). In addition, the number and type of trauma exposures have important implications for the behavioral and mental health functioning of adolescent female offenders (see Kerig & Becker, 2012; Kerig et al., 2009). For adolescent female offenders in particular, lifetime trauma exposure is associated with increased risk for PTSD, which in turn is comorbid with other disorders (Abram et al., 2003, 2004), including major depression and substance use disorders. In fact, patterns of comorbidity are found among 57% of adolescent female detainees (Teplin et al., 2013), with substance use, conduct, and anxiety problems being common comorbid diagnoses that are also documented as correlates of recidivism risk (Cottle

et al., 2001). Patterns of comorbidity have also been found to predict an escalating pattern of more frequent and severe future offenses relative to nondisordered adolescent offenders (Hoeve, McReynolds, Wasserman, & McMillan, 2013) and differentially affect adolescent females, with the presence of mental health disorders being a stronger predictor of multiple delinquency outcomes (e.g., number of offenses, days in detention) for adolescent female offenders relative to their male counterparts (Welch-Brewer, Stoddard-Dare, & Mallett, 2011).

Personality disorders and psychopathy.   Although all personality disorder typologies are represented in female offender populations, the two most prevalent diagnoses are ASPD and borderline personality disorder (BPD; Lewis, 2006; Teplin et al., 1996). Research indicates that between 13.8% and 43.0% of incarcerated female offenders present with ASPD (Lewis, 2004, 2006; Warren et al., 2002; Zlotnick, 1999), and 28% present with BPD (Jordan et al., 1996). In addition to the elevated suicide risk, ASPD is associated with earlier onset (poly) substance dependence, as well as poor clinical outcomes (Lewis, 2006), and BPD has been linked to self-harm, impulsivity, anger, emotional lability, and high psychiatric comorbidity in female offenders (D. W. Black et al., 2007).

In addition to personality disorders, psychopathy (a potent predictor of institutional misconduct, poor adjustment and treatment response, recidivism, general and sexual offending, and violence (McKeown, 2010; Warren et al., 2003) is also seen in female offenders at a rate ranging from 7.5% to 31% (Dolan, Fullam, Logan, & Davies, 2008; Lewis, 2006; see Bourque case illustration). Though findings regarding gender differences in psychopathy on offender/inmate samples are mixed, generally speaking, it appears as though there is a trend towards lower rates in women than in men (10%–15% vs. 25%–30%; Nicholls, Ogloff, Brink, & Spidel, 2005; Nicholls & Petrila, 2005; Strand & Belfrage, 2005; Vitale, Smith, Brinkley, & Newman, 2002).

Adolescent female offenders are diagnosed with disruptive behavior disorders (45.6%) at slightly higher rates relative to adolescent male offenders (41.4%), with this pattern being evident across conduct disorder (40.6% vs. 378%), oppositional defiant disorder (17.5% vs. 14.5%), and attention deficit disorder (21.4% vs. 16.6%; Teplin et al., 2002). The evidence of incremental risk associated with BPD among adult women has also been extended to adolescent females (see Muehlenkamp, Ertelt, Miller, & Claes, 2011; Trupin, Stewart, Beach, & Boesky, 2002). Common characteristics of BPD, including emotion dysregulation, defiance, and impulsivity, are identified as common risk factors contributing to serious conduct problems and depression among adolescent females (Hipwell et al., 2007, 2011). Additionally, the presence of BPD in clinical samples of adolescent females accounted for increased risk for suicide ideation and deliberate self-harm above and beyond the risk associated with major depression (Crowell et al., 2012; Sharp et al., 2012).

Similar evidence exists supporting psychopathy, as measured by the Psychopathy Checklist: Youth Version (PCL:YV; Forth, Kosson, & Hare, 2003), as a predictor of both violent, general, and nonviolent recidivism (Edens, Campbell, & Weir, 2007; Marshall, Egan, English, & Jones, 2006; Olver, Stockdale, & Wormith, 2009) in juvenile offenders, but caution has been raised about weaker predictive validity for adolescent female offenders relative to adolescent male offenders in some samples (Murrie, Boccaccini, McCoy, & Cornell, 2007). The PCL:YV is a developmentally anchored version of the adult instrument and contains items measuring the interpersonal, affective, and behavioral dimensions of the psychopathy construct with empirical evidence supporting the underlying factor structure in at-risk and justice-involved adolescent females across North American and European samples (Kosson et al., 2013). Broader concern about the misinterpretation and misuse of the psychopathy evidence in legal proceedings involving adolescents has also been documented (Viljoen, MacDougall, Gagnon, & Douglas, 2010). Additionally, there is evidence suggesting that psychopathy factors demonstrate differential associations with internalizing disorders and suicide among adolescent female offenders compared to adolescent male offenders (Sevecke, Lehmkuhl, & Krischer, 2009), and the predictive utility of the PCL:YV is diminished when victimization experiences of adolescent females are factored into re-offending models (Odgers, Reppucci, & Moretti, 2005). These findings reinforce caution when applying the PCL:YV to clinical decision-making regarding risk in general and for adolescent female offenders specifically (Murrie et al., 2007; Viljoen et al., 2010).

Callous-unemotional (CU) traits are a developmental extension of the construct of psychopathy focused on children's and adolescents' affective and interpersonal styles that are related to, but not synonymous with, conduct problems. Frick, Ray, Thornton, and Kahn (2014) provided a comprehensive review of the empirical evidence supporting the contribution of CU traits to distinct causal pathways to serious conduct problems in children and adolescents. Their review documented that between 20% and 50% of youth with serious conduct problems also exhibit nonnormative levels of CU traits (see Kahn, Frick, Youngstrom, Findling, & Youngstrom, 2012) that are subsequently associated with more severe, persistent, and violent patterns of aggression and offending behavior; there is also evidence supporting these associations among child and adolescent females (Pardini, Stepp, Hipwell, Stouthamer-Loeber, & Loeber, 2012).

Substance use/dependence. Rates of drug and alcohol use, abuse, and dependence in female offender populations are extremely high, certainly exceed community rates, and in some cases surpass those of male offenders (Blanchette & Brown, 2006; Derkzen, Booth, Taylor, & McConnell, 2013; Lewis, 2006). As discussed previously in this chapter, women are more likely than men to use substances as a coping mechanism to alleviate distress associated with high rates of psychological, physical, and sexual victimization suffered in and out of custody (Chesney-Lind & Pasko, 2004; Sorbello et al., 2002). This association between substances and victimization has been theorized to serve as a gendered etiological conduit in female offenders whereby drug use mediates the relationship between trauma and aggression, which serves to perpetuate criminalization (Javdani et al., 2011). Furthermore, substance-using incarcerated women have been shown to have suffered poorer childhood family and adult social environments, poorer education, and poorer physical health, as compared to their non–substance-using counterparts (N. Langan & Pelissier, 2001).

Teplin et al. (2002) reported alcohol use (26.5%) and marijuana use (40.5%) among adolescent female detainees at rates comparable to adolescent male detainees. Similarly, male and female youth with comorbid substance use and mental health disorders were at highest risk to commit future property offenses compared to youth without substance use disorders (Hoeve et al., 2013). When controlling for gender, strong support for factors such as intrinsic gratification, thrill seeking, and negative peer group influence are identified as contributing to adolescent substance use (see Cooper, May, Soderstrom, & Jarjoura, 2009). Some evidence of gender-specific predictors exists. Exposure to adverse life events (family-related adversity, household dysfunction, and violence exposure) was associated with increased marijuana use for adolescent female offenders with no evidence that coping styles mediated the stressor-substance use relationship (Robertson, Xu, & Stripling, 2010). Further research is needed, however, these results reinforce that drug use may serve as an escape from uncontrollable adverse events, particularly traumatic events, for adolescent female offenders (Molidor, Nissen, & Watkins, 2002).

Unique risk factors. Research has identified a multitude of factors, or *criminogenic needs*, purported to be of specific relevance to the risk of offending in women (Hollin & Palmer, 2006). Most variables identified as gender-specific are to some degree subsumed by what Blanchette (2002) calls *personal/emotional* level factors, and include issues relating to trauma and abuse, self-esteem, medical and mental health status and care, substance use, parenting and childcare, and interpersonal relationships (also see de Vogel et al., 2012; Garcia & Lane, 2013; van Voorhis & Presser, 2001). Furthermore, complex interactions between some of these factors such as substance misuse and childhood and adulthood victimization, depression and other psychiatric disorders, family difficulties, and sexual risk-taking have also been described as potent determinants of female offending (Cotten-Oldenburg, Jordan, Martin, & Kupper, 1999; Martin & Hesselbrock, 2001; Peugh & Belenko, 1999). Some more recent research has found important associations between prison misconduct and child abuse, self-efficacy, and relationship instability, as well as risk of recidivism and mental illness, low self-esteem, poor family support, financial problems, and substance use (Salisbury, van Voorhis, & Spiropoulos, 2009; Salisbury, van Voorhis, & Wright, 2006). Such findings highlight the fact that the predictive accuracy of preferred assessment practices currently utilized with offender populations may be hampered by ignorance of risk factors unique to women and girls, although there remains considerable debate and more research is needed (Andrews et al., 2012; Emeka & Sorensen, 2009; Heilbrun et al., 2008).

Suicide and self-harm. Suicide and self-harming behaviors are increasingly common in offender populations (Perry & Olason, 2009). Although male offenders show higher rates of completed suicides, females reportedly attempt suicide more frequently (O'Connor & Sheehy, 1997; Zhang, Liang, Zhou, & Brame, 2010). Rates for lifetime suicide attempts in female offenders range from 25% to 50% (Verona, Hicks, & Patrick, 2005). Suicide is also a concern among adolescent female offenders, who have been found to be three times more likely to endorse a recent ($OR = 2.88$) or lifetime ($OR = 3.26$) suicide attempt relative to adolescent male offenders (Wasserman et al., 2010). Although many risk factors for self-harm and suicide generalize across men and women, research has demonstrated that there do exist certain factors that appear to be of particular relevance for women and girls. These include history of suicide (Chapman, Specht, & Cellucci, 2005; Shreeram & Malik, 2008), abuse (Duke, Pettingell, McMorris, & Borowsky, 2010; Kimonis et al., 2010), emotional/interpersonal components of psychopathy (Verona et al., 2005), and diagnosis with substance abuse/dependence, and antisocial and BPDs (D. W. Black et al., 2007; Lewis, 2006). Nonsuicidal self-injury (NSSI) has been documented as a specific concern for adolescent female offenders at rates varying from 9% to

75% in detained samples (Cuellar & Curry, 2007; Kenny, Lennings, & Munn, 2008; Penn, Esposito, Schaeffer, Fritz, & Spirito, 2003). Risk factors for suicide overlap with risk factors for NSSI (Hawton, Saunders, & O'Connor, 2012; Kenny et al., 2008; Tørmoen, Rossow, Larsson, & Mehlum, 2013), reinforcing the need for careful assessment and management in correctional settings (Dixon-Gordon, Harrison, & Roesch, 2012; Nicholls, Roesch, Olley, Ogloff, & Hemphill, 2005).

Posttraumatic stress disorder.   Studies have shown that PTSD is one of the most prevalent psychiatric illnesses in female offender populations (Jordan et al., 1996; Lewis, 2006; Teplin et al., 1996). Although research on PTSD in female inmate populations is surprisingly scant, a few studies estimate point prevalence rates ranging from 16.6% to 28.6% (Simpson, Brinded, Laidlaw, Fairley, & Malcolm, 1999; Butler & Allnut, 2003) and lifetime prevalence rates as high as 33.5% (Teplin et al., 1996). For sufferers, trauma often dates back to childhood and frequently includes repeated and severe physical and sexual abuses (Lewis, 2006). Female offenders diagnosed with PTSD show elevated risk of depression, suicide, risky sexual behavior, substance abuse, and continued victimization (Kessler et al., 1995; Lewis, 2005; Zlotnick, 1997). In many cases, the relationship between these latter two adverse outcomes is cyclical such that substance use leaves women vulnerable to victimization; women, more than men, tend to cope with distress associated with victimization by using substances (Javdani et al., 2011; Lewis, 2006). Comorbid PTSD and substance use also fosters even greater comorbidity with affective, anxiety, and personality disorders (Lewis, 2005; Najavits et al., 1998), bearing consequences for management and treatment in correctional settings.

Studies also consistently document a high prevalence of PTSD in adolescents within the juvenile justice system (see Dierkhising et al., 2013 for a review) with rates varying from 10% to 30% among youth across detention and secure custody or correctional settings (Ford, Chapman, Connor, & Cruise, 2012a). PTSD among adolescent female offenders are at the upper end of this range within the United States and internationally (see Ariga et al., 2008; Dixon et al., 2005; Foy, Ritchie, & Conway, 2012). For instance, Abram et al. (2004) reported a past 12-month prevalence rate of 14.7% in a large sample of detained female adolescents and no significant differences across race/ethnicity and age groups. Rates can vary according to time frame, assessment measures, and juvenile justice setting (see Abram et al., 2004); however, PTSD is often comorbid with other internalizing and substance use disorders among adolescent females in community and juvenile justice settings (Danielson et al., 2010; Foy et al., 2012). Polyvictimization in particular has been identified as a potential risk marker for this comorbid pattern and delinquent behaviors, suggesting the relevance of screening and assessment specifically among adolescent female offenders (see Ford, Elhai, Connor, & Frueh, 2010; Ford et al., 2012a).

Parenting.   Poehlmann, Dallaire, Loper, and Shear (2010) estimated that as many as 1.7 million children in the United States have parents who are incarcerated in prisons, and suggested that millions more children have a parent incarcerated in jails; however, the researchers noted that exact figures are unavailable because jails, prisons, schools, and other relevant systems do not systematically collect this information. The Bureau of Justice Statistics reported that 7 of 10 women offenders criminally sanctioned in the United States have minor children (in excess of 1,300,000 children; Greenfield & Snell, 1999). Bloom et al. (2003) similarly concluded that as many as half the women in federal prisons and more than half of women in state prisons have dependent children. Glaze and Maruschak (2008) conducted a national survey of state and federal prisoners in the United States in 2007. They found that of the estimated 74 million children (<18 years) in the United States on July 1, 2007, 2.3% had a parent in prison. Black children (6.7%) were 7.5 times more likely than White children (0.9%) to have a parent in prison. Hispanic children (2.4%) were >2.5 times more likely than White children to have a parent in prison. Twenty-two percent of children with parents in state prison and 16% of children with parents in federal prison were 4 years of age or younger. Of particular note, the number of children under the age of 18 who have a mother in prison has more than doubled since 1991 (up 131%; Glaze & Maruschak, 2008). Fathers in prison reported having 1,559,200 children; mothers reported 147,400.

Not only are incarcerated men comparatively less likely to have children (51.2% of men vs. 61.7% of women in state prisons were parents), those who do are less likely than incarcerated women to have (primary) custody of their children. Glaze and Maruschak (2008) reported that female inmates who had children were more likely than male inmates with children to report living with at least one child prior to their incarceration. Specifically, more than half of mothers held in state prison reported living with at least one of their children in the month before arrest, compared to 36% of fathers. Glaze and Maruschak (2008) also found that imprisoned mothers more frequently reported at least monthly phone calls (47% vs. 38%) and mail correspondence with children (65% vs. 51%) than did imprisoned fathers (also see Loper, Carlson, Levitt, & Scheffel, 2009). However, no gender differences in frequency of visits with children emerged (Glaze & Maruschak, 2008). Parenthood also appears to be more central to the experience of being incarcerated (e.g., separation from children being described as the most difficult aspect of incarceration) and (to aspirations for) desistance for women than for men (for discussions, see Broidy & Cauffman, 2006; Poehlman et al., 2010). The literature on contact with children during incarceration is, however, quite equivocal. For instance, some studies demonstrate reduced mental health problems and associated distress among women who have visits with their children, whereas other studies reveal higher rates of violent infractions, which are postulated to reflect the distress of having little control over their children's lives and the "emotional upheaval" associated with the contact (e.g., Poehlman et al., 2010, p. 588).

Significant gaps in the empirical literature exist regarding teen parents and risk for entering the juvenile justice system (Pinderhughes, Craddock, & Fermin, 2011). Black adolescent females were three times more likely to have histories of being pregnant relative to European American offenders (Khurana, Cooksey, & Gavazzi, 2011) with rates of health-related and substance-related risky behaviors differentiating adolescent females with and without

pregnancy histories. Positive attitudes toward being a parent, substance use, and risky sexual behavior significantly predict pregnancy in adolescent female offenders (Kelly, Lesser, & Paper, 2008). Additionally, researchers have documented that becoming a parent substantially reduces trajectories of delinquent behavior among adolescent females (Hope, Wilder, & Watt, 2003).

Populations and Offense Categories

The following section will discuss categories of crimes that are of particular interest in a chapter on female offenders because they are evidently rare among females (e.g., sexual offending), as well as several categories of offenses that are unique because they are commonly committed by female offenders (e.g., IPV, child abuse, filicide, and neonaticide).

Sexual offending.   Research consistently demonstrates that sexual offending is predominantly perpetrated by male offenders. Federal Bureau of Investigation (2006) statistics suggest that as much as 90% of sexual offending is committed by men. International estimates place the prevalence of female offenders at as low as 5% of all sex offenders (Cortoni et al., 2010). Experts caution, however, that prevalence rates are likely vastly underestimated given that assessors tend to focus on women as victims and neglect to assess for male victimization and female perpetration (Anderson & Struckman-Johnson, 1998). Despite increasing interest in the topic of female sexual offending (e.g., Nathan & Ward, 2001), there remains a societal presumption that sexual offending by women is not harmful (Anderson & Struckman-Johnson, 1998; Nathan & Ward, 2001; West et al., 2011). Nathan and Ward (2001) recently concluded that the evidence base for female sexual offending remains very much in its infancy, noting that the bulk of work in the field has only emerged since the mid-1980s, and "the knowledge base is still tentative and equivocal" (p. 213). Wijkman, Bijleveld, and Hendriks (2010) examined the characteristics of all adult female sex offenders in the Netherlands between 1994 and 2005 ($N = 111$). In the majority of cases, the women had abused their own children (77%) and often offended with a male co-offender (nearly two thirds of women offended with another person; in 75% of those cases, the co-offender was the woman's husband or intimate partner), characteristics that are common according to the literature (Wijkman et al., 2010). Female sexual offenders tend to come from highly dysfunctional childhood homes characterized by (sexual) abuse and conflict, and they often present with mental disorders (Strickland, 2008; Wijkman et al., 2010; Wijkman, Bijleveld, & Hendriks, 2011). For instance, Weijkman and colleagues concluded that just one fourth of the women in their sample *did not* report mental disorder; personality disorder; drug use; a current violent partner; or past physical, sexual, or psychological abuse, neglect, or prostitution.

The field is growing, however, and research has started to move beyond a consideration of the prevalence of female-perpetrated sexual offending and the characteristics of female sexual offenders to begin to examine whether women who commit sexual offenses are specialists or generalists. For instance, using latent class analysis, Wijkman et al. (2011) identified three subgroups: (a) one-time only sex offenders; (b) generalists, women who perpetrated the sexual offense, often against nonrelatives in combination with a record for other frequent serious offenses; and (c) specialists, women who commit multiple sex offenses, often in combination with some minor offenses (shoplifting, receiving stolen goods). The recidivism rates of female sexual offenders have been found to be very low. A meta-analysis of 10 studies including 2,490 offenders with an average follow-up period of 6.5 years concluded that less than 3% of the women reoffended, and approximately 1.5% sexually reoffended (Cortoni et al., 2010).

Similar to adult females, arrest rates for sexual offenses by adolescent females are extremely low relative to arrests for sexual offenses by adolescent males. In 2009, adolescent females accounted for only 2% of juvenile forcible rape arrests (62 out of 3,100 arrests) and for 11% of other sex offenses excluding forcible rape and prostitution (1,474 out of 13,400 arrests; see Puzzanchera & Adams, 2011). As such, far less is known about the background, clinical characteristics, and risk patterns of problem sexual behavior for adolescent female

sexual offenders relative to their male counterparts. Limited data suggest that adolescent female sexual offenders are younger than male sexual offenders at time of arrest and more likely to offend against both male and female victims (Vandiver & Teske, 2006). Existing research suggests that adolescent females charged with sexual offenses are not a homogenous group and are likely differentiated by histories of child maltreatment. Female juvenile sexual offenders with histories of child maltreatment have greater mental health difficulties (anger, anxiety, depression), report greater use of coercion in their offenses (Roe-Sepowitz & Krysik, 2008), and engage in repetitive patterns of antisocial sexual behavior prior to detection (Matthews, Hunter, & Vuz, 1997). Little is known about the recidivism risk for adolescent females charged with sexual offenses. To illustrate, recent reviews of specialized risk assessment instruments used with juvenile sex offenders were based exclusively on adolescent male samples (Hempel, Buck, Cima, & van Marle, 2013; Viljoen, Mordell, & Beneteau, 2012).

Intimate partner violence. As discussed in the IPV chapter (see Volume 1, Chapter 12, this handbook), there are now more than 200 studies documenting gender symmetry in IPV perpetration rates. Not only do men and women perpetrate partner violence at nearly equal rates and severity levels, they do so for similar reasons (Fiebert, 2012; Follingstad, Wright, Lloyd, & Sebastian, 1991). The most commonly reported proximate motivations for use of violence among both men and women are coercion, anger, and punishing misbehavior by their partner (Follingstad et al., 1991; Kernsmith, 2005; Stets & Hammons, 2002). Follingstad, Bradley, Helff, and Laughlin (2002) reported that anxious attachment and angry temperament predicted dating violence in both sexes. As violence escalates, there are greater gender differences in the use of violence in self-defense; however, self-defense is still a relatively uncommon motivation for IPV (Straus, 2009). The CDC National Intimate Partner Violence and Sexual Violence Survey (M. C. Black et al., 2011) reported that 81% of women and 35% of men who experienced rape, physical violence, or stalking by an intimate partner reported at least one impact related to the IPV experiences, such as fear, concern for safety, injury, or having missed at least one day of work or school. Data from the National Crime Victimization Survey (Rennison & Welchans, 2000) indicated that, between 1993 and 1998, 47,000 men were injured by their partner, 18,910 of whom received medical treatment. Straus's (2011) meta-analytic review of 91 empirical studies compared rates of *clinical-level* IPV perpetrated by men and women (defined as severe assaults such as punching, choking, and attacks with objects or physical acts resulting in injury) demonstrated that the median percentage of clinical-level IPV perpetrated by women was higher (7%) than by men (5%). The median percentage of individuals who injured a partner was 14% for men compared to 7% for women (Straus, 2011). Based on the extant literature, three conclusions seem reasonable: (a) Women are injured more than men, but men are injured, too, and are not immune to being seriously injured; (b) attacks by men cause more fear and injury, including more deaths; and (c) simply because the injury rates are lower, men should not be denied protection (Dutton & Nicholls, 2005; Nicholls, 2011, 2012; Straus, 2009; also see Volume 1, Chapter 12, this handbook).

Dating violence. A unique form of violence applicable to adolescent females is dating violence. Data obtained for the 2011 Youth Risk Behavior Survey (YRBS) indicated that 9.4% of high school students reported being hit, slapped, or physically hurt on purpose by a romantic partner (boyfriend or girlfriend) within the past 12 months. Reported rates were comparable across adolescent females and males and varied little across grades (7.6%–10.7% across 9th through 12th grades for females; 7.4%–11.2% across 9th through 12th grades for males). Black and Hispanic females reported slightly higher rates (11.8% and 10.6%, respectively) than White females (7.7%; Eaton et al., 2012). Concern has been raised that the juvenile justice system is failing to recognize and address dating violence (Zosky, 2010), even with the available evidence indicating that delinquency violence and dating violence are influenced by common factors (Brendgen, Vitaro,

Tremblay, & Wanner, 2002). Similar to IPV, Vagi et al. (2013) supported a "background-situational model of dating violence" (p. 646), indicating that general violence risk factors (e.g., childhood physical abuse, mental health problems) and contextual factors (e.g., conflictual dating relationship) are associated with adolescent dating violence. Chiodo et al. (2012) focused exclusively on patterns of dating violence and perpetration in adolescent females over a two year time period to identify profiles of dating violence. Mutual violence (victim and perpetrator) was identified in 15.6% of the adolescent females, with smaller percentages of victim-only (7.5%) and perpetrator-only (6.2%) being found. Histories of delinquency, parental rejection, and sexual harassment predicted classification in the mutual dating violence group in the 11th grade, with this group reporting a host of psychosocial risks including peer aggression, delinquent behaviors, sexual risk-taking, and histories of suicide ideation. While debate exists regarding operational definitions and the most appropriate measurement strategy, the existing research linking dating violence to delinquency indicates that screening, assessment, and management strategies should incorporate a focus on this specific form of violence with adolescent female offenders (Hamby & Turner, 2013).

Child abuse. Women's violent offending also frequently targets their biological children, at rates nearly identical to those of fathers. National and state child abuse statistics derived from protective agencies (U.S. Department of Health and Human Services) reveal there were 9.3 unique victims of child maltreatment per 1,000 children in the U.S. population in 2009. In the majority of cases, the perpetrator was a parent, and most often it was the mother acting alone (37.7%; father alone, 18.6%; mother and father, 18.0%; mother and other, 5.5%; father and other, 0.9%). Similarly, child fatalities were most likely perpetrated by parents (75.8%), and the mother was again the most likely perpetrator (27.3%; mother and father, 22.5%; father, 14.8%; mother and other, 9.8%; father and other, 1.4%).

A U.S. National Incidence study reported that biological parents inflicted abuse on children at similar rates, with 54% of children reporting abuse by a father and 51% reporting abuse by a mother (Sedlak et al., 2010).[1] Women, both biological and nonbiological caregivers, are more commonly the perpetrators of neglect, with 86% of children reporting a perpetrator of neglect being a female and 38% reporting a male as a perpetrator of neglect (Sedlak et al., 2010).[2] When all abuse and neglect are factored together, 75% of children reported that the biological mother was the perpetrator, and 43% identified the biological father. Sedlak et al. (2010) also found that women were predominantly responsible for serious offenses: Children suffering fatal/serious maltreatment are more often injured or killed at the hands of the mother (75%) rather than the father (45%).

Filicide. Daly and Wilson (1988) asserted that the relationship between the victim and the killer is a useful basis for categorizing violent interpersonal crimes. Homicide by family members is a common cause of death among children, especially if death due to neglect is included (Harris, Hilton, Rice, & Eke, 2007). *Filicide* is a generic term describing the deliberate act of a parent or parents, including step-parents, of killing their child(ren) (Resnick, 1969). At their youngest ages, mothers represent the greatest risk to children, and the risk presented by mothers subsequently declines until approximately 6 years of age (Harris et al., 2007). Among children under 5 years of age in the United States who were murdered in the last quarter of the 20th century, 61% were killed by their own parents: 30% by their mothers, and 31% by their fathers (Finkelhor, 1997; Friedman, Hrouda, Holden, Noffsinger, & Resnick, 2005). Research suggests that, compared to other developed nations, the United States has the highest rates: 8.0/100,000 for infants; 2.5/100,000 for 1–4 years; 1.5/100,000 for 5–14 years. Canada's rate of child homicide is less than half that of the U.S. rate (2.9/100,000 for infants; Finkelhor, 1997; Friedman et al., 2005). Contemporary data from the western world suggests that filicide represents 5% to 10% of solved homicides (Léveillée, Marleau, & Dubé, 2007).

Bourget, Grace, and Whitehurst (2007) found that some studies have noted that mothers

commit filicide more often than fathers (Bourget & Bradford, 1990; Copeland, 1985; Harder, 1967; Jason, Gilliland, & Tyler, 1983; Kaplun & Reich, 1976; Myers, 1970; Resnick, 1969), and other research has shown that paternal filicide is as common or more common than maternal filicide (Adelson, 1961, 1991; Bourget & Gagné, 2002; Fornes, Druilhe, & Lecomte, 1995; Krugman, 1985; Lucas et al., 2002; Marks & Kumar, 1993, 1996; Somander & Rammer, 1991; Wright & Leroux, 1991). The authors concluded that reports of a higher proportion of maternal filicides most likely reflect the inclusion of neonaticides in some studies (Bourget et al., 2007). Harris et al. (2007) used the Violent Crime Linkage Analysis System (ViCLAS) to extract all Canadian cases involving the homicide of a person <12 years old, which included 385 fatal cases from 1997 to 2003 ($N = 378$). Results indicated that women were nearly equally likely to have been perpetrators of filicide as men: 111 (29%) by genetic mothers; 86 (22%) by genetic fathers; 16 (4%) by stepmothers; 62 (16%) by stepfathers; 103 (27%) by nonrelatives. Stepparents, particularly stepmothers, are more likely to have physically assaulted the child previously (Harris et al., 2007; M. Wilson et al., 1995). Children killed by stepmothers have been found to have experienced "much worse ongoing abuse and neglect than any other victims" (Harris et al., 2007, p. 92). A significant minority of killings by stepmothers also reflected "active assistance or complicity" of the victim's genetic father (Harris et al., 2007).

Resnick (1969) was the first to propose a classification based on motive: altruism, acute psychosis, unwanted child, accident, and spousal revenge. This categorization has been replicated in research, and some distinct gender differences have been noted. Women who commit filicide for altruistic reasons have been found to be particularly likely to commit a self-destructive act (69% of women vs. 29% of men; Léveillée et al., 2007), whereas men who perpetrate filicide as a means of reprisal against their partner appear to be much more likely to attempt suicide than women who do so (women, 6%; men, 57%;

---

[1]This rate includes physical, emotional, and sexual abuse.
[2]This rate includes physical, emotional, and educational neglect.

Léveillée et al., 2007). An in-depth examination of child abuse homicide cases in Kansas from 1994 to 2007 indicates that filicide was most commonly perpetrated at nearly equal rates by the victim's biological father (26.6%) and the victim's biological mother (24.9%).[3] Men appear to be far more likely to commit retaliatory filicides than women (Daly & Wilson, 1988, pp. 213–219; Harris et al., 2007; Léveillée et al., 2007; Wilczynski, 1997).

Neonaticide.   Resnick (1970) coined the term *neonaticide* to describe the killing of a child less than 24 hours old. Unique from the term filicide, neonaticide encompasses all potential offenders, including parents. Although neonaticide is not uncommon among mothers, it is an exceptionally rare event among fathers. Neonaticidal mothers are generally young (between 16 and 38 years of age, with as many as 90% being 25 years of age or younger) and unmarried (less than 20% are married). Less than 30% of female neonaticide perpetrators are seen as psychotic or depressed; they are however noted to be lacking interpersonal support, experiencing stressors, or have denied or concealed the pregnancy since conception. They frequently give birth alone and dispose of the baby as an abortion that occurs "too late." Mothers who kill newborns often are charged with a lesser offense than murder (Uniform Crime Reports; see Harris et al., 2007; Shelton, Muirhead, & Canning, 2010).

Much of the data and discussion in this chapter focuses on the fact that women perpetrate substantially less societal violence than men, representing a drastically smaller proportion of offenders and inmates. A consideration of the offenses that female offenders perpetrate, however, reveals little evidence of less injury sustained by the victims, regardless of whether the perpetrator was a man or a woman. Specifically, Kong and AuCoin (2008) reported that data from 121 police services showed that half (51%) of women's victims sustained no injury, 43% experienced a minor injury, and 2% suffered a major physical injury, numbers nearly identical to the proportion of male-perpetrated violence victims resulting in injury (54%, 38%, and 4%, respectively; see Figures 4.1 and 4.2). Data specific to adolescents also supports that adolescent females represent a smaller proportion of the overall juvenile justice population. Representation within specific offending categories (e. g., sexual offending) reflects this gender gap. Despite smaller numbers, limited data reflect heterogeneity among adolescent females who engage in dating violence and problem sexual behavior with the existing research supporting that early adversity (e.g., child maltreatment, interpersonal trauma exposure), psychosocial risk factors (e.g., peer aggression, histories of general delinquent behavior), and psychopathology (e.g., anger, depression, suicide ideation) are associated with these specific offending patterns among adolescent females. Clearly more research is needed to better understand the backgrounds and risk profiles of adolescent females who engage in specific forms of violence.

PRACTICE AND POLICY ISSUES

Central to planning treatment and the provision of services for offenders and inmates is the assessment of risk and mental health needs. The female offender assessment literature continues to be dominated by debates about, (a) the extent to which gender is central to informing the identification of variables of importance to women's future risk, (b) the absence of sufficient research to test women-specific needs, and (c) insufficient research to evaluate the psychometric properties of existing measures. We begin with a discussion of assessment-related issues and then move to treatment-related issues.

Given the disproportionate risk of offending presented by males, most forensic and correctional assessment technologies routinely implemented in offender populations were originally developed, validated, and normed on male, or predominately male, samples (Blanchette & Brown,

---

[3] Defined as homicides as a result of abuse from caretakers (inflicting injury with malicious intent, usually as a form of discipline or punishment) or neglect (failing to provide shelter, safety, reasonable supervision, and nutritional needs).

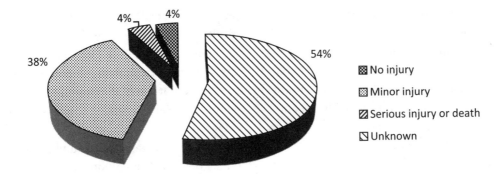

FIGURE 4.1.   Injuries resulting from violent crimes committed by males.

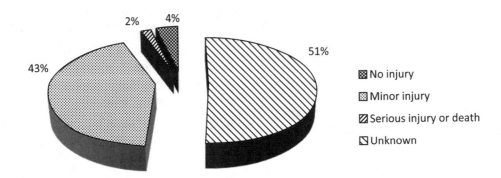

FIGURE 4.2.   Injuries resulting from violent crimes committed by females.

2006; Garcia-Mansilla, Rosenfeld, & Nicholls, 2009; Hardyman & van Voorhis, 2004). Despite the advancement of knowledge on the putatively unique pathways to offending behavior in women (Leschied, 2011), a substantial body of research continues to support a nongendered (or gender-neutral) perspective relevant to many assessment approaches (Andrews & Dowden, 2006; Nicholls & Petrila, 2005; Schwalbe, 2008). Proponents of a more gender-neutral perspective assert that similar offense-related risk factors are found in both male and female offenders, and that pronounced gender differences in offending base rates are attributable to the differential prevalence of these factors in men and women (Cale & Lilienfeld, 2002; Loucks & Zamble, 2000; Nicholls, Ogloff, & Douglas, 2004). Supporters of a gendered, or gender-sensitive, approach (see Emeka & Sorensen, 2009; Leschied, 2011) to assessment acknowledge important differences in the nature, severity, frequency, and etiology

of women's violence (Odgers, Moretti, & Reppucci, 2005; Robbins, Monahan, & Silver, 2003; Teasdale, Silver, & Monahan, 2006), and suggest that risk of offending-related behaviors is inextricably determined by women's unique person- and context-level experiences (Garcia-Mansilla et al., 2009; Funk, 1999). Accordingly, some experts insist that assessment procedures used with women must take such unique factors into account (de Vogel et al., 2012; Garcia-Mansilla et al., 2009; Logan & Blackburn, 2009).

Risk Assessment Measures

Over the past four decades substantial progress has been made in the assessment and management of violence risk (Monahan et al., 2001; Otto & Douglas, 2010; see Volume 1, Chapter 3, this handbook). Despite those advancements, a critical limitation in the violence risk assessment field to date has been the failure to integrate in a systematic way a consideration of the unique profile of women offenders and the extant literature on the unique offending trajectories of females into risk assessment and risk management research and clinical practice. There also remain large gaps in knowledge as to the clinical relevance of such efforts (i.e., do female-specific risk items add incremental validity once established gender-neutral risk variables are considered?). Here we discuss a handful of some of the most commonly used violence risk assessment measures and consider the empirical evidence to support their implementation in correctional populations of women.

Psychopathy Checklist: Revised. Although not a violence risk assessment measure, considerable research points to a significant association between psychopathy, criminal offending, recidivism, and violence (Hare, 1996; Hart, 1998; Hemphill, Hare, & Wong, 1998). The Psychopathy Checklist—Revised (PCL–R; Hare, 1991, 2003; see Volume 1, Chapter 9, this handbook) is considered by some to be applicable across genders (Hart, 1998); however, more recent reviews of the literature have found that psychopathy may not be as potent a risk factor for women as it is for men (see Logan, 2009; Nicholls et al., 2005; Strand & Belfrage, 2005). These reviews describe important gender differences in psychopathy prevalence, symptomology, and mental disorder comorbidity. Nevertheless, while it is appropriate to use caution when using the PCL–R to assess violence risk in women (Falkenbach, 2008), there is sufficient empirical evidence in the literature to suggest that the tool is, by and large, equally predictive of antisocial and criminal behavior for men and women (Hare, 2003; Nicholls et al., 2004; Vitale & Newman, 2001; C. D. Webster, 1999), and thus a valuable addition to any comprehensive risk assessment conducted with men or women. That being said, considerable caution should be used, and cutoff scores based on norms with men should be avoided (Forouzan & Cooke, 2005; Nicholls et al., 2004).

Historical, Clinical, Risk Management—20. The generalizability of one of the gold standard violence risk assessment tools, the Historical Clinical Risk Management—20 (HCR–20; C. D. Webster, Douglas, Eaves, & Hart, 1997; see also Volume 1, Chapter 3, this handbook), across gender is a debate that continues to divide the literature. Despite an impressive body of work examining the scheme's performance in civil psychiatric, forensic, juvenile, and correctional samples, surprisingly few studies have explored potential gender differences, especially in offenders. Despite this, it is useful to note that the some work supports the applicability of the HCR–20 across genders in women sampled from psychiatric settings (Nicholls et al., 2004; Strand & Belfrage, 2001), whereas others have noted differences such that women tended scored lower than men (Bauer & Knörnschild, 2010; de Vogel & de Ruiter, 2005; Nicholls et al., 2004; Strand & Belfrage, 2001). In a large offender sample, Coid and colleagues (2009) found that the HCR–20 predicted violent reconviction as well in women as it did in men, if not better, and meta-analyses of mixed samples have revealed few gender differences (Guy, 2008; Singh, Grann, & Fazel, 2011; Yang, Wong, & Coid, 2010). Though the results of investigations into the applicability of the HCR–20 to women are mixed, there exists important evidence suggesting that the scheme is appropriate for use with women, and specifically with female offenders.

Female Additional Manual. In response to perceived equivocal findings with respect to the applicability of the HCR–20 to women, and to address the field's total lack of risk assessment schemes developed specifically for use in adult women, the Female Additional Manual (FAM; de Vogel et al., 2012) has recently been developed. Serving as an addendum to the HCR–20, the FAM provides additional guidelines for seven and nine additional risk factors identified in the literature. Such risk factors include problematic circumstances and behavior during childhood, prostitution, parenting difficulties, pregnancy at young age, suicidality/self-harm, victimization after childhood, covert/manipulative behavior, low self-esteem, problematic childcare responsibility, and problematic intimate relationships. Research into the psychometric properties, predictive accuracy, and utility of the FAM is thus far virtually nonexistent, as the tool has yet to be examined outside of the developer's pilot studies with mentally disordered offenders.

Level of Service Inventory—Revised. Considerable research has explored gender differences in the performance of the Level of Service Inventory-Revised (LSI-R), which is an actuarial assessment of general recidivism, (Andrews & Bonta, 1995; see Volume 1, Chapter 3, this handbook). In recent years the LSI-R has been subject to critique for being male-specific in that critics assert that it relies too heavily on gender-neutral criminogenic predictors. Although a number of meta-analyses provide evidence for the applicability of the measure across genders (Gendreau, Goggin, & Law, 1997; Gendreau, Goggin, & Smith, 2003; Smith et al., 2009), there is research that has also demonstrated that the LSI-R may not perform as well for those female offenders who enter the correctional system through "gendered pathways" (Holtfreter & Cupp, 2007; Reisig, Holtfreter, & Morash, 2006). Researchers supporting the gender-specific model of risk assessment have adapted the LSI-R for use with women, and results from empirical investigations into its performance show that both gender-neutral and gender-sensitive factors significantly predict prison misconduct and general recidivism (Salisbury et al., 2009; van Voorhis et al., 2010).

Violence Risk Scale—Second Edition. The Violence Risk Scale—Second Edition (VRS–2; Wong & Gordon, 2000; see Volume 1, Chapter 3, this handbook) is being utilized with female offenders in both forensic and correctional settings, but there have been few empirical investigations into the applicability of the measure across genders (Logan, 2002; McKeown, 2010). One study of 147 offenders found that women scored lower than men on the measure's static factors, but not the dynamic factors (Dolan et al., 2008), however the sample contained only 11 women. The most significant contribution to the small body of work on the VRS–2 and its use with female offenders noted that women's scores were somewhat lower than previously reported men's scores (consistent with research with comparing men and women on other measures such as the PCL measures [Hare, 2003] and the HCR–20, [e.g., Douglas & Reeves, 2010; Nicholls et al., 2004; Nicholls & Petrila, 2005]), but the measure still demonstrated good risk-level differentiation as well as predictive validity for violent recidivism in women (Stewart, 2011).

Adolescent-specific risk measures. Specific advancements have been made in the development and validation of risk assessment tools for adolescents (see Viljoen, Cruise, Nicholls, Desmarais, & Webster, 2012 for a review). Survey results support that the available tools are being actively incorporated into clinical practice (Viljoen, McLachlan, & Vincent, 2010). However, the empirical evidence supporting reliability and validity with adolescent males far surpasses the evidence supporting use with adolescent female offenders. Therefore, it is important to evaluate the existing literature highlighting measures that have tested and replicated findings specific to adolescent females. Six published studies specifically report predictive validity results for adolescent females using the Structured Assessment of Violence Risk in Youth (SAVRY; Borum, Bartel, & Forth, 2003). These studies span settings including juvenile assessment centers (Meyers & Schmidt, 2008), psychiatric facilities (Gammelgård, Koivisto, Eronen, & Kaltiala-Heino, 2008), and juvenile correctional/residential centers (Lodewijks et al., 2008; Penney, Lee, & Moretti, 2010), testing predictive validity from 6 months (Gammelgård, Weizmann-Henelius, Koivisto, Eronen, & Kaltiala-Heino, 2012) to 10 years (Schmidt, Campbell, & Houlding, 2011). Area under the curve (AUC) values reflecting predictive validity for violent offending ranged from 0.72 to 0.84 and from 0.65 to 0.67 for nonviolent offending. Although these initial findings are promising, average sample sizes of adolescent female offenders in these studies was 50 females suggesting the need for additional research with larger samples.

Support for the Youth Level of Service/Case Management Inventory (YLS/CMI; Hoge & Andrews, 2006) has been primarily tested on adolescent males and mixed-gender samples. Olver et al. (2009) conducted a meta-analysis and reported female specific predictive validity estimates for general recidivism ($k = 9, n = 992, r_w = 0.36$) and violent recidivism ($k = 4, n = 350, r_w = 0.24$). Olver, Stockdale, and Wong (2012) reported AUCs for general (0.71 = youth; 0.71 = adult), nonviolent (0.71 = youth; 0.70 = adult), and violent (0.65 = youth; 0.75 = adult) recidivism for 74 adolescent female offenders who varied little based on age (categorized as early and late adolescent).

As such, the overall research base for the YLS/CMI surpasses the SAVRY with comparable results.

While not a risk assessment instrument per se, the PCL:YV (Forth et al., 2003) has been utilized to predict recidivism in adolescent females. Edens et al. (2007) conducted a meta-analysis and reported gender-specific estimates for general recidivism ($k = 5$, $n = 207$, $r_w = 0.13$) and violent recidivism ($k = 5$, $n = 228$, $r_w = 0.10$), and they concluded that results were discouraging regarding the instrument's predictive validity with adolescent females. In a head-to-head comparison within the same studies ($k = 5$), Olver et al. (2009) found that that YLS/CMI and PCL:YV performed similarly in predicting general ($r_w = 0.35$ and 0.39, respectively) and violent ($r_w = 0.29$ and 0.29, respectively) recidivism. These estimates, however, were based on mixed-gender samples. Shepherd, Luebbers, and Dolan (2013) concluded that, on the basis of published meta-analyses and independent studies (e.g., Vincent, Odgers, McCormick, & Corrado, 2008), there is only modest evidence supporting the PCL:YV's predictive validity for adolescent female offenders.

Assessment of psychopathology. As noted, female offenders are more likely to experience psychopathology than male offenders, with the reported prevalence of psychiatric disorders in female inmate populations ranging as high as 80% (DiCataldo, Greer, & Profit, 1995; Maden, Swinton, & Gunn, 1994; Teplin et al., 1996). As suggested by Sorbello et al. (2002) and others, mental disorder compounds the trauma, emotional distress, and adverse outcomes often experienced by incarcerated offenders, and the effects have been shown to be particularly deleterious for women. Accordingly, a wide range of mental health screening tools and assessment schemes are available and routinely used in offender populations, some of which are intended to assess for specific disorders (e.g., Briere's Trauma Screening Inventory [TSI], Inventory of Altered Self Capacities [IASC]), whereas others are used for general screening purposes. Although these and other measures have been demonstrated to perform well psychometrically, and there are obvious difficulties in conducting time-consuming and costly clinical interviews with entire inmate populations, some scholars call

the use of such brief screening measures inherently problematic (Boothby, Mulholland, Cases, Carrington, & Bolger, 2010; Grisso, 2006), particularly with women. Some of these measures include the Brief Jail Mental Health Screen (BJMHS), the Jail Screening Assessment Tool (JSAT), the Offender Assessment System (OASys), and the Brief Mental Health Screening Instrument for Newly Incarcerated Adults (BMHSINIA). Results from studies looking at the reliability of some of these tools across gender, while mixed, do in some cases demonstrate insensitivity to gender and details relevant to programming decision-making (Fitzgibbon & Green, 2006), high diagnostic false-negatives (Steadman, Scott, Osher, Agnese, & Robbins, 2005), and unsatisfactory accuracy in identifying mental disorder (Ford, Trestman, Wiesbrock, & Zhang, 2007). Importantly, the JSAT, while not a psychometric instrument, does take into account factors identified as relevant to female offenders with mental illness (Martin, Colman, Simpson, & McKenzie, 2013; Nicholls, Roesch, Olley, Ogloff, & Hemphill, 2005).

Comparable mental health prevalence rates for adolescent female offenders also reinforce the need for systemic and universal mental health screening and follow-up assessment of adolescent females who come into contact with the juvenile justice system (Cruise, Marsee, Dandreaux, & DePrato, 2007; Teplin et al., 2002; Wasserman et al., 2003). Mental health screening practices include a focus on identifying both emergent (e.g., suicide) and common mental health needs (i.e., depression, substance use, trauma exposure) that identify youth in need of further assessment. Mental health screening is a process that should be standardized, incorporate tools with demonstrated reliability and validity, be supported by decisions or structured rules that screen in and screen out youth for further evaluation, and supported by policies that communicate results and protect confidentiality (see Grisso, 2007; Williams, 2007). Example tools with demonstrated empirical support for adolescent female offenders include the Massachusetts Youth Screening Instrument Version 2 (MAYSI-2), Problem-Oriented Screening Instrument for Teenagers (POSIT), Substance Abuse Subtle Screening Inventory for Adolescents—Second Version (SASSI–A2), and the Global Appraisal of Individual

Needs Short Screener (GAIN-SS). A wide variety of mental health assessment tools are available to assist mental health professionals in conducting further assessments of adolescent female offenders, with some tools focusing specifically on targeted symptoms (e.g., UCLA Posttrauamtic Stress Disorder Index for *DSM-5*) or multiple mental health domains (e.g., Minnesota Multiphasic Personality Inventory–Adolescent; MMPI-A). As referenced above in the review of adolescent risk assessments, it is critical to review the available empirical literature and determine that psychometric properties often derived on adolescent males or mixed-gender samples are replicated and reported specific to adolescent female offenders with results predicting relevant information about mental health functioning (see Cruise et al., 2007; Goldstein et al., 2003). Despite advances, it is clear from the available literature that screening standards for justice-involved youth are not being met in daily practice, with only 70% of juvenile residential facilities reporting screening of all youth at intake (Hockenberry, Sickmund, & Sladky, 2013).

Assessment summary. In a survey from February to May, 2000, the Federal Bureau of Prisons found that 92% of respondents from 50 state correctional agencies reported that, in their opinions, women offenders have unique needs that should be addressed in correctional settings (van Voorhis & Presser, 2001). Yet, 3 years later Hardyman and van Voorhis (2004) found that many correctional services continued to utilize gender-neutral assessments with women. The absence of a gender-informed assessment paradigm has unknown but potentially dramatic implications for efforts to successfully prevent and treat women's crime and violence. Despite the fact that clinicians, researchers, and decision-makers alike have denounced the absence of woman-centered services (Pollock & Davis, 2005), experts caution that there is an absence of a strong empirical basis to support novel gendered approaches (Havens, Ford, Grasso, & Marr, 2012; Heilbrun et al., 2008; Odgers, Schmidt, & Reppucci, 2004).

Treatment

The objective of correctional programming is two-pronged: (a) to ensure the safe management of institutions, and (b) to facilitate the safe reintegration of offenders into the community (Gendreau & Smith, 2012; Serin, 2005). As Serin (2005) outlined, the continuum of correctional services is such that improved outcomes in community corrections, jails, and prisons are predictably interconnected such that reduced severity and prevalence of adverse events (e.g., institutional infractions, recidivism) and increasing positive events (e.g., adherence to treatment and sustained behavioral changes) will have positive implications for staff, administrators, and the community across diverse settings.[4] We would add that the success of correctional programming will invariably have implications for other related systems as well, such as in emergency rooms, tertiary psychiatric settings, and forensic psychiatric hospitals. Despite the therapeutic nihilism that pervaded much of correctional history, there is firm and convincing evidence that treatment and correctional programming has been found to reduce institutional misconduct and recidivism (by as much as 20%–40% (Serin, 2005; for an excellent review of cost effectiveness of correctional treatment, see Gendreau & Smith, 2012). As such, it should come as little surprise that effective correctional programming is estimated to be highly cost effective. To illustrate, Serin (2005) estimated that "a 1% improvement in community supervision outcomes would reduce the number of readmissions by 1,423 inmates ($459,000 \times 0.31 \times 0.01$). At $54.11 daily cost ($63.57 daily cost in BOP facility − $9.46 daily cost for probation), this equates to a savings of $28.1 million dollars yearly" (p. 2). It is important to note, however, that effective services to reduce criminal recidivism are "services," and that reductions in offending have been demonstrated for treatment approaches that are consistent with evidence-based human services, not punishment (Brown, 2000; Dvoskin et al., 2012). Moreover, these more effective interventions do not appear to cost more. Romani, Morgan, Gross, and McDonald (2012) concluded,

---

[4]For instance, treatment adherence can result in reduced adverse events in institutional settings which often are reflected in decreased rates and severity of injuries to staff and other inmates, and ultimately in shorter prison stays and thus reduced prison crowding and recidivism which is subsequently reflected in improved cost effectiveness and enhanced community safety.

"appropriate correctional services (services that adhered to RNR [Risk Needs Responsivity]) were not significantly more expensive than inappropriate correctional services (services that did not adhere to RNR) or traditional criminal sanctions" (p. 144). We have concentrated our review on general correctional programming and recommend that readers interested in services specific to mentally disordered inmates consider Latessa (2014), Leschied (2011), and Lowenkamp, Latessa, and Holsinger (2006).

Criteria guiding effective programming. In order to be effective, correctional programming must adhere to strict criteria (Gendreau, Little, & Goggin, 1996). Several authorities have proposed various rubrics summarizing the essential principles of (nongendered) effective correctional services (e.g., Livingston, 2009; McGuire, 2002; Serin, 2005). A particularly well-researched and influential paradigm is the Risk Need Responsivity (RNR) model (Andrews et al., 2012; Andrews & Bonta, 1994; now in its fifth edition, Andrews & Bonta, 2010). Correctional rehabilitation in North America (van Voorhis et al., 2010) and internationally (Polaschek, 2012) has been strongly influenced by the work of people like Don Andrews, James Bonta, and Paul Gendreau. The RNR approach recommends a consideration of the importance of targeting interventions to match the level of risk presented by the offender (the *risk* principle—the "who"), focusing treatment to target criminogenic needs (the *need* principle—the "what") and being sensitive to other individual differences (the *responsivity* principle—the "how"; e.g., language, Hills, Siegfried, & Ickowitz, 2004; see Andrews et al., 2012). To date, "the RNR model remains the only empirically validated guide for criminal justice interventions that aim to help offenders to depart from that system" (Polaschek, 2012, p. 1).[5]

A long-standing and central tenet of mental health treatment has been the need to be attentive to diversity in an attempt to reduce inequities between various groups (e.g., ethnicity, gender, disability; U.S. Department of Health and Human Services, 1999). Despite increasing attention to diversity, a common critique leveled at women's corrections is that programs developed for men have often been applied to women without due consideration to the unique psychosocial presentation of women and the exceptional circumstances that bring them into conflict with the law (e.g., Bloom et al., 2003; Caulfield, 2012). Following from this perspective is the assertion that we need to consider the extent to which interventions should be gender-specific or gender-sensitive and a call for research that evaluates the relevance of the three prongs of the RNR model for female offenders (e.g., Blanchette, 2000).

Early research investigations into the extent to which the etiology of women's offending and thus the appropriate assessment, management, and treatment of female offenders differs from what we deliver to male offenders has yielded mixed results. In one of the first available studies, Koons et al. (1997) conducted a qualitative survey of correctional administrators to identify promising approaches relevant to female offenders. An interesting finding was the lack of consistency between the results of the survey by Koons et al. and the targets traditionally identified by scholars (i.e., criminogenic needs by correctional treatment experts (e.g., Andrews & Bonta, 2010). In comparison, one of the early empirical studies to test well established (male) criminogenic needs found that many of the variables known to predict reconviction in males were also predictive with females (Bonta et al., 1995). This has been the backdrop to a small but rapidly expanding field of research testing the RNR principles with women.

RNR and female offenders: Risk principle. The first RNR principle is concerned with *who* should be considered as treatment priorities and states that the nature of the intervention should match the degree of risk presented by the offender. Specifically, more intensive services should be reserved for use with high-risk offenders, and low-risk offenders tend to fare better with minimal or no intervention (Andrews, Bonta, & Hoge, 1990; Dvoskin et al., 2012). This principle resonates with the importance of diversity and the unique presentation of women

---

[5]Despite its empirically demonstrated efficacy Polaschek (2012) provides an excellent critique of remaining areas of implementation and practice that remain to be further developed in the model and supporting documents.

in conflict with law. Given, as we have demonstrated, that women tend to perpetrate primarily minor/nonviolent offenses and there have been concerns expressed that female offenders are at risk of being managed at unnecessarily high security levels. In an early influential paper on the topic, Dowden and Andrews (1999) tested the applicability of the RNR principles to female offenders using meta-analytic techniques. A total of 26 unique studies (reporting 45 effect sizes) were examined in the meta-analysis. The overall conclusion of the authors was that the RNR principles are particularly relevant to reductions in reoffending in women. The study revealed several noteworthy findings, including the fact that, when the analysis was focused only on studies with exclusively women offenders, the mean effect size (+0.17; *SD* = 0.24) was larger than when studies sampling both men and women were included (+0.14; *SD* = 0.24). Dowden and Andrews (1999) also concluded that stronger treatment effects were found for programs that targeted high-risk women versus low-risk women. Lovins, Lowenkamp, Latessa, and Smith (2007) similarly tested the risk principle in community corrections for a sample of female offenders (*N* = 1,340). Lovins et al. (2007) also concluded that the risk principle is as applicable to women as it is to men. Despite promising findings demonstrating the relevance of the risk principle, experts caution that predictive validity might differ systematically by gender. Consider for instance that Andrews et al. (2012) found that the base rates of recidivism of low-risk women were substantially lower than those of low-risk men. Similarly, Hardyman and van Voorhis (2004) found that the rates of recidivism and serious prison misconducts are generally lower for high-risk women than for high-risk men.

A particularly novel finding in the field of corrections treatment is the extent to which treatment and intervention with low-risk populations are not only ineffective but may actually hinder progress (Lowekamp & Latessa, 2004; see Dvoskin et al., 2012, for a discussion); given the low rate of violence by women in general and the low rate of recidivism by women offenders specifically, this is an area in particular need of further research (Andrews & Bonta, 1998; Dvoskin et al., 2012).

There is an important caveat to consider; despite evidence that correctional interventions for low-risk women should be minimized, this is not to suggest that women (or men for that matter) with noncriminogenic needs are not in need of services (Lovins et al., 2007). In fact, to the contrary, the need for comprehensive and integrated evidence-informed services with women offenders is well established (e.g., Andrews et al., 2012, p. 130; also see Salina, Lesondak, Razzano, & Parenti, 2011; Teplin et al., 1996).

RNR and female offenders: Need principle. The need principle of the RNR model is concerned with *what* should be the target of treatment. Essentially, if the objective of treatment is to reduce offending, then the criminogenic needs of offenders must be emphasized and less promising targets (i.e., noncriminogenic needs) that have not been found to lead to significant reductions in offending should not be prioritized, or at a minimum should not be anticipated to have any effect on recidivism (e.g., self-esteem; Andrews & Bonta, 1998). Andrews and Bonta (1994, 2010) identified eight central risk factors. These eight are proposed to be composed of the "big four" (e.g., a history of antisocial behavior, antisocial personality pattern, antisocial cognitions, and antisocial associates) and the "modest four" (family/marital, school/work, leisure/recreation, substance abuse).

Taken together, research to date largely demonstrates that women offenders' needs are similar but distinct from those of male offenders (de Vogel et al., 2012; Nicholls et al., 2008). Even when gender differences are evident there is often considerable overlap, but policymakers and treatment providers will need to be attentive to the nuances of how these variables are reflected in treatment needs. For instance, although relationships (Alarid, Burton, & Cullen, 2000; Heilbrun et al., 2008) and employment/reliance on social services (Greenfield & Snell, 1999) are relevant to both genders, they appear to be particularly salient for females and thus may present a focal point for intervention. Critics of gender-neutral treatment for offenders assert that different pathways are believed to bring men and women into contact with the criminal justice system, and, as such, unique variables will be required to inform risk management and intervention planning to ensure women's successful recovery and safe community (re)entry (Holtfreter & Cupp, 2007). As is evident from the discussion to this point, there is substantial evidence to support a consideration of feminine-specific risk factors for girls and women to enter into criminality and engage in aggressive and antisocial behavior (e.g., FAM, de Vogel et al., 2012). As we have discussed, women tend to present with disproportionately high rates of mental illness (Lewis, 2006; Warren et al., 2002), and these often are comorbid with chronic and severe substance use problems (Sacks et al., 2008). Victimization rates and secondary substance abuse, dependence, depression, and PTSD symptoms have also been found to distinguish male offenders from female offenders (Teplin et al., 1996). As much as minorities are overrepresented among male offenders, the discrepancy consistently remains substantially greater among female offenders (e.g., U.S. Department of Justice, 2011), and the importance of social support is particularly salient to women (Salina et al., 2011). Given the presenting profile of female offenders, the importance of multimorbidity treatment modalities that address diverse and overlapping needs has been identified as a priority (e.g., Sacks et al., 2008). This approach has been affirmed through empirical studies demonstrating that "the seriously troubled marginalized woman was at highest risk for future (criminal) involvement" (van Voorhis et al., 2010, p. 282).

There is also considerable evidence to suggest commonalities in terms of protective factors that might deter women from crime and offending (e.g., social support, employment; de Vogel et al., 2012; C. D. Webster, Martin, Brink, Nicholls, & Desmarais, 2009; C. D. Webster, Martin, Brink, Nicholls, & Middleton, 2004). Based on their meta-analysis, Dowden and Andrews (1999) concluded that the RNR need principle also applies to the treatment of female offenders. More recently, Andrews and Dowden (2006) completed another extensive meta-analysis and concluded that the evidence for this facet of the RNR model actually performed much more strongly for female offenders than for male offenders. The authors caution, however, that due to the small number of studies, the interaction

should be considered unstable. The authors further noted that the empirical support did not vary as a function of study quality (randomized design, attrition problems, rated comparability of groups, independent evaluator), setting (e.g., community or institutional, restorative or nonrestorative), ethnicity of offender (majority or minority), or history of violence (Andrews & Dowden, 2006). Examining aggregated data from five data sets, Andrews et al. (2012, p. 127) concluded that "gender neutrality appears to be the rule in regard to the predictive validity of risk/need factors in the analysis of criminal recidivism." The authors went on to conclude by asking "that gender-informed positions be enhanced still further by attention to considerations beyond the major risk/need factors and adherence with the risk/need principles" (Andrews et al., 2012, p. 130). In general, there appears to be agreement that what is relevant to men is also relevant to women, but there is little evidence to suggest that gender-neutral approaches could not potentially be improved by expanding treatment to include a consideration of variables of particular relevance to female offenders.

RNR and female offenders: Responsivity principle. Responsivity, the third RNR principle, is concerned with *how* treatment is delivered. The responsivity principle suggests that treatment services should be provided in a manner that is conducive to the learning styles and characteristics of the individual. The model encompasses both general responsivity factors (e.g., theoretical foundations of effective interventions such as cognitive behavioral approaches) and specific responsivity factors (e.g., the gender, culture, mental health, literacy, sexual orientation, or disability of the individual client). The RNR evaluation literature has demonstrated that there is support for the responsivity principle, in general (i.e., the vast majority of the literature has involved male participants). The meta-analysis of Andrews et al. (1990) revealed that the correctional treatment programs that best reflected the priorities of the RNR model (comparing criminal sanctions, inappropriate service, unspecified service, and appropriate service) yielded the best outcomes (see Andrews et al., 2012 for a recent review).

Despite the promise of the responsivity principle, scholars have noted that this aspect of the RNR model is among its weakest and least developed components (see Dowden & Andrews, 2004, for an exception). For instance, Polaschek (2012) asserted that it remains unclear why demographic variables such as gender and ethnicity are important. Similarly, although there are widespread and diverse approaches for integrating gender considerations into treatment advances, advocates of a gender-responsive approach to women's treatment concede that there is "no uniform procedure or instrument for identifying women's needs, nor is there a commonly accepted theory-based method for matching clients to programs and services" (Prendergast, Wellisch, & Falkin, 1995, p. 252; Blanchette, 2000).

Matching adolescent female offenders to effective treatments. The application of the RNR model to adolescent offenders in general, and female offenders specifically, has been examined in the professional literature (Hubbard & Matthews, 2008; Koehler, Lösel, Akoensi, & Humphreys, 2013; H. Wilson & Hoge, 2013) reflecting many of the themes and findings identified above for adult female offenders. For example, Hubbard and Pratt (2002) supported the conclusion that risk factors central to the RNR model (antisocial peers, antisocial personality factors) were strong predictors of recidivism in both adolescent males and females. The authors noted that factors identified in the gender responsive literature (school/family relationships, trauma histories) had moderate to strong effect sizes as well. Vincent, Paiva-Salisbury, Cook, Guy, and Perrault (2012) demonstrated that field-based implementation of risk/need assessment tools in juvenile probation settings altered juvenile probation officers' decision-making to be more consistent with the RNR model (e.g., assigning supervision based on risk level, making service referrals based on identified needs) but did not directly address differences by gender. Utilizing the YLS/CMI, Vitopoulos, Peterson-Badali, and Skilling (2012) investigated the utility of treatment matching for adolescent male and female offenders to community-based services. The researchers supported the finding that similar percentages of male and female offenders were matched to services based on risk level and specific need areas. After controlling for risk level, level of service matching significantly predicted recidivism reduction in males but not in females, calling into question the efficacy of reducing recidivism through matching services to recommendations generated from the YLS/CMI. This research raises at least two critical questions. First, are risk/need instruments used with adolescent females signaling the presence of gender-specific needs that could improve gender-specific treatment matching? Second, are treatment programs serving adolescent females using models developed and tested for males and/or failing to consider the need for gender responsive-adaptations? Unfortunately, much like the adult literature, the adolescent risk assessment literature provides little guidance as to the reliable and valid identification of gender-specific risk/need factors (Penney et al., 2010; Schinke, Fang, & Cole, 2008; Vincent, Terry, & Maney, 2009). Fortunately, researchers are addressing the effectiveness of broad treatment models (e.g., Multidimensional Treatment Foster Care, Multisystemic Therapy) to determine that delinquent behavior reductions found for adolescent males are also found for females (see Leve, Chamberlain, & Reid, 2005; Ogden & Amlund Hagen, 2009). Evidence of positive intervention outcomes with adult females (e.g., Dialectical Behavior Therapy) has also been reported when the intervention is tested with adolescent female offenders (Trupin et al., 2002). Similarly, advances are being made in testing the efficacy of gender-sensitive, adolescent-specific treatment models that address salient delinquency risk factors such as anger management (Goldstein et al., 2013), substance use (Welch, Roberts-Lewis, & Parker, 2009), and trauma (Ford, Steinberg, Hawke, Levine, & Zhang, 2012b).

Gender responsive treatment. In recent years there has been an increasing focus on the potential contributions to be made by integrating *gender-responsive* or *gender-specific* programming for women offenders (e.g., Bloom et al., 2003; Hannah-Moffat, 2009). Advancing gender-informed interventions is in part in recognition of the sheer increasing prevalence of women in contact with the criminal justice system. Given exceptionally high rates of victimization, mental health problems, poverty, physical illness, and drug abuse among women offenders, it stands to reason that multimorbidity may be of particular concern to this population, suggesting that the benefits of interventions that are particularly attentive to women's needs in these domains are more likely to lead to healthy outcomes and reduced recidivism (e.g., Bloom et al., 2003; Sacks et al., 2008; Salisbury & van Voorhis, 2009).

A gender-responsive approach is defined as programming that supports *empowerment* (supports skill building, competencies, and independence), *meaningful and responsible choices* (providing women with options and the ability to make choices that relate to their needs), *respect and dignity* (reflects the importance of reciprocal respect that is needed among and between staff and offenders; reflects women's orientation toward, and the importance they place on, relationships), *supportive environment* (promoting physical, psychological, and personal development), and *shared responsibility* (all levels of government, corrections, volunteer organizations, businesses, private sector, and community have a role; e.g., Correctional Service of Canada Task Force on Federally Sentenced Women, 1990). Although measures like the HCR–20 and LSI appear comprehensive, critics maintain that these types of measures fail to take into consideration many of the risk/need factors central to female offenders (e.g., relationships, poverty, depression, parental issues, substance abuse, self-esteem, self-efficacy, trauma, and victimization; Blanchette & Brown, 2006; Reisig et al., 2006; van Voorhis & Presser, 2001; van Voorhis et al., 2010).

It is important that treatment programs for adolescent females do not merely add female-specific activities to empirically supported treatments for adolescent males, but take into account unique and complex needs of females (Molidor et al., 2002) to ensure gender responsiveness. Many programs are modified from existing programs for adolescent males, however, making it difficult to determine if gender-specific components influence effectiveness (Cauffman, 2008). Ethnic and cultural factors, as well as age and race, must be taken into account in gender-responsive programing for adolescent females. Building relational skills; strengthening

connections to family and community; and enhancing self-esteem, self-sufficiency, and socialization are recommended as gender-responsive targets for adolescent female offenders (Emerson & Shelton, 2001; Guthrie & Low, 2006). Focus should also be given to the unique needs surrounding pregnancy and running away (Bloom, Owen, Deschenes, & Rosenbaum, 2002). These specific factors must also be viewed through a broader lens of effective principles in program design, implementation, and outcomes. For example, Matthews and Hubbard (2008) suggested that the essential elements of working with adolescent females offenders include (a) using gender-specific assessments to guide program planning and evaluation, (b) ensuring a healthy therapeutic or helping alliance, (c) incorporating cognitive behavioral approaches that targets both the process (greater support and desire for intimacy) and content (gender-specific cognitive distortions) found among adolescent females, (d) promoting healthy connections throughout the social ecology of adolescent females, and (e) recognizing the heterogeneity found within adolescent female offenders.

Experts caution, however, that the theoretical foundation to support "gender-specific rehabilitation needs" is not firmly established despite substantial and growing pressure to implement gender-sensitive programming (Heilbrun et al., 2008). Men and women share many vulnerabilities that lead to antisocial and criminal behaviors (Dowden & Andrews, 1999; Moffitt et al., 2001; see also Volume 1, Chapter 12, this handbook). In fact, the predictive strength of many of the risk/need factors that have been proposed as promising gender-informed variables have been found to have minimal predictive validity. For instance, Andrews et al. (2012; also see Andrews et al., 2011) reported the validity estimates for variables such as poverty and victimization are "minimal to mild at best (below 0.19)" (p. 119).

Treatment summary. As much as feminist insights (Blanchette & Brown, 2006; Hannah-Moffat, 2009; Holtfreter & Cupp, 2007) and well-established theory (i.e., RNR; Andrews & Bonta, 1994) converge to support the potential value of gender-informed services, we agree with Andrews et al. (2012) who cautioned that we not misrepresent these variables as central risk factors (i.e., key needs relevant to reducing recidivism, violence) given the state of the extant literature. Rather, until empirical evidence demonstrates their centrality to offending and their incremental validity (also see van Voorhis et al., 2010), they might best be acknowledged as important to engaging women (e.g., motivation) and central to delivering ethical, respectful interventions (i.e., the responsivity principle).

SUMMARY AND CONCLUSION'S

Female offenders represent the fastest growing population of inmates worldwide, yet they remain a subgroup for whom we have limited theoretical development and empirical evidence. An enhanced understanding of female offending is important given that data across international borders suggest that the growth rate in the number of individuals in prisons and jails is substantially higher among women than among men (Nicholls et al., 2008). For instance, the proportion of Canadian women charged with criminal offenses has increased steadily over the past three decades, up from 15% in 1979 to 21% in 2009 (Hotton Mahoney, 2009). A similar trend is seen in the arrest rates of American women, which has shown a 57% increase between 1998 and 2010 (Bureau of Justice Statistics, 2010). Between 1985 and 2010, the number of delinquency cases in the United States involving the arrest of an adolescent female increased 69% (from 225,800 to 381,5000 cases; Puzzanchera & Adams, 2011). Importantly, these increases in female offending have been seen at a time when evidence suggests parallel decreasing rates of offending among males (e.g., Federal Bureau of Investigation, 2005; Glaze, 2011; Hotton Mahoney, 2009; Puzzanchera & Adams, 2011). Despite this unexpected pattern, women and girls continue to represent a small proportion of individuals charged with criminal offenses, and as such they remain a small minority of other relevant populations (e.g., approximately 15% of inpatient forensic hospitals; Crocker et al.,

2013) and a postscript to assessment and treatment development and program evaluation work.

As the number of women in conflict with the law has continued to rise, there has been an increasingly urgent call from decision makers (Auditor General of Canada, 2003) and academics alike (Hannah-Moffat, 2004; C. M. Webster & Doob, 2004) to avoid what some consider systematic bias against minority groups (women as well as ethnic minorities) in violence risk assessments and the need for a woman-wise agenda (Heilbrun et al., 2008; Hubbard & Pratt, 2002).

Although it has been a prominent aspect of the criminological literature for several decades (e.g., Correctional Service of Canada Task Force on Federally Sentenced Women, 1990; Corston, 2007; C. D. Webster, 1999), the extent to which gender should be reflected in the development and implementation of unique assessment and treatment for female offenders remains a complex and unresolved issue. There is a burgeoning literature on female offending, but concrete advancements reflected in the development and validation of woman-centered or gender-informed assessment and treatment approaches have been relatively rare. There remains considerable debate with regard to the extent to which clinicians working with women can comfortably rely on current assessment measures, ostensibly constructed with men in mind (Garcia-Mansilla et al., 2009), yet, with the exception of a handful of recently introduced measures and interventions developed from the outset to inform evaluations and treatment with female populations, gender-informed approaches remain an essential deficiency in the tool kit and repertoire of most clinicians. There remains considerable room for advancements in both the assessment and treatment literatures. That being said, the publications of measures such as the FAM (de Vogel et al., 2012) and the EARL-G (Levene et al., 2001) as well as treatment modalities such as Seeking Safety (Najavits, 2002), Holistic Enrichment for At-Risk Teens (HEART; Welch et al., 2009), and the Juvenile Justice Anger Management (JJAM) Treatment for Girls (Goldstein et al., 2013) signify paradigmatic shifts and may represent meaningful advances, pending further empirical validation.

References

Abram, K. M., Teplin, L. A., Charles, D. R., Longworth, S. L., McClelland, G. M., & Dulcan, M. K. (2004). Posttraumatic stress disorder and trauma in youth in juvenile detention. *Archives of General Psychiatry, 61,* 403–410. doi:10.1001/archpsyc.61.4.403

Abram, K. M., Teplin, L. A., & McClelland, G. M. (2003). Comorbidity of severe psychiatric disorders and substance use disorders among women in jail. *American Journal of Psychiatry, 160,* 1007–1010. doi:10.1176/appi.ajp.160.5.1007

Adelson, L. (1961). Slaughter of the innocents. A study of forty-six homicides in which the victims were children. *New England Journal of Medicine, 264,* 1345–1349. doi:10.1056/NEJM19610629 2642606

Adelson, L. (1991). Pedicide revisited: The slaughter continues. *American Journal of Forensic Medicine and Pathology, 12,* 16–26. doi:10.1097/00000433-199103000-00003

Alarid, L., Burton, V., & Cullen, F. (2000). Gender and crime among felony offenders: Assessing the generality of social control and differential association theories. *Journal of Research in Crime and Delinquency, 37,* 171–199. doi:10.1177/0022427800037002002

American Correctional Association. (1990). *The female offender.* Washington, DC: St. Mary's Press.

Anderson, P. B., & Struckman-Johnson, C. (Eds.). (1998). *Sexually aggressive women: Current perspectives and controversies.* New York, NY: The Guilford Press.

Andrews, D. A., & Bonta, J. (1994). *The psychology of criminal conduct.* Cincinnati, OH: Anderson.

Andrews, D. A., & Bonta, J. (1995). *LSI-R: The Level of Service Inventory-Revised.* Toronto, Ontario, Canada: Multi-Health Systems.

Andrews, D. A., & Bonta, J. (2010). *The psychology of criminal conduct* (5th ed.). New Providence, NJ: LexisNexis/Matthew Bender.

Andrews, D. A., Bonta, J., & Hoge, R. D. (1990). Classification for effective rehabilitation: Rediscovering psychology. *Criminal Justice and Behavior. 17,* 19–52.

Andrews, D. A., Bonta, J., Wormith, J. S., Guzzo, L., Brews, A., Rettinger, J., & Rowe, R. (2011). Sources of variability in estimates of predictive validity a specification with level of service general risk and need. *Criminal Justice and Behavior, 38,* 413–432.

Andrews, D. A., & Dowden, C. (2006). Risk principle of case classification in correctional treatment: A meta-analytic investigation. *International Journal of Offender Therapy and Comparative Criminology, 50,* 88–100. doi:10.1177/0306624X05282556

Andrews, D. A., Guzzo, L., Raynor, P., Rowe, R. C., Rettinger, L. J., Brews, A., & Wormith, J. S. (2012). Are the major risk/need factors predictive of both female and male reoffending? A test with the eight domains of the level of service/case management inventory. *International Journal of Offender Therapy and Comparative Criminology, 56,* 113–133. doi:10.1177/0306624X10395716

Andrews, D. A., Zinger, I., Hoge, R. D., Bonta, J., Gendreau, P., & Cullen, F. T. (1990). Does correctional treatment work? A clinically relevant and psychologically informed meta-analysis. *Criminology, 28,* 369–404.

Antonishak, J., Reppucci, N., & Mulford, C. (2004). Girls in the justice system: Treatment and intervention. In M. M. Moretti, C. L. Odgers, & M. A. Jackson (Eds.), *Girls and aggression: Contributing factors and intervention principles* (pp. 165–180). New York, NY: Kluwer Academic/Plenum. doi:10.1007/978-1-4419-8985-7_12

Archer, J. (2000). Sex differences in aggression between heterosexual partners: A meta-analytic review. *Psychological Bulletin, 126,* 651–680. doi:10.1037/0033-2909.126.5.651

Ariga, M., Uehara, T., Takeuchi, K., Ishige, Y., Nakano, R., & Mikuni, M. (2008). Trauma exposure and posttraumatic stress disorder in delinquent female adolescents. *Journal of Child Psychology and Psychiatry, 49,* 79–87. doi:10.1111/j.1469-7610.2007.01817.x

Auditor General of Canada. (2003). *Report of the Auditor General of Canada to the House of Commons: A message from the Auditor General.* Ottawa, Ontario, Canada: Minister of Public Works and Government Services Canada.

Augimeri, L. K., Enebrink, P., Walsh, M., & Jiang, D. (2010). Gender specific risk assessment tools: Early assessment risk list for boys (EARL-20B) and girls (EARL-21G). In R. K. Otto & K. S. Douglas (Eds.), *Handbook of violence risk assessment: International perspectives on forensic mental health* (pp. 43–62). New York, NY: Routledge.

Austin, J., Bloom, B., & Donahue, T. (1992). *Female offenders in the community: An analysis of innovative strategies and programs.* Washington, DC: National Institute of Corrections.

Baglivio, M. T. (2009). The assessment of risk to recidivate among a juvenile offending population. *Journal of Criminal Justice, 37,* 596–607. doi:10.1016/j.jcrimjus.2009.09.008

Bauer, P., & Knörnschild, C. (2010, May). The ignored female minority: Do women have differentiated needs in the forensic setting? In R. Müller-Isberner (Chair), *Forensic patients with special needs.* Symposium conducted at the annual conference of the International Association of Forensic Mental

Health Services, Vancouver, British Columbia, Canada.

Bennett, S., Farrington, D. P., & Huesmann, L. R. (2005). Explaining gender differences in crime and violence: The importance of social cognitive skills. *Aggression and Violent Behavior, 10*, 263–288. doi:10.1016/j.avb.2004.07.001

Black, D. W., Gunter, T., Allen, J., Blum, N., Arndt, S., Wenman, G., & Sieleni, B. (2007). Borderline personality disorder in male and female offenders newly committed to prison. *Comprehensive Psychiatry, 48*, 400–405. doi:10.1016/j.comppsych.2007.04.006

Black, M. C., Basile, K. C., Breiding, M. J., Smith, S. G., Walters, M. L., Merrick, M. T. . . . Stevens, M. R. (2011). *The National Intimate Partner and Sexual Violence Survey (NISVS): 2010 Summary Report.* Atlanta, GA: National Center for Injury Prevention and Control, Centers for Disease Control and Prevention. Retrieved from: http://www.cdc.gov/ViolencePrevention/pdf/NISVS_Executive_Summary-a.pdf

Blanchette, K. (2000). Effective correctional practice with women offenders. In L. Motiuk & R. Serin (Eds.), *Compendium 2000 on effective correctional programming.* Retrieved from http://www.csc-scc.gc.ca/research/comm2000-chap_20-eng.shtml

Blanchette, K. (2002). Classifying female offenders for effective intervention: Application of the case-based principles of risk and need. *Forum on Corrections Research, 14*, 31–35.

Blanchette, K., & Brown, S. L. (2006). *The assessment and treatment of woman offenders.* Chichester, England: Wiley. doi:10.1002/9780470713013

Bloom, B. E. (1996). *Triple jeopardy: race, class, and gender as factors in women's imprisonment* (Unpublished doctoral dissertation, University of California, Riverside).

Bloom, B. B., Owen, B., & Covington, S. (2003). *Gender-responsive strategies: research, procedures and guiding principles for women offenders.* Washington, DC: U.S. Department of Justice National Institute on Corrections.

Bloom, B., Owen, B., Deschenes, E., & Rosenbaum, J. (2002). Moving toward justice for female juvenile offenders in the new millennium: Modeling gender-specific policies and programs. *Journal of Contemporary Criminal Justice, 18*, 37–56. doi:10.1177/1043986202018001004

Bonta, J., Pang, B., & Wallace-Capretta, S. (1995). Predictors of recidivism among incarcerated female offenders. *Prison Journal, 75*, 277–294. doi:10.1177/0032855595075003002

Boothby, M., Mulholland, I., Cases, A., Carrington, K., & Bolger, T. (2010). Towards mental health promotion in prisons: The role of screening for emotional distress. *Procedia: Social and Behavioral Sciences, 5*, 90–94. doi:10.1016/j.sbspro.2010.07.056

Borum, R., Bartel, P., & Forth, A. (2003). *Manual for the Structured Assessment for Violence Risk in Youth (SAVRY).* Sarasota, FL: Professional Assessment Resources.

Bourget, D., & Bradford, J. M. (1990). Homicidal parents. *Canadian Journal of Psychiatry, 35*, 233–238.

Bourget, D., & Gagné, P. (2002). Maternal filicide in Quebec. *Journal of the American Academy of Psychiatry and the Law, 30*, 345–351.

Bourget, D., Grace, J., & Whitehurst, L. (2007). A review of maternal and paternal filicide. *Journal of the American Academy of Psychiatry and the Law, 35*, 74–82.

Brendgen, M., Vitaro, F., Tremblay, R. E., &Wanner, B. (2002). Parent and peer effects on delinquency-related violence and dating violence: A test of two mediational models. *Social Development, 11*, 225–244. doi:10.1111/1467-9507.00196

Broidy, L. M., & Cauffman, E. E. (2006). *Understanding the female offender.* Washington, DC: U.S. Department of Justice. Retrieved from https://www-ncjrs-gov.ezproxy.library.ubc.ca/pdffiles1/nij/grants/216615.pdf

Brown, S. L. (2000). *Cost effective correctional treatment.* Ottawa, Ontario, Canada: Correctional Service of Canada. Retrieved from http://www.csc-scc.gc.ca.ezproxy.library.ubc.ca/publications/forum/e122/122n_e.pdf

Browne, A., Miller, B., & Maguin, E. (1999). Prevalence and severity of lifetime physical and sexual victimization among incarcerated women. *International Journal of Law and Psychiatry, 3–4*, 301–322. doi:10.1016/S0160-2527(99)00011-4

Butler, T., & Allnut, S. (2003). *Mental Illness among New South Wales' Prisoners.* New South Wales, Australia: New South Wales Corrections Health Service.

Byrne, M., & Howells, K. (2000). *Key issues in the provision of correctional services of women.* Paper presented at the Women in Corrections: Staff and Clients Conference, Australian Institute of Criminology, Adelaide, Australia.

Cale, E. M., & Lilienfeld, S. O. (2002). Sex differences in psychopathy and antisocial personality disorder: A review and integration. *Clinical Psychology Review, 22*, 1179–1207. doi:10.1016/S0272-7358(01)00125-8

Carr, N. T., Hudson, K., Hanks, R. S., & Hunt, A. N. (2008). Gender effects along the juvenile justice system: Evidence of a gendered organization. *Feminist Criminology, 3*, 25–43. doi:10.1177/1557085107311390

Carter, C. O. (1973). Multifactorial genetic disease. In V. A. McKusick, & R. Claiborne (Eds.), *Medical genetics* (pp. 199–208). New York, NY: HP Publishing.

Cauffman, E. (2008). Understanding the female offender. *Future of Children, 18*, 119–142. doi:10.1353/foc.0.0015

Caulfield, L. (2012). Life histories of women who offend: A study of women in English prosons (Doctoral dissertation). Retrieved from https://dspace.lboro.ac.uk/dspace-jspui/handle/2134/10178

Chapman, A. L., Specht, M. W., & Cellucci, T. (2005). Factors associated with suicide attempts in female inmates: The hegemony of hopelessness. *Suicide and Life-Threatening Behavior, 35*, 558–569. doi:10.1521/suli.2005.35.5.558

Chauhan, P., Reppucci, N., & Turkheimer, E. N. (2009). Racial differences in the associations of neighborhood disadvantage, exposure to violence, and criminal recidivism among female juvenile offenders. *Behavioral Sciences and the Law, 27*, 531–552. doi:10.1002/bsl.868

Chesney-Lind, M., & Pasko, L. (2004). *Girls, women, and crime*. Thousand Oaks, CA: Sage.

Chesney-Lind, M., & Shelden, R. G. (2004). *Girls, delinquency, and juvenile justice* (3rd ed.). Belmont, CA: Thompson Wadsworth.

Chiodo, D., Crooks, C. V., Wolfe, D. A., McIsaac, C., Hughes, R., & Jaffe, P. G. (2012). Longitudinal prediction and concurrent functioning of adolescent girls demonstrating various profiles of dating violence and victimization. *Prevention Science, 13*, 350–359. doi:10.1007/s11121-011-0236-3

Cohen, M. A., Piquero, A. R., & Jennings, W. G. (2010). Monetary costs of gender and ethnicity disaggregated group-based offending. *American Journal of Criminal Justice, 35*, 159–172. doi:10.1007/s12103-010-9071-5

Coid, J., Yang, M., Ullrich, S., Zhang, T., Sizmur, S., Roberts, C., . . . Rogers, R. D. (2009). Gender differences in structured risk assessment: Comparing the accuracy of five instruments. *Journal of Consulting and Clinical Psychology, 77*, 337–348. doi:10.1037/a0015155

Collie, R., & Polaschek, D. (2003). Sorting women's risk: New Zealand Women prisoners' misconducts and internal security risk. *New Zealand Journal of Psychology, 32*(2), 101–109.

Conrad, S. M., Tolou-Shams, M., Rizzo, C. J., Placella, N., & Brown, L. K. (2013). Gender differences in recidivism rates for juvenile justice youth: The impact of sexual abuse. *Law and Human Behavior*. doi:10.1037/lhb0000062

Cooper, K., May, D., Soderstrom, I., & Jarjoura, G. (2009). Examining theoretical predictors of substance use among a sample of incarcerated youth. *Journal of Offender Rehabilitation, 48*, 669–695. doi:10.1080/10509670903287675

Copeland, A. R. (1985). Homicide in childhood: The Metro-Dade County experience from 1956 to 1982. *American Journal of Forensic Medicine and Pathology, 6*, 21–24.

Correctional Service of Canada Task Force on Federally Sentenced Women. (1990). *Creating choices: the report of the Task Force on Federally Sentenced Women*. Ottawa, Ontario, Canada: Author.

Corston, J. (2007). *The Corston report: A report by Baroness Jean Corston of a review of women with particular vulnerabilities in the criminal justice system*. London, England: The Home Office.

Cortoni, F., & Hanson, R. K. (2005). *A review of recidivism rates of adult female sexual offenders*. Ottawa, Ontario, Canada: Correctional Service of Canada.

Cortoni, F., Hanson, R. K., & Coache, M. È. (2010). The recidivism rates of female sexual offenders are low: A meta-analysis. *Sexual Abuse: Journal of Research and Treatment, 22*, 387–401.

Cotten-Oldenburg, N., Jordan, B. K., Martin, S. L., & Kupper, L. (1999). Women inmates' risky sex and drug behaviours: Are they related? *American Journal of Drug and Alcohol Abuse, 25*, 129–149. doi:10.1081/ADA-100101850

Cottle, C. C., Lee, R. J., & Heilbrun, K. (2001). The prediction of criminal recidivism in juveniles: A meta-analysis. *Criminal Justice and Behavior, 28*, 367–394. doi:10.1177/0093854801028003005

Crocker, A. G., Nicholls, T. L., Seto, M. C., Charette, Y., Cote, G., & Caulet, M. (2013). *The national trajectory project of individuals found not criminally responsible on account of mental disorder in Canada: Part 2—The "new face" of forensic mental health?* Manuscript in preparation.

Crowell, S. E., Beauchaine, T. P., Hsiao, R. C., Vasilev, C. A., Yaptangco, M., Linehan, M. M., & McCauley, E. (2012). Differentiating adolescent self-injury from adolescent depression: Possible implications for borderline personality development. *Journal of Abnormal Child Psychology, 40*, 45–57. doi:10.1007/s10802-011-9578-3

Cruise, K. R., Marsee, M. A., Dandreaux, D. M., & DePrato, D. K. (2007). Mental health screening of female juvenile offenders: Replication of a subtyping strategy. *Journal of Child and Family Studies, 16*, 615–625. doi:10.1007/s10826-006-9111-4

Cuellar, J., & Curry, T. R. (2007). The prevalence and comorbidity between delinquency, drug abuse, suicide attempts, physical and sexual abuse, and self-mutilation among delinquent Hispanic females. *Hispanic Journal of Behavioral Sciences, 29*, 68–82. doi:10.1177/0739986306295796

Daly, M., & Wilson, M. (1988). *Homicide*. New York, NY: Aldine de Gruyter.

Danielson, C. K., Macdonald, A., Amstadter, A. B., Hanson, R., de Arellano, M. A., Saunders, B. E., & Kilpatrick, D. G. (2010). Risky behaviors and depression in conjunction with—or in the absence of—lifetime history of PTSD among sexually abused adolescents. *Child Maltreatment, 15*, 101–107. doi:10.1177/1077559509350075

Denno, D. W. (1994). Gender, crime, and the criminal law defenses. *Journal of Criminal Law and Criminology, 85*, 80–180. doi:10.2307/1144115

Derkzen, D., Booth, L., Taylor, K., & McConnell, A. (2013). Mental health needs of federal female offenders. *Psychological Services, 10*, 24–36. doi:10.1037/a0029653

Desai, R. A., Falzer, P. R., Chapman, J., & Borum, R. (2012). Mental illness, violence risk, and race in juvenile detention: Implications for disproportionate minority contact. *American Journal of Orthopsychiatry, 82*, 32–40. doi:10.1111/j.1939-0025.2011.01138.x

Desmarais, S. L., Reeves, K., Nicholls, T. L., Telford, R. P., & Fiebert, M. S. (2012a). Prevalence of physical violence in intimate relationships, Part 1: Rates of male and female victimization. *Partner Abuse, 3*, 140–169.

Desmarais, S. L., Reeves, K., Nicholls, T., Telford, R. P., & Fiebert, M. S. (2012b). Prevalence of physical violence in intimate relationships, Part 2: Rates of male and female perpetration. *Partner Abuse, 3*, 170–198.

de Vogel, V., & de Ruiter, C. (2005). The HCR-20 in personality disordered female offenders: A comparison with a matched sample of males. *Clinical Psychology and Psychotherapy, 12*, 226–240. doi:10.1002/cpp.452

de Vogel, V., de Vries Robbé, M., van Kalmthout, W., & Place, C. (2012). *Female Additional Manual (FAM). Additional guidelines to the HCR-20 for assessing risk for violence in women. English version.* Utrecht, the Netherlands: Van der Hoeven Kliniek.

DiCataldo, F., Greer, A., & Profit, W. E. (1995). Screening prison inmates for mental disorder: An examination of the relationship between mental disorder and prison adjustment. *Bulletin of the American Academy of Psychiatry and the Law, 23*, 573–585.

Dierkhising, C. B., Ko, S. J., Woods-Jaeger, B., Briggs, E. C., Lee, R., & Pynoos, R. S. (2013). Trauma histories among justice-involved youth: Findings from the National Child Traumatic Stress Network. *European Journal of Psychotraumatology, 4.*

Dixon, A., Howie, P., & Starling, J. (2005). Trauma exposure, posttraumatic stress, and psychiatric comorbidity in female juvenile offenders. *Journal of the American Academy of Child and Adolescent Psychiatry, 44*, 798–806.

Dixon-Gordon, K., Harrison, N., & Roesch, R. (2012). Non-suicidal self-injury within offender populations: A systematic review. *International Journal of Forensic Mental Health, 11*, 33–50. doi:10.1080/14999013.2012.667513

Dolan, M., Fullam, R., Logan, C., & Davies, G. (2008). The Violence Risk Scale Second Edition (VRS-2) as a predictor of institutional violence in a British forensic inpatient sample. *Psychiatry Research, 158*, 55–65. doi: 10.1016/j.psychres.2006.08.014

Douglas, K., & Reeves, K. (2010). Historical-Clinical-Risk Management–20 (HCR-20) violence risk assessment scheme: Rationale, application, and empirical overview. In R. Otto & K. Douglas (Eds.), *Handbook of violence risk assessment* (pp. 147–186). New York, NY: Routledge.

Dowden, C., & Andrews, D. A. (1999). What works for female offenders: A meta-analytic review. *Crime and Delinquency, 45*, 438–452. doi:10.1177/0011128799045004002

Dowden, C., & Andrews, D. A. (2004). The importance of staff practice in delivering effective correctional treatment: A meta-analytic review of core correctional practice. *International Journal of Offender Therapy and Comparative Criminology, 48*, 203–214. doi:10.1177/0306624X03257765

Duke, N. N., Pettingell, S. L., McMorris, B. J., & Borowsky, I. W. (2010). Adolescent violence perpetration: Associations with multiple types of adverse childhood experiences. *Pediatrics, 125*, e778–e786.

Dutton, D. G., & Nicholls, T. L. (2005). A critical review of the gender paradigm in domestic violence research and theory: Part I—Theory and data. *Aggression and Violent Behavior, 10*, 680–714. doi:10.1016/j.avb.2005.02.001

Dvoskin, J. A., Skeem, J. L., Novaco, R. W., & Douglas, K. S. (2012). What if psychology redesigned the criminal justice system? In J. A. Dvoskin, J. L. Skeem, R. W. Novaco, & K. S. Douglas (Eds.), *Using social science to reduce violent offending* (pp. 291–302). New York, NY: Oxford University Press.

Eaton, D. K., Kann, L., Kinchen, S., Shanklin, S., Flint, K. H., & Wechsler, H. (2012). *Youth risk behavior surveillance, United States 2011.* Atlanta, GA: Centers for Disease Control and Prevention.

Edens, J. F., Campbell, J. S., & Weir, J. M. (2007). Youth psychopathy and criminal recidivism: A meta-analysis of the psychopathy checklist measures. *Law and Human Behavior, 31*, 53–75. doi:10.1007/s10979-006-9019-y

Eme, R. F. (1992). Selective females affliction in the developmental disorders of childhood: A literature review. *Journal of Clinical Child Psychology, 21*, 354–364. doi:10.1207/s15374424jccp2104_5

Emeka, T. Q., & Sorensen, J. R. (2009). Female juvenile risk: Is there a need for gendered assessment instruments? *Youth Violence and Juvenile Justice, 7,* 313–330. doi:10.1177/1541204009334083

Emerson, E., & Shelton, D. (2001). Using creative arts to build coping skills to reduce domestic violence in the lives of female juvenile offenders. *Issues in Mental Health Nursing, 22,* 181–195. doi:10.1080/016128401750063358

Espinosa, E. M., Sorensen, J. R., & Lopez, M. A. (2013). Youth pathways to placement: The influence of gender, mental health need and trauma on confinement in the juvenile justice system. *Journal of Youth and Adolescence, 42,* 1824–1836. doi:10.1007/s10964-013-9981-x

Falkenbach, D. M. (2008). Psychopathy and the assessment of violence in women. *Journal of Forensic Psychology Practice, 8,* 212–224. doi:10.1080/15228930801964125

Federal Bureau of Investigation. (2005). *Uniform crime reports.* Washington, DC: Author.

Federal Bureau of Investigation. (2006). *Uniform crime reports.* Washington, DC: Author.

Federal Bureau of Investigation. (2008). *Crime in the United States, 1980–2000, 2007.* Washington, DC: Author.

Fiebert, M. (2012). *References examining assaults by women on their spouses or male partners: An annotated bibliography.* Retrieved from http://www.csulb.edu/~mfiebert/assault.htm

Finkelhor, D. (1997). The homicides of children and youth: a developmental perspective. In G. K. Kantor & J. L. Jasinski (Eds.), *Out of the darkness: Contemporary perspectives on family violence* (pp. 17–34). Thousand Oaks, CA: Sage. doi:10.4135/9781483328058.n2

Fitzgibbon, D., & Green, R. (2006). Mentally disordered offenders: challenges in using the OASys risk assessment tool. *British Journal of Community Justice, 4,* 33–45.

Follingstad, D. R., Bradley, R. G., Helff, C. M., & Laughlin, J. E. (2002). A model for predicting dating violence: Anxious attachment, angry temperament, and need for relationship control. *Violence and Victims, 17,* 35–47. doi:10.1891/vivi.17.1.35.33639

Follingstad, D. R., Wright, S., Lloyd, S., & Sebastian, J. A. (1991). Sex differences in motivations and effects in dating violence. *Family Relations, 40,* 51–57. doi:10.2307/585658

Ford, J. D., Chapman, J., Connor, D. F., & Cruise, K. R. (2012a). Complex trauma and aggression in secure juvenile justice settings. *Criminal Justice and Behavior, 39,* 694–724. doi:10.1177/0093854812436957

Ford, J. D., Elhai, J. D., Connor, D. F., & Frueh, B. (2010). Poly-victimization and risk of posttraumatic, depressive, and substance use disorders and involvement in delinquency in a national sample of adolescents. *Journal of Adolescent Health, 46,* 545–552. doi:10.1016/j.jadohealth.2009.11.212

Ford, J. D., Hartman, J. K., Hawke, J., & Chapman, J. C. (2008). Traumatic victimization posttraumatic stress disorder, suicidal ideation, and substance abuse risk among juvenile justice-involved youths. *Journal of Child and Adolescent Trauma, 1,* 75–92. doi:10.1080/19361520801934456

Ford, J. D., Steinberg, K. L., Hawke, J., Levine, J., & Zhang, W. (2012b). Randomized trial comparison of emotion regulation and relational psychotherapies for PTSD with girls involved in delinquency. *Journal of Clinical Child and Adolescent Psychology, 41,* 27–37. doi:10.1080/15374416.2012.632343

Ford, J. D., Trestman, R. L., Wiesbrock, V., & Zhang, W. (2007). Development and validation of a brief mental health screening instrument for newly incarcerated adults. *Assessment, 14,* 279–299. doi:10.1177/1073191107302944

Fornes, P., Druilhe, L., & Lecomte, D. (1995). Childhood homicide in Paris, 1990–1993: A report of 81 cases. *Journal of Forensic Sciences, 40,* 201–204.

Forouzan, E., & Cooke, D. J. (2005). Figuring out la femme fatale: Conceptual and assessment issues concerning psychopathy in females. *Behavioral Sciences and the Law, 23,* 765–778. doi:10.1002/bsl.669

Forth, A. E., Kosson, D. S., & Hare, R. D. (2003). *Hare Psychopathy Checklist Youth Version: PCL:YV user manual.* Toronto, Ontario, Canada: Multi-Health Systems.

Foy, D. W., Ritchie, I. K., & Conway, A. H. (2012). Trauma exposure, posttraumatic stress, and comorbidities in female adolescent offenders: Findings and implications from recent studies. *European Journal of Psychotraumatology, 3.*

Franklin, C. A. (2008). Women offenders, disparate treatment, and criminal justice: A theoretical, historical, and contemporary overview. *Criminal Justice Studies, 21,* 341–360.

Frick, P. J., Ray, J. V., Thornton, L. C., & Kahn, R. E. (2014). Can callous-unemotional traits enhance the understanding, diagnosis, and treatment of serious conduct problems in children and adolescents? A comprehensive review. *Psychological Bulletin, 140,* 1–57. doi:10.1037/a0033076

Friedman, S. H., Hrouda, D. R., Holden, C. E., Noffsinger, S. G., & Resnick, P. J. (2005). Filicide-suicide: Common factors in parents who kill their children and themselves. *Journal of the American Academy of Psychiatry and the Law, 33,* 496–504.

Funk, S. J. (1999). Risk assessment for juveniles on probation: A focus on gender. *Criminal Justice and Behavior, 26*, 44–68. doi:10.1177/0093854899026001003

Gammelgård, M., Koivisto, A., Eronen, M., & Kaltiala-Heino, R. (2008). The predictive validity of the Structured Assessment of Violence Risk in Youth (SAVRY) among institutionalised adolescents. *Journal of Forensic Psychiatry and Psychology, 19*, 352–370. doi:10.1080/14789940802114475

Gammelgård, M., Weizmann-Henelius, G., Koivisto, A., Eronen, M., & Kaltiala-Heino, R. (2012). Gender differences in violence risk profiles. *Journal of Forensic Psychiatry and Psychology, 23*, 76–94. doi:10.1080/14789949.2011.639898

Garcia, C. A., & Lane, J. (2013). What a girl wants, what a girl needs: Findings from a gender-specific focus group study. *Crime and Delinquency, 59*, 536–561. doi:10.1177/0011128709331790

Garcia-Mansilla, A., Rosenfeld, B., & Nicholls, T. L. (2009). Risk assessment: Are current methods applicable to women? *International Journal of Forensic Mental Health, 8*, 50–61. doi:10.1080/14999010903014747

Gendreau, P., Goggin, C. E., & Law, M. A. (1997). Predicting prison misconducts. *Criminal Justice and Behavior, 24*, 414–431. doi:10.1177/0093854897024004002

Gendreau, P., Goggin, C., & Smith, P. (2003). Is the PCL-R really the 'unparalleled' measure of offender risk? A lesson in knowledge cumulation: Erratum. *Criminal Justice and Behavior, 30*, 722–724. doi:10.1177/0093854803256464

Gendreau, P., Little, T., & Goggin, C. (1996). A meta-analysis of the predictors of adult offenders recidivism: What works! *Criminology, 34*, 575–608. doi:10.1111/j.1745-9125.1996.tb01220.x

Gendreau, P., & Smith, P. (2012). Assessment and treatment strategies for correctional institutions. In J. A. Dvoskin, J. L. Skeem, R. W. Novaco, & K. S. Douglas (Eds.), *Using social science to reduce violent offending* (pp. 157–177). New York, NY: Oxford University Press.

Glaze, L. E. (2011). *Correctional populations in the United States, 2010*. Washington, DC: U.S. Department of Justice, Bureau of Justice Statistics. Retrieved from http://www.bjs.gov/content/pub/pdf/cpus10.pdf

Glaze, L. E., & Maruschak, L. M. (2008). *Parents in prison and their minor children*. Washington, DC: U.S. Department of Justice. Retrieved from http://www.bjs.gov/content/pub/pdf/pptmc.pdf

Goldstein, N. E., Arnold, D. H., Weil, J., Mesiarik, C. M., Peuschold, D., Grisso, T., & Osman, D. (2003). Comorbid symptom patterns in female juvenile offenders. *International Journal of Law and Psychiatry, 26*, 565–582. doi:10.1016/S0160-2527(03)00087-6

Goldstein, N. S., Kemp, K. A., Leff, S. S., & Lochman, J. E. (2012). Guidelines for adapting manualized interventions for new target populations: A step-wise approach using anger management as a model. *Clinical Psychology: Science and Practice, 19*, 385–401. doi:10.1111/cpsp.12011

Goldstein, N. S., Serico, J. M., Riggs Romaine, C. L., Zelechoski, A. D., Kalbeitzer, R., Kemp, K., & Lane, C. (2013). Development of the juvenile justice anger management treatment for girls. *Cognitive and Behavioral Practice, 20*, 171–188. doi:10.1016/j.cbpra.2012.06.003

Grayston, A. D., & De Luca, R. V. (1999). Female perpetrators of child sexual abuse: A review of the clinical and empirical literature. *Aggression and Violent Behavior, 4*, 93–106. doi:10.1016/S1359-1789(98)00014-7

Greenfield, L. A., & Snell, T. L. (1999). *Women offenders: Bureau of Justice Statistics Special Report (NCJ175688)*. Rockville, MD: U.S. Department of Justice, Bureau of Justice Statistics.

Grisso, T. (2006). Review of the jail screening assessment tool (JSAT): Guidelines for mental health screening in jails. *Psychiatric Services, 57*, 1049. doi:10.1176/appi.ps.57.7.1049-a

Grisso, T. (2007). *Implementing mental health screening. Mental Health Screening and Juvenile Justice: The Next Frontier*. Delmar, NY: National Center for Mental Health and Juvenile Justice.

Guthrie, B. J., & Low, L. (2006). Moving beyond the trickle-down approach: Addressing the unique disparate health experiences of adolescents of color. *Journal for Specialists in Pediatric Nursing, 11*, 3–13. doi:10.1111/j.1744-6155.2006.00038.x

Guy, L. S. (2008). *Performance indicators of the structured professional judgment approach for assessing risk for violence to others: A meta-analytic survey*. (Unpublished doctoral dissertation). Simon Fraser University, Burnaby, British Columbia, Canada.

Hamby, S., & Turner, H. (2013). Measuring teen dating violence in males and females: Insights from the national survey of children's exposure to violence. *Psychology of Violence, 3*, 323–339. doi:10.1037/a0029706

Hamel, J., & Nicholls, T. L. (Eds.). (2007). *Family interventions in domestic violence: A handbook of gender-inclusive theory and treatment*. London, England: Springer.

Hannah-Moffat, K. (2004). Losing ground: Gendered knowledges, parole risk, and responsibility. *Social Politics: International Studies in Gender, State and Society, 11*, 363–385.

Hannah-Moffat, K. (2009). Gridlock or mutability: Reconsidering "gender" and risk assessment.

Criminology and Public Policy, 8, 209–219. doi:10.1111/j.1745-9133.2009.00549.x

Hanson, R. K., & Morton-Bourgon, K. E. (2009). The accuracy of recidivism risk assessments for sexual offenders: A meta-analysis of 118 prediction studies. *Psychological Assessment, 21*, 1. doi:10.1037/a0014421

Harder, T. (1967). The psychopathology of infanticide. *Acta Psychiatrica Scandinavica, 43*, 196–245. doi:10.1111/j.1600-0447.1967.tb11026.x

Hardyman, P. L., & van Voorhis, P. (2004). *Developing gender-specific classification systems for women offenders.* Washington, DC: U.S. Department of Justice, National Institute of Corrections. doi:10.1037/e308982005-001

Hare, R. D. (1991). *The Hare psychopathy checklist—Revised manual.* North Tonawanda, NY: Multi-Health Systems.

Hare, R. D. (1996). Psychopathy a clinical construct whose time has come. *Criminal Justice and Behavior, 23*, 25–54. doi:10.1177/0093854896023001004

Hare, R. D. (2003). *Hare psychopathy checklist—revised (PCL–R), 2nd ed.* Technical manual. North Tonawanda, NY: Multi-Health Systems.

Harris, G. T., Hilton, N. Z., Rice, M. E., & Eke, A. W. (2007). Children killed by genetic parents versus stepparents. *Evolution and Human Behavior, 28*, 85–95. doi:10.1016/j.evolhumbehav.2006.08.001

Hart, S. D. (1998). The role of psychopathy in assessing risk for violence: Conceptual and methodological issues. *Legal and Criminological Psychology, 3*, 121–137. doi:10.1111/j.2044-8333.1998.tb00354.x

Havens, J. F., Ford, J., Grasso, D., & Marr, M. (2012). Opening Pandora's box: The importance of trauma identification and intervention in hospitalized and incarcerated adolescent populations. *Adolescent Psychiatry, 2*, 309–312. doi:10.2174/2210676611202040309

Hawton, K., Saunders, K. A., & O'Connor, R. C. (2012). Self-harm and suicide in adolescents. *Lancet, 379*, 2373–2382. doi:10.1016/S0140-6736(12)60322-5

Heilbrun, K., Dematteo, D., Fretz, R., Erickson, J., Yasuhara, K., & Anumba, N. (2008). How specific are gender-specific rehabilitation needs? An empirical analysis. *Criminal Justice and Behavior, 35*, 1382–1397. doi:10.1177/0093854808323678

Hempel, I., Buck, N., Cima, M., & van Marle, H. (2013). Review of risk assessment instruments for juvenile sex offenders: What is next? *International Journal of Offender Therapy and Comparative Criminology, 57*, 208–228. doi:10.1177/0306624X11428315

Hemphill, J. F., Hare, R. D., & Wong, S. (1998). Psychopathy and recidivism: A review. *Legal and Criminological Psychology, 3*, 139–170. doi:10.1111/j.2044-8333.1998.tb00355.x

Hills, H., Siegfried, C., & Ickowitz, A. (2004). *Effective prison mental health services: Guidelines to expand and improve treatment.* Washington, DC: U.S. Department of Justice.

Hipwell, A. E., Pardini, D. A., Loeber, R., Sembower, M., Keenan, K., & Stouthamer-Loeber, M. (2007). Callous-unemotional behaviors in young girls: Shared and unique effects relative to conduct problems. *Journal of Clinical Child and Adolescent Psychology, 36*, 293–304. doi:10.1080/15374410701444165

Hipwell, A. E., Stepp, S., Feng, X., Burke, J., Battista, D. R., Loeber, R., & Keenan, K. (2011). Impact of oppositional defiant disorder dimensions on the temporal ordering of conduct problems and depression across childhood and adolescence in girls. *Journal of Child Psychology and Psychiatry, 52*, 1099–1108. doi:10.1111/j.1469-7610.2011.02448.x

Hockenberry, S. (2013). *Juveniles in residential placement, 2010. Juvenile court statistics 2010.* Washington, DC: Office of Juvenile Justice and Delinquency Prevention.

Hockenberry, S., Sickmund, M., & Sladky, A. (2013). *Juvenile residential facility census, 2010: Selected findings.* Washington, DC: Office of Juvenile Justice and Delinquency Prevention.

Hodgins, S., Calem, M., Shimel, R., Williams, A., Harleston, D., Morgan, C. . . . Jones, P. (2011). Criminal offending and distinguishing features of offenders among persons experiencing a first episode of psychosis. *Early Intervention in Psychiatry, 5*, 15–23. doi:10.1111/j.1751-7893.2010.00256.x

Hoeve, M., McReynolds, L. S., Wasserman, G. A., & McMillan, C. (2013). The influence of mental health disorders on severity of reoffending in juveniles. *Criminal Justice and Behavior, 40*, 289–301. doi:10.1177/0093854812459639

Hoge, R. D., & Andrews, D. A. (2006). *Youth Level of Service/Case Management Inventory users manual.* New York, NY: Multi-Health Systems.

Hollin, C. R., & Palmer, E. J. (2006). Criminogenic need and women offenders: A critique of the literature. *Legal and Criminological Psychology, 11*, 179–195. doi:10.1348/135532505X57991

Holtfreter, K., & Cupp, R. (2007). Gender and risk assessment: The empirical status of the LSI-R for women. *Journal of Contemporary Criminal Justice, 23*, 363–382. doi:10.1177/1043986207309436

Hope, T. L., Wilder, E. I., & Watt, T. (2003). The relationships among adolescent pregnancy, pregnancy resolution, and juvenile delinquency. *Sociological Quarterly, 44*, 555–576. doi:10.1111/j.1533-8525.2003.tb00525.x

Hotton Mahoney, T. (2009). *Women and the criminal justice system*. Ottawa, Ontario, Canada: Statistics Canada.

Howell, J. C. (2003). *Preventing and reducing juvenile delinquency: A comprehensive framework*. Thousand Oaks, CA: Sage.

Hubbard, D., & Matthews, B. (2008). Reconciling the differences between the "gender-responsive" and the "what works" literatures to improve services for girls. *Crime and Delinquency, 54*, 225–258. doi:10.1177/0011128706296733

Hubbard, D., & Pratt, T. C. (2002). A meta-analysis of the predictors of delinquency among girls. *Journal of Offender Rehabilitation, 34*, 1–13. doi:10.1300/J076v34n03_01

Huesmann, L. R., & Guerra, N. G. (1997). Children's normative beliefs about aggression and aggressive behavior. *Journal of Personality and Social Psychology, 72*, 408. doi:10.1037/0022-3514.72.2.408

Jason, J., Gilliland, J. C., & Tyler, C. W. (1983). Homicide as a cause of pediatric mortality in the United States. *Pediatrics, 72*, 191–197.

Javdani, S., Sadeh, N., & Verona, E. (2011). Gendered social forces: A review of the impact of institutionalized factors on women and girls' criminal justice trajectories. *Psychology, Public Policy, and Law, 17*, 161–211. doi:10.1037/a0021957

Jordan, B. K., Schlenger, W. E., Fairbank, J. A., & Caddell, J. M. (1996). Prevalence of psychiatric disorders among incarcerated women: Convicted felons entering prison. *Archives of General Psychiatry, 53*, 513–519. doi:10.1001/archpsyc.1996.01830060057008

Kahn, R. E., Frick, P. J., Youngstrom, E., Findling, R. L., & Youngstrom, J. (2012). The effects of including a callous–unemotional specifier for the diagnosis of conduct disorder. *Journal of Child Psychology and Psychiatry, 53*, 271–282. doi:10.1111/j.1469-7610.2011.02463.x

Kaplun, D., & Reich, R. (1976). The murdered child and his killers. *American Journal of Psychiatry, 133*, 809–813.

Kelly, P. J., Lesser, J., & Paper, B. (2008). Detained adolescents' attitudes about pregnancy and parenthood. *Journal of Pediatric Health Care, 22*, 240–245. doi:10.1016/j.pedhc.2007.07.005

Kenny, D. T., Lennings, C. J., & Munn, O. A. (2008). Risk factors for self-harm and suicide in incarcerated young offenders: Implications for policy and practice. *Journal of Forensic Psychology Practice, 8*, 358–382. doi:10.1080/15228930802199317

Kerig, P. K., & Becker, S. P. (2012). Trauma and girls' delinquency. In S. Miller, L. D. Leve, P. K. Kerig (Eds.), *Delinquent girls: Contexts, relationships, and adaptation* (pp. 119–143). New York, NY: Springer Science + Business Media.

Kerig, P. K., Ward, R., Vanderzee, K. L., & Moeddel, M. (2009). Posttraumatic stress as a mediator of the relationship between trauma and mental health problems among juvenile delinquents. *Journal of Youth and Adolescence, 38*, 1214–1225. doi:10.1007/s10964-008-9332-5

Kernsmith, P. (2005). Exerting power or striking back: A gendered comparison of motivations for domestic violence perpetration. *Violence and Victims, 20*, 173–185. doi:10.1891/0886-6708.2005.20.2.173

Kessler, R. C., Avenevoli, S., Costello, J., Green, J., Gruber, M. J., McLaughlin, K. A. . . . Merikangas, K. (2012). Severity of 12-month DSM-IV disorders in the National Comorbidity Survey Replication Adolescent Supplement. *Archives of General Psychiatry, 69*, 381–389. doi:10.1001/archgenpsychiatry.2011.1603

Kessler, R. C., Sonnega, A., Bromet, E., Hughes, M., & Nelson, C. B. (1995). Posttraumatic stress disorder in the National Comorbidity Survey. *Archives of General Psychiatry, 52*, 1048. doi:10.1001/archpsyc.1995.03950240066012

Khurana, A., Cooksey, E. C., & Gavazzi, S. M. (2011). Juvenile delinquency and teenage pregnancy: A comparison of ecological risk profiles among midwestern White and Black female juvenile offenders. *Psychology of Women Quarterly, 35*, 282–289. doi:10.1177/0361684310384103

Kimonis, E. R., Skeem, J. L., Edens, J. F., Douglas, K. S., Lilienfeld, S. O., & Poythress, N. G. (2010). Suicidal and criminal behavior among female offenders: The role of abuse and psychopathology. *Journal of Personality Disorders, 24*, 581–609. doi:10.1521/pedi.2010.24.5.581

Koehler, J. A., Lösel, F., Akoensi, T. D., & Humphreys, D. K. (2013). A systematic review and meta-analysis on the effects of young offender treatment programs in Europe. *Journal of Experimental Criminology, 9*, 19–43. doi:10.1007/s11292-012-9159-7

Kong, R., & AuCoin, K. (2008). *Female Offenders in Canada*. Ottawa, Ontario, Canada: Statistics Canada. Retrieved from http://www.statcan.gc.ca/pub/85-002-x/2008001/article/10509-eng.htm

Koons, B. A., Burrow, J. D., Morash, M., & Bynum, T. (1997). Expert and offender perceptions of program elements linked to successful outcomes for incarcerated women. *Crime and Delinquency, 43*, 512–532. doi:10.1177/0011128797043004007

Kosson, D. S., Neumann, C. S., Forth, A. E., Salekin, R. T., Hare, R. D., Krischer, M. K., & Sevecke, K. (2013). Factor structure of the Hare Psychopathy Checklist: Youth Version (PCL:YV) in adolescent females. *Psychological Assessment, 25*, 71–83. doi:10.1037/a0028986

Krugman, R. D. (1985). Fatal child abuse: Analysis of 24 cases. *Pediatrician, 12*, 68–72.

Laishes, J. (2002). *The 2002 mental health strategy for women offenders*. Ottawa, Ontario, Canada: Correctional Service of Canada. Retrieved from http://www.csc-scc.gc.ca/text/prgrm/fsw/mhealth/toc-eng.shtml

Langan, N. P., & Pelissier, B. M. M. (2001). Gender differences among prisoners in drug treatment. *Journal of Substance Abuse, 13*, 291–301. doi:10.1016/S0899-3289(01)00083-9

Langan, P. A., & Levin, D. J. (2002). *Recidivism of prisoners released in 1994*. Washington, DC: U.S. Department of Justice, Bureau of Justice Statistics.

Latessa, E. (2014). *What works and what dosen't work in reducing recidivism: Some lessons learned from evaluating correctional programs*. Paper presented at the American Psychology-Law Society Conference, New Orleans, LA.

Lauritsen, J. L., Heimer, K., & Lynch, J. P. (2009). Trends in the gender gap in violent offending: New evidence from the National Crime Victimization Survey. *Criminology, 47*, 361–399. doi:10.1111/j.1745-9125.2009.00149.x

Leschied, A. W. (2011). *The treatment of incarcerated mentally disordered women offenders: A synthesis of current research*. Ottawa, Ontario, Canada: Public Safety Canada. Retrieved from http://www.publicsafety.gc.ca/res/cor/rep/_fl/2011-03-imdwo-eng.pdf

Leve, L. D., Chamberlain, P., & Reid, J. B. (2005). Intervention outcomes for girls referred from juvenile justice: Effects on delinquency. *Journal of Consulting and Clinical Psychology, 73*, 1181–1185. doi:10.1037/0022-006X.73.6.1181

Léveillée, S., Marleau, J. D., & Dubé, M. (2007). Filicide: A comparison by sex and presence or absence of self-destructive behavior. *Journal of Family Violence, 22*, 287–295. doi:10.1007/s10896-007-9081-3

Levene, K. S., Augimeri, L. K., Pepler, D. J., Walsh, M. M., Webster, C. D., & Koegl, C. J. (2001). *Early Assessment Risk List for Girls: EARL-21G, Version 1, Consultation Edition*. Toronto, Ontario, Canada: Earlscourt Child and Family Center.

Lewis, C. (2006). Treating incarcerated women: Gender matters. *Psychiatric Clinics of North America, 29*, 773–789. doi:10.1016/j.psc.2006.04.013

Lewis, C. F. (2000). Successfully treating aggression in mentally ill prison inmates. *Psychiatric Quarterly, 71*, 331–343. doi:10.1023/A:1004684223522

Lewis, C. F. (2004, May). *Ethnicity, diagnosis and healthcare utilization in incarcerated women*. Paper presented at the American Psychiatric Association Annual Meeting, New York, NY.

Lewis, C. F. (2005). Post-traumatic stress disorder in HIV-positive incarcerated women. *Journal of the American Academy of Psychiatry and the Law, 33*, 455–464.

Livingston, J. (2009). *Mental health and substance use services in correctional settings: A review of minimum standards and best practices*. Vancouver, British Columbia, Canada: International Centre for Criminal Law Reform and Justice Policy.

Lodewijks, H. B., de Ruiter, C., & Doreleijers, T. H. (2008). Gender differences in violent outcome and risk assessment in adolescent offenders after residential treatment. *International Journal of Forensic Mental Health, 7*, 133–146. doi:10.1080/14999013.2008.9914410

Logan, C. (2002). *Dangerous and severe personality disorder women's services pre-assessment pilot* (Unpublished academic report). London, England: Home Office and Her Majesty's Prison Service.

Logan, C. (2009). Psychopathy in women: Conceptual issues, clinical presentation and management. *Neuropsychiatrie (Deisenhofen), 23*, 1–9.

Logan, C., & Blackburn, R. (2009). Mental disorder in violent women in secure settings: Potential relevance to risk for future violence. *International Journal of Law and Psychiatry, 32*, 31–38. doi:10.1016/j.ijlp.2008.11.010

Loper, A., & Levitt, L. (2011). Mental health needs of female offenders. In T. J. Fagan & R. K. Ax (Eds.), *Correctional mental health: From theory to best practice* (pp. 214–234). Thousand Oaks, CA: Sage.

Loper, A. B., Carlson, L. W., Levitt, L., & Scheffel, K. (2009). Parenting stress, alliance, child contact, and adjustment of imprisoned mothers and fathers. *Journal of Offender Rehabilitation, 48*, 483–503.

Loucks, A. D., & Zamble, E. (2000). *Predictors of criminal behaviour and prison misconduct in serious female offenders*. Unpublished manuscript, Queen's University, Kinston, Ontario, Canada.

Lovins, L. B., Lowenkamp, C. T., Latessa, E. J., & Smith, P. (2007). Application of the risk principle to female offenders. *Journal of Contemporary Criminal Justice, 23*, 383–398.

Lowenkamp, C. T., & Latessa, E. J. (2004). Understanding the risk principle: How and why correctional interventions can harm low-risk offenders. *Topics in Community Corrections, 2004*, 3–8.

Lowenkamp, C. T., Latessa, E. J., & Holsinger, A. M. (2006). The risk principle in action: What have we learned from 13,676 offenders and 97 correctional programs? *Crime & Delinquency, 52*, 77–93.

Lucas, D. R., Wezner, K. C., Milner, J. S., McCanne, T. R., Harris, I. N., Monroe-Posey, C., & Nelson, J. P. (2002). Victim, perpetrator, family, and incident characteristics of infant and child homicide in the United States Air Force. *Child Abuse and Neglect, 26,* 167–186. doi:10.1016/S0145-2134(01)00315-5

Maden, T., Swinton, M., & Gunn, J. (1994). Psychiatric disorder in women serving a prison sentence. *British Journal of Psychiatry, 164,* 44–54. doi:10.1192/bjp.164.1.44

Marks, M. N., & Kumar, R. (1993). Infanticide in England and Wales. *Medicine, Science, and the Law, 33,* 329–339.

Marks, M. N., & Kumar, R. (1996). Infanticide in Scotland. *Medicine, Science, and the Law, 36,* 299–305.

Marshall, J., Egan, V., English, M., & Jones, R. M. (2006). The relative validity of psychopathy versus risk/needs-based assessments in the prediction of adolescent offending behaviour. *Legal and Criminological Psychology, 11,* 197–210. doi:10.1348/135532505X68719

Martin, M. E., & Hesselbrock, M. N. (2001). Women Prisoners' Mental Health: Vulnerabilities, Risks and Resilience. *Journal of Offender Rehabilitation, 34,* 25–43. doi:10.1300/J076v34n01_03

Martin, M. S., Colman, I., Simpson, A. I., & McKenzie, K. (2013). Mental health screening tools in correctional institutions: A systematic review. *BMC Psychiatry, 13,* 275.

Matthews, B., & Hubbard, D. (2008). Moving ahead: Five essential elements for working effectively with girls. *Journal of Criminal Justice, 36,* 494–502. doi:10.1016/j.jcrimjus.2008.09.011

Matthews, R., Hunter, J., & Vuz, J. (1997). Juvenile female sexual offenders: Clinical characteristics and treatment issues. *Sexual Abuse: Journal of Research and Treatment, 9,* 187–199.

McGuire, J. (2002). Integrating findings from research reviews. In J. McGuire (Ed.), *Offender rehabilitation and treatment: Effective programmes and policies to reduce re-offending* (pp. 3–38). Chichester, England: Wiley.

McKeown, A. (2010). Female offenders: Assessment of risk in forensic settings. *Aggression and Violent Behavior, 15,* 422–429. doi:10.1016/j.avb.2010.07.004

McReynolds, L. S., Schwalbe, C. S., & Wasserman, G. A. (2010). The contribution of psychiatric disorder to juvenile recidivism. *Criminal Justice and Behavior, 37,* 204–216. doi:10.1177/0093854809354961

Mears, D. P., Ploeger, M., & Warr, M. (1998). Explaining the gender gap in delinquency: Peer influence and moral evaluations of behavior. *Journal of Research in Crime and Delinquency, 35,* 251–266. doi:10.1177/0022427898035003001

Meloy, J. R., & Boyd, C. (2003). Female stalkers and their victims. *Journal of the American Academy of Psychiatry and the Law, 31,* 211–219.

Meyers, J. R., & Schmidt, F. (2008). Predictive validity of the Structured Assessment for Violence Risk in Youth (SAVRY) with juvenile offenders. *Criminal Justice and Behavior, 35,* 344–355. doi:10.1177/0093854807311972

Miller, S., Leve, L. D., & Kerig, P. K. (2012). *Delinquent girls: Contexts, relationships, and adaptation.* New York, NY: Springer Science + Business Media.

Minor, K. I., Wells, J. B., & Angel, E. (2008). Recidivism among juvenile offenders following release from residential placements: Multivariate predictors and gender differences. *Journal of Offender Rehabilitation, 46,* 171–188. doi:10.1080/10509670802143474

Moffitt, T. E., Caspi, A., Rutter, M., & Silva, P. A. (2001). *Sex differences in antisocial behaviour: Conduct Disorder, delinquency, and violence in the Dunedin longitudinal study.* Cambridge, England: Cambridge University Press. doi:10.1017/CBO9780511490057

Molidor, C. E., Nissen, L. B., & Watkins, T. R. (2002). The development of theory and treatment with substance abusing female juvenile offenders. *Child and Adolescent Social Work Journal, 19,* 209–225. doi:10.1023/A:1015528031152

Monahan, J., Steadman, H. J., Silver, E., Appelbaum, P. S., Robbins, P. C., Mulvey, E. P., & Banks, S. (2001). *Rethinking risk assessment: The MacArthur study of mental disorder and violence.* New York, NY: Oxford University Press.

Morash, M., Bynum, T., & Koons, B. (1998). *Women offenders: Programming needs and promising approaches.* Washington, DC: National Institute of Justice.

Muehlenkamp, J. J., Ertelt, T. W., Miller, A. L., & Claes, L. (2011). Borderline personality symptoms differentiate non-suicidal and suicidal self-injury in ethnically diverse adolescent outpatients. *Journal of Child Psychology and Psychiatry, 52,* 148–155. doi:10.1111/j.1469-7610.2010.02305.x

Mulvey, E. P., Steinberg, L., Piquero, A. R., Besana, M., Fagan, J., Schubert, C., & Cauffman, E. (2010). Trajectories of desistance and continuity in antisocial behavior following court adjudication among serious adolescent offenders. *Development and Psychopathology, 22,* 453–475. doi:10.1017/S0954579410000179

Murdoch, S., Vess, J., & Ward, T. (2012). A descriptive model of female violent offenders. *Psychiatry, Psychology and Law, 19,* 412–426. doi:10.1080/13218719.2011.589942

Murphy, D. A., Brecht, M., Huang, D., & Herbeck, D. M. (2012). Trajectories of delinquency from age 14 to 23 in the National Longitudinal Survey of Youth sample. *International Journal of Adolescence and Youth, 17*, 47–62. doi:10.1080/02673843.2011.649401

Murrie, D. C., Boccaccini, M. T., McCoy, W., & Cornell, D. G. (2007). Diagnostic labeling in juvenile court: How do descriptions of psychopathy and conduct disorder influence judges? *Journal of Clinical Child and Adolescent Psychology, 36*, 228–241. doi:10.1080/15374410701279602

Myers, S. A. (1970). Maternal filicide. *American Journal of Diseases of Children, 120*, 534–536. doi:10.1001/archpedi.1970.02100110082008

Najavits, L. M. (2002). *Seeking safety: A treatment manual for PTSD and substance abuse.* New York, NY: Guilford Press.

Najavits, L. M., Weiss, R. D., Reif, S., Gastfriend, D. R., Siqueland, L., Barber, J. P. . . . Blaine, J. (1998). The Addiction Severity Index as a screen for trauma and posttraumatic stress disorder. *Journal of Studies on Alcohol, 59*, 56–62.

Nathan, P., & Ward, T. (2001). Females who sexually abuse children: Assessment and treatment issues. *Psychiatry, Psychology and Law, 8*, 44–55. doi:10.1080/13218710109525003

National Commission on Correctional Health Care. (2011). *Standards for health services in juvenile detention and confinement facilities.* Chicago, IL: National Commission on Correctional Health Care.

National Council on Crime and Delinquency. (2006, December). *Reducing the incarceration of women: Community-based alternatives.* Retrieved from http://www.nccdglobal.org/sites/default/files/publication_pdf/special-report-women-incarceration.pdf

Nicholls, T. L. (2011, July). *The emperor has no clothes: The glaring gap between what we know and what we deliver in the domestic violence field.* Keynote Lecture delivered at the annual meeting of the International Association of Forensic Mental Health Services. Barcelona, Spain.

Nicholls, T. L. (2012, November 22–25). *The top 10 "hits" in the intimate partner violence literature.* Keynote Lecture delivered at the annual meeting of the Australian and New Zealand Association of Psychiatry, Psychology and Law, Melbourne, Australia.

Nicholls, T. L., Greaves, C., & Moretti, M. M. (2008). Aggression: Gender differences. In A. Jamieson & A. Moenssens (Eds.), *Wiley encyclopedia of forensic science.* Hoboken, NJ: Wiley.

Nicholls, T. L., Ogloff, J. R. P., Brink, J., & Spidel, A. (2005). Psychopathy in women: A review of its clinical usefulness for assessing risk for aggression and criminality. *Behavioral Sciences and the Law, 23*, 779–802. doi:10.1002/bsl.678

Nicholls, T. L., Ogloff, J. R. P., & Douglas, K. S. (2004). Assessing risk for violence among male and female psychiatric patients: The HCR-20, PCL:SV, and VSC. *Behavioral Sciences and the Law, 22*, 127–158. doi:10.1002/bsl.579

Nicholls, T. L., & Petrila, J. (2005). Gender and psychopathy: An overview of important issues and introduction to the special issue. *Behavioral Sciences and the Law, 23*, 729–741. doi:10.1002/bsl.677

Nicholls, T. L., Roesch, R., Olley, M. C., Ogloff, J. R. P., & Hemphill, J. F. (2005). *Jail Screening Assessment Tool (JSAT).* Burnaby, British Columbia, Canada: Mental Health, Law and Policy Institute.

O'Connor, R. C., & Sheehy, N. P. (1997). Suicide and gender. *Mortality, 2*, 239–254. doi:10.1080/714892786

Odgers, C. L., Moretti, M. M., & Reppucci, N. D. (2005). Examining the science and practice of violence risk assessment with female adolescents. *Law and Human Behavior, 29*, 7–27. doi:10.1007/s10979-005-1397-z

Odgers, C. L., Reppucci, N., & Moretti, M. M. (2005). Nipping psychopathy in the bud: An examination of the convergent, predictive, and theoretical utility of the PCL-YV among adolescent girls. *Behavioral Sciences and the Law, 23*, 743–763. doi:10.1002/bsl.664

Odgers, C. L., Schmidt, M. G., & Reppucci, N. (2004). Reframing violence risk assessment for female juvenile offenders. In M. M. Moretti, C. L. Odgers, & M. A. Jackson (Eds.), *Girls and aggression: Contributing factors and intervention principles* (pp. 195–210). New York, NY: Kluwer Academic/Plenum. doi:10.1007/978-1-4419-8985-7_14

Ogden, T., & Amlund Hagen, K. (2009). What works for whom? Gender differences in intake characteristics and treatment outcomes following multisystemic therapy. *Journal of Adolescence, 32*, 1425–1435. doi:10.1016/j.adolescence.2009.06.006

Olver, M. E., Stockdale, K. C., & Wong, S. P. (2012). Short and long-term prediction of recidivism using the youth level of service/case management inventory in a sample of serious young offenders. *Law and Human Behavior, 36*, 331–344. doi:10.1037/h0093927

Olver, M. E., Stockdale, K. C., & Wormith, J. (2009). Risk assessment with young offenders: A meta-analysis of three assessment measures. *Criminal Justice and Behavior, 36*, 329–353. doi:10.1177/0093854809331457

Otto, R. K., & Douglas, K. S. (2010). *Handbook of violence risk assessment*. New York, NY: Routledge/Taylor & Francis Group.

Owen, B., & Bloom, B. (1995). Profiling women prisoners: Findings from national surveys and a California sample. *Prison Journal, 75,* 165–185. doi:10.1177/0032855595075002003

Pardini, D., Stepp, S., Hipwell, A., Stouthamer-Loeber, M., & Loeber, R. (2012). The clinical utility of the proposed DSM-5 callous-unemotional subtype of conduct disorder in young girls. *Journal of the American Academy of Child and Adolescent Psychiatry, 51,* 62–73. doi:10.1016/j.jaac.2011.10.005

Peled, E. (2011). Abused women who abuse their children: A critical review of the literature. *Aggression and Violent Behavior, 16,* 325–330. doi:10.1016/j.avb.2011.04.007

Penn, J. V., Esposito, C. L., Schaeffer, L. E., Fritz, G. K., & Spirito, A. (2003). Suicide attempts and self-mutilative behavior in a juvenile correctional facility. *Journal of the American Academy of Child and Adolescent Psychiatry, 42,* 762–769. doi:10.1097/01.CHI.0000046869.56865.46

Penney, S. R., Lee, Z., & Moretti, M. M. (2010). Gender differences in risk factors for violence: An examination of the predictive validity of the Structured Assessment of Violence Risk in Youth. *Aggressive Behavior, 36,* 390–404. doi:10.1002/ab.20352

Perry, A. E., & Olason, D. T. (2009). A new psychometric instrument assessing vulnerability to risk of suicide and self-harm behaviour in offenders: Suicide Concerns for Offenders in Prison Environment (SCOPE). *International Journal of Offender Therapy and Comparative Criminology, 53,* 385–400. doi:10.1177/0306624X08319418

Peugh, J., & Belenko, S. (1999). Substance-involved women inmates: Challenges to providing effective treatment. *Prison Journal, 79,* 23–44. doi:10.1177/0032885599079001003

Pinderhughes, E. E., Craddock, K. T., & Fermin, L. L. (2011). Adolescent parents and the juvenile justice system: Toward developmentally and socioculturally based provision of services. In F. T. Sherman & F. H. Jacobs (Eds.), *Juvenile justice: Advancing research, policy, and practice* (pp. 174–196). Hoboken, NJ: Wiley. doi:10.1002/9781118093375.ch9

Poehlmann, J., Dallaire, D., Loper, A. B., & Shear, L. D. (2010). Children's contact with their incarcerated parents: Research findings and recommendations. *American Psychologist, 65,* 575–598.

Polaschek, D. L. L. (2012). An appraisal of the risk-needs-responsivity (RNR) model of offender rehabilitation and its application in correctional treatment.

Legal and Criminological Psychology, 17, 1–17. doi:10.1111/j.2044-8333.2011.02038.x

Pollock, J. M., & Davis, S. M. (2005). The continuing myth of the violent female offender. *Criminal Justice Review, 30,* 5–29. doi:10.1177/0734016805275378

Prendergast, M. L., Wellisch, J., & Falkin, G. P. (1995). Assessment of and services for substance-abusing women offenders in community and correctional settings. *Prison Journal, 75,* 240–256. doi:10.1177/0032855595075002007

Puzzanchera, C., & Adams, B. (2011). *Juvenile arrests 2009.* Washington, DC: Office of Juvenile Justice and Delinquency Prevention.

Puzzanchera, C., & Hockenberry, S. (2013). *Juvenile court statistics 2010.* Pittsburgh, PA: National Center for Juvenile Justice.

Reisig, M., Holtfreter, K., & Morash, M. (2006). Assessing recidivism risk across female pathways to crime. *Justice Quarterly, 23,* 384–405. doi:10.1080/07418820600869152

Rennison, C. M., & Welchans, S. (2000). *Intimate partner violence.* Washington, DC: U.S. Department of Justice, Bureau of Justice Statistics. Retrieved from http://www.bjs.gov/content/pub/pdf/ipv.pdf

Resnick, P. J. (1969). Child murder by parents: A psychiatric review of filicide. *American Journal of Psychiatry, 23,* 325–334.

Resnick, P. J. (1970). Murder of the newborn: A psychiatric review of neonaticide. *American Journal of Psychiatry, 126,* 1414–1420.

Robbins, P. C., Monahan, J., & Silver, E. (2003). Mental disorder, violence, and gender. *Law and Human Behavior, 27,* 561–571. doi:10.1023/B:LAHU.0000004886.13268.f2

Robertson, A. A., Xu, X., & Stripling, A. (2010). Adverse events and substance use among female adolescent offenders: Effects of coping and family support. *Substance Use and Misuse, 45,* 451–472. doi:10.3109/10826080903452512

Roe-Sepowitz, D., & Krysik, J. (2008). Examining the sexual offenses of female juveniles: The relevance of childhood maltreatment. *American Journal of Orthopsychiatry, 78,* 405–412. doi:10.1037/a0014310

Roe-Sepowitz, D. E. (2009). Comparing male and female juveniles charged with homicide: Child maltreatment, substance abuse, and crime details. *Journal of Interpersonal Violence, 24,* 601–617. doi:10.1177/0886260508317201

Romani, C. J., Morgan, R. D., Gross, N. R., & McDonald, B. R. (2012). Treating criminal behavior: Is the bang worth the buck? *Psychology, Public Policy, and Law, 18,* 144–165.

Rowe, D. C., Vazsonyi, A. T., & Flannery, D. J. (1995). Sex differences in crime: Do means and within-sex variation have similar causes? *Journal of Research in Crime and Delinquency, 32*, 84–100. doi:10.1177/0022427895032001004

Sacks, J. Y., McKendrick, K., Hamilton, Z., Cleland, C. M., Pearson, F. S., & Banks, S. (2008). Treatment outcomes for female offenders: Relationship to number of axis I diagnoses. *Behavioral Sciences and the Law, 26*, 413–434.

Salina, D. D., Lesondak, L. M., Razzano, L. A., & Parenti, B. M. (2011). Addressing unmet needs in incarcerated women with co-occurring disorders. *Journal of Social Service Research, 37*, 365–378.

Salisbury, E. J., & van Voorhis, P. (2009). Gendered pathways: A quantitative investigation of women probationers' paths to incarceration. *Criminal Justice and Behavior, 36*, 541–566. doi:10.1177/0093854809334076

Salisbury, E. J., van Voorhis, P., & Spiropoulos, G. V. (2009). The predictive validity of a gender-responsive needs assessment: An exploratory study. *Crime and Delinquency, 55*, 550–585. doi:10.1177/0011128707308102

Salisbury, E. J., van Voorhis, P., & Wright, E. (2006). *Construction and validation of a gender responsive risk/needs instrument for women offenders in Missouri and Maui.* Presented at the Annual Meeting of the American Society of Criminology, Los Angeles, CA.

Schinke, S. P., Fang, L., & Cole, K. A. (2008). Substance use among early adolescent girls: Risk and protective factors. *Journal of Adolescent Health, 43*, 191–194. doi:10.1016/j.jadohealth.2007.12.014

Schmidt, F., Campbell, M., & Houlding, C. (2011). Comparative analyses of the YLS/CMI, SAVRY, and PCL: YV in adolescent offenders: A 10-year follow-up into adulthood. *Youth Violence and Juvenile Justice, 9*, 23–42. doi:10.1177/1541204010371793

Schufelt, J., & Coccoza, J. J. (2006). *Youth with mental health disorders in the juvenile justice system: Results from a multi-state prevalence study.* Delmar, NY: National Center for Mental Health and Juvenile Justice.

Schwalbe, C. S. (2008). A meta-analysis of juvenile justice risk assessment instruments: Predictive validity by gender. *Criminal Justice and Behavior, 35*, 1367–1381. doi:10.1177/0093854808324377

Sedlak, A. J., Mettenburg, J., Basena, M., Petta, I., McPherson, K., Greene, A., & Li, S. (2010). *Fourth national incidence study of child abuse and neglect (NIS-4): Report to Congress.* Washington, DC: U.S. Department of Health and Human Services, Administration for Children and Families. Retrieved from http://www.acf.hhs.gov/sites/default/files/opre/nis4_report_congress_full_pdf_jan2010.pdf

Serbin, L. A., & Karp, J. (2004). The intergenerational transfer of psychosocial risk: Mediators of vulnerability and resilience. *Annual Review of Psychology, 55*, 333–363.

Serin, R. C. (2005). *Evidence-based practice: Principles for enhancing correctional results in prisons.* Washington, DC: National Institute of Corrections.

Sevecke, K., Lehmkuhl, G., & Krischer, M. K. (2009). Examining relations between psychopathology and psychopathy dimensions among adolescent female and male offenders. *European Child and Adolescent Psychiatry, 18*, 85–95. doi:10.1007/s00787-008-0707-7

Sharp, C., Green, K. L., Yaroslavsky, I., Venta, A., Zanarini, M. C., & Pettit, J. (2012). Incremental validity of borderline personality disorder relative to major depressive disorder for suicidal ideation and deliberate self-harm in adolescents. *Journal of Personality Disorders, 26*, 927–938. doi:10.1521/pedi.2012.26.6.927

Shelton, J. L. E., Muirhead, Y., & Canning, K. E. (2010). Ambivalence toward mothers who kill: An examination of 45 U.S. cases of maternal neonaticide. *Behavioral Sciences and the Law, 28*, 812–831.

Shepherd, S. M., Luebbers, S., & Dolan, M. (2013). Gender and ethnicity in juvenile risk assessment. *Criminal Justice and Behavior, 40*, 388–408. doi:10.1177/0093854812456776

Shreeram, S. S., & Malik, A. (2008). Suicidality in the juvenile justice environment. *International Journal of Child Health and Human Development, 1*, 245–260.

Simpson, A. I. F., Brinded, P. M., Laidlaw, T. M., Fairley, N., & Malcolm, F. (1999). *The national study of psychiatric morbidity in New Zealand prisons.* Auckland, New Zealand: Department of Corrections.

Singh, J. P., Grann, M., & Fazel, S. (2011). A comparative study of violence risk assessment tools: A systematic review and metaregression analysis of 68 studies involving 25,980 participants. *Clinical Psychology Review, 31*, 499–513. doi:10.1016/j.cpr.2010.11.009

Singleton, N., Meltzer, H., Gatward, R., Coid, J., & Deasey, D. (1998). *Psychiatric morbidity among prisoners in England and Wales.* London, England: The Stationery Office.

Smith, P., Cullen, F. T., & Latessa, E. J. (2009). Can 14,737 women be wrong? A meta-analysis of the LSI-R and recidivism for female offenders. *Criminology and Public Policy, 8*, 183–208. doi:10.1111/j.1745-9133.2009.00551.x

Somander, L. K., & Rammer, L. M. (1991). Intra- and extrafamilial child homicide in Sweden

1971–1980. *Child Abuse and Neglect, 15*, 45–55. doi:10.1016/0145-2134(91)90089-V

Sorbello, L., Eccleston, L., Ward, T., & Jones, R. (2002). Treatment needs of female offenders: A review. *Australian Psychologist, 37*, 198–205. doi:10.1080/00050060210001706876

Spjeldnes, S., & Goodkind, S. (2009). Gender differences and offender reentry: A review of the literature. *Journal of Offender Rehabilitation, 48*, 314–335. doi:10.1080/10509670902850812

Statistics Canada. (2011). *Women and the criminal justice system*. Ottawa, Ontario, Canada: Author. Retrieved from http://www.statcan.gc.ca/pub/89-503-x/2010001/article/11416-eng.pdf

Steadman, H. J., Scott, J. E., Osher, F., Agnese, T. K., & Robbins, P. C. (2005). Validation of the brief jail mental health screen. *Psychiatric Services, 56*, 816–822. doi:10.1176/appi.ps.56.7.816

Steffensmeier, D., & Allan, E. (1988). Sex disparities in crime by population subgroup: Residence, race, and age. *Justice Quarterly, 5*, 53–80. doi:10.1080/07418828800089611

Steffensmeier, D., & Allan, E. (1995). Gender, age, and crime. In J. Sheley (Ed.), *Handbook of contemporary criminology*. New York, NY: Wadsworth.

Steffensmeier, D., Allan, E., & Streifel, C. (1989). Modernization and female crime: A cross-national test of alternative explanations. *Social Forces, 68*, 262–283.

Stets, J. E., & Hammons, S. A. (2002). Gender, control, and marital commitment. *Journal of Family Issues, 23*, 3–25. doi:10.1177/0192513X02023001001

Stewart, C. (2011, November). *Risk assessment of federal female offenders*. (Unpublished doctoral dissertation). University of Saskatchewan, Saskatoon, Saskatchewan, Canada. Retrieved from http://hdl.handle.net/10388/ETD-2011-11-248

Stith, S.M., Smith, D. B., Penn, C. E., Ward, D. B., & Tritt, D. (2004). Intimate partner physical abuse perpetration and victimization risk factors: A meta-analytic review. *Aggression and Violent Behavior: A Review Journal, 10*, 65–98. doi: 0.1016/j.avb.2003.09.001

Strand, S., & Belfrage, H. (2001). Comparison of HCR-20 scores in violent mentally disordered men and women: Gender differences and similarities. *Psychology, Crime & Law, 7*, 71–79. doi:10.1080/10683160108401784

Strand, S., & Belfrage, H. (2005). Gender differences in psychopathy in a Swedish offender sample. *Behavioral Sciences and the Law, 23*, 837–850. doi:10.1002/bsl.674

Straus, M. A. (1999). The controversy over domestic violence by women: A methodological, theoretical, and sociology of science analysis. In X. Arriaga & S. Oskamp (Eds.), *Violence in intimate relationships* (pp. 17–44). Thousand Oaks, CA: Sage. doi:10.4135/9781452204659.n2

Straus, M. A. (2009). Why the overwhelming evidence on partner physical violence by women has not been perceived and is often denied. *Journal of Aggression, Maltreatment and Trauma, 18*, 552–571. doi:10.1080/10926770903103081

Straus, M. A. (2011). Gender symmetry and mutuality in perpetration of clinical-level partner violence: Empirical evidence and implications for prevention and treatment. *Aggression and Violent Behavior, 16*, 279–288. doi:10.1016/j.avb.2011.04.010

Straus, M. A. (2012). Blaming the messenger for the bad news about partner violence by women: The methodological, theoretical, and value basis of the purported invalidity of the Conflict Tactics Scale. *Behavioral Sciences and the Law, 30*, 538–556. doi:10.1002/bsl.2023

Strickland, S. M. (2008). Female sex offenders exploring issues of personality, trauma, and cognitive distortions. *Journal of Interpersonal Violence, 23*, 474–489.

Teasdale, B., Silver, E., & Monahan, J. (2006). Gender, threat/control-override delusions and violence. *Law and Human Behavior, 30*, 649–658. doi:10.1007/s10979-006-9044-x

Teplin, L. A., Abram, K. M., & McClelland, G. M. (1996). Prevalence of psychiatric disorders among incarcerated women: Pretrial jail detainees. *Archives of General Psychiatry, 53*, 505–512. doi:10.1001/archpsyc.1996.01830060047007

Teplin, L. A., Abram, K. M., McClelland, G. M., Dulcan, M. K., & Mericle, A. A. (2002). Psychiatric disorders in youth in juvenile detention. *Archives of General Psychiatry, 59*, 1133–1143. doi:10.1001/archpsyc.59.12.1133

Teplin, L. A., Abram, K. M., Washburn, J. J., Welty, L. J., Hershfield, J. A., & Dulcan, M. K. (2013). *The Northwestern Juvenile Project: Overview*. Washington, DC: U.S. Department of Justice. Retrieved from http://www.ojjdp.gov/pubs/234522.pdf

Thomas, A., & Pollard, J. (2001). *Substance abuse, trauma and coping: A report on women prisoners at the Dame Phyllis Frost Centre for Women*. Unpublished report, Caraniche Pty Ltd, Melbourne, Australia.

Tørmoen, A. J., Rossow, I., Larsson, B., & Mehlum, L. (2013). Nonsuicidal self-harm and suicide attempts in adolescents: Differences in kind or in degree? *Social Psychiatry and Psychiatric Epidemiology, 48*, 1447–1455. doi:10.1007/s00127-012-0646-y

Tracy, P. E., Kempf-Leonard, K., & Abramoske-James, S. (2009). Gender differences in delinquency and juvenile justice processing: Evidence from national data. *Crime and Delinquency*, *55*, 171–215. doi:10.1177/0011128708330628

Truman, J. L., & Planty, M. (2012). *Criminal victimization, 2011* (Report No. NCJ 239437). U.S. Department of Justice, Bureau of Justice Statistics. Retrieved from http://bjs.ojp.usdoj.gov/content/pub/pdf/cv11.pdf

Trupin, E. W., Stewart, D. G., Beach, B., & Boesky, L. (2002). Effectiveness of dialectical behaviour therapy program for incarcerated female juvenile offenders. *Child and Adolescent Mental Health*, *7*, 121–127. doi:10.1111/1475-3588.00022

UN Office on Drugs and Crime. (2008, September). *Handbook for prison managers and policymakers on women and imprisonment*. Retrieved from http://www.refworld.org/docid/4a096b0a2.html

U.S. Department of Health and Human Services (1999). *Mental health: A report of the Surgeon General*. Rockville, MD: U.S. Department of Health and Human Services, Substance Abuse and Mental Health Services Administration, Center for Mental Health Services.

U.S. Department of Justice, Bureau of Justice Statistics Bulletin. (2010). *Federal criminal case processing statistics*. Washington, DC: Author. Retrieved from http://www.bjs.gov/fjsrc/

U.S. Department of Justice, Bureau of Justice Statistics Bulletin. (2011). *Homicide trends in the United States, 1980–2008*. Washington, DC: Author. Retrieved from http://www.bjs.gov/index.cfm?ty=pbdetail&iid=2221

Vagi, K. J., Rothman, E. F., Latzman, N. E., Tharp, A. T., Hall, D. M., & Breiding, M. J. (2013). Beyond correlates: A review of risk and protective factors for adolescent dating violence perpetration. *Journal of Youth and Adolescence*, *42*, 633–649.

Vandiver, D. M., & Teske, R. R. (2006). Juvenile female and male sex offenders: A comparison of offender, victim, and judicial processing characteristics. *International Journal of Offender Therapy and Comparative Criminology*, *50*, 148–165. doi:10.1177/0306624X05277941

van Marle, H., & van der Kroft, P. (2007). Research issues in forensic psychiatry. *Current Opinion in Psychiatry*, *20*, 511–515. doi:10.1097/YCO.0b013e32826fb345

van Voorhis, P. V., & Presser, L. (2001). *Classification of women offenders: A national assessment of current practices*. Washington, DC: U.S. Department of Justice, National Institute of Corrections. Retrieved from http://static.nicic.gov/Library/017082.pdf

van Voorhis, P., & Salisbury, E. (2013). *Correctional counseling and rehabilitation*. Boston, MA: Newnes.

van Voorhis, P., Wright, E. M., Salisbury, E., & Bauman, A. (2010). Women's risk factors and their contributions to existing risk/needs assessment the current status of a gender-responsive supplement. *Criminal Justice and Behavior*, *37*, 261–288. doi:10.1177/0093854809357442

van Wormer, K. (2010). *Working with female offenders: A gender sensitive approach*. Mississauga, Ontario, Canada: Wiley. doi:10.1002/9781118265581

Vazsonyi, A. T., & Chen, P. (2010). Entry risk into the juvenile justice system: African American, American Indian, Asian American, European American, and Hispanic children and adolescents. *Journal of Child Psychology and Psychiatry*, *51*, 668–678. doi:10.1111/j.1469-7610.2010.02231.x

Verona, E., Hicks, B. M., & Patrick, C. J. (2005). Psychopathy and suicidal behavior in female offenders: Mediating influences of personality and abuse history. *Journal of Consulting and Clinical Psychology*, *73*, 1065–1073. doi:10.1037/0022-006X.73.6.1065

Viljoen, J. L., Cruise, K. R., Nicholls, T. L., Desmarais, S. L., & Webster, C. D. (2012). Taking stock and taking steps: The case for an adolescent version of the short-term assessment of risk and treatability. *International Journal of Forensic Mental Health*, *11*, 135–149. doi:10.1080/14999013.2012.737406

Viljoen, J. L., MacDougall, E. M., Gagnon, N. C., & Douglas, K. S. (2010). Psychopathy evidence in legal proceedings involving adolescent offenders. *Psychology, Public Policy, and Law*, *16*, 254–283. doi:10.1037/a0019649

Viljoen, J. L., McLachlan, K., & Vincent, G. M. (2010). Assessing violence risk and psychopathy in juvenile and adult offenders: A survey of clinical practices. *Assessment*, *17*, 377–395. doi:10.1177/1073191109359587

Viljoen, J. L., Mordell, S., & Beneteau, J. L. (2012). Prediction of adolescent sexual reoffending: A meta-analysis of the J-SOAP-II, ERASOR, J-SORRAT-II, and Static-99. *Law and Human Behavior*, *36*, 423–438. doi:10.1037/h0093938

Vincent, G. M., Odgers, C. L., McCormick, A. V., & Corrado, R. R. (2008). The PCL:YV and recidivism in male and female juveniles: A follow-up into young adulthood. *International Journal of Law and Psychiatry*, *31*, 287–296. doi:10.1016/j.ijlp.2008.04.012

Vincent, G. M., Paiva-Salisbury, M. L., Cook, N. E., Guy, L. S., & Perrault, R. T. (2012). Impact of risk/needs assessment on juvenile probation officers' decision making: Importance of implementation. *Psychology, Public Policy, and Law*, *18*, 549–576. doi:10.1037/a0027186

Vincent, G. M., Terry, A. M., & Maney, S. M. (2009). Risk/needs tools for antisocial behavior and violence among youthful populations. In J. T. Andrade (Ed.), *Handbook of violence risk assessment and treatment:*

New approaches for mental health professionals (pp. 377–423). New York, NY: Springer.

Vitale, J. E., & Newman, J. P. (2001). Using the Psychopathy Checklist—Revised with female samples: Reliability, validity, and implications for clinical utility. *Clinical Psychology: Science and Practice, 8,* 117–132. doi:10.1093/clipsy.8.1.117

Vitale, J. E., Smith, S. S., Brinkley, C. A., & Newman, J. P. (2002). The reliability and validity of the Psychopathy Checklist—Revised in a sample of female offenders. *Criminal Justice and Behavior, 29,* 202–231.

Vitopoulos, N. A., Peterson-Badali, M., & Skilling, T. A. (2012). The relationship between matching service to criminogenic need and recidivism in male and female youth: Examining the RNR principles in practice. *Criminal Justice and Behavior, 39,* 1025–1041. doi:10.1177/0093854812442895

Warren, J. I., Burnette, M., South, S. C., Chauhan, P., Bale, R., & Friend, R. (2002). Personality disorders and violence among female prison inmates. *Journal of the American Academy of Psychiatry and the Law, 30,* 502–509.

Warren, J. I., Burnette, M. L., South, S. C., Chauhan, P., Bale, R., Friend, R., & Van Patten, I. (2003). Psychopathy in women: Structural modeling and comorbidity. *International Journal of Law and Psychiatry, 26,* 223–242. doi:10.1016/S0160-2527(03)00034-7

Wasserman, G. A., Jensen, P. S., Ko, S. J., Cocozza, J., Trupin, E., Angold, A., Cauffman, E., & Grisso, T. (2003). Mental health assessments in juvenile justice: Report on the Consensus Conference. *Journal of the American Academy of Child and Adolescent Psychiatry, 42,* 752–761. doi:10.1097/01.CHI.0000046873.56865.4B

Wasserman, G. A., & McReynolds, L. S. (2011). Contributors to traumatic exposure and posttraumatic stress disorder in juvenile justice youths. *Journal of Traumatic Stress, 24,* 422–429.

Wasserman, G. A., McReynolds, L. S., Schwalbe, C. S., Keating, J. M., & Jones, S. A. (2010). Psychiatric disorder, comorbidity, and suicidal behavior in juvenile justice youth. *Criminal Justice and Behavior, 37,* 1361–1376. doi:10.1177/0093854810382751

Webster, C. D. (1999, December). *Risk assessment and risk management with women offenders.* Report to the National Parole Board, Ottawa, Ontario, Canada.

Webster, C. D., Douglas, K. S., Eaves, D., & Hart, S. D. (1997). *HCR-20: Assessing risk for violence (Version 2).* Vancouver: Simon Fraser University and Forensic Psychiatric Services Commission of British Columbia.

Webster, C. D., Martin, M. L., Brink, J., Nicholls, T. L., & Desmarais, S. (2009). *Manual for the Short-Term Assessment of Risk and Treatability (START) (Version 1.1).*

Port Coquitlam, British Columbia, Canada: Forensic Psychiatric Services Commission; Odessa, FL: St. Joseph's Healthcare.

Webster, C. D., Martin, M. L., Brink, J., Nicholls, T. L., & Middleton, C. (2004). *Manual for the Short-Term Assessment of Risk and Treatability (START) (Version 1.0 Consultation Edition).* Port Coquitlam, British Columbia, Canada: Forensic Psychiatric Services Commission; Hamilton, Ontario, Canada: St. Joseph's Healthcare.

Webster, C. M., & Doob, A. N. (2004). Classification without validity or equity: An empirical examination of the Custody Rating Scale for federally sentenced women offenders in Canada. *Canadian Journal of Criminology and Criminal Justice, 46,* 395–422.

Welch, C. L., Roberts-Lewis, A. C., & Parker, S. (2009). Incorporating gender specific approaches for incarcerated female adolescents: Multilevel risk model for practice. *Journal of Offender Rehabilitation, 48,* 67–83. doi:10.1080/10509670802572292

Welch-Brewer, C. L., Stoddard-Dare, P., & Mallett, C. A. (2011). Race, substance abuse, and mental health disorders as predictors of juvenile court outcomes: Do they vary by gender? *Child and Adolescent Social Work Journal, 28,* 229–241.

West, S. G., Hatters, S., Friedman, M. D., & Kim, K. D. (2011). Women accused of sex offenses: A gender-based comparison. *Behavioral Sciences and the Law, 29,* 728–740. doi:10.1002/bsl.1007

Wijkman, M., Bijleveld, C., & Hendriks, J. (2010). Women don't do such things! Characteristics of female sex offenders and offender types. *Sexual Abuse: A Journal of Research and Treatment, 22,* 135–156.

Wijkman, M., Bijleveld, C., & Hendriks, J. (2011). Female sex offenders: Specialists, generalists and once-only offenders. *Journal of Sexual Aggression, 17,* 34–45.

Wilczynski, A. (1997). Mad or bad? Child-killers, gender and the courts. *British Journal of Criminology, 37,* 419–436.

Williams, V. (2007). *Procedures and policies: Good practices and appropriate use of screening results.* Mental Health Screening and Juvenile Justice: The Next Frontier. Delmar, NY: National Center for Mental Heath and Juvenile Justice.

Wilson, H. A., & Hoge, R. D. (2013). The effect of youth diversion programs on recidivism: A meta-analytic review. *Criminal Justice and Behavior, 40,* 497–518. doi:10.1177/0093854812451089

Wilson, M., Daly, M., & Daniele, A. (1995). Familicide: The killing of spouse and children. *Aggressive Behavior, 21,* 275–291. doi:10.1002/1098-2337(1995)21:4<275::AID-AB2480210404>3.0.CO;2-S

Wong, S. C. P., & Gordon, A. (2000). *Violence risk scale.* Unpublished manuscript, Saskatoon, Saskatchewan, Canada.

Wright, C., & Leroux, J. P. (1991). Les enfants victimes d'actes criminels violents [Child victims of violent criminal acts]. *Juristat, 11,* 1–13.

Yang, M., Wong, S. C. P., & Coid, J. (2010). The efficacy of violence prediction: A meta-analytic comparison of nine risk assessment tools. *Psychological Bulletin, 136,* 740–767. doi:10.1037/a0020473

Zhang, J., Liang, B., Zhou, Y., & Brame, W. (2010). Prison inmates' suicidal ideation in China: A study of gender differences and their impact. *International Journal of Offender Therapy and Comparative Criminology, 54,* 959–983. doi:10.1177/0306624X09348200

Zlotnick, C. (1997). Posttraumatic stress disorder (PTSD), PTSD comorbidity, and childhood abuse among incarcerated women. *Journal of Nervous and Mental Disease, 185,* 761–763. doi:10.1097/00005053-199712000-00007

Zlotnick, C. (1999). Antisocial personality disorder, affect dysregulation and childhood abuse among incarcerated women. *Journal of Personality Disorders, 13,* 90–95. doi:10.1521/pedi.1999.13.1.90

Zosky, D. L. (2010). Accountability in teenage dating violence: A comparative examination of adult domestic violence and juvenile justice systems policies. *Social Work, 55,* 359–368. doi:10.1093/sw/55.4.359

CHAPTER 5

RACE IN THE JUSTICE SYSTEM

Jennifer S. Hunt

This chapter will provide an overview of the growing literature on race, ethnicity, and culture in the justice system, focusing primarily on research within forensic psychology, but also including scholarship from other fields, such as law, criminology, and sociology, when possible. After discussing some highly publicized cases and statistics suggesting racial disparities in criminal justice and legal outcomes, I will review important psychological theories and concepts related to prejudice, stereotyping, and discrimination that inform research on bias in the justice system. Then I will discuss research examining how race and ethnicity influence judgments and behaviors in the criminal justice and legal contexts, leading to significant disparities in outcomes. This research shows that (a) police officers engage in racial profiling and are more likely to stop, search, and arrest Blacks and Latinos; (b) police officers' decisions to shoot are influenced by race, such that they are quicker to shoot armed Black individuals; (c) attorneys, especially prosecutors, often use peremptory challenges during the jury selection process to strike racial and ethnic minorities, leading to nonrepresentative juries; (d) jurors may make more favorable verdicts for same-race defendants and show racial biases in their evaluation of trial evidence; (e) even after controlling for legally relevant variables, Black and Latino defendants are more likely to receive

sentences involving incarceration; and (f) the death penalty is most likely to be imposed in cases in which Black defendants are convicted of killing White victims. I also will review research on the influence of race and ethnicity on ordinary citizens' views of and interactions with the justice system, showing that Blacks and, to a lesser extent, Latinos have more negative attitudes toward the police and justice system, which may contribute to negative interactions with justice professionals. I will conclude the chapter with a discussion about some ways that forensic psychologists can disseminate research on these issues to the courts and policymakers as well as contribute to the development of training and interventions to reduce racial bias in the justice system.

IMPORTANCE OF THE PROBLEM

Yes, Black America still lives on the brink of fear. For all the progress we have made, dues we have paid, degrees we have acquired and presidencies we have won, we can all recite the story of the father, son, daughter or niece who has gone from citizen to suspect in an instant—the son frisked, the cousin shoved against the car, the uncle badly beaten—and, more often than should

I gratefully acknowledge Sam Sommers, Dennis Devine, and Evelyn Maeder for sharing their knowledge and providing valuable feedback on this chapter.

http://dx.doi.org/10.1037/14462-005
APA Handbook of Forensic Psychology: Vol. 2. Criminal Investigation, Adjudication, and Sentencing Outcomes,
B. L. Cutler and P. A. Zapf (Editors-in-Chief)
Copyright © 2015 by the American Psychological Association. All rights reserved.

be, the nephew convicted of a crime he didn't commit or, worse, shot dead by the police. (Dreyfuss, 2011)

Although the 14th Amendment of the U.S. Constitution guarantees equal protection of law to all U.S. citizens, individual cases as well as aggregate statistics reveal that, too often, race plays an important role in criminal justice and legal outcomes. Individuals from racial and ethnic minority groups are more likely to be suspected of criminal behavior, stopped by the police, and even targeted with deadly force. In criminal trials, defendant race can affect the evaluation of evidence, likelihood of conviction, and severity of sentencing, with minority defendants usually receiving harsher outcomes. Given these patterns, it is not surprising that individuals from racial and ethnic minority groups tend to have more negative attitudes toward the criminal justice and legal systems as well as more negative expectations about interacting with them. Indeed, as the quote at the beginning of this section suggests, there may be deep fissures across racial and ethnic groups that reflect differences in perceived treatment by the justice system and beliefs about the system as a source of ongoing inequality and oppression.

To highlight the importance of race in criminal justice and legal outcomes, it is instructive to consider a few cases. The influence of a suspect's race on police officers' decisions to use force became an issue of widespread concern after the 1999 death of Amadou Diallo, a 22-year-old immigrant from Guinea living in the Bronx. Diallo was standing outside his apartment building when he was approached by four police officers who were searching for a rapist. Diallo, who was unarmed, pulled out his wallet to get identification. The police officers responded by firing 41 shots, killing Diallo (Cooper, 1999). A similar case occurred in 2006, when Queens police officers fired over 50 shots at a 23-year-old Black man, Sean Bell, who was supposed to get married later that day (McFadden, 2006). After these deaths, psychologists began to study racial biases in decisions to shoot. This research revealed a pattern of bias in which police officers and lay people tend to be faster to shoot armed

Black individuals and, conversely, to decide not to shoot unarmed White individuals (e.g., Correll, Park, Judd, Wittenbrink, et al., 2007).

Another issue of considerable concern is the influence of race in decisions involving the death penalty. In 2011, there was widespread outrage about Georgia's execution of a Black man named Troy Davis. Davis was convicted of the 1989 murder of a White, off-duty police officer named Mark MacPhail. Although nine eyewitnesses testified against Davis at his trial, seven of those individuals later recanted their testimony. Some identified another man—who also testified against Davis—as the actual killer (Liptak, 2009). Despite these revelations and numerous calls for clemency, the U.S. Supreme Court declined to stay his execution (Severson, 2011). Many believe that the fact that Davis was a Black man accused of murdering a White police officer played an important role in his sentence as well as the refusal of the Georgia Parole Board to grant him clemency. In fact, several archival analyses reveal that death sentences are more likely to be given in cases in which Black defendants are convicted of killing White individuals, even after controlling for numerous other elements of the cases (e.g., Baldus, Brain, Weiner, & Woodworth, 2009; S. L. Johnson, Blume, Eisenberg, Hans, & Wells, 2012). These data have contributed to decisions to abolish the death penalty in 16 states, most recently Illinois (J. Schwartz & Fitzsimmons, 2011); however, in *McCleskey v. Kemp* (1987), the U.S. Supreme Court held that aggregate racial disparities in the imposition of the death penalty do not provide evidence that discrimination occurred in any single case.

In addition to high-profile cases such as Diallo, Bell, and Davis, it is useful to consider data on issues such as incarceration rates. According to the Bureau of Justice Statistics (Glaze, 2011), in 2010 the rate of incarceration per 100,000 U.S. residents was 678 for White men, 1,775 for Latinos, and 4,347 for Black men. In other words, Latinos were 2.6 times and Black men were 6.4 times more likely than White men to be incarcerated. Similar patterns were found for women, although the disparities were smaller in magnitude. Although many factors are likely to contribute to racial disparities in sentencing (e.g., crime characteristics, socioeconomic status [SES]), controlling for these variables does not eliminate the effect of race, strongly suggesting that racial bias has an influence on sentencing judgments (e.g., O. Mitchell, 2005).

Finally, it is important to examine policies, statutes, and organizational practices that, intentionally or unintentionally, have racially disparate impacts, creating institutional racism within the criminal justice and legal systems. For example, an important contributor to racial disparities in incarceration involves sentencing guidelines that mandate far more severe sentences for crack cocaine than for powder cocaine. Under the Anti-Drug Abuse Act of 1986, sentencing guidelines equated possession of one gram of crack cocaine, which is more likely to be used by racial minorities, to 100 grams of powder cocaine, which is more likely to be used by White people. Although the Fair Sentencing Act of 2010 reduced this discrepancy, an 18:1 ratio for crack versus powder cocaine remains, perpetuating a system in which racial minorities are far more likely than White individuals to receive jail time for drug use (Davis, 2011).

Institutional bias also can be found in police procedures. In recent years, there has been a great deal of concern about the use of racial profiling, such as decisions by police officers to stop individuals that are based, at least in part, on race. In 2010, this issue was extended to the realm of immigration when Arizona enacted a new law (SB1070) requiring police officers to check the immigration status of any individuals suspected of being illegally in the United States. This law has been widely criticized as a mechanism for the police to target Latinos (Archibold, 2010). In addition to concerns about fairness, legality, and public perceptions the use of racial profiling has been challenged due to its potential to increase racial disparities in incarceration (e.g., Glaser, 2006).

The cases, statistics, and policies discussed in this section provide only a glimpse into the many important ways in which race and ethnicity can influence criminal justice and legal outcomes. Given that equality before the law is a central legal principle in the United States, it is critical for forensic psychologists to systematically examine the role of

race and ethnicity in the justice system, identify circumstances in which racial bias may affect legally relevant judgments and outcomes, and develop interventions to reduce those effects.

In the following sections, I will review research from forensic psychology and related fields that examines the effects of race and ethnicity on police officers' behaviors, including their use of force, jury selection, jury decision making, sentencing, including the death penalty, and other legal outcomes. I also will discuss the ways that race and ethnicity influence lay people's attitudes, expectations, and interactions with the justice system. Given space limitations, there are several topics related to race in the justice system that will not be addressed in this chapter, although some of them are addressed in other chapters of this text. These topics include the effects of race on eyewitness identification (see Chapter 7, this volume), racial bias in forensic assessment (see Volume 1, Chapter 1, this handbook), associations between race and criminal behavior (see Volume 1, Chapter 8, this handbook), racial conflict in prisons (Chapter 15, this volume), and hate crime (e.g., Gerstenfeld, 2010). In addition, the legal aspects of racial inequalities and discrimination in domains such as employment and education are discussed in Volume 1, Chapter 15, this handbook.

RELEVANT PSYCHOLOGICAL THEORY AND PRINCIPLES

In order to determine how, when, and why race influences judgments and behaviors in criminal justice and legal contexts, it is necessary to understand some basic concepts and theories from social psychological research on prejudice, stereotyping, and discrimination. In this section, I will provide a brief overview of this literature (for more extensive reviews, see Dovidio & Gaertner, 2010; Nelson, 2009). Theories of prejudice, stereotyping, and discrimination are also addressed in Volume 1, Chapter 15, this handbook.

Basic Terminology and Concepts

In this chapter, the term *racial bias* will be used as a general label for any psychological process or behavior that disadvantages members of a particular race or ethnic group. More precise terminology will be used when referring to specific psychological processes. *Prejudice* refers to a negative attitude or evaluation about a racial or ethnic group, that is, a tendency to dislike a certain race, to evaluate it negatively, or to consider it to be inferior to other racial groups. Prejudice often has a strong emotional or affective component, with people experiencing negative feelings toward members of certain groups. *Stereotyping*, in contrast, refers to cognitive beliefs and generalizations about members of a particular group; for example, many people believe that Black individuals are hostile and aggressive (Stangor & Schaller, 1996; Welch, 2007). The use of stereotypes may lead perceivers to make different judgments about individuals, including verdicts and sentencing judgments, based on their race. Finally, *discrimination* occurs when people treat others differently based on group membership. The tendency for people to be quicker to shoot Black than White individuals, even when both are armed (e.g., Correll, Park, Judd, & Wittenbrink, 2007), is an extreme example of discrimination. Although prejudice, stereotyping, and discrimination often are used synonymously in everyday discourse, psychological research has shown that they are only moderately correlated with each other (Stangor & Schaller, 1996). For example, people may be prejudiced against members of a certain race, but not discriminate against them, due to situational constraints (e.g., workplace policies) or fear of social disapproval.

Categorization

Early theories about racial prejudice conceptualized it as a pathology found in individuals with maladaptive personality traits or as an unconscious, psychodynamic process used as a defense against frustration and threat (Duckitt, 1992). Since the 1970s, however, prejudice and stereotyping have been seen as consequences of normal and in fact universal cognitive processes. Humans have a fundamental need to categorize people and objects in their environments. Categorization occurs automatically, enabling people to quickly and efficiently ascertain the nature of a target and access related information that is stored in memory (Fiske & Neuberg, 1990).

When categories such as "human" are large and heterogeneous, categorization often occurs at the level of subgroups that are seen as more meaningful and informative. In particular, people tend to be categorized according to demographic characteristics such as race, gender, and age (Fiske & Neuberg, 1990). Thus, the natural tendency to categorize underlies the tendency for people to judge, evaluate, and treat individuals differently due to their race or ethnicity.

Prejudice

Over the past 50 years, the nature of racial prejudice has shifted considerably. So called "old-fashioned racism" was characterized by openly negative attitudes and hostility toward members of racial minority groups; for example, many White Americans considered Black and Native Americans to be morally and intellectually inferior and felt justified in engaging in cruel and dehumanizing practices such as slavery, segregation, and forced relocation. After the Civil Rights Movement, however, cultural beliefs about racial inferiority increasingly have been replaced by ideologies of equality and tolerance, and the expression of prejudice has shifted from a ubiquitous practice to a source of social disapproval and condemnation (Gaertner & Dovidio, 1986). These changes have led to a decline in old-fashioned racism, but not an end to prejudice. Instead, racial prejudice has taken on new, more nuanced and conditional, forms.

Aversive racism theory (Gaertner & Dovidio, 1986; Pearson, Dovidio, & Gaertner, 2009) asserts that, in contemporary society, most people want to be nonprejudiced, but many people continue to harbor unwanted negative associations and discomfort with racial minorities due to psychological processes that differentiate between groups as well as exposure to prejudicial statements and stereotypical imagery. According to aversive racism theory, the tension between egalitarian beliefs and negative racial associations leads individuals to engage in racial bias under a predictable set of conditions. When aversive racists are aware that their judgments or behaviors may be influenced by race, they act in a nonprejudiced matter, and in some cases may even show favoritism to racial minorities. However, when race is not salient, situations are ambiguous, or judgments can be justified with nonracial explanations, aversive racists may be influenced by negative racial associations and make biased judgments about minorities without realizing it. For example, jurors may be more likely to ignore instructions to disregard damaging inadmissible evidence, and thus be more likely to render guilty verdicts, when defendants are Black (Hodson, Hooper, Dovidio, & Gaertner, 2005).

Other theories about the contemporary manifestation of prejudice emphasize its relation to "traditional" (generally conservative) American values as well as the potential for prejudice to be expressed symbolically. For example, according to symbolic racism theory (Sears & Henry, 2005), traditional moral values, such as the Protestant ethic and individualism, often are accompanied by negative views about racial minorities, who are seen as a threat to those values. Symbolic racists often express negative racial attitudes by opposing social policies, such as affirmative action, that are seen as violating traditional values and benefiting minorities. Although aversive and symbolic racism theories differ in their conceptualizations of prejudice, both theories assert that racial bias is likely to be expressed in subtle and potentially indirect ways, which can make it difficult to identify, even for the individuals engaging in bias.

Complementing these theories of prejudice, research on intergroup relations indicates that a substantial contributor to racial bias involves the tendency to show ingroup favoritism by making judgments and engaging in behaviors (e.g., resource allocation) that benefit members of one's own group (Brewer, 1999). In order to survive, humans have had to cooperate with and rely upon close social networks (e.g., kin) for food, information, and protection. As a result, the tendency to favor members of one's ingroup—which may be inferred based on race—may be an evolved psychological mechanism. Notably, ingroup favoritism can exist even without active feelings of hostility toward outgroups; thus, in some cases, favoritism toward same-race individuals may be a stronger contributor to racial disparities than negative attitudes toward other-race individuals. The similarity-leniency effect, in which mock jurors are less likely to convict members of their own racial group, may be an example of

ingroup favoritism (T. L. Mitchell, Haw, Pfeifer, & Meissner, 2005).

Stereotyping

As discussed earlier, stereotypes are generalized beliefs about the characteristics, such as traits and social roles, of a particular group. Although many racial and ethnic stereotypes have become more positive over time (Madon et al., 2001), minority groups such as Blacks and Latinos continue to be associated with negative characteristics and criminality (Eberhardt, Goff, Purdie, & Davies, 2004; Niemann, 2001; Welch, 2007). In contrast, Asian Americans often are seen as a "model minority" that is intelligent, hardworking, and successful, although not interpersonally skilled (Chao, Chiu, Chan, Mendoza-Denton, & Kwok, 2012). Because many racial and ethnic groups are seen as heterogeneous, perceivers often categorize and stereotype at the level of subgroups. For example, perceivers may distinguish between group members based on characteristics like occupation (e.g., separating Black professionals from poor Blacks; Fiske, Cuddy, Glick, & Xu, 2002) or other demographic characteristics such as gender. In addition, certain crimes tend to be associated with specific racial and ethnic groups; for instance, violent crimes such as assault are associated with Blacks and Latinos, whereas embezzlement is associated with Whites (Esqueda, 1997).

Importantly, stereotypes can serve to both legitimize and perpetuate social power and hierarchy (Pratto & Pitpitan, 2008). If members of social groups are believed to have traits and characteristics consistent with their roles in society, disparities in power, status, resources, and outcomes appear rational and even natural. For example, stereotypes associating Blacks and Latinos with crime may make racial disparities in incarceration seem justified.

Stereotypes are a form of schema, that is, cognitive representations used to organize and store information in memory (Schneider, 2004). When perceivers encounter a group-relevant cue, such as skin tone, the information stored in associated stereotypes can become automatically activated and able to influence perceptions and judgments. Relying on stereotypes allows perceivers to simplify and expedite judgments, rather than spend time and energy to form individualized impressions of every person in their social environment (Macrae, Milne, & Bodenhausen, 1994).

Like other schemas, stereotypes serve as a filter or framework that can direct virtually all aspects of information processing (Schneider, 2004). In general, stereotypes bias perceivers toward congruency; perceivers often are more likely to attend to information that is consistent with stereotypical expectations and to interpret ambiguous information as being more stereotype-consistent than it objectively may be. For example, perceivers may be more likely to notice gang insignia and interpret behavior as aggressive when a youth is Black rather than White (Duncan, 1976; Eberhardt et al., 2004). On the other hand, attributes that are highly inconsistent with stereotypes can attract special attention because they seem novel and informative. Stereotypes also affect attributions, or explanations for behavior. Perceivers often make personal (internal) attributions for stereotype-consistent behavior, but situational (external) attributions for stereotype-inconsistent behavior (Schneider, 2004). For example, when explaining why a juvenile engaged in a petty crime, a perceiver might infer that a racial minority "is destructive and defiant," but a White youth "succumbed to peer pressure in the moment" (Rattan, Levine, Dweck, & Eberhardt, 2012). Finally, perceivers often are more likely to encode and retrieve information from memory when it is consistent with group stereotypes (Fyock & Stangor, 1994). There are, however, many situational factors that moderate (influence) the use of stereotypes. Perceivers are less likely to use stereotypes when they have adequate time and information to make judgments, when they are motivated to make good judgments, and, in some cases, when they will be held accountable to others (Martell, 1991; Neuberg & Fiske, 1987).

Discrimination

Discrimination occurs when individuals or groups are treated unfairly or unfavorably due to group membership. Discrimination can take a wide range of forms, from interpersonal behaviors to allocation of resources and opportunities. It can involve either the imposition of negative outcomes (e.g., use of force by police) or the failure to receive positive outcomes (e.g., denial of parole). Discrimination can be overt, such as use of racial epithets, or subtle, such as failing to maintain eye contact with racial minorities. As social norms have become more egalitarian and disapproval of racism has increased, discrimination is increasingly occurring in subtle ways (Gaertner & Dovidio, 1986).

Notably, discrimination can occur at both individual and institutional levels. Individual discrimination occurs when a specific actor engages in behavior based on group membership, for example, when jurors' decisions to impose the death penalty are influenced by defendant race (e.g., Baldus, Broffitt, Weiner, Woodworth, & Zuckerman, 1998). In contrast, institutional discrimination occurs when policies, practices, and statutes have disproportionately negative effects on certain groups. As discussed earlier, federal sentencing guidelines that impose harsher sentences for crack cocaine than for powder cocaine can be seen as a form of institutional bias because they disproportionately affect racial minorities (Davis, 2011).

Implicit Bias

Recent research emphasizes that prejudice, stereotyping, and discrimination can occur in either an explicit or implicit manner. Explicit bias is characterized by intentionality, awareness, control, or deliberate engagement; for example, someone who considers whether Asians are more likely to be trustworthy when making a parole decision is engaging in explicit stereotyping. In contrast, implicit bias tends to be unintentional and automatic, and perceivers may be unaware that they are being influenced by race; for example, someone who "just gets a bad feeling" from a Latino defendant may be experiencing implicit prejudice. Implicit biases may occur when racial cues, such as ethnically distinctive names, prime racial stereotypes or prejudice and make them cognitively accessible (Andersen, Moskowitz, Blair, & Nosek, 2007). Once activated, these biases may act as a filter for interpreting and acting upon new information. The automatic activation and use of racial biases depends on several factors, including perceivers' motivations and the situational context (Andersen et al., 2007); for example, negative stereotypes of Black individuals are more likely to be activated in situations perceived as threatening (Wittenbrink, Judd, & Park, 2001). However, because even low-prejudice individuals have been exposed to cultural stereotypes and negative racial associations, implicit biases may occur frequently (Nosek et al., 2007). In fact, recent refinements to aversive racism theory suggest that it may reflect a combination of explicit egalitarianism with implicit prejudice (Pearson et al., 2009).

The fact that contemporary racial biases often are implicit and expressed in subtle ways poses several important challenges for the justice system. Implicit and subtle biases are difficult to detect and control. When racial prejudice or stereotyping is implicit, decision makers such as police, prosecutors, and jurors may be unaware that race is affecting their judgments. As a result, there may be aggregate racial disparities (e.g., in capital sentences) without clear evidence of improper discrimination in most individual cases (see *McCleskey v. Kemp*, 1987). A growing literature informed by the legal movements of Critical Race Theory and Critical Race Realism is grappling with whether and how discriminatory outcomes that result from implicit biases can be addressed and remediated under legal doctrines that are structured around intentionality (Hunt, 2007; Levinson & Smith, 2012; Parks, Jones, & Cardi, 2008).

Sociological and Criminological Theories

Although the focus of this chapter is on psychological research and theory, it is important to recognize that research on racial bias in the justice system also is heavily informed by theories from the fields of sociology and criminology. For example, focal concerns theory asserts that, when making sentencing judgments, decision makers are influenced by three overarching concerns: the defendants' blameworthiness, community protection, and practical constraints and outcomes (e.g., costs of incarceration). Given the amount and complexity of information that is relevant to those concerns, however, decision makers may use demographic characteristics such as race as a "perceptual shorthand" to facilitate judgments, leading to bias against minority defendants

(Steffensmeier & Demuth, 2001). This theory is highly consistent with the psychological research on stereotyping discussed earlier. Another influential theory is racial threat theory, which predicts that bias against minorities will be strongest in contexts in which their racial or ethnic groups are perceived as a threat to the majority, especially in terms of crime (Crawford, Chiricos, & Kleck, 1998). For example, racial threat may be higher in areas with growing minority populations, high economic inequality, or high crime rates, resulting in larger disparities in criminal justice and legal outcomes.

RESEARCH REVIEW

In this section, I will provide an overview of the literature on the effects of race and ethnicity on the judgments and behavior of police, juries, judges, and other legal actors. This research provides empirical evidence that racial bias occurs at many stages in the justice system, from racial profiling and police officers' decisions to use force, to juries' determinations of guilt in criminal trials, to sentencing outcomes, including the imposition of the death penalty. Each of these biases can have life-altering effects on the individuals, usually racial and ethnic minorities, who experience them. In addition, these biases have a cumulative impact, with small biases at each stage of the process aggregating into substantial racial and ethnic disparities in ultimate legal outcomes. After reviewing the literature on racial bias, I will discuss research examining how race and ethnicity influence attitudes and expectations about the justice system among lay people, affecting their interactions with the system.

The Influence of Race and Ethnicity on Police Behavior

In recent decades, there has been considerable concern about whether and how police officers' behaviors are influenced by the race and ethnicity of the people they serve, especially when those people are seen as potential suspects. These concerns have been extended to a variety of police behaviors, including traffic stops, pedestrian stops (e.g., "stop and frisk"), decisions to conduct searches, and decisions to make arrests. Because police officers frequently serve as the gatekeepers to the justice system, racial bias in any of these domains can be an important contributor to subsequent disparities in conviction and incarceration (Glaser, 2006). In addition, questions have been raised about whether police officers are more likely to use force, including gunfire, against minority suspects, potentially leading to injury or death.

Racial profiling.   There is a common belief that racial and ethnic minorities are targeted for stops by police officers (Weitzer & Tuch, 2005). For example, the expression "driving while Black" refers to the belief that Black drivers are pulled over simply because of their race. Concerns also have been raised about the use of race, ethnicity, and religion in profiles of potential criminals (e.g., drug couriers, terrorists). In general, racial profiling refers to any instance in which the administration of criminal justice is based on a person's race or ethnicity rather than his or her behavior.

The first major study of racial profiling occurred in response to complaints that, as part of the "war on drugs," racial and ethnic minorities driving on the New Jersey Turnpike were disproportionately likely to be pulled over, searched, and arrested by state troopers. As part of the landmark case, *State of New Jersey v. Pedro Soto* (1996), a New Jersey judge commissioned an empirical study of police stops. The study found that police were more likely to stop minority drivers due to the use of drug courier profiles that included race. This finding led to the dismissal of charges against the 17 defendants in the case, as well as a Department of Justice investigation that resulted in significant fines and oversight of the New Jersey State Police (Tillyer, Engel, & Wooldredge, 2008).

Following this case, dozens of studies have been conducted by state and police agencies as well as academic researchers to determine whether racial profiling occurs in various geographical areas. Many of these studies rely on police records of the race and ethnicity of individuals who are stopped, comparing those numbers against a baseline or benchmark to see if minorities are stopped at a rate that exceeds their representation in the relevant population. Other research uses survey methodology to compare the frequency of police encounters across members of different racial and ethnic groups, but these studies are subject to the limits of self-reported data (e.g., socially desirable responses).

As a whole, research on racial profiling indicates that, compared to White individuals, Black individuals are disproportionately likely to be stopped by the police while driving (for reviews, see Engel, Calnon, & Bernard, 2002; Withrow, 2006). For example, studies in Maryland, Ohio, New Jersey, New York City, Philadelphia, and San Diego have found evidence of racial disparities in police stops or other outcomes, such as searches. Although data from the 2008 Police-Public Contact Survey, administered by the Department of Justice, did not show statistically significant differences in traffic stops across Whites, Blacks, and Latinos, once stopped, Black drivers (12.3%) were substantially more likely than White (3.9%) and Latino (5.8%) drivers to be searched (Eith & Durose, 2011). A recent lawsuit in New York City (*Floyd et al. v. City of New York et al.*, 2013) relied heavily on data showing that more than 85% of individuals stopped by New York City police officers were Black or Latino, with most of those searches failing to produce evidence of weapons or criminal behavior. There has been less research focused on racial profiling targeting Latinos, although it is commonly believed to occur due to stereotypes about drug involvement and immigration status (Reitzel, Rice, & Piquero, 2004). For example, a recent Justice Department investigation found that deputies in the sheriff's office in Alamance County, North Carolina, were four to ten times more likely to pull over Latinos than non-Latinos, positioned vehicle checkpoints in locations that disproportionately affected Latinos, and were more likely to check identification for Latino than non-Latino drivers (U.S. Department of Justice, 2012).

Racial profiling can vary considerably across contexts. For example, consistent with racial threat theory, racial profiling may be more likely to occur in neighborhoods with more Black and Latino residents as well as neighborhoods with higher crime rates (Petrocelli, Piquero, & Smith, 2003; Roh & Robinson, 2009). In addition, certain officers ("repeat offenders") may account for a disproportionate number of racial profiling incidents (Bostaph, 2007). In a few jurisdictions, research has failed to find evidence of racial profiling; for instance, racial disparities in traffic stops were not found in Knoxville, Tennessee (Scheb, Lyons, & Wagers, 2009) or Syracuse, New York (Worden, McLean, & Wheeler, 2012).

Research on racial profiling has been criticized on several dimensions. It often lacks a theoretical framework and fails to provide information about the factors that lead police officers to stop racial and ethnic minorities (Engel et al., 2002; Novak & Chamlin, 2012; Tillyer & Hartley, 2010). There is considerable variability in the nature and quality of the data that are collected (e.g., what variables and outcomes are recorded, how race is assessed; Engel et al., 2002). Also, even though studies have used a variety of benchmarks from census estimates to direct observations of the driving population (e.g., from traffic cameras), these benchmarks have been criticized for failing to provide a true baseline comparison (Tillyer & Hartley, 2010). More recent research has attempted to address these concerns. For example, testing predictions derived from racial threat theory, Novak and Chamlin (2012) found evidence that racial profiling is more likely to occur when individuals are driving in neighborhoods that police officers associate with other races (e.g., when White individuals are in "Black neighborhoods") because their race becomes salient and raises suspicions about criminal activity. Other research has used multivariate statistical analyses to control for factors other than race that may influence police stops (e.g., neighborhood type; Tillyer & Hartley, 2010). More research is needed to develop a thorough understanding of how, when, and why racial profiling occurs.

Racial profiling also is difficult to prove in legal cases. Despite the early victory in *State of New Jersey v. Pedro Soto*, most plaintiffs and appellants alleging racial profiling have failed to convince courts of their claims. Courts have expressed skepticism about the accuracy of benchmark data, and plaintiffs and appellants have struggled to establish the discriminatory effect and intent required for an Equal Protection claim. Courts also have shown deference to police officers' subjective assessments of the need

to conduct pat-downs or frisks (Withrow & Dailey, 2012). Perhaps most damaging is the outcome of *Whren et al. v. United States* (1996), in which the Supreme Court held that searches are permissible if there was any objective reason for police to stop a driver, even that reason was clearly pretextual, such as failure to signal a lane change. This decision made it substantially easier for police officers to engage in and justify racially motivated stops.

Decisions to arrest. In addition to being more likely to make stops, police officers are more likely to arrest racial and ethnic minorities than White people. A meta-analysis of 27 studies by Kochel, Wilson, and Mastrofski (2011) found overall odds ratios of 1.32–1.52, indicating that minorities are approximately 30% more likely than White individuals to be arrested. This effect is consistent across a number of potential moderators, including characteristics of the offense, suspect behavior, criminal history, and study methods. Further, the effects of race continue to be significant even when multivariate analyses control for these factors. Other research shows bias in decisions to arrest related to victim race, with crimes involving Black and Latino victims being less likely to result in arrests (e.g., Briggs & Opsal, 2012). Given that arrest is the entry point to legal proceedings that may result in sanctions such as incarceration, it is important to expand our understanding of the ways that race and ethnicity influence police officers' decisions to make arrests.

Use of force. In Section I, I discussed the case of Amadou Diallo, a West African immigrant who was shot 41 times by New York City police officers after putting his hand into his pocket to reach for his wallet. Many observers questioned the role of race in Diallo's death, wondering whether the officers would have waited longer before shooting or fired fewer rounds if Diallo had been White instead of Black.

Statistical analyses of police records provide evidence that race influences decisions to use force. For example, data collected by the U.S. Department of Justice from the late 1970s to mid-2000s indicate that a disproportionate number of deaths caused by police officers involve Black men (J. M. Brown & Langan, 2001; Mumola, 2007). Recent studies show that police officers are more likely to use Tasers on minority suspects (Gau, Mosher, & Pratt, 2010), especially when those suspects are attempting to flee (Crow & Adrion, 2011). Evidence of racial bias in police officers' use of force also comes from surveys of U.S. residents; for example, in the 2008 Police-Public Contact Survey, Black respondents were more likely than Whites and Latinos to indicate that force had been used against them (Eith & Durose, 2011).

After the death of Amadou Diallo, psychologists began to conduct simulation studies to develop a fuller understanding of the effects of race on decisions to shoot. These studies generally use variants on a research paradigm developed by Correll, Park, Judd, and Wittenbrink (2002) in which participants, either police officers or lay people, engage in a computerized first-person shooter task similar to a video game. In the task, participants are exposed to a series of images of White and Black individuals who are holding objects that either are guns or non-weapons (e.g., cell phones). After each image, participants press one of two keys to indicate whether they would "shoot" or "not shoot" the individual. Both the accuracy of their judgments (i.e., shooting armed individuals, not shooting unarmed individuals) and the time required to make them are recorded and analyzed to determine whether they are influenced by race.

Research using this paradigm consistently has found evidence of shooter bias in both police officers and lay participants. Two patterns of bias have emerged. Biases in reaction time show that participants make quicker decisions about stereotype-consistent targets; that is, they are faster to shoot armed individuals when they are Black and to not shoot unarmed individuals when they are White (Correll et al., 2002; Correll, Park, Judd, & Wittenbrink, 2007; Sadler, Correll, Park, & Judd, 2012). Some studies also have found biases in accuracy in which participants are more likely to mistakenly shoot unarmed Black targets and fail to shoot armed White targets (Correll et al., 2002; Greenwald, Oakes, & Hoffman, 2003; Plant & Peruche, 2005; Plant, Peruche, & Butz, 2005). The evidence for accuracy biases is less consistent, however, with some research suggesting

that police officers actually may be more accurate at distinguishing guns from other objects when targets are Black or Latino (Sadler et al., 2012). Across studies, signal detection analyses indicate that police and lay participants tend to have a lower threshold for deciding to shoot Black rather than White targets.

Although most research on shooter bias has focused on comparisons between Black and White male targets, two recent studies have extended this scope. Sadler et al. (2012) compared shooting decisions for Black, Latino, Asian, and White men. Response time bias was strongest for Black men; however, police officers also were quicker to shoot armed Latinos than Whites, and they were especially slow to shoot Asian targets. Plant, Goplen, and Kunstman (2011) examined the role of gender in shooter bias and found that lay participants often failed to respond appropriately (i.e., had lower accuracy) when women were holding weapons. Combining gender and race, lay people produced the highest number of errors by shooting unarmed Black men and failing to shoot armed White women. This finding suggests that, at least for lay people, stereotypes about gender differences in aggression and protective attitudes towards women can moderate the effects of race on shooting decisions.

Contextual factors also moderate the magnitude of shooter bias. Shooter bias may diminish with practice in contexts in which race is not diagnostic of weapon possession (e.g., when White and Black individuals are equally likely to have guns; Plant & Peruche, 2005; Plant et al., 2005). In contrast, shooter bias does not diminish (Plant et al., 2005) and in fact may become stronger (Correll, Park, Judd, & Wittenbrink, 2007) in contexts in which members of a particular group actually are more likely to have weapons. This finding may occur because participants see race as diagnostic (Plant et al., 2005) or because seeing Black individuals with guns primes racial stereotypes (Correll, Park, Judd, & Wittenbrink, 2007). In addition, shooter bias is stronger in neutral contexts than in threatening contexts (e.g., near dilapidated buildings), although this difference reflects an increased likelihood of shooting White targets in threatening contexts (Correll, Wittenbrink, Park, Judd, & Goyle, 2011). One interpretation of this effect is that Black targets may be perceived as threatening even in neutral contexts, whereas White targets may require additional cues to be perceived as a danger.

Research also has investigated personal characteristics associated with shooter bias. Shooter bias does not tend to vary based on the race or gender of the actor (Correll et al., 2002; Sadler et al., 2012). It does, however, tend to be stronger among police officers who work in cities that are large, have more violent crime, or have larger minority populations (Correll, Park, Judd, Wittenbrink, et al., 2007). The evidence linking shooter bias to racial attitudes is somewhat inconsistent. Some research indicates that individuals with greater racial prejudice and stereotypes about Black criminality show stronger shooter bias, at least before practice (Peruche & Plant, 2006), whereas other research suggests that shooter bias is not related to personal views (Correll et al., 2002; Correll, Park, Judd, Wittenbrink, et al., 2007). Likewise, some research shows that police officers who have had more positive contact with Black people show less shooter bias (Peruche & Plant, 2006), whereas other research shows no relation (Correll, Park, Judd, Wittenbrink, et al., 2007) or even the reverse pattern (Correll et al., 2002).

Overall, there is substantial evidence that police officers' decisions to use force are influenced by racial associations with criminality and danger. Analyses of police records, large-scale surveys, and simulation studies all show that police officers are more likely to use force, including firing weapons, when suspects are Black. Although there is less research, disparities may occur for other groups, such as Latinos, as well. Because decisions to use force can have life or death consequences, it is critical to continue studying racial biases in this domain so that effective training and interventions can be developed.

Jury Selection

During the process of jury selection (*voir dire*), potential jurors (venire members) can be excused for two reasons. Challenges for cause can be used to remove jurors who indicate that they cannot be impartial in a given case, due to familiarity with the parties or personal biases. In addition, attorneys can use a limited number of peremptory challenges to remove jurors who they do not believe will be sympathetic to their case. There is a longstanding concern that attorneys may use peremptory challenges in a racially discriminatory manner to exclude Black and other minority venire members from juries. Such exclusions may reflect concerns that Black jurors will be more lenient in cases involving same-race defendants. They also may be based on stereotypes about the influence of race on jurors' judgments, such as beliefs that Whites are softer on corporate crime and Black people distrust police officers (Sommers & Norton, 2008). For more on jury selection and decision making, see Chapter 10, this volume.

Case law. The U.S. Supreme Court first addressed the use of race in jury selection in the case *Swain v. Alabama* (1965), in which a Black defendant in Talladega County, Alabama, was convicted of rape and sentenced to death by an all-White jury. At the time, 26% of the population of Talladega County was Black, yet no Black person had been selected for a jury in over a decade. Although the Court acknowledged that it would be unconstitutional to systematically exclude venire members on the basis of race, it affirmed Swain's conviction and held that defendants must provide evidence of an ongoing pattern of purposeful discrimination in order to challenge a prosecutor's use of peremptory challenges.

This threshold proved exceedingly difficult to meet, and the Court revisited the issue in the case, *Batson v. Kentucky* (1986). In *Batson*, the Court held that the use of race in peremptory challenges violated the Equal Protection Clause and outlined a less stringent process for establishing racial bias. The defense must make a *prima facie* ("at first look") case that racial discrimination may have occurred. If that argument is accepted, the prosecution must provide race-neutral justifications for challenging each potential juror. The trial court then must determine whether discrimination occurred (i.e., whether the explanations are actually race-neutral or simply pretextual).

The *Batson* decision soon was followed by other cases that extended its scope (e.g., to civil cases, *Edmonson v. Leesville Concrete Co.*, 1991, and women, *J. E. B. v. Alabama*, 1994). Subsequent cases also have provided more guidance about how to determine whether a justification is race-neutral. For example, *Miller-El v. Dretke* (2005) established that potential jurors from one racial group cannot be excused for reasons that do not lead to challenges for potential jurors from other racial groups. Other cases, however, such as *Hernandez v. New York* (1991), have upheld the use of questionably neutral peremptory challenges, such as excusing Latino jurors who speak Spanish on the basis that they might not rely on the translations of witness testimony provided by a court interpreter.

Research on the effects of race on peremptory challenges. Despite legal prohibitions, archival research provides strong evidence that race influences the use of peremptory challenges. A common finding is that prosecutors are more likely to strike Black potential jurors, whereas defense attorneys are likely to excuse White potential jurors (Baldus, Woodworth, Zuckerman, Weiner, & Broffitt, 2001; Clark, Boccaccini, Caillouet, & Chaplin, 2007; Rose, 1999). For example, Baldus et al. (2001) found that, over a 16-year period, prosecutors in Philadelphia County struck approximately twice as many Black as non-Black potential jurors, with defense attorneys showing the reverse pattern. The tendency for prosecutors to excuse Black potential jurors was strongest in cases involving a Black defendant and non-Black murder victim. Because of differences in population size and the fact that Blacks tend to be underrepresented in venires (Fukurai & Krooth, 2003), bias in prosecutors' use of peremptory challenges may eliminate most or all of the potential Black jurors from a trial. A recent report by the Equal Justice Initiative (2010) found evidence of substantial racial discrimination in jury selection in eight southern states, including evidence that Black potential jurors were systematically excluded from death penalty cases involving Black defendants. In some counties, almost no Black individuals were selected as jurors, leading most juries to be nonrepresentative of their communities.

Challenges alleging the race-based use of peremptory challenges frequently are unsuccessful.

An analysis of every published *Batson* challenge from 1986 to 1993 revealed that *prima facie* cases of racial bias were established in only 62.2% of the cases, and actual violations were found in only 17.6% of the cases (Melilli, 1996). A more recent analysis of 184 federal appeals from 2002 to 2006 found that only 12.3% of the appeals were completely successful. In 79% of the cases, the higher courts held that the proffered justifications were race-neutral (Gabbidon, Kowal, Jordan, Roberts, & Vincenzi, 2008). In both studies, common justifications for peremptory challenges that were accepted by judges as race-neutral included behavior during *voir dire* (e.g., body language), criminal record, assumptions about bias toward one side of the case, assumptions of economic hardship, and personal characteristics, such as marriage, age, or employment. The strongest predictor of successful challenges was disparate treatment of Black (or other minority) versus White potential jurors; other predictors included insufficient questioning (i.e., not gaining enough information before striking jurors) and inability to explain challenges or provide race-neutral justifications (Gabbidon et al., 2008; Melilli, 1996). The low rate of successful *Batson* challenges may reflect courts' deference to attorneys as well as defense attorneys' lack of comfort and training in pursuing these challenges (Equal Justice Initiative, 2010).

Experimental research suggests that both legal professionals and lay people are facile at generating race-neutral explanations for decisions to excuse Black potential jurors. In an experiment by Sommers and Norton (2007), practicing attorneys, advanced law students, and college students were asked to act as a prosecutor with one remaining peremptory challenge in a trial involving a Black defendant. Participants read about two potential jurors, one who was skeptical of forensic science and statistics, and another who had written about police misconduct as a journalist. The races of the potential jurors were manipulated across conditions, such that one was presented as White and the other as Black. Regardless of the information they were given, the majority of participants used their peremptory to strike the Black juror. When asked to explain their decision, however, participants used the personal information to provide an ostensibly race-neutral justification. Notably, the investigation by the Equal Justice Initiative (2010) found that some district attorneys' offices provide training for new prosecutors about how to generate race-neutral justifications.

Conclusion and implications. In sum, archival and experimental research suggests that, despite *Batson* prohibitions, peremptory challenges often are influenced by race, leading to nonrepresentative juries. Attorneys are able to generate explanations for their challenges based on ostensibly nonracial factors, and judges seem inclined to accept them, resulting in a low success rate for *Batson* challenges. It is important to note that the exclusion of racial and ethnic minorities from jury service can lead to a range of negative outcomes beyond violating the rights of potential jurors. Discrimination in jury selection can diminish public confidence in the jury system; people are less likely to view verdicts as fair and just when juries are predominantly or entirely White (Diamond & Ellis, 2003; Fukurai & Krooth, 2003; MacCoun & Tyler, 1988). In addition, the presence of an all-White jury may encourage subtle expressions of bias, such as arguments based on racial stereotypes, by attorneys and judges during trials (Fukurai & Krooth, 2003).

The Effects of Race, Ethnicity, and Culture on Jury Functioning

Another important argument for the inclusion of racial and ethnic minorities on juries is that their participation may change the nature and potentially the outcome of jury deliberation. A small body of research has addressed this issue and related questions about the influence of race, ethnicity, and culture on jurors' behaviors and judgments.

Racial composition of juries. In the case *Peters v. Kiff* (1972), the Supreme Court ruled that excluding Black jurors constitutes a violation of due process for defendants, even if those defendants are White. The Court held, "When any large and identifiable segment of the community is excluded from jury service, the effect is to remove from the jury room qualities of human nature and varieties of human experience" (p. 503). In other words,

diverse juries may have advantages over more homogeneous juries that affect the nature and quality of their verdicts. Diverse juries may contain a wider range of attitudes and experiences, generating more perspectives from which to view the case and evidence as well as greater information exchange. In addition, the inclusion of racial and ethnic minorities may sensitize jurors to the possibility of racial bias and lead to the inhibition of prejudice (Sommers & Adekanmbi, 2008).

Empirical support for these arguments was produced by Sommers (2006), who compared mock juries that consisted of either six White jurors or four White and two Black jurors. In a case involving a Black defendant, the diverse juries deliberated for a longer period of time, discussed more of the evidence presented, and made fewer factual errors in their discussions. They also were more likely to consider the role of the defendant's race in the case. Notably, these patterns were found for both Black and White jurors, suggesting that diverse juries promote more systematic processing and deliberation in all jurors.

Jury participation. A few studies also have examined how race, ethnicity, and culture may influence participation in deliberation by individual jurors, although the results have been somewhat mixed. In a sample of jurors from trials held in diverse, urban jurisdictions, self-reported participation in deliberation was highest for Black jurors, followed by White and Latino jurors, whose participation did not differ significantly. The lowest levels of participation were reported by Asian American women (Cornwell & Hans, 2011). Self-reported participation did not vary based on the juries' racial or gender composition. In contrast, research analyzing jurors' perceptions of their peers found that race and gender did not predict jury participation or influence over and above upper class status (York & Cornwell, 2006). The discrepancies between these findings may reflect differences in their methods or the jurisdictions studied.

Cultural values and practices also may affect the communication strategies jurors use in deliberation. People with more independent (individualist) self-construals tend to engage in more direct communication behaviors (e.g., clear statements of one's opinion, even in the face of disagreement) than do people with more interdependent (collectivist) self-construals (Gudykunst, Matsumoto, Ting-Toomey, & Nishida, 1996). Consistent with this finding, a survey of U.S. jurors found that White, Latino, and Black jurors reported higher levels of participation and direct communication in jury deliberation than did Asian and East Indian jurors (Hunt, 2014). Mediational analyses indicated that racial and ethnic group predicted independent self-construal and direct communication style, which in turn predicted deliberation behavior. Thus, jurors with certain cultural orientations may express their views more strongly and potentially exert more influence in deliberations.

Cultural influences on juror judgments. The cultural backgrounds of jurors also may influence the judgments they make about cases. Levinson and Peng (2004) argued that, although psychological researchers and legal scholars tend to assume that judgment biases in civil cases are similar across jurors, this assumption contradicts the sizable body of research on cultural psychology. For example, when explaining the causes of behavior, Westerners (individualists) tend to overweigh personal factors and underweigh situational factors, leading them to be disproportionately likely to make internal attributions (i.e., the fundamental attribution error). In contrast, due to their collectivist orientation, East Asians pay more attention to situational influences and therefore do not show this bias (Morris & Peng, 1994). As a result, European American jurors might overweigh a civil defendant's causal responsibility in a torts case, whereas Asian Americans might, if anything, underweigh it. Another possibility is that, because collectivists place a greater emphasis on social norms and collective well-being, they might have more negative reactions to crimes that reflect immoral behavior that could harm the community, such as drug dealing or sexual offenses (Levinson & Peng, 2004). Despite the strength of these theoretical arguments, there has been little empirical research applying cultural psychology to juror decision making.

Given the increasing diversity of the jury pool, more research is needed to examine cultural, as well as racial and ethnic, influences on juror judgments (for a similar argument about Latino jurors, see Padilla, Miller, & Broadus, 2008).

Juror and Jury Decision Making

Once jurors have been selected, concern shifts to their ability to accurately and impartially evaluate evidence and render fair and appropriate verdicts. In particular, it is important to determine whether jurors' judgments are influenced by the race of defendants, witnesses, or legal professionals, such as attorneys. In this section, I will review research examining the effects of race on jurors' verdicts and related judgments, emphasizing factors that moderate the impact of race and psychological processes that may underlie those effects. Research on jurors' recommendations for sentencing will be discussed in the next section.

Most research on juror decision making conducted by forensic psychologists has relied on experimental mock juror paradigms in which lay participants read about or watch part or all of a criminal trial, then render verdicts and make other judgments (e.g., defendant ratings; see Chapter 10, this volume). These analog experiments have many strengths. They provide researchers with the opportunity to manipulate key variables (e.g., defendant race) while holding constant and controlling all other aspects of the trial. They also allow for measures that assess the judgment processes underlying verdict decisions. Experimental research has been criticized, however, for lacking construct validity (e.g., realistic trial materials and procedures) and external validity (i.e., generalizability to real-world contexts; for reviews of these arguments, see Devine, 2012; Wiener, Krauss, & Lieberman, 2011). In addition, many studies use college students rather than community participants and do not provide jurors with the opportunity to engage in deliberation. Although most scholars believe that research using student samples and individual judgments produces results similar to studies with community samples and deliberation, differences have emerged in some contexts (Bornstein, 1999; Wiener et al., 2011).

Focusing on race, two other important concerns emerge. First, the vast majority of experimental research has involved comparisons between White and Black defendants. There is a strong need for more research examining judgments about defendants from other racial and ethnic groups, such as Latinos, indigenous populations, and individuals of Middle Eastern descent. Second, virtually all research investigating the effects of race on juror judgments has involved criminal rather than civil contexts (for exceptions, see Foley & Pigott, 2002; S. L. Schwartz & Hunt, 2011). The lack of research investigating the effects of race and ethnicity on judgments about liability, damages, and other civil issues creates an important limitation in our understanding of race in the justice system.

Experimental research. The most basic question about race addressed in mock juror studies is whether, holding other elements of a trial constant, the race of a criminal defendant influences jurors' verdicts. Notably, racial bias can be indicated by different patterns of verdicts. One possibility is a consistent tendency for jurors to be more likely to make guilty verdicts for defendants from racial or ethnic minority groups, due to prejudice, stereotyping, or related processes (see Section II). A variant on this pattern is the similarity-leniency effect, in which jurors make more favorable judgments about defendants from their own racial or ethnic group (i.e., show ingroup favoritism). A third pattern, known as the black sheep effect, occurs when jurors make harsher judgments about ingroup members who engage in extremely negative behavior, presumably to distance themselves from those individuals and maintain the positivity of the ingroup (Kerr, Hymes, Anderson, & Weathers, 1995).

Research has provided support for each of these patterns of bias, although the strongest support in the experimental literature is for the similarity-leniency effect. Three meta-analyses have examined the effects of race on mock jurors' guilt judgments for Black versus White defendants. The earliest meta-analysis (Mazzella & Feingold, 1994) did not find evidence of an overall bias in verdicts against Black defendants among 21 studies including participants from different racial and ethnic backgrounds.

The more recent meta-analyses (Devine & Caughlin, 2014; T. L. Mitchell et al., 2005) both found evidence of a small overall similarity-leniency effect (ds = 0.06, 0.09, respectively), with jurors making more favorable judgments about same-race defendants. These meta-analyses, however, did not test for general bias against Black defendants. Importantly, all three meta-analyses found substantial variability in the effects produced across studies, indicating that other factors moderate racial bias in juror judgments (see below). Finally, the black sheep effect has been demonstrated by Kerr et al. (1995), who found that jurors made harsher judgments of same-race defendants when trial evidence was strong rather than weak. Notably, this effect only occurred when jurors anticipated deliberating in a jury in which their race would be in the numerical minority, suggesting that the black sheep effect may occur primarily when jurors anticipate having to "defend their race" to others and potentially explaining why other research has not found the effect (Taylor & Hosch, 2004).

A much smaller number of studies have investigated bias against defendants from non-Black minority groups. Based on seven studies (some unpublished), the Devine and Caughlin (2014) meta-analysis found that White jurors made significantly higher guilt judgments (d = 0.11) for Latino than White defendants. Again, there was substantial variability within the effects; for example, Esqueda, Espinoza, and Culhane (2008) found that White mock jurors were only more likely to convict Mexican American defendants if they also were portrayed as low SES. With respect to defendants of Middle Eastern descent, one study found that jurors were more likely to find Middle Eastern defendants guilty when they were primed with stereotypes related to terrorism (Adams, Bryden, & Griffith, 2011), but another study failed to find overall evidence of bias against this group (Maeder, Dempsey, & Pozzulo, 2012). More research is clearly needed to provide a stronger understanding of bias against non-Black minorities.

Moderators of racial bias in verdicts. Research indicates that the magnitude of racial biases in juror verdicts is influenced by a number of factors. As discussed earlier, a key moderator involves juror race, with jurors tending to make more favorable judgments of same-race than other-race defendants (similarity-leniency effect). This pattern has been found in judgments made by individual jurors (Devine & Caughlin, 2014; T. L. Mitchell et al., 2005), as well as verdicts reached by deliberating juries (Bradbury & Williams, 2013; Perez, Hosch, Ponder, & Trejo, 1993). The effect appears to be particularly strong for Black jurors (Devine & Caughlin, 2014; T. L. Mitchell et al., 2005), who, in addition to showing ingroup favoritism, may try to safeguard against the possibility of institutional bias against Black defendants (Sommers & Adekanmbi, 2008).

Other moderators of racial bias involve individual differences among jurors. For example, individuals who are high in social dominance orientation (SDO) support hierarchical relations in which certain social groups are dominant and have greater access to resources and opportunities. These individuals tend to endorse the status quo and subscribe to beliefs that justify group inequalities, including racial prejudice (Pratto, Sidanius, & Levin, 2006). In contrast, individuals who are low in SDO tend to have more egalitarian views and hold beliefs that challenge existing social hierarchies. Consistent with these ideologies, mock jurors who are high in SDO make harsher judgments of Black versus White defendants, whereas jurors low in SDO actually may make more lenient judgments of Black defendants (Kemmelmeier, 2005). Although it would be reasonable to expect that direct measures of racial prejudice would show similar patterns, clear relationships between racial prejudice and juror judgments are not always found, potentially because contextual factors may increase or decrease the degree to which individuals act on prejudiced views (e.g., Cohn, Bucolo, Pride, & Sommers, 2009).

Racial bias also can be moderated by characteristics of the crime, such as type of offense. Jurors are more likely to convict defendants who commit crimes that are stereotypically associated with their race. For example, Black defendants are more likely to be convicted of violent crimes, whereas White defendants are more likely to be convicted of crimes like fraud and embezzlement (Gordon, Bindrim, McNicholas, & Walden, 1988; Jones & Kaplan, 2003).

An important contextual moderator involves racial salience. Aversive Racism Theory (Gaertner & Dovidio, 1986; Pearson et al., 2009) posits that most White individuals want to be nonprejudiced, and when they are aware of the potential for bias, they try to avoid it. Accordingly, Sommers and Ellsworth (2000, 2001) predicted that juror bias should be reduced when criminal trials are racially charged and the potential for discrimination is salient. They tested this prediction by manipulating the presence of racially charged language (e.g., "you know better than to talk that way about a Black man") or allegations of discrimination in mock trials. Results were consistent with aversive racism, indicating that, when cases were racially charged, White jurors made comparable judgments for Black and White defendants, but when racial issues were not made salient, they made harsher judgments of the Black defendant.

Although a broader range of manipulations is needed (Sommers & Ellsworth, 2009), the concepts of aversive racism and racial salience may explain several moderators of juror bias. For example, studies that provide judicial instructions and use dichotomous verdicts rather than scale ratings of guilt show weaker effects for race compared to studies that do not (T. L. Mitchell et al., 2005; Pfeifer & Bernstein, 2003). These findings suggest that reminding jurors of the need for fairness and reducing the ambiguity of trial judgments may reduce racial bias.

Psychological processes underlying juror bias. Some studies also have assessed the influence of defendant race on other judgments by jurors, which may serve as mechanisms through which race influences final verdicts. One mechanism involves attributions or inferences about the causes of behavior. When criminal behaviors are assumed to reflect the defendant's stable disposition rather than unstable situational factors, jurors may be more likely to convict and support severe punishment. Jurors may show ingroup favoritism by making situational attributions for criminal behavior in ingroup members, but dispositional attributions for the same behavior in outgroup members, especially when racial salience is low (Sommers & Ellsworth, 2000). In addition, jurors may be more likely to make dispositional attributions when criminal behavior is consistent with racial stereotypes (Bodenhausen & Wyer, 1985; Jones & Kaplan, 2003). A related mechanism involves judgments about the blameworthiness of defendants. Holding behavior constant, jurors may see minority defendants as more blameworthy or culpable than White defendants (Esqueda et al., 2008; Rattan et al., 2012).

In addition, jurors may process trial information in a manner that supports harsher judgments of Black defendants. For example, Hodson et al. (2005) found that White mock jurors were influenced by incriminating but inadmissible DNA evidence when the defendant was portrayed as Black, but not when he was portrayed as White. In another study involving a murder trial with a Black defendant, White mock jurors judged prosecution witnesses to be more credible than did Black jurors and subsequently were more likely to render guilty verdicts (Abshire & Bornstein, 2003). Jurors who make race-based dispositional attributions about a defendant's behavior may be especially likely to engage in biased processing of trial evidence (Bodenhausen & Wyer, 1985)

Not all research shows that biases in jurors' processing of trial information disadvantage minority defendants. In some cases, jurors show a "watchdog" effect, giving greater scrutiny to the strength of evidence when defendants are Black rather than White (Sargent & Bradfield, 2004). This attention may stem from a desire to avoid making biased judgments against Black defendants. Jurors also may consider evidence more carefully in cases involving crimes that are inconsistent with stereotypes about a defendant's race (Jones & Kaplan, 2003). Similarly, in some cases, stereotype-inconsistent evidence may be more powerful than stereotype-consistent evidence. Maeder and Hunt (2011) found that mock jurors were more influenced by character evidence when it challenged racial expectations, such that positive character evidence had a greater influence on judgments about a Black defendant, but negative character evidence had a stronger effect on judgments about a White defendant. Because jurors may base initial impressions of defendants on racial stereotypes, stereotype-inconsistent character evidence

may appear to be more informative or novel than stereotype-confirming character evidence. Thus, in at least some situations, jurors may be attuned to evidence that suggests minority defendants are not guilty.

Conclusions. In sum, research shows a small tendency for jurors' verdicts to be influenced by defendant race, with the most common pattern involving more favorable judgments for same-race defendants. The strongest influence on jurors' verdicts, however, is the strength of the evidence rather than the race of the defendant. Although several factors influence the magnitude of juror bias, common themes emerge. Consistent with Aversive Racism Theory, many moderators of juror bias involve characteristics of the case, juror, or decision-making context that affect jurors' sensitivity to bias or appear to provide nonracial justifications for biased judgments (Cohn, Bucolo, & Sommers, 2012); in addition, factors such as type of crime may appear to justify the use of stereotypes or prejudice. Overall, it seems likely that race generally exerts relatively subtle effects on verdicts, with stereotypes, prejudice, and ingroup favoritism acting as frameworks that can influence the ways jurors interpret and organize the evidence, make inferences about the defendant, and determine which of the competing "stories" about the events in question is most plausible (Pennington & Hastie, 1986).

Non-Capital Sentencing Decisions

As discussed in the Importance of the Problem section, there are substantial racial and ethnic disparities in the rate of incarceration in the United States, especially for men. Controlling for the size of each group in the general population, in 2010, Latinos were 2.6 times more likely and Black men were 6.4 times more likely than White men to be incarcerated (Glaze, 2011). Similar but smaller disparities exist for the incarceration rates of women. Given these statistics, it is important to determine whether and how race and ethnicity affect sentencing decisions (for a review of research on sentencing, see Chapter 14, this volume). In particular, it is critical to assess whether racial and ethnic minorities are more likely to be incarcerated and/or receive more severe sentences than are White defendants after controlling for legally relevant factors such as type of offense, crime characteristics, and criminal history.

These issues have been examined in a substantial number of studies conducted by forensic psychologists, criminologists, and sociologists. As discussed earlier, research by forensic psychologists tends to rely on experimental paradigms in which mock jurors make sentencing recommendations after reading about or viewing a trial. Despite their many strengths (see earlier discussion), the generalizability of such experiments to real-world criminal sentencing has been questioned given the lack of consequences for mock jurors' judgments, as well as the fact that sentencing decisions usually are made by judges (for reviews of these arguments, see Devine, 2012; Wiener et al., 2011). In contrast, most of the research conducted by criminologists and sociologists has involved archival analyses of actual criminal outcomes, for which important variables related to the defendant, crime, jurisdiction, etc., have been coded from case records. Using this strategy, researchers can compare outcomes in a large sample of cases involving defendants from different racial and ethnic groups while statistically controlling for legally relevant factors that may vary across cases. Experimental and archival studies have complementary strengths and weaknesses, and together they provide converging evidence about racial disparities in sentencing.

Experimental research.   Three meta-analyses have assessed the effects of defendant race, operationalized as Black versus White, on sentencing judgments made by mock jurors. The earliest meta-analysis (Sweeney & Haney, 1992) found a small but significant tendency ($d = 0.17$) for White mock jurors to give harsher punishments to Black than White defendants. Two years later, another meta-analysis (Mazzella & Feingold, 1994) failed to show support ($d = 0.06$) for a general bias against Black defendants. Instead, sentencing biases varied by crime, with Black defendants receiving harsher punishments for negligent homicide and White defendants receiving harsher punishments for fraud. There are several reasons for these differences; perhaps most importantly, the Mazzella and Feingold

(1994) meta-analysis included participants from different racial and ethnic backgrounds, whereas the Sweeney and Haney analysis focused on judgments made by White participants, which may have resulted in stronger racial bias.

The more recent meta-analysis (T. L. Mitchell et al., 2005) operationalized sentencing bias as recommending more severe sentences for outgroup members (i.e., individuals of another race) and therefore did not report an overall comparison of sentences recommended for Black versus White defendants. Consistent with guilt judgments (see previous section), there was a small but significant effect ($d = 0.18$) in which mock jurors recommended harsher sentences for defendants from other racial groups or, conversely, showed a similarity-leniency effect for same-race defendants. This effect was stronger among Black rather than White mock jurors and community members rather than student samples.

Thus, experimental research provides evidence that defendant race has a small effect on sentencing recommendations made by mock jurors. However, differences in operational definitions of bias as well as samples make it difficult to generalize across the three meta-analyses. In addition, all of the meta-analyses found that the magnitude of sentencing bias varied substantially as a result of other factors. Thus, additional research is needed to provide a more complete understanding of racial and ethnic bias in lay judgments about criminal sentencing.

Archival research.   The most rigorous meta-analysis of archival research on sentencing disparities comes from O. Mitchell (2005), who synthesized 116 independent effects from 71 published and unpublished studies that compared sentences for Black and White defendants while controlling for both offense severity and criminal history. Overall results indicated that Black defendants tended to receive more severe sentences than did White defendants in both non-federal and federal courts; however, the effects were small and variable. There were larger effects when outcomes measures involved the decision to incarcerate or discretionary punitiveness rather than sentence severity (e.g., length). In addition, there were smaller effects for studies that more precisely measured other important case factors, such as criminal history, offense severity, type of counsel, and defendant SES. However, racial disparities in sentencing persisted even when analyses controlled for all of these factors. Further, although the magnitude of racial disparities was greater in cases prior to 1970, there was no evidence that disparities had decreased since that time.

Despite their growing representation in the U.S. population, there are fewer studies that have examined sentencing outcomes for other racial and ethnic minority groups, such as Latinos. An analysis of case outcomes for nearly 10,000 felony defendants in large, urban counties found that, controlling for offense severity, criminal history, and other relevant factors, Latino defendants were 45% more likely than White defendants to receive sentences involving incarceration (Demuth & Steffensmeier, 2004a). The likelihood of incarceration for Latino defendants was slightly slower than, but not significantly different from, the likelihood for Black defendants. Other studies have found that Latino drug court defendants in North Carolina were actually more likely than Black or White defendants to receive incarceration (Brennan & Spohn, 2008), and that Latino and Black defendants in Florida were approximately 20% more likely than White defendants to be designated as "habitual offenders," which is a discretionary sentencing enhancement (Caravelis, Chiricos, & Bales, 2011). In addition, Latinos may face challenges in court due to both actual and assumed citizenship status and English language ability. Although judges are prohibited from considering national origin when making sentencing decisions, they still may be affected by common views of immigrants as threatening and prone to committing crime (Wolfe, Pyrooz, & Spohn, 2011). An analysis of over 58,000 federal cases in 2006 found higher incarceration rates for immigrants who were illegally in the United States, the majority of whom were Latinos, followed by immigrants who were legally in the country, followed by U.S. citizens. Notably, the reverse pattern was found for sentence length, perhaps due to expectations that non-citizens would be deported. Thus, although more studies are needed, research suggests that Latinos experience sentencing

disparities at a level that may be comparable to disparities found for Black individuals. These findings also suggest that analyses that do not include ethnicity and therefore classify the majority of Latino defendants as "White" may underestimate true sentencing disparities between Black and non-Latino White defendants (Demuth & Steffensmeier, 2004a).

In contrast, an analysis of more than 165,000 cases from 1997 to 2000 found that, controlling for relevant factors, Asian defendants were actually less likely to be incarcerated than White, Black, or Latino defendants (B. D. Johnson & Betsinger, 2009). They also were significantly more likely to receive substantial assistance departures, that is, reduced sentences in return for providing information to prosecutors, although those departures did not account for the difference in rate of incarceration. This research indicates that racial disparities in sentencing may depend on the nature of stereotypical assumptions about specific groups, with Asians receiving less severe sentences in part due to the perception that they are a "model minority."

Since the Sentencing Reform Act of 1984, sentencing guidelines, including sentencing enhancements and mandatory terms, have been enacted in many jurisdictions in order to reduce judicial discretion and variability in sentencing. Although in theory such policies should reduce racial disparities, many argue that they actually increase disparities because racial and ethnic minorities may be disproportionately likely to commit certain crimes with high mandatory sentences (e.g., possession of crack cocaine) and to meet certain sentencing enhancements (e.g., proximity to protected public spaces, possession of a weapon; Davis, 2011; Schlesinger, 2011). For example, longitudinal analyses for male defendants in the states of Alabama, California, Illinois, New Jersey, and Texas found that, when sentencing enhancements and mandatory terms were introduced, incarceration rates increased across racial groups, but the changes disproportionately impacted Black defendants (Schlesinger, 2011). Likewise, the O. Mitchell (2005) meta-analysis found that racial disparities in federal cases increased after the introduction of federal sentencing guidelines. Although not every study has produced consistent evidence (e.g., Wooldredge, Griffin, & Rauschenberg, 2005), overall, the data suggest that sentencing reforms may disadvantage minority defendants and increase racial disparities, thereby constituting an important form of institutionalized racism (for reviews, see Free, 1997; Schlesinger, 2011; Volume 1, Chapter 7, this handbook; Chapter 17, this volume).

Moderators of sentencing disparities. As mentioned earlier, there is substantial variability in the size of racial and ethnic disparities in sentencing (Mazzella & Feingold, 1994; O. Mitchell, 2005; T. L. Mitchell et al., 2005). A number of studies have investigated potential moderators related to the defendant, decision-maker, crime, and broader context of the case.

Starting with defendant characteristics, individuals whose appearance is more consistent with the prototype for a minority group tend to receive harsher sentences. For example, analyses of case records reveal that individuals receive more severe sentences when they have more Afrocentric facial features (Blair, Judd, & Chapleau, 2004) and darker skin tones (Viglione, Hannon, & DeFina, 2011). Also, consistent with prison population statistics (Glaze, 2011), defendant gender moderates sentencing bias, such that racial and ethnic disparities tend to be larger for men than women (Brennan & Spohn, 2009; Steffensmeier & Demuth, 2006).

Characteristics of the decision maker also moderate sentencing disparities. As discussed earlier, experimental studies indicate that mock jurors often show a similarity-leniency effect, recommending less severe sentences for defendants from their own racial group (T. L. Mitchell et al., 2005). The converse pattern of outgroup punitiveness was shown by Daudistel and colleagues (Daudistel, Hosch, Holmes, & Graves, 1999), who found that juries with larger proportions of Latinos recommended harsher sentences for White defendants. Again, the similarity-leniency effect tends to be stronger for Black jurors, who, in addition to ingroup favoritism, may be influenced by a desire to protect against institutional bias (Sommers & Adekanmbi, 2008). Likewise, racial bias in sentencing may be lower in jurisdictions with greater numbers of Black prosecutors (Ward, Farrell, & Rousseau, 2009); however, the involvement of Black judges does not appear to have a strong effect (Steffensmeier & Britt, 2001; Ward et al., 2009).

The nature and characteristics of a crime can impact the magnitude and even direction of sentencing disparities. Biases against Black and Latino defendants are stronger for drug crimes (Crow, 2008; O. Mitchell, 2005). Disparities also tend to be stronger for crimes that are stereotypically associated with a defendant's racial or ethnic group, such as violent crimes for Black defendants and "white collar" crimes for White defendants (Gordon et al., 1988; Mazzella & Feingold, 1994). Another important factor is the race of the victim, with harsher sentences given in cases involving White victims (Mazzella & Feingold, 1994); this factor will be discussed in more detail in the next section.

Finally, racial threat theory predicts that sentencing disparities will be strongest in contexts in which racial or ethnic groups are perceived as a threat to the majority, due to growing minority populations, high economic inequality, or high crime rates (Crawford et al., 1998). Support for these predictions has been mixed. In the O. Mitchell (2005) meta-analysis, there were not significant differences in the size of sentencing disparities as a function of racial composition or economic inequality. Counter to predictions, sentencing disparities were stronger in areas with low crime rates. Likewise, in a sample of federal cases, sentencing disparities against Latinos actually were smaller in areas with large Latinos populations (Feldmeyer & Ulmer, 2011). A recent study suggests that it may be useful to take a dynamic approach when assessing racial threat; Caravelis et al. (2011) found that measures of the extent to which Florida counties were experiencing an increase in their minority populations predicted disparities in sentencing Latino and Black defendants as habitual offenders better than static measures of the size of minority populations. Additional research is needed to better understand how perceptions of threat relate to sentencing disparities and how they are best operationalized.

Capital (Death) Sentencing

Although racial disparities in any aspect of criminal sentencing are cause for concern, disparities in capital sentences elicit the greatest alarm because they involve the ultimate, irreversible penalty of death. However, archival analyses provide strong evidence that racial disparities exist in the administration of the death penalty. Capital sentencing is discussed separately in this chapter because it differs from non-capital sentencing in meaningful ways. Decisions to impose the death penalty usually are made by juries, rather than judges. After rendering a guilty verdict, jurors hear additional evidence relevant to sentencing in the penalty phase of the trial. Specifically, jurors are asked to consider aggravating factors (i.e., factors that suggest a more severe punishment is appropriate, such as lack of remorse and victim impact) and mitigating factors (i.e., factors that suggest a less severe punishment is appropriate, such as childhood abuse). They then engage in a second deliberation to determine the defendant's sentence. See Volume 1, Chapter 7, this handbook and Chapter 6, this volume for more research and practice issues associated with capital cases.

Archival research. The most common procedure for assessing racial disparities in death sentences was established by Baldus, Pulaski, and Woodworth (1983). Using a sample of 594 murder defendants in the state of Georgia, the researchers coded more than 200 variables related to characteristics of the crime, defendant, victim, and broader case context that may have affected sentencing. This sample was later expanded to include nearly 2,500 cases (Baldus, Woodworth, & Pulaski, 1990). Analyses revealed that, controlling for numerous legally relevant factors, death sentences were 4.3 times more likely to be given in cases in which a defendant was accused of killing a White rather than Black victim, suggesting racial bias in the perceived "worth" of a murder victim.

Subsequent research using similar methodologies has continued to provide evidence of racial bias in capital sentences, although the specific pattern of disparities varies across jurisdictions. An analysis of 707 cases in Philadelphia found that, again considering hundreds of relevant factors, Black defendants were 3.8 times more likely than White defendants to receive death sentences (Baldus et al., 1998). The most consistent pattern of disparities involves an

interaction between defendant and victim race, with a significantly higher rate of death sentences in cases involving Black defendants accused of killing White victims. This pattern has been found in several studies, including analyses of cases in Arkansas (Baldus et al., 2009), Delaware (S. L. Johnson et al., 2012), Kentucky (Keil & Vito, 1995), Maryland (Paternoster & Brame, 2008), North Carolina (Unah, 2009), and South Carolina (Songer & Unah, 2006; for a review, see Baldus & Woodworth, 2003). Although there is substantially less research, it appears that there are similar disparities in cases involving Latinos, with the death penalty more likely to be imposed in cases involving Latino defendants and White victims and less likely to be imposed in cases involving Latino victims (Lee, 2007; Thomson, 1997).

Despite the abundance of research showing racial bias in capital sentencing, it has received mixed reactions from policymakers and the courts. On one hand, this research has been influential in individual states' decisions to abolish capital punishment (J. Schwartz & Fitzsimmons, 2011) as well as in the development of reform laws, such as North Carolina's Racial Justice Act of 2009, which, before it was repealed in 2013, expanded defendants' options for appealing death sentences that may have been influenced by race. On the other hand, in *McCleskey v. Kemp* (1987), the Supreme Court dismissed evidence of aggregate racial disparities in capital sentences as irrelevant, stating that it did not show that race had influenced decisions in the case at hand.

Moderators of racial bias in capital sentences. Racial bias in death penalty judgments may be strongest when juries contain greater numbers of White individuals, especially men. In an analysis of 340 trials from the Capital Jury Project, Bowers, Steiner, and Sandys (2001) found that Black defendants were 41% more likely to receive a death sentence when juries contained five or more White men (*White male dominance* pattern). When there were no Black men on a jury, Black defendants were 34% more likely to be sentenced to death (*Black male presence* pattern). Similarly, an analysis of cases in Philadelphia found that juries with greater numbers of White individuals were more likely to give the death penalty, particularly in cases involving Black defendants and White victims (Baldus et al., 2001). The finding that White men are more likely to impose the death penalty in cases involving Black defendants is especially problematic, given that death qualification procedures are more likely to eliminate women and minorities from the jury pool due to their greater opposition to capital punishment (e.g., Summers, Hayward, & Miller, 2010); thus, the jurors most likely to be seated on capital juries also appear to be the ones most likely to show racial bias in their sentencing judgments.

Psychological processes underlying racial bias in capital sentences. Several psychological processes may contribute to racial disparities in death sentences, as well as the increased likelihood of bias in sentences made by White male jurors. Both archival analyses and jury simulation research show that, in the penalty phase, jurors may give less weight to evidence about mitigating factors—that is, factors that suggest the death penalty is inappropriate—when defendants are Black and victims are White (Baldus et al., 1998; Lynch & Haney, 2000, 2009). Jurors' lack of comprehension of judicial instructions for sentencing may contribute to this bias. Jury simulation research indicates that participants who understand judicial instructions do not show racial bias in their use of mitigating evidence or sentencing recommendations. In contrast, participants who do not understand those instructions give less weight to mitigating evidence and are substantially more likely to recommend the death penalty for Black defendants, especially when victims are White (Lynch & Haney, 2000, 2009). These effects are especially pronounced in White male jurors, with White women and minority jurors showing little bias. Notably, deliberation may increase the tendency for Black defendants to receive the death penalty, especially when there are more White men in the juries (Lynch & Haney, 2009).

Differences in emotional and empathic responses between White and Black male jurors also may underlie race of juror effects in death penalty judgments, such as the White male dominance and Black male presence patterns (Bowers et al., 2001). Interviews of jurors in the Capital Jury Project found that

White jurors reported more anger and less empathy toward the defendants in their trials, seeing them as more dangerous and "cold-blooded" and less remorseful and likeable than did Black jurors (Bowers, Brewer, & Sandys, 2004; Garvey, 2000). Likewise, an analysis of cases in South Carolina found that Black male jurors were less likely than White male jurors to support a death sentence during the initial vote, shaping the course of deliberation and final sentencing decisions of their juries (Eisenberg, Garvey, & Wells, 2001).

In addition, disparities in capital sentences may reflect racial prejudice, stereotypes associating Black people with criminality and dangerousness, and the tendency to make internal attributions for criminal behavior by minorities (for a review, see Lynch & Haney, 2011). For example, mock jurors with higher scores on measures of racial prejudice show greater bias in death penalty recommendations (Dovidio, Smith, Donnella, & Gaertner, 1997). Recent research suggests that implicit racial biases also may contribute to capital sentences. Research based on the Philadelphia cases analyzed by Baldus et al. (1998) suggests that death sentences may be more likely to be given when defendants have a more stereotypically Black appearance and are depicted using ape-like imagery. Specifically, defendants whose mugshots were rated as more stereotypically Black (e.g., in terms of facial features and skin tone) were more likely to receive the death penalty in cases involving White (but not Black) victims (Eberhardt, Davies, Purdie-Vaughns, & Johnson, 2006). An analysis of newspaper articles related to the cases found that Black defendants were more likely than White defendants to have been described with words that evoke ape, rather than human, status. Black defendants who were depicted with the most ape imagery were significantly more likely to have received the death penalty (Goff, Eberhardt, Williams, & Jackson, 2008). These findings suggest that capital sentencing judgments may be affected by implicit racial biases that dehumanize Black defendants or make them seem more "deathworthy" to jurors.

Notably, there is evidence suggesting that defense attorneys who work on death penalty cases also may possess implicit racial biases. White defense attorneys who took a paper and pencil version of the Implicit Association Test were able to categorize words and faces more quickly when "Black" was paired with the concept "bad" and "White" was paired with the concept "good," showing an automatic preference for White people. In contrast, Black defense attorneys showed an automatic preference for Black people, but the magnitude of the bias was much weaker (Eisenberg & Johnson, 2004). These findings suggest that, despite their role as advocates and safeguards for defendants, defense attorneys in capital cases may have implicit racial biases that, if unchecked, could influence their behaviors, judgments, and interactions.

Overall Conclusions About Sentencing

In sum, there is strong evidence that defendant race and ethnicity influence sentencing judgments, with Black and Latino defendants being more likely and Asian defendants being less likely to be incarcerated. There also is evidence that Blacks and Latinos who kill White victims are more likely to receive the ultimate sentence of death. Thus, sentencing disparities reflect biases against minority defendants, as well as the devaluation of non-White victims. As with juror decision making, it is important to realize that legally relevant variables, such as offense severity and criminal history, consistently have larger effects on sentencing judgments than do either defendant or victim race. This pattern suggests that decision makers are attempting to focus on the most important variables, but their final sentencing judgments may be colored by racial bias. Any effect of race and ethnicity, however, that leads to the deprivation of liberty or even life itself is a serious challenge to the constitutional right of equality before the law, as well as a threat to the actual and perceived integrity of the justice system.

Other Legal Judgments

Although the majority of research on racial disparities by forensic psychologists has focused on police behavior, jury decision making, and sentencing, biases also have been found at other stages of the legal process. Numerous studies have found evidence of discrimination against racial and ethnic

minorities in pretrial judgments, including determinations about pretrial release and bail and decisions to file capital charges (for a review, see Free, 2002). For example, Blacks and Latinos, especially men, may be less likely than Whites to be released while awaiting trial (e.g., Demuth & Steffensmeier, 2004b; Freiburger, Marcum, & Pierce, 2010). This disparity is highly important because defendants who are not released before their trials are substantially more likely to receive sentences involving incarceration, even controlling for personal history and case variables (e.g., Tartaro & Sedelmaier, 2009). Racial disparities also have been found in postconviction judgments, such as parole decisions (see Chapter 13, this volume for research on parole and probation decisions). Again controlling for personal and offense characteristics, racial and ethnic minorities may spend significantly more time in prison before being granted parole compared to White individuals (e.g., Huebner & Bynum, 2008). In addition, racial and ethnic minorities are significantly more likely to have their parole revoked (i.e., be reimprisoned) if they engage in additional criminal violations (Lin, Grattet, & Petersilia, 2010). These pre- and posttrial judgments provide fruitful areas for forensic psychologists to expand their research on racial biases in legal decision making.

Racial and Ethnic Variability in Attitudes and Expectations About the Justice System

The majority of the research in this chapter has examined the way that criminal justice and legal professionals, as well as jurors, treat criminal suspects and defendants from different racial and ethnic backgrounds. Although there has been less research on these issues, it also is important to consider how race and ethnicity can affect lay people's attitudes, beliefs, and expectations about the justice system, as well as their behaviors during interactions with justice professionals, such as police officers.

Attitudes and beliefs about the justice system.
Given the pervasiveness of racial disparities across a wide range of criminal justice and legal outcomes, it is perhaps not surprising that survey research shows sizable differences in attitudes,

beliefs, and expectations about the justice system across members of different racial and ethnic groups (for a review, see B. Brown & Benedict, 2002). A growing number of large-scale surveys, including studies with nationally representative samples, provide evidence that Black individuals tend to have more negative attitudes and beliefs about police officers and the criminal justice system than do Latinos, who in turn tend to have more negative views than do White individuals. Unfortunately, there has been relatively little research examining the views of other racial and ethnic groups.

The majority of Blacks and Latinos believe that the police treat minorities worse than White individuals, whereas the majority of Whites believe that the police treat people equally, regardless of race or ethnicity (Weitzer & Tuch, 2005). A similar pattern is found for beliefs about the way that police treat neighborhoods with large minority populations versus neighborhoods that are predominantly White. Blacks and Latinos are more likely than Whites to report that police officers in their community are racially prejudiced (Weitzer & Tuch, 1999, 2005) and to report fears that they or their children will be mistreated by the police (Schuck, Rosenbaum, & Hawkins, 2008). They are more likely to believe that racial profiling occurs in their community and that they or people they know have been targeted (Reitzel et al., 2004; Weitzer & Tuch, 2005). Blacks and Latinos also are substantially more likely than Whites to believe that the police engage in misconduct, such as corruption, use of excessive force, and use of insulting language when dealing with minority suspects (Weitzer & Tuch, 2004).

The tendency for Blacks and Latinos to have more negative attitudes toward the police may, in part, reflect previous negative experiences with the police (Schuck et al., 2008; Weitzer & Tuch, 2005). Blacks and Latinos are more likely than Whites to report both direct and vicarious (i.e., within their social network) negative experiences with police officers (Weitzer & Tuch, 1999). For example, one study found that 37% of Blacks, 23% of Latinos, but only 1% of Whites reported an experience in which they were unfairly treated by the police due to their race or ethnicity (Weitzer & Tuch, 2005). Differences in attitudes also may reflect the greater

likelihood for racial and ethnic minorities to live in disadvantaged or high-crime neighborhoods. Attitudes toward the police tend be more negative among individuals who live in such neighborhoods, even if those individuals are middle-class themselves (Schuck et al., 2008; Weitzer & Tuch, 2004; Weitzer, Tuch, & Skogan, 2008). Findings on the effects of education are mixed; some studies show that, regardless of race, individuals with lower levels of education have more negative views of the police (Weitzer et al., 2008), whereas other studies find that better-educated Black individuals are especially likely to perceive police misconduct and discrimination (Weitzer & Tuch, 1999).

Notably, multivariate analyses show that racial and ethnic differences in attitudes toward the justice system tend to persist even when these factors are statistically controlled, suggesting that group membership itself may be an important influence (Weitzer & Tuch, 1999, 2005). This possibility is consistent with group position theory, which suggests that majority groups see the police as an ally in preserving their groups' dominant position in society and maintaining social control and safety, whereas minority groups often view the police as a means of oppression and source of mistreatment (Weitzer & Tuch, 2005). These differences also are consistent with procedural justice theory (Tyler, 2001; see also Chapter 12, this volume), which asserts that attitudes toward the police and legal system are strongly influenced by beliefs about whether individuals are treated in a fair and just manner. As shown in this section, Blacks and Latinos are substantially less likely to hold such views.

There is less research on racial and ethnic variability in attitudes toward the courts. Research by the National Center for State Courts (National Center for State Courts, 1999; Rottman, Hansen, Mott, & Grimes, 2003) shows that Black individuals are less likely than White individuals to perceive the courts, as well as their procedures and decisions, as being fair. Black respondents are more likely to believe that minorities are treated negatively by the courts, and they express more concerns about disrespectful treatment, level of citizen participation, and lack of cultural sensitivity. Latinos tend to express overall views of the courts that are at least as positive as the views of White respondents, but they also indicate concerns about issues such as differential treatment and lack of representative juries (see also de la Garza & DeSipio, 2001).

Interactions with the police.   Racial and ethnic differences in attitudes and expectations about the justice system are important in part because they may influence actual interactions between lay people and the police or other justice professionals. If members of racial and ethnic minority groups have negative attitudes about the police and believe that they are likely to engage in misconduct or unfair treatment, they may avoid interacting with the police (e.g., fail to report crime) and act in a guarded, disrespectful, or even hostile manner when such interactions are unavoidable (Weitzer & Tuch, 2005). Because police officers expect to be treated in a respectful and deferent manner, such behavior may elicit suspicion and negative responses, creating a cycle that may lead to hostile interactions as well as consequences such as arrest.

Relatively little research has examined how attitudes and expectations about the police affect interactions in members of different racial and ethnic groups. An analysis of recordings from 194 traffic stops in Cincinnati found that, controlling for characteristics of the stop and officer behavior, Black drivers engaged in less positive communication behavior with the police than did White drivers (Dixon, Schell, Giles, & Drogos, 2008). Specifically, they were less respectful, polite, pleasant, and apologetic, and they were more belligerent, especially when the stops were more extensive (e.g., longer, involving searches). This tendency for Black drivers to engage in more negative communication behavior potentially reflects negative attitudes and expectations about the police. The study also found that, controlling for relevant variables, police officers used less positive communication in interracial traffic stops; they were less approachable and respectful, more indifferent and dismissive, and more likely to act in a superior manner (see also Huggins, 2012). Because there are substantially more White police officers than Black police officers, this pattern suggests that Black drivers may be especially likely to

have negative police encounters that reinforce their existing views.

Converging evidence comes from qualitative interviews of teenage boys and parents in East St. Louis (Brunson & Weitzer, 2011; Weitzer & Brunson, 2009). Both groups expressed considerable distrust of police officers and concerns about interacting with them, including personal safety. The boys indicated that they try to avoid interactions with police officers, even running away from them. They expressed concerns about sharing information (in part due to concerns about being seen as a snitch) and, based on previous experiences, expected negative treatment, including offensive name-calling, to occur during encounters (Weitzer & Brunson, 2009). Likewise, the parents said that they cautioned their children to avoiding interacting with the police or attracting their attention. If encounters happened, they stressed the need to be respectful and compliant, but urged their children not to volunteer information or make movements that might lead to aggressive responses (Brunson & Weitzer, 2011).

In addition to influencing noncustodial interactions, expectations about the police may affect minority individuals' behavior in interrogation contexts. A phenomenon known as *stereotype threat* occurs when individuals are in situations in which they are reminded about a negative stereotype related to their group (e.g., race). They become highly motivated not to support or confirm the stereotype; however, those concerns increase arousal and consume cognitive resources, impairing their performance (Schmader, Johns, & Forbes, 2008). Applied to interrogation settings, innocent Black suspects may believe that, due to racial stereotypes, the police assume that they are guilty. As a result, they may work hard to establish their innocence, leading to high levels of arousal and self-regulation, which in turn may increase speech errors and nonverbal behaviors, such as fidgeting (Najdowski, 2011). In fact, an initial study showed that Black individuals who were questioned by a White security guard reported more concerns about racial stereotyping and appeared more nervous than did White individuals in the same situation (Najdowski, 2012). An important implication is that, if minority suspects appear nervous, interrogators may infer guilt and apply more pressure, creating a vicious cycle that may result in false confessions (Najdowski, 2011). Given the stakes involved in interrogation and confession, it is important for forensic psychologists to continue to investigate how race and ethnicity may affect behavior during police interrogation.

Conclusion.   Research examining how race and ethnicity influence views of the justice system and behavior during legally relevant encounters has the potential to substantially increase our understanding of the ways that people negotiate the justice system in their daily lives, as well as elucidate additional sources of disparities in criminal justice and legal outcomes. To date, most of the research on these issues has been conducted by sociologists, criminologists, and political scientists. Given psychologists' expertise on attitudes and behavior, expanding research in this area seems like a natural fit. More generally, forensic psychologists would do well to ask more questions about racial and ethnic minorities as *actors* in justice contexts, instead of continuing to primarily study them as the *targets* of others' behaviors and judgments.

PRACTICE AND POLICY ISSUES

Forensic psychologists, along with scholars in the fields of sociology, criminology, and law, have produced important evidence of racial biases in the criminal justice and legal systems. As described in the previous section, psychologists have made particular contributions in terms of explaining the psychological processes involved with racial bias and identifying contextual factors that make racial bias more or less likely to occur. In many cases, however, forensic psychologists have not been as effective as they could be in getting this information to policymakers. To maximize the practical impact of their research, forensic psychologists need to expand their efforts to disseminate their findings to justice professionals, as well as become more actively involved in the development of policies and training programs that may reduce racial bias in criminal justice and legal outcomes. Effective

strategies may include expert testimony, *amicus curiae* briefs, participation in jury composition challenges, and participation in policy and training initiatives.

Expert Testimony

Forensic psychologists may share research findings with the courts through expert testimony in pre- or post-trial hearings involving allegations of racial bias in the investigation and/or adjudication of a case. For example, psychologists may testify about racial bias in the use of peremptory challenges in jury selection, as well as differences in deliberation and verdicts that may occur if juries are entirely or predominantly White instead of racially diverse. A recent case, *North Carolina v. Robinson* (2012), involved an appeal of the death sentence of Marcus Robinson, a Black man who was convicted of murdering a White victim. During jury selection, Black venire members were struck more than three times as often as White venire members, resulting in a predominantly White jury. A hearing under the state's now repealed Racial Justice Act of 2009 included both psychological testimony and statistical evidence of racial bias in jury selection (*North Carolina v. Robinson*, 2012; S. R. Sommers, personal communication, Nov. 6, 2012). Based on that evidence, the Cumberland County Superior Court changed Robinson's sentence from death to life in prison without parole, stating "the persistent, pervasive, and distorting role of race in jury selection . . . requires relief in his case and should serve as a clear signal of the need for reform in capital jury proceedings in the future" (*North Carolina v. Robinson*, 2012, p. 3).

In addition, forensic psychologists may serve as expert witnesses in criminal or civil trials in which racial bias is an issue, such as cases involving alleged hate crimes or employment discrimination. In such cases, expert testimony is likely to take the form of social framework evidence (Walker & Monahan, 1987), in which social scientists discuss research findings related to prejudice, stereotyping, and discrimination in order to provide jurors with appropriate context for evaluating the facts of a case. This form of expert testimony is discussed in more detail in Volume 1, Chapter 15, this handbook.

Amicus Briefs

Forensic psychologists also may share their knowledge about racial bias by acting as "friends of the court" and submitting written *amicus curiae* briefs. These briefs present information (e.g., research findings) and arguments that may be relevant for a court in deciding a particular case. Organizations such as the American Psychological Association (APA) have been active in submitting *amicus* briefs in appellate cases related to psychological issues. For example, the APA has submitted *amicus* briefs discussing research about racial bias and the positive effects of diversity in affirmative action cases such as *Fisher v. University of Texas at Austin* (2013; Brief for APA, 2013), the stigmatization of gay and lesbian relationships in same-gender marriage cases such as *Perry v. Schwarzenegger* (2010; Brief for APA, 2010), and the use of gender stereotypes in employment discrimination cases such as *Price Waterhouse v. Hopkins* (1989; Brief for APA, 1989).

To date, the APA has not submitted *amicus* briefs in cases involving alleged racial bias in the justice system; however, some psychologists have contributed to *amicus* briefs submitted by other professional organizations, such as the "Brief for Social Scientists, Statisticians, and Law Professors" submitted by the American Bar Association (ABA) in the jury composition case, *Berghuis v. Smith* (2010; Brief for ABA, 2010). As cases involving racial bias come before the higher courts, it would behoove forensic psychologists to be more proactive about submitting *amicus* briefs to inform the courts about research findings that may shape their understanding of and judgments in those cases.

Jury Composition Challenges

Another professional activity through which forensic psychologists can help to reduce racial biases in the justice system involves assisting with jury composition challenges. Under the Sixth Amendment, defendants have the right to an impartial jury drawn from "a fair cross section" of their community. Accordingly, the venires used to select juries need to reflect the demographic composition of the relevant jurisdiction. If defendants believe that certain groups are excluded from or underrepresented in the jury pool, either intentionally or due to the procedures used to create the venire, they may engage in a jury composition challenge. Based on procedures established by the Supreme Court in *Duren v. Missouri* (1979), to initiate such a challenge, a defendant must demonstrate that the representation of a "distinctive" or "cognizable" group in the jury pool is unreasonable based on the demographics of the community, and systematic procedures in jury selection are leading to the discrepancy. Establishing these requirements is difficult, with considerable debate about the best way to assess disparities between venire and community demographics, especially for groups with small populations (Hannaford-Agor & Waters, 2011). In addition, because it is reasonable to expect some variability in the jury pool, composition challenges are likely to require assessments of the representativeness of a jury pool at multiple time points (H. Fukurai, personal communication, Sept. 29, 2012). Given their extensive methodological and statistical training, forensic psychologists are well-equipped to contribute to jury composition challenges, and their involvement may enhance the potential for these challenges to be successful and promote greater diversity in jury participation.

Policy and Training Initiatives

Forensic psychologists should strive to be more involved in the development of policies, legislation, and training procedures designed to reduce racial disparities at various stages in the criminal justice and legal process. At the most basic level, psychologists should be clear about discussing the policy implications of their own research. As an example, Sommers and Norton (2008) outline and evaluate potential policy implications of research on racial bias in jury selection, such as developing selection procedures that mask the race of potential jurors and using affirmative strategies to increase jury diversity.

However, it is important for psychologists to increase their scope of dissemination beyond journals, so that justice professionals, legislators, and policymakers are more likely to encounter and use the information. Psychologists may share research findings by testifying in hearings held by policy groups and legislative bodies. Likewise, professional organizations such as the APA and American Psychology-Law Society can develop and disseminate policy statements and position papers. For example, the APA (2001) developed a policy statement calling for a moratorium on the death penalty until procedures are developed to resolve the problems in its administration identified by social science research. Psychologists also can become more active in policy development by participating in interdisciplinary policy teams, advisory groups, commissions, or task forces focused on racial disparities in the justice system.

Finally, forensic psychologists should be more actively engaged in using research on prejudice, stereotyping, and discrimination to develop training and other initiatives that may minimize racial bias in the criminal justice and legal system. To maximize potential effectiveness, psychologists should work closely with law enforcement and legal professionals in both developing and assessing new training protocols and procedures. The Consortium for Police Leadership in Equity at UCLA is an example of an ongoing collaboration in which psychologists are part of an interdisciplinary team that works with police departments to conduct research on racial and gender equity and provide training on issues such as racial profiling.

SUMMARY AND CONCLUSIONS

The following points summarize the most important conclusions from this chapter:

- High profiles cases, such as the shooting death of Amadou Diallo and execution of Troy Davis, as well as statistics showing racial disparities in important legal outcomes, such as incarceration and the death penalty, strongly suggest that police behavior and legal judgments are influenced by race and ethnicity.
- Psychological theories provide a means of understanding how prejudice against racial and ethnic minorities and stereotypes associating minorities with crime and danger can influence judgments and behavior, leading to discriminatory outcomes. Recent research emphasizes that contemporary racial bias often occurs in a subtle

rather than overt manner. It also may occur without conscious awareness or intent, even by people who hold egalitarian beliefs, which may put many acts of bias outside of the purview of legal standards requiring discriminatory intent.

- Forensic psychologists have conducted a great deal of research on bias against Blacks, and to a lesser extent, Latinos, in police officers' decisions to shoot, juror decision making, and capital sentencing. There is a need for more forensic psychology research examining bias against other racial and ethnic groups as well as other criminal justice and legal outcomes. There also is a need for more research examining the ways that race and ethnicity influence lay people's beliefs about and interactions in the criminal justice and legal systems.
- Consistent with the notion of "driving while Black," there is evidence that police officers engage in racial profiling and are more likely to stop, search, and arrest Black and Latino individuals. Racial profiling may be especially likely to occur in situations in which minorities seem "out of place" or are perceived as a threat to the majority.
- Race also may affect police officers' decisions to use force. Research on shooter bias indicates that, consistent with stereotypical assumptions, police officers are quicker to decide to shoot armed Black individuals and to decide not to shoot unarmed White individuals.
- Although it is prohibited by cases such as *Batson v. Kentucky* (1986), attorneys' use of peremptory challenges may be influenced by race, with minority jurors being more likely to be struck from jury pools, especially by prosecutors.
- Diverse juries may deliberate longer, discuss evidence more accurately, and render less biased verdicts than all-White juries.
- Jurors show a small tendency to be more lenient in their judgments about same-race defendants. Race also may influence their evaluation and use of evidence. The magnitude of racial bias in juror decision making is influenced by several factors, with stronger effects occurring when characteristics of the case, juror, or decision

making context decrease sensitivity to bias or appear to provide non-racial justifications for biased judgments.

■ Archival analyses provide evidence of racial bias in criminal sentencing, with Black and Latino defendants being more likely and Asian defendants being less likely to be incarcerated. Racial disparities are stronger for drug-related and stereotype-consistent crimes. Sentencing reforms such as mandatory terms and sentencing enhancements actually may increase racial disparities.

■ The death penalty is more likely to be imposed in cases involving Black or Latino defendants and White victims, indicating biases as a function of defendant race as well as the perceived worth of minority victims. Racial bias is more likely to be found in sentencing recommendations by White male jurors, due in part to their underuse of mitigating evidence as well as negative emotional reactions to defendants.

■ Black and Latino individuals tend to have more negative attitudes about the police than do White individuals. This pattern reflects their greater likelihood of personal or vicarious negative experiences with police officers, as well as their greater likelihood of residing in disadvantaged neighborhoods. These negative attitudes may contribute to negative interactions with justice professionals.

■ Forensic psychologists can help to reduce and remedy racial biases in the justice system by sharing these research findings through expert testimony and *amicus curiae* briefs. They also can use their expertise to contribute to jury composition challenges, policy development, and the creation of training programs targeting racial bias in the police and other criminal justice and legal professionals.

In conclusion, empirical research clearly shows that "equality before the law" remains a Constitutional ideal rather than a reality for racial and ethnic minorities. Racial bias in criminal justice and legal outcomes can forever alter the lives of the individuals who experience it; it also threatens the integrity of the justice system and has a negative impact upon society as a whole. Forensic psychologists have much to contribute to the further development of a scientific understanding of when and how race influences judgments and outcomes at various stages of the criminal justice and legal process. They are especially well-equipped to help elucidate the psychological processes that underlie racial biases, contributing to the development of training procedures and other interventions that can reduce racial disparities. Given the critical nature of these issues, it is important for forensic psychologists to increase their focus on race and ethnicity and help to turn the concept of "justice for all" into an actuality.

References

Abshire, J., & Bornstein, B. H. (2003). Juror sensitivity to the cross-race effect. *Law and Human Behavior*, 27, 471–480. doi:10.1023/A:1025481905861

Adams, L. T., Bryden, M. W., & Griffith, J. D. (2011). Middle Eastern racial bias and the impact of jury deliberation. *American Journal of Forensic Psychology*, 29(3), 41–59.

American Psychological Association. (2001). *The death penalty in the United States*. Retrieved from http://www.apa.org/about/policy/death-penalty.aspx

Andersen, S. M., Moskowitz, G. B., Blair, I. V., & Nosek, B. A. (2007). Automatic thought. In A. W. Kruglanski & E. T. Higgins (Eds.), *Social psychology: Handbook of basic principles* (2nd ed., pp. 138–175). New York, NY: Guilford Press.

Archibold, R. C. (2010, April 24). Arizona enacts stringent law on immigration. *New York Times*. Retrieved from http://www.nytimes.com/2010/04/24/us/politics/24immig.html

Baldus, D. C., Brain, J., Weiner, N. A., & Woodworth, G. (2009, Spring). Evidence of racial discrimination in the use of the death penalty: A story from Southwest Arkansas (1990–2005) with special reference to the case of death row inmate Frank Williams, Jr. *Tennessee Law Review*, 76, 555–613.

Baldus, D. C., Broffitt, B., Weiner, N. A., Woodworth, G., & Zuckerman, D. (1998). Racial discrimination and the death penalty in the post-Furman era: An empirical and legal overview, with recent findings from Philadelphia. *Cornell Law Review*, 83, 1638–1770.

Baldus, D. C., Pulaski, C., & Woodworth, G. (1983). Comparative review of death sentences: An empirical study of the Georgia experience. *Journal of Criminal Law and Criminology*, 74, 661–753. doi:10.2307/1143133

Baldus, D. C., & Woodworth, G. (2003). Race discrimination in the administration of the death penalty: An overview of the empirical evidence with special emphasis on the post-1990 research. *Criminal Law Bulletin, 39,* 194–226.

Baldus, D. C., Woodworth, G., & Pulaski, C. (1990). *Equal justice and the death penalty: A legal and empirical analysis.* Boston, MA: Northeastern University Press.

Baldus, D. C., Woodworth, G., Zuckerman, D., Weiner, N. A., & Broffitt, B. (2001). The use of peremptory challenges in capital murder trials: A legal and empirical analysis. *University of Pennsylvania Journal of Constitutional Law, 3,* 3–172.

Batson v. Kentucky, 476 U.S. 79 (1986).

Berghuis v. Smith, 130 S.Ct. 1382 (2010).

Blair, I. V., Judd, C. M., & Chapleau, K. M. (2004). The influence of Afrocentric facial features in criminal sentencing. *Psychological Science, 15,* 674–679. doi:10.1111/j.0956-7976.2004.00739.x

Bodenhausen, G. V., & Wyer, R. S. (1985). Effects of stereotypes in decision making and information-processing strategies. *Journal of Personality and Social Psychology, 48,* 267–282. doi:10.1037/0022-3514.48.2.267

Bornstein, B. H. (1999). The ecological validity of jury simulations: Is the jury still out? *Law and Human Behavior, 23,* 75–91. doi:10.1023/A:1022326807441

Bostaph, L. G. (2007). Race and repeats: The impact of officer performance on racially biased policing. *Journal of Criminal Justice, 35,* 405–417. doi:10.1016/j.jcrimjus.2007.05.005

Bowers, W. J., Brewer, T. W., & Sandys, M. (2004). Crossing racial boundaries: A closer look at the roots of racial bias in capital sentencing when the defendant is black and the victim is white. *De Paul Law Review, 53,* 1497–1538.

Bowers, W. J., Steiner, B. D., & Sandys, M. (2001). Death sentencing in black and white: An empirical analysis of the role of jurors' race and jury racial composition. *University of Pennsylvania Journal of Constitutional Law, 3,* 171–274.

Bradbury, M. D., & Williams, M. R. (2013). Diversity and citizen participation: The effect of race on juror decision making. *Administration and Society, 45,* 563–582. doi: 10.1177/0095399712459729

Brennan, P. K., & Spohn, C. (2008). Race/ethnicity and sentencing outcomes among drug offenders in North Carolina. *Journal of Contemporary Criminal Justice, 24,* 371–398. doi:10.1177/1043986208322712

Brennan, P. K., & Spohn, C. (2009). The joint effects of offender race/ethnicity and sex on sentence length decisions in federal courts. *Race and Social Problems, 1,* 200–217. doi:10.1007/s12552-009-9016-0

Brewer, M. B. (1999). The psychology of prejudice: Ingroup love or outgroup hate? *Journal of Social Issues, 55,* 429–444. doi:10.1111/0022-4537.00126

Brief for the American Bar Association as Amicus Curiae, Berghuis v. Smith, 130 S.Ct. 1382 (2010).

Brief for the American Psychological Association as Amicus Curiae, Price Waterhouse v. Hopkins, 490 U.S. 228 (1989).

Brief for the American Psychological Association as Amicus Curiae, Perry v. Schwarzenegger, 704 F. Supp. 2d 921 (2010).

Brief for the American Psychological Association as Amicus Curiae, Fisher v. University of Texas at Austin, 631 F. 3d 213 (2013).

Briggs, S., & Opsal, T. (2012). The influence of victim ethnicity on arrest in violent crimes. *Criminal Justice Studies, 25,* 177–189.

Brown, B., & Benedict, W. R. (2002). Perceptions of the police: Past findings, methodological issues, conceptual issues and policy implications. *Policing, 25,* 543–580. doi:10.1108/13639510210437032

Brown, J. M., & Langan, P. A. (2001). *Policing and homicide, 1976–98: Justifiable homicide of felons by police and murder of police by felons.* Washington, DC: Bureau of Justice Statistics.

Brunson, R. K., & Weitzer, R. (2011). Negotiating unwelcome police encounters: The intergenerational transmission of conduct norms. *Journal of Contemporary Ethnography, 40,* 425–456. doi:10.1177/0891241611409038

Caravelis, C., Chiricos, T., & Bales, W. (2011). Static and dynamic indicators of minority threat in sentencing outcomes: A multi-level analysis. *Journal of Quantitative Criminology, 27,* 405–425. doi:10.1007/s10940-011-9130-1

Chao, M. M., Chiu, C.-y., Chan, W., Mendoza-Denton, R., & Kwok, C. (2012). The model minority as a shared reality and its implication for interracial perceptions. *Asian American Journal of Psychology, 4,* 84–92. doi:10.1037/a0028769

Clark, J., Boccaccini, M. T., Caillouet, B., & Chaplin, W. F. (2007). Five-Factor Model personality traits, jury selection, and case outcomes in criminal and civil cases. *Criminal Justice and Behavior, 34,* 641–660. doi:10.1177/0093854806297555

Cohn, E. S., Bucolo, D., Pride, M., & Sommers, S. R. (2009). Reducing white juror bias: The role of race salience and racial attitudes. *Journal of Applied Social Psychology, 39,* 1953–1973. doi:10.1111/j.1559-1816.2009.00511.x

Cohn, E. S., Bucolo, D., & Sommers, S. R. (2012). Race and racism. In B. L. Butler (Ed.), *Conviction of the* innocent: *Lessons from psychological research* (pp. 279–301). Washington, DC: American Psychological Association. doi:10.1037/13085-013

Cooper, M. (1999, February 5). Officers in Bronx fire 41 shots, and an unarmed man is killed. *New York Times*. Retrieved from http://www.nytimes.com/1999/02/05/nyregion/officers-in-bronx-fire-41-shots-and-an-unarmed-man-is-killed.html

Cornwell, E. Y., & Hans, V. P. (2011). Representation through participation: A multilevel analysis of jury deliberations. *Law and Society Review, 45,* 667–698.

Correll, J., Park, B., Judd, C. M., & Wittenbrink, B. (2002). The police officer's dilemma: Using ethnicity to disambiguate potentially threatening individuals. *Journal of Personality and Social Psychology, 83,* 1314–1329. doi:10.1037/0022-3514.83.6.1314

Correll, J., Park, B., Judd, C. M., & Wittenbrink, B. (2007). The influence of stereotypes on decisions to shoot. *European Journal of Social Psychology, 37,* 1102–1117. doi:10.1002/ejsp.450

Correll, J., Park, B., Judd, C. M., Wittenbrink, B., Sadler, M. S., & Keesee, T. (2007). Across the thin blue line: Police officers and racial bias in the decision to shoot. *Journal of Personality and Social Psychology, 92,* 1006–1023. doi:10.1037/0022-3514.92.6.1006

Correll, J., Wittenbrink, B., Park, B., Judd, C. M., & Goyle, A. (2011). Dangerous enough: Moderating racial bias with contextual threat cues. *Journal of Experimental Social Psychology, 47,* 184–189. doi:10.1016/j.jesp.2010.08.017

Crawford, C., Chiricos, T., & Kleck, G. (1998). Race, racial threat, and sentencing of habitual offenders. *Criminology, 36,* 481–512. doi:10.1111/j.1745-9125.1998.tb01256.x

Crow, M. S. (2008). The complexities of prior record, race, ethnicity, and policy: Interactive effects in sentencing. *Criminal Justice Review, 33,* 502–523. doi:10.1177/0734016808320709

Crow, M. S., & Adrion, B. (2011). Focal concerns and police use of force: Examining the factors associated with Taser use. *Police Quarterly, 14,* 366–387. doi:10.1177/1098611111423740

Daudistel, H. C., Hosch, H. M., Holmes, M. D., & Graves, J. B. (1999). Effects of defendant ethnicity on juries' dispositions of felony cases. *Journal of Applied Social Psychology, 29,* 317–336. doi:10.1111/j.1559-1816.1999.tb01389.x

Davis, L. (2011). Rock, powder, sentencing: Making disparate impact evidence relevant in crack cocaine sentencing. *Journal of Gender, Race, and Justice, 14,* 375–404.

de la Garza, R. O., & DeSipio, L. (2001). A satisfied clientele seeking more diverse services: Latinos and the courts. *Behavioral Sciences and the Law, 19,* 237–248. doi:10.1002/bsl.436

Demuth, S., & Steffensmeier, D. (2004a). Ethnicity effects on sentence outcomes in large urban courts: Comparisons among White, Black, and Hispanic defendants. *Social Science Quarterly, 85,* 994–1011. doi:10.1111/j.0038-4941.2004.00255.x

Demuth, S., & Steffensmeier, D. (2004b). The impact of gender and race-ethnicity in the pretrial release process. *Social Problems, 51,* 222–242. doi:10.1525/sp.2004.51.2.222

Devine, D. J. (2012). *Jury decision making: The state of the science.* New York: New York University Press.

Devine, D. J., & Caughlin, D. E. (2014). Do they matter? A meta-analytic investigation of individual characteristics and guilt judgments. *Psychology, Public Policy, and Law, 20,* 109–134. doi: 10.1037/law0000006

Diamond, S., & Ellis, L. (2003). Race, diversity, and jury composition: Battering and bolstering legitimacy. *Chicago-Kent Law Review, 78,* 1033–1058.

Dixon, T. L., Schell, T. L., Giles, H., & Drogos, K. L. (2008). The influence of race in police-civilian interactions: A content analysis of videotaped interactions taken during Cincinnati police traffic stops. *Journal of Communication, 58,* 530–549. doi:10.1111/j.1460-2466.2008.00398.x

Dovidio, J. F., & Gaertner, S. L. (2010). Intergroup bias. In S. T. Fiske, D. T. Gilbert & G. Lindzey (Eds.), *Handbook of social psychology* (5th ed., Vol. 2, pp. 1084–1121). Hoboken, NJ: Wiley.

Dovidio, J. F., Smith, J. K., Donnella, A. G., & Gaertner, S. L. (1997). Racial attitudes and the death penalty. *Journal of Applied Social Psychology, 27,* 1468–1487. doi:10.1111/j.1559-1816.1997.tb01609.x

Dreyfuss, J. (2011). *Why we cared so much about Troy Davis.* Retrieved from http://www.theroot.com/views/why-we-cared-so-much-about-troy-davis

Duckitt, J. H. (1992). Psychology and prejudice: A historical analysis and integrative framework. *American Psychologist, 47,* 1182–1193. doi:10.1037/0003-066X.47.10.1182

Duncan, B. L. (1976). Differential social perception and attribution of intergroup violence: Testing the lower limits of stereotyping of Blacks. *Journal of Personality and Social Psychology, 34,* 590–598. doi:10.1037/0022-3514.34.4.590

Duren v. Missouri, 439 U.S. 357 (1979).

Eberhardt, J. L., Davies, P. G., Purdie-Vaughns, V. J., & Johnson, S. L. (2006). Looking death-worthy: Perceived stereotypicality of Black defendants predicts capital-sentencing outcomes. *Psychological Science, 17,* 383–386. doi:10.1111/j.1467-9280.2006.01716.x

Eberhardt, J. L., Goff, P. A., Purdie, V. J., & Davies, P. G. (2004). Seeing Black: Race, crime, and visual processing. *Journal of Personality and Social Psychology*, 87, 876–893. doi:10.1037/0022-3514.87.6.876

Edmonson v. Leesville Concrete Co., 500 U.S. 614 (1991).

Eisenberg, T., Garvey, S. P., & Wells, M. T. (2001). Forecasting life and death: Juror race, religion, and attitude toward the death penalty. *Journal of Legal Studies*, 30, 277–311. doi:10.1086/322060

Eisenberg, T., & Johnson, S. L. (2004). Implicit racial attitudes of death penalty lawyers. *De Paul Law Review*, 53, 1539–1556.

Eith, C., & Durose, M. R. (2011). *Contacts between police and the public, 2008* (NCJ 234599). Washington, DC: Bureau of Justice Statistics. Retrieved from http://bjs.ojp.usdoj.gov/content/pub/pdf/cpp08.pdf

Engel, R. S., Calnon, J. M., & Bernard, T. J. (2002). Theory and racial profiling: Shortcomings and future directions in research. *Justice Quarterly*, 19, 249–273. doi:10.1080/07418820200095231

Equal Justice Initiative. (2010). *Illegal racial discrimination in jury selection: A continuing legacy*. Montgomery, AL: Equal Justice Initiative.

Esqueda, C. W. (1997). European American students' perceptions of crimes committed by five racial groups. *Journal of Applied Social Psychology*, 27, 1406–1420. doi:10.1111/j.1559-1816.1997.tb01605.x

Esqueda, C. W., Espinoza, R. K. E., & Culhane, S. E. (2008). The effects of ethnicity, SES, and crime status on juror decision making: A cross-cultural examination of European American and Mexican American mock jurors. *Hispanic Journal of Behavioral Sciences*, 30, 181–199. doi:10.1177/0739986308315319

Feldmeyer, B., & Ulmer, J. T. (2011). Racial/ethnic threat and federal sentencing. *Journal of Research in Crime and Delinquency*, 48, 238–270. doi:10.1177/0022427810391538

Fisher v. University of Texas at Austin, 631 F. 3d 213 (2013).

Fiske, S. T., Cuddy, A. J. C., Glick, P., & Xu, J. (2002). A model of (often mixed) stereotype content: Competence and warmth respectively follow from perceived status and competition. *Journal of Personality and Social Psychology*, 82, 878–902. doi:10.1037/0022-3514.82.6.878

Fiske, S. T., & Neuberg, S. L. (1990). A continuum model of impression formation, from category-based to individuating processes: Influences of information and motivation on attention and interpretation. In M. P. Zanna (Ed.), *Advances in social psychology* (Vol. 23, pp. 1–74). San Diego, CA: Academic Press.

Floyd et al. v. City of New York et al., No. 1:08-cv-01034-SAS-HBP (S.D.N.Y. 2013).

Foley, L. A., & Pigott, M. A. (2002). Race, self presentation and reverse discrimination in jury decisions. *American Journal of Forensic Psychology*, 20(3), 37–52.

Free, M. D., Jr. (1997). The impact of federal sentencing reforms on African Americans. *Journal of Black Studies*, 28, 268–286.

Free, M. D., Jr. (2002). Race and presentencing decisions in the United States: A summary and critique of the research. *Criminal Justice Review*, 27, 203–232. doi:10.1177/073401680202700202

Freiburger, T. L., Marcum, C. D., & Pierce, M. (2010). The impact of race on the pretrial decision. *American Journal of Criminal Justice*, 35, 76–86. doi:10.1007/s12103-009-9069-z

Fukurai, H., & Krooth, R. (2003). *Race in the jury box: Affirmative action in jury selection*. Albany: State University of New York Press.

Fyock, J., & Stangor, C. (1994). The role of memory biases in stereotype maintenance. *British Journal of Social Psychology*, 33, 331–343. doi:10.1111/j.2044-8309.1994.tb01029.x

Gabbidon, S. L., Kowal, L. K., Jordan, K. L., Roberts, J. L., & Vincenzi, N. (2008). Race-based peremptory challenges: An empirical analysis of litigation from the U.S. Court of Appeals, 2002–2006. *American Journal of Criminal Justice*, 33, 59–68. doi:10.1007/s12103-007-9027-6

Gaertner, S. L., & Dovidio, J. F. (1986). The aversive form of racism. In J. F. Dovidio & S. L. Gaertner (Eds.), *Prejudice, discrimination, and racism* (pp. 61–89). San Diego, CA: Academic Press.

Garvey, S. P. (2000). The emotional economy of capital sentencing. *New York University Law Review*, 75, 26–73.

Gau, J. M., Mosher, C., & Pratt, T. C. (2010). An inquiry into the impact of suspect race on police use of tasers. *Police Quarterly*, 13, 27–48. doi:10.1177/1098611109357332

Gerstenfeld, P. B. (2010). Hate crimes. In C. J. Ferguson (Ed.), *Violent crime: Clinical and social implications* (pp. 257–275). Thousand Oaks, CA: Sage.

Glaser, J. (2006). The efficacy and effect of racial profiling: A mathematical simulation approach. *Journal of Policy Analysis and Management*, 25, 395–416. doi:10.1002/pam.20178

Glaze, L. E. (2011). *Correctional population in the United States, 2010* (NCJ 236319). Washington, DC: Bureau of Justice Statistics. Retrieved from http://www.bjs.gov/content/pub/pdf/cpus10.pdf

Goff, P. A., Eberhardt, J. L., Williams, M. J., & Jackson, M. C. (2008). Not yet human: Implicit knowledge, historical dehumanization, and contemporary consequences.

Journal of Personality and Social Psychology, 94, 292–306. doi:10.1037/0022-3514.94.2.292

Gordon, R. A., Bindrim, T. A., McNicholas, M. L., & Walden, T. L. (1988). Perceptions of blue-collar and white-collar crime: The effect of defendant race on simulated juror decisions. *Journal of Social Psychology, 128*, 191–197. doi:10.1080/00224545.1988.9711362

Greenwald, A. G., Oakes, M. A., & Hoffman, H. G. (2003). Targets of discrimination: Effects of race on responses to weapons holders. *Journal of Experimental Social Psychology, 39*, 399–405. doi:10.1016/S0022-1031(03)00020-9

Gudykunst, W. B., Matsumoto, Y., Ting-Toomey, S., & Nishida, T. (1996). The influence of cultural individualism-collectivism, self construals, and individual values on communication styles across cultures. *Human Communication Research, 22*, 510–543. doi:10.1111/j.1468-2958.1996.tb00377.x

Hannaford-Agor, P., & Waters, N. L. (2011). Safe harbors from fair-cross-section challenges? The practical limitations of measuring representation in the jury pool. *Journal of Empirical Legal Studies, 8*, 762–791. doi:10.1111/j.1740-1461.2011.01240.x

Hernandez v. New York, 500 U.S. 352 (1991).

Hodson, G., Hooper, H., Dovidio, J. F., & Gaertner, S. L. (2005). Aversive racism in Britain: The use of inadmissible evidence in legal decisions. *European Journal of Social Psychology, 35*, 437–448. doi:10.1002/ejsp.261

Huebner, B. M., & Bynum, T. S. (2008). The role of race and ethnicity in parole decisions. *Criminology, 46*, 907–938. doi:10.1111/j.1745-9125.2008.00130.x

Huggins, C. M. (2012). Traffic stop encounters: Officer and citizen race and perceptions of police propriety. *American Journal of Criminal Justice, 37*, 92–110. doi:10.1007/s12103-010-9097-8

Hunt, J. S. (2007). Implicit bias and hate crimes: A psychological framework and Critical Race Theory analysis. In R. L. Wiener, B. H. Bornstein, R. Schopp & S. L. Willborn (Eds.), *Social consciousness in legal decision making: Psychological perspectives* (pp. 247–265). New York, NY: Springer Science + Business Media.

Hunt, J. S. (2014, May). *Race, ethnic, and cultural influences on jury experiences and deliberation strategies.* Paper presented at the meeting of the Law and Society Association, Minneapolis, MN.

J. E. B. v. Alabama, 511 U.S. 127 (1994).

Johnson, B. D., & Betsinger, S. (2009). Punishing the "model minority": Asian-American criminal sentencing outcomes in federal district courts. *Criminology, 47*, 1045–1090. doi:10.1111/j.1745-9125.2009.00169.x

Johnson, S. L., Blume, J. H., Eisenberg, T., Hans, V. P., & Wells, M. T. (2012). The Delaware death penalty: An empirical study. *Iowa Law Review, 97*, 1925–1964.

Jones, C. S., & Kaplan, M. F. (2003). The effects of racially stereotypical crimes on juror decision-making and information-processing strategies. *Basic and Applied Social Psychology, 25*, 1–13. doi:10.1207/S15324834BASP2501_1

Keil, T. J., & Vito, G. F. (1995). Race and the death penalty in Kentucky murder trials: 1976–1991. *American Journal of Criminal Justice, 20*, 17–36. doi:10.1007/BF02886116

Kemmelmeier, M. (2005). The effects of race and social dominance orientation in simulated juror decision making. *Journal of Applied Social Psychology, 35*, 1030–1045. doi:10.1111/j.1559-1816.2005.tb02158.x

Kerr, N. L., Hymes, R. W., Anderson, A. B., & Weathers, J. E. (1995). Defendant-juror similarity and mock juror judgments. *Law and Human Behavior, 19*, 545–567. doi:10.1007/BF01499374

Kochel, T. R., Wilson, D. B., & Mastrofski, S. D. (2011). Effect of suspect race on officers' arrest decisions. *Criminology: An Interdisciplinary Journal, 49*, 473–512. doi:10.1111/j.1745-9125.2011.00230.x

Lee, C. (2007). Hispanics and the death penalty: Discriminatory charging practices in San Joaquin County, California. *Journal of Criminal Justice, 35*, 17–27. doi:10.1016/j.jcrimjus.2006.11.012

Levinson, J. D., & Peng, K. (2004). Different torts for different cohorts: A cultural psychological critique of tort law's actual cause and foreseeability inquiries. *Southern California Interdisciplinary Law Journal, 13*, 195–226.

Levinson, J. D., & Smith, R. J. (Eds.). (2012). *Implicit racial bias across the law.* Cambridge, England: Cambridge University Press. doi:10.1017/CBO9780511820595

Lin, J., Grattet, R., & Petersilia, J. (2010). "Back-end sentencing" and reimprisonment: Individual, organizational, and community predictors of parole sanctioning decisions. *Criminology, 48*, 759–795. doi:10.1111/j.1745-9125.2010.00201.x

Liptak, A. (2009, August 18). Supreme Court orders new look at death row case. *New York Times.* Retrieved from http://www.nytimes.com/2009/08/18/us/18scotus.html

Lynch, M., & Haney, C. (2000). Discrimination and instructional comprehension: Guided discretion, racial bias, and the death penalty. *Law and Human Behavior, 24*, 337–358. doi:10.1023/A:1005588221761

Lynch, M., & Haney, C. (2009). Capital jury deliberation: Effects on death sentencing, comprehension, and discrimination. *Law and Human Behavior, 33,* 481–496. doi:10.1007/s10979-008-9168-2

Lynch, M., & Haney, C. (2011). Mapping the racial bias of the white male capital juror: Jury composition and the "empathic divide". *Law and Society Review, 45,* 69–102. doi:10.1111/j.1540-5893.2011.00428.x

MacCoun, R. J., & Tyler, T. R. (1988). The basis of citizens' perceptions of the criminal jury: Procedural fairness, accuracy, and efficiency. *Law and Human Behavior, 12,* 333–352. doi:10.1007/BF01044389

Macrae, C. N., Milne, A. B., & Bodenhausen, G. V. (1994). Stereotypes as energy-saving devices: A peek inside the cognitive toolbox. *Journal of Personality and Social Psychology, 66,* 37–47. doi:10.1037/0022-3514.66.1.37

Madon, S., Guyll, M., Aboufadel, K., Montiel, E., Smith, A., Palumbo, P., & Jussim, L. (2001). Ethnic and national stereotypes: The Princeton trilogy revisited and revised. *Personality and Social Psychology Bulletin, 27,* 996–1010. doi:10.1177/0146167201278007

Maeder, E., Dempsey, J., & Pozzulo, J. (2012). Behind the veil of juror decision making: Testing the effects of Muslim veils and defendant race in the courtroom. *Criminal Justice and Behavior, 39,* 666–678. doi:10.1177/0093854812436478

Maeder, E. M., & Hunt, J. S. (2011). Talking about a black man: The influence of defendant and character witness race on jurors' use of character evidence. *Behavioral Sciences and the Law, 29,* 608–620. doi:10.1002/bsl.996

Martell, R. F. (1991). Sex bias at work: The effects of attentional and memory demands on performance ratings of men and women. *Journal of Applied Social Psychology, 21,* 1939–1960. doi:10.1111/j.1559-1816.1991.tb00515.x

Mazzella, R., & Feingold, A. (1994). The effects of physical attractiveness, race, socioeconomic status, and gender of defendants and victims on judgments of mock jurors: A meta-analysis. *Journal of Applied Social Psychology, 24,* 1315–1338. doi:10.1111/j.1559-1816.1994.tb01552.x

McCleskey v. Kemp, 481 U.S. 279 (1987).

McFadden, R. D. (2006, November 26). Police kill man after a Queens bachelor party. *New York Times.* Retrieved from http://www.nytimes.com/2006/11/26/nyregion/26cops.html

Melilli, K. J. (1996). Batson in practice: What we have learned about Batson and peremptory challenges. *Notre Dame Law Review, 71,* 447–503.

Miller-El v. Dretke, 545 U.S. 231 (2005).

Mitchell, O. (2005). A meta-analysis of race and sentencing research: Explaining the inconsistencies. *Journal of Quantitative Criminology, 21,* 439–466. doi:10.1007/s10940-005-7362-7

Mitchell, T. L., Haw, R. M., Pfeifer, J. E., & Meissner, C. A. (2005). Racial bias in mock juror decision-making: A meta-analytic review of defendant treatment. *Law and Human Behavior, 29,* 621–637. doi:10.1007/s10979-005-8122-9

Morris, M. W., & Peng, K. (1994). Culture and cause: American and Chinese attributions for social and physical events. *Journal of Personality and Social Psychology, 67,* 949–971. doi:10.1037/0022-3514.67.6.949

Mumola, C. J. (2007). *Arrest-related deaths in the United States, 2003–2005.* Washington, DC: Bureau of Justice Statistics. doi:10.1037/e719082007-001

Najdowski, C. J. (2011). Stereotype threat in criminal interrogations: Why innocent Black suspects are at risk for confessing falsely. *Psychology, Public Policy, and Law, 17,* 562–591. doi:10.1037/a0023741

Najdowski, C. J. (2012). *Stereotype threat in police encounters: Why African Americans are at risk of being targeted as suspects* (Unpublished doctoral dissertation). University of Illinois–Chicago.

National Center for State Courts. (1999, May). *How the public views the state courts: A 1999 national survey.* Paper presented at the National Conference on Public Trust and Confidence in the Justice System, Washington, DC.

Nelson, T. D. (2009). *Handbook of prejudice, stereotyping, and discrimination.* New York, NY: Psychology Press.

Neuberg, S. L., & Fiske, S. T. (1987). Motivational influences on impression formation: Outcome dependency, accuracy-driven attention, and individuating processes. *Journal of Personality and Social Psychology, 53,* 431–444. doi:10.1037/0022-3514.53.3.431

Niemann, Y. F. (2001). Stereotypes about Chicanas and Chicanos: Implications for counseling. *Counseling Psychologist, 29,* 55–90. doi:10.1177/0011000001291003

North Carolina Racial Justice Act, N.C. Gen. Stat., §§ 15A-2010 to 2012 (2009).

North Carolina v. Robinson, No. 91 CRS 23143 (N.C. Super. Ct. Apr. 20, 2012).

Nosek, B. A., Smyth, F. L., Hansen, J. J., Devos, T., Lindner, N. M., Ranganath, K. A., . . . Banaji, M. R. (2007). Pervasiveness and correlates of implicit attitudes and stereotypes. *European Review of Social Psychology, 18,* 36–88. doi:10.1080/10463280701489053

Novak, K. J., & Chamlin, M. B. (2012). Racial threat, suspicion, and police behavior: The impact of race and place in traffic enforcement. *Crime and Delinquency, 58,* 275–300. doi:10.1177/0011128708322943

Padilla, J. B., Miller, M. K., & Broadus, A. D. (2008). Analysis of Hispanic representation and conceptualization in psychology and law research. *Behavioral Sciences and the Law, 26,* 655–670. doi:10.1002/bsl.818

Parks, G. S., Jones, S., & Cardi, W. J. (Eds.). (2008). *Critical race realism: Intersections of psychology, race, and law.* New York, NY: New Press.

Paternoster, R., & Brame, R. (2008). Reassessing race disparities in Maryland capital cases. *Criminology, 46,* 971–1008. doi:10.1111/j.1745-9125.2008.00132.x

Pearson, A. R., Dovidio, J. F., & Gaertner, S. L. (2009). The nature of contemporary prejudice: Insights from aversive racism. *Social and Personality Psychology Compass, 3,* 314–338. doi:10.1111/j.1751-9004.2009.00183.x

Pennington, N., & Hastie, R. (1986). Evidence evaluation in complex decision making. *Journal of Personality and Social Psychology, 51,* 242–258. doi:10.1037/0022-3514.51.2.242

Perez, D. A., Hosch, H. M., Ponder, B., & Trejo, G. C. (1993). Ethnicity of defendants and jurors as influences on jury decisions. *Journal of Applied Social Psychology, 23,* 1249–1262. doi:10.1111/j.1559-1816.1993.tb01031.x

Perry v. Schwarzenegger, 704 F. Supp. 2d 921 (2010).

Peruche, B. M., & Plant, E. A. (2006). The correlates of law enforcement officers' automatic and controlled race-based responses to criminal suspects. *Basic and Applied Social Psychology, 28,* 193–199. doi:10.1207/s15324834basp2802_9

Peters v. Kiff, 407 U.S. 493 (1972).

Petrocelli, M., Piquero, A. R., & Smith, M. R. (2003). Conflict theory and racial profiling: An empirical analysis of police traffic stop data. *Journal of Criminal Justice, 31,* 1–11. doi:10.1016/S0047-2352(02)00195-2

Pfeifer, J. E., & Bernstein, D. J. (2003). Expressions of modern racism in judgments of others: The role of task and target specificity on attributions of guilt. *Social Behavior and Personality, 31,* 749–765. doi:10.2224/sbp.2003.31.8.749

Plant, E. A., Goplen, J., & Kunstman, J. W. (2011). Selective responses to threat: The roles of race and gender in decisions to shoot. *Personality and Social Psychology Bulletin, 37,* 1274–1281. doi:10.1177/0146167211408617

Plant, E. A., & Peruche, B. M. (2005). The consequences of race for police officers' responses to criminal suspects. *Psychological Science, 16,* 180–183. doi:10.1111/j.0956-7976.2005.00800.x

Plant, E. A., Peruche, B. M., & Butz, D. A. (2005). Eliminating automatic racial bias: Making race non-diagnostic for responses to criminal suspects. *Journal of Experimental Social Psychology, 41,* 141–156. doi:10.1016/j.jesp.2004.07.004

Pratto, F., & Pitpitan, E. V. (2008). Ethnocentrism and sexism: How stereotypes legitimize six types of power. *Social and Personality Psychology Compass, 2,* 2159–2176. doi:10.1111/j.1751-9004.2008.00148.x

Pratto, F., Sidanius, J., & Levin, S. (2006). Social dominance theory and the dynamics of intergroup relations: Taking stock and looking forward. *European Review of Social Psychology, 17,* 271–320. doi:10.1080/10463280601055772

Price Waterhouse v. Hopkins, 490 U.S. 228 (1989).

Rattan, A., Levine, C. S., Dweck, C. S., & Eberhardt, J. L. (2012). Race and the fragility of the legal distinction between juveniles and adults. *PLoS ONE, 7*(5), e36680. doi:10.1371/journal.pone.0036680

Reitzel, J. D., Rice, S. K., & Piquero, A. R. (2004). Lines and shadows: Perceptions of racial profiling and the Hispanic experience. *Journal of Criminal Justice, 32,* 607–616. doi:10.1016/j.jcrimjus.2004.08.011

Roh, S., & Robinson, M. (2009). A geographic approach to racial profiling: The microanalysis and macroanalysis of racial disparity in traffic stops. *Police Quarterly, 12,* 137–169. doi:10.1177/1098611109332422

Rose, M. R. (1999). The peremptory challenge accused of race or gender discrimination? Some data from one county. *Law and Human Behavior, 23,* 695–702. doi:10.1023/A:1022393506784

Rottman, D. B., Hansen, R., Mott, N., & Grimes, L. (2003). *Perceptions of the courts in your community: The influence of experience, race, and ethnicity.* Williamsburg, VA: National Center for State Courts.

Sadler, M. S., Correll, J., Park, B., & Judd, C. M. (2012). The world is not Black and White: Racial bias in the decision to shoot in a multiethnic context. *Journal of Social Issues, 68,* 286–313. doi:10.1111/j.1540-4560.2012.01749.x

Sargent, M. J., & Bradfield, A. L. (2004). Race and information processing in criminal trials: Does the defendant's race affect how the facts are evaluated? *Personality and Social Psychology Bulletin, 30,* 995–1008. doi:10.1177/0146167204265741

Scheb, J. M., Lyons, W., & Wagers, K. A. (2009). Race, gender, and age discrepancies in police motor vehicle stops in Knoxville, Tennessee: Evidence of racially biased policing? *Police Practice and Research: An International Journal, 10,* 75–87. doi:10.1080/15614260802674081

Schlesinger, T. (2011). The failure of race neutral policies: How mandatory terms and sentencing enhancements contribute to mass racialized incarceration. *Crime and Delinquency, 57,* 56–81. doi:10.1177/0011128708323629

Schmader, T., Johns, M., & Forbes, C. (2008). An integrated process model of stereotype threat effects on performance. *Psychological Review, 115*, 336–356. doi:10.1037/0033-295X.115.2.336

Schneider, D. J. (2004). *The psychology of stereotyping.* New York, NY: Guilford Press.

Schuck, A. M., Rosenbaum, D. P., & Hawkins, D. F. (2008). The influence of race/ethnicity, social class, and neighborhood context on residents' attitudes toward the police. *Police Quarterly, 11*, 496–519. doi:10.1177/1098611108318115

Schwartz, J., & Fitzsimmons, E. G. (2011, March 10). Illinois governor signs capital punishment ban. *New York Times.* Retrieved from http://www.nytimes.com/2011/03/10/us/10illinois.html

Schwartz, S. L., & Hunt, J. S. (2011). Considering her circumstances: How ethnicity and cultural relativist arguments affect sexual harassment judgments by undergraduate and community mock jurors. *Behavioral Sciences and the Law, 29*, 419–438. doi:10.1002/bsl.972

Sears, D. O., & Henry, P. J. (2005). Over thirty years later: A contemporary look at symbolic racism. In M. P. Zanna (Ed.), *Advances in experimental social psychology* (Vol. 37, pp. 95–150). San Diego, CA: Elsevier Academic Press.

Severson, K. (2011, September 22). Georgia inmate executed; raised racial issues in death penalty. *New York Times.* Retrieved from http://query.nytimes.com/gst/fullpage.html?res=9F06E5D61F3FF931A1575AC0A9679D8B63

Sommers, S. R. (2006). On racial diversity and group decision making: Identifying multiple effects of racial composition on jury deliberations. *Journal of Personality and Social Psychology, 90*, 597–612. doi:10.1037/0022-3514.90.4.597

Sommers, S. R., & Adekanmbi, O. O. (2008). Race and juries: An experimental psychology perspective. In G. S. Parks, S. Jones, & W. J. Cardi (Eds.), *Critical race realism: Intersections of psychology, race, and law* (pp. 78–93). New York, NY: New Press.

Sommers, S. R., & Ellsworth, P. C. (2000). Race in the courtroom: Perceptions of guilt and dispositional attributions. *Personality and Social Psychology Bulletin, 26*, 1367–1379. doi:10.1177/0146167200263005

Sommers, S. R., & Ellsworth, P. C. (2001). White juror bias: An investigation of prejudice against Black defendants in the American courtroom. *Psychology, Public Policy, and Law, 7*, 201–229. doi:10.1037/1076-8971.7.1.201

Sommers, S. R., & Ellsworth, P. C. (2009). "Race salience" in juror decision-making: Misconceptions, clarifications, and unanswered questions. *Behavioral Sciences and the Law, 27*, 599–609. doi:10.1002/bsl.877

Sommers, S. R., & Norton, M. I. (2007). Race-based judgments, race-neutral justifications: Experimental examination of peremptory use and the Batson Challenge procedure. *Law and Human Behavior, 31*, 261–273. doi:10.1007/s10979-006-9048-6

Sommers, S. R., & Norton, M. I. (2008). Race and jury selection: Psychological perspectives on the peremptory challenge debate. *American Psychologist, 63*, 527–539. doi:10.1037/0003-066X.63.6.527

Songer, M. J., & Unah, I. (2006). The effect of race, gender, and location on prosecutorial decisions to seek the death penalty in South Carolina. *South Carolina Law Review, 58*, 161–210.

Stangor, C., & Schaller, M. (1996). Stereotypes as individual and collective representations. In C. N. Macrae, C. Stangor, & M. Hewstone (Eds.), *Stereotypes and stereotyping* (pp. 3–37). New York, NY: Guilford Press.

State of New Jersey v. Pedro Soto, A734A. 2d 350 (N.J. Super. Ct. Law Div. 1996).

Steffensmeier, D., & Britt, C. L. (2001). Judges' race and judicial decision making: Do Black judges sentence differently? *Social Science Quarterly, 82*, 749–764. doi:10.1111/0038-4941.00057

Steffensmeier, D., & Demuth, S. (2001). Ethnicity and judges' sentencing decisions: Hispanic-Black-White comparisons. *Criminology, 39*, 145–178. doi:10.1111/j.1745-9125.2001.tb00919.x

Steffensmeier, D., & Demuth, S. (2006). Does gender modify the effects of race-ethnicity on criminal sanctioning? Sentences for male and female White, Black, and Hispanic defendants. *Journal of Quantitative Criminology, 22*, 241–261. doi:10.1007/s10940-006-9010-2

Summers, A., Hayward, R. D., & Miller, M. K. (2010). Death qualification as systematic exclusion of jurors with certain religious and other characteristics. *Journal of Applied Social Psychology, 40*, 3218–3234. doi:10.1111/j.1559-1816.2010.00698.x

Swain v. Alabama, 380 U.S. 202 (1965).

Sweeney, L. T., & Haney, C. (1992). The influence of race on sentencing: A meta-analytic review of experimental studies. *Behavioral Sciences and the Law, 10*, 179–195. doi:10.1002/bsl.2370100204

Tartaro, C., & Sedelmaier, C. M. (2009). A tale of two counties: The impact of pretrial release, race, and ethnicity upon sentencing decisions. *Criminal Justice Studies, 22*, 203–221. doi:10.1080/14786010902975507

Taylor, T. S., & Hosch, H. M. (2004). An examination of jury verdicts for evidence of a similarity-leniency effect, an out-group punitiveness effect or a black sheep effect. *Law and Human Behavior, 28*, 587–598. doi:10.1023/B:LAHU.0000046436.36228.71

Thomson, E. (1997). Discrimination and the death penalty in Arizona. *Criminal Justice Review, 22*, 65–76. doi:10.1177/073401689702200106

Tillyer, R., Engel, R. S., & Wooldredge, J. (2008). The intersection of racial profiling research and the law. *Journal of Criminal Justice, 36*, 138–153. doi:10.1016/j.jcrimjus.2008.02.004

Tillyer, R., & Hartley, R. D. (2010). Driving racial profiling research forward: Learning lessons from sentencing research. *Journal of Criminal Justice, 38*, 657–665. doi:10.1016/j.jcrimjus.2010.04.039

Tyler, T. R. (2001). Public trust and confidence in legal authorities: What do majority and minority group members want from the law and legal institutions? *Behavioral Sciences and the Law, 19*, 215–235. doi:10.1002/bsl.438

Unah, I. (2009). Choosing those who will die: The effect of race, gender, and law in prosecutorial decision to seek the death penalty in Durham County, North Carolina. *Michigan Journal of Race and Law, 15*, 135–179.

U.S. Department of Justice. (2012, September 18). *Letter of findings to Alamance County, N.C., Sheriff's Office.* Retrieved from http://www.justice.gov/iso/opa/resources/171201291812462488198.pdf

Viglione, J., Hannon, L., & DeFina, R. (2011). The impact of light skin on prison time for Black female offenders. *Social Science Journal, 48*, 250–258. doi:10.1016/j.soscij.2010.08.003

Walker, L., & Monahan, J. (1987). Social frameworks: A new use of social science in law. *Virginia Law Review, 73*, 559–598. doi:10.2307/1072923

Ward, G., Farrell, A., & Rousseau, D. (2009). Does racial balance in workforce representation yield equal justice? Race relations of sentencing in federal court organizations. *Law and Society Review, 43*, 757–806. doi:10.1111/j.1540-5893.2009.00388.x

Weitzer, R., & Brunson, R. K. (2009). Strategic responses to the police among inner-city youth. *Sociological Quarterly, 50*, 235–256. doi:10.1111/j.1533-8525.2009.01139.x

Weitzer, R., & Tuch, S. A. (1999). Race, class, and perceptions of discrimination by the police. *Crime and Delinquency, 45*, 494–507. doi:10.1177/0011128799045004006

Weitzer, R., & Tuch, S. A. (2004). Race and perceptions of police misconduct. *Social Problems, 51*, 305–325. doi:10.1525/sp.2004.51.3.305

Weitzer, R., & Tuch, S. A. (2005). Racially biased policing: Determinants of citizen perceptions. *Social Forces, 83*, 1009–1030. doi:10.1353/sof.2005.0050

Weitzer, R., Tuch, S. A., & Skogan, W. G. (2008). Police-community relations in a majority-Black city. *Journal of Research in Crime and Delinquency, 45*, 398–428. doi:10.1177/0022427808322617

Welch, K. (2007). Black criminal stereotypes and racial profiling. *Journal of Contemporary Criminal Justice, 23*, 276–288. doi:10.1177/1043986207306870

Whren et al. v. United States, 517 U.S. 806 (1996).

Wiener, R. L., Krauss, D. A., & Lieberman, J. D. (2011). Mock jury research: Where do we go from here? *Behavioral Sciences and the Law, 29*, 467–479. doi:10.1002/bsl.989

Withrow, B. L. (2006). *Racial profiling: From rhetoric to reason.* Upper Saddle River, NJ: Pearson/Prentice-Hall.

Withrow, B. L., & Dailey, J. D. (2012). Racial profiling litigation: Current status and emerging controversies. *Journal of Contemporary Criminal Justice, 28*, 122–145. doi:10.1177/1043986211425731

Wittenbrink, B., Judd, C. M., & Park, B. (2001). Spontaneous prejudice in context: Variability in automatically activated attitudes. *Journal of Personality and Social Psychology, 81*, 815–827. doi:10.1037/0022-3514.81.5.815

Wolfe, S. E., Pyrooz, D. C., & Spohn, C. C. (2011). Unraveling the effect of offender citizenship status on federal sentencing outcomes. *Social Science Research, 40*, 349–362. doi:10.1016/j.ssresearch.2010.09.013

Wooldredge, J., Griffin, T., & Rauschenberg, F. (2005). (Un)anticipated effects of sentencing reform on the disparate treatment of defendants. *Law and Society Review, 39*, 835–874. doi:10.1111/j.1540-5893.2005.00246.x

Worden, R. E., McLean, S. J., & Wheeler, A. P. (2012). Testing for racial profiling with the veil-of-darkness method. *Police Quarterly, 15*, 92–111. doi:10.1177/1098611111433027

York, E., & Cornwell, B. (2006). Status on trial: Social characteristics and influence in the jury room. *Social Forces, 85*, 455–477. doi: 10.1353/sof.2006.0150

PART II

CRIMINAL INVESTIGATIONS AND JURY TRIALS

CHAPTER 6

INVESTIGATIVE PSYCHOLOGY

Paul J. Taylor, Brent Snook, Craig Bennell, and Louise Porter

Investigative psychology seeks to improve our understanding of criminal behavior and the investigative process. It emerged in response to early experiential approaches to offender profiling and a desire to formulate an alternative, empirical method of supporting police investigations (Canter, 2000). From the beginning, investigative psychology distinguished itself from other forms of profiling by relying on the systematic exploration of how offenders and investigators behaved during their offenses and investigations. This empirical approach led researchers to utilize novel data on offenders' behavior (e.g., derived from case files) and to develop new ways of analyzing this "real-world" data. It also required theoretical developments, such as a specification of the conditions necessary to allow accurate inferences from snapshots of offender behavior. This historical background and the unique conceptual contributions of investigative psychology are discussed in the first two sections of this chapter.

The third section of this chapter expands on these foundations by discussing four prominent areas of investigative psychology research. The first area, arguably most synonymous with investigative psychology, concerns the differentiation of offenders on the basis of their offense behavior, and the association of such distinctions to offender characteristics. We review the unique methodology that researchers have used to analyze offense behavior, and the common behavioral tendencies that have emerged across different types of crime. The second area concerns the social psychology of criminal groups and the process of leadership within such groups. This work

has contributed to our understanding of the processes that compel and inhibit gang crime and, by drawing on the sociological technique of social network analysis, it has shed light on how online and offline networks structure criminal activities.

The third and fourth areas of research we discuss move away from offender behavior and concern themselves with the investigative process. We begin with research that has examined investigators' expertise and decision making. Drawing on cognitive theories of reasoning, this research has challenged the view that investigative judgments are often flawed, showing instead that many decisions are fueled by appropriate heuristics that suffice in a world of heightened time pressure and high stakes. Finally, we consider a number of contributions that have used empirical data to develop specific investigative practices, such as crime linkage and the negotiation tactics used in hostage situations. We show how a combination of experimental research and field studies has enabled investigative psychology to develop solutions to real-world problems while making important contributions to psychological science.

We conclude by examining the impact of investigative psychology on policy and practice. We contrast examples of investigative interviewing and hostage negotiations, where research has had a dramatic impact, with major crime linkage systems, where research has raised concerns over reliability but has not yet led to changes in practice. We argue that such latter examples exist, in part because of a disconnect between the nature of experiments and

http://dx.doi.org/10.1037/14462-006
APA Handbook of Forensic Psychology: Vol. 2. Criminal Investigation, Adjudication, and Sentencing Outcomes,
B. L. Cutler and P. A. Zapf (Editors-in-Chief)
Copyright © 2015 by the American Psychological Association. All rights reserved.

what occurs in practice, and we conclude by discussing how investigative psychology has sought to breach this divide.

IMPORTANCE OF THE PROBLEM

The contribution of psychology to the investigations of law enforcement and security organizations is not new. During the 1970s, the U.S. Federal Bureau of Investigation (FBI) provided 192 recommendations about the characteristics and motives of perpetrators of serious crimes, by means of an "examination of the crime scene and the extrapolation of certain relevant psychological material" (Pinizzotto, 1984). By the 1980s, psychologists had begun not only to give advice on cases but also proposed new techniques that were based on psychological principles. Frank Boltz and Harvey Schlossberg drew on clinical principles of therapeutic listening and persuasion to define an approach to negotiating with hostage takers that now forms the basis of modern crisis negotiation practice (Vecchi, Van Hasselt, & Romano, 2005; Wells, Taylor, & Giebels, 2013). Fisher and Geiselman's (1992) analysis of police interviewing led to the development of the cognitive interview, which utilizes principles of memory to enhance the recall of witnesses (see Chapter 7, this volume for a review of research on eyewitness memory).

While there was clear value in applying cognitive and social psychology to the investigative process, the integration of psychology into practice did not come without its problems. The use of offender profiling, in part spurred on by media portrayals (e.g., the film *Silence of the Lambs*), popularized a form of consulting that took good deductive inference to the level of unsubstantiated claims and personal opinion. In the United Kingdom, this was exemplified by the case of murdered Rachel Nickell, where a clinical psychologist's profile of Nickell's killer made some arguably gratuitous assertions that led to an undercover investigation against an innocent man (Alison, Bennell, Mokros, & Ormerod, 2002). Such reliance on unsubstantiated inference has since been shown to be common within major UK investigations (Alison, Smith, Eastman, & Rainbow, 2003). By coding each statement in the profiles using Toulmin's (1958) method of categorizing argument,

Alison et al. (2003) showed that of the 4,000 claims made, nearly 80% were unsubstantiated and less than 31% were falsifiable. It is not surprising, then, that Torres, Boccaccini, and Miller's (2006) survey revealed that fewer than 25% of trained psychologists and psychiatrists viewed profiling as scientifically reliable or valid.

Investigative psychology emerged in response to the issues surrounding offender profiling and as part of an effort by a number of psychologists to ensure that future contributions were grounded in theoretically and empirically informed analysis. Indeed, the term investigative psychology was coined by David Canter to reflect the growing contributions of psychology to police investigations. The early focus of investigative psychology was the differentiation of serious crime offenders based on their behavior at the crime scene: a scientific offender profiling (Snook, Cullen, Bennell, Taylor, & Gendreau, 2008). The field has since grown to make significant contributions to our understanding of gang violence and property crime, investigator reasoning and decision making, and investigative techniques such as crime linkage and hostage negotiation. Its scope remains related to, but distinct from, forensic psychology because it is concerned with what happens prior to the penal systems and not with how offenders are treated once convicted. It is also defined, at least in part, by its innovative use of archival material (e.g., police investigative files) as the basis for data on offenders, and by its techniques for quantifying and analyzing this data in a way that allows for meaningful inferences about otherwise hard-to-reach populations (Alison, Snook, & Stein, 2001).

Alongside providing insights that improve investigations, investigative psychology has also been instrumental in highlighting dubious practices. One area of such contributions concerns the early framework for offender profiling. For example, Canter, Alison, Alison, and Wentink (2004) showed that the FBI's method of classifying murderers as "organized" or "disorganized" was not consistent with the behavior of 100 offenders, who exhibited behaviors characteristic of organized offending and disorganized offending in the same offense. Other work has sought to provide retrospective evaluation of actuarial aids deployed in investigations. For example,

Snook, Taylor, and Bennell (2004) showed that predictions about a serial offender's home location based on the location of the crime sites—a technique known as geographic profiling—can be made accurately by students, without the help of expensive computer software. On the basis of these results, they argued that police services should be open to trusting investigators' judgments when the utilization of computer solutions is not viable.

RELEVANT PSYCHOLOGICAL THEORY AND PRINCIPLES

The theoretical underpinnings of investigative psychology are drawn from many areas of social science. Contributions to our understanding of offender behavior have drawn on theories from social and personality psychology and related disciplines such as criminology and geography. For example, the ideas that underpin geographic profiling rest on criminological work on crime pattern theory (Brantingham & Brantingham, 1981) and routine activity theory (Cohen & Felson, 1979). Similarly, efforts to understand the factors that draw people into terrorism are grounded in social psychological theories (e.g., social identity theory; Ysseldyk, Matheson, & Anisman, 2010) and clinical perspectives (e.g., static and dynamic risk factors; Jacques & Taylor, 2013). Contributions to our understanding of investigative processes have drawn on theories from cognitive psychology. For example, much of the research on investigator decision making considers the role of heuristics (Gilovich, Griffin, & Kahneman, 2002) or uses concepts of situation awareness and assessment (Klein, 1989). Similarly, research on interrogation has embraced cognitive load as an explanation for why suspects find it difficult to lie when giving their account in reverse order (Vrij, Granhag, Mann, & Leal, 2011; see also Chapter 8, this volume) or when challenged with actual evidence in a strategic way (Hartwig, Granhag, Stromwall, & Kronkvist, 2006).

Alongside embracing theories from other areas of psychology, investigative psychology has also been instrumental in clarifying thinking about the link between an offender's behavior and his or her characteristics (see Volume 1, Chapter 8, this handbook for a review of theories of crime and criminal behavior). This actions-to-characteristics relationship, often referred to as a profiling equation (Canter, 2000), hypothesizes that actions at a crime scene reflect more fundamental interpersonal tendencies of the offender, which will be born out in how she or he acts in other contexts of life. This account of criminality is different from explanations that focus on psychological deficiencies or the life events that provide the tipping point into crime (Loeber & Dishion, 1983). Thus, unlike forensic psychology, which usually concerns itself with the factors that predict crime in order to provide risk assessments and therapeutic interventions, investigative psychology focuses on uncovering the relationship between aspects of offending and aspects of the offender's noncriminal life.

As Alison et al. (2002) identified, this focus implies two conditions about the nature of offense behavior. The first condition is that offenders must act in a way that is consistent enough to allow them to be differentiated from other offenders. If the behavior of the same offender varies more than the behavior of multiple offenders, then classification based on behavior would be illogical. This condition is often referred to as the consistency assumption. The second condition is that differences in offense behavior must relate in a predictable way to distinctions in offenders' characteristics or broader pattern of life. If information about an offender (e.g., occupation) cannot be inferred from his or her crime scene behavior in an organized and consistent manner, then the profiling equation breaks down because there is no clear link between the actions and characteristics. This condition is often referred to as the homology assumption.

The importance of these assumptions becomes clear when considering some of the tasks undertaken by investigators. One task, known as crime linkage, involves determining whether a single offender is responsible for a series of offenses on the basis of the existence of a discernable and common pattern in behavior across the offenses (Bennell, Snook, MacDonald, House, & Taylor, 2012). If there were no patterns of consistent and differentiable behavior over a series of offenses, then any attempt at crime linkage would be fruitless because it would not be possible to differentiate the offenses of one offender from those of another.

RESEARCH REVIEW

Although the topics of research in investigative psychology are diverse, most of the studies fall into three broad areas: the nature of offender behavior, the social psychology of group crime, and the cognitive psychology of investigator decision making. We review contributions in each of these areas in this section.

Offender Differentiation

Investigative psychology was originally motivated by the problem of differentiating the ways in which offenders behave during their offenses, on the basis that these variations may reflect underlying differences in the offender's motivations or interpersonal tendencies (Canter, 2000). This required an identification of the salient behavioral features of the offense and then an attempt to relate these behavioral features to specific offender characteristics. In the first published study to use the methodology synonymous with investigative psychology, Nutch and Bloombaum (1968) examined 37 observed behaviors of 598 members of delinquent gangs. By exploring the intercorrelations of gang behaviors through multidimensional scaling, they found that gang members could be classified as one of three distinct types: the "retreatist," the "authority-protest," and the "good-boy activities and developing alienation." Each type was associated with a cluster of background features, previous convictions, and an approach toward life that distinguished it from the other two types. Thus, Nutch and Bloombaum's analysis encapsulates the notion that offense behaviors instantiate the offenders' wider approach to social interactions.

Since this early work, researchers have classified the offense behavior of many offense types, including homicide (Salfati, 2000), rape (Canter, Bennell, Alison, & Reddy, 2003), arson (Canter & Fritzon, 1998), hostage taking (Wilson, 2000), and computer hacking (Kjaerland, 2005). The approach taken in the majority of this work follows Nutch and Bloombaum's method of coding information about the offense behavior and examining the co-occurrences of these behaviors to identify types of offending. A popular method of performing such analyses, which in many ways is quite unique to investigative psychology, is to use multidimensional scaling. In this approach, the behaviors that occur and do not occur in an offense are coded as variables, and the multidimensional scaling analysis produces a visual presentation of the aggregate pattern of co-occurrences among the behaviors across multiple offenses. Behaviors that regularly co-occur in offenses appear close together in the visual presentation, while those that seldom co-occur appear further apart. This makes it possible to identify groups of behaviors that may be interpreted as reflecting a common approach to offending. Predictions about offenders' motivations for offending can then be tested by searching for evidence or otherwise of regions of highly co-occurring behaviors that instantiate the underpinning motivation. Such regions typically occur as wedge-like divisions, with behaviors central to the majority of offenses appearing at the mid-point where all the wedges touch, and behaviors specific to the styles of offenders appearing toward the outer edge of each wedge. In the literature, these divisions are typically described as themes to denote them as fuzzy sets of behavior rather than absolute classifications, in the same way that the colors red, green, and blue are labels used to define segments of a color wheel rather than exact sections of the wheel.

As research on offender differentiation has matured, it has become clear that the co-occurrence of behaviors across a variety of crime types is remarkably consistent. This has allowed researchers to propose metatheories of the different themes that distinguish offender behavior and motivations (Canter & Fritzon, 1998; Salfati & Taylor, 2006). One compelling account argues for three themes, which reflect the various destructive personal narratives that drive offenders' behavior (e.g., Canter, 1995; Canter & Youngs, 2012). These themes are *victim as an object*, characterized by indifferent and often frenzied, excessively violent actions; *victim as vehicle*, characterized by self-serving actions made possible through the victim, such as sexual acts; and *victim as a person*, characterized by pseudo-intimate behaviors in which the offender plays out a desire for personal closeness or control. Each of these narratives reflects a fundamental difference in how offenders think about their interpersonal lives, which is instantiated in different behaviors at the crime scene.

Although this systematic approach to understanding criminal behavior is more robust than early descriptive accounts, it is not without limitations. One common concern is the high number of offenses that involve behaviors from multiple themes within a model. This is a concern because it brings into question the extent to which the classifications offered by thematic models provide the basis for a homogenous link between type of actions and type of characteristics. For example, using the criterion that two thirds of the behaviors in an offense had to be associated with one theme over the other themes, Salfati and Bateman (2005) were only able to assign 41% of murder cases to a particular theme. Conversely, in their analysis of homicide offenders, Trojan and Salfati (2011) found evidence of the behavioral themes described above, but also found that 95% of their single offenders fell into only one theme. In this case, the thematic classification of the behaviors was not able to usefully differentiate offenders.

There have also been some direct tests of whether the homology assumption holds when using thematic models. These studies often fail to find compelling evidence of a link between actions and characteristics (e.g., Häkkänen, Puolakka, & Santtila, 2004; Santtila, Häkkänen, Canter, & Elfgren, 2003; Woodhams & Toye, 2007). For example, conceptualizing homology as a dimension, Mokros and Alison (2002) reasoned that there should be a positive association between the similarity of offenders' crime scene behaviors and the similarity of their background characteristics. In this clever design, the homology assumption is tested by the degree of similarity across offenders, with a greater similarity affording more support to the idea that certain types of offenders use certain groups of behavior. In their examination of 100 male rapists, however, Mokros and Alison did not find a positive relationship between the similarity in rapists' offending patterns and the rapists' age, sociodemographic features, or

criminal records. More recently, Doan and Snook (2008) classified 87 arsonists and 177 robbers using established thematic models and then compared the background characteristics of these classified offenders. Their analysis found that the homology assumption was violated in 56% of comparisons for arsonists and in 67% of comparisons for robbers.

A second set of problems with the thematic models stem from the data and the analytical approach used in their derivation. In many studies, the data that researchers examine comes from police reports captured in crime databases such as the Homicide Investigation Tracking System (HITS) and Violent Crime Linkage Analysis System (ViCLAS), yet the reliability and validity of these databases has not been robustly examined, opening up the possibility that published research and the resulting knowledge is based on a "nonsense in, nonsense out" analysis (Bennell et al., 2012). Indeed, in a recent study of this issue, Canadian police officers using the ViCLAS system to code a crime scene report managed to achieve an acceptable level of interrater agreement on only 10% of offense behaviors (Snook, Luther, House, Bennell, & Taylor, 2012). This low reliability raises questions about the legitimacy of using such data for research.

In terms of an analytical approach, Taylor, Donald, Jacques, and Conchie (2012) have demonstrated that the method typically used to measure the co-occurrence of behaviors within offenses operates in a way that is not independent of the frequency with which behaviors occur across offenses. Specifically, most studies measure the association among offense behaviors using the Jaccard coefficient because it omits joint nonoccurrences in its calculation. The rationale for this is that Jaccard reduces the potential bias that occurs when nonoccurrences in data reflect a failure to observe the behavior at the crime scene, rather than actual nonoccurrence. This omission, however, means that Jaccard's measure of co-occurrence is linked with variable frequency, with high-frequency variables having a greater opportunity to co-occur. In this circumstance, the outcome of a multidimensional scaling analysis is in part driven by the artifact of using the Jaccard coefficient and does not solely reflect the behavioral tendencies of offenders.

A number of researchers have worked around such limitations by using alternative methodological and conceptual approaches. For example, Goodwill, Alison, and Beech (2009) compared the degree to which three established methods of classifying offender behavior were able to predict the criminal history of 85 stranger rapists. Their results revealed a clear difference in effectiveness, with the FBI's power and anger model (Hazelwood, 1987) outperforming both the MTC:R3 (Knight & Prentky, 1990) and the thematic model proposed by Canter et al. (2003). Interestingly, however, they also found that a regression of single behaviors on characteristics outperformed the predictions of the three classification models (see also Goodwill, Stephens, Oziel, Yapp, & Bowes, 2012). This, they argue, suggests that more effort should be made to understand the links between individual behaviors and background characteristics because the link between the two may be more idiosyncratic than first assumed. In this spirit, researchers have been isolating the links between offender characteristics and key offense behaviors such as degree of violence (Beauregard, Lussier, & Proulx, 2005) and offense planning (Goodwill & Alison, 2007). Others have argued that the assumption of consistency may be relaxed to one in which offenders must show predictable change or development in their offending over time (Sorochinski & Salfati, 2010). This opens up the possibility of finding discrete classes of offending trajectories—a possibility that resonates with research on criminal careers (Sampson & Laub, 1993).

Groups and Networks

While much of investigative psychology considers crimes that are social in nature, most studies of such crimes (including those considered so far) treat offenders at the individual level. This is, of course, a simplification of reality, because offenders often act in concert, be it as dyads, groups, or structured criminal networks. This social dynamic is important to the nature of offending, and it introduces a layer of complexity to investigations of offender consistency and homology. A researcher may take the group as the unit of analysis and make comparisons across groups. The researcher also may consider individual members as the unit of analysis and make comparisons both within and across groups. Both approaches are relevant to practice. Investigators may need to know the behaviors that distinguish a particular criminal group (e.g., which terrorist group is responsible for an attack?), or they may need to identify a specific member from within a group (e.g., who perpetrated an armed robbery?).

Just as psychological principles have informed studies of individual offending, so social and organizational psychology has informed our understanding of group offending. Indeed, research in these areas points to properties of groups that may in fact increase the applicability of investigative psychology principles. For example, group formation seldom occurs at random but is instead the result of a process of social selection where those with similarities, such as interpersonal attractions or a common goal, come together (Forsyth, 2009; Glueck & Glueck, 1950). Similarly, group members do not act in isolation but rather socialize one another into a set of behavioral norms that produce an internal order to their behavior (Donald & Wilson, 2000; Stott, Adang, Livingstone, & Schreiber, 2008). Given these dynamics, it is perhaps not surprising that studies drawing on theories relating to social identity (Mullins, 2009), leadership (Porter, 2008), and work team cohesion (Donald & Wilson, 2000) have observed empirically the kinds of stable patterns in behavior that define investigative psychology research. Moreover, other studies have turned these principles on their head by showing that offenders can be identified precisely because they do not conform to the social norm displayed by other group members (Rashid, Greenwood, Walkerdine, Baron, & Rayson, 2012; Taylor, Tomblin, Conchie, & van der Zee, in press).

So what of investigative psychology's consistency and homology assumptions at the group level? Examining offender consistency within groups introduces a further complexity of within-group behavior. For example, inconsistency arises if half of the group members behave in a gratuitously aggressive manner while the other half act in a more intimate or pseudocooperative way. One way to address this question is to examine whether individual group members are consistent in taking on particular task roles within offenses or have their own place in an internal hierarchy. Task roles between criminal group members have been identified in property crimes such as robbery (Einstadter, 1969; McCluskey & Wardle, 2000) and ram raiding (Donald & Wilson, 2000). Power differentiation, or leadership, has also been demonstrated in criminal groups, leading researchers to produce a method for identifying criminal leadership behavior. Porter and Alison (2001, 2005, 2006b; see also Porter, 2008; Woodhams, Cooke, Harkins, & da Silva, 2012) developed a scale of influence that identified leaders in approximately 98% of rape and robbery groups by coding group members in terms of their decision making, actions, and order-giving behaviors. Group members who score higher on the scale are considered more influential and leader-oriented in their offense behavior.

A second way to address this question is to examine whether groups demonstrate consistent behavior. To date, this group-level analysis has been conducted for robbery co-offenders (Porter & Alison, 2006a) and rape co-offenders (Porter & Alison, 2004). In these studies, the behavior of offenders was coded at the level of the offense and examined for evidence of themes equivalent to those observed for single-offender crimes. However, critically, in this case, such themes would only emerge if the offenders of the same group showed a degree of consistency in their behaviors that was greater than the between-group differences. In both studies, Porter and Alison (2004, 2006a) found this to be the case. They showed not only that there are specific themes of behavior in these crimes, but also that offenders from the same group act in thematically consistent ways within any one offense.

Interestingly, the themes identified by Porter and Alison (2004, 2006a) were different from the narrative explanations that dominate single offender models. Given the social nature of the crime, they tested the structure proposed by Leary's (1957) interpersonal circumplex theory. This structure proposes that behavior differs along the dimensions of dominance-submission and cooperation-hostility, which intersect at right angles to form four behavioral themes: cooperative-dominance, cooperative-submission, hostile-dominance, and hostile-submission. As with other behavioral

models, the circumplex is intended to be thematic rather than typological. Thus, while the groups in these studies show behavioral consistency to the point of forming the hypothesized behavioral structure, the structure does not necessarily allow groups to be classified as a specific type. The implication of this characteristic becomes particularly apparent when group consistency is considered across offenses. Many criminal groups, particularly delinquent groups, are not stable in their membership over time (Sarnecki, 1990). Changes in membership can seed changes in the group's dynamics, which in turn can affect the behavior of group members (Jordan, 2009; Warr, 1996). This will likely affect the consistency of behavior over time and, therefore, reduce the possibility of differentiating one group from the next.

Group consistency over time has been shown for some more formal groups. For example, Wilson (2000) found similarities between incidents of terrorism carried out by the same terrorist organization. She found that multiple barricade siege incidents by the same group showed similarities in the way they were conducted, to the point that organizations could be differentiated based on their behavior. Consistent with Wilson's results, Prentice, Taylor, Rayson, Hoskins, and O'Loughlin (2011) have shown that terrorist groups such as Al-Qa'ida, Hamas, and Hezbollah are differentiable based on the kinds of rhetoric they use to argue for their cause and promote violence. Similarly, Bohm and Alison (2001) demonstrated that it is possible to differentiate destructive cults according to their articulated beliefs and practices. In a very different area, Canter (2004) explored the possibility of differentiating criminal groups based on six structural properties of social network. He identified three levels of organizational structure—ad hoc groups, oligarchies, and organized criminals—that were characterized by differences in relative group size and centrality of leadership. Interestingly, these types were also somewhat related to the criminal activities of the group, with hooligans tending to be loosely structured and drug networks the most structured.

There is some tentative evidence to suggest that group-level behavioral consistency relates systematically with aspects of offenders' lives. Leaders in multiple-perpetrator rapes have been shown to experience significantly higher levels of emotional problems compared to followers ('t Hart-Kerkhoffs, Vermeiren, Jansen, & Doreleijers, 2011). Similarly, members who fulfill particular roles in ram raiding teams tend to have commensurate criminal histories (Donald & Wilson, 2000). Specifically, in Donald and Wilson's (2000) study, those who took on the violent roles of controlling and intimidating victims/bystanders tended to have more convictions for violent offenses than those with other roles (e.g., drivers). Such findings point to the possibility of identifying clear and stable patterns in the social dynamics of group offending, though the complexities of such analyses and the difficulties of obtaining group level data make this area of investigative psychology a particular challenge.

Investigative Expertise

A substantial portion of investigative psychology research considers the nature of investigative decisions and the contextual factors that influence them. Much has been learned through systematic observation of investigators performing their tasks. For example, Morley, Ball, and Ormerod (2006; see also Ormerod, Ball, & Morley, 2012) performed ethnographic studies of insurance fraud investigations and identified three elements that impact investigator's decisions. These ranged from organizational influences, such as the companies' priorities on customer satisfaction, to individual influences, such as the extent to which the investigator operated within a hypothesis-testing framework. Barrett and Hamilton-Giachritsis (2013) had detectives express their thoughts about documents drip-fed to them as part of a simulated rape investigation. They found that detectives orientated toward the victim as a source of information rather than a person in need of emotional support. This behavior was not due to a lack of awareness of the victim's needs, but was a decision to address such needs through a professional and thorough investigation.

One observation that stems from this research is the importance of studying investigative decisions as a process, where prior knowledge and expectations are important. Investigators view evidence inconsistent with their working hypothesis as less reliable

(Marksteiner, Ask, Reinhard, & Granhag, 2011), they change their depth of processing to match implied occupational norms (Ask, Granhag, & Rebelius, 2011), and they are most likely to shift their mindset with regard to the guilt of an offender when confronted with specific individual and situational events (e.g., information availability; see Fahsing & Ask, 2013). Ormerod, Barrett, and Taylor (2008) refer to the process of assimilating and evaluating evidence as investigative sense-making. Across three investigative tasks (e.g., homicide investigations), they showed that sense-making is driven by a combination of internalized cognitive frames and externally imposed legal scripts that determine the likely courses of events.

A second observation made in many of the descriptive accounts, and implied by the analysis by Ormerod et al. (2008), is that investigators do not always engage in a methodical analysis of all the available evidence. They often appear to use heuristics, or simple mental strategies that operate through principles such as salience, anchoring, and representativeness rather than through an exhaustive evaluation of information. For a long time, cognitive psychology was dominated by a "heuristics are bad" view that stemmed from research showing that people's decisions often deviate from idealistic, statistics-based solutions (Kahneman, Slovic, & Tversky, 1982; Nisbett & Ross, 1980). This negative view of heuristics permeated investigative psychology. For example, the use of heuristics was assumed to produce reasoning errors that contributed to investigative failures (e.g., Findley & Scott, 2006), and this led researchers to heavily promote sophisticated actuarial solutions as the alternative (e.g., Canter, Coffey, Huntley, & Missen, 2000; Rossmo, 2000).

Inspired by research showing that heuristics work well in natural environments (Gigerenzer, 2000; Todd, Gigerenzer, & the ABC Research Group, 2000), investigative psychology researchers have also studied the positive side of heuristics. One task that has received much attention is the geographic profiling task, which involves using information about the location of a series of crimes to predict the offender's home location. In the first of a series of studies, Snook, Canter, and Bennell (2002) found that untrained university students could make predictions about where a serial offender lived with a level of accuracy equal to the predictions of a sophisticated software algorithm. More importantly, they showed that almost everybody achieved this performance when taught two heuristic principles about offender spatial behavior. Their finding has since been replicated with different types of crimes (Snook et al., 2004), different numbers of crimes (Taylor, Snook, & Bennell, 2009), the inclusion of topological information (Bennell, Snook, Taylor, Covey, & Keyton, 2007), police officers as participants (Bennell et al., 2007), and with prediction techniques of varying complexity (Paulsen, 2006; Snook, Zito, Bennell, & Taylor, 2005). Critically, these studies have also shown that people adapt to different distributions of crime scenes by using different heuristics. When these adaptations were ecologically valid in the sense that they fit the nature of the offenders' behavior, then their predictions were accurate. More recent research on this task has examined the extent to which humans are also able to make judgments about search patterns and take into account crime ordering. Taylor et al. (2009) found that people can go beyond making "X marks the spot" predictions and make accurate predictions using search areas, in the same way as the geographic profiling software produces a likelihood surface. Bennell, Emeno, Snook, Taylor, and Goodwill (2009) demonstrated that simple prediction strategies were able under some conditions to make spatial predictions that match the performance of novel, yet complex, approaches, such as Bayesian methods.

Investigative psychologists have also recently shown that heuristic models capture the decision making of offenders and police officers. For example, Snook, Dhami, and Kavanagh (2010) found that a noncompensatory decision strategy (i.e., matching heuristic) was a better predictor of burglars' judgments about residential occupancy than a compensatory strategy that considered all information (i.e., Franklin's rule; see also Garcia-Retamero & Dhami, 2009). Burglars were able to predict occupancy beyond chance levels, and cue use in the simple heuristic model corresponded better with how they achieved this. In a similar fashion, Snook and Mercer (2010) found that the matching heuristic outperformed Franklin's rule when modeling

investigators' decisions about the veracity of suicide notes. Their finding is compelling because they avoided the use of unrepresentative stimuli (e.g., where cue values are equally distributed), which allowed participants to demonstrate their natural decision policies. When decisions are studied in this more ecologically valid way, heuristics appear to give a very strong account of the decisions made by investigators and offenders.

Investigative Practices

By contributing to the three areas of research described above, investigative psychologists have not only sought to make fundamental conceptual contributions, but they have also sought to make direct and useful contributions to law enforcement practice. This has typically taken the form of providing new solutions to discrete investigative tasks. We describe research on these tasks in this section.

Linking crimes.   Crime linkage uses offense behaviors to identify crimes that have been committed by the same offender (Grubin, Kelly, & Brunsdon, 2001). The technique has proven especially useful when hard physical evidence, such as DNA, is not available at the crime scene. The goal when conducting linkage analysis is to identify patterns within the actions of offenders that allow crimes committed by different offenders to be distinguished from one another. For the necessary patterns to emerge, offenders must exhibit similar behaviors across their crime series (i.e., behavioral stability) while also exhibiting behaviors that are different from other offenders (i.e., behavioral distinctiveness; Bennell & Canter, 2002). Effective crime linkage can increase the efficiency of criminal investigations by allowing evidence to be pooled from multiple crime scenes (Labuschagne, 2006), and it is a precursor to the effective use of other investigative tools such as geographic profiling (Rossmo, 2000).

Like offender profiling, early attempts at crime linkage analysis were experiential in nature and largely relied on a detective's ability to recognize similarities in the modus operandi (MO) or behavioral signatures of offenders (Gross, 1906; Keppel, 1995). To systematize the analysis of offense behaviors, sophisticated computer databases were constructed to facilitate cross-crime comparisons of behavioral information (Bennell et al., 2012). With the advent of standardized data collection protocols came the possibility for researchers to examine empirically the degree to which behavioral information coded from crime scenes could be used to reliably link crimes to the same offender (Bennell, Woodhams, & Mugford, 2014). Much of this research has focused on determining whether evidence exists to support the primary assumptions underlying crime linkage analysis (i.e., behavioral consistency and distinctiveness). Across a range of crime types, this evidence is beginning to emerge (Bennell, Mugford, Ellingwood, & Woodhams, 2014; Woodhams, Hollin, & Bull, 2007), although not necessarily in relation to the kinds of MO behaviors that investigators have historically used.

In one of the first studies to address this issue empirically, Bennell and Canter (2002) found only low levels of linking accuracy when using behaviors related to standard MO domains such as entry decisions, property stolen, and target selection. When the average distance between offense locations was considered, however, high levels of linking accuracy were observed (i.e., crime committed by the same offender were characterized by shorter intercrime distances). The value of intercrime distance as a predictor has since been replicated in studies of different crime types (e.g., Tonkin, Grant, & Bond, 2008) and with alternative methodologies (e.g., Goodwill & Alison, 2006). Bennell et al. (2014) suggest that the effectiveness of intercrime distance is a product of two factors. The first, in line with findings from the field of personality psychology (e.g., Funder & Colvin, 1991), is that intercrime distance is largely under the control of the offender (e.g., where to commit a crime) rather than a product of the situation (e.g., property stolen). The second is that intercrime distance may be coded by the police in an accurate and reliable fashion, whereas coding offense behaviors such as type of entry typically relies on potentially problematic data sources, such as testimony of victims or inferences drawn from evidence at the crime scene (Alison et al., 2001).

The observations of Bennell, Bloomfield, Snook, Taylor, and Barnes (2010) may explain why investigators experience difficulties linking serial crimes (i.e., they may rely on nondiagnostic behaviors). Indeed, investigators tend to perform relatively poorly in laboratory-based linking tasks. For example, Santtila, Korpela, and Häkkänen (2004) examined the ability of experienced car crime investigators, experienced and novice general investigators, and naive participants to correctly link mock car crimes. They found that investigators were significantly more accurate than naive participants, but that there were no differences in accuracy among the different types of investigators. Each group identified about half of all possible links. Performance on mock linking tasks can be improved, however, when people are trained to focus their decision-making strategies on ecologically valid heuristics. For example, Bennell et al. (2010) examined the performance of university students, police professionals, and a logistic regression model on a linking task involving burglaries. As well as giving all participants information about offense behavior, Bennell et al. informed half of the participants about the value of intercrime distance to linking. Participants who were taught to use intercrime distance made more accurate predictions compared to participants who did not receive this information, although even the trained participants were outperformed by a purely statistical approach. In crime linkage there may be value in using the actuarial solutions that investigative psychologists are currently developing (e.g., Yokota & Watanabe, 2002).

Investigative interviewing. The interviews that police officers carry out with victims, witnesses, and suspects often provide the foundation for successful criminal investigations. The information elicited from witnesses and victims can lead to the identification of suspects and the gathering of leads, while the information provided by suspects allows investigators to obtain evidence and seek the truth about criminal offenses (Kebbell & Milne, 1998; Milne & Bull, 2003). Given the central role of interviews, it is not surprising that a great deal of effort has been put into developing, implementing, and evaluating interview protocols (e.g., Dando, Wilcock, Benkle, & Milne, 2011;

Fahsing & Rachlew, 2009; Snook, Eastwood, Stinson, Tedeschini, & House, 2010).

Perhaps the most well recognized and studied protocol is the cognitive interview (CI; Fisher & Geiselman, 1992). Briefly, at its heart, the CI uses four retrieval prompts that are designed to restore the original state in which the experience was encoded, and tap into multiple parts of the same memory. These prompts—report everything, reinstatement of context, describe the event in reverse order, and describe the event from other perspectives—have been shown to be effective at improving the memory of a witness under a variety of conditions. In their meta-analysis of 55 comparisons between CIs and control interviews, Köhnken, Milne, Memon, and Bull (1999) found a large overall effect size ($d =$ 0.87) for the amount of correct information recalled by the CI. A decade later, Memon, Meissner, and Fraser (2010) found a similar increase in the amount of correct information elicited by a CI ($d = 1.20$), but also a small but significant increase of incorrect information recalled ($d = 0.24$).

One ongoing line of research in investigative psychology involves isolating the factors that contribute to the elicitation of incorrect information without negatively affecting the amount of correct information recalled. This work has developed along three strands. One target of this analysis is the individual effect of each mnemonic. For example, Boon and Noon (1994) explored the functional utility of each individual mnemonic component and found that all but the *change perspective* mnemonic was able to elicit additional information from interviewees after an initial attempt with the *report everything* approach. A second target of this analysis is the police interviewer and how to ensure the interviewer applies the full CI protocol appropriately (Dando, Wilcock, & Milne, 2008; Kebbell & Milne, 1998; Memon, Holley, Milne, Koehnken, & Bull, 1994). Dando, Wilcock, Milne, and Henry (2009) found that modifying the CI by asking witnesses first to talk through a sketch of the witnessed event and then recall the event again produced as many details of the event as the full CI. A third target of this analysis has been the adaptation of the CI for different contexts. Hope, Gabbert, and Fisher (2011) have developed the self-administered interview

(SAI), which allows witnesses to write their own statement, and this is particularly useful when a traditional interview is not possible (e.g., multiple witnesses of a pub fire). Hope et al. (2011) report that the SAI is effective at both eliciting a comprehensive initial account from witnesses and, critically, at inoculating them against loss of memory associated with delayed interview.

In undertaking analyses in each of these areas, researchers are also uncovering other benefits of the CI approach. For example, Powell, Hughes-Scholes, and Sharman (2012) demonstrated that interviewers skilled in the use of the open-ended questions were less likely to seek to confirm what they already knew (i.e., they avoided a confirmation bias). Vrij et al. (2008) found that police officers were more accurate at spotting liars when suspects were telling their lie under the "reverse-order recall" mnemonic than when telling their lie in chronological order. This was because liars' accounts contained more cues to deception under the reverse-order condition, arguably because of the additional cognitive load associated with backward fabrication (see Chapter 7, this volume for a review of research on eyewitness memory).

Another interesting line of CI research pertains to the use of a strategic use of evidence (SUE) technique to detect deception. Users of the SUE technique follow up their initial open-ended questions (e.g., the report everything mnemonic) with a series of specific questions pertaining to the available evidence, without revealing the exact nature of the evidence. It is assumed that liars will avoid talking spontaneously about the evidence and will contradict themselves if they deny the evidence, while truth tellers will do the opposite. Hartwig et al. (2006) experimentally tested the SUE technique and found that SUE-trained interviewers were 85% accurate, whereas their naïve counterparts were merely 56% accurate. Similar results have been reported in subsequent studies (see Clemens et al., 2010; Hartwig, Granhag, & Strömwall, 2007; see Chapter 8, this volume for a review of research on the detection of deception).

Interviewing child witnesses is arguably a special case within investigative interviewing (Hagborg, Stromwall, & Tidefors, 2012; see also Chapter 1, this volume). The National Institute of Child and

Human Development (NICHD) protocol was developed to ensure that child witnesses are interviewed in a way that makes their testimony useful and reliable (Lamb, Hershkowitz, Orbach, & Esplin, 2008). The protocol is based on what psychologists know about children's memory, social norms, suggestibility, and language development. Interviewers are instructed to move through 11 phases of interaction that, among other things, ensure that the child understands what it means to tell the truth, attempt to build rapport, familiarize the child with open-ended prompts, and move the child through a series of progressively more suggestive prompts that seek a free narrative account. Lamb et al. (2008) found that 50% of forensically relevant information and 80% of disclosure of child abuse were provided in response to the kinds of open-ended prompts incorporated in the NICHD protocol. Such open-ended prompts are used rarely with children, however (e.g., Myklebust & Alison, 2000). Lamb et al. (1996) found that only 2% of dialogue in interviews conducted by Israeli youth investigators was open-ended in nature, and that most questions were directive or option-posing questions (e.g., forced-choice). Lamb et al. (2002) suggest that this problem may be overcome by having interviewers regularly attend workshops, discuss best practices, and review their own interviews.

Crisis negotiations and terrorism. The systematic examination of offense behavior has also contributed to our understanding of terrorism and crisis/hostage negotiation. One set of contributions has examined the motivations and cognitions that surround such offenses, either by examining the public statements of parties (Saucier, Akers, Shen-Miller, Knezevic, & Stankov, 2009) or by interviewing those involved (Post, Sprinzak, & Denny, 2003). For example, Sarangi and Alison's (2005) narrative interviews of left-wing terrorists identified a common narrative (i.e., life story) that showed coherence with the propaganda that was likely consumed by the interviewees. Similarly, in interviews with hostages, Giebels, Noelanders, and Vervaeke (2005) identified a number of distinct "periods of feelings" that might be the focus of particular interventions by authorities seeking to improve victim well-being.

Studies in this area have also utilized open-source data. For example, Jacques and Taylor (2013) examined the growing involvement of females in terrorism by examining nearly 500 case histories of male and female terrorists (see Chapter 4, this volume for a review of research on female offenders). They found that females are more likely to be motivated by personal events than males (e.g., death of a loved one; Jacques & Taylor, 2008), but that, in contrast to popular myths, females who become involved in terrorism do not differ from the general population in terms of their age, education, employment, and criminal history (Jacques & Taylor, 2013). These broad findings are important because they provide an evidence base from which to begin to think about investigative and treatment interventions.

A second set of contributions in this area looks for patterns in the behavioral make-up of incidents using the same kinds of methodology as those used to examine consistency and homology in offender behavior. For example, in their examination of UK prison sieges, Harvey-Craig, Fisher, and Simpson (1997) coded the occurrence and nonoccurrence of behaviors such as the nature of the threats made, the degree of agitation and mood swings, and the type of weapons used. Their examination suggested that some incidents involve mainly expressive behaviors, such as verbal aggression and discussions of family issues, while others involve mainly instrumental behaviors, such as demands and more rational discussion. Several authors have also shown how such behavioral differences can be used to predict the outcome of a crisis negotiation (Taylor, 2002b; Yokota, Iwami, Watanabe, Fujita, & Watanabe, 2004). All crisis negotiations move through periods of escalating hostility and cooperation, but some cross a behavioral threshold that leads to an increased risk of deaths and the likely need for a tactical resolution (Taylor, 2002b).

The behavioral approach has also proven fruitful for understanding terrorist incidents. Wilson (2000) found strong evidence of a consistency in the resources used and demands made by different terrorist groups, which she attributed to differences in the social and historic roots of the groups. Wilson, Scholes, and Brocklehurst (2010) took this analysis one step further by showing that the behavior exhibited by terrorists depended on the type of victim that was targeted. This suggests that there is some regularity with respect to the kinds of attack used in various circumstances, implying a degree of planning and goal-driven behavior behind such incidents. Their finding is consistent with comparisons by Donohue and Taylor (2003) of the tactics that terrorists and governments use in aerial hijackings. They showed that aerial hijackings involved more overt power strategies than barricade-siege incidents, and that terrorists with a religious fundamentalist ideology typically used more violence and less compromising behaviors than terrorists with other ideological backgrounds.

A third set of contributions in this area has focused on the language used while negotiating hostage and terrorist incidents (Richardson, Taylor, Snook, Conchie, & Bennell, in press). As with the research on investigative interviewing, the contribution here comes from a systematic analysis of the language used over time and its relationship with outcome. For example, Taylor (2002a; see also Bilsky, Tebrugge, & Webel-Therhorn, 2010; Taylor & Donald, 2004, 2007) demonstrated that the way in which perpetrators and negotiators use language falls into a consistent structure that can be anticipated by negotiators (Taylor & Thomas, 2008). Specifically, Taylor showed that, at any one time, police negotiators and hostage takers adopt an avoidant, competitive, or cooperative orientation to interaction and pursue either identity, instrumental, or relational goals with varying degrees of intensity. As an incident progresses, they move through these different regions of discussion, ideally moving towards a cooperative interaction. On some occasions, for example, a hostage taker may yell abuse and insults as he vents his frustration. At other moments, perhaps when discussing his love for his child, he may revert to more cooperative, instrumental behavior.

A number of studies have evaluated the communicative strategies that negotiators use to navigate this structure. This work has typically coded transcripts for influence strategies using classification schemes such as the Table of Ten (Giebels, 2002). For example, Kamphuis, Giebels, and Noelanders (2006) compared the use of influence strategies in three negotiation phases (initial encounter,

problem-solving, and resolution) for crisis negotiations considered effective and ineffective. They found that strategy use differed as a function of outcome across all three periods of interaction, and that some of these variations were dependent on the type of incident being negotiated. Giebels and Taylor (2009) have extended this work to cross-cultural hostage crises. They suggest that many of the strategies used to resolve hostage crises, such as rational persuasion and empathizing with the others face, are rooted in a Western, low-context perspective and may be less applicable in negotiations with those from high-context cultures where message meaning is more implicit and connected to the social context. Consistent with this idea, they found that high-context hostage takers were less likely to engage in persuasive arguments or respond to them positively, and they were more likely to reciprocate threats, particularly those made about self. This, they argue, is because high-context communicators expect dialogue to emphasize relationship and identity over the exchange of rational arguments, such that they fail to engage in the rational persuasion and respond negatively when the identity dynamic is challenged. These early findings highlight the challenge that police negotiators face in an increasingly global world.

PRACTICE AND POLICY ISSUES

As noted at the outset of this chapter, one of the motivations of investigative psychology is to produce a scientific contribution to law enforcement practice that delivers both evidence-based advice to ongoing investigations and the improvement of investigative strategies and policies. In relation to ongoing investigations, investigative psychology has helped move the contribution of psychology away from experiential offender profiling and toward a multidisciplinary approach that relies on behavioral analysis alongside tacit expertise (Alison, Goodwill, Almond, van den Heuvel, & Winter, 2010). The contributions of this approach now include suspect prioritization, crime linkage, geographic profiling, providing advice on interview strategies, and risk assessments (e.g., in hostage crises). Indeed, within the United Kingdom at least, this change in scope is captured by the use of the term *behavioral investigative advice* (Association of Chief Police Officers, 2006), which also reflects the fact that efforts have been made to professionalize the field and the nature of its contributions.

In relation to investigative techniques, it is also possible to identify some significant contributions. In investigative interviewing, the development of the cognitive interview and the examination of what occurs in practice have helped shape the training received by law enforcement and promoted a culture of continuous, supportive evaluation and development (Oxburgh & Dando, 2011). This continues to be the case as researchers and practitioners work together to address new challenges in the area of investigative interviewing. For example, working with a Dutch police force, Beune, Giebels, and Taylor (2010) examined transcripts of within- and between-culture interviews, showing that some of the strategies often adopted when interviewing were not as effective at eliciting information when used across cultures. This kind of evidence provides a basis for the development of training geared toward raising awareness and reducing the potential misunderstandings that come from the use of inappropriate investigative strategies (Taylor et al., in press). Similarly, the development of the Self-Administered Interview by Hope et al. (2011) was a direct response to a need identified by law enforcement practitioners. The development of this tool was only possible because of the integration of expertise in the cognitive psychology of memory and the opportunity to trial the tool in real investigative situations.

There are also examples of investigative psychologists contributing their particular methodological approach to collaborations that were traditionally found at the periphery of the discipline. For example, by drawing on investigative psychology practices for examining archival data, Porter and various colleagues have begun to test social-psychological explanations for the occurrence of police misconduct (Porter & Warrender, 2009). By working with police forces on this issue, researchers have been able to identify the organizational and professional development strategies that are effective at reducing police complaints (Porter, Prenzler, & Fleming, 2012). In the corporate domain, there is also increasing application of investigative psychology techniques, particularly in the area of cyber security. For example, Taylor et al. (2013) hypothesized that it should be possible to identify insiders trying to steal sensitive information from an organization based on changes in the way in which they interacted with colleagues. Utilizing email behavior as a data source, they showed that insiders' language contained more self-focus and more negative affect compared to the language of coworkers. They also showed that the natural process of language accommodation was lower for insiders interacting with coworkers compared to coworkers interacting amongst themselves. This difference, which suggests an inadvertent social distancing by the insiders, increased over time and was sufficient to allow 92.6% of insiders to be identified.

There are, however, limits to investigative psychology's contribution. In large part these limits are characterized by two kinds of disconnect between research and practice. The first kind of disconnect relates to the way in which findings are described by researchers and what users infer from such descriptions. This issue is illustrated elegantly by Johnson's (1973) study of how 23 NATO officers interpreted different statements such as "highly likely," "improbably," and "little chance." Johnson found that the officers gave widely different estimates of the meaning of particular statements on a probability scale of 0%–100%. Some statements, such as "we believe" and "probable," were associated with differences in interpretation of over 50%. This heterogeneity in interpretation has more recently been shown in the interpretation of offender profiles. Villejoubert, Almond, and Alison (2009) found not only that participants reported a diverse range of interpretations, but also that their interpretations were affected by the framing of the claim and the nature of the object about which the claim was being made. This has implications for those producing specific investigative psychology products, such as offender profiles, because their writing may influence how their research is understood and utilized. It also has wider implications for how researchers convey and translate their findings for different audiences across all areas of forensic psychology.

The second disconnect relates to a gap between how research is conducted and what occurs in practice. For example, some researchers and practitioners understood the results of the studies by Snook and various colleagues (e.g., Snook et al., 2004) as indicating that modern geographic profiling procedures had little to offer (Rossmo, 2005). However, as Bennell et al. (2007) clarified, this is not the message behind such research, not least because the geographic profiling task involves a range of contributions (e.g., qualitative interpretations of evidence by a geographic profiler) that were not examined as part of those studies. Rather, this research suggests that it may be possible to take an alternative, quicker, and more cost-effective approach to completing one aspect of a geographic profile. More importantly, this research also suggests that there may be value in conducting a detailed, *in vivo* evaluation of the wider practice of geographic profiling. This latter message is common to many areas of investigative psychology where experimental research hints at possible areas for the testing and development of existing practice. The clear communication of research findings, therefore, is immensely important, not only for furthering research, but also for the development of good practice and for the maintenance of good relationships between researchers and practitioners. Ultimately, undertaking such collaborative *in vivo* studies will serve the common ambition of both investigative psychologists and law enforcement practitioners: to use robust evaluation techniques to identify ways to improve current practice so that offenders are caught and innocents go free.

SUMMARY AND CONCLUSIONS

The breadth of the issues tackled in investigative psychology has grown significantly over the last decade. The initial studies of serious crime have been overtaken by research on other forms of offending, a focus on investigative techniques, and a broadening in methodological approach. For example, early studies of criminal differentiation are now embedded in studies of crime linkage, which continues to test the behavioral stability/distinctiveness principles while also contributing to linkage techniques. Alongside this, a number of researchers are

using sequence-analysis techniques that enable offender–victim interactions to be examined as an unfolding series of cues and responses (Fossi, Clarke, & Lawrence, 2005; Taylor et al., 2008). This kind of development is allowing researchers to ask a more sophisticated set of questions about offender behavior, and, in doing so, challenge some of the early models that emerged from the field.

In addition to a growing sophistication in the research addressing core questions, there is a growth in the breadth of the field's interests. For example, there are now emerging lines of research in counter-intelligence interviewing (Granhag, Montecinos, & Oleszkiewicz, 2013), the detection of fabricated intentions (Warmlink, Vrij, Mann, & Granhag, 2013), the use of Bayes methods of analysis for linking crimes (Salo et al., 2013), the effect of police warning complexity on the comprehension of legal rights (Eastwood & Snook, 2012; Eastwood, Snook, & Luther, 2012) and the application of geographic profiling methodologies in military and counter-terrorism contexts (Rossmo, 2012).

The nature of the partnerships between researchers and practitioners has also grown significantly with the field. Investigative psychologists have always placed value on the insights of practitioners, but partnerships with practitioners are now becoming more formal and, as a result, more beneficial. For example, the Crime Linkage International Network (C-LINK) brings together academic researchers and police practitioners from seven different countries to jointly develop a strategy for carrying out crime-linkage research and a research agenda for the future. Such partnerships ensure not only that researchers are undertaking research that is relevant to the user community, but that they also ensure an efficient use of available data and available expertise, and that they provide a clear mechanism for the user community to stay up to date with research developments in their field.

Finally, the growth of investigative psychology is apparent in the emergence of dedicated research centers around the world, in the increasing number of graduate programs that have an investigative focus, and in dedicated outlets such as a periodic journal and biannual conference. The reason for such growth is a desire to undertake rigorous testing of psychological theory in a way that has implications for law enforcement practice, which is attributable to the underlying principles of the field. This synergy of theory and practice is timely given the current demand on policing to be evidence-based, and for research to have a discernable value for society. For it to continue, researchers must strive to communicate the contributions and limitations of their research effectively and understand the varied ways that different audiences can receive their work. In return, practitioners must strive to engage with and shape research agendas, record and provide access to research-relevant data, and be positive about the benefits of allowing an evaluation of their practices.

References

Alison, L., Goodwill, A., Almond, L., van den Heuvel, C., & Winter, J. (2010). Pragmatic solutions to offender profiling and behavioural investigative advice. *Legal and Criminological Psychology, 15*, 115–132.

Alison, L. J., Bennell, C., Mokros, A., & Ormerod, D. (2002). The personality paradox in offender profiling: A theoretical review of the processes involved in deriving background characteristics from crime scene actions. *Psychology, Public Policy, and Law, 8*, 115–135.

Alison, L. J., Smith, M. D., Eastman, O., & Rainbow, L. (2003). Toulmin's philosophy of argument and its relevance to offender profiling. *Psychology, Crime & Law, 9*, 173–183.

Alison, L. J., Snook, B., & Stein, K. L. (2001). Unobtrusive measures: Using police information for forensic research. *Qualitative Research, 1*, 241–254.

Ask, K., Granhag, P. A., & Rebelius, A. (2011). Investigators under influence: How social norms activate goal-directed processing of criminal evidence. *Applied Cognitive Psychology, 25*, 548–553.

Association of Chief Police Officers. (2006). *Murder investigation manual*. Bedford, England: National Centre for Policing Excellence.

Barrett, E. C., & Hamilton-Giachritsis, C. (2013). The victim as a means to an end: Detective decision making in a simulated investigation of attempted rape. *Journal of Investigative Psychology and Offender Profiling, 10*, 200–218.

Beauregard, E., Lussier, P., & Proulx, J. (2005). The role of sexual interests and situational factors on rapists' modus operandi: Implications for offender profiling. *Legal and Criminological Psychology, 10*, 265–278.

Bennell, C., Bloomfield, S., Snook, B., Taylor, P. J., & Barnes, C. (2010). Linkage analysis in cases of serial burglary: Comparing the performance of university students, police professionals, and a logistic regression model. *Psychology, Crime & Law, 18*, 507–524.

Bennell, C., & Canter, D. V. (2002). Linking commercial burglaries by modus operandi: Tests using regression and ROC analysis. *Science and Justice, 42*, 153–164.

Bennell, C., Emeno, K., Snook, B., Taylor, P. J., & Goodwill, A. M. (2009). The precision, accuracy and efficiency of geographic profiling predictions: A simple heuristic versus mathematical algorithms. *Crime Mapping: A Journal of Research and Practice, 1*, 65–84.

Bennell, C., Mugford, R., Ellingwood, H., & Woodhams, J. (2014). Linking crimes using behavioral clues: Current levels of linking accuracy and strategies for moving forward. *Journal of Investigative Psychology and Offender Profiling, 11*, 29–56.

Bennell, C., Snook, B., MacDonald, S., House, J., & Taylor, P. J. (2012). Computerized crime linkage analysis systems: A critical review and research agenda. *Criminal Justice and Behavior, 39*, 616–630.

Bennell, C., Snook, B., Taylor, P. J., Covey, S., & Keyton, J. (2007). It's no riddle, choose the middle: The effect of number of crimes and topographical detail on police officer predictions of serial burglars' home locations. *Criminal Justice and Behavior, 34*, 119–132.

Bennell, C., Woodhams, J., & Mugford, R. (2014). Linkage analysis for crime. In G. J. N. Bruinsma & D. L. Weisburd (Eds.), *Encyclopedia of criminology and criminal justice* (pp. 2947–2953). New York, NY: Springer.

Beune, K., Giebels, E., & Taylor, P. J. (2010). Patterns of interaction in police interviews: The role of cultural dependency. *Criminal Justice and Behavior, 37*, 904–925.

Bilsky, W., Tebrugge, B., & Webel-Therhorn, D. (2010). Escalation and deescalation in hostage-negotiation. In R. G. Rogan & F. J. Lanceley (Eds.), *Contemporary theory, research and practice of crisis and hostage negotiation* (pp. 119–140). Cresskill, NJ: Hampton Press.

Bohm, J., & Alison, L. J. (2001). An exploratory study in methods of distinguishing destructive cults. *Psychology, Crime & Law, 7*, 133–165.

Boon, J., and Noon, E. (1994). Changing perspectives in cognitive interviewing. *Psychology, Crime & Law, 1*, 59–69.

Brantingham, P. J., & Brantingham, P. L. (Eds.). (1981). *Environmental criminology*. Prospect Heights, IL: Waveland Press.

Canter, D. V. (1995). *Criminal shadows*. London, England: Harper Collins.

Canter, D. V. (2000). Offender profiling and criminal differentiation. *Legal and Criminological Psychology, 5*, 23–46.

Canter, D. V. (2004). A partial order scalogram analysis of criminal network structures. *Behaviormetrika, 31,* 131–152.

Canter, D. V., Alison, L., Alison, E., & Wentink, N. (2004). The organised/disorganised typology of serial murder: Myth or model? *Psychology, Public Policy, and Law, 10,* 292–320.

Canter, D. V., Bennell, C., Alison, L., & Reddy, R. (2003). Differentiating sex offences: A behaviorally based thematic classification of stranger rapes. *Behavioral Sciences and the Law, 21,* 157–174.

Canter, D. V., Coffey, T., Huntley, M., & Missen, C. (2000). Predicting serial killers' home base using a decision support system. *Journal of Quantitative Criminology, 16,* 457–478.

Canter, D. V., & Fritzon, K. (1998). Differentiating arsonists: A model of firesetting actions and characteristics. *Legal and Criminological Psychology, 3,* 73–96.

Canter, D. V., & Youngs, D. (2012). Sexual and violent offenders' victim role assignments: A general model of offending style. *Journal of Forensic Psychiatry and Psychology, 23,* 297–326.

Clemens, F., Granhag, P. A., Strömwall, L. A., Vrij, A., Landström, S., Roos af Hjelmäter, E., & Hartwig, M. (2010). Skulking around the dinosaur: Eliciting cues to children's deception via strategic disclosure of evidence. *Applied Cognitive Psychology, 24,* 925–940.

Cohen, L. E., & Felson, M. (1979). Social change and crime rate trends: A routine activity approach. *American Sociological Review, 44,* 468–608.

Dando, C., Wilcock, R., Benkle, C., & Milne, R. (2011). Modifying the cognitive interview: Countenancing forensic application by enhancing practicability. *Psychology, Crime & Law, 17,* 491–511.

Dando, C. J., Wilcock, R., & Milne, R. (2008). Victims and witnesses of crime: Police officers' perceptions of interviewing practices. *Legal and Criminological Psychology, 13,* 59–70.

Dando, C. J., Wilcock, R., Milne, R., & Henry, L. (2009). An adapted cognitive interview procedure for frontline police investigators. *Applied Cognitive Psychology, 23,* 698–716.

Doan, B., & Snook, B. (2008). A failure to find empirical support for the homology assumption in criminal profiling. *Journal of Police and Criminal Psychology, 23,* 61–70.

Donald, I. J., & Wilson, A. (2000). Ram raiding: Criminals working in groups. In D. V. Canter & L. J. Alison (Eds.), *The social psychology of crime: Groups, teams, and networks* (pp. 191–246). Dartmouth, England: Ashgate.

Donohue, W. A., & Taylor, P. J. (2003). Testing the role effect in terrorist negotiations. *International Negotiation, 8,* 527–547.

Eastwood, J., & Snook, B. (2012). The effect of listenability factors on the comprehension of police cautions. *Law and Human Behavior, 36,* 117–183.

Eastwood, J., Snook, B., & Luther, K. (2012). Measuring the reading complexity and oral comprehension of Canadian youth waiver forms. *Crime and Delinquency.* Advance online publication. doi: 10.1177/0011128712453689

Einstadter, W. J. (1969). The social organization of armed robbery. *Social Problems, 17,* 64–83.

Fahsing, I., & Ask, K. (2013). Decision making and decisional tipping points in homicide investigations: An interview study of British and Norwegian detectives. *Journal of Investigative Psychology and Offender Profiling, 10,* 155–165.

Fahsing, I. A., & Rachlew, A. A. (2009). Investigative interviewing in the Nordic region. In B. Milne & S. Savage (Eds.), *International developments in investigative interviewing* (pp. 39–65). Devon, England: Willan.

Findley, K. A., & Scott, M. S. (2006). The multiple dimensions of tunnel vision in criminal cases. *Wisconsin Law Review, 291,* 291–397.

Fisher, R. P., & Geiselman, R. E. (1992). *Memory-enhancing techniques for investigative interview: The cognitive interview.* Springfield, IL: Charles C. Thomas.

Forsyth, D. R. (2009). Group dynamics. In H. T. Reis & S. Sprecher (Eds.), *Encyclopedia of human relationships* (pp. 777–780). Thousand Oaks, CA: Sage.

Fossi, J., Clarke, D. D., & Lawrence, C. (2005). Bedroom rape: Sequences of sexual behavior in stranger assaults. *Journal of Interpersonal Violence, 20,* 1444–1466.

Funder, D. C., & Colvin, C. R. (1991). Explorations in behavioral consistency: Properties of persons, situations, and behaviors. *Journal of Personality and Social Psychology, 60,* 773–794.

Garcia-Retamero, R., & Dhami, M. K. (2009). Take-the-best in expert-novice decision strategies for residential burglary. *Psychonomic Bulletin and Review, 16,* 163–169.

Giebels, E. (2002). Beïnvloeding in gijzelingsonderhandelingen: De tafel van tien. [Influencing in hostage negotiations: The table of ten]. *Nederlands Tijdschrift voor de Psychologie, 57,* 145–154.

Giebels, E., Noelanders, S., & Vervaeke, G. (2005). The hostage experience: Implications for negotiation strategies. *Clinical Psychology and Psychotherapy, 12,* 241–253.

Giebels, E., & Taylor, P. J. (2009). Interaction patterns in crisis negotiations: Persuasive arguments and cultural differences. *Journal of Applied Psychology, 94,* 5–19.

Gigerenzer, G. (2000). *Adaptive thinking: Rationality in the real world*. Oxford, England: Oxford University Press.

Gilovich, T., Griffin, D., & Kahneman, D. (2002). *Heuristics and biases: The psychology of intuitive judgment*. Cambridge, England: Cambridge University Press.

Glueck, S., & Glueck, E. (1950). *Unraveling juvenile delinquency*. Cambridge, MA: Harvard University Press.

Goodwill, A. M., & Alison, L. J. (2006). The development of a filter model for prioritizing suspects in burglary offences. *Psychology, Crime & Law, 12*, 395–416.

Goodwill, A. M., & Alison, L. J. (2007). When is profiling possible? Offence planning and aggression as moderators in predicting offender age from victim age in stranger rape. *Behavioral Sciences and the Law, 25*, 823–840.

Goodwill, A. M., Alison, L. J., & Beech, A. R. (2009). What works in offender profiling? A comparison of typological, thematic and multivariate models. *Behavioral Sciences and the Law, 27*, 507–529.

Goodwill, A. M., Stephens, S., Oziel, S., Yapp, J., & Bowes, N. (2012). Multidimensional latent classification of 'street robbery' offences. *Journal of Investigative Psychology and Offender Profiling, 9*, 93–109.

Granhag, P. A., Montecinos, S. C., & Oleszkiewicz, S. (2013). Eliciting intelligence from sources: The first scientific test of the Scharff technique. *Legal and Criminological Psychology*. Advance online publication. doi: 10.1111/lcrp.12015

Gross, H. (1906). *Criminal investigation*. Masdras, India: G. Ramasawmy Chetty.

Grubin, D., Kelly, P., & Brunsdon, C. (2001). *Linking serious sexual assaults through behaviour*. London, England: Home Office.

Hagborg, J. M., Stromwall, L. A., & Tidefors, I. (2012). Prosecution rate and quality of the investigative interview in child sexual abuse cases. *Journal of Investigative Psychology and Offender Profiling, 9*, 161–173.

Häkkänen, H., Puolakka, P., & Santtila, P. (2004). Crime scene actions and offender characteristics in arsons. *Legal and Criminological Psychology, 9*, 1–18.

Hartwig, M., Granhag, P. A., & Strömwall, L. A. (2007). Guilty and innocent suspects' strategies during police interrogations. *Psychology, Crime & Law, 13*, 213–227.

Hartwig, M., Granhag, P. A., Stromwall, L. A., & Kronkvist, O. (2006). Strategic use of evidence during police interviews: When training to detect deception works. *Law and Human Behavior, 30*, 603–619.

Harvey-Craig, A., Fisher, N. J., & Simpson, P. (1997). An explanation of the profiling of hostage incidents in HM prison services. *Issues in Criminological and Legal Psychology, 29*, 41–46.

Hazelwood, R. R. (1987). Analyzing the rape and profiling the offender. In R. R. Hazelwood & A. W. Burgess (Eds.), *Practical aspects of rape investigation: A multidisciplinary approach* (pp. 169–199). New York, NY: Elsevier.

Hope, L., Gabbert, F., & Fisher, R. P. (2011). From laboratory to the street: Capturing witness memory using the self-administered interview. *Legal and Criminological Psychology, 16*, 211–226.

Jacques, K., & Taylor, P. J. (2008). Male and female suicide bombers: Different sexes, different reasons? *Studies in Conflict and Terrorism, 31*, 304–326.

Jacques, K., & Taylor, P. J. (2013). Myths and realities of female-perpetrated terrorism. *Law and Human Behavior, 37*, 35–44.

Johnson, E. M. (1973). *Numerical encoding of qualitative expressions of uncertainty*. Army Research Institute for the Behavioral and Social Sciences, National Technical Information Service.

Jordan, J. (2009). When heads role: Assessing the effectiveness of leadership decapitation. *Security Studies, 18*, 719–755.

Kahneman, D., Slovic, P., & Tversky, A. (1982). *Judgment under uncertainty: Heuristics and biases*. New York, NY: Cambridge University Press.

Kamphuis, W., Giebels, E., & Noelanders, S. (2006). Effective influencing in crisis negotiations: the role of type of incident and incident phase [in Dutch]. *Nederlands Tijdschrift voor de Psychologie, 21*, 83–100.

Kebbell, M., & Milne, R. (1998). Police officers' perception of eyewitness factors in forensic investigations. *Journal of Social Psychology, 138*, 323–330.

Keppel, R. D. (1995). Signature murders: A report of several related cases. *Journal of Forensic Sciences, 40*, 670–674.

Kjaerland, M. (2005). A classification of computer security incidents based on reported attack data. *Journal of Investigative Psychology and Offender Profiling, 2*, 105–120.

Klein, G. (1989). Recognition-primed decisions. In W. B. Rouse (Ed.), *Advances in man–machine systems research* (Vol. 5, pp. 47–92). Greenwich, CT: JAI Press.

Knight, R. A., & Prentky, R. A. (1990). Classifying sexual offenders: The development and corroboration of taxonomic models. In W. L. Marshall, D. R. Laws, & H. E. Barbaree (Eds.), *Handbook of sexual assault: Issues, theories, and treatment of the offenders* (pp. 23–52). New York, NY: Plenum Press.

Köhnken, G., Milne, R., Memon, A., & Bull, R. (1999). The cognitive interview: A meta-analysis. *Psychology, Crime & Law, 5*, 3–28.

Labuschagne, G. (2006). The use of linkage analysis as evidence in the conviction of the Newcastle serial murderer, South Africa. *Journal of Investigative Psychology and Offender Profiling, 3,* 183–191.

Lamb, M. E., Hershkowitz, I., Orbach, Y., & Esplin, P. W. (2008). *Tell me what happened: Structured investigative interviews of child victims and witnesses.* Chichester, England: Wiley.

Lamb, M. E., Herskowitz, I., Sternberg, K. J., Esplin, P. W., Hovav, M., Manor, T., & Yudilevitch, L. (1996). Effects of investigative utterance types on Israeli children's responses. *International Journal of Behavioral Development, 19,* 627–637.

Lamb, M. E., Sternberg, K. J., Orbach, Y., Hershkowitz, I., Horowitz, D., & Esplin, P. W. (2002). The effects of intensive training and ongoing supervision on the quality of investigative interviews with alleged sex abuse victims. *Applied Developmental Science, 6,* 114–125. doi:10.1207/S1532480XADS0603_2

Leary, T. (1957). *Interpersonal diagnosis of personality.* New York, NY: Ronald Press.

Loeber, R., & Dishion, T. (1983). Early predictors of male delinquency: A review. *Psychological Bulletin, 94,* 68–99.

Marksteiner, T., Ask, K., Reinhard, M.-A., & Granhag, P. A. (2011). Asymmetrical skepticism toward criminal evidence: The role of goal- and belief-consistency. *Applied Cognitive Psychology, 25,* 541–547.

McCluskey, K., & Wardle, S. (2000). The social structure of robbery. In D. V. Canter & L. J. Alison (Eds.), *The social psychology of crime: Groups, teams, and networks* (pp. 249–285). Dartmouth, England: Ashgate.

Memon, A., Holley, A., Milne, R., Koehnken, G., & Bull, R. (1994). Towards understanding the effects of interviewer training in evaluating the cognitive interview. *Applied Cognitive Psychology, 8,* 641–659.

Memon, A., Meissner, C., & Fraser, J. (2010). The cognitive interview: A meta-analytic review and study space analysis of the past 25 years. *Psychology, Public Policy, and Law, 6,* 340–372.

Milne, R., & Bull, R. (2003). Does the cognitive interview help children to resist the effects of suggestive questioning? *Legal and Criminological Psychology, 8,* 21–38.

Mokros, A., & Alison, L. J. (2002). Is offender profiling possible? Testing the predicted homology of crime scene actions and background characteristics in a sample of rapists. *Legal and Criminological Psychology, 7,* 25–43.

Morley, N. J., Ball, L. J., & Ormerod, T. C. (2006). How the detection of insurance fraud succeeds and fails. *Psychology, Crime & Law, 12,* 163–180.

Mullins, S. (2009). Parallels between crime & terrorism: A social-psychological perspective. *Studies in Conflict and Terrorism, 32,* 811–830.

Myklebust, T., & Alison, L. J. (2000). The current state of police interviews with children in Norway: How discrepant are they from models based on current issues in memory and communication? *Psychology, Crime & Law, 6,* 331–351.

Nisbett, R. E., & Ross, L. D. (1980). *Human inference: Strategies and shortcomings of social judgment.* Englewood Cliffs, NJ: Prentice-Hall.

Nutch, F. J., & Bloombaum, M. (1968). A smallest space analysis of gang boy behaviors. *Pacific Sociological Review, 11,* 116–122.

Ormerod, T., Barrett, E., & Taylor, P. J. (2008). Investigative sense-making in criminal contexts. In J. M. Schraagen, L. G. Militello, T. Ormerod, & R. Lipshitz (Eds.), *Naturalistic decision making and macrocognition* (pp. 81–102). Aldershot, England: Ashgate.

Ormerod, T. C., Ball, L. J., & Morley, N. J. (2012). Informing the development of a fraud prevention toolset through a situated analysis of fraud investigation expertise. *Behaviour and Information Technology, 31,* 371–381.

Oxburgh, G., & Dando, C. J. (2011). Psychology and interviewing: What direction now in our quest for reliable information? *British Journal of Forensic Practice, 13,* 135–147.

Paulsen, D. J. (2006). Connecting the dots: Assessing the accuracy of geographic profiling software. *Policing: An International Journal of Police Strategies and Management, 29,* 306–334.

Pinizzotto, A. J. (1984). Forensic psychology: Criminal personality profiling. *Journal of Police Science and Administration, 12,* 32–40.

Porter, L. E. (2008). Using archival data and multidimensional scaling to explore leadership: Examples from group crime. *Issues in Forensic Psychology, 8,* 31–42.

Porter, L. E., & Alison, L. J. (2001). A partially ordered scale of influence in violent group behavior: An example from gang rape. *Small Group Research, 32,* 475–497.

Porter, L. E., & Alison, L. J. (2004). Behavioural coherence in violent group activity: An interpersonal model of sexually violent gang behaviour. *Aggressive Behavior, 30,* 449–468.

Porter, L. E., & Alison, L. J. (2005). Decisions, actions and orders as influence strategies employed by leaders of violent gangs. *Small Group Research, 36,* 188–207.

Porter, L. E., & Alison, L. J. (2006a). Behavioral coherence in group robbery: A circumplex model of offender and victim interactions. *Aggressive Behavior, 32,* 330–342.

Porter, L. E., & Alison, L. J. (2006b). Leadership and hierarchies in criminal groups: Scaling degrees of leader behavior in group robbery. *Legal and Criminological Psychology, 11,* 245–265.

Porter, L. E., Prenzler, T., & Fleming, J. (2012). Complaint reduction in the Tasmania police. *Policing and Society, 22,* 426–447.

Porter, L. E., & Warrender, C. (2009). A multivariate model of police deviance: Examining the nature of corruption, crime and misconduct. *Policing and Society, 19,* 79–99.

Post, J., Sprinzak, E., & Denny, L. (2003). The terrorists in their own words: Interviews with 35 incarcerated Middle Eastern terrorists. *Terrorism and Political Violence, 15,* 171–184.

Powell, M. B., Hughes-Scholes, C. H., & Sharman, S. J. (2012). Skill in interviewing reduces confirmation bias. *Journal of Investigative Psychology and Offender Profiling, 9,* 126–134.

Prentice, S., Taylor, P. J., Rayson, P., Hoskins, A., & O'Loughlin, B. (2011). Analyzing the semantic content and persuasive composition of extremist media: A case study of texts produced during the Gaza conflict. *Information Systems Frontiers, 13,* 61–73.

Rashid, A., Greenwood, P., Walkerdine, J., Baron, A., & Rayson, P. (2012). Technological solutions to offending. In E. Quayle & K. Ribisl (Eds.), *Understanding and preventing online sexual exploitation of children* (pp. 228–243). London, England: Willan.

Richardson, B., Taylor, P. J., Snook, B., Conchie, S. M., & Bennell, C. (in press). Language style matching and confessions in police interrogations. *Law and Human Behavior.* doi:10.1037/lhb0000077

Rossmo, K. (2000). *Geographic profiling.* Boca Raton, FL: CRC Press.

Rossmo, K. (2005). Geographic heuristics or shortcuts to failure? Response to Snook et al. *Applied Cognitive Psychology, 19,* 651–654.

Rossmo, K. (2012). Recent developments in geographic profiling. *Policing: A Journal of Policy and Practice, 6,* 144–150.

Salfati, C. G. (2000). Profiling homicide: A multidimensional approach. *Homicide Studies, 4,* 265–293.

Salfati, C. G., & Bateman, A. (2005). Serial homicide: An investigation of behavioral consistency. *Journal of Investigative Psychology and Offender Profiling, 2,* 121–144.

Salfati, C. G., & Taylor, P. J. (2006). Differentiating sexual violence: A comparison of sexual homicide and rape. *Psychology, Crime & Law, 12,* 107–125.

Salo, B., Sirén, J., Corander, J., Zappalà, A., Bosco, D., Mokros, A., & Santtila, P. (2013). Using Bayes' theorem in behavioural crime linking of serial homicide. *Legal and Criminological Psychology, 18,* 356–370.

Sampson, R. J., & Laub, J. H. (1993). *Crime in the making: Pathways and turning points through life.* Cambridge, MA: Harvard University Press.

Santtila, P., Häkkänen, H., Canter, D. V., & Elfgren, T. (2003). Classifying homicide offenders and predicting their characteristics from crime scene behavior. *Scandinavian Journal of Psychology, 44,* 107–118.

Santtila, P., Korpela, S., & Häkkänen, H. (2004). Expertise and decision-making in the linking of car crime series. *Psychology, Crime & Law, 10,* 97–112.

Sarangi, S., & Alison, L. J. (2005). Life story accounts of left wing terrorists in India. *Journal of Investigative Psychology and Offender Profiling, 2,* 69–86.

Sarnecki, J. (1990). Delinquent networks in Sweden. *Journal of Quantitative Criminology, 6,* 31–50.

Saucier, G., Akers, L. G., Shen-Miller, S., Knezevic, G., & Stankov, L. (2009). Militant extremist mindset. *Perspectives in Psychological Science, 4,* 256–271.

Snook, B., Canter, D. V., & Bennell, C. (2002). Predicting the home location of serial offenders: A preliminary comparison of the accuracy of human judges with a geographic profiling system. *Behavioural Sciences and the Law, 20,* 109–118.

Snook, B., Cullen, R. M., Bennell, C., Taylor, P. J., & Gendreau, P. (2008). The criminal profiling illusion: What's behind the smoke and mirrors? *Criminal Justice and Behavior, 35,* 1257–1276.

Snook, B., Dhami, M. K., Kavanagh, J. M. (2010). Simply criminal: Predicting burglars' occupancy decisions with a simple heuristic. *Law and Human Behavior, 35,* 316–326.

Snook, B., Eastwood, J., Stinson, M., Tedeschini, J., & House, J. C. (2010). Reforming investigative interviewing in Canada. *Canadian Journal of Criminology and Criminal Justice, 52,* 203–217.

Snook, B., Luther, K., House, J. C., Bennell, C., & Taylor, P. J. (2012). The violent crime linkage analysis system: A test of its interrater reliability. *Criminal Justice and Behavior, 39,* 607–619. doi:10.1177/0093854811435208

Snook, B., & Mercer, J. C. (2010). Modelling police officers' judgments of the veracity of suicide notes. *Canadian Journal of Criminology and Criminal Justice, 52,* 79–95.

Snook, B., Taylor, P. J., & Bennell, C. (2004). Geographical profiling: The fast, frugal, and accurate way. *Applied Cognitive Psychology, 18,* 105–121.

Snook, B., Zito, M., Bennell, C., & Taylor, P. J. (2005). On the complexity and accuracy of geographic profiling strategies. *Journal of Quantitative Criminology, 21,* 1–26.

Sorochinski, M., & Salfati, C. G. (2010). The consistency of inconsistency in serial homicide: Patterns of behavioural change across series. *Journal of Investigative Psychology and Offender Profiling*, 7, 109–136.

Stott, C., Adang, O., Livingstone, A., & Schreiber, M. (2008). Tackling football hooliganism: A quantitative study of public order, policing and crowd psychology. *Psychology, Public Policy, and Law*, 14, 115–141.

Taylor, P. J. (2002a). A cylindrical model of communication behavior in crisis negotiations. *Human Communication Research*, 28, 7–48.

Taylor, P. J. (2002b). A partial order scalogram analysis of communication behavior in crisis negotiation with the prediction of outcome. *International Journal of Conflict Management*, 13, 4–37.

Taylor, P. J., Dando, C., Ormerod, T., Ball, L., Jenkins, M., Sandham, A., & Menacere, T. (2013). Detecting insider threats to organizations through language change. *Law and Human Behavior*, 37, 267–275.

Taylor, P. J., & Donald, I. J. (2004). The structure of communication behavior in simulated and actual crisis negotiations. *Human Communication Research*, 30, 443–478.

Taylor, P. J., & Donald, I. J. (2007). Testing the relationship between local cue-response patterns and global dimensions of communication behavior. *British Journal of Social Psychology*, 46, 273–298.

Taylor, P. J., Donald, I., Jacques, K., & Conchie, S. (2012). Jaccard's heel: Are radex models of criminal behaviour falsifiable when derived using Jaccard coefficient? *Legal and Criminological Psychology*, 17, 41–58.

Taylor, P. J., Jacques, K., Giebels, E., Levine, M., Best, R., Winter, J., & Rossi, G. (2008). Analysing forensic processes: Taking time into account. *Issues in Forensic Psychology*, 8, 45–57.

Taylor, P. J., Snook, B., & Bennell, C. (2009). The bounds of cognitive heuristic performance on the geographic profiling task. *Applied Cognitive Psychology*, 23, 410–430. doi:10.1002/acp.1469

Taylor, P. J., & Thomas, S. (2008). Linguistic style matching and negotiation outcome. *Negotiation and Conflict Management Research*, 1, 263–281.

Taylor, P. J., Tomblin, S., Conchie, S. M., & van der Zee, S. (in press). Cross-cultural deception detection. In P. A. Granhag, A. Vrij, & B. Verschuere (Eds.), *Deception detection: Current challenges and new approaches*. London, England: Wiley.

't Hart-Kerkhoffs, L. A., Vermeiren, R. R. J. M., Jansen, L. M. C., & Doreleijers, T. A. H. (2011). Juvenile group sex offenders: A comparison of group leaders and followers. *Journal of Interpersonal Violence*, 26, 3–20. doi:10.1177/0886260510362882

Todd, P. M., Gigerenzer, G., & the ABC Research Group. (2000). How can we open up the adaptive toolbox? *Behavioral and Brain Sciences*, 23, 767–780.

Tonkin, M., Grant, T., & Bond, J. W. (2008). To link or not to link: A test of the case linkage principles using serial car theft data. *Journal of Investigative Psychology and Offender Profiling*, 5, 59–77.

Torres, A. N., Boccaccini, M. T., & Miller, H. A. (2006). Perceptions of the validity and utility of criminal profiling among forensic psychologists and psychiatrists. *Professional Psychology: Research and Practice*, 37, 51–58.

Toulmin, S. (1958). *The uses of argument*. Cambridge, England: Cambridge University Press.

Trojan, C., & Salfati, C. G. (2011). Linking criminal history to crime scene behavior in single-victim serial homicide: Implications for offender profiling research. *Homicide Studies*, 15, 3–31. doi:10.1177/1088767910397281

Vecchi, G. M., van Hasselt, V. B., & Romano, S. J. (2005). Crisis (hostage) negotiation: Current strategies and issues in high-risk conflict resolution. *Aggression and Violent Behavior*, 10, 533–551.

Villejoubert, G., Almond, L., & Alison, L. (2009). Interpreting claims in offender profiles: The role of probability phrases, base-rates and perceived dangerousness. *Applied Cognitive Psychology*, 23, 36–54.

Vrij, A., Granhag, P. A., Mann, S., & Leal, S. (2011). Outsmarting the liars: Towards a cognitive lie detection approach. *Current Directions in Psychological Science*, 20, 28–32.

Vrij, A., Mann, S., Fisher, R., Leal, S., Milne, B., & Bull, R. (2008). Increasing cognitive load to facilitate lie detection: The benefit of recalling an event in reverse order. *Law and Human Behavior*, 32, 253–265.

Warmlink, L., Vrij, A., Mann, S., & Granhag, P. A. (2013). Spatial and temporal details in intentions: A cue to detecting deception. *Applied Cognitive Psychology*, 27, 101–106.

Warr, M. (1996). Organization and instigation in delinquent groups. *Criminology*, 34, 11–37.

Wells, S., Taylor, P. J., & Giebels, E. (2013). Crisis negotiations. In M. Olekalns & W. L. Adair (Eds.), *Handbook of research on negotiation* (pp. 473–498). London, England: Edward Edgar.

Wilson, M. A. (2000). Toward a model of terrorist behavior in hostage-taking incidents. *Journal of Conflict Resolution*, 44, 403–424.

Wilson, M. A., Scholes, A., & Brocklehurst, E. (2010). A behavioural analysis of terrorist action: The assassination and bombing campaigns of ETA between 1989 and 2007. *British Journal of Criminology*, 50, 690–707.

Woodhams, J., Cooke, C., Harkins, L., & da Silva, T. (2012). Leadership in multiple perpetrator stranger rape. *Journal of Interpersonal Violence*, 27, 728–752.

Woodhams, J., Hollin, C. R., & Bull, R. (2007). The psychology of linking crimes: A review of the evidence. *Legal and Criminological Psychology, 12,* 233–249.

Woodhams, J., & Toye, K. (2007). An empirical test of the assumptions of case linkage and offender profiling with serial commercial robberies. *Psychology, Public Policy, and Law, 13,* 59–85.

Yokota, K., Iwami, H., Watanabe, K., Fujita, G., Watanabe, S. (2004). High-risk factors of hostage barricade incidents in a Japanese sample. *Journal of Investigative Psychology and Offender Profiling, 1,* 131–151.

Yokota, K., & Watanabe, S. (2002). Computer-based retrieval of suspects using similarity of *modus operandi. International Journal of Police Science and Management, 4,* 5–15.

Ysseldyk, R., Matheson, K., & Anisman, H. (2010). Religiosity as identity: Toward an understanding of religion from a social identity perspective. *Personality and Social Psychology Review, 14,* 60–71.

CHAPTER 7

EYEWITNESS MEMORY

Nancy K. Steblay

Human memory has been studied by psychologists for more than 100 years, providing a deep theoretical and empirical foundation for understanding memory processes of interest to the legal system—in particular, the eyewitness experience. Psychology's specific interest in the topic of eyewitness memory spans 100 years as well. The writings of Munsterberg (1908) brought early attention to intriguing intersections between the young science of psychology and the established discipline of law. The most recent 35 years have seen intense experimental examination of eyewitness issues and the productive application of memory science to legal cases and policy. The audience for eyewitness research includes lawyers, judges and juries, legislators and policymakers, law enforcement, and the media.

Eyewitness reports are essential for criminal and civil investigations, for development of evidence in support of or against a defendant, and for courtroom testimony before judge and jury—and yet, one of the most important outcomes of memory research is an appreciation of the substantial vulnerabilities for eyewitness memory. Scientists now recognize that the legal system's expectations for eyewitness memory may well exceed witness memory capability. Intrusions from outside sources—including the very procedures used by police to collect memory evidence—can dramatically alter witness memory in ways often unrecognized by investigators and legal decision makers or by witnesses themselves. Misplaced confidence in witness memory subsequently may undermine effective jury decisions. This chapter begins with the problem, the most brutal

consequence of memory error in the legal system: wrongful conviction. From there, the content of a massive research effort in the domain of eyewitness memory will be briefly summarized with specific attention to two central challenges for eyewitness evidence integrity: witness accuracy and confidence. Procedures developed by scientists to avoid error in the collection of eyewitness evidence will be detailed. The chapter will also highlight changes in legal policy spurred by collaboration between scientists and legal professionals, and will discuss challenges ahead for research and its application to public policy.

IMPORTANCE OF THE PROBLEM

The news headline is familiar by now: An innocent person vindicated by DNA evidence, released from prison at last, reunited with family. The happy resolution of an individual case is eclipsed, however, by realization of the scope of the atrocity: years of justice denied, ever-increasing numbers of demonstrated wrongful convictions, and guilty perpetrators left on the street to commit additional offenses when innocents are imprisoned. The Innocence Project recently documented its 300th exoneration, a man named Damon Thibodeaux, who served 15 years on death row in Louisiana for the murder of his cousin before being exonerated by DNA evidence in September 2012. Factors contributing to conviction included a false confession and two eyewitnesses who mistakenly identified Thibodeaux from a photo lineup and again in court (Innocence Project, 2012).

http://dx.doi.org/10.1037/14462-007
APA Handbook of Forensic Psychology: Vol. 2. Criminal Investigation, Adjudication, and Sentencing Outcomes,
B. L. Cutler and P. A. Zapf (Editors-in-Chief)
Copyright © 2015 by the American Psychological Association. All rights reserved.

False arrest and wrongful conviction can stem from many kinds of errors. If there were no discernible patterns of risk factors, the justice system would likely be at a loss to offer solutions for these problems, perhaps judging them to be the unavoidable fallout of an imperfect system. The growing list of exonerations does present clear patterns, however, in particular the problem of eyewitness error. The oft-quoted figure from the Innocence Project is that approximately 75% of their successfully resolved wrongful conviction cases have involved mistaken eyewitness identification. In all but two of the hundreds of mistaken identifications (some cases involve multiple witnesses), the eyewitness was facing a culprit-absent lineup; certainly the lineup contained a police suspect, but the suspect was not the culprit. Nonetheless, rather than responding with "I don't know" or "I don't see him," these witnesses identified an innocent suspect and went on to testify against that defendant. As strikingly noted by Wells, Cutler, and Hasel (2009), "The question of why honest eyewitnesses mistakenly identify someone, rather than refuse to make an identification, is one of the most fundamental questions that eyewitness scientists have faced" (p. 310).

The greater availability of DNA in rape cases compared to other crimes likely explains the preponderance of rape cases among DNA exonerations. Hence, it can be argued that cases in which false convictions are exposed by DNA are the "tip of the iceberg" in miscarriages of justice. Gross, Jacoby, Matheson, Montgomery, and Patil (2005) remind us that there are likely to be large numbers of undetected wrongful convictions in rape cases without testable DNA, and some larger number of undetected false convictions in robberies and serious violent crimes for which DNA collection is not possible. The National Registry of Exonerations, maintained as a joint project between the University of Michigan and Northwestern University Schools of Law, lists 973 cases since 1989 that each presented strong evidence of actual innocence. The Registry reports that mistaken identifications have been involved in approximately 43% of cases and in 80% of robbery and sexual assault cases (National Registry of Exonerations, 2012).

The revelation of postconviction DNA exoneration cases beginning in the 1990s corresponded well to the emerging eyewitness literature of that time, and research by eyewitness scientists gained attention from media and the legal community. These cases highlighted the relevance of laboratory findings to the memory experiences of real eyewitnesses to real crimes. Psychological scientists have brought forward a century of research that has explored the strengths and weaknesses of memory and produced principles of memory operation common to human experience, among them errors of omission in which we forget what we need to remember and errors of commission in which we remember things that are not so. Scientists also recognize that eyewitness experience is not just a memory phenomenon. Social psychology has enhanced the understanding of memory processes with an empirical accounting of social influences that impact memory and decision making. Indeed, the social world provides the context through which humans orient their attention, find meaning in what they see and experience, and assess past, present, and future events. In addition, the social psychology literature has provided an instructive parallel between a social psychology experiment and a lineup procedure, also known as the lineup-as-experiment analogy (Wells & Luus, 1990), discussed later in this chapter.

In the domain of criminal and civil justice procedures, eyewitnesses are called upon to report who and what they have seen. How did the accident happen? Who cashed the check? What did he look like? Who threw the first punch? Was there a weapon? Eyewitnesses are also asked to state their level of confidence in these memory reports, and witness confidence often serves as a marker of memory accuracy (*Manson v. Brathwaite*, 1977). Investigators, cowitnesses, and juries react favorably to confident eyewitnesses (Brewer & Burke, 2002; Cutler, Penrod, & Dexter, 1990; Semmler, Brewer, & Douglass, 2012).

Eyewitnesses to crimes are no less subject than others to basic processes of cognition and social influence, nor are they less vulnerable to serious lapses in accuracy and misapplied confidence. The difference for eyewitnesses is the greater likelihood that the experience will entail an unexpected and emotion-laden event and an unusually intense postevent examination of episodic memory, frequently under external pressure (e.g., a cowitness, a family member, a police investigator) to retrospectively produce a cohesive, detailed, and forensically useful narrative of the event. External and self-imposed expectations together with an often limited memory of the event may pose an unreasonable challenge for the human memory system.

The perfect storm of memory dysfunction is revealed in eyewitness misidentification of innocent suspects. In these cases, the confluence of cognitive processes and social influence is readily observable. A witness's error—the selection of an innocent suspect from a police show-up or lineup—is exacerbated with the inflation of eyewitness confidence subsequent to the identification. Eyewitness accuracy and confidence are not always appropriately aligned, frequently due to the interplay of memory with external influences, yet the confidence of the witness will drive the investigation forward and provide strong testimony at trial. DNA exoneration cases reveal that most mistaken eyewitnesses have been compelling and unshakably confident at trial, even if not always so confident at the time of the identification (Garrett, 2011). It is very difficult for jurors to distinguish mistaken from accurate identification testimony, particularly when an eyewitness is confident regarding the guilt of the defendant (Semmler et al., 2012).

RELEVANT PSYCHOLOGICAL THEORY AND PRINCIPLES

It is useful to begin by placing eyewitness memory within the broader narrative of psychological principles. As specific eyewitness phenomena are described throughout the chapter, basic cognitive and social processes will be played out repeatedly.

The phrase "memory's fragile power" (Schacter, 2001) denotes the paradox of human memory: Memory is the foundation for learning, reasoning, knowledge, creativity, and for each person's unique history and identity, but it also allows for substantial frailties in these psychological endeavors. In fact, adaptive mechanisms that allow memory to work as it should most of the time also generate memory

glitches that plague us in systematic and sometimes perplexing ways. Schacter (2001) has categorized *seven sins* of memory: absent-mindedness (not paying attention in the first place), transience (memory loss), blocking (difficulty in retrieval), misattribution (confusion about the source of the memory), suggestibility (influence from external sources), bias (rewriting previous experiences with benefit of what we know now), and persistence (repeated recall of what we wish we could forget). The seven sins set the stage for eyewitness error.

Cognitive Resources

A core principle of memory science is that the resources of our cognitive system are limited, and we therefore must attend to and use information selectively in a manner that efficiently and effectively allows us to engage with the environment (Kahneman, 2011). Our cognitive system manages trade-offs regarding what to attend to and what to remember. In the eyewitness world, for example, action is more likely to draw priority attention than are details peripheral to that action (clothing, setting, other people); a threatening object similarly garners more cognitive resources. In what may be an evolution-based tendency, attention to peripheral detail and metacognition ("I wish I had a better view of the criminal") are far less likely than attention to the situation at hand (to escape harm).

Indeed, a cognitive system that attends closely to peripheral details (What was George wearing today? How far away was he standing from me?) or metacognition (How focused was my attention during our conversation?) would be inefficiently cluttered with (usually) irrelevant information. The legal system, however, may request such information and judgments from witnesses: How long was the culprit within view? Were you paying close attention?

Acquisition of New Information

As information is incorporated into personal knowledge, a new memory trace may be generated, an earlier memory altered, or an original memory may simply become less easily accessible (Loftus, 2005; Schacter, 2001). Whatever the case, this adjustment is often useful and efficient: As I finally acquire the skill to solve a difficult equation, learn to use my new cell phone, or find a faster route to navigate the subway system to a frequent destination, outdated information fades. In like manner, an attempt to recall your mother's appearance when you were age 10 is likely to be futile (setting aside recalled photos—that's cheating); instead the image that likely comes to mind is a more recent (and aged) mother. This is helpful as a means to recognize Mom without undue surprise when you meet her next week at the train station.

In a spectacular twist of memory, however, an eyewitness may replace (or confuse) a perpetrator's face with another image—of an innocent lineup member, a police composite, or a face seen in a mug-shot or other postevent context (see, e.g., Deffenbacher, Bornstein, & Penrod, 2006; Loftus, 1976). The subsequent "memory" is often quite compelling both to the eyewitness and to a jury (see Chapter 10, this volume for a review of research on juries). One of the most riveting and well-publicized DNA exoneration cases—the rape conviction of Ronald Cotton—includes a chain of identification tasks during which the face of the rapist, Bobby Poole, was replaced in the victim's memory with that of innocent Ronald Cotton. With 100% confidence at trial, Jennifer Thompson called the day of Cotton's conviction "the happiest day of my life" and failed to recognize Poole when she finally was confronted with him (Thompson, 2000; Thompson-Cannino, Cotton, & Torneo, 2010). An otherwise useful cognitive function that purges or updates old information in favor of new may present difficulties for the eyewitness of crime interviewed at a later date. Can a witness be expected to effectively retain and parse information based on when it was acquired (pre-, during, or postevent) and report only time-linked impressions?

Retrospective Narrative

Eyewitness testimony is heavily dependent on the retrospective piecing together of what was often a fast-paced, emotional and novel experience. External influences may be most intrusive when a witness's memory is weak and the witness is highly motivated to remember. Thus, the quality of interviewing practice and integrity of identification procedure may matter the most when weak eyewitness memory does not support a clear internal rendition of events.

Long-standing theories of social psychology tell us that a person comes to know his or her internal states (e.g., motivation, beliefs, abilities) at least in part by inferring them from present behavior. Bem's self-perception theory (1972) posits that an individual will often seek and rely on external sources of information to infer an internal state, particularly to the extent that internal cues are weak or ambiguous. Thus, if a witness does not have a strong memory or a feeling of familiarity (as in the case of an identification), the pull toward external information may be quite powerful as a means to make sense of the crime event: information from a lineup administrator, a police investigator, a family member, or from less personal but relevant sources (e.g., news reports). This shortcoming in memory integrity may be exacerbated by the fact that people tend to more quickly forget the source of information than the information itself (Brown, Deffenbacher, & Sturgill, 1977).

Memory conformity among cowitnesses is a forceful example of the way in which eyewitness narratives can be shaped by external information. Festinger's (1954) social comparison theory specifies that we inform and evaluate subjective opinions through comparisons with others. A cowitness who has shared the experience of a crime can be an especially compelling source of information. Thus, the "John Doe" sought in a costly FBI manhunt after the Oklahoma bombing of 1995 is now believed to have been nonexistent, although three eyewitnesses described Timothy McVeigh's "accomplice" at the time. The co-witnesses at a truck rental shop were apparently influenced by one employee who recalled confidently that Timothy McVeigh was with another man when he rented the truck used in the bombing. All three witnesses described the accomplice to investigators—after they first shared their recall with one another (Memon & Wright, 1999; Schacter, 2001).

Best practices for police require that witnesses be separated as soon as possible in order to avoid memory contamination (Technical Working Group for Eyewitness Evidence, 1999; hereinafter as the NIJ Eyewitness Evidence Guide). In many cases, however, multiple witnesses to a crime frequently share their impressions before police have a chance to interview them (Paterson & Kemp, 2006; Skagerberg & Wright, 2008). The results can be the transfer of relevant information (correct or incorrect) to produce a seemingly consistent and corroborative story across witnesses. Gabbert, Memon, and Allan (2003) used two versions of a video crime event that allowed pairs of witnesses to unknowingly view slightly different accounts. Of those witnesses who discussed the crime with a cowitness, 71% later reported "memory" of information that had in fact only been presented to their cowitness. Perhaps it is not surprising that cowitnesses are more affected by acquaintances than strangers (Hope, Ost, Gabbert, Healey, & Lenton, 2008), by others who are confident (Allan & Gabbert, 2008), or by those who possess greater source credibility (Skagerberg & Wright, 2009). Memory conformity is impelled by the same triggers that produce behavioral conformity.

The upshot is that expectations for the fidelity of eyewitness memory may well exceed memory capabilities. The cognitive and social processes that humans use to effectively navigate their daily lives may not always serve the justice system's expectation for eyewitness performance. It behooves scientists and legal professionals to better understand eyewitness memory and derive procedures to more effectively access and protect the true memories that can help investigations and courtroom decisions.

RESEARCH REVIEW

The basic processes of memory and social cognition described above are revealed in specific and systematic ways in the experiences of eyewitnesses. Laboratory research in recent decades has sharply defined strengths and weaknesses of eyewitness memory.

Specific Vulnerabilities for Eyewitness Memory

Consider the ideal eyewitness: All sensory systems operate optimally (including required eyewear and absence of the ubiquitous ear-buds), in an attentive, calm, and nonintoxicated witness, within a situation that provides an unobstructed, well illuminated view at a distance and for a duration of time that allows a reasonable study of the culprit and circumstances. The ideal witness will attend to and perceive all that transpires; encode this information completely, meaningfully, and accurately into memory; retain the information across time; and then retrieve and report it faithfully and fully when requested by investigators. This ideal witness has passed through four steps of a simple model akin to the operation of our memory system. That is, eyewitnesses perceive, encode, store, and retrieve information and images. This simple model is an appealing device for grasping the witness experience and for understanding what can go wrong in the eyewitness account of a crime because, alas, this ideal witness does not exist (see Loftus & Palmer, 1974; Wells & Loftus, 2013).

Attention: Guns and Gorillas

An elegant pair of laboratory experiments provided early empirical support for a phenomenon called the *weapon focus effect*. Loftus, Loftus, and Messo (1987) reported increased eye fixations and duration times for a weapon (a gun) compared to a neutral object (a check) when witnesses viewed a slide-show presentation of an exchange between a customer and cashier in a fast-food restaurant. Memory was worse for witnesses who viewed the weapon than for witnesses who viewed the check when they later attempted to describe the customer and identify him in a 12-person photo lineup. Here was a demonstrated link between visual attention to a weapon and its consequences for eyewitnesses: a reduced ability to accurately describe and recognize the perpetrator of the crime. The article by Loftus et al. (1987) highlighted research questions that would dominate exploration of the eyewitness experience for the decades that followed: What factors have a reliable impact on eyewitness perception and encoding? How, specifically, does witness memory suffer? Why does a weapon (or other factor) affect the memory performance of an eyewitness? As other lines of research expanded, an applied question arose: Is there a way to share this information in legal settings or perhaps to even prevent and overcome disruptive influences on eyewitness memory?

The weapon focus effect provides a useful illustration of attention in the eyewitness experience. Weapon focus begins with a simple orienting response. The cumulative body of weapon focus research provides support for the claim that the presence of a weapon draws the attention of an eyewitness, preempts encoding of other details, and thereby diminishes the ability of the eyewitness to later recognize ($g = 0.22$) and describe the culprit ($g = 0.75$; Fawcett, Russell, Peace, & Christie, 2013; N. M. Steblay, 1992). A recent line of investigation has explored whether the presence of a threat (or even a weapon per se) is necessary to draw visual attention and to produce memory effects parallel to the weapon focus effect. Pickel (1999) found that attention effects can be produced by objects that are simply unusual within a given context. Hope and Wright (2007) employed a clever means to further explore the weapon focus effect using a secondary cognitive task. They found that both threatening and unusual objects commanded attention and slowed reaction time in the secondary task, but the weapon generated a greater impairment in confidence and accuracy. These authors posit that a weapon threat is a uniquely emotion-based attentional drain—a conceptually loaded target object with impact far beyond the simple orienting response.

The weapon focus effect can be placed within the broader context of inattentional blindness that pervades the cognitive functioning of all humans. Simons and Chabris (1999) asked research participants to count the number of basketball passes between white-shirted players in a short video. Approximately 50% of viewers did not even notice an actor in a gorilla costume who strolled into the scene, thumped her chest, and sauntered off-camera. The attention devoted to the central action made these observers blind to the gorilla. Chabris and Simons (2010) further note the surprise of viewers when told there was a gorilla in the scene: an illusion of attention. We experience far less of our visual world than we think we do.

Encoding: Beyond the Gist of It

A popular exercise in introductory psychology textbooks or with audiences for memory experts is the *penny lineup*, a display of six drawings of a penny, each with a different configuration of wording and positioning of Lincoln's profile. With the possible exception of coin collectors, most people have difficulty recognizing the correct version of an item that they have used effectively in social and financial transactions since elementary school. The core characteristics of a penny—size, shape, color—have been encoded and retained successfully, but specific details are not accessible, even if they were at one time encoded into memory. In miserly style, our cognitive system operates on limited information; peripheral details are not necessary nor particularly useful. If one is asked to identify the penny in a lineup of coins, the solution is easy; we have encoded the gist of a penny enough to distinguish it from a nickel, a dime, or a quarter. On the other hand, the lineup of six pennies can be impossibly difficult. In lineup terms, the failure to discern the one penny of interest from among others of similar general characteristics means that you are not a very helpful memory witness.

In a similar manner, an eyewitness may encode the basics of a perpetrator's physical presence—size, skin and hair color, gender, race—as we often do in social interactions, but not attend to or encode specific details. Furthermore, what we do encode is not uniformly an objective record of "what is there" but instead is based on knowledge and past experience. An example of this is the cross-race effect, long recognized in eyewitness memory research. In a meta-analysis of cross-race effect studies spanning 30 years and encompassing the laboratory experiences of nearly 5,000 research participants, Meissner and Brigham (2001b) found that witnesses were 1.40 times more likely to correctly identify a previously seen face of their own race compared to a face of another race, and 1.56 times more likely to falsely identify an other-race face never seen before. The authors cogently present the results as a *mirror effect* in which other-race faces receive both a lower proportion of hits and a higher proportion of false alarms when compared with own-race faces. Time available for encoding moderates the strength of the cross-race effect: longer encoding tends to diminish the effect.

Theoretical explanations for the cross-race effect have emphasized an encoding process that is general rather than specific for the "other" race. Outgroup members are frequently categorized more superficially than ingroup members, with less expenditure of cognitive resources. Very little individuating information is attended to or stored beyond racial categorization (Brigham, Bennett, Meissner, & Mitchell, 2007; MacLin & Malpass, 2003). The cross-race effect can also be a function of how one has learned to differentially attend to social cues that provide the best basis for discrimination between same-race faces, cues that do not work equally well for encoding faces of another race (Chance, Turner, & Goldstein, 1982). Sporer (2001) predicts a related response bias such that witnesses are generally more apt to choose other-race than same-race faces in an identification task. From a signal detection framework, this implies a more lax response criterion for cross-race identification decisions (Meissner & Brigham, 2001b; see Chapter 5, this volume for a review of additional research on race and the justice system).

Retention: Postevent Information and Memory Malleability

Information encoded into memory at the time of a crime is not stored in pristine or immutable condition, rather it is quite vulnerable to revision, contrary to a common-sense assumption of an image "burned into memory." Eyewitnesses forget both important and unimportant details as time goes by (Shapiro & Penrod, 1986); eyewitness memory also can err through commission, i.e., incorporating new information that may seemingly sharpen the experience or shape the narrative for the witness in ways that, even if factually correct, change the memory such that it is no longer a veridical report of that eyewitness's original experience. Witnesses may second-guess their own version of events under pressure from cowitnesses or a case investigator (normative social influence) or accept information from other sources that is assumed to be true (informational social influence; Deutsch & Gerard, 1955).

One of the most important experimental research programs of the past three decades is the explication of the misinformation effect and the cognitive and

social influences underlying that phenomenon, from Elizabeth Loftus and her research colleagues (e.g., Loftus, 2005). The misinformation effect refers to the impairment in memory for the past that occurs after exposure to misleading information. This seminal research provided the cornerstone for eyewitness memory science and for understanding of the puzzling and destructive circumstance of false memory, that is, "memories" in the absence of direct perception of a real event (Loftus, 1997; Loftus & Ketcham, 1994).

Hundreds of experiments have established beyond question that information from outside of memory can be incorporated into a convincing "memory experience" as memory gaps are unknowingly and effortlessly filled. Explicit or even subtle exposure to incorrect information can alter witness memory for events and faces. In experiments that document this occurrence, participants exposed to misleading information incorporate it into their versions of events and—with a little prompting by credible sources such as parents—even create false renditions of autobiographical events (Braun, Ellis, & Loftus, 2002; Loftus & Pickrell, 1995). Participants have been led to believe that, in childhood, they were lost in a shopping mall, broke a window and cut themselves, were attacked by an animal, or endured other emotionally painful experiences. To counter the possibility that these rich false beliefs may stem from true experiences recalled with experimental cues, Braun et al. (2002) demonstrated how subjects can recall that they met Bugs Bunny at a Disney resort—Bugs Bunny (a Warner Brothers character) does not visit Disney.

There are common outcome patterns in misinformation research. An example is an experiment by Stark, Okado, and Loftus (2010), who showed participants sequential photos of a theft of a wallet. Participants then heard recorded narratives describing the photos. When asked later about the photos, witnesses incorporated wrong details implanted by the narratives (e.g., the wallet hidden in pants pocket versus jacket) and misremembered where they had secured that information (photos versus narrative), illustrating a combination of misinformation effects and source confusion. Recall of public events is also vulnerable to memory distortion.

Ost, Granhag, Udell, and Roos af Hjelmsäter (2008) found that 40% of their subjects reported having seen film footage of a bus exploding in the 2005 London terrorist attacks. These reports of (nonexistent) film were prompted by a simple suggestive question regarding whether subjects had seen videos of the recent newsworthy event.

In a related domain, Hasel and Kassin (2009) offer a disturbing demonstration of the undermining of eyewitness evidence fidelity by misinformation. Eyewitnesses to a staged but realistic live theft were asked to identify the thief from a six-person lineup. Two days later, the witness-participants returned for a follow-up interview and reconsideration of their lineup decision. The experimenter relayed to the witness the pertinent information that one of the lineup members had in fact confessed, a suspect not identified by the witness. Of those witnesses who had made an identification of a lineup member two days earlier, 61% revised their identification in line with the "confession" of this nonselected lineup member. Some offered a rationale: "His face now looks more familiar than the one I chose before." Of those witnesses who had not made an identification at the first session, 50% changed their nonidentification decision to identify the confessor.

The practical implications of this study—and of the misinformation effect more broadly—are significant: An eyewitness's new knowledge regarding one type of evidence, such as case information or a confession, can corrupt another type of evidence, the eyewitness identification. In addition, potentially exculpatory evidence (a witness's initial failure to identify the suspect) is undermined by the confession. As discussed by Hasel and Kassin (2009), this finding challenges the presumption in law that evidence is independent, as in the "harmless error" rule of appeals courts that relies on the assumed independence of confession and eyewitness evidence (see Chapter 9, this volume for a review of research on interrogations and confessions).

Retrieval and Reconstruction: Memory Strength and Reasoning Processes

As has been cautioned now for decades, eyewitness memory is not like a play-back system that can be accessed for a veridical version of an event. Equally important is the fact that an eyewitness brings a store of knowledge and experience to the crime event that will direct the witness's attention and color the meaning of the experience and how it is encoded. The subsequent retrieval of this information likewise will be affected by the meaning the witness can place around the event. Memories are not so much *retrieved* as they are *reconstructed*, often using current knowledge to understand the past event or fill in a gap in the story. Information from external sources will become a part of this narrative, as will internal scripts regarding how the witnessed scene played out and how it makes sense.

A challenge for eyewitness researchers and the legal system is to assess the level of reconstruction that afflicts an eyewitness's memory report. In the words of writer Tim O'Brien (1990), the simple difference is between happening-truth (what objectively occurred) and story-truth (what the witness believes and feels must have occurred), a boundary that quickly becomes very blurry. The potential errors that developed at earlier stages of memory (perception, encoding, and retention) cumulate as the story-truth is relayed by the eyewitness to investigators in the narrative of what occurred and who is responsible.

Eyewitnesses are often called upon to report whether they recognize a suspect at a show-up (presentation of a single suspect), or from a lineup (physical or photo). Charman and Wells (2006, 2012) posit that a witness may have an immediate ecphoric experience, a fast automatic recognition of the offender that results in a positive identification. Ecphory is a function of good memory strength and a reasonable likeness of the offender in the lineup. The absence of an ecphoric experience, however, such as when memory for the culprit is not strong, culprit appearance has changed, or the culprit is not in the lineup, will prompt secondary processes, slower, more effortful and deliberative modes of decision-making (see also Dunning & Stern, 1994). Charman and Wells (2006) state that these psychological processes involve a continuum of judgment from automatic to deliberative processes, the latter being critically less sensitive to the actual presence of the culprit in the lineup. It is during a deliberative search to explain and correct for the absence of ecphory that contextual aspects of the lineup matter most.

One secondary strategy is reliance on an *intuitive heuristic* (Kahneman, 2011). We often respond to a difficult question by answering an easier one, usually without noticing the change in tack. That is, we fully intend to address the target question, but if the answer is not immediately accessible, a simpler question is substituted, especially one with an intuitively adequate response. This may be a suitable cognitive strategy at times, and it is rather effortless. For example, when we try to locate a vaguely remembered server mid-meal in a restaurant (Was that the young man who took my order?), the answer to an alternative question may easily suffice (Which of these servers is *closest* to what I remember?).

A process of choosing the closest to memory is well known in the lineup literature: Relative judgment is the comparison of lineup members to one another in order to select the one who looks most like the offender relative to the other lineup members (Wells, 1984). Other secondary strategies may include a process of elimination, imagining each lineup member with a different hairstyle, or otherwise arriving at a lineup decision in the absence of immediate recognition.

R. C. L. Lindsay and Wells (1985) suspected that a witness who moves from an absolute (this is the guy!) to a relative (closest!) judgment strategy places an innocent suspect at risk. In his now classic removal-without-replacement experiment, Wells (1993) compared two groups of witnesses who viewed a staged crime and then were shown one of two versions of a lineup. Wells compared the lineup selections of witnesses who saw a culprit-present lineup to those who viewed a lineup from which the culprit had been removed. When the culprit was present, 54% of witnesses correctly identified the culprit (21% rejected the lineup). The central question for the study rested with the witnesses who viewed the culprit-absent lineup. If 54% of witnesses truly can recognize the culprit when he is present (absolute judgment), this 54%, who would have identified the culprit had he been in the lineup, should join the 21% in the "no-pick" category because now the culprit is absent, to produce a 75% lineup rejection rate. Importantly, all witnesses

were warned that the offender might not be in the lineup. Even with this explicit warning, only 32% correctly rejected the culprit-absent lineup. The remaining 68% of witnesses shifted their pick to another lineup member. One lineup member went from second to first choice, a change in the selection rate from 13% to 38%, when the culprit was not available.

The intuitive "correctness" of relative judgment for the witness produces a dangerous situation when police place an innocent suspect in a lineup who more closely resembles the true culprit than other lineup members. This straightforward conceptualization of relative judgment is rich in its implications for lineup procedural revisions and has provided the basis for new lineup procedure recommendations discussed later in this chapter.

Eyewitness Evidence and the Supreme Court: *Perry v. New Hampshire*

The U.S. Supreme Court revisited eyewitness identification for the first time since 1977 in *Perry v. New Hampshire* (2012). The case is illustrative of the Court's approach to eyewitness evidence and of the need for procedural safeguards that can reduce suggestiveness and the likelihood of misidentification. The latter two topics (policy and procedural safeguards) will be covered later in this chapter, but the Perry case can first provide a useful example of the many complex factors that may affect eyewitness memory.

On an August night in 2008, Nashua New Hampshire police responded to a call from an eyewitness in an apartment overlooking a parking lot. The caller reported that a man was attempting to break into cars. At the apartment, police asked the witness to describe the man. She moved to her apartment window and pointed at a Black man standing below with a police officer. Barion Perry was arrested on the basis of this identification. At trial, Mr. Perry's attorney moved unsuccessfully to suppress the identification, claiming a violation of due process. After Perry's conviction and appeal, the case was ultimately heard by the nation's highest court. Mr. Perry contended that the trial court wrongly denied his pretrial motion to suppress the identification evidence.

Early in the development of eyewitness literature, Wells (1978) pointed out two categories of influence on eyewitness memory: estimator variables and system variables. At the time of the crime, the witness's attention, perception, and encoding of memory can be inhibited by aspects of the scene (e.g., lighting, distance), characteristics of the offender (e.g., race, disguise), and by personal characteristics of the witness (e.g., visual acuity, stress). The impact of such factors on an individual witness's memory representation for the event can only be estimated post hoc by the criminal justice system, and therefore estimator variables do not lend themselves well to systemic change. In contrast, once police have arrived at the crime scene to collect information from witnesses, the manner in which the investigation proceeds can be controlled by the criminal justice system. System variables, such as interview techniques and identification procedures, enormously affect eyewitness memory and decision making, and research knowledge on these topics can help prevent eyewitness error from occurring in the first place. Recommendations from a system variable approach are primarily directed toward law enforcement within the useful framework that eyewitness memory can be likened to physical trace evidence that must be carefully collected and evaluated using science-based procedures (Wells, 1995).

To return to Mr. Perry's case (*Perry v. New Hampshire*, 2012), there are a number of relevant estimator variables that may have influenced the eyewitness's perception and encoding of information at the scene. The witness and culprit were of different races. The crime occurred near 3:00 a.m. in relative darkness. Although there were building lights and nearby street lights (somewhat obscured by tree branches), parts of the parking lot were in darkness. The witness viewed the events from a distance—upper-floor apartment window—with a view partly obstructed by a parked van. The witness conceded to being "so scared [she] really didn't pay attention" to what Perry was wearing, nor could the witness describe the culprit's facial features or any other identifying marks, only describing him as a "tall Black man" (American Psychological Association, 2012, p. 35). At trial, the witness stated that she could not clearly see the face. Although not

intentional, the de facto identification procedure was a one-person show-up (a system variable). Perry was the only Black man at the scene and stood next to a uniformed police officer. At the time of a full photo lineup a month later, the witness was unable to identify Mr. Perry.

The question for the Supreme Court was whether Mr. Perry's due process rights should extend to a suggestive identification procedure not intentionally orchestrated by the police. The Court ruled against Perry, stating that "the due process check for reliability, *Brathwaite* made plain, comes into play only after the defendant establishes improper police conduct" (*Perry v. New Hampshire*, 2012, p. 3). The Court recognized witness memory fallibility, but ruled that the reliability of the eyewitness testimony was for the jury to consider (*Perry v. New Hampshire*, 2012, p. 14).

Estimator Variables

Estimator variables cannot be controlled by the criminal justice system because they largely operate as the witness encodes memory at the time of the crime event. Estimator variables can, however, signal initial eyewitness memory strength, an accurate and accessible memory representation. For both practical and theoretical purposes, memory strength can be viewed as a moderator of procedural (system) factors. For example, witnesses with low memory strength may be more likely to engage in secondary processes of decision making and be particularly vulnerable to the external influence of biased or suggestive procedures.

Earlier in this chapter, attention and encoding issues were discussed with examples of weapon focus and cross-race effects, as well as problems of misinformation and influence incurred during the retention interval between viewing and subsequent memory retrieval. In the following section, a nonexhaustive subset of estimator variables is summarized from the large volume of empirical work on these topics, variables most heavily examined with experimental laboratory tests (see also Wells & Loftus, 2013).

Exposure duration and retention interval.
Studies of exposure duration and retention interval support intuitive notions that longer exposure to the

crime stimulus allows for a stronger memory trace, and that memory will fade over the retention period between the crime event and recall. Two meta-analyses speak to these issues. Bornstein, Deffenbacher, Penrod, and McGorty (2012) reviewed studies involving almost 3,000 witness-participants and found that longer exposure to the culprit reliably aided correct culprit identifications from a culprit-present lineup ($d = 0.69$) and correct rejections of the culprit-absent lineup ($d = 0.22$) compared to a shorter exposure. (Compared exposure times differed in seconds or minutes, similar to the brief exposures that are common to crime events.) What is not intuitively obvious is that the effect of exposure duration is nonlinear and most influential at the low end of the distribution; that is, the authors concluded that the benefit of increased exposure time is greatest up to about 30 seconds.

Deffenbacher, Bornstein, McGorty, and Penrod (2008) reviewed 53 facial identification studies and found a reliable, if small, association ($r = 0.18$) between a longer retention interval and forgetting of once-seen faces. The effect size was similar for the facial recognition studies typical of cognitive psychology and the tests of single-event person memory common to applied eyewitness experimentation. Memory for an unfamiliar face drops off steeply right after the encounter and then levels off over time, a forgetting function that the authors reported as "Ebbinghausian in nature" (p. 148), in a nod to the historically familiar forgetting curve. A delay of even a few hours can be detrimental to accuracy.

These data prompt recommendations for system variables, e.g., that investigators talk to witnesses as soon as possible and secure an estimate (from the witness or corroborative sources) about the amount of time the culprit was in view and the length of the retention interval. At the same time, investigators must be cautious because of the known difficulty for witnesses in retrospectively assessing time lapses (Douglass & Steblay, 2006).

Encoding processes, appearance changes, and disguises. Bornstein et al. (2012) meta-analyzed the impact of witness encoding processes on identification accuracy. When participant-witnesses used a holistic encoding strategy rather than focusing on specific facial features, correct identifications were significantly higher ($d = 0.52$). This follows expectations from a levels-of-processing theory that social judgments are more likely to be deeper and holistic, whereas discrete feature judgments are relatively shallow (Craik & Lockhart, 1972; Olsson & Juslin, 1999).

When an eyewitness views a perpetrator in disguise, subsequent identification errors depend both on the degree of disguise and the part of the face covered. Upper portions of the face, hair, and eyes are essential for accurate recognition (Shepherd, Davies, & Ellis, 1978). Deliberate disguises such as sunglasses, masks, and hats generally impede later identification accuracy (Mansour et al., 2012; see meta-analysis by Shapiro & Penrod, 1986). For example, Cutler, Penrod, & Martens (1987) compared participants' ability to identify a robber in a video crime scene when the culprit wore a hat pulled over his hair or was hatless. Correct identification dropped significantly (from 45% to 27%) for the witnesses who viewed the hatted robber at the crime scene. Similarly, intentional appearance change between crime event and lineup reduces recognition accuracy. A feature change (e.g., hairstyle) can make a face appear quite different, disrupting recognition for faces that were encoded holistically (Wells & Hryciw, 1984). Pozzulo and Marciniak (2006) found significantly lower correct identifications when a perpetrator changed his hairstyle between crime and lineup, as did Patterson and Baddeley (1977).

The intoxicated witness. Eyewitnesses may be intoxicated at the time of the crime event, at the later interview, or both. Alcohol is presumed to affect memory by interfering with encoding and consolidation, specifically the transfer of information from short-term to long-term memory (Ray & Bates, 2006). The degree of memory impairment appears to be dose-dependent, that is, it increases with amount and duration of alcohol ingestion. Read, Yuille, and Tollestrup (1992) found that a moderate blood alcohol concentration (BAC) affected recall for a staged crime event after a one-week delay (participants were sober at the recall test). Compared with subjects who were sober at the time of encoding, intoxication at .11% BAC reduced recall of correct details and lowered the rate of correct identifications. Subjects at .08% BAC did not differ significantly from the nonintoxicated control group, and false identification rates were similar for intoxicated and sober participants. Compo et al. (2012) also saw no differences in memory recall of a staged theft between intoxicated witnesses (.07% BAC) and sober controls.

Van Oorsouw and Merckelbach (2012) assessed the impact of higher levels of alcohol intoxication, up to a mean BAC of .17%, by recruiting participants in bars (level of intoxication was not a manipulated variable). Subjects were asked to watch a mock crime video. Three to five days later, when subjects were sober, they responded to free and cued recall questions. Intoxicated participants, compared to sober controls, were 33% less complete in free recall recollections of central crime details and generated more dose-dependent errors for cued recall of salient features. Dysart, Lindsay, MacDonald, and Wicke (2002) explored the impact of witness intoxication at both encoding and retrieval. They found that more highly intoxicated participants approached at a bar (average BAC of .09%) made more false identifications from a culprit-absent show-up than less intoxicated subjects (average BAC of .02%), 52% versus 22%, although the two groups were equally able to identify the culprit when he was presented at the show-up. Dysart et al. suggested that "alcohol myopia" was produced from higher alcohol consumption: Alcohol narrows attention to a few salient features (such as hair or clothing), and witnesses fail to attend to other details (Steele & Josephs, 1990). In short, the research indicates that moderate to higher levels of intoxication can impair memory encoding to a nontrivial degree. Sober witnesses will encode more information. To the extent that encoding produces a weak memory, perhaps intoxication also sets up witnesses to be suggestible to outside influence.

Stress. Common sense imparts that a very stressful event is likely to be well-remembered, a notion that is only partly correct. Although one may never forget the event (sufferers of posttraumatic stress often wish they could), the stress of a crime event often evokes the opposite problem for memory of details. The human defensive response to a stressful condition is a physical readiness for action ("fight or flight") that conflicts with metacognition and deep encoding. Details of the crime often are not always well-remembered, including the face of the culprit, especially under the complex conditions of a typical crime in which a threatening stranger is seen for a very short time.

Even longer encounters with an offender under stressful conditions may disrupt memory. Morgan et al. (2004) presented a lineup identification task to active-duty personnel of a military survival training camp. The participants had undergone an intensive 40-minute interrogation, with prior 12-hour confinement in the mock prisoner-of-war camp, sleep and food deprivation, and both verbal and physical confrontation during the interrogation. This study included a physiological measure of cortisol (stress) level that corroborated participant conditions of high versus low stress. Compared with soldiers who experienced a less stressful interrogation (no physical confrontation), the high-stress group was significantly impaired in their ability to recognize their interrogator in a lineup one day after the interrogation. One outcome is particularly striking: Of participants who viewed a live lineup in the low-stress condition, most were able to correctly identify their interrogator (62%), and 35% made a wrong identification. Rates for witnesses in the high-stress condition were flipped: only 27% picked the correct lineup member, and 73% made an identification error.

Hope, Lewinski, Dixon, Blocksidge, and Gabbert (2012) recently conducted a fascinating field experiment in which law enforcement officers' memory was tested after their interaction in a realistic staged training environment (a trailer with weapons and a target individual). One of two groups of officers was assigned to a condition in which they exerted themselves to the point of fatigue during a high-intensity assault exercise just prior to the critical interactive (trailer) scenario. Compared to officers who did not experience the assault exercise, those who had physically exerted themselves displayed impaired recall about the target individual and were significantly less accurate in recognizing the target in a lineup. To explain their results, Hope et al. (2012)

called upon a compensatory control model: When processing resources are compromised because of arousal, adjustments maintain high-priority tasks but also produce decrements for secondary tasks (Robert & Hockey, 1997). In a differential display of the weapon focus effect, participants did not differ in their detection of the weapons, but the exerted participants seemingly diverted their limited resources to the weapons, thereby diminishing encoding of the critical target. This finding supports the notion that stress (arousal) produces a generalized attentional impairment.

The ecologically valid field settings of the studies by Morgan et al. (2004) and Hope et al. (2012) are important for the study of stress. Ethical considerations prohibit laboratory studies from creating stress beyond the lower range of the continuum, so, field experiments complement (and confirm) findings of laboratory tests (see meta-analysis of Deffenbacher, Bornstein, Penrod, & McGorty, 2004). In the lab, higher stress negatively impacts both recall of event details ($d = -0.31$) and correct identifications from culprit-present lineups ($h = -0.52$) compared to lower stress conditions. Effect sizes are notably larger for eyewitness identification (event) studies and with staged (more realistic) crime scenes than for facial recognition studies.

Witness age and personality. Witness age has been explored as a moderator for most of the eyewitness principles discussed in this chapter. In general, elderly witnesses tend to remember event details less accurately even at immediate recall, suggesting a less complete initial encoding (Bornstein, Witt, Cherry, & Greene, 2000) and tend to perform worse on source monitoring tasks (Mitchell, Johnson, & Mather, 2003). The elderly are more susceptible to misinformation, recall errors, and misidentifications (Davis & Loftus, 2005; see Chapter 3, this volume for a review of research on aging and the justice system). Very young children also are more susceptible to misinformation than older children (Ceci & Bruck, 1993; see Chapter 1, this volume for a more detailed review of the topic of children as eyewitnesses).

Frenda, Nichols, and Loftus (2011) reiterate an important point: Nobody is immune to memory error. Vulnerability to misinformation is more likely, however, when a person's attentional resources are limited. In that respect, individuals who doubt their own memory (e.g., experience memory lapses or unusual levels of forgetfulness or are simply not paying attention) will be more likely to seek out external help or to rely on another's version of an event. Frenda et al. (2011) also report that subjects of higher intelligence, greater perceptual abilities, greater working memory capacities, and greater performance on facial recognition tasks are more resistant to misinformation and false memory errors (Zhu et al., 2010a). Particularly among persons of lesser cognitive ability, those low in fear of negative evaluation and high in cooperativeness, reward dependence, and self-directedness are more vulnerable to misinformation effects (Zhu et al., 2010b).

It is important to note that Bornstein et al. (2012) report that no meta-analysis of estimator variables shows statistically reliable effects that are smaller for more ecologically valid (event memory) versus less ecologically valid (facial recognition) research paradigms, including stress, cross-race, and weapon focus effects. When an effect occurs, the impact of a tested independent variable (estimator or system) on facial identification is larger in more naturalistic eyewitness scenarios (Penrod & Bornstein, 2007).

PRACTICE AND POLICY ISSUES

In what has been described as one of the most successful applications of experimental psychology to practice (Doyle, 2005), psychological scientists have used a system variable approach to develop a set of recommendations to improve the reliability of identification procedures (see Wells et al., 1998). The NIJ Eyewitness Evidence Guide (1999) and its associated training materials provide a concise summary of psychological principles, including interview procedures and better ways to construct lineups, to instruct witnesses, and to take a certainty statement at the time of identification. These recommendations have been informed by the expertise of law enforcement and legal professionals as well as empirical evidence. At the time it was published, the

NIJ Eyewitness Evidence Guide noted with interest but did not endorse two additional aspects of lineup procedure: double-blind administration and sequential lineup presentation. In subsequent years, these two components have become part of lineup procedural recommendations (Wells, 2006).

Memory for Events: The Cognitive Interview

Witnesses are inevitably asked "What happened?" The goal for investigators is to ascertain the course of events and to gather enough information to further the investigation and to generate leads about a suspect. For reasons discussed earlier, witnesses may come up short on details. In years past, forensic hypnosis was sometimes used to procure information from eyewitnesses. Hypnosis presents a host of problems, however, not the least of which is that it produces more of both accurate and inaccurate details from witnesses who become quite confident in erroneous memory (N. M. Steblay & Bothwell, 1994). Hypnotized witnesses have been found to be particularly vulnerable to leading questions and memory confabulation (N. M. Steblay & Bothwell, 1994).

At the same time, standard police interviews are not always productive: Investigators tend to be overly directive in their questioning, interrupt much too frequently, and sometimes use repetitive and misleading questions or confusing lines of inquiry (Ceci & Bruck, 1993; Fisher, Geiselman, & Raymond, 1987). Concern about the corrosive impact of misinformation requires a technique that can prompt accurate recall but tamp down guessing, false recall, and false confidence. In answer to shortcomings of standard interviewing techniques, Geiselman, Fisher, MacKinnon, and Holland (1985) applied principles of memory and social interaction to develop an innovative method for effective forensic interviews. The Cognitive Interview (CI) was first supported in scientific tests with real witnesses and real investigators, where it increased accurate information gain by 35%–75%. The CI also used a structure to limit information transfer from interviewer to witness as a means to reduce memory contamination and witness guessing. The revised ("enhanced") Cognitive Interview combines components for effective communication, interaction, and cognition in a four-step procedure (Fisher & Geiselman, 1992).

The bookends of the CI emphasize rapport-building (Step 1) and closure (Step 4), with control of memory retrieval handed over to the witness, who in point of fact holds the memory. The interviewer is relegated to a role of active listener, allowing the witness to choose the speed, direction, and wording of recall. The questioning itself (Steps 2 and 3) relies on a reinstatement of the crime context and urges witness recall to flow in a narrative from that starting point. The interviewer may use open-ended questions and prompts in a "witness-compatible" format as a means to more extensively search memory and clarify witness responses without leading the witness (Fisher, 1995; Wells, Memon, & Penrod, 2006).

The rationale for this nondirective interview strategy rests primarily on two cognitive principles. First, the encoding specificity hypothesis (Tulving & Thomson, 1973) holds that memory accessibility is heightened when there is overlap between encoded information and retrieval cues. Thus, the reinstatement of original encoding context should provide retrieval cues for stored information. Second, multiple trace theory (Bower, 1967) maintains that memory is made up of a network of associations, and so a variety of cues can be used to trigger recall of a specific event. The CI encourages witnesses to report everything that comes to mind, whether seemingly trivial or incomplete, with the expectation that even partial or out-of-order details may trigger recall of other, more relevant items. The witness may be asked to recall the event in reverse chronological order or from another visual perspective, again with the expectation that different memory cues may be productive. These techniques attempt to minimize witness guessing and self-imposed editing.

The CI addresses police complaints that eyewitnesses fail to provide sufficient information to assist an investigation and has been successful in prompting information from witnesses. Two additional questions arise: What is the quality of this additional information? Which components of the CI are prime contributors to its impact? A meta-analysis of 53 studies (Köhnken, Milne, Memon, & Bull, 1999) found that the CI increased recall of correct information by a median 34% compared to control conditions; a small increase in incorrect details was also reported. Individual studies offer mixed results from the CI (e.g., Memon, Wark, Holley, Bull, & Köhnken, 1997). Comparative effectiveness of the CI's four mnemonic components ("report everything"; context reinstatement; change of chronological order; change of perspective) remains a topic of discussion, particularly as to cumulative and interactive effects (e.g., Colomb & Ginet, 2012). The report everything and context reinstatement principles appear to be more consistently effective in increasing recall of correct information.

The CI is generally established in the literature as a means to elicit significantly more correct information at a minor cost of increased errors. Despite the longevity of the CI in the research literature and its presence in many police training manuals, however, very few law enforcement agencies in the United States or the United Kingdom have adjusted their interview techniques accordingly (Fisher & Schreiber, 2007).

Memory for People: Eyewitness Identification

A number of police jurisdictions in the United States, Canada, and the United Kingdom have adopted lineup procedural revisions recommended by scientists. For example, U.S. states such as Connecticut, New Jersey, North Carolina, Ohio, and Wisconsin have adopted statewide reforms, as have jurisdictions in major cities such as Boston, Minneapolis/St. Paul, Denver, Dallas, and Tampa. The summary below focuses on what can be called the package of lineup procedural recommendations from eyewitness science.

The development of lineup procedural revisions has followed a logic both practical and theoretical. The need to reduce false identifications of an innocent suspect has been the pragmatic basis for many experimental tests. The goal is to increase the likelihood that a witness selection from the lineup is a guilty rather than an innocent suspect, i.e., a lineup procedure's diagnosticity (Wells & Lindsay, 1980). At the same time, an understanding of why revisions to lineup procedures produce changes in witness performance is equally important (Wells, Steblay, & Dysart, 2012). Thus, the recommendations are anchored in a deep research literature about human memory, social influence, suggestiveness, and decision making.

Whether conducted for investigative or evidentiary purposes, the core objective of a lineup is for law enforcement officers to have more reliable information about their hypothesis of suspect guilt after the lineup than they had before the lineup. The memory of the witness can offer support for or against the supposition of "suspect as culprit" as a means to reduce uncertainty about the offender's identity. To achieve this objective, a single suspect is presented along with "fillers" (known innocents) of similar physical attributes (Wells, Rydell, & Seelau, 1993). An eyewitness with a strong memory of the culprit should be able to recognize the perpetrator if he is in the lineup or to reject a lineup that includes an innocent suspect. A witness's firm rejection of a lineup (e.g., "He's not there") in fact suggests a strong memory trace that should cause the police to reevaluate their suspicion about the suspect (Wells & Olson, 2002).

Beyond this straightforward rationale, however, is a complication: The identification task for the witness is supposed to be one of recognition, not reasoning. Otherwise stated, the charge is to determine if a member of the lineup is familiar as the perpetrator (recognition), not to figure out whom the police suspect (reasoning). The former is based on a strong memory trace for the culprit at the crime scene; the latter draws on nonmemory factors, i.e., social, motivational, and metacognitive influences. A legitimate identification is based on recognition (Wells et al., 2012).

The legal system is similarly very clear in its expectation for eyewitness identification evidence. An identification should be the result of an independent recollection by the witness and must not be influenced by administrator cues, suggestive procedures, case evidence, or any form of external intrusion. In *Perry v. New Hampshire* (2012), the U.S. Supreme Court strongly reiterated that unnecessary suggestiveness in police procedures is a constitutional issue of due process that gives rise to judicial review and possible suppression of the evidence. A lineup must fairly secure the identification of a culprit or exonerate an innocent suspect based on the witness's memory alone. This basic legal premise underlies reforms for eyewitness evidence procedures.

The challenge for researchers and for the legal system therefore has been to develop identification procedures that tap witness recollection of the culprit and avoid extraneous influences that may compromise witness reliance on memory alone. Although identification is seemingly a direct matter of memory, Wells and Luus (1990) highlighted decades ago the similarity of a lineup to a social psychology experiment, with its great potential for social influences of experimenter-expectancy effects, demand characteristics, and cross-subject contamination. An analogous principle for lineup reform is that all the things that can go wrong in an experiment can also go wrong when police conduct a lineup. Investigators have a hypothesis regarding the suspect and pressure to move the investigation forward. Witnesses have expectations and beliefs about the task (e.g., the police have caught the guy; I just need to find him in the lineup), motivation to help the investigation and to take the bad guy off the street, and substantial interest in what others have to say about this crime and culprit.

A "biased" lineup procedure is one that can influence a witness through nonmemory factors: aspects of the lineup construction and presentation, instructions to the witness, and investigator cues. Lineup bias may operate as general or specific: General impairment factors urge witnesses to make identifications, but the push is not necessarily directed against the suspect, whereas specific bias variables are those that point the witness toward the suspect and away from the fillers (Brewer & Wells, 2011; Wells & Loftus, 2013). For example, a policy of biased lineup instruction ("Which of these is the person?") may prompt more identifications and thus incur a general increase in witness choosing that does not explicitly implicate the suspect. On the other hand, poorly constructed lineups in which only the suspect bears resemblance to the witness's description of the culprit will prompt more witnesses to specifically pick the suspect. In either case,

laboratory research has ferreted out the impact of bias factors, whether subtle or blatant. Eyewitness scientists have built a set of recommendations for effective lineup practice centered on the requirement that the lineup provide a test of recognition memory alone, circumventing problems of biased procedures.

Lineup construction. The lineup (live or photo) presents a challenge for the witness to discern the perpetrator's face from others with similar characteristics. An eyewitness whose memory is weak should be dissuaded by the many unfamiliar faces in the lineup from falsely claiming recognition of the suspect. Fillers also help ensure that the lineup does not suggest to the witness who the police suspect is. In this way, effective lineup fillers can inhibit demand characteristics of the identification procedure (Wells & Olson, 2002). If a witness with a very limited memory nevertheless makes a lineup pick (akin to a best guess), the risk to an innocent suspect is diminished if spread across lineup fillers. The recommendation that only one suspect be included in a lineup is based on this logic as well, that risk from an unreliable witness can and should be spread away from an innocent suspect. This rationale also exposes the problem of a show-up, in which a single suspect is unprotected from a simple guess (see meta-analysis of N. Steblay, Dysart, Fulero, & Lindsay, 2003).

The extreme end of a contrary lineup construction strategy—an all-suspect lineup—can be seen in the Duke University lacrosse team rape case that came to attention in 2006. The witness, who described the multiple offenders as lacrosse team members, was shown a series of lineups with all team members, including one display with all 46 lacrosse players; there were no fillers (Wells et al., 2009). Any witness pick would incriminate that selected team member, just as throwing a dart at the photos would have netted a suspect hit. In short, the procedures used were nondiagnostic for the guilt or innocence of the young men in the lineup. It is important to note that the absence of fillers in the lineups also meant that the witness's credibility could not be challenged; she could not make a "wrong" pick.

Alternative explanations for a witness's positive identification of a suspect must also be ruled out, such as suspect position in the lineup, photo quality and size, clothing, or other nonmemory cues. To this end, the photo context must be consistent across lineup members, and all members of the lineup must be plausible picks based on the description provided by the witness—but only one can be the suspect. A witness's initial verbal description of a stranger is likely to be relatively generic and limited to a small number of salient features: gender, race, build, age, and hair color. Even familiar persons are hard to describe; holistic facial processing is difficult to capture in discrete descriptors of language (a problem for creating composites). Beyond an unusual facial feature such as tattoo or scar, recognition will be holistic as well. A witness is likely to recall the earlier statement to police and expect a guilty member in the lineup who possesses the described attributes. In fact, when the identification shortly follows the verbal description, identification accuracy may be hindered to a small but significant extent—the overshadowing effect—such that participants who describe the target are 1.27 times more likely to misidentify the target compared with witnesses in a no-description control condition (Meissner & Brigham, 2001a).

Police do not know if the suspect is the culprit when they build the lineup. Therefore, a method of fit-to-description (as opposed to a fit-to-suspect) is necessary to limit bias against a suspect who may be innocent (Wells et al., 1998). Variability in lineup member appearance is allowed around the core verbal descriptors provided by the witness, a method that avoids both an impossible "clone" lineup and one that unfairly flags the suspect (Wells & Bradfield, 1999b). A lineup constructed to increase physical similarity beyond the level of witness description provides no additional protection to the innocent suspect and can harm the eyewitness's ability to identify the perpetrator. Clark and Tunnicliff (2001) have uncovered the danger of using the suspect as the reference point to select fillers: a backfire effect in which an innocent suspect has an increased chance of being identified as the culprit.

This rationale for a match-to-description method with just one suspect per lineup also underlies

procedures to assess lineup quality after the fact. The mock witness method (Doob & Kirshenbaum, 1973) at first seems counterintuitive: Persons who did not witness the crime—in fact, have no knowledge of it—view the lineup and hazard a best guess as to who the suspect is. The mock witness is given only one clue: the real witness's verbal description of the perpetrator. Wells and Bradfield (1999b) recommend use of the specific question "Which person is the accused?" instead of "Which person best fits the description?" to capture the mock witness's use of any nonmemory information available to the eyewitness (e.g., aspects of the display that make the suspect stand out). The quality of the lineup then is assessed in the context of mock witness selections. If a six-person lineup is fairly constructed, no more than one sixth of mock witness guesses should land on the suspect. On the other hand, if a significant proportion of mock witnesses can reason their way to the suspect with exactly no memory of the crime, the lineup is clearly unfair. Evaluation of the real witness's true memory (and pick of the suspect) is now confounded by nonmemory factors (Wells, Luus, & Windschitl, 1994).

The mock witness method generates metrics of lineup quality (see Brigham, Meissner, & Wasserman, 1999 for a review). Functional size is an index of the number of plausible choices for the witness, calculated as the reciprocal of the proportion of mock witnesses choosing the suspect (Wells & Turtle, 1986). Effective size indicates the number of plausible lineup members without specific reference to the suspect (Malpass, Tredoux, & McQuiston-Surrett, 2007). These metrics are used for evaluation of lineup construction effectiveness for both laboratory and real lineups. As illustration, the original work by Doob and Kirshenbaum (1973) involved a case selected because of suspicion of bias, as have many others. Actual cases generally reveal that lineups are frequently biased against suspects, who are picked twice as often (relative to the fillers) as one would expect by chance alone (Brigham et al., 1999; Wells & Bradfield, 1999b).

An additional use of the mock witness procedure is to ascertain typical lineup quality in a police jurisdiction averaged across the sample set. Valentine and Heaton (1999) used this method to compare the quality of 25 live and 16 video lineups. N. K. Steblay (2007) examined the lineup quality of 37 six-person sequential lineups in an urban jurisdiction (see also Klobuchar, Steblay, & Caligiuri, 2006). The lineups produced a mean functional size of 4.54 and effective size of 3.96. N. K. Steblay (2011) also calculated average functional size (5.05) and effective size (4.1) for six-person simultaneous and sequential lineups from Evanston, Illinois. Both field and lab tests reveal that lineups rarely function with effective or functional sizes equal to nominal size.

Lineup instructions.   A lineup instruction provides information to the witness that cannot improve memory but may affect the identification decision. The recommendation is for an explicit instruction to the witness that the offender may or may not be in the lineup, thereby also allowing for rejection of the lineup to be a reasonable response to the lineup (informational and normative social influence). The NIJ Eyewitness Evidence Guide solidified this recommendation, and this cautionary instruction has become a noncontroversial policy reform in many U.S. jurisdictions. It has been required police procedure in England and Wales since 1986.

A meta-analytic review (N. M. Steblay, 1997) confirmed findings of earlier single studies that biased instructions produce a significant average increase (25%) in identification errors when the lineup does not include the true offender, and has minimal impact on correct identifications when the culprit is in the lineup, compared to a condition of unbiased instruction. The studies of this early meta-analysis (and later analysis by Clark, 2005) included a variety of operational definitions for biased and unbiased instructions because research teams had explored different means to influence witness selection rates. For example, encouraging (e.g., "We're sure you'll be able to recognize him"), discouraging (e.g., "You only saw him for a short time, your memory may play tricks"), or neutral instructions were compared, with no significant differences (Hilgendorf & Irving, 1978). In another study, an instruction that revealed police uncertainty ("It might be the guy, but we can't be sure") decreased choosing rates from both culprit-present and culprit-absent lineups compared to an instruction that implied that the police were certain about the suspect (Malpass, Devine, & Bergen, 1980). Explicit response options were tested by O'Rourke, Penrod, Cutler, and Stuve (1989): "Write the number of the suspect" versus "Write the number of the suspect or indicate that the robber is not present by writing *not present*".

As the research developed, the key experimental manipulation coalesced around the intent to disabuse the witness of the notion that the perpetrator had to be in the lineup. Thus the unbiased instruction clearly provided an additional consideration for the witness, i.e., that the culprit may be not present. N. K. Steblay (2013) recently reevaluated the lineup instruction literature with a narrowed focus on experimental studies that specifically tested the presence versus absence of a "may or may not be present" instruction. The 16 tests included more than 3,000 adult eyewitnesses who viewed an event and attempted a lineup identification of the culprit. The "may or may not be present" instruction significantly reduced (from 70% to 43%) identification errors when the culprit was missing from the lineup, and a designated innocent suspect was picked by half as many witnesses (19% vs. 40%) after hearing a "may or may not be present" instruction. This instruction also led to a 5% loss of correct identifications, but the confidence interval for this number included zero. The research is clear: An instruction that specifically alerts the witness to the possibility that the true perpetrator may not be in the lineup significantly decreases witness picks from the lineup, compared to an instruction that suggests culprit presence in the array. The primary impact of the admonition is to inhibit choosing by witnesses who otherwise would make identification errors.

The NIJ Eyewitness Evidence Guide (1999) also recommends a prelineup instruction that offender features may have changed over time: "Individuals depicted in lineup photos may not appear exactly as they did on the date of the incident because features such as head and facial hair are subject to change" (pg. 32). The appearance change instruction (ACI) has been tested only minimally. Charman & Wells (2007) found that an ACI overall increased false alarms and had a slight impact on culprit identifications only in a condition in which appearance change was greatest. It might be expected that the ACI will influence witnesses to more closely examine the photos in an attempt to imagine changes in hairstyle, skin tone, or age. This strategy may be productive if the culprit is in the lineup, but potentially dangerous for an innocent suspect. It remains necessary to determine whether the ACI prompts selective picks of the culprit or merely more picks from the lineup.

Witness confidence statements. Best practices recommend that a confidence statement in the witness's own words be secured immediately at the time of the identification and before feedback about the correctness of that decision arrives from any source, particularly from the case investigator. Charman, Carlucci, Vallano, and Gregory (2010) use a selective cue integration framework to explain the process that a witness goes through when asked: "How confident are you?" The basics of this framework echo the broad principles described earlier in this chapter, now specific to the witness's self-report of confidence in an identification decision. A witness may derive immediate confidence from the internal cue of a strong recognition for the culprit. If internal cues are weak, a witness then may search for external information from a lineup administrator. External cues are quickly evaluated (e.g., Is the source credible or not?). This three-stage process—assessment, search, evaluation—indicates how eyewitness confidence can depend on a lineup administrator's feedback, especially when memory strength is weak.

How influential is feedback from a lineup administrator? A sizable body of research literature has revealed the astonishing power of a casual comment from a lineup administrator to affect eyewitness confidence. In the first study to examine this phenomenon, Wells and Bradfield (1998) showed witness-participants a security video and asked them to identify the offender from a lineup. The lineup did not include the offender, yet all witnesses made a selection. Immediately after these mistaken identifications, confirming feedback was provided to a randomly assigned group of witnesses: "Good. You identified the actual suspect." Witnesses assigned to the control group were told nothing about their identification accuracy. Confirming feedback significantly inflated witnesses' retrospective confidence reports compared to the control group. Furthermore, an extensive range of variables was inflated in conjunction with retrospective certainty, including witnesses' positive evaluation of their viewing experience for the crime. Importantly, the witnesses believed that the feedback did not affect their perceptions.

The postidentification feedback effect (PIFE) is robust across studies and noteworthy for multiple reasons (see meta-analyses by Douglass & Steblay, 2006; N. K. Steblay, Wells, & Dysart, 2014). First, witnesses whose decisions were confirmed became more certain of their identification both at the time of the feedback (perhaps not surprisingly) but also retrospectively for the time of the identification ($d = 0.98$). Importantly, these witnesses typically have made identifications from culprit-absent lineups; hence, their distorted reports correspond to mistaken identifications of innocent suspects, a forensically relevant scenario of critical importance. This dramatic effect is produced by a simple, casual, even seemingly helpful, comment from the lineup administrator.

Second, the PIFE is more than a simple hindsight bias (e.g., "I knew it all along"; Fischhoff, 1975). Witness memory is distorted beyond the boundaries of misremembering an earlier decision; rather, memory of the circumstances surrounding the identification task and the crime itself has been altered. After confirming feedback, witnesses recalled greater ease and speed of the identification and reported having had a better view of the perpetrator, having paid more attention, having had a better basis to identify the suspect, and having greater clarity of the offender's image in mind. These aspects of eyewitness experience are the very attributes that are likely to bolster eyewitness credibility in the eyes of investigators, prosecutors, and juries.

Additionally, witnesses who received confirming feedback showed elevation in broader subjective measures, such as a belief that they possess good memory for strangers, greater trust in eyewitnesses with similar experiences, and an increased willingness to testify about their eyewitness experience. These witnesses are more willing to bring their testimony to a jury ($d = 0.98$). This combination—that jurors are especially willing to believe a confident witness and that lineup administrators can influence a witness's confidence—poses a serious problem for courtroom evidence. The confidence of the witness can be misaligned with accuracy (Sporer, Penrod, Read, & Cutler, 1995), yet a witness who is truly convinced of the correctness of the testimony will not exude cues of deception or insincerity.

Finally, attempts to remedy or prevent the PIFE have met with only limited success (see, e.g., Lampinen, Scott, Leding, Pratt, & Arnal, 2007; Wells & Bradfield, 1999a). A *confidence prophylactic* of requiring the witness to think about confidence and testimony-relevant factors prior to the feedback can somewhat reduce the PIFE, as can strategies to undo the feedback by suggesting that it was random, erroneous, or suspicious in its intent. A recent study (Dysart, Lawson, & Rainey, 2012) supports the most frequently offered advice to law enforcement as to how to avoid PIFE: Have a blind lineup administrator secure the confidence rating from the witness at the time of the lineup.

Double-blind lineup administration. A standard protective measure of experimental research design is a double-blind procedure, in which neither the research participant nor the experimenter knows whether the participant is in the treatment or control group. An enormous empirical literature provides support for the pervasiveness of experimenter expectancy effects on participant behavior, exposing the need for a double-blind procedure (see Harris & Rosenthal, 1985; Rosenthal & Rubin, 1978). In police investigations, the case investigator has a hypothesis about the suspect-as-culprit that may have an impact on the direction of the investigation and the assessment of case evidence (Findley & Scott, 2006). A double-blind lineup keeps both eyewitness and lineup administrator unaware of which lineup member is the police suspect. The blind status of the eyewitness is a given in the lineup procedure; there is no point to a lineup if the eyewitness is told which member is the suspect. Forensic interest rests with the blind lineup administrator. For

brevity's sake, in subsequent discussion the term *blind* rather than *double-blind* refers to the lineup administrator's status regarding knowledge of the suspect's identity.

The recommendation for a blind identification procedure was issued over two decades ago and has long been endorsed by eyewitness scientists (Wells, 1988; Wells et al., 1998). A primary reason for this advice is the potential for influence on a witness identification decision by a lineup administrator who knows the identity of the suspect. Beyond the worry of direct influence during the lineup procedure, there are additional negative effects of the nonblind lineup administration after the lineup decision is made.

Laboratory research on blind lineup procedures began with Phillips, McAuliff, Kovera, and Cutler (1999), who found that lineup administrators (research participants) with knowledge of the suspect's identity had a significant influence on eyewitness identification decisions compared to blind administrators, even in the presence of a neutral observer who was placed in the room as a means to tamp down overt attempts at administrator influence. The research revealed that a lineup administrator may divulge suspect information to a witness through unobtrusive and unintentional ways. Garrioch and Brimacombe (2001) reported witness confidence inflation as well when the lineup administrator possessed suspect information. Subtle and presumably unintentional nonverbal cues from the nonblind lineup administrator resulted in more confident witnesses for both correct and incorrect witness decisions. Douglass, Smith, and Fraser-Thill (2005) further found that a blind administrator who develops a suspicion about suspect identity in the course of showing a lineup to one witness can then influence a second witness based on that suspicion.

Identifications from lineups conducted by blind administrators have been found to be more diagnostic of suspect guilt than those conducted according to nonblind procedures (Greathouse & Kovera, 2009). An exploration of the underlying conditions for witness vulnerability to influence found that the impact from nonblind administrators was greatest when the lineup procedure was biased by general impairment factors of biased lineup instructions and simultaneous lineup format. Nonblind administrators behaved differently toward witnesses, in ways that were consistently detected by neutral observers (Greathouse & Kovera, 2009; see also Haw & Fisher, 2004).

Clark, Marshall, and Rosenthal (2009) studied different categories of influence as another facet of nonblind administration: overt (e.g., "Does anyone look more like him than anyone else?"), and covert (e.g., "Look at each photo carefully."). Administrator influence was evident for both overt and covert influence, despite the fact that most witnesses reported no awareness of the influence attempt. Research has established that both witnesses and administrators may be unaware of administrator influence (Garrioch & Brimacombe, 2001).

A blind lineup administrator in the field does not simply present the lineup to the witness. This administrator can (and should) converse with the witness for clarification of responses and record the witness's decision along with witness comments, qualifiers, and expressed certainty about an identification. Rodriguez and Berry (2014) report an experimental lab study in which blind versus nonblind lineup administrators presented a photo lineup to a confederate witness who identified either the suspect or a filler. Nonblind lineup administrators (the subjects in this study) were more likely than blind administrators to record the witness pick as a positive identification and to rate the witness as credible when the witness chose the suspect rather than a filler. Under a blind procedure, the recording of suspect responses and witness's credibility rating was not influenced by the witness's choice of suspect or filler.

An administrative reporting difference was also documented in real field lineups (N. K. Steblay, 2011). Analysis of 87 lineups from Evanston, Illinois, indicated that nonblind investigators administering simultaneous lineups were 44% less likely to report verbatim witness comments (e.g., "That's him, I recognize the crooked teeth.") than were blind investigators administering sequential lineups. Nonblind administrators more frequently reported in third-person form (e.g., "The witness identified the suspect."), revealing an interpretation of the lineup outcome filtered through the lens of

investigator knowledge. In this field comparison, blind status of the lineup was confounded with lineup format. Nevertheless, the take-away point is that a blind lineup administrator, by virtue of the lack of knowledge about the suspect, is unable to interject conclusions based on case information.

Lineup administrator knowledge can also affect subsequent witness interviews and the further investigation. MacLean, Brimacombe, Allison, Dahl, and Kadlec (2011) found that participant-investigators who learned about the witness's pick of the suspect from a lineup were significantly more likely to use positive leading questions in a follow-up interview (defined as a query that suggests confidence; e.g., "So you are pretty confident in the choice you made?") compared to a control condition in which the investigator had not been tipped off to the witness's lineup selection. The nonblind and blind participant-investigators were equally likely to ask leading questions, but nonblind investigators were more likely to phrase the question with the positive frame.

Dysart et al. (2012) led participant-witnesses to presume that the lineup administrator was blind or nonblind to the suspect's identity. When witnesses were provided positive although nonspecific feedback after their identification decision (e.g., "You've been a really great witness."), confidence and other testimony-relevant judgments were inflated only in the "presumed nonblind" condition and only for inaccurate witnesses. The results point to a practical recommendation: Blind lineup administrators may serve as a prophylactic against the negative effects of PIFE, but also, no feedback, even benign, should be given to eyewitnesses before confidence is recorded. The results of this study by Dysart et al. (2012) fit nicely with the selective cue integration theory in that inaccurate witnesses seemingly assessed their confidence using feedback from a lineup administrator whom they presumed had knowledge of the suspect.

Sequential lineup procedure.   A traditional identification procedure presents all lineup members at the same time (simultaneously), yet there is no logical or empirical basis to assume that a reliable witness's memory of the culprit can be improved by side-by-side comparison of lineup members, nor is there a financial benefit of a simultaneous display (Klobuchar et al., 2006). There is also a risk in the traditional procedure: Simultaneous lineup presentation allows witnesses to engage in relative judgment, thereby incurring a general impairment bias. A greater reliance on absolute judgment should produce better accuracy than relative judgments (Clark, Erickson, & Breneman, 2011; Wells, 1984). The current recommendation is that all lineups, photographic or live, be presented to the witness one member at a time (R. C. L. Lindsay & Wells, 1985; N. K. Steblay, Dysart, & Wells, 2011).

Nonetheless, concerns have been raised about the sequential lineup. For example, the sequential presentation may produce an order effect if a "stopping rule" is applied. The stopping rule can be problematic for several reasons. A witness may expend his or her pick on a filler early in the lineup display, and if the lineup ends at that point, a suspect identification is impossible (Memon & Gabbert, 2003). A case detective will no doubt be frustrated that the witness never viewed the suspect. If the early pick is the suspect, a defense lawyer will object to an identification from a truncated lineup. The solution is to use a "continuation rule" that requires the witness to continue to the end of the lineup, as was the original intent for the sequential lineup procedure (R. C. L. Lindsay & Wells, 1985).

The sequential procedure is a combination of prescribed components that each contributes to making relative judgment less likely. The witness views each lineup member only once, with no option to return to an earlier lineup member or to view members side-by-side. The witness does not know how many lineup members will be in the series and must make a decision for each member before moving to the next (a "sequential-only, let them see them once, must decide before proceeding, can't know how many people they will see" lineup; R. C. L. Lindsay, Mansour, Beaudry, Leach, & Bertrand, 2009, p. 32). Some take the position that the impact of each of these components should be isolated prior to a policy recommendation (Malpass, Tredoux, & McQuiston-Surrett, 2009). There may be theoretical and practical use in estimating the impact of each component, and some of this work

has been done, but whether such research is necessary for policy can be debated.

Additional concerns include the possibilities that the sequential procedure may simply make witnesses more cautious, and that a reduction in false alarms will be offset by a reduction in correct culprit identifications. This notion stems from a signal detection framework, an assessment of lineup technique that focuses on the change in a witness's decision criterion (responses to the lineup) as the lineup procedure is manipulated. This approach has been useful in many research contexts but is more controversial when applied to the lineup procedures discussed in this chapter (see Clark, 2012; Wells et al., 2012). To that point, Palmer and Brewer (2012) have recently used a compound signal detection model to better fit the scenario of eyewitness identification decisions.

Empirical data are essential to address these issues, as are field tests that incorporate the realities of how lineups are conducted by case investigators. The most recent published meta-analysis of lab studies included 72 tests of the sequential versus simultaneous procedure (N. K. Steblay, Dysart, & Wells, 2011). The core analysis was from a "diagnostic dataset" of 22 published tests. Each test in this subset was weighted equally (contributing one effect size to the calculation), and each involved a full 2x2 design to guarantee equivalence across testing conditions (sequential vs. simultaneous lineup; culprit present vs. absent). This allowed a straightforward evaluation of the comparative advantages of the two lineup procedures. The simultaneous lineup showed an average 8% benefit in correct identifications; the sequential procedure showed an average 22% benefit of lower misidentifications. The risk to a designated innocent suspect in a culprit-absent lineup was cut almost in half (from 28% to 15%) with use of a sequential versus a simultaneous procedure. The superior performance for the sequential procedure was due to the greater ratio of culprit identifications to misidentifications of an innocent suspect (diagnosticity), not simply a reduction in choosing.

The meta-analysis also clarified the specific components of the sequential lineup that produced favorable results, beginning with a single-suspect lineup with at least four (usually five) fillers, a restriction to a first identification attempt, and a cautionary instruction to the witness that the true perpetrator may or may not be in the lineup. Specific to the sequential procedure, the witness was prohibited from side-by-side comparison of lineup members or returning to previous photos, and was required to give a yes/no decision for each photo before moving to the next. A continuation rule (discussed above) was associated with a smaller discrepancy between sequential and simultaneous lineups in correct identification rate (5%). This specified set of procedures became important as the investigation of sequential lineups moved into field testing.

Sequential and simultaneous lineup procedures were directly compared in a controlled, randomized field experiment sponsored by the American Judicature Society (AJS), involving almost 500 lineups from real witnesses to real crimes (from fraud to murder) in four U.S. police jurisdictions (Wells, Steblay, & Dysart, 2011; in press). The lineups were randomly assigned to simultaneous versus sequential lineup procedures. Results were in concert with laboratory findings, in that sequential lineups generated significantly fewer (11%) filler identifications compared to simultaneous lineups (18%), with no loss of suspect identifications.

For police, the critical question is whether the identification is a good predictor of the suspect's guilt. The meta-analysis by N. K. Steblay, Dysart, and Wells (2011) showed that once a witness has made a positive identification from the lineup, the likelihood that this pick is correct is better if the lineup was sequential rather than simultaneous. These results are now echoed with the AJS field data. Although suspect identifications did not differ between sequential and simultaneous field lineups, 41% of witness selections from simultaneous field lineups were filler picks compared to 31% of witness picks from sequential lineups. In this way, the sequential procedure increases the probative value of the identification evidence.

Repeated identification tasks. John Jerome White served 22 years of a life sentence for burglary and rape before he was exonerated by DNA evidence in 2007. The victim was "almost positive" when she identified White in a photo lineup. A week later, White was placed in a live lineup of five men. This time, the witness was positive of her identification, a false identification that was remarkable in that the police had unknowingly placed her real attacker in that same physical lineup (Wells, 2010). Garrett (2011) reports that, in at least 14 DNA-exoneration cases, the exoneree was the only person repeated in multiple viewings by the same eyewitness. These cases have the common thread of mistaken identification by eyewitnesses who became increasingly but erroneously convinced of the culprit's identity across two or more identification tasks.

One reason that a suspect may stand out in a lineup (a specific-bias) is that he has appeared in a prior identification context: a mugshot book, a show-up, an earlier lineup. The lineup identification procedures recommended by eyewitness scientists have been developed for a witness's *first* identification attempt (Wells, 2006). This is the test that can best determine whether recognition memory supports police suspicions about the identity of the perpetrator. Conversely, influences inherent to repeated identifications challenge the fidelity of the witness's memory at a second identification task or beyond. Repeated identification tasks are not uncommon in practice (Behrman & Davey, 2001; N. K. Steblay, 2011), yet few jurisdictions have written policies about repeated identification practices.

Experimental work on this topic has been reviewed in a meta-analysis of laboratory tests for the mugshot exposure effect (Deffenbacher et al., 2006). Mugshot exposure of a suspect to a witness prior to a lineup resulted in decreased identification accuracy, with reductions in both correct identifications and correct rejections of a culprit-absent lineup and an increase in false alarms. A witness's selection of the suspect at a second identification task may stem from exposure to the same person at the first identification task rather than at the crime scene. A memory failure for the circumstances of the previous encounter (source confusion) results in the witness's sense that the face is familiar although the correct context for that memory has been lost (Brown et al., 1977). Recent research provides evidence of neurological alterations that underlie memory changes

under conditions of repeated retrieval
(Bridge & Pallen, 2012).

Along with misplaced familiarity, witness motivation may drive decision-making with repeated identifications. The witness may have heightened expectations that the suspect in a show-up will be in the subsequent lineup (Godfrey & Clark, 2010), and the witness may feel committed to stick with an early pick, presumably to reduce dissonance or to help the investigation. This commitment will be revealed in consistent picks of the same suspect across identification tasks. A commitment effect can also be inferred when choosers continue to choose or when nonchoosers continue to not choose; in this case, the commitment is to a decision strategy rather than to a specific suspect (Goodsell, Neuschatz, & Gronlund, 2009). Finally, the very presence of the same suspect at both identifications may suggestively signal to the witness that the police believe this is the perpetrator.

Available research shows increased positive lineup identifications (correct and incorrect) after show-ups (Valentine, Davis, Memon, & Roberts, 2012) or a previous lineup (Hinz & Pezdek, 2001). In short, legal concern about repeated identification is well placed. Misidentifications from show-ups or culprit-absent lineups at a first identification task set the stage for these errors to be carried through to a second lineup decision (N. K. Steblay, Tix, & Benson, 2013).

Postdiction of Witness Accuracy

A system-variable approach attempts to prevent misidentification problems. Nevertheless, it is inevitable that investigators, attorneys, judges, and juries will continue to be placed in the unenviable position of assessing the credibility of eyewitness testimony after the fact.

Confidence and accuracy. As already noted, a confident eyewitness can be very convincing to a jury. Thirty-five years ago, the U.S. Supreme Court appeared to be similarly convinced about the diagnostic value of witness confidence, ruling in *Manson v. Brathwaite* (1977) that eyewitness confidence provides an acceptable index of reliability for identification accuracy. Subsequent laboratory outcomes decidedly tamped down enthusiasm among

scientists for confidence as a marker of accuracy. A set of meta-analytic reviews reported modest average confidence-accuracy (CA) correlations, in the range of $r = 0.25$ (Bothwell, Deffenbacher, & Brigham, 1987; Sporer et al., 1995), although the average correlation coefficient was larger for witnesses who made a pick from the lineup (0.37) compared to nonchoosers (0.12; Sporer et al., 1995).

D. S. Lindsay, Nilsen, and Read (2000) documented a stronger CA relationship ($r = 0.68$) when they allowed for a moderating impact of witness encoding memory strength. This report underscored that the CA connection can be viewed as an index of process subject to varying conditions of witness exposure to the crime. Brewer and Wells (2011), among others, have fleshed out this notion by using a calibration statistic to assess identification accuracy at varying levels of witness confidence (100%, 90%, etc.) under differing conditions of eyewitness encoding. When measured immediately after an identification, confidence can provide a meaningful but not infallible index of accuracy. Witnesses become overconfident under some conditions, with confidence levels of 90%–100% associated with accuracy rates around 75%–90%. An implication from this calibration approach is that police should closely investigate a suspect identified by a highly confident eyewitness, but react to a report of low witness confidence with reconsideration of their hypothesis regarding the suspect's guilt rather than simply with a dismissal of the witness's memory as uninformative. Brewer and Weber (2008) furthermore claim that an eyewitness's confidence in memory may shape the retrieval process itself, that is, the reporting or withholding of information by an eyewitness.

Perhaps the strongest message at this point for law enforcement practice and evidentiary concerns has been that the CA relationship can so easily be corrupted, particularly in the direction of inflated retrospective confidence for an inaccurate memory. Disassociation between accuracy and confidence is not unexpected when one considers the discordant factors that influence these two variables. Accuracy is a function of subject and event factors at the time of the crime (e.g., visual acuity and illumination), whereas confidence can be dramatically altered by postevent information (e.g., a news report or postidentification feedback from law enforcement) and extraneous social factors (e.g., cowitness sharing or repeated public testimony) without a concomitant rise in accuracy.

Eyewitness confidence for identification decisions has drawn the bulk of research attention, but some scientists have explored the CA relationship for witness reports of event memory, finding weak to moderate links between the two (Smith, Kassin, & Ellsworth, 1989; Perfect, 2002). It should be noted that another potential indicator of accuracy—consistency of witness memory report—has not been found to be a reasonable substitute for accuracy (Fisher & Cutler, 1996).

Identification response latency. In cognitive psychology, response latency (reaction time) has long been an indicator of memory strength. The time needed for a witness to make an identification decision has been measured against the accuracy of that decision (a latency-accuracy index). Accurate identifications from simultaneous lineup displays tend to occur more rapidly than inaccurate identifications (Brewer, Caon, Todd, & Weber, 2006; Sporer, 1992). And, the latency-accuracy relationship is more reliable for witnesses who choose a member of the lineup compared to witnesses who do not pick from the lineup (similar to the CA relationship). As discussed by Brewer and Weber (2008), the latency-accuracy relationship has not yet generated a great deal of research attention, nor a way of bringing this measure to applied practice. Response latency can vary enormously among witnesses, and a useful application of the latency-accuracy relationship would depend on finding a temporal cutoff that could sort accurate from inaccurate witness identifications (Brewer et al., 2006; Weber, Brewer, Wells, Semmler, & Keast, 2004). Furthermore, postevent contamination can undermine the usefulness of a witness's retrospective report of confidence.

Witness self-reports of familiarity with the culprit. A witness who cites prior familiarity with a culprit (e.g., "I've seen him around before.") would seem to be a good bet for identification accuracy. One laboratory study involved witnesses who self-reported a naturally occurring prior familiarity

with the culprit (a recent-past student at the college). This "familiar perpetrator" condition revealed the link between witness-reported memory strength (prior exposure) and identification accuracy. Witnesses without prior culprit familiarity had great difficulty recognizing him, with 10% correct culprit identifications. As might be expected, witnesses with reported prior familiarity were significantly more likely to make a correct identification (59%) and less likely to misidentify (4% from a culprit-present lineup, 8% from a culprit-absent lineup; N. K. Steblay, Dietrich, Ryan, Raczynski, & James, 2011). That said, claims of prior familiarity were certainly not a perfect indicator of identification accuracy.

Eyewitness Identification in Archival and Field Studies

A substantial base of laboratory research is now available to aid our understanding of eyewitness identification processes and to support recommendations for lineup reform. There are, however, a limited number of peer-reviewed published studies that measure eyewitness performance in real police cases. Field studies bring unique strengths and weaknesses to research efforts, capturing eyewitness decisions in the most forensically relevant settings but under circumstances that lack the control and precision of the lab. Field studies are enormously important to connect laboratory outcomes with real investigations.

Each witness decision for a field lineup falls into one of three response categories: a suspect identification, a filler selection, or a nonidentification from the lineup. A perplexing component of research with real cases is that suspect guilt is unknowable in most cases, unlike lab studies with defined culprit-absent and culprit-present lineups. Some unknown percentage of real lineups do not include the perpetrator, and suspect identifications likely include some innocent suspects. Thus, identification of a police suspect cannot be directly equated with a correct identification of the guilty. Likewise, the rejection of a lineup by an eyewitness may in fact be a correct answer if the true culprit is not in the lineup. Only filler picks are known to be definite errors (N. K. Steblay, 2008; Wells, 2008). All said, the precise interpretation of witness accuracy is difficult.

In the few available archival studies, a consistency in outcomes is apparent. In England and Wales, three studies of live, simultaneous identity parades produced approximately 40% suspect identifications, 20% filler picks, and 40% nonidentifications (Slater, 1994; Valentine, Pickering, & Darling, 2003; Wright & McDaid, 1996). In the United States, Behrman and Davey (2001) and Behrman and Richards (2005) reported 48%–52% suspect identification rates in simultaneous photo and live lineups; where filler picks could be tallied, rates ranged from 15% to 24%. In Canada, Tollestrup, Turtle, and Yuille (1994) detailed 170 identification attempts, primarily from simultaneous photo lineups and reported suspect identification rates for robbery victims (46%) and for fraud victims (25%).

A number of observations can be made about these eyewitness identifications from real crimes. First, suspect identification rates hover around 40%–50% for nonblind simultaneous procedures, but field lineup data can conceal rates of prior familiarity (where the witness knew the suspect prior to the crime) and of witnesses who had already identified the suspect in a prior photo lineup or show-up. Both of these factors elevate suspect identification rates and reduce filler pick rates (N. K. Steblay, 2011). For example, Valentine et al. (2003) documented real witnesses who attempted lineup identification of a perpetrator who was a stranger at the time of the crime. These witnesses produced a suspect identification rate of 41% and a filler pick rate of 21%. In comparison, lineups in which witnesses attempted to identify a perpetrator who was familiar prior to the crime produced a much higher suspect identification rate (73%) and a lower filler pick rate (5%). Twenty-one percent of the witnesses who reported prior familiarity with the culprit did not choose from the lineup (Valentine et al., 2003); perhaps the culprit was not in the lineup or the witness misjudged familiarity (as in N. K. Steblay, Dietrich, et al., 2011). A field study of double-blind sequential photo lineups, in which all the perpetrators were strangers to the witnesses and all lineups were the first identification task for the witness, yielded a suspect identification rate of 35% and a filler rate of 11% (Klobuchar et al., 2006).

With the exception of the study Klobuchar et al. (2006), filler selection rate in field studies runs at approximately 20%, a number that can be viewed as frightening high. Filler picks frequently account for one in three positive identifications (also true of the study by Klobuchar et al., 2006). Keep in mind that these are results from witnesses who presumably self-selected for the identification procedure because they felt capable of recognizing the culprit. Many witnesses clearly are not overly cautious about choosing from the lineup, dispelling a frequent criticism of laboratory results that the seriousness of the identification task for real eyewitnesses would inhibit errors.

The level of filler picks in the field may be even higher than reported. Many police reports neglect to differentiate between a filler pick and a nonidentification, reporting instead that the witness could not identify the suspect (Behrman & Davey, 2001; Pike, Brace, & Kyman, 2002; Tollestrup et al. 1994). In the archival studies, eyewitnesses abstained from lineup picks in sizable proportions (25%–40%). There is no way to know exactly how many nonidentifications are unrecorded filler selections. Nonidentifications also are ambiguous in that we do not know if witnesses were unable to remember or unwilling to choose, or if the lineups did not include the culprit.

A final difficulty is common to all archival studies: the multicollinearity of situation and witness factors that are not experimentally (orthogonally) manipulated. Researchers must be careful of the dangers of comparing quasi-experimental conditions. For example, weapon presence may be confounded with crime type (robbery vs. fraud) and therefore also with differential witness attention, quality of culprit description, and delay prior to lineup. In the study by Tollestrup et al. (1994), type of crime was confounded with delay, in that robbery cases were brought for victim identification more quickly. Another example is in the Behrman and Davey (2001) data, where show-ups produced a very high suspect identification rate (76%), significantly higher than rates for the full lineup. The difficulty for interpreting these comparative results (show-ups work better than lineups?) is in the multicollinearity within the suggestive context for a show-up as well as differential features, such as shorter retention intervals and crime type (Dysart & Lindsay, 2007).

In 2006, the AJS brought together a group of eyewitness scientists, attorneys, and law enforcement professionals in Greensboro, North Carolina. The purpose of the meeting was to plan and design an experimental protocol for testing sequential versus simultaneous lineup procedures in the field with real eyewitnesses to real crimes. A primary achievement of the AJS study (beyond the results discussed earlier in this chapter) was to bring a lineup protocol to the field in a manner that aligned with both police investigative procedures and with rigorous experimental protocol, thereby achieving interpretable and trustworthy results from the field (Wells et al., 2011; Wells, Steblay, & Dysart, in press).

An enormous challenge for this group was the fact that dozens of case detectives in four U.S. cities (Charlotte–Mecklenburg, NC; Austin, TX; Tucson, AZ; and San Diego, CA) would deliver the lineups, in all types of environments—station interview rooms, victim homes, public places—and with all types of witnesses. How can a field test maintain consistency in instructions, blind presentation to witnesses, and in interaction and verbal exchanges? How can true random assignment to lineup conditions be accomplished? How can documentation be maintained in a thorough and consistent manner? What became dubbed as "the Greensboro Protocol" was a remarkable advancement in experimental field protocol: double-blind administration of lineups delivered via standardized software on laptop computers that could meet the rigorous requirements of true random assignment to experimental conditions and complete documentation of the experimental session.

SUMMARY AND CONCLUSIONS

Policy changes in lineup practice began to show up nationally a little over a decade ago. The implementation of eyewitness science into law has been a remarkably successful phenomenon, with change occurring through a variety of avenues: executive mandate, legislation, study commissions, case law, and law enforcement initiatives from detectives, police chiefs, or county attorneys in individual

jurisdictions. A wealth of information on these issues is available from the Innocence Project website (http://www.innocenceproject.org). As we look to the future, these strategies will continue to be important, as will be continuing eyewitness memory research. Specific issues on the horizon are discussed below.

Policy and Practice

Changes in policy and practice illustrate a continuum of strategies, from local law enforcement ("bottom-up") to state and national ("top-down"). The highest authority, the U.S. Supreme Court, has been largely silent on the eyewitness issue for three decades. More prominent have been changes initiated at state and local levels.

The U.S. Supreme Court. The U.S. Supreme Court delivered the *Manson v. Brathwaite* (1977) decision prior to an avalanche of eyewitness research studies that occurred in its wake. The Court established a two-pronged strategy for the evaluation of eyewitness reliability. First was a determination of whether the identification procedure was unnecessarily suggestive. (Recall that the *Perry* decision recently clarified that suggestiveness must be linked to intentional police procedure in order to merit possible suppression of eyewitness evidence.) If the police procedure is not unduly suggestive, the identification evidence is allowable at trial. When the procedure is deemed too suggestive, the second prong of the strategy is invoked, in which the reliability of the evidence is weighed against five criteria: the witness's opportunity to view the offender, degree of attention during the crime, certainty at the time of the identification, the accuracy of the witness's description of the defendant, and the amount of time elapsed between the crime and the identification.

The *Manson v. Brathwaite* criteria have not fared well under empirical scrutiny over the past 35 years. The relationship between retention interval and accuracy is not strong, and the interval can be plagued by the intrusion of postevent information. Description accuracy and correct identification are not tightly linked (Pigott & Brigham, 1985; Wells, 1985). In fact, this specific *Manson v. Brathwaite* criterion exposes an odd logic in that police typically will find a suspect based on the witness's prelineup description, and the witness will tend to select a member of the lineup who fits that description. Thus, consistency between description and the defendant can exist even if the defendant is innocent. Of greater concern, however, is that three of the five *Manson v. Brathwaite* criteria are secured through retrospective self-report of the witness. Postidentification feedback can significantly inflate witness reports of certainty, quality of view, and attention to the crime. Wells and Quinlivan (2009) point out an unfortunate deficit in the *Manson v. Brathwaite* criteria, that a suggestive police procedure (first prong) can prompt distortion of the eyewitness's memory in the very direction that will "pass" the second prong. A *Manson v. Brathwaite* inquiry is unlikely to detect the unreliable witness at a pretrial hearing, nor does *Manson v. Brathwaite* incentivize law enforcement to avoid suggestive procedures.

Many scientists and legal scholars have called for a new legal framework for the evaluation of eyewitness reliability based more tightly on scientific research. The reason for this, as articulated in the *Perry v. New Hampshire* scientific brief prepared by the American Psychological Association (2012), includes the fact that traditional tools of the court—pretrial evidentiary hearings, cross-examination, jury instructions, and expert testimony—appear to inadequately protect against unreliable eyewitness testimony (Devenport, Stinson, Cutler, & Kravitz, 2002; Garrett, 2011). The problem often rests with a confident and entirely sincere eyewitness who is nevertheless incorrect.

The New Jersey Supreme Court took unprecedented action in the 2011 case of *State v. Henderson*, appointing a Special Master to review the extant eyewitness research. The Court determined that the existing legal standard does not adequately meet its goals because it does not offer an adequate measure of eyewitness evidence reliability, does not sufficiently deter inappropriate police conduct, and relies too heavily on the jury's ability to evaluate identification evidence. The ruling revised the legal framework for evaluating and admitting eyewitness identification evidence, requiring examination of relevant estimator and system variables, and directed that revised jury charges be prepared to help jurors evaluate the reliability of such evidence.

Eyewitness memory and juries. A central point of this chapter is that the legal system may have unreasonable expectations for eyewitness memory. This is also true for juries. Schmechel, O'Toole, Easterly, and Loftus (2006) are among researchers who have documented that jurors typically do not understand eyewitness memory principles, and in fact may hold beliefs contrary to scientific principles (see also Kassin, Tubb, Hosch, & Memon, 2001). Nor does it appear that lay persons appreciate the implications of police procedure for eyewitness accuracy (Devenport et al., 2002). Wright, Carlucci, Evans, and Compo (2009) asked experiment participants to judge the guilt of a suspect when the identification procedure had been conducted blind or not-blind. Participants were found to be unaware of the bias that can be incurred with nonblind lineups. This concurs with many research findings that show great weight attached to eyewitness identification evidence (Winter & Greene, 2007) but little downward adjustment on the part of the people when they learn that the identification is unreliable (Loftus, 1974). Wright et al. (2009) reiterate the need to correct misperceptions through courtroom methods of expert testimony and jury instructions.

A troubling fact is that even eyewitnesses themselves are relatively insensitive to the quality of encoding conditions under which they formed a memory of an offender or of the impact of police procedures on their identification decisions (R. C. L. Lindsay, Semmler, Weber, Brewer, & Lindsay, 2008; Wells & Bradfield, 1998). Eyewitness scientists play an important role in helping legal decision makers assess eyewitness credibility and even train or prepare potential witnesses (e.g., bank tellers) to exert some control over cognitive processes of attention and encoding (Bornstein et al., 2012). Video-recording of the witness's identification attempt may be helpful in jurors' assessment of eyewitness accuracy (Reardon & Fisher, 2011). Legal remedies for eyewitness issues are discussed more broadly by Smalarz and Wells (2012), including reconsideration of *Manson v. Brathwaite* criteria, suppression of identification evidence, motions in limine to limit testimony (e.g., on confidence), judicial instructions, and expert testimony.

Law enforcement. The International Association of Chiefs of Police (IACP) has endorsed recommended identification procedures, including sequential double-blind lineups. Nevertheless, a recent survey of law enforcement by the Police Executive Research Forum (2013) found a minority of jurisdictions fully using these best practices. Wise, Safer, and Maro (2011) surveyed 532 U.S. law enforcement officers and found that very few had knowledge of eyewitness factors or of how memory works. It goes without saying that education and training are necessary components for policy change.

Observations for Eyewitness Research

The system-variable approach has generated extremely useful empirically supported methods to increase the reliability of eyewitness evidence, yet the job is not done. The AJS field experiment in 2011 exposed a substantial level of eyewitness error in real police identification procedures despite the use of best practices recommended by eyewitness research. There is a need for additional innovative approaches for securing eyewitness evidence (see Brewer & Wells, 2011). Three questions for further study can be offered.

Under which conditions is a specific procedure of memory evidence collection most likely to affect witness memory and decisions? Research will benefit from considering the interactions among estimator and system variables (e.g., Greathouse & Kovera, 2009). The conceptualization of suspect-bias and general impairment factors (Wells & Loftus, 2013) can be a catalyst to strengthen identification procedures. For example, suspect-bias variables may have more impact in the presence of general impairment factors. This approach also may help to more clearly address eyewitness issues in court. As explained by Wells and Loftus (2013), a jury may hear a case in which encoding and retention conditions were clearly substandard (e.g., a witness with a poor view who makes a cross-race identification long after the event), yet the jury may be little impressed by

warnings about a raft of general impairment concerns, because, after all, the witness still picked the defendant from a lineup. General impairment variables can only take the courtroom argument so far. Suspect-bias variables, on the other hand, can provide an answer to the pressing question of why the witness picked this defendant if he is not guilty (see also Brewer & Wells, 2011)

How are memory evidence procedures in field practice necessarily different from the lab? Close attention to the realities and nuances of the field can guide theoretical work and directly enhance the external validity and applied value of research. One shortcoming in laboratory and even field studies is the lack of attention to the verbal exchange between witness and lineup administrator, a seemingly rich source of information about the decision-making process. To access these potentially informative witness and administrator behaviors we must measure more than final lineup decisions. Admittedly, witness–administrator interaction can be tough to accomplish in the lab, where the tools that help to avoid experimenter expectancy effects also limit our interactions with participants. A blinded lineup administrator achieved with a laptop computer and audio/visual capture of the interview for blind coding will facilitate this endeavor.

Aspects of field protocol that at first may appear troublesome from a lab perspective (e.g., a second "lap" through a sequential lineup, multiple lineup picks from a witness, an "I'm not sure" response option) can be reconciled as useful practice especially when paired with full documentation and a recorded interview between blind administrator and witness. Similarly, lineup order effects that usually denote something in need of a fix in experimental design can be seen differently from an evidentiary perspective in which the purpose of a lineup is to weed out witnesses with weak memories (Steblay, Dysart, & Wells, 2011).Some established lab components can be confirmed as essential for field lineup practice (e.g., the continuation rule for sequential lineups). New laboratory research has already begun to address these issues (see, e.g., N. K. Steblay, Dietrich, et al., 2011; N. K. Steblay & Phillips, 2011; Weber & Perfect, 2012).

What is occurring outside the span of our current observations? It is useful to step back and take a long view of the identification and interview processes within the context of the broader police investigation. For example: How did this suspect get in the lineup to begin with? How did the case detective decide how the investigation should proceed, given this identification evidence? Up to 40% of officers report that they would place a suspect in a lineup with no evidence of guilt but by simply playing a hunch (Wise et al., 2011), an unwritten policy with direct implications for the rate of culprit-absent lineups in the field and inherent risks for innocent suspects (Wells, 2006). The 2009 DNA exoneration of Thomas McGowan revealed that the witness had initially picked McGowan's photo, saying she "thought" he was the attacker. Police told her that she had to be certain, say yes or no, and "couldn't just think it was him." She then said McGowan was "definitely" her attacker (*Monterey Herald*, 2009). We have very little information about how investigators respond to nonidentifications, to contradictory eyewitness evidence, or to witness qualifiers of an identification, and whether evidentiary standards influence detective decisions and eyewitness decisions.

These are three modest suggestions for research. Fortunately, eyewitness memory research is sustained by an international and interdisciplinary cadre of exceptional scientists and informed legal professionals, who regularly bring forth innovative ways to understand the many aspects of eyewitness experience. To that point, two recent examples involve a self-administered interview as a protection against postevent information memory contamination (Gabbert, Hope, Fisher, & Jamieson, 2012), and a novel lineup procedure in which witness confidence judgments about each sequential lineup member rather than a dichotomous decision are assessed under a constrained time limit of three seconds per photo (Brewer, Weber, Wootten, & Lindsay, 2012).

The central importance of eyewitness memory evidence in the legal system, and its substantial weight and significant consequences in criminal convictions and monetary awards, mean that eyewitness science must be an informed and informing partner to law. Scientific evaluation of legal assumptions about the strengths and limitations of human memory remains essential, as do continued advances in empirically based remedies to protect witness memory from disruption and contamination.

References

Allan, K., & Gabbert, F. (2008). I still think it was a banana: Memorable "lies" and forgettable "truths." *Acta Psychologica, 127,* 299–308. doi:10.1016/j.actpsy.2007.06.001

Behrman, B. W., & Davey, S. L. (2001). Eyewitness identification in actual criminal cases: An archival analysis. *Law and Human Behavior, 25,* 475–491. doi:10.1023/A:1012840831846

Behrman, B. W., & Richards, R. E. (2005). Suspect/foil identification in actual crimes and in the laboratory: A reality monitoring analysis. *Law and Human Behavior, 29,* 279–301. doi:10.1007/s10979-005-3617-y

Bem, D. J. (1972). Self-perception theory. *Advances in Experimental Social Psychology, 6,* 1–62. doi:10.1016/S0065-2601(08)60024-6

Bornstein, B. H., Deffenbacher, K. A., Penrod, S. D., & McGorty, E. K. (2012). Effects of exposure time and cognitive operations on facial identification accuracy: A meta-analysis of two variables associated with initial memory strength. *Psychology, Crime & Law, 18,* 473–490. doi:10.1080/1068316X.2010.508458

Bornstein, B. H., Witt, C. J., Cherry, K. E., & Greene, E. (2000). The suggestibility of older witnesses. In M. B. Rothman, B. D. Dunlop, & P. Entzel (Eds.), *Elders, crime, and the criminal justice system.* New York, NY: Springer.

Bothwell, R. K., Deffenbacher, K. A., & Brigham, J. C. (1987). Correlations of eyewitness accuracy and confidence: Optimality hypothesis revisited. *Journal of Applied Psychology, 72,* 691–695. doi:10.1037/0021-9010.72.4.691

Bower, G. (1967). A multicomponent theory of memory trace. In K. W. Spence & J. T. Spence (Eds.), *The psychology of learning and motivation* (Vol. 1, pp. 229–325). New York, NY: Academic Press.

Braun, K. A., Ellis, R., & Loftus. (2002). Make my memory: How advertising can change our memories of the past. *Psychology and Marketing, 19,* 1–23. doi:10.1002/mar.1000

Brewer, N., & Burke, A. (2002). Effects of testimonial inconsistencies and eyewitness confidence on mock-juror judgments. *Law and Human Behavior, 26,* 353–364. doi:10.1023/A:1015380522722

Brewer, N., Caon, A., Todd, C., & Weber, N. (2006). Eyewitness identification accuracy and response latency. *Law and Human Behavior, 30,* 31–50. doi:10.1007/s10979-006-9002-7

Brewer, N., & Weber, N. (2008). Eyewitness confidence and latency: Indices of memory processes not just markers of accuracy. *Applied Cognitive Psychology, 22,* 827–840. doi:10.1002/acp.1486

Brewer, N., Weber, N., Wootten, D., & Lindsay, D. S. (2012). Identifying the bad guy in a lineup using confidence judgments under deadline pressure. *Psychological Science.* Advance online publication. doi:10.1177/0956797612441217

Brewer, N., & Wells, G. L. (2011). Eyewitness identification. *Current Directions in Psychological Science, 20,* 24–27. doi:10.1177/0963721410389169

Bridge, D. J., & Pallen, K. A. (2012). Neural correlates of reactivation and retrieval-induced distortion. *Journal of Neuroscience, 32,* 12144–12151. doi:10.1523/JNEUROSCI.1378-12.2012

Brief of the American Psychological Association as Amicus Curiae, Perry v. New Hampshire, 132 S.Ct. 716 (2012).

Brigham, J. C., Bennett, L. B., Meissner, C. A., & Mitchell, T. L. (2007). The influence of race on eyewitness memory. In R. Lindsay, D. Ross, J. Read, & M. Toglia (Eds.), *Handbook of eyewitness psychology: Vol. 2. Memory for people* (pp. 257–281). Mahwah, NJ: Erlbaum.

Brigham, J. C., Meissner, C. A., & Wasserman, A. W. (1999). Applied issues in the construction and expert assessment of photo lineups. *Applied Cognitive Psychology, 13,* S73–S92. doi:10.1002/(SICI)1099-0720(199911)13:1+<S73::AID-ACP631>3.3.CO;2-W

Brown, E., Deffenbacher, K., & Sturgill, W. (1977). Memory for faces and circumstances of encounter. *Journal of Applied Psychology, 62,* 311–318. doi:10.1037/0021-9010.62.3.311

Ceci, S. J., & Bruck, M. (1993). The suggestibility of the child witness: A historical review and synthesis. *Psychological Bulletin, 113,* 403–439. doi:10.1037/0033-2909.113.3.403

Chabris, C. F., & Simons, D. J. (2010). *The invisible gorilla and other ways our intuitions deceive us.* New York, NY: Crown.

Chance, J. E., Turner, A. L., & Goldstein, A. G. (1982). Development of differential recognition of own- and other-race faces. *Journal of Psychology: Interdisciplinary and Applied, 112,* 29–37. doi:10.1080/00223980.1982.9923531

Charman, S., & Wells, G. L. (2006). Applied lineup theory. In R. C. L. Lindsay, D. F. Ross, J. D. Read, & M. P. Toglia (Eds.), *The handbook of eyewitness psychology: Vol. 2. Memory for people* (pp. 219–254). Mahwah, NJ: Erlbaum.

Charman, S. D., Carlucci, M., Vallano, J., & Gregory, A. H. (2010). The selective cue integration framework: A theory of witness confidence assessment following post-identification feedback. *Journal of Experimental Psychology: Applied, 16,* 204–218. doi:10.1037/a0019495

Charman, S. D., & Wells, G. L. (2007). Eyewitness lineups: Is the appearance-change instruction a good idea? *Law and Human Behavior, 31,* 3–22. doi:10.1007/s10979-006-9006-3

Charman, S. D., & Wells, G. L. (2012). The moderating effect of ecphoric experience on post-identification feedback: A critical test of the cues-based inference conceptualization. *Applied Cognitive Psychology, 26,* 243–250. doi:10.1002/acp.1815

Clark, S. E. (2005). A re-examination of the effects of biased lineup instructions in eyewitness identification. *Law and Human Behavior, 29,* 575–604. doi:10.1007/s10979-005-7121-1

Clark, S. E. (2012). Costs and benefits of eyewitness identification reform: Psychological science and public policy. *Perspectives on Psychological Science, 7,* 238–259. doi:10.1177/1745691612439584

Clark, S. E., Erickson, M. A., & Breneman, J. (2011). Probative value of absolute and relative judgments in eyewitness identification. *Law and Human Behavior, 35,* 364–380. doi:10.1007/s10979-010-9245-1

Clark, S. E., Marshall, T. E., & Rosenthal, R. (2009). Lineup administrator influences on eyewitness identification decisions. *Journal of Experimental Psychology: Applied, 15,* 63–75. doi:10.1037/a0015185

Clark, S. E., & Tunnicliff, J. L. (2001). Selecting lineup foils in eyewitness identification experiments: Experimental control and real-world simulations. *Law and Human Behavior, 25,* 199–216. doi:10.1023/A:1010753809988

Colomb, C., & Ginet, M. (2012). The cognitive interview for use with adults: An empirical test of an alternative mnemonic and of a partial protocol. *Applied Cognitive Psychology, 26,* 35–47. doi:10.1002/acp.1792

Compo, N. S., Evans, J. R., Carol, R. N., Villalba, D., Ham, L. S., Garcia, T., & Rose, S. (2012). Intoxicated eyewitnesses: Better than their reputation? *Law and Human Behavior, 36,* 77–86. doi:10.1037/h0093951

Craik, F. I. M., & Lockhart, R. S. (1972). Levels of processing: A framework for memory research. *Journal of Verbal Learning and Verbal Behavior, 11,* 671–684. doi:10.1016/S0022-5371(72)80001-X

Cutler, B. L., Penrod, S. D., & Dexter, H. R. (1990). Juror sensitivity to eyewitness identification evidence. *Law and Human Behavior, 114,* 185–191. doi:10.1007/BF01062972

Cutler, B. L., Penrod, S. D., & Martens, T. K. (1987). The reliability of eyewitness identification: The role of system and estimator variables. *Law and Human Behavior, 11*, 233–258. doi:10.1007/BF01044644

Davis, D., & Loftus, E. F. (2005). Age and functioning in the legal system: Perception memory and judgment in victims, witnesses, and jurors. In I. Noy & W. Karwowski (Eds.), *Handbook of human factors in litigation* (pp. 11–53). New York, NY: CRC Press.

Deffenbacher, K. A., Bornstein, B. H., McGorty, E. K., & Penrod, S. D. (2008). Forgetting the once-seen face: Estimating the strength of an eyewitness's memory representation. *Journal of Experimental Psychology: Applied, 14*, 139–150. doi:10.1037/1076-898X.14.2.149.

Deffenbacher, K. A., Bornstein, B. H., & Penrod, S. D. (2006). Mugshot exposure effects: Retroactive interference, source confusion, and unconscious transference. *Law and Human Behavior, 30*, 287–307. doi:10.1007/s10979-006-9008-1

Deffenbacher, K. A., Bornstein, B. H., Penrod, S. D., & McGorty, E. K. (2004). A meta-analytic review of the effects of high stress on eyewitness memory. *Law and Human Behavior, 28*, 687–706. doi:10.1007/s10979-004-0565-x

Deutsch, M., & Gerard, H. B. (1955). A study of normative and informational social influence upon individual judgment. *Journal of Abnormal and Social Psychology, 51*, 629–636. doi:10.1037/h0046408

Devenport, J. L., Stinson, V., Cutler, B. L., & Kravitz, D. A. (2002). How effective are the cross-examination and expert testimony safeguards? Jurors' perceptions of the suggestiveness and fairness of biased lineup procedures. *Journal of Applied Psychology, 87*, 1042–1054. doi:10.1037/0021-9010.87.6.1042

Doob, A. N., & Kirshenbaum, H. M. (1973). Bias in police lineups—partial remembering. *Journal of Police Science and Administration, 1*, 287–293. doi:10.1016/0022-1031(73)90062-0

Douglass, A., & Steblay, N. K. (2006). Memory distortion in eyewitnesses: A meta-analysis of the post-identification feedback effect. *Applied Cognitive Psychology, 20*, 859–869. doi:10.1002/acp.1237

Douglass, A. B., Smith, C., & Fraser-Thill, R. (2005). A problem with double-blind photospread procedures: Photospread administrators use one eyewitness's confidence to influence the identification of another witness. *Law and Human Behavior, 29*, 543–562. doi:10.1007/s10979-005-6830-9

Doyle, J. (2005). *True witness: Cops, courts, science and the battle against misidentification.* New York, NY: Palgrave Macmillan.

Dunning, D., & Stern, L. B. (1994). Distinguishing accurate from inaccurate eyewitness identifications via inquiries about decision processes. *Journal of Personality and Social Psychology, 67*, 818–835. doi:10.1037/0022-3514.67.5.818

Dysart, J. E., Lawson, V. Z., & Rainey, A. (2012). Blind lineup administration as a prophylactic against the postidentification feedback effect. *Law and Human Behavior, 36*, 312–319. doi:10.1037/h0093921

Dysart, J. E., & Lindsay, R. C. L. (2007). Show-up identifications: Suggestive technique or reliable method? In R. C. L. Lindsay, D. R. Ross, J. D. Read, & M. P. Toglia (Eds.), *The handbook of eyewitness psychology: Vol. 2. Memory for people* (pp. 137–153). Mahwah, NJ: Erlbaum.

Dysart, J. E., Lindsay, R. C. L., MacDonald, T. K., & Wicke, C. (2002). The intoxicated witness: Effects of alcohol on identification accuracy from show-ups. *Journal of Applied Psychology, 87*, 170–175. doi:10.1037/0021-9010.87.1.170

Fawcett, J. M., Russell, E. J., Peace, K. A., & Christie, J. (2013). Of guns and geese: A meta-analytic review of the 'weapon focus' literature. *Psychology, Crime & Law, 19*, 35–66. doi:10.1080/1068316X.2011.599325

Festinger, L. (1954). A theory of social comparison processes. *Human Relations, 7*, 117–140. doi:10.1177/001872675400700202

Findley, K. A., & Scott, M. S. (2006). The multiple dimensions of tunnel vision in criminal cases. *Wisconsin Law Review, 2*, 291–397.

Fischhoff, B. (1975). Hindsight is not equal to foresight: The effect of outcome knowledge on judgment under uncertainty. *Journal of Experimental Psychology: Human Perception and Performance, 1*, 288–299. doi:10.1037/0096-1523.1.3.288

Fisher, R. P. (1995). Interviewing victims and witnesses of crime. *Psychology, Public Policy, and Law, 1*, 732–764. doi:10.1037/1076-8971.1.4.732

Fisher, R. P., & Cutler, B. L. (1996). The relation between consistency and accuracy of eyewitness testimony. In G. Davies, S. Lloyd-Bostock, M. McMurran, & C. Wilson (Eds.), *Psychology, law, and criminal justice: International developments in research and practice* (pp. 21–28). Oxford, England: Walter De Gruyter. doi:10.1515/9783110879483.21

Fisher, R. P., & Geiselman, R. E. (1992). *Memory enhancing techniques for investigative interviewing: The cognitive interview.* Springfield, IL: Charles C. Thomas.

Fisher, R. P., Geiselman, R. E., & Raymond, D. S. (1987). Critical analysis of police interview techniques. *Journal of Police Science and Administration, 15*, 177–185.

Fisher, R. P., & Schreiber, N. (2007). Interviewing protocols to improve eyewitness memory. In M. Toglia,

R. Lindsay, D. Ross, & J. Reed (Eds.), *The handbook of eyewitness psychology: Vol. 1. Memory for events* (pp. 53–80). Mahwah, NJ: Erlbaum.

Frenda, S. J., Nichols, R. M., & Loftus, E. F. (2011). Current issues and advances in misinformation research. *Current Directions in Psychological Science, 20,* 20–23. doi:10.1177/0963721410396620

Gabbert, F., Hope, L., Fisher, R. P., & Jamieson, K. (2012). Protecting against misleading post-event information with a self-administered interview. *Applied Cognitive Psychology, 26,* 568–575. doi:10.1002/acp.2828

Gabbert, F., Memon, A., & Allan, K. (2003). Memory conformity: Can eyewitnesses influence each other's memories for an event? *Applied Cognitive Psychology, 17,* 533–543. doi:10.1002/acp.885

Garrett, B. L. (2011). *Convicting the innocent: Where criminal prosecutions go wrong.* Cambridge, MA: Harvard University Press. doi:10.4159/harvard.9780674060982

Garrioch, L., & Brimacombe, C. A. E. (2001). Lineup administrators' expectations: Their impact on eyewitness confidence. *Law and Human Behavior, 25,* 299–315. doi:10.1023/A:1010750028643

Geiselman, R. E., Fisher, R. P., MacKinnon, D. P., & Holland, H. L. (1985). Eyewitness memory enhancement in the police interview. *Journal of Applied Psychology, 70,* 401–412. doi:10.1037//0021-9010.70.2.401

Godfrey, R. D., & Clark, S. D. (2010). Repeated eyewitness identification procedures: Memory, decision making, and probative value. *Law and Human Behavior, 34,* 241–258. doi:10.1007/s10979-009-9187-7

Goodsell, C. A., Neuschatz, J. S., & Gronlund, S. D. (2009). Effects of mugshot commitment on lineup performance in young and older adults. *Applied Cognitive Psychology, 23,* 788–803. doi:10.1002/acp.1512

Greathouse, S. M., & Kovera, M. (2009). Instruction bias and lineup presentation moderate the effects of administrator knowledge on eyewitness identification. *Law and Human Behavior, 33,* 70–82. doi:10.1007/s10979-008-9136-x

Gross, S., Jacoby, K., Matheson, D. J., Montgomery, N., & Patil, S. (2005). Exonerations in the United States, 1989 through 2003. *Journal of Criminal Law and Criminology, 95,* 523–531.

Harris, M. J., & Rosenthal, R. (1985). Mediation of interpersonal expectancy effects: 31 meta-analyses. *Psychological Bulletin, 97,* 363–386. doi:10.1037/0033-2909.97.3.363

Hasel, L. E., & Kassin, S. M. (2009). On the presumption of evidentiary independence: Can confessions corrupt eyewitness identifications? *Psychological Science, 20,* 122–126. doi:10.1111/j.1467-9280.2008.02262.x

Haw, R. M., & Fisher, R. P. (2004). Effects of administrator–witness contact on eyewitness identification accuracy. *Journal of Applied Psychology, 89,* 1106–1112. doi:10.1037/0021-9010.89.6.1106

Hilgendorf, E. L., & Irving, B. L. (1978). False positive identification. *Medicine, Science, and the Law, 18,* 255–262.

Hinz, T., & Pezdek, K. (2001). The effect of exposure to multiple lineups on face identification accuracy. *Law and Human Behavior, 25,* 185–198. doi:10.1023/A:1005697431830

Hope, L., Lewinski, W., Dixon, J., Blocksidge, D., & Gabbert, F. (2012). Witnesses in action: The effect of physical exertion on recall and recognition. *Psychological Science, 23,* 386–390. doi:10.1177/0956797611431463

Hope, L., Ost, J., Gabbert, F., Healey, S., & Lenton, E. (2008). "With a little help from my friends . . .": The role of co-witness relationship in susceptibility to misinformation. *Acta Psychologica, 127,* 476–484. doi:10.1016/j.actpsy.2007.08.010

Hope, L., & Wright, D. B. (2007). Beyond unusual? Examining the role of attention in the weapon focus effect. *Applied Cognitive Psychology, 21,* 951–961. doi:1002/acp.1307

Innocence Project. (2012). *Meet Damon Thibodeaux.* Retrieved from http://www.innocenceproject.org/300/index.php

Kahneman, D. (2011). *Thinking, fast and slow.* New York, NY: Farrar, Straus & Giroux.

Kassin, S. M., Tubb, V. A., Hosch, H. M., & Memon, A. (2001). On the "general acceptance" of eyewitness testimony research: A new survey of the experts. *American Psychologist, 56,* 405–416. doi:10.1037/0003-066X.56.5.405

Klobuchar, A., Steblay, N., & Caligiuri, H. (2006). Improving eyewitness identifications: Hennepin County's Blind Sequential Lineup Pilot Project. *Cardozo Public Law, Policy, and Ethics Journal, 4,* 381–413.

Köhnken, G., Milne, R., Memon, A., & Bull, R. (1999). A meta-analysis on the effects of the cognitive interview. *Psychology, Crime & Law, 5,* 3–27. doi:10.1080/10683169908414991

Lampinen, J. M., Scott, J., Leding, J. K., Pratt, D., & Arnal, J. D. (2007). "Good, you identified the suspect . . . but please ignore this feedback": Can warnings eliminate the effects of post-identification feedback? *Applied Cognitive Psychology, 21,* 1037–1056. doi:10.1002/acp.1313

Lindsay, D. S., Nilsen, E., & Read, J. D. (2000). Witnessing-condition heterogeneity and witnesses' versus investigators' confidence in the accuracy of witnesses' identification decisions. *Law and Human Behavior, 24*, 685–697. doi:10.1023/A:1005504320565

Lindsay, R. C. L., Mansour, J. K., Beaudry, J. L., Leach, A. M., & Bertrand, M. I. (2009). Beyond sequential presentation: Misconceptions and misrepresentations of sequential lineups. *Legal and Criminological Psychology, 14*, 31–34. doi:10.1348/135532508X382104

Lindsay, R. C. L., Semmler, C., Weber, N., Brewer, N., & Lindsay, M. R. (2008). How variations in distance affect eyewitness reports and identification accuracy. *Law and Human Behavior, 32*, 526–535. doi:10.1007/s10979-008-9128-x

Lindsay, R. C. L., & Wells, G. L. (1985). Improving eyewitness identification: Simultaneous versus sequential lineup presentations. *Journal of Applied Psychology, 70*, 556–564. doi:10.1037/0021-9010.70.3.556

Loftus, E. F. (1974). Reconstructing memory: The incredible eyewitness. *Psychology Today, 8*, 116–119.

Loftus, E. F. (1976). Unconscious transference in eyewitness identification. *Law and Psychology Review, 2*, 93–98.

Loftus, E. F. (1997). Creating false memories. *Scientific American, 277*, 70–75. doi:10.1038/scientificamerican0997-70

Loftus, E. F. (2005). Planting misinformation in the human mind: A 30-year investigation of the malleability of memory. *Learning and Memory, 12*, 361–366. doi:10.1101/lm.94705

Loftus, E. F., & Ketcham, K. (1994). *The myth of repressed memory: False memory and allegations of sexual abuse.* New York, NY: St. Martin's Press.

Loftus, E. F., Loftus, G. R., & Messo, J. (1987). Some facts about "weapon focus." *Law and Human Behavior, 11*, 55–62. doi:10.1007/BF01044839

Loftus, E. F., & Palmer, J. C. (1974). Reconstruction of auto-mobile destruction: An example of the interaction between language and memory. *Journal of Verbal Learning and Verbal Behavior, 13*, 585–589. doi:10.1016/S0022-5371(74)80011-3

Loftus, E. F., & Pickrell, J. E. (1995). The formation of false memories. *Psychiatric Annals, 25*, 7 720–725.

MacLean, C. L., Brimacombe, C. A. E., Allison, M., Dahl, L. C., & Kadlec, H. (2011). Post-identification feedback effects: Investigators and evaluators. *Applied Cognitive Psychology, 25*, 739–752. doi:10.1002/acp.1745

MacLin, O. H., & Malpass, R. S. (2003). The ambiguous-race face illusion. *Perception, 32*, 249–252. doi:10.1068/p5046

Malpass, R. S., Devine, P. G., & Bergen, G. T. (1980). *Eyewitness identification: Realism vs. the laboratory.* Unpublished manuscript, State University of New York, Plattsburg.

Malpass, R. S., Tredoux, C. G., & McQuiston-Surrett, D. (2007). Lineup construction and lineup fairness. In R. Lindsay, D. Ross, J. D. Read, & M. P. Toglia (Eds.), *Handbook of eyewitness psychology: Vol. 2. Memory for people* (pp. 155–178). Mahwah, NJ: Erlbaum.

Malpass, R. S., Tredoux, C. G., & McQuiston-Surrett, D. (2009). Public policy and sequential lineups. *Legal and Criminological Psychology, 14*, 1–12. doi:10.1348/135532508X384102

Manson v. Brathwaite, 432 U.S. 98, 114 (1977).

Mansour, J. K., Beaudry, J. L. Bertrand, M. I., Kalmet, N., Melsom, E. I., & Lindsay, R. C. L. (2012). Impact of disguise on identification decisions and confidence with simultaneous and sequential lineups. *Law and Human Behavior, 36*, 513–26. doi:10.1037/h0093937

Meissner, C. A., & Brigham, J. C. (2001a). A meta-analysis of the verbal overshadowing effect in face identification. *Applied Cognitive Psychology, 15*, 603–616. doi:10.1002/acp.728

Meissner, C. A., & Brigham, J. C. (2001b). Thirty years of investigating the own-race bias in memory for faces: A meta-analytic review. *Psychology, Public Policy, and Law, 7*, 3–35. doi:10.1037/1076-8971.7.1.3

Memon, A., & Gabbert, F. (2003). Unravelling the effects of sequential presentation in culprit present lineups. *Applied Cognitive Psychology, 17*, 703–714. doi:10.1002/acp.909

Memon, A., Wark, L., Holley, A., Bull, R., & Köhnken, G. (1997). Eyewitness performance in cognitive and structured interviews. *Memory, 5*, 639–656. doi:10.1080/741941481

Memon, A., & Wright, D. B. (1999). Eyewitness testimony and the Oklahoma bombing. *Psychologist, 12*, 292–295.

Mitchell, K. J., Johnson, M. K., & Mather, M. (2003). Source monitoring and suggestibility to misinformation: Adult age-related differences. *Applied Cognitive Psychology, 17*, 107–119. doi:10.1002/acp.857

Monterey Herald. (2009, August 24). Dallas police pioneering new photo lineup approach. Retrieved from http://www.montereyherald.com/news/ci_13175601

Morgan, C. A., Hazlett, G., Doran, A., Garrett, S., Hoyt, G., Thomas, P., . . . Southwick, S. M. (2004). Accuracy of eyewitness memory for persons encountered during exposure to highly intense stress. *International Journal of Law and Psychiatry, 27*, 265–279. doi:10.1016/j.ijlp.2004.03.004

Munsterberg, H. (1908). *On the witness stand*. New York, NY: Doubleday.

National Registry of Exonerations. (2012). *Exonerations in the United States, 1989–2012*. Retrieved from http://www.law.umich.edu/special/exoneration/Documents/exonerations_us_1989_2012_key_figures.pdf

O'Brien, T. (1990). *The things they carried*. New York, NY: Broadway Books.

Olsson, N., & Juslin, P. (1999). Can self-reported encoding strategy and recognition skill be diagnostic of performance in eyewitness identifications? *Journal of Applied Psychology, 84*, 42–49. doi:10.1037/0021-9010.84.1.42

O'Rourke, T. E., Penrod, S. D., Cutler, B. L., & Stuve, T. E. (1989). The external validity of eyewitness identification research: Generalizing across subject populations. *Law and Human Behavior, 13*, 385–395. doi:10.1007/BF01056410

Ost, J., Granhag, P., Udell, J., & Roos af Hjelmsäter E. (2008). Familiarity breeds distortion: The effects of media exposure on false reports concerning media coverage of the terrorist attacks in London on 7 July 2005. *Memory, 16*, 76–85. doi:10.1080/09658210701723323

Palmer, M. A., & Brewer, N. (2012). Sequential lineup presentation promotes less-biased criterion setting but does not improve discriminability. *Law and Human Behavior, 36*, 247–255. doi:10.1037/h0093923

Paterson, H. M., & Kemp, R. I. (2006). Comparing methods of encountering post-event information: The power of co-witness suggestion. *Applied Cognitive Psychology, 20*, 1083–1099. doi:10.1002/acp.1261

Patterson, K. E., & Baddeley, A. D. (1977). When face recognition fails. *Journal of Experimental Psychology: Human Learning and Memory, 3*, 406–417. doi:10.1037/0278-7393.3.4.406

Penrod, S. D., & Bornstein, B. H. (2007). Generalizing eyewitness reliability research. In R. C. L. Lindsay, D. Ross, D. Read, & M. Toglia (Eds.), *Handbook of eyewitness psychology: Vol. 2. Memory for people* (pp. 529–558). Mahwah, NJ: Erlbaum.

Perfect, T. J. (2002). When does eyewitness confidence predict performance? In T. J. Perfect & B. L. Schwartz (Eds.), *Applied metacognition* (pp. 95–120). Cambridge, England: Cambridge University Press. doi:10.1017/CBO9780511489976.006

Perry v. New Hampshire, 132 S.Ct. 716 (2012).

Phillips, M. R., McAuliff, B. D., Kovera, M. B., & Cutler, B. L. (1999). Double-blind photoarray administration as a safeguard against investigation bias. *Journal of Applied Psychology, 84*, 940–951. doi:10.1037/0021-9010.84.6.940

Pickel, K. L. (1999). The influence of context on the weapon focus effect. *Law and Human Behavior, 23*, 299–311. doi:10.1023/A:1022356431375

Pike, G., Brace, N., & Kyman, S. (2002). *The visual identification of suspects: procedures and practice*. Briefing note 2/02, Policing and Reducing Crime Unit, Home Office Research Development and Statistics Directorate. Retrieved from http://www.homeoffice.gov.uk/rds/prgbriefpubs1.html

Pigott, M. A., & Brigham, J. C. (1985). Relationship between accuracy of prior description and facial recognition. *Journal of Applied Psychology, 70*, 547–555. doi:10.1037/0021-9010.70.3.547

Police Executive Research Forum. (2013). *A national survey of eyewitness identification procedure in law enforcement agencies*. Washington, DC: Author. Retrieved from http://www.policeforum.org/free-online-documents

Pozzulo, J. D., & Marciniak, S. (2006). Comparing identification procedures when the perpetrator has changed appearance. *Psychology, Crime & Law, 12*, 429–438. doi:10.1080/10683160500050690

Ray, S., & Bates, M. E. (2006). Acute alcohol effects on repetition priming and word recognition memory with equivalent memory cues. *Brain and Cognition, 60*, 118–127. doi:10.1016/j.bandc.2005.07.009

Read, J. D., Yuille, J. C., & Tollestrup, P. (1992). Recollections of a robbery: Effects of arousal and alcohol upon recall and person identification. *Law and Human Behavior, 16*, 425–446. doi:10.1007/BF02352268

Reardon, M. C., & Fisher, R. P. (2011). Effect of viewing the interview and identification process on juror perceptions of eyewitness accuracy. *Applied Cognitive Psychology, 25*, 68–77. doi:10.1002/acp.1643

Robert, G., & Hockey, J. (1997). Compensatory control in the regulation of human performance under stress and high workload: A cognitive-energetical framework. *Biological Psychology, 45*, 73–93. doi:10.1016/S0301-0511(96)05223-4

Rodriguez, D. N., & Berry, M. A. (2014). The effect of line-up administrator blindness on the recording of eyewitness identification decisions. *Legal and Criminological Psychology, 19*, 69–79. doi:10.1111/j.2044-8333.2012.02058x

Rosenthal, R., & Rubin, D. B. (1978). Interpersonal expectancy effects: The first 345 studies. *Behavioral and Brain Sciences, 1*, 377–386. doi:10.1017/S0140525X00075506

Schacter, D. L. (2001). *The seven sins of memory (how the mind forgets and remembers)*. Boston: Houghton Mifflin.

Schmechel, R. S., O'Toole, T. P., Easterly, C. E., & Loftus, E. F. (2006). Beyond the ken? Testing jurors' understanding of eyewitness reliability evidence. *Jurimetrics, 46*, 177–214.

Semmler, C., Brewer, N., & Douglass, A. B. (2012). Jurors believe eyewitnesses. In B. L. Cutler (Ed.), *Conviction of the innocent: Lessons from psychological research* (pp. 185–209). Washington, DC: American Psychological Association. doi:10.1037/13085-009

Shapiro, P. N., & Penrod, S. D. (1986). Meta-analysis of facial identification studies. *Psychological Bulletin, 100*, 139–156. doi:10.1037/0033-2909.100.2.139

Shepherd, J. W., Davies, G. M., & Ellis, H. D. (1978). How best shall a face be described? In M. M. Gruneberg, P. E. Morris, & R. N. Sykes (Eds.), *Practical aspects of memory* (pp. 278–285). London: Academic Press.

Simons, D. J., & Chabris, C. F. (1999). Gorillas in our midst: Sustained inattentional blindness for dynamic events. *Perception, 28*, 1059–1074. doi:10.1068/p2952

Skagerberg, E. M., & Wright, D. B. (2008). The presence of co-witnesses and co-witness discussions in real eyewitnesses. *Psychology, Crime & Law, 14*, 513–521. doi:10.1080/10683160801948980

Skagerberg, E. M., & Wright, D. B. (2009). Susceptibility to post-identification feedback is affected by source credibility. *Applied Cognitive Psychology, 23*, 506–523. doi:10.1002/acp.1470

Slater, A. (1994). Identification parades: A scientific evaluation. *Police Research Award Scheme*. London: Police Research Group, Home Office.

Smalarz, L., & Wells, G. L. (2012). Eyewitness-identification evidence: Scientific advances and the new burden on trial judges. *Court Review: The Journal of the American Judges Association, 48*, 14–21.

Smith, V. L., Kassin, S. M., & Ellsworth, P. C. (1989). Eyewitness accuracy and confidence: Within versus between-subjects correlations. *Journal of Applied Psychology, 74*, 356–359. doi:10.1037/0021-9010.74.2.356

Sporer, S. L. (1992). Post-dicting eyewitness accuracy: Confidence, decision-times and person descriptions of choosers and nonchoosers. *European Journal of Social Psychology, 22*, 157–180. doi:10.1002/ejsp.2420220205

Sporer, S. L. (2001). Recognizing faces of other ethnic groups: An integration of theories. *Psychology, Public Policy, and Law, 7*, 36–97. doi:10.1037/1076-8971.7.1.36

Sporer, S. L., Penrod, S. D., Read, J. D., & Cutler, B. L. (1995). Choosing, confidence, and accuracy: A meta-analysis of the confidence-accuracy relation in eyewitness identification studies.

Psychological Bulletin, 118, 315–327. doi:10.1037/0033-2909.118.3.315

Stark, C. E. L., Okado, Y., & Loftus, E. F. (2010). Imaging the reconstruction of true and false memories using sensory reactivation and the misinformation paradigms. *Learning and Memory, 17*, 485–488. doi:10.1101/lm.1845710

State v. Henderson, 27 A.3d 872 (N.J. 2011).

Steblay, N., Dysart, J., Fulero, S., & Lindsay, R. C. L. (2003). Eyewitness accuracy rates in police showup and lineup presentations: A meta-analytic comparison. *Law and Human Behavior, 27*, 523–540. doi:10.1023/A:1025438223608

Steblay, N. K. (2007). *Double-blind sequential police lineup procedures: Toward an integrated laboratory and field practice perspective*. National Institute of Justice, Final report Grant No. 2004-IJ-CX-0044. Retrieved from http://web.augsburg.edu/~steblay/March2007_Final_NIJ_report.pdf

Steblay, N. K. (2008). Commentary on "Studying eyewitness investigations in the field": A look forward. *Law and Human Behavior, 32*, 11–15. doi:10.1007/s10979-007-9105-9

Steblay, N. K. (2011). What we know now: The Evanston Illinois lineups. *Law and Human Behavior, 35*, 1–12. doi:10.1007/s10979-009-9207-7

Steblay, N. K. (2013). Lineup instructions. In B. Cutler (Ed.), *Reform of eyewitness identification procedures* (pp. 65–81). Washington, DC: American Psychological Association.

Steblay, N. K., Dietrich, H. L., Ryan, S. L., Raczynski, J. L., & James, K. A. (2011). Sequential lineup laps and eyewitness accuracy. *Law and Human Behavior, 35*, 262–274. doi:10.1007/s10979-010-9236-2

Steblay, N. K., Dysart, J. E., & Wells, G. L. (2011). Seventy-two tests of the sequential lineup superiority effect: A meta-analysis and policy discussion. *Psychology, Public Policy, and Law, 17*, 99–139. doi:10.1037/a0021650

Steblay, N. K., & Phillips, J. (2011). The not-sure response option in sequential lineup practice. *Applied Cognitive Psychology, 25*, 768–774. doi:10.1002/acp.1755

Steblay, N. K., Tix, R. W., & Benson, S. L. (2013). Double exposure: The effects of repeated identification lineups on eyewitness accuracy. *Applied Cognitive Psychology, 27*, 644–654. doi:10.1002/acp.2944

Steblay, N.K., Wells, G. L., & Douglass, A. B. (2014). The eyewitness post-identification feedback effect 15 years later: Theoretical and policy implications. *Psychology, Public Policy, and Law, 20*, 1–18. doi:10.1037/1aw0000001

Steblay, N. M. (1992). A meta-analytic review of the weapon-focus effect. *Law and Human Behavior, 16*, 413–424. doi:10.1007/BF02352267

Steblay, N. M. (1997). Social influence in eyewitness recall: A meta-analytic review of lineup instruction effects. *Law and Human Behavior, 21*, 283–297. doi:10.1023/A:1024890732059

Steblay, N. M., & Bothwell, R. (1994). Evidence for hypnotically refreshed testimony: The view from the laboratory. *Law and Human Behavior, 18*, 635–651. doi:10.1007/BF01499329

Steele, C. M., & Josephs, R. A. (1990). Alcohol myopia: Its prized and dangerous effects. *American Psychologist, 45*, 921–933. doi:10.1037/0003-066X.45.8.921

Technical Working Group for Eyewitness Evidence. (1999). *Eyewitness evidence: A guide for law enforcement.* Washington, DC: National Institute of Justice (NCJ 178240).

Thompson, J. (2000, June 18). I was certain, but I was wrong. *New York Times.* Retrieved from http://www.nytimes.com/2000/06/18/opinion/i-was-certain-but-i-was-wrong.html

Thompson-Cannino, J., Cotton, R., & Torneo, E. (2010). *Picking Cotton.* New York, NY: St. Martin's Press.

Tollestrup, P. A., Turtle, J. W., & Yuille, J. C. (1994). Actual witnesses to robbery and fraud: An archival analysis. In D. F. Ross, J. D. Read, & M. P. Toglia (Eds.), *Adult eyewitness testimony: Current trends and developments* (pp. 144–160). New York, NY: Cambridge University Press. doi:10.1017/CBO9780511759192.008

Tulving, E., & Thomson, D. M. (1973). Encoding specificity and retrieval processes in episodic memory. *Psychological Review, 80*, 352–373. doi:10.1037/h0020071

Valentine, T., Davis, J. P., Memon, A., & Roberts, A. (2012). Live show-ups and their influence on a subsequent video lineup. *Applied Cognitive Psychology, 26*, 1–23. doi:10.1002/acp.1796

Valentine, T., & Heaton, P. (1999). An evaluation of the fairness of police line-ups and video identifications. *Applied Cognitive Psychology, 13*, S59–S72. doi:10.1002/(SICI)1099-0720(199911)13:1+<S59::AID-ACP679>3.0.CO;2-Y

Valentine, T., Pickering, A., & Darling, S. (2003). Characteristics of eyewitness identification that predict the outcome of real lineups. *Applied Cognitive Psychology, 17*, 969–993. doi:10.1002/acp.939

van Oorsouw, K., & Merckelbach, H. (2012). The effects of alcohol on crime-related memories: A field study. *Applied Cognitive Psychology, 26*, 82–90. doi:10.1002/acp.1799

Weber, N., Brewer, N., Wells, G. L., Semmler, C., & Keast, A. (2004). Eyewitness identification accuracy and response latency: The unruly 10–12 second rule. *Journal of Experimental Psychology: Applied, 10*, 139–147. doi:10.1037/1076-898X.10.3.139

Weber, N., & Perfect, T. J. (2012). Improving eyewitness identification accuracy by screening out those who say they don't know. *Law and Human Behavior, 36*, 28–36. doi:10.1037/h0093976

Wells, G. L. (1978). Applied eyewitness testimony research: System variables and estimator variables. *Journal of Personality and Social Psychology, 36*, 1546–1557. doi:10.1037/0022-3514.36.12.1546

Wells, G. L. (1984). The psychology of lineup identifications. *Journal of Applied Social Psychology, 14*, 89–103. doi:10.1111/j.1559-1816.1984.tb02223.x

Wells, G. L. (1985). Verbal descriptions of faces from memory: Are they diagnostic of identification accuracy? *Journal of Applied Psychology, 70*, 619–626. doi:10.1037/0021-9010.70.4.619

Wells, G. L. (1988). *Eyewitness identification: A system handbook.* Toronto, Ontario, Canada: Carswell.

Wells, G. L. (1993). What do we know about eyewitness identification? *American Psychologist, 48*, 553–571. doi:10.1037/0003-066X.48.5.553

Wells, G. L. (1995). Scientific study of eyewitness memory: Implications for public and legal policy. *Psychology, Public Policy, and Law, 1*, 726–731. doi:10.1037/h0092727

Wells, G. L. (2006). Eyewitness identification: Systemic reforms. *Wisconsin Law Review, 2*, 615–643.

Wells, G. L. (2008). Field experiments on eyewitness identification: Towards a better understanding of pitfalls and prospects. *Law and Human Behavior, 32*, 6–10. doi:10.1007/s10979-007-9098-4

Wells, G. L. (2010). *The mistaken identification of John Jerome White.* Retrieved from http://www.psychology.iastate.edu/~glwells/The_Misidentification_of_John_White.pdf

Wells, G. L., & Bradfield, A. L. (1998). "Good, you identified the suspect": Feedback to eyewitnesses distorts their reports of the witnessing experience. *Journal of Applied Psychology, 83*, 360–376. doi:10.1037/0021-9010.83.3.360

Wells, G. L., & Bradfield, A. L. (1999a). Distortions in eyewitnesses' recollections: Can the postidentification-feedback effect be moderated? *Psychological Science, 10*, 138–144. doi:10.1111/1467-9280.00121

Wells, G. L., & Bradfield, A. L. (1999b). Measuring the goodness of lineups: Parameter estimation, question effects, and limits to the mock witness paradigm. *Applied Cognitive Psychology, 13*, S27–S39. doi:10.1002/(SICI)1099-0720(199911)13:1+<S27::AID-ACP635>3.3.CO;2-D

Wells, G. L., Cutler, B. L., & Hasel, L. E. (2009). The Duke lacrosse rape investigation: How not to do eyewitness-identification procedures. In M. L. Siegel

(Ed.), *Race to injustice: Lessons learned from the Duke lacrosse rape case* (pp. 307–321). Durham, NC: Carolina Academic Press.

Wells, G. L., & Hryciw, B. (1984). Memory for faces: Encoding and retrieval operations. *Memory and Cognition, 12*, 338–344. doi:10.3758/BF03198293

Wells, G. L., & Lindsay, R. C. L. (1980). On estimating the diagnosticity of eyewitness nonidentifications. *Psychological Bulletin, 88*, 776–784. doi:10.1037/0033-2909.88.3.776

Wells, G. L., & Loftus, E. F. (2013). Eyewitness memory for people and events. In R. K. Otto & I. B. Weiner (Eds.), *Handbook of psychology: Vol. 11. Forensic psychology* (2nd ed., pp. 617–629). Hoboken, NJ: Wiley.

Wells, G. L., & Luus, C. A. E. (1990). Police lineups as experiments: Social methodology as a framework for properly conducted lineups. *Personality and Social Psychology Bulletin, 16*, 106–117. doi:10.1177/0146167290161008

Wells, G. L., Luus, C. A. E., & Windschitl, P. D. (1994). Maximizing the utility of eyewitness identification evidence. *Current Directions in Psychological Science, 3*, 194–198. doi:10.1111/1467-8721.ep10770833

Wells, G. L., Memon, A., & Penrod, S. D. (2006). Eyewitness evidence: Improving its probative value. *Psychological Science in the Public Interest, 7*, 45–75. doi:10.1111/j.1529-1006.2006.00027.x

Wells, G. L., & Olson, E. (2002). Eyewitness identification: Information gain from incriminating and exonerating behaviors. *Journal of Experimental Psychology: Applied, 8*, 155–167. doi:10.1037/1076-898X.8.3.155

Wells, G. L., & Quinlivan, D. S. (2009). Suggestive eyewitness identification procedures and the Supreme Court's reliability test in light of eyewitness science: 30 years later. *Law and Human Behavior, 33*, 1–24. doi:10.1007/s10979-008-9130-3

Wells, G. L., Rydell, S. M., & Seelau, E. P. (1993). On the selection of distractors for eyewitness lineups. *Journal of Applied Psychology, 78*, 835–844. doi:10.1037/0021-9010.78.5.835

Wells, G. L., Small, M., Penrod, S., Malpass, R. S., Fulero, S. M., & Brimacombe, C. A. E. (1998). Eyewitness identification procedures: Recommendations for lineups and photospreads. *Law and Human Behavior, 22*, 603–647. doi:10.1023/A:1025750605807

Wells, G. L., Steblay, N. M., & Dysart, J. E. (2011). *A test of the simultaneous vs. sequential lineup methods: An initial report of the AJS national eyewitness identification field studies.* Des Moines, IA: American Judicature Society.

Wells, G. L., Steblay, N. K., & Dysart, J. E. (2012). Eyewitness identification reforms: Are suggestiveness-induced hits and guesses true hits? *Perspectives on Psychological Science, 7*, 264–271. doi:10.1177/1745691612443368

Wells, G. L., Steblay, N. K., & Dysart, J. E. (in press). Double-blind photo lineups using actual eyewitnesses: An experimental test of the sequential versus simultaneous lineup procedure. *Law and Human Behavior.*

Wells, G. L., & Turtle, J. W. (1986). Eyewitness identification: The importance of lineup models. *Psychological Bulletin, 99*, 320–329. doi:10.1037/0033-2909.99.3.320

Winter, R. J., & Greene, E. (2007). Juror decision making. In F. T. Durso, R. S. Nickerson, S. T. Dumais, S. Lewandosky, & T. J. Perfect (Eds.), *Handbook of applied cognition* (2nd ed., pp. 739–761). Hoboken, NJ: Wiley. doi:10.1002/9780470713181.ch28

Wise, R. A., Safer, M. A., & Maro, C. M. (2011). What U.S. law enforcement officers know and believe about eyewitness factors, eyewitness interviews, and identification procedures. *Applied Cognitive Psychology, 25*, 488–500. doi:10.1002/acp.1717

Wright, D. B., Carlucci, M., Evans, J., & Compo, N. S. (2009). Turning a blind eye to double blind line-ups. *Applied Cognitive Psychology, 23*, 1–19. doi:10.1002/acp.1592

Wright, D. B., & McDaid, A. T. (1996). Comparing system and estimator variables using data from real lineups. *Applied Cognitive Psychology, 10*, 75–84. doi:10.1002/(SICI)1099-0720(199602)10:1<75::AID-ACP364>3.0.CO;2-E

Zhu, B., Chen, C., Loftus, E. F., Lin, C., He, Q., Chen, C., . . . Dong, Q. (2010a). Individual differences in false memory from misinformation: Cognitive factors. *Memory, 18*, 543–555. doi:10.1080/09658211.2010.487051

Zhu, B., Chen, C., Loftus, E. F., Lin, C., He, Q., Chen, C., . . . Dong, Q. (2010b). Individual differences in false memory from misinformation: Personality characteristics and their interactions with cognitive abilities. *Personality and Individual Differences, 48*, 889–894. doi:10.1016/j.paid.2010.02.016

CHAPTER 8

DECEPTION DETECTION

Aldert Vrij

The importance of detecting deceit in police or intelligence interviews is paramount. Unsurprisingly, throughout history people have attempted to detect deception through observing behavior and analyzing speech, and several nonverbal and verbal lie-detection tools have been developed for this purpose. This chapter describes the two nonverbal tools, the Behavior Analysis Interview (BAI) and lie detection through observing facial emotional expressions, and the two verbal tools, Statements Validity Analysis (SVA) and Scientific Content Analysis (SCAN), that are predominantly used at this point in time.

The BAI is a standardized interview protocol and forms an important first step in police interviewing in the United States. Investigators conduct a BAI to obtain insight into the guilt or innocence of suspects. If the investigator judges the suspect to be guilty, an interrogation may follow. Observing facial emotional expressions, including microexpressions, forms part of security programs implemented in the United States at some international airports. SVA is a systematic method to assess the credibility of children of alleged sexual abuse, and SVA assessments are used as evidence in criminal courts in several West European countries. SCAN is a method to assess written statements produced by suspects, witnesses, or alleged victims and is used by law enforcement, military, and intelligence services across the world.

It will become clear that each of these tools has limitations and that they are not as accurate as their developers claim them to be. In fact, there is no evidence that guilty and innocent suspects respond to the BAI questions in the way BAI investigators claim they do, and research has yet to show that SCAN actually works. SVA can classify truth tellers and liars at accuracy levels above chance but below "reasonable doubt," the standard of proof typically set in criminal courts. A lie-detection tool based on the observation of microexpressions of facial emotions is largely ineffective.

During the last 10 years, two new research trends have become apparent. First, research has emerged demonstrating that interviewers can elicit and enhance nonverbal and verbal cues to deceit via specific questioning techniques. This new wave of "interviewing to detect deception" research is summarized in this chapter. This new research represents a paradigm shift: In the past, anxiety-based lie detection was dominant, but the new literature is predominantly cognitively based. The rationale behind this paradigm shift is also discussed in this chapter.

The second new research trend is a focus on lie detection in intelligence interviews. The occurrence of terrorist attacks and the continuing threat of terrorism have sparked interest in this area, which in several ways differs from lie detection in police interviews about criminal activities, the traditional area of research. This chapter outlines the available intelligence lie detection research. The Practice and Policy Issues section of this chapter includes thoughts about whether the cognitive lie detection approach is too lenient on suspects and the desirability to establish clear decision rules in lie-detection tools.

http://dx.doi.org/10.1037/14462-008
APA Handbook of Forensic Psychology: Vol. 2. Criminal Investigation, Adjudication, and Sentencing Outcomes,
B. L. Cutler and P. A. Zapf (Editors-in-Chief)
Copyright © 2015 by the American Psychological Association. All rights reserved.

The focus of this chapter is lie detection through observation of nonverbal and verbal cues, but lies can also be detected in other ways, such as by measuring people's physiological responses (e.g., skin response, heart rate, blood pressure) or brain activity (brain waves or neural activities). These measurements are intrusive as examinees need to be attached to a polygraph machine to measure heart rate, blood pressure, and skin responses; must undergo electroencephalograms (EEGs) to measure event-related potentials such as the P300 brain wave; or must undergo functional magnetic resonance imaging (fMRI) brain scans to measure neural brain activity. This makes measuring physiological responses and brain activity inapplicable to many real life situations; therefore, they will not be discussed in this chapter. Comprehensive reviews of the polygraph research (Kleiner, 2002; Verschuere, Ben-Shakhar, & Meijer, 2011), P300 research (Rosenfeld, 2011; Vrij & Verschuere, 2013), and fMRI research (Christ, van Essen, Watson, Brubaker, & McDermott, 2009; Gamer, 2011; Vrij & Verschuere, 2013) are available elsewhere.

IMPORTANCE OF THE PROBLEM

In virtually all interviews that the police and intelligence services conduct, investigators need to determine whether a suspect is lying. Those assessments are used to determine further actions. If the police believe that a suspect is lying, they may expose him or her to interrogation techniques meant to break resistance, or they may invest considerable investigative resources into the case to search for conclusive evidence that the suspect is lying. If the SVA expert comes to the conclusion that the child's statement about the alleged sexual abuse is truthful, the alleged perpetrator runs a serious risk of being found guilty in a criminal court, whereas this is less likely to happen if the SVA expert concludes that the statement was fabricated. If intelligence services believe that they can trust an informant, they may act upon the information provided by that informant; if intelligence services do not believe that they can trust a suspect, they may decide not to pay further attention to his or her actions that initially may have been seen as suspicious or odd.

Incorrect veracity judgements can do irreparable harm. Take as example the loss of seven U.S. Central Intelligence Agency (CIA) agents and one Jordanian intelligence officer in Afghanistan on 30 December 2009. The CIA agents were killed in a suicide attack by the informant al-Balawi, who had been recruited by Jordanian intelligence. They thought that al-Balawi was going to give them information about Taliban and Al-Qaeda targets in Pakistan's tribal areas, including Ayman al-Zawahiri, the Al-Qaeda leader at the time. The CIA trusted al-Balawi and therefore did not strip-search him when he arrived at the highly secured CIA base on the Afghan-Pakistan border. The CIA was aware that al-Balawi had posted extreme anti-American views on the internet, but it was decided that the views he had expressed were part of a good cover, and the possibility that they were his real views was discounted (Granhag, 2010; Leal, Vrij, Mann, & Fisher, 2010). Another example is Mohammed Merah, the 23-year-old man who killed three unarmed French soldiers as well as a rabbi, three small children, and a Jewish school teacher in southwest France in March 2012. Merah had long been known as a petty criminal, but his visits to Pakistan and Afghanistan and his links to Islamist extremism drew attention. He was brought in for questioning by French intelligence services in November 2011, but, according to the head of France's intelligence services, his story had been convincing and Merah had shown excellent cooperation, education, and courtesy ("Obituary: Toulouse gunman," 2012; Willsher, 2012).

RELEVANT PSYCHOLOGICAL THEORY AND PRINCIPLES

Traditionally, verbal and nonverbal lie detection has focused on the difference in emotions that liars and truth tellers experience. The core of this anxiety-based approach is that liars are more nervous than truth tellers and therefore will show more nervous behaviors. Ekman's (1985/2001) analysis of facial expressions of emotions is a prime example; the Behavior Analysis Interview is also, in part, based on this premise. The anxiety-approach has not only dominated verbal and nonverbal lie detection, it is also the main approach in physiological polygraph testing. Emotion/anxiety is generally considered as one of the main correlates of deception (Zuckerman, DePaulo, & Rosenthal, 1981), and there is empirical evidence that liars sometimes do come across as being more nervous than truth tellers (DePaulo et al., 2003), but the approach has serious limitations. First, experiencing emotions is not the sole domain of liars: Truth tellers can experience the same emotions, particularly if they know that they are scrutinized or are afraid of not being believed (Bond & Fahey, 1987; Ofshe & Leo, 1997). Second, if emotional displays or cues of nervousness per se do not reliably distinguish between truth tellers and liars, perhaps questions can be asked that will elicit such cues in liars but not in truth tellers or, alternatively, that will enhance such cues more in liars than in truth tellers. No such questioning technique exists to date, and it is doubtful that it can ever be developed (National Research Council, 2003).

In recent years, researchers have concentrated on cognitive lie detection. The premise is that lying is mentally more taxing than truth telling (Vrij, Fisher, Mann, & Leal, 2006). Cognition is also considered as one of the main correlates of deception (Zuckerman et al., 1981), and there is empirical evidence that liars sometimes do show signs of thinking hard (DePaulo et al., 2003). This approach shares one limitation with the emotion approach: Cues of cognitive load are not the sole domain of liars either; truth tellers also may have to think hard, and therefore they may display cues of being mentally taxed (DePaulo et al., 2003). Unlike the emotion approach, however, interview protocols that elicit and enhance cues of cognitive load more in liars than in truth tellers can be developed, making it possible to discriminate between the two (Vrij & Granhag, 2012a). Three approaches discussed in this chapter—imposing cognitive load, asking unanticipated questions, and the strategic use of evidence—are examples of cognitive lie-detection techniques. The latter technique also takes into account the notion that liars use different strategies to avoid detection than do truth tellers (Granhag & Hartwig, 2008). In sum, in verbal and nonverbal lie detection, the emphasis has moved in recent years from emotion-based lie-detection techniques to cognitive-load lie-detection techniques that focus on liars' and truth tellers' different psychological states and take their differential strategies into account.

Apart from the fact that liars may experience emotions and cognitive load, a third aspect often plays a role in lie-detection techniques: Liars are more concerned than truth tellers with impression management and are therefore, compared to truth tellers, keener to construct a report or show behavior that they believe will make a credible impression on others and will leave out information or avoid showing behavior that, in their view, will damage their image of being a sincere person (Zuckerman et al., 1981). This leads to liars attempting to show responses that they believe appear honest and to avoid showing responses that they believe appear suspicious (Hocking & Leathers, 1980; Köhnken, 2004). This impression management approach is particularly present in the SVA verbal veracity tool.

RESEARCH REVIEW

This section summarizes the available nonverbal and verbal lie detection research. First, the two nonverbal tools, the Behavior Analysis Interview (BAI) and lie detection through observing facial emotional expressions, and the two verbal tools, Statements Validity Analysis (SVA) and Scientific Content Analysis (SCAN), that are mostly used at this point in time are discussed. This is followed by a discussion of two new and promising trends in (non) verbal deception research: Interviewing to detect deception, and lie detection in intelligence interviews.

Nonverbal Lie-Detection Tools

Analyses of nonverbal behavior have a long history, and the assumption was that fear of being detected was an essential element of deception and lie detection. In a Hindus writing from 900 BC, it is mentioned that liars rub the great toe along the ground and shiver, and that they rub the roots of their hair with their fingers (Trovillo, 1939). More detailed and systematic analyses of nonverbal cues to deceit emerged in the second half on the twentieth century, with Reid and Arther's (1953) analysis of the behavior of more than 800 suspects being one of the front runners. Reid and Arther's observations, together with Horvath's (1973) work regarding nonverbal cues to deceit, resulted in the development of the BAI, the nonverbal lie-detection tool that will be described first.

Behavior Analysis Interview. The BAI is developed and taught by John E. Reid and Associates, a U.S. firm that provides training in interrogation and interviewing. The BAI is described in John E. Reid and Associates' manual (Inbau, Reid, Buckley, & Jayne, 2013), which is now in its fifth edition. On their website, John E. Reid and Associates report that, since it was first offered in 1974, more than 300,000 professionals have attended the three-day interviewing and interrogation training of which BAI forms a part. Trainees come from the private and public sector and are from across the world.

Different rationales exist as to why truth tellers and liars would display different responses in a BAI. One explanation is that liars feel less comfortable than truth tellers during an investigative interview (Inbau et al., 2013); other explanations are that liars lack understanding of how truth tellers actually behave and that liars are reluctant to share much information out of fear that it will lead to deception detection (Horvath, Blair, & Buckley, 2008).

The BAI forms an important first step in U.S. police interviewing. Police investigators who are reasonably certain of a suspect's guilt may submit the suspect to persuasive interrogation techniques meant to break down resistance (see Chapter 9, this volume for a review of interrogations and confessions). Because such interrogation techniques may lead to false confessions, it is important to avoid submitting innocent suspects to these techniques. Therefore, investigators conduct a BAI to obtain insight into the innocence or guilt of suspects. Investigators form a judgement about this based on the suspect's nonverbal and verbal responses during the BAI. If the investigator judges the suspect to be deceptive, an interrogation may follow.

The BAI protocol includes asking investigative, nonthreatening questions and behavior-provoking questions (Buckley, 2012). The former type of question forms part of most interview protocols, and it is the latter type of question that makes the BAI stand out from other interview protocols. There are 14 predetermined and standardized behavior-provoking questions, including a question whether the suspect committed the crime him/herself and a question whether the suspect knows who has committed the crime. In the BAI it is assumed that guilty suspects are more likely than truth tellers to display nervous or anxiety-reducing behavior, such as crossing their legs, shifting about in their chair, and performing grooming behavior while answering the question, whereas innocent suspects are more likely than guilty suspects to lean forward, establish eye contact, and use illustrators to reinforce their confidence in their statements. In addition, guilty suspects are more likely to answer quickly, and their answers will sound less sincere.

Horvath, Jayne, and Buckley (1994) tested the efficiency of the BAI in a field study. The study included 60 videotaped interviews with real suspects in which the BAI protocol was used and the investigators made veracity judgments. When inconclusive outcomes were disregarded, an overall accuracy rate of 86% was obtained. This is an impressive accuracy rate, but the study had an important limitation in that the ground truth was unclear. That is, it could not be established with certainty that the innocent suspects were truly innocent and the guilty suspects were truly guilty, a widespread and well documented problem in deception field studies (Iacono, 2008). In fact, Horvath et al. (1994) reported that the ground truth was established by "incontrovertible evidence" in only two of the 60 cases that they analyzed. They concluded that, "if it were possible to develop ground truth criteria in a large number of cases such as occurred in these two instances, the interpretation of findings would be less problematic" (p. 805). This conclusion probably does not go far enough. The results of a study in which the ground truth is established in only 3% of the cases (two out of 60 cases) are simply unreliable.

Other studies provide less flourishing results for the BAI both in terms of the nonverbal cues to deceit that emerge in (BAI) interviews and the ability to detect deceit when paying attention to the BAI cues.

We tested the working of BAI in a controlled laboratory experiment, and our results directly refuted Inbau et al.'s (2013) predictions about how liars behave: Liars were less likely to cross their legs and less likely to shift posture than truth tellers (Vrij, Mann, & Fisher, 2006). In addition, Inbau et al.'s (2013) predictions about how liars behave are not supported by DePaulo et al.'s (2003) meta-analysis of more than 150 studies about nonverbal and verbal cues to deception. Inbau et al.'s (2013) predictions are, however, in alignment with how observers believe liars behave (Masip, Barba & Herrero, 2012; Masip & Herrero, 2013; Masip, Herrero, Garrido, & Barba, 2011). Moreover, in Kassin and Fong's (1999) experiment, half of the observers received training in the visual BAI cues. The trained observers' performance on a subsequent lie-detection test was worse than that of untrained participants. This finding, that paying attention to the visual BAI cues impairs lie detection performance, was supported by a field study where police officers judged the veracity of statements made by murder, rape, and arson suspects who told the truth and lied during their real-life (videotaped) police interviews (Mann, Vrij, & Bull, 2004). The police officers were also asked which cues they pay attention to when they attempt to detect deceit. Mann et al. (2004) found a negative relationship between officers reportedly attending to the BAI cues (e.g., averting gaze, shifting posture, making self-adaptors, etc.) and accuracy in the lie-detection task. That is, the more the officers endorsed the BAI's view on cues to deception, the worse they became at distinguishing between truths and lies. In other words, there is evidence that endorsing the information about visual cues to deception discussed in the BAI protocol is counterproductive and makes people worse lie detectors.

Lie detection through the observation of facial expressions. Over the years, Paul Ekman, an American psychologist and pioneer in the study of emotions and their relation to facial expressions, has argued that facial expressions of emotion betray liars (Ekman, 1985/2001). According to Ekman (Henig, 2006), aspects of facial communication are beyond control and can betray a deceiver's true emotion via

microexpressions (lasting 1/25 to 1/5 of a second) of that emotion. Ekman has claimed that his system of lie detection, which includes the observation of facial expressions of emotions, including microexpressions, can be taught to anyone with an accuracy of more than 95%. Ekman's lie detection method forms part of the security program SPOT (Screening Passengers by Observational Techniques), which is implemented in the United States, including at Boston's Logan International Airport (Ekman, 2006).

Worryingly, Ekman has never published empirical data showing that facial (micro)expressions of emotions are diagnostic indicators of deceit or that observers achieve 95% accuracy when paying attention to such expressions. The former has been investigated by a group of Canadian researchers: In an experimental laboratory study, Porter and ten Brinke (2008) found that microexpressions of emotions occurred in only 14 out of the 697 analyzed facial expressions, and that six of those 14 microexpressions were displayed by truth tellers. In a second experimental laboratory study, microexpressions again only occurred in a minority of cases and were again equally common in truth tellers and liars (ten Brinke, MacDonald, Porter, & O'Connor, 2012). Those findings suggest that a lie-detection tool based on microexpressions of facial emotions is largely ineffective.

Someone may argue that facial (micro)expressions of emotions only occur when there are severe consequences for the liar when the lie fails, which is never the case in laboratory studies. In another research project, the same group of Canadian researchers examined the facial expressions (rather than microexpressions) of 52 individuals who pleaded on television to the public for the return of their missing relative, half of whom were convicted of murdering that person. In other words, this was a true high-stakes situation. Muscles associated with grief (*corrugator supercilii* and *depressor anguli oris*) were more often contracted in genuine pleaders than in deceptive pleaders, and full contractions of the *frontalis* (failed attempts to appear sad) occurred more frequently in liars than in truth tellers. On the basis of these behaviors, however, only a modest number of liars (around 56%) and more truth tellers (around 82%) were classified correctly, resulting in a modest 69% overall accuracy (ten Brinke, Porter, & Baker, 2012). In a second paper about this high-stakes situation, the facial expressions of 78 individuals (including the 52 individuals from ten Brinke, Porter, & Baker, 2012) were examined (ten Brinke & Porter, 2012). More liars than truth tellers expressed disgust, surprise, and happiness, whereas more truth tellers than liars expressed sadness. The percentages were not impressive, however, and the total classifications of truth tellers and liars based on these expressions fell in the 60%–70% range. Those findings do not support Ekman's claim that facial (micro)expressions of emotions can classify correctly more than 95% of truth tellers and liars. In addition, the high-stakes situation in which the facial expressions of emotion were examined create optimum conditions for these expressions to occur. Many real-life situations involve lower stakes, and in such situations facial expressions of emotions will occur less frequently (or not at all), leading to less than 60%–70% accuracy.

Verbal Lie Detection

There is not much history in analyzing speech. A Hindus writing of 900 BC referred to speech by saying that liars do not answer questions or are evasive (Trovillo, 1939). In other words, it refers to the absence of speech. The notion that the presence of speech can indicate deceit arose much later, and early systematic analyses of speech started to arrive in the 1950s in Germany (Undeutsch, 1982) and Sweden (Trankell, 1972). In 1954 the Supreme Court of West Germany summoned a small number of experts to a hearing. The Court wanted to assess to what extent psychologists could help in determining the credibility of child witnesses' testimonies, particularly in trials for sexual offences (see Volume 1, Chapter 11, this handbook for a review of sexual offending and Chapter 1, this volume for a review of child witnesses). The forensic psychologist Udo Undeutsch (1989) reported the case of a 14-year-old alleged victim of rape that he had investigated, and the five Justices of the Senate were impressed by his analysis. Subsequently a ruling was made in 1955 by the German Supreme Court that required the use of psychological interviews and assessments of credibility in virtually all contested cases of child sexual

abuse. This led to numerous cases in which psychologists were called on as experts. Arntzen (1982) estimated that by 1982 expert testimony had been offered in more than 40,000 cases.

In West Germany and Sweden, this resulted in the further development of various content criteria to assess the credibility of statements made by alleged victims of sexual abuse. Undeutsch (1982) was the first to compile a comprehensive list of criteria, but others have published similar lists (Vrij, 2008). The German scholars Günter Köhnken and Max Steller took statement analysis a step further. They refined the available criteria and integrated them into a formal assessment procedure, the SVA, which they published in English (Köhnken & Steller, 1988; Steller & Köhnken, 1989). Of the nonverbal and verbal veracity tools, SVA assessment outcomes are the only ones accepted as evidence in some North American courts and in criminal courts in several West-European countries, including Germany, the Netherlands, and Sweden (Vrij, 2008). The introduction of SVA has resulted in a large number of experimental studies examining one stage of this tool, criteria-based content analysis (CBCA). This section presents an outline of SVA and a discussion of the results of these experimental CBCA studies.

During the late 1980s, another verbal veracity tool originated, Scientific Content Analysis (SCAN). This tool has attracted considerably less interest from researchers, and there is very little SCAN research to date. SCAN is frequently used by practitioners, however, which makes it appropriate for discussion in this chapter. This section briefly outlines SCAN together with the available SCAN research.

Statement Validity Analysis. SVA was designed to determine the credibility of child witnesses' testimonies in trials for sexual offences. It is not surprising that a technique has been developed to verify whether a child has been sexually abused. It is often difficult to determine the facts in an allegation of sexual abuse, because often there is no medical or physical evidence. Frequently the alleged victim and the defendant give contradictory testimony, and often there are no independent witnesses to give an objective version of events. This makes the perceived credibility of the defendant and alleged victim important. The alleged victim is in a disadvantageous position if he or she is a child, as adults have a tendency to mistrust statements made by children.

SVA consists of four stages (Vrij, 2008): (1) a case-file analysis, (2) a semistructured interview, (3) a CBCA that systematically assesses the quality of the transcribed interviews, and (4) an evaluation of the CBCA outcome via a set of questions (Validity Checklist).

The case-file analysis (stage 1) considers information about the child witness (e.g., age, cognitive abilities, relationship to the accused person), the nature of the event in question, and previous statements of the child and other parties involved. This gives the SVA expert insight into what may have happened and the issues under dispute. The three subsequent stages focus on these disputed elements. In stage 2, the interview, the child provides his or her own account of the allegation. Interviewing young children is difficult, because their descriptions of past events are notably incomplete. Special interview techniques based upon psychological principles have been designed to obtain as much information as possible from interviewees in a free narrative style (see Bull, 2010; Fisher, 2010).

The core of the technique is stage 3, in which trained evaluators perform the CBCA to assess the presence of 19 different criteria in the transcribed interview (Köhnken & Steller, 1988; Steller & Köhnken, 1989). Each of these 19 criteria is assumed to occur more frequently in truthful than in deceptive accounts. According to CBCA/SVA theory, some criteria are likely to indicate genuine experiences because these criteria are typically too difficult to fabricate (Köhnken, 1996, 2004). Therefore, statements that are coherent and consistent (logical structure), whereby the information is not provided in a chronological time sequence (unstructured production) and which contain a significant amount of detail (quantity of detail) are more likely to be true. CBCA makes a further distinction between 10 different types of detail (criteria 4–13), which are also considered indicators of truthfulness. Criteria include contextual embeddings (references

to time and space: "He approached me for the first time in the garden during the summer holidays."), descriptions of interactions (statements that link at least two actors with each other: "The moment my mother came into the room, he stopped smiling."), reproduction of speech (speech in its original form: "And then he asked: Is that your coat?"), accounts of subjective mental state (when the witness describes his or her feelings or thoughts experienced at the time of the incident), and attribution of perpetrator's mental state (when the witness gives their interpretation of the perpetrator's feelings, thoughts, or motives during the incident).

Other criteria (criteria 14–18) are more likely to occur in truthful statements for motivational reasons. Truthful persons will not be as concerned with impression management as deceivers. Compared to truth tellers, deceivers will be keener to construct a report that they believe will make a credible impression on others, and will leave out information that, in their view, will damage their image of being a sincere person (Köhnken, 1996, 2004). As a result, a truthful statement is more likely to contain information that is inconsistent with the stereotypes of truthfulness. The CBCA list includes five of these so-called "contrary-to-truthfulness-stereotype" criteria (Ruby & Brigham, 1998), including: spontaneous corrections (corrections made without prompting from the interviewer), and admitting lack of memory (expressing concern that some parts of the statement may be incorrect: "I think," "Maybe," "I am not sure," etc.). Although SVA is designed to evaluate children's testimonies in alleged sexual abuse cases, some scholars have argued that the technique can also be used to evaluate the testimonies of adults who talk about issues other than sexual abuse as the underlying factors of cognitive load and impression management also apply to adults (Köhnken, 2004; Porter & Yuille, 1996; Ruby & Brigham, 1997). Research findings have supported this view (Vrij, 2008)

CBCA has been widely researched, and more than 50 empirical studies about this method have been published to date (Vrij, 2008). Those studies demonstrate that CBCA analyses can be useful for lie-detection purposes. In 20 studies, researchers computed total CBCA scores and compared these scores for truth tellers and liars. In 16 of 20 studies (80%), the hypothesis that truth tellers will obtain significantly higher total CBCA scores than liars was supported. Regarding the individual criteria, criterion 3 (quantity of details) received the most support. The amount of details was calculated in 29 studies, and in 22 of those (76%) truth tellers included significantly more details in their accounts than liars. Moreover, in not a single study did truth tellers include significantly less details in their statements than liars. Finally, the extent to which CBCA analyses can discriminate liars from truth tellers was examined in 24 studies. The average accuracy rate in these studies was 71%. In other words, there is evidence that CBCA can be effective in discriminating between truths and lies.

All of these studies were laboratory studies, however, and there are reasons to believe that the use of SVA is more difficult in real life. The problem is that CBCA scores are affected by factors other than the veracity of the statement. For example, older children produce statements that typically contain more CBCA criteria than younger children (Buck, Warren, Betman, & Brigham, 2002), statements are unlikely to contain many CBCA criteria if the interviewer did not give the child enough opportunity to tell the whole story (Hershkowitz, Lamb, Sternberg, & Esplin, 1997), and highly suggestible children may give an inaccurate account when leading questions are asked (Bull, 2010; Fisher, 2010). The fourth and final phase of the SVA method is to examine whether any of these alternative explanations may have affected the presence of the CBCA criteria in the transcripts. For this purpose, the Validity Checklist has been compiled and comprises 11 factors that are thought to possibly affect CBCA scores. By systematically addressing each of the factors addressed in the Validity Checklist, the evaluator explores and considers alternative interpretations of the CBCA outcomes.

There are reasons to believe that applying the Validity Checklist can be problematic. Some factors, such as susceptibility to suggestion, are difficult to measure. To examine a child's susceptibility to suggestion, the interviewer should ask the witness a few leading questions at the end of the interview (Yuille, 1988; see Chapter 1, this volume for a review of

children as witnesses). At this point, interviewers should only ask questions about irrelevant peripheral information, because asking questions about central information could damage the quality of the statement. Being allowed only to ask questions about peripheral information is problematic, as it may say little about the witness' suggestibility regarding core issues of his or her statement, because children show more resistance to suggestibility for central parts than peripheral parts of an event (Dalton & Daneman, 2006). In addition, it is difficult, if not impossible, to determine the exact impact of many factors on CBCA scores. For example, in one study SVA raters were instructed to take the age of the child into account (a factor that appears on the Validity Checklist) when calculating CBCA scores (Lamers-Winkelman & Buffing, 1996). Nevertheless, several criteria positively correlated with age.

Given these difficulties in measuring the factors and in examining the exact impact of these factors on CBCA scores, it is clear that the Validity Checklist procedure is more subjective and less formalized than the CBCA procedure. It is therefore not surprising that, if two experts disagree about the truthfulness of a statement in a German criminal case, they are likely to disagree about the likely impact of Validity Checklist issues on that statement (Vrij, 2008). One field study revealed that Swedish experts sometimes use the Validity Checklist incorrectly, which could be due to the difficulties with applying it (Gumpert & Lindblad, 2000). First, although SVA experts sometimes highlight the influence of Validity Checklist factors on children's statements in general, they do not always discuss how these factors may influence the statement of the particular child they are asked to assess. Second, although experts sometimes indicate possible external influence on statements, they are inclined to rely upon the CBCA outcome and tend to judge high-quality statements as truthful and low-quality statements as fabricated.

In sum, although SVA assessments are used as evidence in (criminal) courts to evaluate the veracity of child witnesses' testimonies in trials for sexual offences, the accuracy of these assessments is unknown. Research has shown that CBCA assessments distinguish truths from lies with 71%

accuracy, but the use of the Validity Checklist is problematic for a variety of reasons.

Scientific Content Analysis. Scientific Content Analysis (SCAN) was developed by the former Israeli police lieutenant and polygraph examiner Avioam Sapir (1987/2000). SCAN is used all over the world (Vrij, 2008) by federal law enforcement (including the U.S. Federal Bureau of Investigation), military agencies (including the U.S. Army Military Intelligence), secret services (including the CIA), and other types of investigators (including social workers, lawyers, fire investigators, and the American Society for Industrial Security; Bockstaele, 2008).

Typically, a SCAN analysis starts with asking the suspect, witness, or alleged victim to write down "everything that happened" during a particular time frame. This account is referred to as a pure version of the event and has to be produced without the presence and interference of an investigator to minimize investigator influences. The SCAN expert then evaluates the statement. There is no standardized set of SCAN criteria, but 12 criteria have been used in research (Nahari, Vrij, & Fisher, 2012).

Sapir (1987/2000) claims that some SCAN criteria are more likely to occur in truthful than in deceptive statements (e.g., denial of allegations, use of self-references), whereas other criteria are more likely to occur in deceptive than in truthful statements (e.g., change in language, missing information). The SCAN literature does not mention an underlying theoretical rationale for these predictions or a rationale for why criteria are included in the SCAN list. Examination of the SCAN criteria gives the impression that SCAN is based at least in part on a motivational approach in which liars attempt strategically to select the exact words that reflect their knowledge but hide their guilt. For example, at least four criteria explicitly deal with what the examinee did not say or concealed. Within the missing information criterion, SCAN experts look for words or phrases such as "finally," "later on," or "some time after," which can imply that some information is left out. Another SCAN criterion referring to hiding guilt is objective and subjective time. Here, the proportions of the actual durations of the activities (objective time) are compared with the number of words that the examinee used to describe these activities (subjective time). When the subjective time is shorter than the objective time, it may imply that the examinee is attempting to conceal information regarding that activity.

SCAN users refer to Driscoll's (1994) field study as evidence that SCAN works. Indeed, the accuracy rate obtained in that study was high at 83%, but a serious limitation of the study was that the ground truth could not be established. Nahari et al. (2012) tested the efficiency of SCAN in a laboratory experiment. Truth tellers truthfully wrote down their activities during the last half hour, whereas liars were asked to fabricate a story. The statements were analyzed with SCAN and, by way of comparison, also with Reality Monitoring (RM), a verbal veracity tool used by deception researchers but not used in the field (Masip, Sporer, Garrido, & Herrero, 2005; Vrij, 2008). SCAN did not distinguish truth tellers from liars above the level of chance but RM did. With RM analyses, 71% of truth tellers and liars were correctly classified.

Smith (2001) also published a SCAN field study in which she asked SCAN users and experienced detectives not trained in SCAN to judge 27 statements. The SCAN users could give truthful, deceptive, or inconclusive verdicts, and correctly classified 80% of the truths and 75% of the lies. This sounds impressive, but the group of experienced detectives untrained in SCAN obtained accuracy rates that did not differ significantly from these accuracy rates. In other words, knowledge of SCAN did not lead to a superior ability in distinguishing truths from lies. Moreover, as in Driscoll's study, the ground truth for all cases was uncertain. Armistead (2011) claims that Smith's (2001) conclusion that SCAN users were as accurate as experienced detectives untrained in SCAN was not supported by her data, but the lack of ground truth makes interpreting the accuracy rates problematic anyway.

Smith (2001) further examined whether different SCAN users were using the same criteria when applying SCAN. This is an important standardization question and a lack of ground truth does not affect the results. Smith found that different experts used different SCAN criteria to justify their decision of whether a statement was deceptive. In other words, there was a lack of consistency in the application of SCAN amongst SCAN users.

There is some overlap between SCAN and CBCA in the criteria that are examined. For example, the spontaneous corrections, lack of memory, and extraneous information criteria appear on both lists. Intriguingly, the predictions about how these criteria differ between truth tellers and liars vary. In CBCA the occurrence of those cues are perceived as indictors of truth, whereas in SCAN the same criteria are seen as indicators of deceit. Research regarding these individual criteria gives support only to the CBCA assumptions (Vrij, 2008).

In sum, SCAN is popular among practitioners and is widely used, but there is not much SCAN research available, and the research that exists has yet to demonstrate that SCAN analyses can distinguish truth tellers from liars. In addition, there are reasons to believe that there is a lack of consistency among SCAN users in applying the method.

Interviewing to Detect Deception

In physiological lie detection it has been acknowledged for a long time that the type of questioning matters. For example, the Relevant–Irrelevant polygraph test is widely criticized for asking the wrong questions (Kleiner, 2002). The rationale behind the Relevant–Irrelevant test is that deception will increase arousal. This increased arousal becomes apparent in increased heart rate, blood pressure, and skin response that will be detected by the polygraph machine. As such, the Relevant–Irrelevant Test is an anxiety-based lie-detection test. In the test, physiological responses to relevant questions (e.g., "On March 13, 2011, did you kill Julie Appletoddler?") are compared with physiological responses to irrelevant questions (e.g., "Is it today Tuesday?"), to which the examinee is instructed to give a truthful answer. Guilty examinees who deny their guilt will lie in response to the relevant question and will tell the truth in response to the irrelevant question. The relevant question should thus result in higher arousal levels than the neutral question according to the Relevant–Irrelevant test's "deception increases arousal" rationale. Truth tellers will tell the truth in response to both questions and their arousal levels should therefore not differ between the two types of

question. The test is highly criticized because it puts truth tellers at risk. There are good reasons why truth tellers might react strongly to the relevant questions, such as out of fear not to be believed. In the polygraph community the debate is ongoing whether an anxiety-based physiology test can be devised that resolves the problem of truth tellers also showing increased arousal to the relevant questions than the control questions. Most people in the academic world think that such a test cannot be composed (Iacono & Lykken, 1997), and the National Research Council (2003) is skeptical.

Only in the last 10 years it has been acknowledged that questioning also matters in nonverbal and verbal lie detection, and research about effective interview techniques has started to emerge. Based on the problems associated with anxiety-based tests that emerged in the physiological lie-detection debate, a new, cognitive approach is pursued. The assumption is that it is possible to ask questions that raise cognitive load more in liars than in truth tellers. Three cognitive lie detection approaches have emerged to date, the imposing cognitive load, asking unanticipated questions, and strategic use of evidence approaches. They are outlined in this section.

Imposing cognitive load.   Sources varying from self-reports to fMRI research have shown that lying is often more cognitively demanding than truth telling (Vrij, Fisher, et al., 2006; Vrij, Granhag, Mann, & Leal, 2011; Vrij, Granhag, & Porter, 2010). Factors that contribute to the increased cognitive load include formulating the lie; the liar's inclination to monitor and control his demeanor in order to appear honest to the investigator; the liar's inclination to monitor the investigator's reactions carefully in order to assess whether he appears to be getting away with the lie; the liar's need to suppress the truth whilst he is fabricating; and the fact that activation of the truth often happens automatically, whereas activation of the lie is more intentional and deliberate.

An investigator could exploit the differential levels of cognitive load that truth tellers and liars experience to discriminate more effectively between them. Liars who require more cognitive resources than truth tellers will have fewer cognitive resources left over. If cognitive demand is further raised, which could be achieved by making additional requests such as telling a story in reverse order or maintain eye contact with the interviewer, liars do not cope with these additional tasks as well as truth tellers. As a result, more cues to deception occur, and observers are better at detecting deceit (Vrij et al., 2008; Vrij, Mann, Leal, & Fisher, 2010). For example, in the reverse-order experiment in which truth tellers and liars either recalled an alleged activity in reverse order or in normal chronological time order (Vrij et al., 2008), nine cues to deceit emerged in the reverse-order condition compared to one cue in the chronological time order (control) condition. In the reverse-order condition, observers could detect lies with 60% accuracy compared to a 42% accuracy rate in the control condition.

An alternative way to impose cognitive load on liars is to ensure that truth tellers will provide more information in a given interview setting. Talkative truth tellers raise the standard for liars, who also need to become more talkative to match truth tellers. Liars may be reluctant to add more information out of fear that it gives their lies away. They also may find it too difficult or lack the imagination to add as many details as truth tellers do, or what information they do add may be of lesser quality or may sound less plausible. We recently successfully tested one way of increasing the amount of detail truth tellers generate. In the experiment, two interviewers were used (Mann et al., 2013). The second interviewer was silent but showed different demeanors during the interview. In one condition he was supportive throughout (e.g., nodding his head and smiling); in a second condition he was neutral, and in a third condition he was suspicious (e.g., frowning). Being supportive during an interview facilitates talking and encourages cooperative witnesses (e.g., truth tellers) to talk (Memon, Meissner, & Fraser, 2010; Bull, 2010; Fisher, 2010). Indeed, truth tellers provided most detail in the supportive condition, and only in that condition did they provide significantly more detail than liars (Mann et al., 2013). Based on detail, 71% of truth tellers and liars were correctly classified in the supportive condition compared to 55% in the neutral condition.

In sum, imposing cognitive load can be achieved in two different ways: first, by using interventions that increase the difficulty to recall information (reverse order and maintaining eye contact), and, second, by using interventions that makes examinees more talkative.

Asking unanticipated questions.   A consistent finding in deception research is that liars prepare themselves when anticipating an interview (Hartwig, Granhag, & Strömwall, 2007). This strategy makes sense. Planning makes lying easier, and planned lies typically contain fewer cues to deceit than do spontaneous lies (DePaulo et al., 2003). The positive effects of planning, however, will only emerge if liars correctly anticipate the questions that will be asked. Investigators can exploit this limitation by asking questions that liars do not anticipate. Though liars can refuse to answer unanticipated questions, such "I don't know" or "I can't remember" responses will create suspicion if the questions are about central (but unanticipated) aspects of the target event. To test the unanticipated-questions technique, pairs of liars and truth tellers were interviewed individually about an alleged visit to a restaurant (Vrij et al., 2009). The conventional opening questions (e.g., "What did you do in the restaurant?") were anticipated, whereas spatial questions (e.g., "Where did you and your friend sit?") and the request to sketch the layout of the restaurant were not. (Anticipation was established with the interviewees after the interview.) Based on the overlap (similarity) in the pair members' drawings, 80% of the liars and truth tellers were classified correctly (the drawings were less alike for the pairs of liars than pairs of truth tellers), whereas on the basis of the conventional questions the pairs were not classified above chance level. A difference in overlap between anticipated and unanticipated questions further indicated deceit. Pairs of truth tellers showed the same amount of overlap in their answers to the anticipated and unanticipated questions, whereas liars showed significantly more overlap in their answers to the anticipated questions than in their answers to the unanticipated questions.

Comparing the answers to anticipated and unanticipated questions can also be used to detect deceit in individual liars. In an experiment by Warmelink, Vrij, Mann, Jundi, and Granhag (2012), truth tellers and liars (who were given the opportunity to prepare themselves) were interviewed about their alleged forthcoming trip. Expected questions about the purpose of the trip (e.g., "What is the main purpose of your trip?") were followed by unexpected questions about transport (e.g., "How are you going to travel to your destination?"), planning ("What part of the trip was easiest to plan?"), and the core event ("Keep in mind an image of the most important thing you are going to do at this trip. Please describe this mental image in detail."). The hypothesis was that liars are likely to have prepared answers to the expected questions and may therefore be able to answer them in considerable detail. Liars will not have prepared answers for the unexpected questions and may therefore struggle to generate detailed answers to them. Indeed, compared to truth tellers, liars gave significantly more detail to the expected questions and significantly less detail to the unexpected questions.

The strategic use of evidence.   Lying and truthful suspects enter police interviews with different mental states (Granhag & Hartwig, 2008). Guilty suspects will often have unique knowledge about the crime, which, if recognized by the interviewer, makes it obvious that they are the perpetrators. Their main concern will be to ensure that the interviewer does not gain that knowledge. In contrast, innocent suspects face the opposite problem, fearing that the interviewer will not learn or believe what they did at the time of the crime. These different mental states result in different counter-interrogation strategies for liars and truth tellers (Hartwig et al., 2007). Guilty suspects are inclined to use avoidance strategies (e.g., in a free recall, they may avoid mentioning that they were at a certain place at a certain time) or denial strategies (e.g., they may deny having been at a certain place at a certain time when directly asked). In contrast, innocent suspects neither avoid nor escape but are forthcoming and "tell the truth like it happened" (Granhag & Hartwig, 2008).

When investigators possess critical and possibly incriminating background information (evidence) in a case, they can exploit these differential truth tellers' and liars' strategies by introducing the available evidence during the interview in a strategic manner, known as the Strategic Use of Evidence technique (SUE). When questions about the evidence are asked, the forthcoming innocent suspects will be more consistent with the available evidence than the avoidant/denying guilty suspects.

In the SUE technique, three groups of tactics are relevant: evidence tactics, question tactics, and disclosure tactics (Granhag, Strömwall, Willén, & Hartwig, 2013). The evidence tactics are used primarily to assess the evidence in the planning phase; the question tactics are used systematically to exhaust the alternative explanations that a suspect may have to account for the evidence; and the disclosure tactics are used to maximise the diagnostic value of the evidence. Granhag et al. (2013) tested the so-called Evidence Framing Matrix, which is an example of a disclosure tactic. This matrix suggests that when one piece of evidence is disclosed, two dimensions are particularly helpful in illuminating the different framing alternatives that exist: the strength of the source of the evidence, which can vary from weak to strong, and the degree of precision of the evidence, which can vary from low to high. Granhag et al. (2013) found that using this matrix to reveal the evidence in a stepwise manner, moving from the most indirect form of framing (weak source/low specificity, e.g., "We have information telling us that you recently visited the central station.") to the most direct form of framing (strong source/high specificity, e.g., "We have CCTV footage showing that you collected a package from a deposit box at the central station, ground floor level, on the 24th of August at 7.30 p.m."), elicited more and stronger cues to deception than using the most direct form of framing only. In other words, it was found that both when and how the evidence was disclosed moderated the effectiveness of disclosure. It was most effective to disclose the evidence late rather than early in the interview, and it was most effective when the evidence became progressively stronger and more precise.

Hartwig, Granhag, Strömwall, and Kronkvist (2006) tested the SUE technique at a Swedish police academy. Swedish police trainees, half of whom were trained in the SUE technique, interviewed mock suspects who had or had not stolen a wallet from a briefcase. The SUE trained interviewers obtained 85.4% accuracy, whereas the untrained interviewers obtained 56.1% accuracy. In addition, the liars' answers were more inconsistent with the evidence than the truth tellers' answers. The SUE technique has been found to be successful in eliciting cues to deception for lying adults and lying children, for lying single suspects and lying multiple suspects, and for suspects lying about their past actions and lying about their intentions (Vrij & Granhag, 2012a).

Lie Detection in Intelligence Interviews

Terrorist attacks across the world and the continuing threat of such attacks have made the urge to prevent them paramount. Gathering information to prevent terrorist attacks often comes from interviewing people (Loftus, 2011), and in such interviews lie detection can be important (Loftus, 2011). It requires interviewing known and potential terrorists, or other people who may possess valuable information. The threat of terrorism has further led to an increased emphasis on the detection of deception in public spaces, such as country borders, security checkpoints, bus terminals, train stations, shopping malls, and sports venues (Cooke & Winner, 2008; Driskell, Salas, & Driskell, 2012). Deception detection in intelligence interviews differs in several ways from deception detection in police suspect interviews, the traditional domain of forensic deception research (Vrij & Granhag, 2012a; Vrij, Granhag, & Porter, 2010). For example, in police interviews investigators typically focus on a suspect's past activities, but in intelligence interviews investigators are often interested in someone's future activities (e.g., intentions). Another difference in intelligence interviews is that investigators, particularly those who are working in an undercover capacity, sometimes have good reason not to tell the interviewees that the "chat" they have with them is in fact an interview. A third difference is that terrorist acts are often planned and executed by groups rather than individuals. A fourth difference is that police suspect interviews are typically focused on solving crimes through obtaining admissions or confessions from suspects, whereas intelligence interviews are more about gathering information (Brandon, 2011).

Intentions.   Most forensic deception research deals with lying about past activities. This makes sense because most of that research focuses on police interviewing, and the police mostly interview suspects about their alleged past activities. In counterterrorism, however, being able to discriminate between true and false accounts about future activities (e.g., intentions) is of paramount importance, as this addresses the issue of preventing criminal acts from occurring. An example of the negative consequences that arise if an offender is falsely believed is given in the Importance of the Problem section.

Deception research about intentions has commenced (see Granhag, 2010, for an overview), and the pattern that emerges from these experiments is that intentions reveal different verbal cues to deceit than past activities. For example, the verbal criterion "detail," a diagnostic cue to deceit when interviewees discuss their past activities, is less likely to emerge as a cue to deceit when interviewees discuss their future activities (Vrij, Leal, Mann, & Granhag, 2011). One aspect that often makes truth tellers' stories about past activities more detailed than liars' is that there is a wealth of perceptual details that truth tellers have experienced during these past activities that they can recall (if they still remember them; see Chapter 7, this volume for a review of eyewitness memory). In contrast, when discussing their intentions about a forthcoming activity, truth tellers have not yet experienced anything that restricts the amount of detail in their recall of intentions.

There may be a diagnostic cue to deceit that is uniquely related to lying about intentions: the elicitation of mental images. In Granhag and Knieps's (2011) experiment, participants who told the truth about their intentions agreed more frequently that planning their future actions evoked mental images than did participants who lied about their intentions. In addition, liars who claimed to have activated a mental image during the planning phase provided verbal descriptions of it that were less rich in detail than truth tellers. Those findings are in alignment with the concept of episodic future thought, which represents the ability to mentally pre-experience a one-time personal event that may occur in the future (Schacter & Addis, 2007). People who make up a plan for a future event that they intend to execute seem to activate a more concrete (detailed) mental image of the upcoming scenario than do those who adopt a plan that they do not intend to execute (Watanabe, 2005).

Undercover interviewing. In some investigative contexts, law enforcement and security personnel may have good reason to extract information from suspects without them actually being aware that they are under investigation. In particular, law enforcement officers working in an undercover capacity and interacting with potential suspects in informal settings will not wish to draw attention to themselves or to arouse suspicion about their motives by using direct question formats. For example, in settings where an undercover officer has become embedded within a criminal gang or is required to interact with suspects in order to collect intelligence, the ability to elicit relevant and usable information without detection is critical. In addition, in the United Kingdom the police were accused of misuse of terror laws when they stopped innocent photographers taking pictures of tourist attractions (see Jundi, Vrij, Mann, Hillman, & Hope, in press).

A possible solution in such situations is to conduct interviews without the suspect actually knowing they are being interviewed (so-called undercover interviewing). For example, an undercover interviewer could pose as a tourist pretending to take pictures of tourist attractions. Undercover interviewing may shed light on whether an individual has criminal intentions without arousing their suspicion in such circumstances. To date one undercover interviewing deception experiment has been published, and, encouragingly, that experiment demonstrated that undercover interviews can reveal deceit (Vrij, Mann, Jundi, Hope, & Leal, 2012). Liars (posing as tourists) and actual tourists were interviewed in a seemingly innocuous manner about their travel plans by an undercover investigator. Truth tellers and liars provided different responses, particularly to spatial questions (e.g., "Show me on this map the locations you just said you are going to visit?"). Liars were less accurate than truth tellers in pointing out the locations they claimed they would visit. This is an example of an effective unanticipated question: Liars do not expect spatial questions and have not prepared answers to them.

Lying by networks. Most deception research addresses individual truth tellers and liars, but terrorists often act in pairs or larger groups. For example, the London 7/7 bombers entered the Underground together, and the 9/11 bombers worked together to plan and execute the attacks. Groups of people can be interviewed in two different ways, separate or together. In the previous section, we discussed an efficient way of interviewing pairs of suspects separately by asking them unanticipated questions. Liars who have not prepared answers to those questions are more likely to show less overlap in their responses than truth tellers who can search their memory for the answers.

When people travel together, or in other situations when they are together, it may be convenient to interview them together. Recent research has shown that this method results in diagnostic cues to deceit. In one experiment, pairs of truth tellers were interviewed together about a visit to a restaurant. The liars did not visit the restaurant but had to pretend that they did visit the restaurant together. They were given time to prepare themselves for the interview. Memory research has shown that when pairs of truth tellers recall a jointly experienced event during an interview, they communicate substantially with each other in an attempt to collectively recall all the details they know, and to correct each other's stories. In this respect, Hollingshead (1998) refers to transaction information search. Consistent with this view, pairs of truth tellers interrupted and corrected each other more, and added more information to each other's stories than liars (Vrij, Jundi, et al., 2012). Two other experiments also found support for the idea that truth tellers communicate more with each other. Jundi et al. (2013) found that pairs of truth tellers looked more at each other and less at the interviewer than pairs of liars; and Driskell et al. (2012) found that pairs of truth tellers made more speech transitions than pairs of liars (one person's speech immediately follows the other's within the flow of the conversation).

PRACTICE AND POLICY ISSUES

In this section the implications of the research review in terms of application of the various lie-detection techniques are briefly summarized. This section further contains two final thoughts. One addresses the idea whether cognitive lie detection strategies are not "too lenient" on suspects to obtain useful results. The second addresses the urge to establish clear decision rules in lie-detection tools.

Nonverbal Lie Detection

There is no evidence that guilty and innocent suspects respond to the BAI questions in the way BAI investigators believe they do. Regarding observing facial expressions of emotions, microexpressions hardly occur, and there is no empirical evidence available to date showing that they distinguish truth tellers from liars. Although facial expressions of emotions do differentiate truth tellers from liars, observing such expressions will lead to a considerably lower accuracy rate (60%–70% in high-stakes situations, lower in other situations) than the 95% claimed by Paul Ekman. The findings that truth tellers can also show signs of nervousness and that no questions can be asked that makes liars necessarily more nervous than truth tellers makes the use of anxiety-based lie nonverbal detection techniques problematic.

Verbal Lie Detection

SVA is the only tool among the verbal and nonverbal veracity tools that is used as evidence in criminal courts. Research into CBCA, the key part of SVA, has revealed an error rate of 29%. This implies that CBCA assessments are not made "beyond reasonable doubt," which is the standard of proof typically set in criminal courts. In other words, the research accumulated to date does not justify the use of CBCA/SVA as evidence in criminal courts. CBCA assessments do result in approximately 71% accuracy in classifying truth tellers and liars, however, which makes CBCA a useful tool to apply in investigative interviewing situations—considerably more

useful than SCAN, which failed to accumulate any empirical support to date.

Interviewing to Detect Deception

Research during the last 10 years has indicated that investigators can improve their ability to detect deceit by applying specific questioning techniques. The three approaches reported in the interviewing to detect deception section, imposing cognitive load, asking unanticipated questions and the strategic use of evidence, have in common that they are based on the assumption that interviewers can use techniques that liars find more difficult to address than truth tellers. This cognitive lie detection approach is now the dominant approach in lie detection research (Evans, Houston, & Meissner, 2012; Kassin, 2012; Lane & Vieira, 2012; Vrij & Granhag, 2012a, 2012b), and practitioners are encouraged to use it by both scholars (Kassin, 2012) and practitioners (Tedeschini, 2012).

Lie Detection in Intelligence Interviewing

Lie detection in intelligence interviewing differs in certain aspects from lie detection in police interviewing, the more traditional forensic context. There are some unique challenges for lie detection in intelligence interviews, and three of them have been discussed: lying about intentions, and undercover and collective interviewing. Research has commenced in all these areas with some promising results, but more research is needed.

Are Cognitive Lie Detection Approaches Too Lenient?

The stereotypical view, often addressed in police manuals, is that suspects are reluctant to talk and that the investigator needs to use an accusatory approach to get them to talk. This approach is characterized by accusation, the use of minimization and maximization techniques, and the disallowing of denials (Inbau et al., 2013). The view that such techniques are needed is not shared by all practitioners in the field. Ali Soufan (2011), a successful U.S. Federal Bureau of Investigation interrogator who gathered a substantial amount of valuable information when interrogating al-Qaeda terrorists, did not use an accusatory approach. Instead he used a cognitive, information-gathering approach characterized by rapport building, truth seeking, and listening. For example, he noticed that spatial questions are difficult to address by liars, a finding that also emerged from experimental laboratory research discussed above. The question of whether accusatory techniques are needed to obtain valuable results can be answered better via research than via anecdotal evidence. Such research has shown that the idea that suspects in police interviews are unwilling to talk in information-gathering interviews is a myth rather than fact. A systematic analysis of more than 1067 such police interviews in the United Kingdom has shown that only 5% of the suspects remained silent (Moston, Stephenson, & Williamson, 1993). In addition, in his analysis of 600 information-gathering police interviews, Baldwin (1993) found that 80% of the suspects were thoroughly cooperative and answered police questions of significance.

Furthermore, a recent meta-analysis of field and laboratory studies about the influence of the interview/interrogation method on confession outcomes revealed that cognitive information-gathering approaches elicited more diagnostic cues to deception and more diagnostic information in general than accusatorial methods (Meissner, Redlich, Bhatt, & Brandon, 2012). In summary, research findings do not support the idea that accusatory techniques are needed to yield success in interviews. On the contrary, cognitive information-gathering styles yield better results in terms of obtaining information and eliciting cues to deceit.

Clear Decision Rules in Lie-Detection Tools

For a lie-detection technique to be useful in the field, it is desirable that it includes a clear decision rule indicating when someone is truthful or deceptive. Such scores are often not available. Take for example CBCA: The CBCA rater will calculate a final CBCA score with the assumption that the higher the score the more likely it is that the person is telling the truth. There is no decision rule, however, that informs the investigator which scores indicate truth and which indicate lie. This is due to the fact that CBCA scores are influenced by factors

other than veracity, such as the quality of the interview style. The BAI shares this problem and also has no clear decision rule. In contrast, the SUE technique has a decision rule (contradicting the evidence means deception), which makes the technique easier to use. Other ways of creating decision rules is to break the interview into two parts and compare the responses of the interviewee to those two parts. As discussed above, interviewees can be asked a mixture of anticipated and unanticipated questions. Liars have in all likelihood prepared answers to the anticipated questions but will not have prepared answers to the unanticipated questions. They are likely to be more detailed in answering the anticipated questions than the unanticipated questions. In contrast, truth tellers can search their memory for both sets of questions and are likely to be able to answer the two sets of questions in the same amount of detail.

SUMMARY AND CONCLUSIONS

In an attempt to catch liars, nonverbal and verbal lie-detection tools have been developed and are used in the field. Research has demonstrated that some of these tools, and CBCA in particular, can distinguish truth tellers and liars above chance. Research has yet to show that other tools, and SCAN and BAI in particular, actually work. In recent years a shift took place in nonverbal and verbal lie detection research, with a strong emphasis on cognitive-based interview protocols. Research has shown that such interview protocols can improve an investigator's ability to detect deceit. A new domain of research examines deception in intelligence interviews, which differs in several aspects from traditional police interviews and therefore requires new deception detection techniques. The emerging literature showed promising results for the ability to detect lies in this important area.

References

Armistead, T. W. (2011). Detecting deception in written statements: The British Home Office study of scientific content analysis (SCAN). *Policing, 34,* 588–605. doi:10.1108/13639511111180225

Arntzen, F. (1982). Die Situation der Forensischen Aussagenpsychologie in der Bundesrepublik

Deutschland. In A. Trankell (Ed.), *Reconstructing the past: The role of psychologists in criminal trials* (pp. 107–120). Deventer, the Netherlands: Kluwer.

Baldwin, J. (1993). Police interview techniques. *British Journal of Criminology, 33*, 325–352.

Bockstaele, M. (2008). Scientific Content Analysis (SCAN). Een nutting instrument by verhoren? In L. Smets & A. Vrij (Eds.), *Het analyseren van de geloofwaardigheid van verhoren* (pp. 105–156). Brussels, Belgium: Politeia.

Bond, C. F., & Fahey, W. E. (1987). False suspicion and the misperception of deceit. *British Journal of Social Psychology, 26*, 41–46. doi:10.1111/j.2044-8309.1987.tb00759.x

Brandon, S. E. (2011). Impacts of psychological science on national security agencies post-9/11. *American Psychologist, 66*, 495–506. doi:10.1037/a0024818

Buck, J. A., Warren, A. R., Betman, S., & Brigham, J. C. (2002). Age differences in Criteria-Based Content Analysis scores in typical child sexual abuse interviews. *Journal of Applied Developmental Psychology, 23*, 267–283. doi:10.1016/S0193-3973(02)00107-7

Buckley, J. P. (2012). Detecting of deception researchers need to collaborate with experienced practitioners. *Journal of Applied Research in Memory and Cognition, 1*, 126–127. doi:10.1016/j.jarmac.2012.04.002

Bull, R. (2010). The investigative interviewing of children and other vulnerable witnesses: Psychological research and working/professional practice. *Legal and Criminological Psychology, 15*, 5–23. doi:10.1348/014466509X440160

Christ, S. E., van Essen, D. C. Watson, J. M., Brubaker, L. E., & McDermott, K. B. (2009). The contributions of prefrontal cortex and executive control to deception: Evidence from activation likelihood estimate meta-analyses. *Cerebral Cortex, 19*, 1557–1566. doi:10.1093/cercor/bhn189

Cooke, N. J., & Winner, J. L. (2008). Human factors of homeland security. In D. A. Boehm-Davis (Ed.), *Reviews of human factors and ergonomics* (Vol. 3, pp. 79–110). Santa Monica, CA: Human Factors and Ergonomics Society.

Dalton, A. L., & Daneman, M. (2006). Social suggestibility to central and peripheral misinformation. *Memory, 14*, 486–501. doi:10.1080/09658210500495073

DePaulo, B. M., Lindsay, J. L., Malone, B. E., Muhlenbruck, L., Charlton, K., & Cooper, H. (2003). Cues to deception. *Psychological Bulletin, 129*, 74–118. doi:10.1037/0033-2909.129.1.74

Driscoll, L. N. (1994). A validity assessment of written statements from suspects in criminal investigations using the SCAN technique. *Police Studies, 17*, 77–88.

Driskell, J. E., Salas, E., & Driskell, T. (2012). Social indicators of deception. *Human Factors, 54*, 577–588.

Ekman, P. (2001). *Telling lies: Clues to deceit in the marketplace, politics, and marriage.* New York, NY: Norton. (Original work published 1985)

Ekman, P. (2006, October 29). How to spot a terrorist on the fly. *Washington Post.* Retrieved from http://www.washingtonpost.com/wp-dyn/content/article/2006/10/27/AR2006102701478_2.html

Evans, J. R., Houston, K. A., & Meissner, C. A. (2012). A positive collaborative, and theoretically-based approach to improving deception detection. *Journal of Applied Research in Memory and Cognition, 1*, 122–123. doi:10.1016/j.jarmac.2012.04.007

Fisher, R. P. (2010). Interviewing cooperative witnesses. *Legal and Criminological Psychology, 15*, 25–38. doi:10.1348/135532509X441891

Gamer, M. (2011). Detection of deception and concealed information using neuroimaging techniques. In B. Verschuere, G. Ben-Shakhar, & E. Meijer (Eds.), *Memory detection: Theory and application of the concealed information test* (pp. 90–113). Cambridge, England: Cambridge University Press. doi:10.1017/CBO9780511975196.006

Granhag, P. A. (2010). On the psycho-legal study of true and false intentions: Dangerous waters and some stepping stones. *Open Criminology Journal, 3*, 37–43. doi:10.2174/1874917801003020037

Granhag, P. A., & Hartwig, M. (2008). A new theoretical perspective on deception detection: On the psychology of instrumental mind-reading. *Psychology, Crime & Law, 14*, 189–200. doi:10.1080/10683160701645181

Granhag, P. A., & Knieps, M. (2011). Episodic future thought: Illuminating the trademarks of forming true and false intentions. *Applied Cognitive Psychology, 25*, 274–280. doi:10.1002/acp.1674

Granhag, P. A., Strömwall, L. A., Willén, R., & Hartwig, M. (2013). Eliciting cues to deception by tactical disclosure of evidence: The first test of the Evidence Framing Matrix. *Legal and Criminological Psychology, 18*, 341–355. doi:10.1111/j.2044-8333.2012.02047.x

Gumpert, C. H., & Lindblad, F. (2000). Expert testimony on child sexual abuse: A qualitative study of the Swedish approach to statement analysis. *Expert Evidence, 7*, 279–314. doi:10.1023/A:1016657130623

Hartwig, M., Granhag, P. A., & Strömwall, L. (2007). Guilty and innocent suspects' strategies during interrogations. *Psychology, Crime & Law, 13*, 213–227. doi:10.1080/10683160600750264

Hartwig, M., Granhag, P. A., Strömwall, L., & Kronkvist, O. (2006). Strategic use of evidence during police interrogations: When training to detect deception works. *Law and Human Behavior, 30*, 603–619. doi:10.1007/s10979-006-9053-9

Henig, R. M. (2006, February 5). Looking for the lie. *New York Times Magazine*. Retrieved from http://www.nytimes.com/2006/02/05/magazine/05lying.html

Hershkowitz, I., Lamb, M. E., Sternberg, K. J., & Esplin, P. W. (1997). The relationships among interviewer utterance type, CBCA scores and the richness of children's responses. *Legal and Criminological Psychology, 2*, 169–176. doi:10.1111/j.2044-8333.1997.tb00341.x

Hocking, J. E., & Leathers, D. G. (1980). Nonverbal indicators of deception: A new theoretical perspective. *Communication Monographs, 47*, 119–131. doi:10.1080/03637758009376025

Hollingshead, A. B. (1998). Retrieval processes in transactive memory systems. *Journal of Personality and Social Psychology, 74*, 659–671. doi:10.1037/0022-3514.74.3.659

Horvath, F. (1973). Verbal and nonverbal cues to truth and deception during polygraph examinations. *Journal of Police Science and Administration, 1*, 138–152.

Horvath, F., Blair, J. P., & Buckley, J. P. (2008). The behavioral analysis interview: Clarifying the practice, theory and understanding of its use and effectiveness. *International Journal of Police Science and Management, 10*, 101–118. doi:10.1350/ijps.2008.10.1.101

Horvath, F., Jayne, B., & Buckley, J. (1994). Differentiation of truthful and deceptive criminal suspects in behavioral analysis interviews. *Journal of Forensic Sciences, 39*, 793–807.

Iacono, W. G. (2008). Accuracy of polygraph techniques: Problems using confessions to determine ground truth. *Physiology and Behavior, 95*, 24–26. doi:10.1016/j.physbeh.2008.06.001

Iacono, W. G., & Lykken, D. T. (1997). The validity of the lie detector: Two surveys of scientific opinion. *Journal of Applied Psychology, 82*, 426–433. doi:10.1037/0021-9010.82.3.426

Inbau, F. E., Reid, J. E., Buckley, J. P., & Jayne, B. C. (2013). *Criminal interrogation and confessions* (5th ed.). Burlington, MA: Jones & Bartlett Learning.

Jundi, S., Vrij, A., Mann, S., Hillman, J., & Hope, L. (in press). "I'm a photographer, not a terrorist": The use of photography to detect deception. *Psychology, Crime & Law*.

Jundi, S., Vrij, A., Mann, S., Hope, L., Hillman, J., Warmelink, L., & Gahr, E. (2013). Who should I look at? Eye contact during collective interviewing as a cue to deceit. *Psychology, Crime & Law, 19*, 661–771. doi:10.1080/1068316X.2013.793332

Kassin, S. M. (2012). Paradigm shift in the study of human lie-detection: Bridging the gap between science and practice. *Journal of Applied Research in Memory and Cognition, 1*, 118–119. doi:10.1016/j.jarmac.2012.04.009

Kassin, S. M., & Fong, C. T. (1999). "I'm innocent!": Effects of training on judgments of truth and deception in the interrogation room. *Law and Human Behavior, 23*, 499–516. doi:10.1023/A:1022330011811

Kleiner, M. (2002). *Handbook of polygraph testing*. San Diego, CA: Academic Press.

Köhnken, G. (1996). Social psychology and the law. In G. R. Semin & K. Fiedler (Eds.), *Applied social psychology* (pp. 257–281). London, Great Britain: Sage Publications. doi:10.4135/9781446250556.n10

Köhnken, G. (2004). Statement validity analysis and the detection of the truth. In P. A. Granhag & L. A. Strömwall (Eds.), *Deception detection in forensic contexts* (pp. 41–63). Cambridge, England: Cambridge University Press. doi:10.1017/CBO9780511490071.003

Köhnken, G., & Steller, M. (1988). The evaluation of the credibility of child witness statements in German procedural system. In G. Davies & J. Drinkwater (Eds.), *The child witness: Do the courts abuse children?* (Issues in Criminological and Legal Psychology, No. 13; pp. 37–45). Leicester, United Kingdom: British Psychological Society.

Lamers-Winkelman, F., & Buffing, F. (1996). Children's testimony in the Netherlands: A study of Statement Validity Analysis. In B. L. Bottoms & G. S. Goodman (Eds.), *International perspectives on child abuse and children's testimony* (pp. 45–61). Thousand Oaks, CA: Sage Publications. doi:10.4135/9781483327501.n3

Lane, S. M., & Vieira, K. M. (2012). Steering a new course for deception detection research. *Journal of Applied Research in Memory and Cognition, 1*, 136–138. doi:10.1016/j.jarmac.2012.04.001

Leal, S., Vrij, A., Mann, S., & Fisher, R. (2010). Detecting true and false opinions: The devil's advocate approach as a lie detection aid. *Acta Psychologica, 134*, 323–329. doi:10.1016/j.actpsy.2010.03.005

Loftus, E. F. (2011). Intelligence gathering post-9/11. *American Psychologist, 66*, 532–541. doi:10.1037/a0024614

Mann, S., Vrij, A., & Bull, R. (2004). Detecting true lies: Police officers' ability to detect deceit. *Journal of Applied Psychology, 89*, 137–149. doi:10.1037/0021-9010.89.1.137

Mann, S., Vrij, A., Shaw, D. J., Leal, S., Ewans, S., Hillman, J., . . . Fisher, R. P. (2013). Two heads are better than one? How to effectively use two interviewers to elicit cues to deception. *Legal and Criminological Psychology, 18*, 324–340. doi:10.1111/j.2044-8333.2012.02055.x

Masip, J., Barba, A., & Herrero, C. (2012). Behaviour analysis interview and common sense. A study with novice and experienced officers. *Psychiatry, Psychology and Law, 19*, 21–34. doi:10.1080/13218719.2010.543402

Masip, J., & Herrero, C. (2013). What would you say if you were guilty? Suspects' strategies during a hypothetical behavior analysis interview concerning a serious crime. *Applied Cognitive Psychology, 27*, 60–70. doi:10.1002/acp.2872

Masip, J., Herrero, C., Garrido, E., & Barba, A. (2011). Is the behaviour analysis interview just common sense? *Applied Cognitive Psychology, 25*, 593–604. doi:10.1002/acp.1728

Masip, J., Sporer, S., Garrido, E., & Herrero, C. (2005). The detection of deception with the reality monitoring approach: A review of the empirical evidence. *Psychology, Crime & Law, 11*, 99–122. doi:10.1080/10683160410001726356

Meissner, C. A., Redlich, A. D., Bhatt, S., & Brandon, S. (2012). Interview and interrogation methods and their effects on true and false confessions. *Campbell Systematic Reviews, 8*(13). doi:10.4073/csr.2012.13

Memon, A., Meissner, C. A., & Fraser, J. (2010). The cognitive interview: A meta-analytic review and study space analysis of the past 25 years. *Psychology, Public Policy, and Law, 16*, 340–372. doi:10.1037/a0020518

Moston, S. J., Stephenson, G. M., & Williamson, T. M. (1993). The incidence, antecedents and consequences of the use of the right to silence during police questioning. *Criminal Behaviour and Mental Health, 3*, 30–47.

Nahari, G., Vrij, A., & Fisher, R. P. (2012). Does the truth come out in the writing? SCAN as a lie detection tool. *Law and Human Behavior, 36*, 68–76. doi:10.1037/h0093965

National Research Council. (2003). The polygraph and lie detection. *Committee to Review the Scientific Evidence on the Polygraph.* Washington, DC: The National Academic Press.

Obituary: Toulouse gunman Mohamed Merah. (2012, March 22). *BBC World News.* Retrieved from http://www.bbc.com/news/world-europe-17456541

Ofshe, R. J., & Leo, R. A. (1997). The decision to confess falsely: Rational choice and irrational action. *Denver University Law Review, 74*, 979–1112.

Porter, S., & ten Brinke, L. (2008). Reading between the lies: Identifying concealed and falsified emotions in universal facial expressions. *Psychological Science, 19*, 508–514. doi:10.1111/j.1467-9280.2008.02116.x

Porter, S., & Yuille, J. C. (1996). The language of deceit: An investigation of the verbal clues to deception in the interrogation context. *Law and Human Behavior, 20*, 443–458. doi:10.1007/BF01498980

Reid, J. E., & Arther, R. O. (1953). Behavior symptoms of lie-detector subjects. *Journal of Criminal Law, Criminology, and Police Science, 44*, 104–108. doi:10.2307/1139477

Rosenfeld, J. P. (2011). P300 in detecting concealed information. In B. Verschuere, G. Ben-Shakhar, & E. Meijer (Eds.), *Memory detection: Theory and application of the concealed information test* (pp. 63–89). Cambridge, England: Cambridge University Press.

Ruby, C. L., & Brigham, J. C. (1997). The usefulness of the criteria-based content analysis technique in distinguishing between truthful and fabricated allegations. *Psychology, Public Policy, and Law, 3*, 705–737. doi:10.1037/1076-8971.3.4.705

Ruby, C. L., & Brigham, J. C. (1998). Can criteria-based content analysis distinguish between true and false statements of African-American speakers? *Law and Human Behavior, 22*, 369–388. doi:10.1023/A:1025766825429

Sapir, A. (2000). *The LSI course on scientific content analysis (SCAN).* Phoenix, AZ: Laboratory for Scientific Interrogation. (Original work published 1987)

Schacter, D. L., & Addis, D. R. (2007). The cognitive neuroscience of constructive memory: Remembering the past and imagining the future. *Philosophical Transactions of the Royal Society, 392*, 773–786. doi:10.1098/rstb.2007.2087

Smith, N. (2001). *Reading between the lines: An evaluation of the scientific content analysis technique (SCAN).* London, England: Research, Development and Statistics Directorate, Home Office.

Soufan, A. H. (2011). *The black banners: The inside story of 9/11 and the war against al-Qaeda.* New York, NY: Norton.

Steller, M., & Köhnken, G. (1989). Criteria-based content analysis. In D. C. Raskin (Ed.), *Psychological methods in criminal investigation and evidence* (pp. 217–245). New York, NY: Springer-Verlag.

Tedeschini, J. (2012). Overcoming roadblocks to reform. *Journal of Applied Research in Memory and Cognition, 1*, 134–135. doi:10.1016/j.jarmac.2012.04.008

ten Brinke, L., MacDonald, S., Porter, S., & O'Connor, B. (2012). Crocodile tears: Facial, verbal and body language behaviours associated with genuine and fabricated remorse. *Law and Human Behavior, 36*, 51–59. doi:10.1037/h0093950

ten Brinke, L., & Porter, S. (2012). Cry me a river: Identifying the behavioural consequences of extremely high-stakes interpersonal deception. *Law and Human Behavior, 36*, 469–477. doi:10.1037/h0093929

ten Brinke, L., Porter, S., & Baker, A. (2012). Darwin the detective: Observable facial muscle contractions reveal emotional high-stakes lies. *Evolution and Human Behavior, 33*, 411–416. doi:10.1016/j.evolhumbehav.2011.12.003

Trankell, A. (1972). *Reliability of evidence.* Stockholm, Sweden: Beckmans.

Trovillo, P. V. (1939). A history of lie detection, I. *Journal of Criminal Law and Criminology, 29*, 848–881. doi:10.2307/1136489

Undeutsch, U. (1982). Statement reality analysis. In A. Trankell (Ed.), *Reconstructing the past: The role of psychologists in criminal trials* (pp. 27–56). Deventer, the Netherlands: Kluwer.

Undeutsch, U. (1989). The development of statement reality analysis. In J. C. Yuille (Ed.), *Credibility assessment* (pp. 101–119). Dordrecht, the Netherlands: Kluwer. doi:10.1007/978-94-015-7856-1_6

Verschuere, B., Ben-Shakhar, G., & Meijer, E. (Eds.). (2011). *Memory detection: Theory and application of the concealed information test.* Cambridge, England: Cambridge University Press. doi:10.1017/CBO9780511975196

Vrij, A. (2008). *Detecting lies and deceit: Pitfalls and opportunities* (2nd ed.). Chichester, England: Wiley.

Vrij, A., Fisher, R., Mann, S., & Leal, S. (2006). Detecting deception by manipulating cognitive load. *Trends in Cognitive Sciences, 10,* 141–142. doi:10.1016/j.tics.2006.02.003

Vrij, A., & Granhag, P. A. (2012a). Eliciting cues to deception and truth: What matters are the questions asked. *Journal of Applied Research in Memory and Cognition, 1,* 110–117. doi:10.1016/j.jarmac.2012.02.004

Vrij, A., & Granhag, P. A. (2012b). The sound of critics: New tunes, old tunes and resistance to play. *Journal of Applied Research in Memory and Cognition, 1,* 139–143. doi:10.1016/j.jarmac.2012.05.001

Vrij, A., Granhag, P. A., Mann, S., & Leal, S. (2011). Outsmarting the liars: Towards a cognitive lie detection approach. *Current Directions in Psychological Science, 20,* 28–32. doi:10.1177/0963721410391245

Vrij, A., Granhag, P. A., & Porter, S. B. (2010). Pitfalls and opportunities in nonverbal and verbal lie detection. *Psychological Science in the Public Interest, 11,* 89–121. doi:10.1177/1529100610390861

Vrij, A., Jundi, S., Hope, L., Hillman, J., Gahr, E., Leal, S., . . . Granhag, P. A. (2012). Collective interviewing of suspects. *Journal of Applied Research in Memory and Cognition, 1,* 41–44. doi:10.1016/j.jarmac.2011.12.002

Vrij, A., Leal, S., Granhag, P. A., Mann, S., Fisher, R. P., Hillman, J., & Sperry, K. (2009). Outsmarting the liars: The benefit of asking unanticipated questions. *Law and Human Behavior, 33,* 159–166. doi:10.1007/s10979-008-9143-y

Vrij, A., Leal, S., Mann, S., & Granhag, P. A. (2011). A comparison between lying about intentions and past activities: Verbal cues and detection accuracy. *Applied Cognitive Psychology, 25,* 212–218. doi:10.1002/acp.1665

Vrij, A., Mann, S., & Fisher, R. (2006). An empirical test of the behaviour analysis interview. *Law and Human Behavior, 30,* 329–345. doi:10.1007/s10979-006-9014-3

Vrij, A., Mann, S., Fisher, R., Leal, S., Milne, B., & Bull, R. (2008). Increasing cognitive load to facilitate lie detection: The benefit of recalling an event in reverse order. *Law and Human Behavior, 32,* 253–265. doi:10.1007/s10979-007-9103-y

Vrij, A., Mann, S., Jundi, S., Hope, L., & Leal, S. (2012). Can I take your picture? Undercover interviewing to detect deception. *Psychology, Public Policy, and Law, 18,* 231–244. doi:10.1037/a0025670

Vrij, A., Mann, S., Leal, S., & Fisher, R. (2010). "Look into my eyes": Can an instruction to maintain eye contact facilitate lie detection? *Psychology, Crime & Law, 16,* 327–348. doi:10.1080/10683160902740633

Vrij, A., & Verschuere, B. (2013). Lie detection in a forensic context. *Oxford Bibliographies Online: Psychology.* doi:10.1093/abo/9780199828340-0122

Warmelink, L., Vrij, A., Mann, S., Jundi, S., & Granhag, P. A. (2012). Have you been there before? The effect of experience and question expectedness on lying about intentions. *Acta Psychologica, 141,* 178–183.

Watanabe, H. (2005). Semantic and episodic predictions of memory for plans. *Japanese Psychological Research, 47,* 40–45. doi:10.1111/j.1468-5584.2005.00271.x

Willsher, K. (2012, March 25). Failure to find first chosen target led assassin to a Jewish school. *Observer,* pp. 24–25.

Yuille, J. C. (1988). The systematic assessment of children's testimony. *Canadian Psychology, 29,* 247–262. doi:10.1037/h0079769

Zuckerman, M., DePaulo, B. M., & Rosenthal, R. (1981). Verbal and nonverbal communication of deception. In L. Berkowitz (Ed.), *Advances in experimental social psychology* (Vol. 14, pp. 1–57). New York, NY: Academic Press.

CHAPTER 9

CONFESSIONS

Saul M. Kassin, Jennifer T. Perillo, Sara C. Appleby, and Jeff Kukucka

The 2012 film *The Central Park Five* tells the story of five African- and Hispanic-American boys, 14 to 16 years old, who in 1989 confessed to the brutal assault and rape of a female jogger in New York City's Central Park. Solely on the basis of these confessions, four of which were videotaped, the boys were convicted and sentenced to prison. The tapes themselves were compelling, as every one of the defendants described in vivid—though often erroneous—detail how the jogger was attacked. Thirteen years later, Matias Reyes, in prison for three rapes and a murder committed subsequent to the jogger attack, stepped forward to claim that he was the Central Park jogger rapist and that he acted alone. Reinvestigating the case, the Manhattan district attorney's office questioned Reyes and discovered that he had accurate and independently corroborated guilty knowledge—and that the DNA samples originally recovered from the victim's body belonged to him. In 2002, the defendants' convictions were vacated. The Central Park jogger case now stands as a shocking demonstration of five false confessions resulting from a single investigation (for an overview of this case, see Burns, 2011).

As illustrated by the infamous Central Park jogger case, the use of DNA testing to exonerate innocent people who were wrongfully convicted has shed new light on the problem of false confessions. On the basis of classic principles of psychology found in experimental, social, cognitive, and developmental domains, and using a variety of case study, archival, laboratory, and field research methods, psychologists and other social scientists have sought to better understand the causes and consequences of confession evidence.

One line of research has focused on the methods and processes of police interrogation that are used to procure confessions from crime suspects. As commonly practiced, police often conduct a preinterrogation interview to determine whether a suspect is telling the truth or lying. Although police exhibit confidence in their ability to make these judgments at high levels of accuracy, controlled experiments have shown that their judgments are often erroneous and that they exhibit a bias toward seeing deception (see Chapter 8, this volume for a review of research on the detection of deception). As a result, interrogation itself is by definition a guilt-presumptive process aimed at producing confessions. Most U.S. police use the Reid technique, a confrontational approach designed to get suspects to confess by increasing the anxiety associated with denial and decreasing the anxiety associated with confession. Importantly, a vast majority of suspects waive their *Miranda* rights to silence and to counsel, their only means of legal protection. Some people waive their rights due to a lack of comprehension; others do so because they are convinced it is in their best interest. Believing they have nothing to fear or to hide, innocent people in particular are likely to waive their rights.

Focusing on false confessions, a number of researchers have found that specific tactics used to manipulate anxiety in the interrogation room—in particular, isolation and questioning for lengthy periods of time, presentations of false evidence, and

http://dx.doi.org/10.1037/14462-009
APA Handbook of Forensic Psychology: Vol. 2. Criminal Investigation, Adjudication, and Sentencing Outcomes,
B. L. Cutler and P. A. Zapf (Editors-in-Chief)
Copyright © 2015 by the American Psychological Association. All rights reserved.

minimization themes that provide moral justification and imply leniency upon confession—can put innocent people at risk to confess. Research also shows that certain types of suspects—namely, adolescents and people who are intellectually impaired or diagnosed with a psychological disorder—are particularly vulnerable to these types of manipulation.

Whereas a good deal of research has focused on the causes of true and false confessions, an important second direction has been to consider the consequences of confessions both in the courtroom and during the criminal investigation process. In the courtroom, it is clear that judges and juries intuitively trust confessions, as seen in their verdicts, even when they realize that the confessions were coerced by police, uncorroborated, contradicted by other evidence, and otherwise compromised. Part of the problem is that common sense tells us that people do not confess to crimes they did not commit; part of the problem is that most confessions, including false confessions, are highly detailed narratives that contain a number of credibility cues. Recent research also suggests that confessions can corrupt eyewitnesses and forensic examiners, thereby fostering an illusion that the confession is corroborated by independent evidence.

The literature reviewed in this chapter, and the continued discovery of false confessions in actual cases, has inspired various calls for reform. In particular, research has compelled the conclusion that the video recording of interrogations is a necessary safeguard (both to prevent coercive police tactics and to provide judges and juries with an objective record of the process by which the confession was produced); that serious consideration be given to the reform of police interrogations (in particular, the use of tactics that put innocent people at risk to confess); and that psychological experts be permitted to testify at trial, giving testimony that would draw from generally accepted research and assist the trier of fact.

IMPORTANCE OF THE PROBLEM

A confession is an admission of guilt followed by a narrative statement of what, how, and why the confessor committed the crime. In criminal law,

confession evidence is highly regarded but fallible. Dating back to the Salem witch trials of 1692, countless numbers of people have been wrongfully convicted after confessing to crimes they did not commit. In 1989, Gary Dotson became the first wrongfully convicted person to be exonerated by DNA testing. Since that time, the Innocence Project has reported on more than 300 postconviction DNA exonerations. In more than 25% of these cases, false confessions were a contributing factor (Garrett, 2011). Importantly, the population of DNA exoneration cases represents only a fraction of all wrongful convictions.

Over the years, DNA testing has provided only one method by which false confessions have been uncovered. Confessions have been proven false in other ways as well—as when it is discovered that the confessed crime was never committed; when new evidence shows it was physically impossible for the confessor to have committed the crime; when the real perpetrator, having no connection to the defendant, is captured and implicated; and when other non-DNA evidence affirmatively establishes the confessor's innocence. Contrary to the widespread belief that people do not confess to crimes they did not commit, large numbers of such cases have been exposed throughout history (for reviews, see Gudjonsson, 2003; Kassin, 1997, 2005; Kassin et al., 2010; Kassin & Gudjonsson, 2004; Warden & Drizin, 2009; Wrightsman & Kassin, 1993). To make matters worse, research shows that confessions are so potent that, once taken, they often lead police to close investigations, bias lay and expert witnesses, and lead prosecutors, judges, and juries to presume the confessor guilty—frequently resulting in wrongful convictions (Drizin & Leo, 2004; Kassin, 2012; Leo & Ofshe, 1998).

RELEVANT PSYCHOLOGY THEORY AND PRINCIPLES

By necessity, the scholarly study of confession evidence has drawn content from the broad discipline of basic psychology and has used a wide range of empirical methodologies.

To understand why someone would confess to a crime, it is necessary to draw on basic theories and research in psychology that were developed long before the first empirical studies of confessions were conducted. Perhaps the most basic area of relevance concerns the behaviorist principles of reinforcement and decision making. Dating back to Thorndike's (1911) law of effect, research has shown that people are highly responsive to reinforcement and subject to the laws of conditioning, and that behavior is influenced more by perceptions of short-term than of long-term consequences. Relevant to a psychological analysis of interrogation are the classic operant animal studies of reinforcement schedules, punishment, and appetitive, avoidance, and escape learning, as well as behavioral modification applications in clinics, schools, and workplaces (e.g., Herrnstein, 1970; Skinner, 1938).

Of particular relevance to an analysis of choice behavior in the interrogation room are studies of human decision-making in a behavioral economics paradigm. An extensive body of research has shown that people make choices that they think will maximize their outcomes given the constraints they face, making the best of the situation they are in—what Herrnstein has called the "matching law" (Herrnstein, Rachlin & Laibson, 1997). With respect to a suspect's response to interrogation, studies on the discounting of rewards and costs show that people tend to be impulsive in their orientation, preferring outcomes that are immediate rather than delayed, with delayed outcomes depreciating over time in their subjective value (Rachlin, 2000; in the context of confessions, see Madon, Guyll, Scherr, Greathouse, & Wells, 2012; for a self-regulation perspective, see Davis & Leo, 2012).

As humans are inherently social beings, a second set of core principles pertains to the fact that people are vulnerable to various forms of influence from others. Of direct relevance to an analysis of interrogation is the extensive social psychology literature on attitudes and persuasion (Petty & Cacioppo, 1986), informational and normative influences (e.g., Asch, 1956; Sherif, 1936), the use of direct request strategies, as in the foot-in-the-door technique (Cialdini, 2001), and the gradual escalation of commands, issued by figures of authority, that can elicit unconscionable acts of obedience (Milgram, 1974). Conceptually, Latané's (1981) social impact theory provides a predictive mathematical model that can

account for the influence of police interrogators, who bring power, proximity, and number to bear on their interactions with suspects (for social psychological perspectives on interrogation, see Bem, 1966; Davis & O'Donohue, 2004; Zimbardo, 1967).

Two additional bodies of research are also brought to bear on the psychology of confessions. One concerns the cognitive psychology literature on misinformation effects on the formation of biased and illusory memories (Loftus, 2005; Schacter, 2001). Over the years, a number of cases have been identified involving innocent people who not only confessed to a crime but went on as a result of highly suggestive interrogation tactics to internalize a belief in their own culpability, often confabulating false memories in the process (see Kassin & Wrightsman, 1985; for reviews, see Gudjonsson, 2003; Kassin, 2007). A second relevant literature concerns the developmental psychology of adolescence. In general, there is a good deal of concern about juveniles within the criminal justice system—and the number who have confessed to crimes they did not commit (Drizin & Leo, 2004). Over the years, basic research has shown that children and adolescents are cognitively and psychosocially less mature than adults, and that this immaturity fosters impulsive decision making and a relative lack of regard for long-term consequences (e.g., Steinberg, 2007). Drawing on this work, there is now a wealth of forensically oriented research indicating that juvenile suspects are particularly vulnerable to manipulation in an interrogation setting (Owen-Kostelnik, Reppucci, & Meyer, 2006).

The study of confessions also involves a wide range of methodologies. One approach has involved a focus on singular instances of proven false confessions, producing a vast literature of individual and aggregated case studies. As reported in books, newspapers, TV news shows, documentaries, and analyses of actual case files, these stories reveal that false confessions occur with some frequency, that they share certain common features, and that they seem to occur in some types of people and in some circumstances more than others (e.g., Drizin & Leo, 2004; Gudjonsson, 2003; Leo & Ofshe, 1998). Although case studies cannot be used to prove what causes false confessions, they have been useful in the development of this area. By comparing and contrasting several known cases, for example, Kassin and Wrightsman (1985) introduced a taxonomy that distinguished among three types of false confessions: voluntary (where people claim responsibility for crimes they did not commit without prompting or pressure from police), coerced-compliant (where people capitulate during a police interrogation in order to escape the stress, avoid physical or legal punishment, or gain a promised or implied reward), and coerced-internalized (where innocent people under interrogation come to believe they committed the crime in question, a belief produced by presentations of false evidence and sometimes accompanied by false memories).

Other empirical methods are also used to investigate the processes of police interviewing, interrogation, the elicitation of confessions, and the consequences of those confessions. These include naturalistic observations of live and videotaped police interrogations (e.g., Feld, 2013; Leo, 1996b; Moston, Stephenson, & Williamson, 1992); self-report methods used to examine correlations between various personal suspect characteristics—such as interrogative compliance and suggestibility—and the tendency to confess or resist confession (Gudjonsson, 1992, 2003); and laboratory and field experiments conducted to assess preinterrogation judgments of truth and deception (Kassin & Fong, 1999; Meissner & Kassin, 2002; Vrij, Granhag & Porter, 2010; for a recent review, see Chapter 8, this volume), the effects of certain interrogation tactics (Kassin & Kiechel, 1996; Russano, Meissner, Narchet, & Kassin, 2005), and the impact of confession evidence on juries (Kassin & Neumann, 1997; Kassin & Sukel, 1997), judges (Wallace & Kassin, 2012), eyewitnesses (Hasel & Kassin, 2009), and various types of forensic examiners (Kassin, Dror, & Kukucka, 2013).

RESEARCH REVIEW

To fully understand the psychology of confession evidence, researchers have studied (a) the processes of police interrogation (i.e., the use of preliminary interviews to assess whether suspects are telling the truth or lying, the presentation of *Miranda* warnings,

and the interrogation techniques used to elicit confessions), (b) the problem of false confessions (i.e., the types of suspects who are most vulnerable, the interrogation techniques that increase the risk, and the role that innocence plays in the mind of the innocent suspect), and (c) the consequences of confession evidence once taken (i.e., as it affects judges and juries in the courtroom as well as lay and expert witnesses during criminal investigations). In the coming pages, we will review empirical research addressing each of these areas.

Police Interrogation Practices

During the course of investigating crimes, police often identify one or more suspects for interrogation—the primary goal of which is to produce an admission of guilt or even a full confession. Sometimes this identification is based on witnesses, informants, a suspect's own history, or other extrinsic evidence. Often, however, it is based on a clinical hunch that police form during a preinterrogation interview. In *Criminal Interrogations and Confessions*, an influential manual on interrogation first published in 1962 and now in its fifth edition, Inbau, Reid, Buckley, and Jayne (2013) propose a two-step process by which the highly confrontational, accusatory process of interrogation is preceded by a neutral, information-gathering interview, the purpose of which is to help determine whether the suspect is being deceptive and, hence, is likely to be guilty. Although interviewing and interrogation are not so impeccably discrete in practice, we will treat these two processes in sequence separated by the process of informing the suspect of his or her *Miranda* rights to silence and to counsel.

The preinterrogation interview. To determine whether suspects are telling the truth or lying, Inbau et al. (2013) train investigators in the use of the Behavior Analysis Interview (BAI). Using this approach, investigators are advised to ask special "behavior-provoking questions," the responses to which are taken to be indicative of guilt and innocence (e.g., "Do you know who took the money?", "What do you think should happen to the person who took the money?"). They are also trained to observe changes from baseline in the suspect's verbal and nonverbal behavior (e.g., eye contact, pauses, qualified denials, posture, and fidgety movements). This judgment of truth or deception becomes a critical point in an investigation because it determines whether a suspect should be released or held for interrogation.

The creators of the Reid technique, both in their manual and in actual training sessions, claim that interrogators can be trained to make judgments of truth and deception with a high level of accuracy. To support this claim, proponents point to a single highly flawed study. In that study, Horvath, Jayne, and Buckley (1994) selected—through an unspecified nonrandom process—60 interviews from their collection, the ground truths of which could not be established with certainty. For 34 of the interviews, guilt or innocence was inferred by confession; for 24 interviews, it was inferred by a "factual analysis" of the case files (which included the interviews themselves). The authors then edited the tapes, showed these edited tapes to four experienced employees of John E. Reid and Associates, and concluded from their judgments that training in the Reid technique yields an 85% level of accuracy. No comparison group of untrained or lay evaluators was included in the design.

Apart from this study, research in the field of deception detection contradicts this claim. Research has consistently shown that laypersons on average distinguish between truth and deception at only a 54% rate of accuracy, that the behavioral cues recommended by the Reid technique are weak or not diagnostic, and that training in general does not appreciably improve performance (for reviews, see Bond & DePaulo, 2006; Hartwig & Bond, 2011; Vrij, 2008). Empirical research specifically testing the BAI has failed to support the efficacy of the approach. In one study, Vrij, Mann, and Fisher (2006) had some participants commit a mock crime while others did not. All participants, who were incentivized to appear innocent, were then interviewed about the crime using the BAI questions. Overall, the results showed that verbal and behavioral responses to the questions did not significantly distinguish between truth tellers and liars in the Reid-predicted manner. Of the significant differences that were found, innocent participants were more likely than their guilty counterparts to display behaviors that are supposed to be associated with

deception (i.e., crossing legs, shifting posture). In short, there is no evidence to suggest that the behavior-provoking questions of the BAI interview produce diagnostic responses.

There is also no evidence that suggests that the verbal and nonverbal cues upon which Reid-trained investigators are instructed to rely have any diagnostic value. For example, Kassin and Fong (1999) randomly trained some college students but not others in the use of "behavioral symptoms" cited by the Reid technique. The training was achieved through use of tapes and written materials purchased from John E. Reid and Associates and verified in a subsequent test. All students then watched videotaped interviews of mock suspects, some of whom committed one of four mock crimes (shoplifting, breaking and entering, vandalism, and computer break-in), others of whom did not. During questioning, all suspects denied their involvement. As in the typical laboratory experiment, observers could not reliably differentiate between the two groups of suspects. In fact, those who underwent training were significantly less accurate, more confident, and more biased toward seeing deception. Using these same taped interviews, Meissner and Kassin (2002) next tested experienced samples of police detectives and found that they exhibited these same erroneous and biased tendencies. Other research as well suggested that police tend to make prejudgments of guilt, with confidence, that are frequently in error (e.g., Elaad, 2003; Garrido, Masip, & Herrero, 2004; Leach, Talwar, Lee, Bala, & Lindsay, 2004).

One additional point concerning this process is worth noting. In light of the consistent finding that laypeople are not accurate lie detectors on the basis of intuition, recent research provides a possible explanation for the empirical failures of the BAI—namely, that in suggesting that deception is betrayed by gaze avoidance, fidgeting, changes in posture, and other nondiagnostic behaviors, the BAI merely formalizes the folk wisdom and common-sense misconceptions already used by laypeople and police (Masip, Barba, & Herrero, 2012; Masip, Herrero, Garrido, & Barba, 2011). In contrast, researchers have identified other ways to improve police lie-detection performance. Representing one line of research, Hartwig, Granhag, Strömwall, and

Vrij (2005) found that interviewers make more accurate judgments by withholding crime details while questioning suspects, a strategy that traps guilty liars in discernible inconsistencies when these facts are later disclosed. Interviewers who are trained in this "strategic disclosure" technique thus become more accurate in their judgments (Hartwig, Granhag, Strömwall, & Kronkvist, 2006). In a second line of research, Vrij, Fisher, Mann, and Leal (2006) theorized that lying is more effortful than telling the truth, so interviewers should tax a suspect's cognitive load and attend to cues that betray effort. Hence, when interviewers had truth tellers and liars recount their stories in reverse chronological order, they became more accurate in their ability to distinguish between the truthful and deceptive accounts (Vrij et al., 2008; for an overview, see Vrij, Granhag, & Porter, 2010).

The *Miranda* warning and waiver. Before transitioning from interview to an accusatory interrogation aimed at confession, police must inform all suspects who are in custody of their constitutional rights. In *Miranda v. Arizona* (1966), the U.S. Supreme Court ruled that police must inform suspects in custody of their constitutional rights to silence (e.g., "You have the right to remain silent; anything you say can and will be held against you in a court of law.") and to counsel (e.g., "You are entitled to consult with an attorney; if you cannot afford an attorney, one will be appointed for you."). Only if suspects waive these rights "voluntarily, knowingly, and intelligently" as determined by consideration of "a totality of the circumstances" can the statements they produce be admitted into evidence. In *Dickerson v. United States* (2000), the U.S. Supreme Court upheld the basic warning-and-waiver requirements of *Miranda v. Arizona*. In general, however, it is clear from post-1966 case rulings that the Court has narrowed the scope of *Miranda v. Arizona* and minimized the consequences for police noncompliance (for a review, see Wrightsman, 2010).

Despite the influence of *Miranda v. Arizona* in criminal justice, its benefits are unclear for two reasons. First, a voluminous body of research shows that many suspects lack the capacity to understand and apply these rights. Many years ago, Grisso

(1981) reasoned that a person's capacity to make an informed waiver requires three abilities: an understanding of the words and phrases contained in the warnings, an accurate perception of their intended functions, and a capacity to reason about the likely consequences of the decision to waive or invoke these rights. Since that time, empirical studies have shown that adolescents under age 15 do not comprehend their rights as fully or know how to apply them as well as older adolescents and adults (Goldstein, Condie, Kalbeitzer, Osman, & Geier, 2003; McLachlan, Roesch, & Douglas, 2011; Oberlander & Goldstein, 2001; Viljoen, Zapf, & Roesch, 2007). The same is true of adults who are mentally retarded (Clare & Gudjonsson, 1995: Everington & Fulero, 1999; O'Connell, Garmoe, & Goldstein, 2005; Salseda, Dixon, Fass, Miora, & Leark, 2011). To further complicate matters, it is now clear that *Miranda* warnings differ markedly from one police department to another in their content, wording, format, and difficulty level (Rogers et al., 2012; Rogers, Harrison, Shuman, Sewell, & Hazelwood, 2007; Rogers, Hazelwood, Sewell, Harrison, & Shuman, 2008) and that a suspect's comprehension may also be compromised by interrogation stress and other situational factors (Rogers, Gillard, Wooley, & Fiduccia, 2011; Scherr & Madon, 2012).

Comprehension notwithstanding, a second reason that *Miranda* warnings may not adequately protect the accused is that most people tend to waive their rights. In an observational study of 122 live interrogations and 60 videotaped interrogations, Leo (1996b) observed that 78% of suspects waived their rights. Cassell and Hayman (1996) reported a similar waiver rate of 79.8% during a six-week period in Salt Lake City. Kassin et al. (2007) found that 631 North American police officers recently surveyed estimated on average that approximately 81% of suspects waive their rights. Over the years, archival studies in Great Britain have revealed a similar waiver rate (Baldwin, 1993; Moston et al., 1992).

Different explanations have been put forth to explain this pattern of resuts. Leo (1996a) noted that police detectives are highly effective at persuading suspects to waive their rights. He likened the persuasive process to a confidence game in which detectives establish rapport with the suspect and present the warning-and-waiver requirement as a mere formality (in some cases, police conduct noncustodial interrogations, which do not trigger a warning-and-waiver requirement; Frantzen, 2010). Another reason for the high waiver rate may be that suspects labor under the misconception that invoking *Miranda* will prove ineffective or, worse, yield negative consequences such as a perception of guilt that can be used to incriminate them at trial (Rogers et al., 2010). A third reason relates to innocence. Based on Leo's (1996a) observation that individuals without a prior record were more likely than those with a felony record to waive their *Miranda* rights, Kassin (2005) proposed that innocence itself is a state of mind that would lead innocent people—believing that they have nothing to fear or to hide—to waive their rights. Kassin and Norwick (2004) tested this hypothesis in a mock crime study and found that 81% of innocent participants signed a waiver compared to only 36% of those who were guilty (see also Moore & Gagnier, 2008).

The processes of interrogation. During the early part of the twentieth century, police in the United States often extracted confessions by using coercive "third-degree" methods of interrogation. These methods involved prolonged confinement and isolation; explicit threats of harm or punishment; deprivations of sleep, food, and other needs; extreme sensory discomfort (e.g., shining a bright, blinding strobe light on the suspect's face); and physical violence and torture (e.g., simulated drownings, or beatings with a rubber hose, which seldom left visible marks). In *Brown v. Mississippi* (1936), the U.S. Supreme Court signaled a change in direction designed to deter oppressive police practices. In that case, three black tenant farmers who had been accused of murdering a white farmer were whipped, pummeled, and tortured until they gave detailed confessions. The Court unanimously reversed the convictions of these defendants and held that statements extracted by physical abuse were involuntary and inadmissible as evidence at trial. Except for the torturous "enhanced interrogation" techniques used on terrorist suspects after the terror attack on September 11, 2001, third-degree methods of interrogation thus declined precipitously and were replaced by a

psychological approach to interrogation—one that relies heavily on tactics that are designed to induce confession by manipulating a suspect's cognitive, motivational, and emotional state (for an historical overview and analysis, see Leo, 2008).

This psychological approach to interrogation is designed to increase the anxiety associated with denial and to decrease the anxiety associated with confession—in short, to make it easier for a suspect to confess as a means of coping with the interrogation. In the Reid technique, as described in Inbau et al.'s (2013) *Criminal Interrogation and Confessions*, this objective is achieved by isolating the suspect in a small, bare, soundproof room to create a nonsupportive environment, and then engaging in a nine-step process that combines the use of positive and negative incentives referred to broadly as *maximization* and *minimization* (Kassin & McNall, 1991). Maximization involves a cluster of tactics designed to convey the interrogator's strong and certain belief that the suspect is guilty and that all denials will fail. Such tactics include making an accusation, interrupting denials, overriding objections, and citing evidence, real or manufactured, to shift the suspect's mental state from confident to hopeless. At the same time, minimization tactics are designed to provide the suspect with moral justification and face-saving excuses for having committed the crime in question. Using this approach, the interrogator offers sympathy and understanding; normalizes and minimizes the crime, often suggesting that he or she would have behaved similarly; and offers the suspect a choice of alternative explanations—for example, suggesting to the suspect that the murder was spontaneous, provoked, peer-pressured, or accidental rather than the premeditated work of a cold-blooded killer. As we will see later, research has shown that this tactic communicates by implication that the crime was justifiable and that leniency in punishment is forthcoming upon confession. The process as a whole is designed to lead suspects to see confession as their most expedient means of "escape." Once the suspect is persuaded to admit guilt, the trained interrogator seeks to convert that admission into a narrative confession, on tape or in writing.

Both observational and police self-report studies suggest that the recommended techniques are commonly employed. Leo (1996b) reported on his observations of live and videotaped interrogations at three police departments in California and found that detectives used, on average, 5.62 different techniques per interrogation and that Reid-like approaches were common. Similar results were obtained in observational studies of adult interrogations in Canada (King & Snook, 2009) and juvenile interrogations in Minnesota (Feld, 2013). Moreover, police investigators who were surveyed estimated that their most frequent tactics, in order, were to physically isolate the suspect from family and friends, typically in a small private room; identify contradictions in the suspect's account; try to establish rapport in order to gain the suspect's trust; confront the suspect with evidence of his or her guilt; and appeal to his or her self-interests (Kassin et al., 2007).

False Confessions

In recent years, false confessions have been uncovered in a number of cases involving innocent people who were wrongfully convicted—and these cases represent the tip of an iceberg. As a consequence of these miscarriages of justice, researchers have sought to identify risk factors: Are some people more malleable than others in an interrogation setting and more vulnerable to giving a false confession? Do some conditions and interrogation tactics in particular put people at risk to confess? Does being innocent necessarily protect people from giving false confessions? Empirical research has sought answers to these questions.

Dispositional risk factors. Not everyone is equally resistant to influence during an interrogation. Dispositional risk factors refer to the stable personal characteristics of suspects that increase their risk of a false confession relative to the general population. In particular, research has focused on youth, cognitive impairments, and psychopathology, all characteristics that are associated with compliance, suggestibility, and other types of social influence.

Childhood and adolescence. In an interrogation setting, youth is a strong dispositional risk factor and has been acknowledged as such by many researchers in the field (Kassin et al., 2010; for reviews, see Drizin & Colgan, 2004; Owen-Kostelnik et al., 2006; Scott-Hayward, 2007) and by interrogation specialists (Inbau et al., 2013; but see Meyer & Reppucci, 2007). As illustrated by the Central Park jogger case described earlier, in which five teenagers—all 14 to 16 years old—confessed an assault they did not commit, juveniles are overrepresented in populations of known false confessions. In Drizin and Leo's (2004) sample of 125 cases, youth under the age of 18 years comprised 32 percent of known false confessors; the National Registry of Exonerations (2012) reports a similar rate of 28 percent. These confessions are typically to violent crimes (Drizin & Leo, 2004; Owen-Kostelnik et al., 2006), though the Office of Juvenile Justice and Delinquency Prevention (2012) reports that juveniles commit only 11% of violent crimes overall (see also Puzzanchera & Adams, 2011). Juveniles are overall more likely to be wrongfully convicted based on confessions as well; indeed, 42% of juvenile exonerees had falsely confessed compared to only 13% of adult exonerees (Gross, Jacoby, Matheson, Montgomery, & Patel, 2005). The youngest exonerees, between 12 and 15 years old, exhibited an even higher false confession rate of 75%.

These criminal justice statistics are supported by other types of research. In one study, Redlich and Goodman (2003) examined variation in the age of participants using a popular laboratory paradigm for studying false confessions. As predicted, false confession rates varied as a function of age: 78% among 12 and 13 year olds compared to 72% among 15 and 16 year olds and 59% of young adults. A long line of research has also produced largely consistent self-reported rates of false confessions among youths in the United States and across Europe, ranging from 6% to 19% (Gudjonsson, 2010; Gudjonsson, Sigurdsson, & Sigfusdottir, 2009; Steingrimsdottir, Hreinsdottir, Gudjonsson, Sigurdsson, & Nielsen, 2007; Viljoen, Klaver, & Roesch, 2005). In the largest study of self-reported false confessions among youth, Gudjonsson et al. (2009) collected reports of interrogation experiences from 23,771 adolescents across seven European countries: Iceland, Norway, Finland, Latvia, Lithuania, Russia, and Bulgaria.

Overall, 11.5% of participants reported experience being interrogated by the police. Of those participants, roughly 14% reported having given a false confession to the police, typically to protect someone else. Supporting the vulnerability of juveniles, these self-reported confession rates were higher than among university students and adults (Gudjonsson, 2010; also see Goldstein et al., 2003; Viljoen et al., 2005).

Developmental research explains why juveniles may be disproportionately more vulnerable to false confession. According to the National Institute of Mental Health (2001), children's brains are not fully formed until young adulthood, a finding supported by neurological research (Steinberg, 2007). With their brains being works in progress, juveniles tend to exhibit immaturity of judgment (Cauffman & Steinberg, 2000; Steinberg & Cauffman, 1996). In particular, they tend to be focused myopically on short-term gains and losses rather than the longer-term consequences for their actions (Steinberg & Scott, 2003). This tendency manifests itself in a variety of risky tendencies, including a lack of impulse control, sensitivity to immediate rewards, inability to accept delayed gratification, and the discounting of delayed rewards (Reyna et al., 2011; Ripke et al., 2012; Steinberg, 2007). Of relevance to decision-making in the interrogation room, research shows that juveniles are even more likely to make myopic decisions when they are under stress (Galván & McGlennen, 2012).

As if adolescence did not constitute enough of an impairment, it turns out that juveniles in the criminal justice system exhibit a high incidence rate of mental illness, with some estimates as high as 70%–100%, far exceeding the 20% incidence rate for youth in the general population (Redlich, 2007; Shufelt & Cocozza, 2006). In fact, a recent prevalence study found that 27% of the juveniles who were diagnosed with mental illness (70.4% of the overall sample) had a severe disorder, and 79% met criteria for comorbid diagnoses (Shufelt & Cocozza, 2006). Redlich (2007) used the term *double jeopardy* to describe the two-fold risk of false confessions among juveniles with mental illness (see Chapter 2, this volume for a review of research on youth in the justice system).

Intellectual impairments. People diagnosed as mentally retarded or having other intellectual deficits are also overrepresented in the population of known false confessions (Gudjonsson, 2003). Twenty-eight of the 125 cases described by Drizin and Leo (2004) involved defendants who suffered from intellectual disability—and this number may well underestimate the population (intelligence test scores were not available or reported in most cases).

When it comes to false confessions, there are several reasons for concern about people who are mentally retarded. One is that they tend to have poor comprehension of their *Miranda* rights. Using standardized tests that measure *Miranda* comprehension, research shows that comprehension scores correlate significantly with IQ; most people who are mentally retarded do not adequately comprehend their rights or know how to apply them in their own actions (Everington & Fulero, 1999; Fulero & Everington, 1995; O'Connell et al., 2005). Specifically addressing this lack of competency, Appelbaum and Appelbaum (1994) noted that people who are mentally retarded might confess to a crime merely to avoid the discomfort of police interrogation—that "friendliness, as well as threats and coercion, can result in waivers and confessions" (p. 493). In one study, a majority of intellectually disabled individuals who were tested indicated the belief that having an attorney would have a negative impact on their case, and only two percent realized they could remain silent without penalty, leading the researchers to describe the *Miranda* warnings to mentally retarded suspects as "words without meaning" (Cloud, Shepherd, Barkoff, & Shur, 2002, p. 495).

A lack of understanding of criminal justice consequences in general is also a source of concern. In England, Clare and Gudjonsson (1995) showed a videotaped police interrogation to intellectually disabled and non-disabled participants, followed by a series of decision-making questions. They found that those who were intellectually disabled were more likely to think that a false confession could be credibly retracted; they were more likely to believe the suspect would be allowed to go home while awaiting trial; and they were less likely to believe that the suspect should have had legal advice at the start of the interview.

A third basis for concern with regard to false confessions is that people who are mentally retarded are more susceptible to social influences. Research shows they are more compliant toward authority figures (Appelbaum & Appelbaum, 1994), and they exhibit a high need for approval, particularly from others in positions of authority, which reveals itself in an acquiescence response bias (Shaw & Budd, 1982). Indeed, people who are mentally retarded tend to answer "yes" to a wide range of questions—even when an affirmative response is incorrect and inappropriate, and even in response to absurd questions such as "Does it ever snow here in the summer?" (Finlay & Lyons, 2002). Importantly, people who are mentally retarded are also more suggestible than others (Everington & Fulero, 1999; Gudjonsson, 2003; O'Connell et al., 2005). Research shows that they are more malleable and more likely to incorporate incorrect information from misleading questions into their reported memories (Perlman, Ericson, Esses, & Isaacs, 1994). Hence, people with intellectual disabilities score higher on the Gudjonsson Suggestibility Scale, or GSS, a standardized test of interrogative suggestibility (Everington & Fulero, 1999; Gudjonsson & Henry, 2003).

Psychopathology. In terms of susceptibility to false confession, it is important to consider other individual factors of relevance to a person's decision to confess. In particular, people with mental illness are overrepresented in these cases. Noting that psychological disorders are often accompanied by faulty reality monitoring, distorted perception, impaired judgment, anxiety, mood disturbance, poor self-control, and feelings of guilt, Gudjonsson (2003) described several cases in which false confessions were directly related to specific disorders.

There are many possible mechanisms by which this can happen. For example, research shows that defendants suffering from psychotic disorders are less likely to comprehend their constitutional rights compared to psychologically normal suspects (Viljoen, Roesch, & Zapf, 2002); people diagnosed with autism spectrum disorders tend to be highly compliant, anxious, and fearful of negative social evaluation (North, Russell, & Gudjonsson, 2008); and prisoners who are symptomatic for

attention-deficit/hyperactivity disorder (ADHD) score high on measures of compliance and are more likely to self-report having given a false confession compared to other prisoners (41% vs. 18%; Gudjonsson, Sigurdsson, Bragason, Newton, & Einarsson, 2008; Gudjonsson, Sigurdsson, Einarsson, Bragason, & Newton, 2010; Gudjonsson, Sigurdsson, Sigfusdottir, & Young, 2012). Still other symptoms of psychopathology, such as thought disorganization, impaired judgment, mood disturbance, anxiety, and difficulty with reality monitoring, may also increase the likelihood of false confession (Davis & O'Donohue, 2004; Redlich, 2004; Wolfradt & Meyer, 1998). Thus, when people are asked if they have ever confessed to a crime they did not commit, those with mental health problems are more likely to self-report false confessions and even to give false guilty pleas (Redlich, Kulish, & Steadman, 2011; Redlich, Summers, & Hoover, 2010).

Situational risk factors. Being designed to procure confessions by heightening the anxiety associated with denial and reducing the anxiety associated with confession, the practice of interrogation involves three essential elements that can sometimes induce innocent people to confess: isolation, the presentation of false evidence, and minimization.

The first risk factor concerns physical custody and interrogation time. Over the years, observational studies in the United States have shown that most interrogations last from 30 minutes up to two hours (Feld, 2013; Leo, 1996b; Wald, Ayres, Hess, Schantz, & Whitebread, 1967). In a self-report survey, 631 North American police investigators estimated from their experience that the mean length of a typical interrogation is 1.60 hours and that their longest interrogations lasted an average of 4.21 hours (Kassin et al., 2007). It appears that cases involving false confessions contrast sharply with these norms. In their study of 125 proven false confessions, Drizin and Leo (2004) thus found, in cases in which interrogation time was recorded, that 34% lasted 6 to 12 hours, that 39% lasted 12 to 24 hours, and that the mean length of interrogation was 16.3 hours.

It is not surprising that people can be induced to capitulate after long periods of time, indicating a dogged persistence in the face of denial. The needs for belonging, affiliation, and social support, especially in times of stress, are a fundamental human motive (Baumeister & Leary, 1995). People under stress seek out others for the psychological and physiological benefits that social support provides (Rofé, 1984; Schachter, 1959; Uchino, Cacioppo, & Kiecolt-Glaser, 1996). Prolonged isolation in this situation can thus be considered a form of deprivation. Depending on the number of hours and conditions of interrogation, sleep deprivation may also become a source of concern. Research in the laboratory and in field settings has shown that sleep deprivation can lower people's resistance to influence and impair their decision-making in complex tasks. The range of effects is varied, with studies showing that sleep deprivation impairs sustained attention, flexibility of thinking, and suggestibility in response to leading questions (Blagrove, 1996; for a review, see Harrison & Horne, 2000). Combining the results in a meta-analysis, Pilcher and Huffcutt (1996) thus concluded that sleep deprivation strongly impairs human functioning.

A second interrogation tactic that can induce confessions from innocent people is the presentation of false evidence. In the process of confronting suspects and refusing to accept their denials, U.S. police will sometimes present supposedly incontrovertible evidence of guilt (e.g., a fingerprint, blood or hair sample, eyewitness identification, or failed polygraph)—even if that evidence does not exist—as a way to convince suspects that resistance is futile and that confession is their best option. In the United States, it is permissible for police to outright lie to suspects about the evidence (*Frazier v. Cupp*, 1969). Empirical research, however, warns clearly of the risk.

There are two types of evidence for this conclusion. First, many proven false confession cases featured the use of the false evidence ploy. In one case, 17-year-old Marty Tankleff was accused of murdering his parents despite a complete absence of evidence against him. Tankleff denied the accusation for several hours. Then his interrogator told him that his hair was found on his mother, that a crime scene investigation test indicated he had showered (hence the lack of blood on him), and that his

hospitalized father had emerged from his coma to identify Marty as his assailant (in fact, the father never regained consciousness and died shortly thereafter). As a result of these lies, Tankleff became disoriented and confessed—then quickly retracted it. Solely on the basis of that confession, however, he was convicted in 1989, a conviction that was vacated in 2008 after he spent eighteen years in prison (Firstman & Salpeter, 2008). Tankleff's reaction to the outright lies about evidence is not surprising. In self-report studies, many actual suspects reported that the reason they confessed is that they perceived themselves to be trapped by the weight of evidence (Moston et al., 1992; Gudjonsson & Sigurdsson, 1999).

A number of laboratory experiments also indicate that the presentation of false evidence increases the rate of false confessions. In the first of these studies, Kassin and Kiechel (1996) accused participants of hitting a forbidden key during a computer-typing task and crashing a computer. Some participants but not others were also presented with false evidence in the form of a confederate eyewitness who claimed to have seen the participant hit the key. Despite their innocence and initial denials, subjects were then asked to sign a confession and queried to determine if they also had internalized a belief in their own culpability. The effect was dramatic: The presentation of false evidence nearly doubled the number of students who signed a written confession and internalized the belief in their guilt.

Follow-up studies have replicated this finding, to the extent that the alleged transgression was plausible (Horselenberg et al., 2006; Klaver, Lee, & Rose, 2008), even when the confession was said to bear a financial or other consequence (Horselenberg, Merckelbach, & Josephs, 2003; Redlich & Goodman, 2003), and even among informants who were pressured to report on a confession supposedly made by another person (Swanner, Beike, & Cole, 2010). Using a different paradigm, Nash and Wade (2009) used digital editing software to fabricate video evidence of participants in a computerized gambling experiment "stealing" money from the "bank" during a losing round. Presented with this false evidence, all participants confessed and most internalized the confession.

A third situational risk factor concerns the use of minimization. In addition to using the processes of confrontation, interrogators are trained to minimize the crime through "theme development," a process of providing moral justification or face-saving excuses, suggesting to suspects that their actions were spontaneous, accidental, provoked, pressured by others, induced by hormones or drugs, or otherwise justifiable by external factors. These themes are designed to lessen the anxiety associated with confession, but by what mechanism? Kassin and McNall (1991) proposed that minimization induces suspects to confess by implying leniency in consequences. To test this hypothesis, they had participants read a transcript of an interrogation of a murder suspect (the text was taken from an actual interrogation). The transcripts were edited to produce three versions in which the detective made a contingent explicit promise of leniency, used the technique of minimization by blaming the victim, or did not use either technique. Participants read one version and then estimated the sentence that they thought would be imposed on the suspect. The result: As if explicit promises had been made, minimization lowered sentencing expectations compared to conditions in which no technique was used.

Research has further shown that minimization can also lead innocent people to confess. Russano et al. (2005) devised a laboratory paradigm to not only assess the behavioral effects of minimization but to assess the diagnosticity of the resulting confession (a technique has *diagnosticity* to the extent that it increases the ratio of true to false confessions). In their study, subjects were paired with a confederate for a problem-solving study and instructed to work alone on some problems and jointly on others. In the guilty condition, the confederate sought help on a problem that was supposed to be solved alone, inducing commission of a "crime." In the innocent condition, the confederate did not make this request. The experimenter soon "discovered" a similarity in their solutions, separated the participant and confederate, and accused the participant of cheating. The experimenter then tried to get the participant to sign a confession by making an explicit promise of leniency (offering an opportunity to return for a second session), making

minimizing remarks (e.g., "I'm sure you didn't realize what a big deal it was."), using both tactics, or using no tactics. Overall, the confession rate was higher among guilty participants than innocent, when leniency was promised than when it was not, and when minimization was used than when it was not. Diagnosticity—defined as the rate of true confessions to false confessions—was highest when no tactics were used (46% of guilty suspects confessed vs. only 6% of innocents) and minimization—like an explicit offer of leniency—reduced diagnosticity by increasing not only the number of true confessions but even more so the rate of false confessions. In short, minimization statements may not offer explicit promises of leniency but they do lead people to infer that leniency will be forthcoming and confess as a result. It is important to note that minimization and the risk it engenders is not a mere laboratory phenomenon. Analyzing more than 125 electronically recorded interrogations and transcripts, Ofshe and Leo (1997) found that police often use these techniques that serve to communicate promises and threats by implication.

Innocence as a risk factor. On the basis of anecdotal evidence indicating that innocent people think and behave differently from guilty suspects in the interrogation room, Kassin (2005) proposed that innocence itself could be a risk factor for confession. Noting that innocent people believe that the truth—and their innocence—will prevail, Kassin and Norwick (2004) found, in a mock crime experiment, that innocent suspects are more likely to waive their *Miranda* rights to silence and to counsel even when in the presence of an officer who appears guilt-presumptive, hostile, and closed-minded (Kassin & Norwick, 2004; also see Moore & Gagnier, 2008). Still other research shows that innocent people do not use self-presentation "strategies" in their narratives when talking to police (Hartwig et al., 2005); they offer up alibis freely, without regard for the fact that police would view minor inaccuracies with suspicion (Olson & Charman, 2012); and they become less physiologically aroused in response to the stress of interrogation (Guyll et al., 2012). The sense of reassurance that accompanies innocence may reflect a generalized and perhaps motivated belief in a just world in which human beings get what they deserve and deserve what they get (Lerner, 1980). It may also occur because of an "illusion of transparency," a tendency for people to overestimate the extent to which their true thoughts, emotions, and other inner states can be seen by others (Gilovich, Savitsky, & Medvec, 1998; Miller & McFarland, 1987). Whatever the reason, a good deal of research now supports the hypothesis.

Feeling reassured and being forthright can have unintended consequences for the innocent suspect who is interrogated. As a natural consequence of the two-step process in which investigators make an initial judgment before interrogating a suspect, research shows that police presume guilt when questioning suspects and that this guilt bias can lead them to engage in more aggressive interrogations with innocent suspects who vigorously deny involvement (Kassin, Goldstein, & Savitsky, 2003). To innocent people, even apparently benign interrogation tactics can induce them to confess. Perillo and Kassin (2011) examined the bluff technique by which interrogators pretend to have evidence without the added lie that this evidence implicates the suspect (e.g., stating that biological evidence was collected and sent to a laboratory for testing). In theory, the bluff should threaten guilty suspects with certain detection, leading them to cooperate to cut their losses, without similarly affecting innocent people who have nothing to fear from this future evidence. In two experiments, Perillo and Kassin found that innocent participants were more likely to confess to pressing a forbidden key and causing a computer to crash when told that their keystrokes had been recorded for later review. In a third experiment, innocent participants were more likely to confess to willful cheating when told that a surveillance camera had taped their session. In both sets of studies, these participants reported afterward that the bluff had represented a promise of future exoneration despite confession, which paradoxically made it easier to confess.

The Consequences of Confession

A good deal of research has focused on the *causes* of true and false confessions, where agreement to sign a confession has served as the dependent measure. An important second direction has been to consider the *consequences* of confession in studies in which confession has served as an independent variable. In particular, research has focused on two criminal justice venues in which confession evidence is potent: in the courtroom, and during the criminal investigation process.

Confessions in the courtroom. Confession evidence is potent throughout the criminal justice system. Its impact begins with the police, who often close investigations rather than pursue exculpatory evidence or other possible suspects (Drizin & Leo, 2004; Leo & Ofshe, 1998), and extends to prosecutors, who sometimes maintain their beliefs in a confessor's guilt even after DNA evidence has established his or her innocence (Findley & Scott, 2006; Martin, 2011). Confessions are especially devastating in the courtroom. When a suspect retracts a confession—sometimes immediately after the pressure of interrogation has subsided—pleads not guilty, and goes to trial, a judge determines at a pretrial suppression hearing whether the confession was voluntary and hence admissible as evidence. There are no simple criteria for making this judgment, but the courts have made it clear that, although forms of trickery and deception are permissible, confessions are to be excluded if extracted by physical violence, threats of harm or punishment, explicit promises of leniency or immunity from prosecution, or—barring exceptional circumstances—if police failed to notify the suspect of his or her *Miranda* rights (for reviews, see Kassin et al., 2010; White, 2001). Whatever the criteria, confessions ruled voluntary are admitted at trial. Hearing the admissible confession, the jury then determines whether the defendant is guilty beyond a reasonable doubt. Are people truly accurate judges of confessions? What effect does this evidence have in the full context of a trial?

To assess whether police can distinguish between true and false confessions to actual crimes, Kassin, Meissner, and Norwick (2005) recruited male prison inmates to take part in a pair of videotaped interviews. Each inmate gave both a true narrative confession to the crime for which he was incarcerated and a newly concocted false confession to a crime he did not commit. Using this procedure, Kassin et al. compiled a videotape of ten confessions known to be true or false. College students and police investigators judged these statements, and the results showed that neither group exhibited significant accuracy, although police investigators were more confident in their judgments.

Research on the impact of confessions at trial is not more encouraging. Archival analyses show that when false confessors have pleaded not guilty and proceeded to trial, 73%–81% of cases result in conviction, even when there was scant corroboration and even when the confessions were inconsistent or contradicted by other evidence (Drizin & Leo, 2004; Leo & Ofshe, 1998). These figures led Drizin and Leo (2004) to describe confessions as "inherently prejudicial and highly damaging to a defendant, even if it is the product of coercive interrogation, even if it is supported by no other evidence, and even if it is ultimately proven false beyond any reasonable doubt" (p. 959).

Mock jury studies have also shown that confessions have more impact on verdicts than eyewitness and character testimony (Kassin & Neumann, 1997), and that people do not adequately discount confession evidence even when retracted confessions are perceived to have been coerced by police (Kassin & Wrightsman, 1980; Kassin & Sukel, 1997); even when jurors are told that the defendant suffers from a psychological illness or interrogation-induced stress (Henkel, 2008); even when the defendant is a juvenile (Redlich, Ghetti, & Quas, 2008; Redlich, Quas, & Ghetti, 2008); even when the confession was given not by the defendant but by a secondhand informant incentivized to lie (Neuschatz, Lawson, Swanner, Meissner, & Neuschatz, 2008; Neuschatz et al., 2012); and even when the confession is contradicted by exculpatory DNA that is explained away by the prosecutor (Appleby & Kassin, 2011; see Chapter 10, this volume for a review of research on jury decision making).

In a study that illustrates the potency of confession evidence, Kassin and Sukel (1997) presented subjects with one of three versions of a murder trial transcript. In a low-pressure version, the defendant was said to have confessed to police immediately upon questioning. In a high-pressure version, participants read that the suspect was in pain and interrogated aggressively by a detective who brandished

his gun. A control version contained no confession in evidence. In some ways, participants presented with the high-pressure confession responded in a legally appropriate manner: They judged the statement involuntary and said it did not influence their decisions. This confession, however, significantly boosted the conviction rate.

This pattern of results was recently replicated in a study involving judges. Wallace and Kassin (2012) presented 132 experienced judges with a case summary with strong or weak evidence and a confession elicited by either high- or low-pressure interrogation tactics, plus a no control group that did not include a confession. As expected, judges were less likely to see the confession as voluntary, and hence as properly admitted into evidence, when it resulted from a high-pressure than a low-pressure interrogation (29% vs. 84%, respectively). As in past research on mock juries, however, even the high-pressure confession significantly increased their guilty verdicts. In the weak-evidence condition, which produced a mere 17% conviction rate in the absence of a confession, a significant increase was produced not only by the low-pressure confession (96%) but by the high-pressure confession as well (69%). As with lay juries, it appears that judges are influenced by confession evidence such that they do not discount it when it is legally and logically appropriate to do so.

It is important to note that innocent people who confess are disadvantaged often by relinquishing their right to a jury trial. On the basis of the DNA exoneration cases from the Innocence Project database, Redlich (2010) found that exonerees who falsely confessed were four times more likely to plead guilty than those who had not confessed. Although these numbers are based on a small number of guilty pleas, this difference has persisted. Through the first 289 DNA exonerations, false confession cases were far more likely to be resolved by a guilty plea than were non-confession cases (26% vs. 4%; Kassin, 2012). Similar numbers appear in a larger database not restricted to convictions overturned by DNA (National Registry of Exonerations, 2012). Although more research is needed to shed light on the plea process, it appears that, relative to other innocents, those who confess are later more likely to surrender rather than assert a defense.

This is no small matter. Pleading guilty preempts the safeguards that come with a trial by jury in which a defendant is presumed innocent, the burden of proof is on the state, and accusing witnesses can be cross-examined. Pleading guilty also makes it more difficult later for a defendant to gain post-conviction scrutiny and assert factual innocence.

The various findings on the power of confession evidence through the stages of criminal justice raise a question: Why are confessions so persuasive? There are two reasons. First, common sense in general leads us to trust people's self-reports, especially when it comes to statements against self-interest. Hence, research shows that people are more likely to believe peoples' admissions of guilt than denials (Levine, Kim, & Blair, 2010; for an overview of the basic social psychology underlying this phenomenon, see Kassin, 2012). Surveys show that most people believe that they would never confess to a crime they did not commit and they evaluate others accordingly (Henkel, Coffman, & Dailey, 2008; Leo & Liu, 2009). Part of the problem is that people have only a rudimentary understanding of police interrogation tactics and the dispositional and situational risk factors that would lead someone to make a false confession (Blandón-Gitlin, Sperry, & Leo, 2011; Henkel et al., 2008; Leo & Liu, 2009).

Another reason that people trust confessions is that police are trained to convert initial admissions of guilt into credible narrative confessions that detail what, when, where, how, and even why the crime was committed and other content cues commonly associated with guilty knowledge and truth telling (Inbau et al., 2013). Garrett (2010) compared 38 proven false confessions from the Innocence Project DNA exoneration case files to the actual crime facts and found that 36 (95%) contained accurate details about the crime that were not in the public domain. Often the details served as a centerpiece for the prosecution at trial, with interrogating detectives testifying that these facts could have only been known by the perpetrator. The confessors in these cases have been proved innocent, so they could not have had a firsthand basis for guilty knowledge. Thus, it appears that police had communicated these details—purposefully or not—by asking leading questions, making factual assertions, showing photographs, or taking the suspect to the crime scene.

In a content analysis of 20 known false confessions, Appleby, Hasel, and Kassin (2013) found that most false confessions contained vivid sensory details about the crime and how, when, and where it was committed, including descriptions of the crime scene and the victim. Eighty percent also contained motive statements as to why the confessor allegedly committed the crime, often accompanied by a minimization theme that justified, excused, mitigated, or externalized blame. Half of the false confessors asserted that their statements were voluntary; 40% expressed remorse; and 25% outright apologized. Still others contained "illustrators" (e.g., a hand-drawn map or physical reenactment) and deliberately inserted errors that were corrected by the confessor. The contents of false confessions—present as a function of the interrogations through which they were produced—enhance perceptions of their credibility. To follow up on their content analysis, Appleby et al. (2013) varied the presence or absence of details, motive statements, and apologies in a mock jury experiment on the effects of confession evidence. Results showed that elaborate narrative confessions containing details about what happened, how, and why, increased perceptions of guilt and jurors' confidence in their convictions relative to a simple admission of guilt.

To summarize, confession evidence is highly persuasive and trusted by judges and juries alike, even when it is not appropriate to do so. Research suggests that confessions are believed as a matter of common sense and because of the ways that police convert admissions of guilt into full narrative confessions. In these regards, future research should examine feasible ways, to be described later, of increasing the accuracy with which triers of fact make judgments of guilt and innocence from confession evidence.

Confession effects on criminal investigations.
Just as confessions are trusted by judges and juries, often providing a sufficient basis for conviction, basic research in social cognition suggests the possibility that confessions may also have an impact on

how other evidence is collected and interpreted by tainting the perceptions of eyewitnesses, forensic scientists, and others. Basic cognitive and social psychological literature on confirmation biases suggests that one's preexisting expectations can affect subsequent perceptions and behaviors in a self-perpetuating cycle (see Nickerson, 1998, for a review). Findley and Scott (2006) described the phenomenon of "tunnel vision," whereby investigators identify a suspect and then rigidly focus on gathering additional inculpatory evidence against that suspect, overlooking or discounting exculpatory information. While one might argue tunnel vision is generally a useful heuristic for investigators (e.g., Snook & Cullen, 2008), such a process may well increase the likelihood of wrongful convictions. In an archival analysis of 125 known false confession cases, for example, Drizin and Leo (2004) noted that often once a confession is obtained, investigators "make no effort to pursue other possible leads" (p. 920). This creates what Risinger, Saks, Thompson, and Rosenthal (2002) called an "investigative echo chamber" (p. 29), where a narrowed focus on limited evidence makes it difficult to discover the suspect's innocence. With this in mind, research suggests that confessions, which create a particularly strong expectation of guilt, can trigger bias and thereby contribute to wrongful convictions by corrupting other evidence and creating an illusion of corroboration (Kassin, 2012). As indicated by basic research in social perception and cognition, as well as the recent forensic studies described below, the result is an investigative process that is tainted by forensic confirmation biases (see Kassin et al., 2013).

In one study, Hasel and Kassin (2009) had participants witness a staged theft and then make an identification decision from a target-absent lineup. Two days later, they were given additional information and an opportunity to change their decision. When told that another suspect had confessed, 61% of participants changed their initial decision and identified the suspect who had allegedly confessed. Those who were told that the individual they had identified confessed became more confident in their decision. Among participants who at first correctly rejected the lineup, indicating that the culprit was

not present, nearly half went on to identify an innocent person after being told that someone had confessed. In short, eyewitness identifications were corrupted by the confession.

Elaad, Ginton, and Ben-Shakhar (1994) observed a similar effect of confession evidence on polygraph examiners. In their experiment, 10 examiners analyzed records from polygraph interviews of suspects that had been deemed inconclusive by independent experts. When told that the suspect later confessed, examiners were more likely to judge the suspect as deceptive (9%) than truthful (4%). Conversely, when told that someone else later confessed, the suspect was more often judged as truthful (21%) than as deceptive (0%). Thus, professional examiners tended to score ambiguous polygraph charts in accordance with a confession-based expectation of the suspect's guilt or innocence.

Kukucka and Kassin (2014) found that knowledge of a recanted confession can also taint evaluations of handwriting evidence. In this study, lay participants read a bank robbery case in which the perpetrator gave a handwritten note to a bank teller. Soon afterward, they were told that a suspect was apprehended and interrogated, at which point he gave a handwritten *Miranda* waiver. Participants were asked to compare the handwriting samples taken from the perpetrator (the bank note) and the defendant (the *Miranda* waiver). When told that the defendant had confessed—even though he later recanted his confession and claimed it was coerced—participants perceived the handwriting samples as more similar and were more likely to conclude, erroneously, that they were authored by the same individual.

Dror and Charlton (2006) sought to examine the influence of contextual bias on latent fingerprint experts. Six experienced examiners were shown eight pairs of fingerprints that they had unknowingly examined earlier in their career. Half were previously judged a match, half a non-match. The prints were now presented with biasing contextual information—either that the suspect confessed (suggesting a match) or that he was in custody and had an alibi (suggesting a non-match). Strikingly, 17% of the examiners' judgments changed after exposure to the biasing alibi information. Half of the experts changed at least one of their previous judgments. This study is particularly troubling because the change as a function of context was obtained among experienced examiners, in a highly trusted forensic science, and in a within-subject experimental design. Moreover, this finding may extend to visual similarity judgments in other forensic science domains such as ballistics; hair and fiber analysis; impression evidence involving shoeprints, bite marks, tire tracks; and bloodstain pattern analysis (Dror & Cole, 2010). Even the interpretation of complex DNA mixtures is subject to bias (Dror & Hampikian, 2011).

In addition to the results of laboratory and field experiments, archival data also support the notion that confessions can corrupt other evidence. In an analysis of the first 241 DNA exonerations from the Innocence Project, Kassin, Bogart, and Kerner (2012) tested the hypothesis that confessions prompt additional evidentiary errors by examining whether other contributing factors were present in DNA exoneration cases containing a false confession. The results showed that additional errors were present in 78% of these cases. More specifically, false confessions were accompanied by invalid or improper forensic science (63%) and mistaken eyewitness identifications (29%) and snitches or informants (19%). Consistent with the causal hypothesis that the false confessions had influenced the subsequent errors, the confession was obtained first rather than later in the investigation in 65% of these cases.

By creating a strong expectation of guilt, confessions can taint the perceptions, memories, and judgments of lay and expert witnesses, corrupting other evidence and creating an illusion of corroboration for the confession itself. It is important to note that although confessions create a uniquely strong expectation of guilt, evidence can be tainted by other contextual information as well. For example, studies have shown that mock investigators judge facial composites as more similar to a suspect when told that he had been identified by an eyewitness (Charman, Gregory, & Carlucci, 2009; see also Chapter 7, this volume); people hear more incrimination in degraded audiotapes when told that the tapes depict an interview with a criminal suspect (Lange, Thomas, Dana, & Dawes, 2011); and

fingerprint experts more often judge ambiguous prints as a match when told that the prints came from a murder case than from a theft (Dror, Peron, Hind, & Charlton, 2005).

PRACTICE AND POLICY ISSUES

The literature on police interviews, interrogations, and confessions, the consequences of these confessions, and analyses of false confession-based wrongful convictions, have inspired various calls for systemic reform. In particular, research has compelled the conclusion that the video recording of interrogations is a necessary safeguard—indeed, it is the primary recommendation in the recent American Psychology-Law Society white paper—as a means of deterring coercive police tactics, lessening the risk of false confessions, and preserving the factual record for judges and juries empowered to assess the voluntariness and reliability of the confessions that are produced (see Kassin et al., 2010). At present, a number of states require the recording of interrogations in major felony investigations. A survey of 465 law enforcement agencies in states that do not require electronic recording of interrogations has revealed that the practice is widespread elsewhere as well. In these latter states, the reaction among police has been uniformly favorable (Sullivan, 2004; Sullivan, Vail, & Anderson, 2008).

Other recommendations have focused on the protection of highly vulnerable suspect populations and the reform of certain police interrogation practices. In light of the numerous false confession cases that have surfaced in recent years, one wonders on a macro level if the confrontational approach to interrogation commonly employed in the United States is inherently flawed. Recent history in Great Britain is instructive in this regard. Several years ago, after a number of high-profile false confessions, the British transitioned police from a classic interrogation to a process of "investigative interviewing," the primary purpose of which is fact-finding, not confession. The Police and Criminal Evidence Act of 1984 (Home Office, 1985) thus sought to reduce the use of psychological coercion. In 1993, the Royal Commission on Criminal Justice further reformed the practice of interrogation by proposing the PEACE model, using this mnemonic to describe the five parts of this approach—Preparation and Planning (i.e., organizing the evidence and planning the interview), Engage and Explain (i.e., establishing a rapport and communicating the purpose of the interview to the suspect), Account (conducting a "cognitive interview" to get the compliant suspect to speak freely and "conversation management" to open up the non-compliant suspect), Closure (addressing discrepancies that may appear in the suspect's narrative account), and Evaluation (comparing the suspect's final statement to evidence, trying to resolve inconsistencies, and drawing conclusions). On the question of whether investigative interviewing may prove an effective replacement for confrontational interrogation, preliminary naturalistic research is encouraging but more is needed (for an overview, see Clarke & Milne, 2001; Williamson, 2006).

A third issue concerns expert testimony. There is now a wealth of science in place to inform the courts on the dispositional and suspect factors that put innocent people at risk to confess. Research has shown that laypeople do not fundamentally understand false confessions as a matter of common sense, nor do they understand the processes of police interrogation that can put innocent people at risk. Over the years, the U.S. courts have proved inconsistent in their willingness to permit confession experts to testify at trial (Fulero, 2004). Indeed, the American Psychological Association has opined in two recently submitted *amicus* briefs (*Rivera v. Illinois*, 2011; *Michigan v. Kowalski*, 2012) that judges and juries have difficulty assessing confession evidence, that the phenomenon of false confession is counterintuitive, and that psychological experts should be permitted to testify at trial because their testimony would draw from generally accepted research and would assist the trier of fact. As always, more research will prove useful to address specific issues (e.g., how to increase the accuracy of interview-based judgments of truth and deception; how to protect vulnerable suspects; whether PEACE elicits more diagnostic interview outcomes than the Reid technique; whether suspects are affected in their behavior by knowing that their interrogations are being recorded). The literature that currently exists, however, some of which has been described

in this chapter, leads us to agree with the American Psychological Association that the necessary criteria for expert testimony on the psychology of confessions have been met.

SUMMARY AND CONCLUSIONS

Inspired by a number of cases involving people who were wrongfully convicted because of false confessions, researchers have drawn from basic psychology and research methods to understand the causes and consequences of confession evidence.

One line of research has focused on the methods of police interviewing and interrogation that are used to evaluate crime suspects and to elicit confessions from those presumed to be guilty. Importantly, most suspects waive their *Miranda* rights to silence and to counsel, their only means of legal protection, which allows this process of social influence to continue. Focusing on false confessions, a number of researchers have found that specific tactics used to manipulate anxiety in the interrogation room (e.g., isolation and questioning for lengthy periods of time, presentations of false evidence, and minimization themes that imply leniency upon confession) can cause innocent people to confess. In addition, certain types of suspects (e.g., juveniles as well as people who are intellectually impaired psychologically disordered) are particularly vulnerable to these types of manipulation.

A second line of research has focused on the consequences of confessions both in the courtroom and during the criminal investigation process. In court, judges and juries intuitively trust confessions, as seen in their guilty verdicts, even when they realize that the confessions were coerced by police and not corroborated by other evidence. Part of the problem is that common sense tells us that people do not confess to crimes they did not commit. In addition, research shows that most confessions, including false confessions, contain vivid crime details and other credibility cues. Recent research also shows that confessions can corrupt eyewitnesses and forensic examiners, thereby fostering an illusion that the confession is corroborated by independent evidence.

The literature reviewed in this chapter has motivated various calls for criminal justice reform. In particular, research has compelled the conclusion that the video recording of interrogations is an important means both to prevent coercive police tactics and to provide judges and juries with an accurate record of the process by which the confession was produced. Research also suggests that serious consideration be given to the reform of police interrogations, the recognition by the courts that confessions can corrupt other evidence, and the admissibility of psychological expert testimony at trial that would communicate this research and assist the trier of fact.

References

Appelbaum, K. L., & Appelbaum, P. S. (1994). Criminal justice-related competencies in defendants with mental retardation. *Journal of Psychiatry and Law, 22,* 483–503.

Appleby, S. C., Hasel, L. E., & Kassin, S. M. (2013). Police-induced confessions: An empirical analysis of their content and impact. *Psychology, Crime & Law, 19,* 111–128. doi:10.1080/1068316X.2011.613389

Appleby, S. C., & Kassin, S. M. (2011). *When confessions trump DNA: Relative impacts of self-report and DNA evidence on juror decisions.* Paper presented at the annual meeting of the American Psychology-Law Society, Miami, FL.

Asch, S. E. (1956). Studies of independence and conformity: A minority of one against a unanimous majority. *Psychological Monographs, 70,* 1–70. doi:10.1037/h0093718

Baldwin, J. (1993). Police interviewing techniques: Establishing truth or proof? *British Journal of Criminology, 33,* 325–352.

Baumeister, R. F., & Leary, M. R. (1995). The need to belong: Desire for interpersonal attachments as a fundamental human motivation. *Psychological Bulletin, 117,* 497–529. doi:10.1037/0033-2909.117.3.497

Bem, D. J. (1966). Inducing belief in false confessions. *Journal of Personality and Social Psychology, 3,* 707–710. doi:10.1037/h0023226

Blagrove, M. (1996). Effects of length of sleep deprivation on interrogative suggestibility. *Journal of Experimental Psychology: Applied, 2,* 48–59. doi:10.1037/1076-898X.2.1.48

Blandón-Gitlin, I., Sperry, K., & Leo, R. (2011). Jurors believe interrogation tactics are not likely to elicit false confessions: Will expert witness testimony inform them otherwise? *Psychology, Crime & Law, 17,* 239–260. doi:10.1080/10683160903113699

Bond, C. F., Jr., & DePaulo, B. M. (2006). Accuracy of deception judgments. *Personality and Social Psychology Review, 10,* 214–234. doi:10.1207/s15327957pspr1003_2

Brief for the American Psychological Association as Amicus Curiae, Rivera v. Illinois, 962 N.E.2d 53 (2011).

Brief for the American Psychological Association as Amicus Curiae, Michigan v. Kowalski, 492 Mich. 106 (2012).

Brown v. Mississippi, 297 U.S. 278 (1936).

Burns, S. (2011). *The Central Park Five: A chronicle of city wilding.* New York, NY: Knopf.

Cassell, P. G., & Hayman, B. S. (1996). Police interrogation in the 1990s: An empirical study of the effects of *Miranda. UCLA Law Review, 43,* 893–931.

Cauffman, E., & Steinberg, L. (2000). (Im)maturity of judgment in adolescence: Why adolescents may be less culpable than adults. *Behavioral Sciences and the Law, 18,* 741–760. doi:10.1002/bsl.416

Charman, S. D., Gregory, A. H., & Carlucci, M. (2009). Exploring the diagnostic utility of facial composites: Beliefs of guilt can bias perceived similarity between composite and suspect. *Journal of Experimental Psychology: Applied, 15,* 76–90. doi:10.1037/a0014682

Cialdini, R. B. (2001). *Influence: Science and practice* (4th ed.). Needham Heights, MA: Allyn & Bacon.

Clare, I., & Gudjonsson, G. H. (1995). The vulnerability of suspects with intellectual disabilities during police interviews: A review and experimental study of decision-making. *Mental Handicap Research, 8,* 110–128. doi:10.1111/j.1468-3148.1995.tb00149.x

Clarke, C., & Milne, R. (2001). *National evaluation of the PEACE investigative interviewing course. Police Research Award Scheme.* London, England: Home Office.

Cloud, M., Shepherd, G. B., Barkoff, A. N., & Shur, J. V. (2002). Words without meaning: The Constitution, confessions, and mentally retarded suspects. *University of Chicago Law Review, 69,* 495–624. doi:10.2307/1600500

Davis, D., & Leo, R. A. (2012). Interrogation-related regulatory decline: Ego depletion, failures of self-regulation, and the decision to confess. *Psychology, Public Policy, and Law.* Advance online publication. doi:10.1037/a0027367

Davis, D., & O'Donohue, W. (2004). The road to perdition: "Extreme influence" tactics in the interrogation room. In W. O'Donohue, P. Laws, & C. Hollin (Eds.), *Handbook of forensic psychology* (pp. 897–996). New York, NY: Basic Books.

Dickerson v. United States, 530 U.S. 428 (2000).

Drizin, S. A., & Colgan, B. (2004). Tales from the juvenile confession front: A guide to how standard police interrogation tactics can produce coerced and false confessions from juvenile suspects. In G. D. Lassiter (Ed.), *Interrogations, confessions, and entrapment* (pp. 127–162). New York, NY: Kluwer Academic/Plenum Press. doi:10.1007/978-0-387-38598-3_6

Drizin, S. A., & Leo, R. A. (2004). The problem of false confessions in the post-DNA world. *North Carolina Law Review, 82,* 891–1004.

Dror, I. E., & Charlton, D. (2006). Why experts make errors. *Journal of Forensic Identification, 56,* 600–616.

Dror, I. E., & Cole, S. A. (2010). The vision in "blind" justice: Expert perception, judgment, and visual cognition in forensic pattern recognition. *Psychonomic Bulletin and Review, 17,* 161–167. doi:10.3758/PBR.17.2.161

Dror, I. E., & Hampikian, G. (2011). Subjectivity and bias in forensic DNA mixture interpretation. *Science and Justice, 51,* 204–208. doi:10.1016/j.scijus.2011.08.004

Dror, I. E., Peron, A. E., Hind, S.-L., & Charlton, D. (2005). When emotions get the better of us: The effect of contextual top-down processing on matching fingerprints. *Applied Cognitive Psychology, 19,* 799–809. doi:10.1002/acp.1130

Elaad, E. (2003). Effects of feedback on the overestimated capacity to detect lies and the underestimated ability to tell lies. *Applied Cognitive Psychology, 17,* 349–363. doi:10.1002/acp.871

Elaad, E., Ginton, A., & Ben-Shakhar, G. (1994). The effects of prior expectations and outcome knowledge on polygraph examiners' decisions. *Journal of Behavioral Decision Making, 7,* 279–292. doi:10.1002/bdm.3960070405

Everington, C., & Fulero, S. (1999). Competence to confess: Measuring understanding and suggestibility of defendants with mental retardation. *Mental Retardation, 37,* 212–220. doi:10.1352/0047-6765(1999)037<0212:CTCMUA>2.0.CO;2

Feld, B. C. (2013). *Kids, cops, and confessions: Inside the interrogation room.* New York: New York University Press.

Findley, K. A., & Scott, M. S. (2006). The multiple dimensions of tunnel vision in criminal cases. *Wisconsin Law Review, 2,* 291–397.

Finlay, W. M. L., & Lyons, E. (2002). Acquiescence in interviews with people who have mental retardation. *Mental Retardation, 40,* 14–29. doi:10.1352/0047-6765(2002)040<0014:AIIWPW>2.0.CO;2

Firstman, R., & Salpeter, J. (2008). *A criminal injustice: A true crime, a false confession, and the fight to the free Marty Tankleff.* New York, NY: Ballantine Books.

Frantzen, D. (2010). Interrogation strategies, evidence, and the need for *Miranda:* A study of police ideologies. *Police Practice and Research: An International Journal, 11,* 227–239. doi:10.1080/15614260902830005

Frazier v. Cupp, 394 U.S. 731 (1969).

Fulero, S., & Everington, C. (1995). Assessing competency to waive *Miranda* rights in defendants with mental retardation. *Law and Human Behavior, 19,* 533–543. doi:10.1007/BF01499342

Fulero, S. M. (2004). Expert psychological testimony on the psychology of interrogations and confessions. In G. Lassiter (Ed.), *Interrogations, confessions, and entrapment* (pp. 247–263). New York, NY: Kluwer Academic/Plenum Press. doi:10.1007/978-0-387-38598-3_11

Galván, A., & McGlennen, K. M. (2012). Daily stress increases risky decision-making in adolescents: A preliminary study. *Developmental Psychobiology, 54,* 433–440. doi:10.1002/dev.20602

Garrett, B. L. (2010). The substance of false confessions. *Stanford Law Review, 62,* 1051–1119.

Garrett, B. L. (2011). *Convicting the innocent: Where criminal prosecutions go wrong.* Cambridge, MA: Harvard University Press. doi:10.4159/harvard.9780674060982

Garrido, E., Masip, J., & Herrero, C. (2004). Police offers' credibility judgments: Accuracy and estimated ability. *International Journal of Psychology, 39,* 254–275. doi:10.1080/00207590344000411

Gilovich, T., Savitsky, K., & Medvec, V. (1998). The illusion of transparency: Biased assessments of others' ability to read one's emotional states. *Journal of Personality and Social Psychology, 75,* 332–346. doi:10.1037/0022-3514.75.2.332

Goldstein, N. E. S., Condie, L. O., Kalbeitzer, R., Osman, D., & Geier, J. L. (2003). Juvenile offenders' *Miranda* rights comprehension and self-reported likelihood of offering false confessions. *Assessment, 10,* 359–369. doi:10.1177/1073191103259535

Grisso, T. (1981). *Juveniles' waiver of rights: Legal and psychological competence.* New York, NY: Plenum Press. doi:10.1007/978-1-4684-3815-4

Gross, S. R., Jacoby, K., Matheson, D. J., Montgomery, N., & Patel, S. (2005). Exonerations in the United States 1989 through 2003. *Journal of Criminal Law and Criminology, 95,* 523–553.

Gudjonsson, G. H. (1992). *The psychology of interrogations, confessions, and testimony.* London, England: Wiley.

Gudjonsson, G. H. (2003). *The psychology of interrogations and confessions: A handbook.* Chichester, England: Wiley.

Gudjonsson, G. H. (2010). The psychology of false confessions: A review of the current evidence. In G. D. Lassiter & C. A. Meissner (Eds.), *Police interrogations and false confessions: Current research, practice, and policy recommendations* (pp. 31–47). Washington, DC: American Psychological Association. doi:10.1037/12085-002

Gudjonsson, G. H., & Henry, L. A. (2003). Child and adult witnesses with learning disabilities: The importance of suggestibility. *Legal and Criminological Psychology, 8,* 241–252. doi:10.1348/135532503322363013

Gudjonsson, G. H., & Sigurdsson, J. F. (1999). The Gudjonsson Confession Questionnaire-Revised (GCQ-R): Factor structure and its relationship with personality. *Personality and Individual Differences, 27,* 953–968. doi:10.1016/S0191-8869(98)00278-5

Gudjonsson, G. H., Sigurdsson, J. F., Bragason, O. O., Newton, A. K., & Einarsson, E. (2008). Interrogative suggestibility, compliance and false confessions among prisoners and their relationship with attention deficit hyperactivity disorder (ADHD) symptoms. *Psychological Medicine, 38,* 1037–1044. doi:10.1017/S0033291708002882

Gudjonsson, G. H., Sigurdsson, J. F., Einarsson, E., Bragason, O. O., & Newton, A. K. (2010). Inattention, hyperactivity/impulsivity, and antisocial personality disorder. Which is the best predictor of false confession? *Personality and Individual Differences, 48,* 720–724. doi:10.1016/j.paid.2010.01.012

Gudjonsson, G. H., Sigurdsson, J. F., & Sigfusdottir, I. D. (2009). False confessions among 15 and 16 year olds in compulsory education and their relationship with adverse life events. *Journal of Forensic Psychiatry and Psychology, 20,* 950–963. doi:10.1080/14789940903174212

Gudjonsson, G. H., Sigurdsson, J. F., Sigfusdottir, I. D., & Young, S. (2012). False confessions to police and their relationship with conduct disorder, ADHD, and life adversity. *Personality and Individual Differences, 52,* 696–701. doi:10.1016/j.paid.2011.12.025

Guyll, M., Madon, S., Yang, Y., Scherr, K. C., Lannin, D., Smalarz, L., . . . Greathouse, S. (2012, March). *Physiologic reactions to interrogation stress: Differences between the innocent and the guilty.* Paper presented at the Annual Conference of the American Psychology-Law Society, San Juan, Puerto Rico.

Harrison, Y., & Horne, J. A. (2000). The impact of sleep deprivation on decision making: A review. *Journal of Experimental Psychology: Applied, 6,* 236–249. doi:10.1037/1076-898X.6.3.236

Hartwig, M., & Bond, C. F., Jr. (2011). Why do lie-catchers fail? A lens model of human lie judgments. *Psychological Bulletin, 137,* 643–659. doi:10.1037/a0023589

Hartwig, M., Granhag, P., Strömwall, L. A., & Kronkvist, O. (2006). Strategic use of evidence during police interviews: When training to detect deception works. *Law and Human Behavior, 30,* 603–619. doi:10.1007/s10979-006-9053-9

Hartwig, M., Granhag, P., Strömwall, L. A., & Vrij, A. (2005). Detecting deception via strategic disclosure of evidence. *Law and Human Behavior, 29,* 469–484. doi:10.1007/s10979-005-5521-x

Hasel, L. E., & Kassin, S. M. (2009). On the presumption of evidentiary independence: Can confessions corrupt eyewitness identifications? *Psychological Science, 20,* 122–126. doi:10.1111/j.1467-9280.2008.02262.x

Henkel, L. A. (2008). Jurors' reactions to recanted confessions: Do the defendant's personal and dispositional characteristics play a role? *Psychology, Crime & Law, 14,* 565–578. doi:10.1080/10683160801995247

Henkel, L. A., Coffman, K. A. J., & Dailey, E. M. (2008). A survey of people's attitudes and beliefs about false confessions. *Behavioral Sciences and the Law, 26,* 555–584. doi:10.1002/bsl.826

Herrnstein, R. J. (1970). On the law of effect. *Journal of the Experimental Analysis of Behavior, 13,* 243–266. doi:10.1901/jeab.1970.13-243

Herrnstein, R. J., Rachlin, H., & Laibson, D. I. (Eds.). (1997). *The matching law: Papers in psychology and economics.* New York, NY: Russell Sage Foundation.

Home Office. (1985). *Police and Criminal Evidence Act 1984.* London, England: HMSO.

Horselenberg, R., Merckelbach, H., & Josephs, S. (2003). Individual differences and false confessions: A conceptual replication of Kassin and Kiechel (1996). *Psychology, Crime & Law, 9,* 1–8. doi:10.1080/1068316030308141

Horselenberg, R., Merckelbach, H., Smeets, T., Franssens, D., Peters, G., & Zeles, G. (2006). False confessions in the lab: Do plausibility and consequences matter? *Psychology, Crime & Law, 12,* 61–75. doi:10.1080/1068310042000303076

Horvath, F., Jayne, B., & Buckley, J. (1994). Differentiation of truthful and deceptive criminal suspects in behavior analysis interviews. *Journal of Forensic Sciences, 39,* 793–807.

Inbau, F. E., Reid, J. E., Buckley, J. P., & Jayne, B. C. (2013). *Criminal interrogation and confessions* (5th ed.). Burlington, MA: Jones & Bartlett Learning.

Kassin, S. M. (1997). The psychology of confession evidence. *American Psychologist, 52,* 221–233. doi:10.1037/0003-066X.52.3.221

Kassin, S. M. (2005). On the psychology of confessions: Does innocence put innocents at risk? *American Psychologist, 60,* 215–228. doi:10.1037/0003-066X.60.3.215

Kassin, S. M. (2007). Internalized false confessions. In M. Toglia, J. Read, D. Ross, & R. Lindsay (Eds.), *Handbook of eyewitness psychology: Vol. 1. Memory for events* (pp. 175–192). Mahwah, NJ: Erlbaum.

Kassin, S. M. (2012). Why confessions trump innocence. *American Psychologist, 67,* 431–445. doi:10.1037/a0028212

Kassin, S. M., Bogart, D., & Kerner, J. (2012). Confessions that corrupt: Evidence from the DNA exoneration case files. *Psychological Science, 23,* 41–45. doi:10.1177/0956797611422918

Kassin, S. M., Drizin, S. A., Grisso, T., Gudjonsson, G. H., Leo, R. A., & Redlich, A. D. (2010). Police-induced confessions: Risk factors and recommendations. *Law and Human Behavior, 34,* 3–38. doi:10.1007/s10979-009-9188-6

Kassin, S. M., Dror, I. E., & Kukucka, J. (2013). The forensic confirmation bias: Problems, perspectives, and proposed solutions. *Journal of Applied Research in Memory and Cognition, 2,* 42–52. doi:10.1016/j.jarmac.2013.01.001

Kassin, S. M., & Fong, C. T. (1999). "I'm innocent!": Effects of training on judgments of truth and deception in the interrogation room. *Law and Human Behavior, 23,* 499–516. doi:10.1023/A:1022330011811

Kassin, S. M., Goldstein, C. C., & Savitsky, K. (2003). Behavioral confirmation in the interrogation room: On the dangers of presuming guilt. *Law and Human Behavior, 27,* 187–203. doi:10.1023/A:1022599230598

Kassin, S. M., & Gudjonsson, G. H. (2004). The psychology of confessions: A review of the literature and issues. *Psychological Science in the Public Interest, 5,* 33–67. doi:10.1111/j.1529-1006.2004.00016.x

Kassin, S. M., & Kiechel, K. L. (1996). The social psychology of false confessions: Compliance, internalization, and confabulation. *Psychological Science, 7,* 125–128. doi:10.1111/j.1467-9280.1996.tb00344.x

Kassin, S. M., Leo, R. A., Meissner, C. A., Richman, K. D., Colwell, L. H., & Leach, A. M. (2007). Police interviewing and interrogation: A self-report survey of police practices and beliefs. *Law and Human Behavior, 31,* 381–400. doi:10.1007/s10979-006-9073-5

Kassin, S. M., & McNall, K. (1991). Police interrogations and confessions: Communicating promises and threats by pragmatic implication. *Law and Human Behavior, 15,* 233–251. doi:10.1007/BF01061711

Kassin, S. M., Meissner, C. A., & Norwick, R. J. (2005). "I'd know a false confession if I saw one": A comparative study of college students and police investigators. *Law and Human Behavior, 29,* 211–227. doi:10.1007/s10979-005-2416-9

Kassin, S. M., & Neumann, K. (1997). On the power of confession evidence: An experimental test of the "fundamental difference" hypothesis. *Law and Human Behavior, 21,* 469–484. doi:10.1023/A:1024871622490

Kassin, S. M., & Norwick, R. J. (2004). Why suspects waive their *Miranda* rights: The power of innocence. *Law and Human Behavior, 28,* 211–221. doi:10.1023/B:LAHU.0000022323.74584.f5

Kassin, S. M., & Sukel, H. (1997). Coerced confessions and the jury: An experimental test of the "harmless error" rule. *Law and Human Behavior, 21,* 27–46. doi:10.1023/A:1024814009769

Kassin, S. M., & Wrightsman, L. S. (1980). Prior confessions and mock juror verdicts. *Journal of Applied Social Psychology, 10,* 133–146. doi:10.1111/j.1559-1816.1980.tb00698.x

Kassin, S. M., & Wrightsman, L. S. (1985). Confession evidence. In S. M. Kassin & L. S. Wrightsman (Eds.), *The psychology of evidence and trial procedure* (3rd ed., pp. 67–94). Beverly Hills, CA: Sage.

King, L., & Snook, B. (2009). Peering inside a Canadian interrogation room: An examination of the Reid model of interrogation, influence tactics, and coercive strategies. *Criminal Justice and Behavior, 36,* 674–694. doi:10.1177/0093854809335142

Klaver, J., Lee, Z., & Rose, V. G. (2008). Effects of personality, interrogation techniques and plausibility in an experimental false confession paradigm. *Legal and Criminological Psychology, 13,* 71–88. doi:10.1348/135532507X193051

Kukucka, J., & Kassin, S. M. (2014). Do confessions taint juror perceptions of handwriting evidence? An empirical test of the forensic confirmation bias. *Law and Human Behavior, 38,* 56–70.

Lange, N. D., Thomas, R. P., Dana, J., & Dawes, R. M. (2011). Contextual biases in the interpretation of auditory evidence. *Law and Human Behavior, 35,* 178–187. doi:10.1007/s10979-010-9226-4

Latané, B. (1981). The psychology of social impact. *American Psychologist, 36,* 343–356. doi:10.1037/0003-066X.36.4.343

Leach, A.-M., Talwar, V., Lee, K., Bala, N., & Lindsay, R. L. (2004). "Intuitive" lie detection of children's deception by law enforcement officials and university students. *Law and Human Behavior, 28,* 661–685. doi:10.1007/s10979-004-0793-0

Leo, R. A. (1996a). The impact of *Miranda* revisited. *Journal of Criminal Law and Criminology, 86,* 621–692. doi:10.2307/1143934

Leo, R. A. (1996b). Inside the interrogation room. *Journal of Criminal Law and Criminology, 86,* 266–303. doi:10.2307/1144028

Leo, R. A. (2008). *Police interrogation and American justice.* Cambridge, MA: Harvard University Press.

Leo, R. A., & Liu, B. (2009). What do potential jurors know about police interrogation techniques and false confessions? *Behavioral Sciences and the Law*, 27, 381–399. doi:10.1002/bsl.872

Leo, R. A., & Ofshe, R. J. (1998). The consequences of false confessions: Deprivations of liberty and miscarriages of justice in the age of psychological interrogation. *Journal of Criminal Law and Criminology*, 88, 429–496. doi:10.2307/1144288

Lerner, M. J. (1980). *The belief in a just world*. New York, NY: Plenum Press. doi:10.1007/978-1-4899-0448-5

Levine, T. R., Kim, R. K., & Blair, J. P. (2010). (In)-accuracy at detecting true and false confessions and denials: An initial test of a projected motive model of veracity judgments. *Human Communication Research*, 36, 82–102. doi:10.1111/j.1468-2958.2009.01369.x

Loftus, E. F. (2005). Planting misinformation in the human mind: A 30-year investigation of the malleability of memory. *Learning and Memory*, 12, 361–366. doi:10.1101/lm.94705

Madon, S., Guyll, M., Scherr, K., Greathouse, S., & Wells, G. L. (2012). Temporal discounting: The differential effect of proximal and distal consequences on confession decisions. *Law and Human Behavior*, 36, 13–20. doi:10.1037/h0093962

Martin, A. (2011, November 27). The prosecution's case against DNA. *New York Times Magazine*, p. MM44.

Masip, J., Barba, A., & Herrero, C. (2012). Behavioral Analysis Interview and common sense: A study with novice and experienced officers. *Psychiatry, Psychology and Law*, 19, 21–34. doi:10.1080/13218719.2010.543402

Masip, J., Herrero, C., Garrido, E., & Barba, A. (2011). Is the Behavior Analysis Interview just common sense? *Applied Cognitive Psychology*, 25, 593–604. doi:10.1002/acp.1728

McLachlan, K., Roesch, R., & Douglas, K. S. (2011). Examining the role of interrogative suggestibility in Miranda rights comprehension in adolescents. *Law and Human Behavior*, 35, 165–177. doi:10.1007/s10979-009-9198-4

Meissner, C. A., & Kassin, S. M. (2002). "He's guilty!": Investigator bias in judgments of truth and deception. *Law and Human Behavior*, 26, 469–480. doi:10.1023/A:1020278620751

Meyer, J. R., & Reppucci, N. D. (2007). Police practices and perceptions regarding juvenile interrogation and interrogative suggestibility. *Behavioral Sciences and the Law*, 25, 757–780. doi:10.1002/bsl.774

Milgram, S. (1974). *Obedience to authority: An experimental view*. New York, NY: Harper & Row.

Miller, D. T., & McFarland, C. (1987). Pluralistic ignorance: When similarity is interpreted as dissimilarity. *Journal of Personality and Social Psychology*, 53, 298–305. doi:10.1037/0022-3514.53.2.298

Miranda v. Arizona, 384 U.S. 436 (1966).

Moore, T. E., & Gagnier, K. (2008). "You can talk if you want to": Is the police caution on the right to silence comprehensible? *Criminal Reports*, 5, 233–249.

Moston, S., Stephenson, G. M., & Williamson, T. (1992). The effects of case characteristics on suspect behaviour during police questioning. *British Journal of Criminology*, 32, 23–39.

Nash, R. A., & Wade, K. A. (2009). Innocent but proven guilty: Eliciting internalized false confessions using doctored-video evidence. *Applied Cognitive Psychology*, 23, 624–637. doi:10.1002/acp.1500

National Institute of Mental Health (2001). *Teenage brain: A work in progress*. Bethesda, MD: Author.

National Registry of Exonerations. (2012). Retrieved from http://www.law.umich.edu/special/exoneration

Neuschatz, J. S., Lawson, D. S., Swanner, J. K., Meissner, C. A., & Neuschatz, J. S. (2008). The effects of accomplice witnesses and jailhouse informants on jury decision making. *Law and Human Behavior*, 32, 137–149. doi:10.1007/s10979-007-9100-1

Neuschatz, J. S., Wilkinson, M. L., Goodsell, C. A., Wetmore, S. A., Quinlivan, D. S., & Jones, N. J. (2012). Secondary confessions, expert testimony, and unreliable testimony. *Journal of Police and Criminal Psychology*, 27, 179–192. doi:10.1007/s11896-012-9102-x

Nickerson, R. S. (1998). Confirmation bias: A ubiquitous phenomenon in many guises. *Review of General Psychology*, 2, 175–220. doi:10.1037/1089-2680.2.2.175

North, A. S., Russell, A. J., & Gudjonsson, G. H. (2008). High functioning autism spectrum disorders: An investigation of psychological vulnerabilities during interrogative interview. *Journal of Forensic Psychiatry and Psychology*, 19, 323–334. doi:10.1080/14789940701871621

Oberlander, L. B., & Goldstein, N. E. (2001). A review and update on the practice of evaluating *Miranda* comprehension. *Behavioral Sciences and the Law*, 19, 453–471. doi:10.1002/bsl.453

O'Connell, M. J., Garmoe, W., & Goldstein, N. E. S. (2005). *Miranda* comprehension in adults with mental retardation and the effects of feedback style on suggestibility. *Law and Human Behavior*, 29, 359–369. doi:10.1007/s10979-005-2965-y

Office of Juvenile Justice and Delinquency Prevention. (2012). *OJJDP statistical briefing book*. Retrieved from http://www.ojjdp.gov/ojstatbb/offenders/qa03105.asp?qaDate=2010

Ofshe, R. J., & Leo, R. A. (1997). The social psychology of police interrogation: The theory and classification of true and false confessions. *Studies in Law, Politics, and Society*, 16, 189–251.

Olson, E. A., & Charman, S. D. (2012). "But can you prove it?" Examining the quality of innocent suspects' alibis. *Psychology, Crime & Law, 18*, 453–471.

Owen-Kostelnik, J., Reppucci, N. D., & Meyer, J. R. (2006). Testimony and interrogation of minors: Assumptions about maturity and morality. *American Psychologist, 61*, 286–304. doi:10.1037/0003-066X.61.4.286

Perillo, J. T., & Kassin, S. M. (2011). Inside interrogation: The lie, the bluff, and false confessions. *Law and Human Behavior, 35*, 327–337. doi:10.1007/s10979-010-9244-2

Perlman, N. B., Ericson, K. I., Esses, V. M., & Isaacs, B. J. (1994). The developmentally handicapped witness: Competency as a function of question format. *Law and Human Behavior, 18*, 171–187. doi:10.1007/BF01499014

Petty, R. E., & Cacioppo, J. T. (1986). *Communication and persuasion: Central and peripheral routes to attitude change.* New York, NY: Springer-Verlag. doi:10.1007/978-1-4612-4964-1

Pilcher, J. J., & Huffcutt, A. J. (1996). Effects of sleep deprivation on performance: A meta-analysis. *Sleep, 19*, 318–326.

Puzzanchera, C., & Adams, B. (2011). *Juvenile arrests 2009.* Washington, DC: Office of Juvenile Justice and Delinquency Prevention.

Rachlin, H. (2000). *The science of self-control.* Cambridge, MA: Harvard University Press.

Redlich, A. D. (2004). Mental illness, police interrogation, and the potential for false confession. *Psychiatric Services, 55*, 19–21. doi:10.1176/appi.ps.55.1.19

Redlich, A. D. (2007). Double jeopardy in the interrogation room for youths with mental illness. *American Psychologist, 62*, 609–611. doi:10.1037/0003-066X62.6.609

Redlich, A. D. (2010). False confessions and false guilty pleas: Similarities and differences. In G. D. Lassiter & C. Meissner (Eds.), Police *interrogations and* false *confessions: Current research, practice, and policy recommendations* (pp. 49–66). Washington, DC: American Psychological Association. doi:10.1037/12085-003

Redlich, A. D., Ghetti, S., & Quas, J. A. (2008). Perceptions of children during a police interview: A comparison of alleged victims and suspects. *Journal of Applied Social Psychology, 38*, 705–735. doi:10.1111/j.1559-1816.2007.00323.x

Redlich, A. D., & Goodman, G. S. (2003). Taking responsibility for an act not committed: Influence of age and suggestibility. *Law and Human Behavior, 27*, 141–156. doi:10.1023/A:1022543012851

Redlich, A. D., Kulish, R., & Steadman, H. J. (2011). Comparing true and false confessions among persons with serious mental illness. *Psychology, Public Policy, and Law, 17*, 394–418. doi:10.1037/a0022918

Redlich, A. D., Quas, J. A., & Ghetti, S. (2008). Perceptions of children during a police interrogation: Guilt, confessions, and interview fairness. *Psychology, Crime & Law, 14*, 201–223. doi:10.1080/10683160701652542

Redlich, A. D., Summers, A., & Hoover, S. (2010). Self-reported false confessions and false guilty pleas among offenders with mental illness. *Law and Human Behavior, 34*, 79–90. doi:10.1007/s10979-009-9194-8

Reyna, V. F., Estrada, S. M., DeMarinis, J. A., Myers, R. M., Stanisz, J. M., & Mills, B. A. (2011). Neurobiological and memory models of risky decision making in adolescents versus young adults. *Journal of Experimental Psychology: Learning, Memory, and Cognition, 37*, 1125–1142. doi:10.1037/a0023943

Ripke, S., Hübner, T., Mennigen, E., Müller, K. U., Rodehacke, S., Schmidt, D., . . . Smolka, M. N. (2012). Reward processing and intertemporal decision making in adults and adolescents: The role of impulsivity and decision consistency. *Brain Research, 1478*, 36–47. doi:10.1016/j.brainres.2012.08.034

Risinger, D. M., Saks, M. J., Thompson, W. C., & Rosenthal, R. (2002). The Daubert/Kumho implications of observer effects in forensic science: Hidden problems of expectation and suggestion. *California Law Review, 90*, 1–56. doi:10.2307/3481305

Rofé, Y. (1984). Stress and affiliation: A utility theory. *Psychological Review, 91*, 235–250. doi:10.1037/0033-295X.91.2.235

Rogers, R., Blackwood, H. L., Fiduccia, C. E., Steadham, J. A., Drogin, E. Y., & Rogstad, J. E. (2012). Juvenile *Miranda* warnings: Perfunctory rituals or procedural safeguards? *Criminal Justice and Behavior, 39*, 229–249. doi:10.1177/0093854811431934

Rogers, R., Gillard, N. D., Wooley, C. N., & Fiduccia, C. E. (2011). Decrements in *Miranda* abilities: An investigation of situational effects via a mock-crime paradigm. *Law and Human Behavior, 35*, 392–401. doi:10.1007/s10979-010-9248-y

Rogers, R., Harrison, K. S., Shuman, D. W., Sewell, K. W., & Hazelwood, L. L. (2007). An analysis of *Miranda* warnings and waivers: Comprehension and coverage. *Law and Human Behavior, 31*, 177–192. doi:10.1007/s10979-006-9054-8

Rogers, R., Hazelwood, L. L., Sewell, K. W., Harrison, K. S., & Shuman, D. W. (2008). The language of *Miranda* warnings in American jurisdictions: A replication and vocabulary analysis. *Law and Human Behavior, 32*, 124–136. doi:10.1007/s10979-007-9091-y

Rogers, R., Rogstad, J. E., Gillard, N. D., Drogin, E. Y., Blackwood, H. L., & Shuman, D. W. (2010). "Everyone knows their *Miranda* rights": Implicit assumptions and countervailing evidence.

Psychology, Public Policy, and Law, 16, 300–318. doi:10.1037/a0019316

Russano, M. B., Meissner, C. A., Narchet, F. M., & Kassin, S. M. (2005). Investigating true and false confessions within a novel experimental paradigm. *Psychological Science, 16*, 481–486.

Salseda, L. M., Dixon, D. R., Fass, T., Miora, D., & Leark, R. A. (2011). An evaluation of *Miranda* rights and interrogation in autism spectrum disorders. *Research in Autism Spectrum Disorders, 5*, 79–85. doi:10.1016/j.rasd.2010.06.014

Schachter, S. (1959). *The psychology of affiliation: Experimental studies of the sources of gregariousness.* Palo Alto, CA: Stanford University Press.

Schacter, D. L. (2001). *The seven sins of memory: How the mind forgets and remembers.* Boston, MA: Houghton Mifflin.

Scherr, K. C., & Madon, S. (2012). You have the right to understand: The deleterious effect of stress on suspects' ability to comprehend *Miranda. Law and Human Behavior, 36*, 275–282. doi:10.1037/h0093972

Scott-Hayward, C. S. (2007). Explaining juvenile false confessions: Adolescent development and police interrogation. *Law and Psychology Review, 31*, 53–76.

Shaw, J. A., & Budd, E. D. (1982). Determinants of acquiescence and nay saying of mentally retarded persons. *American Journal of Mental Deficiency, 87*, 108–110.

Sherif, M. (1936). *The psychology of social norms.* New York, NY: Harper.

Shufelt, J. L., & Cocozza, J. J. (2006). *Youth with mental health disorders in the juvenile justice system: Results from a multi-state prevalence study.* Retrieved from http://www.ncmhjj.com/pdfs/publications/PrevalenceRPB.pdf

Skinner, B. F. (1938). *The behavior of organisms.* New York, NY: Appleton-Century-Crofts.

Snook, B., & Cullen, R. M. (2008). Bounded rationality and criminal investigations: Has tunnel vision been wrongfully convicted? In D. K. Rossmo (Ed.), *Criminal investigative failures* (pp. 71–98). Boca Raton, FL: CRC Press. doi:10.1201/9781420047523.ch6

Steinberg, L. (2007). Risk taking in adolescence: New perspectives from brain and behavioral science. *Current Directions in Psychological Science, 16*, 55–59. doi:10.1111/j.1467-8721.2007.00475.x

Steinberg, L., & Cauffman, E. (1996). Maturity of judgment in adolescence: Psychosocial factors in adolescent decision making. *Law and Human Behavior, 20*, 249–272. doi:10.1007/BF01499023

Steinberg, L., & Scott, E. (2003). Less guilty by reason of adolescence: Developmental immaturity, diminished responsibility, and the juvenile death penalty.

American Psychologist, 58, 1009–1018. doi:10.1037/0003-066X.58.12.1009

Steingrimsdottir, G., Hreinsdottir, H., Gudjonsson, G. H., Sigurdsson, J. F., & Nielsen, T. (2007). False confessions and the relationship with offending behaviour and personality among Danish adolescents. *Legal and Criminological Psychology, 12*, 287–296. doi:10.1348/135532506X153380

Sullivan, T. P. (2004). *Police experiences with recording custodial interrogations.* Chicago, IL: Northwestern University Law School Center on Wrongful Convictions.

Sullivan, T. P., Vail, A. W., & Anderson, H. W. (2008). The case for recording police interrogations. *Litigation, 34*, 1–8.

Swanner, J. K., Beike, D. R., & Cole, A. T. (2010). Snitching, lies and computer crashes: An experimental investigation of secondary confessions. *Law and Human Behavior, 34*, 53–65. doi:10.1007/s10979-008-9173-5

Thorndike, E. L. (1911). *Animal intelligence: Experimental studies.* New York, NY: Macmillan. doi:10.5962/bhl.title.55072

Uchino, B. N., Cacioppo, J. T., & Kiecolt-Glaser, J. K. (1996). The relationship between social support and physiological processes: A review with emphasis on underlying mechanisms and implications for health. *Psychological Bulletin, 119*, 488–531. doi:10.1037/0033-2909.119.3.488

Viljoen, J. L., Klaver, J., & Roesch, R. (2005). Legal decisions of preadolescent and adolescent defendants: Predictors of confessions, pleas, communication with attorneys, and appeals. *Law and Human Behavior, 29*, 253–277. doi:10.1007/s10979-005-3613-2

Viljoen, J. L., Roesch, R., & Zapf, P. A. (2002). An examination of the relationship between competency to stand trial, competency to waive interrogation rights, and psychopathology. *Law and Human Behavior, 26*, 481–506. doi:10.1023/A:1020299804821

Viljoen, J. L., Zapf, P., & Roesch, R. (2007). Adjudicative competence and comprehension of Miranda rights in adolescent defendants: A comparison of legal standards. *Behavioral Sciences and the Law, 25*, 1–19. doi:10.1002/bsl.714

Vrij, A. (2008). *Detecting lies and deceit: Pitfalls and opportunities.* Chichester, England: Wiley.

Vrij, A., Fisher, R., Mann, S., & Leal, S. (2006). Detecting deception by manipulating cognitive load. *Trends in Cognitive Sciences, 10*, 141–142. doi:10.1016/j.tics.2006.02.003

Vrij, A., Granhag, P. A., & Porter, S. (2010). Pitfalls and opportunities in nonverbal and verbal lie detection. *Psychological Science in the Public Interest, 11*, 89–121. doi:10.1177/1529100610390861

Vrij, A., Mann, S., & Fisher, R. P. (2006). An empirical test of the Behaviour Analysis Interview. *Law and Human Behavior, 30*, 329–345. doi:10.1007/s10979-006-9014-3

Vrij, A., Mann, S. A., Fisher, R. P., Leal, S., Milne, R., & Bull, R. (2008). Increasing cognitive load to facilitate lie detection: The benefit of recalling an event in reverse order. *Law and Human Behavior, 32*, 253–265. doi:10.1007/s10979-007-9103-y

Wald, M., Ayres, R., Hess, D. W., Schantz, M., & Whitebread, C. H. (1967). Interrogations in New Haven: The impact *Miranda. Yale Law Journal, 76*, 1519–1648. doi:10.2307/795054

Wallace, D. B., & Kassin, S. M. (2012). Harmless error analysis: How do judges respond to confession errors? *Law and Human Behavior, 36*, 151–157. doi:10.1037/h0093975

Warden, R., & Drizin, S. A. (Eds.). (2009). *True stories of false confessions.* Evanston, IL: Northwestern University Press.

White, W. S. (2001). Miranda's *waning protections: Police interrogation practices after Dickerson.* Ann Arbor: University of Michigan Press.

Williamson, T. (Ed.). (2006). *Investigative interviewing: Rights, research, regulation.* Devon, England: Willan.

Wolfradt, U., & Meyer, T. (1998). Interrogative suggestibility, anxiety and dissociation among anxious patients and normal controls. *Personality and Individual Differences, 25*, 425–432. doi:10.1016/S0191-8869(98)00023-3

Wrightsman, L. S. (2010). The Supreme Court on *Miranda* rights and interrogations: The past, the present, and the future. In G. D. Lassiter & C. A. Meissner (Eds.), *Police interrogations and false confessions: Current research, practice, and policy recommendations* (pp. 161–177). Washington, DC: American Psychological Association. doi:10.1037/12085-010

Wrightsman, L. S., & Kassin, S. M. (1993). *Confessions in the courtroom.* Newbury Park, CA: Sage.

Zimbardo, P. G. (1967, June). The psychology of police confessions. *Psychology Today, 1*, 17–20, 25–27.

CHAPTER 10

JURY DECISION MAKING

Margaret Bull Kovera and Lora M. Levett

The Constitution of the United States guarantees its citizens a right to a trial by jury. Article III, Section 2 provides that anyone facing criminal charges is entitled to a jury trial. The Seventh Amendment extended this right to civil actions in which more than twenty dollars is in dispute. Thus, the jury is a crucial decision-making body within the U.S. judicial system. Although some have lamented the research attention lavished on jury decision making because the cases that are resolved through plea bargaining or settlement outnumber the cases that juries decide (Galanter, 2004), data collected by the National Center for State Courts in 2006 suggest that more than a hundred thousand jury trials are held each year in the United States alone, with more than 1.5 million citizens serving as jurors (Mize, Hannaford-Agor, & Waters, 2007).

The United States is not the only country that relies on the participation of lay citizens to resolve legal questions. Some countries, like the United Kingdom, have had jury systems for hundreds of years. Other countries, such as Japan, Korea, Russia, and Venezuela, have more recently introduced lay participation into their legal systems either through the adoption of juries composed entirely of laypeople or of tribunals that have a mixed composition of laypeople and professional judges (Hans, 2008). In comparison to the substantial literature on jury decision making in the United States (D. J. Devine, 2013; Vidmar & Hans, 2007), there is relatively little research on juries or other models of lay participation in legal decision making in other countries. The limited research that is available on lay participation

in other countries is often more sociological in nature, consisting of surveys examining fact finders' and citizens' perceptions of mixed tribunals and other quasi-jury systems (Fukurai, 2007; Ivković, 2007) or verdict agreement between judges and juries (Kim, Park, Park, & Eom, 2013) rather than empirical examinations of the factors that influence jury decisions and behavior. For the purposes of this chapter, we will focus our review on the more established literature on juries operating in the United States or similar systems.

To that end, we will discuss the importance of identifying the factors that influence jury decision making. Examining these factors allows us to evaluate whether juries are competent to make appropriate legal decisions that follow from the presented evidence and the relevant laws. The types of decisions that juries make vary depending upon whether the dispute to be resolved is criminal or civil in nature, with juries deciding criminal responsibility and guilt in criminal trials, determining defendant liability and monetary awards to compensate the injured party, and to punish reprehensible defendants in civil cases. In these types of cases, there are similar opportunities for juror error, with extralegal information, internal biases, or the misapplication of law inappropriately influencing juror decisions.

In the next section of the chapter, we will review the psychological theory and principles that contribute to our understanding of jury decision making. Some researchers have relied on general social psychological theories of persuasion to identify variables that should influence jurors' evaluation of the

http://dx.doi.org/10.1037/14462-010
APA Handbook of Forensic Psychology: Vol. 2. Criminal Investigation, Adjudication, and Sentencing Outcomes,
B. L. Cutler and P. A. Zapf (Editors-in-Chief)
Copyright © 2015 by the American Psychological Association. All rights reserved.

arguments presented at trial. Others have developed theories of individual juror decision making specifically designed to understand how jurors integrate information to arrive at a verdict. Still others have designed theoretical models of group decision making and behavior designed to capture the influence of group dynamics on the decision-making process facing jurors. We will argue that this theoretical work on jury decision making lacks a model that coherently synthesizes what we know about individual and group decision making and will propose some research questions that should be addressed before we can fully integrate individual and group models of jury decision making.

Next we will review the empirical research on jury decision making, starting with studies that examine how jurors evaluate different types of evidence, such as eyewitness identifications, confessions, DNA and other forensic evidence, and expert testimony. We will also review studies examining whether jury-level variables like jury size, jury composition, and decision rule (unanimity vs. majority) affect juror decision making. Finally, we will consider the evidence for whether juries are able to competently execute their duty to render a verdict that is fair and impartial, based on the evidence, and conforming to the applicable law. Although extralegal biases undoubtedly influence juror decisions and there are times when jurors misapply or ignore relevant laws, trial evidence remains a strong predictor of juror verdicts and agreement between judge and jury verdicts is high.

In the final section of the chapter, we will address practice and policy issues as they relate to jury decision making. In terms of practice, the field of trial consulting is burgeoning, as is the empirical study of jury selection, including whether juror characteristics predict verdicts, the jury selection process can rehabilitate potential jurors who express bias or partiality, jury selection is free from racial bias, and pretrial publicity (PTP) biases potential jurors against defendants. Jury researchers have also actively evaluated potential reforms to the jury system, including allowing jurors to take notes during trial, to submit questions to be asked of witnesses, and to discuss trial evidence as it is presented rather than admonishing them to wait for the start of

deliberation to begin discussions. Because many of these reforms stem from suggestions from members of the legal profession rather than from an analysis of psychological mechanisms underlying the problem the reforms are intended to address, many of the reforms do not seem to improve the quality of juror decisions even if they do not appear to be harmful either. We end the chapter by addressing the question of whether juries are competent decision making bodies in light of the empirical evidence presented in the chapter.

IMPORTANCE OF THE PROBLEM

There is no question that 29-year-old George Zimmerman fatally shot 17-year-old Trayvon Martin as he was walking home from a convenience store, armed with only his cell phone, a bag of Skittles, and an iced tea. Yet a Florida jury composed of six women acquitted Zimmerman, a former neighborhood watch volunteer, of all charges related to the shooting, accepting the defense claim that Zimmerman shot Martin in self-defense. In the days after the acquittal, there was a public outcry over a perceived injustice in the outcome of this case. Zimmerman is Hispanic and had a history of physical aggression, including resisting arrest. Martin was black, walking at night with a hoodie pulled around his head, with a record clean of violence (Campo-Flores & Waddell, 2013). Was this a case of a racist man, carrying a legal firearm, stalking and killing a boy whom he judged was up to no good? Would Zimmerman have been acquitted if he had been Black and the boy whom he killed had been White?

In the aftermath of Zimmerman's acquittal, many questioned the competence of the jury who heard the case and the justice provided by jury trials more generally. Did the races of the defendant and the victim improperly influence the jury's verdict? Did the jury render an appropriate verdict given the evidence and Florida's particular version of self-defense law that allows people to defend themselves even when standing their ground in contrast to many states' self-defense laws that allow people to use force to defend themselves only when retreat or escape is not possible? Although it is impossible to know with certainty whether the jury in the

Zimmerman case impartially weighed the evidence, was uninfluenced by racial bias, and followed the law as it was given to them, empirical research can shed light on the extent to which personal biases (e.g., attitudes, stereotypes) or extralegal information (e.g., PTP, inadmissible evidence) is likely to improperly influence jury verdicts. Empirical research can also assess whether jurors are likely to understand the law and apply it correctly.

Juries operate in both the criminal and civil justice systems, and jurors have different duties in each system, sometimes requiring different competencies. In both systems, juries must evaluate the reliability of evidence and the extent to which it makes a fact at issue in a case more or less probable. Some types of evidence, such as confessions of guilt, are specific to the criminal context; other types of evidence, such as eyewitness testimony, expert testimony, or statistical evidence, may be proffered in either type of trial. The standards of proof that jurors use in the two types of systems also differ, with criminal trials requiring that juries decide a defendant's guilt beyond a reasonable doubt and civil trials often using the standard that something must be proven by a preponderance of the evidence (i.e., more likely than not), which is a less stringent standard.

Sometimes these differences between the two systems can make it appear that juries are illogical decision-making bodies. One high-profile example comes from the criminal and civil actions brought against former football star O. J. Simpson for the death of his wife, Nicole Brown Simpson, and her friend, Ronald Goldman. The criminal jury that tried Simpson on first-degree murder charges acquitted him, yet a civil jury found that he was responsible for causing the deaths of his ex-wife and Goldman and awarded their families many millions of dollars in compensatory and punitive damages (Ayres, 1997). How can two competent juries come to different conclusions about whether Simpson was responsible for the death of his ex-wife? It is easy to understand the differences between these juries' decisions if one considers that all twelve jurors in the Simpson case had to find him guilty of his wife's murder beyond a reasonable doubt, whereas only nine of the twelve jurors on the civil jury had to find that there was more evidence than not that Simpson

was responsible for her death. The differences in the requirements for unanimity plus the differences in the decision rules in the two cases, with a much more stringent requirement in the criminal case, provide reasons for the differences in the two juries' verdicts without any need to invoke jury incompetence as an explanation.

In criminal cases, judging the competence of a jury centers on whether juries make accurate judgments about the guilt of defendants. In civil cases, jurors do not decide the guilt of a defendant but decide whether a defendant is liable for a wrong suffered by another party, called the plaintiff; if the defendant is found to be liable, jurors may also award the plaintiff damages to compensate them for any injuries that they have suffered as a result of the defendant's conduct and possibly to punish the defendant if the conduct was reprehensible. Some critics have raised concerns about whether juries can make appropriate decisions about these types of damage awards, especially in light of some highly publicized cases that were deemed outlandish by some. In one particularly ridiculed outcome, a jury awarded Stella Liebeck close to $3 million due to injuries she sustained when she spilled a cup of hot McDonald's coffee on her lap (*Liebeck v. McDonald's Restaurant*, 1994). What was less likely to be reported in the media is that Ms. Liebeck sustained fourth-degree burns that required multiple surgical procedures to heal, that McDonald's operating manuals required franchises to hold their coffee at temperatures of 180°–190°F, a temperature known to create severe burns if the liquid comes into contact with the skin, and McDonald's had already received numerous complaints about injuries resulting from their coffee coming into contact with customers' skin. In addition, Ms. Liebeck was awarded just $200,000 to compensate her for the injury, the cost of her medical care, and her surgeries (which was reduced to $160,000 because the jury found her partially responsible for her injuries). The remainder of the award, $2.7 million, was intended to punish McDonald's for their failure to adjust their operations in the face of evidence that their coffee temperatures were causing harm and was the equivalent of just two days of revenue from coffee sales at McDonald's. Thus, what at first appears to be a classic example of jury awards run amok, after further consideration seems as if it could be a reasonable outcome based on the evidence and the applicable law.

Although juries sometimes, maybe even often, make competent decisions, there are clearly cases in which there is no doubt that juries made the wrong decisions. The Innocence Project, a non-profit organization with a mission to use DNA to exonerate people who have been wrongfully convicted, has identified 310 people who have been wrongfully convicted by juries (http://www.innocenceproject.org/know). The causes of these wrongful convictions vary but include mistaken eyewitness identifications, false confessions, jailhouse snitches, invalid scientific evidence, and prosecutorial misconduct? To be sure, it is difficult for juries provided with poor evidence to make good decisions, but are there factors other than unreliable evidence that can lead juries to make better (or worse) decisions. To understand the factors that influence whether juries are competent decision-making bodies, we must consider relevant social psychological theories of individual and group decision making as well as empirical research on jury and juror decision making.

RELEVANT PSYCHOLOGICAL THEORY AND PRINCIPLES

In rendering a decision, the jury is called to evaluate and weigh evidence from both sides, first determining what behavior occurred in the dispute. The jury then evaluates the behavior according to the law governing the case and the standard of proof. In most cases, the jury renders a decision that reflects their beliefs about the evidence, the law, and whether the standard of proof has been met in that case. Trial events (opening and closing statements, presentation of evidence) can be conceptualized as persuasive arguments made to a group of people that must evaluate whether the evidence supports a particular verdict.

What determines whether a jury will be persuaded by the arguments presented? How does the jury ultimately weigh evidence and render a verdict? Researchers have developed theories explaining both jury and juror decision making; that is, they

have examined the decision making process on the group and individual levels. Presumably, jurors form opinions about the evidence and verdict prior to beginning deliberation. During deliberation, these opinions are combined into the group verdict. Thus, our exploration of the relevant psychological theories underpinning jury decision making will begin with a review of how general psychological theories might explain jurors' decisions, followed by a discussion of individual theories of juror decision making and a summary of the group models and dynamics in jury decision making to understand how jurors may be persuaded at trial.

Applying Basic Theories to Jurors' Decisions in Specific Cases

In addition to using theory to understand the processes of juror and jury decision making, researchers have used basic social or cognitive psychological theory to understand and explain how jurors make decisions in several different types of cases. The theory used is usually dependent on the specific issues in the case. For example, some research has examined how the types of questions that attorneys ask during the jury selection process, called *voir dire*, affects jurors' trial decisions (Haney, 1984). In capital cases, jurors are typically asked whether they can find the defendant guilty knowing that the death penalty is a possible punishment. To help explain how answering these types of questions may affect jurors' decisions or pretrial verdict preferences, researchers have relied on basic social psychological theory on the availability heuristic, which shows that when a person imagines doing something, it increases the person's expectation that the event will occur in the future (Tversky & Kahneman, 1973). Thus, in capital cases, jurors who answer those *voir dire* questions affirmatively and are chosen for trial are more prone toward conviction than jurors who are not asked these questions prior to the start of trial because jurors who are asked the questions have already imagined finding the defendant guilty (Haney, 1984; see also Chapter 17, this volume).

Similar examples can be found in other literature. Social psychological literature on stereotyping and prejudice has helped us understand how race may affect decision making (see Sommers, 2007;

Chapter 5, this volume), reactance theory has been used to explain how jurors may process inadmissible evidence (see Lieberman, Arndt, & Vess, 2009), and the fundamental attribution error or correspondence bias has been used to understand how jurors perceive and use an involuntary confession in their decision making (see Kassin & Wrightsman, 1980; Chapter 9, this volume). Other work in the field has relied on theoretical principles from other disciplines to explain how jurors make decisions. For example, one study cited political science work on agenda-setting to provide the theoretical backdrop in work on PTP (Kovera, 2002). In this case, the theory helped explain how news broadcasts on rape may affect jurors' decisions in a rape case. Similarly, cultivation theory from the communications field has informed how watching shows like *CSI* might affect jurors' decisions (Hayes-Smith & Levett, 2011; see also Chapter 11, this volume).

Certainly, not all work in jury and juror decision making is theoretically based. Researchers have often asked practical research questions about the jury that are interesting for legal or other reasons. In this and most juror and jury decision-making work, however, social psychological models on persuasion may provide an overarching understanding of what generally drives jurors' decisions. The heuristic-systematic and the elaboration likelihood models of persuasion suggest that jurors make decisions about information using one of two routes to persuasion (Chaiken, Liberman, & Eagly, 1989; Petty & Wegener, 1998). The first route is termed the systematic or central route to persuasion. In using the central route, decision makers carefully consider the information in question, deliberately evaluating the content of the message to determine whether they are persuaded by that information. The ability to process information centrally depends on two factors: the decision maker's motivation and ability (Petty & Wegener, 1998). Presumably, jurors are highly motivated to make a good decision, but they might not always have the ability to evaluate the information in question, as might be the case with complex evidence like expert testimony (Levett & Kovera, 2008).

If jurors do not process systematically, they may use the second route to persuasion, termed the heuristic or peripheral route to persuasion (Petty & Wegener, 1998). Decision makers using the peripheral route to process information use heuristics or factors other than the information conveyed in the message to evaluate the message. For example, instead of attending to the quality of the argument proffered by an expert, jurors may attend to peripheral qualities of the testimony like the ecological validity of the research (Kovera, McAuliff, & Hebert, 1999) or the qualifications of an expert (Cooper, Bennett, & Sukel, 1996). Thus, these models suggest that jurors who have the ability and motivation will be persuaded by the content of the message conveyed at trial, whereas those who lack either the ability or motivation to directly evaluate the information will be persuaded by the peripheral characteristics of the message or the messenger. Moreover, jurors can use peripheral and central routes simultaneously in evaluating information (Levett & Kovera, 2009).

Researchers have used the models of persuasion to explain and predict jurors' decisions in evaluating expert testimony (see, for examples, Kovera et al., 1999; Levett & Kovera, 2008; McAuliff & Kovera, 2008). In addition, these models of persuasion have also been used to evaluate the messages used by jurors in persuading their fellow jurors during deliberation (Salerno, Bottoms, & Peter-Hagene, 2012). In general, when processing trial information, the models and this research suggest that jurors are persuaded by the content of the messages and pieces of evidence at trial (as long as they have the ability and motivation to do so), as well as the heuristics surrounding the message or piece of evidence.

Thus, general theories of persuasion and the broader psychological literature can inform how jurors make decisions in several different types of cases. The theory chosen to explain jurors' decisions may change based on the issues under question in the particular case. Next, we turn to a review of the research on jury and juror decision making, bearing in mind these theoretical underpinnings.

Individual Theories of Juror Decision Making

Much of the research in jury decision making has focused on individual jurors' decisions. There are several good empirical and practical reasons to explore individual decisions even though groups ultimately render verdicts. First, the biggest predictor of the jury's postdeliberation verdict is the initial verdict distribution of the individual jurors (Davis, 1980; Kalven & Zeisel, 1966; Sandys & Dillehay, 1995), and most jurors enter deliberation with a predeliberation verdict preference (Hannaford-Agor, Hans, Mott, & Munsterman, 2002; Hastie, Penrod, & Pennington, 1983). Thus, it is worthwhile to understand what jurors bring into the deliberation process at the individual level, knowing that these individual preferences are predictive of the group outcome.

Second, the methodological and logistical difficulties of studying group decision making make studying individual jurors more attractive for many researchers. For example, a researcher studying a group-level decision needs a jury made up of at least six members to record one data point for verdict; the same number of jurors results in six data points for verdict at the individual level. Certainly, studying group-level jury decision making is more ecologically valid than studying individual-level juror decision making, and this may sometimes be necessitated by the research question. Given these practical and theoretical considerations, however, it may be sensible to begin testing most research questions by studying individual juror decision making and examining the group level in later stages of research. As with all research, however, the research question should drive the research; if the question centers on deliberation or group processes, then one should begin by studying the group.

Broadly, individual theories of juror decision making fall under two categories: (1) mathematical models and (2) explanation-based or cognitive models (Greene et al., 2002; Hastie, 1993). The goal of all of these models is to develop a comprehensive, unified theory of juror decision making that allows prediction of how jurors will make decisions in mock jury simulations and actual trials (Hastie, 1993). Mathematical models generally describe a juror's decision by using a mathematical formula that mimics how jurors weigh different pieces of evidence throughout the trial. These models vary on the basis of the formula used for adjusting a juror's overall verdict testimony based on additional evidence (e.g., algebraic, probabilistic). Explanation-based or cognitive models are more likely to account for a juror's multifaceted, active role in the decision-making process. In our discussion of individual models of juror decision making, we will discuss the mathematical models (Bayesian, algebraic, and stochastic process models) and the most popular explanation-based model (the story model for juror decision making).

The Bayesian model. Like other mathematical models, the Bayesian model assumes jurors make decisions along a single mental meter; according to this model, the meter represents the juror's belief in the probability that an event occurred (i.e., that the defendant is guilty) at a certain point in time (i.e., the beginning, middle, or end of trial; Hastie, 1993). The juror starts the trial with an a priori belief in the defendant's guilt, presumably based on judicial instructions, beliefs about the trial actors, and personal values (Hastie, 1993). Jurors then interpret, weigh, and process each piece of information that informs the belief in the defendant's guilt (e.g., witness testimony and trial exhibits), one piece at a time. Jurors combine each piece of information with their a priori beliefs in the probability of the defendant's guilt to update their beliefs about the defendant's guilt. This cycle continues throughout the trial as new information is acquired (Hastie, 1993).

The equation that describes this process is based in probability theory and is multiplicative. Thus, if the belief in the probability that the defendant is guilty ever shifts to an extreme probability of 0 or 1, the mental meter will freeze; any new information, regardless of weight, will not change the a priori belief (Hastie, 1993). At the end of trial, presumably, jurors compare their posterior belief in the probability the defendant is guilty with their decision criterion to convict, which is likely created through judicial instructions, crime severity, and personal beliefs or attitudes about the justice system. If their posterior belief exceeds the threshold, the jurors would convict (Hastie, 1993).

Using a Bayesian model to describe jurors' decisions has been criticized for a few reasons. First, using a single mental meter to describe the jurors' decision-making processes most likely simplifies the multidimensional process (Hastie, 1993). For example, in the judicial instructions, jurors are told they must believe that each element of the crime has been satisfied by the evidence beyond a reasonable doubt; even if the decision-making process mirrors a mental meter, it probably involves multiple mental meters representing the different elements of the crime. Bayesian theory does not specify how these meters should be combined (Hastie, 1993). In addition, Bayesian theory does not specify how jurors identify and define units of information, construct their a priori probabilities, or construct their threshold for conviction. Thus, although Bayesian models may account for the manner in which jurors reason about evidence, they do not account for other complexities in jurors' decisions.

Algebraic models. Similar to Bayeisan models, algebraic models assume that jurors make decisions on a single mental meter. Again, the meter represents the probability that the defendant is guilty, but algebraic models differ from Bayesian models in the method of calculation used to combine different pieces of evidence; Bayesian models use multiplication, whereas algebraic models use weighted averaging or addition to calculate the influence of new evidence on the juror's evaluation of the defendant's guilt (Hastie, 1993). In algebraic models, jurors first identify probative pieces of evidence (e.g., those that could affect the outcome judgment). Then, those pieces of evidence are weighed according to their importance, reliability, credibility, and relevance (Hastie, 1993).

For example, in a trial, a juror may identify testimony from a witness who corroborates the defendant's alibi as a piece of evidence affecting the probability that the defendant is guilty. The juror assigns a weight to that evidence; an alibi corroborator may be important for establishing the guilt or innocence of the defendant, but a corroborator who is good friends with the defendant may be weighed less than a corroborator who only knows the defendant casually (Olson & Wells, 2004).

All identified pieces of evidence are similarly weighed and averaged in the equation until the end of trial. Unlike Bayesian models, extreme judgments or weights do not freeze the mental meter. At the end of trial, the juror's final opinion about defendant guilt is presumably compared to the decision criterion (similar to Bayesian models). If the opinion exceeds the threshold created by the decision criterion, the juror votes to convict.

Criticisms of algebraic models for juror decision making are similar to those of the Bayesian models; the most significant criticism is that the algebraic equation simplifies the multidimensional juror decision-making process (Hastie, 1993). There is evidence, however, that the model can describe jurors' decisions (e.g., Moore & Gump, 1995), and the simple model can be expanded to apply to jurors' complex task (Hastie, 1993).

Stochastic process models. Researchers have also used stochastic models in describing individual jurors' decisions. Similar to the algebraic and Bayesian models, current stochastic process models assume jurors make decisions along a single mental meter. Some previous versions of these models included multiple meters to account for evidentiary and non-evidentiary information or information supporting guilt and information supporting innocence (Hastie, 1993). The evolution of the model has led to the elimination of these multiple meters in favor of a single meter representing the probability of a defendant's guilt.

One of the major differences between stochastic process models and those previously discussed is that stochastic models include an element of randomness in jurors' decisions. Instead of calculating a single outcome based on the input variables, stochastic process models give a distribution of possible outcomes, thus accounting for the uncertainty in each individual juror's response. This uncertainty can be attributed to a variety of things, such as the individual differences between jurors or nuances of the particular case (Hastie, 1993).

According to stochastic process models describing jurors' decisions, there are three basic subprocesses involved in juror decision making (Hastie, 1993; Kerr, 1993; Thomas & Hogue, 1976). First, there is a process by which jurors evaluate evidence. Evidence evaluation occurs in real time as the jurors hear each piece of evidence. Second, stochastic process models postulate that a critical event occurs at trial, and this critical event freezes the evidence evaluation process. Thus, the final outcome value is equivalent to the value at the time of the presentation of the critical evidence. Third, this final value is compared to the decision criterion to render a verdict decision; the jurors also indicate their confidence in that verdict.

Because of the inclusion of the random element, stochastic process models account for differences among jurors' decisions in ways unaccounted for by other mathematical models. In addition, it accounts for jurors' evaluation of evidentiary information and extralegal information (Hastie, 1993). Similar to other mathematical models, however, it does not capture the complexities of jurors' decisions largely because of the use of a single mental meter. Despite these shortcomings, research has shown support for stochastic process models in describing jurors' decisions (Kerr, 1978; Kerr, Harmon, & Graves, 1982; Thomas & Hogue, 1976).

The story model. The story model of juror decision making is the most endorsed model of individual juror decision making (Pennington & Hastie, 1988, 1992, 1993). It is an explanation-based model and rests on the assumption that jurors actively organize evidence they hear during trial in a narrative, story-like format. According to the story model, the process of decision making takes place in three steps: story construction, learning verdict alternatives, and rendering a verdict. The story model not only provides a description of the processes jurors undertake when making a decision in a trial but also posits that the story constructed by the juror ultimately determines the verdict chosen by the juror (Pennington & Hastie, 1993).

During story construction, jurors use three things: the evidence presented at trial, personal knowledge of similar situations, and knowledge about the elements that make a complete story (Pennington & Hastie, 1993). When jurors hear evidence in a trial, it is usually presented in a disconnected format, meaning that they usually do not hear the evidence presented in a logical, temporally accurate order. In addition, witnesses are testifying in a question and answer format in which they are not allowed to elaborate or speculate on why certain

actions occurred (Pennington & Hastie, 1993). Thus, the presentation of evidence and information at trial is largely disconnected and could be incomplete.

Given that the information connecting the pieces of evidence may be missing from trial presentation, jurors may use their own personal knowledge and experiences to fill gaps left in the story. Thus, different jurors may create different stories, and one way to account for these differences is by understanding the personal experiences that jurors use to fill in gaps in story creation. That is, jurors generally will hear the same evidence at trial and have the same expectations about what makes a complete story; differences arise because of differences in beliefs, attitudes, or past experiences (Pennington & Hastie, 1993).

The story model posits that jurors play an active role in the trial by listening to the evidence and actively organizing it into narrative with a story-like, causal structure that accounts for the events that occurred (Pennington & Hastie, 1993). The story that the juror creates is made of units termed episodes. An episode is a series of events or an event that is paired with either intentions or motivations to result in action that results in consequences. Elements of episodes can be taken either from the trial evidence or from jurors' personal knowledge. Episodes are then hierarchically organized to create the story, and this organization accounts for jurors' weightings of the pieces of evidence (Pennington & Hastie, 1993).

According to the story model, jurors can create more than one story, but one story usually emerges as the best explanation for the events in question. To explain how jurors choose the most acceptable story (and subsequently, how confident the juror is in the chosen story), the story model proposes three certainty factors: coverage, coherence, and uniqueness (Pennington & Hastie, 1993). Coverage refers to the amount of evidence accounted for by a particular story. The greater the coverage, the more likely the story will be chosen and the more confidence a juror will have in that particular story. Story coherence is determined by the consistency, plausibility, and completeness of the story. A consistent story contains neither internal contradictions nor contradictions with evidence the juror believes. A plausible story contains all the elements that a juror believes typically happen in similar situations, and a complete story contains all the elements of a story as determined by the juror. If more than one story is deemed high in both coherence and coverage, the uniqueness of either story is compromised, and jurors' confidence in either story is weakened (Pennington & Hastie, 1993).

In the second stage of the story model, jurors learn possible verdict options. This process is difficult given that jurors typically do not receive judicial instructions containing the verdict options until the end of the trial, and learning the definitions of the possible verdicts is a one-trial task (Pennington & Hastie, 1993). Generally speaking, jurors do not comprehend all of the instructions given to them at trial (Diamond & Levi, 1996; Reifman, Gusick, & Ellsworth, 1992), and jurors' preconceived knowledge about such events interferes with learning and comprehending verdict instructions (V. L. Smith, 1991).

In the last stage of the story model, jurors map their chosen story onto the verdict options available and determine the verdict that best matches their chosen story (Pennington & Hastie, 1993). Once jurors determine the best match, they apply the judicial instructions to make a final decision. For example, if the best match between verdict and story is for a verdict of guilty of murder in the first degree, the juror will apply the judicial instructions on reasonable doubt to this match to determine if the match between the story and the verdict exceeds the threshold of reasonable doubt. If this threshold were met, then the juror would render a verdict of guilty of murder in the first degree. If the threshold were not met, the juror will render a verdict of not guilty. The jurors' confidence in their story and subsequent verdict decision is affected by the story's coherence, coverage, and uniqueness, and by the goodness-of-fit match between verdict and story (Pennington & Hastie, 1993).

Research has generally shown support for the story model for juror decisions in a variety of civil and criminal cases (e.g., murder, rape, sexual harassment; Huntley & Costanzo, 2003; Olsen-Fulero & Fulero, 1997; Pennington & Hastie, 1993). Furthermore, the chosen story mediates the influence of evidence on jurors' decisions, i.e., jurors first hear evidence, then spontaneously generate the story, and finally choose the verdict (Huntley & Costanzo, 2003; Pennington & Hastie, 1993). The story model is the theory of juror decision making that currently has the most empirical support; this model, however, and all other individual models, are missing an understanding of how jurors combine their individual stories and verdict preferences with those of other jurors into a group verdict during the deliberation process. Thus, we will next turn to the group literature to explore how researchers have explained jury decision making at the group level.

Group Dynamics in Jury Decision Making

In studying juries' (rather than jurors') decisions, researchers have generally focused on developing mathematical models of jury decision making or studying the group processes that occur as a jury deliberates to a verdict. Thus, the theory that drives this research is either mathematical in nature or is driven by more basic social psychological theory on deliberating groups.

Mathematical models of jury decision making.

During deliberation, the jurors' individual preferences and decisions are combined into one unanimous verdict. As previously stated, the biggest predictor of postdeliberation verdict is the predeliberation verdict preferences of the individuals within the jury (Kalven & Zeisel, 1966). Therefore, it follows that mathematical models using the predeliberation preferences of individual jurors are predictive of the jury's final verdict. Thus, the predeliberation verdict distribution of the jury provides information about what verdict the jury may render independent of the deliberation process. Several mathematical based models describe how those preferences are combined into one verdict (see D. J. Devine, 2013, for a thorough review of all these models).

The Social Decision Scheme (SDS; Davis, 1973) model is one of the most popular general theories of group decision making that has been applied to the jury's decision. SDS is a stochastic model that uses the distribution of initial verdict preferences of the group members and the rule or decision scheme used by the group to combine those initial preferences into a final verdict. In the model, the possible predeliberation verdict preferences are represented in a matrix indicating the number of guilty and not guilty verdict preferences in the jury. For example, a six-person jury would be represented with the following possibilities: (6, 0), (5, 1), (4, 2), (3, 3), (2, 4), (1, 5), and (0, 6). The final verdict is calculated by using an equation that applies the decision rule or scheme to combine the preferences into a verdict (Davis, 1973; Kerr et al., 1976).

In criminal jury decision making, the decision scheme used in SDS modeling has been described as a majority rules primary scheme with an asymmetric sub scheme (Kerr, Niedermeier, & Kaplan, 1999). That is, if the majority of jurors agree on a particular verdict, this verdict will likely be the final verdict. This decision rule is consistent with evidence that juries beginning with a clear majority are likely to render a verdict in favor of that majority (D. J. Devine, Clayton, Dunford, Seying, & Pryce, 2001; Kerr et al., 1976; Stasser, Kerr, & Bray, 1982). The strongest majorities, however, are those favoring acquittal (Kerr et al., 1999; Stasser, Kerr, & Davis, 1989), with majorities favoring acquittal more likely to prevail over the minority faction than are majorities favoring conviction. The asymmetry is generally attributed to the standard of proof in criminal cases; jurors must believe the defendant is guilty beyond a reasonable doubt to find the defendant guilty (Kerr et al., 1999). The SDS model frequently predicts the decisions rendered by juries (e.g., Davis, Tindale, Nagao, Hinsz, & Robertson, 1984; Kerr et al., 1976, 1999).

Researchers have also used probability or Bayesian models to model juries' decisions, again calculating final verdicts based on predeliberation preferences of the individual jury members (Penrod & Hastie, 1979). With these models, researchers have investigated how changing procedural aspects of the deliberation may alter decision making, such as by changing the decision rule (majority rules vs. a unanimous decision) or jury size. Similarly, computer simulation models also have successfully described some deliberation factors that influence juries' final decisions. For example, in one study the number of straw polls in deliberation influenced the probability the majority will increase in number (Penrod & Hastie, 1979).

Generally, the mathematical group models of jury decision making do not account for the deliberation process or, at best, account for a small part of the deliberation process (e.g., the number of straw polls in deliberation). The deliberation process itself, however, may affect the final jury verdict. In addition, these models may not describe how jurors adopt verdict positions during jury decision making when they previously were undecided (Diamond, 1997; Salerno & Diamond, 2010). In one study, 20% of jurors interviewed after deliberation reported that they did not have a clear verdict preference prior to deliberation, and when asked to rate which side they favored prior to deliberation, 38% of jurors chose numbers near the middle of a continuous scale (Hannaford-Agor et al., 2002). A number of undecided jurors do not undermine the predictive ability of the SDS model (Kerr & MacCoun, 2012), although the process of how and why those initially undecided jurors eventually come to adopt a final verdict has been explained using a solely mathematical explanation. In addition, the traditional mathematical models do not provide information about the dynamics of deliberation that could affect the quality of the deliberation process and ultimately the outcome of deliberation. For example, mathematical models do not provide information about why the majority is so influential or the conditions that lead to a successful minority (Salerno & Diamond, 2010). Thus, it is worthwhile to explore the deliberation process to fully understand how the jury arrives at a collective verdict.

Group processes and deliberation. As a whole, the studies that have examined the role of the deliberation process in jury decision making suggest that the deliberation process matters in the group decision. For example, the deliberation process mediates the relationship between jurors' individual predeliberation verdict preferences and final verdict (Tanford & Penrod, 1986), and deliberation accounts for a significant amount of the variance in modeling the final jury verdict (Hastie, Schkade, & Payne, 1999). In one study, accounting for deliberation variables almost doubled the amount of variance explained in final verdict (Hastie, Schkade, & Payne, 1998). In addition, there are sometimes differences between the decisions of deliberating groups and individual jurors. For example, two studies have shown that deliberating juries awarded different damage award amounts compared to individual jurors (Diamond & Casper, 1992; Schkade, Sunstein, & Kahneman, 2000).

The deliberation process can also improve the quality of juries' decisions. For example, deliberating mock juries in one study were more likely than nondeliberating individuals to follow a judicial admonition to disregard inadmissible evidence (Kerwin & Shaffer, 1994; Wheatman & Shaffer, 2001). In another study, jurors who deliberated were better at understanding and remembering trial evidence than were individual jurors who did not deliberate (Ellsworth, 1989). Deliberating increased jurors' confidence levels in a verdict that was more in line with an accurate expert (Salerno & McCauley, 2009). In contrast, however, deliberation in another study either did not correct for improper effects of PTP on juror judgment or even magnified the effect of emotional PTP (Kramer, Kerr, & Carroll, 1990; see Chapter 11, this volume for a review of research on the impact of PTP). Collectively, these deliberation studies suggest that the deliberation process has the potential to affect, and in at least some cases, improve the quality of juries' decisions.

Early observations of the deliberation process suggest that jurors spend most of the time in deliberation discussing evidence and a significant portion of the time discussing the law, and that juries tend to have legally relevant and accurate discussions (Ellsworth, 1989; Kessler, 1973; Simon, 1967). Other observations suggest three stages of deliberation: orientation, open conflict, and reconciliation (Costanzo, 2003; Stasser, 1992). During orientation, the jury discusses general procedural and trial issues, elects a foreperson, and begins deliberation. During open conflict, jurors engage in discussions with the goal of persuading fellow jury members to adopt a particular verdict preference. During reconciliation, jurors attempt to ensure the outcome of the deliberation is satisfactory to each member of the jury (Costanzo, 2003; Stasser, 1992).

Deliberation usually starts in one of two deliberation styles (or a mixture of these two styles). The first deliberation style is a verdict-driven style. Verdict-driven juries typically begin deliberation by taking an initial straw poll of the individual jurors (Hastie et al., 1983). After the initial poll establishes which jurors are leaning in either direction, deliberation is then oriented around these preferences, with jurors attempting to use the evidence and their experiences to show support for their verdict preferences and persuade their fellow jurors.

The second deliberation style is an evidence-driven style (Hastie et al., 1983). In the evidence-driven jury, the deliberation initially is centered on reviewing the different pieces of trial evidence, with the jury discussing and agreeing on the evaluation of each piece of evidence. After a thorough discussion of the evidence, jurors discuss the different verdict choices, matching verdict options to the agreed-upon evidence. Jurors may take a straw poll in an evidence-driven jury but usually only late in the process after most evidence has been discussed and agreed upon. Verdict-driven juries complete deliberation more quickly than evidence-driven juries (Hastie et al., 1983). Evidence-driven juries, however, engage in a more thorough examination of the evidence than verdict-driven juries, and jurors who participate in evidence-driven juries report feeling more satisfied with the task than jurors who participate in verdict-driven juries (Hastie et al., 1983).

The social-psychological literature on group decision making can be applied to the open conflict stage of jury decision making to understand what happens during this process and how jurors persuade one another to adopt different viewpoints, interpretations of evidence, and verdicts. Generally, persuasion in small groups takes place through two processes: informational and normative influence (Cialdini & Trost, 1998; Deutsch & Gerard, 1955; Kaplan & Miller, 1987). If a juror changes her mind through the process of informational influence, the juror adopts a new viewpoint both publicly and privately, changing her beliefs in response to compelling information or data communicated by another juror. Thus, change represents a desire to be correct in one's decisions (Cialdini & Trost, 1998;

Deutsch & Gerard, 1955). If jurors change their minds because of normative influence, the jurors adopt a new viewpoint publicly, but privately maintain their previous beliefs. Thus, change in this case represents compliance and a desire to be consistent or harmonious with the group (Kaplan & Miller, 1987; Moscovici & Lage, 1976).

The type of information under scrutiny affects whether jurors use normative or informational arguments in attempting to persuade their fellow jurors (Kaplan & Miller, 1987). Kaplan and Miller (1987) found that jurors deciding on more intellective issues, defined as compensatory damages, were more likely to use informational influence than jurors deciding on more judgmental issues, defined as punitive damage awards. This effect was stronger for juries deliberating under a unanimous decision rule than juries using a majority decision rule. Another study showed that deliberating juries who were given a dynamite charge (i.e., a judicial instruction compelling the jury to reach a unanimous verdict after a period of deliberation) were more likely be influenced via normative processes than informational processes (V. L. Smith & Kassin, 1993).

Social psychological research on minority and majority influence suggests that persuasion in open conflict and the type of influence that occurs in jury deliberations is also partially a product of the size of the faction doing the persuading. A consistent minority or majority faction is more likely to be successful in persuading other jurors than an inconsistent minority or majority (Moscovici & Lage, 1976); consistent with mathematical model predictions, the majority faction is more likely to prevail than the minority faction (Kalven & Zeisel, 1966). In conditions in which the majority prevails, normative influence is likely to be at work. That is, basic social psychological literature suggests that jurors who are part of the minority and change their opinions to be consistent with the majority likely change their manifest opinion but retain their latent belief, termed compliance in the literature (Moscovici & Lage, 1976; Moscovici & Personnaz, 1980).

Recall that the influence of the majority is asymmetric in that the strongest majorities are those that favor acquittal (Kerr et al., 1999). Thus, the strongest minorities in criminal juries are also those that favor acquittal. In conditions in which the minority prevails, the process by which change occurs is likely informational influence. That is, jurors who are part of the majority and change their opinions to be consistent with the minority likely change both their manifest and latent beliefs, termed conversion in the literature (Moscovici & Lage, 1976; Moscovici & Personnaz, 1980). Thus, the basic social psychological literature on group processes can be applied to the jury's task to help us understand how the jury deliberates and ultimately renders a verdict. Next, we will consider the possibility that using the information gained by exploring individual models of juror decision making could combine with these group variables to further explain the group's decision making process.

Integrating Group and Individual Models

As previously discussed, research at the group level has largely focused on input-output variables in the mathematical modeling literature and on the group processes during deliberation (type of influence, group dynamics, etc.). At the individual level, literature has focused on how various pieces of evidence or testimony influences jurors' decisions, describing that process with either mathematical equations or the story model for jurors' decisions. To date, however, no research has attempted to integrate the individual models for how jurors make decisions with the group literature on jury decision making. Integration of these two areas could be beneficial for understanding more about how and why the jury arrives at a verdict decision and could account for what jurors bring into the deliberation process (i.e., individual stories) and the group dynamics that lead the jury to render a particular verdict.

At the group level, researchers have reported observing processes in deliberation similar to the processes individual jurors engage in according to the story model of juror decision making, implying that perhaps the story model could explain how jurors arrive at a group decision (Hastie, 2009; Hastie et al., 1998). In addition, other research on the deliberation process could be reinterpreted to show support for the idea that the story model may operate on a group level as well (Holstein, 1985). In this study, the author coded jury deliberations for discussions of what he termed *schematic interpretations*, which were defined as jurors' assertions about "what really happened" (p. 88) in the case combined with their own unique knowledge and experiences. These schematic interpretations could be interpreted as stories or story episodes through a story model lens.

In this study, jurors generated up to 15 schematic interpretations and revised their own schematic interpretations to integrate other jurors' viewpoints. As the number of schematic interpretations in any given jury increased, the probability that the jury would hang also increased (Holstein, 1985). Again, these findings could be understood using principles operating in the story model. That is, in the story model, as the number of stories high in coverage and coherence increases, the uniqueness of any one story decreases. Thus, the juror with many stories is more likely to render a not guilty verdict. In the case of the group deliberation, it could be that the number of stories (or schematic interpretations) presented is directly related to the probability the jury will hang because the uniqueness of any one story is compromised. Given the small number of cases in this study, however, it is difficult to make generalizations about the deliberation process or the story model applied to the group's decision from this data alone.

Whether and how stories are shared during deliberation and the group decides on a collective story may be dependent on the group dynamic variables at play during deliberation. For example, in the general social psychological group literature, the social sharedness of information (defined as the opinions and preferences that group members share) predicts how influential that information will be in the group's decision making (Kameda, Takezawa, Tindale, & Smith, 2002). In the context of the jury, the social sharedness of various stories or story episodes may also predict how influential those stories will be in the group's final verdict. Other factors, such as the size of the factions lobbying for each story, the type of influence being used by jurors, the number of stories, and the deliberation style of the jury may also play into whether or how the story model applies to the group decision. Future research could address these possibilities.

RESEARCH REVIEW

Since the publication of Kalven and Zeisel's (1966) *The American Jury*, there has been an explosion of research on the jury. The Web of Science database lists more than 4,300 articles on the subject of jurors or juries. In the PsycInfo database, which only covers articles in psychology, there are more than 3,600 articles on juror or jury behavior. Given the extensive literature on juries, we have chosen to focus our coverage on certain areas that have received significant attention and are more likely than others to provide insight into whether juries are making competent decisions. For example, although there are studies evaluating jurors' decisions about many types of evidence (e.g., alibi witnesses, battered women's syndrome, DNA), we have focused our review on jurors' evaluations of eyewitness, confession, and expert evidence, as the research on these topics is the most comprehensive and robust. We will also review evidence regarding whether internal and external biases influence jurors' decisions and whether there are any procedures that help minimize the effects of these biases. Next, we discuss the research on the decision-making capabilities of civil juries, which have the responsibility of deciding both the liability of the defendant and what compensation the plaintiff should receive if they find the defendant liable. Finally, we will discuss research related to how group variables influence jury decision making, including research on jury size, decision rule, and composition.

How Well Do Jurors Evaluate Evidence?

One organizing theme of the research conducted on juror and jury decision making is an examination of the competence of juries to make decisions that serve justice. Can jurors appropriately weigh evidence, giving more weight to evidence that is more reliable and less weight to evidence that is unreliable? There is considerable evidence that specific characteristics of the witnessing conditions and the procedure through which eyewitness evidence is collected influence its reliability (for a review, see Cutler & Kovera, 2010). Similarly, there are a number of factors that influence the likelihood that confessions obtained from suspects through police interrogations are false (for a review, see Kassin et al., 2010). There may also be variability in the reliability of expert scientific evidence presented in court. To what extent are jurors sensitive to the variations in the reliability of these forms of evidence, and does the relative reliability of the evidence appropriately influence jurors' verdict decisions?

Jurors' evaluations of eyewitness evidence.
According to examinations of the cases against defendants who were wrongfully convicted by juries and later exonerated through DNA, three quarters of the cases contained at least one eyewitness identification of the defendant (Garrett, 2011), an identification that was demonstrably wrong. The accuracy of eyewitness identifications is dependent on the conditions under which the witness viewed the crime and the procedures the police used to collect their identifications (see Chapter 7, this volume for a review of research on eyewitness memory). Features of the witnessed event that cannot be controlled by the criminal justice system but allow people to estimate the accuracy of witnesses' identifications are known as estimator variables (Wells, 1978) and include variables such as the presence of a weapon, duration of the exposure to the perpetrator, the time between the event and the identification procedure (i.e., retention interval), and cross-racial identification. Features of the identification procedure that are under the control of the justice system are known as system variables (Wells, 1978) and include variables such as lineup instructions, lineup composition, and whether the lineup members are presented simultaneously or sequentially. Eyewitness experts believe that the effects of these variables on eyewitness accuracy are reliable (Kassin, Tubb, Hosch, & Memon, 2001), yet surveys of laypeople eligible to serve as jurors suggest that they may be unaware of the influence of many of these variables on memory. A meta-analysis of many of these surveys, representing the responses of thousands of laypeople, showed that many potential jurors are less certain about the influence on eyewitness accuracy of many estimator variables (e.g., exposure duration, retention interval, cross-race identification) and some system variables (e.g., bias from mugshot exposure, simultaneous

versus sequential presentation) than are experts (Desmarais & Read, 2011). Although these findings suggest that laypeople may be aware of other variables affecting eyewitness accuracy (e.g., alcohol intoxication), it is unclear whether any of this juror knowledge about the reliability of eyewitness identifications affects their assessments of eyewitness reliability in a trial context or their verdicts in a case resting on identification evidence.

In contrast to survey methods, trial simulation methodology allows for an assessment of jurors' sensitivity to the factors that influence the reliability of eyewitness identification. In general, eyewitness identification evidence has a significant effect on jurors' decisions (Loftus, 1980). Jurors' reliance on eyewitness evidence when rendering verdicts does not appear shaken by evidence suggesting that the identification may be unreliable. In two studies, variations in the presence of a weapon, the quality of the witnessing conditions, length of the interval between the event and the identification did not influence mock jurors' trial judgments (Cutler, Penrod, & Dexter, 1990; Cutler, Penrod, & Stuve, 1988). There is inconsistency in the findings related to jurors' sensitivity to the role of system variables in eyewitness accuracy. In one study, jurors were insensitive to the effects of biased instructions and the method of presenting lineup members (i.e., simultaneous versus sequential presentation); in contrast, bias in the composition of the lineup (i.e., biased foils) appropriately influenced jurors' ratings of lineup suggestiveness and, to some extent, verdicts (Devenport, Stinson, Cutler, & Kravitz, 2002). In another study, both variations in the fairness of the lineup composition and bias in the instructions affected jurors' ratings of the suggestiveness of the lineup, but only variations in instructions influenced ratings of the accuracy of the identification (Devenport & Cutler, 2004). Neither of these variables influenced defendant culpability ratings or verdict, and expert testimony intended to educate jurors on the role of these variables in eyewitness accuracy had no effect on juror judgments (Devenport & Cutler, 2004).

Although there are some inconsistencies in the findings, overall the estimator and system variables that are related to the accuracy of eyewitness identifications do not reliably influence jurors' judgments of defendant guilt. In contrast, there is one estimator variable that does influence jurors' assessments of eyewitness accuracy and their verdicts: witness confidence. Jurors who hear the testimony from a 100% confident witness rate that witness to be more accurate and are more likely to vote to convict the identified defendant than are jurors who hear testimony from a witness who is only 80% confident in the accuracy of the identification (Cutler et al., 1988, 1990). Unfortunately, witness confidence is not strongly related to witness accuracy (Sporer, Penrod, Read, & Cutler, 1995) and is malleable, changing as a function of lineup administrator feedback about the witness's ability to identify the suspect (Douglass & Steblay, 2006). Thus, the one estimator variable that is not a reliable indicator of witness accuracy is the one variable that reliably influences jurors' evaluations of eyewitness evidence.

Although jurors' judgments in eyewitness cases are not influenced by factors that affect the reliability of an eyewitness identification, these studies had actors playing the role of witnesses. Thus, jurors were judging the credibility of actors and not true witnesses to a crime. Perhaps real witnesses emit behavioral cues to their accuracy during their testimony, and jurors could rely on these cues to make better judgments about eyewitness accuracy. In a laboratory simulation, accurate and inaccurate witnesses were cross-examined about their identifications (Wells, Lindsay, & Ferguson, 1979). Mock jurors who watched these cross-examinations were unable to distinguish between accurate and inaccurate witnesses. Instead, consistent with prior research, jurors judged confident witnesses to be more accurate even though confidence was unrelated to accuracy. Overall, jurors do not appear equipped to judge the reliability of eyewitness evidence, and neither expert testimony on eyewitness accuracy (Devenport & Cutler, 2004) nor cross-examination (Devenport et al., 2002) appear to improve jurors' ability to make these discriminations.

Jurors' evaluations of confession evidence.

Data gleaned from the DNA exonerations of the wrongfully convicted revealed that false confessions were also present in a number of wrongful conviction cases (Garrett, 2011; see Chapter 9, this volume for a review of research on interrogations and confessions). It must be compelling for jurors to hear evidence that the defendant actually confessed to the crime of which he is accused, because it is difficult to comprehend why people would confess to committing crimes that they did not commit. Yet it is clear there are people who do falsely confess to even serious crimes, like the five young men who initially confessed to the brutal beating and rape of the Central Park jogger but later recanted their confessions (Kassin et al., 2010). DNA evidence eventually implicated another man as the rapist, but not before the Central Park Five spent years in prison after being convicted by a jury (*People of the State of New York v. Kharey Wise et al.*, 2002). Was this case an anomaly, or do jurors have difficulty determining whether confessions are true or false?

Once a judge admits a defendant's confession into evidence, jurors have the duty to evaluate the confession for its voluntariness by examining the conditions under which the confession was obtained. If the confession is deemed voluntary, then it is almost a foregone conclusion that the jury will vote to convict the defendant. If the jury determines that the police engaged in coercive behaviors, then they have to determine how much weight they will give to the confession. Jury simulation studies suggest that jurors find confession evidence to be very persuasive (Appleby, Hasel, & Kassin, 2013), even more convincing than eyewitness or character evidence (Kassin & Neumann, 1997).

Jurors often fail to adjust their judgments of the voluntariness of confessions or their verdicts when there are situational pressures on suspects to confess (Kassin & Sukel, 1997; Kassin & Wrightsman, 1980), except for when the pressure is applied through threats of physical harm (Kassin & Wrightsman, 1980). Effects of confessions on verdicts are seen even when jurors believe that a confession is involuntary and assert that the confession had no effect on their verdicts (Kassin & Sukel, 1997). The effects of confessions on jurors' verdicts persist even when jurors are given the chance to deliberate to a group verdict (Kassin & Wrightsman, 1985) and when they hear judicial instructions to disregard confessions that are involuntarily given (Kassin & Wrightsman, 1981).

If jurors view a videotape of a confession that focuses solely on the suspect (i.e., only the suspect but not the interrogator is in the frame of the camera shot), they are less likely to consider the role of the interrogator in eliciting a confession compared to if jurors view a perspective that is equally focused on the interrogator and the suspect (Lassiter & Irvine, 1986; Lassiter, Slaw, Briggs, & Scanlan, 1992). When jurors watch a videotaped confession that contains both the interrogator and the suspect in the frame, situational factors in the interrogation are more likely to influence their beliefs about the voluntariness of the confession and their verdicts (Lassiter, Geers, Handley, Weiland, & Munhall, 2002; Lassiter, Geers, Munhall, Handley, & Beers, 2001). These findings may not extend to all suspects, however. Some research shows that when viewing a camera perspective equally focused on the suspect and interrogator, White participants judged racial minority suspects who were interrogated by a White interrogator as more likely to be guilty and to have given voluntary confessions compared to White suspects (Pickel, Warner, Miller, & Barnes, 2013; Ratcliff et al., 2010). Similarly, sexual-orientation minority suspects who confessed in an equal-focused video were more likely to be viewed as guilty and their confessions as voluntary compared to sexual-orientation majority suspects (Pickel et al., 2013). Eye-tracking data confirms that jurors' bias against considering situational information when evaluating confession voluntariness is at least in part perceptually based (Ratcliff, Lassiter, Schmidt, & Snyder, 2006), with jurors spending less time looking at the suspect (and more time looking at the interrogator) when both actors are in the camera frame and the suspect and interrogator are the same race or ethnicity (Ware, Lassiter, Patterson, & Ransom, 2008).

Like much of the trial simulation research examining whether factors that affect eyewitness accuracy influence jurors' evaluations of the reliability of an identification and their verdicts, these studies suggest that factors that influence the voluntariness of confessions do not influence jurors' evaluations of confessions or their verdicts. A known shortcoming of these studies, however, is

that they did not allow jurors to view actual confessions to determine whether they were true or false. Although it is often impossible to determine whether confessions obtained in the field are true, the ground truth of confessions made in laboratory studies is known. Lay people who viewed confessions from innocent and guilty mock suspects who had participated in an experimental simulation of confession behavior could not distinguish the guilt or innocence of the suspects at rates better than chance (Lassiter, Clark, Daniels, & Soinski, 2004). Other participants were unable to judge with any accuracy whether confessions made by prison inmates—who had confessed to the crime for which they were serving time or to the crime committed by another inmate—were true or false (Kassin, Meissner, & Norwick, 2005). Jurors appear to be limited in their ability to spot false confessions even in real cases, with 73% (Leo & Ofshe, 1998) to 81% (Drizin & Leo, 2004) of the juries hearing confessions later proven to be false returning guilty verdicts.

Jurors' evaluations of expert evidence. Early studies of jury decisions about expert evidence examined whether the testimony of an expert affected verdicts in a variety of different trial contexts. As intended, expert testimony presented by the defense typically decreased the probability that mock jurors or juries voted to convict the defendant across a number of types of testimony, including eyewitness reliability (Fox & Walters, 1986), battered woman syndrome (Schuller, 1992), children's cognitive development (Crowley, O'Callaghan, & Ball, 1994), and child sexual abuse accommodation syndrome (Kovera, Levy, Borgida, & Penrod, 1994). Similarly, expert evidence presented by the prosecution, such as evidence on rape trauma syndrome, increased the probability that mock jurors would render guilty verdicts (Brekke & Borgida, 1988). Once researchers established that expert testimony affected jurors' verdicts, they began to explore whether certain conditions moderated its influence. Expert testimony that appears early rather than later in the trial has greater influence, perhaps because the early presentation provides jurors a framework for understanding the other evidence yet to be presented at trial (Brekke & Borgida, 1988;

Schuller & Cripps, 1998). Expert testimony has a greater impact on juror decisions if the expert concretely links the scientific research to the facts of the case (Brekke & Borgida, 1988; Schuller, 1992). In addition, information related to the expert witness can increase or decrease the expert's influence, with superior credentials increasing influence (Cooper et al., 1996) and high rates of pay decreasing influence (Cooper & Neuhaus, 2000).

The design of many of these early studies provided information about whether and when expert testimony had its intended effect of swaying jurors toward the side presenting the testimony, but the results did not speak to whether expert testimony sensitized jurors to important trial information that they otherwise would have ignored. As noted earlier, jurors left to their own knowledge were insensitive to variations in estimator variables that affect the accuracy of eyewitness identifications (Cutler et al., 1988), but if jurors heard expert testimony about the factors that influence eyewitness reliability, then evidence of witnessing conditions that decrease the accuracy of eyewitness identifications caused jurors to be less likely to convict the defendant; jurors were not sensitive to the effects of witnessing conditions on eyewitness accuracy in the absence of this expert testimony (Cutler, Penrod, & Dexter, 1989). Similarly, expert testimony on child witnesses increased jurors' sensitivity to the quality of the forensic interview conducted with a child victim (Buck, London, & Wright, 2011; see Chapter 1, this volume for a review of research on child witnesses). Jurors are more likely to be sensitized to important trial evidence when the expert explicitly links the scientific research and the facts of the case (Kovera, Gresham, Borgida, Gray, & Regan, 1997).

Thus, expert testimony often influences jurors' decisions in the ways intended by the party in the case who called the expert, and such testimony sometimes sensitizes jurors to important case evidence that they should consider when rendering verdicts. All of the research discussed until now assumes that expert testimony should influence jurors' decisions because it can help jurors make better decisions and that the expert testimony proffered is based on sound science. It appears, however, that judges, who are responsible for determining

whether expert testimony is admissible at trial, are unfamiliar with the scientific principles that are important for evaluating expert evidence reliability despite the standard that the evidence should be reliable and will assist jurors in their decision-making process (Gatowski et al., 2001). Judges sometimes will admit expert evidence based on flawed research into evidence (Kovera & McAuliff, 2000). Given that it would not be desirable for jurors to base their verdicts on flawed expert evidence, it is important to consider whether jurors are able to differentiate flawed from valid science.

In the first study to examine this question, jurors' decisions were unaffected by variations in the construct validity in the research on which the expert based her opinion, instead relying on information about the ecological validity and the general acceptance of her work when forming their verdict opinions (Kovera et al., 1999). In another study, jurors were similarly unaffected by some design features that threatened the internal validity of the expert's research, namely an experimenter who was not blind to experimental condition and a confound (McAuliff & Duckworth, 2010; McAuliff, Kovera, & Nunez, 2009). Jurors are more likely to discount an expert's research when it is missing a critical control group than when it is not (McAuliff & Duckworth, 2010; McAuliff et al., 2009), especially when the jurors are high in "Need for Cognition" and therefore enjoy thinking and reasoning about difficult issues (McAuliff & Kovera, 2008). These findings question the ability of jurors to evaluate scientific evidence and are consistent with other research showing that jurors have difficulty reasoning about statistical evidence (Kaasa, Peterson, Morris, & Thompson, 2007; Schklar & Diamond, 1999; B. C. Smith, Penrod, Otto, & Park, 1996).

In the landmark U.S. Supreme Court decision *Daubert v. Merrell Dow Pharmaceuticals* (1993), the justices held that even if judges admitted unreliable expert evidence at trial, the procedural safeguards of cross-examination, opposing expert testimony, and judicial instruction on the standard of proof would help jurors identify flaws that exist in the evidence. It is unclear how instructions on the standard of proof would sensitize jurors to the importance of methodological flaws that exist in scientific research rather than merely alter jurors' criterion for judging that a defendant is guilty or liable (for a more complete discussion of this argument, see Kovera, Russano, & McAuliff, 2002). Moreover, in one trial simulation that manipulated whether the research on which an expert based her opinion had an experimenter who was blind to condition, judicial instructions tailored to educate jurors about the problems associated with non-blind experimenters did not cause jurors to judge the valid research to be of higher quality than the flawed research or render verdicts that reflected the different quality of the expert evidence (Berman, Austin, Levett, & Kovera, 2013).

Cross-examination also appears to be an ineffective method of sensitizing jurors to methodological problems underlying expert evidence. Jurors who heard expert testimony on the risk that the defendant would be dangerous in the future preferred testimony that rested on clinical opinion rather than on an actuarial prediction of risk, despite the stronger scientific basis for the actuarial expert's opinion (Krauss & Lee, 2003; Krauss & Sales, 2001; see Volume 1, Chapter 3, this handbook for a review of research on risk assessment and communication). Cross-examination caused the jurors to view the expert less positively and to believe that the defendant was less likely to be dangerous in the future but did not change jurors' preference for the clinical opinion testimony over the more evidence-based actuarial prediction (Krauss & Lee, 2003; Krauss & Sales, 2001).

Although jurors in these studies showed a clear preference for clinical opinion testimony rather than actuarial data, it is not clear whether cross-examination might help sensitize jurors to methodological flaws in the research underlying an expert's opinion. Jurors who heard a scientifically informed cross-examination (i.e., questions that specifically address the methodological features of the research) were no more likely to render decisions that differentiated between expert evidence that had high or low construct validity than were jurors who heard a scientifically naive cross-examination that focused on the expert's qualifications and credibility (Kovera et al., 1999). Although a scientifically informed cross-examination did help jurors recognize that a missing control group in an expert's research

made it less valid than research that contained a control group, this recognition did not influence jurors' verdicts (Austin & Kovera, 2013).

Perhaps cross-examination does not help jurors evaluate the quality of scientific evidence and weigh it appropriately in their verdicts because a partisan party, the attorney, delivers the intended education. If so, then it is possible that similar educational material from a respected scientist in the form of opposing expert testimony might have the intended effect of sensitizing jurors to variations in the validity of expert evidence. This possibility has been tested in trial simulation studies with different fact patterns. In a child sexual abuse case, the defense expert testified about the suggestibility of child witnesses, relying on a study that she had conducted that varied in its internal validity across conditions (Levett & Kovera, 2008). Some versions of the trial had an opposing prosecution expert who attacked the defense expert's willingness to generalize from laboratory studies to real world contexts only, or who also testified about the internal validity of the defense expert's study, stating that the research was valid or flawed (based on condition). The opposing expert did not sensitize jurors to the quality of the defense expert's study, even when directly addressing the internal validity of the study. Instead, the opposing expert made the jurors skeptical of the defense expert's research, irrespective of the quality of that research. These findings were replicated in a sexual harassment trial simulation (in which the opposing expert testified for the defense), which further demonstrated that the skepticism caused by the opposing defense expert was mediated by juror beliefs about the general acceptance of the plaintiff expert (Levett & Kovera, 2009; see Volume 1, Chapter 15, this handbook for a review of research in employment law).

Although these findings suggest that the opposing expert safeguard is also ineffective, there are two alterations to the traditional use of opposing expert testimony that may increase its ability to sensitize jurors to flaws in expert evidence: a court-appointed opposing expert or the use of a demonstrative illustrating the opposing expert's testimony. In a robbery trial, the use of the opposing expert produced a replication of the skepticism effect seen in earlier research, with jurors more likely to vote guilty after hearing either an adversarial or a court-appointed opposing prosecution expert than after hearing judicial instructions on how to evaluate experimental methods (Berman et al., 2013). Jurors who heard from the court-appointed opposing expert, however, rated an expert's research to be less valid when the experimenter knew which conditions the participants were in when conducting the research sessions than when the experimenter was blind to condition, suggesting that court-appointed opposing experts may be a more effective method of educating jurors about the quality of another expert's research. In another study, jurors who heard an adversarial prosecution opposing expert testify using a visual demonstrative to illustrate how to evaluate the quality of the defense expert's research methods were more likely to vote guilty when the defense expert's research methods lacked internal validity than when they were valid (Yarbrough & Kovera, 2013).

Why were these modes of presenting opposing expert testimony more effective than traditional adversarial opposing expert testimony? Relying on the elaboration likelihood models (Petty & Wegener, 1998) to provide an explanatory framework, perhaps these forms of opposing expert testimony better motivated or enabled jurors to understand the methodological arguments made by the expert. For example, maybe jurors were more trusting of the court-appointed than the adversarial opposing expert and therefore were more motivated to process the testimony and the arguments contained in the testimony. Alternatively, the presence of the demonstrative may have given the jurors extra skills to evaluate the quality of the expert evidence. Further research is needed to test these possibilities.

Bias in Juror Decision Making

The Sixth Amendment of the U.S. Constitution guarantees defendants the right to be tried by a fair and impartial jury. The jury selection process, known as *voir dire*, is intended to provide judges and attorneys an opportunity to evaluate the impartiality of prospective jurors (i.e., venirepersons) after asking them questions intended to reveal bias. Venirepersons can be eliminated from jury service through challenges for cause or peremptory challenges. Judges will grant challenges for cause when venirepersons exhibit clear bias against one of the parties in the case; judges may grant as many challenges for cause as they believe necessary to remove biased venirepersons from the jury. Attorneys may use a limited number of peremptory challenges to remove from service venirepersons whom they believe to be biased.

These procedures are in place to ensure the seating of an impartial jury, but their success depends on jurors being forthcoming while answering *voir dire* questions and the ability of judges and attorneys to detect bias in venirepersons. Venirepersons do not always answer voir dire questions honestly, especially when the questions are asked in open court (Seltzer, Venuti, & Lopes, 1991) or by a judge rather than an attorney (Jones, 1987), and attorneys are not able to reliably detect juror bias (Olczak, Kaplan, & Penrod, 1991). Judges' decisions to grant challenges for cause are predicted by the confidence with which a venireperson asserts their impartiality (Rose & Diamond, 2008), even though jurors' assessments of their impartiality appear to be unrelated to their level of bias (Moran & Cutler, 1991). Thus it is likely that some biased jurors will be seated on juries despite these selection procedures. Bias can come in a variety of forms, including jurors' attitudes about the legitimacy of certain legal defenses (Crocker & Kovera, 2010; Skeem, Louden, & Evans, 2004) and previous crime victimization (Culhane, Hosch, & Weaver, 2004). Two forms of bias that have received considerable scholarly attention in the jury literature are racial bias and bias resulting from exposure to PTP.

Racial bias in juror decision making. If jurors were truly impartial, then similar verdicts would be obtained in cases irrespective of the race of the defendant or the race of the victim (see Chapter 5, this volume for a review of research on race and the justice system). Meta-analyses of laboratory research suggest, however, that defendant race does influence juror decisions (Sweeney & Haney, 1992), albeit in seemingly complex ways, often interacting with other variables that affect jurors' judgments (Mazzella & Feingold, 1994; Sommers, 2007). In one capital trial simulation, defendant race had a very small effect on participants' sentencing decisions (life without parole vs. death), but this effect was magnified among participants who manifested poor comprehension of the sentencing instructions (Lynch & Haney, 2000; see Chapter 17, this volume for a review of research on capital cases). Instead of correcting for this bias, deliberation exacerbated it (Lynch & Haney, 2009). Moreover, defendant race interacts with juror race to influence both verdicts and sentencing in laboratory studies. The most recent meta-analysis of juror decision-making research containing experimental manipulations of defendant race found that jurors were more likely to convict defendants of another race than their own and that there was a similar pattern for sentencing decisions, although the effect size was smaller (Mitchell, Haw, Pfeifer, & Meissner, 2005).

Effects of defendant race appear in archival studies of real sentencing decisions as well, but again race effects often appear only when the victim of the crime is White. For example, Black defendants were more likely to receive the death penalty in Georgia than were White defendants, but only when their victims were White; when victims were Black, there was no effect of defendant race on sentencing decisions (Baldus, Woodworth, & Pulaski, 1990). This effect is particularly pronounced for some Black defendants as opposed to others. When murder victims were White, Black defendants convicted of killing them were more likely to receive the death penalty (as opposed to life without possibility of parole) if independent raters judged the defendants' facial features to be more stereotypically Black (Eberhardt, Davies, Purdie-Vaughns, & Johnson, 2006). Stereotypicality did not play a role in the sentencing of Black defendants who had been convicted of killing Black victims.

One possible explanation for these racial biases in juror decisions is that jurors hold stereotypes about the criminality of Blacks that they are unwilling or unable to set aside when deciding a case. There certainly is evidence that stereotypes about Blacks contain information that would lead jurors to convict them at greater rates. The notion that people associate Blacks with crime is not new (Allport & Postman, 1947; P. G. Devine, 1989). Studies have shown that many people believe that neighborhoods

with a greater proportion of young Black men have higher crime rates, and the association holds even after controlling for actual rates of crime (Quillian & Pager, 2001, 2010). More recent research demonstrates that the association between the constructs "Black" and "crime" is bidirectional, with exposure to crime-related images directing participants' visual attention in a subsequent task toward Black rather than White faces (Eberhardt, Goff, Purdie, & Davies, 2004). Some people also associate Blacks with apes, and this association allows for the dehumanization of Black defendants (Goff, Eberhardt, Williams, & Jackson, 2008). These studies provide support for the notion that jurors' attitudes about the criminality of Blacks may explain the disparity in jurors' racially biased decisions.

Is it possible to reduce this racial bias in jury decision making? Basic social psychological research suggests that making individuals low in prejudice aware of the content of their racial stereotypes causes them to work harder to avoid discriminating against Blacks (P. G. Devine, 1989). Thus, although counterintuitive, perhaps making jurors aware of race would make them less likely to discriminate against Black defendants (Sommers & Ellsworth, 2001). Indeed, trial simulation studies suggest that when race was not made salient in an interracial assault trial, Whites were more likely to convict Black defendants than White defendants; in contrast, when race was salient, Whites convicted Black and White defendants at equal rates (Sommers & Ellsworth, 2000). Race salience has the ability to reduce racial bias in White jurors even when the jurors harbor high levels of prejudice (Cohn, Bucolo, Pride, & Sommers, 2009; for more on race salience and related phenomena, see Chapter 5, this volume).

Effects of exposure to PTP on juror decisions.
Although some forms of juror bias are dispositional (e.g., attitudes and stereotypes), other forms of bias are situationally induced by exposure to extralegal information that creates a prejudice that subsequently influences jurors' decisions at trial (see Chapter 11, this volume for a review of research on pretrial publicity and other aspects of media and law). The American Bar Association (2000)

has identified several classes of information that, if released to the public before the start of the trial, may unfairly prejudice the jury pool against the defendant. Information deemed prejudicial includes but is not limited to information about the defendant's prior criminal record, character or reputation, and confession or admission against interest if one was made. Information of this type is problematic because, although it is often inadmissible as trial evidence, it can lead potential jurors to infer that the defendant is guilty. Therefore, exposure to media reports of this prejudicial yet inadmissible information may interfere with jurors' ability to presume that the defendant is innocent until proven guilty by trial evidence, which is required under the law.

Exposure to proprosecution PTP adversely affects jurors' pretrial and posttrial judgments of defendant guilt (Studebaker & Penrod, 1997, 2005). The phenomenon has been studied using laboratory simulations as well as surveys of communities in which PTP is prevalent. In the laboratory simulations, participants are exposed to varied amounts of PTP, watch or read a trial simulation, and render trial judgments. In field research, people in the community are surveyed about their naturally occurring exposure to PTP and their pretrial evaluations of the defendant's guilt. The prejudicial effects of PTP on jurors' judgments of defendant guilt manifest in both contexts.

The only published meta-analysis of the PTP literature suggests that exposure to negative publicity about a defendant has a small to moderate effect on jurors' judgments of defendant guilt, but that the size of the effect varied as a function of participants, settings, PTP types, and research methods (Steblay, Besirevic, Fulero, & Jimenez-Lorente, 1999). PTP effects were larger when conducted using survey rather than laboratory simulation methods, jurors read or heard about multiple categories of prejudicial information, and community members rather than college students participated in the studies. Because many of these methodological features are confounded with each other (survey studies were more likely to include more types of prejudicial information and have community members as participants), it is hard to know which of these variables is responsible for the variability in the size of

PTP effects in the literature. It is clear, however, that the effects are robust, obtaining across a variety of conditions. For example, negative effects of media exposure occurred even when jurors were exposed to media that was not specific to the case they are trying. Media that was topically related to a case but did not include prejudicial information about the defendant in the specific case being tried (known as general PTP) increased the likelihood that jurors convicted (Greene & Loftus, 1984; Greene & Wade, 1988; Kovera, 2002).

Although some have raised concerns about the applicability of PTP studies using survey methods to understanding decisions in actual cases because they typically do not hear trial evidence, receive judicial instruction, or deliberate, mock jurors exposed to negative PTP about a defendant were more likely than those not exposed to believe that the defendant was guilty not only before hearing trial evidence but also after hearing the trial evidence, receiving judicial instruction, and participating in deliberation. Thus PTP effects survive the presentation of trial evidence (Chrzanowski, 2005; Otto, Penrod, & Dexter, 1994; Ruva, McEvoy, & Bryant, 2007). Indeed, deliberation may even magnify the effect of PTP when the PTP is intended to evoke a negative emotional response toward the defendant (Kramer et al., 1990) or when the evidence against the defendant is more ambiguous (Kerr et al., 1999).

How is it that PTP effects can survive the presentation of trial evidence, judicial instruction, and deliberation? Exposure to prejudicial information about the defendant appears to change the way that jurors process trial evidence, causing them to adopt a proprosecution bias when evaluating the evidence that they hear at trial (Hope, Memon, & McGeorge, 2004). This predecisional distortion reinforced rather than mitigated the effects of PTP, providing an explanation for how PTP effects can survive and even thrive despite the presentation of trial evidence. If the PTP is prejudicial, the distortion is proprosecution; if the PTP presents prodefense information, then the decisional distortion favors the defense (Ruva, Guenther, & Yarbrough, 2011). Overall, this research suggests that the justice system cannot count on deliberation to correct for the effects of PTP exposure, and therefore it is important to consider the efficacy of other potential remedies.

If deliberation does not eliminate the effects of PTP on juror judgments, are there other procedural safeguards that could help jurors overcome the bias introduced by PTP and render fair and impartial decisions? Some suggested remedies include judicial instructions to ignore PTP, delays of the trial (i.e., continuances), extended *voir dire* proceedings in which the judge allows for expansive questioning of venirepersons, and either importing jurors from another community that had less PTP exposure (i.e., change of venire) or moving the trial to another, less tainted community (i.e., a change of venue; American Bar Association, 2000). Does the use of these safeguards ensure that defendants who were the subject of extensive media coverage receive a fair trial from an impartial jury? For many of these safeguards, the answer is no.

Judges may try to reduce the effects of PTP exposure by instructing jurors to ignore information about the case that they heard about before the trial and was not entered into evidence. These types of instructions do not eliminate PTP effects in well-conducted laboratory studies (Fein, McCloskey, & Tomlinson, 1997; Sue, Smith, & Gilbert, 1974). Instructions fail to prevent either PTP that presents facts or PTP that arouses emotion by affecting jurors' judgments of defendant culpability (Kramer et al., 1990). Most of these studies failing to find a curative effect of judicial instructions were conducted in a criminal trial context, but they do not appear to work in civil contexts either (Bornstein, Whisenhunt, & Nemeth, 2002).

It is not surprising that this type of instruction does not reduce PTP effects, as a meta-analysis revealed that jurors also do not follow instructions to disregard inadmissible evidence that is wrongfully presented at trial (Steblay, Hosch, Culhane, & McWethy, 2006). Moreover, mock jurors who heard PTP were more likely to report that they heard information from the PTP during the presentation of trial evidence than were those who were not exposed (Ruva et al., 2007), suggesting that jurors have difficulty monitoring whether information comes from PTP or trial evidence. If they cannot identify known information as coming from PTP

rather than from the trial, instructions to disregard PTP information will prove hard to follow.

Judges often rely on extended *voir dire* to remedy the effects of extensive PTP exposure. Extended *voir dire* is presumed to combat PTP bias by allowing extensive questioning of prospective jurors in an attempt to elicit information that will help judges and attorneys identify biased jurors and by providing an opportunity to educate prospective jurors about their duty to disregard prejudicial PTP if they are chosen to serve and to seek their commitment to perform that duty. First, for extended *voir dire* to serve as an effective remedy for PTP, judges and attorneys must be able to identify biased jurors. Although no data exist on judges' capabilities, the limited data on attorneys' abilities is mixed. For example, in one study, attorneys removed venirepersons who were more biased against their side, but the attitudes of the jurors they selected were no different than the attitudes held by a randomly selected group of people from the community or from the first 12 people to report for jury service (Johnson & Haney, 1994). Second, although increasing venirepersons' exposure to PTP strengthens their belief in the defendant's guilt (Moran & Cutler, 1991), there is no correlation between jurors' self-reported ability to remain impartial and their pretrial judgments of a defendant's guilt (Kerr, Kramer, Carroll, & Alfini, 1991; Moran & Cutler, 1991). Social desirability concerns may cause venirepersons to attempt to hide any PTP bias they may have during *voir dire*, with venirepersons in a venue with extensive PTP exposure under reporting their inability to hear the case fairly in contrast with a community survey of residents in the same venire (Chrzanowski, 2005). These attempts to cover signs of bias will further inhibit attorneys' and judges' abilities to identify biased venirepersons.

Only one study has tested whether exposure to the *voir dire* process itself might eliminate or at least minimize PTP effects on jurors' decisions (Dexter, Cutler, & Moran, 1992). In this simulation, attorneys conducted either a standard *voir dire* or an extended *voir dire* with participants who either had or had not read PTP. The extended *voir dire* was designed to educate venirepersons about PTP effects, to make them feel accountable for their decisions, and to urge them to admit to any effects of the PTP on their pretrial verdict preferences and beliefs about defendant guilt. After watching the trial, as would be expected, those jurors who had PTP exposure were more likely to vote guilty than those who did not. Jurors subjected to the extended *voir dire* were less likely to convict the defendant than those subjected to a standard *voir dire*. Most important, there was no interaction of PTP exposure and type of *voir dire*, so an extended voir did not minimize or eliminate the effects of PTP.

A continuance, or a delay of the start of the trial, is another proposed method for eliminating PTP effects because the delay presumably puts distance between jurors' exposure to media reports about the case and the start of trial. In one study, starting the trial several days after PTP expsoure (as opposed to immediately) eliminated the effects of factual PTP but not emotional PTP (Kramer et al., 1990). The delay in this study was rather short—only several days. Continuances are often granted for many months, so it is possible that longer delays could counteract even emotional PTP. Meta-analytic findings found that delays of seven days increased PTP effects. This effect should be viewed cautiously, however, as there were very few studies in the meta-analysis that actually manipulated the length of time between PTP exposure and trial (Steblay et al., 1999). Thus, other characteristics may have systematically varied with delay, although none were readily apparent, to produce what appeared to be an increased effect of PTP with longer delay, or perhaps jurors were less able to remember the source of information about the case (PTP vs. trial evidence) with longer delays between PTP exposure and trial (Ruva & McEvoy, 2008). Whether continuances increase or decrease PTP effects, there remain concerns that pretrial media attention to the case will reemerge when the trial resumes at the later date, thus effectively eliminating the effect of the continuance while abrogating the defendant's right to a speedy trial.

The most effective method of eliminating PTP effects from a jury is for a trial to be moved to a different community in which PTP exposure has not prejudiced the citizens, or at least a community that has had less media attention on the case, a procedure

known as a change of venue. Community surveys have repeatedly shown that community members in venues with a highly publicized trial are more likely to believe that a defendant is guilty than are citizens from nearby venues in which the trial received far less media attention (Moran & Cutler, 1991; Nietzel & Dillehay, 1983; Vidmar & Judson, 1981). Although changes of venue are effective methods of ensuring a jury pool that is less prejudiced against the defendant, judges rarely grant motions to move trials unless they are convinced that there is no possible way to seat a fair jury. Such determinations are rarely reached without data on the community sentiments toward the defendant from citizens living in the current trial venue and at least one alternative venue (Nietzel & Dillehay, 1983), or without a systematic content analysis of local media coverage of the case in the different venues (Studebaker, Robbennolt, Pathak-Sharma, & Penrod, 2000).

Summary. There are many possible biases, some from sources internal to the juror (e.g., stereotypes, attitudes) and some from sources external to the juror (e.g., pretrial media coverage) that can interfere with jurors' ability to render decisions based solely on the evidence and the laws applicable to a case. These biases are sometimes hard to overcome. Even procedural safeguards intended to remedy juror bias may not fully protect defendants against the problems stemming from a partial jury that is unable to set aside extraevidentiary considerations.

Decision Making in Civil Cases

Much of the research discussed until now has addressed jury decision making in criminal cases in which jurors are deciding whether a defendant is guilty of a criminal offense. Defendants also have a right to a jury trial in civil cases, guaranteed by the Seventh Amendment, in which there is more than twenty dollars in dispute. In civil cases, juries are not deciding the guilt of a defendant but whether the defendant is liable for a harm that a plaintiff has suffered. If the jury deems that the defendant has some liability for the harm, it then determines what type of compensation the plaintiff should receive from the defendant in the form of monetary damages. Compensatory damages are intended to make plaintiffs whole by compensating them for economic losses (e.g., medical bills, lost wages) and noneconomic losses (e.g., pain and suffering, loss of companionship); punitive damages are awarded to punish the defendant for egregious behavior and to deter the defendant and others from behaving similarly in the future (Greene & Bornstein, 2000). Claims that civil juries are out of control, awarding damages that are not supported by the trial evidence, are relatively common in the media (Robbennolt & Studebaker, 2003). How well do jurors follow the law when making decisions in civil cases?

The defendant's conduct should determine whether jurors find a defendant liable. For example, when a defendant has been accused of negligence, the reasonableness of the defendant's conduct, but not the consequences of that conduct, should influence liability judgments. A direct test of juror comprehension of judicial instructions on the legal standards for negligence using a multiple choice format suggested that comprehension was relatively poor; deliberation modestly improved comprehension, but access to written instructions during decision making did not (Greene & Johns, 2001). Trial simulation studies that manipulated variables that should or should not affect liability judgments tested whether jurors could accurately apply the law in a given case. In accordance with the law, jurors were more likely to find a defendant liable if his conduct was careless rather than reasonable (Greene, Johns, & Bowman, 1999). The consequences of defendant conduct such as injury severity also influence liability judgments, even though they should not (Bornstein, 1998; Greene et al., 1999). Repeated instructions to disregard the severity of harm when deciding liability also had no effect on juror judgments (A. C. Smith & Greene, 2005). The procedural modification that has proven most successful for reducing the influence of plaintiff harm on liability decisions is bifurcation, or the withholding of information about injury severity before liability is decided. When information about the severity of harm experienced by the plaintiff was withheld, mock jurors judged a defendant to be less negligent than did mock jurors who heard about the consequences of the defendant's conduct (A. C. Smith & Greene, 2005).

In contrast to judgments of liability, juror awards of compensatory damages should be based on the severity of the harm experienced by the plaintiff but not the conduct of the defendant. In several jury analogue studies, defendant conduct improperly influenced damage awards in trial simulation studies (e.g., Greene, Johns, & Smith, 2001; Sommer, Horowitz, & Bourgeois, 2001). Moreover, jurors awarded less to a plaintiff who had contributed to the negligence that caused the tortious harm than to a plaintiff who made no contribution to causing the harm, even though judicial instructions state that jurors are to ignore the plaintiff's role in causing the harm when deciding damages (Zickafoose & Bornstein, 1999). Like with liability decisions, bifurcation—in this case withholding information about the defendant's conduct—caused jurors to rate that the plaintiff had experienced less severe harm, to be less likely to award damages, and to award less money for economic damages than jurors who heard evidence about the defendant's negligent conduct (A. C. Smith & Greene, 2005).

The amount of damages requested by the plaintiff's attorney—known as *ad danums*—also influences jurors' decisions about compensatory awards. In jury analogue studies, *ad danums* served as anchors for compensatory awards, with larger *ad danums* producing larger compensatory awards (Chapman & Bornstein, 1996; Raitz, Greene, Goodman, & Loftus, 1990), except when they were extreme requests (Chapman & Bornstein, 1996). The method of quantifying the request (per diem based on an hourly rate vs. a monthly rate) also affected juror awards, even when the resulting dollar amount of the award would be the same, with jurors viewing per diem requests at a monthly rate as more extreme than the same request made as a lump sum or as a per diem at an hourly rate (McAuliff & Bornstein, 2010). Finally, jurors in real cases were more likely to object in deliberation to the size of a plaintiff attorney's request for compensation for pain and suffering than for compensation for economic losses that have a demonstrated value (Diamond, Rose, Murphy, & Meixner, 2011).

Much of the debate on whether jury damage awards are outlandish focuses on the awarding of punitive damages, with concerns that jurors will make larger awards when defendants have "deep pockets." In real cases, however, jurors rarely made punitive awards. When they have, the award amount did not vary as a function of whether the defendant was an individual or a corporation (Eisenberg, Goerdt, Ostrom, Rottman, & Wells, 1997). Judges and juries awarded similar amounts of punitive damages, and the relationship between the sizes of the compensatory and punitive damage awards was similar for the two groups (Eisenberg, LaFountain, Ostrom, Rottman, & Wells, 2002). Moreover, punitive awards were larger when defendant behavior was more reprehensible and compensatory awards were higher (Choi & Eisenberg, 2010). As is the case for compensatory damages, however, the amount of a plaintiff's request for punitive damages influenced the size of mock jurors' punitive damage awards, with larger requests producing larger awards (Hastie et al., 1999).

Because of concerns about the size and variability of punitive damage awards, some courts and legislatures have enacted reforms to cap the amount of punitive damages that a jury can award. Rather than limiting punitive awards in all circumstances, caps served as an anchor for punitive awards, with punitive award amounts increasing as caps increased in a trial simulation study (Robbennolt & Studebaker, 1999). Moreover, punitive awards in the high-cap condition were larger than those in a control condition in which there was no cap on punitive awards (Robbennolt & Studebaker, 1999). Thus, caps on punitive awards may not work as intended.

Group Dynamics and the Rules of Deliberation

In examining jury decision making at the group level, there are several procedural rules governing the deliberation process and the composition of the jury that may affect how the jury renders a verdict. In these rules, the law makes several assumptions about human behavior. Thus, the rules became a natural source of research questions for psychologists. Are the law's assumptions about human behavior valid? In this section, we will review the law regarding jury size, decision rule, and jury composition. Then we will review the psychological literature testing the assumptions behind these rules.

Jury size.   In *Williams v. Florida* (1970), the United States Supreme Court (USSC) ruled that juries in criminal cases could consist of six jurors instead of the traditional 12 jurors. In the ruling, the justices asserted that juries consisting of six members were "functionally equivalent" to juries consisting of 12 members. This decision was later extended to include civil juries (*Colgrove v. Battin*, 1973) and was limited in *Ballew v. Georgia* (1978), which held that juries of fewer than six jurors were prohibited. Currently, many states and federal courts allow jury trials with juries consisting of fewer than 12 members (however, juries consisting of 12 members are required for capital cases).

The major assumption underlying this series of cases is that a six-member jury is functionally equivalent to a 12-member jury. Many scholars tackled this research question after *Williams v. Florida* (1970). Combining 17 studies, a meta-analysis of the literature examining the effects of jury size on jury behavior showed that the deliberation processes of six and 12 person juries differed in several areas (Saks & Marti, 1997). Larger juries tended to deliberate for longer, recall evidence more accurately, and had more thorough discussions than smaller juries. Later research showed similar effects; among juries who took notes during trial, larger juries recalled more facts postdeliberation than six-person juries (Horowitz & Bordens, 2002).

In addition, in the meta-analysis, larger juries were more likely to represent the minority viewpoint and were more diverse than smaller juries. In the four studies included in the meta-analysis that dealt with civil juries, the majority of studies showed that smaller juries rendered higher damage awards than larger juries (Saks & Marti, 1997). This result is consistent with later studies on jury size and damage awards (Davis, Au, Hulbert, Chen, & Zarnoth, 1997; Horowitz & Bordens, 2002), although one of those studies only showed the effect in conditions in which the jurors could not take notes during trial (Horowitz & Bordens, 2002).

Despite these differences between six- and 12-member juries, Saks and Marti (1997) showed that smaller and larger juries rendered similar verdicts. In conditions in which the juries were deliberating under a requirement to reach a unanimous verdict, however, larger juries were more likely than smaller juries to hang, or not reach a decision (Saks & Marti, 1997). So, even though smaller and larger juries differ in the quality of deliberation, time devoted to deliberation, damage awards rendered, diversity, and representation of the minority viewpoint, the outcome (verdict) is likely to be similar in larger or smaller juries. Thus, the USSC's assumption of "functional equivalence" may be somewhat true for verdict outcomes (with the exception of the occurrence of the hung jury), but the quality of the processes is different between juries differing in size.

Jury decision rule.   Similar to the USSC's decisions about jury size, the USSC addressed the constitutionality of using a non-unanimous decision rule (as opposed to a unanimous requirement) in two decisions. In *Apodaca, Cooper, & Madden v. Oregon* (1972) and *Johnson v. Louisiana* (1972), the court ruled that a non-unanimous verdict decision was constitutional. In the decisions, the justices opined that using a majority decision rule instead of a unanimous decision rule did not affect the function of the jury to use their commonsense judgment in rendering a decision, and that the meaningful participation of the minority segment of the jury was not compromised by using a majority decision rule. These decisions were later limited in *Burch v. Louisiana* (1979), which required unanimous decisions from six-person juries. Currently, many states allow for a non-unanimous decision in several types of jury trials, but 26 states require a unanimous verdict in all trials, 44 states require a unanimous verdict in criminal felony trials, and all states with capital punishment as an option require a unanimous verdict in capital trials (D. J. Devine, 2013).

Similar to the research spawned by the USSC's decisions on six- versus 12-member juries, these decisions prompted researchers to explore the assumptions underlying the USSC's reasoning regarding allowing a majority decision rule. In one study, six-person juries in a mock robbery trial deliberated to a verdict under a unanimous decision rule or were told that, even though ideally all jurors would agree, a majority consisting of five jurors in agreement was an acceptable decision (Hans, 1978). The videotaped discussions revealed that in

unanimous decision juries, the members of the jury holding minority positions took more active roles in deliberation, participated more, and were more influential than in majority decision juries (Hans, 1978).

Similarly, in another extensive study, researchers instructed 12-person juries in a mock murder trial to deliberate to a unanimous verdict or a majority decision verdict requiring either a 10-person or eight-person majority (Hastie et al., 1983). Again, the deliberation process differed based on decision rule. Unanimous decision juries were more likely to be evidence-driven, spent more time discussing evidence, and were more likely to use informational influence to persuade fellow jurors than were majority decision juries. In addition, once majority decision juries reached the correct number of votes required by the decision rule, deliberation stopped, regardless of the minority's views. Unanimous juries were also more likely than majority decision juries to hang and took longer to make a decision. Last, juror satisfaction was higher in unanimous juries than in majority decision juries (Hastie et al., 1983). Thus, based on the psychological research, it appears that the court's assumption that the minority would meaningfully participate in deliberation in a majority decision context similar to a unanimous decision rule context may not be valid.

Jury composition.   As previously noted, the Sixth Amendment of the U.S. Constitution guarantees defendants the right to a trial "by an impartial jury of the State and district wherein the crime shall have been committed." The Seventh Amendment further extends this right to defendants in civil cases. These rights have been interpreted by the USSC to mean that the jury pool must be drawn from a representative cross-section of the community (see Hans & Vidmar, 1982, for an overview of those decisions; *Strauder v. West Virginia*, 1880). In these decisions, the USSC forbade excluding potential jurors on the basis of membership in a racial, religious, or other cognizable group (a common trait or characteristic of the group that distinguishes the group from others). The assumptions behind a representative jury is that a jury consisting of members who have a wide variety of backgrounds, experiences, and knowledge would result in a better decision and would be more likely to include minority group members' opinions than a more homogenous group (Hans & Vidmar, 1982). In addition, including minority group members should inhibit majority group members from acting on their own prejudices during decision making (Hans & Vidmar, 1982).

These assumptions were tested in a study in which the demographic makeup of deliberating mock juries in a rape case were varied to consist of either all White jurors or four White jurors and two Black jurors (Sommers, 2006). Diverse juries deliberated for longer and exchanged more information than all-White juries. The increase in information exchange, however, was not just due to the inclusion and participation of Black jurors. The quality of the White jurors' participation changed as a function of being included in a diverse jury. Specifically, White jurors participating in diverse juries referenced more case facts, were less likely to make errors, and were more likely to discuss racism than White jurors participating in homogenous juries. Thus, this study suggests that a representative, diverse jury actually engages in a superior decision-making process than a homogenous jury. In addition to these benefits, a decision made by a jury that is representative of the community is more likely to be accepted by the community and perceived as fair than a decision made by a more homogenous jury (Ellis & Diamond, 2003).

Despite the research suggesting that diverse juries make better decisions and the legal doctrine suggesting that juries should be drawn from a representative cross-section of the community, there are special cases in which the representativeness of the jury may be compromised. As previously mentioned, in capital cases, jurors are typically asked during *voir dire* if their attitudes about the death penalty would interfere with their abilities to follow the law and be impartial in considering the trial evidence (see Chapter 17, this volume for a review of research on death penalty cases). This process is termed death qualification (Haney, 1984; *Wainwright v. Witt*, 1985; *Witherspoon v. Illinois*, 1968). Jurors who would not impose the death penalty or who could not fairly consider all the evidence knowing that the defendant could be sentenced to death upon conviction are excluded from serving in a capital case.

Thus, those jurors are not death-qualified. Jurors who answer the *voir dire* questions affirmatively are considered death-qualified jurors.

Several studies have shown that the death-qualification process alters the composition of the jury, resulting in juries that are more homogenous than juries in non-capital cases (Fitzgerald & Ellsworth, 1984; Haney, Hurtado, & Vega, 1994; Moran & Comfort, 1986). In these studies, researchers surveyed community members and impaneled felony jurors and found that Black jurors and female jurors were significantly more likely than White jurors and male jurors to hold attitudes that would exclude them from serving in a capital case. In addition, Democrats and the poor were more likely than Republicans and the wealthy to hold attitudes that would exclude them. A meta-analysis confirmed the finding that women and minorities are more likely than men and Whites to hold attitudes that would systematically exclude them from serving in a capital jury (Filkins, Smith, & Tindale, 1998). Thus, it is likely that in capital cases, the jury is more homogenous than juries typically seated in non-capital cases.

In addition to altering the demographic composition of the jury, death qualification also alters the attitudinal composition of the jury. Death-qualified jurors are more likely than those excluded because of their attitudes toward the death penalty to be prosecution-oriented, more punitive, less trusting of criminal defendants, and more concerned with crime control (Fitzgerald & Ellsworth, 1984). In addition, other research shows that death-qualified jurors are more likely than excluded jurors to have high beliefs in a just world, hold legal authoritarian attitudes, exhibit an internal locus of control (Butler & Moran, 2007), and exhibit higher levels of homophobia, modern racism, and modern sexism (Butler, 2007). Thus, the death-qualification process changes the attitudinal composition of the jury to become more homogenous in several undesirable ways.

Similar to the research on the decision-making processes of racially diverse versus racially homogenous juries (Sommers, 2006), the decision processes of death-qualified versus non–death-qualified juries also differs. One study showed that juries containing jurors with mixed attitudes toward the death penalty were better at remembering evidence, were more critical of witnesses, and thought the case was more difficult to decide compared to juries containing only death-qualified jurors (Cowan, Thompson, & Ellsworth, 1984). Thus, a death-qualified jury may not examine evidence as critically as a jury composed of jurors with mixed attitudes toward the death penalty. In addition, death-qualified jurors are more conviction-prone than jurors who would be excluded in the death-qualification process (Cowan et al., 1984; Moran & Comfort, 1986). Three different meta-analyses have confirmed that there is a significant relationship between death penalty attitudes and verdict (Allen, Mabry, & McKelton, 1998; Filkins et al., 1998; Nietzel, McCarthy, & Kern, 1999). These studies have shown that a juror who favors the death penalty is 25%–44% more likely to convict a defendant than a juror who is against the death penalty.

The literature examining death qualification shows that the process alters the demographic and attitudinal composition of the jury, creating a jury that is less likely to consider all the evidence critically and more likely to convict the defendant than a jury made up of jurors with mixed attitudes toward the death penalty. Until recently, researchers believed that this type of qualification process was unique to capital cases, but examination of the voir dire process in juvenile waiver cases reveals a similar type of juvenile-qualification process in which jurors are asked about their attitudes toward juvenile waiver (Greathouse, Sothmann, Levett, & Kovera, 2011). In this process, jurors who voice concern about trying juveniles as adults are typically excluded from serving in a juvenile waiver case, similar to how jurors who express concern about considering the death penalty as a punishment are excluded in a capital case (Danielsen, Levett, & Kovera, 2004).

Similar to the death-qualification process, the juvenile-qualification process in juvenile waiver cases alters the demographic composition of the jury in that Black jurors are more likely than other jurors to be excluded based on attitudes toward juvenile waiver (Levett, Otis, & Kovera, 2013). In addition, analysis of community members' jury deliberations in a difficult to decide mock-juvenile waiver case

revealed that juries composed of jurors with mixed attitudes toward juvenile waiver used higher levels of reasoning and were less conviction-prone than juries composed of juvenile-qualified jurors (Levett, Greathouse, Sothmann, Copple, & Kovera, 2006, 2007).

In summary, the research on jury composition suggests that a diverse jury will deliberate at a higher level than a more homogenous jury. Thus, the USSC's assumptions in requiring that the jury be chosen from a sample that is representative of the community are well founded. There are special cases (capital cases and juvenile waiver cases) in which the composition of the jury may be altered due to the *voir dire* process required or typically used. In these cases, it is likely the jury is rendering a lower-quality decision, most likely because the jury selected is more demographically and attitudinally homogenous than juries seated in other types of cases.

PRACTICE AND POLICY ISSUES

Some of the research conducted on juror and jury decision making has implications for the practice of psychology and for public policy regarding juries. Practice in the area of jury behavior takes the form of litigation consulting, in which psychologists advise attorneys on the psychology of evidence evaluation or provide information to help attorneys conduct *voir dire* and exercise their peremptory challenges. The motivation behind jury practice is not to improve juror decision making but to influence decision making in a direction desired by the hired attorneys. In contrast, jury research that is relevant for public policy is motivated by the desire to identify alternative procedures that will improve the quality of the decisions that juries make. Because of space constraints, we will not review the extensive research literature on jury selection (for a review, see Kovera & Cutler, 2013), but we will provide an overview of psychologists' activities in jury selection and policy reform.

Jury Selection

In the early 1970s, social scientists began studying the relationship of juror characteristics that were predictive of verdict, ultimately using that knowledge in an attempt to influence the outcome of a case (Schulman, Shaver, Colman, Emrich, & Christie, 1973). Since that time, the trial-consulting industry has grown from groups of politically active social scientists working to level the playing field for anti-war activists whom they believed the government was persecuting to multimillion dollar businesses that are more likely to represent defendants in civil rather than criminal cases (Seltzer, 2006; Strier & Shestowsky, 1999).

The first systematic application of social science methods to jury selection was in the conspiracy trial of the Harrisburg Seven, members of a group of anti-war activists. The government chose to try the Harrisburg Seven in a venue that was known to be conservative, Republican, Catholic, and friendly to defense contractors (Schulman et al., 1973). Social scientists joined forces to interview community members to develop a profile of the ideal defense juror, identifying venireperson characteristics that predicted verdict preferences and attitudes toward the defendants. Defense attorneys used this information to exercise their peremptory challenges to eliminate jurors who did not fit the profile. The jury hung after seven days of deliberation, with the majority of jurors favoring acquittal. Schulman et al. continued to apply behavioral science methods to assist attorneys in jury selection, founding the first trial-consulting company (Lieberman & Sales, 2007). Other companies followed, as did consulting departments within law firms.

In 1982, a couple dozen practicing trial consultants founded a professional society, the American Society of Trial Consultants (ASTC), for the purpose of providing an outlet for the discussion of trial-consulting methods, the development of ethical standards, and the promotion of the profession (American Society of Trial Consultants, 2011). The society now has more than 500 members, an annual conference, and online publications that cover issues related to jury selection and litigation strategy. The members of the society have also adopted a set of professional guidelines for trial consultants. According to these guidelines, jury consultants should only provide services that they have the required education, training, or experience to perform and for which they have no conflict of interest. The guidelines also urge consultants to practice

social responsibility by providing pro bono services for indigent clients and training for law students and professionals. The guidelines specify how the consultant's duties differ depending on whether the client is an attorney, a litigant, or an insurer. The guidelines also place restrictions on how consultants may advertise their services, specifically prohibiting the publication of win–loss records because it is impossible to know whether the trial consultant's services had a causal role in the trial outcome.

Jury Reforms

In contrast to an interest in identifying methods to influence trial outcomes in a particular direction, psychologists involved in jury reform are motivated to identify procedures that will improve the process of jury decision making, presumably resulting in more just outcomes. One suggested reform has received considerable empirical attention: allowing jurors to take notes during trial. It was hoped that juror note-taking would improve jurors' attention during the trial and consequently improve their memory for the evidence (Heuer & Penrod, 1994; Penrod & Heuer, 1997). Although in some laboratory studies note-taking improved juror memory for complex evidence (Forsterlee, Horowitz, & Bourgeois, 1994; Forsterlee, Kent, & Horowitz, 2005; Rosenhan, Eisner, & Robinson, 1994) and reduced the variability of jury awards made by smaller juries (Horowitz & Bordens, 2002), note-taking did not improve understanding of DNA evidence in one jury analogue study (Dann, Hans, & Kaye, 2007), and data from several large field studies showed no improvement in memory for the evidence and no increase in juror satisfaction with their jury service (Heuer & Penrod, 1988, 1994).

Another procedural innovation to receive empirical attention is allowing jurors to ask questions of witnesses during the trial. Although some have expressed concerns that jurors will ask inappropriate questions that the judge will not permit to be posed to the witnesses, and that jurors will consequently become angry or frustrated, about three quarters of questions posed by jurors in one field study were allowed by the judge (Diamond, Rose, Murphy, & Smith, 2006). Jurors asked questions to gain clarification about evidentiary issues

(Diamond et al., 2006; Heuer & Penrod, 1988). Jurors were more satisfied with the questioning of the witnesses (Heuer & Penrod, 1988) but not with their overall trial experience (Heuer & Penrod, 1988, 1994) when they were allowed to ask questions. Moreover, judges and attorneys felt that the questions that jurors asked were not helpful (Heuer & Penrod, 1988, 1994).

Some courts have been the driving force behind proposed jury reforms, with psychologists serving as the evaluators of the success of those reforms. For instance, Arizona became the first state that allowed jurors to discuss the trial evidence before the start of deliberations in civil trials as long as all jurors were present for the discussion (Dann & Logan, 1996). The Pima County Superior Court authorized an evaluation of the effects of this innovation (Diamond, Vidmar, Rose, Ellis, & Murphy, 2003). In this evaluation, the original intention was to randomly assign 30 of the 50 civil trials in the sample to the discussion condition and the remaining trials to the no-discussion condition. Random assignment broke down and other trials were removed from the sample because of the nature of the trial; the final sample contained only 12 trials without discussion (compared to 30 discussion trials). The trial, all juror discussions, and the jury deliberations were videotaped and later evaluated to test a variety of empirical questions.

Jurors discussed the case in two thirds of the trials in which the jurors were admonished not to discuss the case, suggesting that the manipulation of discussion was not strong or clean. Moreover, the breakdown in random assignment and the small number of trials in the no-discussion condition make it difficult to draw strong inferences from the comparisons between the two conditions. For example, although a higher proportion of juries who were allowed to discuss the trial before deliberation took initial votes within the first ten minutes of deliberation than juries who could not discuss before deliberation, this difference was not statistically significant. There was also no difference in the prevalence of plaintiff verdicts in the two conditions, despite critics' fears that early discussion would cause the jurors to prematurely accept the plaintiff's version of events.

Thus, many of the studies of jury reform suggest that the reforms do not make much of a difference. Although the reforms do not result in the types of improvements intended by those implementing them, neither do they produce the types of harms that critics propose they will. There are problems associated with many of the studies that have been conducted to date. In some studies, lack of true random assignment and small sample sizes often make it difficult to draw conclusions about the effectiveness of the reform, especially as so many of these studies have produced null effects. Moreover, many suggested reforms stem from legal analysis of problems rather than an understanding of the psychological mechanisms that may produce the identified problem the reform is intended to solve, which may contribute further to the failure in identifying successful reforms.

SUMMARY AND CONCLUSIONS

In this chapter, we have reviewed the research on juror and jury decision making. After reading this review, one may be struck with all of the errors that jurors make when deciding cases. Jurors are overwhelmed by eyewitness and confession evidence. They have difficulty recognizing flawed expert testimony. There are a variety of biases that affect their decision making that are hard to overcome. Their decisions about liability and damages in civil cases are influenced by considerations that are improper according to the law, and some court rulings actually make it more difficult for juries to make good decisions by allowing smaller juries, non-unanimous decision rules, and practices that bias the composition of the jury.

Despite these problems with jury decision making, there are reasons to be optimistic about the competence of juries. After all, evidence strength is a strong predictor of verdicts in criminal cases (D. J. Devine, Buddenbaum, Houp, Studebaker, & Stolle, 2009; Visher, 1987). In civil cases, injury severity is the best predictor of compensatory damages and defendant conduct influences liability judgments, as they should (Greene & Bornstein, 2003). These findings demonstrate that jurors do attend to the evidence they are supposed to consider, as instructed by the law. When they do make errors, the errors are often the result of basic cognitive biases that plague decision making of all types of people, in all types of situations (Bornstein & Greene, 2011).

If we are to rid of ourselves of juries because of their errors in decision making, what is our alternative? At present, the only alternative to a trial by jury is a bench trial in which a judge is the sole determiner of the facts and the verdict. Is this a desirable alternative? Judges are prone to many of the same cognitive errors that jurors are (e.g., Wistrich, Guthrie, & Rachlinski, 2005). Moreover, there is substantial agreement between the decisions made by judges and juries (Eisenberg et al., 2005), and when their decisions do differ, it is likely due to differences in the evidence heard by judges and juries (Eisenberg & Heise, 2011). There is no question that continued research is needed to identify procedures that improve jury decision making, but in the meantime there is no other identifiable system in existence that works better to resolve disputes between the government and its citizens and among the citizens themselves.

References

Allen, M., Mabry, E., & McKelton, D. (1998). Impact of juror attitudes about the death penalty on juror evaluations of guilt and punishment: A meta-analysis. *Law and Human Behavior, 22,* 715–731. doi:10.1023/A:1025763008533

Allport, G. W., & Postman, L. J. (1947). *The psychology of rumor.* New York, NY: Russell & Russell.

American Bar Association. (2000). *Model rules of professional conduct.* Chicago, IL: Author.

American Society of Trial Consultants. (2011). *History and goals of the American Society of Trial Consultants.* Retrieved from http://www.astcweb.org/public/article.cfm/society-goals

Apodaca, Cooper, & Madden v. Oregon, 406 U.S. 404 (1972).

Appleby, S. C., Hasel, L. E., & Kassin, S. M. (2013). Police-induced confessions: An empirical analysis of their content and impact. *Psychology, Crime & Law, 19,* 111–128. doi:10.1080/10683 16X.2011.613389

Austin, J. L., & Kovera, M. B. (2013). *Examining the effectiveness of inquisitorial and adversarial cross-examinations in educating jurors about scientific validity.* Manuscript under review.

Ayres, B. D., Jr. (1997, February 11). Jury decides Simpson must pay $25 million in punitive damages. *New York Times.* Retrieved from http://www.nytimes.com/1997/02/11/us/jury-decides-simpson-must-pay-25-million-in-punitive-award.html

Baldus, D. C., Woodworth, G., & Pulaski, C. A., Jr. (1990). *Equal justice and the death penalty: A legal and empirical analysis.* Boston, MA: Northeastern University Press.

Ballew v. Georgia, 435 U.S. 223 (1978).

Berman, M. K., Austin, J. L., Levett, L. M., & Kovera, M. B. (2013). *Do court-appointed experts or educational instructions safeguard against junk science?* Manuscript under review.

Bornstein, B. H. (1998). From compassion to compensation: The effect of injury severity on mock jurors' liability judgments. *Journal of Applied Social Psychology, 28,* 1477–1502. doi:10.1111/j.1559-1816.1998.tb01687.x

Bornstein, B. H., & Greene, E. (2011). Jury decision making: Implications for and from psychology. *Current Directions in Psychological Science, 20,* 63–67. doi:10.1177/0963721410397282

Bornstein, B. H., Whisenhunt, B. L., & Nemeth, R. J. (2002). Pretrial publicity and civil cases: A two-way street? *Law and Human Behavior, 21,* 3–17. doi:10.1023/A:1013825124011

Brekke, N., & Borgida, E. (1988). Expert psychological testimony in rape trials: A social cognitive analysis. *Journal of Personality and Social Psychology, 55,* 372–386. doi:10.1037/0022-3514.55.3.372

Buck, J. A., London, K., & Wright, D. B. (2011). Expert testimony regarding child witnesses: Does it sensitize jurors to forensic interview quality? *Law and Human Behavior, 35,* 152–164. doi:10.1007/s10979-010-9228-2

Burch v. Louisiana, 441 U.S. 130 (1979).

Butler, B. (2007). Death qualification and prejudice: The effects of implicit racism, sexism, and homophobia on capital defendants' right to due process. *Behavioral Sciences and the Law, 25,* 857–867. doi:10.1002/bsl.791

Butler, B., & Moran, G. (2007). The impact of death qualification, belief in a just world, legal authoritarianism, and locus of control on venirepersons' evaluations of aggravating and mitigating circumstances in capital trials. *Behavioral Sciences and the Law, 25,* 57–68. doi:10.1002/bsl.734

Campo-Flores, A., & Waddell, L. (2013, July 14). Jury acquits Zimmerman of all charges. *Wall Street Journal.* Retrieved from http://online.wsj.com/article/SB10001 424127887324879504578603562762064502.html

Chaiken, S., Liberman, A., & Eagly, A. (1989). Heuristic and systematic information processing within and beyond the persuasion context. In J. S. Uleman & J. A. Bargh (Eds.), *Unintended thought* (pp. 212–251). New York, NY: Guilford Press.

Chapman, G. B., & Bornstein, B. H. (1996). The more you ask for, the more you get: Anchoring in personal injury verdicts. *Applied Cognitive Psychology, 10,* 519–540. doi:10.1002/(SICI)1099-0720(199612)10:6<519::AID-ACP417>3.0.CO;2-5

Choi, S. J., & Eisenberg, T. (2010). Punitive damages in securities arbitration: An empirical study. *Journal of Legal Studies, 39,* 497–546. doi:10.1086/649601

Chrzanowski, L. M. (2005). *Rape, truth, and the media: Laboratory and field assessments of pretrial publicity in a real case* (Unpublished doctoral dissertation). City University of New York, New York.

Cialdini, R. B., & Trost, M. R. (1998). Social influence: Social norms, conformity and compliance. In D. T. Gilbert, S. T. Fiske, & G. Lindzey (Eds.), *The handbook of social psychology* (4th ed., pp. 151–192). New York, NY: McGraw-Hill.

Cohn, E. S., Bucolo, D., Pride, M., & Sommers, S. R. (2009). Reducing White juror bias: The role of race salience and racial attitudes. *Journal of Applied Social Psychology, 39,* 1953–1973. doi:10.1111/j.1559-1816.2009.00511.x

Colgrove v. Battin, 413 U.S. 149 (1973).

Cooper, J., Bennett, E. A., & Sukel, H. L. (1996). Complex scientific testimony: How do jurors make decisions? *Law and Human Behavior, 24,* 149–171. doi:10.1023/A:1005476618435

Cooper, J., & Neuhaus, I. M. (2000). The "hired gun" effect: Assessing the effect of pay, frequency of testifying, and credentials on the perception of expert testimony. *Law and Human Behavior, 24,* 149–171. doi:10.1023/A:1005476618435

Costanzo, M. (2003). *Psychology applied to law.* Belmont, CA: Wadsworth.

Cowan, C. L., Thompson, W., & Ellsworth, P. C. (1984). The effects of death qualification on jurors' predisposition to convict and on the quality of deliberation. *Law and Human Behavior, 8,* 53–79. doi:10.1007/BF01044351

Crocker, C. B., & Kovera, M. B. (2010). The effects of rehabilitative voir dire on juror bias and decision making. *Law and Human Behavior, 34,* 212–226. doi:10.1007/s10979-009-9193-9

Crowley, M. J., O'Callaghan, M. G., & Ball, P. J. (1994). The juridical impact of psychological expert testimony in a simulated child sexual abuse trial. *Law and Human Behavior, 18,* 89–105. doi:10.1007/BF01499146

Culhane, S. E., Hosch, H. M., & Weaver, G. (2004). Crime victims serving as jurors: Is there bias present?

Law and Human Behavior, 28, 649–659. doi:10.1007/s10979-004-0792-1

Cutler, B. L., & Kovera, M. B. (2010). *Evaluating eyewitness identification.* New York, NY: Oxford University Press.

Cutler, B. L., Penrod, S. D., & Dexter, H. R. (1989). The eyewitness, the expert psychologist, and the jury. *Law and Human Behavior, 13,* 311–332. doi:10.1007/BF01067032

Cutler, B. L., Penrod, S. D., & Dexter, H. R. (1990). Juror sensitivity to eyewitness identification evidence. *Law and Human Behavior, 14,* 185–191. doi:10.1007/BF01062972

Cutler, B. L., Penrod, S. D., & Stuve, T. E. (1988). Juror decision making in eyewitness identification cases. *Law and Human Behavior, 12,* 41–55. doi:10.1007/BF01064273

Danielsen, E., Levett, L. M., & Kovera, M. B. (2004, March). *When juveniles are tried as adults: What happens in voir dire?* Paper presented at the annual meeting of the American Psychology-Law Society, Scottsdale, AZ.

Dann, B. M., Hans, V. P., & Kaye, D. H. (2007). Can jury trial innovations improve juror understanding of trial evidence? *Judicature, 90,* 152–156.

Dann, B. M., & Logan, G. (1996). Jury reform: The Arizona experience. *Judicature, 79,* 280–286.

Daubert v. Merrell Dow Pharmaceuticals, Inc., 509 U.S. 579 (1993).

Davis, J. H. (1973). Group decision and social interaction: A theory of social decision schemes. *Psychological Review, 80,* 97–125. doi:10.1037/h0033951

Davis, J. H. (1980). Group decision and procedural justice. In M. Fishbein (Ed.), *Progress in social psychology* (pp. 157–229). Hillsdale, NJ: Erlbaum.

Davis, J. H., Au, W. T., Hulbert, L. G., Chen, X. P., & Zarnoth, P. (1997). The effects of group size and procedural influence on consensual judgments of quantity: The example of damage awards and mock civil juries. *Journal of Personality and Social Psychology, 73,* 703–718. doi:10.1037/0022-3514.73.4.703

Davis, J. H., Tindale, R. S., Nagao, D. H., Hinsz, V. B., & Robertson, B. (1984). Order effects in multiple decisions by groups: A demonstration with mock juries and trial procedures. *Journal of Personality and Social Psychology, 47,* 1003–1012. doi:10.1037/0022-3514.47.5.1003

Desmarais, S. L., & Read, J. D. (2011). After 30 years, what do we know about what jurors know? A meta-analytic review of lay knowledge regarding eyewitness factors. *Law and Human Behavior, 35,* 200–210. doi:10.1007/s10979-010-9232-6

Deutsch, M., & Gerard, H. B. (1955). A study of normative and informational social influences upon individual judgment. *Journal of Abnormal and Social Psychology, 51,* 629–636. doi:10.1037/h0046408

Devenport, J. L., & Cutler, B. L. (2004). The impact of defense-only and opposing eyewitness experts on juror judgments. *Law and Human Behavior, 28,* 569–576. doi:10.1023/B:LAHU.0000046434.39181.07

Devenport, J. L., Stinson, V., Cutler, B. L., & Kravitz, D. A. (2002). How effective are the cross-examination and expert testimony safeguards? Jurors' perceptions of the suggestiveness and fairness of biased lineup procedures. *Journal of Applied Psychology, 87,* 1042–1054. doi:10.1037/0021-9010.87.6.1042

Devine, D. J. (2013). *Jury decision making: The state of the science.* New York: New York University Press.

Devine, D. J., Buddenbaum, J., Houp, S., Studebaker, N., & Stolle, D. P. (2009). Strength of evidence, extraevidentiary influence, and the liberation hypothesis: Data from the field. *Law and Human Behavior, 33,* 136–148. doi:10.1007/s10979-008-9144-x

Devine, D. J., Clayton, L. D., Dunford, B. B., Seying, R., & Pryce, J. (2001). Jury decision making: 45 years of empirical research on deliberating groups. *Psychology, Public Policy, and Law, 7,* 622–727. doi:10.1037/1076-8971.7.3.622

Devine, P. G. (1989). Stereotypes and prejudice: Their automatic and controlled components. *Journal of Personality and Social Psychology, 56,* 5–18. doi:10.1037/0022-3514.56.1.5

Dexter, H. R., Cutler, B. L., & Moran, G. (1992). A test of voir dire as a remedy for the prejudicial effects of pretrial publicity. *Journal of Applied Social Psychology, 22,* 819–832. doi:10.1111/j.1559-1816.1992.tb00926.x

Diamond, S. S. (1997). Illuminations and shadows from jury simulations. *Law and Human Behavior, 21,* 561–571. doi:10.1023/A:1024831908377

Diamond, S. S., & Casper, J. D. (1992). Blindfolding the jury to verdict consequences: Damages, experts, and the civil jury. *Law and Society Review, 26,* 513–563. doi:10.2307/3053737

Diamond, S. S., & Levi, J. N. (1996). Improving decisions on death by revising and testing jury instructions. *Judicature, 79,* 224–232.

Diamond, S. S., Rose, M. R., Murphy, B., & Meixner, J. (2011). Damage anchors on real juries. *Journal of Empirical Legal Studies, 8,* 148–178. doi:10.1111/j.1740-1461.2011.01232.x

Diamond, S. S., Rose, M. R., Murphy, B., & Smith, S. (2006). Juror questions during trial: A window into juror thinking. *Vanderbilt Law Review, 59,* 1927–1972.

Diamond, S. S., Vidmar, N., Rose, M., Ellis, L., & Murphy, B. (2003). Juror discussions during civil trials: Studying an Arizona innovation. *Arizona Law Review, 45,* 1–81.

Douglass, A. B., & Steblay, N. (2006). Memory distortion in eyewitnesses: A meta-analysis of the post-identification feedback effect. *Applied Cognitive Psychology, 20,* 859–869. doi:10.1002/acp.1237

Drizin, S. A., & Leo, R. A. (2004). The problem of false confessions in the post-DNA world. *North Carolina Law Review, 82,* 891–1007.

Eberhardt, J. L., Davies, P. G., Purdie-Vaughns, V. J., & Johnson, S. L. (2006). Looking deathworthy: Perceived stereotypicality of black defendants predicts capital-sentencing outcomes. *Psychological Science, 17,* 383–386. doi:10.1111/j.1467-9280.2006.01716.x

Eberhardt, J. L., Goff, P. A., Purdie, V. J., & Davies, P. G. (2004). Race, crime, and visual processing. *Journal of Personality and Social Psychology, 87,* 876–893. doi:10.1037/0022-3514.87.6.876

Eisenberg, T., Goerdt, J., Ostrom, B., Rottman, D., & Wells, M. T. (1997). The predictability of punitive damages. *Journal of Legal Studies, 26,* 623–661. doi:10.1086/468010

Eisenberg, T., Hannaford-Agor, P. L., Hans, V. P., Waters, N. L., Munsterman, G. T., Schwab, S. J., & Wells, M. T. (2005). Judge-jury agreement in criminal cases: A partial replication of Kalven and Zeisel's *The American Jury. Journal of Empirical Legal Studies, 2,* 171–207. doi:10.1111/j.1740-1461.2005.00035.x

Eisenberg, T., & Heise, M. (2011). Judge-jury difference in punitive damages awards: Who listens to the Supreme Court? *Journal of Empirical Legal Studies, 8,* 325–357. doi:10.1111/j.1740-1461.2011.01211.x

Eisenberg, T., LaFountain, N., Ostrom, B., Rottman, D., & Wells, M. T. (2002). Juries, judges, and punitive damages: An empirical study. *Cornell Law Review, 87,* 743–782.

Ellis, L., & Diamond, S. S. (2003). Race, diversity and jury composition. *Chicago-Kent Law Review, 78,* 1033–1058.

Ellsworth, P. C. (1989). Are twelve heads better than one? *Law and Contemporary Problems, 52,* 205–224. doi:10.2307/1191911

Fein, S., McCloskey, A. L., & Tomlinson, T. M. (1997). Can the jury disregard that information? The use of suspicion to reduce the prejudicial effects of pretrial publicity and inadmissible testimony. *Personality and Social Psychology Bulletin, 23,* 1215–1226. doi:10.1177/01461672972311008

Filkins, J., Smith, C. M., & Tindale, R. S. (1998). The fairness of death qualified juries: A meta-analytic/simulation approach. In R. S. Tindale, J. E. Edwards, L. Heath, E. J. Posavac, F. B. Bryant, E. Henderson-King, . . . Myers, J. (Eds.), *Social psychological applications to social issues: Vol. 4. Applications of theory and research on groups* (pp. 1–8). New York, NY: Plenum Press.

Fitzgerald, R., & Ellsworth, P. C. (1984). Due process vs. crime control: Death qualification and attitudes. *Law and Human Behavior, 8*, 31–51. doi:10.1007/BF01044350

Forsterlee, L., Horowitz, I. A., & Bourgeois, M. (1994). Effects of notetaking on verdicts and evidence processing in a civil trial. *Law and Human Behavior, 18*, 567–578. doi:10.1007/BF01499175

Forsterlee, L., Kent, L., & Horowitz, I. A. (2005). The cognitive effects of jury aids on decision making in complex civil litigation. *Applied Cognitive Psychology, 19*, 867–884. doi:10.1002/acp.1124

Fox, S. G., & Walters, H. A. (1986). The impact of general versus specific expert testimony and eyewitness confidence upon mock juror judgment. *Law and Human Behavior, 10*, 215–228. doi:10.1007/BF01046211

Fukurai, H. (2007). The rebirth of Japan's petit quasi-jury and grand jury systems: A cross-national analysis of legal consciousness and the lay participatory experience in Japan and the U.S. *Cornell International Law Journal, 40*, 315–354.

Galanter, M. (2004). The vanishing trial: An examination of trials and related matters in federal and state courts. *Journal of Empirical Legal Studies, 1*, 459–570. doi:10.1111/j.1740-1461.2004.00014.x

Garrett, B. L. (2011). *Convicting the innocent: Where criminal prosecutions go wrong.* Cambridge, MA: Harvard University Press. doi:10.4159/harvard.9780674060982

Gatowski, S. I., Dobbin, S. A., Richardson, J. T., Ginsburg, G. P., Merlino, M. L., & Dahir, V. (2001). Asking the gatekeepers: A national survey of judges on judging expert evidence in a post-*Daubert* world. *Law and Human Behavior, 25*, 433–458. doi:10.1023/A:1012899030937

Goff, P. A., Eberhardt, J. L., Williams, M. J., & Jackson, M. C. (2008). Not yet human: Implicit knowledge, historical dehumanization, and contemporary consequences. *Journal of Personality and Social Psychology, 94*, 292–306. doi:10.1037/0022-3514.94.2.292

Greathouse, S. M., Sothmann, F. C., Levett, L. M., & Kovera, M. B. (2011). The potentially biasing effects of voir dire in juvenile waiver cases. *Law and Human Behavior, 35*, 427–439. doi:10.1007/s10979-010-9247-z

Greene, E., & Bornstein, B. (2000). Precious little guidance: Jury instruction on damage awards. *Psychology, Public Policy, and Law, 6*, 743–768. doi:10.1037/1076-8971.6.3.743

Greene, E., & Bornstein, B. H. (2003). *Determining damages: The psychology of jury awards.* Washington, DC: American Psychological Association. doi:10.1037/10464-000

Greene, E., Chopra, S. R., Kovera, M. B., Penrod, S. D., Rose, V. G., Schuller, R., & Studebaker, C. A. (2002). Jurors and juries: A review of the field. In J. R. P. Ogloff (Ed.), *Taking psychology and law into the twenty-first century* (pp. 225–284). New York, NY: Kluwer Academic/Plenum Press.

Greene, E., & Johns, M. (2001). Jurors' use of instructions on negligence. *Journal of Applied Social Psychology, 31*, 840–859. doi:10.1111/j.1559-1816.2001.tb01416.x

Greene, E., Johns, M., & Bowman, J. (1999). The effects of injury severity on jury negligence decisions. *Law and Human Behavior, 23*, 675–693. doi:10.1023/A:1022341522714

Greene, E., Johns, M., & Smith, A. (2001). The effects of defendant conduct on jury damage awards. *Journal of Applied Psychology, 86*, 228–237. doi:10.1037/0021-9010.86.2.228

Greene, E., & Loftus, E. F. (1984). What's new in the news? The influence of well-publicized news events on psychological research and courtroom trials. *Basic and Applied Social Psychology, 5*, 211–221. doi:10.1207/s15324834basp0503_4

Greene, E., & Wade, R. (1988). Of private talk and public print: General pre-trial publicity and juror decision-making. *Applied Cognitive Psychology, 2*, 123–135. doi:10.1002/acp.2350020204

Haney, C. (1984). On the selection of capital juries: The biasing effects of the death-qualification process. *Law and Human Behavior, 8*, 121–132. doi:10.1007/BF01044355

Haney, C., Hurtado, A., & Vega, L. (1994). Modern death qualification: New data on its biasing effects. *Law and Human Behavior, 18*, 619–633. doi:10.1007/BF01499328

Hannaford-Agor, P. L., Hans, V. P., Mott, N. L., & Munsterman, G. T. (2002). *Are hung juries a problem?* Retrieved from http://www.ncsonline.org/WC/Publications/Res_Juries_HungJuriesProblemPub.pdf

Hans, V. P. (1978). *The effects of the unanimity requirement on group decision processes in simulated juries* (Unpublished doctoral dissertation). University of Toronto, Toronto, Ontario, Canada.

Hans, V. P. (2008). Jury systems around the world. *Annual Review of Law and Social Science, 4*, 275–297. doi:10.1146/annurev.lawsocsci.4.110707.172319

Hans, V. P., & Vidmar, N. (1982). Jury selection. In N. L. Kerr & R. M. Bray (Eds.), *The psychology of the courtroom* (pp. 39–82). New York, NY: Academic Press.

Hastie, R. (1993). Algebraic models of juror decision processes. In R. Hastie (Ed.), *Inside the juror: The psychology of juror decision making* (pp. 84–115). New York, NY: Cambridge University Press. doi:10.1017/CBO9780511752896.006

Hastie, R. (2009). What's the story? Explanations and narratives in civil jury decisions? In B. H. Bornstein, R. L. Wiener, R. Schopp, & S. L. Willborn (Eds.), *Civil juries and civil justice: Psychological and legal perspectives* (pp. 23–34). New York, NY: Springer Verlag.

Hastie, R., Penrod, S. D., & Pennington, N. (1983). *Inside the jury*. Cambridge, MA: Harvard University Press. doi:10.4159/harvard.9780674865945

Hastie, R., Schkade, D. A., & Payne, J. W. (1998). A study of juror and jury judgments in civil cases: Deciding liability for punitive damages. *Law and Human Behavior, 22*, 287–314. doi:10.1023/A:1025754422703

Hastie, R., Schkade, D. A., & Payne, J. W. (1999). Juror judgments in civil cases: Effects of plaintiff's requests and plaintiff's identity on punitive damage awards. *Law and Human Behavior, 23*, 445–470. doi:10.1023/A:1022312115561

Hayes-Smith, R. M., & Levett, L. M. (2011). The jury is still out: The CSI effect on juror decisions. *Applied Psychology in Criminal Justice, 7*, 29–46.

Heuer, L., & Penrod, S. (1988). Increasing jurors' participation in trials: A field experiment with jury notetaking and question asking. *Law and Human Behavior, 12*, 231–261. doi:10.1007/BF01044383

Heuer, L., & Penrod, S. (1994). Juror notetaking and question asking during trials: A national field experiment. *Law and Human Behavior, 18*, 121–150. doi:10.1007/BF01499012

Holstein, J. A. (1985). Jurors' interpretations and jury decision making. *Law and Human Behavior, 9*, 83–100. doi:10.1007/BF01044291

Hope, L., Memon, A., & McGeorge, P. (2004). Understanding pretrial publicity: Predecisional distortion of evidence by mock jurors. *Journal of Experimental Psychology: Applied, 10*, 111–119. doi:10.1037/1076-898X.10.2.111

Horowitz, I. A., & Bordens, K. S. (2002). The effects of jury size, evidence complexity, and note taking on jury process and performance in a civil trial. *Journal of Applied Psychology, 87*, 121–130. doi:10.1037/0021-9010.87.1.121

Huntley, J. E., & Costanzo, M. (2003). Sexual harassment stories: Testing a story-mediated model of juror decision-making in civil litigation. *Law and Human Behavior, 27*, 29–51. doi:10.1023/A:1021674811225

Ivković, S. K. (2007). Exploring lay participation in legal decision-making: Lessons from mixed tribunals. *Cornell International Law Journal, 40*, 429–453.

Johnson, C., & Haney, C. (1994). Felony voir dire: An exploratory study of its content and effect. *Law and Human Behavior, 18*, 487–506. doi:10.1007/BF01499170

Johnson v. Louisiana, 406 U.S. 356 (1972).

Jones, S. E. (1987). Judge- versus attorney-conducted voir dire: An empirical investigation of juror candor. *Law and Human Behavior, 11*, 131–146. doi:10.1007/BF01040446

Kaasa, S. O., Peterson, T., Morris, E. K., & Thompson, W. C. (2007). Statistical inference and forensic evidence: Evaluating a bullet lead match. *Law and Human Behavior, 31*, 433–447. doi:10.1007/s10979-006-9074-4

Kalven, H., Jr., & Zeisel, H. (1966). *The American jury.* Chicago, IL: University of Chicago Press.

Kameda, T., Takezawa, M., Tindale, R. S., & Smith, C. M. (2002). Social sharing and risk reduction: Exploring a computational algorithm for the psychology of windfall gains. *Evolution and Human Behavior, 23*, 11–33. doi:10.1016/S1090-5138(01)00086-1

Kaplan, M. F., & Miller, C. E. (1987). Group decision making and normative versus informational influence: Effects of type of issue and assigned decision rule. *Journal of Personality and Social Psychology, 53*, 306–313. doi:10.1037/0022-3514.53.2.306

Kassin, S. M., Drizin, S. A., Grisso, T., Gudjonsson, G. H., Leo, R. A., & Redlich, A. D. (2010). Police-induced confessions: Risk factors and recommendations. *Law and Human Behavior, 34*, 3–38. doi:10.1007/s10979-009-9188-6

Kassin, S. M., Meissner, C. A., & Norwick, R. I. (2005). "I'd know a false confession if I saw one": A comparative study of college students and police investigators. *Law and Human Behavior, 29*, 211–227. doi:10.1007/s10979-005-2416-9

Kassin, S. M., & Neumann, K. (1997). On the power of confession evidence: An experimental test of the "fundamental difference" hypothesis. *Law and Human Behavior, 21*, 469–484. doi:10.1023/A:1024871622490

Kassin, S. M., & Sukel, H. (1997). Coerced confessions and the jury: An experimental test of the "harmless error" rule. *Law and Human Behavior, 21*, 27–46. doi:10.1023/A:1024814009769

Kassin, S. M., Tubb, V. A., Hosch, H. M., & Memon, A. (2001). On the "general acceptance" of eyewitness testimony research. *American Psychologist, 56*, 405–416. doi:10.1037/0003-066X.56.5.405

Kassin, S. M., & Wrightsman, L. S. (1980). Prior confessions and mock juror verdicts. *Journal of Applied Social Psychology, 10*, 133–146. doi:10.1111/j.1559-1816.1980.tb00698.x

Kassin, S. M., & Wrightsman, L. S. (1981). Coerced confessions, judicial instruction, and mock juror verdicts. *Journal of Applied Social Psychology, 11*, 489–506. doi:10.1111/j.1559-1816.1981.tb00838.x

Kassin, S. M., & Wrightsman, L. S. (1985). Confession evidence. In S. M. Kassin & L. S. Wrightsman (Eds.), *The psychology of evidence and trial procedure* (pp. 67–94). Beverly Hills, CA: Sage.

Kerr, N. (1993). Stochastic models of juror decision making. In R. Hastie (Ed.), *Inside the juror: The psychology of juror decision making* (pp. 116–135). New York, NY: Cambridge University Press. doi:10.1017/CBO9780511752896.007

Kerr, N. L. (1978). Severity of prescribed penalty and mock jurors' verdicts. *Journal of Personality and Social Psychology, 36,* 1431–1442. doi:10.1037/0022-3514.36.12.1431

Kerr, N. L., Atkin, R., Stasser, G., Meek, D., Holt, R., & Davis, J. H. (1976). Guilt beyond a reasonable doubt: Effects of concept definition and assigned decision rule on the judgment of mock jurors. *Journal of Personality and Social Psychology, 34,* 282–294. doi:10.1037/0022-3514.34.2.282

Kerr, N. L., Harmon, D. L., & Graves, J. K. (1982). Independence of multiple verdicts by jurors and juries. *Journal of Applied Social Psychology, 12,* 12–29. doi:10.1111/j.1559-1816.1982.tb00845.x

Kerr, N. L., Kramer, G. P., Carroll, J. S., & Alfini, J. J. (1991). On the effectiveness of voir dire in criminal cases with prejudicial pretrial publicity: An empirical study. *American University Law Review, 40,* 665–701.

Kerr, N. L., & MacCoun, R. (2012). Is the leniency asymmetry really dead? Misinterpreting asymmetry effects in criminal jury deliberation. *Group Processes and Intergroup Behavior, 15,* 585–602. doi:10.1177/1368430212441639

Kerr, N. L., Niedermeier, K. E., & Kaplan, M. F. (1999). Bias in jurors vs. bias in juries: New evidence from the SDS perspective. *Organizational Behavior and Human Decision Processes, 80,* 70–86. doi:10.1006/obhd.1999.2855

Kerwin, J., & Shaffer, D. R. (1994). Mock jurors versus juries: The role of deliberations in reactions to inadmissible testimony. *Personality and Social Psychology Bulletin, 20,* 153–162. doi:10.1177/0146167294202002

Kessler, J. (1973). An empirical study of six- and twelve-member jury decision making processes. *University of Michigan Journal of Law Reform, 6,* 712–734.

Kim, S., Park, J., Park, K., & Eom, J. S. (2013). Judge-jury agreement in criminal cases: The first three years of the Korean jury system. *Journal of Empirical Legal Studies, 10,* 35–53. doi:10.1111/jels.12001

Kovera, M. B. (2002). The effects of general pretrial publicity on juror decisions: An examination of moderators and mediating mechanisms. *Law and Human Behavior, 26,* 43–72. doi:10.1023/A:1013829224920

Kovera, M. B., & Cutler, B. L. (2013). *Jury selection.* New York, NY: Oxford University Press.

Kovera, M. B., Gresham, A. W., Borgida, E., Gray, E., & Regan, P. C. (1997). Does expert testimony inform or influence juror decision-making? A social cognitive analysis. *Journal of Applied Psychology, 82,* 178–191. doi:10.1037/0021-9010.82.1.178

Kovera, M. B., Levy, R. J., Borgida, E., & Penrod, S. D. (1994). Expert testimony in child sexual abuse cases: Effects of expert evidence type and cross-examination. *Law and Human Behavior, 18,* 653–674. doi:10.1007/BF01499330

Kovera, M. B., & McAuliff, B. D. (2000). The effects of peer review and evidence quality on judge evaluations of psychological science: Are judges effective gatekeepers? *Journal of Applied Psychology, 85,* 574–586. doi:10.1037/0021-9010.85.4.574

Kovera, M. B., McAuliff, B. D., & Hebert, K. S. (1999). Reasoning about scientific evidence: Effects of juror gender and evidence quality on juror decisions in a hostile work environment case. *Journal of Applied Psychology, 84,* 362–375. doi:10.1037/0021-9010.84.3.362

Kovera, M. B., Russano, M. B., & McAuliff, B. D. (2002). Assessment of the commonsense psychology underlying *Daubert*: Legal decision makers' abilities to evaluate expert evidence in hostile work environment cases. *Psychology, Public Policy, and Law, 8,* 180–200. doi:10.1037/1076-8971.8.2.180

Kramer, G. P., Kerr, N. L., & Carroll, J. S. (1990). Pretrial publicity, judicial remedies, and jury bias. *Law and Human Behavior, 14,* 409–438. doi:10.1007/BF01044220

Krauss, D. A., & Lee, D. H. (2003). Deliberating on dangerousness and death: Jurors' ability to differentiate between expert actuarial and clinical predictions of dangerousness. *International Journal of Law and Psychiatry, 26,* 113–137. doi:10.1016/S0160-2527(02)00211-X

Krauss, D. A., & Sales, B. D. (2001). The effects of clinical and scientific expert testimony on juror decision making in capital sentencing. *Psychology, Public Policy, and Law, 7,* 267–310. doi:10.1037/1076-8971.7.2.267

Lassiter, G. D., Clark, J. K., Daniels, L. E., & Soinski, M. (2004, March). *Can we recognize false confessions and does the presentation format make a difference?* Paper presented at the annual meeting of the American Psychology-Law Society, Scottsdale, AZ.

Lassiter, G. D., Geers, A. L., Handley, I. M., Weiland, P. E., & Munhall, P. J. (2002). Videotaped confessions and interrogations: A simple change in camera perspective alters verdicts in simulated trials. *Journal of Applied Psychology, 87,* 867–874. doi:10.1037/0021-9010.87.5.867

Lassiter, G. D., Geers, A. L., Munhall, P. J., Handley, I. M., & Beers, M. J. (2001). Videotaped confessions: Is guilt in the eye of the camera? *Advances in Experimental Social Psychology, 33*, 189–254. doi:10.1016/S0065-2601(01)80006-X

Lassiter, G. D., & Irvine, A. A. (1986). Videotaped confessions: The impact of camera point of view on judgments of coercion. *Journal of Applied Social Psychology, 16*, 268–276. doi:10.1111/j.1559-1816.1986.tb01139.x

Lassiter, G. D., Slaw, R. D., Briggs, M. A., & Scanlan, C. R. (1992). The potential for bias in videotaped confessions. *Journal of Applied Social Psychology, 22*, 1838–1851. doi:10.1111/j.1559-1816.1992.tb00980.x

Leo, R. A., & Ofshe, R. J. (1998). The consequences of false confessions: Deprivations of liberty and miscarriages of justice in the age of psychological interrogation. *Journal of Criminal Law and Criminology, 88*, 429–496. doi:10.2307/1144288

Levett, L. M., Greathouse, S. M., Sothmann, F. K., Copple, R., & Kovera, M. B. (2006, March). When juveniles are tried as adults: Does the juvenile qualification process result in a bias jury? In E. M. Brank & L. M. Levett (Co-Chairs), *Players in the juvenile justice puzzle: From public sentiment to putting it into practice.* Symposium conducted at the annual meeting of the American Psychology-Law Society, St. Petersburg, FL.

Levett, L. M., Greathouse, S. M., Sothmann, F. K., Copple, R., & Kovera, M. B. (2007). *Juvenile waiver attitudes and the quality of deliberation.* Poster presented at the meetings of the American Psychological Association, San Francisco, CA.

Levett, L. M., & Kovera, M. B. (2008). The effectiveness of opposing expert witnesses for educating jurors about unreliable expert evidence. *Law and Human Behavior, 32*, 363–374. doi:10.1007/s10979-007-9113-9

Levett, L. M., & Kovera, M. B. (2009). Psychological mediators of the effects of opposing expert testimony on juror decisions. *Psychology, Public Policy, and Law, 15*, 124–148. doi:10.1037/a0016309

Levett, L. M., Otis, C. C., & Kovera, M. B. (2013). *The development of the attitudes toward adjudicating juveniles as adults scale.* Unpublished manuscript.

Liebeck v. McDonald's Restaurants, 23 N.M. Dist. Ct. 360309 (1994).

Lieberman, J. D., Arndt, J., & Vess, M. (2009). Inadmissible evidence and pretrial publicity: The effects (and ineffectiveness) of admonitions to disregard. In J. D. Lieberman & D. A. Krauss (Eds.), *Jury psychology: Social aspects of trial processes: Psychology in the courtroom* (pp. 67–95). Burlington, VT: Ashgate.

Lieberman, J. D., & Sales, B. D. (2007). *Scientific jury selection.* Washington, DC: American Psychological Association. doi:10.1037/11498-000

Loftus, E. F. (1980). Impact of expert psychological testimony on the unreliability of eyewitness identification. *Journal of Applied Psychology, 65*, 9–15. doi:10.1037/0021-9010.65.1.9

Lynch, M., & Haney, C. (2000). Discrimination and instructional comprehension: Guided discretion, racial bias, and the death penalty. *Law and Human Behavior, 24*, 337–358. doi:10.1023/A:1005588221761

Lynch, M., & Haney, C. (2009). Capital jury deliberation: Effects on death sentencing, comprehension, and discrimination. *Law and Human Behavior, 33*, 481–496. doi:10.1007/s10979-008-9168-2

Mazzella, R., & Feingold, A. (1994). The effects of physical attractiveness, race, socioeconomic status, and gender of defendants and victims on judgments of mock jurors: A meta-analysis. *Journal of Applied Social Psychology, 24*, 1315–1344. doi:10.1111/j.1559-1816.1994.tb01552.x

McAuliff, B. D., & Bornstein, B. H. (2010). All anchors are not created equal: The effects of per diem versus lump sum requests on pain and suffering awards. *Law and Human Behavior, 34*, 164–174. doi:10.1007/s10979-009-9178-8

McAuliff, B. D., & Duckworth, T. D. (2010). I spy with my little eye: Jurors' detection of internal validity threats in expert evidence. *Law and Human Behavior, 34*, 489–500. doi:10.1007/s10979-010-9219-3

McAuliff, B. D., & Kovera, M. B. (2008). Juror need for cognition and sensitivity to methodological flaws in expert evidence. *Journal of Applied Social Psychology, 38*, 385–408. doi:10.1111/j.1559-1816.2007.00310.x

McAuliff, B. D., Kovera, M. B., & Nunez, G. (2009). Can jurors recognize missing control groups, confounds, and experimenter bias in psychological science? *Law and Human Behavior, 33*, 247–257. doi:10.1007/s10979-008-9133-0

Mitchell, T., Haw, R. M., Pfeifer, J. E., & Meissner, C. A. (2005). Racial bias in mock juror decision-making: A meta-analytic review of defendant treatment. *Law and Human Behavior, 29*, 621–637. doi:10.1007/s10979-005-8122-9

Mize, G. E., Hannaford-Agor, P., & Waters, N. L. (2007). *The state-of-the-states survey of jury improvement efforts: A compendium report.* Retrieved from http://www.ncsc-jurystudies.org/~/media/Microsites/Files/CJS/SOS/sos_exec_sum.ashx

Moore, P. J., & Gump, B. B. (1995). Information integration in juror decision making. *Journal of Applied Social Psychology, 25*, 2158–2179. doi:10.1111/j.1559-1816.1995.tb01831.x

Moran, G., & Comfort, J. C. (1986). Neither "tentative" nor "fragmentary": Verdict preference of impaneled felony jurors as a function of attitude toward capital punishment. *Journal of Applied Psychology, 71*, 146–155. doi:10.1037/0021-9010.71.1.146

Moran, G., & Cutler, B. L. (1991). The prejudicial impact of pretrial publicity. *Journal of Applied Social Psychology, 21*, 345–367. doi:10.1111/j.1559-1816.1991.tb00524.x

Moscovici, S., & Lage, E. (1976). Studies in social influence: III. Majority versus minority influence in a group. *European Journal of Social Psychology, 6*, 149–174. doi:10.1002/ejsp.2420060202

Moscovici, S., & Personnaz, B. (1980). Studies in social influence: V. Minority influence and conversion behavior in a perceptual task. *Journal of Experimental Social Psychology, 16*, 270–282. doi:10.1016/0022-1031(80)90070-0

Nietzel, M. T., & Dillehay, R. C. (1983). Psychologists as consultants for changes in venue. *Law and Human Behavior, 7*, 309–335. doi:10.1007/BF01044735

Nietzel, M. T., McCarthy, D. M., & Kern, M. J. (1999). Juries: The current state of the empirical literature. In R. Roesch, S. D. Hart, & J. R. Ogloff (Eds.), *Psychology and law: The state of the discipline* (pp. 23–52). New York, NY: Kluwer Academic/Plenum Press. doi:10.1007/978-1-4615-4891-1_2

Olczak, P. V., Kaplan, M. F., & Penrod, S. (1991). Attorney's lay psychology and its effectiveness in selecting jurors: Three empirical studies. *Journal of Social Behavior and Personality, 6*, 431–452.

Olsen-Fulero, L., & Fulero, S. M. (1997). Commonsense rape judgments: An empathy-complexity theory of rape juror story making. *Psychology, Public Policy, and Law, 3*, 402–427. doi:10.1037/1076-8971.3.2-3.402

Olson, E. A., & Wells, G. L. (2004). What makes a good alibi? A proposed taxonomy. *Law and Human Behavior, 28*, 157–176. doi:10.1023/B:LAHU.0000022320.47112.d3

Otto, A. L., Penrod, S., & Dexter, H. R. (1994). The biasing impact of pretrial publicity on juror judgments. *Law and Human Behavior, 18*, 453–469. doi:10.1007/BF01499050

Pennington, N., & Hastie, R. (1988). Explanation-based decision making: Effects of memory structure on judgment. *Journal of Experimental Psychology: Learning, Memory, and Cognition, 14*, 521–533. doi:10.1037/0278-7393.14.3.521

Pennington, N., & Hastie, R. (1992). Explaining the evidence: Tests of the story model for juror decision making. *Journal of Personality and Social Psychology, 62*, 189–206. doi:10.1037/0022-3514.62.2.189

Pennington, N., & Hastie, R. (1993). The story model for juror decision making. In R. Hastie (Ed.), *Inside the juror: The psychology of juror decision making* (pp. 192–222). New York, NY: Cambridge University Press. doi:10.1017/CBO9780511752896.010

Penrod, S., & Hastie, R. (1979). Models of jury decision-making: A critical review. *Psychological Bulletin, 86*, 462–492. doi:10.1037/0033-2909.86.3.462

Penrod, S. D., & Heuer, L. (1997). Tweaking commonsense: Assessing aids to jury decision making. *Psychology, Public Policy, and Law, 3*, 259–284. doi:10.1037/1076-8971.3.2-3.259

People of the State of New York v. Kharey Wise, Kevin Richardson, Antron McCray, Yusef Salaam, & Raymond Santana: Affirmation in Response to Motion to Vacate Judgment of Conviction (2002). Indictment No. 4762/89, December 5, 2002.

Petty, R. E., & Wegener, D. T. (1998). Attitude change: Multiple roles for persuasion variables. In D. T. Gilbert, S. T. Fiske, & G. Lindzey (Eds.), *The handbook of social psychology* (pp. 323–390). Boston: McGraw Hill.

Pickel, K. L., Warner, T. C., Miller, T. J., & Barnes, Z. T. (2013). Conceptualizing defendants as minorities leads mock jurors to make bias evaluations in retracted confession cases. *Psychology, Public Policy, and Law, 19*, 56–69. doi:10.1037/a0029308

Quillian, L., & Pager, D. (2001). Black neighbors, higher crime? The role of racial stereotypes in evaluations of neighborhood crime. *American Journal of Sociology, 107*, 717–767. doi:10.1086/338938

Quillian, L., & Pager, D. (2010). Estimating risk: Stereotype amplification and the perceived risk of criminal victimization. *Social Psychology Quarterly, 73*, 79–104. doi:10.1177/0190272509360763

Raitz, A., Greene, E., Goodman, J., & Loftus, E. F. (1990). Determining damages: The influence of expert testimony on jurors' decision-making. *Law and Human Behavior, 14*, 385–395. doi:10.1007/BF01068163

Ratcliff, J. J., Lassiter, G. D., Jager, V. M., Lindberg, M. J., Elek, J. K., & Hasinski, A. E. (2010). The hidden consequences of racial salience in videotaped interrogations and confessions. *Psychology, Public Policy, and Law, 16*, 200–218. doi:10.1037/a0018482

Ratcliff, J. J., Lassiter, G. D., Schmidt, H. C., & Snyder, C. J. (2006). Camera perspective bias in videotaped confessions: Experimental evidence of its perceptual basis. *Journal of Experimental Psychology: Applied, 12*, 197–206. doi:10.1037/1076-898X.12.4.197

Reifman, A., Gusick, S. M., & Ellsworth, P. C. (1992). Real jurors' understanding of the law in real cases. *Law and Human Behavior, 16*, 539–554. doi:10.1007/BF01044622

Robbennolt, J. K., & Studebaker, C. A. (1999). Anchoring in the courtroom: The effects of caps on punitive damages. *Law and Human Behavior, 23*, 353–373. doi:10.1023/A:1022312716354

Robbennolt, J. K., & Studebaker, C. A. (2003). News media reporting on civil litigation and its influence on civil justice decision making. *Law and Human Behavior, 27*, 5–27. doi:10.1023/A:1021622827154

Rose, M. R., & Diamond, S. S. (2008). Judging bias: Juror confidence and judicial rulings on challenges for cause. *Law and Society Review, 42,* 513–549. doi:10.1111/j.1540-5893.2008.00350.x

Rosenhan, D. L., Eisner, S. L., & Robinson, R. J. (1994). Notetaking can aid juror recall. *Law and Human Behavior, 18,* 53–61. doi:10.1007/BF01499143

Ruva, C. L., Guenther, C. C., & Yarbrough, A. (2011). Positive and negative pretrial publicity: The roles of impression formation, emotion, and predecisional distortion. *Criminal Justice and Behavior, 38,* 511–534. doi:10.1177/0093854811400823

Ruva, C. L., & McEvoy, C. (2008). Negative and positive pretrial publicity affect juror memory and decision making. *Journal of Experimental Psychology: Applied, 14,* 226–235. doi:10.1037/1076-898X.14.3.226

Ruva, C. L., McEvoy, C., & Bryant, J. B. (2007). Effects of pre-trial publicity and jury deliberation on juror bias and source memory errors. *Applied Cognitive Psychology, 21,* 45–67. doi:10.1002/acp.1254

Saks, M. J., & Marti, M. W. (1997). A meta-analysis of the effects of jury size. *Law and Human Behavior, 21,* 451–467. doi:10.1023/A:1024819605652

Salerno, J. M., Bottoms, B. L., & Peter-Hagene, C. L. (2012, March). Peripheral arguments can sometimes help juries evaluate expert witness quality. Paper presented at the annual meeting of the American Psychology-Law Society, San Juan, Puerto Rico.

Salerno, J. M., & Diamond, S. S. (2010). The promise of a cognitive perspective on jury deliberation. *Psychonomic Bulletin and Review, 17,* 174–179. doi:10.3758/PBR.17.2.174

Salerno, J. M., & McCauley, M. R. (2009). Mock jurors' judgments about opposing scientific experts: Do cross-examination, deliberation and need for cognition matter? *American Journal of Forensic Psychology, 27,* 37–60.

Sandys, M., & Dillehay, R. C. (1995). First-ballot votes, predeliberation dispositions, and final verdicts in jury trials. *Law and Human Behavior, 19,* 175–195. doi:10.1007/BF01499324

Schkade, D., Sunstein, C. R., & Kahneman, D. (2000). Deliberating about dollars: The severity shift. *Columbia Law Review, 100,* 1139–1175. doi:10.2307/1123539

Schklar, J., & Diamond, S. S. (1999). Juror reactions to DNA evidence: Errors and expectancies. *Law and Human Behavior, 23,* 159–184. doi:10.1023/A:1022368801333

Schuller, R. A. (1992). The impact of battered woman syndrome evidence on jury decision-processes. *Law and Human Behavior, 16,* 597–620. doi:10.1007/BF01884018

Schuller, R. A., & Cripps, J. (1998). Expert evidence pertaining to battered women: The impact of

gender of expert and timing of expert testimony. *Law and Human Behavior, 22,* 17–31. doi:10.1023/A:1025772604721

Schulman, J., Shaver, P., Colman, R., Emrich, B., & Christie, R. (1973, May). Recipe for a jury. *Psychology Today,* 37–44, 77, 79–84

Seltzer, R. (2006). Scientific jury selection: Does it work? *Journal of Applied Social Psychology, 36,* 2417–2435. doi:10.1111/j.0021-9029.2006.00110.x

Seltzer, R., Venuti, M., & Lopes, G. (1991). Juror honesty during the voir dire. *Journal of Criminal Justice, 19,* 451–462. doi:10.1016/0047-2352(91)90019-R

Simon, R. J. (1967). *The jury and the defense of insanity.* Boston, MA: Little, Brown and Company.

Skeem, J. L., Louden, J. E., & Evans, J. (2004). Venirepersons' attitudes toward the insanity defense: Developing, refining, and validating a scale. *Law and Human Behavior, 28,* 623–648. doi:10.1007/s10979-004-0487-7

Smith, A. C., & Greene, E. (2005). Conduct and its consequences: Attempts at debiasing jury judgments. *Law and Human Behavior, 29,* 505–526. doi:10.1007/s10979-005-5692-5

Smith, B. C., Penrod, S. D., Otto, A. L., & Park, R. C. (1996). Jurors' use of probabilistic evidence. *Law and Human Behavior, 20,* 49–82. doi:10.1007/BF01499132

Smith, V. L. (1991). Prototypes in the courtroom: Lay representations of legal concepts. *Journal of Personality and Social Psychology, 61,* 857–872. doi:10.1037/0022-3514.61.6.857

Smith, V. L., & Kassin, S. M. (1993). Effects of the dynamite charge on the deliberations of deadlocked mock juries. *Law and Human Behavior, 17,* 625–643. doi:10.1007/BF01044686

Sommer, K. L., Horowitz, I. A., & Bourgeois, M. J. (2001). When juries fail to comply with the law: Biased evidence in individual and group decision making. *Personality and Social Psychology Bulletin, 27,* 309–320. doi:10.1177/0146167201273005

Sommers, S. R. (2006). On racial diversity and group decision making: Identifying multiple effects of racial composition on jury deliberations. *Journal of Personality and Social Psychology, 90,* 597–612. doi:10.1037/0022-3514.90.4.597

Sommers, S. R. (2007). Race and the decision making of juries. *Legal and Criminological Psychology, 12,* 171–187. doi:10.1348/135532507X189687

Sommers, S. R., & Ellsworth, P. C. (2000). Race in the courtroom: Perceptions of guilt and dispositional attributions. *Personality and Social Psychology Bulletin, 26,* 1367–1379. doi:10.1177/0146167200263005

Sommers, S. R., & Ellsworth, P. C. (2001). White juror bias: An investigation of prejudice against black defendants in the American courtroom. *Psychology, Public Policy, and Law, 7,* 201–229. doi:10.1037/1076-8971.7.1.201

Sporer, S. L., Penrod, S., Read, D., & Cutler, B. (1995). Choosing, confidence, and accuracy: A meta-analysis of the confidence-accuracy relation in eyewitness identification studies. *Psychological Bulletin, 118,* 315–327. doi:10.1037/0033-2909.118.3.315

Stasser, G. (1992). Information salience and the discovery of hidden profiles by decision-making groups: A "thought experiment." *Organizational Behavior and Human Decision Processes, 52,* 156–181. doi:10.1016/0749-5978(92)90049-D

Stasser, G., Kerr, N., & Bray, R. M. (1982). The social psychology of jury deliberations: Structure, process, and product. In N. Kerr & R. M. Bray (Eds.), *The psychology of the courtroom* (pp. 221–256). New York, NY: Academic Press.

Stasser, G., Kerr, N. L., & Davis, J. H. (1989). Influence processes and consensus models in decision making groups. In P. Paulus (Ed.), *Psychology of group influence* (2nd ed., pp. 279–326). Hillsdale, NJ: Erlbaum.

Steblay, N., Hosch, H. M., Culhane, S. E., & McWethy, A. (2006). The impact on juror verdicts of judicial instruction to disregard inadmissible evidence: A meta-analysis. *Law and Human Behavior, 30,* 469–492. doi:10.1007/s10979-006-9039-7

Steblay, N. M., Besirevic, J., Fulero, S. M., & Jimenez-Lorente, B. (1999). The effects of pretrial publicity on juror verdicts: A meta-analytic review. *Law and Human Behavior, 23,* 219–235. doi:10.1023/A:1022325019080

Strauder v. West Virginia, 100 U.S. 303 (1880).

Strier, F., & Shestowsky, D. (1999). Profiling the profilers: A study of the trial consulting profession, its impact on trial justice, and what, if anything to do about it. *Wisconsin Law Review, 1999,* 441–499.

Studebaker, C. A., & Penrod, S. D. (1997). Pretrial publicity: The media, the law, and common sense. *Psychology, Public Policy, and Law, 3,* 428–460. doi:10.1037/1076-8971.3.2-3.428

Studebaker, C. A., & Penrod, S. D. (2005). Pretrial publicity and its influence on juror decision making. In N. Brewer & K. D. Williams (Eds.), *Psychology and law: An empirical perspective* (pp. 254–275). New York, NY: Guilford Press.

Studebaker, C. A., Robbennolt, J. K., Pathak-Sharma, M. K., & Penrod, S. D. (2000). Assessing pretrial publicity effects: Integrating content analytic results. *Law and Human Behavior, 24,* 317–336. doi:10.1023/A:1005536204923

Sue, S., Smith, R., & Gilbert, R. (1974). Biasing effects of pretrial publicity on judicial decisions. *Journal of Criminal Justice, 2,* 163–171. doi:10.1016/0047-2352(74)90007-5

Sweeney, L. T., & Haney, C. (1992). The influence of race on sentencing: A meta-analytic review of experimental studies. *Behavioral Sciences and the Law, 10,* 179–195. doi:10.1002/bsl.2370100204

Tanford, S., & Penrod, S. (1986). Jury deliberations: Discussion content and influence processes in jury decision-making. *Journal of Applied Social Psychology, 16,* 322–347. doi:10.1111/j.1559-1816.1986.tb01144.x

Thomas, E. A., & Hogue, A. (1976). Apparent weight of evidence, decision criteria and confidence ratings in juror decision making. *Psychological Review, 83,* 442–465. doi:10.1037/0033-295X.83.6.442

Tversky, A., & Kahneman, D. (1973). Availability: A heuristic for judging frequency and probability. *Cognitive Psychology, 5,* 207–232. doi:10.1016/0010-0285(73)90033-9

Vidmar, N., & Hans, V. P. (2007). *American juries: The verdict.* New York, NY: Prometheus Books.

Vidmar, N., & Judson, J. W. T. (1981). The use of social-science data in a change of venue application: A case study. *Canadian Bar Review, 59,* 76–102.

Visher, C. A. (1987). Juror decision making: The importance of evidence. *Law and Human Behavior, 11,* 1–17. doi:10.1007/BF01044835

Wainwright v. Witt, 469 U.S. 412 (1985).

Ware, L. J., Lassiter, G. D., Patterson, S. M., & Ransom, M. R. (2008). Camera perspective bias in videotaped confessions: Evidence that visual attention is a mediator. *Journal of Experimental Psychology: Applied, 14,* 192–200. doi:10.1037/1076-898X.14.2.192

Wells, G. L. (1978). Applied eyewitness-testimony research: System variables and estimator variables. *Journal of Personality and Social Psychology, 36,* 1546–1557. doi:10.1037/0022-3514.36.12.1546

Wells, G. L., Lindsay, R. C. L., & Ferguson, T. J. (1979). Accuracy, confidence, and juror perceptions in eyewitness identification. *Journal of Applied Psychology, 64,* 440–448. doi:10.1037/0021-9010.64.4.440

Wheatman, S. R., & Shaffer, D. R. (2001). On finding for defendants who plead insanity: The crucial impact of dispositional instructions and opportunity to deliberate. *Law and Human Behavior, 25,* 167–183. doi:10.1023/A:1005645414992

Williams v. Florida, 399 U.S. 78 (1970).

Wistrich, A. J., Guthrie, C., & Rachlinski, J. J. (2005). Can judges ignore inadmissible information? The difficulty of deliberately disregarding. *University of Pennsylvania Law Review, 153,* 1251–1345. doi:10.2307/4150614

Witherspoon v. Illinois, 391 U.S. 510 (1968).

Yarbrough, A. M., & Kovera, M. B. (2013). *Do demonstratives increase the effectiveness of the opposing expert safeguard against unreliable scientific evidence?* Manuscript under review.

Zickafoose, D. J., & Bornstein, B. J. (1999). Double discounting: The effects of comparative negligence on mock juror decision making. *Law and Human Behavior, 23,* 577–596. doi:10.1023/A:1022300313628

CHAPTER 11

MEDIA AND THE LAW

Jennifer Groscup

Media in its various forms is omnipresent in modern life. It can shape our attitudes, perceptions, and behaviors in a variety of ways. One arena in which the media can exert a variety of influences is the legal system. The media, psychology, and the law intersect in a wide variety of contexts. Exposure to media, such as violent video games and pornography, can increase legally relevant behaviors such as aggression and criminal behaviors. Media can be used to facilitate or engage in criminal activity, such as pedophiles' use of social media to access children and the use of the internet for cyberbullying. Increasingly, the media has also been used in crime-solving, with police and laypersons engaging in cyber-sleuthing, raising questions about the validity of this type of investigation and about expectations of privacy.

This chapter will review some of the ways in which media can influence behaviors within the legal system itself. The media can influence how people perceive crime, criminals, and the effectiveness of the legal system. The media also can influence how laypersons behave within the legal system and make legal decisions. This chapter will review research related to the influence of the media on these noncriminal behaviors. First, theoretical underpinnings for research on media and law are presented. Then, the research investigating the intersection of media and the law is presented. Topics include the media's influence on perceptions of criminals, crime, and the legal system. This research indicates that media portrayals of crime and criminals tend to give an unrealistic view of who commits crimes, how they commit crimes, and with what frequency. This research also indicates that crime portrayals in the media, accurate or not, can increase fear of crime and affect other legally relevant attitudes. Research on how media can influence trials also will be covered, including the influence of pretrial publicity (PTP), the "CSI Effect," and social media. PTP has a demonstrated negative influence on juror impartiality and can potentially affect trial fairness. Jurors exposed to PTP are more likely to hold biased pretrial opinions about a defendant, and this negative influence can be increased by the type of publicity. Although its existence is widely accepted in the media and in the legal world, little research has found a significant link between crime drama viewership (watching shows like *CSI: Crime Scene Investigation*) and jury decision making in trials. On the other hand, crime drama viewership can increase jurors' expectations about the type of evidence that will be proffered in trials. Social media is also widely discussed by legal practitioners as a problematic influence on trials, but research has not thoroughly investigated this issue. Because most of the media effects on trials tend to be negative, leading to potentially biased jury decision making, research also has extensively investigated corrective measures that the legal system can take to minimize the media's negative impact on trial fairness. The last section of this chapter will review the research on legal safeguards against the media's influence on trials. Overall, this research indicates that current solutions to the problem of media and the law may be ineffective.

http://dx.doi.org/10.1037/14462-011
APA Handbook of Forensic Psychology: Vol. 2. Criminal Investigation, Adjudication, and Sentencing Outcomes,
B. L. Cutler and P. A. Zapf (Editors-in-Chief)
Copyright © 2015 by the American Psychological Association. All rights reserved.

IMPORTANCE OF THE PROBLEM

The First Amendment of the U.S. Constitution prohibits governmental restriction of the freedom of the press and the freedom of expression more broadly. It also prohibits restricting access to forms of the press and expression, except in extraordinary circumstances. The freedom of the press and expression includes all forms of media, such as newspapers, television, and the internet. Therefore, it is the fundamental right of the media to report and to comment on issues that are important to society, such as crime and the legal system. Access to the media by the people is at an all-time high. Recently, there has been a steady increase in the number and availability of media outlets for information, including crime reporting and fiction about crime. On television, there are more networks creating more news shows and more scripted dramas about crime than in the past. News outlets have also increased including print media, internet news sources, news networks, and internet blogs. Technology allowing for the access to media is advancing, giving people more access to the media and more ways to interact with it than ever before. This increase in technology has spawned the world of social media, the use of which continues to increase. Therefore, access to and interaction with the media is ever increasing, exposing more people at a higher rate to a potentially greater saturation of information on a variety of topics.

Although it is a fundamental right, unfettered access to the media creates specific problems for the legal system. Another fundamental right—the Sixth Amendment right to a fair trial by an impartial jury—can be violated when potential trial decision makers are exposed to legally relevant media. General fictional and nonfictional information about the legal system available through the media can influence attitudes, perceptions, and behaviors about the legal system. This influence could, in turn, affect decision making in actual trials. Media also has the potential to directly influence decision making in cases. Overall, the guarantees of the rights in the First Amendment can come in conflict with the rights guaranteed to criminal defendants in the Sixth Amendment. This conflict has serious implications

for constitutionally guaranteed trial fairness, making this a grave problem for the legal system. The trial of George Zimmerman for the shooting death of Trayvon Martin and the trial of Casey Anthony for the murder of her two-year-old daughter exemplify this conflict between the omnipresent media and the legal system. Both cases were highly and nationally publicized, with media appearing not only in traditional news sources but also in internet blogs, Wikipedia, reality crime shows, dedicated Facebook pages, and other social media outlets. These cases were tried simultaneously by the jurors in the courtrooms and by society through the media. Cases like these are affected by the media, but their presence in the media also has the potential to affect perceptions of the legal system.

One solution would be to restrict the media from reporting on issues related to crime, criminals, and the legal system. This type of restriction would prevent people from exposure to the media material that could affect the right to a fair trial. Not only is this impractical given nationwide interest in both real and fictional crime, it would also violate the First Amendment. Censorship of the media is not accomplished lightly, as evidenced by recent Supreme Court cases limiting restrictions on the media such as network television programming and video games (*Brown v. Entertainment Merchants Association*, 2011; *FCC v. Fox Television Stations, Inc.*, 2012). Therefore, the legal system must determine how to guarantee trial fairness while accommodating omnipresent media coverage. The problems of how the media influences perceptions of the legal system, how the media influences actual trial decision making, and the effectiveness of potential safeguards against unfair trials are the important issues addressed in this chapter.

RELEVANT PSYCHOLOGICAL THEORY AND PRINCIPLES

Many theories have been used to explain the influence of media on attitudes toward the criminal justice system and on legal decision making, but much of the research in this area is purely applied or atheoretical. Of the theories that have been used in this area, some specifically attempt to explain how media can influence the ways in which we behave. Social learning theory has commonly been applied to explain the link between media exposure and a variety of behaviors. According to social learning theory, behaviors are learned by observing the behaviors of others and modeling those behaviors (Bandura, 1973, 1977, 1986). According to social learning theory, if a behavior is attended to and the memory of it retained, that behavior may later be modeled or repeated. If the performed behavior is reinforced, it is likely to be performed again and thus learned (Bandura, 1986). The media can be a source of these observed and modeled behaviors and can also be a source of attitudes and feelings about behaviors (Bandura, 1973; Dill & Burgess, 2012; Oates, 2012). Most research on social learning from the media has focused on the link between exposure to violent or obscene material and the development of later aggressive, deviant, or criminal behavior patterns (Bandura, 1973; Cohan & Cook, 2013). For example, research has linked children's exposure to violent television and video games to adult aggression and violence (Huesmann, Moise-Titus, Podolski, & Eron, 2003). On the other hand, social learning theory could be used to explain the acquisition of many other behaviors and viewpoints from the media.

Some theories are used to explain how the media develops our thinking about the world, including our thinking about the legal system. From the field of media studies, cultivation theory is a popular explanation for the influence of television and print media on general attitudes about the legal system and crime (Hayes-Smith & Levett, 2011; Romer, Jamieson, & Aday, 2003; Schweitzer & Saks, 2007). According to cultivation theory, what people see in the media cultivates their global view of the world (Gerbner, Gross, Morgan, Signorielli, & Shanahan, 2002; Potter, 1988). The world on television is presented as more menacing than the real world, so cultivation theorists tend to hypothesize that heavy television viewers will view the world as more dangerous and criminal than it is in reality (Gerbner & Gross, 1976; Gerbner et al., 2002). Critics of the theory cite small or nonexistent effect sizes and a lack of accounting for other variables that could intervene in the relationship between television

viewership and world view (Romer et al., 2003). Cultivation has been used in an attempt to explain the influence of media on perceptions of crime and criminals (Gerbner & Gross, 1976; Gross & Aday, 2003; Romer et al., 2003) and on the development of attitudes and expectations about the legal system that are related to the CSI Effect (Hayes-Smith & Levett, 2011; Podlas, 2006b; Schweitzer & Saks, 2007).

Other theories have been used to explain media's influence on related and potentially unrelated trial tasks. Many of the problems created during trials are related to jurors' inappropriate use of information learned outside the courtroom in their decision making. Various types of media are major sources of this extralegal information, including news, other television, and social media. Theories of memory can help explain why these media sources are relied on during trials, potentially without the conscious awareness of the decision maker. Specifically, source monitoring has been applied to explain the influence of the news, scripted television dramas, and PTP (Ruva & McEvoy, 2008; Ruva & Hudak, 2013). Research on memory suggests that it is sometimes difficult to properly identify the source of information in memory (Johnson, Hashtroudi, & Lindsay, 1993). When making decisions during trials, jurors may misattribute information learned from the media as having been presented in the trial evidence (Ruva & McEvoy, 2008). If source-monitoring errors are occurring, it becomes more difficult for jurors to disregard extralegal information from the media because they do not identify it as coming from an inappropriate source (Ruva & McEvoy, 2008; Ruva & Hudak, 2013; see Chapter 10, this volume for a review of research on jury decision making).

Additional theories have attempted to explain the type of influence the media has on trial decision making. In the specific area of PTP, predecisional distortion has been used to explain how the exposure to media may influence orientations toward the case prior to the introduction of case evidence (Hope, Memon, & McGeorge, 2004; Ruva, Guenther, & Yarbrough, 2011). In predecisional distortion, it is hypothesized that perceptions of the trial evidence become distorted before trial or early in the trial process. The perception of and weight given to evidence proffered at trial is distorted to favor the side of the case that is favored in the initial distortion (Carlson & Russo, 2001; Hope et al., 2004; Ruva et al., 2011). Although this theory has only been applied to PTP effects in the legal system, it could explain the influence of other extralegal media information on trials. Overall, there are no consistently used theories in the area of media and the law, and the theories that have been used have not been universally applied even within topic areas.

RESEARCH REVIEW

Given the clear importance of the topic, psychological research has extensively investigated the relationship between media and the legal system. Research has investigated a wide array of relationships between media consumption and behavior related to legally relevant behaviors, including its influence on the development of aggression, deviant behavior, and criminal behavior. Research also probed how media exposure can influence the general public's perceptions of the legal system and laypersons' decision making within the legal system. The following research review will focus on how the media affects noncriminal individuals' perceptions of and decision making within the legal system, including fear of crime and the effect of PTP, crime drama viewership, and social media use.

Media Portrayals of the Legal System and Effects of Media on Perceptions of Criminals, Crime, and the Legal System

Media has the potential to influence a variety of social, political, and legally relevant attitudes. In terms of legally relevant attitudes, media can influence how viewers perceive crime, criminals, and the criminal justice system. More specifically, television viewership, a very common source of information from the media, could influence these perceptions in ways that are consistent with the media coverage of crime-related issues. Television programming that is related to crime and the legal system primarily comes from three types of programming: news programs, nonfiction reality police/crime programs (e.g., *America's Most Wanted, Cops*), and fictional scripted crime dramas (e.g., *Law & Order, CSI: Crime Scene Investigation*). Research on all three of these types of

programs indicates that they can all affect perceptions of criminals, crime, and the legal system.

Local and national television news programs are a primary source of actual information about criminals and the legal system. A first step to understanding the influence of this form of media on perceptions of the legal system is examining the content presented on the news, and research has investigated how perpetrators, victims, and police officers are portrayed in the news, particularly in regard to portrayals of race. Several studies investigating television news content, specifically examining the relationship between race and the portrayals of crime victims, lawbreakers, and law defenders have been conducted (Dixon, Azocar, & Casas, 2003; Dixon & Linz, 2000a, 2000b). In two studies, Dixon and Linz (2000a, 2000b) content coded local news for portrayals of crime and race, and they compared the frequencies they observed to crime statistics. In their 2000b study comparing portrayals of crime victims and perpetrators on Los Angeles local news, they found that Whites were portrayed as victims more than they were portrayed as perpetrators, were portrayed as victims more than Blacks and Latinos, and were overrepresented as victims as compared to actual crime victim statistics. In contrast, Blacks and Latinos were more likely to be portrayed as perpetrators than as victims, with Blacks overrepresented as perpetrators as compared to reality (Dixon & Linz, 2000b). Dixon and Linz (2000a) also compared portrayals of lawbreakers and defenders in Los Angeles and found that Blacks and Latinos were more likely than Whites to be portrayed as lawbreakers, and they were more likely to be portrayed as lawbreakers overall than as law defenders. In contrast, Whites were more likely to be portrayed as law defenders and less likely to be portrayed as law breakers. Blacks were overrepresented as lawbreakers, and Whites were overrepresented as law defenders as compared to reality (Dixon & Linz, 2000a). Dixon et al. (2003) coded national nightly news programs by content and found that Whites and Blacks were portrayed as lawbreakers in frequencies that were consistent with crime statistics on perpetrator race, but Whites were overrepresented and Blacks were underrepresented as victims and police officers as compared to reality (Dixon et al., 2003). Finding similar results to

Dixon's research, Chiricos and Eschholz (2002) content-coded news in Orlando, Florida, and found that Blacks and Latinos were represented more often than Whites as the suspect in crimes, and when they were presented as suspects, the representation was more threatening than the representation of Whites as suspects (Chiricos & Eschholz, 2002).

Research on the content of news portrayals of crime has also focused on more specific types of crime and news reports. Dixon and Azocar (2006) specifically examined portrayals of crimes committed by juveniles in Los Angeles area local news and found that Black juveniles were overrepresented as lawbreakers and Latino juveniles were underrepresented as lawbreakers. Dixon and Linz (2002) investigated the presence of prejudicial PTP in the news and found that prejudicial pretrial statements were two times more likely to be associated with Black and Latino defendants than they were to be associated with White defendants (Dixon & Linz, 2002). Dowler (2006) investigated portrayals of sex crimes on television news and found that the news was more likely to present fear and information about victim credibility for sex crimes than for other types of crimes. Overall, the research on the portrayal of crime in the news indicates that it may be biased in terms of race and based on the type of crime being reported.

Some research also has investigated the content of police reality television shows and found similar representations of perpetrator, victim, and police officer race (Oliver, 1994). Blacks are underrepresented as police officers, and Whites are overrepresented as police officers. Additionally, violent crime and the percentage of crimes solved by the police tend to be overrepresented in police reality television (Oliver, 1994). Other research on the content of information presented in police reality television indicates that it may be an accurate portrayal of the job duties of the police and in what activities police typically engage as part of their jobs (Soulliere, 2004). This limited research raises questions about the type of information about crime and the police the public might be exposed to by viewing crime reality television.

The content of information about the legal system presented during scripted crime dramas also has been investigated and provides an essential context to understanding the influence of crime drama viewership on perceptions of and attitudes about the legal system. Podlas (2006a) content-coded the first two seasons of *CSI: Crime Scene Investigation* for the type of forensic evidence presented and found that fingerprint and blood analysis were the most commonly presented types of forensic evidence. In their content analysis of the first seasons of *CSI: Crime Scene Investigation* and *CSI: Miami*, Smith, Stinson, and Patry (2011) found that DNA and fingerprint evidence were the most frequently used types of forensic evidence, consistent with Podlas (2006a). Smith et al. also found that the perpetrator was almost always caught, and errors were rarely made by the forensic scientists. Additionally, they surveyed a small group of actual forensic scientists who rated the accuracy of the forensic science presented on *CSI: Crime Scene Investigation* as "low." Desmarais, Price, and Read (2008) also investigated the accuracy of the portrayal of forensic investigation techniques on television. They examined several crime dramas including *CSI: Crime Scene Investigation* for the accuracy of their portrayal of eyewitness reliability and found that depictions of eyewitnesses on television have increased with the proliferation of crime dramas and that representations of eyewitnesses' abilities are largely inaccurate, giving an impression that they are more reliable than they are in reality (Desmarais et al., 2008). DeGarmo (2011) content-coded two seasons each of *CSI: Crime Scene Investigation*, *Criminal Minds*, and *Law & Order: SVU* and found several overall themes were present in these shows, including the portrayal of the criminal as "evil" and the police as "heroes." Overall, examinations of crime drama content indicate that forensic science is featured prominently, is portrayed as infallible, and is usually prosecution-oriented. This research provides support for Tyler's (2006) argument that this genre of shows presents a one-sided view of crime and the legal system.

Given that research has generally found an overrepresentation of Whites as victims and law defenders in the news and an overrepresentation of Blacks and Latinos as perpetrators, research has investigated the impact of these representations on perceptions of crime and race. Dixon (2008) found that exposure to typical newscasts increased participants' concern about crime and perceptions that Blacks are violent. Participants exposed to the news also gave higher ratings of potential criminal culpability to a hypothetical Black or racially unidentified suspect than to a White suspect (Dixon, 2008). In a mock news story about the murder of a police officer, Dixon (2007) manipulated the race of the perpetrator and the officer to be either Black, White, or unidentified. Participants who were heavy news viewers generally were more likely to believe the racially unspecified officer was White and rated the officers they perceived as being White positively, whereas participants were more likely to perceive the unidentified perpetrator as being Black regardless of viewing habits (Dixon, 2007). Dixon (2006) manipulated whether participants watched a newscast about a Black or a racially unidentified crime suspect. Participants who were heavy news viewers who saw a newscast about a Black suspect were more likely to perceive the world as dangerous (Dixon, 2006). Dixon and Azocar (2007) presented participants with a noncrime news story or a news story about crime featuring Black, White, or racially unidentified suspects. Ratings of potential culpability for the Black suspect were higher than other suspects for typically heavy news viewers (Dixon & Azocar, 2007). Dixon and Maddox (2005) further investigated the influence of race by manipulating the skin tone of a news story suspect to be either White or Black (light, medium, or dark skin tone). For all participants, the suspect with dark skin tone was the most memorable, but participants who were heavy news viewers also perceived the crime victim more favorably when the perpetrator in the news story they watched was Black (Dixon & Maddox, 2005). Together, this research indicates that racially biased news portrayals of crime may affect people's attitudes about crime and perceptions of alleged suspects and that this effect may increase as typical news viewing increases.

In addition to these race-related news programming effects, research has found that exposure to various types of television programming can influence subjective perceptions of legal issues, such as fear of crime, and can influence attitudes related to the legal system, such as attitudes toward the death penalty. Many studies have demonstrated

the influence of media exposure on fear of crime. Most of this research relates measurements of fear of crime to viewership of various law-related media such as television news, nonfictional or police reality crime shows, and scripted crime dramas. Although much of the research demonstrates an association between crime-related television news viewership and increased fear of crime generally (Callanan, 2012; Holbert, Shah, & Kwak, 2004; Romer et al., 2003) and situational fear of crime specifically (Custers & van den Bulck, 2011), other research has found no effect of television news viewership on increased fear of crime (Grabe & Drew, 2007; Kort-Butler & Hartshorn, 2011; Lane & Meeker, 2003). Limited research has found that increased television news viewership may decrease fear of crime (Custers & van den Bulck, 2013). Similarly inconsistent effects have been found for the relationship between reality crime and crime drama viewership and fear of crime. Viewing police reality shows typically increases fear of crime (Callanan, 2012; Eschholz, Chiricos, & Gertz, 2003; Kort-Butler & Hartshorn, 2011), but some research found no link between watching these programs and fear of crime (Holbert et al., 2004). Most research found that crime drama viewership does not affect fear of crime (Callanan, 2012; Grabe & Drew, 2007; Kort-Butler & Hautshorn, 2011), but some research indicates that watching crime dramas may increase perceived risk of sexual violence victimization (Custers & van den Bulck, 2013) or may increase fear of crime when participants perceive that they live in a racially diverse neighborhood (Eschholz et al., 2003).

Research also has demonstrated a link between television exposure and other legally relevant attitudes and behaviors, such as attitudes toward the criminal justice system, support of the death penalty, and actual gun ownership. Some research shows that television viewing, specifically police reality shows, can decrease overall support for the criminal justice system (Kort-Butler & Hartshorn, 2011) and can increase negative perceptions of police and police fairness (Dirikx, Gelders, & van den Bulck, 2013; Reith, 1999). In contrast, other research has found that news and police reality television exposure increases confidence in the police (Callanan & Rosenberger, 2011). Research results on the effects of television viewing on support for the death penalty are mixed. Some research demonstrates that watching the news (Dixon, 2006; Holbert et al., 2004), police reality programs (Holbert et al., 2004), and crime dramas (Holbert et al., 2004; Kort-Butler & Hartshorn, 2011) increases support for the death penalty. For example, Slater, Rouner, and Lang (2006) experimentally manipulated whether participants watched *Law & Order* or an episode of *If These Walls Could Talk* about gay rights and measured support for the death penalty and for gay rights. Watching *Law & Order* increased support for the death penalty regardless of prior political ideology, but neither television program affected support for gay rights (Slater et al., 2006). Other research, however, found no effect of television exposure on support for the death penalty (Dixon & Azocar, 2007). Finally, television news and police reality television viewing may increase support for gun ownership and actual gun ownership (Holbert et al., 2004), although no relationship between crime drama viewership and either attitudes about or actual gun ownership has been established (Grabe & Drew, 2007).

Overall, television media about crime, criminals, and the legal system may present an inaccurate and potentially biased view of the realities of the criminal justice system. Television news presents a skewed perception of who is committing crimes and who is defending against them, which results in viewer misperceptions about crime. Exposure to television news, police reality shows, and scripted crime dramas also influences attitudes about the criminal justice system and other legally relevant attitudes. Exposure generally increases fear of crime, support of the death penalty, and support for gun ownership. All of these attitudes are consistent with the high-crime, prosecution-oriented nature of the legal system's portrayal in the media.

Effects of Media on Trials

A large portion of the psychological study of media and the law has focused on the influence of media exposure on jurors. This research has primarily examined the influence of PTP on juror decision making. Research

also has examined the validity of the CSI Effect. More recently, commentary has focused on the influence of social media usage on juror decision making.

Pretrial publicity.　The right to a trial by an impartial jury is guaranteed under the Sixth Amendment to the U.S. Constitution. The right to freedom of speech and freedom of the press is also guaranteed in the U.S. Constitution under the First Amendment. In cases with extensive media coverage, these Constitutional rights may come into conflict. The media have the right to cover the content of legal cases and trials, but extensive media coverage or PTP may interfere with a defendant's right to an impartial jury. PTP is often biased against a defendant and may include a variety of inadmissible information maligning the character of the defendant and reporting the existence of incriminating evidence. In cases with extensive PTP, it is possible that potential jurors in the trial venue have formed opinions about the guilt of a defendant based on information reported by the media.

Research indicates that PTP is a real and growing problem in the legal system. Trial motions regarding the negative effects of PTP on a defendant's Sixth Amendment right to a fair trial are frequent and have been increasing over time. Minow and Cate (2001) investigated the number of motions made by defendants claiming an inability to receive a fair trial in the trial venue due to the presence of significant, negative PTP about their cases in the 1980s, and they estimated that at least 3,100 defendants made such claims (Minow & Cate, 2001). Between the years of 1996 and 2006, defendant motions about PTP and trial fairness increased to over 7,000 (Spano, Groscup, & Penrod, 2011).

Most of the research on the effects of PTP on decision making has investigated how PTP affects decision making and what makes this influence more or less powerful. Research on PTP effects has been conducted using a variety of methodological approaches. The most commonly used methods are experimental methods, which investigate PTP effects in a laboratory (Spano et al., 2011). In a laboratory study of PTP, participants are typically exposed to various types and amounts of PTP and then asked to render a verdict in the mock trial. More complex designs may also include *voir dire*, judicial instructions, and jury deliberations. In these experimental studies, there can be wide variation in the source of the participants (i.e., college students versus jury-eligible community members), the realistic quality of the PTP and the mock trial, and the level of experimental control. These methodological variations can affect both the validity of the study and its generalizability to the real world. Another commonly used methodological approach to studying PTP effects is to conduct research in the field using real cases. The primary benefit of this type of study is that participants have been naturally exposed to PTP and they tend to be jury-eligible community members, so there is a more direct connection to the real world. Field research provides valuable information about juror perceptions of PTP in a real-life setting, but it may lack experimental control (Spano et al., 2011). The method and the materials used to investigate PTP effects may influence the size of the effect observed in the research. For example, the meta-analysis of PTP effects by Steblay, Besirevic, Fulero, and Jimenez-Lorente (1999) found larger associations between PTP and case prejudgment when the research was a survey rather than an experiment, when the participants were community members rather than college students, when the PTP was from actual articles instead of fictionalized, and when the crime was for sexual abuse, drugs, or murder versus other crimes (Steblay et al., 1999).

Regardless of the method used to investigate the impact of PTP on jury decision making, the research overall demonstrates that PTP providing negative information about the defendant results in increased presumptions of guilt and guilty verdicts. The majority of the extant research on the effect of PTP exposure has demonstrated that prejudicial PTP in criminal cases can influence jurors' perceptions of the likeability of the defendant, the amount of sympathy felt about the defendant, and the criminal nature of the defendant, and PTP can also create prejudgment guilt and increase guilty verdicts (Studebaker & Penrod, 1997). Early research on the influence of PTP, primarily conducted on real cases in the field, found that increased knowledge about a case from PTP can result in prejudgment of

the case. Specifically, case studies and survey research demonstrated that jury-eligible adult participants exposed to negative PTP were more likely to have knowledge about the case, to have proprosecution attitudes, and to prejudge the defendant as guilty than participants who were not exposed to PTP (Costantini & King, 1980–1981; Nietzel & Dillehay, 1983; Simon & Eimermann, 1971). Prejudgment of the cases by participants in these studies was not related to their reported ability to be impartial jurors, indicating that jurors may be unaware of the effects of PTP on their impartiality (Costantini & King, 1980–1981; Moran & Cutler, 1991; Simon & Eimermann, 1971). These effects have been found across a variety of case types (Costantini & King, 1980–1981; Moran & Cutler, 1991). These results indicate that knowledge about a case originating in PTP can create an antidefendant bias in trials, that potential jurors may be unaware of this bias, and that this bias may occur regardless of the type of case.

Researchers have also investigated how various types and amounts of negative PTP affect juror impartiality. Some research indicates that attending to more media sources (Costantini & King, 1980–1981) and exposure to a variety of types of information about the defendant (Tans & Chaffee, 1966) increases the negative influence of PTP. Previous research has also shown that negative information about the defendant from the media that would be inadmissible in court influences juror decision making in trials. In particular, research demonstrates that information about the defendant's bad character, prior criminal record, gang membership, and polygraph results influence juror decision making although they were not part of the trial evidence (DeLuca, 1979; Hvistendahl, 1979; Otto, Penrod, & Dexter, 1994). The presence of these types of information in PTP makes the PTP more influential because inadmissible information tends to be the most prejudicial towards the defendant. Exposure to inadmissible information is also problematic because it cannot be taken into account in the verdict and is difficult to disregard. PTP about the prior criminal record of the plaintiff (Otto et al., 1994) and of the defendant (Kline & Jess, 1966) can also influence decision making in civil cases. For example, Otto et al. (1994) exposed participants to negative information about the plaintiff's character and prior criminal record. When exposed to this PTP, jurors were less likely to find the defendant negligent, more likely to perceive the defendant and the defense witnesses positively, and more likely to perceive the plaintiff negatively. The vast majority of the extant research shows that PTP containing substantive negative information about the defendant results in an antidefendant bias that persists throughout the presentation of trial evidence, resulting in more guilty verdicts. Overall, the association between PTP and guilty verdicts is on average a correlation equaling 0.16, according to a meta-analysis (Steblay et al., 1999). More recent research has continued to find an association between negative PTP and guilty verdicts, demonstrating that negative media about a defendant can influence trial fairness (Ruva et al., 2011; Ruva & Hudak, 2013; Ruva & McEvoy, 2008).

Given the large body of research indicating that negative PTP can increase guilty verdicts, much recent research has investigated the impact of PTP that portrays the criminal defendant in a positive manner to determine if positive pretrial information could create a positive bias toward the defendant at trial. Early research not specifically contrasting positive versus negative PTP indicated that PTP could influence jurors' verdicts in a way that was beneficial for the defendant (Otto & Penrod, 1991). In the context of an insanity case where judgments of "insanity" are positive for the defendant, PTP indicating the defendant was "insane" was associated with judgments that the defendant was insane, while PTP indicating the defendant was "sane" had the opposite, detrimental effect (Otto & Penrod, 1991). More recent research has specifically investigated the influence of positive versus negative PTP. Some of this research has found no beneficial effect of positive PTP. Woody and Viney (2007) exposed participants to either proprosecution or prodefense general PTP in a sexual assault case and found that both positive and negative PTP increased guilty verdicts, but there were no differences in verdicts between the positive and negative PTP (Woody & Viney, 2007). In contrast, other studies have found differences between the influence of positive and

negative PTP, indicating that positive PTP could benefit the defendant. Ruva and McEvoy (2008) exposed jurors to PTP about the defendant: PTP was positive, negative, or unrelated to the defendant prior to watching a prerecorded mock trial. Negative PTP resulted in more guilty verdicts than neutral PTP, and both negative and neutral PTP resulted in more guilty verdicts than positive PTP (Ruva & McEvoy, 2008). Ruva et al. (2011) found similar effects of positive versus negative PTP. They exposed participants to positive and negative PTP. Negative PTP resulted in more guilty verdicts, increases in ratings of defendant culpability, increases in predecisional distortion favoring the prosecution, and decreases in ratings of defendant credibility. Positive PTP had the opposite effect and resulted in jurors rendering more not guilty verdicts, decreases in ratings of defendant culpability, and increases in ratings of defendant credibility (Ruva et al., 2011). In addition to finding that positive PTP overall led to positive outcomes for and perceptions of the defendant, Ruva and Hudak (2013) also found that the effect of positive versus negative PTP may depend on the age of the juror, such that older mock jurors were more influenced by positive PTP and younger mock jurors were more influenced by negative PTP. Older mock jurors exposed to positive PTP were more likely to render not guilty verdicts and have positive impressions of the defendant, whereas younger mock jurors exposed to negative PTP were more likely to render guilty verdicts and have negative impressions of the defendant. They also found that source memory errors were more likely when jurors were exposed to negative than positive PTP (Ruva & Hudak, 2013). The effects of positive PTP on criminal defendants have also been investigated in the context of real-world cases. Jacquin and Hodges (2007) exposed mock jurors to unbiased PTP, sympathetic PTP, unsympathetic PTP, or no PTP from the Andrea Yates murder case prior to their reading a shortened version of the trial. Unsympathetic PTP, like negative PTP, increased guilty verdicts and the recommended sentence, and sympathetic PTP, like positive PTP, increased positive attitudes about post-partum depression and mentally ill offenders (Jacquin & Hodges, 2007). The effects of positive

PTP have also been examined in the context of civil cases. Bornstein, Whisenhunt, Nemeth, and Dunnaway (2002) presented participants with positive, negative, or neutral PTP about the defendant in a personal injury case. Participants were influenced by the negative PTP in their decision making, such that participants who read negative PTP about the defendant were more likely to find the defendant liable for the plaintiff's injury. Positive PTP, however, did not influence participants in their decision making (Bornstein, et al., 2002). The results of this area of research indicate that, while negative PTP can bias trial decision making against the subject of the PTP, positive PTP may create the opposite, positive bias toward the subject of the PTP at trial.

Research has also investigated the influence of the emotional content of PTP. Kramer, Kerr, & Carroll (1990) exposed mock jurors to either high or low amounts of factual or emotional PTP prior to watching a mock trial. The factual publicity contained information about the defendant's prior criminal record. The emotional publicity provided information about the defendant's involvement in an unrelated hit-and-run accident in which a child was killed. Results indicated that emotional PTP may bias jurors against the defendant more than negative, factual information about the defendant. Although there were no PTP effects on jurors' predeliberation verdicts, mock jurors exposed to emotional PTP were more likely to render guilty verdicts postdeliberation than jurors not exposed to this information. This indicates that emotionally evocative PTP can bias jurors against the defendant, even more so than negative but nonemotional PTP, which did not influence verdict in this research. In contrast, J. R. Wilson and Bornstein (1998) found that both factual and emotional PTP created bias against the defendant, including increased guilty verdicts. Emotional memory about and reactions to nonemotional PTP have also been investigated. Honess, Charman, and Levi (2003) investigated whether factual or emotional recall of PTP affected decision making. Emotionally laden recall of PTP increased proprosecution reasoning, decreased prodefense reasoning, and increased confidence in guilty verdicts. These effects were partially mediated by trial facts. Factual recall of PTP did not influence reasoning or

verdict (Honess et al., 2003). Ruva et al. (2011) examined the emotionality of recall for PTP and emotional reactions to PTP. They exposed jurors to positive, negative, or neutral PTP prior to their watching a prerecorded mock trial and measured jurors' recall for the PTP and emotional reactions. Jurors who were exposed to both negative and positive PTP used more emotional words in their recall of the PTP than jurors exposed to neutral PTP. Negative emotional words were used more often in recall and were associated with guilty verdicts when the PTP was negative, and positive emotional words were used more often in recall and were associated with not guilty verdicts when the PTP was positive. The type of PTP also affected jurors' emotional reactions to the trial. Negative PTP increased jurors' level of anger, and the increased levels of anger resulted in more guilty verdicts, higher culpability ratings, and reduced defendant credibility (Ruva et al., 2011). Overall, the research on emotional PTP indicates that it might exert a greater impact on decision making than factual PTP either directly, by increasing the amount of emotion in jurors' memory of the PTP, or by influencing the emotions experienced by the jurors.

The research described above demonstrates that PTP providing details about specific cases and defendants can affect perceptions of the defendants and decision making in those cases. While this is referred to as "case-specific PTP," information in the media about the legal system more broadly may also influence decision making in trials. This type of PTP is referred to as "general PTP" and can include information about similar cases, similar defendants, or the functioning of the legal system in general (Greene, 1990). Although the Steblay et al. (1999) meta-analysis found larger effect sizes for the relationship between PTP and guilty verdicts when the PTP was case-specific than when the PTP was more general in nature, general PTP also exerts a biasing impact on juror decision making. The first research to investigate the impact of general PTP found that both naturally occurring and experimentally manipulated PTP about mistaken eyewitness identifications reduced guilty verdicts in a mock trial involving an eyewitness (Greene & Loftus, 1984). The impact of stories about wrongful convictions has also been investigated in the research on general PTP. Greene and Wade (1988) presented participants with publicity about either a wrongful conviction due to an eyewitness misidentification, publicity about a serial killer committing heinous crimes, or unrelated publicity prior to rendering verdicts in an unrelated, armed-robbery trial. Publicity about wrongful conviction decreased guilty verdicts in the mock trial, but guilty verdicts were not more likely when participants read inflammatory information about a serial killer. Greene and Wade (1988) also found that general PTP affected decision making in an unrelated case more when the crimes described in the PTP and the crime being tried in the case were more similar (Greene & Wade, 1988). Woody and Viney (2007) investigated the impact of general PTP about wrongful conviction in the context of a sexual assault trial. They presented mock jurors in a sexual assault case with no PTP or general PTP about sexual assault that either favored the prosecution by describing a mistaken acquittal that resulted in additional sexual assaults or favored the defense by describing a wrongful conviction sexual assault. Contrary to expectation, jurors presented with both types of general PTP rendered more guilty verdicts than jurors presented with no PTP (Woody & Viney, 2007). Other studies have investigated the influence of general PTP about sexual assault on decision making in sexual assault cases. Kovera (2002) showed mock jurors televised stories that were unrelated to rape or were about rape and had either a prodefense or a proprosecution slant. The general PTP in the form of the rape stories influenced the participants' ratings of the witnesses and the amount of evidence required for a conviction. Specifically, participants exposed to prodefense general PTP required more evidence in order to convict a rape defendant (Kovera, 2002). Finally, Mullin, Imrich, and Linz (1996) compared the influence of antidefendant, case-specific PTP and prosecution-oriented, general PTP about acquaintance rape in a sexual assault case. Contrary to their hypothesis, they found that the general PTP resulted in male participants making more prodefense attributions and decisions, but the case-specific did not exert an impact on decision making (Mullin et al., 1996). Overall, this research demonstrates that general PTP can also influence jurors, more so when it is similar to the case at hand or about failures of the legal system such as wrongful convictions.

Overall, research on PTP indicates that it can affect jurors' evaluations of the evidence and verdict decision making in both civil and criminal cases. Jurors exposed to PTP are more likely to hold biased pretrial opinions about a defendant. Additionally, jurors who are able to recall more and more detailed information from the media are significantly more likely to perceive a defendant as guilty when compared to individuals who are unable to recall as many case details. The content of PTP can make it more influential. Negative PTP, case-specific PTP, PTP including inadmissible information, and emotionally laden PTP have the potential to influence jurors' perceptions of defendant culpability, which may lead to a significantly greater chance that a defendant is ultimately found guilty. In particular, negative information about the defendant's character or about a defendant's prior criminal history is particularly problematic. Jurors exposed to these types of PTP are more likely to perceive a defendant as guilty both pretrial and posttrial.

The CSI Effect. Procedural crime dramas that depict a group of police detectives or lawyers solving different cases each week are not new to television. This type of television show typically features a solved crime, with the team of investigators always "getting their man." Since the days of *Perry Mason*, American TV viewers have made this type of show popular. In 2000, *CSI: Crime Scene Investigation* (*CSI*) premiered. *CSI* is a procedural crime drama that provided the unique combination of crime fighting and science (Cole & Dioso-Villa, 2007). Instead of relying solely on their detective skills to solve crimes, *CSI*'s protagonists solve crimes with forensic science evidence, of which they typically find in abundance at their crime scenes. CSI has spawned several equally popular spin-offs (*CSI: Miami* and *CSI: New York*), and they were recognized as the most-watched television shows in the world in 2006 through 2009 (Gorman, 2010).

The prevalence and popularity of shows like *CSI* resulted in media discussions of the impact *CSI* viewership could have on decision making in real criminal cases, dubbed the *CSI Effect*, beginning in 2002 (Cole & Dioso-Villa, 2007). The CSI Effect, broadly defined, is the potential for crime dramas such as *CSI* and its progeny to provide viewers with unrealistic expectations about criminal investigations and forensic science, which may in turn influence perceptions of the legal system and jury decision making in real cases (Cole & Dioso-Villa, 2007; Tyler, 2006). Several studies have investigated the content of media reports on the CSI Effect. Harvey and Derksen (2009) content-coded popular media articles about the CSI Effect published from 2002 to 2005. The majority of the articles in their sample asserted that the CSI Effect exists and that it exerts a negative effect on jurors. Specifically, the media reported that the CSI Effect leads viewers to have unreasonably high expectations about forensic evidence, and the media asserted that this increase in expectations would result in more acquittals (Harvey & Derksen, 2009). Extending that research, Cole and Dioso-Villa (2009) content-coded popular media articles to examine the media's description of the CSI Effect. Consistent with the findings of Harvey and Derksen (2009), they found overwhelming evidence that the media believes in the CSI Effect, with very few articles expressing any doubt in the existence of the CSI Effect. They also found that the media overwhelmingly asserted that the effect of viewership on trials would be increased acquittals, not increased convictions (Cole & Dioso-Villa, 2009). Smith et al. (2011) also report content-coding news reports on the CSI Effect. Consistent with other research, they observed the news reporting that crime drama viewing makes jurors more likely to acquit. Additionally, they found media asserting that lawyers are changing the way that they try cases in response to this effect, that crime drama viewership increases student interest in obtaining a forensic science education, and that shows like *CSI* increase criminals' knowledge about forensic evidence (Smith et al., 2011). Overall, this research indicates that the media consistently proclaims the existence of the CSI Effect and that the outcome of the CSI Effect will be increased wrongful acquittals.

Consistent with the media reports, scholars also argue that these types of shows could negatively affect the criminal justice system. Arguments include that the shows present an unrealistic view of science (Kruse, 2010). The science presented in fictional dramas provides the absolute truth about a crime or a criminal suspect, which is equated with justice, whereas science in the real world provides information about probabilities, not absolutes (Kruse, 2010). Additional arguments for why these shows might be dangerous are that crime drama shows, especially those featuring forensic evidence, present a one-sided, prosecution-oriented view of the legal system because only the prosecution perspective on the cases is presented (Tyler, 2006). This type of information has the potential to affect jurors in trials in a manner similar to negative PTP about a defendant (Tyler, 2006). Although most of the media regarding the CSI Effect frames it in terms of a problem that results in wrongful acquittals, it is clear that there are other equally plausible negative effects of crime drama viewership on perceptions of the legal system. Contrary to the media representations of the CSI Effect, some commentators argue that shows like *CSI* could have positive effects on the legal system, such as a creating a well-informed jury, requiring the prosecution to explain and justify forensic evidence choices, and "return[ing] the focus to exonerating the innocent" (Catalani, 2006, p. 77). Tyler (2006) argued that it was equally plausible that effects favoring the defense could occur, such as lowered thresholds for convictions. *CSI*-like shows could also result in increased reliance on scientific evidence and increased perceptions of its credibility so that convictions become more likely when it is presented (Tyler, 2006).

The media and researchers use the general term CSI Effect to refer to a variety of possible effects on a variety of possible participants in the legal system, although it is clear that the CSI Effect may manifest itself in several ways. Cole and Dioso-Villa (2007) argue that discussion of and research on the CSI Effect should be specific about what legal players are being influenced and in what ways. In order to clarify descriptions of and research about the CSI Effect, they describe six potential types of CSI Effects that represent the different kinds of impact that crime drama viewership can potentially have on the legal system. The first is the *strong prosecutor effect*, in which a wrongful acquittal occurs when there is a lack of forensic evidence. In contrast, the *weak prosecutor effect* is defined as remedial steps taken by prosecutors to decrease the potential strong prosecutor effect, such as addressing issues of forensic science during *voir dire*, opening statements, and closing arguments. The weak prosecutor effect could also be exemplified by prosecutors introducing *negative witnesses*, whose purpose is to provide information about the reasonableness of the lack of forensic evidence (see also, Stevens, 2008). The *defense effect*, also called the "reverse CSI Effect" by Tyler (2006), is an increase in perceptions of the credibility of prosecution witnesses. This increase in the believability of prosecution witnesses, especially those presenting forensic science, could increase convictions and possibly wrongful convictions. The *producer's effect* is the potential for *CSI*-like shows to increase laypersons' knowledge about forensic evidence, which may result in a jury that is savvier about forensic evidence. The *professor's effect* is the potential for increased interest in forensic science programs by students, resulting in more people being educated as forensic scientists. Finally, the *police effect* is an increase in criminals' knowledge about forensic science resulting from viewership of shows featuring forensic science. This increased knowledge might result in crimes committed that leave less evidence to be analyzed by forensic science (Cole & Dioso-Villa, 2007). Cole and Dioso-Villa later added a seventh type of CSI Effect that they termed the *victim effect*, in which victims are more likely to expect that forensic evidence will be collected during the investigation of their cases, resulting in certain expectations about the police and the legal system as it relates to the prosecution of their cases (Cole & Dioso-Villa, 2009). Cole and Dioso-Villa argue that the strong prosecutor, defense, and police effects would be the most dangerous for the functioning of the legal system (Cole & Dioso-Villa, 2009). They also suggest that researchers, scholars, and commentators should be specific about which effect they predict when discussing and researching the CSI Effect (Cole & Dioso-Villa, 2007).

Despite the voluminous discussion about the existence of the CSI Effect and the media's proclamation of its existence, many researchers question whether it exists in any of its potential forms. As Tyler highlights, most of the data supporting the existence of the CSI Effect is anecdotal evidence obtained from surveys of attorneys about their perceptions of their courtroom experiences (Tyler, 2006). Survey research conducted on attorneys indicates that attorneys believe the CSI Effect influences their cases even though there may be no actual impact of crime drama viewership on real cases. Podlas (2006b) conducted a short survey of prosecutors, 50% of whom identified specific cases in which they thought the CSI Effect had influenced the verdict. When these cases were examined, all but one resulted in guilty verdicts indicating that the CSI Effect did not result in the predicted high number of acquittals in these cases (Podlas, 2006b). Survey research not only indicates that attorneys believe the CSI Effect exists but also that attorneys have modified their litigation strategies to compensate for this perceived effect. Maricopa County, Arizona (2005) conducted a survey of prosecuting attorneys on their beliefs about the CSI Effect and their observations of it in their own cases. The majority of attorney respondents thought jurors expected forensic evidence to be presented and were disappointed when it was not presented. Thirty-eight percent of prosecutors believed they got a not guilty verdict in a case due to a lack of forensic evidence. The majority of prosecutors reported changing their practice to include asking questions related to the CSI Effect during *voir dire* and discussing the CSI Effect in their opening statements and closing arguments (Maricopa County, 2005). A survey of attorneys in Florida also indicated that attorneys believe crime shows create jurors' expectations that forensic evidence will be presented and that attorneys modify their trial strategies to account for this expectation (Watkins, 2004). Stevens (2008) surveyed prosecutors on how the CSI Effect influences prosecutorial decisions. The majority of prosecutors in this survey believed that jurors are always influenced by forensic evidence, regardless of its quality. Despite this belief, they did not think that the availability of forensic evidence or the perceived presence of CSI Effect affected their decisions about whether to prosecute in their cases. They reported using "negative evidence witnesses" to compensate for a lack of forensic evidence (Stevens, 2008). Overall, this research indicates that attorneys believe that the CSI Effect exists, that the impact of the effect is to increase jurors' expectations for the presentation of forensic evidence and improperly increases acquittals, and that attorneys have modified their litigation strategies to combat these perceived effects.

Other players in the criminal justice system may also believe the CSI Effect exists, and that belief may have real or perceived effects on their jobs within the legal system. Stinson, Patry, and Smith (2007) surveyed police about their observations of the CSI Effect. Police respondents believed that crime drama shows affected the public's perceptions of the police, police procedures, and the criminal justice system. They thought crime drama shows increased public knowledge about investigative techniques. Police observed that the public expected investigations to be faster than how they proceed in reality and that the public expected forensic evidence to be available more often than it is in reality. The police surveyed also observed that jurors were more informed about forensic evidence, which affected how they presented their testimony in court (Stinson et al., 2007). These results provide some evidence that Cole and Dioso-Villa's (2007) police effect and producer's effect have been observed in police practice. Weaver, Salamonson, Koch, and Porter (2012) surveyed forensic science students about the CSI Effect, finding that although crime dramas inaccurately and sometimes unprofessionally portray the field of forensic science, they are influencing more students to enter forensic science programs and act as a recruitment tool, providing evidence for Cole and Dioso-Villa's (2007) professor effect. Providing evidence of a belief in the producer's effect (Cole & Dioso-Villa, 2007), Hayes and Levett (2013) surveyed community members about the CSI Effect and found that they believed people who watch crime dramas have more knowledge about crime scene investigation.

Even though the media consistently proclaims that the CSI Effect poses a real-world problem for the legal system (Cole & Dioso-Villa, 2007, 2009), it has been argued that there is a lack of empirical data demonstrating that the CSI Effect actually exists or

demonstrating what type of effect on jurors is most likely to occur (Tyler, 2006). The biggest question raised in the media about the CSI Effect is how it will influence juror decision making in real trials. One of the claims about the CSI Effect is that crime drama viewership will increase expectations about the presentation of forensic science evidence and about the quality of that forensic evidence. Confirming the media's suspicions, several studies have demonstrated that crime drama viewership increases expectations about forensic science in the courtroom. Baskin and Sommers (2010) conducted a public opinion poll of 1,201 registered California voters in which they asked how reliable participants thought various types of evidence were (i.e., DNA, fingerprints, and testimony by police, victims, medical experts, and eyewitnesses). Participants judged the scientific evidence, such as DNA and fingerprint evidence, as more reliable than testimony by police, victims, and eyewitnesses. The scientific evidence was rated as even more reliable by TV viewers watching more than three hours per week of crime dramas. These participants also reported that they would be less likely to convict a rape or murder defendant without forensic evidence, providing evidence of Cole and Dioso-Villa's strong prosecutor effect (Baskin & Sommers, 2010). Other researchers have found increases in expectations about forensic science evidence across several studies (Kim, Barak, & Shelton, 2009; Shelton, 2010; Shelton, Kim, & Barak, 2006, 2009). In several surveys of community members, crime drama viewers had higher expectations that forensic science evidence would be presented in trials than nonviewers (Kim et al., 2009; Shelton, 2010; Shelton et al., 2006, 2009), and expectations for the presence of forensic science at trial were higher in cases involving violent crimes (Shelton et al., 2006). Across two dissertation studies, Tapscott (2012) observed that high levels of crime drama viewing were related to increased knowledge about the criminal justice system and to increased expectations that scientific evidence would be presented in trials, particularly DNA evidence, consistent with other research on raised expectations (Tapscott, 2012). Overall, the research on the effect of crime drama viewership and expectations about trials provides evidence that jurors may expect forensic evidence to be presented more often than it actually is, especially in trials for violent crimes.

Perhaps the most important question about the CSI Effect is whether exposure to shows like *CSI* can influence jury verdicts in real court cases. Little research has been conducted on the influence of the CSI Effect on verdict decisions in actual cases, but the extant research does not provide consistent evidence of an impact on verdicts in real trials. Cole and Dioso-Villa (2007; 2009) investigated whether there was an actual increase in acquittals after the creation and airing of *CSI*. They investigated acquittal rates in federal courts from 1945 to 2005, finding a decrease in acquittals over time but not finding any significant increase in acquittals in the ten years surrounding the premiere of *CSI* until a decrease occurred in 2005 (Cole & Dioso-Villa, 2007). They also investigated changes in acquittal rates in cases from eight states. They found an increase in acquittals just after *CSI* first appeared on television in 2001 and 2002, but the amount of acquittals decreased again to pre-*CSI* levels. Their findings agree with research demonstrating no change in acquittal rates in several states post-*CSI* (Loeffler, 2006, as cited in Cole & Dioso-Villa, 2007). Cole and Dioso-Villa argued for the possibility that acquittals were already rising prior to *CSI*, which would account for the brief post-*CSI* increase they observed (Cole & Dioso-Villa, 2007). They also argue that just looking at acquittal rates over time ignores the potential that *CSI* has a variety of effects on verdicts. For example, in some cases the CSI Effect could be the strong prosecutor effect, resulting in increased acquittals, whereas in other cases it could be the defense effect, resulting in decreased acquittals (Cole & Dioso-Villa, 2007, 2009). The variety of effects could be cancelling each other out in the measurement of base acquittal rates. Thus, evaluating acquittal rates in real cases alone may be missing some of the more nuanced consequences of the CSI Effect in real cases (Cole & Dioso-Villa, 2009). Overall, they conclude that research on actual acquittal rates provides very limited evidence of a "strong prosecutor" type of CSI Effect (Cole & Dioso-Villa, 2007, 2009).

Experimental, laboratory research on the CSI Effect may be able to address the more complex issues of whether and how the CSI Effect influences verdicts. Although some laboratory research has examined the relationship between crime drama viewership and juror verdicts, this research has found little evidence that watching crime dramas influences juror verdicts. Cole and Dioso-Villa (2007) argue that, for research to demonstrate a CSI Effect on jury decision making that is consistent with the media concern, such research would have to include a mock trial containing adequate, nonforensic evidence of guilt in which mock jurors who are CSI-type viewers would acquit the defendant at higher rates than mock jurors who are nonviewers. Several studies have exposed mock jurors to a mock trial containing forensic evidence and measured participants' viewership of crime dramas to determine if increased viewership affects jury verdicts. Most of the research on the CSI Effect, however, has used trials containing forensic evidence and has found no effect of crime drama viewership on verdict. For example, Schweitzer and Saks (2007) had jurors read a transcript for a murder trial with forensic evidence about hair found in the perpetrator's ski mask and rendered a verdict. They also measured perceptions of the trial evidence and crime drama viewership. Participants who viewed scientifically oriented crime dramas reported a perceived increase in their understanding of the scientific evidence, were more critical of the forensic evidence in the trial, and found the forensic evidence less believable, but there were no differences in verdicts based on viewership (Schweitzer & Saks, 2007). Mancini (2011) measured crime drama viewership and presented jurors with a mock trial including potentially tainted forensic evidence, and jurors rendered verdicts and answered questions about their opinions of the prosecution's forensic evidence (Mancini, 2011). Although heavy crime drama viewers reported requiring a higher percentage of guilt to find a guilty verdict, there were no differences in verdict decisions in the mock trial based on crime drama viewership. Increased viewership influenced perceptions of the forensic evidence in the case. Heavier viewers were less satisfied with the prosecution's evidence and reported problems with or a lack of forensic evidence more often than lighter viewers. There were no differences, however, between heavy and light crime drama viewers in how familiar they thought they were with forensic evidence (Mancini, 2011). Shelton et al. (2006, 2009) presented two large, community-member mock-juror samples with several types of mock criminal trials and measured willingness to convict in the mock trials, in addition to participants' crime drama viewership and expectations about forensic science evidence, as discussed above. Although crime drama viewership increased expectations about the presentation of forensic science, crime drama viewership had no relationship to willingness to convict in any of the trials in either study (Shelton et al., 2006, 2009). Shelton (2010) combined the data from these previous studies and reported that there was no overall difference in actual verdicts between viewers and nonviewers, further indicating that viewership of crime dramas does not have a direct effect on verdict decision making. In contrast, Podlas (2006a) exposed mock juror participants to a rape trial with no forensic evidence. Consistent with other research, there was no relationship between crime drama viewership and verdict. In a separate study, Podlas (2006b) exposed mock jurors to a variety of cases containing no forensic evidence and again found no relationship between crime drama viewership and verdict across these case types.

Other research has found a limited effect of crime drama viewership on verdicts. For example, Hayes-Smith and Levett (2011) manipulated the amount of forensic evidence presented to jurors during a mock trial and measured crime drama viewership and verdict. Amount of forensic evidence did not affect verdict, nor was there an interaction between forensic evidence and crime drama viewership. As the amount of general television viewing increased, however, guilty verdicts decreased and confidence in verdict increased. In addition, heavy viewers presented with no forensic evidence were less confident in their verdicts and more confident when there was forensic evidence (Hayes-Smith & Levett, 2011). Kim et al. (2009) reanalyzed the data from one of their earlier studies (Shelton et al., 2006) to investigate potential indirect effects of viewership on verdict. They again found no direct effect of crime drama viewership on verdict, but they did find an indirect effect of crime

drama viewership on verdict in cases involving only nonscientific, circumstantial evidence. Crime drama viewership increased expectations for the presentation of forensic science evidence, and the increased expectations led to fewer convictions in circumstantial cases in which forensic science was not presented (Kim et al., 2009). Therefore, there is some evidence that general television viewing can affect verdicts, and crime drama viewing can indirectly affect verdicts by increasing expectations.

All of the research on the CSI Effect described so far has measured crime drama viewership and attempted to determine whether that viewership was associated with evidentiary perceptions and verdict decisions. Few published studies to date have experimentally manipulated exposure to *CSI*-type shows to determine if there is a causal relationship between viewership and legal decision making. Some unpublished research manipulating type and amount of exposure to crime dramas indicates that these factors do not relate to mock juror verdicts. For example, in addition to examining the effect of viewership on expectations as described above, Tapscott's dissertation (2012) also manipulated type of television exposure by exposing participants to four episodes of crime dramas, medical dramas, or no television prior to rendering verdicts in a mock trial. Using the same case scenarios as Shelton et al. (2006, 2009), Tapscott (2012) also found no effect of crime viewership, or more specifically type of television viewership, on verdicts in these cases (Tapscott, 2012). In a review article, Smith et al. (2011) mention conducting a study in which jurors watched zero, four, or eight episodes of *CSI* in which they found that participants who watched either four or eight episodes rated DNA evidence as more accurate and reliable than participants who watched no *CSI*; however, this study has not yet been published on its own.

Given the limited effects of crime drama viewership on expectations for the presentation of forensic evidence and on actual or mock jury verdicts, Shelton et al. (2006) argue that the CSI Effect may be better conceptualized as a "tech effect." In the tech effect, they propose that effects on juror behavior that have been attributed to *CSI*-type shows may not be caused solely by viewership of the shows. Instead, they may be caused by the development of the underlying technology that is depicted in the program. Information about developments in this technology is widely available, and they argue it is part of our culture in ways that extend beyond viewing a certain type of television show (Shelton et al., 2006). This information about forensic science capabilities, accurate or not, can influence expectations about forensic science in court and potentially jury verdicts. Jurors may assume the technology exists and that it will be used in trials (Shelton et al., 2009). Therefore, referring to any influence of expectations about science in the courtroom as a CSI Effect narrows and simplifies a complex problem by ignoring a multitude of sources for information about forensic science (Shelton et al., 2006). This may partially account for the lack of CSI Effect found in empirical studies. On that topic, similar to their arguments that researchers should carefully distinguish among types of CSI Effects, Cole and Dioso-Villa also argue that research on the various CSI Effects should be careful to distinguish them from the tech effect described by Shelton (Cole & Dioso-Villa, 2009). Shelton et al. (2009) found some evidence of the tech effect. Participants in their survey were very familiar with technology like smart phones and computers, indicating access to the information on technology. The vast majority of participants thought police departments had the capabilities to perform tests like ballistics, fingerprints, and DNA analysis; and almost half of the participants thought these technologies should be used in every case. However, personal use of technology and exposure to general media about forensic technology increased expectations about the use of forensic evidence in trials less than crime drama viewership, indicating the presence of a tech effect on expectations that is weaker than the CSI Effect on expectations (Shelton et al., 2009).

Overall, it is clear from the research that many people in the media and in the criminal justice system believe that prosecution-oriented, science-heavy shows like *CSI* are influencing how jurors understand evidence and make decisions in real trials. The media portrays this effect mainly as an increased likelihood for wrongful acquittals, but various potential effects have been identified. Although the media is confident in the existence of some

influence of crime drama viewership on the legal system, research has demonstrated very limited effects of viewership on the jury. Crime drama viewership may increase expectations people have about the presentation of forensic evidence, especially in certain types of cases, but research has shown that these raised expectations do not necessarily affect case verdicts.

The influence of social media.   The use of social media and social networking sites like Facebook, Twitter, LinkedIn, and others has risen dramatically and continues to rise (St. Eve & Zuckerman, 2012). This has created a variety of issues in the legal system. For example, potential employers and educational institutions have used information posted by applicants on social media sites during the hiring process, leading to claims of employment discrimination and invasion of privacy (Brutocao, 2012). Social media posts have also been identified as a potential ethical problem for lawyers and judges in terms of what they post to the internet, comments that are made on their posts, and who they "friend" on these sites (Criss, 2012; Pitluk, 2012). Social media websites are used as a source of information on suspects and crimes during an investigation, but issues have arisen about the reliability and admissibility of evidence gathered from social media sites (Morales, 2012). Finally, multiple intersections between social media and jurors have been identified, and most of the research attention in the area has been focused on the problems associated with them, which will be summarized here.

One intersection between social media and jurors is when social media is used as a tool by attorneys to research jurors either prior to or during *voir dire*. Internet investigation of the venire by attorneys prior to *voir dire* is common when the names of venirepersons are made available (Hoffmeister, 2011). Information found on social media sites also could be used by attorneys to tailor their case themes, opening statements, and closing arguments (Babcock & Gilman, 2012; Hoffmeister, 2011). It has been argued that using social media to investigate jurors could have several positive effects on the trial process. Social media content could be used to uncover juror fraud from dishonesty during *voir dire* or to uncover juror misconduct or favoritism (Hoffmeister, 2011). Biases that could affect trial fairness may be more easily uncovered on social media sites than during a traditional *voir dire* because jurors may be more honest online (Babcock & Gilman, 2012; Hoffmeister, 2011) and attorneys will be able to track potential jurors' likes and dislikes over time (Babcock & Gilman, 2012). Assuming jurors are aware of these investigations, they may be more honest in their responses during *voir dire* (Babcock & Gilman, 2012; Hoffmeister, 2011), and they may be less likely to engage in inappropriate posting about the trial if they are under the impression that their online activity is being monitored (Hoffmeister, 2011). Social media sites also allow for investigations of juror misconduct, which could help increase trial fairness if discovered and reported (Babcock & Gilman, 2012; Hoffmeister, 2011). Misconduct could be either active in which jurors are intentionally seeking information about the trial and inappropriately posting about it, or passive in which jurors are exposed to information on these sites during their normal usage of them (Hecht & Secco, 2012).

Of course, legal players using information about jurors found on social media sites for these purposes raises significant issues of invasion of privacy (Hoffmeister, 2011). Currently, there is no prohibition against attorneys using publically available information posted on social media sites to inform their decision making during jury selection. As long as they are generally following the rules of ethics that govern professional legal practice, this procedure is permissible (Babcock & Gilman, 2012; Hoffmeister, 2011). Therefore, this use of social media is not a paramount concern for courts at this time. On the other hand, jurors' access to outside information or potentially engaging in misconduct during a trial is of concern to courts.

The most commonly raised problem with social media and the jury is the potential for risk to trial fairness associated with jurors' online activity (Dunn, 2011; Hecht & Secco, 2012; Hoffmeister, 2012; Munisteri, 2012; Simpler, 2012; St. Eve & Zuckerman, 2012). Jurors' use of social media sites during the course of a trial poses the risk of exposing jurors to outside information similar to PTP, to watching the news, or to conducting internet searches (Simpler, 2012). Concerns about jurors' use of social media have also been raised regarding jurors' release of confidential information about the trial or about the deliberations in posts written on social media sites (Simpler, 2012). These problems can also occur simultaneously. When considering whether a juror's tweets during the trial interfered with the defendant's right to an impartial jury, the court in the Third Circuit described the multiple problems created by social media as follows:

> Not unlike a juror who speaks with friends or family members about a trial before the verdict is returned, a juror who comments about a case on the internet or social media may engender responses that include extraneous information about the case, or attempts to exercise persuasion and influence. If anything, the risk of such prejudicial communication may be greater when a juror comments on a blog or social media website than when she has a discussion about the case in person, given that the universe of individuals who are able to see and respond to a comment on Facebook or a blog is significantly larger. (*United States v. Fumo*, 2011, p. 305)

Concerns raised about social media additionally include that its use by jurors will "chill" discussions during deliberations because jurors will be afraid that what they say will be broadcast on the internet (Hoffmeister, 2012; Simpler, 2012; St. Eve & Zuckerman, 2012).

Some surveys of judges have been conducted to examine the extent to which these problems have been observed in real courtrooms and what remedies judges are currently using; however, there is little research on this topic. The Federal Judicial Center conducted the most extensive of these surveys asking judges to report on the frequency of problems associated with social media, their reactions to uncovering problems, and any preventative measures they use (Dunn, 2011). Judges reported that juror misconduct on social media sites was rare, but when it occurred it comprised a variety of behaviors including posting information about the trial, posting information about other jurors, and "friending" trial players. They admit juror misconduct of this type is difficult to discover, and mostly they learn of it because another juror or a lawyer reports it to them. When misconduct is discovered, the judges reported using a variety of responses depending on the severity of the misconduct, which included removal of the juror, cautioning the juror, and declaring a mistrial (Dunn, 2011).

Overall, the use of social media by various participants in the legal system, especially by jurors during a trial, has the potential to seriously affect the fairness of the legal system. There are a variety of ways these types of media and communication outlets are being used in courts that stretch the bounds of ethical and legal responsibility. Many commentators have expressed concerns over the perceived influence social media has and will have on the trial process. Although some survey research has been conducted on its presence in the courtroom, there is very little empirical information indicating if and how social media is exerting an influence on the courtroom. Further research in this area is needed.

PRACTICE AND POLICY ISSUES

Media exposure and use have several implications for the practice of law and for legal policies. As already discussed, media can influence perceptions of others, perceptions of the legal system, perceptions of evidence during trials, and decision making during trials. Although media is related to the law in a variety of ways, the proposed solutions to these various problems are similar. One overarching theme in the response to media by the law is selective censorship. This can include either preventing the public from exposure to the media entirely or limiting the exposure by public policy. This approach happens very infrequently because of First Amendment protections. A second theme in the response policies are techniques used in the various settings to prevent exposure from affecting critical behaviors. Examples of this include limiting children's exposure to violent television or limiting jurors' exposure to news accounts during a trial. Finally, media itself could be used as a means to reduce unwanted behaviors or change behavior. For

example, people could be exposed to media intended to make desired behaviors more likely. Although much of the research has focused on the negative effects of the media on perceptions of the court system and its participants, some research has investigated the power of the media to positively influence perceptions of the legal system. B. J. Wilson, Linz, Donnerstein, and Stipp (1992) found that participants who were randomly assigned to watch a movie on date rape had less acceptance of rape myths and were more likely to perceive rape as a social problem than participants who did not view the movie. Positive PTP as a means to counteract the effect of negative PTP is another example of the use of media itself to counteract the effects of media (Ruva et al., 2011; Ruva & Hudak, 2013; Ruva & McEvoy, 2008). Presenting material in the media that is likely to counteract negative media influences on the legal system may be effective, but it may not be practical to implement from a policy perspective.

Practice and policy issues related to media and trials mostly focus on strategies that courts can use to reduce the impact of various media influences on legal decision making. There are common approaches courts take when attempting to mitigate the effect of media exposure on trial decision making, whether that exposure is to PTP, crime dramas, or social media. One option is restricting exposure to the offending media generally, which is often impractical or impossible to accomplish. The first line of defense against the influence of the media during a trial is the *voir dire* process. A second approach is for attorneys to tailor their cases to counteract potential media influences. Trial procedures also can be used that might minimize media effects. Finally, jury instructions that specifically target inappropriate reliance on media sources in the jury decision are commonly used. The research on the manifestation and effectiveness of these strategies in cases involving various types of media exposure is described below.

Safeguards against the influence of PTP are the most thoroughly researched responses to the effects of media on trials. The research on the influence of PTP on trial decision making clearly demonstrates that PTP has the potential to negatively impact defendants' constitutionally guaranteed trial fairness, therefore research has also examined strategies to counteract the influence of PTP on trials. One option to prevent this problem is to reduce the information that is available to the public about defendants and trials, but courts have been very reluctant to restrict the press's coverage of and access to trials because of the First Amendment right to a free press. In *Sheppard v. Maxwell* (1966), the Supreme Court suggested that some limits on the press may be necessary to ensure trial fairness. Since then, however, the Supreme Court has ruled several times that restraining the press is an unacceptable violation of the First Amendment. For example, the Supreme Court ruled that gag orders preventing the media from publishing information about the trial violate the First Amendment (*Nebraska Press Association v. Stuart*, 1976). The Court has also ruled that courtrooms should not be closed to either the press or the general public (*Richmond Newspapers v. Virginia*, 1980).

Although courts may be prevented from restricting the media's access to a trial, judges do have the capacity to discourage or to prevent the attorneys and witnesses in their courtrooms from providing prejudicial information about their cases to the media, as was done in the Andrea Yates case (CNN, 2007). The American Bar Association's (ABA) *Model Rules of Professional Conduct* (2006) suggests restricting the type of information attorneys can provide to the media about their cases. Under the Model Rules, attorneys are prohibited from making public statements about information that would have a substantial likelihood of prejudicing a legal proceeding. The Model Rules specifically mention statements about the defendant's character, prior criminal record, confessions, and polygraph results. The Model Rules also prohibit attorneys from sharing their own opinions on the defendant's guilt or innocence and from providing information to the media that would likely be inadmissible at trial (ABA, 2006). Research indicates that these guidelines do not eliminate the publication of prejudicial PTP. Imrich, Mullin, and Linz (1995) investigated how frequently ABA-prohibited information was published in newspapers and found that proscribed statements appeared in the media for 27% of criminal suspects, particularly information about the

defendant's prior criminal record and confessions. Dixon and Linz (2002) expanded this investigation to television and found that 19% percent of the stories contained an ABA-prohibited statement. In this body of research, however, there were few prohibited statements that were specifically attributable to attorneys in the cases (Dixon & Linz, 2002; Imrich et al., 1995). These studies indicate that the ABA guidelines for attorneys do not by themselves eradicate prejudicial information about trials from the media.

Several legal and courtroom procedures exist that may be effective safeguards against the effects of PTP on juror decision making. These safeguards include individual *voir dire*, extended *voir dire*, judicial admonitions to disregard PTP information, the deliberation process, continuance, and change of venue (Lieberman & Arndt, 2000; Studebaker & Penrod, 1997). Much of the research done on these potential safeguards indicates, however, that they are not effective and that they may even magnify the biasing influence of PTP (Kramer et al., 1990; Lieberman & Arndt, 2000; Studebaker & Penrod, 1997). For example, the research investigating *voir dire* as a safeguard against PTP indicates that it may not be effective. In *Mu'Min v. Virginia* (1991), the U.S. Supreme Court affirmed that an abbreviated *voir dire* may be appropriate even in cases involving extensive PTP. It is theorized that an extended *voir dire*, which includes more involved questioning of venirepersons about their exposure to and willingness to set aside PTP information, will enable attorneys to uncover bias resulting from PTP exposure, but research on the effectiveness of extended *voir dire* demonstrates that it may not be effective. People are sometimes not forthcoming, and when they are, they do not recognize that they are biased by it or they want to appear impartial (Studebaker & Penrod, 1997).

Early research on *voir dire* and PTP found low percentages of jurors that were exposed to negative PTP reported being biased in the case in response to a typical *voir dire* type of question. Exposure to negative PTP was related to verdicts, however, even though participants reported impartiality, indicating that jurors may be unaware of this bias or unwilling to report it during *voir dire* (Sue, Smith, & Pedroza, 1975). Other early research indicated that *voir dire* might be an effective remedy (Padawer-Singer, Singer, & Singer, 1974). This study examined jurors who were exposed or were not exposed to negative publicity about the defendant and then either selected for a jury with no *voir dire* or with a traditional, attorney-conducted *voir dire*. When participants were selected via *voir dire*, the exposed jurors were less likely to vote guilty than the exposed jurors who were not selected through *voir dire*. Unexposed jurors who were selected via *voir dire* were more likely to vote guilty than those who were not selected through *voir dire*, indicating that the *voir dire* process may have created some bias for unexposed jurors (Padawer-Singer et al., 1974). Moran and Cutler (1991) surveyed potential jurors exposed to natural PTP in real drug distribution and murder cases about their knowledge of the cases and their ability to be impartial. The amount of knowledge jurors reported having about the cases was related to their judgments of the defendants' culpability, but it was not related to their self-reported ability to be impartial (Moran & Cutler, 1991).

Judges' and attorneys' ability to uncover juror bias through extended *voir dire* has also been examined. As part of their study on the impact of factual versus emotional PTP and the effectiveness of various safeguards against PTP, Kramer et al. (1990) recorded the mock jurors during a *voir dire* after they were exposed to PTP or not exposed. Kerr, Kramer, Carroll, and Alfini (1991) sent the *voir dire* videos, information about the trial, and information about the PTP in the case to defense attorneys, prosecutors, and trial judges. The attorneys and judges were asked to indicate which jurors they would excuse based on their responses during the *voir dire*. Jurors' self-reports of being definitely biased, possibly biased, not biased by the PTP during the *voir dire* were related to whether defense attorneys and judges exercised challenges against them, but these self-reports of bias were not related to prosecutors' exercise of challenges. Of the jurors exposed to PTP, there were no differences in verdict between jurors who were not excused during *voir dire* and those who were either excused by judges for cause or by defense attorneys exercising peremptory challenges. Only prosecutorial peremptory challenges were related to verdict, with challenged jurors being less

likely to favor a guilty verdict. Seventy-two percent of attorneys believed they accurately asserted their challenges when only 45% of the challenges were actually accurate, indicating the attorneys had an inflated perception of their ability to detect and eliminate biased jurors. Together these results indicate that challenges during *voir dire* might not eliminate jurors who have prejudged the case (Kerr et al., 1991). Dexter, Cutler, and Moran (1992) investigated whether a more extensive *voir dire* would reduce the bias created by the PTP by manipulating the length and content of the *voir dire* process (either 60 or 15 minutes). They found that the longer, more involved *voir dire* did not reduce PTP bias more than the shorter *voir dire* (Dexter et al., 1992). Overall, this research indicates that *voir dire* may not effectively distinguish between potential jurors who have been biased by PTP and those who have not.

Judicial instructions admonishing the jury to disregard PTP information in their decision making have also been suggested as a potential PTP remedy. In these judicial admonitions, jurors are told that they should not rely on PTP as a source of information or influence in their decisions, but research demonstrates that instructions may not effectively reduce PTP bias (Studebaker & Penrod, 1997). Early research including judicial instructions to disregard still found effects of biasing PTP in juror decision making (see, e.g., Kline & Jess, 1966; Padawer-Singer et al., 1974; Padawer-Singer, Singer, & Singer, 1977; Sue, Smith, & Gilbert, 1974). Kramer et al. (1990) investigated whether judicial admonitions about PTP presented as jury instructions were able to decrease the negative effects of PTP they observed. Judicial admonitions did not decrease the negative impact of PTP or affect jury verdicts. In fact, instructions increased the biasing effect of factual PTP (Kramer et al., 1990). Bornstein et al. (2002) also investigated the impact of judicial admonitions while varying the presence or absence of biasing PTP. Participants did not receive a PTP admonition, received one after trial only, or received one both before and after trial. The admonition did not decrease the effect of negative PTP; however, the admonition reduced the perceived culpability of the defendant regardless of the PTP presence when presented both before and after trial (Bornstein et al.,

2002). Kline and Jess (1966) and Ruva and LaVasseur (2012) found that even when jurors were instructed to disregard the PTP, they still discussed the PTP during deliberations. Freedman, Martin, and Mota (1998) admonished jurors to disregard information from outside of the trial after exposing jurors to negative and neutral PTP. The admonition reduced guilty verdicts regardless of type of PTP exposure (Freedman et al., 1998). Results from these studies indicate that judicial admonitions to ignore biasing PTP may be an ineffective safeguard. Some researchers argue that admonitions are ineffective because the information jurors are instructed to ignore is emotional, and it may be difficult to consciously disregard this type of information (Kramer et al., 1990).

Research also has investigated the effectiveness of deliberations as a safeguard against PTP. Deliberations might decrease PTP effects because they provide the opportunity for jurors to reprimand each other for relying on information from PTP that was not part of the trial evidence. Research on deliberations and PTP, however, indicates that they might increase the impact of PTP instead of decrease it. For example, Kramer et al. (1990) found that deliberations increased the impact of emotional PTP on verdict, resulting in more postdeliberation convictions than those not exposed to this information. Additionally, jurors exposed to high levels of emotional PTP who favored conviction were more persuasive during deliberations (Kramer et al., 1990). Ruva, McEvoy, and Bryant (2007) manipulated whether jurors deliberated after being exposed to PTP that was negative or neutral toward the defendant and watching a prerecorded trial. Exposure to PTP increased the number of guilty verdicts overall, but deliberations did not decrease guilty verdicts on the group level, although they did reduce the number of postdeliberation guilty verdicts at the individual level. Deliberations reduced assessments of the credibility of the defendant, and they did not decrease the number of source-monitoring errors for information provided in the PTP (Ruva et al., 2007). Ruva and LeVasseur (2012) content-coded 30 jury deliberations and found that PTP was discussed even though jurors were instructed not to discuss the PTP, and jurors did not often admonish each other not to discuss the PTP, which is one of the

potential benefits of deliberations. PTP also influenced the deliberations by increasing the discussion of and the persuasiveness of ambiguous prosecution facts but not of ambiguous defense facts (Ruva & LeVasseur, 2012). The Steblay et al. (1999) meta-analysis provides additional evidence for the potential backfire effect of deliberations. The average relationship between PTP and verdict was stronger after deliberations than before deliberations, indicating that PTP exerts even more effect after deliberations (Steblay et al., 1999).

The use of a continuance, or a delay between the appearance of PTP in the media and the start of the trial, has also been suggested as a viable safeguard against PTP (Studebaker & Penrod, 1997). A continuance would theoretically reduce the influence of PTP due to normal forgetting or due to a decrease in the salience of the information. For example, Davis (1986) found that the relationship between negative PTP and guilty decisions was smaller after a one-week delay than with no delay. Kramer et al. (1990) also found some evidence that a continuance may be an effective remedy. Delay between exposure to PTP and the trial decreased the negative impact of exposure to factual PTP. Such delay, however, did not attenuate the negative effect of exposure to emotional PTP (Kramer et al., 1990). The results of the Steblay et al. (1999) meta-analysis also indicated that continuance increased the size of the effect between PTP and guilty verdicts, with the largest effects occurring when the delay was longer than one week. Therefore, some research on the effectiveness of continuance indicates that delay might actually magnify PTP effects. Other research has found that delay may increase source-memory errors even when verdicts are not affected. Delay may make it more likely for jurors to misidentify facts as having been presented during the trial when they were actually presented in the PTP (Ruva & McEvoy, 2008). Overall, the research on the effectiveness of continuance is mixed. Even assuming continuance was an effective remedy for PTP effects, the potential for mid-trial publicity to occur (see Vidmar, 2002) may make it ineffective to implement as a safeguard in real-world cases.

Although experimental research has not been conducted on the effectiveness of change of venue, case study research indicates that it may be an effective safeguard unless the publicity is extensive and nationwide. Nietzel and Dillehay (1983) reported the results of community surveys conducted in five separate murder cases that were used to support change of venue motions in those cases. In all five surveys, more respondents in the trial venue had case-related knowledge than respondents in alternative locations. Additionally, respondents in the trial venue were more likely to perceive the defendant as guilty compared to respondents in alternative locations, indicating that a change of venue to the alternate locations would reduce antidefendant bias (Nietzel & Dillehay, 1983). Arbuthnot, Myers, and Leach (2002) argue that actual knowledge of the case, which may be higher in the original venue where publicity is high, has the biggest impact on prejudgment and should be measured in a change of venue survey. They conducted a change of venue survey for a murder case and found that actual case knowledge was a significant predictor of prejudgment of the defendant's guilt, and knowledge was a better predictor than demographics, attitudes, or perceived familiarity with the case (Arbuthnot et al., 2002). These two case studies indicate that change of venue may be a viable safeguard against PTP and suggest ways to identify bias and good alternate venues. In nationally publicized cases, however, change of venue may not be a viable safeguard. Vidmar (2003) studied the effects of PTP on jurors' prejudgment in a nationally publicized and emotionally charged case, the trial of John Phillip Walker Lindh, in support of a potential change of venue. As in many nationally publicized cases, participants who were exposed to more PTP and who recalled more information about the case held unfavorable opinions about the defendant. In addition, the amount of prejudgment about the case was relatively consistent across potential venues. These results indicate that national PTP has the potential to bias the potential jurors in many locations, making a change of venue less effective as a safeguard against PTP-related bias. Overall, although several safeguards against PTP have been suggested, research indicates that they may not be effective at reducing bias created by PTP and may even exacerbate the problems created by PTP.

Assuming that there is some consistent, negative effect of crime drama viewership on jury decision making, the legal system should be interested in minimizing its influence on trial fairness. Many solutions to this potential negative impact on the criminal justice system have been proposed and used. The most commonly used tool to counteract the influence of the CSI Effect on jury decision making is jury instructions. Many jurisdictions now have pattern instructions that include reference to the CSI Effect. For example, the Ohio State Bar Association recently added reference to television shows as prohibited outside resources for information about the trial in Section 3 of its pattern jury instructions (Ohio State Bar Association, 2010). The new instruction specifies that television shows are fictional, portray an inaccurate view of the legal system, and should not be relied on in decision making. Prosecutors also report changing their case strategies to account for the CSI Effect (Podlas, 2006b; Stevens, 2008). Prosecutors may also change their case strategy in terms of whether to present forensic science evidence. Kim et al. (2009) argue that prosecutors should always present forensic science evidence when they have it and that defense attorneys should always stress the lack of forensic science evidence when it is not presented by the prosecution to capitalize on the small effects that the research indicates. They may use several techniques during a case to counteract the potential negative impact on their cases such as using *voir dire* to eliminate jurors who report high crime-drama viewership, addressing the inappropriateness of relying on television to form perceptions of the case in opening statements and closing arguments (Maricopa County, 2005), and proffering negative witnesses, experts who testify about forensic science evidence (Stevens, 2008). Courts are already beginning to grapple with the issues raised by these strategies. Some courts have questioned whether instructing the jury about the CSI Effect is appropriate or prejudicial (*Stabb v. Maryland*, 2011), and others have considered the appropriateness of *voir dire* on CSI Effect issues (*Maryland v. Stringfellow*, 2011). Although these strategies are all being used by attorneys and judges to some degree, no research has been conducted on their effectiveness. Overall, attorneys and courts have used a variety of techniques to counteract the potential for a CSI Effect in their cases, despite a lack of empirical evidence on the effectiveness of these alternative strategies.

Commentators also have suggested several potential solutions to the problems created by social media in the courtroom. Of all the suggested remedies, judicial instructions and admonitions are reported as the most popular and commonly used safeguards (Dunn, 2011; Hecht & Secco, 2012; Hoffmeister, 2012; Munisteri, 2012; Simpler, 2012; St. Eve & Zuckerman, 2012). It is argued that they are a practical and effective means of reducing misconduct while being as minimally intrusive and as respectful of jurors as possible (St. Eve & Zuckerman, 2012). Proponents of instructions to avoid social media exposure and use during a trial argue that they effectively decrease social media misconduct by jurors (Dunn, 2011; Hecht & Secco, 2012; Hoffmeister, 2012; Munisteri, 2012; St. Eve & Zuckerman, 2012). In the only research on jurors' use of social media during trials to date, two federal district court judges surveyed jurors from their own courtrooms about whether they were tempted to communicate information about the case on social media sites and what prevented them from doing so (St. Eve & Zuckerman, 2012). Results indicated that inappropriate use of social media during trial was very rare. The majority of jurors cited the judge's instructions as the reason they did not engage in inappropriate online behavior. The researchers concluded that judicial instructions are effective (St. Eve & Zuckerman, 2012). The judges in the Federal Judicial Center survey also perceived their instructions as effective (Dunn, 2011).

Although instructions about the use of social media are common, they vary widely in their timing, frequency, and content across jurisdictions and courtrooms. In terms of timing and frequency, it has been recommended that judges instruct jurors at the beginning of the trial, throughout the trial, and prior to deliberations (St. Eve & Zuckerman, 2012). Most judges in the Federal Judicial Center survey reported instructing throughout the trial and using frequent reminders of the instructions (Dunn, 2011). It is also recommended that instructions should be very specific and specifically

mention examples of inappropriate social media use (St. Eve & Zuckerman, 2012). For example, California has added specific reference to electronic communications in their preliminary admonitions section of the pattern civil jury instructions (California Civil Jury Instructions, 2013). The Texas civil jury instructions similarly specifically mention avoiding social media (Hecht & Secco, 2012), as does the proposed Federal pattern jury instruction (Federal Evidence Review, 2010). Some recommend that the instructions provide an explanation of why it is important to trial fairness to refrain from posting during the trial to make jurors understand the prohibition and accept the reduced freedom (Hoffmeister, 2012; Simpler, 2012; St. Eve & Zuckerman, 2012). The pattern instruction used in New York State provides an explanation of why the use of social media during the trial interferes with Constitutional rights (New York Jury Instructions, 2009), and the pattern civil jury instructions in California have a special section also providing an explanation about why this deprivation of freedom is important to protect trial fairness (California Civil Jury Instructions, 2013). Other scholars suggest that the information on the punishment for violating such admonitions should be included in the instructions (Simpler, 2012). For example, California's pattern criminal jury instructions specify the range of punishments available for violating the prohibition against communicating about or conducting research on a trial, including the use of electronic communications (California Criminal Jury Instructions, 2013).

Commentators have proffered a variety of additional suggestions for courts to manage the problems associated with social media use by jurors. These include conducting a "modernized" *voir dire* that probes social media use (Munisteri, 2012; Simpler, 2012), sequestration (Hoffmeister, 2012; Simpler, 2012), monitoring jurors' online activity during the trial (Hoffmeister, 2012; Munisteri, 2012), banning electronic devices at trial (the "Luddite" solution; Hoffmeister, 2012; Munisteri, 2012), and making jurors take an extra oath not to use social media (Hoffmeister, 2012). A minority of judges in the Federal Judicial Center survey reported routinely confiscating electronic devices as a remedy (Dunn, 2011). In Hoffmeister's survey of federal judges and attorneys, judges reported using all of these potential solutions in addition to relying on jury instructions (Hoffmeister, 2012). Although all of these strategies are potentially viable solutions to the problem of social media in the courtroom, their effectiveness has not been empirically evaluated.

Overall, research on safeguards against media exposure influencing trials indicates that the safeguards used to date may not effectively counteract media influences. Pretrial, it is nearly impossible to either identify problematic media or constitutionally restrict its dissemination. Research demonstrates that techniques used during trials have limited effectiveness. Even specialized versions of *voir dire* do not eliminate the influence of PTP, the CSI Effect, and social media. Attorneys' modifications to their case strategies, such as specially selected witnesses and arguments targeting media effects, are either underresearched or ineffective. Trial procedures such as continuances and deliberations could potentially reduce some media effects, but research shows that they may actually increase the impact of the media on trials. The most commonly used and researched response to the media are jury instructions admonishing jurors to disregard information gleaned from media sources, but the research that has been conducted on such instructions indicates that their effects may be minimal.

The complicated problem of the media and the law is that the proposed solutions to the negative effects of the media on the legal system (procedures that would prevent its negative impact on people's behavior and trials) simultaneously violate rights protected by the Constitution such as freedom of speech and privacy. Eliminating exposure to the offending media at its source such that people are never exposed to it is problematic because these types of censorship policies tend to violate the First Amendment. It is also difficult or even impossible to identify what media sources will become problematic for the public or in individual trials. Therefore, policies cannot just stop the media; they must instead assume that legally problematic media will be present and then attempt to minimize its impact. The research that has been conducted on trial tactics

that may counteract media influences indicate that their effectiveness is limited. Therefore, more research is required, particularly research that investigates antidotes to a broad array of media influences.

SUMMARY AND CONCLUSIONS

Media plays an important and increasingly large part in the lives of many people. As access to and opportunities for interaction with media increase, the amount of information that people experience about the legal system also increases. Research demonstrates that there are many ways that legally relevant media affect perceptions of and decision making in the legal system. Television presents a skewed impression of the nature and frequency of crime. Regardless of the type of programming, portrayals of crime on television tend to be presented from the orientation of the prosecution and the police. That skewed presentation affects how people perceive criminals. It can also affect legally relevant attitudes such as increasing fear of crime, increasing support for the death penalty, and decreasing trust in the criminal justice system. More importantly, media can influence behavior and decision making during actual trials. Exposure to PTP that represents a defendant negatively leads to biased pretrial opinions about that defendant and prejudgments of the defendant's culpability for the crime. This biasing effect is magnified when the media contains case-specific, inadmissible, or emotionally laden information. The bias created by this media exposure is generally not decreased by the presentation of trial evidence. This has serious implications for the Sixth Amendment guarantee of trial fairness.

On the other hand, not all media has a largely biasing effect on the legal system. Although many people in the media and in the criminal justice system believe that prosecution-oriented, science-heavy shows like *CSI* are influencing how jurors understand evidence and make decisions in real trials, research does not clearly demonstrate this effect. Crime drama viewership may increase expectations people have about the presentation of forensic evidence, especially in certain types of cases, but research has shown that these raised expectations do not necessarily affect case verdicts. Courts and commentators have also been concerned about the influence of social media on trials, but little research has investigated whether this concern is valid. Therefore, not all legally relevant media is necessarily negatively impacting trial fairness.

Because censorship or selected limitation of media exposure is constitutionally and practically difficult, the legal system must pursue alternative means of combatting any negative impact of the media on trial fairness. No matter what the media source, similar solutions have been proposed and investigated. Principal among these solutions are instructions to disregard extralegal media information, *voir dire* on exposure to and use of media, and changes to lawyers' strategies in case presentation. When research has been done on their use, primarily in the context of PTP, none of these safeguards have been particularly effective. The legal system would benefit from more empirical research on safeguard effectiveness, particularly in the underresearched areas of the CSI Effect and the influence of social media. Because currently used safeguards have not been found to be overwhelmingly effective in research, considering truly alternative approaches to the problem of media and the law would benefit the legal system. As media becomes more ingrained in the trial process, it will become even more crucial for the legal system to be able to counteract its influence on trials and trial fairness.

References

American Bar Association. (2006). *Model rules of professional conduct.* Chicago, IL: Author.

Arbuthnot, J., Myers, B., & Leach, J. (2002). Linking juror prejudgment and pretrial publicity knowledge: Some methodological considerations. *American Journal of Forensic Psychology, 20,* 53–71.

Babcock, C., & Gilman, L. (2012). Use of social media in *voir dire. The Advocate: State Bar Litigation Section Report, 60,* 44–49.

Bandura, A. (1973). *Aggression: A social learning analysis.* Oxford, England: Prentice-Hall.

Bandura, A. (1977). *Social learning theory.* Oxford, England: Prentice-Hall.

Bandura, A. (1986). *Social foundations of thought and action: A social cognitive theory.* Englewood Cliffs, NJ: Prentice-Hall.

Baskin, D. R., & Sommers, I. B. (2010). Crime-show-viewing habits and public attitudes toward forensic evidence: The "CSI effect" revisited. *Justice System Journal, 31,* 97–113.

Bornstein, B. H., Whisenhunt, B. L., Nemeth, R. J., & Dunaway, D. L. (2002). Pretrial publicity and civil cases: A two-way street? *Law and Human Behavior, 26,* 3–17. doi:10.1023/A:1013825124011

Brown v. Entertainment Merchants Association, 131 S.Ct. 2729 (2011).

Brutocao, S. (2012). Issue spotting: The multitude of ways social media impacts employment law and litigation. *The Advocate: State Bar Litigation Section Report, 60,* 8–17.

California Civil Jury Instructions. (2013). Retrieved from http://www.courts.ca.gov/partners/documents/caci_2013_edition.pdf

California Criminal Jury Instructions. (2013). Retrieved from http://www.courts.ca.gov/partners/documents/calcrim_juryins.pdf

Callanan, V. J. (2012). Media consumption, perceptions of crime risk and fear of crime: Examining race/ethnic differences. *Sociological Perspectives, 55,* 93–115. doi:10.1525/sop.2012.55.1.93

Callanan, V. J., & Rosenberger, J. S. (2011). Media and public perceptions of the police: Examining the impact of race and personal experience. *Policing and Society, 21,* 167–189. doi:10.1080/10439463.2010.540655

Carlson, K. A., & Russo, J. E. (2001). Biased interpretation of evidence by mock jurors. *Journal of Experimental Psychology: Applied, 7,* 91–103. doi:10.1037/1076-898X.7.2.91

Catalani, R. (2006). A *CSI* writer on the CSI effect. *Yale Law Journal Pocket Part, 115,* 76–78.

Chiricos, T., & Eschholz, S. (2002). The racial and ethnic typification of crime and the criminal typification of race and ethnicity in local television news. *Journal of Research in Crime and Delinquency, 39,* 400–420. doi:10.1177/002242702237286

CNN. (2007). *Andrea Yates case: Yates found not guilty by reason of insanity.* Retrieved from http://www.cnn.com/2007/US/law/12/11/court.archive.yates8

Cohan, M., & Cook, K. E. (2013). Two sides of the same coin: The sociological and psychological social psychology of crime. In J. B. Helfgott (Ed.), *Criminal psychology: Theory and research* (Vol. 1, pp. 163–188). Santa Barbara, CA: Praeger/ABC-CLIO.

Cole, S. A., & Dioso-Villa, R. (2007). *CSI* and its effects: Media, juries, and the burden of proof. *New England Law Review, 41,* 435–469.

Cole, S. A., & Dioso-Villa, R. (2009). Investigating the "CSI effect" effect: Media and litigation crisis in criminal law. *Stanford Law Review, 61,* 1335–1373.

Costantini, E., & King, J. (1980–1981). The partial juror: Correlates and causes of prejudgment. *Law and Society Review, 15,* 9–40. doi:10.2307/3053221

Criss, S. (2012). The use of social media by judges. *The Advocate: State Bar Litigation Section Report, 60,* 18–20.

Custers, K., & van den Bulck, J. (2011). The relationship of dispositional and situational fear of crime with television viewing and direct experience with crime. *Mass Communication and Society, 14,* 600–619. doi:10.1080/15205436.2010.530382

Custers, K., & van den Bulck, J. (2013). The cultivation of fear of sexual violence in women: Processes and moderators of the relationship between television and fear. *Communication Research, 40,* 96–124. doi:10.1177/0093650212440444

Davis, R. W. (1986). Pretrial publicity, the timing of the trial, and mock jurors' decision processes. *Journal of Applied Social Psychology, 16,* 590–607. doi:10.1111/j.1559-1816.1986.tb01161.x

DeGarmo, E. L. (2011). *Knights battling monsters: A content analysis of television crime dramas* (Doctoral dissertation). Available from ProQuest Dissertations and Theses database. (Accession No. 853627720)

DeLuca, A. J. (1979). *Tipping the scales of justice: The effects of pretrial publicity* (Unpublished master's thesis). Iowa State University, Ames.

Desmarais, S. L., Price, H. L., & Read, J. D. (2008). 'Objection, your honor! Television is not the relevant authority.' Crime drama portrayals of eyewitness issues. *Psychology, Crime & Law, 14,* 225–243. doi:10.1080/10683160701652583

Dexter, H. R., Cutler, B. L., & Moran, G. (1992). A test of voir dire as a remedy for the prejudicial effects of pretrial publicity. *Journal of Applied Social Psychology, 22,* 819–832. doi:10.1111/j.1559-1816.1992.tb00926.x

Dill, K. E., & Burgess, M. C. R. (2012). Seeing is believing: Toward a theory of media imagery and social learning. In L. J. Shrum (Ed.), *The psychology of entertainment media: Blurring the lines between entertainment and persuasion* (2nd ed., pp. 195–225). New York, NY: Routledge.

Dirikx, A., Gelders, D., & van den Bulck, J. (2013). Adolescent perceptions of the performance and fairness of the police: Examining the impact of television exposure. *Mass Communication and Society, 16,* 109–132. doi:10.1080/15205436.2011.650341

Dixon, T., & Maddox, K. (2005). Skin tone, crime news, and social reality judgments: Priming the stereotype of the dark and dangerous Black criminal. *Journal of Applied Social Psychology, 35,* 1555–570. doi:10.1111/j.1559-1816.2005.tb02184.x

Dixon, T. L. (2006). Psychological reactions to crime news portrayals of black criminals: Understanding the moderating roles of prior news viewing and stereotype endorsement. *Communication Monographs, 73,* 162–187. doi:10.1080/03637750600690643

Dixon, T. L. (2007). Black criminals and white officers: The effects of racially misrepresenting law breakers and law defenders on television news. *Media Psychology, 10,* 270–291. doi:10.1080/15213260701375660

Dixon, T. L. (2008). Crime news and racialized beliefs: Understanding the relationship between local news viewing and perceptions of African Americans and crime. *Journal of Communication, 58,* 106–125. doi:10.1111/j.1460-2466.2007.00376.x

Dixon, T. L., & Azocar, C. L. (2006). The representation of juvenile offenders by race on Los Angeles area television news. *Howard Journal of Communications, 17,* 143–161. doi:10.1080/10646170600656896

Dixon, T. L., & Azocar, C. L. (2007). Priming crime and activating blackness: Understanding the psychological impact of the overrepresentation of blacks as lawbreakers on television news. *Journal of Communication, 57,* 229–253. doi:10.1111/j.1460-2466.2007.00341.x

Dixon, T. L., Azocar, C. L., & Casas, M. (2003). The portrayal of race and crime on television network news. *Journal of Broadcasting and Electronic Media, 47,* 498–523. doi:10.1207/s15506878jobem4704_2

Dixon, T. L., & Linz, D. (2000a). Overrepresentation and underrepresentation of African Americans and Latinos as lawbreakers on television news. *Journal of Communication, 50,* 131–154. doi:10.1111/j.1460-2466.2000.tb02845.x

Dixon, T. L., & Linz, D. (2000b). Race and the misrepresentation of victimization on local television news. *Communication Research, 27,* 547–573. doi:10.1177/009365000027005001

Dixon, T. L., & Linz, D. (2002). Television news, prejudicial pretrial publicity, and the depiction of race. *Journal of Broadcasting and Electronic Media, 46,* 112–136. doi:10.1207/s15506878jobem4601_7

Dowler, K. (2006). Sex, lies, and videotape: The presentation of sex crime in local television news. *Journal of Criminal Justice, 34,* 383–392. doi:10.1016/j.jcrimjus.2006.05.004

Dunn, M. (2011). *Jurors' use of social media during trials and deliberations: A report to the Judicial Conference Committee on court administration and case management.* Retrieved from http://www.fjc.gov/public/pdf.nsf/lookup/dunnjuror.pdf/$file/dunnjuror.pdf

Eschholz, S., Chiricos, T., & Gertz, M. (2003). Television and fear of crime: Program types, audience traits, and the mediating effect of perceived neighborhood racial composition. *Social Problems, 50,* 395–415. doi:10.1525/sp.2003.50.3.395

FCC v. Fox Television Stations, Inc., 132 S.Ct. 2307 (2012).

Federal Evidence Review. (2013). *Model jury instruction recommended to deter juror use of electronic communication technologies during trial.* Retrieved from http://federalevidence.com

Freedman, J. L., Martin, C. K., & Mota, V. L. (1998). Pretrial publicity: Effects of admonition and expressing pretrial opinions. *Legal and Criminological Psychology, 3*, 255–270. doi:10.1111/j.2044-8333.1998.tb00365.x

Gerbner, G., & Gross, L. (1976). Living with television: The violence profile. *Journal of Communication, 26*, 173–191. doi:10.1111/j.1460-2466.1976.tb01397.x

Gerbner, G., Gross, L., Morgan, M., Signorielli, N., & Shanahan, J. (2002). Growing up with television: Cultivation processes. In J. Bryant & D. Zillmann (Eds.), *Media effects: Advances in theory and research* (2nd ed., pp. 43–67). Mahwah, NJ: Erlbaum.

Gorman, B. (2010). *CSI: Crime Scene Investigation is the most watched show in the world!* Retrieved from http://tvbythenumbers.zap2it.com/2010/06/11/csi-crime-scene-investigation-is-the-most-watched-show-in-the-world/53833

Grabe, M. E., & Drew, D. G. (2007). Crime cultivation: Comparisons across media genres and channels. *Journal of Broadcasting and Electronic Media, 51*, 147–171. doi:10.1080/08838150701308143

Greene, E. (1990). Media effects on jurors. *Law and Human Behavior, 14*, 439–450. doi:10.1007/BF01044221

Greene, E., & Loftus, E. F. (1984). What's new in the news? The influence of well-publicized news events on psychological research and courtroom trials. *Basic and Applied Social Psychology, 5*, 211–221. doi:10.1207/s15324834basp0503_4

Greene, E., & Wade, R. (1988). Of private talk and public print: General pre-trial publicity and juror decision-making. *Applied Cognitive Psychology, 2*, 123–135. doi:10.1002/acp.2350020204

Gross, K., & Aday, S. (2003). The scary world in your living room and neighborhood: Using local broadcast news, neighborhood crime rates, and personal experience to test agenda setting and cultivation. *Journal of Communication, 53*, 411–426. doi:10.1111/j.1460-2466.2003.tb02599.x

Harvey, E., & Derksen, L. (2009). The CSI effect: Science fiction or social fact? In V. M. Johnson & M. Byers (Eds.), *Deconstructing the CSI effect: Producing narratives of justice and science, producing television drama* (pp. 25–26). Lanham, MD: Lexington Books.

Hayes, R. M., & Levett, L. M. (2013). Community members' perceptions of the CSI effect. *American Journal of Criminal Justice, 38*, 216–235. doi:10.1007/s12103-012-9166-2

Hayes-Smith, R., & Levett, L. M. (2011). Jury's still out: How television and crime show viewing influences jurors' evaluations of evidence. *Applied Psychology in Criminal Justice, 7*, 29–46.

Hecht, N. L., & Secco, M. (2012). Juries and technology: Revised Texas civil jury instructions include warnings about the internet and social media. *The Advocate: State Bar Litigation Section Report, 60*, 50–54.

Hoffmeister, T. (2011). Applying rules of discovery to information uncovered about jurors. *UCLA Law Review Discourse, 59*, 28–42.

Hoffmeister, T. (2012). Google, gadgets, and guilt: Juror misconduct in the digital age. *University of Colorado Law Review, 83*, 409–470. doi:10.2139/ssrn.1668973

Holbert, R. L., Shah, D. V., & Kwak, N. (2004). Fear, authority, and justice: Crime-related viewing and endorsements of capital punishment and gun ownership. *Journalism and Mass Communication Quarterly, 81*, 343–363. doi:10.1177/107769900408100208

Honess, T. M., Charman, E. A., & Levi, M. (2003). Factual and affective/evaluative recall of pretrial publicity: Their relative influence on juror reasoning and verdict in a simulated fraud trial. *Journal of Applied Social Psychology, 33*, 1404–1416. doi:10.1111/j.1559-1816.2003.tb01955.x

Hope, L., Memon, A., & McGeorge, P. (2004). Understanding pretrial publicity: Predecisional distortion of evidence by mock jurors. *Journal of Experimental Psychology: Applied, 10*, 111–119. doi:10.1037/1076-898X.10.2.111

Huesmann, L. R., Moise-Titus, J., Podolski, C., & Eron, L. D. (2003). Longitudinal relations between children's exposure to TV violence and their aggressive and violent behavior in young adulthood: 1977–1992. *Developmental Psychology, 39*, 201–221. doi:10.1037/0012-1649.39.2.201

Hvistendahl, J. K. (1979). The effect of placement of biasing information. *Journalism Quarterly, 56*, 863–865. doi:10.1177/107769907905600425

Imrich, D. I., Mullin, C., & Linz, D. (1995). Measuring the extent of prejudicial pretrial publicity in major American newspapers: A content analysis. *Journal of Communication, 45*, 94–117. doi:10.1111/j.1460-2466.1995.tb00745.x

Jacquin, K. M., & Hodges, E. P. (2007). The influence of media messages on mock juror decisions in the Andrea Yates trial. *American Journal of Forensic Psychology, 25*, 21–40.

Johnson, M. K., Hashtroudi, S., & Lindsay, D. (1993). Source monitoring. *Psychological Bulletin, 114*, 3–28. doi:10.1037/0033-2909.114.1.3

Kerr, N. L., Kramer, G. P., Carroll, J. S., & Alfini, J. J. (1991). On the effectiveness of *voir dire* in criminal cases with prejudicial pretrial publicity: An empirical study. *American University Law Review, 40*, 665–701.

Kim, Y. S., Barak, G., & Shelton, D. E. (2009). Examining the "CSI effect" in the cases of circumstantial evidence and eyewitness testimony: Multivariate and path analyses. *Journal of Criminal Justice, 37*, 452–460. doi:10.1016/j.jcrimjus.2009.07.005

Kline, F. G., & Jess, P. H. (1966). Prejudicial publicity: Its effects on law school mock juries. *Journalism Quarterly, 43*, 113–116. doi:10.1177/107769906604300115

Kort-Butler, L., & Hartshorn, K. J. S. (2011). Watching the detectives: Crime programming, fear of crime, and attitudes about the criminal justice system. *Sociological Quarterly, 52*, 36–55. doi:10.1111/j.1533-8525.2010.01191.x

Kovera, M. B. (2002). The effects of general pretrial publicity on juror decisions: An examination of moderators and mediating mechanisms. *Law and Human Behavior, 26*, 43–72. doi:10.1023/A:1013829224920

Kramer, G. P., Kerr, N. L., & Carroll, J. S. (1990). Pretrial publicity, judicial remedies, and jury bias. *Law and Human Behavior, 14*, 409–438. doi:10.1007/BF01044220

Kruse, C. (2010). Producing absolute truth: CSI science as wishful thinking. *American Anthropologist, 112*, 79–91. doi:10.1111/j.1548-1433.2009.01198.x

Lane, J., & Meeker, J. W. (2003). Ethicity, information sources, and fear of crime. *Deviant Behavior, 24*, 1–26. doi:10.1080/10639620390117165

Lieberman, J. D., & Arndt, J. (2000). Understanding the limits of limiting instructions: Social psychological explanations for the failures of instructions to disregard pretrial publicity and other inadmissible evidence. *Psychology, Public Policy, and Law, 6*, 677–711. doi:10.1037/1076-8971.6.3.677

Mancini, D. E. (2011). The CSI effect reconsidered: Is it moderated by need for cognition? *North American Journal of Psychology, 13*, 155–174.

Maricopa County. (2005). *The CSI effect and its real-life impact on justice: A study by the Maricopa County Attorney's Office.* Retrieved from http://www.maricopacountyattorney.org/Press/PDF/CSIReport.pdf

Maryland v. Stringfellow, 28 A.3d 644 (2011).

Minow, N. N., & Cate, F. H. (2001). Who is an impartial juror in an age of mass media? *American University Law Review, 40*, 631–664.

Morales, L., II. (2012). Social media evidence: "What you post or tweet can and will be used against you in a court of law." *The Advocate: State Bar Litigation Section Report, 60*, 32–43.

Moran, G., & Cutler, B. L. (1991). The prejudicial impact of pretrial publicity. *Journal of Applied Social Psychology, 21*, 345–367. doi:10.1111/j.1559-1816.1991.tb00524.x

Mullin, C., Imrich, D. J., & Linz, D. (1996). The impact of acquaintance rape stories and case-specific pretrial publicity on juror decision making. *Communication Research, 23*, 100–135. doi:10.1177/009365096023001004

Mu'Min v. Virginia, 500 U.S. 415 (1991).

Munisteri, J. (2012). Use of social media by jurors: Death knell or paper cut to jury trial integrity? *The Advocate: State Bar Litigation Section Report, 60*, 55–58.

Nebraska Press Association v. Stuart, 427 U.S. 539 (1976).

New York Jury Instructions. (2009). *New York jury admonitions in preliminary instructions.* Retrieved from http://www.nycourts.gov/judges/cji/1-General/CJI2d.Jury_Admonitions.pdf

Nietzel, M. T., & Dillehay, R. C. (1983). Psychologists as consultants for changes of venue: The use of public opinion surveys. *Law and Human Behavior, 7*, 309–335. doi:10.1007/BF01044735

Oates, J. (2012). Learning from watching. In N. Brace & J. Byford (Eds.), *Investigating psychology: Key concepts, key studies, key approaches* (pp. 100–138). New York, NY: Oxford University Press.

Ohio State Bar Association. (2010). *OSBA jury instructions.* Retrieved from http://federalevidence.com/downloads/blog/2010/OSBA.Jury.Instructions.pdf

Oliver, M. B. (1994). Portrayals of crime, race, and aggression in 'reality-based' police shows: A content analysis. *Journal of Broadcasting and Electronic Media, 38*, 179–192. doi:10.1080/08838159409364255

Otto, A. L., & Penrod, S. D. (1991, August). *Assessing mediators of pre-trial publicity effects.* Paper presented at the annual meeting of the American Psychological Association, San Francisco, CA.

Otto, A. L., Penrod, S. D., & Dexter, H. R. (1994). The biasing impact of pretrial publicity on juror judgments. *Law and Human Behavior, 18*, 453–470. doi:10.1007/BF01499050

Padawer-Singer, A. M., Singer, A. N., & Singer, R. L. (1974). *Voir dire* by two lawyers: An essential safeguard. *Judicature, 57*, 386.

Padawer-Singer, A. M., Singer, A. N., & Singer, R. L. (1977). Legal and social-psychological research in the effects of pre-trial publicity on juries, numerical makeup of juries, non-unanimous verdict requirements. *Law and Psychology Review, 3*, 71–79.

Pitluk, E. E. (2012). Ethical issues for lawyers involving the internet. *The Advocate: State Bar Litigation Section Report, 60*, 21–27.

Podlas, K. (2006a). "The CSI effect": Exposing the media myth. *Fordham Intellectual Property, Media, and Entertainment Law Journal, 16*, 431–465.

Podlas, K. (2006b). The "CSI effect" and other forensic fictions. *Loyola of Los Angeles Entertainment Law Review, 27*, 87–124.

Potter, W. J. (1988). Perceived reality in television effects research. *Journal of Broadcasting and Electronic Media, 32,* 23–41. doi:10.1080/08838158809386682

Reith, M. (1999). Viewing of crime drama and authoritarian aggression: An investigation of the relationship between crime viewing, fear, and aggression. *Journal of Broadcasting and Electronic Media, 43,* 211–221. doi:10.1080/08838159909364485

Richmond Newspapers v. Virginia, 448 U.S. 555 (1980).

Romer, D., Jamieson, K. H., & Aday, S. (2003). Television news and the cultivation of fear of crime. *Journal of Communication, 53,* 88–104. doi:10.1111/j.1460-2466.2003.tb03007.x

Ruva, C., McEvoy, C., & Bryant, J. B. (2007). Effects of pre-trial publicity and jury deliberation on juror bias and source memory errors. *Applied Cognitive Psychology, 21,* 45–67. doi:10.1002/acp.1254

Ruva, C. L., Guenther, C. C., & Yarbrough, A. (2011). Positive and negative pretrial publicity: The roles of impression formation, emotion, and predecisional distortion. *Criminal Justice and Behavior, 38,* 511–534. doi:10.1177/0093854811400823

Ruva, C. L., & Hudak, E. M. (2013). Pretrial publicity and juror age affect mock-juror decision making. *Psychology, Crime, and Law, 19,* 179–202. doi:10.1080/1068316X.2011.616509

Ruva, C. L., & LeVasseur, M. A. (2012). Behind closed doors: The effect of pretrial publicity on jury deliberations. *Psychology, Crime & Law, 18,* 431–452. doi:10.1080/1068316X.2010.502120

Ruva, C. L., & McEvoy, C. (2008). Negative and positive pretrial publicity affect juror memory and decision making. *Journal of Experimental Psychology: Applied, 14,* 226–235. doi:10.1037/1076-898X.14.3.226

Schweitzer, N. J., & Saks, M. J. (2007). The CSI effect: Popular fiction about forensic science affects the public's expectations about real forensic science. *Jurimetrics Journal, 47,* 357–364.

Shelton, D. E. (2010). Juror expectations for scientific evidence in criminal cases: Perceptions and reality about the "CSI effect" myth. *Thomas M. Cooley Law Review, 27,* 1–35.

Shelton, D. E., Kim, Y. S., & Barak, G. (2006). A study of juror expectations and demands concerning scientific evidence: Does the "CSI effect" exist? *Vanderbilt Journal of Entertainment and Technology Law, 9,* 331–368.

Shelton, D. E., Kim, Y. S., & Barak, G. (2009). An indirect-effects model of mediated adjudication: The CSI myth, the tech effect, and metropolitan jurors' expectations for scientific evidence. *Vanderbilt Journal of Entertainment and Technology Law, 12,* 1–43.

Sheppard v. Maxwell, 384 U.S. 333 (1966).

Simon, R. J., & Eimermann, T. (1971). The jury finds not guilty: Another look at media influence on the jury. *Journalism Quarterly, 48,* 343–344.

Simpler, M. F. (2012). The unjust "web" we weave: The evolution of social media and its impact on juror impartiality and fair trials. *Law and Psychology Review, 36,* 275–296.

Slater, M. D., Rouner, D., & Long, M. (2006). Television dramas and support for controversial public policies: Effects and mechanisms. *Journal of Communication, 56,* 235–252. doi:10.1111/j.1460-2466.2006.00017.x

Smith, S. M., Stinson, V., & Patry, M. W. (2011). Fact or fiction? the myth and reality of the CSI effect. *Court Review, 47,* 4–7.

Soulliere, D. M. (2004). Policing on prime-time: A comparison of television and real-world policing. *American Journal of Criminal Justice, 28,* 215–233. doi:10.1007/BF02885873

Spano, L. M., Groscup, J. L., & Penrod, S. D. (2011). Pretrial publicity and the jury: Research and methods. In R. Weiner & B. Bornstein (Eds.), *Trial consulting: A psychological handbook* (pp. 217–234). New York, NY: Springer. doi:10.1007/978-1-4419-7569-0_11

Stabb v. Maryland, 31 A.3d 922 (2011).

Steblay, N. M., Besirevic, J., Fulero, S. M., & Jimenez-Lorente, B. (1999). The effects of pretrial publicity on juror verdicts: A meta-analytic review. *Law and Human Behavior, 23,* 219–235. doi:10.1023/A:1022325019080

St. Eve, A. J., & Zuckerman, M. A. (2012). Ensuring an impartial jury in the age of social media. *Duke Law and Technology Journal, 11,* 1–29.

Stevens, D. J. (2008). Forensic science, wrongful convictions, and American prosecutor discretion. *Howard Journal of Criminal Justice, 47,* 31–51. doi:10.1111/j.1468-2311.2008.00495.x

Stinson, V., Patry, M. W., & Smith, S. M. (2007). The CSI effect: Reflections from police and forensic investigators. *Canadian Journal of Police and Security Services, 5,* 1–9.

Studebaker, C. A., & Penrod, S. D. (1997). Pretrial publicity: The media, the law and commonsense. *Psychology, Public Policy, and Law, 3,* 428–460. doi:10.1037/1076-8971.3.2-3.428

Sue, S., Smith, R., & Gilbert, R. (1974). Biasing effects of pretrial publicity on judicial decisions. *Journal of Criminal Justice, 2,* 163–171. doi:10.1016/0047-2352(74)90007-5

Sue, S., Smith, R., & Pedroza, G. (1975). Authoritarianism, pretrial publicity, and awareness of bias in simulated jurors, *Psychological Reports, 37,* 1299. doi:10.2466/pr0.1975.37.3f.1299

Tans, M., & Chaffee, S. (1966). Pretrial publicity and juror prejudice. *Journalism Quarterly, 43*, 647–654. doi:10.1177/107769906604300403

Tapscott, R. L. (2012). *Media effects and the criminal justice system: An experimental test of the CSI effect* (Doctoral dissertation). Available from ProQuest Dissertations and Theses database. (Accession No. 894769470)

Tyler, T. R. (2006). Viewing CSI and the threshold of guilt: Managing truth and justice in reality and fiction. *Yale Law Journal, 115*, 1050–1085. doi:10.2307/20455645

United States v. Fumo, 655 F.3d 288 (2011).

Vidmar, N. (2002). Case studies of pre- and midtrial prejudice in criminal and civil litigation. *Law and Human Behavior, 26*, 73–105. doi:10.1023/A:1013881208990

Vidmar, N. (2003). When all of us are victims: Juror prejudice and "terrorist" trials. *Chicago–Kent Law Review, 1143*, 1–42.

Watkins, M. (2004). *Forensics in the media: Have attorneys reacted to the growing popularity of forensic crime dramas?* (Unpublished master's thesis). Florida State University, Tallahassee.

Weaver, R., Salamonson, Y., Koch, J., & Porter, G. (2012). The CSI effect at university: Forensic science students' television viewing and perceptions of ethical issues. *Australian Journal of Forensic Sciences, 44*, 381–391. doi:10.1080/00450618.2012.691547

Wilson, B. J., Linz, D., Donnerstein, E., & Stipp, H. (1992). The impact of social issue television programming on attitudes toward rape. *Human Communication Research, 19*, 179–208. doi:10.1111/j.1468-2958.1992.tb00299.x

Wilson, J. R., & Bornstein, B. H. (1998). Methodological considerations in pretrial publicity research: Is the medium the message? *Law and Human Behavior, 22*, 585–597. doi:10.1023/A:1025743614951

Woody, W., & Viney, W. (2007). General pretrial publicity in sexual assault trials. *Psychological Reports, 101*, 527–530. doi:10.2466/PR0.101.2.527-530

CHAPTER 12

PROCEDURAL JUSTICE

Diane Sivasubramaniam and Larry Heuer

The procedural justice field explores the role of decision-making processes and their outcomes in determining individuals' perceptions of justice and satisfaction. Dominant theoretical models in this field describe fairness and satisfaction judgments as being determined primarily by treatment concerns rather than by outcomes: When individuals feel that they have been treated fairly in a decision-making procedure, they judge those procedures and their outcomes to be more just, and they are more satisfied with those procedures and their outcomes.

In this chapter, we will describe several recent studies in the procedural justice field that document a disparity between decision makers and non–decision makers in the importance they place on treatment versus outcomes. These recent findings indicate that, when determining the fairness and propriety of decision-making procedures, decision makers are more concerned than non–decision makers about ensuring that decision-making procedures result in just outcomes. We will also discuss potential motivators that lead to this disparity, such as the perception that the target of a procedure deserves respectful treatment, and the responsibility placed on decision makers for protecting the social group.

Throughout the chapter, we consider the ways in which these recent developments in procedural justice may inform forensic psychology researchers and legal practitioners about the fundamental psychological mechanisms in operation among decision makers in the legal system. We conclude by offering suggestions about the ways in which recent work on the basic social psychology of procedural justice

might strengthen our understanding of the behavior of jurors, police officers, interrogators, judges, and other decision makers in the legal system, and how this research may even be leveraged to influence or modify the behavior of these decision makers.

IMPORTANCE OF THE PROBLEM

Procedural justice refers to perceptions of fair treatment during a decision-making procedure, and *distributive justice* (or outcome fairness) refers to perceived fairness of the outcomes resulting from that procedure (Tyler, Degoey, & Smith, 1996). Procedural justice researchers examine the factors that influence people's judgments about the fairness of the treatment and outcomes that they receive in social interactions. The procedural justice literature is a large body of work, with hundreds of studies investigating the way in which people form these judgments about procedural and distributive justice, and the factors that affect those judgments.

The application of procedural justice to the legal context involves the investigation of justice reasoning in legal processes and in response to legal outcomes. Research in this field studies the way in which disputants and other actors in the legal system determine that the processes and outcomes they have experienced are just (Thibaut & Walker, 1975). The scholarship of procedural justice therefore investigates fundamental questions to do with the administration of justice: To what extent do the processes and outcomes intended to produce justice actually do so in the minds of those who are subject

http://dx.doi.org/10.1037/14462-012
APA Handbook of Forensic Psychology: Vol. 2. Criminal Investigation, Adjudication, and Sentencing Outcomes,
B. L. Cutler and P. A. Zapf (Editors-in-Chief)
Copyright © 2015 by the American Psychological Association. All rights reserved.

to those processes and outcomes? Do societal justice structures elicit subjective perceptions that justice has been done? As we will discuss later in this chapter, more recent procedural justice research poses additional and fundamental questions about the administration of justice: How do decision makers in the legal system perceive procedural and distributive justice, and to what extent do the subjective justice perceptions of decision makers in the legal system determine the procedures that they will actually endorse and administer to achieve justice?

Aside from addressing fundamental questions about perceptions of justice themselves, the procedural justice field serves an important practical purpose: When procedures are judged to be fair and just, the outcomes they generate are seen to be more fair and satisfactory, people are more likely to comply with the outcomes of those processes, people are more likely to cooperate in the future with the authorities who enacted those procedures, and people are more likely to view those authorities to be more legitimate (Sunshine & Tyler, 2003). Investigating the antecedents to justice perceptions is therefore important partly because of the consequences of justice perceptions: If we are able to increase procedural justice judgments, then we have a noncoercive means of increasing disputants' compliance with the law, cooperation with legal authorities, and perceived legitimacy of those authorities.

RELEVANT PSYCHOLOGICAL THEORY AND PRINCIPLES

Thibaut and Walker (1975, 1978) were the first to systematically investigate procedural justice perceptions in the context of the legal system. Their findings demonstrated that satisfaction with the outcomes of legal disputes is strongly influenced by treatment as well as by outcomes. Thibaut and Walker also contributed significantly to the development of procedural justice theory by delineating two types of control available to disputants in decision-making procedures: process control and decision control. *Process control* (subsequently referred to as *voice*; Folger, 1977) describes the level of control that disputants have over the procedure itself, referring to the amount of input that

disputants have into the process overall, as well as the extent to which they are able to control particular aspects of the procedure, such as the presentation of evidence. *Decision control* describes the level of control disputants have over the outcome of the process. For example, disputants in the adversarial legal system have process control (i.e., they may present evidence in support of their case, or have other input into the procedure itself), but they do not hold decision control. In the traditional, adversarial legal system, the judge or jury (or another independent third party) makes the final decision about the outcome of the case. In other words, disputants in an adversarial legal procedure retain process control, but they have relinquished decision control to a third party.

Thibaut and Walker's (1975, 1978) main proposition was that people's perceptions of procedural justice would be influenced by the allocation of process control and decision control in a decision-making interaction. When disputants are involved in intractable conflict, which they cannot resolve, they often turn to a third party (e.g., legal authorities) with a request for that third party to administer a binding decision and thereby resolve the dispute. In such situations, disputants are willing to relinquish decision control.

Even when disputants are willing to relinquish decision control in this way, however, Thibaut and Walker (1975, 1978) demonstrated that disputants still valued process control, or voice. Several studies have supported this proposition, demonstrating that disputants perceive legal and other decision-making procedures to be fairer when they have been allowed voice than when they have not been permitted voice (Platow, Filardo, Troselj, Grace, & Ryan, 2006; Tyler, 1989; Van Prooijen, Van den Bos, & Wilke, 2007).

Thibaut and Walker's early findings were therefore important for two major insights they provided into human justice reasoning in the legal system: (1) Disputants' perceptions of justice are not dominated solely by outcomes, but are strongly influenced by voice, or process control; and (2) voice during a decision-making procedure increases disputants' perceptions that the outcomes they receive from that procedure are fair and satisfactory. This second insight, that voice, independent of absolute outcome or outcome fairness, increases perceived fairness of outcomes and satisfaction with them, has become known as the *fair process effect*, and has been replicated across many studies in several contexts (Greenberg & Folger, 1983; Hui, Au, & Zhao, 2007; Leung, Tong, & Lind, 2007).

Initially, the fair process effect was attributed to disputants' perceptions that voice would lead to instrumental benefit: Thibaut and Walker (1975) posited that disputants valued voice because of their perception that the opportunity to communicate their input to a decision maker would ultimately translate into outcomes that were fairer to them. These researchers argued that, when disputants had relinquished decision control to a third party, process control or voice was the mechanism by which they felt they could maximize the likelihood of a fair decision from that third party.

Thibaut and Walker's (1975) initial interpretation of the fair process effect was later superseded by research demonstrating that those waiting to receive a decision from a third party do still value voice even when there is no possibility that it may improve the third party's decision (Lind, Kanfer, & Earley, 1990). In their seminal research, Lind et al. (1990) presented participants with one of three levels of voice: No voice (participants were assigned a particular task to complete, and they were given no input into the workload involved); predecision voice (participants were allowed to express an opinion about their assigned workload, and the experimenter then delivered his workload decision to them); postdecision voice (the experimenter delivered his workload decision to participants, but then allowed the participants to express their opinion about the workload assignment). Participants judged procedures to be fairest in the condition where they were allowed voice prior to the delivery of the decision (predecision voice), but they also considered the postdecision voice procedure to be significantly fairer than the no-voice procedure in which they were allowed no voice at all.

The findings of this study by Lind et al. (1990) demonstrated that participants still valued the opportunity to express their opinion, even when they knew that the expression of their opinion could have no impact at all on the authority's decision. These data posed a considerable challenge to Thibaut and Walker's (1975) control theory of procedural justice, because they indicated that people valued voice for noninstrumental reasons; voice was important independent of its ability to shape third-party decisions. Findings such as these led to the formulation of the group value model (Lind & Tyler, 1988; Tyler, 1989; Tyler & Lind, 1992).

The group value model explains the importance of voice in justice judgments via relational, rather than instrumental, priorities. In this model, the central motivator driving justice reasoning is concern for social relationships. The group value model was initially based on social identity theory (Tajfel, 1982; Tajfel & Turner, 1986) and argues that people are strongly motivated to be valued members in social groups that are of importance to them. When people interact with their social groups, or the authorities representing them, they look for signals indicating that they are valued by that group. If a person is being asked for their input or opinion about an event or about the distribution of a resource, this is taken as a sign of one's value to the social group, and an indication of the person's favorable standing in the group. In the earlier procedural justice theory, Thibaut and Walker (1975, 1978) had construed voice as a form of process control, important for its ability to result in instrumental benefit. With the emergence of the group value model, the construal of voice shifted; in the group value model (Lind & Tyler, 1988), voice was now construed as respect: a relational signal, important for the information that it conveyed about one's value to the social group.

The group value model proposes that three variables are central for shaping procedural justice reasoning due to their role in communicating favorable group standing: respectful treatment, neutral processes, and trustworthy authorities. These three procedural features (respect, neutrality and trust) are often termed the relational variables (Tyler & Lind, 1992). Therefore, if an individual's rights are generally respected (respect) during a procedure, if the procedure itself allows all relevant facts to come to light (neutrality), and the authority appears to have the individual's best interests in mind (trust), the procedure conveys to the individual that he is highly valued by the social group. According to the group value model, when a procedure effectively conveys to people that they are valued members of their valued social groups, they will judge that procedure to be fairer.

The central tenet of the group value model, therefore, is not that we judge procedures to be fair because of the promise of instrumental benefit, nor that we value voice because of the possibility of instrumental benefit. According to the group value model, we consider procedures to be fair when they convey perceptions of social value, and we consider voice to be important because of the message that it communicates about the regard in which we are held by the social group. The group value model has come to dominate scholarship on procedural justice, and much of the procedural justice field is shaped around this model. An extensive body of research provides strong support for these central tenets of the group value model (De Cremer & Blader, 2006; MacCoun, 2005).

RESEARCH REVIEW

The strength of these tenets as a foundation of the procedural justice field depends on the validity of the research investigating their effects. The internal and external validity of procedural justice research is supported by the replication of these central theoretical findings across multiple methods and contexts.

Research Methods in Procedural Justice

Since the earliest days of justice research, researchers have tested their research questions using laboratory experiments in which particular independent variables were manipulated to investigate their effects on justice-related affect, cognitions, and behaviors. Although the procedures used in these studies varied (e.g., asking participants to assume the roles of various actors in a fictitious legal dispute, or deceiving undergraduate research participants into believing that they were completing an interview task in exchange for pay on the first day of a new job), the experimental method has always been utilized widely in the procedural justice field. Some of the earliest and seminal studies in

procedural justice research were experimental, including Thibaut and Walker's (1975, 1978) research program, which demonstrated the importance of input or process control, and research by Lind et al. (1990), which provided an explanation for the importance of process control to disputants.

Since these early days of justice research, however, the procedural justice field has expanded to include a wide range of investigative methods. In fact, the procedural justice field is notable for the breadth of methodologies used and the robustness of its central findings across research contexts, methodologies, and populations. Laboratory experiments continue to be prevalent, and while many of these laboratory experiments include fictitious vignettes, asking participants to imagine themselves in particular situations and to assume certain roles, many studies in the procedural justice field are laboratory experiments that utilize deception to engage participants in what they believe to be circumstances that evoke actual justice judgments and related emotions and behaviors. Field surveys are also conducted regularly, and cross-sectional data from these surveys demonstrate the generalizability of laboratory-based findings to naturalistic field settings. For example, research has demonstrated that procedural justice perceptions affect participants' ratings of the legitimacy of authorities and their intentions to comply with the instructions of those authorities in real citizen–police encounters as well as in laboratory studies (Sunshine & Tyler, 2003; Tyler, 1989). Although such cross-sectional data leave questions about direction of causality unanswered, these concerns are addressed in the research field in other ways. For example, panel data demonstrate that use of fair processes (incorporating variables such as voice, neutrality, respect, and trustworthiness) at one time point increase citizens' reports of perceived legitimacy and (self-reported) compliance at a later time point (Murphy, 2005). The causal directions postulated by researchers in these field studies are also corroborated by laboratory experiments in which independent variables were manipulated to demonstrate causal effects with stronger internal validity (e.g., Gangl, 2003; Murphy, Hinds, & Fleming, 2008).

The procedural justice field also regularly uses both quasiexperiments and true experiments in naturalistic field settings, and many of these studies support the generalizability of results from laboratory settings to real-world contexts (e.g., Wenzel, 2006). These convergent results across various methods are key to enhancing our confidence in the central findings of the procedural justice field.

Hundreds of studies demonstrate that perceptions of fair process increase satisfaction with legal decision-making procedures and the decision makers themselves, and such perceptions also increase compliance with the law and cooperation with legal institutions such as the police. Aside from these demonstrations in legal contexts (e.g., Tyler, 1990; Tyler & Huo, 2002), justice research has been conducted in political (Leung et al., 2007), educational (Tyler & Caine, 1981), family (Brubacher, Fondacaro, Brank, Brown, & Miller, 2009), organizational (Cohen-Charash & Spector, 2001), medical (Poythress, Schumacher, Wiener, & Murrin, 1993), and interpersonal settings (Davis-Lipman, Tyler, & Andersen, 2007). In this body of research, the procedural aspects that are manipulated as independent variables in experimental studies, or measured in nonexperimental field studies, include voice (Van Prooijen, Van den Bos, & Wilke, 2002), accuracy (De Cremer, 2004), respect (Tyler et al., 1996), and neutrality (Lind, Tyler, & Huo, 1997). The measurement of procedural justice also varies markedly across these studies, alternately conceptualized as a general judgment about process fairness (e.g., whether an individual judges that he was treated fairly in a procedure; Heuer, Penrod, Hafer, & Cohn, 2002) or as specific and objectively defined aspects of process criteria (e.g., objectivity and impartiality of the authority figure; Van Prooijen et al., 2002). Several other dependent variables are also measured commonly in this field, including satisfaction with the decision-making process (Tyler & Folger, 1980), negative behaviors like stealing (Colquitt & Greenberg, 2003), and positive behaviors such as compliance with regulations and good organizational citizenship (Sunshine & Tyler, 2003; Van Prooijen et al., 2008).

Recently, meta-analyses have also helped further buttress claims about the reliability and validity of justice effects. For example, two meta-analyses examining justice questions in organizational contexts have provided strong support for the claim that procedurally fair treatment has positive influences on people's behavioral and affective reactions to decision making in organizational settings (Cohen-Charash & Spector, 2002; Colquitt, Conlon, Wesson, Porter, & Ng, 2001). Although these studies examined justice reasoning in organizational, not legal, settings, the measures in question were similar to those often examined in legal procedural justice research. For example, whereas organizational procedural justice researchers might examine affective reactions to outcomes in an organizational context, those in the legal domain would examine satisfaction with the outcomes of legal encounters (e.g., Tyler, 1984). Those in the organizational domain would investigate support for the organization or organizational authorities, whereas those in legal contexts would measure support for legal institutions and legal authorities (e.g., Tyler, 1984, 1989). The consistency in procedural justice effects demonstrated across organizational and legal contexts adds to the evidence for the generality of procedural justice effects.

Despite this variation in methodologies, research questions, independent and dependent variables, contexts, and populations, findings regarding the importance of treatment and procedural concerns in formulating perceptions of justice and satisfaction are remarkably consistent. Cohen-Charash and Spector's (2002) meta-analysis examined the effects of particular study characteristics on results and reported that field studies and laboratory studies produce consistent results concerning the effect of procedural justice on satisfaction with authorities and work performance. This finding, in conjunction with the wider consistency in findings across varying methodologies in the field, strengthens the case for the external validity of procedural justice research beyond its laboratory-based experimental origins.

Overall, the generalizability of findings across contexts, populations, and methodologies in this field should be viewed from a theoretical, rather than purely methodological, perspective. From its origins, the procedural justice field has been one in which theoretical development has driven research directions and interpretation of findings (Heuer & Sivasubramaniam, 2011). Whereas applied research in psychology and law more broadly may focus heavily on the quality of specific links between particular studies and the context of their practical application, the nature of procedural justice research, as an endeavor of basic social psychology, is driven more strongly by attention to external validity as defined by Kruglanski and Kroy (1976). In this regard, justice theories have played a crucial role in the generalization of findings of specific studies in restricted contexts to the more varied settings where justice processes are applied in everyday legal interactions.

Moderators of Procedural Justice Judgments

As noted above, the group value model dominates scholarship on procedural justice, and an extensive body of research provides strong support for its central claims (MacCoun, 2005). As moderators of procedural justice effects have been discovered, however, a more nuanced understanding of procedural fairness has emerged. Recently, evidence has suggested that some factors suppress the effects of fair procedures, decreasing the importance of procedural features in formulating justice perceptions. Some early studies showed that decision makers in organizational (e.g., employers; Lissak & Sheppard, 1983) and legal settings (e.g., judges; Houlden, LaTour, Walker, & Thibaut, 1978) were more strongly influenced by instrumental concerns such as financial considerations than by relational concerns such as respectful treatment, but this finding has received little attention. Recent research has expanded the focus of procedural justice investigation to include decision makers, examining justice reasoning among judges. Judges describe their decision-making processes as a utilitarian balance of outcome considerations; a process of weighing societal benefits against individual harms (Monahan & Walker, 1994). This self-report of justice reasoning as a cost–benefit calculation focused on outcome concerns does not fit well with the dominant models of procedural justice, which focus on the importance of treatment and the centrality of

relational concerns in people's decisions about the fairness and propriety of decision-making procedures (e.g., Lind & Tyler, 1988; Tyler & Lind, 1992).

Most justice scholars have focused primarily on decision recipients (those awaiting a decision from a third party at the end of a decision-making procedure) and have paid very little attention to justice reasoning among decision makers (such as judges, police officers, and employers). The nearly exclusive focus in the procedural justice literature on decision recipients (such as disputants in court, citizens in interactions with police, and employees in encounters with their employers) has produced justice reasoning models that emphasize the dominance of procedures in people's justice concerns. To a large extent, these are the models to which forensic psychologists have been exposed, and which have been adopted by various actors in the legal system (e.g., police departments, judges), who are aware of research demonstrating the ability of procedural justice to enhance perceptions of the legitimacy of legal authorities and to encourage compliance with their instructions and cooperation with their future requests (Sunshine & Tyler, 2003).

Until recently, there was little investigation into whether one's status as a decision maker might moderate justice reasoning processes and priorities. In 2007, Heuer, Penrod, and Kattan examined the moderating effects of decision-making status on justice reasoning in four studies, and they concluded that the weight accorded to procedures versus outcomes is moderated by whether those making the judgments are decision makers or decision recipients (Heuer, Penrod, & Kattan, 2007). This implies that the role in which participants operate when they evaluate decision-making procedures might contribute to the discrepancy between judges' self-reports of their justice reasoning and the findings of much procedural justice research.

Three of these studies by Heuer et al. (2007) are valuable for their investigation of decision-maker populations (appellate court judges in Study 1 and state court judges in Study 2), and for their direct comparison of decision makers' and non–decision makers' justice reasoning (restaurant managers versus employees in Study 4). The remaining study, Study 3, furthered this contribution by randomly assigning participants to either a decision-maker or non–decision-maker role. In Study 3 by Heuer et al. (2007), undergraduate participants read a fictional scenario about a campus housing dispute, in which an undergraduate's room was searched in a contested procedure. In an experimental design, participants were randomly assigned to either a decision-maker role (i.e., they were a member of the board that would make a decision about the case) or non–decision-maker role (i.e., they were either the offending student, a student representative on the housing board, or another student resident of university housing). In addition to manipulating the perspective from which participants read this scenario, Heuer et al. (2007) also manipulated the respect with which the student had been treated during the search procedure (respectful vs. disrespectful procedure), as well as the societal benefits of the search outcome (so that the search revealed cocaine in the student's room in the high-benefit condition, and burning incense in the student's room in the low-benefit condition). The findings of this study were consistent with those of the other studies in this research program: Among participants who were in the authority role, the outcome of the search procedure (high- or low-benefit) had a stronger effect on decisions to uphold or overturn convictions than did the respect with which the search was conducted. Among those in the non–decision-maker role, the respect with which the search was conducted had a stronger effect than outcomes on the recommendation to uphold or overturn the sanction.

Reasons for the Disparity Between Decision Maker and Decision Recipient

In four studies, Heuer et al. (2007) demonstrated that decision makers were more influenced by outcomes, rather than by treatment and relational concerns, when evaluating the fairness and propriety of decision-making procedures. While no research has directly investigated the mediators driving this effect, there are several theoretical explanations as to why it might occur.

First, as outlined above, the group value model states that procedures shape fairness judgments because those procedural features offer information

about one's value and standing in social groups (Lind & Tyler, 1988). Thus, respectful treatment is important, not because it is assumed to lead to beneficial outcomes, but because it conveys information about group membership. This analysis of justice motivations might be well-suited to non–decision makers, who often occupy low status in a group and seek information about group standing from an authority figure representing the social group and with whom the low status non–decision maker interacts. The "group value" mechanism is less applicable, however, to decision makers who are interacting with non–decision makers. Generally, decision makers occupy clearly high-status positions in the social group (e.g., they have been vested with decision-making authority, which is itself a symbol of group standing) and therefore may be less motivated to search for these signs of relational value, as it is already clear to them that they are held in high regard by the social group (De Cremer & Tyler, 2005). As well as offering a suggestion as to why decision makers are less concerned with procedural justice, it is also important to consider what decision makers are concerned about. Decision makers may be motivated by different concerns than those that drive non–decision makers, such as the motivation to protect the group. Motivation to protect the group has been described as a fundamental human motivation (Stangor & Leary, 2006), thus it is likely to be of particular concern to group authorities (such as authorities in political, organizational, and legal contexts), who often hold their high-status position for the specific purpose of protecting the group (e.g., the CEO of a company is responsible for the financial viability of a company, whereas the midlevel employee has less responsibility in this regard; a police officer is responsible for protecting the safety of his or her jurisdiction, whereas an ordinary citizen has less responsibility in this regard; Sivasubramaniam & Heuer, 2008.) This increased responsibility for protecting the safety of the group may be one feature that differentiates decision makers from non–decision makers and would lead to an emphasis by decision makers on instrumental, rather than relational, priorities in procedural evaluations. Preliminary data support the notion that perceived responsibility to protect the social group is a mediator driving authorities' decreased concern for respectful procedures (Sivasubramaniam, Heuer, Becker, Hobgood, & Newkirk, 2008).

Second, it may be the case that decision makers are less likely to judge the targets of decision-making procedures as deserving of respectful treatment. This explanation is supported by research indicating that people judge procedures to be fair to the extent that they feel an individual is treated as he or she deserves (Heuer, Blumenthal, Douglass, & Weinblatt, 1999), and some data indicate that decision makers judge negative treatment of suspects in an interrogation to be more deserved than non–decision makers (Sivasubramaniam, Heuer, Schmidt, & Silva, 2009). If decision makers consider the target of a procedure to be less deserving of respectful treatment than do non–decision makers, this would explain the discrepancy between decision makers' and non–decision makers' justice reasoning: Decision makers judge procedures disrespectful to a target to be fairer, to the extent that they believe the target is undeserving of respectful treatment.

Third, it should be noted that a confound exists in the situations in which decision makers and non–decision makers operate: Decision makers are normally the source, rather than the target, of the procedure being enacted. This confound means that a decision maker is often evaluating the treatment of another person, while a non–decision maker is evaluating another person's treatment of himself or herself. For example, a police officer asked to evaluate the fairness or propriety of a recent traffic stop in which he was involved will evaluate the way in which he treated a citizen, whereas a citizen asked to evaluate that traffic stop process will evaluate the way that he was treated by the police officer. This source–target distinction may drive the reduced concern for respectful treatment shown by decision makers—people may be more concerned about respect when they are evaluating their own treatment than when they are evaluating another person's treatment, perhaps because they feel that they are more deserving of respectful treatment than another (Heuer et al., 1999). Further clarification is therefore required regarding this confound: Investigations into the justice reasoning of decision makers should determine whether decision makers

approach justice reasoning with qualitatively different motivations from decision recipients, or whether this is simply an artifact of being the source rather than the target of the treatment.

The research and theory reviewed above offers suggestions about the mediators driving the disparity between decision makers and non–decision makers as revealed by Heuer et al. (2007). Further research is needed to establish support for any of these theoretical possibilities and to replicate the findings of Heuer et al. (2007) across more contexts, both within and outside of the legal system.

PRACTICE AND POLICY ISSUES

The findings of Heuer et al. (2007) are distinct from the majority of the procedural justice literature. This large body of work focuses on decision recipients and demonstrates the importance of respectful treatment for justice reasoning, in support of the group value model (Lind & Tyler, 1988) and related, subsequent models (e.g., the relational model; Tyler & Lind, 1992). Although the group value model has been developed on the basis of justice reasoning among decision recipients, its application in the legal system has had an important impact on the enactment of justice procedures, encouraging the use of fair procedures by legal decision makers not only for reasons of objective fairness, but also to elicit perceived legitimacy and compliance among decision recipients. This represents only one side of justice reasoning, however, and modern legal practice would benefit by attending to this basic social psychology research on justice reasoning among decision makers. The procedural justice literature is an area of basic social psychology research with broad and important applications to the legal system. The recent developments in procedural justice research, and the various theoretical perspectives outlined above, can offer valuable insight into the motivations driving decision makers in the legal system.

Relevance of Procedural Justice in Modern Courtroom Practice

Cognitive psychology refers to the processes by which sensory input is received, processed, stored, and used (Neisser, 1967). Many areas of forensic psychology research have strong foundations in cognitive psychology, applying cognitive principles in various legal arenas. A central concern of research on false memories, flashbulb memories, and eyewitness memories is the encoding, storage, and retrieval of information. Research on eyewitness identification encompasses memory research as well as the cognitive psychology of attention and perception. In jury decision-making research, the story model (Pennington & Hastie, 1986) describes the process by which jurors integrate information to form a cohesive narrative about an event. Cognitive perspectives in psychology and law are primarily concerned with human ability to meet the processing challenges presented by the legal system—whether humans encode, integrate, store, retrieve, and weigh information according to the aims and principles articulated by the justice system.

Social psychology, on the other hand, is the study of ways in which the thoughts, feelings, and behaviors of individuals are influenced by the actual, imagined, or implied presence of other people (Allport, 1954). Several areas of forensic psychology can essentially be considered as applied social psychology. Psychologists studying race and ethnicity in the legal system apply social psychology research on prejudice and discrimination to investigate the ways in which race affects attitudes towards suspects, victims, and defendants (see Chapter 5, this volume). Social psychologists study the causes and consequences of violence and aggression, and they draw on research about prosocial behavior and altruism to explain phenomena relevant to the legal system, such as the bystander effect. In jury research, social psychologists examine how particular situational factors affect jurors' attitudes toward defendants, and principles of group behavior are applied to investigate the dynamics of juror interactions and decision making (see Chapter 10, this volume). Social psychology perspectives in psychology and law are primarily concerned with particular situations central to the justice system and how those situations influence human affect, behavior, and cognition.

Many areas of forensic psychology research incorporate both cognitive and social psychology perspectives. For example, research on eyewitness identification encompasses both cognitive challenges (i.e., encoding, storage, and retrieval of identification-relevant information) and social aspects (e.g., cues and feedback from lineup administrators) of the identification task (see Chapter 7, this volume). Some areas of forensic psychology research, however, have come to be dominated by one or the other of these perspectives. For example, research on jurors' use of inadmissible evidence has tended toward cognitive explanations focused on juror abilities and reasoning, but there is reason to believe that the social psychological perspective warrants more attention in this area of research.

In the Canadian case of *R. v. Khan* (2001), the accused was convicted of the first-degree murder of his wife. During deliberations, the jury had been given transcripts of the pathologist's testimony, but more than six hours later it was discovered that the transcripts contained a record of matters discussed in *voir dire* (in the absence of the jury), and defense counsel moved for a mistrial. The trial judge denied the request for a mistrial, and instead issued clean transcripts to the jury, along with a curative instruction to rely solely on the admissible evidence that had been placed before them. The defendant was convicted, and the defense appealed the conviction on the grounds that the jury had viewed tainted evidence and could draw adverse inferences against the accused on the basis of that evidence. The Court of Appeal upheld the conviction, affirming the trial judge's decision to issue a curative instruction rather than declare a mistrial, and stated that "the admonition issued by the trial judge to the jury was sufficient to remedy any ill effect that the unedited transcripts might have had on the jury" (*R. v. Khan*, 2001, para. 36).

A central role of the court system is to ensure the fair conduct of jury trials and to ensure that the information that jurors evaluate in arriving at a verdict decision is screened appropriately for its probative versus prejudicial value. Cases such as *R. v. Khan* (2001) demonstrate the faith that Canadian courts (and courts worldwide) place in the *curative instruction*—an instruction to jurors that they should disregard evidence that has been ruled inadmissible. If jurors continue to consider inadmissible evidence, despite these instructions to disregard it, this poses a fundamental challenge to the proper administration of justice in that jurors would be formulating a verdict based on information that the court has deemed inappropriate (because, for example, it is unreliable or improperly obtained), leading to potential miscarriages of justice. It is therefore a central concern of the legal system and the behavioral scientists who study it to ensure that jurors only consider evidence the court has deemed admissible.

Behavioral scientists have consistently demonstrated the need to be skeptical of the effectiveness of these curative instructions, showing that jurors continue to use inadmissible evidence despite instructions to disregard it (e.g., Doob & Kirshenbaum, 1972; Wissler & Saks, 1985). Dozens of studies on juror decision making have demonstrated that, when mock jurors are exposed to incriminating, contested evidence against a defendant that is ruled admissible, there is a greater tendency to convict that defendant, compared to control conditions in which no contested evidence was revealed (Greene & Dodge, 1995; Hans & Doob, 1976; Schuller, 1995). The impact of inadmissible evidence on juror decision making is well established: Steblay, Hosch, Culhane, and McWethy (2006) conducted a meta-analysis of research in the field, in which they analyzed findings from 48 studies involving 8,474 participants, and found that exposure to inadmissible evidence increases convictions, and that it does so even when accompanied by an immediate instruction by a judge to disregard the inadmissible evidence. Research also shows that jurors are not aware of the biasing effects of this evidence. Jurors are more likely to convict a defendant when they have seen (and have been instructed to disregard) inadmissible evidence that the defendant confessed during a coercive interrogation, yet jurors do not accurately self-report that the inadmissible evidence influenced their verdicts (Kassin & Sukel, 1997; for more detail on jury decision-making research, see Chapter 10, this volume).

Many researchers who have demonstrated the effects of inadmissible evidence on jury decision making have relied overwhelmingly on cognitive explanations for these phenomena. For example, Greene and Dodge (1995) ask, "Why weren't these instructions more effective? One possibility is that jurors simply *did not understand* [emphasis added] that they could use prior record information only to determine identity and not for other purposes" (p. 77). Similarly, London and Nunez (2000) state that "the *ability* or *inability* [emphasis added] of jurors to disregard inadmissible evidence has important judicial implications" (p. 932). In discussing the findings of their meta-analysis, Steblay et al. (2006) note that the data are consistent with research on common deficits in information processing, and they highlight the high cognitive load under which jurors must comply with instructions to disregard specific pieces of information. Cumulatively, these explanations focus on juror competence: Researchers note that jurors are unable to disregard evidence to which they have been exposed and which has been ruled inadmissible. Thus, juror use of inadmissible evidence is one example of a problem in legal practice that has primarily been addressed by forensic psychology researchers from a cognitive perspective.

The procedural justice literature, as a social psychology perspective, can and should be leveraged to illuminate motivational mechanisms that also operate in juror (and other) decision making in the legal system. The research on procedural justice that we have outlined in this chapter has the potential to offer a novel insight into this problem of juror consideration of inadmissible evidence. In particular, the recent evidence regarding decision makers' justice reasoning lends support to a motivational, rather than cognitive, explanation for the impact of inadmissible evidence on juror decision making. Evidence from the procedural justice research shows that decision makers adhere more to outcome concerns in their judgments about the fairness and propriety of decision-making procedures, while non–decision makers adhere more to procedural concerns. While Heuer et al. (2007) demonstrate the replicability of this finding across several studies, the finding merits study in some additional contexts to determine its generalizability. Importantly, this generalizability can be tested with an application of the principle to jurors in the courtroom: Jurors are the decision makers in a jury trial—they are charged with the responsibility of making the final verdict decision, and the defendant will either be convicted (and likely incarcerated) or acquitted (and freed into the community) on the basis of their decision. Therefore, when jurors (decision makers) view inadmissible evidence, we argue that they may continue to consider inadmissible evidence in their verdict decisions, despite the judge's instruction to disregard it, if they believe that the evidence will help them reach a just verdict. If people are not in a decision maker role, they will adhere to procedural justice concerns and disregard inadmissible evidence when instructed to do so. As we have outlined above, there are several possible mediators of this effect; for example, jurors could be motivated in their justice reasoning by a perceived need to protect the social group, or by an increased perception that the defendant deserves to be convicted, based on information gleaned from the inadmissible evidence.

Random assignment is an important methodological feature of an experimental study. It should be noted that participants in Study 3 by Heuer et al. (2007) were randomly assigned to one of two roles, and that this random assignment produced differences between decision makers and non–decision makers in justice reasoning. Simply instructing participants to assume the role of a decision maker in these scenarios alters the way that these participants considered the justice and propriety of a procedure and its outcomes. This has direct implications for jury decision making: Stepping into the decision maker role itself changes what people consider to be a fair and acceptable procedure. The research described in this chapter suggests that jurors, who are in a decision-making role with a responsibility to protect the wider social group, are less concerned than non–decision makers (e.g., trial observers, defendants) about the procedural aspects of the decision-making process, such as instructions to disregard inappropriate or unfairly obtained evidence, and are more concerned about ensuring that a just and appropriate outcome results from the procedure. By virtue of being decision makers, and for the possible motivations theorised above, jurors might adopt a different notion of the appropriate balance of procedural and distributive justice as the key to satisfactory procedures, which may explain why they are

disinclined to adhere to judicial admonitions about inappropriate evidence. These recent developments in procedural justice literature therefore illuminate an alternative to the cognitive explanations for jurors' low responsiveness to curative instructions, framing jurors' consideration of inadmissible evidence as a motivational challenge: Jurors may be unwilling to disregard evidence that is ruled inadmissible after they have already been exposed to that evidence.

Relevance in Court Decisions and Legislation

It should be noted that other forensic psychology researchers have considered the possibility of a motivational, rather than a cognitive, explanation for juror consideration of inadmissible evidence. Kassin and Sommers (1997) have argued that jurors are motivated to obtain just outcomes, and they showed that jurors will disregard inadmissible evidence when they are provided with a legitimate reason for the judge's instruction to disregard it, such as a ruling that the evidence itself is unreliable (and therefore is not more likely to lead to a just outcome if considered). While the findings of Kassin and Sommers (1997) demonstrate support for a motivational explanation, the reasoning that we outline in this chapter advances the field further by suggesting a basis for this motivation, that is, decision-making status. This research highlights a key point for forensic psychology researchers who have documented juror consideration of inadmissible evidence and the motivational explanations for it: It is not simply the case that jurors disregard their instructions from judges based on defiance or a decision to sacrifice fair procedures for just outcomes; rather the procedural justice research suggests that jurors (and other decision makers) may construe the fairness of these procedures differently than defendants and other observers, in that they actually perceive a procedure to be fairer when it leads to a just outcome. To an outside observer, who is not in a decision-making role, it may be evident that inappropriately obtained evidence should not be used and would decrease the fairness of the decision-making procedure, whereas to jurors this is less evident.

Therefore, rather than framing juror use of inadmissible evidence as a cognitive issue, or even a broad motivational issue, research in forensic psychology might benefit from more work specifically devoted to understanding decision makers' perceptions of justice, which a few initial studies suggest might be more outcome-driven than the justice perceptions of decision recipients. Testing the decision maker–decision recipient disparity in the jury decision-making context could involve the replication of previous research on inadmissible evidence (in which participants are often asked to read accounts of trials from the perspective of a juror), along with a manipulation of a participant's role: juror versus nonjuror. According to the procedural justice research reviewed in this chapter, participants in a juror (decision maker) role might be expected to behave as participants have done in previous studies on inadmissible evidence, ignoring judicial instructions to disregard inadmissible evidence. The motivational explanation derived from the decision maker–decision recipient disparity in the procedural justice research suggests that this effect will be attenuated among non–decision makers (e.g., defendants, outside observers), with these non–decision makers less concerned about distributive justice and more willing to adhere to judicial instructions about procedural justice.

Applications of this research can then be more effectively devoted to changing jurors' evaluations of these decision-making procedures, so the benefit of this more basic, social psychological analysis is an insight regarding a practical intervention in an important legal problem. Interventions that aim to change behavior are more effective when they target the determinants of that behavior (Michie, Johnston, Francis, Hardeman, & Eccles, 2008). With a greater understanding of juror motivations as decision makers, we may be able to more effectively intervene in the phenomenon, possibly by modifying curative instructions so that they are more aligned with jurors' outcome-driven concerns. The research reviewed in this chapter suggests that the more successful approach would be to make decision makers more aware of unjust outcomes that could result from consideration of inadmissible evidence, rather than instructing them about the importance of adhering to procedural fairness. According to the research that we have reviewed here, successfully convincing jurors that consideration of inadmissible evidence is a threat to just outcomes should lead jurors not only to disregard the inadmissible evidence when instructed, but also to perceive the consideration of inadmissible evidence as procedurally unfair.

Procedural Justice and Other Decision Makers in the Legal System

In this chapter, we have discussed the way in which the application of the procedural justice literature to the jury decision-making field can advance our inquiry into the inadmissible evidence problem in jury decision making. We have applied the research on justice reasoning among decision makers to juror decision making, as one demonstration of its ability to explain established effects in a given domain. The procedural justice research could be applied much more broadly, however, so that the advantage of returning to basic research on the social psychology of procedural justice is to shed light on the behavior of a range of decision makers in the legal system.

The generalizability of the decision maker–decision recipient disparity may be tested among any legal actors who assume an authority role at any stage of the legal process. For example, judges appear to evaluate procedures based on outcome-driven rather than procedural concerns (Heuer et al., 2007), which should prompt further investigation of this phenomenon in judicial decision making as well as juror decision making. Interrogators' decisions about the fairness and propriety of interrogation techniques may be heavily influenced by their role as authorities in the interaction and the responsibility they hold for protecting the social group (Sivasubramaniam & Heuer, 2012; see Chapter 9, this volume for a review of interrogations and confessions). It may be the case that police officers evaluate the fairness of arrest procedures from a decision maker's perspective, and lineup administrators may do the same. Parole boards are subject to many of the concerns that may influence decision makers, particularly a responsibility to protect the community, and thus the motivational pressures in operation among decision makers are likely to affect these authorities as well. These pressures may even operate in forensic assessment decisions, where experts are called on for a recommendation about the threat that a defendant or prisoner poses to the community; to the extent that these experts feel that their decisions will affect the outcome of a case, their recommendations may be influenced by their role as decision makers and the motivational pressures that accompany that role. The social psychology of justice reasoning is therefore a research field that could be applied to decision makers across all stages and domains of the legal system.

SUMMARY AND CONCLUSIONS

Previous procedural justice research has demonstrated the importance of respectful treatment in justice reasoning across a variety of contexts and methodologies. The research that we have reviewed in this chapter indicates that the meaning and importance of procedural justice is moderated by role. We have outlined four studies by Heuer et al. (2007) that demonstrate differences between decision makers and non–decision makers in the factors governing justice reasoning. Overall, this research demonstrates that decision makers' procedural justice reasoning is driven more strongly by outcome concerns, and less strongly by relational concerns, when compared to non–decision makers. We have speculated about possible reasons for this discrepancy (including different levels of perceived responsibility among decision makers and non–decision makers for the protection of the social group; differences between decision makers and non–decision makers in the extent to which the target of a procedure is perceived to deserve respectful treatment; and greater concern for respect when one is the target, rather than the source, of the treatment in question), and we have discussed the implications of this discrepancy for decision making in the legal system. In particular, we have noted that jurors' consideration of inadmissible evidence may be due not to cognitive limitations, and not to a sacrifice of procedural justice in pursuit of just outcomes, but to a basic difference in the meaning of procedural justice

itself: use of inadmissible evidence may be considered by jurors to be procedurally fair, to the extent that it is believed to lead to just outcomes. This social psychological analysis allows forensic psychology researchers to design curative instructions that are more effective in discouraging juror use of inadmissible evidence, because they more effectively target the determinants of jurors' behavior. Similarly, we have argued that procedural justice research indicating a discrepancy between decision makers and decision recipients in procedural justice reasoning could be applied to decision makers across the legal system, which would help forensic psychology researchers and legal practitioners explain and influence the behavior of those decision makers.

In this chapter, we have framed procedural justice research as foundational social psychology, which has a long and established history of empirical testing according to a strong theoretical foundation. As such, this is a rich resource of theory that can be applied across several domains of psychology and law, which can serve to guide forensic psychology research questions. As we have sought to demonstrate here in the case of jury decision making, basic social psychology research on procedural justice can also provide explanations for effects observed in the legal system and can direct our interventions in those effects. As illustrated in our analysis of procedural justice reasoning in juror (and other legal) decision making, it remains important for forensic psychology to continually return to these basic science principles as a touchstone for application to the legal context.

References

Allport, G. W. (1954). The historical background of modern social psychology. In G. Lindzey (Ed.), *Handbook of social psychology* (Vol. 1, pp. 3–56). Reading, MA: Addison-Wesley.

Brubacher, M. R., Fondacaro, M. R., Brank, E. M., Brown, V. E., & Miller, S. A. (2009). Procedural justice in resolving family disputes: Implications for childhood bullying. *Psychology, Public Policy, and Law, 15,* 149–167. doi:10.1037/a0016839

Cohen-Charash, Y., & Spector, P. E. (2001). The role of justice in organizations: A meta-analysis. *Organizational Behavior and Human Decision Processes, 86,* 278–321. doi:10.1006/obhd.2001.2958

Cohen-Charash, Y., & Spector, P. E. (2002). The role of justice in organizations: A meta-analysis: Erratum. *Organizational Behavior and Human Decision Processes, 89*, 1215. doi:10.1016/S0749-5978(02)00040-7

Colquitt, J. A., Conlon, D. E., Wesson, M. J., Porter, C. O., & Ng, K. Y. (2001). Justice at the millennium: A meta-analytic review of 25 years of organizational justice research. *Journal of Applied Psychology, 86*, 425–445. doi:10.1037/0021-9010.86.3.425

Colquitt, J. A., & Greenberg, J. (2003). Organizational justice: A fair assessment of the state of the literature. In J. Greenberg (Ed.), *Organizational behavior: The state of the science* (2nd ed., pp. 165–210). Mahwah, NJ: Erlbaum.

Davis-Lipman, A., Tyler, T. R., & Andersen, S. M. (2007). Building community one relationship at a time: Consequences for the seeking and acceptance of help. *Social Justice Research, 20*, 181–206. doi:10.1007/s11211-007-0038-8

De Cremer, D. (2004). The influence of accuracy as a function of leader's bias: The role of trustworthiness in the psychology of procedural justice. *Personality and Social Psychology Bulletin, 30*, 293–304. doi:10.1177/0146167203256969

De Cremer, D., & Blader, S. L. (2006). Why do people care about procedural fairness? The importance of belongingness in responding and attending to procedures. *European Journal of Social Psychology, 36*, 211–228. doi:10.1002/ejsp.290

De Cremer, D., & Tyler, T. R. (2005). *Managing* group behaviour: The interplay between procedural justice, sense of self, and cooperation. In M. P. Zanna (Ed.), *Advances in experimental social psychology* (pp. 151–218). San Diego, CA: Elsevier Academic Press.

Doob, A. N., & Kirshenbaum, H. M. (1972). Some empirical evidence of the effect of s. 12 of the Canada Evidence Act upon an accused. *Criminal Law Quarterly, 15*, 88–96.

Folger, R. (1977). Distributive and procedural justice: Combined impact of "voice" and improvement on experienced inequity. *Journal of Personality and Social Psychology, 35*, 108–119. doi:10.1037/0022-3514.35.2.108

Gangl, A. (2003). Procedural justice theory and evaluations of the lawmaking process. *Political Behavior, 25*, 119–149. doi:10.1023/A:1023847829172

Greenberg, J., & Folger, R. (1983). Procedural justice, participation, and the fair process effect in groups and organizations. In P. B. Paulus (Ed.), *Basic Group Processes* (pp. 235–256). New York, NY: Springer. doi:10.1007/978-1-4612-5578-9_10

Greene, E., & Dodge, M. (1995). The influence of prior record evidence on juror decision-making. *Law and Human Behavior, 19*, 67–78. doi:10.1007/BF01499073

Hans, V. P., & Doob, A. N. (1976). Section 12 of the Canada Evidence Act and the deliberation of simulated juries. *Criminal Law Quarterly, 18*, 235–253.

Heuer, L., Blumenthal, E., Douglas, A., & Weinblatt, T. (1999). A deservingness approach to respect as a relationally based fairness judgment. *Personality and Social Psychology Bulletin, 25*, 1279–1292. doi:10.1177/0146167299258009

Heuer, L., Penrod, S., Hafer, C. L., & Cohn, I. (2002). The role of resource and relational concerns for procedural justice. *Personality and Social Psychology Bulletin, 28*, 1468–1482. doi:10.1177/014616702237575

Heuer, L., Penrod, S., & Kattan, A. (2007). The role of societal benefits and fairness concerns among decision makers and decision recipients. *Law and Human Behavior, 31*, 573–610. doi:10.1007/s10979-006-9084-2

Heuer, L., & Sivasubramaniam, D. (2011). Procedural justice: Theory and method. In B. Rosenfeld, & S. D. Penrod (Eds.), *Research methods in forensic psychology* (pp. 283–305). Hoboken, NJ: Wiley.

Houlden, P., LaTour, S., Walker, L., & Thibaut, J. (1978). Preference for modes of dispute resolution as a function of process and decision control. *Journal of Experimental Social Psychology, 14*, 13–30. doi:10.1016/0022-1031(78)90057-4

Hui, M. K., Au, K., & Zhao, X. (2007). Interactional justice and the fair process effect: The role of outcome uncertainty. *Journal of Experimental Social Psychology, 43*, 210–220. doi:10.1016/j.jesp.2006.02.014

Kassin, S. M., & Sommers, S. R. (1997). Inadmissible testimony, instructions to disregard, and the jury: Substantive versus procedural considerations. *Personality and Social Psychology Bulletin, 23*, 1046–1054. doi:10.1177/01461672972310005

Kassin, S. M., & Sukel, H. (1997). Coerced confessions and the jury: An experimental test of the "harmless error" rule. *Law and Human Behavior, 21*, 27–46. doi:10.1023/A:1024814009769

Kruglanski, A. W., & Kroy, M. (1976). Outcome validity in experimental research: A conceptualization. *Representative Research in Social Psychology, 7*, 166–178.

Leung, K., Tong, K.-K., & Lind, E. (2007). Realpolitik versus fair process: Moderating effects of group identification on acceptance of political decisions. *Journal of Personality and Social Psychology, 92*, 476–489. doi:10.1037/0022-3514.92.3.476

Lind, E. A., Kanfer, R., & Earley, P. C. (1990). Voice, control, and procedural justice: Instrumental and noninstrumental concerns in fairness judgments. *Journal of Personality and Social Psychology, 59*, 952–959. doi:10.1037/0022-3514.59.5.952

Lind, E. A., & Tyler, T. R. (1988). *The social psychology of procedural justice.* New York, NY: Plenum Press. doi:10.1007/978-1-4899-2115-4

Lind, E. A., Tyler, T. R., & Huo, Y. J. (1997). Procedural context and culture: Variation in the antecedents of procedural justice judgments. *Journal of Personality and Social Psychology, 73,* 767–780. doi:10.1037/0022-3514.73.4.767

Lissak, R. I., & Sheppard, B. H. (1983). Beyond fairness: The criterion problem in research on dispute intervention. *Journal of Applied Social Psychology, 13,* 45–65. doi:10.1111/j.1559-1816.1983.tb00886.x

London, K., & Nunez, N. (2000). The effect of jury deliberations on jurors' propensity to disregard inadmissible evidence. *Journal of Applied Psychology, 85,* 932–939. doi:10.1037/0021-9010.85.6.932

MacCoun, R. J. (2005). Voice, control and belonging: The double-edged sword of procedural fairness. *Annual Review of Law and Social Science, 1,* 171–201. doi:10.1146/annurev.lawsocsci.1.041604.115958

Michie, S., Johnston, S., Francis, J., Hardeman, W., & Eccles, M. (2008). From theory to intervention: Mapping theoretically derived behavioural determinants to behaviour change techniques. *Applied Psychology: An International Review, 57,* 660–680. doi:10.1111/j.1464-0597.2008.00341.x

Monahan, J., & Walker, L. (1994). *Social science and law: Cases and materials* (3rd ed.). Mineola, NY: Foundation Press.

Murphy, K. (2005). Regulating more effectively: The relationship between procedural justice, legitimacy, and tax non-compliance. *Journal of Law and Society, 32,* 562–589. doi:10.1111/j.1467-6478.2005.00338.x

Murphy, K., Hinds, L., & Fleming, J. (2008). Encouraging public cooperation and support for police. *Policing and Society, 18,* 136–155. doi:10.1080/10439460802008660

Neisser, U. (1967). *Cognitive psychology.* New York, NY: Meredith.

Pennington, N., & Hastie, R. (1986). Evidence evaluation in complex decision making. *Journal of Personality and Social Psychology, 51,* 242–258. doi:10.1037/0022-3514.51.2.242

Platow, M. J., Filardo, F., Troselj, L. G., Grace, D. M., & Ryan, M. K. (2006). Non-instrumental voice and extra-role behavior. *European Journal of Social Psychology, 36,* 135–146. doi:10.1002/ejsp.293

Poythress, N. G., Schumacher, J., Wiener, R., & Murrin, M. (1993). Procedural justice judgments of alternative procedures for resolving medical malpractice claims. *Journal of Applied Social Psychology, 23,* 1639–1658. doi:10.1111/j.1559-1816.1993.tb01059.x

R. v. Khan, 3 S.C.R. 823 (2001).

Schuller, R. A. (1995). Expert evidence and hearsay: The influence of "secondhand" information on jurors' decisions. *Law and Human Behavior, 19,* 345–362. doi:10.1007/BF01499136

Sivasubramaniam, D., & Heuer, L. (2008). Decision makers and decision recipients: Understanding disparities in the meaning of fairness. *Court Review, 44,* 62–71.

Sivasubramaniam, D., & Heuer, L. (2012). Procedural justice evaluations in interrogations. In B. L. Cutler (Ed.), *Conviction of the innocent: Lessons from psychological research* (pp. 79–102). Washington, DC: American Psychological Association. doi:10.1037/13085-004

Sivasubramaniam, D., Heuer, L., Becker, S., Hobgood, C., & Newkirk, L. (2008, March). *Respect and threat: Authority–subordinate disparities in justice reasoning.* Paper presented at the annual meeting of the American Psychology-Law Society, Jacksonville, FL.

Sivasubramaniam, D., Heuer, L., Schmidt, H., & Silva, H. (2009, March). *Authorities' perceptions of fairness as a cause of wrongful conviction.* Paper presented at the annual meeting of the American Psychology-Law Society, San Antonio, TX.

Stangor, C., & Leary, S. P. (2006). Intergroup beliefs: Investigations from the social side. In M. Zanna (Ed.), *Advances in experimental social psychology* (Vol. 38, pp. 243–281). San Diego, CA: Elsevier Academic Press.

Steblay, N., Hosch, H. M., Culhane, S. E., & McWethy, A. (2006). The impact of juror verdicts of judicial instruction to disregard inadmissible evidence: A meta-analysis. *Law and Human Behavior, 30,* 469–492. doi:10.1007/s10979-006-9039-7

Sunshine, J., & Tyler, T. R. (2003). The role of procedural justice and legitimacy in shaping public support for policing. *Law and Society Review, 37,* 513–548. doi:10.1111/1540-5893.3703002

Tajfel, H. (1982). The social psychology of intergroup relations. *Annual Review of Psychology, 33,* 1–39. doi:10.1146/annurev.ps.33.020182.000245

Tajfel, H., & Turner, J. (1986). The social identity theory of intergroup behavior. In S. Worchel (Ed.), *Psychology of Intergroup Relations* (pp. 7–24). Chicago, IL: Nelson Hall.

Thibaut, J., & Walker, L. (1975). *Procedural justice: A psychological analysis.* Hillsdale, NJ: Erlbaum.

Thibaut, J., & Walker, L. (1978). A theory of procedure. *California Law Review, 66,* 541–566. doi:10.2307/3480099

Tyler, T. R. (1984). The role of perceived injustice in defendants' evaluations of their courtroom experience. *Law and Society Review, 18,* 51–74. doi:10.2307/3053480

Tyler, T. R. (1989). The psychology of procedural justice: A test of the group-value model. *Journal of Personality and Social Psychology, 57*, 830–838. doi:10.1037/0022-3514.57.5.830

Tyler, T. R. (1990). *Why people obey the law*. New Haven, CT: Yale University Press.

Tyler, T. R., & Caine, A. (1981). The influence of outcomes and procedures on satisfaction with formal leaders. *Journal of Personality and Social Psychology, 41*, 642–655. doi:10.1037/0022-3514.41.4.642

Tyler, T. R., Degoey, P., & Smith, H. J. (1996). Understanding why the justice of group procedures matters: A test of the psychological dynamics of the group value model. *Journal of Personality and Social Psychology, 70*, 913–930. doi:10.1037/0022-3514.70.5.913

Tyler, T. R., & Folger, R. (1980). Distributional and procedural aspects of satisfaction in citizen-police encounters. *Basic and Applied Social Psychology, 1*, 281–292. doi:10.1207/s15324834basp0104_1

Tyler, T. R., & Huo, Y. J. (2002). *Trust in the Law*. New York, NY: Sage.

Tyler, T. R., & Lind, E. A. (1992). *A relational model of authority in groups*. In M. P. Zanna (Ed.), *Advances in experimental social psychology* (Vol. 25, pp. 115–192). New York, NY: Academic Press. doi:10.1016/S0065-2601(08)60283-X

Van Prooijen, J.-W., De Cremer, D., Van Beest, I., Ståhl, T., Van Dijke, M., & Van Lange, P. A. (2008). The egocentric nature of procedural justice: Social value orientation as moderator of reactions to decision-making procedures. *Journal of Experimental Social Psychology, 44*, 1303–1315. doi:10.1016/j.jesp.2008.05.006

Van Prooijen, J.-W., Van den Bos, K., & Wilke, H. A. M. (2002). Procedural justice and status: Status salience as antecedent of procedural fairness effects. *Journal of Personality and Social Psychology, 83*, 1353–1361. doi:10.1037/0022-3514.83.6.1353

Van Prooijen, J.-W., Van den Bos, K., & Wilke, H. A. M. (2007). Procedural justice in authority relations: The strength of outcome dependence influences people's reactions to voice. *European Journal of Social Psychology, 37*, 1286–1297. doi:10.1002/ejsp.435

Wenzel, M. (2006). A letter from the tax office: Compliance effects of informational and interpersonal justice. *Social Justice Research, 19*, 345–364. doi:10.1007/s11211-006-0011-y

Wissler, R. L., & Saks, M. J. (1985). On the inefficacy of limiting instructions: When jurors use prior conviction evidence to decide on guilt. *Law and Human Behavior, 9*, 37–48. doi:10.1007/BF01044288

PART III

SENTENCING AND INCARCERATION

CHAPTER 13

PROBATION AND PAROLE

Jill Viglione and Faye S. Taxman

Approximately seven million adult offenders are under correctional supervision (Glaze & Parks, 2011), with more than five million under some form of community supervision (Clement, Schwarzfeld, & Thompson, 2011). Probation is the most commonly used form of criminal sentencing in the United States (Petersilia, 1997), with approximately 84% of adults on community supervision or probation and 16% on parole (Glaze & Parks, 2011). Similar trends are present in the juvenile justice system, with the majority of youth also on probation (Chiancone, 2010). Despite the breadth of community supervision in the United States, there is little evidence that traditional models of probation and parole are effective in reducing recidivism (Bonta, Rugge, Scott, Bourgon, & Annie, 2008; Taxman, 2002, 2012).

IMPORTANCE OF THE PROBLEM

With the added intrusion of high prison populations and associated costs (Rhine, Mawhorr, & Parks, 2006), and the problems associated with penal severity, evidence-based practices (EBPs), or practices scientifically proven to be effective (Sherman, 1998), are promoted as a tool to provide for better, more fair outcomes. The current emphasis on EBPs shifts the pendulum back toward emphasizing the "people changing" instead of "people processing" outcome that is more compatible with the rehabilitative goal of the justice system. These shifts have

meaningful impacts on probation and parole organizations, often challenging how probation and parole officers (POs) approach their jobs. An unresolved issue is the frequently cited tension between the two distinct goals of the criminal justice system: punishment and rehabilitation.

While traditional probation/parole practice emphasized supervision and control (Taxman, 2008, 2012), the EBP movement introduces new concepts and practices to the community supervision field. Increasingly gaining attention is the risk–needs–responsivity (RNR) model, which combines an actuarial, managerial approach with a rehabilitative, clinical model for supervision (Andrews & Bonta, 2010a; Taxman, 2008). Transforming the justice system to accommodate EBPs has resulted in new methods of knowledge generation and diffusion. Relatively new curriculums and organizational development approaches geared toward probation/parole practice have been advanced to change practice and integrate RNR concepts in the daily work of POs. These approaches have major implications for the field of probation/parole and greatly shift how POs think about and carry out their jobs. The use of EBPs and the RNR model in probation/parole practice is crucial to better serve the millions of probationers in the United States and produce better outcomes.

This chapter presents a historical background on the roles of probation/parole officers and then discusses how the current push for EBPs might shift

We thank Judy Sachwald, Ralph Serin, and Stephanie Maass for their contributions.

http://dx.doi.org/10.1037/14462-013
APA Handbook of Forensic Psychology: Vol. 2. Criminal Investigation, Adjudication, and Sentencing Outcomes,
B. L. Cutler and P. A. Zapf (Editors-in-Chief)
Copyright © 2015 by the American Psychological Association. All rights reserved.

these roles in the 21st century and create new challenges. The remainder of the chapter outlines the various curriculums and models that have been developed and implemented in probation/parole settings to promote and generate changes in the way POs do their jobs. Finally, the chapter concludes with a discussion of the implications for probation/parole practice.

RELEVANT PSYCHOLOGICAL THEORY AND PRINCIPLES

Early practices of probation surfaced in the 1900s, with all U.S. states passing adult and juvenile probation laws by 1956 (Latessa & Allen, 1997). The first POs worked directly for judges and were often recruited from law enforcement (Dressler, 1962). From the start, unclear and often inconsistent missions and goals characterized the field of probation. Contradictory goals of reformation/rehabilitation and law enforcement/control were present since the inception of probation. Prior to the 1970s, rehabilitation and social work strategies dominated the field, with POs focusing on linking probationers to resources and services in the community (Taxman, 2008). A shift toward the more punitive goals of criminal justice occurred after the publication of several reports that drew national attention to the apparent failings of correctional, probation, and treatment interventions and programming (Bailey, 1966; Cullen & Gendreau, 2000). The attack on rehabilitation in the mid-1970s challenged the field of probation and parole. The pendulum swung toward enforcement, which resulted in the permeation of punishment ideals in probation, shifting the focus of POs to monitoring and enforcement in their daily operations (Taxman, 2002, 2008).

The evolution of parole saw similar trends, with the earliest form of parole seen in the mid-1800s (Petersilia, 2002; Walker, 1998). Originally, parole was thought of as a means to encourage reform as individuals were granted parole after earning "marks" or points for good behavior. The possibility of receiving early release on parole was thought to incentivize parolees to participate in rehabilitation programs (Rothman, 1980). In practice, the existence of parole and the opportunity for early release

gave correctional officers a tool for maintaining power and control over inmates (Rothman, 1980). Critics of parole believed that it was not strict enough and offered too many opportunities for early release. Heavy criticism of parole practices led to its eventual abolishment from the federal criminal justice system by 1997 (Adams & Roth, 1998) and many state systems (Petersilia, 2003).

Pendulum shifts between rehabilitation and punishment infiltrate the probation and parole system with competing and contradictory goals. This overarching goal structure influences many aspects of probation and parole work today, affecting how individual POs decide to carry out their job. Previous literature on the "working philosophy" (Klockars, 1972, p. 550) or roles of POs cites the existence of three commonly discussed strategies associated with probation practice: social service, resource broker, and law enforcement (Abadinsky, 2006; Clear & Latessa, 1993; Klockars, 1972). The social service role most closely aligns with a counseling approach, in which POs attempt to intervene in the lives of their clients through treatment, support, and guidance techniques (Abadinsky, 2006; Clear & Latessa, 1993; Klockars, 1972). This differs from the resource broker role as, under this orientation, POs do not provide direct counseling but assess the needs of their clients and refer them to the appropriate services and resources (Abadinsky, 2006; Clear & Latessa, 1993; Klockars, 1972). Lastly, the law enforcement role is the most different, as POs who fall under this working philosophy emphasize surveillance, monitoring, and enforcement of conditions of supervision above all else (Abadinsky, 2006; Clear & Latessa, 1993; Klockars, 1972).

The existence of differing PO roles illustrates the influence the competing goal structure can have on workers and how they operate in practice. Rather than a consistent and preferred philosophy of supervision, there are several roles POs can fulfill, each of which has the potential to provide different experiences and outcomes for probationers or parolees. Researchers examining how POs at the individual level align with these different role orientations find that POs often emphasize rehabilitation and social service orientations while deemphasizing punishment (Sluder, Shearer, & Potts, 1991;

Whitehead & Lindquist, 1985). Similarly, research finds that POs who work with youthful populations are even more likely to emphasize the social service aspect of their job (Sluder & Reddington, 1993). There is also some evidence that POs are able to take an individualistic approach to their job, emphasizing interactions with the probationers on their caseload (Lynch, 1998). More recent research also finds that juvenile POs enact a balanced approach when working with youth on their caseloads (Schwalbe & Maschi, 2009; Ward & Kupchik, 2010), and adult POs enact both law enforcement– and social service–related tasks regardless of their preferences (Clear & Latessa, 1993). The ability to individualize their responses and act in accordance with more than one role is potentially a result of the many different circumstances and offenders POs encounter on a daily basis (Murphy & Lutze, 2009). Although there is not an abundance of research on how these roles play out at the individual level, studies provide evidence that POs often align themselves with one goal (rehabilitation or punishment) more closely instead of fulfilling multiple roles simultaneously. Recent research identifies an approach that does not closely align with either a rehabilitative or a punishment ideology, but is akin to an administrative role (Viglione, Rudes, Nightingale, Watson, & Taxman, 2014). POs associated with this role often focus on "paper processing," such as paperwork and completing supervision reports, instead of "offender change" provisions that include engaging offenders in terms of referral, and compliance procedures as well as both directive and motivational communication strategies. Administrative POs view offenders as required contacts (Viglione et al., 2014) and behave more in line with a bureaucratic role in which the focus is on carrying out the policies of the probation agency (Clear & Latessa, 1993). Table 13.1 presents the PO roles and descriptions of the strategies in use.

Recent theorists define a theoretical framework to explain the pendulum shifts between rehabilitation and punishment as creating a managerial justice. Feeley and Simon (1992) illustrate how the shift in organizational culture to accommodate the new pendulum swing (punishment) creates a demand to manage the caseloads based on level of risk to society. Under this perspective, POs reasonably deploy control strategies to manage their caseloads (Feeley & Simon, 1992), and probation and parole agencies focus on managing offenders to minimize risk while setting aside the goals of reintegration and rehabilitation (Rudes & Viglione, 2014). Presentence reports, risk assessments, monitoring risk, and case planning are all major components of the probation/parole process, and all require the systematic classification and regulation of risk levels (Kemshall, Parton, Walsh, & Waterson, 1997; Lynch, 1998). Some scholars illustrate how the emphasis on these risk-management practices and strategies have hindered the ability of POs to provide or utilize rehabilitative services and meet the individual needs of their clients (Kemshall et al., 1997).

The goal of corrections appears to have shifted again toward decreasing recidivism rates, and many correctional agencies are implementing EBPs that use cognitive–behavioral approaches (Andrews, Bonta, & Hoge, 1990; Cullen & Gendreau, 2000) and risk management strategies (Taxman, Sheperdson, & Byrne, 2004). Although this coupling of practices results in correctional models that incorporate both rehabilitation and punishment (Lerch, James-Andrews, Eley, & Taxman, 2009), this shift creates a new, complex goal structure that requires correctional organizations and POs to change the way they supervise individuals on probation and parole (see Table 13.2).

RESEARCH REVIEW

The present focus on integrating rehabilitative strategies within correctional models has led to an emphasis on using EBPs, or practices that are scientifically proven to be effective (Sherman, 1998) in reducing recidivism and its associated costs (Rhine et al., 2006; Taxman, 2002). The importance placed on the EBP movement is based largely on the fact that there is little evidence that traditional probation and parole practices are effective (under both the clinical and managerial models) in reducing recidivism (Bonta et al., 2008). Increasingly gaining attention in the field of corrections is the RNR model, which combines an actuarial, managerial approach with a rehabilitative, clinical model.

TABLE 13.1

Professional Role Orientations of Probation
and Parole Officers

Role	Strategy
Law enforcement	Emphasizes legal authority and enforcement; concerned with control, compliance and punishment
Social service	Case manager, therapeutic agent; emphasizes rehabilitation, client needs and treatment; concerned with motivation, support, guidance
Resource broker	Concerned with assessing probationer needs and linking them to appropriate services and resources in the community
Balanced	Blends social service and law enforcement; often uses an individualized approach to make decisions based on the unique situation or probationer
Administrative	Concerned with paperwork and supervision reports; engages and communicates very little with offenders in either an authoritarian or rehabilitative manner
Risk management	Concerned with assessing risk, monitoring risk level and case planning strategies, and classifying and sorting probationers; focused on managerial goals and managing the potential threats someone may offer; emphasizes classification and efficiency

The RNR strategy outlines the basic principles of risk, need, and responsivity to generate effective interventions for offender populations, with the ultimate goals of improving treatment for offenders and reducing recidivism (Andrews & Bonta, 2010a). The risk principle states that the level of service should be matched to the offender's level of risk; high-risk offenders are better suited for treatment programming. The needs principle identifies what treatment programs should focus on, specifically offenders' criminogenic needs, or those needs that are directly related to offending behavior. The responsivity principle states that treatment using a cognitive–behavioral approach should be matched to the abilities, motivation, and learning style of the offender (Andrews & Bonta, 2010a). Andrews, Zinger, et al. (1990) test the validity of the

components of the RNR model in a meta-analysis that synthesizes the findings from 80 studies of adult and juvenile treatment interventions and drug treatment programs. Results indicate that the effectiveness of treatment interventions vary based on their adherence to RNR principles. Treatment interventions that follow the RNR model more closely result in greater recidivism reduction, whereas interventions that fail to adhere to the model result in increased recidivism (Andrews, Zinger, et al., 1990). More recent meta-analyses confirm these findings, with treatment adhering to the RNR model resulting in greater reductions in recidivism (Andrews, Bonta, & Wormith, 2010; Prendergast, Pearson, Podus, Hamilton, & Greenwell, 2013).

Despite evidence supporting the RNR model for effective intervention, it is only recently that these principles have been applied to probation and parole settings (Taxman, 2002; Taxman, Henderson, & Lerch, 2010), whereas earlier research was applied to treatment in prison settings (Andrews & Kiessling, 1980). As stated earlier, application of the RNR model to probation and parole bridges actuarial, managerial techniques and rehabilitative, clinical techniques. This shifts the purpose and goals of probation/parole from focusing on surveillance and control to the integration of interventions, programming, and treatment (Taxman, 2008). For example, under the RNR approach, POs use actuarial risk and needs assessment instruments to determine risk and need levels. While use of these actuarial tools could potentially result in a people-processing approach by placing people into categories to manage their risk, probation and parole officers can use this information to inform rehabilitative strategies (Hannah-Moffat, 2005). Once risk level is determined, POs should consider offenders' criminogenic needs and match them to appropriate treatment programming and services. This transforms the people-processing approach, because POs consider individual characteristics and attempt to match offenders to appropriate treatments. Targeting the needs of individual offenders in an attempt to reduce recidivism is vastly different from assigning an individual a risk level and managing risk.

The individualization of supervision on the basis of risk and need factors presents insurmountable

TABLE 13.2

Probation/Parole Curricula

Curriculum	Focus	RNR adherence	Training	Effectiveness: PO	Effectiveness: Probationer
Motivational Interviewing (MI)	Interactions between PO and probationer	Client-centered counseling, tool to address ambivalence toward change, adheres to responsivity principle based on interpersonal communication style emphasis	Varies; introduction to MI should last two hours to one full day; advanced training should last two to four days; training should include role play, vignettes, training videos, and practice sessions	Improvement in PO MI skills, including the use of affirmations, reflections, reframing, and emphasizing client control	Improvement in treatment engagement and retention, increased ability to recognize problems
Proactive Community Supervision (PCS)	Shift role of PO to that of a change agent	Emphasis on communication strategies, cognitive–behavioral interventions, use of actuarial assessments, case planning process based on assessment results emphasizing collaboration between PO and probationer	Long-term implementation: (1) introduced MI and other communication strategies; (2) established guidelines, policies, and procedures; (3) developed coaching model to provide feedback to staff; (4) LSI–R and case planning training; (5) development of performance indicators	PO's perceived job is to be facilitator of offender change and was more likely to work with offenders to improve supervision outcomes, better able to work with difficult cases	Less likely to be rearrested and less likely to have a warrant issued for technical violations
Strategic Training Initiative in Community Supervision (STICS)	Shift role of PO to that of a change agent	Addresses risk (services directed to higher-risk offenders), needs (services target criminogenic needs), responsivity (emphasize relationship between PO and probationer, use of cognitive–behavioral techniques, concepts, and tools are taught to probationer in a clear way, opportunities given for probationer to practice)	Three-day training with ten modules, monthly follow-up meetings, audiotapes	PO to focus more on criminogenic needs and procriminal attitudes, higher quality of RNR-based skills and interventions	Lower rates of reoffending and reconviction
Effective Practices in Community Supervision (EPICS)	Interactions between PO and probationer, social learning	Integration of EBPs and cognitive–behavioral strategies into case management skills, focusing on use of actuarial assessments, provision of interventions by PO, intervention matching based on risk and needs, target criminogenic needs	Four-day training session, demonstrations, follow-up coaching sessions, peer coaching, audiotapes	No evaluation study yet	No evaluation study yet

TABLE 13.2

Probation/Parole Curricula

Staff Training Aimed at Reducing Rearrest (STARR)	Interactions between PO and probationer	Emphasis on a variety of skills: active listening, role clarification, problem solving skills, and teaching, applying, and reviewing the cognitive model	3½-day classroom training, demonstrations, audiotape interactions, four follow-up training sessions	Trained POs used more reinforcement and disapproval skills, more likely to discuss cognitions, peers, and impulsivity, more likely to use cognitive techniques with probationers; trained POs used skills more often, but still only did so in 50 percent of interactions with clients	Reduced failure rates (but effect diminishes once controlling for risk level)
Skills for Offender Assessment and Responsivity in New Goals (SOARING2)	Train POs on effective practices; shift role to change agent	Emphasis on identifying and appropriately using risk and needs assessments, building motivation to change, developing individualized case plans based on assessment results, problem-solving, supporting desistance	Five-module online course with interactive simulations, real-time feedback, printable resources, audio and video demonstrations, and internal coaching	No evaluation study yet, but initial evidence finds positive effects of internal coaching and feedback component	No evaluation study yet

Note. RNR = risk–needs–responsivity; PO = parole officer; LSI–R = Level of Service Inventory; EBP = evidence-based practice.

challenges to moving toward a people-processing mode. POs use various techniques to assess the criminogenic needs of offenders and assign offenders to risk categories (Oleson, VanBenschoten, Robinson, Lowenkamp, & Holsinger, 2012). Oleson et al. (2012) find that 66% of the POs in their sample overclassify offenders according to perceived risk. Risk estimates then shape PO perceptions of the criminogenic needs of the offender. When POs classify an offender as low or moderate risk, they are more likely to identify a criminogenic need than if they classify them as moderate or high risk (Oleson et al., 2012). Many other studies document the inconsistencies across decision-making and in anticipating offender outcomes that are associated with gut-level decision making (Andrews & Bonta, 2010a; Andrews et al. 2010; Gottfredson &

Moriarty, 2006). J. Miller and Maloney (2013) find that officers complete risk and needs instruments most of the time when they are required to, but a large portion of staff only minimally satisfies agency requirements for performing an assessment. Officers commonly make decisions that deviate from the recommendations based on the instrument, seeking options that are more restrictive than indicated or services not highlighted by the risk and needs assessment (J. Miller & Maloney, 2013). Officers also rarely determine the frequency of contact with probationers on the basis of their assessed risk level and pay little attention to criminogenic needs (Bonta et al., 2008). Practitioners often underutilize risk and needs assessments (Schwalbe, 2004) because they do not trust the psychometric properties of the instrument (Krysik & LeCroy, 2002) or prefer to use their own clinical judgment, despite a vast amount of research questioning the validity of gut-level decision making (Hilton & Simmons, 2001). Although the appropriate use of risk and needs instruments can contribute to reductions in recidivism, the positive effects are heavily dependent on practitioner use of the tool (Harris, Gingerich, & Whittaker, 2004; Luong & Wormith, 2011).

The responsivity principle poses additional challenges for POs. To align with the principle, POs should utilize techniques such as motivational interviewing, prosocial modeling, empathy, and problem solving (Robinson, VanBenschoten, Alexander, & Lowencamp, 2011; Trotter, 1996). The responsivity principle suggests POs should be facilitators of offender change and should exercise cognitive–behavioral skills while interacting with offenders (Bourgon & Gutierrez, 2012); this represents a major change in the traditional supervision and control focus in probation/parole settings. Research finds POs rarely use cognitive–behavioral techniques in their interactions with offenders (Bonta et al., 2008); POs do so in approximately 1% of their interactions, and they discuss procriminal attitudes and cognitions with offenders in 5% of interactions (Bourgon & Gutierrez, 2012). Shifting behaviors and interactional styles to align with the responsivity principle may pose the greatest challenge to practitioners in adhering to the RNR model.

Most probation and parole agencies do not prepare officers to fulfill a change agent role and often do not focus on the skills needed to facilitate change. This led researchers to develop a series of in-depth skill development strategies to help POs handle complex psychosocial development issues. Most of these training initiatives emphasize EBPs, such as using a risk and needs assessment instrument in case planning, use of cognitive–behavioral techniques to teach offenders how to problem solve, use of rewards and positive incentives to shape behavior, and use of case-planning strategies to teach offenders problem-solving skills. Most of these training initiatives are delivered in brief, one-time workshops, which is ineffective in enacting lasting change in individuals and organizations (R. A. Baer, 2006; W. R. Miller, Yahne, Moyers,

Martinez, & Pirritano, 2004; Taxman, Henderson, Young, & Farrell, 2012). One-time training initiatives do not allow sufficient time for staff to understand the new information and apply the skills to routine practice (Porporino, 2001). While adoption of EBPs has the potential to improve outcomes, including a 26% reduction in recidivism rates (Andrews & Bonta, 2010b), it is challenging to move in this direction.

Generating change within organizations is a complex process that requires thorough planning (J. S. Baer et al., 2007; Simpson, 2002; Taxman & Belenko, 2011). Organizational culture (Schein, 1990) and staff resistance to change are two major barriers to adoption of EBPs in justice environments, particularly community corrections (Rudes, Viglione, & Taxman, 2014; Taxman et al., 2010). Successfully adopting EBPs or revising current practices requires a shift in both daily operations and business mentality (Taxman, 2002; Clawson, Bogue, & Joplin, 2005; Joplin et al., 2004). Shifting the current organization in ways that support new practices is one of the biggest challenges when implementing EBPs. In probation and parole agencies, this means shifting the agency's core ideology and mission from a focus on surveillance and control to a rehabilitative, service-oriented environment. The culture of an organization, or "the way things get done" (Deal & Kennedy, 2000, p. 90), can serve as a barrier or facilitator to change (Rudes et al., 2014), and often signals to staff what is expected of them (S. G. Scott & Bruce, 1994). Correctional organizations that have open learning environments and focus on performance are more likely to implement EBPs (Friedmann, Taxman, & Henderson, 2007). POs with lower levels of cynicism for change and more positive perceptions of leadership are more likely to use EBP reforms implemented by their organization (Farrell, Young, & Taxman, 2011). Probation staff employed in organizations that are better integrated with community-based service providers are also more likely to use service-oriented practices (Taxman, Henderson, & Belenko, 2009). The culture of an organization can hinder change attempts when staff are not prepared for change (Rudes, Lerch, & Taxman, 2011). In addition, there is a positive relation between resources and culture such that more resources, such as time and money, are spent on activities that align with the existing cultural norms of the organization (Oser, Knudsen, Staton-Tindall, & Leukefeld, 2009).

Equally, changes in organizational culture can facilitate change. Staff resistance to change, a major barrier in implementing EBPs, can be moderated by aligning organizational goals and ideologies with new or changing ones, as well as new procedures (Lin, 2000; Ohlin, Coates, & Miller, 1974). Resistance to change often occurs informally, via "routine resistance" (J. C. Scott, 1985, p. 255), which is often unplanned and covert (Hodson, 1991; Nord & Jermier, 1994; A. Prasad & Prasad, 1998; P. Prasad & Prasad, 2000) and a response to conflicts between the "old way of doing things" and new demands. As previously discussed, staff often align with one role orientation more closely than the others. When changes in overarching probation/parole ideologies occur, staff may feel conflicted and attempt to reconcile the differences, eliminate the strain, or identify ways in which the new processes fit within the existing operations (Bazemore, Dicker, & Al-Gadheeb, 1994; Farabee et al., 1999; Zald, 1962). POs often continue prechange behavioral structures and decisions despite change attempts (Turpin-Petrosino, 1999; Lawrence & Johnson, 1990; Lynch, 1998; McCorkle & Crank, 1996; Steiner, Travis, & Makarios, 2011). When reform does not address the needs (Lawrence & Johnson, 1990; McCorkle & Crank, 1996), wishes (Ekland-Olson & Martin, 1988), or prior decision-making patterns of POs (Lynch, 1998; Steiner et al., 2011), they are more likely to perceive the reform as ineffective. Often resistance occurs indirectly through negative perceptions of change, mistrust, and lack of buy-in. Regardless of its form, resistance can undermine change efforts. A major challenge in the organizational change process is how managers and supervisors frame and communicate change to staff. Staff are more likely to understand reform efforts if change is framed positively and communicated in a way that demonstrates how the changes will benefit their work (Ferguson, 2002; Latessa, 2004). In addition, specifically addressing staff concerns and uncertainties can improve staff

understanding and perceptions regarding change (Ferguson, 2002).

One mechanism to promote and support change and increase adherence to the RNR model in correctional organizations is through formal training curriculums. There have been several attempts to integrate the principles of effective interventions into community supervision settings via specialized curriculums for probation and parole officers (Bonta et al., 2010; Robinson et al., 2011; Taxman et al., 2012). These curriculums attempt to translate the principles of the RNR model into concrete training programs and practices to increase the knowledge, understanding, and application of RNR principles in daily practice. Preliminary results suggest that the use of principles of effective interventions based on the RNR model are associated with recidivism reductions (Bonta et al., 2010; Bourgon, Bonta, Rugge, & Scott, 2010; Robinson et al., 2011; Taxman, 2008). A steady conclusion from the existing research suggests that the effectiveness of probation and parole practice is reliant on the extent to which it addresses the risk, needs, and responsivity of each offender (Andrews & Bonta, 2010a).

Research on organizational change within probation and parole organizations finds that POs trained specifically on the principles of RNR demonstrate better adherence to those principles and more frequently use cognitive–behavioral techniques than POs who are not trained on the RNR model. In turn, offenders supervised by officers trained in new skills are likely to have better outcomes (Bonta et al., 2011; Young, Farrell, & Taxman, 2012). Training focused on the RNR principles is critical in skill development, because adherence to the RNR model requires important behavioral changes in POs and the probationers they supervise. The following section outlines the major curriculums that have been developed to translate the RNR principles into probation/parole practice. Discussion of these curriculums is critical because they serve as a primary tool for probation and parole agencies to generate and sustain change in the roles and behaviors of line-staff. They offer comprehensive skill development, providing a framework for probation and parole agencies and staff to align with changing roles and expectations as a result of scientific evidence on effective practices.

PRACTICE AND POLICY ISSUES

Since the commencement of probation and parole in the United States, POs have relied on various techniques for doing their work, most of which results in learned or tacit knowledge passed down via formal and informal socialization and professionalization strategies. Most of these practices are unsupported by research and are built on a logic of the way it has always been done (Rudes & Viglione, 2014). The increasing emphasis on EBPs has shifted the way we think about probation and parole and how POs think about and perform their work (Sachwald, 2001; Taxman, 2002, 2008). The RNR model in particular has influenced several training curriculums and models that have been applied to probation and parole settings. The overarching goal of these curriculums is to increase the knowledge, understanding, and application of the principles of effective interventions. The following section outlines the background and purpose of each curriculum, how the curriculum is applied in probation/parole settings, and available evidence on the effectiveness of the curriculums.

Motivational Interviewing

Motivational interviewing (MI) draws from client-centered counseling (Rogers, 1961) and uses a directive method for enhancing the intrinsic motivation to change by exploring and resolving ambivalence (W. R. Miller & Rollnick, 2002). MI emphasizes empathy, optimism, and respect for client choice (Rogers, 1961) and is used as a tool to address reluctance or ambivalence toward change (W. R. Miller & Rollnick, 2009). Traditionally, MI is used in healthcare settings where the practice has strong support as an intervention for alcohol and drug use, smoking cessation, medication compliance, HIV risk behaviors, and diet/exercise (Lundahl, Tollefson, Kunz, Brownell, & Burke, 2010). With the emphasis on interpersonal communication style, MI falls under the RNR principle of responsivity (Walters, Vader, Nguyen, Harris, & Eells, 2010).

MI is generally taught to staff in several stages. The first stage focuses on the concepts of autonomy, collaboration, and evocation (ACE), and the principles of expressing empathy, amplifying ambivalence, rolling with resistance, and supporting self-efficacy (EARS; W. R. Miller & Moyers, 2006). This stage in the learning process provides a guide for staff on how to use core counseling skills in practice and helps them understand why autonomy is important in promoting behavior change. The second stage of training allows staff to practice the client-centered counseling skills: open-ended questions, affirmations, reflective listening, and summarization (OARS). During this stage, staff practice these skills in their interactions with clients. Later phases of training include teaching the staff how to recognize change talk and potential resistance, develop a change plan, increase commitment, and how to integrate MI with the use of other intervention strategies. The later stages of the training protocol are often provided in follow-up or booster sessions as a means to gradually build staff skills (W. R. Miller & Moyers, 2006).

The recommended length of training for an introduction to MI skills is between two hours and one day, while more advanced training sessions require two- to four-day workshops. Training should include role play, vignettes, training videos of what MI counseling sessions should look like, and practice sessions that engage staff in the learning process (W. R. Miller, 2004). Generally, training involves taping the individual and having a coach grade the tapes. This provides a feedback loop to the officer on their use of the skills. The tapes and associated feedback are important to staff development of MI skills.

In criminal justice settings, a few studies find improved treatment engagement and retention when staff use MI with offender populations (McMurran, 2009). In probation settings, one study finds that when POs used MI, probationers are more capable of recognizing problems in their lives (Harper & Hardy, 2000), but another study reports no difference in probationer outcomes (Walters et al., 2010). Walters et al. (2010) finds training in MI results in improvements in PO skills. Other studies examine solely PO skills as a result of MI training but do not evaluate the impact of MI use by officers on probationer outcomes (Hohman, Doran, & Koutsenok, 2009; W. R. Miller & Mount, 2001). These studies also find improvements in POs' MI skills after training (Hohman et al., 2009; W. R. Miller & Mount, 2001). In a study of juvenile probation agencies, PO use of MI communication strategies results in positive improvements in the officer's skills and reductions in negative youth behavior (Young et al., 2012). Despite the small body of research on outcomes, MI is recommended as a supervision style in probation settings (Walters et al., 2010) in order to increase compliance with court mandates and encourage other changes in behavior (Alexander, VanBenschoten, & Walters, 2008; Clark, Walters, Gingrich, & Meltzer, 2006; Ginsburg, Mann, Rotgers, & Weekes, 2002; Wormith et al., 2007).

Proactive Community Supervision

In 1999–2002, Maryland experimented with the Proactive Community Supervision (PCS) model, which focuses on shifting the role of the PO to a facilitator of offender change (Taxman, 2008). The PCS model borrows heavily from RNR but is translated into a probation and parole environment. The PCS model has seven key tenets: identify risk and criminogenic need factors; target interventions to higher-risk offenders; minimize contact and services/programming for low-risk offenders; use of cognitive–behavioral interventions; use of rewards; focus on short-term change; and engage social supports and geographic-center supports in interventions (Taxman, 2008; Taxman et al., 2004). The PCS approach includes screening, assessment, assigning a typology that is tied to certain supervision goals, using available programs and services, and monitoring outcomes. Practitioners first use a five-item risk screen to determine whether a more detailed assessment is needed. Practitioners then evaluate offenders assessed as moderate- to high-risk using a comprehensive assessment standardized tool such as the Level of Service Inventory (LSI–R) in addition to assessing the offender's environment/residence and reviewing the offender's behavioral patterns to determine a typology of criminogenic behavior. This

typology then drives the case-planning process, which is a collaborative process between the PO and the offender. The collaborative nature of the case-planning process differentiates the PCS model from previous supervision models (particularly enforcement models where offenders are told what to do) and is designed to engage the offender in the supervision process and promote ownership over their supervision experience. This shifts the role of both the PO and the offender and changes the way in which they interact (Taxman, 2008). The collaborative case plan should reflect the goals and tasks needed to be successful on probation, and it should be broken down into small segments.

The PCS model attempts to make officers active in facilitating offender change through staff training on the use of communication strategies (modeled after MI) and the RNR model. The goals are to create a social learning environment between the officer and the offender, promote the use of performance measures for officers, emphasize regular reviews of case plans by officers, clients, and supervisors, and aid in the development of an organizational learning environment to promote continual development and growth of staff and the organization as a whole. Cognitive–behavioral strategies and skills are key components of the PCS training for officers. Emphasis is placed on setting goals that are dependent on criminogenic needs as a means to emphasize cognitive restructuring. The training process involves three steps: a comprehensive three-day training on communication strategies; a comprehensive three-day training on using the risk screener, LSI–R, and case planning that integrates communication skills; and the use of the Quality Contact Standards (QCS) where on-site coaching occurs with supervision. The organizational development for the PCS model involves the agency partnering with academic institutions, using professional development strategies (including PCS 101) for all employees, skilled coaching in field offices, development of a learning environment in each office, town hall meetings open to all staff, leadership development program for managers, an internal "what works" committee, a management advisory committee that develops new chain-of-command policy, and constant feedback loops to the organization on progress.

Using a random selection-individual match design, Taxman (2008) evaluated the PCS model. Findings suggest that offenders who were supervised under the PCS model of supervision were less likely to be rearrested and less likely to have a warrant issued for technical violations. In addition, probation staff are more likely to perceive their job to be facilitators of offender change and are more likely to work with offenders to improve supervision outcomes. POs display the ability to work on difficult cases for longer periods of time compared to non-PCS supervision cases (268 days versus 210 days). Thus, probation staff develop and use tools to work with offenders who are slower in the change process and who need more guidance after PCS training (Taxman, 2008).

Strategic Training Initiative in Community Supervision

The Strategic Training Initiative in Community Supervision (STICS) project was piloted and then conducted in three Canadian provinces (Bonta et al., 2010, 2011). STICS redefines the role of probation and parole officers to be active and direct in the change process (Bourgon, Gutierrez, & Ashton, 2011). At the heart of these training courses are fundamental therapeutic concepts, cognitive–behavioral intervention techniques, and structuring skills. STICS teaches officers to be a "change agent," where the dominant task is to engage actively with the client instead of using traditional case-management techniques. This new approach challenges officers to work with clients in a therapeutic manner and to use skills and techniques firmly rooted in RNR principles to directly facilitate personal, attitudinal, and behavioral change (Bourgon et al., 2011). Like PCS, the ultimate goal of the STICS curriculum is to design a model of community supervision consistent with the RNR model, create a means to implement this model in routine practice, and create an evaluation strategy to inform the development of STICS in practice (Bourgon et al., 2010).

The STICS curriculum adheres to the RNR model in several ways. First, to address the risk principle,

STICS focuses on higher-risk offenders, with the dosage of treatment and programming increasing as risk increases (Andrews & Bonta, 2010a). To address the need principle, which indicates that services should target criminogenic needs, officers must assess offender's needs and focus their intervention efforts on these specific needs (Bourgon et al., 2010). Designers of STICS argue that POs must be flexible and able to address the majority of criminogenic needs, but procriminal attitudes is a critical need that affects all other criminogenic needs. STICS focuses on helping POs target procriminal attitudes and cognitions (Bourgon et al., 2010). The STICS Action Plan was created to assist officers in understanding how procriminal attitudes and cognitions are intertwined with all other criminogenic needs and in developing an RNR-based supervision plan using the results of each offender's risk and needs assessment (Bourgon et al., 2010). STICS training incorporates skill-building designed to help POs identify and address expressions of procriminal attitudes and replace them with prosocial attitudes (Bourgon et al., 2010). The most challenging RNR principle is responsivity, which states that services and programming must be tailored to the client's learning style, motivation, abilities, and strengths to promote an effective learning environment. The STICS model incorporates four factors critical to addressing responsivity: a positive officer–client relationship; the use of cognitive–behavioral techniques; simple, understandable, and concrete concepts, tools, and skills to be taught to the offender; and supervision structured to be an effective learning environment.

Shifting from a case-management approach to that of a "change agent" is challenging for POs (Bourgon et al., 2011). Underlying the STICS training curriculum, there are four critical, clinical steps that POs must take to play a direct and active role in facilitating change in the offenders they supervise. POs must work with the client to identify the direct link between his/her thoughts and behavior, help the offender identify their personal thinking patterns that cause their problem behaviors, engage in cognitive restructuring techniques to teach the offender clear and concrete thinking and behavioral skills, and provide opportunities for offenders to practice new skills and provide feedback and reinforcement.

A major challenge is the PO's level of understanding of cognitive–behavioral practices and skills and translating traditional risk/need assessment information into a case plan that guides the offender to directly work on change on a daily basis (Bourgon et al., 2011). Once POs create this plan, they must focus on initiating and facilitating attitudinal and behavioral change in the offender. The use of cognitive–behavioral interventions is a widely accepted practice (Cullen & Gendreau, 1989; Gendreau & Andrews, 1990; Landenberger & Lipsey, 2005; Lipsey, Farran, Bilbrey, Hofer, & Dong, 2011; Wilson, Bouffard, & Mackenzie, 2005) that emphasize attention to triggers, thinking errors, and negative thoughts. Practitioners use cognitive restructuring techniques for reframing and positive self-talk. POs facilitate this process through role playing, in which the POs demonstrate to the offender the direct link between their thoughts and their behavior. STICS teaches POs how to show clients in a concrete and practical manner that "the reason they behave as they do is a direct result of their thoughts alone and for no other reason" (Bourgon et al., 2011, p. 36). Once an offender understands this link, they are able to evaluate the costs and benefits of their behavior and of their thinking, putting them in a position to change their behavior through changing their thoughts first (Bourgon et al., 2011).

The second step for POs is to help the offender identify their personal thinking patterns that cause their problem behaviors. With criminal justice populations, problem behaviors are those related to their criminogenic needs. POs are taught to provide structured activities for offenders to learn and practice self-awareness skills to identify specific thoughts and evaluate their contribution to specific behaviors. This involves recognizing and identifying the consequences of their behaviors using exercises and interventions that increase clients' self-awareness (i.e., their understanding that they are completely responsible for their choices, including the choice to change).

The next step in the process is the cognitive restructuring component, or the "countering" stage in STICS. At this point, the officer works with the offender on how to think differently (cognitive) and act differently (behavioral), translating procriminal thoughts and behaviors to prosocial thoughts and behaviors. In this stage, officers are taught to work with the offender on a variety of prosocial behavioral skills such as resume writing, basic communication skills, and problem-solving skills. Lastly, officers are taught to provide abundant opportunities for offenders to practice the new skills they are learning, providing feedback and reinforcement for new patterns of thinking and behaving (Bourgon et al., 2011).

For a PO to become an effective change agent, they must be able to use risk and needs assessment information to develop an individualized action plan for prosocial change (Bourgon et al., 2011). Rather than identifying criminogenic needs and referring clients to appropriate services, the STICS model requires POs to understand what each individual offender's needs are and what services best meet those needs. In addition, STICS emphasizes understanding how to intervene with each offender, which is especially important when multiple needs are present (Bourgon et al., 2011). The cognitive–behavioral model provides guidance for the PO on how to translate the results of a risk and needs assessment into a strategic, comprehensive, and practical therapeutic plan to facilitate offender change (Bourgon et al., 2011). STICS training focuses on developing a solid understanding of cognitive–behavioral issues, making it easier to understand how criminogenic needs are interrelated (Bourgon et al., 2011). The STICS Action Plan helps POs understand and practically formulate strategic intervention plans with each offender. The Action Plan involves several steps: address appropriate supervision levels and reporting frequency, identify acute needs or crises that require immediate attention, conceptualize the risk–needs profile for intervention planning and ensuring consistency with the cognitive–behavioral model of human behavior and change, and identify specific responsivity issues such as guiding the officer in the way they interact with the offender and how to facilitate learning with attention to addressing noncriminogenic needs such as mental health issues. The ultimate goal of the

Action Plan is to assist POs in the movement from a case management role to that of a change agent by guiding their understanding, planning, and implementation of direct one-on-on cognitive–behavioral interventions (Bourgon et al., 2011).

The STICS curriculum was originally designed to be delivered in a three-day training that includes ten modules covering all aspects of STICS supervision, including information for officers to understand the rationale and background of the STICS model, skills and tools necessary to utilize and implement it, exercises in cognitive restructuring, prosocial modeling, reinforcement, punishment, and role plays (Bourgon et al., 2010). The training has a follow-up skill maintenance plan. POs meet monthly in small groups to discuss their use of the skills and concepts and receive clinical supervision by trainers who review audiotaped sessions between POs and offenders (Bourgon et al., 2010). In addition, a one-day follow-up training workshop is offered one year after the initial three-day training focusing on skill maintenance.

Several studies assess the effectiveness of the STICS curriculum. These studies compare POs who received STICS training and control groups who received no training. These studies find that officers in the experimental group spend significantly more of their sessions focusing on criminogenic needs and procriminal attitudes and demonstrate a higher quality of RNR-based skills and interventions (Bonta et al., 2008, 2011; Bourgon et al., 2010; Bourgon & Gutierrez, 2012). Officers who did not receive STICS training rarely use cognitive–behavioral techniques with offenders and rarely engage in interventions to facilitate changes in attitudes and cognitions. Studies examining the use of skills taught in the STICS model find PO use of skills is related to offender outcomes. The use of cognitive–behavioral techniques is significantly related to lower rates of reoffending (Bonta et al., 2008, 2011; Bourgon & Gutierrez, 2012) and lower rates of reconviction (Bonta et al., 2008, 2011). The more POs focus on court-mandated conditions in their contacts, which is believed to interfere with the establishment of a therapeutic relationship (Bonta et al., 2008), the higher the recidivism rate (Bonta et al., 2008, 2011).

Effective Practices in Community Supervision

Developed by researchers at the University of Cincinnati's Corrections Institute, the Effective Practices in Community Supervision (EPICS) is a curriculum similar to the PCS and STICS models (Smith, Schweitzer, Labrecque, & Latessa, 2012). The focus of the EPICS model is to assist POs in translating the principles of effective interventions into practice, specifically focusing on their face-to-face interactions with offenders (Smith et al., 2012). Traditionally, it is believed that interactions between POs and offenders are ineffective because they are often too brief or focus entirely on monitoring compliance. This results in a relationship that is confrontational and authoritarian versus supportive and helpful (Latessa, 2012). The rationale behind EPICS is social learning, thus teaching POs how to use structured learning and cognitive–behavioral therapies (CBT) in their interactions with offenders is paramount (Latessa, 2012). POs are taught how to integrate EBPs and CBTs into their case-management skills, specifically focusing on six components: use of an actuarial assessment to drive a structured case plan; interventions provided during in-person meetings; offenders are matched to interventions according to their risk and needs; interventions used are based in scientific evidence; targets are criminogenic; and quality assurance processes are in place to ensure fidelity (Latessa, 2012). POs are taught to structure their meetings so as to follow four general steps: check-in, during which any acute needs are identified, compliance issues are discussed, and the PO begins to build rapport and trust with the offender; review, during which skills discussed in previous meetings are reviewed, problems that arise in the use of skills are discussed, and short- and long-term goals are worked toward; intervention, during which the PO identifies continued areas of need, discusses trends in problems the offender experiences, teaches relevant skills, targets problematic thinking, models any skills taught during the intervention, role plays the new skill and offers feedback; and homework, in which the PO assigns the offender homework that focuses on applying the new skill before their next meeting (Latessa, 2012).

Training in EPICS typically involves an initial four-day session that includes several opportunities for POs to practice the skills taught to them, in addition to participation exercises and demonstration of skills. Refresher training is also available through follow-up coaching sessions that involve additional demonstration of skills and the opportunity for POs to practice and receive feedback (Smith et al., 2012). Supervisors and peer coaches are identified and are given additional training to supervise the use of EPICS in practice and provide the infrastructure needed to provide continuous support of line-staff in their use of the EPICS model (Latessa, 2012; Smith et al., 2012). EPICS training often involves the use of audiotapes to record sessions with probationers and to provide to researchers or peers to receive feedback (Latessa, 2012; Smith et al., 2012). POs trained on EPICS use core correctional practices more consistently and are more likely to target the needs of offenders in addition to reinforcing and encouraging prosocial behavior (Smith et al., 2012). Further evaluations of the EPICS model are pending.

Staff Training Aimed at Reducing Rearrest

The Staff Training Aimed at Reducing Rearrest (STARR) curriculum promotes the use of core correctional skills by community supervision officers, focusing on client interactions (Robinson et al., 2012). STARR emphasizes improving the skills of officers in the content and form of their interactions with offenders by using cognitive–behavioral supervision strategies (Robinson et al., 2011, 2012). This curriculum, based on the RNR model, emphasizes several key skills: active listening, role clarification, effective use of authority, effective disapproval, effective reinforcement, effective punishment, problem-solving skills, and teaching, applying, and reviewing the cognitive model (Robinson et al., 2011).

Training for STARR includes a 3.5-day classroom training session that includes information on the development and theory behind STARR, which emphasizes the RNR model. In addition, each of the key skills are demonstrated and officers are provided with opportunities to take part in exercises and practice each skill to receive feedback (Robinson et al., 2011, 2012). As part of the training, skill cards are used to provide strategies regarding specific actions and activities officers can perform to deliver each of the skills taught in the curriculum. Skills are also taught via video examples and in-person demonstrations. Officers also send in audiotape interactions from before the initial training and up to 30 days after the training is completed to demonstrate their understanding and use of skills; this also provides the opportunity for feedback on officer performance. Finally, four follow-up training sessions are held throughout the following year to provide additional training specifically emphasizing challenges that are recognized through the audiotape analysis (Robinson et al., 2011, 2012).

Recent evaluations of the STARR curriculum reports generally positive feedback. POs who went through the training utilize reinforcement and disapproval more than untrained officers, and they are more likely to discuss cognitions, peers, and impulsivity (Robinson et al., 2011). A study of outcomes finds that offenders supervised by POs trained through the STARR curriculum have reduced failure rates, but when examining failure rates by risk level, there are no significant differences for higher-risk offenders (Robinson et al., 2011). In a second evaluation of the STARR curriculum, Robinson et al. (2012) finds a similar trend with regard to offender outcomes. In addition, they report that, while trained POs exhibit significantly greater use of core correctional skills, they still use those skills in fewer than 50% of their interactions with clients (Robinson et al., 2012).

Skills for Offender Assessment and Responsivity in New Goals

Skills for Offender Assessment and Responsivity in New Goals (SOARING2) presents a new, innovative approach to building the skills of officers. Similar to other curriculums, SOARING2 focuses on five key areas: appropriate use of risk and needs assessments, supporting and motivating offenders through the behavior change process and dealing with resistance to change, creating individualized case plans, problem-solving skills, and supporting offender desistance. There are three levels of competency in each of these five areas, therefore providing sufficient opportunity for officers to learn the material.

The expert level requires the officer to evaluate case scenarios and answer associated questions to explain the scenario to others (a judge, supervisor, family member, etc.). The SOARING2 training curriculum is unique as it is an online, interactive system incorporating simulations, real-time feedback, printable resources, audio enhancements, video demonstrations, and an extensive coaching component. Probation officers are able to work through the course materials at their own pace, covering an otherwise four-day training in shorter periods of time. The program includes video and audio components to demonstrate skills as well as simulations that allow POs to practice applying the skills learned with real-time feedback. POs have continued access to all course materials and simulations, which serve as training boosters. The system also has built-in tests to allow officers to assess how well they understand the concepts or ideas.

In addition to the interactive, online component, the SOARING2 model includes internal coaches. With the guidance of the SOARING2 research team, agency leaders identify internal coaches prior to the implementation of SOARING2. Internal coaches are typically supervisors, POs with training experience or designated as leaders, or can be other individuals in the agency. SOARING2 creators train identified coaches to be experts in the SOARING2 system and to help guide POs through the course materials and application of skills into daily practice. Coaches use an internal behavioral rating scale to objectively rate the officers in the use of the RNR skills. Coaches meet with probation staff to discuss their scores on the behavioral rating scale and other course materials, ensure they understand the material, and help POs think about application of newly learned skills to practice while using positive reinforcement (Maass et al., 2013).

The SOARING2 model is currently in the pilot phase, but there is early evidence that the coaching component has positive effects on staff behavior. Through pilot data with three probation sites, observations by internal coaches of officers' skills use finds a significant improvement over time. Furthermore, POs who are observed more frequently and receive more feedback from coaches display better use of skills over time than those who are observed

less frequently (Taxman, Maass, Duhaime, & Serin, 2013). While still in the early phase, SOARING2 provides a promising model for correctional agencies to promote and support behavior change amongst staff. SOARING2 provides POs with the skills they need to understand and adopt EBPs by integrating an online system and in-person component, providing ongoing educational training, opportunities to apply newly learned skills, and ongoing guidance and support from organizational leaders.

SUMMARY AND CONCLUSIONS

The roles of POs in the 21st century involve complex human interaction skills. Rather than fulfilling a pure supervisory (compliance management) and authoritarian role, POs are now expected to integrate multiple strategies and techniques, emphasizing actuarial assessment and appropriate responses with individualized treatment and the utilization of cognitive–behavioral techniques—all while developing positive rapport and encouraging offender engagement in the probation process. Most of the advanced approaches view probation, once considered a one-sided process, as a collaborative partnership between the PO and probationer. This suggests major shifts in the way POs think about and perform their daily responsibilities. The various curriculums and organizational development processes discussed throughout this chapter assist POs in making these changes in their mentality and routine, and generally find positive results. Evaluation research finds that curriculums such as MI, PCS, STICS, and STARR can encourage change in the way POs perform their roles, including increased adherence to the principles of RNR. The research findings are mixed in terms of offender outcomes when officers utilize these various curriculums, but there is a tendency to find positive approaches. Mixed findings are probably due to the degree to which POs use the various components in the supervision process; i.e., POs do not consistently apply newly learned skills. For example, in evaluating the STARR training curriculum, Robinson et al. (2012) find that POs use core correctional skills in fewer than 50% of their interactions with clients. This suggests that PO adherence to new and changing roles varies, and more attention should be devoted to understanding how the principles of RNR can be better integrated and accepted in the field of probation and parole.

Many scholars cite the difficulty associated with workplace change, with staff resistance a common occurrence (Agócs, 1997). Resistance to change occurs when staff exhibit behavior that does not align with the goals of an organizational change attempt (Bartunek, 1993) or, in this instance, a curriculum designed to change probation/parole practice. Staff may resist change when there is a shift from a focus on professional judgment or opinions to guide decision making to a more systematic, scientific approach. The reliance on systematic, actuarial risk and needs assessments promoted by adherence to the RNR model may lead POs to feel they are losing some of their discretionary decision-making abilities. In evaluating the implementation of risk and needs assessments in a probation office, Ferguson (2002) finds that probation staff felt they were losing discretion and felt they no longer had any input in creating supervision plans. These perceptions led probation staff to resist the change and delay the successful implementation of the risk and needs assessments (Ferguson, 2002). An emphasis on altering the organizational mission and goals to be compatible with the RNR principles is an important step to overcoming this resistance and dealing with the staff perception of a loss of autonomy (Taxman, 2013).

Resistance can also occur if there is a mismatch between the goals of the change initiative and the goals of the individual POs. For example, when the California Department of Corrections tried to shift their culture from authoritarian to more therapeutic, staff resisted and viewed the new strategy as "soft" and inadequate to effectively manage offenders (Battalino, Beutler, & Shani, 1996). This highlights the challenge that can arise from attempting to shift the role of criminal justice workers from a traditional, supervisory role to one that incorporates therapeutic strategies encouraged by the RNR model. To promote shifts in the roles of POs, larger changes must be made in the culture of the organization. Change initiatives are often pushed from the top down, without consideration of the opinions and beliefs of line-level workers like POs, which is problematic because policy is most often implemented in practice at the street level (Lipsky, 1980). Staff buy-in at all levels of the organization is necessary for the success of change efforts, especially when it means a shift in the roles of line-level workers. Organizations should use a vertical slice of the organization in planning how they are going to attempt change and in deciding which curriculum to use and how that curriculum will be implemented throughout the organization (Taxman & Belenko, 2011). If staff do not understand or see the alignment of reform attempts with the current organizational culture, they often retain prechange behavioral decision-making patterns and structures (Rudes, 2012; Steiner et al., 2011). Including staff in the change process and allowing them to participate in possibly developing and tailoring one of the several discussed curriculums for their organization can promote understanding and buy-in.

Addressing resistance to change and understanding ways in which changes in the roles of POs in the twenty-first century can be made successfully is important for several reasons. No longer is it adequate for POs to purely supervise, control, and punish probationers. Growing evidence suggests that these strategies are ineffective and can actually worsen offender outcomes (Bonta et al., 2008). With more than five million individuals under community supervision (Clement et al., 2011), probation and parole organizations have a responsibility to change the way they do business to better serve probationers and, in turn, better protect the community. The shift toward the rehabilitative goal of the justice system and the RNR model challenges POs to shift both their mentality and practice. The development of training curriculums and organizational development processes built on scientific evidence is a good first step in generating meaningful shifts in the field of probation and parole, but there is still much work to be done to create lasting changes in the culture of these organizations.

References

Abadinsky, H. (2006). *Probation and parole theory and practice* (9th ed.). Englewood Cliffs, NJ: Prentice-Hall.

Adams, W., & Roth, J. (1998). *Federal offenders under community supervision, 1987–96.* Washington, DC: Bureau of Justice Statistics.

Agócs, C. (1997). Institutionalized resistance to organizational change: denial, inaction and repression. *Journal of Business Ethics, 16,* 917–931. doi:10.1023/A:1017939404578

Alexander, M., VanBenschoten, S. W., & Walters, S. T. (2008). Motivational interviewing training in criminal justice: Development of a plan. *Federal Probation, 72,* 61–66.

Andrews, D. A., & Bonta, J. (2010a). *The psychology of criminal conduct* (5th ed.). New Providence, NJ: LexisNexis Matthew Bender.

Andrews, D. A., & Bonta, J. (2010b). Rehabilitating criminal justice policy and practice. *Psychology, Public Policy, and Law, 16,* 39–55. doi:10.1037/a0018362

Andrews, D. A., Bonta, J., & Hoge, R. (1990). Classification for effective rehabilitation: Rediscovering psychology. *Criminal Justice and Behavior, 17,* 19–52. doi:10.1177/0093854890017001004

Andrews, D. A., Bonta, J., & Wormith, S. (2010). The Level of Service (LS) Assessment of adults and older adolescents. In R. Otto & K. Douglas (Eds.), *Handbook of violence risk assessment tools* (pp. 199–225). New York, NY: Routledge.

Andrews, D. A., & Kiessling, J. J. (1980). Program structure and effective correctional practices: A summary of the CaVIC research. In R. Ross & P. Gendreau (Eds.), *Effective correctional treatment* (pp. 439–463). Toronto, Ontario, Canada: Butterworths.

Andrews, D. A., Zinger, I., Hoge, R. D., Bonta, J., Gendreau, P., & Cullen, F. T. (1990). Does correctional treatment work? A clinically relevant and psychologically informed meta-analysis. *Criminology, 28,* 369–404. doi:10.1111/j.1745-9125.1990.tb01330.x

Baer, J. S., Ball, S. A., Campbell, B. K., Miele, G. M., Schoener, E. P., & Tracy, K. (2007). Training and fidelity monitoring in behavioral interventions in multi-site addictions research. *Drug and Alcohol Dependence, 87,* 107–118. doi:10.1016/j.drugalcdep.2006.08.028

Baer, R. A. (2006). *Mindfulness-based treatment approaches: clinician's guide to evidence base and applications.* New York, NY: Academic Press.

Bailey, W. C. (1966). Correctional outcome: An evaluation of 100 reports. *Journal of Criminal Law, Criminology, and Police Science, 57,* 153–160. doi:10.2307/1141289

Bartunek, J. M. (1993). The multiple cognitions and conflicts associated with second order organizational change. In J. K. Murnighan (Ed.), *Social psychology in organizations: Advances in theory and research* (pp. 322–349). Englewood Cliffs, NJ: Prentice-Hall.

Battalino, J., Beutler, L., & Shani, A. B. (1996). Large-system change initiative: Transformation I progress at the California Department of Corrections. *Public Productivity and Management Review, 20,* 24–44. doi:10.2307/3380601

Bazemore, G., Dicker, T. J., & Al-Gadheeb, H. (1994). The treatment ideal and detention reality: Demographic, professional/occupational and organizational influences on detention worker punitiveness. *American Journal of Criminal Justice, 19,* 21–41. doi:10.1007/BF02887437

Bonta, J., Bourgon, G., Rugge, T., Scott, T. L., Yessine, A. K., Gutierrez, L., & Li, J. (2011). An experimental demonstration of training probation officers in evidence-based community supervision. *Criminal Justice and Behavior, 38,* 1127–1148. doi:10.1177/0093854811420678

Bonta, J., Bourgon, G., Rugge, T., Scott, T. L., Yessine, A. K., Gutierrez, L. K., & Public Safety Canada. (2010). *The strategic training initiative in community supervision: Risk–needs–responsivity in the real world.* Ottawa, Ontario, Canada: Public Safety Canada.

Bonta, J., Rugge, T., Scott, T. L., Bourgon, G., & Annie, K. Y. (2008). Exploring the black box of community supervision. *Journal of Offender Rehabilitation, 47,* 248–270. doi:10.1080/10509670802134085

Bourgon, G., Bonta, J., Rugge, T., & Scott, T. L. (2010). The role of program design, implementation, and evaluation in evidence-based real world community supervision. *Federal Probation, 74,* 2–15.

Bourgon, G., & Gutierrez, L. (2012). The general responsivity principle in community supervision: The importance of probation officers using cognitive intervention techniques and its influence on recidivism. *Journal of Criminal Justice, 35,* 149–166.

Bourgon, G., Gutierrez, L., & Ashton, J. (2011). The evolution of community supervision practice: The transformation from case manager to change agent. *Irish Probation Journal, 8,* 28–48.

Chiancone, J. (2010). *A profile of young people in the juvenile justice system: Data from OJJDP's collections.* Juvenile Justice in the Age of the Second Chance Act, the Youth Promise Act, and the JJDP Reauthorization Bill: Research Guided Policy Implications for Maximizing Reentry Initiatives for Adolescents. Congressional Briefing, October 2010.

Clark, M., Walters, S. T., Gingrich, R., & Meltzer, M. (2006). Motivational interviewing for probation officers: Tipping the balance towards change. *Federal Probation, 70,* 38–44.

Clawson, E., Bogue, B., & Joplin, L. (2005). *Implementing evidence-based practices in corrections.* Washington,

DC: Crime and Justice Institute, National Institute of Corrections.

Clear, T., & Latessa, E. (1993). Probation officer roles in intensive supervision: Surveillance versus treatment. *Justice Quarterly, 10,* 441–462. doi:10.1080/07418829300091921

Clement, M., Schwarzfeld, M., & Thompson, M. (Eds.). (2011). *National Summit on Justice Reinvestment and Public Safety, January 2011: Addressing recidivism, crime, and corrections spending.* New York, NY: Council of State Governments Justice Center.

Cullen, F. T., & Gendreau, P. (1989). The effectiveness of correctional rehabilitation. In L. Goodstein & D. L. MacKenzie (Eds.), *The American prison* (pp. 23–44). New York, NY: Plenum Press.

Cullen, F. T., & Gendreau, P. (2000). Assessing correctional rehabilitation: Policy, practice, and prospects. In J. Horney (Ed.), *Criminal justice: Policies, processes, and decisions of the criminal justice system* (Vol. 3, pp. 109–175). Washington, DC: U.S. Department of Justice, National Institute of Justice.

Deal, T. E., & Kennedy, A. A. (2000). *Corporate cultures: The rites and rituals of corporate life.* Cambridge, MA: Perseus.

Dressler, D. (1962). *Practice and theory of probation and parole.* New York, NY: Columbia University Press.

Ekland-Olson, S., & Martin, S. J. (1988). Organizational compliance with court-ordered reform. *Law and Society Review, 22,* 359–384.

Farabee, D., Prendergast, M., Cartier, J., Wexler, H., Knight, L., & Anglin, M. D. (1999). Barriers to implementing effective correctional drug treatment programs. *Prison Journal, 79,* 150–162. doi:10.1177/0032885599079002002

Farrell, J. L., Young, D. W., & Taxman, F. S. (2011). Effects of organizational factors on use of juvenile supervision practices. *Criminal Justice and Behavior, 38,* 565–583. doi:10.1177/0093854811401786

Feeley, M. M., & Simon, J. (1992). The new penology: Notes on the emerging strategy of corrections and its implications. *Criminology, 30,* 449–474. doi:10.1111/j.1745-9125.1992.tb01112.x

Ferguson, J. L. (2002). Putting the "what works" research into practice. *Criminal Justice and Behavior, 29,* 472–492. doi:10.1177/0093854802029004007

Friedmann, P. D., Taxman, F. S., & Henderson, C. (2007). Evidence-based treatment practices for drug-involved adults in the criminal justice system. *Journal of Substance Abuse Treatment, 32,* 267–277. doi:10.1016/j.jsat.2006.12.020

Gendreau, P., & Andrews, D. A. (1990). Tertiary prevention: What the meta-analyses of the offender treatment literature tell us about what works. *Canadian Journal of Criminology, 32,* 173–184.

Ginsburg, J. I., Mann, R. E., Rotgers, F., & Weekes, J. R. (2002). Motivational interviewing with criminal justice populations. In W. R. Miller & S. Rollnick (Eds.), *Motivational interviewing: Preparing people for change* (2nd ed., 333–346). New York, NY: Guilford Press.

Glaze, L. E., & Parks, E. (2011). *Correctional populations in the United States, 2010.* Washington, DC: Bureau of Justice Statistics. Retrieved from http://bjs.ojp.usdoj.gov/index.cfm

Gottfredson, S. D., & Moriarty, L. J. (2006). Statistical risk assessment: Old problems and new applications. *Crime and Delinquency, 52,* 178–200. doi:10.1177/0011128705281748

Hannah-Moffat, K. (2005). Criminogenic needs and the transformative risk subject: Hybridizations of risk/need in penality. *Punishment and Society, 7,* 29–51. doi:10.1177/1462474505048132

Harper, R., & Hardy, S. (2000). An evaluation of motivational interviewing as a method of intervention with clients in a probation setting. *British Journal of Social Work, 30,* 393–400. doi:10.1093/bjsw/30.3.393

Harris, P. M., Gingerich, R., & Whittaker, T. A. (2004). The "effectiveness" of differential supervision. *Crime and Delinquency, 50,* 235–271. doi:10.1177/0011128703258939

Hilton, N. Z., & Simmons, J. L. (2001). The influence of actuarial risk assessment in clinical judgments and tribunal decisions about mentally disordered offenders in maximum security. *Law and Human Behavior, 25,* 393–408. doi:10.1023/A:1010607719239

Hodson, R. (1991). The active worker: Autonomy and compliance at the workplace. *Journal of Contemporary Ethnography, 20,* 47–78. doi:10.1177/089124191020001003

Hohman, M., Doran, N., & Koutsenok, I. (2009). Motivational interviewing training for juvenile corrections staff in California: One year initial outcomes. *Journal of Offender Rehabilitation, 48,* 635–648. doi:10.1080/10509670903196108

Joplin, L., Bogue, B., Campbell, N., Carey, M., Clawson, E., Faust, D., . . . Woodward, W. (2004). *Using an integrated model to implement evidence-based practices in corrections.* Washington, DC: Crime and Justice Institute, National Institute of Corrections.

Kemshall, H., Parton, N., Walsh, M., & Waterson, J. (1997). Concepts of risk in relation to organizational structure and functioning within the personal social services and probation. *Social Policy and Administration, 31,* 213–232. doi:10.1111/1467-9515.00052

Klockars, C. B., Jr. (1972). A theory of probation supervision. *Journal of Criminal Law, Criminology, and Police Science, 63*, 550–557. doi:10.2307/1141809

Krysik, J., & LeCroy, C. W. (2002). The empirical validation of an instrument to predict risk of recidivism among juvenile offenders. *Research on Social Work Practice, 12*, 71–81. doi:10.1177/104973150201200106

Landenberger, N. A., & Lipsey, M. W. (2005). The positive effects of cognitive–behavioral programs for offenders: A meta-analysis of factors associated with effective treatment. *Journal of Experimental Criminology, 1*, 451–476. doi:10.1007/s11292-005-3541-7

Latessa, E. (2012). *Effective practices in community supervision (EPICS)*. Presentation for the Colorado Alliance for Drug Endangered Children, Denver, CO.

Latessa, E. J. (2004). The challenge of change: Correctional programs and evidence-based practices. *Criminology and Public Policy, 3*, 547–560. doi:10.1111/j.1745-9133.2004.tb00061.x

Latessa, E. J., & Allen, H. E. (1997). *Corrections in the community*. Cincinnati, OH: Anderson.

Lawrence, R., & Johnson, S. L. (1990). Effects of the Minnesota sentencing guidelines on probation agents. *Journal of Criminal Justice, 13*, 77–104.

Lerch, J., James-Andrews, S., Eley, E., & Taxman, F. S. (2009). "Town Hall" strategies for organizational change. *Federal Probation, 73*, 2–9.

Lin, A. C. (2000). *Reform in the making: The implementation of social policy in prison*. Princeton, NJ: Princeton University Press.

Lipsey, M. W., Farran, D. C., Bilbrey, C., Hofer, K. G., & Dong, N. (2011). *Initial results of the evaluation of the Tennessee Voluntary Pre-K Program*. Nashville, TN: Vanderbilt University.

Lipsky, M. (1980). *Street-level bureaucracy: Dilemmas of the individual in public services*. New York, NY: Sage.

Lundahl, B. W., Tollefson, D., Kunz, C., Brownell, C., & Burke, B. (2010). Meta-analysis of motivational interviewing: Twenty-five years of research. *Research on Social Work Practice, 20*, 137–160. doi:10.1177/1049731509347850

Luong, D., & Wormith, J. S. (2011). Applying risk/need assessment to probation practice and its impact on the recidivism of young offenders. *Criminal Justice and Behavior, 38*, 1177–1199. doi:10.1177/0093854811421596

Lynch, M. (1998). Waste managers? The new penology, crime fighting and parole agent identity. *Law and Society Review, 32*, 839–870. doi:10.2307/827741

Maass, S. A., Taxman, F. S., Serin, R., Crites, E., Watson, C. A., & Lloyd, C. (2013, November). *SOARING 2: An eLearning Training Program to Improve Knowledge of EBPs*. Paper presented at the American Society of Criminology Annual Conference, Atlanta, GA.

McCorkle, R., & Crank, J. (1996). Meet the new boss: Institutional change and loose coupling in parole and probation. *American Journal of Criminal Justice, 21*, 1–25. doi:10.1007/BF02887427

McMurran, M. (2009). Motivational interviewing with offenders: A systematic review. *Legal and Criminological Psychology, 14*, 83–100. doi:10.1348/135532508X278326

Miller, J., & Maloney, C. (2013). Practitioner compliance with risk/needs assessment tools: A theoretical and empirical assessment. *Criminal Justice and Behavior, 40*, 716–736. doi:10.1177/0093854812468883

Miller, W. R. (2004). Motivational interviewing in service to health promotion. *American Journal of Health Promotion, 18*, A1–A10.

Miller, W. R., & Mount, K. A. (2001). A small study of training in motivational interviewing: Does one workshop change clinical and client behavior? *Behavioural and Cognitive Psychotherapy, 29*, 457–471. doi:10.1017/S1352465801004064

Miller, W. R., & Moyers, T. B. (2006). Eight stages in learning motivational interviewing. *Journal of Teaching in the Addictions, 5*, 3–17. doi:10.1300/J188v05n01_02

Miller, W. R., & Rollnick, S. (2002). *Motivational interviewing: Preparing people for change*. New York, NY: Guilford Press.

Miller, W. R., & Rollnick, S. (2009). Ten things that motivational interviewing is not. *Behavioural and Cognitive Psychotherapy, 37*, 129–140. doi:10.1017/S1352465809005128

Miller, W. R., Yahne, C. E., Moyers, T. B., Martinez, J., & Pirritano, M. (2004). A randomized trial of methods to help clinicians learn motivational interviewing. *Journal of Consulting and Clinical Psychology, 72*, 1050–1062. doi:10.1037/0022-006X.72.6.1050

Murphy, D., & Lutze, F. (2009). Police-probation partnerships: Professional identity and the sharing of coercive power. *Journal of Criminal Justice, 37*, 65–76. doi:10.1016/j.jcrimjus.2008.12.010

Nord, W. R., & Jermier, J. M. (1994). Overcoming resistance to resistance: Insights from a study of the shadows. *Public Administration Quarterly, 17*, 396–409.

Ohlin, L., Coates, E., & Miller, R. R. (1974). Radical correctional reform: A case study of the Massachusetts youth correctional system. *Harvard Educational Review, 44*, 74–111.

Oleson, J. C., VanBenschoten, S., Robinson, C., Lowenkamp, C. T., & Holsinger, A. M. (2012). Actuarial and clinical assessment of criminogenic needs: Identifying supervision priorities among federal probation officers. *Journal of Crime and Justice, 35*, 239–248

Oser, C., Knudsen, H., Staton-Tindall, M., & Leukefeld, C. (2009). The adoption of wraparound services among substance abuse treatment organizations serving criminal offenders: The role of a women-specific program. *Drug and Alcohol Dependence, 103*, S82–S90. doi:10.1016/j.drugalcdep.2008.12.008

Petersilia, J. (1997). Probation in the United States: Practices and challenges. *National Institute of Justice Journal*, 2–8.

Petersilia, J. (2002). *Reforming probation and parole in the 21st Century*. Lanham, MD: American Correctional Association.

Petersilia, J. (2003). *When prisoners come home: Parole and prisoner reentry*. Oxford, England: Oxford University Press.

Porporino, F. J. (2001). *Getting to 'what works' through organizational responsivity: Engaging staff in organizational change*. Prepared as a Monograph series on What Works to be published by the International Community and Corrections Association.

Prasad, A., & Prasad, P. (1998). Everyday struggles at the workplace: The nature and implications of routine resistance in contemporary organizations. *Research in the Sociology of Organizations, 16*, 225–257.

Prasad, P., & Prasad, A. (2000). Stretching the iron cage. *Organization Science, 11*, 387–403. doi:10.1287/orsc.11.4.387.14597

Prendergast, M. L., Pearson, F. S., Podus, D., Hamilton, Z. K., & Greenwell, L. (2013). The Andrews' principles of risk, needs, and responsivity as applied in drug treatment programs: Meta-analysis of crime and drug use outcomes. *Journal of Experimental Criminology, 9*, 275–300.

Rhine, E. E., Mawhorr, T. L., & Parks, E. C. (2006). Implementation: The bane of effective correctional programs. *Criminology and Public Policy, 5*, 347–358. doi:10.1111/j.1745-9133.2006.00382.x

Robinson, C. R., Lowenkamp, C. T., Holsinger, A. M., VanBenschoten, S., Alexander, M., & Oleson, J. C. (2012). A random study of Staff Training Aimed at Reducing Re-arrest (STARR): Using core correctional practices in probation interactions. *Journal of Criminal Justice, 35*, 167–188.

Robinson, C. R., VanBenschoten, S., Alexander, M., & Lowenkamp, C. T. (2011). A random (almost) study of Staff Training Aimed at Reducing Re-Arrest (STARR): Reducing recidivism through intentional design. *Federal Probation, 75*, 57–63.

Rogers, C. R. (1961). *On becoming a person: A therapist's view of psychotherapy*. Boston, MA: Houghton Mifflin.

Rothman, D. (1980). *Conscience and convenience: The asylum and its alternatives in progressive America*. Boston, MA: Little, Brown and Company.

Rudes, D. S. (2012). Getting technical: Parole officers' continued use of technical violations under California's parole reform agenda. *Journal of Criminal Justice, 35*, 249–268.

Rudes, D. S., Lerch, J., & Taxman, F. S. (2011). Implementing a reentry framework at a correctional facility: Challenges to the culture. *Journal of Offender Rehabilitation, 50*, 467–491. doi:10.1080/10509674.2011.624392

Rudes, D. S., & Viglione, J. (2014). Correctional workers through the change process. In G. Bruinsma & D. Weisburd (Eds.), *Encyclopedia of criminology and criminal justice* (pp. 617–630). New York, NY: Springer.

Rudes, D. S., Viglione, J., & Taxman, F. S. (2014). Professional ideologies in United States probation and parole. In I. Durnescu & F. McNeill (Eds.), *Understanding penal practice* (pp. 11–29). Abingdon, England: Routledge.

Sachwald, J. (2001). *Proactive community supervision: A plan for making Maryland communities safer*. Baltimore, MD: Department of Public Safety and Correctional Services.

Schein, E. H. (1990). Organizational culture. *American Psychologist, 45*, 109–119. doi:10.1037/0003-066X.45.2.109

Schwalbe, C. (2004). Re-visioning risk assessment for human service decision making. *Children and Youth Services Review, 26*, 561–576. doi:10.1016/j.childyouth.2004.02.011

Schwalbe, C. S., & Maschi, T. (2009). Investigating probation strategies with juvenile offenders: The influence of officers' attitudes and youth characteristics. *Law and Human Behavior, 33*, 357–367. doi:10.1007/s10979-008-9158-4

Scott, J. C. (1985). *Weapons of the weak: Everyday forms of peasant resistance*. New Haven, CT: Yale University Press.

Scott, S. G., & Bruce, R. A. (1994). Determinants of innovative behavior: A path model of individual innovation in the workplace. *Academy of Management Journal, 37*, 580–607. doi:10.2307/256701

Sherman, L. W. (1998). Evidence-based policing. *Ideas in American Policing Series*. Washington, DC: Police Foundation.

Simpson, D. D. (2002). A conceptual framework for transferring research to practice. *Journal of Substance*

Abuse Treatment, 22, 171–182. doi:10.1016/S0740-5472(02)00231-3

Sluder, R. D., & Reddington, F. P. (1993). An empirical examination of the work ideologies of juvenile and adult probation officers. *Journal of Offender Rehabilitation, 20,* 115–137. doi:10.1300/J076v20n01_08

Sluder, R. D., Shearer, R. A., & Potts, D. W. (1991). Probation officers' role perceptions and attitudes toward firearms. *Federal Probation, 55,* 3–11.

Smith, P., Schweitzer, M., Labrecque, R. M., & Latessa, E. J. (2012). Improving probation officers' supervision skills: An evaluation of the EPICS model. *Journal of Criminal Justice, 35,* 189–199.

Steiner, B., Travis, L. F., & Makarios, M. D. (2011). Understanding parole officers' responses to sanctioning reform. *Crime and Delinquency, 57,* 222–246. doi:10.1177/0011128709343141

Taxman, F., Maass, S., Duhaime, L., & Serin, R. (2013, September). *SOARING 2 pilot summary.* Presentation given at the International Community Corrections Association Annual Conference, Reno, NV.

Taxman, F. S. (2002). Supervision: Exploring the dimensions of effectiveness. *Federal Probation, 66,* 14–27.

Taxman, F. S. (2008). No illusions: Offender and organizational change in Maryland's Proactive Correctional Facility: Challenges to the culture. *Journal of Offender Rehabilitation, 50,* 467–491.

Taxman, F. S. (2012). Probation, intermediate sanctions, and community-based corrections. In J. Petersilia & K. R. Reitz (Eds.), *The Oxford handbook of sentencing and corrections* (pp. 363–385). New York, NY: Oxford University Press.

Taxman, F. S. (2013). Seven keys to "make EBPs stick": Lessons from the field. *Federal Probation,* 10–25.

Taxman, F. S., & Belenko, S. (2011). *Implementing evidence-based practices in community corrections and addiction treatment.* New York, NY: Springer.

Taxman, F. S., Henderson, C., & Belenko, S. (2009). Organizational context, systems change, and adopting treatment delivery systems in the criminal justice system. *Drug and Alcohol Dependence, 103,* S1–S6. doi:10.1016/j.drugalcdep.2009.03.003

Taxman, F. S., Henderson, C., & Lerch, J. (2010). The socio-political context of reforms in probation agencies: impact on adoption of evidence-based practices. In F. McNeill, P. Raynor, & C. Trotter (Eds.), *Offender supervision. New directions in theory, research, and practice* (pp. 336–378). Cullompton, England: Willan.

Taxman, F. S., Henderson, C., Young, D. W., & Farrell, J. (2012). The impact of training interventions on organizational readiness to support innovations in juvenile justice offices. *Administration of Mental Health Policy and Mental Health Services Research,* 1–12.

Taxman, F. S., Sheperdson, E., & Byrne, J. M. (2004). *Tools of the trade: A guide to incorporating science into practice.* Washington, DC: National Institute of Corrections.

Trotter, C. (1996). The impact of different supervision practices in community corrections. *Australian and New Zealand Journal of Criminology, 29,* 1–19. doi:10.1177/000486589602900103

Turpin-Petrosino, C. (1999). Are limiting enactments effective? An experimental test of decision making in a presumptive parole state. *Journal of Criminal Justice, 27,* 321–332. doi:10.1016/S0047-2352(99)00004-5

Viglione, J., Rudes, D., Nightingale, V., Watson, C., & Taxman, F. S. (2014). *The many hats of juvenile justice: A latent class analysis of juvenile probation officers.* Manuscript in preparation.

Walker, S. (1998). *A history of American criminal justice.* New York, NY: Oxford University Press.

Walters, S., Vader, A., Nguyen, N., Harris, T., & Eells, J. (2010). Motivational interviewing as a supervision strategy in probation: A randomized effectiveness trial. *Journal of Offender Rehabilitation, 49,* 309–323. doi:10.1080/10509674.2010.489455

Ward, G., & Kupchik, A. (2010). What drives juvenile probation officers?: Relating organizational contexts, status characteristics, and personal convictions to treatment and punishment orientations. *Crime and Delinquency, 56,* 35–69. doi:10.1177/0011128707307960

Whitehead, J., & Lindquist, C. (1985). Job stress and burnout among probation/parole officers: Perceptions and causal factors. *International Journal of Offender Therapy and Comparative Criminology, 29,* 109–119. doi:10.1177/0306624X8502900204

Wilson, D. B., Bouffard, L. A., & Mackenzie, D. L. (2005). A quantitative review of structured, group-oriented, cognitive–behavioral programs for offenders. *Criminal Justice and Behavior, 32,* 172–204. doi:10.1177/0093854804272889

Wormith, J. S., Althouse, R., Simpson, M., Reitzel, L. R., Fagan, T. J., & Morgan, R. D. (2007). The rehabilitation and reintegration of offenders—The current landscape and some future directions for correctional psychology. *Criminal Justice and Behavior, 34,* 879–892. doi:10.1177/0093854807301552

Young, D. W., Farrell, J., & Taxman, F. S. (2012). Impacts of juvenile probation training models on youth recidivism. *Justice Quarterly.* Advance online publication. doi:10.1080/07418825.2012.673633

Zald, M. R. (1962). Organizational control structures in five correctional institutions. *American Journal of Sociology, 68,* 335–345. doi:10.1086/223353

CHAPTER 14

SENTENCING

R. Barry Ruback

A criminal sentencing decision brings into a single judgment prior investigative, legal, practical, and policy determinations, as well as predictions about future criminal behavior. Although the sentencing decision is based primarily on two legally relevant factors, the severity of the offense and the offender's prior record, factors about the offender, the victim, the judge, the courtroom workgroup, and the jurisdiction may also affect the type and extent of a criminal sentence. These extralegal factors may, in some instances, lead to sentencing disparity between similarly situated offenders.

Psychological research and theory are important for understanding how judges make sentencing decisions, but because these psychological factors operate within larger social and political contexts, understanding sentencing decisions also requires understanding the social psychological processes within the local criminal justice system and courtroom community, the social and economic characteristics of the communities where crime occurs and offenders are prosecuted, and the broad policy determinations about the purposes of criminal justice.

This chapter describes the nature of sentencing decisions and presents theoretical views, from psychology and criminology, that have been used to explain sentencing decisions. The two research literatures have largely been separate, with psychologists focusing on the process of individual decision making and largely ignoring context, and criminologists focusing on factors about jurisdictional contexts and making inferences about individual judges' decisions based on characteristics of offenders and offenses.

After describing the goals and types of sentences and sentencing statutes, this chapter explains attribution theory and suggests that judges' decisions can be understood as judgments based on whether the offender committed the crime because of factors about the offender or factors about the environment (the internal–external dimension) and because of factors that are likely to continue over time or factors that are variable over time (the stable–unstable dimension). Judges impose more severe sentences if they make an internal attribution to the offender and if they make an attribution to a cause that is stable over time.

This review also suggests that, given the large amount of information and the shortage of time, judges rely on heuristics to simplify their decisions. Judges are generally not aware of how they make their decisions, and, in particular, of the fact that their decisions are basically the same as what probation officers recommend to them. Moreover, judges are unlikely to gain expertise over time because they generally do not receive clear and immediate feedback about their decisions.

In addition to the seriousness of the offense and the offender's prior record, the sentencing decision may be affected by whether the defendant was released from jail before trial and whether the defendant pled guilty. Blacks and males receive longer sentences than Whites and females, and young Black males seem to receive disproportionately severe sentences. There is some disagreement, however, about the size and importance of these disparities, once legally relevant factors are controlled.

http://dx.doi.org/10.1037/14462-014
APA Handbook of Forensic Psychology: Vol. 2. Criminal Investigation, Adjudication, and Sentencing Outcomes,
B. L. Cutler and P. A. Zapf (Editors-in-Chief)
Copyright © 2015 by the American Psychological Association. All rights reserved.

Criminologists have investigated factors about the social, economic, and political context of courts, but these effects are generally small. Relatively more important are factors about the proximal context of courts, especially factors about the courtroom community, which consists of the judge, the prosecuting and defense attorneys, and the probation officer.

IMPORTANCE OF THE PROBLEM

Almost seven million people in the United States are under some sort of correctional supervision, i.e., 1 out of every 34 adults in the country (Glaze & Parks, 2012). Of this total, about two and a quarter million are incarcerated in jail or prison, and almost five million are under community supervision (probation or parole). The United States has the highest incarceration rate in the world (Lynch & Pridemore, 2011), higher than Russia, Rwanda, and Cuba (Walmsley, 2009), and, following China, it has the second highest number of prisoners. This high rate of incarceration is the result of a high violent crime rate and the result of policies that target violence and aggressively criminalize drugs (Lynch & Pridemore, 2011; Tonry, 1996): mandatory sentences requiring incarceration, mandatory minimum sentences requiring a specified number of years of incarceration, and statutes that identify and punish particular types of offenders (e.g., repeat violent offenders, habitual offenders, sexual predators). Although there is some evidence that deterrence works to reduce crime (Wilson, 2011), the marginal effect of incarcerating more individuals depends on the number of offenders already incarcerated, such that the higher the incarceration rate, the lower the deterrence effect for additional incarcerations (Piehl & Useem, 2011).

Blacks are incarcerated at a higher rate than Whites, and males are incarcerated at a higher rate than females. Thus, Black males are disproportionately in prison, at a "disparity ratio" of 6.5:1 compared to White males (Reitz, 2011). Among adult Black males in the United States, 20% have served time in prison (Pettit & Western, 2004), and this figure jumps to 62% for Black men with less than a high school education (Pettit, 2012).

Although the focus of most research and political discussions is incarceration, in fact most convicted offenders are supervised in the community. The goal of this supervision is in part to punish offenders but primarily to reduce recidivism, a goal that has implications for treatment.

Sentencing in the United States

After independence from England, state legislatures severely restricted judicial discretion in sentencing because Americans had been angered by the unlimited discretion English judges had enjoyed during the colonial period. Judges in early America presided over trials, but they had little discretion regarding sentencing because the laws generally specified the penalty for each offense and judges simply imposed that sentence (Gaylin, 1974).

Over time, state legislatures gradually imposed different penalties for different types of what had previously been considered the same offense. Beyond these additional grades of felonies, legislatures continued to give more discretion to judges because the laws did not always fit the particular circumstances of the offense. Judges were given a range of sentence lengths for each crime, from which they could assign the appropriate punishment for the particular criminal (Goldfarb & Singer, 1973). With the creation of the indefinite sentence in 1869 in Michigan, and by 1900 in most states, the actual power to determine the length of incarceration for many offenses had passed into the hands of an executive agency, the parole board. This indeterminate sentencing system, under which courts imposed a minimum and maximum sentence and the parole board fixed the release date from prison, lasted into the 1980s (Morris & Tonry, 1990). Offenders rarely appealed these indeterminate sentences, and even when they did, appellate courts rarely overturned the original sentence. Starting around 1980, states began limiting judges' discretion, primarily through determinate sentencing, in which the legislature clearly specified a sentence for a convicted offender, but also through mandatory minimum sentences, which required minimum terms of imprisonment, and, in many states, through sentencing guidelines.

Goals of Sentencing

Sentencing serves one or more of six goals, four of which are aimed at the offender. *Retribution* refers to punishing the criminal for having broken the law. The assumption is that punishment should be proportionate to the seriousness of the offense, although determining that ratio leaves room for disagreement (Reitz, 2011). *Incapacitation* refers to ensuring that a felon incarcerated in jail or prison will not be committing crimes in the community during the period of incarceration. *Specific deterrence* refers to the expectation that punishing an offender will keep that person from committing future crimes. *Rehabilitation* refers to the goal of the offender not committing any more crimes because of a change in attitude following treatment.

In addition to these four purposes aimed at the individual offender, sentencing serves two other goals. *General deterrence*, aimed at potential offenders, refers to the expectation that punishing a single violator will discourage others who are considering breaking the law from doing so. In contrast to specific deterrence, which is based on the particular individual's experience of punishment, general deterrence is based on the threat of punishment to the population at large (Nagin, Cullen, & Jonson, 2009). *Moral outrage* is aimed at all citizens; it refers to an emphatic statement that the crime is wrong and that sentencing the convicted criminal reflects societal values.

Sentencing disparity may exist because statutes generally give judges little guidance about which objectives are to be accomplished through the imposition of a sentence. Moreover, a specific sentence may serve multiple goals (e.g., punishment and incapacitation) and may interfere with others (e.g., rehabilitation). Thus, judges may give different sentences for the same crime because they have different objectives (see Bottomley, 1973; McFatter, 1978).

Types of Sentences

The sentencing decision involves choices about incarceration versus probation, about intermediate sanctions, about economic sanctions, and about treatment (Blumstein, Cohen, Martin, & Tonry, 1983). Judges can, and generally do, order combinations of these sentences, such as incarceration and economic sanctions or probation and treatment. Judges can also suspend sentences, which means that the felon is released and is not under the supervision of the court, although the sentence can be reimposed if the offender commits violations during the period of release.

Incarceration. Incarceration is the decision that is the primary focus of most research and most discussions in the popular press. An offender can be incarcerated in jail for less serious crimes and in prison for the most serious felonies. Incarceration punishes offenders and prevents them from committing crimes in society, although many prisons also have educational, occupational, and therapeutic programming, which may reduce offenders' likelihood of recidivism (see Volume 1, Chapter 3, this handbook for a review of risk assessment). On the other hand, imprisonment also stigmatizes offenders, separates them from their family and friends, lowers their chances of being employed when released, and increases physical and psychological problems (Massoglia, 2008; Western, 2006). The decision to incarcerate an offender is followed by a decision about the length of time the offender will be incarcerated, although for some crimes, this amount of time may be specified by statute.

Probation. If the judge decides not to incarcerate the offender, the offender is likely to be sentenced to probation in the community for a set period of time. While on probation, the offender must report regularly to a probation officer and must meet the conditions of probation, which usually include programs aimed at rehabilitation and testing for alcohol and drugs. Probation gives lower-risk offenders the opportunity to maintain ties to family and friends and to be employed, while also participating in rehabilitative programming that may reduce their likelihood of committing new crimes (see Chapter 13, this volume for a review of probation).

Intermediate sanctions. Incarceration in prison is at the most restrictive end of the sentencing continuum, and probation is at the least restrictive end of sentencing. In between are what are referred to as intermediate sanctions, which include intensive probation supervision, day reporting centers, halfway houses, boot camps, house arrest/electronic monitoring, and community service (Caputo, 2004). Intensive supervision, day reporting centers, and halfway houses are aimed primarily at rehabilitation, whereas community service and house arrest/electronic monitoring are generally punitive in nature and, as standalone programs, often do not include any treatment options. Boot camps are short-term prisons that incarcerate offenders for terms of a few months and that subject the prisoners to the training and discipline characteristic of programs for new military recruits. These intermediate sanctions can be imposed as a "front-end diversion" to keep offenders from being sent to prison or as a "back-end diversion" after an atypically short stay in prison or jail as a way of limiting offenders' time in incarceration (Caputo, 2004).

Economic sanctions. There are three types of economic sanctions: fines, costs/fees, and restitution (Ruback & Bergstrom, 2006). Typically, economic sanctions in the United States are additional penalties rather than sole sanctions, as they are in Europe (Hillsman, 1990). *Fines* are monetary penalties for crime. In many European countries, fines are the legally presumptive penalty and thus are fairly common (Tonry & Lynch, 1996). There is some evidence, however, that the in-out decision (i.e., incarceration or not) is made first even in the German legal system, where fines are supposed to be the equivalent of imprisonment (von Helversen & Rieskamp, 2009). In the United States, within a jurisdiction, judges usually apply the "going rate" for fines (Hillsman & Greene, 1992). Thus, all violators of a particular offense are obligated to pay the same or similar amounts.

Costs and *fees* refer to court-imposed orders to reimburse jurisdictions (local, county, state) for the administrative cost of operating the criminal justice system. A monthly supervision fee is the most common type of special condition of probation (Bonczar, 1997). Special services, such as electronic monitoring, require additional fees. In recent years, the costs of the criminal justice system have risen substantially; $1 of every $15 in state general funds is spent on corrections (Scott-Hayward, 2009), and courts have cut staff and shortened hours (*New York*

Times, 2009). Making offenders pay for at least part of those costs is one way to reduce the burden on taxpayers.

Restitution refers to a payment by the offender to restore victims to where they were before the crime, or at least as close as is possible with money alone (Ruback & Shaffer, 2005). Because of increasing concern for victims (Office for Victims of Crime, 1998), restitution awards are being imposed more frequently than in the past.

Treatment. Oftentimes, as a condition of probation, judges will order offenders to participate in treatment programs (see Volume 1, Chapter 6, this handbook for a review of forensic treatment). Treatment-based intermediate sanctions are generally more effective at reducing recidivism than are incarceration, non–treatment-based sanctions, and traditional probation (Andrews et al., 1990; Bonta, Wallace-Capretta, & Rooney, 2000; Petersilia & Turner, 1991), and they can be effective in reducing drug use, which is a strong correlate of recidivism (Gendreau, Little, & Goggin, 1996).

Role of Plea Bargaining in Sentencing

In more than 95% of all criminal trials, guilt is determined by a guilty plea rather than by a trial before a jury or judge (Cohen & Kyckelhahn, 2010; United States Sentencing Commission, 2012). Most of these guilty pleas involve the waiver of the right to trial in exchange for a reduction in charges or in the severity of the sentence (O'Hear, 2007). Plea bargaining "is not some adjunct to the criminal justice system; it is the criminal justice system" (Scott & Stuntz, 1992, p. 1912, as cited in *Missouri v. Frye*, 2012).

Plea bargaining helps prosecutors fulfill their four sometimes-conflicting roles: administrator, advocate, judge, and legislator (Alschuler, 1968). As an administrator, the prosecutor's goal is to dispose of as many cases as quickly and efficiently as possible. The major administrative factor in the decision on how to handle a particular case is how much time the case would take if it went to trial. As an advocate, the prosecutor wants to have a high proportion of convictions and to have severe sentences imposed for those convictions. As a judge, the prosecutor seeks to do the "right thing" for the defendant (if the defendant pleads guilty). As a legislator, the prosecutor may decide not to prosecute defendants accused of violating a law that is too harsh, or may charge them with a less serious crime.

Prosecutors use their past experience as the basis for typification (Myers & Hagan, 1979). According to Sudnow (1965), *typifying* a case means defining it in terms of the "normal" crime of that type. Thus, typification is based on "knowledge of the typical manner in which offenses of given classes are committed, the social characteristics of the persons who regularly commit them, the features of the settings in which they occur, the types of victims often involved, and the like" (Sudnow, 1965, p. 259). Because this typification explains the crime in terms of the usual characteristics of the offender and the situation and the usual disposition, it is an efficient means of dealing with a large caseload.

Judges benefit in several ways from a plea bargain. The plea deal can give them psychological satisfaction because they have fewer doubts about the defendant's guilt, greater discretion in sentencing, especially when a plea bargain avoids a statutorily mandated sentence, and a rationale for imposing a lenient sentence in a setting where there is less publicity than at a trial (Newman, 1966). Avoiding trial also spares the victim of the crime from having to testify and being exposed to publicity. Finally, the plea bargain benefits the system as a whole by reducing the backlog of cases and by furthering the objectives of punishment through the prompt imposition of penalties after the defendant's admission of guilt.

Sentencing Disparity

One criticism leveled at judges is that their sentencing decisions are inconsistent from one offender to another, from one judge to another, and from one jurisdiction to another. Although discretion and disparity in decisions are present at many stages of the criminal justice system, disparity in sentencing has received the most publicity, probably because sentencing is highly visible and because it is much easier to quantify the existence of disparity at the sentencing stage (e.g., by the percentage of probation sentences or the average length of prison terms) than at the arrest and prosecution stages (Dawson,

1969). Typically, disparity is examined using multiple regression approaches. All legally relevant factors are entered into the equation, and then legally irrelevant factors (e.g., race) are added. If the legally irrelevant factors are significant, after controlling for the legally relevant factors, the assumption is that there is discrimination in sentencing. Using this approach, research is suggestive of race, gender, and age discrimination, although this conclusion is, as described below, contested.

Disparity in sentences is evident not only from statistics on sentence lengths but also from more tightly controlled studies. For example, in a study by Partridge and Eldridge (1974), 50 federal judges were given identical sets of 20 files drawn from actual cases, with the crimes ranging from embezzlement to robbery. The results showed "glaring disparity" in judicial sentencing decisions. To limit judges' discretion, state legislatures have imposed mandatory sentences for certain crimes and many have established sentencing guidelines.

Sentencing Guidelines

For most of American history, judges had complete discretion in sentencing. That is, they did not have to explain what information they considered, how they weighted that information, or how they combined that information to reach a decision. Moreover, their sentences were generally not reviewable as long as they were within the broad range specified by the statute (Hofer, Blackwell, & Ruback, 1999). Because of the disparity in sentencing that sometimes resulted from this wide discretion, many states and the federal government instituted sentencing guidelines, which were typically developed after research into how sentences had been imposed in the past was combined with policy factors and practical considerations. Many guideline systems were designed explicitly to achieve "truth in sentencing" (i.e., the sentence imposed would be the sentence served) and to reduce unwarranted disparity. More generally, sentencing guidelines serve not only to structure the ways in which sentencing goals are achieved, but also to limit discretion, to structure plea negotiations, to provide standards for appropriate punishment, and to shield judges and prosecutors from political fallout for unpopular decisions (Engen, 2011).

Currently, 20 states, the District of Columbia, and the federal system have sentencing guidelines (Kauder & Ostrom, 2008). Under these guidelines, a range of sentences is specified for a particular type of crime and criminal history, with the goal of treating similar offenders (based on offense and criminal history) in a similar way. State guideline systems differ on several dimensions (e.g., whether they incorporate resource-impact assessments, whether they can be enforced by appeals, whether they cover intermediate sanctions and misdemeanor offenses as well as felonies), and they are quite different from the federal guidelines (Frase, 2005).

Generally, judges may go outside the guidelines if they write an explanation giving the mitigating or aggravating factors that justify doing so. The focus is on the usual case rather than the exception. Because a written explanation is required only in the exceptional cases, the exceptions are likely to be made only with some thought and only in unusual cases.

Sentencing in federal trial courts has been extensively studied. In the federal system, the guidelines are based on a two-dimensional grid, one dealing with factors about the offense and the other dealing with prior criminal history. Under the federal sentencing guidelines, the focus on the offense concerns the defendant's conduct, the harms caused, the amount of money involved, the amount of drugs involved, and the degree of the victim's injury. The focus on criminal history primarily concerns convictions for prior crimes.

In general, the U.S. sentencing guidelines incorporate more factors and consider them in more detail than do the guideline systems in the states (Ruback, 1998). For example, the 43 different categories of offense severity used in the federal guidelines are many more than those used in guidelines in states such as Minnesota (10), Oregon (11), Pennsylvania (14), and Washington (15). The federal guidelines are described in more detail in Ruback and Wroblewski (2001).

Hofer et al. (1999) used a natural experiment to test whether the U.S. sentencing guidelines reduced interjudge sentencing disparity. The assumption underlying their approach was that because cases are assigned randomly to judges, the average sentence for a judge should be the effect of the judge, not the cases. In their comparison of interjudge disparity before and after implementation of the federal sentencing guidelines, Hofer et al. found that overall interjudge disparity decreased from before to after the introduction of sentencing guidelines. In general, they found that the interaction effect for offense type by judges was larger than the primary judge effect, which suggests that knowing the type of case the judge is sentencing gives more information than does knowing the judge's average leniency or severity.

In the past decade the Supreme Court has limited the impact of sentencing guidelines and has given more discretion back to judges. The Court has ruled that only factors that have been considered at trial by a jury can be used to determine the final sentence (*United States v. Booker, United States v. Fanfan*, 2005). Moreover, the Court has ruled that guidelines, both federal and state, cannot be mandatory; they are only advisory.

Even though the U.S. Sentencing Guidelines were made advisory, judges' sentences remained quite similar to what they were prior to the Supreme Court decision in *Booker* (Ulmer, Light, & Kramer, 2011), possibly because most of the judges had long operated under the guidelines and because the judges were still required to consider the same factors that they had prior to *Booker* (Albonetti, 2011). Moreover, local norms probably govern the decision, norms that have incorporated the guidelines (Engen, 2011).

RELEVANT PSYCHOLOGICAL THEORY AND PRINCIPLES

Sentencing is a decision that requires the judge to try both to understand the reasons why the offender committed the crime and to predict the likelihood that the offender will commit another crime in the future. Thus, a sentence represents a choice from multiple alternatives regarding punishment for past behavior and prediction of future risk. Sentencing is of interest to psychologists because variables that are important to psychologists are also important to the criminal justice system: race, gender, and prior criminal behavior.

Several research literatures in psychology are relevant to the sentencing decision, including decision making, attribution and social cognition, and actuarial vs. clinical models of prediction. Moreover, work on fairness—to society, to victims, and to offenders—is useful for understanding the process by which sentencing decisions are made.

Although work by psychologists is relevant to sentencing decisions, almost all of the studies on sentencing have been conducted by criminologists, who have examined sentencing by looking at structural variables (e.g., poverty), demographic characteristics of defendants (especially race and gender), and organizational variables (formal rationality and workgroups). Because most sentencing research has been conducted by criminologists, this theoretical and empirical work is also briefly summarized.

Attribution Theory

The key theory for understanding criminal sentencing is attribution theory, which refers to theoretical approaches to understanding how people try to make sense of their own and others' behavior. The fundamental questions concern the underlying causes of behavior—whether these causes are internal to the person and whether they are stable over time—and the implications of these attributions in terms of reactions to past behavior and predictions about future behavior.

An attribution is a judgment of how much behavior is the product of the environment and how much is due to the person (Heider, 1958). Observers who have enough time and information can conduct a complete analysis of causes that increase the likelihood of a given behavior (facilitative causes) and of causes that decrease the likelihood of a given behavior (inhibitory causes), according to principles described by Kelley (1972a). Many times, though, observers do not have either the right information or enough time for a complete causal analysis. Under those circumstances, they use causal schemas (Kelley, 1972b), which are based on salient cues and past experience. Causal schemas are likely to be used when a quick decision is called for and the perceiver does not have the ability or motivation to acquire all of the information needed for a thorough causal analysis. Schemas are especially likely under conditions of heavy workloads, time pressure, and no feedback (von Helversen & Rieskamp, 2009). Time pressure is particularly problematic because it can exacerbate problems regarding conflicts between searching for and integrating information and between the speed and quality of decisions (Svenson, 1996). Thus, a judge who has only ten minutes to read a presentence report, review an offender's file, and perhaps ask the offender a few questions is likely to rely on causal schemas to make a sentencing judgment.

Weiner et al. (1972) proposed a two-dimensional framework for understanding how people make attributions for success or failure: a locus of control dimension and a stability dimension. The locus of control dimension distinguishes between causes that are believed to be internal to the person, like ability and personality, and causes that are believed to be external to the person (i.e., due to the environment), like the difficulty of the task and the person's good or bad luck. The stability dimension distinguishes between causes that are believed to be relatively stable over time, like ability or personality or the difficulty of a task, and causes that are believed to be changeable over time, such as a person's emotional state or good or bad luck.

Although the framework by Weiner et al. (1972) was developed for understanding attributions about success or failure on a task, it has been extended to understand how decision makers make attributions for criminal behavior (Carroll, 1978; Carroll & Payne, 1977; Greenberg & Ruback, 1982). According to Weiner et al., people attribute a behavior to a stable internal cause if that behavior is consistent with the person's past behavior. Thus, a long record of committing crimes is likely to lead to an attribution of a stable criminal disposition. An attribution to a stable external cause is based on how one person's behavior compares with the behavior of others in the situation. Thus, if most teenagers in a neighborhood are involved in property crime, a perceiver is likely to attribute such behavior to something about the environment, such as a norm of deviant behavior (Greenberg & Ruback, 1982). An attribution to an unstable internal cause is likely if some internal state that changes over time (e.g., a state of anger) is present when the behavior is present and absent when the behavior is absent. Finally, if the person's behavior is part of a pattern of highly variable or random behavior, the likely attribution is to an unstable external cause, like good or bad luck.

According to Weiner et al. (1972), the locus of control dimension determines affective responses to the person (e.g., liking or disliking), and the stability dimension is used in predicting future behavior. In terms of the criminal justice system, if a judge attributes an offender's criminal behavior to an internal cause (a criminal disposition), the judge is likely to have more negative feelings about the offender than if the attribution is to an external cause.

Regarding the stability dimension, if a judge attributes an offender's criminal behavior to a stable cause (the offender's criminal disposition or the crime-ridden neighborhood where the offender lives), the judge is predicting that the criminal behavior is likely to continue over time. If, however, the judge attributes the offender's criminal behavior to unstable causes such as being in the wrong place at the wrong time, the judge is more likely to believe that the criminal behavior will not continue over time.

In actual cases, the attribution of criminality is based primarily on the act for which the defendant was found guilty or pleaded guilty to, which includes the type and seriousness of the crime. Attributions on the stability dimension are based primarily on the prior criminal record. In general, making an attribution to either an internal cause or a stable cause results in a longer sentence. Such a conclusion makes sense, because an attribution to an internal stable cause implies that the criminal justice system cannot change the criminal's disposition and that it should instead try to prevent the criminal behavior that results from that disposition (Greenberg & Ruback, 1982). That is, a judge making an internal stable attribution will probably believe that the criminal justice system should change its focus from rehabilitating the offender (changing a stable disposition) to keeping the defendant in prison so that he or she cannot commit more crimes against the public (preventing the consequences of that disposition).

Using this attributional framework, Carroll and Payne's (1977) experiment with college undergraduates found that attributions to internal causes (e.g., an aggressive nature) led to higher ratings of crime severity and responsibility for the crime, as well as to recommendations for longer prison sentences. Attributions to stable causes (e.g., a criminal disposition, a criminogenic environment) led to higher ratings of criminality and higher expectations for recidivism, higher responsibility for the crime, greater desire to remove the criminal from society, and longer recommended prison sentences. A replication of this study using actual parole board members as participants found that the attributional dimensions of stability and locus of causality were unrelated to sentence length. Carroll and Payne did find, however, the theoretically expected relationship between the attributional dimensions and other types of judgments, including those relating to perceived criminality, responsibility, and crime severity.

Decision Making

Aside from the specific work on attribution theory, there is also more general research on decision making that is relevant to the sentencing decision. Judges generally believe that sentencing is a difficult and complex decision process and that it requires wisdom drawn from years of experience (Ruback & Wroblewski, 2001). Judges also believe that making multiple decisions makes them better decision makers.

Sentencing decisions are indeed complex, based on the criteria used by cognitive psychologists (Funke, 1991). Sentencing involves imprecise definitions of goals, a large number of variables (facts and policy considerations), variables that are highly correlated with each other, time pressures (because at any one time judges usually have many sentencing decisions to make), and delayed effects of the decision, such that judges do not know for a long time, and often never, the effects of their decisions.

Nonrational decision processes. Although judges believe that their decision making process is rational, the sentencing decision does not meet the standards of complete rationality: full information regarding alternatives and outcomes and unlimited time in which to make the decision. Decision makers usually know only some of the possible alternatives and their effects, and they therefore attempt to reduce uncertainty by relying on arrangements such as standard operating procedures, an organizational hierarchy, formal channels of communication, professional training, and indoctrination into the culture and procedures of the organization. That is, decision makers are likely to rely on routine choices that have worked in the past and, they assume, will work in the future. The primary purpose of imposing a structure on a problem is to make it easier to solve, because simplified problems require less memory and less cognitive effort (Ranyard, 1989). These structures are also useful for communicating with others, in that a structured problem is easier to understand, and it is easier to explain why a particular choice was made.

Aside from structuring problems, people also use three heuristics (representativeness, availability, anchoring and adjustment) to help them determine facts in resolving complex problems (Tversky & Kahneman, 1974). Heuristics are shortcuts that simplify decisions. Although these simplifying strategies generally lead to faster decisions, they can also lead to systematic errors because they cause decision makers to disregard or misuse information (Saks & Kidd, 1980–1981).

One heuristic is the *representativeness* bias, by which individuals make judgments of causality or association based on the degree to which one event is similar to another. For example, judges are likely to make predictions of future drug use based in part on how similar a particular individual is to the stereotype of an individual who is currently using drugs. Use of the representativeness heuristic occurs because individuals generally rely on concrete examples rather than base-rate information (i.e., how frequently a behavior occurs in the general population).

A second shortcut to decision making is the *availability* heuristic, which refers to the tendency to estimate the probability of an event based on how easy it is to think about examples of the event. For example, when judges are considering whether a particular type of defendant (e.g., a White female) is likely to commit a crime while on probation, they are likely to base their decision on how easily they can recall instances of White females violating probation. If they have trouble thinking of such instances, they are likely to estimate that the chances that a particular White female defendant will violate her probation are low. This tendency to use available information is also associated with relying on salient cues (i.e., those that are easily noticed) and with looking for information that is consistent with what they already believe (Wilkins, 1975).

In addition, the availability bias means that people generally rely more on specific examples than on statistical data that describe the larger group. Thus, in the case of sentencing, judges would tend not to rely on statistical summaries of actual recidivism rates. This unwillingness or inability to use statistical information means that they are likely to incorrectly estimate the probabilities of recidivism. Furthermore, when they receive new information about probabilities, they are not likely to correctly adjust their estimates.

A third heuristic, *anchoring and adjustment*, refers to the fact that estimates of likelihood start by having some initial value (the anchor) and then adjustments are made from that value on the basis of additional information (Tversky & Kahneman, 1974). The problem is that judgments are heavily influenced by the initial anchor, even if it is irrelevant (Englich, 2006). In addition, there is a tendency not to make appropriate adjustments on the basis of the new information.

That judges rely on heuristics to make their decisions would suggest that they may not always be following the law in their decisions. Consistent with that notion, in their analysis of sentencing decisions in German courts for property crimes, von Helversen and Rieskamp (2009) found that the relevant information for sentencing was not used as specified by German regulations.

Unaware of actual decision making processes. Considering the errors and biases involved in complex decision making, it is not surprising that, in general, individuals are not aware of their actual decision making processes (Hammond, Stewart, Brehmer, & Steinmann,

1975); they instead tend to look at the outcomes of their mental processes and rely on their implicit theories about how they reached those outcomes, given the available information (Nisbett & Wilson, 1977). In other words, decision makers are like observers; they examine publicly available information and make inferences about the processes that were probably involved in reaching the decision (Abelson & Levi, 1985). They also tend to use their implicit theories to help them determine which of the many cues they considered actually affected their decisions.

Judges believe that their sentencing decisions are difficult and complexly determined, but most decisions can be explained by only two or three factors, because of limitations in how much information individuals can remember and process (G. A. Miller, 1956). Moreover, this information appears to be combined in a simple linear fashion rather than in some complex configural pattern involving interactions among the variables (Dawes, Faust, & Meehl, 1989). Thus, decisions can generally be best represented by equally weighting the two or three important variables and simply adding them together (Dawes, 1979). This general work on decision making would suggest that the sentencing decision can also be explained by just a few factors.

Judges make their sentencing decisions on the basis of information in the case file, including the original charges against the defendant, the offenses that the defendant was convicted of, and the defendant's criminal history. For some offenders, there might also be a presentence report prepared by a probation officer assigned to the court, which would contain information about the defendant's general background (such as education, employment history, drug and alcohol use, and family stability) and an evaluation of his or her chances for success on probation. Judges also ask for recommended sentences from the probation officer, the prosecuting attorney, and the defense attorney.

Even though judges believe that sentencing is a difficult decision requiring expertise, years of experience, and the consideration of multiple factors, research indicates that actual decisions by judges can be predicted fairly well by two factors: the conviction offense and the offender's prior record. Thus,

sentencing in actual practice is a simple task, not the complex one that judges describe and believe.

Because of this relative simplicity and because sentencing hearings typically last only a few minutes, Konečni and Ebbesen (1982) characterized these hearings as staged rituals having symbolic value for the defendant and the public at large but serving no actual function. Specifically, they found that no information from the hearings (e.g., the amount and content of what was said and by whom) predicted the final sentence after controlling for all prehearing information (e.g., the probation officer's recommendation, the defendant's jail/bail status). Konečni and Ebbesen (1982) also characterized individualized justice as a myth, since few of the factors that would separate one individual case from another (e.g., employment history, social background) were related to the final decision.

No expertise over time. Aside from relying on nonrational decision shortcuts and not understanding how they make decisions, judges are incorrect to believe that making multiple sentencing decisions makes them better decision makers. Multiple decisions can be informative if they provide useful feedback to the decision maker. Generally, however, recurrent decisions may not be better than single decisions, because the decision makers may have learned the wrong lesson and acting on this incorrect information may result in self-fulfilling prophecies (Abelson & Levi, 1985). Repetitive decisions are likely to lead to better decision making only if the outcomes of the decisions are independent of the decision itself, the outcomes are concrete, and there is clear and immediate feedback. Those conditions are met in the case of weather forecasting, and indeed weather forecasters are generally accurate, especially about forecasting hurricanes (Silver, 2012), but those conditions are not met in the case of criminal sentencing, and therefore probably little learning takes place.

Fairness

One of the primary considerations in a sentencing decision is fairness to the offender. That is, the sentence should be proportionate to the harm done. Under this rule, the basic consideration is the harm done to society. There are two other comparisons, however, that determine whether a sentence is fair. First, a sentence is fair if it is proportionate to the harm done to the victim. Second, a sentence is fair if it is proportionate to sentences given to other offenders (see Chapter 12, this volume for a review of procedural justice research).

Fairness to victims.   Under criminal law, a criminal violation is committed against society, not the individual victim, which is why victims generally play only a minor role in the prosecution and punishment of offenders (Ruback & Thompson, 2001). Judges are also concerned, however, with the harm that victims suffered and are motivated to be fair to victims. Equity theory is relevant to how judges make that determination (Lerner, 1977; Walster, Walster, & Berscheid, 1978). According to equity theory, those who receive less than they deserve from a relationship are likely to be angry and distressed and are motivated to restore equity, either actually by increasing their outcomes or psychologically by justifying what they received.

Observers of inequity also experience distress, although not as much as victims, and they also are motivated to restore equity to the victim–offender relationship. Judges, in their role as third-party observers, can restore equity to crime victims by decreasing the offender's outcomes (e.g., a long prison sentence, a fine) or by increasing the victim's outcomes (e.g., making the offender pay restitution to the victim). Alternatively, judges may restore equity psychologically by, for example, believing that the victim's outcome was fair if the victim was in some way responsible (e.g., by starting a fight).

Fairness to other offenders.   Judges are also concerned with treating in similar fashion offenders who are similar to each other, based on the offense they committed and the length and nature of their prior criminal record. In general, judges are concerned with a rule of equality, such that the same type of offenders would receive the same punishment. This assumption underlies sentencing guidelines, which give a range for sentencing and assume that most offenders will be typical and will receive the same typical sentence.

On the other hand, guidelines also authorize judges to go outside the guidelines if there is something about the offender or the case that makes it more aggravated or more mitigated than the typical case. For such cases, judges would rely on equity (punishment proportional to harm) to enhance or lower the punishment.

Aside from equity and equality, there is a third distribution rule that judges sometimes use—the needs rule (Deutsch, 1975). According to the needs rule, the decision maker responds to the offender's needs rather than to the equitable punishment or to the punishment that is the same as what other offenders receive. In the case of an offender, judges might respond to particular needs and impose a less severe sentence. For example, judges might choose not to incarcerate a female offender if they know that her children would have to be sent to the foster care system.

The theory and research related to attributions, decision making, and fairness are the primary bases on which psychologists have attempted to understand sentencing. In addition to this approach, however, there is interesting work by criminologists who have focused more on structural and social contextual factors like poverty and race to explain aggregate sentencing patterns.

Social Contexts

Sociologically based criminologists have suggested that contextual factors can be useful explanations for sentencing decisions, as there has long been evidence that some jurisdictions impose more severe sentences than others. In particular, criminologists have investigated how the racial, political, and economic composition of a jurisdiction affects sentencing. Other studies have also looked at how factors about the criminal justice system affect sentencing.

The best known theoretical position on how racial composition affects sentencing is the racial threat hypothesis, which relates to the relative proportion of particular racial groups in the total population. According to this hypothesis, a larger percentage of a minority group in the population is likely to be associated with greater economic power and more political influence, which together would constitute a threat to Whites in the community (Blalock, 1967). Under such threat, Whites would be more likely to use formal social controls, including harsher sentencing, to control the minority group. A similar perspective relates to economic threat. The notion is that officials in areas that have higher percentages of residents living in poverty will impose more severe sanctions on impoverished offenders than will officials in wealthier areas (Fearn, 2005). Generally, there is only inconsistent support for racial threat theory and economic threat theory (Ulmer, 2012).

With regard to political orientation, there is evidence that more politically conservative jurisdictions impose harsher sentences than politically liberal jurisdictions (Crow & Gertz, 2008; Helms, 2009). This effect of political orientation may be especially true for drug offenders (Walker, 2005) and Black offenders (Helms & Jacobs, 2002). Religiously conservative areas are likely to be more punitive, especially if they are also politically conservative (Fearn, 2005; Ulmer, Bader, & Gault, 2008).

With regard to the practical question of available criminal justice resources, there is evidence that court caseloads are negatively related to the severity of sentences and that jail space is positively related to incarceration (Kramer & Ulmer, 2009). That is, a sentence of incarceration is less likely if judges have larger caseloads and if there is less jail space. Regarding resources for victims, Haynes (2011) used data from the Pennsylvania Commission on Sentencing for the years 1996–2006 and found that greater resources for victims were positively related to victim participation at sentencing and to longer sentences.

Consistent with what would be predicted by social psychological theory, distal factors about a jurisdiction, such as its age, gender, and race composition, have relatively little impact on sentencing, perhaps accounting for about 5% of the variance in sentencing outcomes (Johnson, 2006). More proximal variables, such as factors about the court (number of judges, type and volume of caseloads, similarity and stability of the courtroom workgroups) do seem to significantly affect sentencing (Haynes, Ruback, & Cusick, 2010; Ulmer & Johnson, 2004).

RESEARCH REVIEW

The research findings on sentencing come from some studies by psychologists, but even more so from studies by criminologists. Psychological research on sentencing is based primarily on experimental simulations using college students, and sometimes criminal justice decision makers, as participants. This research generally lacks the mundane realism of actual decisions and always lacks actual impact (i.e., there are no real-world consequences), but it has the advantage of being able to test theoretical predictions about causal processes. In contrast, the criminological research examines multiple sentencing decisions, generally using computerized archives. Both lines of research focus almost exclusively on the decisions of incarceration and length of incarceration, and they almost never look at issues of treatment and economic sanctions.

Both psychological research and criminological research suggest that crime seriousness and criminal record are the most important determinants of the sentencing decision. Additional information that comes from the presentence report is also likely to affect attributions, including the type of victim, the defendant's prior record, the defendant's status during trial, and the defendant's plea. Observable information about the defendant may also likely affect attributions and thereby sentencing: race, sex, age, and physical attractiveness. Some research also suggests that characteristics of the judge influence sentencing. Fairness with regard to the victim, the community, and other defendants is also important. The judge's interpersonal relations with other actors in the courtroom community matter, especially with the probation officer and the prosecutor. Finally, because they are elected officials in most states, judges are concerned about the community's response to crime and criminals.

Seriousness of the Crime

The central factor in the presentence report is the crime for which the defendant was convicted. The more serious the crime is, the more severe the sentence. There are a number of reasons that legislatures have set higher penalties for more serious crimes. First, longer sentences for serious crimes further the goals of sentencing: individual and general deterrence, incapacitation, retribution, and moral outrage. Second, the more serious the crime, the more likely the criminal is to be judged responsible for the crime (Robbennolt, 2000). When a criminal commits a crime despite social norms to the contrary, observers are more likely to make an internal attribution to the criminal. Research is quite clear that more serious crimes result in more severe penalties, both in terms of the likelihood and length of incarceration (Hofer et al., 1999) and in terms of economic sanctions (Ruback & Clark, 2011).

The type of victim also affects seriousness and therefore sentencing. For example, a classic study examined the proportion or prison sentences imposed by criminal judges for several types of crime, broken down by three factors: the specificity of the victim (i.e., whether the victim was an identifiable person or persons, as opposed to the public in general), personal contact between the offender and the victim, and the extent of bodily harm (Green, 1961). First, the more specific the victim, the more severe was the sentence. Crimes against the public in general—for example, liquor and gambling violations—received the lowest penalties. Second, personal contact produced more severe sentences. Third, crimes that included bodily harm received higher penalties than those that did not, and crimes in which the intention of bodily harm was the primary motive, such as murder, were judged more serious than those in which bodily injury was an incidental by-product of the criminal act, such as robbery.

These patterns make sense because all three factors are directly related to the perceived criminality of the defendant. If the defendant singled out a specific victim, if he or she came in contact with the victim, and if he or she harmed the victim, it is more difficult for a perceiver to find a noncriminal explanation for the behavior. Consequently, as the level of each of these factors increases, the judge becomes more likely to attribute a criminal disposition to the defendant.

Another aspect of the victim that is likely to influence the judge's attribution about the defendant is the victim's defenselessness. A defendant who victimizes someone who is very old, a child, or physically handicapped is likely to be seen as more blameworthy than a defendant whose victim is not as vulnerable. A weak victim is likely to be seen as less blameworthy than a victim who could be perceived as having provoked the crime. Moreover, a defendant whose victim was defenseless is likely to be perceived as more criminal because there are societal norms against victimizing a defenseless person. Committing a crime against a weak victim violates these norms and suggests that the defendant has a very strong criminal disposition. Thus, for example, the federal guidelines make crimes against vulnerable victims an aggravating factor resulting in more punishment.

A final feature of the victim that appears to affect sentence length is whether there was a prior relationship between the victim and the offender. Generally, sentences are more severe when the offender and victim were strangers than when there was a prior relationship. When there was no prior relationship, it is difficult to attribute responsibility to the victim. Thus, judges are likely to attribute causation internally, meaning that the offender is more responsible and should be punished more.

Defendant's Prior Record

If the defendant has prior convictions, a judge is likely to believe that the defendant has a stable criminal disposition because he or she has performed criminal acts in different situations and at different times. Behavior that is consistent across varied contexts suggests that the cause is internal to the person (Kelley, 1972a). Moreover, continued behavior across time is evidence of a stable disposition, meaning that a judge is likely to believe that the behavior will continue in the future.

The greater the number of prior felony convictions, the lower the likelihood of a probation sentence (Dawson, 1969) and the more severe the prison sentence (Green, 1960), relationships that are explicitly included in sentencing guidelines. The judge is also likely to consider, when applicable, the defendant's prior success or failure on probation. A defendant who seriously violated probation in the past is unlikely to be placed on probation again (Dawson, 1969).

Although lengthier prior records are generally predictive of greater likelihood and length of incarceration, they are typically inversely related to the imposition of economic sanctions (Ruback & Clark, 2011), even when controlling for incarceration. Judges appear to be influenced by practical considerations. That is, judges might well conclude that individuals with longer criminal records are less likely to pay any fines, fees, or restitution, and thus judges are less likely to even impose those sanctions.

Defendant's Status Before and During Trial

Sentence leniency is highly correlated with having been released on bail (Ares, Rankin, & Sturz, 1963; Rankin, 1964). Even when one controls for the factors that judges believe affect their bail-setting and sentencing decisions (e.g., the defendant's prior record, family stability, employment stability), the mere fact of having been released on bail or on personal recognizance still results in a less severe sentence.

Two reasons might explain why the defendant's status before and during the trial affects sentencing. First, it could be that persons released prior to trial commit less serious crimes and therefore should receive shorter sentences. When researchers statistically control for seriousness of crime, however, they still find that the defendant's pretrial status significantly affects the sentencing decision (Ares et al., 1963; Rankin, 1964). For example, in her examination of offenders in three federal district courts, Spohn (2009) found, consistent with the thinking about the proper purposes of bail (e.g., Goldkamp & Gottfredson, 1979), that offenders who had ties to the community (employment, marriage) were less likely to be detained before trial. Importantly, she also found that pretrial status affected sentencing, even after controlling for other factors.

A second explanation for the influence of the defendant's pretrial status on sentencing is the result of the setting in which the probation officer interviews the offender. As the National Advisory Commission on Criminal Justice Standards and Goals (1973) reported,

> It is not unreasonable to assume that the attitude of a person detained prior to trial is markedly different from that of a person who was at liberty. The man who has met with the indecent conditions typical of jails is likely to have built up considerable animosity toward the criminal justice system and the society that perpetuates it. (p. 99)

If these negative attitudes are conveyed in the interview with the probation officer, then the officer's perceptions and recommendations, in the presentence report, are likely to be less favorable.

Nature of the Defendant's Plea

Whether the defendant pleaded guilty or was found guilty by a jury or by a judge probably also influences judges' sentencing decisions. Arguably, a guilty plea could be evidence of a change in disposition. However, there are generally compelling reasons for pleading guilty that are likely to lead judges to discount this possible change in disposition.

Many judges believe that a defendant who pleads not guilty forces burdens on the system and the taxpayer, and that, if found guilty, he or she should be punished for causing this added expense. Thus, a guilty plea is one part of a prearranged bargain in which the defendant pleads guilty (usually to a lesser crime) in the expectation of being rewarded with a reduced sentence. Because of this reward, no change in disposition is likely to be inferred from a guilty plea (National Advisory Commission on Criminal Justice Standards and Goals, 1973). Most judges operate in terms of seeing a plea bargain solely as an explicit deal in which a more lenient sentence is exchanged for a guilty plea (*Yale Law Journal*, 1956).

Consistent with this idea, research on mode of conviction suggests that defendants who go to trial suffer a trial penalty (King, Soulé, Steen, & Weidner, 2005), but these studies are limited by the fact that they examine only convicted offenders and do not take into account the original charges (Tinik & Ruback, 2012).

Judge's Personal Observation of the Defendant

In addition to information contained in the presentence report, the judge has the opportunity to collect further information through personal observation of the defendant during the trial. Although some judges believe that seeing the defendant gives them evidence about the defendant's character, the amount of useful information that judges can obtain through personal observation is limited by three factors. First, almost all defendants plead guilty, and therefore the judge's encounter with the defendant at sentencing is brief, perhaps only 10–15 minutes. Second, even if the case goes to trial, the judge may be limited to visual cues because not all defendants testify at the trial. Third, even when the defendant does testify, the impression of the defendant may not be reliable because of situational stress arising from the trial proceedings (Weigel, 1966, cited in Goldfarb & Singer, 1973). Given these limitations in their observations, it is not surprising that judges must often rely on stereotypes associated with gross observable characteristics, such as the defendant's race, sex, age, and physical attractiveness.

Defendant's Race

For decades, and still today, Blacks are more likely than Whites to be incarcerated (Bales & Piquero, 2012; see Chapter 5, this volume for a review of race and the justice system). The first question is whether this effect can be explained by other factors. Assuming that the race effect cannot be explained by other factors, the second question is whether it is a substantively important effect.

With regard to the first question, whether the effect is real or is simply due to factors correlated with race, Blumstein (1982) found that Blacks constituted 43% of individuals arrested in 1974 and 1979 and 49% of the prison population in those years. Thus, he concluded that 80% of the racial disproportionality in prison populations was the result of racial disproportionality in offending. For the year 1991, he found that 76% of the racial disproportionality in prison populations was the result of racial disproportionality in offending (Blumstein, 1993). Thus, at least part of the racial disparity in sentencing is the result of differences in offending.

It may also be that the effect of race on sentencing is indirect. For example, Whites are more likely than Blacks to be released on personal recognizance than on monetary bail and are also more likely to receive less severe sentences (Albonetti, 1991; Wooldredge, 2012). Thus, the effect could be due to pretrial release. In addition, because race is highly correlated with economic status, it may be that White offenders fare better at sentencing because they can afford private attorneys, bail, and private treatment in the community (Spohn, Gruhl, &

Welch, 1981). Moreover, it may be that Blacks and other minority group members are more likely to be arrested and prosecuted and are therefore more likely than Whites to have a criminal record (Black, 1971; Chambliss & Seidman, 1971). Thus, according to this argument, it is the prior criminal record, rather than race per se, that affects the judge's sentencing decision.

Likely, Blacks receive harsher sentences than Whites because of stereotypical associations between Blacks and crime, although the particular racial stereotype may vary depending on the type of crime (Steen, Engen, & Gainey, 2005). Steffensmeier, Ulmer, and Kramer (1998) suggested that judges may believe Blacks are more dangerous than Whites because they lack the social ties to the community (e.g., marriage, employment) that prevent recidivism and they have longer criminal records. Black males may also be perceived as being better able than Whites to tolerate prison.

Consistent with this idea of stereotypes leading to racial disparity in sentencing, Blair, Judd, and Chapleau (2004) suggested that, although group-level racial bias may not be present, after controls for legally relevant factors, racial bias based on Afrocentric features may still exist. In their study, Blair et al. randomly selected samples of Black and White male inmates from a public database maintained by the Florida Department of Corrections. They found that inmates, both Black and White, who had more Afrocentric features received harsher sentences, probably because these features more strongly elicited racial stereotypes of Blacks being dangerous (Blair et al., 2004).

Assuming the race effect is real, the second question is whether it is substantively important. Hagan (1974) argued that statistical significance is heavily influenced by the number of cases in a study. Most of the studies on sentencing use very large samples, so that if a significant effect is discovered, the researcher can be fairly confident that the relationship was not due to chance. In nearly all of the 20 studies Hagan reviewed, however, the strength of the relationship was generally low. A more recent review also concluded that the effects of race on the decision to incarcerate are relatively small (Engen, 2011), although statistically significant because of the large samples involved. It should be noted, however, that some studies have found substantively significant effects. For example, even when relevant legal and extralegal factors were controlled, one study found that minority status increased the odds of incarceration by about 50% (Steffensmeier et al., 1998).

Some theorists have argued that the effect of race is conditional. According to the liberation hypothesis (Kalven & Zeisel, 1966), when the evidence is clear, juries have little discretion and will convict. When the evidence is less conclusive, however, juries are free (liberated) to consider other factors, including those related to sentiment. In the context of sentencing, the rationale would be that the judge is bound to impose a severe punishment for serious crimes, but for less serious crimes, the judge has more discretion and can make a decision based on extralegal factors, including the race of the defendant. Baldus, Pulaski, and Woodworth (1983) made a similar argument regarding the imposition of capital punishment.

Defendant's Gender

Generally, women receive smaller fines, receive less severe sentences, and are more likely than men to be placed on probation (Albonetti, 1997; Doerner & Demuth, 2010; Nagel, 1969; see Chapter 4, this volume for a review of research on female offenders). As is true with race, however, there is a question as to whether gender has an independent effect on sentencing, once other factors are controlled for. Female offenders are more often accomplices to men than the lead offender, and they are often the victims of male-inflicted violent abuse, both of which may serve to reduce their perceived blameworthiness (Steffensmeier et al., 1998). Women generally commit less serious crimes than men and are probably less likely to have a prior record than men, possibly because they receive greater leniency at earlier stages in the criminal justice system. Moreover, women are more likely than men to have dependent children, which judges seem to take into account, both in terms of harm to the children and financial burden to the state (Engen, Gainey, Crutchfield, & Weis, 2003).

Defendant's Age

Both younger and older offenders seem to receive more lenient sanctions than do offenders in the middle range (roughly 25–55 years), who receive the harshest sentences (Steffensmeier et al., 1998). Young defendants also seem to be sentenced less severely than older defendants in experimental studies using college students (Smith & Hed, 1979; see Chapter 3, this volume for a review of elders and the justice system, and Chapter 4, this volume for a review of juvenile offenders).

Young offenders may receive lighter sentences for several reasons. First, younger offenders generally have shorter criminal records. Second, many judges may be reluctant to expose youthful offenders to the dangerous environment of the prison. Third, many judges believe that younger offenders have a better chance than older offenders of being rehabilitated (Dawson, 1969). The exception to younger offenders receiving less punishment is young Black males, who receive the harshest penalties of any group, probably because they are perceived as being more committed to crime, less amenable to reform, and better able to adjust to prison (Spohn, 2000; Steffensmeier et al., 1998).

At the other extreme, older offenders are more likely to have ties to the community, through family and employment, which lowers their risk of recidivism. In addition, older offenders are more likely to have physical health problems, sometimes substantial health problems, which lowers their risk of committing future crimes. Aside from relieving the offender from the problems associated with incarceration, a judge's decision not to imprison an older offender might reflect concern with the financial cost to the state of incarcerating a seriously ill individual.

Defendant's Physical Attractiveness

Race, gender, and age are the most important defendant characteristics that affect the sentencing decision. One other factor that social psychologists have examined is the defendant's physical attractiveness. Compared to unattractive people, physically attractive people are viewed as possessing more positive traits and are evaluated more favorably (Berscheid & Walster, 1974). College students judge physically attractive defendants to be less guilty and assign them less severe sentences, even though they believe attractiveness should not be taken into account in the sentencing decision (Efran, 1974). An observational study of real criminal defendants also found that more attractive defendants were given less severe sentences (Stewart, 1980). This finding suggests another explanation for why defendants detained in jail while awaiting trial are given more severe sentences than those released on bail, since jailed persons are likely to be "unshaven, unwashed, unkempt, and unhappy" (Wald, 1964, p. 632).

Physical attractiveness does not always lead to lower punishment, however. One qualification of the physical attractiveness effect is if offenders use their physical attractiveness to aid them in committing a crime. For such crimes (e.g., swindling), offenders are likely to receive more severe sentences (Sigall & Ostrove, 1975). Downs and Lyons (1991) found that for misdemeanors more attractive defendants received lower bail and fine amounts, but for felonies there was no difference between more and less attractive defendants.

It must be noted that, although physical attractiveness is correlated with interpersonal judgments in general, in actual sentencing decisions, the effect of physical attractiveness is likely to be quite small, once severity of crime and prior criminal record are controlled for.

Characteristics of the Judge

Psychologists have investigated how personality variables relate to the sentencing decision. One personality variable that has been well studied is authoritarianism. People who score high on the California F scale show a general tendency to accept conventional values, to submit to those in authority, and to reject those who violate society's standards. For example, Mitchell and Byrne (1973) found that college students who scored higher on the F scale ("authoritarians") recommended significantly more severe punishments for a law violator than those who scored low on this test ("egalitarians").

Another personality factor relevant to the sentencing decision is Rotter's (1966) locus-of-control construct. Using this scale, Carroll and Payne (1976) found that internals focused on internal causes of the defendant's behavior, such as previous parole and probation difficulties, crime committed, and the defendant's educational level, whereas externals focused on information pertaining to external causes, such as alcohol and drug use (see Volume 1, Chapter 10, this handbook for a review of substance abuse and crime).

Differences in beliefs about locus of control may be related to political ideology. W. Miller (1973) proposed that people who hold a conservative political ideology are likely to focus on the internal responsibility of the criminal, while those who hold a liberal political ideology are likely to focus on external conditions such as societal inequality and discrimination. Consistent with this notion, studies show that Republicans give longer sentences than Democrats. Hagan (1975) found than judges strongly favoring "law and order" sentenced defendants primarily on the basis of legal definitions of the seriousness of their offenses. Although judges less concerned with the maintenance of law and order also emphasized the seriousness of the offense, they were more likely to consider other variables, such as the defendant's race, prior record, and number of charges against the defendant, and they gave more lenient sentences to offenders from minority groups.

Carroll, Perkowitz, Lurigio, & Weaver (1987) found that individual differences, including background and personality, relate to ideology, and this ideology relates, in turn, to how judges think about the causes of crime and the goals of sentencing. Conservative judges tend to be more punitive and are more likely to attribute an individual's criminal involvement to personal choice. In contrast, liberal judges are more concerned with rehabilitating the offender and are more likely to believe that the offender's involvement in crime is the result of factors external to the individual.

Using a sample of 264 federal judges, Forst and Wellford (1981) examined sentencing disparity as a function of sentencing goals. They divided inter-judge disparity into two types: the *primary judge effect*, which referred to the general tendency for "toughness or leniency among the various judges" (p. 813) based on their average sentence lengths; and the *interaction effect*, which referred to disagreement among judges about the seriousness of particular types of cases. Forst and Wellford found that about a fifth of the variance in length of prison terms was explained by the primary judge effect, but that even more was explained by the interaction effect.

Judges in rural areas impose harsher sentences than judges in urban areas (Austin, 1981; Hagan, 1977; Pope, 1976). Research at both the state and federal levels finds that offenders sentenced in large urban courts receive less severe sentences than offenders sentenced in small rural courts (Hofer et al., 1999). Judges in more conservative jurisdictions tend to impose longer sentences, especially on repeat offenders and offenders convicted of more serious offenses (Eisenstein, Flemming, & Nardulli, 1988). Further, a study of 337 jurisdictions in seven states revealed that male offenders and Black offenders received longer sentences in more conservative political environments (Helms & Jacobs, 2002).

Findings regarding the effects of the judge's race on sentencing are mixed. Some studies find that minority judges are more likely to incarcerate offenders (Steffensmeier & Britt, 2001), whereas others find that minority judges are somewhat less punitive (Johnson, 2006). Regarding gender, studies generally find that male and female judges sentence offenders similarly (Spohn et al., 1981). Some evidence suggests that female judges are somewhat harsher toward offenders because they are more influenced than male judges by offender characteristics (Steffensmeier & Hebert, 1999).

Courtroom Social Contexts

Social psychological research suggests that individuals' decisions are affected by others around them. In the case of sentencing, these others constitute the courtroom workgroup, which consists of judges, prosecuting attorneys, and probation officers. These individuals are interdependent and contribute to the sentencing decision (Eisenstein et al., 1988). Courtroom workgroups perceive offenders and cases differently, because of the context in which the court is located and the legal culture of the jurisdiction (i.e., members' shared beliefs about interpersonal relations and the manner in which cases should be disposed of). Even when there are formal sentencing policies, as with sentencing guidelines, sentencing is still filtered through the organizational culture of courts, which determines case-processing norms,

going rates, and use of departures from the guidelines (Kautt, 2002; Ulmer & Kramer, 1996).

Haynes et al. (2010) used data from the Pennsylvania Commission on Sentencing for the years 1990–2000 to examine how three social psychological aspects of courtroom workgroups (similarity, proximity, stability) affect sentencing decisions. Similarity is the degree to which workgroup members have the same characteristics (age, gender, race, political ideology). This factor is important because people are attracted to others who have similar attitudes, beliefs, and personal characteristics (Byrne, 1971; Newcomb, 1961), and they value the contributions of similar others more than the contributions of dissimilar others (Hinds, Carley, Krackhardt, & Wholey, 2000). Proximity is the relation of the workgroup members' offices in relation to one another. Individuals who are physically closer to one another generally interact more and are therefore more likely to like each other than are individuals who are more distant from one another (Festinger, Schachter, & Back, 1950). Stability refers to the number of years the workgroup members worked together in the same jurisdiction. Groups are generally more productive when members' behaviors are predictable, and individuals typically prefer to work with others whose personalities and work practices are familiar to the rest of the group (Hinds et al., 2000).

Haynes et al. (2010) found that most of the courtroom workgroups in the 67 counties in Pennsylvania had high similarity (i.e., members were White and male, and they attended Pennsylvania colleges and law schools). In general, members of homogeneous workgroups are more likely to communicate with each other and to have informal communications with each other because they are more likely to share the same values, attitudes, beliefs, and ideologies. These findings likely explain why Eisenstein et al. (1988) found that homogeneous courtroom workgroups were more likely to dispose of cases through consensus. Haynes et al. also found that both proximity and stability were high in the courtroom communities in Pennsylvania.

Controlling for individual, case, and distal contextual factors, Haynes et al. (2010) found that workgroup factors affected the decision to incarcerate, the decision to impose fines, and the decision to impose restitution. The fact that workgroup characteristics mattered even in a state with relatively structured sentencing suggests that the effects of these factors may be even more robust in states where judges' discretion is less limited.

The most important relationship the judge has is with the probation officer, who has the most influence on the judge at the sentencing stage. The probation officer writes the presentence report, at the conclusion of which the probation officer recommends an appropriate sentence for the defendant. Carter and Wilkins (1967) found that the percentage of agreement between probation officers' recommendations for probation and those of judges in the ten federal judicial circuits ranged from 90% to 99% and that agreement on recommendations for incarceration ranged from 68% to 93%. The same general proportions were observed in California courts (Carter & Wilkins, 1967). These high rates of agreement between judges and probation officers are similar to how bail decisions are made (Dhami, 2003).

Interestingly, judges' rated importance of the probation officer's recommendation in their decisions was virtually unrelated to the actually observed agreement (Konečni & Ebbesen, 1982). That is, judges who rated the recommendation of the probation officer as a very important determinant of their decision making were no more likely to agree with the probation officer's recommendation than were judges who believed the recommendation had no effect on their decisions.

In trying to explain the high percentage of agreement between probation officers and judges, Carter and Wilkins (1967) suggested four possible reasons: the judge could be following the probation officer's recommendation because the probation officer knows more about the defendant; most offenders should obviously be sentenced to prison or probation; the probation officer anticipates what the judge is likely to decide; and both the judge and probation officer use the same factors to reach a sentencing decision.

Carter and Wilkins (1967) concluded that, although all four reasons might be relevant, the first is probably the most important. That judges seem to follow the recommendation of the probation officer

is not surprising, given the small amount of time they have in which to arrive at a sentencing decision. Reliance on others' recommendations is true as well in Germany, where judges' sentencing decisions are virtually perfectly predicted by the prosecutors' recommendations (von Helversen & Rieskamp, 2009).

In addition to the information given by the probation officer at the sentencing hearing, the judge is provided with information by the defense attorney and by the prosecutor. The defense counsel's "primary duty is to ensure that the court and his client are aware of the available sentencing alternative and that the sentencing decision is based on complete and accurate information" (National Advisory Commission on Criminal Justice Standards and Goals, 1973, p. 19). Defense counsel need to present information to explain or contradict information in the presentence report, and if the defense counsel believes probation is an appropriate disposition for his or her client, the counsel should suggest a program of rehabilitation. At the hearing, the defense attorney will try to present the defendant in the best possible light, often by introducing letters or affidavits from members of the community who can attest to the good reputation of the defendant. In addition, witnesses are sometimes called to testify about the defendant's good character. Judges, however, generally place little weight on the presentation of character witnesses because they know that the testimony of such witnesses is motivated more by a desire to present the defendant in the most favorable light than by a desire to present an objective picture of the defendant. In attributional terms, the testimony of witnesses is discounted because of the presence of other facilitative causes (e.g., the witness is a close friend of the defendant).

There is some evidence that judges' decisions are affected by practical constraints, such as the caseload in the prosecutor's office. To meet that need, plea bargaining is encouraged in order to avoid overcrowding of trial dockets and long delays. A second practical concern is the level of crowding in the prison system, which might require probation for some offenders simply because there is no room for them in prison (Twentieth Century Fund Task Force on Criminal Sentencing, 1976). For three reasons, however, the pressure to reduce overcrowding in prisons does not always result in fewer inmates being sent there. First, judges are not always sympathetic to the problems caused by overcrowding. Second, in many jurisdictions at least some term of imprisonment is fixed by statute. Third, public opinion would probably be against a felon's receiving probation simply because of overcrowded prison conditions (Hawkins, 1976).

Community

Because they are generally elected, judges care what voters think. Community interest in sentencing varies with the type of crime, with certain categories of crime, such as sensational murders or sex offenses, generating media attention and community interest and forcing judges to take account of public opinion (Dawson, 1969).

In return for judges' satisfactory performance, which in many communities means being "tough" on criminals, the voters will reelect the judges. Thus, it is not surprising that sentencing decisions usually reflect the attitudes of the communities where the courts are situated. Hogarth (1971), for example, found that the attitudes and penal philosophies of Canadian magistrates reflected the types of communities in which they lived and the problems those communities faced. The fact that sentences often reflect the local community helps explain why there are regional differences in severity of sentences. Thus, courts in the South tend to give more severe punishments than those in the North (Harries & Lura, 1974).

Peers

Judges care what their peers think. If the appeals court reverses them, they have been corrected in front of the entire legal community of the state. If the reversal is on a matter as basic as a sentencing decision not being within legislative guidelines, they are quite likely to lose the respect of their peers.

Another way in which judges are measured by their peers is by the number of cases they process. *Quality judges* are those who dispose of a relatively large number of cases, which is the usual result of imposing reasonable sentences. If judges give unreasonable sentences, defendants will be more likely to go to trial, as there is no incentive to do otherwise.

Thus, *hanging judges* end up disposing of fewer cases and are seen as less competent than quality judges (Silberman, 1978).

Fairness to All Offenders

According to equity theory, observers of an inequitable exchange experience distress very much like that experienced by the participants in the exchange. Equity theorists believe that inequity can be resolved in two ways: restoration of actual equity and restoration of psychological equity.

Fairness to other offenders means that judges are influenced by their previous decisions. After sentencing one defendant, a judge would want to treat a similar defendant in a manner consistent with the way the first defendant was treated. Similarly, judges would expect to treat differently defendants from different backgrounds and those who were guilty of different crimes. Both of these assumptions lead to the conclusion that a judge who wanted to sentence consistently would use a sentence given to one defendant as a reference for making subsequent sentences. Using college students, Pepitone and DiNubile (1976) found that, when a recommended punishment for a first crime was "anchored" (i.e., overtly recorded and thus publicly committed), the recommended punishment for a second offender's crimes was increased or decreased as a function of the contrasted seriousness of the crimes. Thus, a homicide that followed a homicide received a mean sentence of 21.8 years, whereas a homicide that followed an assault received a mean sentence of 33.4 years.

The effect of anchors, numeric standards to which estimates are assimilated, on sentencing decisions may lead to a degree of randomness. Tversky and Kahneman (1974) found that arbitrary numbers could influence estimates when people are uncertain (e.g., the percentage of African countries in the United States). Subsequent work suggests that this effect exists even if the information is not relevant and even for judges with experience (Englich & Mussweiler, 2001). The effect is probably the result of selective accessibility.

One of the implications of this work concerns the impact of the prosecution making the initial sentencing recommendation, in that the recommendation can influence the judge's decision both directly and indirectly because the prosecutor's statement also influences the defense attorney's recommendation. Thus, the defense may be at a disadvantage because the prosecutor has a disproportionate influence (Englich, Mussweiler, & Strack, 2005).

Judges may be lenient with an informant as a reward for cooperating with the police, particularly if the informant's services led to the conviction of an important criminal. In the federal system, this cooperation is institutionalized as substantial assistance, which means that mandatory sentences can be avoided. Furthermore, judges sometimes grant probation to a known addict if his or her information led to the conviction of a drug dealer, even if the chances of a successful probation are slight (Dawson, 1969). Leniency may also be granted to defendants who testify against their codefendants. In situations involving cooperative informants and codefendants, keeping these persons out of prison is a particularly important reward because their safety in prison cannot be guaranteed.

Victims at Sentencing

All states require the defendant to make restitution to the victim. In this way the relationship between the defendant and the victim is restored through actual equity to what it was before the crime occurred. Without a restitution order, the victim would be forced to use a civil remedy, an alternative unlikely to be useful, because the amounts involved are typically not worth the time and expense of a civil suit. Even with a restitution order, few offenders completely reimburse victims for their losses (Ruback, Cares, & Hoskins, 2008).

A victim impact statement allows victims to tell the judge how the crime has affected them. Victim impact statements are allowed in every state (National Center for Victims of Crime, 2012). Victims who participate in the justice process have higher satisfaction with the system than victims who do not participate (Erez & Tontodonato, 1992), and participation in the criminal justice system may indirectly help victims cope with the crime by influencing their sense of justice and fairness (Kelly & Erez, 1997).

There are three reasons why victims should participate in sentencing (Kelly & Erez, 1997). First, participation can promote the victim's psychological healing and can produce greater satisfaction and cooperation with the system. Second, victim participation can promote the offender's rehabilitation by forcing the offender to face the harms the victim suffered. Third, in terms of the system, participation can produce sentences that more fairly and accurately indicate the harms done and that better reflect the community's response to the crime.

The arguments against victim participation relate both to the victim—the process may be traumatic and may create expectations that will not be met—and to the system—the system may become overwhelmed by a large number of victims who want to testify and the presence of victims in court puts pressures on judges that may be inconsistent with justice. Moreover, if judges actually take victim impact statements into account, sentencing would be less predictable, and this unpredictability would undermine plea bargains and prosecutors' ability to control cases and caseloads.

Consistent with the arguments against victim participation, research on victim impact statements generally suggests that on balance they have no effect on sentencing (Kelly & Erez, 1997). In some cases, the sentence might be more severe (e.g., if the harm were especially egregious), and in other cases the sentence might be less severe (e.g., if there were no harm). In most cases, however, the impact statement has no effect because most sentences are based on the seriousness of the offense and the offender's prior record, factors that are known before the sentencing hearing. Although emotional appeals might make the victim feel better, judges prefer to rely on objective information (e.g., the extent of physical injury) and are not generally influenced by impassioned requests. In general, victim impact statements almost never add any new information beyond what is already in the record, meaning that the hearings are largely symbolic occasions in which victims have an opportunity to speak but do not have any real impact on the final sentence.

Moreover, victim impact statements often have little impact because they add little to what judges and prosecutors already know about the features of the typical crime victim (the "normal" victim). Further, information about victims is largely irrelevant when there are organizational pressures toward sentence uniformity (Erez & Rogers, 1999).

PRACTICE AND POLICY ISSUES

This review of the research literature indicates that judges tend to overuse incarceration and underuse intermediate sanctions, particularly treatment. Moreover, even though sentencing is based primarily on the seriousness of the offense and the length of the criminal record, disparity is still present to varying degrees. Finally, judges' estimates of future risk are largely based on heuristics and stereotypes, rather than on empirical data. For psychologists, the research on sentencing has three implications for practice and policy: increasing the use of intermediate sanctions, particularly treatment; reducing disparity; and incorporating actuarial models of risk into the sentencing decision.

Increasing the Use of Intermediate Sanctions

The United States has a high level of incarceration because, compared to other countries, criminal sentences are more likely to involve jail or prison and more likely to involve longer periods of confinement. This high incarceration rate is a serious problem, not only in terms of the lives of inmates and their families but also in terms of the strain that high incarceration rates place on state budgets (Savage, 2011; see Chapter 15, this volume for a review of prison overcrowding). Incarceration takes offenders away from their families and communities, reduces their chances of future employment, and makes reintegration into society more difficult. In addition, high incarceration rates have meant that many state prison systems are severely overcrowded, prompting federal courts to intervene. For example, in *Brown v. Plata* (2011), the U.S. Supreme Court upheld a court order requiring California officials to reduce their prison population by more than 30,000 offenders over a two-year period.

There is strong evidence that judges underuse intermediate punishments (Tonry & Lynch, 1996). For example, in Pennsylvania only 12% of sentences are for intermediate punishment (Pennsylvania Commission on Sentencing, 2013). Offenders especially in need of intermediate sanctions are drug offenders, who account for about one quarter of crimes. Judges tend to imprison these offenders because of their desire to punish them and their fear that drug-involved offenders are at high risk of recidivism.

Psychologists can be involved with the issue in terms of the need to encourage the use of nonincarcerative sanctions as a way reducing prison populations, reducing the long-term harms associated with incarceration, and encouraging more rehabilitative programs. Such involvement might include arguing for lower eligibility requirements, advocating for increased funding for more community treatment programs (e.g., residential substance abuse programs, house arrest with mandatory drug treatment; see Chapter 16, this volume for a review of community corrections), and making it clear to judges that intermediate punishments are feasible. Sentencing guidelines for intermediate punishments might serve as a reminder to judges of these programs and of helping judges to choose which intermediate punishment sanction is the most appropriate (Bowles, 2011). Psychologists could usefully educate judges about treatment resources in their community.

Reducing Disparity

Psychologists are concerned with decision making and with understanding prejudice and discrimination, both overt and nonconscious. In addition, because there is a need to have a better understanding of the sentencing decision-making process in order to help judges reach consistent decisions, psychologists should be involved in research on reducing sentencing disparity.

Ruback and Wroblewski's (2001) application of psychological research and theory to the workings of the federal guidelines suggested three conclusions. First, both policy pressures and psychological research and theory indicate that an actuarial model (i.e., guidelines) is needed to make sentencing more consistent and fair than sentencing under unstructured, indeterminate systems. In virtually all cases of complex decision making, statistical prediction is superior to clinical judgment (Meehl,

1954), regardless of what people believe. It is also true that a statistical model that captures a person's decision making does better than the person himself or herself, because the person is likely to be affected by bias, boredom, or fatigue, whereas the statistical model relies consistently only on the limited number of factors that the person actually uses to make decisions. Second, although an actuarial model is needed to place offenders in broad ranges, it is not evident that additional precision brings an increase in validity. In fact, there is some suggestion that more attempted precision leads to lower validity. Third, within the cells of a sentencing matrix there should be sufficient ranges so that judges can consider the multiplicity of possible aggravating and mitigating factors. In this way, decision making will be structured, but judges will still maintain a level of autonomy and discretion. The result should be more appropriate and just sentences.

Under this framework, a sentence for a convicted criminal is determined by case-specific fact finding within a broad public policy framework. The fact finding, on the one hand, establishes the criminal acts committed by the offender and related acts committed by others, the offender's criminal record, and the offender's social and economic background. All of these findings are determined individually for each particular case, as no two offenders and no two crimes are exactly alike. The policy making, on the other hand, establishes the relative priority of the four purposes of sentencing for individual offenders (i.e., punishment, specific deterrence, incapacitation, and rehabilitation; Graham, Weiner, & Zucker, 1997); the relative seriousness of different criminal acts; and whether and how the offender's social and economic conditions should affect the sentence (Quinney, 1977). The policy making also involves a judgment regarding whether and to what degree human behavior can be changed through criminal sentences generally and for certain criminal offenders in particular.

Fact-finding and policy determinations are different kinds of decisions that are best made by different decision makers. Specific fact-finding decisions relevant to particular cases should be made by judges, who are in the best position to determine the facts involved. In contrast, broad policy decisions for a state should be made by policy makers at the state level.

Incorporating Risk into the Sentencing Decision

The sentencing decision looks backward to punish the offender for the prior criminal behavior, but also forward to reduce future criminal behavior through deterrence, incapacitation, and rehabilitation. Current sentencing practices address the risk of future crime indirectly by focusing on the severity of the present offense and the length of the criminal record. Generally, less serious crimes are more likely to be repeated in the future. Thus, property crimes like theft and drug crimes of use and possession have among the highest recidivism rates of all crimes. Furthermore, in terms of criminal record, offenders with longer records are more likely than those with shorter records to reoffend. Judges know both of these facts and almost certainly incorporate them as part of their sentencing decision.

In the past, the development and use of risk assessment instruments generally focused on "back end" judgments, in which decision makers working in jails and prisons were concerned with determining whether an offender being considered for release was likely to commit a new crime. The current trend among states is to incorporate risk judgments at the "front end," when judges are making the initial sentencing decision. Thus, in recent years, several states have moved from an implicit and indirect use of factors that were related to risk toward explicitly incorporating risk into the sentencing decision. For example, Pennsylvania has mandated the Commission on Sentencing to develop a risk assessment instrument to be used at sentencing (Act 95 of 2010). To date, the Commission has followed the recommended steps for developing a risk instrument: They have obtained a sample of cases with recidivism measured for a three-year period; they have divided the sample into a development sample, to develop the risk scale, and a validity sample, for testing the final model; and they have used multiple methods for creating risk scores. The next step is to test the scale on the validity sample (see Volume 1, Chapters 1–3, this handbook for a review of forensic assessment, instruments, and risk assessment).

The explicit incorporation of risk into the sentencing decision illustrates the need for researchers to provide policy makers with policies that are robust across methods (Spohn, 2011), because errors regarding offenders' lives and taxpayer dollars are highly costly. Aside from using traditional correlation and regression methods to develop risk scores, it is important that future work incorporate advanced methods of analysis. For example, recent work has suggested that Bayesian methods of risk assessment need to be adopted (Berk, 2012; Scurich & St. John, 2012).

SUMMARY AND CONCLUSIONS

Prior investigative, legal, practical, and policy judgments affect, and often determine, the final sentencing decision (Albonetti, 1991; Greenberg & Ruback, 1982). In part, these earlier judgments are based on the same factors as the final sentencing decision, so it is not surprising that the decisions are so similar. In particular, sentencing decisions are based on attributions to internal or external causes and to stable or unstable causes. Thus, harsher sentences are imposed when judges make attributions to criminal dispositions internal to offenders and to stable causes over time. These two dimensions and the two factors of crime and criminal record are the same ones that prior decision makers—police, prosecutors, probation officers—have considered and likely have resolved in the same way that judges do (Greenberg & Ruback, 1982).

The prior judgments of criminal justice actors are important, however, not just because they are considering the same factors as judges. They are also important because relationships with other actors are important. The ongoing nature of courtroom communities—judges, prosecutors, defense attorneys, probation officers—means that judges work together with others and these groups establish norms about "going rates" and appropriate punishments for typical criminals. Because more than 95% of all findings of guilt are based on guilty pleas, prosecutors' determinations about appropriate punishments are especially important to the final sentencing decision. Consistent with this notion, the similarity and proximity of members of

these courtroom communities, two social psychological factors that are important in all relationships, are important predictors of sentences.

At the larger contextual level (e.g., the county), there is evidence that the demographic composition (race, age, gender), the economic composition (poverty and inequality), and the political composition (conservatism) of the area sometimes influence sentencing decisions and must be considered in understanding sentencing. Moreover, at the contextual level are the available criminal justice resources. Judges' decisions are constrained to some degree by limited resources, as there is evidence that judges are influenced by their caseloads, the amount of jail and prison space available, and the number and nature of intermediate sentencing options.

Because the sentencing decision is so visible to the public, certainly more visible than arrest, charging, and bail decisions, it is the one best known to the public. Because sentencing decisions often mirror earlier decisions, however, it is reasonable to ask whether the sentencing decision is a key one. That is, because sentencing and earlier decisions involve the same factors, the same mediating attributional processes, the same community of courtroom actors who have long-term relationships, and the same contextual factors, including resource limitations, sentencing may not be the key decision.

Consistent with this idea, criminological research suggests that charging, bail, and plea bargaining decisions affect sentencing, and many have suggested that discrimination evident at sentencing is simply the result of discrimination at earlier decisions. Further, three decades ago, Konečni and Ebbesen (1982) suggested that judges are essentially unnecessary, not only because their decisions essentially mirror probation officers' recommendations but also because all of the important information that forms the basis of the sentencing decision is known well before the actual sentencing hearing.

Aside from the theoretical work on attributions used by a few criminologists 20 years ago, psychologists have had little impact on the research, theory, and policy associated with sentencing decisions. Future sentencing research needs to combine the methods of psychological and criminological perspectives. We need to know about the demographic, personality, and ideological characteristics of decision makers (judges, probation officers, and prosecuting attorneys), the social psychological characteristics of these decision-making workgroups, and the economic, political, and structural characteristics of the larger context.

References

Abelson, R., & Levi, A. (1985). Decision making and decision theory. In G. Lindzey & E. Aronson (Eds.), *Handbook of social psychology* (3rd ed., Vol. 1, pp. 231–309). New York, NY: Random House.

Albonetti, C. A. (1991). An integration of theories to explain judicial discretion. *Social Problems, 38,* 247–266. doi:10.2307/800532

Albonetti, C. A. (1997). Sentencing under the federal sentencing guidelines: Effects of defendant characteristics, guilty pleas, and departures on sentence outcomes for drug offenses, 1991–1992. *Law and Society Review, 31,* 789–822. doi:10.2307/3053987

Albonetti, C. A. (2011). Judicial discretion in federal sentencing: An intersection of policy priorities and law. *Criminology and Public Policy, 10,* 1151–1155. doi:10.1111/j.1745-9133.2011.00772.x

Alschuler, A. W. (1968). The prosecutor's role in plea bargaining. *University of Chicago Law Review, 36,* 50–112. doi:10.2307/1598832

Andrews, D. A., Zinger, I., Hoge, R. D., Bonta, J., Gendreau, P., & Cullen, F. T. (1990). Does correctional treatment work? A clinically relevant and psychologically informed meta-analysis. *Criminology, 28,* 369–404. doi:10.1111/j.1745-9125.1990.tb01330.x

Ares, C. E., Rankin, A., & Sturz, H. (1963). The Manhattan bail project: An interim report on the use of pre-trial parole. *New York University Law Review, 38,* 71–92.

Austin, T. L. (1981). The influence of court location on type of criminal sentence: The rural–urban factor. *Journal of Criminal Justice, 9,* 305–316. doi:10.1016/0047-2352(81)90003-9

Baldus, D. C., Pulaski, C., & Woodworth, G. (1983). Comparative review of death sentences: An empirical study of the Georgia experience. *Journal of Criminal Law and Criminology, 74,* 661–753. doi:10.2307/1143133

Bales, W. D., & Piquero, A. R. (2012). Racial/ethnic differentials in sentencing to incarceration. *Justice Quarterly, 29,* 742–773. doi:10.1080/07418825.2012.659674

Berk, R. (2012). *Criminal justice forecasts of risk: A machine learning approach.* New York, NY: Springer. doi:10.1007/978-1-4614-3085-8

Berscheid, E., & Walster, E. (1974). Physical attractiveness. In L. Berkowitz (Ed.), *Advances in experimental social psychology* (Vol. 7, pp. 157–215). New York, NY: Academic Press.

Black, D. (1971). The social organization of arrest. *Stanford Law Review, 23,* 1087–1111. doi:10.2307/1227728

Blair, I. V., Judd, C. M., & Chapleau, K. M. (2004). The influence of Afrocentric facial features in criminal sentencing. *Psychological Science, 15,* 674–679. doi:10.1111/j.0956-7976.2004.00739.x

Blalock, H. (1967). *Toward a theory of minority-group relations.* New York, NY: Wiley.

Blumstein, A. (1982). On the racial disproportionality of U.S. prison populations. *Journal of Criminal Law and Criminology, 73,* 1259–1281. doi:10.2307/1143193

Blumstein, A. (1993). Racial disproportionality of U.S. prison populations revisited. *University of Colorado Law Review, 64,* 743–760.

Blumstein, A., Cohen, J., Martin, S., & Tonry, M. (Eds.). (1983). *Research on sentencing: The search for reform.* Washington, DC: National Academy Press.

Bonczar, T. P. (1997). *Characteristics of adults on probation, 1995.* Washington, DC: U.S. Department of Justice.

Bonta, J., Wallace-Capretta, S., & Rooney, J. (2000). A quasi-experimental evaluation of an intensive rehabilitation supervision program. *Criminal Justice and Behavior, 27,* 312–329. doi:10.1177/0093854800027003003

Bottomley, A. K. (1973). *Decisions in the penal process.* London, England: Robertson.

Bowles, S. (2011). Multilevel predictors of the imposition of intermediate punishments. Unpublished master's thesis, Pennsylvania State University, University Park.

Brown v. Plata, 131 S. Ct. 1910 (2011).

Byrne, D. (1971). *The attraction paradigm.* New York, NY: Academic Press.

Caputo, G. (2004). *Intermediate sanctions in corrections.* Denton: University of North Texas Press.

Carroll, J. S. (1978). Causal attributions in expert parole decisions. *Journal of Personality and Social Psychology, 36,* 1512–1520. doi:10.1037/0022-3514.36.12.1512

Carroll, J. S., & Payne, J. W. (1976). The psychology of the parole decision process: A joint application of attribution theory and information processing psychology. In J. S. Carroll & J. W. Payne (Eds.), *Cognition and social behavior* (pp. 13–32). Hillsdale, NJ: Erlbaum.

Carroll, J. S., & Payne, J. W. (1977). Crime seriousness, recidivism risk, and causal attributions in judgments of prison term by students and experts. *Journal of Applied Psychology, 62,* 595–602. doi:10.1037/0021-9010.62.5.595

Carroll, J. S., Perkowitz, W. T., Lurigio, A. J., & Weaver, F. M. (1987). Sentencing goals, causal attributions, ideology, and personality. *Journal of Personality and Social Psychology, 52,* 107–118. doi:10.1037/0022-3514.52.1.107

Carter, R. M., & Wilkins, L. T. (1967). Some factors in sentencing policy. *Journal of Criminal Law, Criminology, and Police Science, 58,* 503–514. doi:10.2307/1141909

Chambliss, W. J., & Seidman, R. B. (1971). *Law, order, and power.* Reading, MA: Addison-Wesley.

Cohen, T. H., & Kyckelhahn, T. (2010). Felony defendants in large urban counties, 2006. *NCJ 228944.* Washington, DC: Bureau of Justice Statistics.

Crow, M. S., & Gertz, M. (2008). Sentencing policy and disparity: Guidelines and the influence of legal and democratic subcultures. *Journal of Criminal Justice, 36,* 362–371. doi:10.1016/j.jcrimjus.2008.06.004

Dawes, R. M. (1979). The robust beauty of improper linear models in decision making. *American Psychologist, 34,* 571–582. doi:10.1037/0003-066X.34.7.571

Dawes, R. M., Faust, D., & Meehl, P. E. (1989). Clinical versus actuarial judgment. *Science, 243,* 1668–1674. doi:10.1126/science.2648573

Dawson, R. O. (1969). *Sentencing: The decision as to type, length, and conditions of sentence.* Boston: Little, Brown and Company.

Deutsch, M. (1975). Equity, equality, and need: What determines which value will be used as the basis for distributive justice? *Journal of Social Issues, 31,* 137–149. doi:10.1111/j.1540-4560.1975.tb01000.x

Dhami, M. K. (2003). Psychological models of professional decision making. *Psychological Science, 14,* 175–180. doi:10.1111/1467-9280.01438

Doerner, J. K., & Demuth, S. (2010). The independent and joint effects of race/ethnicity, gender, and age on sentencing outcome in U.S. federal courts. *Justice Quarterly, 27,* 1–27. doi:10.1080/07418820902926197

Downs, A. C., & Lyons, P. M. (1991). Natural observations of the links between attractiveness and initial legal judgments. *Personality and Social Psychology Bulletin, 17,* 541–547. doi:10.1177/0146167291175009

Efran, M. G. (1974). The effect of physical appearance on the judgment of guilt, interpersonal attraction, and severity of recommended punishment in a simulated jury task. *Journal of Research in Personality, 8,* 45–54. doi:10.1016/0092-6566(74)90044-0

Eisenstein, J., Flemming, R., & Nardulli, P. (1988). *The contours of justice: Communities and their courts.* Boston, MA: Little, Brown and Company.

Engen, R. (2011). Unwarranted disparity in the wake of the *Booker/Fanfan* decision: Making sense of "messy" results and other challenges for sentencing research. *Criminology and Public Policy, 10,* 1139–1149. doi:10.1111/j.1745-9133.2011.00773.x

Engen, R. L., Gainey, R. R., Crutchfield, R. D., & Weis, J. G. (2003). Discretion and disparity under guidelines: The role of departures and structured sentencing alternatives. *Criminology, 38,* 1207–1230. doi:10.1111/j.1745-9125.2003.tb00983.x

Englich, B. (2006). Blind or biased? Justicia's susceptibility to anchoring effects in the courtroom based on given numerical representations. *Law and Policy, 28,* 497–514. doi:10.1111/j.1467-9930.2006.00236.x

Englich, B., & Mussweiler, T. (2001). Sentencing under uncertainty: Anchoring effects in the courtroom. *Journal of Applied Social Psychology, 31,* 1535–1551. doi:10.1111/j.1559-1816.2001.tb02687.x

Englich, B., Mussweiler, T., & Strack, F. (2005). The last word in court—A hidden disadvantage for the defense. *Law and Human Behavior, 29,* 705–722. doi:10.1007/s10979-005-8380-7

Erez, E., & Rogers, L. (1999). Victim impact statements and sentencing outcomes and processes. *British Journal of Criminology, 39,* 216–239. doi:10.1093/bjc/39.2.216

Erez, E., & Tontodonato, P. (1992). Victim participation in sentencing and satisfaction with justice. *Justice Quarterly, 9,* 393–417. doi:10.1080/07418829200091451

Fearn, N. E. (2005). A multilevel analysis of community effects of criminal sentencing. *Justice Quarterly, 22,* 452–487. doi:10.1080/07418820500364668

Festinger, L., Schachter, S., & Back, K. (1950). *Social pressures in informal groups: A study of human factors in housing.* Stanford, CA: Stanford University Press.

Forst, B., & Wellford, C. (1981). Punishment and sentencing: Developing sentencing guidelines empirically from principles of punishment. *Rutgers Law Review, 33,* 799–837.

Frase, R. (2005). State sentencing guidelines: Diversity, consensus, and unresolved policy issues. *Columbia Law Review, 105,* 1190–1232.

Funke, J. (1991). Solving complex problems: Exploration and control of complex social systems. In R. J. Sternberg & P. A. Frensch (Eds.), *Complex problem solving: Principles and mechanisms* (pp. 185–222). Hillsdale, NJ: Erlbaum.

Gaylin, W. (1974). *Partial justice: A study of bias in sentencing.* New York, NY: Knopf.

Gendreau, P., Little, T., & Goggin, C. (1996). A meta-analysis of the predictors of adult offender recidivism: What works! *Criminology, 34,* 575–608. doi:10.1111/j.1745-9125.1996.tb01220.x

Glaze, L. E., & Parks, E. (2012). *Correctional population in the United States, 2011.* Retrieved from http://bjs.ojp.usdoj.gov/content/pub/pdf/cpus11.pdf

Goldfarb, R. L., & Singer, L. R. (1973). *After conviction.* New York, NY: Simon & Schuster.

Goldkamp, J. S., & Gottfredson, M. R. (1979). Bail decision making and pretrial detention: Surfacing judicial policy. *Law and Human Behavior, 3,* 227–249. doi:10.1007/BF01039804

Graham, S., Weiner, B., Zucker, G. S. (1997). An attributional analysis of punishment goals and public reactions to O. J. Simpson. *Personality and Social Psychology Bulletin, 23,* 331–346. doi:10.1177/0146167297234001

Green, E. (1960, July–August). Sentencing practices of criminal court judges. *American Journal of Correction,* 32–35.

Green, E. (1961). *Judicial attitudes in sentencing.* London, England: Macmillan.

Greenberg, M. S., & Ruback, R. B. (1982). *Social psychology of the criminal justice system.* Monterey, CA: Brooks/Cole.

Hagan, J. (1974). Extra-legal attributes and criminal sentencing: An assessment of a sociological viewpoint. *Law and Society Review, 8,* 357–383. doi:10.2307/3053080

Hagan, J. (1975). Law, order, and sentencing: A study of attitude in action. *Sociometry, 38,* 374–384. doi:10.2307/2786171

Hagan, J. (1977). Criminal justice in rural and urban communities: A study of the bureaucratization of justice. *Social Forces, 55,* 597–612.

Hammond, K. R., Stewart, T. R., Brehmer, B., & Steinmann, D. (1975). Social judgment theory. In M. F. Kaplan & S. Schwartz (Eds.), *Human judgment and decision processes* (pp. 271–312). New York, NY: Academic Press. doi:10.1016/B978-0-12-397250-7.50016-7

Harries, K. D., & Lura, R. P. (1974). The geography of justice: Sentencing variations in U.S. judicial districts. *Judicature, 57,* 392–401.

Hawkins, G. (1976). *The prison.* Chicago, IL: University of Chicago Press.

Haynes, S. H. (2011). The effects of victim-related contextual factors on the criminal justice system. *Crime and Delinquency, 57,* 298–328. doi:10.1177/0011128710372190

Haynes, S. H., Ruback, R. B., & Cusick, G. R. (2010). Courtroom workgroups and sentencing: The effects of similarity, proximity, and stability. *Crime and Delinquency, 56,* 126–161. doi:10.1177/0011128707313787

Heider, F. (1958). *The psychology of interpersonal relations.* New York, NY: Wiley.

Helms, R. (2009). Modeling the politics of punishment: A conceptual and empirical analysis of "law in action" in criminal sentencing. *Journal of Criminal Justice, 37,* 10–20. doi:10.1016/j.jcrimjus.2008.12.004

Helms, R., & Jacobs, D. (2002). The political context of sentencing: An analysis of community and individual determinants. *Social Forces, 81,* 577–604. doi:10.1353/sof.2003.0012

Hillsman, S. (1990). Fines and day fines. In M. Tonry & N. Morris (Eds.), *Crime and justice: A review of research* (Vol. 12, pp. 49–98). Chicago, IL: University of Chicago Press.

Hillsman, S., & Greene, J. A. (1992). The use of fines an intermediate sanction. In J. M. Byrne, A. J. Lurigio, & J. Petersilia (Eds.), *Smart sentencing: The emergence of intermediate sanctions* (pp. 123–141). Newbury Park, CA: Sage.

Hinds, P. J., Carley, K. M., Krackhardt, D., & Wholey, D. (2000). Choosing work group members: Balancing similarity, competence, and familiarity. *Organizational Behavior and Human Decision Processes, 81,* 226–251. doi:10.1006/obhd.1999.2875

Hofer, P. J., Blackwell, K. R., & Ruback, R. B. (1999). The effect of the Federal Sentencing Guidelines on inter-judge sentencing disparity. *Journal of Criminal Law and Criminology, 90,* 239–321. doi:10.2307/1144166

Hogarth, J. (1971). *Sentencing as a human process.* Toronto, Ontario, Canada: University of Toronto Press.

Johnson, B. D. (2006). The multilevel context of criminal sentencing: Integrating judge and county level influences in the study of courtroom decision making. *Criminology, 44,* 259–298. doi:10.1111/j.1745-9125.2006.00049.x

Kalven, H., Jr., & Zeisel, H. (1966). *The American jury.* Chicago, IL: University of Chicago Press.

Kauder, N. B., & Ostrom, B. J. (2008). *State sentencing guidelines: Profiles and continuum.* Retrieved from http://www.pewtrusts.org/uploadedFiles/wwwpewtrustsorg/Reports/sentencing_and_corrections/NCSC%20Sentencing%20Guidelines%20profiles%20July%202008.pdf

Kautt, P. M. (2002). Location, location, location: Interdistrict and intercircuit variation in sentencing outcomes for federal drug-trafficking offenses. *Justice Quarterly, 19,* 633–671. doi:10.1080/07418820200095381

Kelley, H. H. (1972a). Attribution in social interaction. In E. E. Jones, D. E. Kanouse, H. H. Kelley, R. E. Nisbett, S. Valins, & B. Weiner (Eds.), *Attribution: perceiving the causes of behavior* (pp. 1–26). Morristown, NJ: General Learning Press.

Kelley, H. H. (1972b). Causal schemata and the attribution process. In E. E. Jones, D. E. Kanouse, H. H. Kelley, R. E. Nisbett, S. Valins, & B. Weiner (Eds.), *Attribution: perceiving the causes of behavior* (pp. 151–174). Morristown, NJ: General Learning Press.

Kelly, D. P., & Erez, E. (1997). Victim participation in the criminal justice system. In R. C. Davis, A. J. Lurigio, & W. G. Skogan (Eds.), *Victims of crime* (2nd ed., pp. 231–244). Thousand Oaks, CA: Sage.

King, N. J., Soulé, D. A., Steen, S., & Weidner, R. R. (2005). When process affects punishment: Differences in sentences after guilty plea, bench trial, and jury trial in five guidelines states. *Columbia Law Review, 105*, 959–1009.

Konečni, V. J., & Ebbesen, E. B. (1982). *The criminal justice system: A social–psychological analysis*. San Francisco, CA: Freeman.

Kramer, J. H., & Ulmer, J. T. (2009). *Sentencing guidelines: Lessons from Pennsylvania*. Boulder, CO: Lynne Rienner.

Lerner, M. J. (1977). The justice motive in social behavior: Some hypotheses as to its origins and forms. *Journal of Personality, 45*, 1–52. doi:10.1111/j.1467-6494.1977.tb00591.x

Lynch, J. P., & Pridemore, A. (2011). Crime in international perspective. In J. Q. Wilson & J. Petersilia (Eds.), *Crime and public policy* (pp. 5–52). New York, NY: Oxford University Press.

Massoglia, M. (2008). Incarceration as exposure: The prison, infectious disease, and other stress-related illnesses. *Journal of Health and Social Behavior, 49*, 56–71. doi:10.1177/002214650804900105

McFatter, R. M. (1978). Sentencing strategies and justice: Effects of punishment philosophy on sentencing decisions. *Journal of Personality and Social Psychology, 36*, 1490–1500. doi:10.1037/0022-3514.36.12.1490

Meehl, P. E. (1954). *Clinical versus statistical prediction: A theoretical analysis and a review of the evidence*. Minneapolis: University of Minnesota Press.

Miller, G. A. (1956). The magical number seven plus or minus two: Some limits on our capacity for processing information. *Psychological Review, 63*, 81–97. doi:10.1037/h0043158

Miller, W. (1973). Ideology and criminal justice policy: Some current issues. *Journal of Criminal Law and Criminology, 64*, 141–162.

Missouri v. Frye, 132 S.Ct. 1399 (2012).

Mitchell, H. E., & Byrne, D. (1973). The defendant's dilemma: Effects of jurors' attitudes and authoritarianism. *Journal of Personality and Social Psychology, 25*, 123–129. doi:10.1037/h0034263

Morris, N., & Tonry, M. (1990). *Between prison and probation: Intermediate punishments in a rational sentencing system*. New York, NY: Oxford University Press.

Myers, M. A., & Hagan, J. (1979). Private and public trouble: Prosecutors and the allocation of court resources. *Social Problems, 26*, 439–451. doi:10.2307/800507

Nagel, S. (1969). *The legal process from a behavioral perspective*. Homewood, IL: Dorsey Press.

Nagin, D. S., Cullen, F. T., & Jonson, C. L. (2009). Imprisonment and reoffending. In M. Tonry (Ed.), *Crime and justice: A review of research* (Vol. 38, pp. 115–200). Chicago, IL: University of Chicago Press.

National Advisory Commission on Criminal Justice Standards and Goals. (1973). *A call for citizen action: Crime prevention and the citizen*. Washington, DC: U.S. Government Printing Office.

National Center for Victims of Crime. (2012). *Victim impact statements*. Retrieved from http://www.victimsofcrime.org/help-for-crime-victims/get-help-bulletins-for-crime-victims/victim-impact-statements

Newcomb, T. M. (1961). *The acquaintance process*. New York, NY: Holt, Rinehart, and Winston. doi:10.1037/13156-000

Newman, D. J. (1966). *Conviction: The determination of guilt or innocence without trial*. Boston: Little, Brown and Company.

New York Times. (2009, November 25). State courts at the tipping point. Retrieved from http://www.nytimes.com/2009/11/25/opinion/25weds1.html

Nisbett, R. F., & Wilson, T. D. (1977). Telling more than we can know: Verbal reports on mental processes. *Psychological Review, 84*, 231–259. doi:10.1037/0033-295X.84.3.231

Office for Victims of Crime. (1998). *New directions from the field: Victims' rights and services for the 21st century*. Washington, DC: U.S. Department of Justice.

O'Hear, M. M. (2007). Plea bargaining and procedural justice. *Georgia Law Review, 42*, 407–470.

Partridge, A., & Eldridge, W. B. (1974). *The Second Circuit sentencing study: A report to the judges of the Second Circuit*. Washington, DC: Federal Judicial Center.

Pennsylvania Commission on Sentencing. (2013). *Sentencing in Pennsylvania: 2012 annual report*. Retrieved from http://pcs.la.psu.edu/publications-and-research/annual-reports

Pepitone, A., & DiNubile, M. (1976). Contrast effects in judgments of crime severity and the punishment of criminal violators. *Journal of Personality and Social Psychology, 33*, 448–459. doi:10.1037/0022-3514.33.4.448

Petersilia, J., & Turner, S. (1991). An evaluation of intensive probation in California. *Journal of Criminal Law and Criminology, 82*, 610–658. doi:10.2307/1143747

Pettit, B. (2012). *Invisible men: Mass incarceration and the myth of black progress*. New York, NY: Sage.

Pettit, B., & Western, B. (2004). Mass imprisonment and the life course: Race and class inequality in U.S. incarceration. *American Sociological Review, 69*, 151–169. doi:10.1177/000312240406900201

Piehl, A. M., & Useem, B. (2011). Prisons. In J. Q. Wilson & J. Petersilia (Eds.), *Crime and public policy* (pp. 532–558). New York, NY: Oxford University Press.

Pope, C. E. (1976). The influence of social and legal factors on sentencing dispositions: A preliminary analysis of offender based transactions statistics. *Journal of Criminal Justice, 4*, 203–221. doi:10.1016/0047-2352(76)90003-9

Quinney, R. (1977). *Class, state, and crime: On the theory and practice of criminal justice.* New York, NY: David McKay.

Rankin, A. (1964). The effect of pretrial detention. *New York University Law Review, 39*, 641–664.

Ranyard, R. (1989). Structuring and evaluating simple monetary risks. In H. Montgomery & O. Svenson (Eds.), *Process and structure in human decision making* (pp. 195–207). Oxford, England: Wiley.

Reitz, K. R. (2011). Sentencing. In J. Q. Wilson & J. Petersilia (Eds.), *Crime and public policy* (pp. 467–498). New York, NY: Oxford University Press.

Robbennolt, J. K. (2000). Outcome severity and judgments of responsibility: A meta-analytic review. *Journal of Applied Social Psychology, 30*, 2575–2609. doi:10.1111/j.1559-1816.2000.tb02451.x

Rotter, J. B. (1966). Generalized expectancies for internal versus external control of reinforcement. *Psychological Monographs: General and Applied, 80*, 1–28. doi:10.1037/h0092976

Ruback, R. B. (1998). Warranted and unwarranted complexity in the federal sentencing guidelines. *Law and Policy, 20*, 357–382. doi:10.1111/1467-9930.00054

Ruback, R. B., & Bergstrom, M. H. (2006). Economic sanctions in criminal justice: Purposes, effects, and implications. *Criminal Justice and Behavior, 33*, 242–273. doi:10.1177/0093854805284414

Ruback, R. B., Cares, A. C., & Hoskins, S. N. (2008). Crime victims' perceptions of restitution: The importance of payment and understanding. *Violence and Victims, 23*, 697–710. doi:10.1891/0886-6708.23.6.697

Ruback, R. B., & Clark, V. A. (2011). Economic sanctions in Pennsylvania: Complex and inconsistent. *Duquesne Law Review, 49*, 751–772.

Ruback, R. B., & Shaffer, J. N. (2005). The role of victim-related factors in victim restitution: A multi-method analysis of restitution in Pennsylvania. *Law and Human Behavior, 29*, 657–681. doi:10.1007/s10979-005-7372-x

Ruback, R. B., & Thompson, M. P. (2001). *Social and psychological consequences of violent victimization.* Thousand Oaks, CA: Sage. doi:10.4135/9781483345413

Ruback, R. B., & Wroblewski, J. (2001). The Federal Sentencing Guidelines: Psychological and policy reasons for simplification. *Psychology, Public Policy, and Law, 7*, 739–775. doi:10.1037/1076-8971.7.4.739

Saks, M. J., & Kidd, R. F. (1980–1981). Human information processing and adjudication: Trial by heuristics. *Law and Society Review, 15*, 123–160. doi:10.2307/3053225

Savage, C. (2011, August 12). Trend to lighten harsh sentences catches on in conservative states. *New York Times.* Retrieved from http://www.nytimes.com/2011/08/13/us/13penal.html

Scott, R. E., & Stuntz, W. J. (1992). Plea bargaining as contract. *Yale Law Journal, 101*, 1909–1968. doi:10.2307/796952

Scott-Hayward, C. S. (2009). *The fiscal crisis in corrections: Rethinking policies and practices.* Retrieved from http://www.vera.org/files/The-fiscal-crisis-in-corrections_July-2009.pdf

Scurich, N., & St. John, R. (2012). A Bayesian approach to the group versus individual prediction controversy in actuarial risk assessment. *Law and Human Behavior, 36*, 237–246. doi:10.1037/h0093973

Sigall, H., & Ostrove, N. (1975). Beautiful but dangerous: Effects of offender attractiveness and nature of the crime on juridic judgment. *Journal of Personality and Social Psychology, 31*, 410–414. doi:10.1037/h0076472

Silberman, C. E. (1978). *Criminal violence, criminal justice.* New York, NY: Random House.

Silver, N. (2012). *The signal and the noise: Why so many predictions fail—but some don't.* New York, NY: Penguin.

Smith, E. D., & Hed, A. (1979). Effects of offenders' age and attractiveness on sentencing by mock juries. *Psychological Reports, 44*, 691–694. doi:10.2466/pr0.1979.44.3.691

Spohn, C. (2000). Thirty years of sentencing reform: The quest for a racially neutral sentencing process. *Criminal Justice, 2000, 3*, 427–501. Retrieved from http://www.justicestudies.com/pubs/livelink3-1.pdf

Spohn, C. (2009). Race, sex, and pretrial detention in federal court: Indirect effects and cumulative disadvantage. *Kansas Law Review, 57*, 879–901.

Spohn, C. (2011). Unwarranted disparity in the wake of the *Booker/Fanfan* decision: Implications for research and policy. *Criminology and Public Policy, 10*, 1119–1127. doi:10.1111/j.1745-9133.2011.00768.x

Spohn, C., Gruhl, J., & Welch, S. (1981). The effect of race on sentencing: A re-examination of an unsettled question. *Law and Society Review, 16*, 71–88. doi:10.2307/3053550

Steen, S., Engen, R., & Gainey, R. (2005). Images of danger and culpability: Racial stereotyping, case processing, and criminal sentencing. *Criminology, 43*, 435–468. doi:10.1111/j.0011-1348.2005.00013.x

Steffensmeier, D., & Britt, C. (2001). Judges' race and judicial decision making: Do black judges sentence differently? *Social Science Quarterly, 82,* 749–764. doi:10.1111/0038-4941.00057

Steffensmeier, D., & Hebert, C. (1999). Women and men policymakers: Does the judge's gender affect the sentencing of criminal defendants? *Social Forces, 77,* 1163–1196.

Steffensmeier, D., Ulmer, J., & Kramer, J. (1998). The interaction of race, gender, and age in criminal sentencing: The punishment cost of being young, black, and male. *Criminology, 36,* 763–798. doi:10.1111/j.1745-9125.1998.tb01265.x

Stewart, J. E., II. (1980). Defendant's attractiveness as a factor in the outcome of criminal trials: An observational study. *Journal of Applied Social Psychology, 10,* 348–361. doi:10.1111/j.1559-1816.1980.tb00715.x

Sudnow, D. (1965). Normal crimes: Sociological features of the penal code in a public defender office. *Social Problems, 12,* 255–276. doi:10.2307/798932

Svenson, O. (1996). Decision making and the search for fundamental psychological regularities: What can be learned from a process perspective? *Organizational Behavior and Human Decision Processes, 65,* 252–267. doi:10.1006/obhd.1996.0026

Tinik, L., & Ruback, R. B. (2012). Is there a trial penalty? An analysis of robbery and burglary cases in Pennsylvania. Unpublished manuscript, Pennsylvania State University.

Tonry, M. (1996). *Sentencing matters.* Oxford, England: Oxford University Press.

Tonry, M., & Lynch, M. (1996). Intermediate sanctions. In M. Tonry (Ed.), *Crime and justice: A review of research* (Vol. 20, pp. 99–144). Chicago, IL: University of Chicago Press.

Tversky, A., & Kahneman, D. (1974). Judgment under uncertainty: Heuristics and biases. *Science, 185,* 1124–1131. doi:10.1126/science.185.4157.1124

Twentieth Century Fund Task Force on Criminal Sentencing. (1976). *Fair and certain punishment.* New York, NY: McGraw Hill.

Ulmer, J. T. (2012). Recent developments and new directions in sentencing research. *Justice Quarterly, 29,* 1–40. doi:10.1080/07418825.2011.624115

Ulmer, J. T., Bader, C., & Gault, M. (2008). Do moral communities play a role in criminal sentencing? Evidence from Pennsylvania. *Sociological Quarterly, 49,* 737–768. doi:10.1111/j.1533-8525.2008.00134.x

Ulmer, J. T., & Johnson, B. (2004). Sentencing in context: A multilevel analysis. *Criminology, 42,* 137–178. doi:10.1111/j.1745-9125.2004.tb00516.x

Ulmer, J. T., & Kramer, J. H. (1996). Court communities under sentencing guidelines: Dilemmas of formal rationality and sentencing disparity. *Criminology, 34,* 383–408. doi:10.1111/j.1745-9125.1996.tb01212.x

Ulmer, J. T., Light, M., & Kramer, J. (2011). Does increased judicial discretion lead to increased disparity? The "liberation" of judicial sentencing discretion in the wake of the *Booker/Fanfan* decision. *Justice Quarterly, 28,* 799–837. doi:10.1080/07418825.2011.553726

United States Sentencing Commission. (2012). *Overview of federal criminal cases, Fiscal Year 2011.* Washington, DC: U.S. Sentencing Commission.

United States v. Booker, 543 U.S. 220 (2005).

von Helversen, B., & Rieskamp, J. (2009). Predicting sentencing for low-level crimes: Comparing models of human judgment. *Journal of Experimental Psychology: Applied, 15,* 375–395. doi:10.1037/a0018024

Wald, P. (1964). Pretrial detention and ultimate freedom: A statistical survey, foreword. *New York University Law Review, 39,* 631–640.

Walker, S. (2005). *Sense and nonsense about crime and drugs: A policy guide* (6th ed.). Belmont, CA: Wadsworth.

Walmsley, R. (2009). *World prison population list* (8th ed.). Retrieved from http://www.prisonstudies.org/info/downloads/wppl-8th_41.pdf

Walster, E., Walster, G. W., & Berscheid, E. (1978). *Equity: Theory and research.* Boston, MA: Allyn & Bacon.

Weiner, B., Frieze, I., Kukla, A., Reed, R., Rest, S., & Rosenbaum, R. M. (1972). Perceiving the causes of success and failure. In E. E. Jones, D. E. Kanouse, H. H. Kelley, R. E. Nisbett, S. Valins, & B. Weiner (Eds.), *Attribution: Perceiving the causes of behavior* (pp. 95–120). Morristown, NJ: General Learning Press.

Western, B. (2006). *Punishment and inequality in America.* New York, NY: Sage.

Wilkins, L. T. (1975). Perspectives on court decision-making. In D. M. Gottfredson (Ed.), *Decision making in the criminal justice system: Reviews and essays* (pp. 59–81). Washington, DC: U.S. Government Printing Office.

Wilson, J. Q. (2011). Crime and public policy. In J. Q. Wilson & J. Petersilia (Eds.), *Crime and public policy* (pp. 619–630). New York, NY: Oxford University Press.

Wooldredge, J. (2012). Distinguishing race effects on pre-trial release and sentencing decisions. *Justice Quarterly, 29,* 41–75. doi:10.1080/07418825.2011.559480

Yale Law Journal. (1956). Comment: The influence of the defendant's plea on judicial determination of sentence. *Yale Law Journal, 66,* 204–222. doi:10.2307/794019

CHAPTER 15

PRISON OVERCROWDING

Craig Haney

Much of the research and scholarship conducted on the criminal justice system has been focused on legal practices and procedures (e.g., eyewitness identification, police interrogation) and the fairness and reliability of its decision-making processes (e.g., jury behavior). Relatively less attention has been devoted to the endpoint of those procedures and processes—the punishments to which they often lead, the nature and quality of prison life, and the consequences of incarceration for the persons who are subjected to it. In recent decades, however, the issue of what happens to people in prison has become increasingly important, largely because of the dramatic rise in the sheer number of persons incarcerated in our society and the corresponding increase in the number who return each year to their communities once their prison terms have been completed.

The expansion of the prison population in the United States occurred so rapidly that even very active programs of prison construction could not keep pace. High levels of prison overcrowding began to occur in prison systems throughout the country, in a several-decade period that many scholars and commentators refer to as an era of "mass incarceration." Prisoners were routinely packed into housing units that were designed to hold many fewer persons and, perhaps even more importantly, spent long prison sentences in facilities that lacked the infrastructure and programming to address many of their preexisting problems and needs. During this period, the sheer press of numbers inside increasingly large prison institutions rendered many prisoners vulnerable to physical attack and to psychological deterioration. The lack of programming and treatment resources meant that their needs often went unaddressed, and they returned in unprecedented numbers to their communities worse off than when they left. In addition to its considerable, direct impact on prisoners and their immediate families, the larger society bore the burden of this dysfunctional state of affairs.

This chapter begins by examining the psychological, social, and societal significance of the problem of prison overcrowding. After defining what *overcrowding* means in the context of a prison environment, it examines some of its most important consequences, especially as it exacerbates the "pains of imprisonment" by intensifying prison stress and generating a range of dysfunctional prison dynamics. Prison overcrowding interferes at multiple levels with the prison's ability to properly address the criminogenic (or crime-producing) needs of prisoners, a fact that compromises their ability to reintegrate into free society once they are released. The chapter ends with a discussion of the broader long-term consequences of prison overcrowding and some of the important policy-related recommendations that have been made to ameliorate this problem.

IMPORTANCE OF THE PROBLEM

Currently, there are well over two million persons incarcerated in the United States, about two thirds of whom are housed in state or federal prisons, and

http://dx.doi.org/10.1037/14462-015
APA Handbook of Forensic Psychology: Vol. 2. Criminal Investigation, Adjudication, and Sentencing Outcomes,
B. L. Cutler and P. A. Zapf (Editors-in-Chief)
Copyright © 2015 by the American Psychological Association. All rights reserved.

about a third of whom are confined to local jails (Glaze & Parks, 2012). In any given year, approximately the same number of persons are released back into the community from state or federal prison as enter them; in 2010, for example, that number was nearly 700,000 (Carson & Sabol, 2012, p. 30). Many more persons are released from local jails, virtually always having spent much less time incarcerated than those returning from prison (Minton, 2011). The size of these numbers is historically unprecedented. It is the product of wide ranging changes in sentencing policies that occurred over the last four decades, resulting in many more people being sent to prison for much longer periods of time.

More specifically, beginning in the mid-1970s, the U.S. prison system began to expand at a rapid rate, and it continued to do so for nearly 40 years. In addition to significant and continuing increases in the absolute number of persons in prison (see Figure 15.1), there was an equally dramatic rise in the rate of incarceration. After a half century of relative stability in the rate at which the nation sentenced persons to prison—hovering at around 100 persons incarcerated for every 100,000 in the population between about 1925 until 1975—the

incarceration rate began to increase dramatically and continued to do so until very recently. Thus, a rate of incarceration that had remained largely stable for the 50-year period between the mid-1920s to the mid-1970s increased approximately five-fold over the next 25-year period.

The United States became an outlier in this regard, having approximately 5% of the world's population but 25% of the world's prisoners (e.g., Liptak, 2008). In fact, in the era of mass incarceration, as Figure 15.2 illustrates, the United States assumed a position of unquestioned "leadership" in the rate at which we imprison our residents. For this reason, if no other, what happens inside our prisons, and with what effect, matters more in the United States simply because we imprison proportionately greater numbers of people and return a correspondingly higher number back into society— literally more than any other nation in the world.

It is also important to acknowledge that, although imprisonment greatly impacts U.S. society in general, it has an especially significant impact on some groups and certain communities. Historically, Blacks have suffered disproportionately high rates of incarceration (e.g., Sabol, 1989). Race-based disproportions in incarceration rates significantly

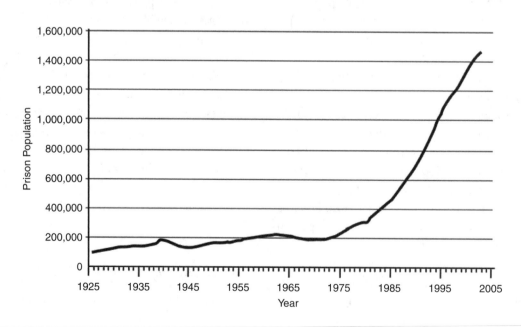

FIGURE 15.1. State and Federal Prisoners (1925–2004). Data from Harrison and Krber (2003); Harrison and Beck (2005).

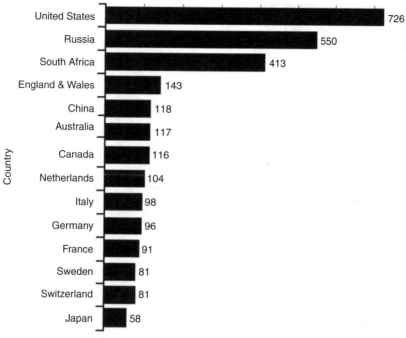

FIGURE 15.2.   Incarceration rate by country. Data from *International Centre for Prison Studies,* calculated from country-specific data obtained for years 2003–2004.

increased over the last several decades, however, in large part as a result of the way in which the so-called "war on drugs" was waged (e.g., Haney, 2006; Tonry, 1995). Over this same time period, the significant increase in Hispanic residents in the United States resulted in a dramatic rise in their number among state and federal prisoners. Thus, the number of Hispanics who reported having been incarcerated in state or federal prison in the United States grew nearly ten-fold between 1974 and 2001 (from 94,000 to 911,000; Bonczar, 2003).

Among other things, these changes made it more likely that persons from different racial and ethnic groups would be incarcerated at some point over the course of their lives. As Figure 15.3 shows, based on 2001 incarceration rates (Bonczar, 2003), one out of three Black men (32.3%) and one in six Hispanics (17.2%) in the United States could expect to be incarcerated in prison at some point in their lifetime, as compared to only a little more than one in 20 White men (5.9%). These differential incarceration rates also mean that the communities in which Blacks and Latinos lived before their imprisonment

will be differentially affected by their absence as well as by their return. For these communities, especially, the issue of whether and how well prison life has prepared prisoners to reintegrate back to society takes on heightened significance.

Understanding the nature and consequences of imprisonment in general is thus important for the larger society and is especially important for the people and communities most directly affected by the high rates of incarceration in the United States. Assessing the overall impact of imprisonment is a challenging task. This is in part because not all prisons are created equal. For one, correctional institutions are categorized and run very differently on the basis of their security or custody level. Moreover, even among prisons at the same level of custody, conditions of confinement can vary widely along critical dimensions—physical layout, staffing levels, resources, correctional philosophy, and administrative leadership—that render one place fundamentally different from another. Social psychological research over the last several decades has underscored the importance of *situational specificity*—the

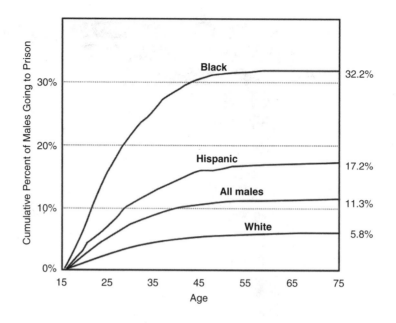

FIGURE 15.3.   Differences in imprisonment over a lifetime. Nearly one in three black males likely to go to prison based on constant 2001 incarceration rates. Data from Bonczar (2003).

extent to which specific aspects of a context or situation can significantly determine its impact or effect on the actors within it (e.g., Ross & Nisbett, 1991). This insight is appropriately applied to prisons and to prison overcrowding. Individual prisons thus vary in their effect depending on the situational specifics, that is, the psychologically important characteristics of the settings that they create and impose on prisoners.

Prisons that have adequate resources and are well run overall do not necessarily, under normal circumstances, inflict harm on literally everyone who is confined in them. For example, as one prison expert summarized the literature on prison effects: "[T]he evidence indicates that imprisonment is not generally or *uniformly devastating* [emphasis added] . . . . Imprisonment, in and of itself, does not seem *inevitably* [emphasis added] to damage individuals" (Porporino, 1990, p. 36). Of course, although incarceration is not uniformly devastating or inevitably damaging, even the best prisons have the potential to do harm. Thus, the same commentator also conceded that "relationships with family and friends can be severed . . . particular vulnerabilities and inabilities to cope and adapt can come to the fore in the prison setting, [and] the behavior patterns and attitudes that emerge can take

many forms, from deepening social and emotional withdrawal to extremes of aggression and violence" (Porporino, 1990, p. 36).

With these things in mind, it is important to acknowledge that prison overcrowding can significantly compromise the operation of even otherwise well-run correctional facilities and jeopardize the well-being of the prisoners who are housed there. It frequently thwarts the delivery of effective programming and treatment, can create and exacerbate dangerous and deprived conditions of confinement, and may precipitate the use of forceful, extreme, and potentially damaging techniques of institutional control.

New prison construction is such a time-consuming process that rapid increases in the number of persons entering prison typically results in widespread overcrowding. This is precisely what occurred in the United States, immediately following increases in rates of incarceration as described earlier. In fact, in 1976—even before mass incarceration had begun in earnest—a national news magazine told readers: "Prisons all across this country are dangerously overcrowded because of a recent, unexpected influx of inmates" ("Yesterday's 'Baby Boom,'" 1976). That influx continued and intensified over the next three decades, and overcrowding-related problems intensified as well.

Correctional administrators have long recognized that overcrowding can jeopardize the safe and effective operation of their institutions. For example, as recently as the late 1970s there was a widespread correctional consensus about the problems that were created by the practice of forced *double-celling*, which is the practice of involuntarily housing two prisoners in a single cell (usually a cell that had been designed to hold one person). Even in jurisdictions that were forced to double-cell from time to time, prison administrators understood that it was problematic, as explained by a 1979 correctional task force that included a number of high-ranking prison officials:

> According to legislative and departmental policy, the Department of Corrections does not sanction double-celling inmates. This task force agrees with the basic premise that *double-celling violates basic standards of decent housing, health, and institutional security* [emphasis added]; however, at present, there is no viable alternative to double-celling inmates as population projections are realized. Thus, while concurring that *double-celling is totally undesirable* [emphasis added], the task force must recommend this, and has attempted to propose gradual population increments and associated staffing to lessen the impact of overpopulation. (Housing Inventory & Population Task Force, 1979, p. iv)

However, beginning in the early the 1980s, correctional officials across the country were forced to accommodate to the "totally undesirable" practice of double-celling, in spite of the earlier acknowledgment that it violated "basic standards of decent housing, health, and institutional security." Eventually, prisons everywhere in the United States became accustomed to double-celling, but not because anything had changed to alter the consensus about its undesirability or the risks that it posed. Instead, the continuing influx of new prisoners forced everyone—including correctional administrators, line staff and, of course, prisoners—to accept it as routine. In fact, many administrators considered themselves fortunate if they were able to maintain a limit of "only" two prisoners to a cell during their worst periods of overcrowding.

Indeed, even by the generous standards by which legally acceptable levels of overcrowding came to be defined—standards that, after the landmark United States Supreme Court case *Rhodes v. Chapman* (1981), did not prohibit or even appear to discourage double-celling—many prison systems remained too overcrowded to function in a constitutional manner. Thus, according to the American Civil Liberty Union's National Prison Project (1995), by the middle of the 1990s there were fully 33 U.S. jurisdictions under court order to reduce overcrowding or improve general conditions in at least one of their major prison facilities. Nine were operating under court orders that covered their entire prison system, and many correctional systems that managed to avoid judicial scrutiny were nonetheless significantly overcrowded and remained so for the next two decades. Even prison systems such as the state of Alabama's, that supposedly "fixed" their overcrowding problem—often under pressure from the courts—found themselves plagued by it and a host of related problems once again (e.g., Cohen, 2004).

Indeed, the massive federal Bureau of Prisons, the largest single prison system in the country, has been plagued with chronic overcrowding. In a report that foreshadows many of the issues that are discussed in this chapter, the Government Accountability Office carefully outlined many of the ways that overcrowding has compromised the operation of the federal prison system and the quality of prison life for the approximately 200,000 prisoners confined in it. The report acknowledged that overcrowding was adversely affecting "inmates' daily living conditions, program participation, meaningful work opportunities, and visitation," including "bring[ing] together for longer periods of time inmates with a higher risk of violence and more potential victims," "waiting lists [for programming] and inmate idleness," the inability to "meet the substance abuse treatment or education needs of inmates," "fewer opportunities . . . to engage in meaningful work," "crowded visiting rooms [that] make it more difficult for inmates to visit with their families," as well as increased "staff stress and over-time hours worked" and "fewer correctional staff on board than needed" (Government Accountability Office, 2012, pp. 18–23).

In addition, of course, "[t]he increased population taxes the infrastructure that was designed for a smaller inmate population, affecting use of toilets, showers, water, and electricity, and wear and tear on food service equipment" (Government Accountability Office, 2012, p. 25). The Government Accountability Office report also noted that "increasing inmate population and staffing ratios negatively affect inmate conduct and the imposition of discipline, thereby affecting security and safety," quoting a 2005 Bureau of Prisons report that concluded that "population pressures on both staffing levels and inmate living space have an upward impact on serious prison violence" (p. 25). The fact that violence rates remained relatively stable in the face of these pressures may have been the result of temporary "augmentation" strategies to mitigate the negative effects of overcrowding, the use of institutional lockdowns to contain violence (which simultaneously terminated inmate programming), and the proliferation of "special management units" that resulted in the around-the-clock lockdown of inmates who were regarded as the most disruptive (Government Accountability Office, 2012, p. 26–27). Nonetheless, Bureau of Prisons officials "raised concern about the possibility of a serious incident occurring," especially at high-security facilities "because these facilities are extremely crowded and house the most serious inmates" (p. 27).

RELEVANT PSYCHOLOGICAL THEORY AND PRINCIPLES

The topic of prison overcrowding implicates and is illuminated by a number of important psychological theories and principles. This section examines the conceptual definitions of prison overcrowding and the various psychological effects that overcrowded prison conditions can produce.

Defining Overcrowding in a Prison Context

It is important to note that prison overcrowding can be calculated in several different ways, depending on exactly how the capacity of an individual prison or prison system is specified. *Design capacity* is the most commonly used and straightforward of these measures; it refers to the number of prisoners that planners or architects designed the prison to hold. *Operational capacity* generally refers to the number of inmates who can be accommodated based on a facility's (or system's) staff, existing programs, and services. Although meaningful in some ways, operational capacity is difficult to calculate in an objective and reliable manner. Finally, the term *rated capacity* is sometimes used to refer to the number of prisoners that a "rating official" in a jurisdiction has indicated the prison or system can or should hold (see Carson & Sabol, 2012, p. 18.).

It is probably fair to assume that the design capacity of a prison has rarely if ever been specified in such a way as to afford prisoners with overly generous amounts of living space. Before prison overcrowding became so widespread in the United States, the average prisoner lived in an approximately 60-square-foot cell—an area slightly larger than the size of a king-sized bed or small bathroom. The cells typically contain a bunk, sink, toilet, a small shelf or desk, and a locker or open space where the prisoner can store all of his worldly possessions while incarcerated (e.g., Branham, 1992). With the advent of double-celling in the mid- to late-1970s, however, most prisoners in the United States had something else with which to contend inside their small cells—at least one other prisoner. By the mid-1980s, available Bureau of Justice Statistics data indicated that only about one third of prisoners in the United States were single-celled (Innes, 1986).

Beyond the basic issue of whether prisoners have adequate cell or living space in which to be humanely housed (i.e., the ratio of prisoners to design capacity), other dimensions of prison life also should be taken into account. A more nuanced view of prison overcrowding would include consideration of the extent to which a prison or prison system houses more prisoners than it has the adequate and comprehensive infrastructure to humanely and effectively care for. Indeed, many prison systems have increased their housing capacity over the last 30 years (by increasing the number of cells or beds) without commensurate increases in programming, medical, and mental health resources. These systems are overcrowded even though, technically, they do not house greater numbers of prisoners than there are cells to hold them.

Before high rates of incarceration became the norm in the United States, most prison administrators agreed that prisons operating at or near their design capacity were approaching dangerous levels of overcrowding. Because prisons are total institutions that operate within closed systems (i.e., prisoners are housed around-the-clock in environments they cannot leave), space is used to separate prisoners and reduce conflict. In addition, when a part of the prison is under repair, being modified, or being repurposed, alternative space within the facility or elsewhere in the prison system must be found to accomplish essential functions (e.g., housing and the delivery of services). Prisons that operate at capacity offer administrators few degrees of freedom for managing inmate populations and implementing initiatives that require the flexible use of space. Although the growth in the overall prison population in the United States has leveled off somewhat in recent years, as Table 15.1 illustrates, there are many prison systems around the country that are still operating at or above their design capacity. In this sense, overcrowded prisons have become the norm in many U.S. prison systems.

The Consequences of Prison Overcrowding

At a macro level, prison overcrowding is a phenomenon that can be understood through principles of organizational behavior, especially the ways that systems and organizations operate in times of stress or crisis, and during periods when the operational demands that they confront exceed their capacity to meet all of them. The topic of stress in organizations—the toll that stress can take on individuals who function inside organizations and institutions, how the stress negatively impacts their behavior, and the means by which it can be reduced in order to maximize performance—is one of long-standing interest in psychology (e.g., McGrath, 1976). The related questions of the effect that stress has on institutions and organizations as entities and how they "behave" under conditions of stress, however, have not been as carefully considered. Although the two levels of analysis are obviously interrelated, they are conceptually distinct. When complex organizations and institutions

TABLE 15.1

Prison Overcrowding: Highest Above Design Capacity

Prison system	Prison population	Percent above design/rated capacity
Alabama	26,268	196
California	147,578	175
Illinois	48,427	163
Hawaii	3,687	161
Delaware	6,546	157
Nebraska	4,657	147
Massachusetts	11,467	143
Federal (Bureau of Prisons)	176,228	138
North Dakota	1,385	132
Wisconsin	22,381	130

Note. Data from Carson and Sabol (2012).

rapidly expand in size, as they do during periods of unprecedented growth, and, in the case of prisons, experience the overcrowding that typically results from such expansion, they not only become stressful places in which to live and work, but they also become difficult to properly manage, oversee, or hold accountable. In fact, the unprecedented growth in the U.S. prison population presented enormous challenges for prison administrators charged with overseeing the management of individual prisons or entire prison systems that suddenly expanded in size and were no longer able to operate as they once had.

Of course, overcrowding has a profound influence on the day-to-day experience of imprisonment. That is, at a more microlevel, there are important social psychological consequences of overcrowding on prisoners' social interactions, adjustment, and personal well-being. Prisoners in overcrowded correctional settings interact with more unfamiliar people, live in extremely close quarters that afford little or no privacy or respite, and must adjust to the fact that fewer of their basic needs are likely to be met. Thus, overcrowding operates at an individual level to worsen the experience of imprisonment and to exacerbate the stress and pain of confinement by literally changing the social context or situation to which prisoners must adapt on a daily basis.

In addition, there are individual differences among prisoners—especially those with certain preexisting vulnerabilities and special needs—that place them especially at risk in overcrowded prisons. Particularly in recent years, as the criminal justice system relinquished any pretense of tailoring prison treatment to the individual needs of the prisoners, those persons with special vulnerabilities were placed in greater jeopardy. Although certain special-needs prisoners have a separate legal status with which to request protection from especially harsh conditions of confinement (e.g., Cohen, 2008), badly overcrowded prison systems are less willing or able to honor their claims. As prison law expert Fred Cohen observed, "inmates who look to litigation to further their desire or need for various forms of help must somehow fit themselves into a variety of 'special needs' groups" (2004, p. 453), yet the outcome of litigation that is conducted on behalf of special-needs prisoners is often uncertain and unpredictable.

Finally, because of the way that imprisonment itself can affect the long-term life trajectories of prisoners—in potentially positive ways if meaningful and effective rehabilitation is accomplished in the course of their imprisonment, or in negative ways if adverse prison effects persist after prisoners are released—prison overcrowding can influence a person's chances for postprison success and, in this way, affect recidivism rates and the overall amount of crime in society (for a review of parole and probation, see Chapter 13, this volume).

There are data that address all of these aspects of prison overcrowding: (a) what overcrowded prisons and prison systems look like and how they function when they must accommodate more prisoners than they were designed to effectively and humanely house and manage, (b) how prisoners are changed and affected by having to live under overcrowded conditions that exacerbate the pains of imprisonment, (c) the plight of vulnerable and special-needs prisoners whose ability to cope with the stress of living under overcrowded prison conditions may be especially limited, and (d) the long-term, postprison consequences of having lived inside overcrowded prisons that not only subject prisoners to heightened levels of disabling stress but also often fail to adequately prepare them for their release.

RESEARCH REVIEW

Contemporary research on prison overcrowding has included the compiled data on the state of the prisons during the era of mass incarceration in the United States. These data are particularly instructive because they illustrate what can happen when overcrowded prisons become the norm. Some provide descriptive accounts of the systemic instability and dysfunction that occurred in at least some prisons and prison systems in response to this overcrowding. In addition, there are more systematic studies of the ways in which individual prisoners and groups of prisoners (including the most vulnerable inmates) can be directly affected by overcrowded conditions of confinement, both in the course of their incarceration and after they have been released from prison and attempted to reintegrate back into free society.

Systemic Instability and Dysfunction

As institutions, prisons are premised on principles and techniques of forceful control. Individual prisons and entire prison systems are designed around the principle of controlling prisoner behavior by using a combination of architectural design, mechanical and technological devices (e.g., cameras, sensors, locking mechanisms, physical restraints), and a complex array of rigidly enforced rules and procedures to enhance and ensure surveillance and regulation at every turn. At a macrolevel, prison overcrowding challenges administrators and prison staff to oversee and manage more prisoners than their facilities were designed to accommodate and, as a result, it taxes every aspect of this control-oriented environment.

Overcrowded prisons and prison systems become difficult to oversee in sheer numerical terms—there are too many people and even too many facilities to effectively manage. In fact, some prison systems in the United States grew so large so quickly during the era of mass incarceration that it was challenging for prison officials to even keep track of the names and locations of all of the facilities in their system, let alone to meaningfully supervise and oversee each of them. For example, by the turn of the twenty-first century, New York operated 70 prisons scattered across the state, 52 of which were built between 1973 and 2000 (Conover, 2000, p. 57). During this same time period the prisoner population in the state increased nearly six-fold, from approximately 12,000 to more than 70,000 (Conover, 2000, p. 57).

The two largest prison systems in the United States, in California and Texas, experienced comparable, remarkable rates of rapid growth. Over a 30-year period beginning in the mid-1970s, California's prisoner population expanded more than eight-fold from roughly 20,000 to more than 170,000 prisoners at its highest mark (Data Analysis Unit, 2009). Funding for prisoner services and programming did not remotely keep pace, which meant that many more prisoners had to make do with much less. In Texas, over just the 11-year period between 1989 and 2000, the prisoner population more than tripled as over 100,000 additional prison beds were added to the prison system (e.g., Turner, Greenwood, Chen, & Fain, 1999, p. 77, n. 21). Indeed, during the mid-1990s Texas achieved one of the highest incarceration rates in the United States, and the number of state prisons swelled to more than 80 facilities to accommodate this rapid expansion in an already sizable prisoner population (Harrison & Beck, 2006). Of course, prison systems that grow at such a pace are at risk of losing their organizational stability, operational oversight, and institutional accountability. In this way, overcrowding changes the way the prison system itself functions. Prison overcrowding makes it difficult to maintain stable norms, to ensure consistent operations and policies across the larger number of facilities, and to monitor the entire system to prevent or correct all but the most egregious problems.

Among other things, procedures and practices intended to facilitate orderly and effective prison operations are sacrificed when they become too time consuming or lead to recommendations that an overcrowded system can no longer follow. Prison systems responding to the press of numbers forgo the careful classification of prisoners, ending the process of carefully screening, monitoring, and managing vulnerable or problematic prisoners. This occurs in part because there are simply too many prisoners to assess in a conscientious (and time consuming) way and in part because overcrowded and underresourced systems lack the capacity to base their housing assignments on the needs of prisoners (rather than simply the availability of bed space). Overcrowded prisons also often cannot maintain a sufficient number of programs (such as educational and vocational training) to match with the many prisoners who badly need them, or to operate the appropriate number of specialized facilities for prisoners who enter the system with special needs. As one group of clinicians conceded at a time when prison overcrowding had become the norm in the United States: "Unfortunately, the prospect of screening inmates for mental disorder and treating those in need of mental health services has become a daunting and nearly impossible task in the present explosion of prison growth" (DiCataldo, Greer, & Profit, 1995, p. 574; for a review of forensic treatment, see Volume 1,

Chapter 6, this handbook). Unidentified and untreated mentally ill prisoners in mainline prison populations are not only more likely to decompensate themselves but also can have a significant adverse effect on the prisoners with whom they must interact and live when they are in crisis (for a review of risk assessment, see Volume 1, Chapter 3, this handbook).

Overall, the overcrowded U.S. prison system has failed to address even the most basic educational needs of many prisoners. Surveys of literacy levels in prisons throughout the United States have documented the magnitude of this problem. One national study concluded that about seven out of ten prisoners were literally or functionally illiterate in 1992 (National Center for Educational Statistics, 1994). Another study reached similar conclusions about the California prisoner population in the mid-1990s. A little more than 20% of California prisoners read at below the third-grade level, and another 30% were only marginally literate by accepted educational standards (Sutherland, 1997). Little was done during the era of mass incarceration and prison overcrowding to remedy these problems. By 2002 the California prison system housed more than 150,000 prisoners, two thirds of whom had been incarcerated before. Yet, according to the prison system itself, those prisoners still read on average at no more than a seventh-grade level (California Department of Corrections and Rehabilitation, 2006). In fact, in part because of prison overcrowding and the lack of adequate resources with which to address the needs of so many prisoners, many of them still routinely leave prison, and return, lacking basic literacy skills.

In addition, prisoners in overcrowded correctional systems often are placed on long waiting lists to obtain prison jobs, and some never obtain them. By the start of the 1990s the Bureau of Justice Statistics reported that nearly 40% of the nation's prisoners had no prison work assignments at all, and another 40% were assigned to "facility support services" that included primarily laundry, kitchen, and building maintenance jobs (Maguire, Pastore, & Flanagan, 1993, p. 640). Only 7% of prisoners were involved in prison industry programs where they were likely to obtain job experience and develop skills that could be transferred to the free world

(Maguire et al., 1993). A decade later a number of large prison systems were reporting the same or similar levels of idleness. For example, only a little more than half of all prisoners in California are employed in prison jobs of any kind. Specifically, only 56% of the more than 150,000 California prisoners were employed in any type of work assignment at the end of 2002 (California Department of Corrections and Rehabilitation, 2006).

In addition to the sheer number of prisoners who go without any assignments, the quality of the programs for those who are assigned is often undermined by the ratio of prisoners to the resources devoted to meeting their needs. For example, here is how sociologist John Irwin characterized the vocational training programs in a badly overcrowded medium-security California prison that he studied—programs in which fewer than 20% of the prisoners were fortunate enough to be involved at any one time:

> Several conditions greatly weaken the efficacy of these vocational training programs, most important, the lack of funds and resources. Instructors report that they have great difficulty obtaining needed equipment and materials. . . . Instructors are fired, or they quit and are not replaced. . . . Further, the training programs are regularly interrupted by lockdowns [and inclement weather] during which prisoners cannot be released to the hill for vocational training. (Irwin, 2005, p. 75)

The effects of prison overcrowding can also reverberate back through the criminal justice system, creating problems in local jails (e.g., Pontell & Welsh, 1994). That is, prison officials may react to overcrowded conditions by attempting to slow the rate at which they are willing or able to receive new prisoners, and in extreme cases, they may refuse to take them at all. The jail overcrowding that results, however, as prisoners back up in the system awaiting transfer to prison, is harmful in its own right. For example, "large jail populations may create a logarithmically increasing demand for services, with overcrowding speeding the deterioration of aging jail facilities and further taxing the ability of institutions to provide for basic human needs" (Welsh, 1992, pp. 604–605).

Unlike prisons, jails are not structured or operated with long-term confinement in mind. Keeping prisoners in jails for longer periods of time means that they have even less access to meaningful activity, programming, or services (e.g., Paulus & McCain, 1983). For some prisoners, the consequences are dire. Researchers have found that suicides are prevalent in jails with high ratios of inmates to staff members (Wooldredge & Winfree, 1992). In addition, the same study found that natural deaths in jail can be reduced when overcrowding is alleviated and other humane standards of confinement are implemented.

In any event, jail crowding has become the norm in the era of mass incarceration. From 1984 to 2000, jails in the United States operated with inmate populations that were at or above 90% of their rated capacity (Maguire & Pastore, 2001, p. 501). Some facilities were more crowded, and there is evidence that the problem has not subsided in recent years (Harrison & Beck, 2006). Jail overcrowding also likely means that increasing numbers of persons will enter the prison system already traumatized by their prior period of incarceration.

Over the last several decades, prison administrators reacted to unprecedented levels of overcrowding in a variety of ways that altered the nature of the prison setting, often making individual prisons more dangerous and psychologically painful places in which to live. For example, the resources that were once devoted to already limited programming and other activities are often reallocated to create bed space and maintain basic security. As many commentators have observed, the prison overcrowding crisis in the United States coincided with the advent of a correctional philosophy that saw deprivation as a legitimate goal rather than a problem to be alleviated. As part of a system that was no longer judged by its ability to rehabilitate but, rather, by its potential to punish, prisons felt little pressure to provide meaningful programming or activities for prisoners. Unprecedented amounts of unproductive inactivity resulted.

Indeed, in the face of extraordinary increases in the number of prisoners, many prison administrators pressed for new tools with which to control and contain them. In most jurisdictions, any pretense of carefully managing the prison "careers" of inmates or effectively monitoring the quality of the conditions under which they were kept was sacrificed during the rapid expansion of the prison population. Feeley and Simon (1992) identified a new penological management style that emerged during the height of prison overcrowding, one in which correctional decision makers began to think about the enormous numbers of prisoners they oversaw only in the aggregate, as dangerous populations that need to be herded, rather than as individuals in need of personal attention. Indeed, in terms that captured both the dehumanizing consciousness of the decision makers and the devalued status of the prisoners under their control, Feeley and Simon analogized the overcrowding-driven new penological ideology as akin to a "waste-management" function (p. 470).

Thus, rather than improving living conditions and investing in prison programs and meaningful activities in which prisoners could participate, many prison systems have committed themselves to harsh policies and procedures designed primarily to maintain order and control. They also now rely increasingly on sophisticated and expensive security hardware and surveillance technology (e.g., Drew, 1999). Metal detectors, x-ray machines, leg irons, waist chains, handcuffs, holding cages, "violent prisoner restraint chairs," psychiatric screens, chain-link fences, concertina wire, Tasers, stun guns, pepper spray, tear gas canisters, gas grenades, and, in some jurisdictions, mini-14 and 9-millimeter rifles, 12-gauge shotguns, and the like now are used inside the cellblocks of a number of maximum-security prisons (see *Madrid v. Gomez*, 1995, p. 1179, n. 52).

Exacerbating the Pains of Imprisonment

The pains of imprisonment derive primarily from the nature of confinement itself. Loss of liberty and privacy, regimentation and routinization, and the deprivation of basic material comforts and psychological sources of support accompany virtually all forms of incarceration. There are various conditions of confinement, however, that exacerbate the painfulness of prison life and, in some instances, places prisoners at grave risk of harm.

Intensifying prison stress and deprivation.
Overcrowding exacerbates the chronic pains of imprisonment. Not surprisingly, a large literature on overcrowding has documented a range of adverse effects that occur when prisons have been filled to capacity and beyond. Much of the empirical literature was compiled years ago, when overcrowding was perceived as a solvable problem rather than an intractable part of the prison system status quo. Although some of the studies are dated, nothing has changed to alter their troubling implications. Thus, as a group of prison researchers summarized in the 1980s, when the overcrowding problem was just beginning to take shape, "crowding in prisons is a major source of administrative problems and adversely affects inmate health, behavior, and morale" (Cox, Paulus, & McCain, 1984, p. 1150). Two other early commentators concluded their review of the literature in much the same way, namely that, "[w]ith few exceptions, the empirical studies indicate that prison overcrowding has a number of serious negative consequences" (Thornberry & Call, 1983, p. 351; see also Ruback & Carr, 1984).

Although under certain circumstances other variables may be able to mediate or reduce the negative effects of overcrowding (e.g., Ekland-Olson, 1986), the psychological toll can still be substantial. Thus, despite an occasional study that yields an inconclusive finding (e.g., Bleich, 1989), there is an empirical consensus that overcrowding significantly worsens the quality of institutional life and increases the destructive potential of imprisonment. Among other things, we know that prison overcrowding increases negative affect among prisoners: "The present study indicates that living under relatively crowded housing conditions in a prison produces both negative affect and a lower criterion of what constitutes overcrowding" (Paulus, Cox, McCain, & Chandler, 1987, p. 90). It also elevates their blood pressure: "[T]he major hypothesis that there would be an association between degree of crowding and blood pressure, systolic and diastolic, was strongly supported" (D'Atri, 1975, p. 247; see also Gaes, 1985; Ostfeld, Dasl, D'Atri, & Fitzgerald, 1987). In

addition, overcrowding leads to greater numbers of prisoner illness complaints (McCain, Cox, & Paulus, 1976; see also Walker & Gordon, 1980).

Not surprisingly, exposure to "long-term, intense, inescapable crowding" of the sort that still characterizes many prison environments results in high levels of stress that "can lead to physical and psychological impairment" (Paulus, McCain, & Cox, 1978, p. 115; see also Ostfeld et al., 1987; Paulus, 1988). In addition, overcrowding has been associated with higher rates of disciplinary infractions. For example, one study concluded that in prisons "where crowded conditions are chronic rather than temporary . . . there is a clear association between restrictions on personal space and the occurrence of disciplinary violations" (Megargee, 1977, p. 295).

Other researchers have found that high levels of perceived crowding in prison were related to increased arousal and stress and decreased psychological well-being (Lawrence & Andrews, 2004). Moreover, the prisoners in this study who experienced crowded prison conditions were more likely to interpret the behavior of other prisoners as aggressive and violent. Other researchers have found that an individual-level factor—the degree of prior street drug use—interacted with the level of prison crowding to explain in-prison drug use. Specifically, "inmates who reported a history of using drugs on the streets prior to incarceration are especially likely to engage in drug abuse inside crowded prisons" (Gillespie, 2005, p. 249).

Studies also have shown that "overcrowding is a critical feature of prison environments that dramatically raises the risk of prison suicide" (Huey & McNulty, 2005, p. 507). Thus, "the reduced risk of suicide found in much prior research to be evident in minimum security facilities"—presumably because of the lower levels of deprivation there—"is in fact voided by the deleterious effects of high overcrowding" (Huey & McNulty, 2005, p. 507). Other researchers have found that overcrowding may lead to higher numbers of prison suicides because it decreases the level of "purposeful activity" in which prisoners are able to engage (Leese, Stuart, & Snow, 2006, p. 359; see also Wooldredge, 1999).

Overcrowding directly affects prisoners' mental and physical health by increasing the level of uncertainty with which they regularly must cope. One useful psychological model of the negative effects of overcrowding emphasizes the way in which being confined in a space that is occupied by too many people increases the sheer number of social interactions persons have that involve "high levels of uncertainty, goal interference, and cognitive load" (Cox, Paulus, & McCain, 1984, p. 1159). Thus, crowded conditions heighten the level of cognitive strain that persons experience by introducing social complexity, turnover, and interpersonal instability into an already dangerous prison world in which interpersonal mistakes or errors in social judgments can be fatal. As noted earlier, overcrowding also raises collective frustration levels inside prisons by generally decreasing the resources available to the prisoners confined in them. The sheer number of things prisoners do or accomplish on a day-to-day basis is compromised by the amount of people in between them and their goals and destinations.

Creating a dysfunctional prison context. One of the most common consequences of prison overcrowding is inmate idleness, obviously caused by an insufficient number of programs and activities for the number of prisoners incarcerated. Idleness in prison, especially when it is persistent, produces negative psychological and behavioral effects. As far back as the 1980s, when trends toward overcrowding and the lack of prison programming had just begun, the U.S. Government Accounting Office noted, "Corrections officials believe that extensive inmate idleness can lead to destructive behavior and increase violence within institutions. Moreover, idleness does little to prepare inmates for re-entry into society" (U.S. General Accounting Office, 1982, p. 2). Other commentators agreed, noting that "[l]ess than 20% of the national prison population works," and expressing concern that most inmates just "sit around, becoming bored, restless[,] and, sometimes, violent" (Mehler, 1984, p. 4). They argued that the best way to keep the costs of incarceration low and the potential for rehabilitation high was to "give inmates a job" (Mehler, 1984, p. 4), but the warning and advice were largely ignored as the trends toward higher rates

of incarceration intensified and prison overcrowding continued over the next several decades.

Thus, as the Office of the Inspector General (2004) acknowledged two decades later, "research conducted by both governmental and private institutions concludes that successful completion of occupational, educational, psychological, and other programs during an inmate's incarceration leads to both a reduction in recidivism and an increase in postrelease employment opportunities" (p. iii). Audits conducted between 1999 and 2002, however, found that between 31% and 69% of institutions examined failed to meet their occupational and educational goals, and that the Bureau did not even "have a standardized process in place" enabling them "to analyze trends related to psychological program performance" (p. iv).

Idleness-related frustration increases the probability of interpersonal conflict and assaults in prison. Overcrowding simultaneously reduces the opportunities for staff to effectively monitor prisoner behavior and drastically limits the options to reduce animosities between prisoners by separating them or sending them to different facilities. Thus, there are fewer things for prisoners to do, fewer outlets to release the resulting tension, a decreased staff capacity to identify prisoner problems, and fewer options to solve them when they do occur. Among the negative behavioral effects that are likely to occur is an increased risk of victimization. For example, one prison researcher has noted that "[i]n less well-regulated institutions in which prisoners have little recourse to protection or in which there may be collusion between dominant prisoners and staff to maintain the peace, sexual violence tends to be greater" (King, 1992, p. 70). Other researchers agreed that overcrowded conditions in which prisoners have a significant amount of idle time can contribute to a higher level of prison rape (e.g., Gunby, 1981, p. 216).

The dynamic by which prison overcrowding changes the context of imprisonment and negatively affects prisoner behavior is complicated by the subsequent actions that prison systems take in response. In many instances, prisons attempt to regain institutional control in the face of prison overcrowding by instituting policies and practices that actually worsen the overall quality of life in prison and provoke even greater levels of prisoner resistance, inadvertently ensuring that this escalating cycle continues. These problematic patterns of actions and reactions can produce a whole host of unintended but harmful long-term consequences.

For example, overcrowding appears to have especially adverse effects on the institutional behavior of younger inmates. Thus, one study of the Texas prison system found that "the greater the proportion of young prisoners housed in the institution, the greater the infraction and assault rates. There is some evidence for an interaction effect between age and prison size. Younger inmates may be more susceptible to the problems and control structures in large prisons than older inmates" (Ekland-Olson, Barrick, & Cohen, 1983, p. 174). Another study obtained similar results, with overall correlations that revealed "a significant association between density and total assaults . . . and assaults on inmates," such that the greater the density the more frequent the assaults (Nacci, Prather, & Teitelbaum, 1977, p. 29) and researchers found that the relationship between crowding and violence was "strongest in the institutions housing young offenders" (Nacci et al., 1977, p. 29).

Age-related crowding effects are not surprising. Younger prisoners tend to be more volatile, sensitive to their surroundings and, in general, more likely to react aggressively to the tensions and conflicts that crowded conditions of confinement generate (e.g., Toch & Adams, 2002). Prison officials and staff members respond to these crowding-related infractions by punishing prisoners, often by placing them in disciplinary segregation units. The heightened reactivity of younger prisoners to their crowded living conditions thus means that greater numbers of them will be exposed to even harsher conditions in the segregated or isolated housing units where many eventually are confined.

A number of adverse consequences are likely to follow from this scenario. Prison officials typically use an inmate's disciplinary segregation status to bar him or her from participation in educational or vocational programming. Moreover, extended time spent in segregation simultaneously places prisoners at risk of developing a host of adverse psychological reactions that are associated with long-term isolation (Grassian, 1983; Haney, 2003; Haney & Lynch, 1997; Smith, 2006). A lack of even minimal forms of programming and exposure to potentially disabling solitary confinement may jeopardize subsequent adjustment in mainline prison housing units as well as in the free world. In addition, if these prisoners return to prison after having been released—something that is unfortunately more likely than not—they often find that their prior disciplinary status leads more readily to their classification as a present security risk, making them prime candidates for assignment to a segregation unit once again.

Failing to address the needs of vulnerable mentally ill prisoners. As noted earlier, the unprecedented influx of prisoners over the last several decades and the levels of overcrowding it has produced have significantly compromised the evaluation and classification of incoming prisoners. The seriousness of a prisoner's commitment offense and the length of his sentence now largely determine classification levels and, as a result, dictate most housing assignments. This means that many fewer new inmates are meaningfully screened or given a careful diagnostic evaluation, or what—in the days of rehabilitation—was referred to as a "needs assessment." The task of assigning prisoners to particular correctional facilities turns largely on whether and where there is available bed space rather than on matching individual prisoner needs with available programming resources.

In turn, this overcrowding-related practice has significantly reduced the ability of prisons and prison systems to even know about the special needs of their prisoners let alone provide them with adequate treatment and programming in response. Remarkably, a number of prison systems have never attempted to systematically and proactively determine exactly how many of their inmates are mentally ill. Some systems use rough estimates obtained from mental health staff, but these estimates are necessarily limited to cases of which the staff is personally aware. Significant underestimates can occur, especially in poorly staffed facilities, which, in turn, may ensure that mental health services and programs will continue to be underfunded and prisoners underserved. California's experience over the last several decades illustrates the pitfalls of this approach. In the late 1980s, the state legislature funded a sophisticated and comprehensive study of mental illness in the state prison system. Its results were both surprising and unsettling. By conducting a series of face-to-face diagnostic interviews with a carefully selected, representative sample of prisoners, the study determined that approximately 7.9% of all of the prisoners incarcerated in California were suffering from one of four "severe mental disorders" (severe organic brain disorder, schizophrenia, major depressive disorder, or bipolar disorder) and had experienced current symptomatology within a month of being interviewed. Another 17% had less severe but still serious mental disorders (Norman & Cotton & Associates, 1989, p. 35, Table 8).

The study also found that nearly 7% of the entire prisoner population had current symptoms and severe mental disorders that were undetected by the prison authorities. Specifically, the study concluded that "a large number of unidentified individuals in the general population, were they to be screened, would be diagnosable with the same serious disorders and exhibit related symptoms. Given the size of the unidentified population (over 57,000 at the time of the survey), even the small base-rate of 7% for the four serious disorders amounts to over 4,000 undetected [seriously mentally disordered] individuals" (Norman & Cotton & Associates, 1989, p. ii, Table 1). Nearly a decade passed from the time of the assessment that led to this finding before the state began to take steps to effectively remedy this problem. Because it was a decade in which there was a significant increase in the prisoner population, a dramatic rise in overcrowding, and no corresponding increase in mental health personnel or services, it is reasonable to assume that the number of seriously mentally disordered prisoners who were undetected by the California Department of Corrections continued to rise.

Of course, mentally ill prisoners who were not classified as needing treatment were not likely to get any, especially in a system that, like many during this period, de-emphasized treatment and therapy. In fact, in 1992, when the study was released, the outpatient clinical staff in the California prison system was less than 20% of what widely accepted

professional guidelines indicated it should have been, given the actual prevalence of mental illness among the prisoners (Specter, 1994). Seven of the state's prisons, most of them large facilities with several thousand prisoners each, did not have a single psychiatrist on staff; six prisons had no mental health professionals of any kind; and ten had less than one full-time mental health clinician (relying only on part-time help).

Thus, treatment resources and staffing levels were woefully inadequate in comparison to the actual magnitude of the need. As a result, many vulnerable prisoners were suffering from painful and potentially disabling psychiatric conditions that were overlooked or disregarded. Treatment resources were stretched so thin that even prisoners who were classified by the prison system as suffering from serious mental disorders were being ignored. In fact, 64% of previously diagnosed prisoners also reported that they had not received professional mental health services at any time during their present incarceration (Specter, 1994, p. 113).

Eventually, litigation was filed to compel the state to provide adequate care for its mentally ill prisoners. At the time, California prisons housed

> almost 10,000 prisoners with a current major mental illness, another 20,000 with other serious mental disorders, while approximately 18,000 prisoners need some form of treatment on any given day. The . . . [California Department of Corrections] currently has the capacity to house only 737 prisoners in a psychiatric hospital and about 3,000 in residential treatment programs. (Specter, 1994, p. 110–111)

Other direct studies of the number of mentally ill prisoners in different jurisdictions in the United States have produced varying but equally unsettling estimates. Consistent with the notion that the prison system has become the default placement for mentally ill persons as resources have been shifted away from the public mental health system, studies suggest that the prevalence rates for major psychiatric disorders in prison continued to increase during the era of mass incarceration and high rates of prison overcrowding (e.g., Jemelka, Trupin, & Giles, 1989).

At the same time, there is evidence that overburdened correctional systems continue to attach low priority to addressing the needs of mentally ill prisoners. According to a Justice Department study published in 2001 that surveyed more than 1500 state public and private adult correctional facilities, more than 20% of state prisons in the United States do not, as a matter of policy, screen inmates at intake to determine their mental health needs (Beck & Maruschak, 2001, p. 1). A similar number of prisons fail to conduct any psychiatric assessments of prisoners, and slightly fewer than 20% of these facilities fail to provide inmates with any therapy or counseling by trained mental health counselors. Slightly less than half of prisons do not have around-the-clock mental health care available for prisoners who may suffer acute psychiatric crises, and a third of them fail to assist inmates in obtaining community mental health services upon release (Beck & Maruschak, 2001, p. 1). Because the study relied entirely on the estimates of the correctional administrators themselves, it likely provides a conservative statement of the magnitude of the problem. Moreover, the survey asked respondents only about the availability of various services; it did not address whether the services, in those cases in which they were provided, were adequate or sufficient overall.

The Justice Department data are admittedly open to interpretation. The tone of the Justice Department report itself suggested that mental health coverage in state prison systems was adequate overall, perhaps even impressive. Thus, at various points the authors noted that nearly all of the facilities accomplished one or another of the important mental health tasks that they identified. Mentally ill prisoners are so numerous in the United States, however, that even attending to "nearly all" of them would still leave tens of thousands of them whose needs were neglected. Moreover, mentally ill prisoners who are in need of therapeutic services but housed in one of the many facilities—between 16% and 29% of state institutions, depending on the type of facility—in which no such services are available (let alone readily accessible or properly provided) represent a serious problem that must be addressed if the overall pains of imprisonment are to be appropriately and

humanely reduced. In addition, the figures were actually less favorable when community-based facilities were taken into account, resulting in the overall calculation that nearly one third of adult correctional facilities in the United States do not screen inmates at intake to determine their mental health needs; about one third fail to conduct any psychiatric assessments of prisoners; nearly 30% fail to provide inmates with any therapy or counseling by trained mental health counselors; nearly half have no around-the-clock mental health care available for prisoners who may suffer acute psychiatric crises; and one third fail to assist inmates in obtaining community mental health services upon release.

Another example is provided by what one commentator has described as the vicious cycle into which mentally ill prisoners can fall (Streeter, 1998). A lack of appropriate treatment and care of the sort that occurs in overburdened and overcrowded prison systems may worsen their condition, "[c]ausing hostile and aggressive behavior to the point that they break prison rules and end up in segregation units as management problems" (Streeter, 1998, p. 167). Because of highly stressful conditions in segregation and the fact that the mental health care that is provided there is often sporadic and of uneven quality, "this regression can go undetected for considerable periods of time before they again receive more closely monitored mental health care" (Streeter, 1998, p. 167). Unfortunately, this is a cycle that can, and often does, repeat.

For example, psychiatrist Terry Kupers has argued that an unusually high number of mentally ill persons in prison are funneled into long-term segregation, "lockup," or so-called supermax prisons, where they are confined to their cells for as many as 23 hours a day. Indeed, my own research and a number of other studies indicate that a high percentage of the prisoners who are confined in these special disciplinary units suffer from serious forms of mental illness (Haney, 2003). For example, a Canadian study estimated that approximately 29% of prisoners in special handling and long-term segregation units suffered from "severe mental disorders" (Hodgins & Côté, 1991). A more recent study conducted by a group of Washington state researchers found the same thing: 29% of intensive management prisoners in the state's correctional system manifested at least one predefined indication of serious mental disorder, such as multiple admissions to an acute care mental care facility, or having been in one of the prison system's residential mental health units (Lovell, Cloyes, Allen, & Rhodes, 2000).

Especially in prison systems that do not have the resources or inclination to adequately treat mentally ill prisoners, disciplinary isolation and supermax confinement offer a short-term (but shortsighted) solution to a difficult long-term problem. Disciplinary units become the default placements for disruptive, troublesome, or inconvenient mentally ill prisoners. Despite the individual level at which these problems are understood and addressed, however, the disproportionately high numbers of vulnerable prisoners in disciplinary segregation reflect a failure of system-wide proportions.

In addition, many persons entering prisons suffering from preexisting psychiatric disorders (who in the past would have been treated elsewhere) may find their problems made worse by the stress of confinement. Indeed, symptoms that may have been muted, kept under control, or have gone into remission may emerge in a more diagnosable, flagrant, and disabling form during imprisonment. The few studies that have attempted to address this issue directly suggest that although prior psychiatric history has some effect on symptomatology during incarceration, conditions of confinement independently contribute to levels of psychopathology. For example, John Gibbs (1987) concluded that "going to jail can substantially increase the severity of some symptoms of psychopathology, and the increase is not accounted for by dramatic changes in symptom levels among those with a history of psychological problems prior to confinement" (p. 307). As Kupers (1998) correctly put it: "Mentally disturbed prisoners have a very difficult time remaining stable in the absence of safe, supervised social interactions and meaningful structured activities. Too many end up confined to their cells, where their condition deteriorates" (p. 82–83). However, that can be true for non-mentally ill prisoners as well.

Long-term consequences. Not surprisingly, several studies have suggested that overcrowding is associated with increased recidivism. For example, at the start of the 1980s David Farrington and his colleagues found a strong relationship between overcrowding and prison ineffectiveness in England (Farrington & Nuttall, 1980). Prisoners released from overcrowded prisons were more likely to be recommitted for subsequent criminal infractions. The relationship could not be explained away by other variables, leading Farrington to recommend a reduction in prison overcrowding in order to improve the ability of prisons to reduce crime. By sending fewer people to prison, or by reducing the effective lengths of prison sentences, he argued, the effectiveness of imprisonment might be enhanced.

Similarly, several years after Farrington's English study, Canadian researchers concluded that placing low-risk offenders in often overcrowded high-security facilities resulted in high rates of reincarceration (Bonta & Motiuk, 1987). The rates were significantly higher than those of comparable low-risk offenders who had been placed in halfway houses (for a review of community corrections, see Chapter 16, this volume). The researchers concluded that the failure to properly divert low-risk offenders from high- to low-security facilities, something that overcrowded prison systems often lack the capacity to do, "may actually increase the risk of future recidivism" (Bonta & Motiuk, 1987, p. 312). Thus, the way officials respond to a structurally caused behavioral problem that they are powerless to control, by reacting to crowding-related disciplinary infractions through the use punitive isolation, can jeopardize the long-term well-being of prisoners, create even more disruptive behavior later on, and, indirectly, increase crime.

PRACTICE AND POLICY ISSUES

Overcrowding—having more prisoners than a facility can accommodate in psychologically healthy and humane ways—changes the behavior of prisons and prison systems, dversely affects the context of imprisonment, and significanity undermines the quality of prison life. It contributes to the failure of many prison systems to address the basic needs of prisoners. Tense prisons, ones that house too many people with too little to do and whose basic needs are not being addressed, present prison administrators with many volatile and potentially explosive situations. In many instances, their reactions to these conflicts and crises have been predictable but problematic, serving to increase the amount of pain dispensed in prison and exacerbating already dangerous situations in the long run. Although it is by no means the only cause of the deprived and dangerous conditions that prevail in many of the nation's prisons or the degrading and harmful treatment to which many prisoners are exposed, overcrowding is a central and critical issue that must be effectively addressed if these other problems are to be solved.

The criminal justice system in general also behaves in response to prison overcrowding in ways that sometimes make its long-term consequences worse. For example, if probation and parole services are also overtaxed by a rapid increase in the number of recently released prisoners—as most studies of these agencies seem to indicate they are—then their agents will be less able to provide guidance and meaningful supervision, or to offer services designed to help probationers avoid prison and assist parolees in making a successful transition back into the free world (e.g., Simon, 1993; Kelly & Ekland-Olson, 1991; and Lemert, 1993; for a review of probation and parole, see Chapter 13, this volume). In this way the effects of overcrowding can become self-perpetuating, through increased rates of reoffending and return to prison.

Correctional administrators have been forced to accommodate an unprecedented press of a growing inmate population over the last several decades. They have responded in predictable but sometimes regrettable and ill-advised ways. Many prisoners lack effective programming or meaningful work during incarceration. Under conditions of unprecedented overcrowding and unheard of levels of idleness, and in an era where prisons were devoted to punishment rather than rehabilitation, prison administrators lacked positive incentives to manage the inevitable tensions and conflicts that festered behind the walls. Supermax prisons and other forms of harsh institutional control that emerged in this context were "seized upon as a technologically-enhanced tightening screw on the pressure cooker-like atmosphere that had been created inside many prison systems in

the United States. As the pressure from overcrowding and idleness increased, the screw was turned ever tighter" (Haney, 2003, p. 49).

There are a number of additional practical and policy implications that stem from these scenarios. For one, not only are an unprecedented number of persons returning to free society each year, having absorbed the psychological and other adverse consequences of incarceration, but the overcrowding-related idleness and lack of effective programming that plague many prison systems mean that these individuals are unlikely to be prepared to successfully reintegrate into their communities. In this context, it is important to underscore that many of the costs of overcrowding will be born not only by prisoners and but also by the larger society to which they return. These costs are rarely factored into crime control calculations or political proposals about how best to address the important goal of public safety.

The potential policy responses to the wide range of problematic individual, social, economic, and even political consequences are important to consider. Policy recommendations to reduce prison overcrowding and reverse the trends of mass incarceration that characterized the last several decades in the United States include (a) a greater emphasis on crime control through programs of primary prevention (by addressing the known criminogenic risk factors associated with criminal behavior); (b) developing alternative responses and placements that handle certain kinds of crime (such as drug offenses or crimes committed by persons who are mentally ill) in treatment-oriented programs and facilities instead of prison; (c) implementing sentencing reform (that lowers both the number of persons who are sent to prison and the amount of time that those who are incarcerated actually spend there); (d) providing more effective and widespread in-prison programming to address the criminogenic needs of incarcerated persons, better prepare them to successfully reenter free society, and reduce the likelihood that they will return to prison after they have been released; and (e) improving transitional services to assist prisoners in moving from prison back into their communities as well as ensuring their access to counseling-, employment-, and housing-related services once they have returned home.

SUMMARY AND CONCLUSIONS

As noted at the outset of this chapter, the massive influx of prisoners that began in the late 1970s and early 1980s in the United States produced a rate of growth in the nation's prison population that scholars and legal commentators repeatedly characterized as unprecedented. Among other things, this unprecedented growth meant that many prison systems became dangerously and destructively overcrowded, and they remained so for several decades, even to the present time.

Prison overcrowding has altered the nature of imprisonment, modified existing correctional norms, placed the well-being of many prisoners and correctional staff members in jeopardy, and contributed little or nothing to the worthy goal of reducing crime rates. Many of the dangerous dynamics created by overcrowded prison conditions have been hidden and repressed by the introduction of harsh and especially forceful mechanisms of institutional control (such as supermax confinement). Like the indirect social and psychological costs that are incurred when such large numbers of prisoners are denied meaningful programs or effective treatment for preexisting problems, the price of this harsh treatment is merely deferred.

Prison overcrowding and the danger, deprivation, and dehumanization that it typically exacerbates, have real consequences, not only for individual prisoners but also for the communities to which the overwhelming majority of them eventually return. Many prisoners find that their chances for successful reentry have been indirectly compromised by their harsh experiences in overcrowded prisons, sometimes because they have suffered adverse psychological effects of confinement under these conditions, in other cases because the idle time they have spent in overcrowded prisons combines with the stigma of incarceration itself to jeopardize their chances for meaningful employment and social acceptance once released. An overall lack of transitional programming and other post-prison resources means that many formerly incarcerated persons must fend for themselves. There are a number of communities where large numbers of returning prisoners place significant strains on existing social service and other already scarce or overtaxed resources.

The sheer size of the prison population in the United States and the correspondingly large number of prisoners who are released back into free society each year underscore the importance of prison overcrowding. It should command the attention of scholars, policymakers, and citizens. In fact, in recent years, attempts to break our nation's heavy dependence on imprisonment by developing various alternatives approaches to crime control—using preventative strategies to reduce crime, developing alternatives to imprisonment, implementing sentencing refrom, emphasizing more extensive and effective prison programming, and making much greater investment in transitional and reentry services before, during, and after prisoners move back into the community—have been proposed. If they are implemented on a widespread and coordinated basis, they are likely to reduce prison overcrowding and simultaneously create more humane and effective prison systems. Otherwise, prison overcrowding is likely to remain a significant problem for the foreseeable future.

References

Beck, A., & Maruschak, L. (2001). *Mental health treatment in state prisons, 2000* (Bureau of Justice Statistics Special Report, NCJ 188215). Washington, DC: U.S. Department of Justice.

Bleich, J. (1989). The politics of prison crowding. *California Law Review, 77,* 1125–1180. doi:10.2307/3480644

Bonczar, T. (2003, August). *Prevalence of imprisonment in the U.S. population, 1974–2001* (Bureau of Justice Statistics Special Report, NCJ 197976). Washington, DC: U.S. Department of Justice.

Bonta, J., & Motiuk, L. (1987). The diversion of incarcerated offenders to correctional halfway houses. *Journal of Research in Crime and Delinquency, 24,* 302–323. doi:10.1177/0022427887024004006

Branham, L. (1992). *The use of incarceration in the United States: A look at the present and the future.* Chicago, IL: American Bar Association.

California Department of Corrections and Rehabilitation. (2006). *Fourth Quarter 2005 Facts and Figures.* Sacramento: California Department of Corrections and Rehabilitation. Retrieved from http://www.cdcr.state.ca.us/DivisionsBoards/AOAP/FactsFiguresArchive/FactsFigures4thQ2005.html

Carson, A., & Sabol, W. (2012, December). *Prisoners in 2011* (Bureau of Justice Statistics Special Report, BJS 239808). Washington, DC: U.S. Department of Justice.

Cohen, F. (2004). The limits of the judicial reform of prisons: What works; what does not. *Criminal Law Bulletin, 40,* 421–465.

Cohen, F. (2008). *The mentally disordered inmate and the law* (2nd ed.). Kingston, NJ: Civic Research Institute.

Conover, T. (2000, April 3). Guarding Sing Sing. *The New Yorker,* 55–57.

Cox, V., Paulus, P., & McCain, G. (1984). Prison crowding research: The relevance for prison housing standards and a general approach to crowding phenomena. *American Psychologist, 39,* 1148–1160. doi:10.1037/0003-066X.39.10.1148

Data Analysis Unit. (2009). *California prisoners and parolees, 2008.* Sacramento: California Department of Corrections and Rehabilitation.

D'Atri, D. (1975). Psychophysiological responses to crowding. *Environment and Behavior, 7,* 237–252. doi:10.1177/001391657500700207

DiCataldo, F., Greer, A., & Profit, W. (1995). Screening prison inmates for mental disorder: An examination of the relationship between mental disorder and prison adjustment. *Bulletin of the American Academy of Psychiatry and the Law, 23,* 573–585.

Drew, C. (1999, November 8). Lockdown—A special report: An iron hand at Rikers Island drastically reduces violence, *New York Times,* p. A1.

Ekland-Olson, S. (1986). Crowding, social control, and prison violence: Evidence from the post-*Ruiz* years in Texas. *Law and Society Review, 20,* 389–421. doi:10.2307/3053581

Ekland-Olson, S., Barrick, D., & Cohen, L. (1983). Prison overcrowding and disciplinary problems: An analysis of the Texas prison system. *Journal of Applied Behavioral Science, 19,* 163–176. doi:10.1177/002188638301900212

Farrington, D., & Nuttall, C. (1980). Prison size, overcrowding, prison violence, and recidivism. *Journal of Criminal Justice, 8,* 221–231. doi:10.1016/0047-2352(80)90002-1

Feeley, M., & Simon, J. (1992). The new penology: Notes on the emerging strategy of corrections and its implications. *Criminology, 30,* 449–474. doi:10.1111/j.1745-9125.1992.tb01112.x

Gaes, G. (1985). The effects of overcrowding in prison. In M. Tonry & N. Morris (Eds.), *Crime and justice: Annual review of research* (pp. 95–146). Chicago, IL: University of Chicago Press.

Gibbs, J. (1987). Symptoms of psychopathology among jail prisoners: The effects of exposure to the jail environment. *Criminal Justice and Behavior, 14,* 288–310. doi:10.1177/0093854887014003003

Gillespie, W. (2005). A multilevel model of drug abuse inside prison. *Prison Journal, 85,* 223–246. doi:10.1177/0032885505277002

Glaze, L., & Parks, E. (2012, November). *Correctional populations in the United States, 2011.* BJS 239972. Washington, DC: U.S. Department of Justice.

Government Accountability Office. (2012, September). *A report to Congressional requesters: Bureau of Prisons. Growing inmate crowding negatively affects inmates, staff, and infrastructure* (GAO-12-743). Washington, DC: Government Accountability Office.

Grassian, S. (1983). Psychopathological effects of solitary confinement. *American Journal of Psychiatry, 140,* 1450–1454.

Gunby, P. (1981). Sexual behavior in an abnormal situation. *JAMA, 245,* 215–220. doi:10.1001/jama.1981.03310280007002

Haney, C. (2003). Mental health issues in long-term solitary and "supermax" confinement. *Crime and Delinquency, 49,* 124–156. doi:10.1177/0011128702239239

Haney, C. (2006). *Reforming punishment: Psychological limits to the pains of imprisonment.* Washington, DC: American Psychological Assocation. doi:10.1037/11382-000

Haney, C., & Lynch, M. (1997). Regulating prisons of the future: A psychological analysis of supermax and solitary confinement. *New York University Review of Law and Social Change, 23,* 477–570.

Harrison, P. M., & Beck, A. J. (2005). *Prison and jail inmates at midyear 2004* (NCJ 208801). Washington, DC: U.S. Department of Justice.

Harrison, P. M., & Beck, A. J. (2006). *Prison and jail inmates at midyear 2005* (NCJ 213133). Washington, DC: U.S. Department of Justice.

Harrison, P. M., & Karberg, J. C. (2003). *Prison and jail inmates at midyear 2002* (NCJ 198877). Washington, DC: U.S. Department of Justice.

Hodgins, S., & Côté, G. (1991). The mental health of penitentiary inmates in isolation. *Canadian Journal of Criminology, 33,* 175–182.

Housing Inventory & Population Task Force. (1979). *Prison overcrowding: A plan for housing felons throughout FY 1986/87.* Sacramento: California Department of Corrections.

Huey, M., & McNulty, T. (2005). Institutional conditions and prison suicide: Conditional effects of deprivation and overcrowding. *Prison Journal, 85,* 490–514. doi:10.1177/0032885505282258

Innes, C. (1986, December). *Population density in state prisons* (NCJ 103204). Washington, DC: U.S. Department of Justice.

Irwin, J. (2005). *The warehouse prison: Disposal of the new dangerous class.* Los Angles, CA: Roxbury.

Jemelka, R., Trupin, E., & Giles, J. (1989). The mentally ill in prison: A review. *Hospital and Community Psychiatry, 40,* 481–491.

Kelly, W., & Ekland-Olson, S. (1991). The response of the criminal justice system to prison overcrowding: Recidivism patterns among four successive parolee cohorts. *Law and Society Review, 25,* 601–620. doi:10.2307/3053728

King, M. (1992). Male rape in institutional settings. In G. Mezey & M. King (Eds.), *Male victims of sexual assault* (pp. 67–74). New York, NY: Oxford University Press.

Kupers, T. (1998). *Prison madness: The mental health crisis behind bars and what we must do about it.* San Francisco, CA: Jossey-Bass.

Lawrence, C., & Andrews, K. (2004). The influence of perceived prison crowding on male inmates' perception of aggressive events. *Aggressive Behavior, 30,* 273–283. doi:10.1002/ab.20024

Leese, M., Stuart, T., & Snow, L. (2006). An ecological study of factors associated with rates of self-inflicted death in prisons in England and Wales. *International Journal of Law and Psychiatry, 29,* 355–360. doi:10.1016/j.ijlp.2005.10.004

Lemert, E. (1993). Visions of social control: Probation considered. *Crime and Delinquency, 39,* 447–461. doi:10.1177/0011128793039004003

Liptak, A. (2008, April 23). U.S. prison population dwarfs that of other nations. *New York Times.* Retrieved from http://www.nytimes.com/2008/04/23/world/americas/23iht-23prison.12253738.html?pagewanted=all&_r=0

Lovell, D., Cloyes, K., Allen, D., & Rhodes, L. (2000). Who lives in super-maximum custody? A Washington State study. *Federal Probation, 64,* 33–38.

Madrid v. Gomez, 889 F. Supp. 1146 (N.D. Cal. 1995), revised and remanded, 150 F.3d 1030 (9th Cir. 1998).

Maguire, K., & Pastore, A. (2001). *Sourcebook of criminal justice statistics—2000* (NCJ 190251). Washington, DC: U.S. Department of Justice.

Maguire, K., Pastore, A., & Flanagan, T. (1993). *Sourcebook of criminal justice statistics—1992* (NCJ 143483). Washington, DC: U.S. Department of Justice.

McCain, G., Cox, V., & Paulus, P. (1976). The relationship between illness complaints and degree of crowding in a prison environment. *Environment and Behavior, 8,* 283–290. doi:10.1177/001391657682006

McGrath, J. (1976). Stress and behavior in organizations. In M. Dunette (Ed.), *Handbook of industrial and organizational psychology* (pp. 1351–1396). Chicago, IL: Rand McNally.

Megargee, E. I. (1977). The association of population density, reduced space, and uncomfortable temperature with misconduct in a prison community. *American Journal of Community Psychology, 5,* 289–298. doi:10.1007/BF00884696

Mehler, G. (1984, July 28). Prisoners need jobs, and we can't afford to let them sit idle. *Los Angeles Daily Journal,* 4.

Minton, T. (2011, June). Jail inmates at midyear 2010: Statistical tables. *BJS 233431.* Washington, DC: U.S. Department of Justice.

Nacci, P., Prather, J., & Teitelbaum, H. (1977). Population density and inmate misconduct rates in the federal prison system. *Federal Probation, 41,* 26–31.

National Center for Educational Statistics. (1994, October). *Literacy behind prison walls.* Washington, DC: U.S. Department of Education. Retrieved from http://nces.ed.gov/pubs94/94102.pdf

National Prison Project. (1995). *Status report: State prisons and the courts.* Washington, DC: ACLU Foundation.

Norman & Cotton & Associates. (1989). *Current description, evaluation, and recommendations for treatment of mentally disordered criminal offenders: Vol. 1. Introduction and prevalence* ("The Stirling Report"). Sacramento: California Department of Corrections, Office of Health Care Services.

Office of the Inspector General. (2004). *The Federal Bureau of Prisons inmate release preparation and transitional reentry programs, audit report 04/16.* Retrieved from http://www.justice.gov/oig/reports/BOP/a0416/final.pdf

Ostfeld, A., Dasl, S., D'Atri, D., & Fitzgerald, E. (1987). *Stress, crowding, and blood pressure in prison.* Hillsdale, NJ: Lawrence Erlbaum.

Paulus, P. (1988). *Prison crowding: A psychological perspective.* New York, NY: Springer-Verlag. doi:10.1007/978-1-4612-3812-6

Paulus, P., Cox, V., McCain, G., & Chandler, J. (1975). Some effects of crowding in a prison environment. *Journal of Applied Social Psychology, 5,* 86–91. doi:10.1111/j.1559-1816.1975.tb00674.x

Paulus, P., & McCain, G. (1983). Crowding in jails. *Basic and Applied Social Psychology, 4,* 89–107. doi:10.1207/s15324834basp0402_1

Paulus, P., McCain, G., & Cox, V. (1978). Death rates, psychiatric commitments, blood pressure, and perceived crowding as a function of institutional crowding. *Environmental Psychology and Nonverbal Behavior, 3,* 107–116. doi:10.1007/BF01135608

Pontell, H., & Welsh, W. (1994). Incarceration as a deviant form of social control: Jail overcrowding in California. *Crime and Delinquency, 40,* 18–36. doi:10.1177/0011128794040001002

Porporino, F. (1990). Difference in response to long-term imprisonment: Implications for the management of long-term offenders. *Prison Journal, 70,* 35–45. doi:10.1177/003288559007000105

Rhodes v. Chapman, 452 U.S. 337 (1981).

Ross, L., & Nisbett, R. (1991). *The person and the situation: Perspectives of social psychology.* New York, NY: McGraw-Hill.

Ruback, B., & Carr, T. (1984). Crowding in a woman's prison: Attitudinal and behavioral effects. *Journal of Applied Social Psychology, 14,* 57–68. doi:10.1111/j.1559-1816.1984.tb02220.x

Sabol, W. (1989). Racially disproportionate prison populations in the United States. *Contemporary Crises, 13,* 405–432. doi:10.1007/BF00729085

Simon, J. (1993). *Poor discipline: Parole and the social control of the underclass, 1890–1990.* Chicago, IL: University of Chicago Press.

Smith, P. (2006). The effects of solitary confinement on prison inmates: A brief review. In M. Tonry (Ed.), *Crime and justice: A review of research* (Vol. 34, pp. 441–528). Chicago, IL: University of Chicago Press.

Specter, D. (1994). Cruel and unusual punishment of the mentally ill in California's prisons: A case study of a class action suit. *Social Justice, 21,* 109–116.

Streeter, P. (1998). Incarceration of the mentally ill: Treatment or warehousing? *Michigan Bar Journal, 77,* 166–169.

Sutherland, G. (1997). *Reading proficiency of inmates in California correctional institutions.* San Marcos: California State University.

Thornberry, T., & Call, J. (1983). Constitutional challenges to prison overcrowding: The scientific evidence of harmful effect. *Hastings Law Journal, 35,* 313–351.

Toch, H., & Adams, K. (2002). *Acting out: Maladaptive behavior in confinement.* Washington, DC: American Psychological Association. doi:10.1037/10494-000

Tonry, M. (1995). *Malign neglect: Race, crime, and punishment in America.* New York, NY: Oxford University Press.

Turner, S., Greenwood, P., Chen, E., & Fain, T. (1999). The impact of truth-in-sentencing and three strikes legislation: Prison populations, state budgets, and crime rates. *Stanford Law and Policy Review, 11,* 75–85.

U.S. General Accounting Office. (1982). *Report to the Attorney General: Improved prison work programs will benefit correctional institutions and inmates.* Washington, DC: Government Accounting Office.

Walker, B., & Gordon, T. (1980). Health risks and high density confinement in jails and prisons. *Federal Probation, 44,* 53–58.

Welsh, W. (1992). The dynamics of jail reform litigation: A comparative analysis of litigation in California counties. *Law and Society Review, 26,* 591–625. doi:10.2307/3053739

Wooldredge, J. (1999). Inmate experiences and psychological well-being. *Criminal Justice and Behavior, 26,* 235–250. doi:10.1177/0093854899026002005

Wooldredge, J., & Winfree, T. (1992). An aggregate-level study of inmate suicides and deaths due to natural causes in U.S. jails. *Journal of Research in Crime and Delinquency, 29,* 466–479. doi:10.1177/0022427892029004004

Yesterday's "Baby Boom" Is Overcrowding Today's Prisons. (1976, March 1). *U.S. News & World Report,* p. 65.

CHAPTER 16

COMMUNITY CORRECTIONS

Erin Crites, Courtney Porter, and Faye S. Taxman

At the end of 2011, there were approximately 6.98 million adults under some form of correctional supervision, with 4.8 million supervised by community corrections agencies (Glaze & Parks, 2012). *Community corrections* is a broad term covering a range of different functions (e.g., alternatives to incarceration, probation, parole/postincarceration supervision, supervised release) for people in various legal statuses (i.e., pretrial, diversion, sentenced, or postincarceration). Goals of community corrections agencies vary by jurisdiction, community expectations, and the local legal system. The original goal was to provide a form of punishment that was less restrictive than incarceration (prison or jail) where individuals with social welfare issues could be treated and monitored. Other goals of community corrections, however, have included serving as an alternative to incarceration, providing accountability for offender behavior, and rehabilitation.

Over the last 50 years, there have been three main reform efforts to expand community corrections in order to reduce the demand for jail and prison beds, including the intermediate sanctions movement of the 1990s, the reentry movement of the 2000s, and the contemporary Justice Reinvestment movement. In each of these eras, the need to reduce the demand on institutions (prisons and jails) has created a need for increased capacity in the community to both safely and effectively (including cost-effectively) manage prison-/jail-bound offenders in community programming. Justice Reinvestment, the most recent effort, has focused on boosting the community and community

correctional agencies as a protective factor against incarceration.

Community corrections is not just an alternative to incarceration. Properly designed and implemented, community corrections programs can be an appropriate punishment option designed to meet the various goals of sentencing from deterrence to rehabilitation. The crime-prevention goals associated with community corrections draw from the use of programs and services that address the risk for reoffending and the criminogenic needs of offenders. Risk can be addressed through social controls such as contacts with supervision officers, drug testing, curfews, house arrest, and global positioning system (GPS) or electronic monitoring. Criminogenic needs, or the drivers of criminal behavior that are changeable, can be handled through the appropriate cadre of services, programs, and interventions that are designed to facilitate offender change. Studies have found that attention to these risk and need factors can reduce recidivism (Taxman & Pattavina, 2013; Taxman, Pattavina, & Caudy, 2013).

This chapter provides a brief overview of community corrections, including how it can be used to prevent crime, the models of treatment provision, and mechanisms to provide needed services used by community corrections agencies. The Justice Reinvestment Initiative will also be discussed, as one of its key goals is to provide resources to community-based organizations. These organizations can fill in the gaps of needed services to reduce the negative effects of incarceration, safely manage offenders in the community, and reduce offenders' engagement in criminal behavior. Finally, we conclude with a discussion of how Justice Reinvestment can be used to engage the community and facilitate effective community corrections practices.

IMPORTANCE OF THE PROBLEM

Community corrections refers to any correctional control that occurs in a community, as opposed to an institutional setting. This can include pretrial (preadjudication), diversion from court, probation (sentencing that involves community control), alternatives to incarceration (some forms of probation), and parole (postincarceration). The early era of probation was essentially an alternative to incarceration that focused on assisting those with needs (mostly alcohol abuse). For over a century, probation served as a tool used by the court for offenders convicted of lesser crimes. Probation was primarily considered a function of social work, where attention is placed on the individual's needs and the probationer is connected to services that can address these needs, such as substance abuse, mental health, employment, and other conditions that affect engagement in criminal behavior. After the Martinson report of 1974, wherein the conclusion was that "nothing works," support for rehabilitation dwindled in the United States and greater emphasis was placed on oversight and enforcement of conditions (a law enforcement approach; Garland, 2001). The emphasis on enforcement was intensified due to the escalation in the number of conditions, stiffening the punishment feasible within the constraints of probation (i.e., general reporting, informing the officer of their whereabouts, restrictions on certain behaviors such as consuming alcohol, and other behavioral controls).

The main component of community supervision is contact with the individual under supervision. This contact-driven approach is designed to reduce criminal behavior by increasing oversight and reducing liberty. While on probation, the offender has a series of liberty restrictions that define the requirements of supervision. The restrictions can be imposed by the court, the parole board, or as part of a standard set of supervision conditions. Standard conditions frequently include reporting requirements, inability to own or possess weapons, and

restrictions on the use of certain recreational substances, among other rules to guide behavior. Enforcement and compliance management are predominant frameworks in the United States, with other countries emulating this style of supervision given the emphasis on offender accountability. The basic idea is to constrain the liberties of individuals and deter them from engaging in criminal behavior with the threat of incarceration and revocation of probation.

RELEVANT PSYCHOLOGICAL THEORY AND PRINCIPLES AND RESEARCH REVIEW

Sentencing individuals to supervision within their own communities has a number of advantages. Individuals can continue employment and care for their loved ones, individuals are provided with the least restrictive sentence, and individuals can use and become familiar with local community resources. The main goals of community corrections are to ensure community safety through surveillance of known offenders and to prevent future crime by assisting individuals in changing behaviors that are likely to lead to instability or criminal involvement. Providing treatment and other programming services in combination with the monitoring function of community supervision is important for achieving successful outcomes in probation (Drake, 2011; MacKenzie, 2006; Taxman, 2008). Depending on the mission of the community corrections organization, officers may take on either a law enforcement or social work role, and these roles affect how the individual is supervised in the community (Taxman, 2012). Regardless of the role of the officer, offenders are often required to use community resources as a part of their conditions of release. Those resources can include treatment for substance abuse and mental health issues, employment services, and community services to achieve goals of restorative justice and paying restitution.

The process for linking offenders to community resources usually requires the officer to use one of three common models: brokerage, direct provision, or referrals (Latessa & Smith, 2011). Others identify these three roles respectively as the case management model, the individualized treatment model, and the nontreatment assistance model (Weiss & Wozner, 2002). The first two (brokerage/case management model and direct services/individualized treatment model) are more in line with a social work model of probation, while providing referrals tends to be associated with law enforcement or a more control-oriented role. The following sections will describe these models in more detail. Each of these different models of service provision requires the supervision officer to take on a different role. Of importance is defining what role a community supervision officer should play in the supervision relationship (Taxman, 2012).

Brokerage Model

The brokerage model of probation, also called a systematic case management approach (Taxman, 1996), is not new to community corrections (Taxman, 2012). Officers have frequently filled the roll of service broker throughout the history of community supervision (Taxman, 2008). This model asks officers to assist treatment providers in screening and placing individuals into treatment, as well as monitoring treatment compliance (Taxman, 2012; Weiss & Wozner, 2002; Whitehead, 1984). A number of theoretical discussions and tests of the brokerage model have occurred in the community corrections field. For example, in their discussion on a number of different models of community supervision, Weiss and Wozner (2002) suggest that "resource brokerage involves meeting the needs of the offender by mediating between him/her and the appropriate welfare services" (p. 90). Whitehead (1984) suggests that this model provides the best benefits for both the client and the officer. Resource brokering creates an opportunity for the officer to develop a strong working relationship with the client, as well as with service providers in the community. The following section discusses a number of tests of the brokerage model in various community corrections agencies.

During a randomized experiment testing the effectiveness of an intensive supervision model, researchers found when officers worked as service brokers—connecting offenders to the services they needed and monitoring compliance—offenders had lower rates of rearrest and technical violations

(Petersilia & Turner, 1993a, 1993b). Taxman (1998) conducted a large-scale test of an enhanced brokerage model in a probation setting. This application created a "seamless system of care" to improve the collaboration between treatment providers and criminal justice agents. Increasing information sharing and including the supervision officer in the treatment process improved collaboration between the officer and the client. The officers' primary roles were to assist the treatment providers in screening and placing offenders into treatment and in monitoring treatment compliance. The seamless system of care model had a retention rate of 85%, which is considerably higher than the average retention rate of around 50%. Clients supervised under this enhanced brokerage model also had lower recidivism rates, defined as rearrest in the first nine months of community supervision, than would be expected (12% compared to the national average of 50%).

Further evaluations of the seamless system approach also found reduced recidivism rates, although this approach is more costly than traditional supervision (Alemi et al., 2006; Alemi, Taxman, Doyon, Thanner, & Baghi, 2004). In their 2006 paper, Alemi and colleagues suggest that increased intensity of services up front and measuring the benefits for longer than three years may adjust the ratio of costs to benefits. Adopting a brokerage model creates an opportunity to help offenders succeed while on community supervision, assists individuals in managing challenging life situations and behaviors, and builds stronger ties between the community corrections agencies and offenders.

Direct Services Model

Providing direct services to offenders in a community corrections context generally includes focusing on the relationship between the offender and the officer, or the officers running group programs. In either case, the officer is expected to take on a role more akin to a social worker than a supervision or law enforcement professional (Taxman, 2002). The following section will discuss in more detail implementation of a direct services model in community corrections and what the empirical literature has to say about its effectiveness.

Relationships between the offender and the officer. A number of discussions have centered on the relationship between the community supervision officer and his or her client (Burnett & McNeill, 2005; Taxman & Ainsworth, 2009; Weiss & Wozner, 2002; Whitehead, 1984). Whitehead (1984) discusses this role of the community supervision officer as one that focuses on rehabilitation, where the officer takes on the role of change agent. This relationship is frequently described as a "soft" technology, called deportment (Taxman, 2002; Taxman, Shepardson, & Byrne, 2004). Specifically, in a discussion explaining the process of moving towards an evidence-based model of supervision, Taxman (2002) notes that the stronger the relationship between the officer and the offender, the greater the chance the offender will comply with a case plan. Deportment, according to Taxman, includes four main components that help build this relationship. These include using eye contact, engaging in "social graces" (i.e., shaking hands, being on time, etc.), openly discussing results of assessments and performance, and displaying empathy (Taxman, 2002).

Focusing on using the relationship between a supervision officer and offender to achieve behavior change can be effective. In Proactive Community Supervision (PCS), officers use a behavioral management model to focus on the needs of offenders and use motivational enhancement strategies to facilitate offender change. In a study of PCS, Taxman (2008) found that offenders randomly assigned to the PCS group had lower recidivism rates (for both rearrest and technical violations) than control groups. This result is noteworthy given that the PCS group was also subject to increased supervision and drug-testing requirements, in addition to the behavioral management approach to supervision. Other studies that have focused on training officers to develop a more active role in helping change offender behavior have also seen positive results. For example, the Step'n Out study tested a supervision model based on a contingency management approach to help improve working relationships between officers and offenders (Friedmann et al., 2008, 2012). Training the officers in this behavioral management style and the subsequent use of the skills with offenders saw a decrease in rearrests and technical violations.

While research finds supervision practices that focus on developing a working alliance between officers and offenders improves outcomes, few officers receive training in these skills when they begin their careers in community corrections (Bonta et al., 2011; Bourgon & Gutierrez, 2012; Robinson et al., 2012). Even though officers do not often begin their careers with the skills to provide direct services (Bonta, Rugge, Scott, Bourgon, & Yessine, 2008), they could, if properly trained and supervised in an environment that encouraged and rewarded them, become proficient in their use (Taxman, 2012). Recent efforts to develop training curricula to assist officers in mastering these relational skills appear to be effective in both increasing the use of these skills in officers' interactions with offenders, and in improving the offenders' outcomes on supervision (Bonta et al., 2011; Bourgon & Gutierrez, 2012; Robinson et al., 2012). Bonta et al. conducted a study of training community supervision officers in an evidence-based supervision model, called the Strategic Training Initiative in Community Supervision (STICS). They trained 80 officers who supervised 143 probationers. The authors tested the officers' use of these new skills (structuring, relationship building, behavioral techniques, and cognitive techniques) by reviewing audiotapes of sessions with offenders. The results of their study suggest that the training did change officer behavior. Specifically, the experimental group receiving the STICS training had more sessions and a greater amount of session time spent discussing the criminogenic needs of the offender. Offenders supervised by officers who had received training in cognitive skills had lower recidivism rates compared to those officers who had not had the STICS training and did not use cognitive skills in their interactions with offenders. Bourgon and Gutierrez (2012) reported similar findings in their review of audio recordings of officers following STICS training. They specifically noted that, officers without training rarely discussed procriminal attitudes (only 5%) or used cognitive interventions (only 1%). Around 39% of officers who participated in the STICS training talked about procriminal attitudes and 42% demonstrated use of cognitive skills.

Providing programming. Another way community supervision officers can engage in direct service provision is through facilitating or running treatment programs. Milkman and Wanberg (2007) provide an extensive report on the use of cognitive-behavior–based treatment programs for correction's professionals. In their report, they discuss six common interventions: T4C (Thinking for a Change), MRT (Moral Reconation Therapy), R & R (Reasoning and Rehabilitation), ART (Aggression Replacement Training), SSC (Criminal Conduct and Substance Abuse Treatment: Strategies for Self Improvement and Change), and RPT (Relapse Prevention Training). Their review provides detailed discussions of each of these interventions and studies of their implementation and outcomes. In the end, they conclude:

> Although meta-analytic studies have conclusively shown that CBT (cognitive-behavioral therapy) significantly reduce recidivism, effect size (i.e., the amount of reduction in recidivism) is affected by multiple variables, such as whether recidivism is defined as rearrest or reconviction, the number of sessions taken, and the level of training for CBT providers. (Milkman & Wanberg, 2007, p. 60)

Their conclusion, while optimistic in suggesting that direct service provision in community corrections can improve outcomes, also suggests a need to place more attention on how providers of these interventions are trained, especially if they are community corrections officers.

After the shift away from a social work model (resource broker and providing services), supervision officers took on a monitoring and law enforcement role, and their only connection to providing services involved handing out referrals (Taxman, 2012). As noted above, providing direct services to offenders, either through developing strong working relationships with the intention to serve as a change agent or by providing treatment programming, requires officers to balance a helping role with a control role (Skeem, Louden, Polaschek, & Camp, 2007; Weiss & Wozner, 2002;

Whitehead, 1984). This is not always easily done and can be a source of job stress (Whitehead, 1984). It is clear that officers are able to engage in this role of direct service provider when provided with the appropriate resources (training, evidence-based and manualized programs, etc.).

Referral Models

A third model for the provision of services within community corrections is a referral model. Weiss and Wozner (2002) describe this as a nontreatment assistance model. This is probably the mechanism most commonly used by community corrections to access programming services. While this model may appear similar to the brokerage model discussed above, it reflects some key differences. First, according to Weiss and Wozner (2002), the aims of probation under a referral model differ from a case management or resource broker model. In the resource broker model, the purpose of probation is to provide clients with services to address conditions related to offending. The aim of probation under the referral model, on the other hand, is to supervise the offender and only provide help for needs identified by the offender. A second related difference in the referral model is the role of the community supervision officer, which is to provide recommendations for services based on identified client needs. In a brokerage model, the officer goes one step further, assisting in the process of assessing client eligibility and ensuring access to services. Whitehead (1984) would describe this model as a bifurcated model, where probation officers provide control and an outside organization provides the services.

One example of this departure from a service broker model into a more referral-based model is TASC, which began as Treatment Alternatives for Street Crime and now refers to Treatment Accountability for Safer Communities. Under the revised model of TASC, community corrections supervision separates itself from the treatment case management process (Taxman, 2002). An evaluation of TASC found that this case management referral model did not show any improvement in outcomes, such as technical violations or access to services (Anglin, Longshore, & Turner, 1999). They found that TASC was only effective in a site that included both referrals and direct provision of treatment services, suggesting that only providing referrals is not an effective model for delivering services in a community corrections setting.

One challenge with referrals is the ability of the individual to access services. While TASC provided an active approach to referrals, Taxman, Perdoni, and Harrison (2007) found that approximately 60% of agencies use "passive referrals," where community corrections officers provide offenders with a list of providers where an offender can obtain an assessment for services. As is evident in the discussion of the brokering services model above, there is much more information available on tests of this more active referral model, compared to the more common passive referral model. This passive model, while attempting to connect the offender to needed resources, does not provide many opportunities for the officer and the offender to develop strategies around accessing services or in determining which of the providers available might best meet the unique needs of the offender.

Focusing on developing relationships (especially through brokerage or direct services models) between community corrections, offenders, and community treatment providers creates a context for engaging the community in the process of reintegrating individuals into their communities after interactions with the criminal justice system. Community corrections has served as one source for facilitating reintegration, as well as helping divert individuals out of incarceration and keeping them in their communities. Community corrections can only help solve part of the mass incarceration problem, however, particularly with the limited resources available. Another strategy designed to reduce the impact of incarceration on the communities most affected by high rates of incarceration is Justice Reinvestment.

Justice Reinvestment

The community corrections system is responsible for a large percentage of offenders in the correctional system. The size and scope of community corrections helps contribute to incarceration rates due to technical violations or failure to meet community requirements. The large size of corrections also contributes to budget constraints and overloaded community supervision organizations, programs, and services. As part of a response to reduce the use of incarceration, balance fiscal resources, and provide for more evidence-based practices, the concept of Justice Reinvestment was born. The Justice Reinvestment Initiative (JRI) is sponsored by the federal government and private foundations to reduce the use of incarceration, provide for a broader array of sentencing options, and advance the use of evidence-based practices. The recession of the mid-2000s offered an opportunity to advance the notion that mass incarceration policies are economically unsustainable, as well as harmful to individuals, communities, and society. Justice Reinvestment offers a perspective wherein resources allocated to prisons should be redistributed to more applicable and cost-effective options that might result in less incarceration and fewer recidivism events.

The current financial challenges faced by many local governments and communities, along with dropping crime rates and new research casting incarceration in a negative light, has created an eagerness on the part of some local governments to accept aid for community-based services, even if it means decreasing spending on correctional institutions (Clear, 2011). Justice Reinvestment set goals to reduce the prison population, and therefore the costs of incarceration. All of this was set in a context to reduce crime and reoffending by addressing community factors associated with high crime and incarceration rates. Research shows that focusing funds on programs that increase public safety will decrease recidivism and reduce spending on corrections in general (Clement, Schwarzfeld, & Thompson, 2011). In a report discussing cost cutting in prisons and increasing public safety, the Justice Policy Institute (2009) indicates that states spending more on education have lower crime rates. For example, one study profiling several cities found a correlation between increased spending on incarceration and decreased educational opportunities (National Association for the Advancement of Colored People [NAACP], 2011). In Houston, Texas, 15 zip codes account for 10% of the city's population but 40% of the city's prison population. In addition, 83% of low-performing schools are in neighborhoods with the highest incarceration rates, and 67% of the highest-performing schools are in areas with the lowest incarceration rates (NAACP, 2011). Philadelphia, Pennsylvania, has a similar profile, with a majority of low-performing schools clustered in or very near neighborhoods with high incarceration rates and about three quarters of the highest-performing schools in neighborhoods with the lowest incarceration rates (NAACP, 2011). The correlation between community-level incarceration rates and negative social indicators fueled an opportunity to rethink the policies associated with mass incarceration and to alter social policy to focus on micro-level changes (i.e., in a community or neighborhood).

Key features of Justice Reinvestment. While the crime prevention component of Justice Reinvestment policies is relatively new (Clear, 2011), the thrust is to "redirect some portion of the billions of dollars spent on prisons to rebuild the human resources and physical infrastructures" (Tucker & Cadora, 2003, p. 3) in communities and neighborhoods. Similarly, the Council of State Governments (CSG; 2012) promotes Justice Reinvestment as "a data-driven approach to reduce corrections spending and reinvest savings in strategies that can decrease crime and strengthen neighborhoods" (p. 1). Justice Reinvestment encompasses a number of different practices (Allen, 2011), but ultimately it is designed to reallocate funds from the prison system into community-based services in neighborhoods where large portions of the population are at risk for incarceration. Clear (2011) proposes that Justice Reinvestment may be best understood as a "broad strategic plan of action" (p. 586), but that many of the details on how to implement a Justice Reinvestment strategy are left undefined. The movement's basic principle includes redefining public safety (Carroll, 2004) to include boosting local communities to serve as protective factors against incarceration. The measures to increase public safety must be tailored to communities and generated locally (Tucker & Cadora, 2003). These community-based programs may include education, housing, vocational training, and other

social services based on the needs of the community. Instead of continuing to be environments that perpetuate the cycle of incarceration and reincarceration, Justice Reinvestment is perceived as a means to rejuvenate these neighborhoods to provide stability and opportunity for success.

Three core steps evolved to define JRI (Allen, 2011; Tucker & Cadora, 2003). First, a jurisdiction looks at the spending associated with incarceration and identifies areas where spending is counterproductive to recidivism reduction. Second, these identified funds are earmarked for alternative programs. Third, JRI reinvests money into programs designed to help improve public safety of specific neighborhoods. Involving communities with the highest rates of incarceration in the process enables reentry from prison to become a shared responsibility among the local government, community, families, and individuals (Tucker & Cadora, 2003). Although the end goal of Justice Reinvestment for many agencies and organizations is to decrease the amount of spending on prisons and incarceration-based punishments, the means to achieve these goals are contained in smaller steps.

How is JRI currently being implemented? The JRI strategies of analyzing spending, identifying alternatives, and reinvesting savings into community programs seem straightforward, but the concept of reinvesting funds from the criminal justice system to local community services can be complex. There is also little empirical evidence offering specific strategies that have been proven effective. Instead, states, counties, and communities have created individualized JRI plans to meet their own needs within their specific political and economic climates.

One example of a program that follows the logic of the Justice Reinvestment philosophy is Hawaii Opportunity Probation With Enforcement (HOPE), which utilizes community corrections and the use of incarceration only after an individual fails the program. More specifically, HOPE is a community supervision program aimed at probationers with substance abuse issues (Hawken & Kleiman, 2009; Kleiman, 2011). Loosely following the three steps of JRI described above (analyzing spending, identifying alternatives, and reinvesting savings into alternatives), Hawaii identified an issue with the current probation system: a lack of swift and certain responses to negative offender behavior, such as compliance with the conditions of release and the failure to respond, reduced the ability to effectively deter probationers from committing additional crimes (Beccaria, 1764/1995; Nagin, 1998; Nagin, Cullen, & Jonson, 2009). The state speculated that if there were more certain and timely sanctions associated with probation violations, fewer probationers would violate conditions of release, resulting in lower recidivism and reduced incarceration rates for probationers (Hawken & Kleiman, 2009), thereby reducing the use of incarceration by program failures. After successful pilot studies, the HOPE model was expanded to other types of probationers, including sex offenders and domestic violence offenders (Hawken & Kleiman, 2009; Kleiman, 2011). Kleiman (2011) speculates that the implementation of a program like HOPE at a national level would save money by increasing the number of individuals on intensive community supervision rather than incarcerating these individuals. In other words, more individuals would be placed on community supervision, thereby reducing the overall number of individuals incarcerated.

Justice Reinvestment is being pursued through various initiatives. The Urban Institute's Justice Policy Center is working with three partner sites, including Alachua County, Florida, Allegheny County, Pennsylvania, and Travis County, Texas, to pilot the Justice Reinvestment model. In each project, the site receives data analysis support and technical assistance from experienced research staff while embarking on an individualized Justice Reinvestment process. For example, Alachua County is focusing on evaluating the effectiveness of existing programs, including bond reduction hearings and pretrial diversion programs (La Vigne, 2010; Urban Partnerships, 2012). The goal is to identify effective alternatives to incarceration that have already been set up in the community, and to use reallocated funds traditionally used to meet the funding demand of jail to increase the capacity of these community-based alternatives. Allegheny County is looking at characteristics of their jail population in an effort to better understand the

causes of its growth and overcrowding. They found a number of repeat jail residents with substance abuse issues, prompting goals surrounding substance abuse treatment (La Vigne, 2010). If these individuals had more successful treatment experiences, they might not be back in jail. Understanding the needs of the jail population and the drivers of recidivism can help Allegheny County transfer money used for jail to increasing the availability of substance abuse treatment services in these offenders' communities. Travis County also found that jail beds are used for "frequent jail residents," many of whom suffer from alcohol addiction (La Vigne, 2010). As a result of this analysis, Travis County is investigating alternatives to incarceration for substance abusers.

The CSG Justice Center also oversees a technical assistance project on Justice Reinvestment. CSG uses their experience with Kansas and Texas as case studies to illustrate the positive outcomes achievable through Justice Reinvestment strategies. In Texas, legislators authorized policies to slow the growth in the prison population by addressing the drug treatment and mental health needs of offenders in prison and in the community. These policies focused on expanding residential and outpatient treatment programs, including increasing substance abuse and mental health services for offenders in halfway houses and in prison- and jail-based programs (Clement et al., 2011). Since the enactment of these new policies, Texas has seen decreasing numbers of probationers and parolees returning to prison, stalling the growth of the prison population. According to Clement et al. (2011), increasing the capacity of substance abuse treatment programs saved the state of Texas $443.9 million in fiscal year 2009 and removed the need for building new prison facilities.

During the data analysis stage (first step) of the Justice Reinvestment process, the state of Kansas became aware that parole and probation revocations accounted for 65% of new prison admissions (CSG, 2010). In response, legislators developed a Risk Reduction Initiative, which provides funding to "county-based programs that emphasize neighborhood revitalization, substance abuse and mental health treatment, and housing options" (Greene & Mauer, 2010, p. 4). Other policy initiatives include changes in sentencing guidelines for drug charges, increasing diversion options instead of incarceration. Between 2007 and 2010, after the legislative changes, Kansas experienced a 4% decrease in the state prison population and a 20% decrease in the number of new prison admissions for probation and parole violations. These decreases allowed the state to close smaller prison facilities, thus "narrowing the state budget gap" (CSG, 2010, p. 3).

Criticisms of current JRIs.   In each of these examples, Justice Reinvestment is achieved using different strategies applied to various mass incarceration practices. Across the sites, the goal is to shift spending from state-sponsored efforts to local initiatives to prevent incarceration (Clear, 2011). Clear identifies two criticisms of the current JRIs. The first is the focus on recidivism, leaving a large portion of the existing incarcerated population untouched, and thus limiting the impact on reinvestment options. By focusing JRIs on reducing community supervision violations that lead to reincarceration, the planners are not attending to existing incarceration policies. Reducing probation/parole violations may decrease the number of individuals sent to prison, but it does not reduce the current budget needs for prison nor does it reduce the number of individuals incarcerated in the first place (Austin et al., 2013). It is also important to look at primary prevention strategies that not only reduce recidivism, but also reduce first-time sentences to incarceration. That is, the strategies do not deal with the "iron-clad" rule of prisons: the size of the population is determined by the number of people in prison and the length of stay (Clear & Austin, 2009). By not reducing the number of people and the length of stay of sentences for current prisoners, it is difficult to reduce expenditures on prisons and move funds to another area. Kleiman (2011) counters this argument, stating that effective community supervision programs can reduce prison expenditures and precipitate the reinvestment of funds into other areas. Using HOPE as an example, Kleiman indicates that, compared with individuals under routine supervision, those in the HOPE program had lower probation revocation rates and conviction rates for new crimes. Although HOPE does not fully address the front-end problem regarding the number of people in prison overall, it may have some impact by diverting certain substance users to probation sentences rather than incarceration, as well as work to limit the number of technical probation violations that result in additional jail or prison time.

The second criticism is that strategies such as JRI end up redirecting government funds into other government-based programs (e.g., court-based diversion programs, community corrections agencies, etc.) rather than into specific local government, community-based programs (Clear, 2011). Implementing JRI in this way moves away from the original purpose proposed by Tucker and Cadora (2003), which was to downsize prison populations and reallocate savings to public and private organizations in communities targeted by the criminal justice system (Austin et al., 2013). The effectiveness of JRI continues to be debated. Policies have yet to yield reductions in incarceration, have failed to affect the practices in geographical areas of high concentration of the community under control of the justice system, and failure to reallocate resources to expand community-based services is negligible (Austin et al., 2013).

The promise of Justice Reinvestment is to boost local communities to better serve as protective factors against incarceration and the consequences of incarceration. It attempts to achieve this by reallocating funds traditionally used to cover the cost of incarceration (prison and jail) toward community-based programs aimed at prevention. One community-based context to which funds can be reinvested is community corrections. While some proponents of Justice Reinvestment may argue that this is inconsistent with the goals of Justice Reinvestment to reinvest in communities rather than other government-based programs, community corrections agencies help prevent incarceration by supervising offenders and providing services to improve the likelihood that they will remain in the community. Placing more offenders on probation as an incarceration alternative does address one half of the "iron-clad" rule to reduce the number of individuals entering prison, allowing saved funds to be reinvested in community-based programs used by community corrections agencies.

Designed to engage communities, Justice Reinvestment helps transfer resources into communities where a high proportion of the population remains at risk for incarceration. Transferring resources from incarceration policies and institutions to the community, including community corrections, can help improve the reach of treatment programming. Specifically, these resources might be put into training community corrections officers in resource brokering (conducting assessments, increasing offender motivation, and contingency management to increase compliance) or to improve the skills of officers at directly providing services to offenders (through improvements in skills necessary for developing a strong working alliance or in facilitating manualized cognitive-behavior–based interventions). Additionally, more resources infused into the local community could improve the ability of offenders to access services to which they are referred. The following section addresses more specifically how community corrections agencies can make better use of community-based resources.

PRACTICE AND POLICY ISSUES

Both Justice Reinvestment and community supervision are designed to improve public safety and reduce incarceration. They rely on community-based resources to meet the needs of individuals involved in the criminal justice system. In both cases, practitioners recognize that incarceration is not always the most appropriate or cost-effective choice for achieving community safety or reducing recidivism. Kleiman (2011) argues this very point:

> Compared with the current system of incarceration for 2.4 million offenders and ineffective community supervision for another 5 million, a much smaller prison system combined with much more effective community supervision could reduce cost and, more importantly, the suffering imposed by incarceration on those incarcerated and those who care about them while shrinking crime. (p. 656)

While, as suggested above, redirecting resources from institutional settings to community corrections

settings was not the intent of Justice Reinvestment, it might be a good way to start (Clear, 2011). Because many jurisdictions find it challenging to begin the process of moving funds out of prisons and directly into community-based services, beginning with the community corrections system can build buy-in for Justice Reinvestment and begin to demonstrate the possible cost savings.

Kleiman (2011) argues that this reinvestment process can begin with grant funding. Agencies would compete for short-term grant funding to develop a probation system that follows practices that are shown to improve client outcomes on supervision. Kleiman focuses on the HOPE model of supervision, but others might be able to adopt a brokerage model or direct services model. As described above, Justice Reinvestment policies and programs can take many forms and be individualized to meet a community's needs. Providing "seed" money through a competitive grant structure with guidelines and requirements that follow a Justice Reinvestment model would allow communities to build the programs that work best for them.

Kleiman (2011) indicates that requiring states or agencies to "reinvest" savings accumulated during the first years of the grant limits indefinite grant funding, taking to heart the core tenant of Justice Reinvestment—to reinvest savings into the community. Projects supported by the Bureau of Justice Assistance, and administered by the Urban Institute and CSG, are designed for this purpose. Through funding from federal partners (e.g., Bureau of Justice Assistance and the Department of Labor), private organizations (e.g., The PEW Center on the States and the Open Society Foundations), and local governmental agencies (e.g., Travis County Adult Probation Department), the Urban Partnerships (2012) and CSG (2012) provide technical assistance to states and counties willing to go through the Justice Reinvestment process identified above. The counties supported by the Urban Partnerships' Justice Reinvestment at the local level were selected through a competitive application process (Urban Partnerships, 2012). In contrast, states and organizations supported by CSG request assistance from the organization when undergoing a JRI (CSG, 2012). Utilizing a competitive grant structure or requiring supplemental funding from the states or counties themselves helps ensure quality services, evaluations, and sustainability of the project among recipients.

Taking a more traditional approach to Justice Reinvestment, reinvesting money that would have been spent on prisons into the community could also be beneficial to both the community and to the ability of community corrections clients to access services. Clear (2011) proposes a voucher system, where communities would receive vouchers for the cost of imprisonment for each offender diverted from incarceration. These vouchers could be used to provide treatment using local community organizations or given to companies employing offenders to use as pay. Tonry (2011) identifies that this may be an "ideal" plan under Justice Reinvestment, but as discussed above, many states and agencies are setting their sights much lower than Clear's lofty goals of giving money directly to community-based programs. The studies reviewed require the need to engage communities through various community supervision strategies that keep offenders engaged in the community, provide treatment and support, and decrease incarceration rates for Justice Reinvestment to be effective.

Community corrections, while often judged as being a stepping stone to incarceration (Kleiman, 2011), can have a positive effect on individual lives. It is well known that punishment without treatment for most offenders will not reduce the likelihood of recidivism (Andrews & Bonta, 2010). As described above, a number of models can be used to provide offenders with the treatment, programming, and resources they need to make positive changes in their lives. The difficulty is often in gaining access to these services because of the dearth of resources available in the community (see Taxman et al., 2013). When community supervision officers only have resources to provide referrals to a few known providers, the likelihood of individuals participating in these services is low (Taxman, 2002). When officers are trained and have the time to develop strong working relationships with clients, however, they can have a strong impact on individual outcomes (Taxman & Ainsworth, 2009). Additionally, when community corrections agencies engage in

brokerage models of service provision, clients are more likely to receive the services they need and benefit from participating in them (Taxman, 2008); when community correction officers can use communication and other skills to engage offenders in problem solving and treatment, reductions in recidivism can occur (see Bonta et al., 2011). These models, as Alemi and colleagues (2006) note, do not come at low financial cost. Justice Reinvestment strategies can be used to help offset some of these initial higher costs. Additionally, benefits from Justice Reinvestment can permeate beyond community corrections or treatment agencies. Helping communities provide services to their own residents can facilitate community engagement in the process of reducing incarceration.

SUMMARY AND CONCLUSIONS

Considering the large number of individuals incarcerated, as well as those under some form of community supervision, it is clear that changes are needed. As with any new idea in the criminal justice system, proposals are generated in an attempt to move from "what" we are trying to accomplish to "how" we will accomplish it (Allen, 2011). Since the inception of Justice Reinvestment, we have seen states and organizations attempt to discover the "right" way to implement programs that meet the criteria of being evidence-based. Looking at the programs and studies described above, there is no clear path to Justice Reinvestment. In fact, it seems that one of the most appealing aspects of Justice Reinvestment is the way states and agencies can individualize plans to meet the needs of their communities rather than forcing a "one size fits all" plan where it might not work. Some agencies might find it beneficial to implement a more intensive community supervision plan, whereas others prefer a direct services model. The goals of community corrections and Justice Reinvestment overlap, as they both aim to reduce the negative effects of incarceration, albeit through different mechanisms. Throughout all of this, community engagement remains at the forefront, with the ultimate goal of Justice Reinvestment being to empower the community as a protective factor against incarceration.

References

Alemi, F., Taxman, F., Baghi, H., Vang, J., Thanner, M., & Doyon, V. (2006). Costs and benefits of combining probation and substance abuse treatment. *Journal of Mental Health Policy and Economics, 9,* 57–70.

Alemi, F., Taxman, F., Doyon, V., Thanner, M., & Baghi, H. (2004). Activity based costing of probation with and without substance abuse treatment: A case study. *Journal of Mental Health Policy and Economics, 7,* 51–57.

Allen, R. (2011). Justice reinvestment and the use of imprisonment: Policy reflections from England and Wales. *Criminology and Public Policy, 10,* 617–627. doi:10.1111/j.1745-9133.2011.00745.x

Andrews, D. A., & Bonta, J. (2010). Rehabilitating criminal justice policy and practice. *Psychology, Public Policy, and Law, 16,* 39–55. doi:10.1037/a0018362

Anglin, M. D., Longshore, D., & Turner, S. (1999). Treatment alternatives to street crime: An evaluation of five programs. *Criminal Justice and Behavior, 26,* 168–195. doi:10.1177/0093854899026002002

Austin, J., Cadora, E., Clear, T. R., Dansky, K., Greene, J., Gupta, V., . . . Young, M. C. (2013). *Ending mass incarceration: Charting a new justice reinvestment.* Washington, DC: The Sentencing Project. Retrieved from http://sentencingproject.org/doc/publications/sen_Charting%20a%20New%20Justice%20Reinvestment.pdf

Beccaria, C. (1995). *On crimes and punishments and other writings* (R. Davies, trans.). Cambridge, England: Cambridge University Press. (Original work published 1764)

Bonta, J., Bourgon, G., Rugge, T., Scott, T.-L., Yessine, A. K., Gutierrez, L., & Li, J. (2011). An experimental demonstration of training probation officers in evidence-based community supervision. *Criminal Justice and Behavior, 38,* 1127–1148. doi:10.1177/0093854811420678

Bonta, J., Rugge, T., Scott, T.-L., Bourgon, G., & Yessine, A. K. (2008). Exploring the black box of community supervision. *Journal of Offender Rehabilitation, 47,* 248–270. doi:10.1080/10509670802134085

Bourgon, G., & Gutierrez, L. (2012). The general responsivity principle in community supervision: The importance of probation officers using cognitive intervention techniques and its influence on recidivism. *Journal of Criminal Justice, 35,* 149–166.

Burnett, R., & McNeill, F. (2005). The place of the officer-offender relationship in assisting offenders to desist from crime. *Probation Journal, 52,* 221–242. doi:10.1177/0264550505055112

Carroll, L. (2004). Prison sitting, rural development, racism and justice reinvestment. *Criminology and Public Policy, 3,* 481–488. doi:10.1111/j.1745-9133.2004.tb00055.x

Clear, T. (2011). A private-sector, incentives-based model for justice reinvestment. *Criminology and Public Policy, 10,* 585–608. doi:10.1111/j.1745-9133.2011.00729.x

Clear, T. R., & Austin, J. F. (2009). Reducing mass incarceration: Implications of the iron law of prison populations. *Harvard Law and Policy Review, 3,* 307–324.

Clement, M., Schwarzfeld, M., & Thompson, M. (2011). *The national summit on justice reinvestment and public safety: addressing recidivism, crime and corrections spending.* Washington, DC: Council of State Governments.

Council of State Governments. (2010). *Justice reinvestment.* Retrieved from http://justicereinvestment.org/about

Council of State Governments. (2012). *Justice reinvestment: A data-driven approach to reduce corrections spending and reinvest savings in strategies that can decrease crime and strengthen neighborhoods.* New York, NY: Author.

Drake, E. K. (2011). *"What works" in community supervision: Interim report* (Document No. 11-12-1201). Olympia: Washington State Institute for Public Policy.

Friedmann, P. D., Green, T. C., Taxman, F. S., Harrington, M., Rhodes, A. G., Katz, E., . . . the Step'n Out Research Group of CJ-DATS. (2012). Collaborative behavioral management among parolees: Drug use, crime and re-arrest in the Step'n Out randomized trial. *Addiction, 107,* 1099–1108. doi:10.1111/j.1360-0443.2011.03769.x

Friedmann, P. D., Katz, E. C., Rhodes, A. G., Taxman, F. S., O'Connell, D., Frisman, L. K., . . . Martin, S. S. (2008). Collaborative behavioral management for drug-involved parolees: Rationale and design of the Step'n Out study. *Journal of Offender Rehabilitation, 47,* 290–318. doi:10.1080/10509670802134184

Garland, D. (2001). *The culture of control.* Chicago, IL: University of Chicago Press.

Glaze, L., & Parks, E. (2012). *Correctional populations in the United States, 2011.* Washington, DC: U.S. Department of Justice, Bureau of Justice Statistics. Retrieved from http://bjs.ojp.usdoj.gov/content/pub/pdf/cpus11.pdf

Greene, J., & Mauer, M. (2010). *Downscaling prisons: Lessons from four states.* Washington, DC: The Sentencing Project.

Hawken, A., & Kleiman, M. (2009). *Managing drug involved probationers with swift and certain sanctions: Evaluating Hawaii's HOPE.* Washington, DC: National Criminal Justice Reference Service. Retrieved from http://www.ncjrs.gov/pdffiles1/nij/grants/230444.pdf

Justice Policy Institute. (2009). *Pruning prisons: How cutting corrections can save money and protect public safety.* Washington, DC: Author.

Kleiman, M. A. R. (2011). Justice reinvestment in community supervision. *Criminology and Public Policy, 10,* 651–659. doi:10.1111/j.1745-9133.2011.00751.x

Latessa, E. J., & Smith, P. (2011). *Corrections in the community* (5th ed.). Burlington, MA: Anderson.

La Vigne, N. (2010). *Statement by Nancy G. La Vigne, PhD, Director, Justice Policy Center, the Urban Institute, at a hearing on H.R. 4080, the "Criminal Justice Reinvestment Act of 2009," and H.R. 4055, the" Opportunity Probation with Enforcement (HOPE) Initiative Act of 2009."* Retrieved from http://www.urban.org/center/jpc/justice-reinvestment/upload/NGL-Testimony.pdf

MacKenzie, D. L. (2006). *What works in corrections: Reducing the criminal activities of offenders and delinquents.* New York, NY: Cambridge University Press.

Milkman, H., & Wanberg, K. (2007). *Cognitive-behavioral treatment: A review and discussion for corrections professionals. (No. 021657).* Washington, DC: National Institute of Corrections.

Nagin, D. (1998). Criminal deterrence research at the outset of the 21st century. *Crime and Justice, 23,* 1–42.

Nagin, D. S., Cullen, F. T., & Jonson, C. L. (2009). Imprisonment and reoffending. *Crime and Justice, 38,* 115–200. doi:10.1086/599202

National Association for the Advancement of Colored People. (2011). *Misplaced priorities: Overincarcerate, undereducate.* Retrieved from http://naacp.3cdn.net/01d6f368edbe135234_bq0m68x5h.pdf

Petersilia, J., & Turner, S. (1993a). *Evaluating intensive supervision probation/parole: Results of a nationwide experiment.* Washington, DC: National Institute of Justice.

Petersilia, J., & Turner, S. (1993b). Intensive probation and parole. *Crime and Justice, 17,* 281–335.

Robinson, C. R., Lowenkamp, C. T., Holsinger, A. M., VanBenschoten, S., Alexander, M., & Oleson, J. C. (2012). A random study of Staff Training Aimed at Reducing Re-arrest (STARR): Using core correctional practices in probation interactions. *Journal of Criminal Justice, 35,* 167–188. doi:10.1080/0735648X.2012.674823

Skeem, J. L., Louden, J. E., Polaschek, D., & Camp, J. (2007). Assessing relationship quality in mandated community treatment: Blending care with control. *Psychological Assessment, 19,* 397–410. doi:10.1037/1040-3590.19.4.397

Taxman, F. S. (1996). *A blueprint for effective offender treatment services: Developing a seamless criminal justice and treatment system for Baltimore City.* College Park: University of Maryland.

Taxman, F. S. (1998). *Reducing recidivism through a seamless system of care: Components of effective treatment, supervision, and transition services in the community.* Washington, DC: Office of National Drug Control Policy, Treatment and Criminal Justice System Conference.

Taxman, F. S. (2002). Supervision: Exploring the dimensions of effectiveness. *Federal Probation, 66,* 14–27.

Taxman, F. S. (2008). No illusions: Offender and organizational change in Maryland's proactive community supervision efforts. *Criminology and Public Policy, 7,* 275–302. doi:10.1111/j.1745-9133.2008.00508.x

Taxman, F. S. (2012). Probation, intermediate sanctions, and community-based corrections. In J. Petersilia, K. R. Reitz (Eds.), *The Oxford handbook of sentencing and corrections* (pp. 363–385). New York, NY: Oxford University Press.

Taxman, F. S., & Ainsworth, S. (2009). Correctional milieu: The key to quality and outcomes. *Victims and Offenders, 4,* 334–340. doi:10.1080/15564880903227347

Taxman, F. S., & Pattavina, A. (Eds.). (2013). *Simulation strategies to reduce recidivism: Risk need responsivity (RNR) modeling in the criminal justice system.* New York, NY: Springer. doi:10.1007/978-1-4614-6188-3

Taxman, F. S., Pattavina, A., & Caudy, M. (2013). Justice reinvestment in the United States: An empirical assessment of the potential impact of increased correctional programming on recidivism. *Victims and Offenders, 9,* 50–75 doi:10.1080/15564886.2013.860934

Taxman, F. S., Perdoni, M. L., & Harrison, L. D. (2007). Drug treatment services for adult offenders: The state of the state. *Journal of Substance Abuse Treatment, 32,* 239–254. doi:10.1016/j.jsat.2006.12.019

Taxman, F. S., Shepardson, E. S., & Byrne, J. M. (2004). *Tools of the trade: A guide to implementing science into practice.* Washington, DC: National Institute of Corrections.

Tonry, M. (2011). Making peace, not a desert: Penal reform should be about values not justice reinvestment. *Criminology and Public Policy, 10,* 637–649. doi:10.1111/j.1745-9133.2011.00757.x

Tucker, S. B., & Cadora, E. (2003). *Justice reinvestment: To invest in public safety by reallocating justice dollars to refinance education, housing, healthcare, and jobs.* Retrieved from http://www.opensocietyfoundations.org/publications/ideas-open-society-justice-reinvestment

Urban Partnerships. (2012). *Justice reinvestment at the social level.* Washington, DC: Urban Institute. Retrieved from http://www.urban.org/center/jpc/justice-reinvestment

Weiss, I., & Wozner, Y. (2002). Ten models for probation supervision compared across eight dimensions. *Journal of Offender Rehabilitation, 34,* 85–105. doi:10.1300/J076v34n03_06

Whitehead, J. T. (1984). Probation mission reform: Implications for the forgotten actor—The probation officer. *Criminal Justice Review, 9,* 15–21. doi:10.1177/073401688400900103

CHAPTER 17

THE DEATH PENALTY

Craig Haney, Joanna Weill, and Mona Lynch

The death penalty occupies a unique position in social science and law. Despite the fact that it directly affects only a relatively small number of people, it is one of the most extensively studied aspects of the criminal justice system. There are several reasons for this high level of scholarly interest, including the fact of what is at stake in death penalty cases could not be more profound—literally life and death. As Supreme Court Justice Potter Stewart expressed it in the landmark *Furman v. Georgia* (1972) case: "The penalty of death differs from all other forms of criminal punishment, not in degree, but in kind. It is unique in its total irrevocability. It is unique in its rejection of rehabilitation of the convict as a basic purpose of criminal justice. And it is unique, finally, in its absolute renunciation of all that is embodied in our concept of humanity" (p. 306).

IMPORTANCE OF THE PROBLEM

Those high stakes and the extraordinary nature of the punishment help to account for the fact that death penalty cases have established many key legal precedents, establishing benchmarks for fairness and due process in the rest of the criminal justice system. In addition to their dramatic stakes and the significance of the legal precedents that they generate, capital cases often involve the highest profile, most sensationalized case facts, sometimes attracting intense public, political, and media interest and, often, the corresponding attention of legal and social science scholars. Scholarly interest also has focused

on another unique aspect of capital punishment—the special set of psychological conditions that must obtain to enable a group of average citizens to rationally authorize the death of another and the various psycho-legal mechanisms that govern this truly extraordinary decision-making process.

We have divided our review of capital punishment-related psychological research into three very broad areas. The first pertains to the overall operation of the death penalty in the United States—more specifically, what our system of capital punishment tells us about the nature of criminal culpability and so-called death eligibility, whether and how the death penalty operates as a deterrent to capital crime, and whether capital punishment is imposed in a racially discriminatory manner. The second broad area of empirical research pertains to death penalty attitudes and the role that they play in the administration of capital punishment. Because capital punishment is both controversial and democratically administered, relative levels of public support versus opposition have special legal and political significance and have been extensively studied. Third, and finally, we examine the operation of the capital jury—the site of a great deal of psychological research. We focus on what is known about the way this unique legal institution is composed and how it functions, including the effects of the special procedures that are used to select capital juries, the unique conditions that are created in capital trials that enable jurors to traverse an otherwise deep-seated moral prohibition against taking a life,

http://dx.doi.org/10.1037/14462-017
APA Handbook of Forensic Psychology: Vol. 2. Criminal Investigation, Adjudication, and Sentencing Outcomes,
B. L. Cutler and P. A. Zapf (Editors-in-Chief)
Copyright © 2015 by the American Psychological Association. All rights reserved.

and the unusual decision-making process in which, supposedly, the jury's decision to render its life and death verdict is simultaneously preserved, yet legally guided. (for a review of research on mental health assessments in capital cases, see Volume 1, Chapter 7, this handbook).

RELEVANT PSYCHOLOGICAL THEORY AND PRINCIPLES

Research on capital punishment implicates a wide range of psychological theories that are often enmeshed with important principles of constitutional law. The theories include the nature of the legal and moral concept of *culpability*, as well as whether and how the discretion of key decision makers can be regulated to ensure that judgments—in this case, judgments about whether a person is "culpable enough" to be sentenced to die—are made in a principled and constitutionally appropriate manner (see Volume 1, Chapter 4, this handbook, for a review of criminal responsibility). In addition, the death penalty raises important theoretical questions about the kinds of punishment that deter the most serious forms of criminal behavior and, in particular, whether capital punishment has a uniquely deterrent effect. Historically, the system of death sentencing in the United States also has highlighted important theoretical questions about the persistence of racial prejudice and its influence on legal decision making, specifically whether, how, and why the application of the ultimate punishment continues to occur in racially disparate ways. In addition, people's attitudes and beliefs about the death penalty—who supports a capital punishment at any given time, how strongly, and why—are long-standing topics of study and have been extensively theorized and researched in the literature on public opinion, posing a number of important conceptual questions about how attitudes about crime and punishment are formed, are interrelated, and change over time. Finally, the special behavior of the capital jury—a group of citizens that is composed in an unusual manner, subjected to a special set of legal procedures, and called upon to engage in an extraordinary decision-making process that is supposed to be guided and regulated by a set of judicial instructions—implicates a number of

psychological theories, including the phenomenon of moral disengagement, the relationship between attitudes and behavior, principles of small group behavior, and whether and how the discretion to select between life and death punishments can be reliably guided (including under conditions where instructional incomprehension and racial discrimination may be implicated).

The Overall Operation of the Death Penalty

In this section we address several psychological aspects of the overall operation of the death penalty, i.e., how it functions in the broadest possible terms, including the process of selecting the persons on whom it is imposed and with what overall societal effect. The first overall aspect involves the way in which a system of capital punishment forces a society and its legal decision makers to address a critically important preliminary or threshold issue: How should we go about identifying and selecting those persons who are eligible for or placed at risk of receiving the death penalty? Especially in a society such as ours in which the exercise of state power is restrained by a set of long-standing constitutional limits, the power to punish—here, to punish by death—cannot run afoul of the prohibition against imposing punishments that are "cruel and unusual." Several approaches to this critical issue involve psychological principles and may be empirically evaluated. A separate aspect of the system of death sentencing involves whether and how it affects the rate of capital crime, which is one of its ostensible justifications. Finally, like all systems of democratically administered punishment and social control, capital punishment is subject to the biases and preconceptions of those who implement it. In the United States, by far the greatest concern involves the racially discriminatory imposition of the death penalty and, appropriately, this is an issue on which much empirical research has been focused.

Culpability. Capital punishment raises important theoretical as well as ethical and moral questions in law and psychology about the nature of legitimate punishment, the basis on which the state is justified in taking the life of one of its citizens, and the circumstances under which a punishment comes to be regarded as so extreme that it is seen as cruel and unusual in constitutional terms. Out of recognition that "death is different"—in its extremity and finality—there is general recognition that truly extraordinary justification must be provided for imposing a death sentence. For the most part, the legal consensus in the United States is that, if capital punishment can ever be justified, it must be reserved for "the worst of the worst." Indeed, as one commentator summarized this consensus, "[l]ike the phrase 'death is different,' 'the worst of the worst' peppers death penalty literature" (Note, 2001). The "worst of the worst" principle not only recurs in the death penalty literature but also has been embraced by the United States Supreme Court, which has explicitly acknowledged that "within the category of capital crimes, the death penalty must be reserved for 'the worst of the worst'" (Justice Souter, in *Kansas v. Marsh*, 2006, p. 206).

Although identifying the way in which death, and therefore, the death penalty, is different is straightforward and perhaps obvious, precisely and meaningfully defining the category of the worst of the worst and doing so in a way that can be reliably implemented and applied by legal decision makers (including capital jurors) are much more challenging tasks. In fact, the Court concluded in the landmark *Furman v. Georgia* (1972) case that the nation's system of death sentencing had failed to accomplish these very tasks, and that the resulting pattern of arbitrary and capricious imposition of the ultimate punishment was therefore unconstitutional.

Several different conceptual and procedural approaches have taken to operationalize the concept of worst of the worst, and each has embodied a somewhat different set of psychological assumptions. The first has been to significantly narrow the class of cases or kinds of crimes for which defendants are eligible to be considered for the death penalty. In this sense, modern death penalty statutes are far more selective than their historical predecessors, and bear little relationship to laws that provided for capital punishment upon conviction for scores of even the most minor or petty offenses. In the post-*Furman* era, that narrowing process supposedly became much more refined, so that "worst of the worst" was defined in terms of the nature of the crime and the presumably heinous features it entailed.

For example, the Supreme Court prohibited the imposition of the death penalty for the crime of rape (e.g., see *Coker v. Georgia*, 1977)—something for which capital punishment had been imposed many times in the past—because a majority of Supreme Court justices concluded that the punishment was categorically disproportionate to the heinousness of the offense. In a related way, the Court held that the death penalty should be reserved only for cases in which the crime itself reflected "a consciousness materially more 'depraved' than that of any person guilty of murder" (*Godfrey v. Georgia*, 1980, p. 433) or, as the Supreme Court justices later summarized, "the culpability of the average murderer is insufficient to justify the most extreme sanction available to the State" (*Atkins v. Virginia*, 2002, p. 319).

To ensure that the death penalty would be reserved for more than just *any* murder committed by a defendant with a merely *average* level of culpability, states passed capital punishment statutes that included threshold requirements making only certain kinds of murders "death-eligible" and excluded all others from consideration as capital cases. Under other kinds of statutory schemes, the narrowing function is accomplished on the basis of a judgment made by the capital jury, whose members are called upon to decide, for example, that at least one "aggravating circumstance" has been proven that allows the defendant to be considered for the death penalty. This part of the capital trial is sometimes referred to as an eligibility phase or stage, whose logic the Court explained this way: "It is in regard to the eligibility phase that we have stressed the need for channeling and limiting the jury's discretion to ensure that the death penalty is a proportionate punishment and therefore not arbitrary or capricious in its imposition" (*Buchanan v. Angelone*, 1998, p. 275–276). In each instance, the narrowing aspects of the statute and eligibility determination are supposed to impose an "inherent restraint on the arbitrary and capricious infliction of the death sentence" (*Godfrey v. Georgia*, 1980, p. 428). Other statutory schemes that are ostensibly designed to reduce the improper exercise of discretion and the arbitrary imposition of the death penalty provide for a postsentencing *proportionality review* in which judges examine individual death verdicts and compare them to others to determine whether some internal standard of proportionate punishment has been violated in any given case.

An entirely different approach, which reflects another set of psychological assumptions, has been to exclude whole categories of persons from the death penalty on the basis of the fact that they presumably cannot, by virtue of their status characteristics, be considered the worst of the worst. To date, there exist two such categories: defendants who are intellectually disabled and those who are juveniles (under the age of 18 years at the time they committed the potentially capital crime). Thus, in *Atkins v. Virginia* (2002) the Supreme Court reversed an earlier position on whether mentally retarded defendants could be eligible for the death penalty, ruling that the cognitive and behavioral limitations of those deemed mentally retarded as well as their difficulties in controlling their impulses meant that they were by definition less culpable than others for the commission of a potentially capital crime. Similarly, in *Roper v. Simmons* (2005) the Court reversed its previous position articulated a decade and a half earlier in *Stanford v. Kentucky* (1989) and ruled that "the diminished culpability of juveniles" (p. 571) precluded them from being punished by death. Specifically, because of their immature judgment, their greater susceptibility to peer influence, and the fact that their personality development was in process and incomplete, the Court found that defendants under the age of 18 at the time they committed the crime of murder were categorically ineligible for the death penalty.

A third and final approach to defining worst of the worst in a capital punishment context involves providing the capital jurors with an instructional framework that is supposed to guide their discretion and regularize the capital decision-making process, in theory eliminating the influence of extralegal factors and ensuring that the death penalty is imposed only when it is legally proper or justified. Thus, the sentencing instructions specify factors, circumstances, or characteristics of the crime and the defendant that jurors are supposed to at least consider or take into account in reaching their life or death sentencing verdicts. The list of factors or circumstances includes ones that supposedly weigh either in favor of imposing the death penalty (aggravating circumstances) or life in prison (mitigating circumstances), and the jurors are instructed to weigh or balance the factors to choose what they believe is the most appropriate sentence. The restrictions on the amount of juror discretion exercised at this final penalty or selection stage of a capital trial, however, must be balanced against the constitutional requirement that individualized determinations be made that pertain to the specific case and specific defendant. This precludes automatic death penalty statutes that mandate death sentences in particular kinds of cases (e.g., *Woodson v. North Carolina*, 1976), and it has also led the Supreme Court to allow defendants wide latitude in the mitigating evidence that they present (e.g., *Lockett v. Ohio*, 1978; and see, more generally, Haney, 2008a). Thus, "in contrast [to the eligibility phase], in the selection phase, we have emphasized the need for a broad inquiry into all relevant mitigating evidence to allow an individualized determination" (*Buchanan v. Angelone*, 1998, p. 276).

In addition, a number of Supreme Court justices have, in a sense, "theorized" some of the psychological linkages that capital jurors should consider in making these individualized determinations, including the adverse effects that an abusive and traumatic background might have on a capital defendant's life chances and adult behavior. They have suggested further that consideration of these adverse effects might well lead a capital jury to assess the defendant's culpability differently and to decide not to sentence him or her to death. These assertions include Justice Powell's statement that "there can be no doubt that evidence of a turbulent family history, of beatings by a harsh father, and of severe emotional disturbance is particularly relevant" to jurors who are determining whether a capital defendant is culpable enough to be sentenced to death (*Eddings v. Oklahoma*, 1982, p. 115), Justice O'Connor's statement that there is a "long held" societal belief that "defendants who commit criminal acts that are attributable to a disadvantaged background, or to emotional and mental problems, may be less culpable than defendants who have no such excuse" (*California v. Brown*, 1987, p. 545), and Justice Souter's statement that "[i]t goes without saying" that evidence about an abusive background "taken as a whole, might well have influenced the jury's appraisal of [a capital defendant's] culpability" (*Rompilla v. Beard*, 2005, p. 393).

Deterrence. The alleged deterrent effect of the death penalty has long been debated. Justice Marshall wrote in *Furman v. Georgia* (1972) that "[t]he most hotly contested issue regarding capital punishment is whether it is better than life imprisonment as a deterrent to crime" (p. 345). Many researchers have sought to empirically determine whether and to what extent the death penalty deters potentially capital crimes, and whether the number of persons who receive the death penalty and are actually executed is offset (and therefore in some way justified) by the number of potential victims whose lives allegedly would be saved by virtue of future perpetrators having been deterred (Ehrlich, 1975; van den Haag, 1969).

Deterrence theory holds generally that potential lawbreakers rationally weigh the estimated costs and benefits of their actions and, accordingly, choose to engage in criminal behavior or not (Bowers & Pierce, 1980b). Theoretically, for an individual to be deterred from committing a crime, the expected punishment or cost of being caught must outweigh the profit or pleasure/benefit to be gained from committing the crime (Bailey & Peterson, 1999). This means that when penalty increases, the number of offenses should decrease, and when penalty decreases, the number of offenses should increase (Archer, Gartner, & Beittel, 1983).

Hjalmarsson (2009) proposed that three conditions must be met for the death penalty to have a deterrent effect: First, there must be a large enough probability that execution will actually occur; second, execution must be considered more severe than life in prison; and third, the person who is to be deterred must be aware of the probability of execution. Hjalmarsson's final criterion is in many ways at the crux of the deterrence debate. While deterrence assumes that people calculate the costs and benefits of committing a crime, many researchers claim that criminal acts, like murder, are, by their nature and their context, not rational. Most crimes of this nature are unplanned or impulsive (Archer et al.,

1983), and they are often driven by emotion or occur when persons are under the influence of drugs or alcohol (Lempert, 1981). In addition, Cochran, Chamlin, and Seth (1994) claim that it is simply impossible for laypeople to conduct an accurate cost–benefit analysis of the possible consequences of their crimes. In *Furman v. Georgia* (1972), which temporarily abolished the death penalty, Justice Brennan acknowledged the problematic nature of deterrence. He noted that the deterrence argument "can apply only to those who think rationally about the commission of capital crimes" (p. 302). Because it assumes rationality, many researchers have argued that deterrence theory is, at its core, illogical.

Racially discriminatory imposition. Capital punishment in the United States has been plagued by racial discrimination since its inception (see Volume 1, Chapter 15, this handbook, for a review of race and the justice system). Before the Civil War, punishments in many states differed based on the race of the defendant. For example, in pre-Civil War West Virginia, 70 crimes were punishable by death for Black defendants while only one was punishable by death for White defendants (Kennedy, 1997). Some of these punishments also differed based on race of the victim of the crime. An 1816 Georgia law required a death sentence if a Black defendant was found guilty of rape or attempted rape of a White victim (Bowers & Pierce, 1980a). The same punishment was not stipulated when there was a Black victim or when the perpetrator was White.

Although many of these explicitly racist death penalty laws were ended in the aftermath of the Civil War, Blacks still suffered starkly discriminatory treatment in the criminal justice system in general and with the death penalty in particular (Bowers & Pierce, 1980a). This included the practice of lynching, in which predominantly White citizens engaged in vigilante justice by executing alleged Black criminals, often as law enforcement and legal authorities stood by (Banner, 2002; Skolnick & Fyfe, 1993).

Although overt racial discrimination has decreased and official or *de jure* racism has been eliminated in more modern times, subtle forms of racial discrimination and race-based decision making persist (Dovidio & Gaertner, 1986), including in the legal and criminal justice systems. This line of research suggests that contemporary discriminatory behavior is more likely when it can be rationalized as race-neutral and in situations involving unclear norms about an appropriate course of action (Dovidio, Pearson, Gaertner, & Hodson, 2008). Indeed, there is a large body of research that suggests that implicit forms of racial bias are relatively widespread, while explicit forms are on the wane. Implicit stereotype biases have been demonstrated to affect perceptions and behavior in ways that are less overt than old-fashioned prejudice, rendering them difficult to recognize and contain (see Lynch & Haney, 2011, for a review).

When the death penalty was temporarily ended in the United States in 1972, the *Furman* Court focused on the arbitrary and "freakish" way in which the death penalty was imposed. Although some justices had concerns about its racially discriminatory imposition, the issue was not determining factor in the Court's decision In the years following *Furman*, a number of states developed new death penalty statutes that provided for guided discretion in the jury's penalty phase decision making. Those statutes that structured the jury's decision-making process by giving them factors or issues to consider in deciding whether a capital defendant should live or die were approved in *Gregg v. Georgia* (1976). In theory, at least, those statutes should have resulted in a reduction in both arbitrary and discriminatory death sentencing, but there is extensive scientific evidence demonstrating that both persist (e.g., Baldus, Woodworth, & Pulaski, 1990). The discriminatory imposition of the death penalty was challenged directly in *McCleskey v. Kemp* (1987), where the Court imposed a very high standard of proof on claims of discriminatory imposition and found that even stark aggregate or systemic patterns of apparent race-based decision making were not enough to render Georgia's death penalty unconstitutional.

Research nonetheless continues to reveal racial disparities in the system of capital punishment, such that murder cases involving White victims are especially likely to be pursued as capital cases and end in death, especially when the defendant is Black. If there were no arbitrariness or discrimination, one would expect similar treatment in similar cases, without regard to defendant or victim race (Bowers, 1983). That these racial characteristics continue to influence charging and sentencing decisions in potentially capital cases implicates both implicit (if not explicit) individual biases as well as institutionalized biases. These patterns have been explained, in part at least, as a function of differential empathy, in that those making judgments are better able to identify with the loss suffered by victims who are similar to them, whereas they are likely to experience an empathic divide that separates them from capital defendants, particularly minority defendants, whose life experiences are starkly different (Haney, 2004).

Attitudes About Capital Punishment

Capital punishment generates a great deal of public debate and controversy. As social psychologists Vidmar & Ellsworth (1974) once noted, "[t]o some extent public opinion has always played a part in modern controversy about the death penalty" (p. 1246). In the United States, average citizens vote for politicians to reject or retain capital punishment and, in perhaps the most democratic of all criminal justice institutions, they sit on criminal juries that, in capital cases, decide not only whether a capital defendant is guilty of a crime for which the death penalty is possible but also determine whether, in fact, he should receive it. Until *Ring v. Arizona* (2002) was decided, a small number of states—Arizona and Colorado, for example—used judge sentencing in capital cases. *Ring* required that juries make the key factual determinations that are the basis for any death sentence, which means that literally every death sentence in the United States now must be handed down by a capital jury. Because the American system of death sentencing is democratically administered in all of these ways, what citizens think about capital punishment (i.e., who supports and opposes it, how strongly, and why) matters a great deal. Attitudes about capital punishment therefore hold special legal and political as well as psychological significance.

Indeed, death penalty attitudes have played a major role in political decisions about capital punishment, helping to shape positions taken by many political candidates and elected officials, having an impact on key legislation that has been enacted into law, and indirectly influencing other political policymaking. For example, writing at a time when death penalty support was at an all-time high, Zeisel and Gallup (1989) observed, "[i]n any legislative debate on the death penalty, one is bound to hear that the great majority of the voters want it" (p. 287). Public opinion about the death penalty has directly affected capital jurisprudence as well. In various Eighth Amendment cases over whether and when the death penalty constitutes cruel and unusual punishment, the United States Supreme Court has made explicit reference to public opinion and has used it as one index of whether the death penalty offends what has been termed *evolving standards of decency*.

The evolution of the legal doctrine connecting death penalty attitudes to the constitutionality of capital punishment began with *Trop v. Dulles* (1958), when the Supreme Court ruled that the prohibition against cruel and unusual punishment "must draw its meaning from the evolving standards of decency that mark the progress of a maturing society" (p. 101). As one commentator suggested, although *Trop* was not a capital case, the logic of the opinion "required the Court to assess punishments with society's changing attitudes," something that, in turn, "called into question, among other things, psychological effects of capital punishment, public opinion, the morality of the death penalty, and its possible deterrence against commission of other heinous crimes" (Bigel, 1991, p. 738).

The Court focused explicitly on attitudes toward capital punishment a decade later when, in *Witherspoon v. Illinois* (1968), it described citizens who supported the death penalty as "a distinct and dwindling minority," and cited public opinion poll data for the proposition that "in a nation less than half of whose people believe in the death penalty, a jury composed exclusively of [death penalty supporters] cannot speak for the community" (p. 520). Public opinion was discussed at some length in five of the nine separate opinions written in *Furman v.*

Georgia (1972). This included Justice Brennan's assertion that capital punishment "must not be unacceptable to contemporary society" (p. 277), Chief Justice Burger's view that the courts should not intervene to end capital punishment because he felt it was the legislature that "responds to public opinion and immediately reflects the society's standards of decency" whenever a particular punishment becomes "basically offensive to the people" (p. 383), and Justice Blackmun's willingness to endorse the proposition that the operative definition of whether the death penalty was cruel and unusual "may acquire meaning as public opinion becomes enlightened by a humane justice" (p. 409) as well as his corresponding concern over "the suddenness of the Court's perception of progress in the human attitude" (p. 410). Although Justice Powell wrote that he found public opinion polls to be "of little probative relevance" (p. 441), he used them to buttress his argument about the existence of widely divided public views about the death penalty, suggesting that "however one may assess the amorphous ebb and flow of public opinion generally on this volatile issue, this type of inquiry lies at the periphery—not the core—of the judicial process in constitutional cases. The assessment of public opinion is essentially a legislative, not a judicial, function" (p. 443). Powell also asserted that "the first indicator of the public's attitude" in a democratic society "must always be found in the legislative judgments of the people's elected representatives" (pp. 436–437) and that an "even more direct source of information reflecting the public's attitude toward capital punishment" (pp. 439–440) existed in the form of the behavior of the capital juries and their willingness to return death verdicts.

Whether at the core or periphery of the judicial process in constitutional cases, or something that is better assessed by legislatures or, notwithstanding the skepticism of various justices, more accurately and reliably measured by scientific opinion polls, the amorphous ebb and flow of people's attitudes toward capital punishment continues to be a significant consideration in our nation's system of death sentencing. Some of the many theoretical and conceptual issues that are implicated in the study of death penalty-related attitudes are discussed below.

Death penalty attitude structure and change. First, public opinion about the death penalty raises questions about the nature of attitude formation and change, particularly in the emotionally charged and politically volatile arena of crime and punishment policy. As noted above, the death penalty in particular has been an especially polarizing topic in American society, dividing many citizens along religious lines as well as serving as the focal point in political debates over crime control. The fact that death penalty attitudes are so legally and politically significant has also meant that they have been carefully studied over time, revealing a historical pattern of change and fluctuation (rather than a consistent evolution). This pattern, in turn, has raised questions both about the underlying structure and stability of death penalty attitudes as well as the methodology used to measure them.

Public support for the death penalty tends to be presented in the media, in public discussions, and political debates as unidimensional (i.e., people are typically depicted as either favoring or supporting the death penalty or as opposing it). The fact that the public's beliefs about the death penalty have most often been measured with a single question also raises the distinct possibility that these beliefs are represented as more unequivocal and indiscriminate than, in fact, they are (cf. Ellsworth & Ross, 1983; Fox, Radelet, & Bonsteel, 1991; Murray, 2003; O'Neil, Patry, & Penrod, 2004). As one public opinion poll expert put it: "Categorizing people as favoring or opposing the death penalty does not take into account the vast heterogeneity of views underlying this simple dichotomy" (Harris, 1986, p. 433).

In addition, surveys rarely collect data that address the strength of respondents' support for the death penalty, or whether that support is based on misunderstanding or misinformation about how the system of capital punishment actually operates. In fact, it was not until 1985 that the Gallup polling organization, which first conducted a national survey that asked a death penalty question as far back as 1936, included a measure of general attitude strength (*very strongly* or *not very strongly*), as well as a few additional questions about the reasons for respondents' death penalty support or opposition, belief in deterrence, and whether their support or

opposition would vary in response to information about deterrence and the alternative sentence of life without parole (Zeisel & Gallup, 1989). Similarly, few studies of death penalty attitudes examine the circumstances under which generalized public support translates into a preference to actually impose the death penalty in particular cases or categories of cases.

The bases and sources of death penalty opinion. The formation and underlying bases for people's death penalty attitudes have been explained by reference to individual-level, social-contextual, historical, and media variables. Thus, some scholars and researchers have suggested that the views that people hold about capital punishment are an extension of other personal characteristics, such as particular personality traits, and belief systems to which they ascribe, such as their broader political orientation, personal prejudices (especially racial prejudice), and certain religious beliefs (e.g., Barkan & Cohn, 1994; Dovidio, Smith, Donnella, & Gaertner, 1997; Harvey, 1986; Miller & Hayward, 2008), as well as specific demographic characteristics such as gender and race (Cochran & Chamlin, 2006; Cochran & Sanders, 2009).

Other scholars have suggested that there are immediate social contextual variables at work in the creation and maintenance of death penalty attitudes, such as the perceived threat of criminal victimization (including actual crime rates, publicity about crime, and neighborhood characteristics that citizens believe are associated with crime). For example, Thomas and Foster (1975) theorized that the public's perception of increasing crime rates should translate directly into support for punitive criminal justice sanctions, including the death penalty: "Under such circumstances, it is quite logical to suppose that the more the public comes to fear victimization, the more it will demand what it believes will be an effective deterrent" (p. 645). Some researchers have hypothesized that certain social contextual variables, such as living in areas with high homicide rates, might be indirectly associated with death penalty support, especially when combined with a conservative political climate (likely to channel fear of crime into punitive responses), a relatively large minority population, and high levels of income inequality (Baumer, Messner, & Rosenfeld, 2003).

In addition, historical forces, traditions, and legacies may shape and condition the death penalty views of individuals (e.g., Banner, 2002), as well as help create lasting cultural or subcultural pockets of support in certain regions of the country (e.g., Borg, 1997; McFeely, 2000; Poveda, 2006). Thus, some scholars have suggested that death penalty support and opposition in some areas of the country might be explained by exposure to and socialization into traditions of vigilantism, ones in which the death penalty is perceived not only as a legitimate action for the state to take, but also one that individual aggrieved citizens could properly participate in and support, as in the case of Southern lynchings (e.g., Brundage, 1993; Zimring, 2003). Obviously, this is an historical legacy that would be expected to create diametrically opposed reactions as a function of race, helping explain support among Whites from the regions in which these outrageous practices were once normalized, and opposition among Blacks whose ancestors were their tragic victims.

In modern society, the mass media wield much influence over whether and how people react to crime, what they understand to be the nature of the "crime problem" in their community, and what particular conclusions they draw about how that problem can best be solved. The process by which the media highlight certain issues around which there is heightened public awareness, debate, and concern has been described as its agenda-setting function and has spawned a substantial amount of academic writing and empirical research (e.g., McCombs & Shaw, 1972; Protess & McCombs, 1991; for a review of research on media and the law, see Volume 1, Chapter 17, this handbook).

The tendency of the media to sensationalize crime news and crime drama and to demonize its perpetrators has been identified as one source of the public's emotional reaction to crime that helped fuel the punitive trends in crime policy that have been pursued over the last several decades, including the increased use of the death penalty (e.g., Beckett, 1997). As one researcher described the phenomenon

during the height of the "tough on crime" era, terrorists and domestic criminals alike were depicted as "isolated from their historical and social context, denied legitimacy of conditions or cause, and portrayed as unpredictable and irrational, if not insane" so that they came to "symbolize a menace that rational and humane means cannot reach or control," (Gerbner, 1992, p. 96). Television drama, at least, "rarely invited the viewer to look for problems within himself. Problems came from the evil of other people, and were solved . . . by confining or killing them" (Barnouw, 1975, p. 214).

Crime news coverage and crime-related drama may have especially powerful effects on the public. As researchers have noted, "[b]ecause most people do not have direct experience with the serious violent crimes that they most fear, the role of the media in generating such fear becomes particularly important" (Cook & Skogan, 1991, pp. 205–206). Because there are so few other sources of information to which the public can turn in attempting to make informed death penalty–related decisions, it is reasonable to think that collective immersion in mass media–based images and storylines leads many persons to develop distorted but influential views of violent crime and criminal defendants. These views, in turn, are likely to affect how subsequently obtained information is processed, including information that is presented as supporting evidence for crime-and-punishment–related political positions and even evidence that is introduced as the basis for capital jury verdicts.

Indeed, some have speculated that media messages about crime are so ubiquitous, consistent, and problematic that many citizens have internalized a form of *media criminology* that systematically miseducates them about the nature of criminality (Haney, 2008b). Precisely because "the public's role in actual capital case decision making is truly unparalleled," the "flawed criminological curriculum and overall media miseducation" may play a role in the administration of the death penalty (Haney, 2008b, p. 691).

The Marshall hypothesis. Justice Thurgood Marshall's concurring opinion in *Furman v. Georgia* (1972) focused very directly on potentially flawed or misinformed public opinion about the death penalty, and did so in a way that spawned a great deal of empirical research. Justice Marshall argued that public opinion about the death penalty was critically important, asserting that even a punishment that served a valid legislative purpose and was otherwise not excessive could still violate the Eighth Amendment if "popular sentiment abhors it" (p. 332). Marshall concluded in *Furman* that the death penalty did in fact violate the Eighth Amendment on precisely these grounds because it had become "morally unacceptable to the people of the United States at this time in their history" (p. 360). He argued, however, that this conclusion about "moral unacceptability" was based on the "opinion of an informed citizenry" (rather than on popular opinion in general). Specifically, he suggested that "whether or not a punishment is cruel and unusual depends, not on whether its mere mention 'shocks the conscience and sense of justice of the people,' but on whether people who were *fully informed* [emphasis added] as to the purposes of the penalty and its liabilities would find the penalty shocking, unjust, and unacceptable" (p. 361).

Marshall argued that if the general public were accurately informed about the workings of the death penalty and were made aware of the evidence concerning its discriminatory imposition and ineffectiveness as a deterrent to murder, then "the great mass of citizens" would conclude it was "immoral" (p. 363). In Marshall's view, because no public opinion poll to date had been able to fully inform its respondents about the actual operation and effects of the death penalty, the results of such polls could not really address the issues in the way that he had posed them. He also suggested that, among the rationales that people had for supporting capital punishment, retribution was nonutilitarian in nature and, therefore, relatively impervious to new or more accurate information. The notion—seemingly a distinctly minority view at the time of *Furman*—that the death penalty should be imposed simply because certain people deserved to be executed, no matter the cost or consequence, was based on a belief that seemed difficult to change, at least with data alone.

Many social scientists have attempted to evaluate the several separate components of what has come to be called *the Marshall hypothesis*. Thus, they have examined whether persons who were better informed about capital punishment were more likely to reject it, whether providing people with more accurate information about the overall system of death sentencing in the United States made them less willing to support it, and whether the retributive rationale for supporting the death penalty was largely impervious to information-based change.

The Nature and Functioning of the Capital Jury

Capital juries, whose members hear evidence in a criminal trial in which the death penalty is a possible outcome, are an unusual and much studied institution in the American legal system. Because they are empowered to render a sentencing verdict that can result in taking the life of a fellow citizen—a unique and daunting power—they are selected in a manner unlike all other juries, and they proceed in response to procedures and instructions that differ from those used in other kinds of cases (for a review of research on jury research in general, see Chapter 8, this volume).

Moral disengagement. Viewed from one perspective, the death penalty represents an apparent inconsistency or contradiction. As Justice Brennan observed, "[f]rom the beginning of our Nation, the punishment of death has stirred acute public controversy . . . . The country has debated whether a society for which the dignity of the individual is the supreme value can, without a fundamental inconsistency, follow the practice of deliberately putting some of its members to death" (*Furman v. Georgia*, 1972, p. 296). This tension between the value modern society places on life on the one hand, and the practice of authorizing and implementing the execution of its citizens on the other, must be resolved if ordinary people are to be regularly called upon to violate the powerful societal prohibition against killing by taking steps that are designed to lead to the death of another. Some scholars have suggested that this tension requires "mechanisms of moral disengagement" (Bandura, 1990, 2002; Bandura,

Barbaranelli, Caprara, & Pastorelli, 1996; Castano, 2011) to be used to systematically distance or disengage citizens, voters, and especially capital jurors from the nature and moral implications of the death sentencing process (Haney, 1997b). In a related way, Cobb (1989) has observed that the "bureaucratization" of capital punishment can seemingly exempt individual decision makers from ever having to confront the personal question of whether and how to extend mercy to capital defendants by "afford[ing] everyone involved in capital sentencing the illusion that no one has decided that any given individual should die; in doing so, it poses the question whether we want a 'headless and soulless' institution sending people to their deaths" (p. 404).

The mechanisms by which this moral distancing is accomplished might include invoking or asserting an apparent moral justification for the actions in question (e.g., the belief that the death penalty, and only the death penalty, is called for), encouraging the dehumanization of the target of the action in question and emphasizing his defects and deficiencies (in this case, the defendant on whom the death sentence would be imposed), desensitizing jurors to the negative consequences of their actions or encouraging them to disregard or distort those consequences (by refusing to fully acknowledge that they will result in the death of another), and diffusing responsibility (e.g., seeing oneself as merely following the law rather than making a personal, moral choice).

Jury selection and death qualification. Although criminal juries in the United States are composed of average citizens, they are selected through a process of *voir dire* in which attorneys and judges question potential jurors. There are a limited number of peremptory challenges that attorneys may use to exclude persons at their discretion. In addition, those persons who hold disqualifying attitudes may be legally eliminated from participation "for cause." For the most part, those disqualifying attitudes are limited to views or points of view commonly understood as bias, perspectives that would prejudice or compromise potential jurors' ability to fairly and impartially judge the facts or the law. The latter kind of bias—bias toward the law—includes an expressed unwillingness to

ascribe to and apply basic legal tenets, such as the presumption of innocence. In practice, the effectiveness of the process may be limited by the fact that many of the persons who harbor the greatest bias and deepest prejudice believe their views to be normative or commonsensical. Other prospective jurors may be aware that they hold problematic counter-normative views, but they are reluctant to express them in open court (e.g., Suggs & Sales, 1981). Finally, people are often unaware of whether and how their beliefs actually shape and affect their judgments, decisions, and behavior (e.g., Nisbett & Wilson, 1977).

In death penalty cases, the *voir dire* process is modified in an unusual way that appears to have important psychological implications for the way in which the resulting juries are composed and function. The special screening process that is used in capital cases is called *death qualification*; it is controversial and has been carefully studied (e.g., Haney, 1984a, 1984d). The perceived need for death qualification is based in part on the fact that jurors in capital cases may be called upon to perform a sentencing function (as well as to decide guilt or innocence), and because moral and religious opposition to the death penalty in the United States has existed on a substantial and organized basis since colonial times. Thus, courts have chosen to qualify all prospective capital jurors by excluding by law those whose attitudes towards the death penalty deem them unfit.

A series of United States Supreme Court cases—*Witherspoon v. Illinois* (1968), *Wainright v. Witt* (1985), *Lockhart v. McCree* (1986), and *Morgan v. Illinois* (1992)—established the constitutional standards that govern this practice. Constitutional law permits the exclusion of persons who are very strongly opposed to the death penalty (i.e., who could never vote to impose it or whose opposition would prevent or substantially impair their ability to function as jurors) as well as also those who are very strongly in favor (i.e., who would always vote to impose it when given the option or whose support would prevent or substantially impair their ability to function as jurors). However, in actual practice there are many more people excluded on the basis of their opposition

461

than support (e.g., Kadane, 1984). The group of death-qualified jurors that remains typically contains few if any death penalty opponents.

The psychological implications of this practice extend beyond the obvious fact that such a group will be composed of persons who are much more inclined to render death than life sentences. This is because death penalty attitudes are correlated with demographic characteristics, measures of racial bias, and a number of other attitudes about criminal justice and social issues. As a consequence, systematically eliminating people on the basis of their beliefs about capital punishment necessarily alters the demographic mix of potential jurors and changes the distribution of the criminal justice attitudes that are represented in the remaining jury pool. This narrowing of the demographic and attitudes range of persons available to be selected may bias the kinds of juries that are seated in capital cases and render them less fair, at least in comparison to the kinds of juries that sit in every other kind of criminal case (i.e., juries from which these distinct groups of people have not been excluded). In addition, the nature of the process by which death qualification is implemented may have its own biasing effects on potential jurors. The unique form of questioning that involves sometimes lengthy discussions with prospective jurors about punishment—indeed, their capacity to impose the death penalty in the case—well in advance of them having heard any evidence or reached any verdict may shape and influence the way they think about the case and their expectations about the likely outcome (Haney, 1984b, 1984c).

The United States Supreme Court did consider a direct constitutional challenge to death qualification that was premised on the psychological data that addressed these conceptual issues. In *Lockhart v. McCree* (1986), the Court decisively rejected the claim that death qualification compromised the fair trial rights of capital defendants. Essentially applying a standard that seemed impossible for any researcher to ever realistically meet—namely, that controlled studies use "actual jurors sworn under oath to apply the law to the facts of an actual case involving the fate of an actual capital defendant" (*Lockhart v. McCree*, 1986, p. 172)—Justice

Rehnquist's majority opinion questioned the validity of all of the data that had been adduced on the effects of death qualification. In addition, Rehnquist's opinion took the further step of ruling that, even if scientifically valid, such research would not be considered to be dispositive of the constitutional issue at hand. This was because juries biased in the ways that death-qualified juries appeared to be could have arisen by chance. In other words, "it is hard for us to understand the logic of the argument that a given jury is unconstitutionally partial when it results from a State-ordained process, yet impartial when exactly the same jury results from mere chance" (*Lockhart v. McCree*, 1986, p. 178). Thus the practice of death qualification continues to operate in virtually every capital case tried in the United States despite all of the attendant biasing effects, which we discuss in the research review portion of this chapter.

Instructional comprehension. We noted earlier that one of the ways in which constitutional concerns over the arbitrary and capricious imposition of the death penalty are addressed is by providing capital juries with a set of specially tailored judicial instructions that are intended to guide the discretion of the capital juries in rendering their penalty phase verdicts. These instructions have taken one of several forms, but in each instance they ostensibly provide jurors with a set of factors, issues, or questions that the jurors are instructed to think about, consider, and take into account when they deliberate and decide what penalty to impose.

A number of theoretical or conceptual questions have been raised that address whether and how these instructions are actually comprehended and applied by jurors, and whether they really do reduce the vast degree of discretion exercised by capital juries that was identified as unconstitutional in *Furman v. Georgia* (1972). Scholars have reasoned that instructions must be comprehended before they can function to affect behavior (Cho, 1994; Diamond, 1993; Haney & Lynch, 1994). A body of research conducted by psychologists and linguists on jury institutions more generally (e.g., Buchanan, Pryor, Taylor, & Strawn, 1978; Charrow & Charrow, 1979; Elwork, Sales, & Alfini, 1982; Lieberman & Sales, 1997) has provided some clues as to why capital penalty instructions have proven so difficult for laypersons to understand and apply. As detailed later in this chapter, there is also a robust body of research assessing the nature and consequences of these linguistic difficulties for capital jury decision making. Some of the key problems include the vocabulary used in standard instructions, which is often legalistic and unfamiliar to laypersons. The sentence structure of the instructions is also problematic, frequently riddled with double negatives, passive phrasing, and convoluted organization (Charrow & Charrow, 1979). Additionally, the mode and timing of delivery adds to comprehension problems, in that they are typically read out loud by a judge and delivered after all of the evidence in the case has been presented. As a consequence, jurors are not aware of the law that frames their decision until after they have heard disjointed and sometimes lengthy presentations of evidence (V. Smith, 1991).

Jury dynamics. In addition to the unique challenges posed by capital jury selection and the distinct difficulties that attend to penalty phase instructions, a number of important social sciences questions revolve around the unique dynamics of the capital jury as a decision-making body (e.g., Bowers, 1995; Haney, 1984b; Haney & Weiner, 2004). The interaction of the factors and forces that drive capital jury composition and its operational parameters—the joint effects of death qualification, intergroup (especially racial) relations and dynamics, instructional comprehension, and decision-making processes and rules—has led to a significant amount of empirical research in which these cross cutting theories and concepts are explored (e.g., Connell, 2009; Haney, 2005; Lynch, 2009). Psychological research on the behavior of the capital jury has begun to evolve from examinations of intrapersonal cognitive processes (i.e., how individuals perceive, make sense of, and judge case factors as a function of their preexisting dispositions and characteristics, cognitive capacities, and affective responses) to the group-level processes that influence penalty phase decision making. This includes the persuasive techniques that influence jury deliberations, whether and how the racial and gendered dynamics of the

jury unit affect the verdicts that are rendered and how they are arrived at, and the role of cognition and emotion in the decision-making process. As we will highlight in the research sections, insights about these phenomena are derived from interview-based studies of former capital juries as well as experimental studies that include small group deliberations and decision making.

RESEARCH REVIEW

As we have tried to show, the death penalty system implicates a number of theoretical propositions and conceptual assumptions, many of which derive as much or more from legal principles and standards as they do from psychological theory. Death sentencing is subject to a complex set of special processes and procedures that raise a number of empirically testable questions about culpability, deterrence, and discrimination, about the relationship between public opinion and legal practice and policy, and about the unique role of the jury in deciding whether someone lives or dies. An extensive amount of research has been conducted on these interrelated theoretical, conceptual, and practical issues and problems.

The Overall Operation of the Death Penalty

Culpability. Empirical research has provided decidedly mixed support for the ability of various approaches to operationalize the worst of the worst, narrowing criteria to do what they are supposed to do in order to maintain a constitutional death penalty process. The different methods of narrowing the categories of cases and defendants that are eligible to receive the death penalty have achieved decidedly different results. Categorical exclusions by offense types (such as exclusion for the crime of rape) accomplish what they set out to do—reduce the number and range of cases and defendants who can be considered for capital punishment—when they are clearly defined and not subject to interpretation.

In the case of the Supreme Court's categorical exclusions from death eligibility based on the reduced culpability of classes of defendants, the criteria for exemption may or may not be as straightforward. In the case of the exemption of juveniles, the *Roper* Court articulated a clear delineating line for determination—whether the offense in question happened before the defendant's eighteenth birthday. The Court made three psychologically based empirical assertions on which it premised its decision about the reduced culpability of juveniles. The Court asserted that juveniles' "lack of maturity" and "underdeveloped sense of responsibility" were more likely to "result in impetuous and ill-considered actions and decisions" (*Roper v. Simmons*, 2005, p. 569); that they were more "vulnerable and susceptible to negative influences and outside pressures" (p. 569), including pressures from peers, and simultaneously less able "to escape negative influences in their whole environment" (p. 570); and that their characters were "not as well formed" as those of adults and that, therefore, there was a greater likelihood their "character deficiencies will be reformed" (p. 570). Although the Court did not explicitly cite it, there is an extensive body of psychological research to support these propositions.

Psychologists Thomas Grisso, Elizabeth Scott, Laurence Steinberg, and their colleagues have both conducted an extensive amount of this primary research themselves and also provided integrative summaries of the larger literature on juvenile culpability (e.g., Scott & Steinberg, 2003; Steinberg & Scott, 2003; see Volume 1, Chapter 12, this handbook). For example, Scott and Grisso (1997) have identified a number of the ways in which adolescent decision-making processes vary from those of adults, Scott, Reppucci, and Woolard (1995) have underscored the tendency of juveniles to conform and comply with peers, and Scott (2000) has explained the well-known tendency for delinquent and criminal behavior to decrease as juveniles move into young adulthood "as a predictable part of the maturation process" (p. 291).

In the case of the intellectually disabled, while the exclusion was explicitly premised on psychological grounds, the *Atkins* Court largely eluded the question of how exactly to determine who belongs in the category of those who are exempt. Thus, the Court decided that, "[b]ecause of their impairments," mentally retarded defendants had

"diminished capacities to understand and process information, to communicate, to abstract from mistakes and learn from experience, to engage in logical reasoning, to control impulses, and to understand the reactions of others" (*Atkins v. Virginia*, 2002, p. 318). These deficiencies, the Court said, did not exempt them from punishment, but did diminish their personal culpability to such a degree that they should not be punished by death (see Volume 1, Chapter 4, this handbook, for a review of research on criminal responsibility, and Volume 1, Chapter 5, this handbook for a review of research on criminal competence).

The Court cited psychological and legal literature that addressed the ways in which intellectual disability compromised defendants' ability to cognitively process information and thereby undermined their capacity for self-regulation, decision making, and moral reasoning (e.g., Ellis & Luckasson, 1990; McGee & Menolascino, 1992; Whitman, 1990). The Court also relied on research that addressed the ways in which intellectual disability undermined a person's cognitive capacity to comprehend basic legal concepts, led to heightened suggestibility, and increased vulnerability to external pressure (e.g., Everington & Fulero, 1999; Levy-Shiff, Kedem, & Sevillia, 1990), as well as the special challenges mentally retarded defendants faced in communicating with others and assisting in their own defense in a criminal proceeding (e.g., Appelbaum & Appelbaum, 1994). All of these things, the Court said, collectively "make these defendants less morally culpable" (*Atkins v. Virginia*, 2002, p. 320).

While the Court was clear on its reasoning for the exemption of the mentally disabled, it provided neither substantive criteria to determine who fits into the category of those exempted, nor any directive as to how the exemption should be determined as a procedural matter. Consequently, states have individually determined their own standards and procedures, resulting in a significant number of substantially cognitively disabled persons who have nonetheless been sentenced to death and face execution (Blume, Johnson, & Seeds, 2009).

Approaches to operationalizing the worst of the worst cases—what the Court has called the "constitutionally necessary narrowing function" (*Pulley v.*

Harris, 1984, p. 50)—by identifying a list of factors or features that render them eligible for the ultimate punishment have proven even less successful. For one, there is really no theoretical underpinning to structure the nature of the narrowing process. In addition, and perhaps because of this, the narrowing principles are difficult to formulate and implement in ways that achieve their ostensible goal. Indeed, the year before *Furman* was decided, Justice Harlan famously opined in *McGautha v. California* (1971) that

> [t]hose who have come to grips with the hard task of actually attempting to draft means of channeling capital sentencing discretion have confirmed the lesson taught by [history] . . . . To identify before the fact those characteristics of criminal homicides and their perpetrators which call for the death penalty, and to express these characteristics in language which can be fairly understood and applied by the sentencing authority, appear to be tasks which are beyond present human ability. (p. 214)

In the face of this seemingly impossible task, and not ready to declare the death penalty unconstitutional, Harlan was willing to continue "committing to the untrammeled discretion of the jury the power to pronounce life or death in capital cases" (*McGautha v. California*, 1971, p. 207), apparently no matter the patterns of arbitrariness and capriciousness that the exercise of such discretion was producing.

The Court reversed itself just a year later, of course, declaring the nation's system of death sentencing unconstitutional in *Furman*, but the justices seemed to ignore Harlan's warning about the difficulty of the task of channeling capital sentencing discretion when it decided *Gregg v. Georgia* (1976) and many subsequent death penalty cases, ones in which the Court repeatedly authorized states to address the arbitrary and capricious imposition of the death penalty by passing statutes that, in Harlan's words, attempted to "identify before the fact those characteristics of criminal homicides and their perpetrators which call for the death penalty"

(*McGautha v. California*, 1971, p. 214) Research seems to have confirmed Harlan's earlier skepticism, if not his preferred solution.

Empirical studies of the actual operation of the statutes that attempt to narrow application of the death penalty to only those cases in which it is at least potentially deserved have found them ill-suited to the task. Research shows that very little narrowing actually takes place, so that only a minute proportion of first-degree murders in some jurisdictions are not death-eligible (e.g. Shatz & Rivkind, 1997); extralegal variables such as race, gender, and geography continue to significantly influence the process of death sentencing, so that the penalty is still inequitably imposed (e.g., Hindson, Potter, & Radelet, 2006); and, in the final analysis, the schemes that are in operation in numerous states fail to effectively narrow the class of death-eligible murders (and, therefore, death-eligible defendants) from all others, so that "there is no meaningful way to distinguish who is eligible for the penalty and the very few who receive it" (Marceau, Kamin, & Foglia, 2013, p. 1074).

The California death sentencing statute is a useful, illustrative example. For a narrowing statute to operate properly in this context, it is supposed to reduce the larger group of persons found guilty of murder to a much smaller group composed of only those likely to be judged the worst of the worst who are supposedly deserving of the death penalty. This means that, once the narrowing has occurred, there should be a fairly high percentage of persons in the remaining group—those who are now eligible to receive the death penalty—who actually do deserve the death penalty (because, by definition, they have been selected by the statute as likely candidates). In *Furman*, for example, the Supreme Court was troubled by the fact that only 15%–20% of defendants who were eligible for the death penalty actually received it, because this suggested that the group at risk of being executed included large numbers of people who should not have been considered among the worst of the worst at all. The Court thought that the failure to narrow the eligible group had helped unleash the unbridled discretion of the jury that rendered the death sentencing process unconstitutional.

465

The California statute attempted to accomplish the necessary post–*Furman* narrowing by requiring that any one of a list of special circumstances must be found true before a capitally charged defendant could be eligible for a death sentence. There is, however, such a large number of these special circumstances written into the statute—including all forms of felony murder—that more than 30 "distinct categories of first-degree murderers" are actually eligible for the death penalty (Shatz & Rivkind, 1997, p. 1318). Beyond the sheer number of categories, the breadth of the cases that they include (especially the fact that any kind of felony murder qualifies and that another special circumstance—lying in wait—is interpreted so broadly that almost every premeditated murder is arguably covered) means that very few—according to Shatz and Rivkind's (1997) empirical analysis, no more than about 1 in 8—first-degree murders in California are noncapital. Thus, a large number of defendants have been placed at risk of receiving the death penalty who presumably should not be. Shatz and Rivkind (1997) found that between 1988 and 1994 fewer than 10% of first-degree murder convictions in the state resulted in death sentences (well below a 15%–20% nationwide figure that had troubled the *Furman* Court more than two decades earlier, before any special narrowing statutes had been put in place). As Shatz and Rivkind concluded their empirical analysis of the effect of this statute: "Succinctly stated, the special circumstances perform no substantial narrowing function" (p. 1327).

The same conclusions have been reached in empirical studies conducted on the actual effects of the narrowing statutes implemented in a number of other states. Studies of judicial proportionality review of death verdicts to determine whether individual death verdicts rendered in a particular case are disproportionate relative to other cases indicate that they too have proven ineffective (e.g., Baldus, Woodworth, Grosso, & Christ, 2002). This is in part because there are few courts that actually conduct such reviews in a meaningful way. In fact, there is no widely agreed upon logic or metric that courts employ in reaching their judgments about proportionality, and reviewing courts almost never find the existence of disproportionality, suggesting

an overall failure to provide rigorous, meaningful review (e.g., Baldus, 1996; Bienen, 1996; Durham, 2004; Kaufman-Osborn, 2008).

The prosecutor's decision as to whether to seek a death sentence is another critical decision point in the narrowing process. In most jurisdictions, prosecutors actually seek death in fewer cases than are potentially eligible, but research indicates that the process by which that selection happens falls short of the narrowing ideals. Thus, evidence suggests that those charging decisions significantly over-value White victims (e.g., Baldus et al., 1990; Paternoster et al., 2003; Songer & Unoh, 2006), and that death notice filings appear to be used to compel guilty pleas (Ehrhard, 2008; Thaxton, 2013).

Finally, capital jurors play a central role in the narrowing process because they ultimately must determine whether they believe that the convicted defendant is culpable enough to be sentenced to death. In the modern era of the death penalty—since *Gregg v. Georgia* (1976) to the present—if there is a conviction in a potentially capital case and a determination made that some aspect of the case renders it death-eligible, the case enters a separate penalty, selection, or sentencing phase. In this phase, capital jurors are typically presented with a wide range of evidence presented by both the prosecution and defense. Prosecutors present aggravating evidence (such as egregious aspects of the crime, prior criminal acts committed by the defendant) that are intended to secure a death verdict, while defense attorneys present mitigating evidence (such as sympathetic aspects the defendant's background or social history, or positive contributions he has or is likely to make in the future) that is intended to secure a life sentence. Under the statutes in operation in most states, judges instruct jurors that they are to consider and take into account both aggravating and mitigating factors, engage in some sort of weighing or balancing process, and reach a sentencing verdict with this evidence in mind. By structuring the decision-making process in this way at this final stage of the capital trial process, the capital jury's discretion is supposed to be properly guided and regularized.

From a psychological perspective, one of the most interesting components of the penalty phase process is the centrality of the defendant's background or social history to the decision-making task. That is, juries are explicitly encouraged to consider the role that the defendant's social history and circumstances have played in shaping or influencing his life trajectory and adult behavior. Moreover, they are instructed to take this information into account in assessing his overall culpability and render a sentencing verdict. This kind of inquiry is rarely even permitted in noncapital criminal cases, much less made the centerpieces of the trial. Research confirms the theoretically soundness of both the social historical inquiry itself (i.e., past events do play an important role in shaping and influencing present and future behavior) and also the relevance of this kind of analysis to the capital jury's task at hand (i.e., jurors can and do use this information to assess culpability). More specifically, much capital mitigation is based on an analysis of the particular criminogenic background factors and forces that helped to shape the capital defendant's life. In addition, research shows that providing decision makers (in this case, capital jurors) with information about these external factors and forces can shift the attributional frame away from purely individual or internal causes, thereby allowing them to contextualize the defendant's behavior and render more informed (and often more lenient) judgments about his fate.

In fact, extensive research has documented the powerful role of criminogenic risk factors in contributing to delinquent, criminal, and violent behavior. Masten and Garmezy (1985) summarized the early research on these issues: "Children who pursue delinquent careers may have been exposed to very severe stresses and harmful life events, genetic disadvantage, inappropriate parental models, selective reinforcement by parents of the child's maladaptive behavior, and chronic low self-esteem" (p. 25). The consequences of exposure to multiple risk factors, aggregated over a long period of time, can negatively shape and affect adult behavior. Broad "contexts of maltreatment" have profound and long-lasting effects over a person's life course (e.g., Belsky, 1993; Briere, 1992; Dutton & Hart, 1992). The field of developmental criminology has relied on many of these social historical and contextual insights to reach conclusions about the origins of criminal behavior (e.g., Loeber, 1996;

Rowe & Farrington, 1997). As Sampson and Laub (1993) noted, "the connection between official childhood misbehavior and [negative] adult outcomes may be accounted for in part by the structural disadvantages and diminished life chances accorded institutionalized and stigmatized youth" (p. 137). The direct application of these psychological insights to understand and explain capital crime has been summarized in a number of publications (e.g., Haney, 1995, 2008a).

Although the psychological connection or link between early traumas and risks and later criminality is empirically well supported, the role that such evidence plays in capital sentencing depends on whether and how jurors use it in assessing a capital defendant's culpability. As we noted earlier, members of the U.S. Supreme Court have suggested over the years—in cases such as *Eddings v. Oklahoma* (1982), *California v. Brown* (1987), and *Rompilla v. Beard* (2005)—that evidence of a capital defendant's abusive and traumatic background and its adverse effects on his life chances and adult behavior might well lead a capital jury to assess his culpability differently and decide not to sentence him or her to death. Much of the research that implicitly supports the justices' assertions about how such evidence is understood is derived from attribution theory. Attribution theory, which dates back to the 1960s, is the notion that people regularly make causal attributions about the behavior they witness others engage in (or when they hear evidence about behavior that has already been engaged in; e.g., Heider, 1958; Jones et al., 1987; Kelley, 1967, 1973; Kelley & Michela, 1980; Ross & Nisbett, 1991).

It is well established in the application of attribution theory to legal settings that jurors engage in a process of analyzing the causes of a defendant's behavior, his intentions in the course of that behavior, and the outcome of the behavior itself in the course of attributing blame, gauging blameworthiness, and assessing culpability. More specifically, depending on whether jurors attribute the causes of the behavior in question to the internal dispositions or willful choices of the actor, or to external circumstances and conditions over which the actor has less control, they judge the behavior and the actor very differently. The nature of the causal attribution affects judgments about the moral quality of the act and the moral culpability of the actor, which then affects perceptions about the nature and severity of the punishment that jurors conclude he deserves (e.g., Albonetti, 1991; Anderson, 1990; Bell, 1989; Cullen, Clark, Cullen, & Mathers, 1985; Hawkins, 1981; Shaver, 1985; Shultz, Schleifer, & Altman, 1981).

Thus, the process of assessing culpability by taking into account the social historical factors and forces that have played a criminogenic role in the lives of capital defendants is grounded in psychological theory and data. There is solid empirical support for the justices' proposition—one that has now become a bedrock principle of capital jurisprudence—that an appreciation of these kinds of mitigating explanations can lead jurors to put capital defendants' lives in context, understand them better, and treat them more leniently. In actual practice, however, the operation of this process and the capital jury's performance in this regard has been extremely uneven and often highly problematic. Here, too, a process that in theory should result in a more rational and principled narrowing of the category of persons on whom the death penalty is actually imposed can and too often does falter at the point of implementation. Obviously, if attorneys fail to discharge their responsibility of competently and conscientiously developing these social historical narratives and effectively presenting them to jurors, then the jurors in turn will lack the information that they need to engage in the most relevant and informed attributional analysis of culpability. In a later section of this chapter we discuss the reasons why this may be so, including the difficulties jurors have in comprehending the instructions that are intended to guide their sentencing discretion and the failure of attorneys to effectively frame and present social historical explanations of their client's lives that correspondingly bear on culpability.

Deterrence. In the early years of death penalty deterrence research, there was a general consensus among researchers that the death penalty did not deter future crimes (Sellin, 1967; van den Haag, 1969). In 1975, however, economist Isaac Ehrlich reached the opposite conclusion when he applied econometric modeling (assuming rationality and the ability of persons to make a cost–benefit analysis) to some of the same data that past researchers had analyzed. In fact, Ehrlich (1975) suggested that each execution deterred seven or eight future murders. Given the timing of Ehrlich's study and his claims about deterrence, which reinvigorated debates about deterrence, U.S. Supreme Court Justice Potter Stewart was able to declare in *Gregg v. Georgia* (1976)—the case that permitted states to reinstitute capital punishment—that there was "no convincing empirical evidence either supporting or refuting" (p. 185) the deterrent effect of capital punishment.

Although the Court did not refute the validity of Ehrlich's conclusions, the research community did. The critical response was swift and vehement. Many researchers identified a number of methodological problems with Ehrlich's analysis (e.g., Beyleveld, 1982; Fox & Radelet, 1989; Knorr, 1979). Perhaps the most significant critique was published by the National Academy of Science (Blumstein, Cohen, & Nagin, 1978). The 1978 National Academy of Science report expressed skepticism about numerous aspects of Ehrlich's research, including doubts about whether the econometric model he used was appropriate in this context. The report pointed out that the model neglected to incorporate important crime-related variables and demonstrated sensitivity to small technical violations, and it stated that Ehrlich's findings were not replicable. The debate over Ehrlich's work also indirectly spurred a number of new studies that demonstrated the lack of a deterrent effect for the death penalty (Archer et al., 1983; Bailey, 1978, 1980, 1983a, 1983b; Forst, 1983).

More recently, another round of deterrence studies was conducted by economists using econometric modeling techniques similar to Ehrlich's, and the research again claimed to demonstrate a significant deterrent effect (Cloninger & Marchesini, 2001; Dezhbakhsh, Rubin, & Shepherd, 2003; Mocan & Gittings, 2003; Shepherd, 2004, 2005; Zimmerman, 2004). They, too, were met with a new set of studies more definitively demonstrating the lack of deterrent effect (Berk, 2005; Cochran & Chamlin, 2000; Donohue & Wolfers, 2005; Fagan, Zimring, & Geller, 2006; Hjalmarsson, 2009; Katz,

Levitt, & Shustorovich, 2003; Stolzenberg & D'Alessio, 2004).

Some of the discrepancies in the results can be attributed to variations in the methods and forms of measurement used (e.g., Knorr, 1979). For example, many of the researchers who have demonstrated a deterrent effect have used aggregated national data (Ehrlich, 1975; Mocan & Gittings, 2003), whereas other researchers have claimed that these data incorrectly assume that executions in jurisdictions with the death penalty affect crime rates in states without a death penalty (Bailey & Peterson, 1989; Knorr, 1979). When more focused jurisdictions are utilized in these studies, however, sample sizes can become very small (Donohue & Wolfers, 2005; Land, Teske, & Zheng, 2009; Lempert, 1983). In addition, different researchers choose to control for different variables, often neglecting variables that are known correlates of crime, such as length of prison sentence and gun accessibility (Blumstein et al., 1978), while including invalid predictors, such as percentage of people who voted Republican in recent elections (Donohue & Wolfers, 2005).

An alternative approach to testing the deterrence hypothesis is to compare homicide rates in states that have the death penalty with neighboring or contiguous states that do not, or to look at single states over time and compare homicide rates in periods when the death penalty was authorized by state law versus rates when it was not (Bailey & Peterson, 1999). These kinds of studies have found no evidence of a deterrent effect for capital punishment (Archer et al., 1983; Bailey, 1983a; Decker & Kohfeld, 1990).

Researchers also have tried to isolate and understand the specific mechanisms that comprise the deterrence model in tests of the theory. For instance, researchers have asked whether relative certainty of execution predicts a deterrent effect. States that have existing death penalty statutes vary in terms of whether and how frequently it is actually carried out. Thus, in states that operate what has been termed a *de facto system of capital punishment*, executions are regularly carried out as the law prescribes, in contrast to states that operate a *de jure system of capital punishment*, where executions are rarely carried out even though the law allows it

(Archer et al., 1983). Again the findings are inconsistent. Some studies have found that executions appear to deter homicide (Cloninger & Marchesini, 2001; Ehrlich, 1975; Shepherd, 2004; Zimmerman, 2004), while others continue to find no significant evidence for deterrence theory (Bailey, 1978, 1980, 1983a; Decker & Kohfeld, 1986, 1990; Donohue & Wolfers, 2005; Lempert, 1983).

Similarly, researchers have examined whether the time-to-execution matters for deterrence. In the context of deterrence, *celerity* refers to the swiftness with which punishment is expected to be applied. Some research suggests that reducing the amount of time between arrest and punishment will lead to lower homicide rates (Bailey & Peterson, 1999). Again, findings are inconsistent, with studies simultaneously finding that homicides are decreased both by a shorter time on death row (Shepherd, 2004) and by a longer time there (Bailey, 1980). A survey of a group of criminology experts indicated that 73.2% disagreed or strongly disagreed with the statement that reducing time spent on death row would reduce homicides (Radelet & Akers, 1996).

Deterrence theory also asserts that for a punishment to deter, it must be known to the population that is to be deterred. This suggests that well publicized executions should have a stronger deterrent effect because of the increased number of persons who will be aware of them (Bailey, 1990; Hjalmarsson, 2009; Stack, 1987). Several studies have examined this possibility, with some finding that highly publicized executions had no deterrent effect (McFarland, 1983) and others reporting that a relationship between execution publicity and subsequent offending did exist (Cochran & Chamlin, 2000; Cochran et al., 1994). Direct comparisons between well and poorly publicized executions yielded similarly inconsistent results, with some support found for a deterrent effect when the executions were more highly publicized (Phillips, 1980; Stack, 1987, 1994) and others finding no such effect (Bailey, 1980, 1990, 1998; Stolzenberg & D'Alessio, 2004). One study (Bailey, 1998) even suggests that execution publicity may increase the number of homicides.

Finally, some researchers have concluded that, far from deterring future homicides, executions may actually increase them through what has been termed a *brutalization effect*. Bowers and Pierce (1980b) suggested that state-sanctioned executions represent an official public statement that devalues life and demonstrates to potential perpetrators that it is appropriate to kill someone who has engaged in wrongdoing. While deterrence theory assumes that potential murderers will identify with the person being executed, and therefore be deterred, brutalization theory suggests that they are more likely to identify with the executioner. Although brutalization, like deterrence, has had inconsistent support, a number of studies have found some evidence of a possible brutalizing effect (Archer et al., 1983; Bailey, 1998; Cheatwood, 1993; Cochran & Chamlin, 2000; Cochran et al., 1994; Forst, 1983; Neumayer, 2003).

A number of researchers have proposed that the inconsistencies found in the empirical data on the deterrent effect of capital punishment stem from differences in the locations, persons, and types of crime being studied. For example, some have suggested that a deterrent effect may exist for capital punishment in Texas, but that these data skew the results for the rest of the country, where no such deterrent effect occurs (Berk, 2005; Cloninger & Marchesini, 2001). Cochran and his colleagues have suggested that there is a deterrent effect for some types of murders but not others. Specifically, his research indicated that when the death penalty was first used after a lapsed time, a brutalization effect seemed to occur in the form of a sudden and permanent increase in the number of murders of strangers (Cochran & Chamlin, 2000; Cochran et al., 1994). However, there appeared to be a corresponding deterrent effect as well, resulting in a reduction in the number of felony-murders of nonstrangers (Cochran & Chamlin, 2000). On the other hand, Shepherd (2004) found no evidence of deterrence or brutalization for stranger murders, although she did find evidence for deterrence in crimes of passion, which are typically thought to be the type of murders that are least likely to be deterred. In many of the studies that parsed out different locations or types of murders, the combined effect tends to be no deterrent effect (Cochran & Chamlin, 2000; Forst, 1983; Land et al., 2009).

Another possible explanation for the inconsistent findings was suggested in an analysis conducted by Shepherd (2005). She found that when initial executions are conducted in a jurisdiction, the first nine have a brutalizing effect; however, after passing that threshold there will begin to be a deterrent effect. Far from encouraging more executions, Shepherd warns of the devastating numbers of homicides that may occur after an initial execution; in Oregon, she found that one execution might have led to as many as 175 murders.

In sum, although the deterrence hypothesis has been tested in multiple ways and across many different time periods and places, there is no definitive proof that executions have any deterrent effect. Consequently, in its 2012 follow-up report on deterrence and the death penalty, the National Research Council concluded that "research to date on the effect of capital punishment on homicide is not informative about whether capital punishment decreases, increases, or has no effect on homicide rates. Therefore, the committee recommends that these studies not be used to inform deliberations requiring judgments about the effect of the death penalty on homicide" (Nagin & Pepper, 2012, p. 102).

Racially discriminatory imposition. The possibility that racial discrimination influences the decision-making processes that produce death verdicts remains central to the debate over capital punishment (e.g., Kotch & Mosteller, 2010). Research that has examined outcomes of capital cases in the post-*Furman* era, having controlled for extraneous variables and taken extralegal and other factors into consideration, continue to find race-based disparities (see Chapter 15, this volume). The distinctive patterns involve the race of the victim as well as that of the defendant. In particular, capital cases in which the victims are White are more likely to result in death sentences than those in which victims are non-White, irrespective of the race of the defendant (Baldus et al., 1990; Paternoster et al., 2003). These findings are consistent with Sundby's (2003) suggestion that capital jurors place murder victims in a hierarchy of intrinsic worth or value, such that the deaths of certain kinds of victims deserve to be vindicated with more serious punishment (i.e., the death penalty), and others deserve less (see also, Kennedy, 1988; Paternoster, 1984). Baldus and his colleagues found that a race-of-defendant effect—e.g., Black defendants are treated more punitively and given the death penalty more often than White defendants—typically only occurred when there was a White victim (Baldus et al., 1990). Others have also found that cases in which there are Black defendants and White victims are more likely than any other racial combination to result in death verdicts (Paternoster & Brame, 2008). Some researchers have suggested that these kinds of interracial cases cross certain racial barriers for predominately White jurors (Bowers & Pierce, 1980a) and play on their perceptions of Black men as more dangerous than others (Bowers, Sandys, & Brewer, 2004).

In addition to the racially disparate patterns of death sentencing, racially discriminatory decision making may occur at earlier stages of a capital case, including the many pretrial and trial decision points at which discretion—and therefore discrimination or bias—may be exercised (Baldus, Woodworth, Zuckerman, & Weiner, 1998). For example, police officers must decide whom to arrest, prosecutors must decide how to charge a defendant and whether to seek the death penalty; judges and jurors must determine whether the defendant is guilty and, under many capital sentencing statutes, decide a threshold question about whether he is eligible to be considered for a death sentence (Thomson, 1997). In addition, there are discretionary decisions that are made after the trial has been concluded and a death verdict rendered, including appellate and habeas review by courts that must evaluate the fairness of the legal proceedings, and sentencing authorities and executive officers who must decide whether to carry out an execution or grant clemency (Thomson, 1997).

A number of studies have identified the importance of prosecutorial discretion in contributing to race-based disparities in death sentencing (Paternoster et al., 2003; Thomson, 1997). Prosecutors must decide who is most worthwhile to prosecute—and to prosecute capitally—with the limited resources they have available (Radelet & Pierce, 1985). These decisions are typically not publicly explained and

are technically not legally reviewable. This means that they may be influenced by a range of possible factors, including prosecutors' own reactions to the racial dynamics of the case. They may also be affected by their interpretation of public outcry over what the community regards as an egregious crime, an especially despised alleged perpetrator, or a particularly sympathetic victim. These community reactions (as well as prosecutors' interpretations of them) may be influenced by racial sentiments (e.g., Paternoster, 1984).

In one study, Baldus et al. found that prosecutorial decision making was significantly associated with victims' race and that death was more likely to be sought in cases with White victims (Baldus et al., 1990). Others have found that prosecutors in cases with White victims were more likely to charge defendants with capital homicide (Lee, 2007), as well as to notify the defense that they would seek the death penalty, to proceed to trial as a death penalty case, and to advance the case to a penalty phase (Paternoster, 1984; Paternoster et al., 2003).

One archival study found evidence of prosecutorial discrimination based on race of the defendant (Baldus et al., 1998); however, mirroring the findings from research done on discrimination in the death sentencing process overall, prosecutorial racial bias was based on the interaction of the defendant's and victim's races. That is, in cases in which defendants were Black and victims White, prosecutors were more likely to charge defendants with capital murder (Paternoster & Brame, 2008), upgrade police classification of cases (Radelet & Akers, 1996), file death notices (indicating that they would seek the death penalty at trial), and continue to pursue the death penalty through subsequent stages of the case (Paternoster et al., 2003).

These overall patterns suggest that although jurors appear to value White victims more overall, race of victim matters even more in a Black defendant case than one in which the defendant is White (Paternoster, 1984). These discrepancies were most pronounced in cases where there was a single aggravated felony, suggesting that there may be a lower threshold to seek the death penalty when there is a Black defendant and a White victim (Paternoster, 1984). Cases with Black defendants and

Black victims seem to attract the least attention from prosecutors, with fewer of these cases being charged capitally (Paternoster, 1984) and fewer death notices being retained as the cases proceed (Paternoster et al., 2003).

Prosecutors and defense lawyers also have influence on later decision points by choosing which individuals will sit on the jury. Research has found that capital jury pools are likely to be less racially diverse than the communities from which they are drawn. Blacks are already less likely to be on the voter and automobile registration lists from which prospective jurors are typically summoned (Baldus et al., 1998). In addition, they are more likely to be removed by death qualification (Haney, 2004; Haney, Hurtado, & Vega, 1994). Finallly, additional racial skewing may occur when trial lawyers choose the jurors they believe will benefit their sides of the case.

Race-based decision making can affect another crucial aspect of a capital trial. During *voir dire*, or jury selection, trial lawyers are allowed a limited number of discretionary peremptory challenges to eliminate potential jurors and they can do so for almost any reason. One exception is the use of peremptory challenges to strike potential jurors on the basis of their race, a practice that was deemed unconstitutional in *Batson v. Kentucky* (1986). Some research has shown that *Batson* has not entirely eliminated this race-based practice (Baldus, Woodworth, Zuckerman, Weiner, & Broffitt, 2001), in part because lawyers who are questioned about their use of peremptory challenges can claim that their strikes were made for other reasons. In examining how race affects jury selection, Baldus et al. (2001) found that prosecuting attorneys strike disproportionate numbers of Black potential jurors, while defense lawyers strike disproportionate numbers of non-Black jurors.

The strikes also specifically varied as a function of the races of the defendant and victim, suggesting that lawyers on both sides considered how the jurors' race might interact with the racial dynamics of the case. These patterns had a much greater impact in reducing the number of potential Black jurors available to serve on a criminal jury (including a death penalty jury). That is, Baldus et al. found that the reduced number of possible Black jurors in

the initial jury pool (Baldus et al., 1998), combined with the prosecutors' tendency to strike Black potential jurors (particularly young Black men), typically resulted in a jury that did not represent the community and was not made up of the defendant's peers (Baldus et al., 2001). For example, in a study of one Pennsylvania jurisdiction, Baldus et al. (2001) found that young Black men, who made up 65% of the capital defendants, had no "closest peer" on their jury in 79% of cases.

The presence of Black peers on the jury matters greatly, as Black jurors have been found to perceive cases differently than White jurors (Bowers, Steiner, & Sandys, 2001). Black jurors feel more empathy, particularly for Black defendants (Garvey, 2000), are more likely to identify with the defendant, their situation, and their family (Bowers et al., 2001), and are less likely to give a death sentence (Lynch & Haney, 2009). Although jurors were more likely to generally agree when they were dominated by White men, more conflict and questioning tended to arise when Black jurors were present (Bowers et al., 2001).

A final component of race-based death sentencing involves the potential effect of what has been termed *biographical racism* (Haney, 2004, 2005). The continued significance of race in the United States means that Black defendants are more likely to have experienced a greater number of accumulated criminogenic risk factors over longer periods of time than other groups. These risk factors may include poverty, child abuse, differential treatment in schools, special education, and confinement in the juvenile justice system (e.g., Haney, 1995, 2008a). Black capital defendants are more likely to have been exposed to a greater number of these risk factors and are therefore more likely to have had their life course affected in these adverse ways (Haney, 2005). These patterns of differential exposure to criminogenic risk factors should serve as a form of built in or structural mitigation that is considered at the sentencing phase of a capital trial, resulting in a greater number of life sentences rather than death sentences (Haney, 2004). However, the racial differentials that continue to occur in the overall rates of death sentencing suggest that these mitigating factors are not having this effect, perhaps because they are fully understood or appreciated, or perhaps because attorneys are failing to properly develop effective mitigating narratives in which biographical racism is highlighted and using them to overcome the empathic divide that otherwise separates Black defendants from the typically White jurors who judge them (Haney, 2004).

Attitudes About Capital Punishment

For all of the reasons that we previously described, public opinion is especially important in the administration of the death penalty and, not surprisingly, has been extensively studied. Although people's attitudes about capital punishment tend to be reported in the media as largely uncomplicated, unidimensional, and stable, they are in fact quite complex, multifaceted, and subject to change. They are also related to a number of demographic characteristics, to other values and beliefs, and to external conditions and influences, including the influence of more accurate information designed to correct some widely held misconceptions about capital punishment.

Death penalty attitude structure and change. As two researchers have noted, "[p]ublic opinion on the death penalty in America over the last 50 years has vacillated" (Radelet & Borg, 2000, p. 44). Actually, this vacillation in death penalty attitudes may have lasted for considerably longer, although it is difficult to be certain. The Gallup organization did not conduct nationwide polls on capital punishment between the mid-1930s and the mid-1950s, so there were few if any reliable national estimates. In the mid-1950s, when regular nationwide polling began again, the percent of the public in favor of the death penalty started a modest but consistent decline. The lowest level of support occurred in 1966, when only 42% of the public supported capital punishment for persons convicted of murder. In fact, this was the only year in which Gallup estimated that the percentage expressing opposition to the death penalty (47%) exceeded those in favor.

This trend soon reversed itself. Reasonably steady increases in death penalty support occurred throughout the 1970s and 1980s. In 1989, for example, the nationwide Gallup Poll reported that nearly 4 out of 5 citizens—what was characterized as the "highest in Gallup annals"—favored capital punishment for persons convicted of murder (Gallup Poll,

1989). Gallup's estimates of death penalty support plateaued at around that time and then, in the mid-1990s, began another modest but consistent decline. According to Gallup, death penalty support reached a 39-year low in 2011, with 61% of respondents to a nationwide survey in favor, and has stabilized at around that number to the present time (Newport, 2011).

What appears to be the most rapid and significant period of change in recent history—the thirty percentage point increase in death penalty support that occurred between 1966 and 1994—coincided with general political campaigns to get tough on criminals by increasing the harshness of the penalties they received. As two commentators put it at the start of this trend of increasing death penalty support: "Support for capital punishment seems to be strongly correlated with 'law and order' campaigns by local, state, and national politicians. It is one stark means a candidate has of displaying that he will 'do something about crime' if elected" (Gelles & Straus, 1975, p. 599).

From the early 1970s until well into the 1990s, very little visible, organized opposition or public debate about the death penalty occurred on a national level in the United States. Moreover, the death penalty continued to serve as an especially potent political symbol. During those decades, as Gross (1998) accurately observed, a "new status quo" had been reached in which the death penalty was regarded as less controversial than at any time in the past and had become simply "an accepted part of our criminal justice system" (p. 1453). Indeed, capital punishment was an issue about which there was little public or political controversy or conflict in part because, as Gross (1998) put it in the late 1990s, "the sides are so severely mismatched" (p. 1453).

In fact, some of the momentum for the new status quo in which the death penalty came to be so widely and unproblematically accepted in the United States may have come from news reporting suggesting that this was the case. That is, to the extent that "[p]eople learn about public opinion from media coverage, and particularly the coverage of public opinion polls" (Gunther, 1998, p. 487), the American public learned a great deal about their own attitudes toward the death penalty during the 1980s and 1990s. These were times when headlines announcing the high levels of support for the death penalty were commonplace in newspapers across the country. Niven (2002) demonstrated that the media's typically unrealistic and simplistic coverage of public opinion about the death penalty suggesting that it was unequivocally supported by large majorities had an impact on individual attitudes and "bolster[ed] a sense of inevitability" about capital punishment. It likely "helped to construct a social reality that support for capital punishment is intractable" (Unnever, Cullen, & Roberts, 2005, p. 187).

As we noted earlier, however, failing to analyze the strength of respondents' support of the death penalty conveyed an all or nothing quality to public sentiments that may have masked significant, underlying ambivalence. As Harris (1986) put it, "[c]ategorizing people as favoring or opposing the death penalty does not take into account the vast heterogeneity of views underlying this simple dichotomy" (p. 433). Neglecting to specify the circumstances under which public support would translate into a recommendation that the death penalty actually should be imposed conveyed an impression of broad, generalized support that may not have extended to all or even most cases in which capital punishment was a possibility. Indeed, in spite of the apparent one-sidedness of public opinion, and perhaps, in an odd way, because of it, it was easy to miss the softness and complexity that characterized at least some people's support of capital punishment. Those complexities were drowned out by all the apparent public enthusiasm and political promotion over the last several decades.

Thus, a number of public opinion surveys showed that, even at the highest point of nationwide support for capital punishment, there were large numbers of people who would not impose it for many kinds of crimes that were technically death-eligible. More specifically, many death penalty supporters nonetheless endorsed a variety of common mitigating factors that they indicated would lead them to impose life rather than death sentences in an actual case, and substantial numbers of those in favor of the death penalty actually preferred a life without parole sentence if it was offered as a

genuine and meaningful alternative to capital punishment (e.g., Bowers, 1993; Fox et al., 1991; Haney, Hurtado, & Vega, 1994).

Bases and sources of death penalty opinion. Numerous studies have attempted to uncover the individual-level variables that appear to influence and direct people's death penalty attitudes. Researchers have identified two demographic characteristics—gender and race—that are consistently related to people's death penalty attitudes. Specifically, studies show that women are significantly less likely to support the death penalty (e.g., Lester, 1998; Stack, 2000). As Cochran and Sanders (2009) summarized, "[a]mong the various known correlates of death penalty support, one of the strongest and most persistent predictors has been respondent's gender" (p. 525). They found that the tendency for women to favor capital punishment significantly less than men has been both enduring and robust, persisting even after controlling for a number of other variables.

Racial differences are equally long-standing and robust and, if anything, even larger (e.g., Bobo & Johnson, 2004; Cochran & Chamlin, 2006; Johnson, 2008; Unnever & Cullen, 2007). For example, Maggard, Payne, and Chappell (2012) found that race was an overriding determinant of death penalty attitudes, with Whites supporting capital punishment in far greater numbers than Blacks, even when a number of other variables were controlled for. Johnson (2008) has reported that this substantial and long-standing racial difference in punitive attitudes may be explained by differences in racial prejudice among Whites, perceived injustice among Blacks, and each group's "social structural location vis-à-vis the criminal justice system" (p. 204). Indeed, there is evidence that Whites' support of the death penalty actually strengthens when they learn of its discriminatory nature (Hurwitz & Peffley, 2010).

Studies that examined the period of increasing crime rates in the United States—the late 1960s and into the early 1970s—suggested that rising crime and perceptions of threat are instrumentally related to death penalty support (e.g., Rankin, 1979; Thomas and Foster, 1975). Other researchers, however, found that death penalty support appeared to be less an instrumental response to crime and more a symbolic attitude held as part of a commitment to a larger set of political and social beliefs (Ellsworth & Gross, 1994; Tyler & Weber, 1982). That is, supporters are more likely to have a political and social commitment to punitiveness in general, of which support for the death penalty is merely a component.

In more recent research, many scholars and researchers have suggested that support for capital punishment is based on people's commitment to a broad personal worldview, including one premised on authoritarianism, fundamentalism and, especially, retributivism (e.g., Bohm, 1987; Finckenauer, 1988; Grasmick, Davenport, Chamlin, & Bursik, 1992). The tendency to cite retribution as an ideological basis for death penalty support has grown during the tough on crime era, while the use of instrumental justifications to explain prodeath penalty sentiments have decreased since 1981 (Ellsworth & Gross, 1994). In a related vein, Harvey (1986) found that persons who supported the death penalty tended to ascribe to the most concrete functioning of the four belief systems he measured. Barkan and Cohn (1994) found that support for the death penalty was associated with political conservatism, antipathy for Blacks, and racial stereotyping. Miller and Hayward (2008) found that a number of personal characteristics were associated with death penalty attitudes, including religious beliefs. Unnever and Cullen (2006) have reported that the relationship between religion and support for the death penalty is far more complex than originally thought, requiring a careful disentangling of specific and potentially countervailing denominational beliefs.

Perhaps not surprisingly, a number of sophisticated analyses have found that death penalty attitudes are influenced by a complicated combination of variables, including demographics, broad values and worldviews, and contextual factors. For example, as Soss, Langbein, and Metelko (2003) concluded from their analysis of White support for the death penalty, "[n]o single factor, taken alone, can explain why most White people support capital punishment or why a dissenting minority stands in opposition" (p. 411). They found that support for the death penalty among White respondents was

influenced by commitment to a broader set of values and perspectives (i.e., trust in government, belief in individual responsibility, order, and deference) and varied significantly by racial prejudice, but that these tendencies were moderated by contextual variables. That is, "[t]wo individuals with similar characteristics can be expected to respond differently [to the death penalty] depending on their surrounding social environments" (p. 414).

Similarly, others have found that although racial differences in death penalty support are very powerful in their own right, they also moderate the effects of a broad historical context (such as a tradition of vigilantism) and contemporary conditions (such as distrust of government) on death penalty support (Messner, Baumer, & Rosenfeld, 2006). However, it is also important to note, that as Unnever, Cullen, and Jonson (2008) concluded in a recent review of empirical studies conducted from the 1980s through the 2000s, "racial animus is one of the most consistent and robust predictors of support for the death penalty. Whites who harbor racial animus toward [Blacks], particularly those who endorse the new form of racism—that is, who are symbolic racists—are significantly more likely to support capital punishment" (p. 69).

Death penalty attitudes also appear to be related to a number of specific legal and criminal justice values and beliefs. Fitzgerald and Ellsworth (1984) studied the ways in which death penalty supporters and opponents systematically differed in their fundamental criminal justice and constitutional values. Using a dichotomy first developed by Packer (1968), which juxtaposed a "due process" perspective that emphasized "the fallibility of the criminal process in correctly apprehending, trying, and convicting lawbreakers" (Fitzgerald & Ellsworth, 1984, p. 33) with a "crime control" perspective that emphasized a belief "that the most important function of the criminal justice system is repressing crime" (p. 34). Fitzgerald and Ellsworth (1984) demonstrated that death penalty supporters were far more likely to be aligned with a crime control perspective, in contrast to death penalty opponents, who were more likely to endorse due process values.

A decade later, when overall support for the capital punishment was at an all-time high, Haney,

Hurtado, and Vega (1994) found much the same thing—that persons who supported the death penalty tended to embrace crime control points of view over the due process perspective that was more likely to be held by death penalty opponents. For example, respondents who disagreed with the basic tenet of American jurisprudence that it is better for society to let some guilty people go free than to risk convicting an innocent person were significantly more likely to support the death penalty, as were those who disagreed with the exclusionary rule and believed that the insanity defense was little more than a loophole that allowed too many guilty persons to go free.

As we noted earlier, in addition to individual-level factors that help account for death penalty attitudes and beliefs, much attention has been paid to the role of external influences, including regional differences that appear to stem from cultural and subcultural practices and norms. Although little psychological research has been conducted to directly explain this phenomenon, a number of researchers have found very reliable and significant geographical variations in both support for the death penalty and in actual death penalty practices (i.e., numbers of persons sentenced to death and numbers of persons actually executed). For example, Borg (1997) found that, although there was little overall difference between southerners and non-southerners in terms of death penalty support, there were very significant differences in regional conditions that translated into much higher percentages of persons who supported capital punishment in some communities or areas than others. To explain these localized differences within a region of the country ordinarily associated with death penalty support, she emphasized the importance of understanding "not only the contextual nature of 'southern violence' but also the variability of 'southern identity,'" (p. 25) from one place to another.

Liebman and Clarke (2011) have found that the variations are much more dramatic when, in addition to attitudes about the death penalty, actual death sentences are taken into account. As they put it: "[N]otwithstanding broad public and statutory support" for capital punishment, "the vast bulk of death sentences are imposed on behalf of a small minority of Americans." Indeed, a "given defendant's likelihood of receiving a sentence of death depends greatly on the county in which he was tried" (p. 265). The small minority of communities that actually use the death penalty were characterized by their high levels of parochialism, or a "tendency to feel embattled from 'outside' influences, including crime" (p. 270) and by their libertarianism, or "a vigilante streak—a willingness to take the law into one's own hands and out of the untrustworthy hands of government" (p. 274).

The mass media are another especially powerful external force that helps to explain death penalty attitudes (see Volume 1, Chapter 17, this handbook, for a review of research on media and the law). Researchers have confirmed the ways in which the media significantly influence how people "frame" and react to certain kinds of criminal justice events, and how they feel about certain crime-related policies. For example, we know that pretrial publicity can shape how people feel about a particular crime, criminal case, and criminal defendant (e.g., Moran & Cutler, 1991; Otto, Penrod, & Dexter, 1994; Sandys & Chermak, 1996). Sherizen (1978) concluded that the "world view or public belief system developed by the media limits the perspectives of the audience to certain limited aspects of the crime phenomena and, in the process of limiting its coverage, certain features of considerable importance are excluded from comprehension" (p. 207).

Studies have documented the relationship between the amount of news coverage that is given to particular topics and the significance that the public subsequently attaches to these same topics (e.g., Iyengar, Peters, & Kinder, 1982; K. Smith, 1987). For example, studies have demonstrated a direct relationship between the amount of newspaper space devoted to violent crime and the likelihood that neighborhood residents selected crime as their community's most serious problem (M. Gordon & Heath, 1991).

With these issues in mind, Haney and Greene (2004) content-analyzed the newspaper coverage of a representative sample of California death penalty cases. They found that the press tended to concentrate more heavily on cases in which a death verdict ultimately was returned (even though, statistically, life verdicts are more common), focus their coverage mostly on the beginning stages of the cases—when little information about the background or social history of the defendant was available—and that the overwhelming majority of the "facts" reported in news stories were details about the crime itself. They also found that the press relied overwhelmingly on the police and other law enforcement agencies as the sources cited for the information contained in the articles that were coded—the so-called subsidized news aspect of crime reporting—and also that the many repeated references to the crime routinely focused the reader's attention on its heinous aspects or features, often with carefully crafted language that further dramatized already emotionally charged events. The stories almost never included even remotely sympathetic background information that might have conveyed an explanation of the defendant's criminal behavior in terms of past trauma, an especially deprived or abusive upbringing, or some other social contextual factors.

Media crime coverage like this not only shapes public perceptions by heightening concerns over the nature and frequency of victimization and the magnitude of the crime problem, but also may influence the judgments that people make about whether to support largely or exclusively punitive strategies (including the death penalty) in order to address these issues. For example, in one study, researchers compared sentencing views among persons who reviewed several case-related court documents with another group who reviewed several newspaper articles about the same case. Those who read the newspaper articles were more than three times as likely to regard the sentence meted out to the defendant as too lenient (Roberts & Doob, 1990). In a separate but related study, Roberts and Edwards (1989) found that crime-related publicity increased participants' recommended levels of punishment even when the crime for which they rendered a sentence (e.g., theft) was very different from the one they read about (e.g., homicide). As one literature review concluded: "[P]references for highly punitive sanctions in the criminal justice system are one consequence of the media's predilection for covering violent and sensational crimes" (Hans & Dee, 1991, p. 142).

Although no researcher has systematically studied whether exposure to media criminology (Haney, 2008b) per se has a direct effect on death penalty attitudes and decision making, Holbert, Shah, and Kwak (2004) conducted a national cross-sectional survey that found that support for the death penalty was positively related to viewing police reality shows and television crime drama. Similarly, Slater, Rouner, and Long (2006) found that viewing a law and order–oriented crime drama suppressed the influence of preexisting liberal ideology among viewers and led them to favor the death penalty and attach greater importance to public safety and crime reduction. More recently, using state-level survey data from Nebraska, Kort-Butler and Hartshorn (2011) found that nonfiction reality crime television viewing significantly contributed to fear of crime and distorted views of crime prevalence, while viewing crime drama television programming directly and significantly predicted support for capital punishment.

One apparent shift in sentiments about capital punishment emerged at a time when support for the death penalty was at or nearing an all-time high. The shift illustrates the potentially complex interplay between political and media influences, general values, and attitudes about the death penalty. Part of the law-and-order political campaigns that were mounted throughout the United States beginning in the 1970s included an intensification of the media's coverage of crime (e.g., Beckett, 1997). The public became increasingly concerned in response, and their anger toward the perpetrators of crime intensified. By the end of the decade, Warr and Stafford (1984) identified an emerging relationship between a belief in retribution as a justification for punishment in general and support for the death penalty in particular: "Retribution is by far the most frequently cited justification of punishment . . . those who view retribution as the most important purpose of punishment overwhelmingly favor capital punishment" (p. 104). A short time later, Harris (1986) reported much the same thing: "[P]oll data are consistent in showing that support for the death penalty is largely a matter of emotion: revenge is a more powerful rationale than any of the utilitarian justifications" (p. 453).

As the decade of the 1990s began, Fox et al. (1991) suggested that "Americans now are unashamed, and perhaps even proud, to verbalize their desire for retribution" (p. 512), and noted that their support for capital punishment was one important way that they were able to give voice to these newly legitimated desires. At around the same time, Ellsworth and Gross (1994) similarly reported that most people's views on capital punishment were now based more on emotional than rational grounds, and that people not only had little accurate knowledge about the death penalty but also were not particularly interested in acquiring more. Near the end of the 1990s, just before support for capital punishment began its slow but steady decline, Simon (1997) correctly observed that the death penalty was no longer being advocated or defended on the basis of its instrumental or social utilitarian value—what it could accomplish—but rather as an "invocation of vengeance" that took the form of a "satisfying personal experience for victims and a satisfying gesture for the rest of the community" (p. 13).

This phenomenon also appeared to be subject to media-driven change. For example, Fan, Keltner, and Wyatt (2002) content-analyzed a very large sample of newspaper stories published about the death penalty between 1977 and 2001, and correlated changes in the content of the reporting to overall changes in public opinion about capital punishment. They found not only that "support for the death penalty could be predicted with good accuracy from press coverage of the death penalty" (p. 446) but also that, as press coverage in the late 1990s shifted the reporting frame to concentrate much more heavily on the wrongful conviction of persons who had been sentenced to death, the shift in coverage was strongly related to a corresponding decrease in nationwide support for capital punishment.

The Marshall hypothesis. Recall that there were essentially three components to the hypothesis that Justice Thurgood Marshall advanced concerning death penalty opinions: the public in general lacks accurate information about capital punishment; a large majority of an informed citizenry would definitively reject the death penalty; and support for the death penalty that was based in whole or in large part on retribution would be relatively impervious to the influence of accurate information (e.g., Sarat & Vidmar, 1976; Vidmar & Ellsworth, 1974). There have been a number of studies of these seemingly straightforward and empirically testable propositions, and they have yielded a somewhat complicated pattern of results.

There is much research that substantiates Marshall's view that the public in general is uninformed or misinformed about capital punishment (e.g., Haney, 2005), relying on what one scholar has called *folk knowledge* rather than actual facts (Steiner, 1999). Perhaps the most consistently studied and identified misconception is the one that pertains to the prevailing alternative to a death sentence—life in prison without possibility of parole. Numerous studies have shown that not only survey respondents but even actual capital jurors misconstrue the meaning of a life without parole sentence. For example, one early study found that some 70% of citizens in a national sample did not believe that defendants sentenced to life without parole would remain in prison for the rest of their lives (Bennack, 1983). Other researchers have noted that "[p]rospective jurors often maintain the common misconception that a life sentence is not, in reality, a *life* sentence" (Dayan, Mahler, & Widenhouse, 1989, p. 166). They highlight one study suggesting that the average juror believed that a life sentence meant the person would be released in seven or eight years. Focusing on actual capital jurors, Paduano and Stafford-Smith (1987) concluded that "the typical juror at the sentencing phase of a capital trial perceives the imposition of a sentence of 'life imprisonment' to mean there is a good chance that the capital defendant will in fact be released from prison on parole" (p. 211). Similarly, the Capital Jury Project, whose researchers interviewed a sample of persons who had actually served as jurors in capital cases in California and 13 other states, reported that only a small percentage—18.4% of the 152 jurors they interviewed—believed that capital defendants who got life without parole sentences actually would spend the rest of their lives in prison (Bowers & Steiner, 1999, p. 653).

This particular misconception is especially important to Marshall's view that misinformation is at the core of much death penalty support. As the Capital Jury Project researchers explained: "Embedded in contemporary cultural common sense about crime and punishment is the tenet of early release, which holds that state policy is too lenient and so ineffective that murderers not condemned to death will be back in society far too soon, even before they actually become eligible for parole" (Steiner, Bowers, & Sarat, 1999, p. 496). Indeed, both having and understanding the option of life without possibility of parole appears to significantly reduce death penalty support. For example, in the 1985 Gallup Poll, nationwide support for the death penalty fell from 72% overall to 56% when respondents were given life without possibility of parole as an explicit alternative (Paduano & Stafford-Smith, 1987). Zeisel and Gallup (1989) aggregated the results of 1985 and 1986 nationwide Gallup polls and showed a slightly larger drop in death penalty support (from 71% to 52%) when the life without parole option was explicitly provided. Similar and in many instances even larger shifts in support (some resulting in sizable majorities favoring life over death) were reported in a number of other studies when this option was given and understood (e.g., Fox et al., 1991; Haney, Hurtado, & Vega, 1994).

A number of studies have suggested that Marshall's second and in many ways key assertion—that knowing more about capital punishment would lead people to support it less—is fundamentally although not uniformly correct (e.g., Bohm, Clark, & Aveni, 1991; Sarat & Vidmar, 1976; Vidmar & Dittenhoffer, 1981). Although one study found that increased information actually polarized people and led them to become even more extreme in their preexisting views (Lord, Ross, & Lepper, 1979), and another showed that short-term information-based changes were not necessarily preserved over much longer terms (Bohm & Vogel, 2004), most studies, including those cited above that focused on life without parole, have indicated that dispelling certain misconceptions about capital punishment—creating an "informed citizenry" on the issue—leads to a decrease in death penalty support. For example, Murray (2003) found that death penalty attitudes were multidimensional and unstable, and that support for capital punishment was reduced when respondents were merely asked a series of questions about how fairly it was being administered. The study by Lambert, Camp, Clarke, and Shanhe (2011) provided nuanced support for Marshall's prediction, showing that accurate information about the death penalty differentially reduced support depending on the demographic characteristics of the recipients and their level of preexisting knowledge about capital punishment.

The final component of the Marshall Hypothesis—that persons who support the death penalty on a primarily or exclusively retributive basis are unlikely to change their views based on new information—was especially relevant in the late 1980s and early 1990s when, as we noted above, high levels of death penalty support were increasingly associated with retributive rationales or justifications for capital punishment. Interestingly, however, a new issue in the death penalty debate emerged at roughly that same time to eventually undermine the nature of that support: wrongful conviction (e.g., Bedau & Radelet, 1987; Gross, Jacoby, Matheson, Montgomery, & Patil, 2005; Huff, 2002; Radelet, Bedau, & Putnam, 1992; Radelet, Lofquist, & Bedau, 1996; Scheck, Neufeld, & Dwyer, 2000). Because the retributive rationale requires that persons unequivocally deserve their punishment, highly publicized cases of death row exonerations of persons convicted and sentenced to death for crimes that they did not commit seemed to call people's confidence in this rationale into question. Studies done more recently, after these exonerations drew increased scrutiny to capital punishment (e.g., Baumgartner, de Boef, & Boydstun, 2008; Tabak, 2001), indicate that even death penalty supporters who base support on retribution are susceptible to information-based change (Cochran & Chamlin, 2005). Current research also indicates that having knowledge about the risk of convicting and executing innocent persons is associated with lower levels of death penalty support (Bobo & Johnson, 2004; Unnever & Cullen, 2005), and that providing persons with information about innocence per se can lead to reductions in number of persons who report favoring capital punishment (e.g., Fan et al., 2002; Lambert et al., 2011).

The Nature and Functioning of the Capital Jury

As a unique institution in the American legal system and the focus of much constitutional jurisprudence, the capital jury has been extensively studied. A variety of different research methods have been used in studies conducted over many decades. The methods used include case studies, analysis of trial transcripts and other archival data, experimental or simulation research, and interview studies of persons who previously served as actual capital jurors.

In the case of interview studies, one major, coordinated research project deserves special mention; its data will be cited extensively in the review below. The Capital Jury Project is an interdisciplinary research project begun in 1991 and composed of research teams in 14 different states selected for their geographical diversity and the representativeness of the capital sentencing statutes and processes (e.g., Bowers, 1995; Bowers, Fleury-Steiner, & Antonio, 2003; Eisenberg & Wells, 1993). The project's core data come from lengthy, semistructured interviews conducted with actual capital jurors. They were sometimes supplemented with data from trial transcripts, interviews with judges, defense attorneys, and prosecutors (e.g., Bowers, 1995), surveys (e.g., Bowers, 1993), and jury simulations (Garvey, Johnson, & Marcus, 2000). By 2002, some 1200 interviews with persons who had served as capital jurors had been completed, and numerous aspects of the jury's decision-making process had been explored and analyzed.

Below we summarize and discuss four broad areas of the psychological research that has been conducted on the capital jury—moral disengagement, jury selection and death qualification, instructional comprehension, and jury dynamics (for more general research on juries, see Volume 1, Chapter 8, this handbook).

Moral disengagement. In its most basic form, the death penalty requires people to transcend a fundamental prohibition against taking a life. Because the death penalty is democratically administered—average citizens are required to make decisions about whether someone lives or dies— "mechanisms of moral disengagement" (Bandura, 1990) appear to play a role in facilitating the death sentencing process:

> Because, under ordinary circumstances, a group of twelve normal, law-abiding persons will not calmly, rationally, and seriously discuss the killing of another, nor will they eventually decide that the person in question should, in fact, die, and then take actions designed to bring that death about, this unique set of conditions is crucial to allow the process of death sentencing to go forward. (Haney, 1997b, p. 1447)

Mechanisms of moral disengagement can change the moral tenor of the decision making in which capital jurors engage, minimize their awareness or appreciation of the full range of consequences that are likely to follow from their actions, and reduce jurors' own sense of personal agency by lessening or displacing responsibility elsewhere. Bandura (1990) has articulated a number of different, specific mechanisms of moral disengagement, and many of them appear to be at work in the death-sentencing process. In fact, Bandura and colleagues have demonstrated the ways in which these mechanisms operate to facilitate not just the legal decision making that makes death sentences possible, but also the actual execution process in which those sentences are finally carried out (Osofsky, Bandura, & Zimbardo, 2005).

One such morally disengaging mechanism is dehumanization. As Bandura put it, "[p]eople seldom condemn punitive conduct—in fact, they create justifications for it—when they are directing their aggression at persons who have been divested of their humanness" (Bandura, 1990, p. 181). The process of dehumanization begins well in advance of a capital trial and pervades mass media depictions of criminal defendants in general. For example, Sloop (1996) analyzed the media's portrayals of criminal offenders over the 40-year period from 1950 to 1993. He found evidence of a dramatic shift away from depicting offenders as redeemable or amenable to personal growth and change. Instead, there was a growing tendency to show prisoners as irrational, predatory, dangerous, and beyond being reformed.

Violent offenders, in particular, tended to be shown as having "animalistic and senseless" characteristics that stemmed from their "warped personalities" (p.142). Similarly, Pillsbury (1989) observed that when media messages encourage the public to "assign the offender the mythic role of Monster," they help simplify the difficult task of assigning moral blame (including the task of condemning to death), making it easier "to ignore the moral complexities [inherent in the process of judging another] and declare the person and his act entirely evil," which in turn "justifies harsh treatment and insulates us from moral concerns about the suffering we inflict" (p. 692). In this context, it becomes justifiable "to kill those who are monsters or inhuman because of their abominable acts or traits, or those who are 'mere animals' (coons, pigs, rats, lice, etc.) . . ." because they have been excluded "from the universe of morally protected entities" (Williams, 1981, p. 34).

The capital trial process builds upon preexisting stereotypes about the inhumanity of persons convicted of murder and helps jurors erect psychological barriers between themselves and the defendant that further this dehumanization. Some of these barriers stem from the formality that attaches to legal language and court proceedings generally. As one legal commentator has noted, "the emotional, physical, and experiential aspects of being human have by and large been banished from the better legal neighborhoods and from explicit recognition in legal discourse . . ." (Henderson, 1987, p. 1575). Because of the way that the capital trial process is structured, opportunities to humanize the capital defendant are typically delayed until the very last phase of the trial itself. As one lawyer put it: "While the state has often presented the evidence in the guilt phase that arguably makes the homicide especially heinous, the penalty phase is usually the defense's first opportunity to present to the factfinder the personal aspects of the defendant's life . . . . [I]t would be an unusual case where the defendant's family history and character were introduced in the guilt phase" (Carter, 1987, p. 101).

Beyond the timing of the defendant's humanizing narrative, other aspects of the capital trial make it difficult to overcome the dehumanization that has preceded it. Thus, "[w]hile the defense will seek to have the jury empathize with the defendant, the defense narrative—unattached to legal form—is a difficult one to convey, and the legalistic formula can provide sanctuary from moral anxiety" (Henderson, 1987, p. 1590). As another legal commentator put it,

> The prosecution will tell a story designed to provoke anger; the defense will respond with one to evoke sympathy. The sentencer must choose between or among them. As the law now stands, this gives the prosecution a significant advantage at the punishment stage. The law's sanction of retribution and the fact of criminal conviction give weight and legitimacy to the prosecution's angry appeal. The defense needs a similar, legally authorized, emotional appeal to check that anger, to keep the debate within moral bounds. (Pillsbury, 1989, p. 607)

Another mechanism of moral disengagement involves minimizing, distorting, or ignoring the full range of consequences that one's actions are likely to bring about. Thus, Bandura (2002) noted that "[i]t is easier to harm others when their suffering is not visible and when destructive actions are physically and temporally remote from their injurious effects" (p. 108). The death qualification process, as discussed in the above section, may contribute to this in several ways. At the very outset of the capital trial—before any evidence has been presented or decisions made, and certainly before any humanizing evidence has been introduced about the defendant—it requires prospective jurors to discuss, reflect on, and imagine a possible execution. In some cases, they are questioned about this issue repeatedly and at length, and in every case they must willingly agree to play some direct role in it if called upon to do so. That is, in order to qualify, prospective jurors must at least express their willingness to impose the death penalty in what they regard as an appropriate case; otherwise they are deemed ineligible to serve and are excused by the judge. This process may desensitize them to the implications of a death sentence because contemplating the imposition of the death penalty—and in some jurors' minds agreeing to it—is a psychological barrier that they have already traversed at the very outset of the trial. It may also lead them to infer that death is the preferred legal outcome because anyone who could not agree to at least consider imposing it has been prohibited from being a capital juror (Haney, 1984b, 1984c).

Capital trials also present jurors with skewed or incomplete narratives of the consequences of violence. On the one hand, a death penalty trial appropriately focuses the jurors' attention on the violence of the defendant. Indeed, as Sarat (1995) put it, "[t]he state compels the juror to view . . . graphic representations [of the defendant's violence] and to grasp the death-producing instrumentalities which are given special evidentiary value in the state's case against the accused" (p. 1124). In addition, the U.S. Supreme Court has sanctioned so-called victim impact testimony in capital penalty trials that allows prosecutors to go even farther and, essentially, to require capital jurors to directly confront and consider the full range of terrible consequences that the defendant's violence has produced (*Payne v. Tennessee*, 1991). On the other hand, however, the law systematically and explicitly prevents capital jurors from learning anything comparable about the violence of the punishment they are being asked to help inflict. For example, as stated in one court's representative ruling on this issue: "Evidence of how the death penalty will be performed, as well as the nature and quality of life for one imprisoned for life without the possibility of parole, is properly excluded" from the jury's consideration (*People v. Fudge*, 1994, p. 1117).

Thus, capital jurors are exposed to—indeed, they are required to view—vivid narratives of the defendant's violence and are systematically excluded from any exposure to the violence that they are being invited to inflict (e.g., Sarat, 1993). The one-sided way in which the law makes one set of consequences salient and another invisible operates to disengage jurors from the full moral implications of their actions. As one legal commentator noted, "[t]he pain of the victims should be brought home to a juror asked to make a moral determination as to appropriate punishment; so should the pain of the defendant, and the violence of the execution being contemplated" (Howarth, 1994, pp. 1393–1394).

In fact, research with capital jurors also shows that not only are the details of the execution ritual systematically hidden from them but that many believe it is unlikely ever to occur. For example, one study of capital jurors in California and Oregon found that *verdict skepticism*—disbelief that the sentencing decisions they reached actually would be imposed—pervaded the deliberation process. As one of the jurors put it,

> We talked about the fact that if you have a hard time voting for the death penalty, are you really not just voting for life imprisonment? Because there hasn't been an execution in over 20 years in California. And so, you know, is it really more a statement than it is an actuality? (Haney, Sontag, & Costanzo, 1994, p. 171)

Similarly, Sarat (1995) found that capital jurors in Georgia were skeptical about whether death actually meant death or, as one of them said: "[T]hey don't put you to death. You sit on death row and get old" (p. 1133).

Another mechanism of moral disengagement involves diffusing or displacing responsibility for one's own actions to others. That is, "[p]eople will behave in ways they normally repudiate if a legitimate authority accepts responsibility for the effects of their conduct" (Bandura, 2002, p. 106). This can take several forms in a capital trial. Research tells us generally that "[t]hrough convoluted verbiage, destructive conduct is made benign and people who engage in it are relieved of a sense of personal agency" (Bandura, 1990, p. 170). As we will discuss later in this chapter, the convoluted verbiage of the capital jury instructions distances jurors from the realities of the decision they are being called upon to make, confuses many of them about the critical concept of mitigation upon which all life verdicts essentially depend, and fails to provide them with an intellectual or moral framework—or even an orderly cognitive process—by which life verdicts can be consistently reached (e.g., Geimer, 1990–1991; Haney & Lynch, 1994, 1997; Haney, Sontag, & Costanzo, 1994; Weisberg, 1984). As one scholar observed: "Under the pre-*Furman* system, the jury rendered a moral decision; it reached into its gut to decide whether death was the appropriate punishment for the defendant. Now, however, the jury is sometimes torn between rendering a moral decision and applying a legal formula they don't quite understand" (White, 1987, p. 69).

Weisberg (1984) suggested that capital jurors might "artificially distance themselves from choices by relying on legal formalities" to help dictate their verdicts (p. 391), and several studies have indicated that they do. For example, one study of Indiana capital jurors uncovered not only "juror misperception of the responsibility for the death sentencing function" (Hoffman, 1995, p. 1138), but also widespread difficulty among jurors in accepting responsibility for the defendant's fate. A study of capital jurors in South Carolina found that penalty instructions not only created false expectations about alternatives to the death penalty but also confused jurors about burdens of proof in the sentencing phase of a capital case (Eisenberg & Wells, 1993). Because of jurors' strong initial inclination to sentence to death following the typical guilt-phase trial, this significantly increased the likelihood that a death verdict would be reached. Indeed, the authors concluded that "[t]he default sentence in a capital case is death . . . . [T]he tilt towards death suggests that a defendant with a confused jury may receive a death sentence by default, without having a chance to benefit from legal standards designed to give him a chance for life" (Eisenberg & Wells, 1993, p. 12).

Thus, many capital jurors readily acknowledge the sense in which condemning someone to death is "not really my decision, it's the law's decision," and they come to believe that they are not personally sentencing someone to die but rather are simply following legal orders—whether in the form of "just weighing the factors" provided in the instructions that prevail in most death penalty states or "just answering the questions" posed in special-issues states like Texas and Oregon (Haney, Sontag, & Costanzo, 1994, pp. 166–167). Similarly, a number of capital jurors in the Indiana study tended to believe inaccurately that,

> [T]he judge's sentencing instructions were intended to define a legally "correct" capital sentencing outcome. These

jurors tended to see the sentencing decision as analogous to the guilt–innocence determination. They interpreted the judge's instructions as eliminating most of their own personal moral responsibility for choosing life or death for the defendant. (Hoffman, 1995, p. 1152)

Jury selection and death qualification. Perhaps because the capital jury's role is so important and unusual, the process by which its members are selected has been subjected to extensive empirical study and analysis. As we noted earlier, jury selection proceeds with prosecution and defense attorneys lodging challenges to prospective jurors that can be either peremptory (essentially, at their discretion) or for cause (alleging a specific legal reason that the person cannot be fair). Although most of the empirical research has focused on the particular cause challenge that is unique to capital cases—death qualification and the elimination of potential jurors on the basis of their death penalty attitudes—the peremptory challenge process has also been studied.

Winick (1982) was among the first to observe that the unique focus on the death penalty attitudes of prospective jurors during capital jury selection allowed for the use of peremptory challenges to bias the composition of the jury that was ultimately selected. He noted that questioning prospective jurors about their death penalty attitudes provided attorneys—in particular, prosecutors—with an opportunity to use peremptory challenges to eliminate persons moderately opposed to the death penalty but otherwise legally qualified to serve. He concluded that this tendency in essence "deprives capital defendants of their due process right to an impartial jury on sentence" (Winick, 1982, p. 82), because even persons moderately opposed to or ambivalent about the death penalty could (and often would) be eliminated. When considered in conjunction with the effects of the exclusions that occur as a result of death qualification (as discussed in more detail below), Winick (1982) concluded that this "produces capital juries that are significantly more prone to convict than would be neutral juries, thereby depriving the capital defendant of his due process right to an impartial jury on guilt" (p. 82).

In a later analysis, Baldus and colleagues reached a number of similar conclusions, including the fact that prosecutors had a significant comparative advantage over defense attorneys in using peremptory challenges to shape the composition of capital juries. Specifically, Baldus et al. (2001) found that prosecutors used this advantage to eliminate larger numbers of Blacks (who are less likely in general to support the death penalty) and that the racial composition of the jury—whether produced by the discriminatory effects of death qualification or the discriminatory use of peremptory challenges—made a difference in death sentencing rates, especially for Black defendants. Thus, although predominately Black juries (with five or more Black members) were significantly less likely to render death sentences than predominately White juries (with four or fewer Black members), the jury selection process ensured that predominately Black juries were very difficult to obtain.

Most of the research on jury selection in capital cases has focused on death qualification, i.e., the practice of excusing persons for cause because of their strong opinions about capital punishment. The early research done on the effects of death qualification focused on the legal standard that was established in *Witherspoon v. Illinois* (1968) and that was in operation in capital cases until 1985. In *Witherspoon*, the United States Supreme Court authorized courts to preclude persons from sitting on capital juries if they expressed an unwillingness to impose the death penalty in any case, no matter the facts and circumstances. In *Wainwright v. Witt* (1985), the standard was changed to exclude persons who said that their death penalty attitudes would prevent or substantially impair them from performing their duties as jurors.

Wainwright appeared to broaden the basis or standard by which a prospective juror could be found excludable, beyond the one articulated in *Witherspoon*, and to correspondingly limit the number of persons whose death penalty attitudes rendered them qualified. Thompson (1989) noted at the time that *Wainwright* "expands the class of individuals who may be excluded from capital juries because of their feelings about the death penalty"

(p. 186), and he and other scholars and researchers expressed concern over the implications of this expansion. Also, by the time *Wainwright* was decided, most states had begun to provide for the exclusion of persons who were so strongly in favor of the death penalty that their extreme views meant that they, too, could not be fair. Although this was ostensibly intended to balance the attitudes represented on the jury, the number of persons excluded on the basis of their extreme support for the death penalty never remotely approximated the number who were disqualified by virtue of their opposition and did not appear to significantly reduce bias (e.g., Kadane, 1984; Luginbuhl & Middendorf, 1988).

In any event, a number of studies have shown that death qualification has a number of deleterious effects overall. It reduces the representativeness of the resulting jury pool, changes its attitudinal mix or composition in ways that render it more oriented toward law enforcement and less sensitive to the due process rights of defendants, and produces a group that is more likely to convict on the basis of the same set of facts and circumstances. In addition, exposure to the process of death qualification itself creates a number of problematic tendencies and expectations, including guilt-proneness. In short, research shows that death qualification creates capital juries that are different from the kind of jury that sits in every other kind of criminal case, and different in ways that are adverse to the interests of capital defendants. As two researchers summarized these studies overall: "At all stages of the trial—jury selection, determination of guilt or innocence, and the final judgment of whether the defendant lives or dies—death qualification results in bias against the capital defendant of a nature that occurs for no other criminal defendant" (Luginbuhl & Middendorf, 1988, p. 279).

More specifically the composition effects of death qualification arise from the fact that people's attitudes about the death penalty are correlated with other things about them. Because persons who strongly oppose the death penalty have many other characteristics and attitudes in common, any procedure that eliminates them also will disproportionately exclude those other characteristics from being represented in the jury pool. Thus, one important way in which the composition of the capital jury is compromised by death qualification concerns the representativeness of the group of eligible, prospective jurors that it creates, and especially the fact that women and Blacks, who are historically more likely to oppose the death penalty than other groups (e.g., T. Smith, 1976; Ziesel & Gallup, 1989), are therefore significantly more likely to be excluded from the capital jury pool. As a result, a process that selects eligible jurors essentially on the basis of their death penalty support will exclude disproportionately greater numbers of women and Blacks (e.g., Bronson, 1970, 1980; Fitzgerald & Ellsworth, 1984; Haney, Hurtado, & Vega, 1994). In addition, because Blacks are already underrepresented on the jury lists in many parts of the country (e.g., Alker, Hosticka, & Mitchell, 1976; Fukurai, Butler, & Krooth, 1993; Fukurai & Krooth, 2003), death qualification may act to compound a preexisting problem.

Studies show that death qualification also biases the composition of the capital jury by skewing attitudinal make-up. Any process that systematically eliminates persons with strong feelings about the death penalty is likely to leave behind a group that differs on a host of other interrelated criminal justice attitudes. Fitzgerald and Ellsworth (1984) captured many of these differences in research that showed that death-qualified jurors were more likely to favor crime control perspectives on criminal justice issues, as opposed to persons excluded by the then-operative *Witherspoon* standard, who tended to endorse a host of due process–related attitudes. Among the beliefs that the death-qualified respondents were significantly more likely to hold are that the failure of a defendant to testify at trial is indicative of guilt, the insanity plea is a loophole, and that defense attorneys "need to be watched."

More recent studies that used the newer *Wainwright* standard, and accounted for the exclusion of extreme prodeath penalty prospective jurors (the requirement in all capital cases after *Morgan v. Illinois*, 1992), found that some attitudinal and other effects were attenuated, but a number of others remained. For example, one study (Haney, Hurtado, & Vega, 1994) using these newer constitutional standards found that, compared to those persons who would be excluded from sitting on a capital jury,

death-qualified persons were less likely to be women or minorities, less concerned about convicting the innocent, more likely to endorse punishment-related polices in general, more likely to find a number of key case facts as aggravating and less likely to find a number of others as mitigating. Death-qualified persons were also less knowledgeable about the system of death sentencing itself (including being significantly less likely to believe that life without parole really meant that a prisoner would not be released from prison), and they had fewer concerns about potential flaws in the system of death sentencing (including being less concerned that innocent people might too often be convicted of capital crimes, or that the death penalty might be unfair to minorities).

In a series of studies regarding the characteristics of death-qualified persons versus those who would be excluded from capital jury service under current legal practices, Butler and colleagues have found that death-qualified jurors are more likely to be male, White, moderately well-educated, politically conservative, Catholic or Protestant, and middle class (Butler & Moran, 2002). Like other researchers (e.g., Cowan, Thompson, & Ellsworth, 1984; Moran & Comfort, 1986; Thompson, Cowan, Ellsworth, & Harrington, 1984), Butler found that death-qualified persons are more likely to find capital defendants guilty and, of course, to sentence them to death (the basis on which they are selected). Butler and colleagues also found the death qualified to be more likely to express racist, sexist, and homophobic views (Butler, 2007a), and to hold what social psychologists have described as a "belief in a just world" that renders them more punitive in capital cases (perhaps because they believe that bad things should always happen to people who have themselves done bad things; Butler & Moran, 2007a). In addition, these jurors are more susceptible to drawing flawed conclusions from flawed science (Butler & Moran, 2007b), are more likely to be skeptical of defenses involving mental illness (including the insanity defense; Butler & Wasserman, 2006), more likely to be influenced by the kind of potentially prejudicial pretrial publicity that often surrounds capital cases (Butler, 2007b), and more likely to be affected by the victim impact statements that may be introduced during the sentencing phase of capital trials (Butler, 2008).

One of the most well-documented and problematic effects of death qualification on the composition of the capital jury pertains to what researchers have termed its conviction proneness. By limiting capital jury participation to only those persons who, among other things, share a pro-prosecution and crime-control perspective and hold more favorable (often erroneous) beliefs about how the system of death sentencing actually functions, death qualification ensures that the evidence presented at trial will be filtered through a particular set of juror predispositions. Surely there are some cases in which the weight of the evidence will completely determine the outcome of the case, and no amount of bias or predisposition will alter the verdict. In other cases, however, even jurors who take seriously their responsibility to base decisions on the evidence and nothing else may be influenced in subtle ways by preexisting attitudes and expectations. Thus, death-qualified jurors may literally see a different case and be "perceptually ready" (Bruner, 1957) to perceive incriminating evidence, give greater credibility and weight to prosecution witnesses, and apply different standards of reasonable doubt and the presumption of innocence than jurors who are more impartial. Ultimately, as the effects of these biases and predispositions accumulate throughout the trial, they may well make their presence felt in changing the likelihood of conviction.

The basic proposition that death-qualified juries might be conviction-prone was first suggested more than 50 years ago (Oberer, 1961). Numerous studies done since then confirmed this (e.g., Bronson, 1970, 1980; Goldberg, 1970; Jurow, 1971). For example, Thompson et al. (1984) found that trial testimony is not only evaluated differently by death-qualified and excludable jurors, but that "death-qualified jurors perceive conflicting, ambiguous testimony in a way that follows the prosecution's version of events, perhaps because that version corresponds to a script that is readily available to them" (p. 111). They also found that death-qualified jurors showed a willingness to convict on a lesser showing of guilt than persons excluded by the death qualification process. Perhaps

not surprisingly, Cowan et al. (1984) found that death-qualified jurors were half as likely as those excluded by death qualification to vote not guilty (22.1% vs. 46.7%) on predeliberation ballots in a potential capital case scenario, and nearly a third as likely to acquit after deliberation had taken place (13.7% vs. 34.5%). Other researchers have reached similar conclusions. In fact, a meta-analysis of studies done through the late 1990s concluded simply: "The results indicate that the more a person favors the death penalty, the more likely that person is to vote to convict a defendant" (Allen, Mabry, & McKelton, 1998, p. 724). Thus, to the extent that death qualification selects jurors on the basis of their willingness to impose the death penalty, it is also likely to produce juries that are conviction-prone.

Death qualification also biases the death-sentencing process is an obvious way: By ensuring that the only jurors who are allowed to decide whether a capital defendant lives or dies are ones that have been selected on the basis of their willingness to impose the death penalty, a capital jury is more likely to actually impose the death penalty than one selected through non–death-qualifying voir dire. Several studies have looked beneath the surface of this obvious fact to explore some of the specific mechanisms by which this occurs, finding that death qualification in essence also selects for persons who are differentially responsive to certain mitigating and aggravating circumstances of the sort that are commonly presented in the penalty phase of a capital trial. That is, death-qualified jurors are not only more in favor of the death penalty in the abstract, but they are also less likely to attend positively to certain mitigating facts about the defendant and are more likely to react negatively to certain aggravating facts about him or his crime (e.g., Haney, Hurtado, & Vega, 1994; Luginbuhl & Middendorf, 1988; Moran & Comfort, 1986). Together these studies suggest that death-qualified jurors not only start out more in favor of the death penalty but, because of their differential sensitivity to different kinds of potential penalty phase evidence, are less likely to be persuaded that life imprisonment is an appropriate sentence.

Finally, Haney (1984b, 1984c) found that merely exposing persons to the unusual and suggestive process of death qualification in which, as we have noted, they are asked to contemplate the defendant's conviction and make a public commitment to be willing to at least consider voting to authorize his execution has independent biasing effects. Haney found that exposure to the process led jurors to be more conviction-prone, to infer that the other major trial participants believed that the defendant was guilty (which would account for their focus on his punishment) in advance of evidence having been presented, and that the law "disapproves" of death penalty opposition (perhaps because death qualification results in those persons who express disapproval being excluded from participating as jurors).

Recall that, in *Lockhart v. McCree* (1986), the United States Supreme Court considered a substantial amount of the research that documented the biasing effects of death qualification and nonetheless refused to prohibit the practice. As one commentator soberly concluded about the decision: "A more complete repudiation of social science research could hardly have been accomplished" (Acker, 1993, p. 76). The decision in effect guaranteed that, at least for the immediate future, death sentences would continue to be meted out by a carefully selected group of jurors who differed along a number of important and problematic dimensions, including being less representative and more guilt- and death penalty–prone than those who decide other kinds of criminal cases.

Instructional comprehension. At least since *Gregg v. Georgia* (1976), the United States Supreme Court has relied very heavily on the use of judicially administered sentencing instructions to attempt to control the previously unbridled and unconstitutional discretion with which capital jurors once acted (e.g., *Furman v. Georgia*, 1972). These instructions are a central feature of the overall system of capital punishment to which the Court has given its approval and continued to confer legitimacy for nearly 40 years. As we have explained, under the post-*Furman* model of death sentencing, if and when a defendant has been convicted of a potentially capital crime, jurors enter a second stage of the trial—a penalty or selection phase—in which they are asked to determine whether the defendant should be sentenced to

death or life in prison without possibility of parole. At this stage, under the sentencing statutes in place in the great majority of jurisdictions, jurors are permitted to hear evidence on both aggravating and mitigating factors or circumstances that are intended to influence them in favor of returning, respectively, either a death or a life verdict. Statutes commonly identify specific aggravating factors that narrow the scope of what can be considered but allow a very broad range of mitigating factors to be introduced and taken into account. Jurors are instructed to consider, take into account, and be guided by this evidence and, usually through some kind of a weighing process, are to a render sentencing verdict by selecting one of the two possible punishments.

Unfortunately, there is much evidence that this guided discretion model does not work as the Court intended. In addition to the way that many statutes fail to adequately narrow the range of death-eligible cases, as we discussed earlier, studies show that capital jury verdicts are still plagued by continued arbitrariness and even racial discrimination. Direct attempts to explain these patterns have focused heavily on the nature and effect of the instructions themselves, especially the extent to which they are poorly comprehended by the persons whose behavior they are supposed to guide. Numerous studies have documented the incomprehensibility of different versions of the capital sentencing instructions that are in use in various jurisdictions across the United States (Diamond, 1993; Diamond & Levi, 1996; Haney & Lynch, 1994; Haney, Sontag, & Costanzo, 1994; Levi, 1993; Luginbuhl & Howe, 1995; Tiersma, 1995; Wiener, Pritchard, & Weston, 1995; Wiener et al., 2004). Because it seems unlikely that jurors can be properly guided by instructions that they are unable to comprehend, this research has raised serious questions about the fairness and reliability of the life-and-death decisions that have been rendered by capital juries in the modern era of death sentencing.

Aside from the limited utility of any instruction that cannot be properly understood by the persons whose discretion is supposed to be guided by it, two additional aspects of this problem bear emphasis. The first is that even confused jurors must render a penalty phase verdict. Their confusion may mean that they are more easily influenced by irrelevant peripheral cues, more likely to fall back on simple judgment heuristics, or more willing to rely on a brand of commonsense justice that includes preexisting stereotypes and prejudices that are scarcely different from the unbridled discretion condemned in *Furman*—save its appearance of having been sanitized by judicial instructions (Haney, 1997a).

The second problematic aspect concerns the asymmetry of the comprehension errors that studies show jurors make. Recall that the penalty-phase instructions in use in most jurisdictions juxtapose two central categories or kinds of evidence— aggravating and mitigating circumstances—and that jurors are supposed to take into account and weigh this opposing evidence to reach their sentencing decisions. These key terms and the weighing process itself are what most studies show jurors simply fail to understand. The errors that occur, however, are much more serious and widespread in the case of one of the key terms—mitigation. In several studies done in California, for example, after having heard the sentencing instructions read several times, not only were comparatively few people able to define the term *mitigation* in even a partially correct manner, but the definitions they did correctly provide tended to relate only to aspects of the crime rather than to the defendant (the opposite of the kind of mitigation that is presented in a typical capital penalty phase). In contrast, the term *aggravation*—the evidence that leads jurors to favor death verdicts—was not only much better understood overall but it was also understood in exactly the crime-related ways in which such evidence typically is introduced at trial (Haney & Lynch, 1994, 1997; Lynch & Haney, 2000).

The crime-focused understanding of these key sentencing terms may help explain the tendencies that were identified by the Capital Jury Project in their postverdict interviews with actual capital jurors. Project researching described an "obsessive focus on the defendant's guilt of the crime" that carried over into the penalty trial and distorted the jurors view of mitigation. As the author put it,

> The jurors do not appear to have grappled with the notion that, despite the defendant's clear guilt of an aggravated murder, they could decide that he deserved a sentence other than death. What is missing from these interviews is any real recognition of a separate choice, an independent decision about whether this defendant should suffer the ultimate penalty of death. (Bentele & Bowers, 2001, p. 1031)

Recall that the Supreme Court mandated that "all relevant mitigating evidence" (*Buchanan v. Angelone*, 1998, p. 276) be allowed to be introduced into the penalty or selection phase of a capital trial in order to ensure the fairness and reliability of the individualized sentencing process. Yet the value of this opportunity to present a wide range of potential mitigation may be compromised by the fact that penalty-phase instructions fail to properly define and explain the meaning of mitigation; jurors unclear on the concept are unlikely to know whether and how to properly make use of whatever mitigating evidence they do receive. These problems may well contribute to what has been called "wrongful condemnations" (Haney, 2006)—the penalty-phase analogue of wrongful convictions in which a capital defendant, sentenced to death, should have and would have been sentenced to life instead if the available mitigation in his case had been effectively presented to a jury that fully comprehended its mitigating significance under applicable constitutional standards.

Finally, we should note that there have been a limited number of attempts to correct at least some of the problems with instructional comprehension by using psycholinguistic principles to rewrite the penalty-phase instructions in ways that are intended to make them clearer and, in some instances, not just easier to understand and to be guided by but also to connect the instructions to the specific facts of the case at hand (e.g., A. Smith & Haney, 2011; Wiener et al., 2004). To date, these attempts have produced limited but promising results. However, they have been used in only a limited number of jurisdictions and typically without any systematic empirical evaluation of whether and how well they are working.

Jury dynamics. Capital juries operate as small groups, ones charged with a unique legal task and daunting moral responsibility. As the Supreme Court itself observed, a "capital sentencing jury is made up of individuals placed in a very unfamiliar situation and called on to make a very difficult and uncomfortable choice" (*Caldwell v. Mississippi*, 1985, p. 242). In fact, researchers have documented some of the emotional impact of serving as a capital juror and discharging these extraordinary duties. Indications of the immense mental and physical strain experienced by capital jurors appear in reports of posttrial personal problems, nightmares, regret, fear, physical illness, and even drug abuse (Antonio, 2006, 2008).

The behavior of the capital jury has been studied not only through the lens of the extraordinary reason for which they have been assembled but also the legal rules that are intended to govern the decisions they make, the composition and characteristics of the jury members who make them, the kind of evidence that is brought to bear on the decision-making process, and the characteristics of the victims and defendants in the cases where a sentencing verdict must be rendered. Because the capital jury's unique legal task and daunting moral responsibility are concentrated primarily in the penalty phase of a capital trial, most of the research focuses on the dynamics and decision making which occur at that stage of the case.

It is worth noting, however, that the Capital Jury Project has found that in some states approximately half of the jurors they interviewed reported discussing punishment during the guilt phase of the trial (Sandys, 1995), and approximately half also revealed that they had personally decided on an appropriate penalty during that first phase (Bowers, Sandys, & Steiner, 1998). Those who had a penalty preference before the penalty phase of the trial commenced were significantly more likely to support a death sentence (Sandys, 1995). In addition, evidence from the guilt phase was not only used in the penalty phase, but many jurors based their penalty decisions largely or exclusively on the facts of the crime or the mere fact that the defendant had been convicted in the first phase of the case (Bentele & Bowers, 2001). Of course, if penalty decisions are made before the presentation of any mitigating and aggravating evidence has occurred, and in

advance of jurors being instructed on how and why such evidence is relevant to and should be considered in making their life-and-death decision, its constitutionally mandated significance will be thwarted (e.g., Bowers et al., 1998).

Consistent with what we said earlier about the role of moral disengagement in the death-sentencing process, the Capital Jury Project also has found that many jurors absolve themselves of personal responsibility for the death verdicts they have rendered by telling interviewers that they felt pressured into voting in favor of the death penalty because they (erroneously) believed that the law required this sentence whenever certain aggravating circumstances had been proven (e.g., Bentele & Bowers, 2001; Garvey et al., 2000). In addition to reporting that the law had somehow compelled them to reach a death verdict, many also explicitly shifted the responsibility for the decision away from themselves and attributed it to others, including the assertion that they were following judicial and even religious mandates (e.g., Bowers, 1995; Bowers, Foglia, Giles, & Antonio, 2006; Hoffman, 1995).

As we noted earlier, in discussing the asymmetry of the narratives of violence that occur in the typical capital trial, the U.S. Supreme Court has permitted the introduction of *victim impact* testimony into the penalty or selection stage of a capital case, allowing family members and others deeply affected by the victim's death to describe that impact to the jury. Much of the research conducted on the nature and effect of victim impact testimony has suggested that jurors are indeed influenced by it (e.g., Greene, 1999; Luginbuhl & Burkhead, 1995). Although it is not necessarily determinative of the outcome of a capital trial, independent of other features of the case and additional evidence that is presented (e.g., T. Gordon & Brodsky, 2007), studies show that victim impact testimony generally generates sympathy and empathy toward victims, and that it provokes anger, hostility, and vengeful feelings toward capital defendants that can lead to increased levels of death sentencing (e.g., Paternoster & Deise, 2011).

Jurors also seem to be influenced by aspects of victim impact testimony that technically should not significantly influence their judgment of the defendant's culpability or *death worthiness*. That is, the power of victim impact testimony to persuade jurors to return death verdicts turns in part on how respectable (e.g., Greene, Koehring, & Quiat, 1998) or valuable (e.g., Eisenberg, Garvey, & Wells, 2003) or innocent as opposed to troubled (e.g., Sundby, 2003) the jurors perceive the victim(s) to be. Specifically, the more respectable or valuable or innocent jurors perceive the victim, the more serious the crime and the more death-worthy the defendant are regarded. Critics have argued that because the potentially emotionally inflammatory nature of victim impact testimony combines with this tendency of jurors to focus on the social value of the victims in judging the defendant's death-worthiness, its use in capital penalty trials actually exacerbates the very kind of arbitrary death sentencing that the Supreme Court has otherwise sought to avoid (e.g., Logan, 1999; Myers & Greene, 2004).

A significant amount of research has been done on the ways in which the composition of the capital jury and the resulting decision-making dynamics affect sentencing outcomes. By looking at the interaction of a number of variables that have been shown separately to influence jury decision making, researchers have gained insights into the way in which the death-sentencing process unfolds and with what consequence. For example, the Capital Jury Project and others have conducted a number of such studies on the racial dynamics that are generated both by the racial dimensions of the case facts (in particular, the race of the defendant and victim) and the demographic characteristics of the jurors. Among other things, they found that the racial make-up of the jury has a large impact on jury dynamics and sentencing decisions (e.g., Bowers et al., 2001), particularly in cases with Black defendants and White victims. In one study, for example, Eisenberg, Garvey, and Wells (2001) found that Black jurors were less likely than Whites to choose death in the first vote taken during penalty deliberations and, although Black and White jurors did not differ by the time of final vote, the first vote was critically important: the proportion of life to death votes at first ballot was the single largest predictor of final sentence.

As we have noted, mitigation plays a special role in capital penalty-phase deliberations because it provides the jurors with crucial information about the defendant's background and character that allows them to more fairly and meaningfully assess his culpability (Haney, 1995; 2008a). A number of studies have examined whether there are racial differences in the way in which this important kind of evidence is handled by jurors. Researchers have reported that Black jurors in general are more likely to feel empathy for the defendant (e.g., Garvey, 2000), potentially making them more sensitive to mitigating evidence (e.g., Bowers et al., 2004; Brewer, 2004). In another study of capital jury dynamics, Baldus et al. (1998) examined whether and how capital juries handled mitigating evidence as a function of the race of the defendant. They found that capital juries were much more likely to give credence to mitigating evidence that was offered on behalf of non-Black defendants, whereas they gave little weight to such evidence when the defendant was Black. The same kind of discounting of mitigation occurred in those cases where there were non-Black victims.

Another capital jury sentencing dynamic that Capital Jury Project researchers have uncovered was termed the *White male dominance effect*. Specifically, they found that the presence of five or more White male jurors on a jury was associated with a significantly higher rate of death sentencing in those cases in which a Black defendant was being punished for having killed a White victim (Bowers et al., 2004). On the other hand, a so-called Black male presence effect occurred when one or more Black male jurors were present in the same kinds of cases, which substantially reduces the chances of a death verdict (Bowers et al., 2004). Their interview data suggested that these overall patterns were a function of the fact that White and Black men typically came to very different conclusions about what they perceived to be the Black defendant's remorsefulness, dangerousness, and his cold-bloodedness (pp. 1531–1532). Moreover, as Brewer (2004) also found, the Black men in this study reported being more empathic toward the defendants in these cases than did any other category of jurors.

In another Capital Jury Project study, Garvey (2000) found that the role that emotion played in death sentencing varied as a function of the race of the jurors. He reported that White jurors expressed much more anger toward defendants overall than Black jurors did, irrespective of the defendants' race. Garvey also found that Black jurors were more able to find something likable about the defendant and to empathize with the defendant than their White counterparts, and concluded that Black jurors were much more likely to "keep the sin separate from the sinner" (Garvey, 2000, p. 47) in both Black and White defendant cases.

Haney and Lynch approached some of these issues with a fundamentally different research method but reached many of the same conclusions. Examining the sentencing implications of their earlier studies (Haney & Lynch, 1994, 1997) showing that capital jury sentencing instructions were difficult to comprehend overall and that the least understood concept in the instructions appeared to be mitigation—the kind of evidence that leads jurors to life sentences rather than death sentences—Haney and Lynch conducted several simulation studies to explore whether instructional comprehension was related to racially discriminatory death sentencing. In the first study, individual jury-eligible, death-qualified adults rendered individual verdicts after viewing one of four simulated penalty trials in which race of defendant and victim were orthogonally varied (Lynch & Haney, 2000). In a follow-up study (Lynch & Haney, 2009), a hundred small group juries comprised of four–seven jurors were randomly assigned to one of the same four conditions and, after viewing the same simulated penalty trial tape, were given an opportunity to deliberate to verdict.

In both studies, Black defendants were significantly more likely to be sentenced to death than White defendants (although in the second study, this occurred only after deliberation), jurors who demonstrated poor comprehension of the instructions were more likely to be influenced by race, and although the understanding of mitigation was poor overall, mitigating evidence was less likely to be given its appropriate weight and actually was more likely to be improperly used in the cases in which a Black defendant was being judged. In the deliberation study, the postdeliberation effect appeared to be driven primarily by the White men on the jury. This White male dominance effect was primarily a function of the divergent ways in which they used the mitigating evidence that was presented to make attributions about the defendant's character as a function of the defendant's race. The researchers concluded that, in addition to racial animus that certain jurors may bring to a capital trial, the jury's inability to cross an "empathic divide" and take into account the life struggles of a Black defendant also appear to be a function of group-level processes and dynamics that occur in the course of deliberation. Those processes and dynamics seemed to activate and exacerbate rather than neutralize or contain preexisting biases.

PRACTICE AND POLICY ISSUES

Capital punishment remains an extremely controversial and intensely criticized practice in the United States and throughout most of the rest of the world. After several decades of successful international abolitionist activity, there are only a very few modern democracies that still retain the practice—notably, the United States, India, and Japan (e.g., Hood, 2001; Hood & Hoyle, 2008). Public opinion in the United States remains extremely divided on the issue of the death penalty, as it has throughout most of the nation's history. Over the last few decades, there has been a trend toward decreased use of the death penalty and, in some places, outright abolition. Fewer death sentences are being returned by capital juries and, at present, only a small percentage of counties in the United States continue to actively utilize capital punishment. These trends appear to be based on a number of factors, including the high cost of the death penalty (especially relative to the minimal or nonexistent return in increased public safety), the surprisingly frequent number of miscarriages of justice that have surfaced in capital cases in recent decades, and the persistence of evidence of arbitrariness and unfairness in the application of the death penalty. The gap appears to be narrowing between the popular and political fictions about capital punishment and what the public and politicians now more accurately understand about its empirical realities.

Most of the research that we have reviewed in this chapter has raised fundamental questions about the utility or purpose of the death penalty and critically examined the manner in which it is administered in the United States. The existence of extensive research that consistently and systematically documents such fundamental flaws and imperfections in our system of death sentencing inevitably raises questions about its moral as well as legal underpinnings. The problems that have been identified with the administration of capital punishment are basic and widespread. For this reason, as we will suggest, they do not lend themselves to piecemeal or partial solutions. Indeed, we believe that this body of research leads very clearly to the conclusion that the death penalty must either be reformed in truly fundamental and comprehensive ways, or it must be abandoned entirely (e.g., Haney, 2005).

In fact, many scholars, researchers, and legal analysts have concluded that the issues and problems that we have identified in the nature and administration of capital punishment simply cannot be addressed effectively enough to ensure fair and equitable administration, and have recommended its abolition. Indeed, Justice Harry Blackmun, who often voted to uphold the death penalty against systemic constitutional challenges during his tenure on the Supreme Court, finally declared that he would "no longer . . . tinker with the machinery of death" (*Callins v. Collins*, 1994, p. 1145) because, after decades of carefully and closely examining the system of death sentencing, he had finally come to the conclusion that "capital punishment cannot morally or constitutionally be imposed" (*McFarland v. Scott*, 1994, p. 1264).

Without presuming to take a moral position on the resolution of these issues, in this section of the chapter we examine the policy implications and recommendations for reform that follow from the empirical study of the system of death sentencing. Moving from the least to most expansive proposals, we first consider attempts to reform especially dysfunctional components of the system, then turn to calls for more comprehensive overhaul, and finally to advocacy of outright abolition. Our policy

suggestions take seriously the challenge to "make law modern" by incorporating "a contemporary contextual, situational, or social–psychological model of behavior [that] will have profound consequences for both the form and substance of our law and legal apparatus" (Haney, 2002, p. 4)

One general set of policy implications and recommendations that emerge from the empirical literature on capital punishment is the need to address the broader context of myth and misinformation in the system of death sentencing. Public opinion is plagued by a relative lack of accurate knowledge about how the death penalty actually is administered and with what consequences. This is all the more problematic because, as Finckenauer (1988) observed, "[p]ublic opinion certainly seems to play a role in the setting of criminal justice policy, including (and perhaps especially) policy regarding capital punishment" (p. 83). Quite apart from what has been empirically documented about the Marshall Hypothesis and the prediction that accurate knowledge invariably leads people to reject capital punishment, it seems clear that, if criminal justice policy is to be shaped by public opinion at all, it should be influenced by public opinion that is well informed rather than based on erroneous factual predicates.

Similar recommendations can be made about the U.S. Supreme Court's analyses of death penalty–related constitutional issues. The Court's long-standing reluctance to rely on and reference social science research has been especially glaring in the case of capital punishment. Although the landmark *Furman v. Georgia* (1972) case was a clear exception to this long-standing tendancy, the Court's record since then has been mixed and problematic. For example, Acker (1993) reviewed some 28 Supreme Court death penalty decisions that were decided between 1986 and 1989 and concluded that "social science evidence had little influence on the Court's death penalty decisions. Lead opinions brushed aside convincing empirical evidence . . . and refused to consider social-scientific evidence relevant to capital punishment" (p. 82). Sometime later, other commentators reached essentially the same conclusion: "Supreme Court justices rarely take into account empirical research when making decisions, and they seem particularly opposed to incorporating social-scientific scrutiny of the death penalty" (Clarke, Lambert, & Whitt, 2000–2001, p. 309). Although the situation improved in the case of two more recent decisions (notably, *Atkins v. Virginia* and *Roper v. Simmons*), there is little to suggest that those cases marked a new commitment to empirical jurisprudence in constitutional decision making about the death penalty.

Turning to more issue-specific policy reforms, attempts to operationalize the legal category of the worst of the worst in order to better define death-eligible levels of culpability have yielded decidedly uneven results, with the Court's research-based categorical exclusions for juvenile defendants (in *Roper v. Simmons*) succeeding in creating a workable, bright-line rule where other approaches to narrow death eligibility have not. One simple and conceptually straightforward solution to the problem of over-breadth in death-eligibility would be the implementation of statutory reform in those jurisdictions (such as California) whose laws are over-inclusive. This would entail drastically reducing the number of death-eligible crimes to include only limited, well-defined acts that are significantly more egregious than common murders (e.g., Alarcón & Mitchell, 2010). At the other end of the death-sentencing process, it would require that enhanced and truly meaningful proportionality reviews be conducted, in which death verdicts are carefully scrutinized to ensure that they have been returned only in cases that are unequivocally regarded as the worst of the worst. Although these reforms appear to be conceptually simple, the strategies that would be required to successfully navigate the complex political dynamics that stand in the way of implementing them seem challenging (but are beyond the scope of our empirically oriented social science analysis.)

With respect to the critical and perennially debated issue of the deterrent effect of the death penalty, as we noted, no conclusive evidence has been produced demonstrating that such an effect exists. We have alluded to the basic psychological reasons why this may be so. At the most fundamental theoretical level, the core assumption that potential lawbreakers are even capable of the complex decision-making processes on which deterrence

depends—let alone whether they actually use them—appears to be misguided. In addition to the questionable psychological assumptions on which it is based, there are seemingly insurmountable methodological limitations to manner in which the deterrent effect of capital punishment can be studied. As Knorr (1979) has suggested, the proper question may not be whether the death penalty deters, but whether researchers have the ability to determine if it does. Either way, an important policy implication of the existing state of research on this question is that capital punishment cannot and should not be justified on the basis of an effect that can only be presumed (i.e., one that empirical research not only has never definitively demonstrated but also never will or can). Moreover, it remains unclear whether and how, in practical terms, such a deterrent effect could actually be created or improved upon. In light of this, a seemingly wiser and empirically more defensible approach to the reduction of capital crime might well be to divert some or all of the substantial resources that are devoted to our system of death sentencing and to invest them instead in efforts aimed at reducing the criminogenic forces—especially exposure to childhood trauma and risk factors—that we now know are so strongly associated with serious violent crime.

Similarly, persistent patterns of racially discriminatory death sentencing provide evidence that the legal system continues to be plagued by the taint of individual and institutional racism. Researchers have effectively documented the myriad and complex ways that race matters in capital cases. To date, however, these insights have been largely ignored, as exemplified by *McCleskey v. Kemp* (1987). Until *McCleskey's* requirement that a successful equal protection claim required proof of an individual intent to discriminate is overturned, systemic remedies to racial discrimination in the administration of capital punishment may have to be pursued in venus beyond or outside the courts. For example, it seems more reasonable at this juncture to seek legislative remedies—perhaps in the form of so-called racial justice acts in which capital defendants are explicitly permitted to use statistical data to establish broad patterns of racially discriminatory charging or death sentencing as the basis for claims of unconstitutionality (e.g., Chemerinsky, 1995). North Carolina's

Racial Justice Act also provided some remedy to the problem of race-based jury selection by allowing county-based challenges based on the patterns of peremptory challenges that are exercised by prosecutors (O'Brien & Grosso, 2013). Admittedly, however, such legislative reforms are also susceptible to political trade-offs and uncertainties; compromises in the drafting of these kinds of laws and threats to repeal them can drastically limit enforcement mechanisms and render them impermanent. At another level, a number of other changes in death penalty procedure and practice that we will discuss below—such as limiting or eliminating death qualification, rewriting capital sentencing instructions to improve their comprehension, and emphasizing the more effective use of mitigation—may have salutary effects on racially discriminatory patterns of death sentencing. Yet many of the race-related problems that continue to plague the administration of capital punishment are widespread, endemic, and seemingly intractable.

With respect to public opinion about the death penalty, the problem for which a policy-related solution seems appropriate and, frankly, long overdue is one to which we have already alluded: even abstract death penalty support tends to be premised on a lack of knowledge or understanding about how the system of capital punishment actually operates. A number of studies have indicated that persons who know the least about how the system of death sentencing actually functions are likely to support it most. We would argue that it is difficult to defend any legal and public policy that is premised so much on widespread ignorance, especially when it is a policy that places individual lives in jeopardy. Thus, the continued collection and analysis of accurate information about the system of death sentencing by social science researchers and the increasingly widespread public dissemination of these findings seem essential. Campaigns of public education that examine and discuss the realities of death sentencing can enhance the general level of debate over whether and how capital punishment should be modified and preserved, and can better ensure that these realities are taken honestly and accurately into account in public policy initiatives. The Marshall Hypothesis notwithstanding, continued public support for the preservation of the death penalty must at least be predicated on accurate views of the way the system actually functions. Otherwise, we belive that it is hard to justify its continued existence.

Death penalty laws may be influenced by myth and misinformation in another way. There is some research to suggest that state lawmakers overestimate the public's demand for capital punishment and then adapt their legislative preferences to those distorted perceptions (Sandys & McGarrell, 1994). Such misperceptions may have catalyzed and facilitated the widespread political manipulation of capital punishment, elevating its stature as a wedge issue in the 1980s and 1990s (Pierce & Radelet, 1990). This possibility underscores the importance of ensuring that lawmakers are optimally informed about a range of death penalty–related topics and issues. They should be targeted by educational campaigns that accurately portray the realities of capital punishment, sensitizing these key decision makers to the true nature of the system of death sentencing they fund and help administer, and keeping them accurately informed about the nature of public opinion on which they ostensibly rely.

Turning to the capital jury, as we have noted, a substantial amount of research has documented numerous, persistent problems in the death-sentencing process. A number of studies—many of them conducted by Capital Jury Project researchers—have underscored the failure of the constitutionally mandated reforms that became the hallmark of the modern system of death sentencing following *Furman v. Georgia*. The findings are so consistent and so damning that they have deepened concerns over whether the challenge of creating a fair and reliable system of death sentencing can ever be achieved. For example, as one commentator concluded, "The best available evidence shows that arbitrariness still runs rampant more than three decades after *Furman v. Georgia*" (McCord, 2005, p. 806) and that, as a result, "much of [the Court's] capital jurisprudence over the last three decades has been a colossal mistake" (McCord, 2005, p. 868). Another argued that "the best description of the capital sentencing pattern the Court's doctrine currently requires . . . is virtually identical to the pattern *Furman* ruled unconstitutional" (Liebman, 2007, p. 12).

Unfortunately, the magnitude and seriousness of these problems are not matched by the promise of available policy-oriented solutions. For example, although there are a number of things that could be done to address the morally disengaging aspects of the capital trial process, these very mechanisms may be part of the foundation on which the viability of capital punishment depends (e.g., Haney, 2005). Possible remedies include broadening the scope of permissible guilt-phase testimony by the defense that humanizes the defendant, providing the defense with the option to request that evidence in the penalty trial be presented in a more chronological sequence, so that the defense could open and perhaps close the penalty trial, balancing the current asymmetries of violence in penalty-phase testimony by permitting capital juries to hear graphic evidence about the realities of both of the sentencing options (life in prison without parole and the death penalty) that they are asked to choose between, explicitly acknowledging the importance of compassion in the meting out of justice by permitting or requiring judges to provide a pre-instruction at the outset of the penalty trial that acknowledges the value that the law requires jurors to attach to the defendant's personhood (e.g., Haney, 2005, p. 228–231). Although these kinds of reforms are likely to have a moderating effect on a number of the problems that we have identified with existing capital trial procedures, they are unlikely ever to be adopted without significant, corresponding shifts in capital jurisprudence. We are left instead with a set of largely practice-oriented implications derived from the research, i.e., attorneys should be trained to effectively overcome moral disengagement and to reduce the empathic divide that separates the jurors from their capital clients. These things may be accomplished by providing jurors with extensive humanizing information about the defendant, emphasizing the commonalities that connect rather than distance them from the personhood of the defendant, and underscoring the deeply personal nature of the decision the jurors are individually responsible for making.

Research has also documented the broad negative consequences of death qualification. The practice significantly skews the composition of the jury panel in ways that make it less representative, balanced, and fair, and the process itself has a biasing effect on those jurors who pass through it. Separately and in combination, these effects appear to facilitate the conviction of capital defendants and the imposition of death sentences. As one commentator put it, "Death qualification as currently practiced tilts the jury first towards guilt and then towards death, both by removing too many of certain kinds of people from the pool, and by affecting the expectations and perceptions of those who remain" (Rozelle, 2002, p. 699). Moreover, because the extent of disqualifying death penalty attitudes varies over time and across jurisdictions, the size of the group challenged for cause on this basis will vary, at any given time and in any given case, so that, ironically, when support for the death penalty wanes, more prospective jurors are likely to be excluded from participation at the outset of trial. Here, too, viable remedies are not difficult to conceptualize but are nearly impossible to implement under current law and policy. They certainly include the outright elimination of death qualification of the guilt-phase jury (for example, by death qualifying the penalty jury if and only if the defendant has been convicted of a death-eligible crime). In addition, much greater emphasis could be placed on what has been called *life qualification*—ensuring that that jurors not only understand mitigation and are willing to consider it in their penalty phase decision-making but also that they "are empowered to react to mitigating evidence in accordance with the dictates of their conscience, even in the face of adverse reactions from other jurors" (Blume, Johnson, & Threlkeld, 2001, p. 1215).

The empirically documented problems with capital jury sentencing instructions are especially vexing given the significance the U.S. Supreme Court seemed to attach to them when it reinstituted the death penalty in 1976. Yet the Court itself has acknowledged that its faith in these instructions was as much a pragmatic necessity as anything else: "The rule that juries are presumed to follow their instructions is a pragmatic one, rooted less in the absolute certitude that the presumption is true than in the belief that it represents a reasonable practical accommodation of the interests of the state and the defendant in the criminal justice process" (*Richardson v. Marsh*, 1987, p. 211). As we noted earlier, the validity of that practical accommodation has been systematically deconstructed in numerous studies documenting the widespread incomprehension of the various jury instructions that govern capital penalty trials in a number of jurisdictions and underscoring the serious consequences that can follow from it. As we also noted, there are a number of promising psycholinguistically inspired revisions of these instructions already in existence, and some have shown a demonstrated potential for improving comprehension. The fact that so few of these science-driven modifications have been attempted or implemented, and none to our knowledge that have been pursued in conjunction with a programmatic and empirical evaluation to document their effects, suggests that the problem of instructional incomprehension is likely to persist (even though potential solutions exist).

Because the capital trial process unfolds sequentially, many of the problematic forces and factors to which capital jurors are exposed will have accumulated by the time the penalty phase and the final jury deliberation stage are reached. As we have noted, this is the stage at which researchers have uncovered what is often a complicated and very troublesome decision-making dynamic at work, one that implicates the moral disengagement that characterizes the proceedings generally, and the continued use of uncorrected myths and misinformation by the previously death-qualified jurors, many of whom fail to fully understand crucial sentencing instructions that are supposed to guide their discretion. The end result is too often unreliable—based on extralegal considerations and erroneous assumptions—and can result in racially discriminatory outcomes.

One doctrinal bright spot in this area of law can be found in the Supreme Court's willingness to broaden the scope of admissible evidence in capital penalty phases, permitting capital juries to consider the background and character of the defendant whose fate they decide (e.g., *Lockett v. Ohio*, 1978; *Eddings v. Oklahoma*, 1982; *Wiggins v. Smith*, 2003; *Rompella v. Beard*, 2005). This important doctrinal innovation provided lawyers with an opportunity to educate jurors in a more comprehensive way about the lives of their clients, to broaden and deepen the psychological analyses to which jurors are exposed that explain the factors and forces that influenced the capital defendants whose fate they must decide, and to provide jurors with accurate knowledge and important insights about the social historical roots of violence by drawing on a growing body of research on the origins of criminal behavior of the sort that can eventually lead to capital murder (e.g., Haney, 2008a).

There are serious problems with the way in which this doctrine is implemented in a number of actual capital cases and, correspondingly, numerous ways that it can and should be improved in practice. Thus, although capital attorneys are now required to conscientiously assemble available mitigation in capital penalty trials, some states still fail to provide attorneys with the level of resources that are necessary to competently investigate, analyze, and present such evidence. In some instances capital cases are tried by attorneys who present only a small portion of the mitigation that actually exists. Indeed, wrongful condemnations—sentencing capital defendants to death who would likely have received life if their cases had been handled competently at the time of trial and adjudicated in a fairer and more just manner (Haney, 2006)—most often occur when attorneys fall short of their duty to effectively educate the jury about their client's social history and fail to provide the jurors with sufficient available information on which to premise a life rather than death sentence. Given the importance of this kind of evidence in deciding the fate of a capital defendant, it would not be unreasonable to require in advance (rather then waiting to correct wrongful condemntions years later on appeal) that a reasonably complete mitigation case be presented in all cases before the jury is permitted to render a death verdict.

In addition, as we have discussed at length, the courts have still done little to insure that capital jurors truly understand the judicial instructions that are supposed to legitimate their use of mitigating evidence. Instead, many capital defendants watch their cases be decided by jurors who have not learned the full truth about the social historical and contextual factors that helped to shape their lives and influence their criminal behavior, and many capital jurors are allowed to muddle through this life and death decision-making process, mired in faulty media-based stereotypes and confused about what if any relevance mitigating evidence has to the issues at hand.

Finally, it is important to acknowledge the many practical and political obstacles to truly fundamental reform that remain in this area of law. Many of the seemingly straightforward policy-related implications of the extensive empirical research that has been done on capital punishment have been effectively resisted to date in a historically conservative legal system where change of any kind is notoriously difficult to bring about. Moreover, the proposals that have the greatest likelihood of being adopted are, frankly, most often mere palliatives—the very kind of "tinkering" that Justice Blackmun warned against. Indeed, many scholars, researchers, and legal analysts have examined the same body of research that we have reviewed in this chapter and reached the conclusion that the problems with our system of death sentencing are so fundamental, endemic, and interconnected that only a truly fundamental and comprehensive program of reform would have any possibility of adequately addressing them.

A number of the policy recommendations that we have made in this concluding section are embodied in various statements by professional organizations concerned with injustices in our nation's system of death sentencing. Many have recommended further that a moratorium should be declared on all executions in the United States until and unless these systemic problems are effectively addressed. Thus, the American Bar Association in 1997 called for a moratorium on executions in order to "ensure that death penalty cases are administered fairly and impartially in accordance with due process" and to "minimize the risk that innocent persons may be executed" (American Bar Association, 1997). A few years later, the American Psychological Association's Council of Representatives (American Psychological Association, 2001) called upon "each jurisdiction in the United States that imposes capital punishment not to carry out the death penalty" until it had implemented "policies and procedures that can be shown through psychological and other social science research to ameliorate the deficiencies" that plague the system of death sentencing. Many of the deficiencies that were listed by the

Council have been discussed in this chapter. As Haney (2005) has argued, however, the effective reform of those policies and procedures that make up the system of capital punishment cannot be accomplished on a piecemeal basis. Rather "[t]he fact that these overarching problems are structural and systemic and that they operate cumulatively and in tandem means that they must be addressed in kind (i.e., through a set of interlocking reforms designed to remedy the entire system of death sentencing rather than one or another faulty component)" (Haney, 2005, p. 214).

In fact, a number of commentators and professional organizations, including the Society for the Psychological Study of Social Issues (2001), have reached the conclusion that it is infeasible to ever bring about a set of structural and systemic reforms that is comprehensive enough to effectively solve the numerous interconnected problems that plague the administration of capital punishment. They have called instead for the abolition of the death penalty, largely on the grounds that its many flaws are simply insurmountable.

SUMMARY AND CONCLUSIONS

Extensive research has been conducted on various aspects of the death penalty. The intense scholarly attention given to this topic is based in part on the magnitude of what is at issue in capital cases, the benchmark status of the legal and constitutional standards that are set in this area of law, and the significance of the moral, societal, and politic issues posed when the state seeks to take the life of one of its citizens. As our review of this literature has underscored, much of the research has focused on the flaws and failures in the system of death sentencing. The empirical realities repeatedly fall short of the symbolic images and aspirations that surround the death penalty, and the constitutional principles that are supposed to govern the application of this extraordinary punishment too often fail to function as they should. There are few if any areas of the criminal justice system that have been subjected to such careful social scientific scrutiny and, correspondingly, few if any parts of the larger system that have been found so consistently wanting.

Capital punishment is thus, in the words of Liebman, Fagan, and West (2000), a "broken system," and the myriad ways that it regularly breaks down have been extensively documented. Much of that research has been reviewed in this chapter, including the various attempts to reliably, meaningfully, and fairly define and refine the nature and amount of personal culpability that warrants a sentence of death, whether and under what circumstances capital punishment achieves the deterrent effect that supposedly provides its most rational and perhaps most often cited justification, the continued legacy of racial discrimination that has plagued this form of punishment throughout its history, the unusually important yet complicated and at times contradictory nature and role of public opinion about the death penalty, and the nature and functioning of the unique and often problematic institution of the capital jury. Even the research that is neutral and dispassionate in tone typically documents the problematic nature of whatever aspect of capital punishment is under study, and our review of this literature has reflected from eprical facts and that perspective.

As we have noted, many of the problems that plague the system of death sentencing are fundamentally psychological in nature. Numerous intra- and interpersonal processes are implicated in the problems that we have described, including unreliable determinations of culpability and deservedness by legislators, prosecutors, and capital jurors, the misperceptions about crime and punishment that shape key judgments that are structured into the death sentencing process, and the operation of bias and error that occurs in the course of emotionally daunting decision-making tasks that are unfamiliar to jurors and for which often incomprehensible instructions provide little useful guidance. There are inherent limitations to the extent to which changes in legal policy and practice alone can effectively resolve these issues.

In fact, as our discussion of policy implications and potential reforms indicates, the many problems that have been empirically documented in the administration of capital punishment do not lend themselves to simple solutions. In some instances, the complexity of the challenge comes about because of political as well as conceptual obstacles that must be overcome. In others—as in the case of

moral disengagement of jurors—the very problem at issue may be instrumental to the preservation of the system of death sentencing itself. That is, implementing policies and practices that truly ensure that individual jurors both fully accept the humanity of a capital defendant and fully appreciate the moral gravity and implications of a decision to sentence that defendant to death would also likely ensure that very few death verdicts are ever rendered. To take a different but related example, as long as perceptions about criminal culpability and victim worthiness are cognitively connected to racial stereotypes and biases—among the general public as well as for key legal decision makers—it is difficult to envision a simple policy directive or legal reform that would effectively neutralize the underlying psychological associations that create and maintain the problem.

These realizations, practicalities, and conundrums help explain why many scholars and professional organizations have concluded that even a comprehensive set of reforms is likely to accomplish no more than modest improvements in the reliability and quality of justice dispensed by our nation's system of death sentencing. The exorbitant costs that are necessary to maintain this system, as compared to its questionable benefits, have led many—even some who support the idea of the death penalty in abstract philosophical terms—to recommend its abolition. In any event, the long and well-documented empirical record of flaws and shortcomings have led scholars and professional organizations to call not only for solutions to the most immediate and glaring problems that plague the death penalty but also for an overarching and systematic overhaul of the system of capital punishment, a moratorium until this kind of comprehensive reform can be completed or, in the alternative, for the abolition of the punishment itself.

References

Acker, J. (1993). A different agenda: The Supreme Court, empirical research evidence, and capital punishment decisions, 1986–1989. *Law and Society Review, 27,* 65–88. doi:10.2307/3053748

Alarcón, A., & Mitchell, P. (2010). Executing the will of the voters? A roadmap to mend or end the California Legislature's multi-billion-dollar death penalty debacle. *Loyola of Los Angeles Law Review, 44,* S41–S223.

Albonetti, C. (1991). An integration of theories to explain judicial discretion. *Social Problems, 38,* 247–266. doi:10.2307/800532

Alker, H., Hosticka, C., & Mitchell, M. (1976). Jury selection as a biased social process. *Law and Society Review, 11,* 9–41.

Allen, M., Mabry, E., & McKelton, D. (1998). Impact of juror attitudes about the death penalty on juror evaluations of guilt and punishment: A meta-analysis. *Law and Human Behavior, 22,* 715–731. doi:10.1023/A:1025763008533

American Bar Association. (1997). *Report with recommendation no. 107.* ABA Midyear Meeting. Retrieved from http://www.abanet.org/irr/rec107.html

American Psychological Association. (2001). *The death penalty in the United States.* Retrieved from http://www.apa.org/about/policy/death-penalty.aspx

Anderson, N. (1990). Psychodynamics of everyday life: Blaming and avoiding blame. In N. Anderson (Ed.), *Contributions to information integration theory* (Vol. I, pp. 243–275). Hillsdale, NJ: Erlbaum.

Antonio, M. E. (2006). I didn't know it'd be so hard-jurors: Emotional reactions to serving on a capital trial. *Judicature, 89,* 282–288.

Antonio, M. E. (2008). Stress and the capital jury: How male and female jurors react to serving on a murder trial. *Justice System Journal, 29,* 396–407.

Appelbaum, K., & Appelbaum, P. (1994). Criminal justice related competencies in defendants with mental retardation. *Journal of Psychiatry and Law, 22,* 483–503.

Archer, D., Gartner, R., & Beittel, M. (1983). Homicide and the death penalty: A cross-national test of a deterrence hypothesis. *Journal of Criminal Law and Criminology, 74,* 991–1013. doi:10.2307/1143141

Atkins v. Virginia, 536 U.S. 304 (2002).

Bailey, W. C. (1978). Some further evidence on imprisonment v. the death penalty as a deterrent to murder. *Law and Human Behavior, 2,* 245–260. doi:10.1007/BF01039082

Bailey, W. C. (1980). Deterrence and the celerity of the death penalty: A neglected question in deterrence research. *Social Forces, 58,* 1308–1333.

Bailey, W. C. (1983a). The deterrent effect of capital punishment during the 1950s. *Suicide and Life-Threatening Behavior, 13,* 95–107.

Bailey, W. C. (1983b). Disaggregation in deterrence and death penalty research: The case of murder in Chicago. *Journal of Criminal Law and Criminology, 74,* 827–859. doi:10.2307/1143136

Bailey, W. C. (1990). Murder, capital punishment, and television: Execution publicity and homicide rates. *American Sociological Review, 55,* 628–633. doi:10.2307/2095860

Bailey, W. C. (1998). Deterrence, brutalization, and the death penalty: Another examination of Oklahoma's return to capital punishment. *Criminology, 36,* 711–734. doi:10.1111/j.1745-9125.1998.tb01263.x

Bailey, W. C., & Peterson, R. D. (1989). Murder and capital punishment: A monthly time-series analysis of execution publicity. *American Sociological Review, 54,* 722–743. doi:10.2307/2117750

Bailey, W. C., & Peterson, R. D. (1999). Capital punishment, homicide, and deterrence: An assessment of the evidence. In M. D. Smith & M. A. Zahn (Eds.), *Studying and preventing homicide: Issues and challenges* (pp. 223–245). Thousand Oaks, CA: Sage. doi:10.4135/9781483328430.n12

Baldus, D. (1996). When symbols clash: Reflections on the future of the comparative proportionality review of death sentences. *Seton Hall Law Review, 26,* 1582–1606.

Baldus, D., Woodworth, G., Grosso, C., & Christ, A. (2002). Arbitrariness and discrimination in the administration of the death penalty: A legal and empirical analysis of the Nebraska experience (1973–1999). *Nebraska Law Review, 81,* 486–756.

Baldus, D. C., Woodworth, G., & Pulaski, C. A. (1990). *Equal justice and the death penalty: A legal and empirical analysis.* Boston, MA: Northeastern University Press.

Baldus, D. C., Woodworth, G., Zuckerman, D., & Weiner, N. A. (1998). Racial discrimination and the death penalty in the post-*Furman* era: An empirical and legal overview with recent findings from Philadelphia. *Cornell Law Review, 83,* 1638–1770.

Baldus, D. C., Woodworth, G., Zuckerman, D., Weiner, N. A., & Broffitt, B. (2001). Symposium race, crime, and the constitution: Article the use of peremptory challenges in capital murder trials: A legal and empirical analysis. *University of Pennsylvania Journal of Constitutional Law, 3,* 3–172.

Bandura, A. (1990). Mechanisms of moral disengagement. In W. Reich (Ed.), *Origins of terrorism: Psychologies, ideologies, theologies, states of mind* (pp. 161–191). New York, NY: Cambridge University Press.

Bandura, A. (2002). Selective moral disengagement in the exercise of moral agency. *Journal of Moral Education, 31,* 101–119. doi:10.1080/0305724022014322

Bandura, A., Barbaranelli, C., Caprara, G., & Pastorelli, C. (1996). Mechanisms of moral disengagement in the exercise of moral agency. *Journal of Personality and Social Psychology, 71,* 364–374. doi:10.1037/0022-3514.71.2.364

Banner, S. (2002). *The death penalty: An American history*. Cambridge, MA: Harvard University Press.

Barkan, S., & Cohn, S. (1994). Racial prejudice and support for the death penalty by Whites. *Journal of Research in Crime and Delinquency, 31*, 202–209. doi:10.1177/0022427894031002007

Barnouw, E. (1975). *Tube of plenty*. Oxford, England: Oxford University Press.

Batson v. Kentucky, 476 U.S. 79 (1986).

Baumer, E., Messner, S., & Rosenfeld, R. (2003). Explaining spatial variation in support for capital punishment: A multilevel analysis. *American Journal of Sociology, 108*, 844–875. doi:10.1086/367921

Baumgartner, F., de Boef, S., & Boydstun, A. (2008). *The decline of the death penalty and the discovery of innocence*. New York, NY: Cambridge University Press.

Beckett, K. (1997). *Making crime pay: Law and order in contemporary American politics*. New York, NY: Oxford University Press.

Bedau, H., & Radelet, M. (1987). Miscarriages of justice in potentially capital cases. *Stanford Law Review, 40*, 21–179. doi:10.2307/1228828

Bell, B. (1989). Distinguishing attributions of causality, moral responsibility, and blame: Perceivers' evaluations of the attributions. *Social Behavior and Personality, 17*, 231–236. doi:10.2224/sbp.1989. 17.2.231

Belsky, J. (1993). Etiology of child maltreatment: A developmental-ecological analysis. *Psychological Bulletin, 114*, 413–434. doi:10.1037/0033-2909. 114.3.413

Bennack, F. A. (1983). The public, the media, and the judicial system: A national survey of citizen's awareness. *State Court Journal, 7*, 4–10.

Bentele, U., & Bowers, W. (2001). How jurors decide on death: Guilt is overwhelming; aggravation requires death; and mitigation is no excuse. *Brooklyn Law Review, 66*, 1011–1079.

Berk, R. (2005). New claims about executions and general deterrence: Déja vu all over again? *Journal of Empirical Legal Studies, 2*, 303–330. doi:10.1111/ j.1740-1461.2005.00052.x

Beyleveld, D. (1982). Ehrlich's analysis of deterrence: Methodological strategy and ethics in Isaac Ehrlich's research and writing on the death penalty as a deterrent. *British Journal of Criminology, 22*, 101–123.

Bienen, L. (1996). The proportionality review of capital cases by state high courts after *Gregg*: Only the "appearance of justice." *Journal of Criminal Law and Criminology, 87*, 130–314. doi:10.2307/1143974

Bigel, A. (1991). William H. Rehnquist on capital punishment. *Ohio Northern University Law Review, 17*, 729–769.

Blume, J., Johnson, S., & Threlkeld, B. (2001). Probing "life qualification" through expanded voir dire. *Hofstra Law Review, 29*, 1209–1264.

Blume, J. H., Johnson, S., & Seeds, C. (2009). Of *Atkins* and men: Deviations from clinical definitions of mental retardation in death penalty cases. *Cornell Journal of Law and Public Policy, 18*, 689–733.

Blumstein, A., Cohen, J., & Nagin, D. (1978). *Deterrence and incapacitation: Estimating the effects of criminal sanctions on crime rates*. Washington, DC: National Academy of Sciences.

Bobo, L., & Johnson, D. (2004). A taste for punishment: Black and White Americans' views on the death penalty and the War on Drugs. *Du Bois Review, 1*, 151–180. doi:10.1017/S1742058X04040081

Bohm, R. (1987). American death penalty attitudes: A critical examination of recent evidence. *Criminal Justice and Behavior, 14*, 380–396. doi:10.1177/0093854887014003008

Bohm, R., Clark, L., & Aveni, A. (1991). Knowledge and the death penalty: A test of the Marshall hypothesis. *Journal of Research in Crime and Delinquency, 28*, 360–387.

Bohm, R., & Vogel, B. (2004). Ten years after: The long-term stability of informed death penalty opinions. *Journal of Criminal Justice, 32*, 307–327. doi:10.1016/j.jcrimjus.2004.04.003

Borg, M. (1997). The Southern subculture of punitiveness? Regional variation in support for capital punishment. *Journal of Research in Crime and Delinquency, 34*, 25–45. doi:10.1177/0022427897034001003

Bowers, W. (1993). Capital punishment and contemporary values: People's misgivings and the Court's misperceptions. *Law and Society Review, 27*, 157–175. doi:10.2307/3053753

Bowers, W. (1995). The Capital Jury Project: Rationale, design, and a preview of early findings. *Indiana Law Journal, 70*, 1043–1102.

Bowers, W., Foglia, W., Giles, J., & Antonio, M. (2006). The decision makers: An empirical examination of the way the role of the judge and the jury influence death penalty decision-making. *Washington and Lee Law Review, 63*, 931–1010.

Bowers, W., Sandys, M., & Steiner, B. (1998). Foreclosed impartiality in capital sentencing: Jurors' predispositions, guilt-trial experiences, and premature decision making. *Cornell Law Review, 83*, 1476–1556.

Bowers, W., & Steiner, B. (1999). Death by default: An empirical demonstration of false and forced choices in capital sentencing. *Texas Law Review, 43*, 606–717.

Bowers, W. J. (1983). The pervasiveness of arbitrariness and discrimination under post-*Furman* capital statutes. *Journal of Criminal Law and Criminology, 74,* 1067–1100. doi:10.2307/1143144

Bowers, W. J., Fleury-Steiner, B., & Antonio, M. E. (2003). The capital sentencing decision: Guided discretion, reasoned moral judgment, or legal fiction. In J. Acker, R. M. Bohm, & C. S. Lanier (Eds.), *America's experiment with capital punishment: Reflections on the past, present, and future of the ultimate penal sanction* (2nd ed., pp. 413–468). Durham, NC: Carolina Academic Press.

Bowers, W. J., & Pierce, G. L. (1980a). Arbitrariness and discrimination under post-*Furman* capital statutes. *Crime and Delinquency, 26,* 563–632. doi:10.1177/001112878002600409

Bowers, W. J., & Pierce, G. L. (1980b). Deterrence or brutalization what is the effect of executions? *Crime and Delinquency, 26,* 453–484. doi:10.1177/001112878002600402

Bowers, W. J., Sandys, M., & Brewer, T. W. (2004). Crossing racial boundaries: A closer look at the roots of racial bias in capital sentencing when the defendant is black and the victim is white. *De Paul Law Review, 53,* 1497–1538.

Bowers, W. J., Steiner, B. D., & Sandys, M. (2001). Death sentencing in black and white: An empirical analysis of the role of jurors' race and jury racial composition. *University of Pennsylvania Journal of Constitutional Law, 3,* 171–274.

Brewer, T. (2004). Race and jurors' receptivity to mitigation in capital cases: The effect of jurors', defendants', and victims' race in combination. *Law and Human Behavior, 28,* 529–545.

Briere, J. (1992). *Child abuse trauma: Theory and treatment of the lasting effects.* Newbury Park, CA: Sage.

Bronson, E. (1970). On the conviction proneness and representativeness of the death-qualified jury: An empirical study of Colorado veniremen. *University of Colorado Law Review, 42,* 1–32.

Bronson, E. (1980). Does the exclusion of scrupled jurors in capital cases make the jury more likely to convict? Some evidence from California. *Woodrow Wilson Journal of Law, 3,* 11–34.

Brundage, W. (1993). *Lynching in the new south: Georgia and Virginia, 1880–1930.* Urbana: University of Illinois Press.

Bruner, J. S. (1957). On perceptual readiness. *Psychological Review, 64,* 123–152. doi:10.1037/h0043805

Buchanan v. Angelone, 522 U.S. 269 (1998).

Buchanan, R., Pryor, B., Taylor, K., & Strawn, D. (1978). Legal communication: An investigation of juror comprehension of pattern instructions. *Communication Quarterly, 26,* 31–35.

Butler, B. (2007a). Death qualification and prejudice: The effect of implicit racism, sexism, and homophobia on capital defendants' right to due process. *Behavioral Sciences and the Law, 25,* 857–867. doi:10.1002/bsl.791

Butler, B. (2007b). The role of death qualification in jurors' susceptibility to pretrial publicity. *Journal of Applied Social Psychology, 37,* 115–123. doi:10.1111/j.0021-9029.2007.00150.x

Butler, B. (2008). The role of death qualification in venirepersons' susceptibility to victim impact statements. *Psychology, Crime & Law, 14,* 133–141. doi:10.1080/10683160701483534

Butler, B., & Moran, G. (2007a). The impact of death qualification, belief in a just world, legal authoritarianism, and locus of control on venirepersons' evaluations of aggravating and mitigating circumstances in capital trials. *Behavioral Sciences and the Law, 25,* 57–68. doi:10.1002/bsl.734

Butler, B., & Moran, G. (2007b). The role of death qualification and need for cognition in venirepersons' evaluations of expert scientific testimony in capital trials. *Behavioral Sciences and the Law, 25,* 561–571. doi:10.1002/bsl.758

Butler, B., & Wasserman, A. (2006). The role of death qualification in venirepersons' attitudes toward the insanity defense. *Journal of Applied Social Psychology, 36,* 1744–1757. doi:10.1111/j.0021-9029.2006.00079.x

Butler, B. M., & Moran, G. (2002). The role of death qualification in venirepersons perceptions of aggravating and mitigating circumstances in capital trials. *Law and Human Behavior, 26,* 175–184. doi:10.1023/A:1014640025871

Caldwell v. Mississippi, 472 U.S. 320 (1985).

California v. Brown, 479 U.S. 538 (1987).

Callins v. Collins, 510 U.S. 1141 (1994).

Carter, L. (1987). Maintaining systemic integrity in capital cases: The use of court-appointed counsel to present mitigating evidence when the defendant advocates death. *Tennessee Law Review, 55,* 95–152.

Castano, E. (2011). Moral disengagement and morality shifting in the context of collective violence. In R. Kramer, F. Leonardelli, & R. Livingston (Eds.), *Social cognition, social identity, and intergroup relations: A Festschrift in honor of Marilynn B. Brewer* (pp. 319–338). New York, NY: Psychology Press.

Charrow, R., & Charrow, V. (1979). Making legal language understandable: A psycholinguistic study of jury instructions. *Columbia Law Review, 52,* 386–407.

Cheatwood, D. (1993). Capital punishment and the deterrence of violent crime in comparable counties. *Criminal Justice Review, 18,* 165–181. doi:10.1177/073401689301800202

Chemerinsky, E. (1995). Eliminating discrimination in administering the death penalty: The need for the Racial Justice Act. *Santa Clara Law Review, 35,* 519–533.

Cho, S. (1994). Capital confusion: The effect of jury instructions on the decision to impose death. *Journal of Criminal Law and Criminology, 85,* 532–561. doi:10.2307/1144109

Clarke, A., Lambert, A., & Whitt, L. (2000–2001). Executing the innocent: The next step in the Marshall Hypothesis. *New York University Review of Law and Social Change, 26,* 309–345.

Cloninger, D. O., & Marchesini, R. (2001). Execution and deterrence: A quasi-controlled group experiment. *Applied Economics, 33,* 569–576. doi:10.1080/00036840122871

Cobb, P. (1989). Reviving mercy in the structure of capital punishment. *Yale Law Journal, 99,* 389–409. doi:10.2307/796590

Cochran, J., & Chamlin, M. (2005). Can information change public opinion? Another test of the Marshall hypotheses. *Journal of Criminal Justice, 33,* 573–584. doi:10.1016/j.jcrimjus.2005.08.006

Cochran, J., & Chamlin, M. (2006). The enduring racial divide in death penalty support. *Journal of Criminal Justice, 34,* 85–99. doi:10.1016/j.jcrimjus.2005.11.007

Cochran, J., & Sanders, B. (2009). The gender gap in death penalty support: An exploratory study. *Journal of Criminal Justice, 37,* 525–533. doi:10.1016/j.jcrimjus.2009.09.001

Cochran, J. K., & Chamlin, M. B. (2000). Deterrence and brutalization: The dual effects of executions. *Justice Quarterly, 17,* 685–706. doi:10.1080/07418820000094721

Cochran, J. K., Chamlin, M. B., & Seth, M. (1994). Deterrence or brutalization? An impact assessment of Oklahoma's return to capital punishment. *Criminology, 32,* 107–134. doi:10.1111/j.1745-9125.1994.tb01148.x

Coker v. Georgia, 433 U.S. 584 (1977).

Connell, N. (2009). *Death by jury: Group dynamics and capital sentencing.* El Paso, TX: LFB Scholarly Publishing.

Cook, F., & Skogan, W. (1991). Agenda setting and the rise and fall of policy issues. In D. Protess & M. McCombs (Eds.), *Agenda setting: Readings on media, public opinion, and policymaking* (pp. 189–209). Hillsdale, NJ: Erlbaum.

Cowan, C. L., Thompson, W. C., & Ellsworth, P. C. (1984). The effects of death qualification on jurors' predisposition to convict and on the quality of deliberation. *Law and Human Behavior, 8,* 53–79. doi:10.1007/BF01044351

Cullen, F., Clark, G., Cullen, J., & Mathers, R. (1985). Attribution, salience, and attitudes toward criminal sentencing. *Criminal Justice and Behavior, 12,* 305–331.

Dayan, M., Mahler, R., & Widenhouse, M. (1989). Searching for an impartial sentencer through jury selection in capital trials. *Loyola of Los Angeles Law Review, 23,* 151–191.

Decker, S. H., & Kohfeld, C. W. (1986). The deterrent effect of capital punishment in Florida: A time series analysis. *Criminal Justice Policy Review, 1,* 422–437. doi:10.1177/088740348600100404

Decker, S. H., & Kohfeld, C. W. (1990). The deterrent effect of capital punishment in the five most active execution states: A time series analysis. *Criminal Justice Review, 15,* 173–191. doi:10.1177/073401689001500203

Dezhbakhsh, H., Rubin, P. H., & Shepherd, J. M. (2003). Does capital punishment have a deterrent effect? New evidence from postmoratorium panel data. *American Law and Economics Review, 5,* 344–376. doi:10.1093/aler/ahg021

Diamond, S. (1993). Instructing on death: Psychologists, juries, and judges. *American Psychologist, 48,* 423–434. doi:10.1037/0003-066X.48.4.423

Diamond, S. S., & Levi, J. N. (1996). Improving decisions on death by revising and testing jury instructions. *Judicature, 79,* 224–232.

Donohue, J. J., & Wolfers, J. J. (2005). Uses and abuses of empirical evidence in the death penalty debate. *Stanford Law Review, 58,* 791–846.

Dovidio, J., Pearson, A., Gaertner, S., & Hodson, G. (2008). On the nature of contemporary prejudice: From subtle bias to severe consequences. In V. Esses & R. Vernon (Eds.), *Explaining the breakdown of ethnic relations: Why neighbors kill* (pp. 41–60). Malden, MA: Blackwell.

Dovidio, J., Smith, J., Donnella, A., & Gaertner, S. (1997). Racial attitudes and the death penalty. *Journal of Applied Social Psychology, 27,* 1468–1487. doi:10.1111/j.1559-1816.1997.tb01609.x

Dovidio, J. F., & Gaertner, S. L. (1986). *Prejudice, discrimination, and racism.* San Diego, CA: Academic Press.

Durham, P. (2004). Review in name alone: The rise and fall of comparative proportionality review of capital sentences by the Supreme Court of Florida. *St. Thomas Law Review, 17,* 299–370.

Dutton, D., & Hart, S. (1992). Evidence for long-term, specific effects of childhood abuse and neglect on criminal behavior in men. *International Journal of Offender Therapy and Comparative Criminology, 36,* 129–137. doi:10.1177/0306624X9203600205

Eddings v. Oklahoma, 455 U.S. 104 (1982).

Ehrhard, S. (2008). Plea bargaining and the death penalty: An exploratory study. *Justice System Journal, 29,* 313–325.

Ehrlich, I. (1975). The deterrent effect of capital punishment: A question of life and death. *American Economic Review, 65,* 397–417.

Eisenberg, T., Garvey, S. P., & Wells, M. T. (2001). Forecasting life and death: Juror race, religion, and attitude toward the death penalty. *Journal of Legal Studies, 30,* 277–311. doi:10.1086/322060

Eisenberg, T., Garvey, S. P., & Wells, M. T. (2003). Victim characteristics and victim impact evidence in South Carolina capital cases. *Cornell Law Review, 88,* 306–342.

Eisenberg, T., & Wells, M. (1993). Deadly confusion: Juror instructions in capital cases. *Cornell Law Review, 79,* 1–17.

Ellis, J., & Luckasson, R. (1990). Mentally retarded criminal defendants. *George Washington Law Review, 53,* 414–493.

Ellsworth, P., & Gross, S. (1994). Hardening of attitudes: Americans' views on the death penalty. *Journal of Social Issues, 50,* 19–52. doi:10.1111/j.1540-4560.1994.tb02409.x

Ellsworth, P., & Ross, L. (1983). Public opinion and capital punishment: A close examination of the views of abolitionists and retentionists. *Crime and Delinquency, 29,* 116–169. doi:10.1177/001112878302900105

Elwork, A., Sales, B., & Alfini, J. (1982). *Making jury instructions understandable.* Charlottesville, VA: Michie.

Everington, C., & Fulero, S. (1999). Competence to confess: Measuring understanding and suggestibility of defendants with mental retardation. *Mental Retardation, 37,* 212–220. doi:10.1352/0047-6765(1999)037<0212:CTCMUA>2.0.CO;2

Fagan, J., Zimring, F. E., & Geller, A. (2006). Capital punishment and capital murder: Market share and the deterrent effects of the death penalty. *Texas Law Review, 84,* 1803–1867.

Fan, D., Keltner, K., & Wyatt, R. (2002). A matter of guilt or innocence: How news reports affect support for the death penalty in the United States. *International Journal of Public Opinion Research, 14,* 439–452. doi:10.1093/ijpor/14.4.439

Finckenauer, J. O. (1988). Public support for the death penalty: Retribution as just deserts or retribution as revenge? *Justice Quarterly, 5,* 81–100. doi:10.1080/07418828800089621

Fitzgerald, R., & Ellsworth, P. (1984). Due process vs. crime control: Death qualification and jury attitudes. *Law and Human Behavior, 8,* 31–51. doi:10.1007/BF01044350

Forst, B. (1983). Capital punishment and deterrence: Conflicting evidence. *Journal of Criminal Law and Criminology, 74,* 927–942. doi:10.2307/1143139

Fox, J., Radelet, M., & Bonsteel, J. (1991). Death penalty opinion in the post-*Furman* years. *New York University Review of Law and Social Change, 28,* 499–528.

Fox, J. A., & Radelet, M. L. (1989). Persistent flaws in econometric studies of the deterrent effect of the death penalty. *Loyola of Los Angeles Law Review, 23,* 29–44.

Fukurai, H., Butler, E., & Krooth, R. (1993). *Race and the jury: Racial disenfranchisement and the search for justice.* New York, NY: Plenum Press. doi:10.1007/978-1-4899-1127-8

Fukurai, H., & Krooth, R. (2003). *Race in the jury box: Affirmative action in jury selection.* Albany: State University of New York Press.

Furman v. Georgia, 408 U.S. 238 (1972).

Gallup Poll. (1989). *Public support for death penalty is highest in Gallup Annals.* Princeton, NJ.

Garvey, S. P. (2000). The emotional economy of capital sentencing. *New York University Law Review, 75,* 26–73.

Garvey, S. P., Johnson, S. L., & Marcus, P. (2000). Correcting deadly confusion: Responding to jury inquiries in capital cases. *Cornell Law Review, 85,* 627–655.

Geimer, W. (1990–1991). Law and reality in the capital penalty trial. *New York University Review of Law and Social Change, 28,* 273–295.

Gelles, R. J., & Straus, M. A. (1975). Family experience and public support of the death penalty. *American Journal of Orthopsychiatry, 45,* 596–613. doi:10.1111/j.1939-0025.1975.tb01190.x

Gerbner, G. (1992). Violence and terror in and by the media. In M. Raboy & B. Dagenais (Eds.), *Media crisis and democracy: Mass communications and the disruption of the social order* (pp. 94–107). London, England: Sage.

Godfrey v. Georgia, 446 U.S. 420 (1980).

Goldberg, F. (1970). Toward expansion of *Witherspoon*: Capital scruples, jury bias, and use of psychological data to raise presumptions in the law. *Harvard Civil Rights-Civil Liberties Law Review, 5,* 53–69.

Gordon, M., & Heath, L. (1991). The news business, crime, and fear. In D. Protess & M. McCombs (Eds.), *Agenda setting: Readings on media, public opinion, and policymaking* (pp. 71–74). Hillsdale, NJ: Erlbaum.

Gordon, T., & Brodsky, S. (2007). The influence of victim impact statements on sentencing in capital jurors. *Journal of Forensic Psychology Practice, 7,* 45–52. doi:10.1300/J158v07n02_03

Grasmick, H., Davenport, E., Chamlin, M., & Bursik, R. (1992). Protestant fundamentalism and the retributive doctrine of punishment. *Criminology, 30,* 21–46. doi:10.1111/j.1745-9125.1992.tb01092.x

Greene, E. (1999). The many guises of victim impact evidence and effects on jurors' judgments. *Psychology, Crime & Law, 5,* 331–348. doi:10.1080/10683169908401776

Greene, E., Koehring, H., & Quiat, M. (1998). Victim impact evidence in capital cases: Does the victim's character matter? *Journal of Applied Social Psychology, 28,* 145–156. doi:10.1111/j.1559-1816.1998.tb01697.x

Gregg v. Georgia, 428 U.S. 153 (1976).

Gross, S. (1998). Update: American public opinion on the death penalty—It's getting personal. *Cornell Law Review, 83,* 1448–1475.

Gross, S., Jacoby, K., Matheson, D., Montgomery, N., & Patil, S. (2005). Exonerations in the United States 1989 through 2003. *Journal of Criminal Law and Criminology, 95,* 523–560.

Gunther, A. (1998). The persuasive press inference. *Communication Research, 25,* 486–504. doi:10.1177/009365098025005002

Haney, C. (1984a). Epilogue: Evolving standards and the capital jury. *Law and Human Behavior, 8,* 153–158. doi:10.1007/BF01044357

Haney, C. (1984b). Examining death qualification: Further analysis of the process effect. *Law and Human Behavior, 8,* 133–151. doi:10.1007/BF01044356

Haney, C. (1984c). On the selection of capital juries: The biasing effects of the death qualification process. *Law and Human Behavior, 8,* 121–132. doi:10.1007/BF01044355

Haney, C. (Ed.). (1984d). Special issue on death qualification. *Law and Human Behavior, 8,* 1–6. doi:10.1007/BF01044348

Haney, C. (1995). The social context of capital murder: Social histories and the logic of capital mitigation. *Santa Clara Law Review, 35,* 547–609.

Haney, C. (1997a). Commonsense justice and capital punishment: Problematizing the "will of the people." *Psychology, Public Policy, and Law, 3,* 303–337. doi:10.1037/1076-8971.3.2-3.303

Haney, C. (1997b). Violence and the capital jury: Mechanisms of moral disengagement and the impulse to condemn to death. *Stanford Law Review, 49,* 1447–1486. doi:10.2307/1229350

Haney, C. (2002). Making law modern: Toward a contextual model of justice. *Psychology, Public Policy, and Law, 8,* 3–63. doi:10.1037/1076-8971.8.1.3

Haney, C. (2004). Condemning the other in death penalty trials: Biographical racism, structural mitigation, and the empathic divide. *De Paul Law Review, 53,* 1557–1590.

Haney, C. (2005). *Death by design: Capital punishment as a social psychological system.* New York, NY: Oxford University Press.

Haney, C. (2006). Exonerations and wrongful condemnations: Expanding the zone of perceived injustice in capital cases. *Golden Gate Law Review, 37,* 131–173.

Haney, C. (2008a). Evolving standards of decency: Advancing the nature and logic of capital mitigation. *Hofstra Law Review, 36,* 835–882.

Haney, C. (2008b). Media criminology and the death penalty. *De Paul Law Review, 58,* 689–740.

Haney, C., & Greene, S. (2004). Capital constructions: Newspaper reporting in death penalty cases. *Analyses of Social Issues and Public Policy (ASAP), 4,* 129–150. doi:10.1111/j.1530-2415.2004.00038.x

Haney, C., Hurtado, A., & Vega, L. (1994). "Modern" death qualification. *Law and Human Behavior, 18,* 619–633. doi:10.1007/BF01499328

Haney, C., & Lynch, M. (1994). Comprehending life and death matters: A preliminary study of California's capital penalty instructions. *Law and Human Behavior, 18,* 411–436. doi:10.1007/BF01499048

Haney, C., & Lynch, M. (1997). Clarifying life and death matters: An analysis of instructional comprehension and penalty phase closing arguments. *Law and Human Behavior, 21,* 575–595. doi:10.1023/A:1024804629759

Haney, C., Sontag, L., & Costanzo, S. (1994). Deciding to take a life: Capital juries, sentencing instructions, and the jurisprudence of death. *Journal of Social Issues, 50,* 149–176. doi:10.1111/j.1540-4560.1994.tb02414.x

Haney, C., & Weiner, R. (2004). Death is different: An editorial introduction to the theme issue. *Psychology, Public Policy, and Law, 10,* 373–378. doi:10.1037/1076-8971.10.4.373

Hans, V., & Dee, J. (1991). Media coverage of law: Its impact on juries and the public. *American Behavioral Scientist, 35,* 136–149. doi:10.1177/0002764291035002005

Harris, P. (1986). Over-simplification and error in public opinion surveys on capital punishment. *Justice Quarterly, 3,* 429–455. doi:10.1080/07418828600089051

Harvey, O. (1986). Belief systems and attitudes toward the death penalty and other punishments.

Journal of Personality, 54, 659–675. doi:10.1111/j.1467-6494.1986.tb00418.x

Hawkins, D. (1981). Causal attribution and punishment for crime. *Deviant Behavior, 2*, 207–230. doi:10.1080/01639625.1981.9967554

Heider, F. (1958). *The psychology of interpersonal relations.* New York, NY: Wiley. doi:10.1037/10628-000

Henderson, L. (1987). Legality and empathy. *Michigan Law Review, 85*, 1574–1653. doi:10.2307/1288933

Hindson, S., Potter, H., & Radelet, M. (2006). Race, gender, region and death sentencing in Colorado, 1980–1999. *University of Colorado Law Review, 77*, 549–574.

Hjalmarsson, R. (2009). Does capital punishment have a "local" deterrent effect on homicides? *American Law and Economics Review, 11*, 310–334. doi:10.1093/aler/ahn004

Hoffman, J. (1995). Where's the buck? Juror misperception of sentencing responsibility in death penalty cases. *Indiana Law Review, 70*, 1137–1160.

Holbert, R., Shah, D., & Kwak, N. (2004). Fear, authority, and justice: Crime-related viewing and endorsements of capital punishment and gun ownership. *Journalism and Mass Communication Quarterly, 81*, 343–363. doi:10.1177/107769900408100208

Hood, R. (2001). Capital punishment: A global perspective. *Punishment and Society, 3*, 331–354. doi:10.1177/1462474501003003001

Hood, R., & Hoyle, C. (2008). *The death penalty: A worldwide perspective.* Oxford, England: Oxford University Press. doi:10.1093/acprof:oso/9780199228478.001.0001

Howarth, J. (1994). Deciding to kill: Revealing the gender in the task handed to capital jurors. *Wisconsin Law Review, 1994*, 1345–1424.

Huff, C. (2002). Wrongful conviction and public policy: The American Society of Criminology presidential address. *Criminology, 40*, 1–18. doi:10.1111/j.1745-9125.2002.tb00947.x

Hurwitz, J., & Peffley, M. (2010). And justice for some: Race, crime, and punishment in the U.S. criminal justice system. *Canadian Journal of Political Science, 43*, 457–479. doi:10.1017/S0008423910000120

Iyengar, S., Peters, M., & Kinder, D. (1982). Experimental demonstrations of the "not-so-minimal" consequences of television news programs. *American Political Science Review, 76*, 848–858. doi:10.2307/1962976

Johnson, D. (2008). Racial prejudice, perceived injustice, and the Black–White gap in punitive attitudes. *Journal of Criminal Justice, 36*, 198–206. doi:10.1016/j.jcrimjus.2008.02.009

Jones, E., Kanouse, D., Kelley, H., Nisbett, R., Valins, S., & Weiner, B. (Eds.). (1987). *Attribution: Perceiving the causes of behavior.* Hillsdale, NJ: Erlbaum.

Jurow, G. (1971). New data on the effect of a "death qualified" jury on the guilt determination process. *Harvard Law Review, 84*, 567–611. doi:10.2307/1339553

Kadane, J. (1984). After Hovey: A note on taking account of the automatic death penalty jurors. *Law and Human Behavior, 8*, 115–120. doi:10.1007/BF01044354

Kansas v. Marsh, 548 U.S. 163 (2006).

Katz, L., Levitt, S. D., & Shustorovich, E. (2003). Prison conditions, capital punishment, and deterrence. *American Law and Economics Review, 5*, 318–343. doi:10.1093/aler/ahg014

Kaufman-Osborn, T. (2008). Proportionality review and the death penalty. *Justice System Journal, 29*, 257–272.

Kelley, H. (1967). Attribution theory in social psychology. *Nebraska Symposium on Motivation, 15*, 192–238.

Kelley, H. (1973). The processes of causal attribution. *American Psychologist, 28*, 107–128. doi:10.1037/h0034225

Kelley, H., & Michela, J. L. (1980). Attribution theory and research. *Annual Review of Psychology, 31*, 457–301. doi:10.1146/annurev.ps.31.020180.002325

Kennedy, R. (1988). *McCleskey v. Kemp*: Race, capital punishment, and the Supreme Court. *Harvard Law Review, 101*, 1388–1443. doi:10.2307/1341399

Kennedy, R. (1997). *Race, crime, and the law.* New York, NY: Pantheon Books.

Knorr, S. J. (1979). Deterrence and the death penalty: A temporal cross-sectional approach. *Journal of Criminal Law and Criminology, 70*, 235–254. doi:10.2307/1142925

Kort-Butler, L. A., & Hartshorn, K. J. S. (2011). Watching the detectives: Crime programming, fear of crime, and attitudes about the criminal justice system. *Sociological Quarterly, 52*, 36–55. doi:10.1111/j.1533-8525.2010.01191.x

Kotch, S., & Mosteller, R. (2010). The Racial Justice Act and the long struggle with race and the death penalty in North Carolina. *North Carolina Law Review, 88*, 2031–2131.

Lambert, E., Camp, S., Clarke, A., & Shanhe, J. (2011). The impact of information on death penalty support, revisited. *Crime and Delinquency, 57*, 572–599. doi:10.1177/0011128707312147

Land, K. C., Teske, R. H. C., & Zheng, H. (2009). The short-term effects of executions on homicides:

Deterrence, displacement, or both? *Criminology, 47,* 1009–1043. doi:10.1111/j.1745-9125.2009.00168.x

Lee, C. (2007). Hispanics and the death penalty: Discriminatory charging practices in San Joaquin County, California. *Journal of Criminal Justice, 35,* 17–27. doi:10.1016/j.jcrimjus.2006.11.012

Lempert, R. O. (1981). Desert and deterrence: An assessment of the moral bases of the case for capital punishment. *Michigan Law Review, 79,* 1177–1231. doi:10.2307/1288113

Lempert, R. O. (1983). The effect of executions on homicides: A new look in an old light. *Crime and Delinquency, 29,* 88–115. doi:10.1177/001112878302900104

Lester, D. (1998). *The death penalty: Issues and answers* (2nd ed.). Springfield, IL: Charles C Thomas.

Levi, J. (1993). Evaluating jury comprehension of Illinois capital-sentencing instructions. *American Speech, 68,* 20–49. doi:10.2307/455834

Levy–Shiff, R., Kedem, P., & Sevillia, Z. (1990). Ego identity in mentally retarded adolescents. *American Journal on Mental Retardation, 94,* 541–549.

Lieberman, J., & Sales, B. (1997). What social science teaches us about the jury instruction process. *Psychology, Public Policy, and Law, 3,* 589–644. doi:10.1037/1076-8971.3.4.589

Liebman, J. (2007). Slow dancing with death: The Supreme Court and capital punishment, 1963–2006. *Columbia Law Review, 107,* 1–130.

Liebman, J., & Clarke, P. (2011). Minority practice, majority's burden: The death penalty today. *Ohio State Journal of Criminal Law, 9,* 255–350.

Liebman, J., Fagan, J., & West, V. (2000). *A broken system: Error rates in capital cases, 1973–1995.* Retrieved from http://www2.law.columbia.edu/instructionalservices/liebman/liebman_final.pdf

Lockett v. Ohio, 438 U.S. 586 (1978).

Lockhart v. McCree, 476 U.S. 162 (1986).

Loeber, R. (1996). Developmental continuity, change, and pathways in male juvenile problem behaviors and delinquency. In J. Hawkins (Ed.), *Delinquency and crime: Current theories* (pp. 1–27). Cambridge, England: Cambridge University Press.

Logan, W. (1999). Through the past darkly: A survey of the uses and abuses of victim impact evidence in capital trials. *Arizona Law Review, 41,* 143–192.

Lord, C., Ross, L., & Lepper, M. (1979). Biased assimilation and attitude polarization: The effects of prior theories on subsequently considered evidence. *Journal of Personality and Social Psychology, 37,* 2098–2109. doi:10.1037/0022-3514.37.11.2098

Luginbuhl, J., & Burkhead, M. (1995). Victim impact evidence in a capital trial: Encouraging votes for death. *American Journal of Criminal Justice, 20,* 1–16. doi:10.1007/BF02886115

Luginbuhl, J., & Howe, J. (1995). Discretion in capital sentencing instructions: Guided or misguided? *Indiana Law Review, 70,* 1161–1181.

Luginbuhl, J., & Middendorf, K. (1988). Death penalty beliefs and jurors' responses to aggravating and mitigating circumstances in capital trials. *Law and Human Behavior, 12,* 263–281. doi:10.1007/BF01044384

Lynch, M. (2009). The social psychology of capital cases. In J. Lieberman & D. Krauss (Eds.), *Jury psychology: Social science aspects of trial processes: Psychology in the courtroom* (Vol. I, pp. 157–181). Burlington, VT: Ashgate.

Lynch, M., & Haney, C. (2000). Discrimination and instructional comprehension: Guided discretion, racial bias, and the death penalty. *Law and Human Behavior, 24,* 337–358. doi:10.1023/A:1005588221761

Lynch, M., & Haney, C. (2009). Capital jury deliberation: Effects on death sentencing, comprehension, and discrimination. *Law and Human Behavior, 33,* 481–496. doi:10.1007/s10979-008-9168-2

Lynch, M., & Haney, C. (2011). Mapping the racial bias of the White male capital juror: Jury composition and the "empathic divide." *Law and Society Review, 45,* 69–102. doi:10.1111/j.1540-5893.2011.00428.x

Maggard, S., Payne, B., & Chappell, A. (2012). Attitudes toward capital punishment: Educational, demographic, and neighborhood crime influences. *Social Science Journal, 49,* 155–166. doi:10.1016/j.soscij.2011.08.016

Marceau, J., Kamin, S., Foglia, W. (2013). Death eligibility in Colorado: Many are called, few are chosen. *University of Colorado Law Review, 84,* 1069–1115.

Masten, A., & Garmezy, N. (1985). Risk, vulnerability and protective factors in developmental psychopathology. In B. Lahey & A. Kazdin (Eds.), *Advances in clinical child psychology* (Vol. 12, pp. 1–52). New York, NY: Plenum Press. doi:10.1007/978-1-4613-9820-2_1

McCleskey v. Kemp, 481 U.S. 279 (1987).

McCombs, M., & Shaw, D. (1972). The agenda-setting function of the mass media. *Public Opinion Quarterly, 36,* 176–188. doi:10.1086/267990

McCord, D. (2005). Lightening still strikes: Evidence from the popular press that death sentencing continues to be unconstitutionally arbitrary more than three decades after *Furman. Brooklyn Law Review, 71,* 797–870.

McFarland v. Scott, 512 U.S. 1256 (1994).

McFarland, S. G. (1983). Is capital punishment a short-term deterrent to homicide? A study of the effects of four recent American executions. *Journal of Criminal Law and Criminology, 74,* 1014–1032. doi:10.2307/1143142

McFeely, W. (2000). *Proximity to death.* New York, NY: W. W. Norton.

McGautha v. California, 402 U.S. 183, 185 (1971).

McGee, J., & Menolascino, F. (1992). The evaluation of defendants with mental retardation in the criminal justice system. In R. Conley, R. Luckasson, & G. Bouthilet (Eds.), *The criminal justice system and mental retardation* (pp. 55–77). Baltimore, MD: Paul Brookes.

Messner, S., Baumer, E., & Rosenfeld, R. (2006). Distrust of government, the vigilante tradition, and support for capital punishment. *Law and Society Review, 40,* 559–590. doi:10.1111/j.1540-5893. 2006.00273.x

Miller, M. K., & Hayward, R. (2008). Religious characteristics and the death penalty. *Law and Human Behavior, 32,* 113–123. doi:10.1007/ s10979-007-9090-z

Mocan, H. N., & Gittings, R. K. (2003). Getting off death row: Commuted sentences and the deterrent effect of capital punishment. *Journal of Law and Economics, 46,* 453–478. doi:10.1086/382603

Moran, G., & Comfort, J. (1986). Neither "tentative" nor "fragmentary": Verdict preference of impaneled felony jurors as a function of attitude toward capital punishment. *Journal of Applied Psychology, 71,* 146–155. doi:10.1037/0021-9010.71.1.146

Moran, G., & Cutler, B. (1991). The prejudicial impact of pretrial publicity. *Journal of Applied Social Psychology, 21,* 345–367. doi:10.1111/j.1559-1816. 1991.tb00524.x

Morgan v. Illinois, 504 U.S. 719 (1993).

Murray, G. R. (2003). Raising considerations: Public opinion and the fair application of the death penalty. *Social Science Quarterly, 84,* 753–769.

Myers, B., & Greene, E. (2004). The prejudicial nature of victim impact statements. *Psychology, Public Policy, and Law, 10,* 492–515. doi:10.1037/ 1076-8971.10.4.492

Nagin, D. S., & Pepper, J. V. (Eds.). (2012). *Deterrence and the death penalty.* Washington, DC: National Academies Press.

Neumayer, E. (2003). Good policy can lower violent crime: Evidence from a cross-national panel of homicide rates, 1980–1997. *Journal of Peace Research, 40,* 619–640. doi:10.1177/00223433030406001

Nisbett, R., & Wilson, T. (1977). Telling more than we can know: Verbal reports on mental process. *Psychological Review, 84,* 231–259. doi:10.1037/ 0033-295X.84.3.231

Niven, D. (2002). Bolstering an illusory majority: The effects of the media's portrayal of death penalty support. *Social Science Quarterly, 83,* 671–689. doi:10.1111/1540-6237.00108

Note. (2001). The rhetoric of difference and the legitimacy of capital punishment. *Harvard Law Review, 114,* 1599–1622.

Oberer, W. (1961). Does disqualification of jurors for scruples against capital punishment constitute denial of fair trial on issue of guilt? *Texas Law Review, 39,* 545–567.

O'Brien, B., & Grosso, C. (2013). Beyond *Batson's* scrutiny: A preliminary look at racial disparities in prosecutorial preemptory strikes following the passage of the North Carolina Racial Justice Act. *U.C. Davis Law Review, 46,* 1623–1654.

O'Neil, K., Patry, M., & Penrod, S. (2004). Exploring the effects of attitudes toward the death penalty on capital sentencing verdicts. *Psychology, Public Policy, and Law, 10,* 443–470. doi:10.1037/1076-8971.10.4.443

Osofsky, M. J., Bandura, A., & Zimbardo, P. (2005). The role of moral disengagement in the execution process. *Law and Human Behavior, 29,* 371–393. doi:10.1007/s10979-005-4930-1

Otto, R., Penrod, S., & Dexter, H. (1994). The biasing effects of pretrial publicity on juror judgments. *Law and Human Behavior, 18,* 453–469. doi:10.1007/ BF01499050

Packer, H. (1968). *The limits of the criminal sanction.* Redwood City, CA: Stanford University Press.

Paduano, A., & Stafford-Smith, C. (1987). Deathly errors: Juror misperceptions concerning parole in the imposition of the death penalty. *Columbia Human Rights Law Review, 18,* 211–257.

Paternoster, R. (1984). Prosecutorial discretion in requesting the death penalty: A case of victim-based racial discrimination. *Law and Society Review, 18,* 437–478. doi:10.2307/3053431

Paternoster, R., & Brame, R. (2008). Reassessing race disparities in Maryland capital cases. *Criminology, 46,* 971–1008. doi:10.1111/j.1745-9125.2008.00132.x

Paternoster, R., Brame, R., Bacon, S., Ditchfield, A., Biere, D., Beckman, K. . . . Murphy, K. (2003). *An empirical analysis of Maryland's death sentencing system with respect to the influence of race and legal jurisdiction: Final report.* Retrieved from http://www.newsdesk. umd.edu/pdf/finalrep.pdf

Paternoster, R., & Deise, J. (2011). A heavy thumb on the scale: The effect of victim impact evidence on capital decision making. *Criminology, 49,* 129–161. doi:10.1111/j.1745-9125.2010.00220.x

Payne v. Tennessee, 501 U.S. 808 (1991).

People v. Fudge, 7 Cal. 4th 1075 (1994).

Phillips, D. P. (1980). The deterrent effect of capital punishment: New evidence on an old controversy. *American Journal of Sociology, 86,* 139–148. doi:10.1086/227206

Pierce, G., & Radelet, M. L. (1990). Role and consequences of the death penalty in American politics. *New York University Review of Law and Social Change, 18,* 711–728.

Pillsbury, S. (1989). Emotional justice: Moralizing the passions of criminal punishment. *Cornell Law Review, 74,* 655–710.

Poveda, T. (2006). Geographic location, death sentences and executions in post-*Furman* Virginia. *Punishment and Society, 8,* 423–442. doi:10.1177/1462474506067566

Protess, D., & McCombs, M. (Eds.). (1991). *Agenda setting: Readings on media, public opinion, and policymaking.* Hillsdale, NJ: Erlbaum.

Pulley v. Harris, 465 U.S. 37 (1984).

Radelet, M., Bedau, H., & Putnam, C. (1992). *In spite of innocence.* Boston, MA: Northeastern University Press.

Radelet, M., & Borg, M. (2000). The changing nature of death penalty debates. *Annual Review of Sociology, 26,* 43–61. doi:10.1146/annurev.soc.26.1.43

Radelet, M., Lofquist, L., & Bedau, H. (1996). Prisoners released from death row because of doubts about their guilt. *Thomas M. Cooley Law Review, 13,* 907–966.

Radelet, M. L., & Akers, R. L. (1996). Deterrence and the death penalty: The views of the experts. *Journal of Criminal Law and Criminology, 87,* 1–16. doi:10.2307/1143970

Radelet, M. L., & Pierce, G. L. (1985). Race and prosecutorial discretion in homicide cases. *Law and Society Review, 19,* 587–622. doi:10.2307/3053422

Rankin, J. (1979). Changing attitudes toward capital punishment. *Social Forces, 58,* 194–211.

Richardson v. Marsh, 481 U.S. 200 (1987).

Ring v. Arizona, 586 U.S. 584 (2002).

Roberts, J., & Doob, A. (1990). News media influences on public views of sentencing. *Law and Human Behavior, 14,* 451–468. doi:10.1007/BF01044222

Roberts, J., & Edwards, D. (1989). Contextual effects in judgments of crimes, criminals, and the purposes of sentencing. *Journal of Applied Social Psychology, 19,* 902–917. doi:10.1111/j.1559-1816.1989.tb01228.x

Rompilla v. Beard, 545 U.S. 374 (2005).

Roper v. Simmons, 543 U.S. 551 (2005).

Ross, L., & Nisbett, R. (1991). *The person and the situation: Perspectives of social psychology.* New York, NY: McGraw-Hill.

Rowe, D., & Farrington, D. (1997). The familial transmissions of criminal convictions. *Criminology, 35,* 177–202. doi:10.1111/j.1745-9125.1997.tb00874.x

Rozelle, S. (2002). The utility of *Witt:* Understanding the language of death qualification. *Baylor Law Review, 54,* 677–699.

Sampson, J., & Laub, J. (1993). *Crime in the making: Pathways and turning points through life.* Cambridge, MA: Harvard University Press.

Sandys, M. (1995). Crossovers—Capital jurors who change their minds about the punishment: A litmus test for sentencing guidelines. *Indiana Law Journal, 70,* 1183–1221.

Sandys, M., & Chermak, C. (1996). A journey into the unknown: Pretrial publicity and capital cases. *Communication Law and Policy, 1,* 533–577. doi:10.1080/10811689609368615

Sandys, M., & McGarrell, E. (1994). Attitudes toward capital punishment among Indiana legislators: Diminished support in light of alternative sentencing options. *Justice Quarterly, 11,* 651–677. doi:10.1080/07418829400092471

Sarat, A. (1993). Speaking of death: Narratives of violence in capital trials. *Law and Society Review, 27,* 19–58. doi:10.2307/3053746

Sarat, A. (1995). Violence, representation and responsibility in capital trials: The view from the jury. *Indiana Law Review, 70,* 1103–1135.

Sarat, A., & Vidmar, N. (1976). Public opinion, the death penalty, and the Eighth Amendment: Testing the Marshall hypothesis. *Wisconsin Law Review, 1976,* 171–207.

Scheck, B., Neufeld, P., & Dwyer, J. (2000). *Actual innocence: Five days to execution, and other dispatches from the wrongly convicted.* New York, NY: Doubleday.

Scott, E. (2000). Criminal responsibility in adolescence: Lessons from developmental psychology. In T. Grisso & R. Schwartz (Eds.), *Youth on trial: A developmental perspective on juvenile justice* (pp. 291–324). Chicago, IL: University of Chicago Press.

Scott, E., & Grisso, T. (1997). The evolution of adolescence: A developmental perspective on juvenile justice reform. *Journal of Criminal Law and Criminology, 88,* 137–189. doi:10.2307/1144076

Scott, E., Reppucci, N., & Woolard, J. (1995). Evaluating adolescent decision-making in legal contexts. *Law and Human Behavior, 19,* 221–244.

Scott, E., & Steinberg, L. (2003). Blaming youth. *Texas Law Review, 81*, 799–840.

Sellin, J. T. (1967). *Capital punishment.* New York, NY: Harper & Row.

Shatz, S., & Rivkind, N. (1997). The California death penalty scheme: Requiem for *Furman. New York University Law Review, 72*, 1283–1335.

Shaver, K. (1985). *The attribution of blame: Causality, responsibility, and blameworthiness.* New York, NY: Springer-Verlag. doi:10.1007/978-1-4612-5094-4

Shepherd, J. M. (2004). Murders of passion, execution delays, and the deterrence of capital punishment. *Journal of Legal Studies, 33*, 283–321. doi:10.1086/421571

Shepherd, J. M. (2005). Deterrence versus brutalization: Capital punishment's differing impacts among states. *Emory School of Law Working Paper Series, 104*, 203–255.

Sherizen, S. (1978). Social creation of crime news: All the news fitted to print. In C. Winick (Ed.), *Deviance and mass media* (pp. 203–224). Beverly Hills, CA: Sage.

Shultz, T., Schleifer, M., & Altman, A. (1981). Judgments of causation, responsibility, and punishment in cases of harm-doing. *Canadian Journal of Behavioural Science/Revue canadienne des sciences du comportement, 13*, 238–253. doi:10.1037/h0081183

Simon, J. (1997). *Violence, vengeance and risk: Capital punishment in the neo-liberal state.* Unpublished manuscript, University of Miami, Miami, FL.

Skolnick, J., & Fyfe, J. J. (1993). *Above the law: Police and the excessive use of force.* New York, NY: The Free Press.

Slater, M., Rouner, D., & Long, M. (2006). Television dramas and support for controversial public policies: Effects and mechanisms. *Journal of Communication, 56*, 235–252. doi:10.1111/j.1460-2466.2006.00017.x

Sloop, J. (1996). *The cultural prison: Discourse, prisoners, and punishment.* Tuscaloosa: University of Alabama Press.

Smith, A. E., & Haney, C. (2011). Getting to the point: Attempting to improve juror comprehension of capital penalty phase instructions. *Law and Human Behavior, 35*, 339–350. doi:10.1007/s10979-010-9246-0

Smith, K. (1987). Newspaper coverage and public concern about community issues. *Journalism Monographs, 101*, 1–32.

Smith, T. (1976). A trend analysis of attitudes toward capital punishment. In J. David (Ed.), *Studies of social change since 1948.* Chicago, IL: National Opinion Research Center Report 127B.

Smith, V. (1991). Impact of pretrial instruction on jurors' information processing and decision making. *Journal of Applied Psychology, 76*, 220–228. doi:10.1037/0021-9010.76.2.220

Society for the Psychological Study of Social Issues. (2001). *SPSSI statement on the death penalty.* Retrieved from http://www.spssi.org/index.cfm?fuseaction=page.viewpage&pageid=1461

Songer, M. J., & Unoh, I. (2006). The effect of race, gender, and location on prosecutorial decisions to seek the death penalty in South Carolina. *South Carolina Law Review, 58*, 161–209.

Soss, J., Langbein, L., & Metelko, A. (2003). Why do White Americans support the death penalty? *Journal of Politics, 65*, 397–421.

Stack, S. (1987). Publicized executions and homicide, 1950–1980. *American Sociological Review, 52*, 532–540.

Stack, S. (1994). Execution publicity and homicide in Georgia. *American Journal of Criminal Justice, 18*, 25–39. doi:10.1007/BF02887637

Stack, S. (2000). Support for the death penalty: A gender-specific model. *Sex Roles, 43*, 163–179.

Stanford v. Kentucky, 492 U.S. 361 (1989).

Steinberg, L., & Scott, E. (2003). Less guilty by reason of adolescence: Developmental immaturity, diminished responsibility, and the juvenile death penalty. *American Psychologist, 58*, 1009–1018. doi:10.1037/0003-066X.58.12.1009

Steiner, B. (1999). Folk knowledge as legal action: Death penalty judgments and the tenet of early release in a culture of mistrust and punitiveness. *Law and Society Review, 33*, 461–496. doi:10.2307/3115171

Steiner, B., Bowers, W., & Sarat, A. (1999). Folk knowledge as legal action: Death penalty judgments and the tenet of early release in a culture of mistrust and punitiveness. *Law and Society Review, 33*, 461–505. doi:10.2307/3115171

Stolzenberg, L., & D'Alessio, S. J. (2004). Capital punishment, execution publicity and murder in Houston, Texas. *Journal of Criminal Law and Criminology, 94*, 351–380. doi:10.2307/3491373

Suggs, D., & Sales, B. (1981). Juror self-disclosure in voir dire: A social science analysis. *Indiana Law Journal, 56*, 245–271.

Sundby, S. E. (2003). Capital jury and empathy: The problem of worthy and unworthy victims. *Cornell Law Review, 88*, 343–381.

Tabak, R. (2001). Finality without fairness: Why we are moving towards moratoria on executions, and the potential abolition of capital punishment. *Connecticut Law Review, 33*, 733–763.

Thaxton, S. (2013). Leveraging death. *Journal of Criminal Law and Criminology, 103*, 475–552.

Thomas, C. W., & Foster, S. (1975). A sociological perspective on public support for capital punishment.

American Journal of Orthopsychiatry, 45, 641–657. doi:10.1111/j.1939-0025.1975.tb01192.x

Thompson, W. (1989). Death qualification after *Wainwright v. Witt* and *Lockhart v. McCree. Law and Human Behavior, 13*, 185–215. doi:10.1007/BF01055923

Thompson, W. C., Cowan, C. L., Ellsworth, P. C., & Harrington, J. C. (1984). Death penalty attitudes and conviction proneness: The translation of attitudes into verdicts. *Law and Human Behavior, 8*, 95–113. doi:10.1007/BF01044353

Thomson, E. (1997). Discrimination and the death penalty in Arizona. *Criminal Justice Review, 22*, 65–76. doi:10.1177/073401689702200106

Tiersma, P. (1995). Dictionaries and death: Do capital jurors understand mitigation? *Utah Law Review, 1*, 1–49.

Trop v. Dulles, 356 U.S. 86 (1958).

Tyler, T., & Weber, R. (1982). Support for the death penalty: Instrumental response to crime, or symbolic attitude? *Law and Society Review, 17*, 21–45. doi:10.2307/3053531

Unnever, J., & Cullen, F. (2005). Executing the innocent and support for capital punishment: Implications for public policy. *Criminology and Public Policy, 4*, 3–38. doi:10.1111/j.1745-9133.2005.00002.x

Unnever, J., & Cullen, F. (2006). Christian fundamentalism and support for capital punishment. *Journal of Research in Crime and Delinquency, 43*, 169–197. doi:10.1177/0022427805280067

Unnever, J., & Cullen, F. (2007). Reassessing the racial divide in support for capital punishment: The continuing significance of race. *Journal of Research in Crime and Delinquency, 44*, 124–158. doi:10.1177/0022427806295837

Unnever, J., Cullen, F., & Jonson, C. (2008). Race, racism, and support for capital punishment. *Crime and Justice, 37*, 45–96. doi:10.1086/519823

Unnever, J., Cullen, F., & Roberts, J. (2005). Not everyone strongly supports the death penalty: Assessing weakly-held attitudes about capital punishment. *American Journal of Criminal Justice, 29*, 187–216. doi:10.1007/BF02885735

van den Haag, E. (1969). On deterrence and the death penalty. *Journal of Criminal Law, Criminology, and Police Science, 60*, 141–147. doi:10.2307/1142233

Vidmar, N., & Dittenhoffer, T. (1981). Informed public opinion and death penalty attitudes. *Canadian Journal of Criminology, 23*, 43–56.

Vidmar, N., & Ellsworth, P. (1974). Public opinion and the death penalty. *Stanford Law Review, 26*, 1245–1270. doi:10.2307/1227989

Wainwright v. Witt, 460 U.S. 412 (1985).

Warr, M., & Stafford, M. (1984). Public goals of punishment and support for the death penalty. *Journal of Research in Crime and Delinquency, 21*, 95–111. doi:10.1177/0022427884021002002

Weisberg, R. (1984). Deregulating death. *Supreme Court Review, 8*, 305–395.

White, W. (1987). *The death penalty in the eighties.* Ann Arbor: University of Michigan Press.

Whitman, T. L. (1990). Self-regulation and mental retardation. *American Journal on Mental Retardation, 94*, 347–362.

Wiener, R., Rogers, M., Winter, R., Hurt, L., Hackney, A., Kadela, K. . . . Morasco, B. (2004). Guided jury discretion in capital murder cases. *Psychology, Public Policy, and Law, 10*, 516–576. doi:10.1037/1076-8971.10.4.516

Wiener, R. L., Pritchard, C. C., & Weston, M. (1995). Comprehensibility of approved jury instructions in capital murder cases. *Journal of Applied Psychology, 80*, 455–467. doi:10.1037/0021-9010.80.4.455

Wiggins v. Smith, 539 U.S. 510 (2003).

Williams, R. (1981). Legitimate and illegitimate uses of violence: A review of ideas and evidence. In W. Gaylin, R. Macklin, & T. Powledge (Eds.), *Violence and the politics of research* (pp. 23–45). New York, NY: Plenum Press. doi:10.1007/978-1-4684-4019-5_2

Winick, B. (1982). Prosecutorial peremptory challenge practices in capital cases: An empirical study and constitutional analysis. *Michigan Law Review, 81*, 1–98. doi:10.2307/1288544

Witherspoon v. Illinois, 391 U.S. 510 (1968).

Woodson v. North Carolina, 428 U.S. 289 (1976).

Zeisel, H., & Gallup, A. (1989). Death penalty sentiment in the United States. *Journal of Quantitative Criminology, 5*, 285–296. doi:10.1007/BF01062741

Zimmerman, P. (2004). State executions, deterrence, and the incidence of murder. *Journal of Applied Econometrics, 7*, 163–193.

Zimring, F. (2003). *The contradictions of American capital punishment.* New York, NY: Oxford University Press.

Index

511